THE OXFORD HANDBOOK OF

MIGRATION CRISES

THE OXFORD HANDBOOK OF

MIGRATION CRISES

Edited by

CECILIA MENJÍVAR

MARIE RUIZ

and

IMMANUEL NESS

OXFORD
UNIVERSITY PRESS

OXFORD
UNIVERSITY PRESS

Oxford University Press is a department of the University of Oxford. It furthers the University's objective of excellence in research, scholarship, and education by publishing worldwide. Oxford is a registered trade mark of Oxford University Press in the UK and certain other countries.

Published in the United States of America by Oxford University Press
198 Madison Avenue, New York, NY 10016, United States of America.

Library of Congress Cataloging-in-Publication Data
Names: Menjívar, Cecilia, editor. | Ruiz, Marie, editor. | Ness, Immanuel, editor.
Title: The Oxford handbook of migration crises /
edited by Cecilia Menjivar, Marie Ruiz, and Immanuel Ness.
Description: New York : Oxford University Press, [2019] |
Includes bibliographical references and index.
Identifiers: LCCN 2018024218 | ISBN 9780190856908 (hardcover)
Subjects: LCSH: Emigration and immigration—History—21st century. |
Population geography—History—21st century. | Refugees—History—21st century.
Classification: LCC JV6033 .O94 2019 | DDC 304.8—dc23
LC record available at https://lccn.loc.gov/2018024218

9 8 7 6 5 4 3 2 1

Printed by Sheridan Books, Inc., United States of America

To all immigrants whose lives are misconstrued as a problem, in hope that they will be treated with respect and dignity in their new homes.

Contents

About the Editors

Cecilia Menjívar holds the Dorothy L. Meier Chair in Social Equities at UCLA, where she is a professor of sociology. Her research focuses on the legal frameworks and enforcement strategies at various levels of government and the effects of such strategies on immigrants' lives. Her recent books include, *Immigrant Families* (Polity, 2016), with Leisy Abrego and Leah Schmalzbauer, and the coedited volumes, *Constructing Immigrant "Illegality": Critiques, Experiences, and Responses* (Cambridge, 2014) with Daniel Kanstroom; and *Deportation and Return in a Border-Restricted World* (Springer, 2017) with Bryan Roberts and Nestor Rodriguez.

Marie Ruiz is an associate professor in British history at the Université de Picardie Jules Verne, Amiens, France. She holds a PhD in British History from the Université Paris Diderot–Sorbonne Paris Cité. Her research focuses on nineteenth-century British female emigration societies. She is the author of *British Female Emigration Societies and the New World, 1860–1914* (Palgrave Macmillan, 2017); editor of *International Migrations in the Victorian Era* (Brill, 2018); and coeditor with Mélanie Grué of the 2017 special issue of *Women's History* entitled "Documents in Women's History. She is the editor of the Anthem Series in British History (Anthem Press).

Immanuel Ness is a professor of political science at Brooklyn College, City University of New York, and a senior research associate at the Centre for Social Change, University of Johannesburg. He is author of *Southern Insurgency* (Pluto, 2015); *Guest Workers and Resistance to U.S. Corporate Despotism* (Univ. of Illinois Press, 2011); and other works on migration, labor movements and political organizations, social change, and imperialism. He is co-editor, with Zak Cope, of the quarterly periodical *Journal of Labor and Society*.

About the Contributors

Dalia Abdelhady is a reader in sociology and the Director of the Centre for Middle Eastern Studies at Lund University. Her work focuses on the experiences of different groups of migrants (and their children) in different national and regional contexts. Specifically, she looks at forms of identification, communal belonging, and cultural expression as aspects of integration trajectories. Additionally, she studies the ways institutions such as labor markets, schools, and media influence the experiences of migration and integration.

Leisy J. Abrego is an associate professor in the Department of Chicana/o Studies at UCLA. Her research and teaching interests are in Central American immigration, Latina/o families, inequalities created by gender, and the production of "illegality" through US immigration laws. Her first book, *Sacrificing Families: Navigating Laws, Labor, and Love Across Borders* (Stanford University Press, 2014), examines the well-being of Salvadoran immigrants and their families—both in the United States and in El Salvador—as these are shaped by immigration policies and gendered expectations. Her second book, co-authored with Cecilia Menjívar and Leah Schmalzbauer, is *Immigrant Families* (Polity, 2016).

Olayinka Akanle, PhD, is a lecturer in the Department of Sociology, University of Ibadan, Nigeria. He is also a postdoctoral fellow at the South African Research Chair Initiative (SARChI) in Social Policy, College of Graduate Studies, University of South Africa (UNISA), South Africa. He has won scholarly awards such as the World Social Science Fellowship (WSSF) of the International Social Science Council (ISSC), Paris, France; Laureate of Council for the Development of Social Science Research in Africa (CODESRIA); and University of Ibadan Postgraduate School Prize for scholarly publication. His research interests include the sociology of development/development studies, social theory, and social policy.

Idil Atak is an associate professor and graduate program director in the Department of Criminology of Ryerson University, Toronto. She is the editor-in-chief of *International Journal for Migration and Border Studies*. Idil is a member of the International Association for the Study of Forced Migration's (IASFM) Executive Committee and the past president of the Canadian Association for Refugee and Forced Migration Studies (CARFMS). She is currently conducting Social Sciences and Humanities Research Council of Canada (SSHRC)-funded research on the intersection of security, irregular migration, and asylum.

Dr. Jen Bagelman is a lecturer at the University of Exeter in the Department of Geography. Her work critically examines how displacement is produced through exclusionary citizenship and bordering practices. She is also deeply interested in how people mobilize to enact more loving geopolitics. She has explored these questions particularly in relation to anticolonial migrant justice movements, such as sanctuary, in her recent book, *Sanctuary City: A Suspended State* (Palgrave, 2016).

Pascale Baligand teaches in the Department of Psychoanalytic Studies at the Université Paris Diderot, Sorbonne Paris Cité. She is an associate professor in social sciences, and a clinical psychologist. Her work brings together the social sciences and psychoanalysis, focusing on subjective relationships to space and the notion of the home.

Tanya Basok is a professor of sociology and anthropology in the Department of Sociology, Anthropology, and Criminology at the University of Windsor. She has conducted research on seasonal Mexican workers in Canada, migrant rights, citizenship, migrant women, refugees, trade unions' solidarity with migrants, migrant "illegality," and status regularization for undocumented workers. Her major publications include *Keeping Heads Above Water: Salvadorean Refugees in Costa Rica* (McGill-Queens University Press, 1993); *Tortillas and Tomatoes: Mexican Transmigrant Harvesters in Canada* (McGill Press, 2002); and *Rethinking Transit Migration: Mobility, Precarity, and Self-Making* (Palgrave Macmillan, 2015, with Danièle Bélanger, Martha Rojas, and Guillermo Candiz).

Danièle Bélanger is a professor of geography at the Université Laval in Québec City, and the holder of the Senior Canada Research Chair in Global Migration Processes. Between 1997 and 2013, she was a professor of sociology at Western University, London, Ontario, Canada. Her research analyzes the relationships between policies and precarious migration status. Her projects have focused on temporary migrant workers, trafficked individuals, undocumented migrants, refugees, asylum-seekers, and marriage migrants. She conducts fieldwork in Asia, Latin America, the Middle East, and Canada. Some of her recent migration research has been published in *The Annals of Social and Political Science, Current Sociology, Asian Population Studies, Asia Pacific Migration Journal*, and *Pacific Affairs*.

Pablo Bose is a migration and urban studies scholar, an associate professor in the Department of Geography and Director of Global and Regional Studies at the University of Vermont. His three main research projects currently are on refugee resettlement in North America and Europe, on environmentally-induced displacement worldwide, and on cities of the global south. He has written *Urban Development in India: Global Indians in the Remaking of Kolkata* (Routledge, 2015) and his articles have appeared in *Urban Geography, Annals of the American Association of Geographers, Refuge*, and *Area*, among others.

Ulbe Bosma is a senior researcher at the International Institute of Social History in Amsterdam and professor of international comparative social history at the VU

University in Amsterdam. He has published extensively on the history of plantation economies and colonial migrations in maritime Southeast Asia. Among his publications are *Postcolonialism in the Netherlands* (Amsterdam University Press, 2012); *The Sugar Plantation in India and Indonesia* (Cambridge University Press, 2013); and "Migration and Colonial Enterprise in Nineteenth Century Java," in *Globalising Migration History* (edited by Leo Lucassen and Jan Lucassen, Brill, 2014).

John R. Campbell teaches in the Department of Anthropology and Sociology at the School of Oriental and African Studies, London. He has conducted fieldwork in Ghana, Tanzania, and the UK and has been involved in international development in Ethiopia, Kenya, and Botswana. His recent work focuses on refugees and migration in the Horn of Africa and on criminal justice in the United Kingdom. His most recent book is *Bureaucracy, Law, and Dystopia in the United Kingdom's Asylum System* (Routledge, 2017).

Céline Cantat is a Marie Curie individual fellow at the Centre for Policy Studies, Central European University, Budapest. She works on *MigSol: Migration Solidarity and Acts of Citizenship along the Balkan Route*, a project which examines solidarity along that route. Céline holds a PhD in Refugee Studies from the University of East London, and spent a year at Migrinter, University of Poitiers, as a Marie Curie early stage researcher. Céline has been involved in several migrant solidarity networks in London and Paris, as well as with refugee groups in Syria. Her interests include globalization and migration, migration solidarity, racism and exclusion in Europe, and state formation and dynamics of mass displacement.

Jock Collins is a professor of social economics in the Management Discipline Group at the UTS Business School, Sydney, Australia. His research interests center on immigration and cultural diversity in the economy and society. His recent research has been on Australian immigration and refugee settlement; refugee, immigrant, and Indigenous entrepreneurship; multiculturalism; immigrants and the built environment; immigrants in regional and rural Australia; and the social use of ethnic heritage. He is the author or co-author of ten books, the most recent of which is *Global Teachers, Australian Perspectives: Goodbye Mr. Chips Hello Ms. Banerjee* (with Carol Reid and Michael Singh, Springer Singapore, 2014).

Laurence Cros is an associate professor in the Department of English Studies at the Université Paris Diderot, where she teaches American and Canadian history and culture. She received the Agrégation d'Anglais in 1991 and a PhD in Canadian studies from the Université Sorbonne Nouvelle in 1998. She received several research grants from the Canadian government and is a board member of the French Association of Canadian Studies. After working on the interaction between the writing of Canadian history and nation building, she now works on the way in which Canadian identity is defined and promoted through Canada's foreign policy.

Heike Drotbohm is a professor of social and cultural anthropology at the University of Mainz. Her area of research includes Afro-Atlantic societies (Caribbean, West-Africa,

Brazil), in which she studied the circulation of care in transnational families and transnational religious networks as well as the social implications of cross-border control and the affective dimensions of humanitarian aid. She is coeditor (with Ines Hasselberg) of *Deportation, Anxiety, Justice: New Ethnographic Perspectives* (Routledge, 2017) and of *Anthropological Perspectives on Care: Work, Kinship, and the Life Course* (with Erdmute Alber, Palgrave Macmillan, 2015). Her research also appears in *Journal of Ethnic and Migration Studies, History of the Family,* and *Citizenship Studies.*

Olugbenga Samuel Falase earned a PhD from the Department of Sociology, University of Ibadan. He is a recipient of the Social Science Research Council (SSRC) Doctoral Fellowships (2014, 2016, and 2017), and Lift Above Poverty Organization (LAPO) Doctoral Research Support Grant, 2015. He is a specialist in contextual sociology, development sociology, and the sociology of natural resources. He is a lecturer at the Department of Sociology and Psychology, Lead City University, Ibadan, Nigeria.

Xavier Casademont Falguera is an assistant professor at the University of Girona and a political scientist. His PhD focuses on the process of integration of internal migration in Catalonia during the Franco regime. His main areas of research are immigrant integration policies and citizenship, social policies, and social services, as well as the crisis of liberal democracies and political participation. He was a civil servant in a town council in Catalonia for thirteen years, and acted as coordinator of the immigrant integration plan.

Carol Farbotko is a researcher in cultural geography and environmental studies, with interests in conceptualizing and testing the ways in which culture shapes, and is shaped by, environmental change. She has studied the cultural politics of a range of human and nonhuman subjects, including climate migrants. She is a research scientist at the Commonwealth Scientific and Industrial Research Organisation (CSIRO), Australia.

Caroline Fleay is an associate professor at the Centre for Human Rights Education, Curtin University in Western Australia. She conducts research into the experiences of people seeking asylum in Australia at sites of immigration detention as well as in the community, and has a range of publications that explore the impacts of government policies on people seeking asylum. She is a board member of the Refugee Council of Australia and has been an active campaigner for the rights of people seeking asylum over the past eighteen years.

Eric Fong is a professor of sociology at the Chinese University of Hong Kong. He is also the inaugural director of the Center on Migration and Mobility at CUHK and Changjiang Chair Professor at Xi'an Jiaotong University. Fong formerly served as President of the Canadian Population Society and the North America Chinese Sociologist Association, as well as chair of the International Migration Section of the American Sociological Association. Fong publishes widely on race and ethnic residential patterns and immigration. His latest book, coauthored with Brent Berry, is *Immigration and the City* (Polity, 2017).

Jane Freedman is a professor at the Université Paris 8 and a member of the Centre de Recherches Sociologiques et Politiques de Paris (CRESPPA). She has researched and published widely on gender, migration, and asylum. Recent publications include *Gendering the International Asylum and Refugee Debate* (Palgrave Macmillan, 2015) and *A Gendered Approach to the Syrian Refugee Crisis* (Routledge, 2017).

Christiane Fröhlich is a research fellow at the GIGA German Institute of Global and Area Studies in Hamburg. She researches human mobility in the context of political and environmental crises with a focus on the Middle East. She has done extensive field research on the impact of a prolonged drought period in prerevolutionary Syria. She also inquires into the role of the Global North in current migration movements from the Global South from a postcolonial perspective. Her work has been published in, among other journals, *Political Geography, Global Policy*, and *Contemporary Levant*, as well as a number of edited volumes.

Ruchira Ganguly-Scrase obtained her PhD in anthropology from the University of Melbourne. She is a development consultant and professor at the Social Global Studies Centre, RMIT (Royal Melbourne Institute of Technology). In 2013–2014 she was a professor of anthropology and National Course Director for Global Studies and International Development Studies, Australian Catholic University. Previously she was the Coordinator of the Centre for Asia Pacific Social Transformation Studies (CAPSTRANS), University of Wollongong, Australia. Her research focuses on the intersections of involuntary mobility and various development narratives, the impact of neoliberal reforms, ethnographic method, and gender relations in Asia. She is currently completing an Australian Research Council Discovery Project, entitled "Contingent Development: The Regional Impacts of Neoliberal Globalisation in India."

Jordi Feu Gelis, sociologist, is a professor in the Department of Pedagogy at the University of Girona. He has focused his research on rural education; poverty, marginalization and social exclusion; social structure and inequality; and identity and immigration. He is currently researching democracy and participation in education. He has taught sociology and social inequality at several Latin American universities. He is a founding member of the Observatory of Rural Education of Catalonia and head of the "Cabinet for Social Mentoring" of the University of Girona, where he conducts research on the social and cultural inclusion of students of foreign origin.

Ines Hasselberg is a postdoctoral research fellow at the Centre for Research in Anthropology. After completing her PhD in anthropology (University of Sussex, 2013) she held a postdoctoral position at the Centre for Criminology, University of Oxford. She has conducted extensive research on punishment, border control, and family life. Her work is published in international peer-reviewed journals such as *Punishment and Society, Criminology and Criminal Justice, JEMS* and *Anthropology Today*. She is the author of *Enduring Uncertainty: Deportation, Punishment and Everyday Life* (Berghahn, 2016) and together with Heike Drotbohm coeditor of *Deportation, Anxiety, Justice: New Ethnographic Perspectives* (Routledge, 2017).

Dirk Hoerder has taught global history of migrations at Arizona State University and at the University of Bremen, as well as at York University, Toronto; Duke University; University of Toronto; and Université de Paris 8-Saint Denis. His publications include *Creating Societies: Immigrant Lives in Canada* (McGill-Queen's University Press, 1999); *Cultures in Contact: World Migrations in the Second Millennium*, winner of the 2003 Sharlin Prize (Duke University Press, 2002); *The Historical Practice of Diversity* (Bergahn, 2003); *What is Migration History?* (Polity, 2009), with Christiane Harzig and Donna Gabaccia; *Connecting Seas and Connected Ocean Rims* (Brill, 2011), co-editor with Donna Gabaccia; and *Towards a Global History of Domestic and Caregiving Workers* (Brill, 2015), with Elise van Nederveen Meerkerk and Silke Neunsinger.

Zeynep Kivilcim is an associate professor of public international law. She received her PhD from University Paris II (Panthéon-Assas). She has taught law and gender; international human rights law; and critical approaches to public international law, gender, and refugee rights at Istanbul University, Gottingen University, and Humboldt University. Her research was recently published in *Feminist Legal Studies* in 2016, and the edited volumes *A Gendered Approach to the Syrian Refugee Crisis* (Routledge, 2017); and *The Politics of Legality in a Neoliberal Age* (Routledge, 2018).

Silja Klepp is a professor of geography at Kiel University. She is a trained social anthropologist. In her current research on climate change migration and adaptation, she integrates postcolonial perspectives and critical theories in the study of the effects of climate change. Silja's field research experience includes countries such as Kiribati, Vanuatu, New Zealand, Italy, Libya, Malta, and Zambia. In 2012, she won the Christiane Rajewsky Award of the German Association for Peace and Conflict Studies for her PhD on refugees and border control in the Mediterranean Sea. Fields of research include migration and refugees, political ecology of climate change, legal anthropology, borders, and STS.

Yingtong Lai is a PhD candidate in the Department of Sociology at the Chinese University of Hong Kong. Her primary areas of research are urban sociology, migration and immigration, and identity and ethnicity. She works on topics of foreign domestic helpers' adaptation with a particular emphasis on their subjective social positions perceived through interaction with the host society.

Rachel A. Lewis earned a PhD from Cornell University and is an associate professor in the Women and Gender Studies Program at George Mason University. Her research and teaching interests include transnational feminisms, queer theory, media and cultural studies, sexuality, race and immigration, human rights, transnational sexualities, and feminist and queer disability studies. Her book projects include *Deportable Subjects: Lesbians and the Political Asylum Process*, which integrates visual and textual criticism with analyses of legal discourses, and *Queer Intimacies: Visualizing Black Lesbian Desire in Post-Apartheid South Africa*, which focuses on media and cultural advocacy produced by lesbian, intersex, and transgender human rights activists in South Africa.

Aijia Li is an MPhil student in the Department of Sociology at the Chinese University of Hong Kong. Her research interest focuses on new immigrants' destinations in the Global South and migrant workers in Asia. Recently she has been working on a project about the health of domestic helpers in Hong Kong.

John Lie teaches social theory at the University of California Berkeley. His most recent book is *The Dream of East Asia* (Association for Asian Studies, 2018).

Domenico Maddaloni is currently an associate professor of sociology at the University of Salerno, Department of Political, Social, and Communication Sciences and head of the Sociology Research Unit of the Athens Institute for Education and Research (ATINER, Athens). He is also a fellow of the Instituto di Ricerche sulla Popolazione e le Politiche Sociali [Italian National Research Council], Rome. He works mainly on social change, migration, welfare, and local development.

Celia McMichael is a senior lecturer in the School of Geography at The University of Melbourne, Australia. She has a background in health social sciences and international development. Celia has conducted applied work in the area of migration and health; this includes work with WHO focused on infectious disease prevention among returning refugees in Angola, and with UNFPA addressing displacement and population health in Sri Lanka following the 2004 tsunami. Her academic research focuses on refugee resettlement in Australia and, more recently, environmental change and planned relocation in Fiji.

Karen E. McNamara is a senior lecturer in the School of Earth and Environmental Sciences, at The University of Queensland, Australia. Karen has qualifications in both environmental science and human geography. Prior to working at UQ, Karen worked at various universities and government offices in Australia and the Pacific region, and she has consulted for UNESCO and UNDP. Karen's research focuses on livelihood vulnerability and sustainability more broadly, and human adaptation to climate change impacts, the sociocultural implications of environmental change, and environmental migration more specifically.

Claudio Minca is a professor and Head of the Department of Geography and Planning at Macquarie University in Sydney, Australia. His current research focuses on three major themes: the spatialization of (bio)politics; tourism and travel theories of modernity; and the relationship between modern knowledge, space, and landscape in postcolonial geography. His most recent books are *On Schmitt and Space* (Routledge, 2015, with R. Rowan); *Hitler's Geographies* (University of Chicago Press, 2016, with P. Giaccaria); *Moroccan Dreams* (I. B. Tauris, 2016, with L. Wagner); and *After Heritage* (Edward Elgar, 2018, with H. Muzaini).

Grazia Moffa is currently an assistant professor of economic sociology at the University of Salerno, Department of Political, Social and Communication Sciences. She is also the director of the recently established UniSa Migration research laboratory. She mainly works on local development, labor market, and migration issues from a gender perspective.

Richard C. M. Mole is a senior lecturer in political sociology and Deputy Director of the School of Slavonic and East European Studies at University College London. He received his PhD in international relations from the London School of Economics in 2003 and was an Andrew W. Mellon Post-Doctoral Research Fellow at UCL from 2003–2005. His research focuses on the relationship between identity and power, with particular reference to nationalism, sexualities, migration, diaspora, and asylum.

Maria Cristina Morales is an associate professor of sociology at the University of Texas at El Paso. Dr. Morales' interests are in Latina/o sociology, international migration, and social inequality, particularly focusing on labor, immigration, and the U.S.-Mexico border. She coauthored the book *Latinos in the United States: Diversity and Change* (Malden, 2015) with Dr. Rogelio Saenz. Dr. Morales' recent research is focusing on immigration and policing.

Stephanie J. Nawyn is the co-director for academic programs at the Center for Gender in Global Context (GenCen) and an associate professor in the Department of Sociology with expertise in gender and migration. Her work has primarily focused on refugee resettlement and protection, as well as the economic advancement of African voluntary migrants in the United States. She was a Fulbright Fellow at Istanbul University for the 2013–2014 academic year, studying the treatment of Syrian refugees in Turkey. Her most recent work appears in *Journal of Refugee Studies* and *Journal of Ethnic and Racial Studies.*

Ayokunle Olumuyiwa Omobowale holds a PhD in sociology. He is a lecturer in sociology at the University of Ibadan, Ibadan. He has won the University of Ibadan Postgraduate School Award for scholarly publication, 2007; IFRA (French Institute for Research in Africa) Research Fellowship, 2009; American Council of Learned Societies-African Humanities Programme Post-Doctoral Fellowship, 2010; and African Studies Association (USA) Presidential Award, 2014. He was also a Visiting Scholar at the Centre for African Studies, Rutgers University, New Jersey, USA in November 2014. He is the author of *The Tokunbo Phenomenon and the Second-hand Economy in Nigeria* (Peter Lang, 2013).

Mofeyisara Oluwatoyin Omobowale holds a PhD in anthropology. Her doctoral research was on space, sexuality, and power at Bodija Market, Ibadan, Nigeria. She was a recipient of the American Council of Learned Societies-African Humanities Program (ACLS-AHP) Doctoral Fellowship, 2012; the Cadbury Fellowship (Department of Anthropology and African Studies, Birmingham University), 2014; and ACLS-AHP Post-Doctoral Fellowship, 2016. Her interests lie in medical anthropology; cultural studies; sexuality issues; and maternal, child, and adolescent studies. She is a research fellow and lecturer at the Institute of Child Health, College of Medicine, University of Ibadan, Nigeria.

William Outhwaite, FAcSS, taught at the universities of Sussex and Newcastle, where he is an emeritus professor of sociology. His interests include the philosophy of social science, social theory, political sociology, sociology of knowledge, and contemporary

Europe. He is the author of *Understanding Social Life: The Method Called Verstehen* (Allen and Unwin, 1975, 2nd edition 1986); *Concept Formation in Social Science* (Routledge, 1983); *New Philosophies of Social Science: Realism, Hermeneutics and Critical Theory* (Macmillan, 1987); *Habermas* (Polity, 1994); *The Future of Society* (Malden, 2006); *European Society* (Wiley, *2008); Critical Theory and Contemporary Europe* (Continuum, 2012); *Social Theory* (Profile, 2015); *Europe Since 1989: Transitions and Transformations* (Routledge, 2016);*Contemporary Europe* (Routledge, 2017); and, with Larry Ray, *Social Theory and Postcommunism* (Malden, 2005).

María Dolores París Pombo is a full-time researcher at the Colegio de la Frontera Norte (or COLEF), in Tijuana, Mexico. She is editor of *Migrantes, desplazados, braceros y deportados: Experiencias migratorias y prácticas políticas* (El Colegio de la Frontera Norte, 2012) and author of Violencias y migraciones centroamericanas en México (El Colegio de la Frontera Norte, 2017). Dr. París Pombo has also been featured in several migration-themed publications, including the *Journal of Borderland Studies, Migrations Société, Latin American Perspectives*, and *Migraciones Internacionales*.

Òscar Prieto-Flores is an associate professor of Sociology at the University of Girona, Spain. His work on Romani and immigrant integration has been published in relevant journals of ethnic and migration studies. He has been visiting scholar at the Center for Comparative Studies in Race and Ethnicity at Stanford University and at the Center for Migration and Development at Princeton. He is leading a research project on undocumented youth and coming of age in Spain focusing on the transition into adulthood of two subgroups that lost their legal status once they turned eighteen.

S. Irudaya Rajan is a professor at the Centre for Development Studies (CDS), Thiruvananthapuram, Kerala, India. He has coordinated seven large-scale migration surveys in Kerala since 1998 (with Professor K. C. Zachariah) including the Goa Migration Survey 2008 and the Tamil Nadu Migration Survey 2015. He was instrumental in conducting the Punjab Migration Survey 2009 and Gujarat Migration Survey 2011. He has published extensively in national and international journals on social, economic, demographic, and political implications of international migration. He is the editor of the *Annual Series India Migration Report* and also editor-in-chief of *Migration and Development* (Taylor and Francis).

Prem Kumar Rajaram is an associate professor in the Department of Sociology and Social Anthropology at Central European University, Budapest. He is the Head of the CEU Open Learning Initiative which offers educational programs for refugees and asylum-seekers. He is the author of *Ruling the Margins: Colonial Power and Administrative Rule in the Past and Present* (Routledge, 2016) and the co-editor (with Carl Grundy-Warr) of *Borderscapes: Hidden Geographies and Politics at Territory's Edge* (University of Minnesota Press, 2008). His research focuses on the common marginalizations of refugees and other subaltern groups particularly in relation to capitalism and the state, and on colonial histories of labor and capitalism. He holds a PhD in International Relations from the London School of Economics.

Smriti Rao is an associate professor in economics and global studies at Assumption College and resident scholar in the Women's Studies Research Center at Brandeis University.

Eric Richards is an emeritus professor of history at Flinders University in Adelaide, and was Carnegie Trust Centenary Professor in Scotland in 2014. His publications include: *Britannia's Children. Emigration from England, Scotland, Wales, and Ireland since 1600* (Bloomsbury, 2012); *Destination Australia: Migration to Australia since 1900* (Manchester University Press, 2008); *The Highland Clearances; People, Landlords and Rural Turmoil* (Edinburgh, Birlinn, 2016); and *The Genesis of International Migration: the British Case 1750–1900* (Manchester University Press, 2018).

Isabelle Rigoni is an associate professor in sociology. She teaches at INS HEA (Suresnes, France) and is currently hosted as a research fellow at the CNRS-Centre Emile Durkheim in Bordeaux. She has received training in politics, law, sociology, and anthropology. During the 2000s, she spent several years in Britain and Germany and won European grants for developing research projects on media and migration. She is currently working on ethnic and cultural diversity in schooling and has contributed to developing collaborative and participative research methods for working with children and young migrants, including visual methods.

Alex Sager is an associate professor and Chair of the Department of Philosophy at Portland State University. He has published widely on the ethics of migration. Recent publications include the monograph *Toward a Cosmopolitan Ethics of Mobility: The Migrant's-Eye View of the World* (Palgrave, 2017) and an edited collection *The Ethics and Politics of Immigration* (Rowman and Littlefield, 2016). He is currently writing a book defending open borders.

Danica Šantić is an assistant professor of geography at the University of Belgrade, Serbia. Her main fields of research are migration and population geography. She is presently involved in several international projects focused on migration in Europe.

Cenk Saraçoğlu is a faculty member in the Faculty of Communication at Ankara University, Turkey. He received his undergraduate diploma from the Bilkent University International Relations Department and earned his MA and PhD degree in sociology from the University of Western Ontario, Canada in 2008. He is interested in migration, nationalism, urban transformation and ethnic relations with a particular focus on Turkey. He is the author of *Kurds of Modern Turkey: Migration, Neoliberalism and Exclusion* (I.B Tauris, 2008) and has published several articles on Turkish society and politics in scholarly journals.

Caress Schenk is an associate professor of political science at Nazarbayev University, Kazakhstan, with teaching and research specialties related to comparative politics, national identity, immigration control, and Eurasian politics. She is a member of the PONARS network and has received research funding from the American Councils for

International Education, the Fulbright Scholar Program, and Nazarbayev University. Her work has been published in *Demokratizatisya*, *Europe-Asia Studies*, and *Nationalities Papers*. Her recent book is entitled *Why Control Immigration? Strategic Uses of Migration Management in Russia* (University of Toronto Press, 2018).

Marlou Schrover is a professor of migration history, and she holds the Chair of Economic and Social History at Leiden University. She is Editor-in-Chief of the *Journal of Migration History*.

Laura Jeanne Sims earned her PhD in History at the University of North Carolina at Chapel Hill. Her research interests include French colonial and postcolonial history, women's and gender history, and museum and migration studies. She has published articles on Harki and Pied-Noir collective memory practices in edited volumes and the peer-reviewed journal *French Politics, Culture & Society*. Laura has taught at several French universities, including the Université de Picardie Jules Verne and the Université du Littoral Côte d'Opale, and currently teaches European History at the American University of Paris.

Ninna Nyberg Sørensen holds a PhD in social anthropology and is a senior researcher at the Danish Institute for International Studies. She has worked on transnational migration issues for most of her career and published widely on migration, development, conflict, and gender, for example *Work and Migration* (Routledge, 2002); *The Migration-Development Nexus* (Oxford Blackwell, 2003); *Living Across Worlds* (Geneva, IOM, 2007); and *The Migration Industry and the Commercialization of International Migration* (Routledge, 2013). Her recent work explores undocumented migration of Central Americans and Dominicans, including the effects of deportation on local communities. She is also involved in policy analysis of the European "migration crisis."

Claudia Tazreiter is an associate professor of sociology at the University of New South Wales, Sydney. Her research focuses on the social and affective impacts of forced and irregular migration, human rights culture, the role of civil society in social change, and gender. She coauthored *Fluid Security in the Asia Pacific: Transnational Lives and State Control* (Palgrave McMillan, 2016). She is Managing Editor of *The Australian Journal of Human Rights*, an associate of the Australian Human Rights Centre, and serves on the management committee of the Gilbert and Tobin Centre for Public Law and the steering committee of the Kaldor Centre for International Refugee Law. She is the convenor of the multidisciplinary Forced Migration Research Network.

Inga K. Thiemann is a lecturer in law at the University of Exeter, UK. Prior to joining Exeter Law School, she was a visiting research fellow at the University of Bristol Law School and a research fellow at St Mary's University's Centre for the Study of Modern Slavery. Her current research focuses on policy and legislation and precarious labor and human trafficking, particularly in the context of sex work and other feminized work sectors. Her wider research interests are in feminist labor law, antidiscrimination law, women's labor migration, rights-based responses to sex work, and the work-life balances of women workers.

Dragan Umek is an assistant professor of geography at the University of Trieste. His research interest focuses on historical cartography and human and cultural geography with a particular focus on the Balkans. He has extensively investigated the "return and relocation" of refugees in former Yugoslavia and, more recently, the migration flows along the "Balkan Route" and the widespread hospitality for asylum-seekers and refugees in Italy.

Vamsi Vakulabharanam is an associate professor of economics at the University of Massachusetts, Amherst. He is also Director of the Asian Political Economy Program at the Political Economy Research Institute of the University of Massachusetts, Amherst.

Marko Valenta is a sociologist and professor at the Norwegian University of Science and Technology (NTNU) in Trondheim, Norway. He received his PhD in sociology at the Norwegian University of Science and Technology. His research interests include ethnic relations, welfare/public policy, and international migrations and migration policies in West-Balkan countries, Scandinavian countries, and the Middle East. He has published articles in leading journals such as *The Journal of Refugee Studies, The Journal of Ethnic and Migration Studies*, and *Ethnicities*. His most recent book (co-edited with Sabrina Ramet) is *Ethnic Minorities and Politics in Southeastern Europe* (Cambridge University Press, 2016).

Floris Vermeulen is an associate professor in the Department of Political Science at the University of Amsterdam. He has been Co-Director of the Institute for Migration and Ethnic Studies (IMES). His research focuses on the civic and political participation of immigrants at the local level and local integration policies and their effects on different domains. His work is published in different international volumes and journals such as *European Union Politics, Journal of Ethnic and Migration Studies, Nonprofit and Voluntary Sector Quarterly, Urban Studies, West European Politics, British Journal of Sociology, Political Psychology*, and *Terrorism and Political Violence.*

Martha Luz Rojas Wiesner holds a PhD in social science with a specialization in sociology from El Colegio de México. She is Senior Researcher in the Department of Society and Culture of El Colegio de la Frontera Sur in San Cristobal de Las Casas, Chiapas, Mexico. She conducts studies on Central American migration and women's migration in particular on the southern border of Mexico, around issues related to social vulnerability, precariousness, and migration, as well as the inclusion and exclusion of migrants.

Ailsa Winton holds a PhD in geography from Queen Mary, University of London; she is currently Senior Researcher in the Department of Society and Culture in El Colegio de la Frontera Sur in Tapachula, Chiapas, and part of the Migration and Border Studies group. Her research interests relate broadly to the critical geographies of marginality and violence. Recently her work has focused specifically on the dynamics and lived repercussions of violence-based displacement in northern Central America and southern Mexico, including research on LGBTQ mobility.

Caroline Zickgraf is Deputy Director of the Hugo Observatory—the world's first scientific research center dedicated to the links between environment, migration, and politics—and is an FNRS postdoctoral fellow in the Department of Geography at the University of Liège. She specializes in African environmental migration, with a particular focus on immobility and transnationalism in areas affected by climate change and other forms of environmental degradation. She currently leads the IMMOBILE project, funded by the Belgian National Scientific Fund (FNRS), in which she has conducted case studies in two African countries, Senegal and Comoros, as well as the Mekong Delta of Viet Nam.

Drago Župarić-Iljić is a sociologist and, currently, a research associate at the Institute for Migration and Ethnic Studies. He also teaches in the Faculty of Humanities and Social Sciences at the University of Zagreb, Croatia. His research within the interdisciplinary fields of forced migration, asylum, ethnicity, and environmental studies focuses on various structural causes and drivers of migration, mobility, and postmigration phenomena, with a special concern for Central and Southeast Europe. He edited the first anthology that analyzed development of asylum protection systems in Croatia and the West Balkan region.

Acknowledgments

We want to thank all the contributors to this volume for their wonderful work, patience, punctuality, and overall enthusiasm for The Handbook. University of Kansas Sociology doctoral student Erin Adamson provided top- notch assistance to the logistics and organization of this project.

Menjívar would like to recognize the institutional support she received at the University of Kansas, where this project was carried out, in particular, resources made available through her Foundation Distinguished Professorship. In addition, as Menjívar is an Andrew Carnegie Fellow, this publication was made possible (in part) by a grant from Carnegie Corporation of New York. The statements made and views expressed are solely the responsibility of the authors and contributors.

We are grateful to Toby Wahl's longstanding support and advice in developing and shepherding *The Oxford Handbook of Migration Crises* through to publication.

The editors would like to pay tribute to Eric Richards, an outstanding historian of migration and contributor to this volume, who passed away in September 2018. His work has been a source of inspiration to generations of migration historians and a remarkable contribution to our understanding of migration processes. His legacy will stand the test of time.

MIGRATION CRISES

Definitions, Critiques, and Global Contexts

CECILIA MENJÍVAR, MARIE RUIZ, AND IMMANUEL NESS

Over time, demographic, economic, religious or political developments, as well as wars and conflicts, have resulted in massive human displacements and have triggered major diasporic movements which have disrupted and reconstituted the social fabric of the sending countries. In such contexts, an upsurge in migration often is both a result of and initiator of crises. *The Oxford Handbook of Migration Crises* focuses on this dual nature of migration crises and proposes to clarify the conceptual links between migration and crisis. The volume examines migratory flows in contexts of crisis in general, but also migrations initiating crises or situations that are constructed as crises. It interrogates why and how some migratory flows are constructed as creating crises (e.g., Central American women or children or both migrating to the United States in recent years) but others are not (e.g., Cubans, migrating in the same numbers as Central Americans). The media and public officials play a major role in framing migratory flows as crises; hence our objective is to deconstruct and question such representations, which offers the opportunity to revisit and redefine, through a critical lens, what is commonly understood as a "migration crisis." From this vantage point, this volume critically examines what is a migration crisis and how this definition is used in the field of migration research and in policy responses. Contributors to this volume also debunk expectations about where crises originate and whom they affect. For instance, in the case of deportation crises, it is the receiving states that create crises, not the migrants seeking to enter nor the sending states.

An emphasis on the contexts, and not individual actors, that generate crises aligns with critical perspectives in research on migration flows. As such, this volume brings together an examination of the contexts of crises within which migratory flows arise, but also how some flows are framed as crises and others are not. Importantly, the *Handbook* seeks to go beyond the common conceptual association between migratory crises and refugee flows, since there are many complex migration situations around the world that are not formally defined as refugee flows, but that take place in the context of crises or give rise to crises. Including refugee flows but also going beyond the commonly understood link between crises and refugee flows, the *Handbook*'s goal is to unveil the significance of migration crises in the context of social change and thus to amplify the analytic lens to examine human migrations in today's rapidly changing political economic, social, and environmental terrain. In this, we follow FitzGerald and Arar's (2018) recent call to question taken-for-granted assumptions about the separation of refugee flows from regular migratory flows. As these authors correctly note, theorizing in the sociology of migration, particularly in the key areas of assimilation and citizenship, can benefit significantly from closer engagement with studies of refugee flows.

Recent research has tended to construe migration crises as reflecting permanent aspects of modernity. This handbook revisits the notion of crisis through the prism of the context in which permanent and nonpermanent migration flows occur. We posit that the term "crisis," is overused in today's society, and its meaning is somehow diffused: are today's crises becoming the "new norm"? How are crises defined, especially at the receiving end? Hence, today's "new norm" may render almost inadequate the use of the term "crisis" to describe migratory flows that new—more permanent—conditions are generating. Therefore, both notions of crisis and transformation are combined in order to take a critical look at what constitutes migration crises and who and what defines them, beyond those that are formally recognized as refugee flows. If crises around the world today appear to be the "new norm," then they need to be examined as a whole to identify what makes them a crisis—and what makes them not a crisis. On this basis, the *Handbook* reexamines the idea of migration crisis based on a wide range of case studies. The purpose of this volume therefore is to identify the contexts in which crises and migratory flows are generated, and how they are dealt with and defined at the receiving end, thus revisiting the definition of crisis from a contextual perspective.

The contributors to this volume were charged with conceptualizing and situating contemporary migrations in relation to crises, and critically examining the notion of crisis in the context of long-term, short-term, as well as temporary migration phenomena. The case studies therefore provide answers and definitions to major worldwide, longstanding migration situations, not only the sudden migratory flows that tend to be defined as crises. The *Handbook* endeavors to examine migration crises conceptually and critically and to reveal the epistemological relationship between migration crises and global social transformations. Taken together, the chapters in this volume offer a fundamental understanding of individuals in sending and receiving societies, socioeconomic structures and unequal power relations, and group processes through the prism of migration and crisis.

This handbook adds a key dimension to an examination of migration crises today: the context that generates certain migratory flows and the context where they arrive, making conceptualizations of the context of exit and reception (see Portes and Rumbaut 2006) central throughout the volume. Thus, in this volume, migration crises are examined in the context of structural and social transformations, hence offering a comprehensive analysis of major migration situations. Studying migrants' departures and arrivals, the *Handbook* brings the topics of crisis and migrations to the fore, to grasp the conceptual rationales of mass human displacements, which have left a heavy imprint on societies worldwide, as phenomena with historical and social roots. Taken together, the chapters advance our understandings of migration crises, providing a sociologically grounded conceptualization of migration and crisis. As migration takes center stage in political and economic debates, this handbook examines how the concept of "crisis" bears on these larger questions.

Migration in Modern Historical Context

Far from unprecedented, human mobility has marked world history. An understanding that intensified periods of migration have existed well before the contemporary era can shift the lens and avoid the framing of contemporary migration as crisis. Undeniably, migration has existed since the dawn of time, yet migration flows intensified during specific intervals—for example, the expansion of European colonialism from 1500 to 1900, the emergence and extension of industrial capitalism from 1750 to the present, world wars, decolonization and regional wars, and the neoliberal era of capital mobility and decline of the state, with paradoxically unprecedented restrictions on human mobility through strict border controls. As such, these specific periods have triggered more stringent control on migration when expanded transnational mobility challenged plans to consolidate emerging nation-states, stability, and perceived security privileged populations. In this context, migrants often become easy targets to weakening states and ruthless politicians; identified as "outsiders," as threats, or simply as problematic. Indeed, as McAdam (2014) notes, some states in receiving countries have shifted strategies away from a focus on the vulnerability of certain migrants to narratives that construct these migrants as threats. Migration "crises" are thus born.

How does the natural phenomenon of human migration become an anomaly and a source of concern in the twenty-first century? Many may argue that the increase in migration flows justifies the definition of migration as problematic today (i.e., "crises"). The chapters in this volume examine the conceptual links between migratory flows and crises, as migration often results from, can create, and often is constructed as, a crisis. Contributors interrogate why and how some migratory patterns are defined as crises while others are not. These are the main questions animating this volume. In addressing them, the contributors go beyond common associations between migration and crises as well as between refugee flows and crises, with a critical emphasis on the language used. As McAdam (2014, 43) observes, " . . . we need to be cautious and precise about how we use the concept of 'migration crisis' . . . there is a risk that the language of 'crisis' may serve to pathologize all movement." She goes on, "This sort of characterization is counterproductive, especially in a climate of general hostility toward 'outsiders.'"

In addressing the first set of links, between migration crises and the conditions that produce them, this volume focuses on the social and structural transformations, protracted conflicts and sudden events that may precipitate population mobility, some of them long-standing and structural and some human-made and more immediate. Moreover, contributors do not aim at determining whether the migratory flows examined are "forced" or "voluntary," as arguably there is a measure of individual volition and of coercive force in all migratory movements and therefore it is a difficult issue to settle (see Martin, Weerasinghe, and Taylor 2014; McAdam 2014; Van Hear 2009). Along these lines, the aim in this volume is not to demarcate precise lines between structural versus human-made factors that can generate a particular population movement. In taking a critical approach, the authors in this volume start out from the premise that structural conditions, policy decisions, and immediate stressors are interrelated. Thus extreme poverty and various forms of inequality are often at the root of political conflicts, health epidemics, and the amplified effects that natural disasters can have. Following this approach, and in line with McAdam's (2014) call for amplifying the lens used to examine migration crises to unsettle traditional notions of what constitutes a "crisis," the focus in this volume is on shedding light on *situations* that sometimes reach a "tipping point" and become a "crisis." As Martin, Weerasinghe, and Taylor (2014, 5) observe, "While events and processes may be the trigger or immediate *cause* of a humanitarian crisis, in most cases, underlying structural factors or contemporaneous stressors provide the context in which they occur. Lack of or poor national and local governance and emergency preparedness, high levels of poverty and inequality, human rights violations, insufficient access to basic services, and weakness in local and national capacity combine to precipitate (and at times perpetuate) humanitarian crises." To this we must add the role of military intervention by hegemonic foreign states, often with the support of local and regional proxies.

In addressing the second set of links, between migration crises and their definition as such in receiving countries, this volume makes use of a constructionist approach. The chapters elucidate the symbolic and political power of words and images in transforming migration flows into crises—in particular the popular and political representations of racial and cultural differences are tools in the social construction of migration as crisis.

Conceptual Explanations to Migration as Crisis

A significant body of research has examined the framing of particular situations as crises or disasters (Altheide 2002; Best 2004; Glassner 2010), and the consequences that such framing has for those deemed to be the problem and for the rest of society as well.

Nowhere is perhaps the Thomas theorem more apt than in this scholarship, as definitions of an issue as a problem or as a crisis have real consequences.[1] From this body of work, we know that the media play a critical role in framing certain migratory flows as a crisis or a problem to be addressed (Haynes, Merolla, and Ramakrishnan 2016), with real, even fatal consequences for those affected (Holmes and Castañeda 2016). A prime example is the US president defining the "caravan" of four hundred Central American women and three hundred children traveling through Mexico to seek protection in the United States as dangerous, inciting hysteria and fear in the American public. Detrimental consequences, especially when the framing comes from government officials, also reach the wider society. Beyond media and political figures and policymakers, there are other actors, such as NGOs and nonprofit organizations, that are involved in constructing crisis narratives as well (Schuetze 2015). As Calhoun (2010) observes more generally in reference to crises, they are constructed by a range of actors, including policymakers, the media, and some interest groups. Thus, recurrent anti-immigration popular narratives have led to many recent works on the linguistic construction of migration crises in the press. Esther Greussing and Hajo G. Boomgaarden (2017) demonstrate that media narratives of the refugees generally fall into three categories: passive victims, national threats, or dehumanized anonymous. Representing refugees as victims can have deleterious consequences. Consequently, migrants are viewed in desperate economic need and are often blamed for taking advantage of the receiving country's benefits.

When migratory movements are conceptualized as crises they also acquire a specific temporal dimension, as immediate and largely disconnected from previous events and history, which directly shapes policies to address these crises. Palliative solutions to address an immediate manifestation, and not a root cause, become policy. As Jane McAdam (2014, 30) notes, "'crises' are posited as exceptions, requiring special solutions. From a policy perspective, this risk sidelining *every day* systemic issues such as poverty, vulnerability, and environmental fragility, which are central to how people experience hazards, and overlooking relevant legal frameworks, such as human rights law" (see also Charlesworth 2002). Such framing of a migratory flow as crisis, as an exceptional event, is bound to deprioritize more thorough (and perhaps more complex) and longer-lasting solutions.

Key to this conceptualization of certain migration flows as crises, McAdam (2014, 31) observes, is that the "potency of this *idea* helps both to constitute the emergency and drive responses to it." This is not to say that catastrophic events around the world, such as the effects of climate change and other natural disasters, are not grave or *real*. The point we make here is that when a migratory flow is understood as a crisis, as a one point in time event, certain responses that focus on the immediacy of the event are activated, which can have counterproductive consequences. These responses may disregard deeper and entrenched inequalities based on class, race, gender, religious affiliation, and sexual orientation, among other social cleavages, and may in fact further cement inequitable power relations between those affected, and seen as weak and vulnerable, and those with the "solutions" to their problems (see Farbotko and Lazarus 2012). Such solutions are often based on an "emergency" frame that by definition seeks to alleviate immediate suffering but cannot attend to deeper structural changes that could prevent some of these urgent situations in the first place (see Charlesworth 2002; McAdam 2014).

As the chapters in this volume demonstrate, the framing of a migration flow will elicit certain responses, and a focus on crisis can produce policy initiatives that do more harm than good, disregarding long-standing social conditions in favor of expediency as well as placing too much emphasis on the individuals who move. A framing of crisis, therefore, must be questioned, as it can easily lead to mischaracterizations of the individuals who move as a problem and in these times of anti-immigrant hostility, as "threats" (see also McAdam 2014). This is the case of the US president defining Central American immigrants seeking protection as *threats* to the nation and as invasions that need to be contained, requiring even military solutions. In the same vein, "transit" countries such as Mexico, those in Southeast Europe and North Africa, which often collaborate closely with the larger receiving countries where migrants are headed, adopt the same narratives and strategies and construct mobile populations who pass through as dangers or threats to be contained. The Brexit referendum gained popular support on the basis of defending British nationalism, and especially British identity and sovereignty, which was under threat by foreign workers employed in low-waged jobs in agriculture and personal services. The supposed national security threat of refugees from South and Southeast Asia and the Pacific arriving in boats to the shores of Australia has buttressed a deportation policy that detains refugees in foreign countries in the region. To legitimate the attack against newcomers therefore, "threats" are constructed in particular temporal and geographic contexts.

Noteworthily, not all migrants are seen as problematic to destination regions; so, who are the migrants targeted by anti-migration discourses and more likely to be framed as problematic or as a crisis? To address this question, we need to examine how race, ethnicity, and regional origin are used to construct national identity, as an integral aspect of constructing a migratory flow as a crisis is the *othering* and boundary drawing of the particular group.

Kristin Surak argues that intolerance toward immigrants shifts depending on the receiving nation's perception of which migrants are desirable and which are not. In turn, new groups are identified as non-welcome. For instance, migrant workers may be conveniently welcome in times of economic growth when a nation's production requires additional labor that is also expected to show rapid adaptation to the nation to blend in and erase signs of otherness (Surak 2013).

Urban Migration

Another type of migration "crisis" concerns rural to urban migration, but in this case, the crisis is especially material, tangible, and *real* for those on the move. The dominant movement of the twentieth century is urbanization, triggered by the application of Newtonian physics to the production of agriculture as commodities and the forced relocation from rural to urban regions as rural regions which supported peasants for thousands of years are commodified. New urban dwellers are integral to urban industrial economies in industrializing countries and this low-cost reserve army of labor is the major factor in foreign direct investments (FDI) to the Global South. The very real economic crisis in the countryside has expanded since the end of the Second World War and the rise of nation-states in the former imperial economies in Asia and Africa (Ness 2015). In Latin America, neoliberal commodification and regional integration has accelerated internal migration among populations unable to survive in poor regions, pushing labor migration to urban centers where the only employment is precarious and highly dependent on foreign markets (Delgado Wise 2013). Moreover, the demands that urban dwellers have placed on basic human needs as food, water, housing, healthcare, education, and beyond have given rise to a material crisis in major urban areas which have expanded from the 1970s to the present. This has resulted in the growth of what Mike Davis calls a "Planet of Slums" as the vast majority of inhabitants in South and Southeast Asia, Africa, and Latin America have moved to rundown squatter settlements with makeshift shelters and unsanitary conditions which ring cities of tens of million dwellers: Karachi, Kolkata, Mumbai, New Delhi, and Jakarta in Asia; Cairo and Lagos in Africa; and Buenos Aires, Lima, Mexico City, Rio de Janeiro, and Sao Paulo in Latin America (Davis 2004, 26).

The new urban poor form part of a global labor force within contemporary capitalism and are responsible for producing consumer products in the Global North, forming profound imbalances and discrepancies in life chances between developing and advanced capitalist regions, where nation-states unable to provide for the basic needs of their populations are required to establish robust and repressive and violent border control agents to prevent migration to the North (Sørensen 2012). Thus, a *real* humanitarian and ecological crisis is taking root in the Global South which is produced in the South by the beneficiaries in Europe and North America where state and public antagonism is most strident.

Nation State, Migration, and Poverty

The construction of xenophobic narratives about immigrants goes hand in hand with questions of assimilation and cultural and ethnic identity, as well as challenges to national unity and national identity. The nation-state ideologies, grounded on ethnic and cultural homogeneity, contradict the historical and contemporary record of migration as a natural human phenomenon and instead posit migration as unnatural and disruptive—a danger to national homogeneity. Indeed, the latter perspective is often a direct result of interventions and foreign meddling by the US and NATO military alliances, which disrupt the lives of residents in North Africa, the Middle East, and Latin America. In the 2010s, public support for nationalistic far-right political parties has grown substantially in destination and transit states of

Europe, North America, and Oceania. Ironically, sentiment in favor of immigrant exclusion has occurred in countries that have higher levels of racial and ethnic homogeneity and are far less diverse. In former European Union countries of Eastern and central Europe—Poland, Hungary, and beyond—liberal, center, and right political parties articulating the most extreme xenophobic positions have gained electoral support through framing of migrants as a threat to a fictitious national identity and unity. This pattern has expanded in the core of Western Europe: Germany, France, Italy, Austria, and Holland. What Leo Lucassen calls "the exclusionary power of the nation-state" is a sense of rooted populations and stable economies, demographics, and culture (Lucassen 2005). This leads to defining migration as crisis. Indeed, official discourses on stability are based on the fear of disruption of ideal national models; "crises" then become catch-all frames to define such disruptions and are often attributed to migrants, who are then seen as threats to idealized national uniformity. Therefore, discourses on migration "crises" often target the migrants themselves as agents of disruption of national ideals and national projects of ethnic and cultural homogenization.

Nation-state ideologies have paved the way for the development of extreme right-wing parties' popularity and xenophobic and anti-immigration political forces worldwide. These political actors officially frame migration as crises by resorting to populist discourses grounded on nations' fears of invasion and disruption of identities. They are echoed in the press and official discourses that resort to the use of cherry-picked statistics to increase global popular fear of otherness, and ultimately of migration itself.

Migration and Crisis, Part Outlines

I. Historical Contexts

Part I examines migratory patterns in different historical periods from antiquity to the present and demonstrates how the conceptual link between migrations and crises is deployed in research, as often migration crises are researched without questioning what constitutes a crisis, whether a particular migratory flow is indeed connected to a crisis, or what the consequences of taking migration crises at face value may be (see for instance, Weiner 1995). The chapters in Part I examine the policy consequences in receiving countries when migratory flows are characterized as crises. A major difference between migration trends in the early twentieth century and today concerns growing global inequality and wage gaps between Northern and Southern countries. From the late nineteenth century to the present, migration restrictions have been set up to limit migration from poorest to richest countries. Stricter restrictions were enforced in Europe between 1880 and 1914; Canada limited Chinese migration in 1901; and Australia raised landing taxes for blacks, Chinese, and southern Europeans. The United

States restricted the immigration of the Chinese in 1882. From the 1970s to 2006, a total of 41 anti-immigration laws were enacted in sending and destination countries to restrict population movement (Gozzini 2006). Thus, while migration is a natural trend resulting from human and natural factors, over the past 150 years states have consistently sought to restrict passage and settlement.

In the framing chapter of Part I, Dirk Hoerder's sweeping examination of the relationship between natural and human crises through the lens of the *longue-durée* demonstrates the significance of disruption through historiographic perspectives which reveal hegemonic discourses established by master narrators that denote migrations as either crises or beneficial to receiving societies. Eric Richards then examines migration in Victorian Britain, which, while mostly voluntary, contributed to forced instances of migration, especially under the extreme conditions of the Irish Famine of the 1840s that exposed the rifts in Victorian society. In the next chapter, Laura Jeanne Sims focuses on postcolonial France's disparate treatment of Harkis compared to to Pied-Noirs descendants of European settlers following the Algerian War of Independence. Shifting to Southeast Asia, Ulbe Bosma explores the disparate treatment of refugees in the wake of the First World War. In contrast to European refugees, those displaced in Southeast Asia were ignored or neglected until the end of the 1990s.

II. Constructions of Crises

In Part II we move from the historical legacy to the contemporary construction of crises by European and North American political actors, demonstrating a shared propensity to manipulate public opinion for political gain, even at the risk of tangibly constructing political-economic crises. In the first chapter, William Outhwaite chronicles the exploitation of migration leading up to Britain's popular referendum to withdraw from the EU in 2016. In the next chapter, Xavier Casademont Falguera, Òscar Prieto-Flores, and Jordi Feu Gelis assess the differential treatment of refugees and Romani immigrant populations in Barcelona. While welcoming refugees, the government encouraged the deportation of Roma people. Isabelle Rigoni then shows us how French authorities have manipulated public unease following terrorist attacks to identify migrants as the enemy and galvanize support for punitive national security laws that severely erode migrant rights and undermine diversity and the idea of universality. Shifting to North America, Maria Cristina Morales provides a historical overview of the public and political discourse that has shaped violence and insecurity for migrant populations on the United States border with Mexico. Paradoxically, border security policies that intensify migrant deaths in the region are utilized to justify extension of exclusionary immigration policies. As Stephanie J. Nawyn demonstrates in the next chapter, drawing on the case of Central American refugees to the United States in the 2010s, the very identification of migration as crisis by those sympathetic to the plight of refugees more often stimulates negative responses than a willingness to protect and assist asylum seekers. Then Céline Cantat and Prem Kumar Rajaram propose an examination of the representation of refugees escaping wars who are only passing through Hungary as a refugee crisis, and demonstrate how state officials use human misery and the deprivation of migrants to marginalize Roma and *other* vulnerable populations. Part II concludes with John Lie's demonstration that migration crises do not affect East Asia as much as Western countries. Drawing on the distinction between the West and East Asia, he unveils the construction of migration crises through the prism of Western ethnocentrism, nation-state ideologies, and the rise of populism. Yet he also shows how populism is on the rise in East Asia, though still far from reaching the levels of Western populist surges. While Lie demonstrates how East Asia seems exempt from migration crisis, he also highlights the rise of anti-immigration rhetoric "in the name of patriotism and the nation."

III. Contexts of Protracted Conflicts: Producing Crises

Part III shifts to the significance of the adverse conditions in countries of origin, frequently fueled by economic, political, and military policies and engagements of destination countries as factors in producing crises. Migration scholars must be apprised of conditions in countries of origin to understand holistically the circumstances which generate mobility. The unambiguous pattern which emerges is that policies of Global North countries produce the conditions for population displacement and mobility. Part III begins with an exposé by Leisy J. Abrego of how US foreign policy fosters conditions of violence and abject poverty in Central America. She argues that US governments aid and abet policies that drive migrant populations from their homelands in Central America to the US border. In turn, upon arrival, these same refugees are detained and expelled by US government authorities. John R. Campbell then analyzes the duplicity of European Union policies. While labeling migration to Europe as a "crisis" the EU misrepresents and misunderstands the factors responsible for large-scale migration in the Horn of Africa, and thus the highly flawed and impracticable EU proposals for border management policies in northeast Africa. Returning to Central America, Martha Luz Rojas Wiesner and Ailsa Winton examine the systemic and permanent crisis among migrants displaced from their homelands, now struggling through precarious existences in a continuous state of uncertainty. In the next chapter on protracted crises in communities of origin, Smriti Rao and Vamsi Vakulabharanam examine urbanization in India, which, along with China, has the world's largest population. Under economic liberalization programs initiated in the early 1990s, urban migration has grown in scale and nature, and is often marked by temporary and circular employment migration, largely owing to the crises emerging from a decisive shift from feudal to capitalist accumulation in rural India. Drawing on the Turkish example of treatment of Syrian refugees, the final chapter of Part III by Danièle Bélanger and Cenk Saraçoğlu questions the use of the term "crisis" in migration situations and argues that structural forces are the creators of migration crises. As such, Syrians forced to migrate continue to be reduced to precariousness and vulnerability in the receiving country (i.e., Turkey in this chapter), a development fueled by rising xenophobic sentiment in Turkish cities.

IV. Climate and Environment

Part IV examines migration as a corollary to changes in climate and environment that are a consequence of global capitalist market pressures to ensure commodities for large markets in economically advanced regions of the world. The first victims of the abrupt and severe climactic shifts are inhabitants in the Global South, as Celia McMichael, Carol Farbotko, and Karen E. McNamara observe in their chapter on the Pacific region. They examine how inhabitants of Pacific island countries are forced to develop response mechanisms to environmental crisis through "migration as climate change adaptation." In the next chapter, Ayokunle Olumuyiwa Omobowale, Olayinka Akanle, Olugbenga Samuel Falase, and Mofeyisara Oluwatoyin Omobowale examine environmental crisis as a force in stimulating transnational migration for the privileged few who have the economic resources to escape to prosperous regions in the global North. Christiane Fröhlich and Silja Klepp investigate the effects of climate change on the migration crises in Oceania and the Pacific region, focusing on the barriers established to prevent entry to secure regions. More and more, the authors assert, states in Oceania resort to border securitization to prevent human mobility for populations displaced through climate change. Part IV concludes with an examination of the relationship between climate change and migration in Africa, by Caroline Zickgraf. The chapter enriches linear perspectives on climate change and migration through examining the multidimensional relationship between human mobility and climate change in Africa social, political, economic, and environmental forces interact with climatic change to intensify vulnerability and migration.

V. Migration Corridors and Transit Countries

The focal point of Part V is the significance of migration corridors and the importance of transit country policy choices in aggravating the conditions of vulnerable refugees and displaced populations. Migrants fleeing war and violence, from the Middle East and Central Asia to Central America, must traverse multiple borders to reach places of destination and are made even more vulnerable by the construction of barriers to prevent egress. For political expediency, political authorities in transit countries have emboldened xenophobia through the construction of crisis narratives, in so doing putting migrants at serious risk. In the first chapter, Drago Župarić-Iljić and Marko Valenta write on the Southeast European West-Balkan corridor in 2015–2016. The authors conclude that rather than providing refugees with access to protection and possible integration into local communities, most governments opted to conflate migrants with crisis, leading to the closing of the passageway. Ninna Nyberg Sørensen explores the disappearance of at-risk populations during war as well as post-conflict migration, revealing that migrants and refugees escaping war also go missing as an effect of stricter border enforcement policies and practices. Thus, the chapter unveils the importance of recognizing the consequences of border enforcement policies toward migrants in conjunction with armed conflict, terrorism and natural disasters. Drawing on empirical research and interviews with Afghan communities forced to flee to Pakistan during the protracted conflict, Ruchira Ganguly-Scrase reveals the complex decision-making processes that involuntary migrants undertake. The chapter shows the importance of ethnographic research of migrants' experiences in producing accurate data that challenges artificially constructed negative discursive stereotypes on asylum seekers and refugees. The next chapter, by Zeynep Kivilcim, examines Turkey's political responses to the influx of the highest number of refugees in the world today, exhibiting how crisis paradigms influence legislation on asylum. The chapter shows how European Union agencies seek to frame migration policies in a period of uncertainty and how the Turkish state, in turn, shapes legal responses toward the "refugee crisis" that bears on Europe. The final chapter of Part V by Claudio Minca, Danica Šantić, and Dragan Umek ends on a positive note. The authors examine the response of Serbian authorities to the refugee crisis, validating that transit states can fashion humanitarian policies toward refugees, showing convincingly that the "refugee crisis" places Serbia in a positive light compared to "relatively unconditional humanitarian support that guides its policy towards these families and individuals on the move." As such, Serbian government officials did not manipulate public opinion for political gain but present a new model European geography of humanitarian management for displaced populations.

VI. Policy Responses: Criminalization, Control, and Detention

It is states and political actions that relegate refugees fleeing harm into the source of crisis by developing securitization measures and criminalizing migrants. Thus, the crisis narrative serves to advance policy responses of criminalization, control, and detention. Indeed, if the EU's twenty-seven member states received 942,400 refugee claims in 2015, the twelve EU states had received as many as 696,500 refugee claims in 1992. Therefore, the EU proportionally received many more refugee claims twenty years ago. As Liliana Lyra Jubilut asserts, "Refugees are not the creators of the crisis. They are the victims" (Jubilut 2017). Part VI begins with Idil Atak's examination of how crisis narratives contribute to the criminalization of asylum-seekers in Canada through the outsized role of the Canada Border Services Agency in the refugee system, which erodes the human rights of refugees. Next, María Dolores París Pombo evaluates how political discourse on violence on the US-Mexico border produces social suffering among migrants. Stated as public policies, the declarations of war against drugs, immigration, and terrorism have legitimized violence at the border, carried out by security forces, state institutions, pressure groups, and organized crime. Turning to the Southern Cone, Tanya Basok examines the decree by Argentina's conservative government to characterize immigrants as "menacing foreigners" and criminals. In a country viewed as welcoming toward migrants, Basok shows how the anti-immigrant decree comports with past measures and attitudes under liberal governments. Next, Caroline

Fleay examines Australia's political consensus which categorizes asylum seekers to its shores as constituting a "crisis" of "illegal" people as the basis for punitive government policies and practices which neglect the human rights of asylum-seekers. Then, Caress Schenk examines the formation of Russian migration management through the political frame of a crisis narrative that is institutionalized into law. Pablo S. Bose focuses on the US government's management of Syrian refugees in the 2010s in the comparative and historical context of refugee resettlement policies in the past, revealing how antimigrant rhetoric frames contemporary debates on refugee resettlement policies. In the final chapter on criminalization of migrants, Heike Drotbohm and Ines Hasselberg examine how deportation has emerged as the inevitable response to "migration crises." The authors resort to the political genealogy of the term "crisis", which they view as used as justification of "emergency" policies and the implementation of new measures of control. Deplorably, government crisis narratives are used to justify criminalization and deportation of migrants and their families. Drotbohm and Hasselberg observe that deportation is "a break of a situation considered normal, stable and healthy" constructed through the rhetorical use of crisis.

VII. Media Constructions and Visual Cultures

Part VII examines recurrent popular discourses in the media and visual culture as principal foundations of the contemporary migration crisis narrative that permeates much the world today. Whether perceived as threats or victims, migrants are regarded as liabilities or dangers to traditional destination states for displaced persons. Alex Sager's chapter maintains that media, popular discourse, and policy research miscategorizes migration as crisis and deprive migrants to the right of safety and asylum. Moreover, as major contributors to crises through foreign and economic policies, countries in the West customarily viewed as receiving states bear particular responsibility for social dislocation that produces refugees. The second chapter, by Domenico Maddaloni and Grazia Moffa, shows how popular debates shape the uneven and disparate treatment of migrants to southern European countries, including country and region of origin, economic status, and refugee and asylum-seeking status. The authors argue that neoliberal globalization provides the basis for constructing migration policies beneficial for privileged classes and deleterious to those who are at greater risk. Claudia Tazreiter focuses on the narratives of crisis migration and the power of visual culture through an examination of asylum-seeker arrivals in Australia. Tazreiter examines the signal role of visual images and cultural markers used by the states to shape public opinion and sentiment in opposition toward asylum-seekers. Dalia Abdelhady then provides comparative analysis of the mainstream print media's role in framing Syrian refugees through content analysis of daily newspapers in Sweden, Jordan, and Turkey. The chapter demonstrates that a common theme in each setting is the equation of refugee migration with crisis and with the attendant uncertainty and demands posed on each society.

VIII. Gendered Constructions of Crises

Part VIII hinges on gender and the construction of crises. A significant feature of the contemporary era is the remarkable expansion of the feminization of migration. Though women have migrated from the onset of the colonial era and through different historical periods, the contemporary era has seen a significant increase in flows dominated by women, as well as migrant women's increased vulnerability, both inside and between national borders. A crucial feature of the contemporary "crisis" is the intensification of women's responsibility and attendant physical and economic risk in the perilous and unpredictable journey from zones of violence in the South to new zones of violence in the North. These chapters in *The Oxford Handbook of Migration Crises* demonstrate the obligations of women in decision-making for family security, engaging in the most onerous and dangerous labor, traversing international boundaries, and negotiating tenuous statuses constituting what Menjívar and Abrego demonstrate as a system of "legal violence" in work, family, and civil society. As the new constitution of crisis expands, immigrant women are increasingly the object of the state's system of criminal law and violence (Menjívar and Abrego 2012). In a wide-ranging examination of twentieth-century migration, Marlou Schrover examines gender, social exclusion, and the construction of crisis in European migration through a sociohistorical perspective. Schrover reveals the differences between men and women refugees in the eyes of advocates for migrant rights, calling attention to the duality that refugee women are used as victims lacking agency, concluding a recurrent dilemma of saving victims in a way that reinforces the popular narratives around women, migration, and crisis. Next, turning to LGBTQ migration, Rachel A. Lewis examines and evaluates the legal and administrative laws and policies that relegate LGBTQ migrants to discrimination, uncertainty, and peril, leaving them permanently vulnerable to detention and deportation. Richard C. M. Mole documents the experiences of Polish LGBTQ migrants in London following the collapse of the Soviet bloc. Viewed as a threat to Polish norms and values, LGBT Poles have moved abroad as homophobic rhetoric, violence, and discrimination have become more palpable. In the next chapter, Jane Freedman examines the experiences of women arriving in Europe during the current dominant narrative of migration as "crisis," exploring the bearing of national and EU policies on women's migration experiences. The chapter highlights how the terminology of crisis and securitization inflects the differential treatment of women refugees. Part VIII concludes with Inga K. Thiemann's chapter on human trafficking and misguided state policies of using border control and anti-immigration as policy. Rather, Thiemann calls for policies that address the root causes of human trafficking and protect vulnerable female workers in private households and in the sex industry where exploitation is intensified by precarious status, insufficient and unsafe migration routes, and lack of labor protection.

IX. Integration, Multiculturalism, and Membership

The closing section of the *Handbook* examines the significance of integration, multiculturalism, and membership as essential societal objectives that are under acute threat in the contemporary era of extremist national rhetoric against migrants. While migration policies in the past century are hardly humanitarian standards, the migration and refugee crisis rhetoric in the neoliberal era that is proffered by states, politicians, and the media is evocative of fascist narratives in 1930s and 1940s Europe. Jen Bagelman's chapter addresses the discursive framing of refugee crisis and the crucial importance of providing sanctuary to migrants through historically accurate narratives that challenge the dominant discourses on migration and crisis which dominate today. Next, on a positive momentary note, Laurence Cros examines the Canadian response to Syrian refugees in the 2010s as a possible prototype for refugee-receiving countries in the contemporary era of austerity. Then, Eric Fong, Yingtong Lai, and Aijia Li turn to the characteristics of the mass internal rural-urban migration in China today, depicted by some as crisis. Turning to Europe, Floris Vermeulen focuses on the narrative of the crisis of multiculturalism which takes for granted a false portrayal of a tolerant and welcoming legacy toward immigrants. Vermeulen depicts a historic legacy of European chauvinism, especially toward migrants from the Muslim world. Rather than encouraging participation, Muslims have been stigmatized in Europe. Jock Collins reveals the relationship between global economic, political, and social crises and Australian migration policies, focusing on the construction of political crisis to restrict migration. Pascale Baligand examines how the construction of "crisis" itself contributes to individual and social trauma among migrant populations in France. S. Irudaya Rajan addresses labor migration to Arab Gulf Cooperation Council (GCC) countries at a time of rising nationalism and the institution of policies to reduce migration and regulate undocumented workers to a region that depends so highly on foreigners. The Arab GCC is an outlier that exposes how financialization of the global economy relentlessly undermines conditions of migrants yet is framed as an issue that impinges on the lives of populations in privileged destination regions.

Conclusion

The significance of political and economic events but also of their construction as crises for contemporary and future research on migration and policy practice is reflected in the wide range of contributions in *The Oxford Handbook of Migration Crises*, which has assembled scholars with a deep geographic and temporal knowledge of the field. Taken together, the contributions to this volume present an in-depth, comprehensive, and critical examination of protracted, structural, and immediate conditions that can result in migration crises as well as constructions of crises and their consequences, all of which contribute to understanding the social forces that shape human mobility: economic dislocation and war as well as violence and the poisonous rhetoric which intensifies the suffering of migrants in transit and destination zones. Moreover, we share a common objective that states and media bear a social and political responsibility to protect and defend the rights of the most vulnerable in society including refugees, asylum-seekers, and other migrant populations. However, the framing of these flows within a securitization paradigm that rests on the construction of borders, increased detention, and expanded deportation have transformative consequences on all inhabitants in nation states and the world system. We trust that the works in this volume will resonate with source countries, transit states, and regions of destination so that actors at each stage will advance policies that acknowledge the plight of migrants and vulnerable populations and create policies focused on their humane treatment. The chapters in the *Handbook* are intended to advance scholarship on this crucial dimension of migration. While the chapters of this collection cover a wide range of themes and concepts across geographic and temporal zones, it is our hope that this volume will encourage empirical and theoretical research on the causes, consequences, and policy responses to migration.

Note

1. The Thomas theorem (William Isaac Thomas and Dorothy Swaine Thomas) states that when people define a situation as real, it is real in its consequences. The definition itself then is more important than actual circumstances.

References

Altheide, D. L. 2002. *Creating Fear: News and the Construction of Crisis.* New York: Aldine De Gruyter.

Best, J. 2004. *More Dammed Lies and Statistics: How Numbers Confuse Public Issues.* Berkeley, CA: University of California Press.

Calhoun, C. 2010. "The Idea of Emergency: Humanitarian Action and Global (Dis)Order." In *Contemporary States of Emergency: The Politics of Military and Humanitarian Interventions*, edited by Didier Fassin and Mariella Pandolfi, 29–59. New York: Zone Books.

Charlesworth, H. 2002. "International Law: A Discipline of Crisis." *Modern Law Review* 65, no. 3: 377–392.

Davis, M. 2004. "Planet of Slums: Urban Involution and the Informal Proletariat," *New Left Review* 26 (March-April 2004): 3–34.

Farbotko, C., and H. Lazarus. 2012. "The First Climate Refugees? Contesting Global Narratives of Climate Change in Tuvalu." *Global Environmental Change* 22, no. 2: 382–390.

FitzGerald, D., and R. Arar. 2018. "The Sociology of Refugee Migration." *Annual Review of Sociology* 44, no. 1. doi:10.1146/annurev-soc-073117-041204

Gozzini, G. "The Global System of International Migrations, 1900 and 2000: A Comparative Approach." *Journal of Global History* 1, no. 3: 321–341.

Glassner, Barry. 2010. *The Culture of Fear: Why Americans Are Afraid of the Wrong Things: Crime, Drugs, Minorities, Teen Moms, Killer Kids, Mutant Microbes, Plane Crashes, Road Rage, & So Much More*. 10th Ed. New York: Basic Books.

Greussing, E., and H. G. Boomgaarden. 2017. "Shifting the Refugee Narrative? An Automated Frame Analysis of Europe's 2015 Refugee Crisis." *Journal of Ethnic and Migration Studies*, 43, no. 11: 1749–1774.

Haynes, C., J. L. Merolla, and S. K. Ramakrishnan. 2016. *Framing Immigrants: News Coverage, Public Opinion, and Policy*. New York: The Russell Sage Foundation.

Holmes, S. M., and H. Castañeda. 2016. "Representing the 'European Refugee Crisis' in Germany and Beyond: Deservingness and Difference, Life and Death." *American Ethnologist* 43, no. 1: 12–24. doi:10.1111/amet.12259

Jubilut, L. L. 2017. "Refugees Are Not the Victims of the Crisis: Not the Creators." World Economic Forum, November 6. https://www.weforum.org/agenda/2017/11/the-refugee-crisis-or-a-crisis-for-refugees/.

Lucassen, L. 2005. *The Immigrant Threat: The Integration of Old and New Migrants in Western Europe since 1850*. Champaign: University of Illinois Press.

Martin, S. F., S. Weerasinghe, and Abbie Taylor, eds. *Humanitarian Crises and Migration: Causes, Consequences and Responses*. London and New York: Routledge, 2014.

McAdam, J. 2014. "Conceptualizing 'Crisis Migration': A Theoretical Perspective." In *Humanitarian Crises and Migration: Causes, Consequences and Responses*, edited by S. F. Martin, S. Weerasinghe and A. Taylor, 28–49. London and New York: Routledge.

Menjívar, C., and L. Abrego. 2012. "Legal Violence: Immigration Law and the Lives of Central American Immigrants." *American Journal of Sociology*, 117, no. 5: 1381–1421.

Ness, I. 2015. *Southern Insurgency: The Coming of the Global Working Class*. London: Pluto.

Portes, A., and R. G. Rumbaut. 2006. *Immigrant America: A Portrait*. 3rd ed. Berkeley: University of California Press.

Schuetze, C. 2015. "Narrative Fortress: Crisis Narratives and Conflict in the Conservation of Mount Gorongosa, Mozambique." *Conservation And Society*. Volume 13, no. 2: 141–153.

Sørensen, N. N. 2012. "Revisiting the Migration–Development Nexus: From Social Networks and Remittances to Markets for Migration Control." *International Migration* 50, no. 3: 61–76.

Surak, K. 2013. "Guestworkers: A Taxonomy." *New Left Review* 84 (November-December): 84–102.

van Hear, Nicholas. 2009. *Managing Mobility for Human Development: The Growing Salience of Mixed Migration*. New York: UNDP, Human Development Research.

Weiner, M. 1995. *The Global Migration Crisis: Challenge to States and to Human Rights. HarperCollins Series in Comparative Politics*. New York: HarperCollins.

Wise, R. D., H. M. Covarrubias, and R. Puentes. 2013. "Reframing the Debate on Migration, Development and Human Rights." *Population, Space and Place* 19, no. 4: 430–443.

PART I

HISTORICAL CONTEXTS

CHAPTER 1

MIGRATIONS AND MACRO-REGIONS IN TIMES OF CRISES

Long-Term Historiographic Perspectives

DIRK HOERDER

Migrations of large numbers of people have often been and still are associated *with* "crises" or *as* crisis. If "crisis" is the interpretive frame, who determines the narrative—migrant groups or receiving societies? Or do competing narratives emerge? Is "crisis" merely a discursive tool of those who benefit from dramatization? If migration-inducing crises may be discerned, are they natural or societal phenomena or both? Who decides whether arriving migrants are labeled as detrimental to social cohesion or as beneficial for labor markets?

Historians have focussed on actual migrations and have analyzed conflict or peaceful insertion after arrival. Thus published scholarly and school-socialized popular memories look at the end of migrants' trajectories. This is not surprising since resident societies experiencing in-migration have the apparatus for reflecting and writing while the migrants themselves are busy rearranging their lives. Only a few of them reflect in later life-writings on departure, actual moves, and reestablishment of life plans. Societies of departure are short of means, in havoc, unwilling to deal with causes pushing "their" people out. Thus, at the starting point, no memory is committed to writing. As a result, sources for historians are produced almost exclusively at the receiving end of the trajectory by nonmovers.

This essay will look at *large* migrations—the label "mass migration" often evokes negative connotations—and choose a *longue durée*-perspective. The latter is a prerequisite to approach societies' and historians' discourses involving terms like "hordes" or "settlers," "entrepreneurs" or "workers," and "women" and "men," loaded with traditional, supposedly age-old meanings. They indicate tropes and preconceptions and each succeeding generation imbues these in the processes of parental and educational socialization. Thus, rather than historical analysis, labels form the implicit mental frame for branding migrant arrivals in the respective present.

In the western world, the usual starting point is the second to sixth century "great migrations", narrated—and judged—to have been destructive of the static and settled Roman Empire. From the early modern period, African "slaves" and "free" European migrants crossed the Atlantic: The processes, enslavement and departure decisions in Europe's economic problem regions vanish behind the terms. National historiographies propound that the Second World War mass refugees were difficult to accommodate but do not analyze willful declaration of warfare as causes of flight. In the present, in the terms of those who master the discourse, refugees from the Afghanistan-to-Syria macro-region constitute a refugee crisis.

This survey will trace actual migrations, ask for causes—whether mobilizing crisis or one of several life-course options—and evaluate perceptions of and discourses about the large migrations. The "cases" or (better) "processes" analysed will cover Eurasia with developments in the Mediterranean macro-region and sub-Saharan Africa.

Scales of Analysis, Types of Migration and Potential Impact

This comprehensive approach requires (a) a usable way of structuring place and space (b) a similarly usable method of structuring historical time, and (c) a way of understanding different types of migration. As to the first, the customary way of approaching the world's vast territorial expanses has been the division into continents, clearly bordered and named entities. However, in the last decades scholarship has become critical of "border*lines*" and for almost a century has been critical of "place". In common discourses, migrants still leave a place such as "the countryside", "Syria" or "Africa," and enter a state such as "Canada", "Germany", or other. Or they depart from underserviced rural regions in China and become, by official label, a "floating population" in cities. Or generic "Africans" head for Europe in large numbers, or Mexican masses to the United States.

This established terminology restricts analytical approaches to physical territory, bordered continents, and states, and it eliminates human conceptualizations, from "land" to explorable space to mental and lived "land-scapes." In addition, it eliminates from consideration water expanses, routes in densely frequented interior seas (whether Southeast Asian seas, Indian littorals, Mediterranean and Baltic or North Sea regions) or across less-frequented oceans. In most of history, mobility across seas and along waterways was faster than step-by-step moves overland. However, seafaring required special knowledge and, for scholars, understanding of seaways. Fixed continents structure the trope "from Europe to America" which involved perhaps 50 million—a mass incursion that only few contemporaries viewed as "migration crisis" and that only recently has been discussed in terms of shipping entrepreneurs and funds for the voyage.

The nineteenth-century discipline of physical geography established continents as unquestioned starting "points" of enquiry, topography immutably fixed in place and "fixism" as methodology. Outside the rigorous "discipline" migrants with open questions perceived lands as forbidding or offering options. This change from place to land-scape was not incorporated by scholars into analysis, nor did they note naturally changing coastlines when, for example, storms and floods induced Angles and Saxons to move from territorially decreasing Jutland to inhabited isles later called British. Elsewhere young people faced lack of cultivable land, migrated, and by hard work built coastline-changing dykes to cultivate lowlands. This future-oriented perspective, the achievement-related view of history, needs to be supplemented by a starting-point perspective: birth families experiencing land shortages as food crises—and, possibly, as crises in family relations and emotions.

When historians adopted the "fixism" approach in the nineteenth century, they divided "their" fixed continent Europe into fixed "nations" stuck to the soil, separated by borderlines, with newly invented "nationals" fixed to each other by unchanging bloodlines. Their colleagues in the Chinese Empire, starting a few centuries earlier, fixed the empire and themselves as "in the middle." These scholar-ideologues or, more cautiously, master-discourse-socialized authors, wrote for the greater glory of "their" nation, but lived, whether in Europe or in China, in multiethnic spaces with shifting borders and vast contact zones. Some constructed departing young men, not women, as crises in terms of a recruitment reservoir for soldiers (needed, interestingly, to change fixed borders aggressively). In contrast, the trajectories and memories of emigrants indicate that they saw the political and social system of their birth-*place* as a socioeconomic *scape*-in-crisis causing havoc in their lives. They saw borders as permeable or as a hindrance to be overcome.

Spaces in or through which migrants move worldwide may, in a human-economy-centered and dynamic approach, be conceptualized in terms of commercial connectivity. This "world systems approach" was pioneered by Immanuel Wallerstein (1974–1988) and differentiated by Janet Abu-Lughod (1989) for the twelfth to fourteenth centuries. World systems are macro-regions connected by traders and merchants exchanging goods intensively within a single system and extensively across the borders of two or more systems. Systems of exchange and the routes established seem to offer a promising approach to migration researchers. However, potential migrants' lifecourse plans and projects did and do not necessarily follow trade. Trade may induce intensification of migrations at the supply-side, where additional producers are needed to satisfy distant demand, or at the destination, where additional transport workers and families are required to service demand. Upswings or downswings in a particular system influenced migrations but did not induce mass migrations.

A more appropriate way of approaching both continuous migrations and those occurring in times of crises divides physical geography into macro-regions of human activity and connectedness—for example the Mediterranean world, coastal regions of the Indian Ocean, Europe north of the Alps, the Yangtze Valley, and the Sahel region. (Those living in the second "Old World," the Americas, also divided the double continent into macro-, meso-, and micro-regions.) Macro-regions are partly defined by natural resources—pastures, arable lands, ore-yielding mountain ranges, and others—which circumscribe, as the scholars of the French School of Annales demonstrated, options of individual human beings and whole societies. They are further defined by the usages sedentary or mobile people make of them, in terms of material products as well as in terms of spirituality and belief systems. People appropriate nature-given landscape—not mere topographic place—to their mentality and this perceived *land*scape, in turn, shapes mentalities and spiritualities: *socio*scapes emerge in which humans stay or from which they depart (Appadurai 1991, 2000; Lefèbvre 1991). Allen Roberts coined the helpful concept of "processual geographies" (2006). The spaces/scapes of departure, in the worldview of migrants, are neither continents nor states but meso-regions of life-supporting economic options from adolescence on, and micro-regions of socialization and networks imbued from infancy on.

The second structuration issue, sequentialization of time, corresponds to macro-regional cultures but not to continents. Periods of empires or of migrations differed between the East Asian Chinese and the Mediterranean Roman Empire; between institutionally structured polities and confederations—usually around a leading core—of people in the regions from Amur River through the lands north of the Himalayas and Alpine Mountains to the Elbe, Rhine, and Loire rivers. The emergences (plural!) of societies and states as well as of (crisis-induced) migrations from Mesopotamia to Egypt follow, again, a different time sequence. The standard Western-imposed sequence of "pre-history"—ancient times, (dark) medieval period, modernity—is mere chronological fixism. Early cultural groups did have a history of their own, ancient and medieval ones were highly mobile, and then globalization began in the sixteenth century with the arrival of armed Europeans as crisis factors for resident peoples in the Americas and Asias. The global mass movements during the "delayed" nineteenth century in Europe extended from the end of the migration-halting trans-European war crises, 1815, to the beginning of the migration-interrupting World War One crisis, 1914, and also in the four Asias—south, southeast, east, north—from the beginning to the end of indentured migrations, 1830s–1930s. Since the introduction of railroads in Europe in the 1830s and the introduction of transoceanic steamships in the 1870s spaces have become increasingly interlinked. Air traffic changed mobility starting in the 1950s.

The third factor in establishing mental and ascriptive connections—or lack of them—between migration and crises involves both type of migrations and the master discourses about them. Sedentary oasis-dwellers lived in symbiosis with mobile caravan-traders but had lifeways disrupted by nomad raiders: such nomads might be called a wandering crisis. In many societies residents in villages, towns, or cities—while depending on structured connectivity between their socioscapes—saw wanderers whether nomads, beggars, or generically constructed "wandering peoples" as threatening. It was the residents who established the master discourse and owned storage space for manuscripts or books; those mobile lacked writing time, writing place, and perhaps literacy. Thus, to the present, historians follow written, situation-specific master discourses that, over time, have become unquestioned narratives based on one-sided sources.

The "standard" approach to migration (i.e., the scholars' master concept) has focused on rural settlement as well as labor migrations, and in some cases elite migrations.[1] Other types of migration and mobility were slotted—by whom and for which purposes?—into different subdisciplines: "slavery" as a fixed regime, "war" as an event of battles and territories gained (or lost) and not related to mobile, warfaring soldiers or force-mobilized refugees. Forced migrations of enslaved as well as coerced workers, men and women, interacted with "free" migrations (see later for the terminological construction). An integrated approach to the forced vs. free dichotomy permits questions about power as inducing crises, whether disruptive slaving raids or sedentary oppressive regimes are the push-factor. As to the subdiscipline of military history: soldiers are conscripted, move to rallying points, are marched to war zones; if not equipped with the necessary provisions, they confiscate them along their route, often sending residents into famine mobility; where they are ordered to take action, they generate refugees; where they are disbanded they may (have to) forage for food as armed vagrants or settle and thus become permanent migrants. War work was the largest labor market for migrant men (and accompanying women and children) in medieval Europe. To separate warfare from "migration proper" serves to prevent analysis of crisis situations inducing mass migrations. Many languages use ideological conventions of speech to separate warfare from other types of mobility—"the war erupted," "the war broke out"—this not only serves to prevent discussion of who declared war but also hinders the connection of refugee movements ("waves of" refugees, refugees that "overrun" settled cultures) to the migration-inducing *man*-made crises.

Migrations may induce crises—the coming of a few hundred Europeans to Caribbean islands and central America resulted in the death of 90 percent or more of the residents of many cultures. Migrations may induce urban growth, as in China since the T'ang period or, perhaps, even earlier. Migrants may create societies as in the United States and Canada, and they may cultivate—relatively—unused arable spaces. In each case-process, the reason for departure requires analysis: economic or other crisis, self-willed moves to additional options, group (troop) movement of heavily armed men, and moves of unarmed families with funds of knowledge or, at least, labor power.

Historiography and the Elimination of Migration from Memory

Long historical memory in the Eastern Mediterranean has "sea peoples," probably from the Aegean, moving against people living in the Levant and Nile Valley, 1200–900 BCE. The migrants were aggressive, and Egyptian rulers reacted with major military and political moves. This aggression (difficult to situate for modern scholars) according to the few sources of the time created a clear sense of crisis among the politically powerful in the pharaonic polity and, probably, among people living close to the coasts and estuaries. In contrast, in long "Western" historical memory, "the Greeks" of the 8th to 4th centuries BCE simply "were there," their in-migration not remembered. And they lived in urban quasi-democracies that served as models for "western democracies." Similarly, "the Romans" built an empire—with conquering legions but no refugees and mass displacement—that historians constructed as model for nineteenth-century empires. Any mention of crises would have undercut the value of the two interlinked narratives, urban democracy and territorial empire, for the nineteenth-century usages in political theory and master-narrated historical memory. A sociological analysis of "the" Greeks and "the" Romans according to status, gender, interest and other parameters would also have been detrimental to the—sleek—uniformity of the construct.

Empirical analysis reveals sequences of crises. The Peloponnesian city elites fought bitter and destructive wars against each other, the respective winning side enslaving whole populations of the vanquished (Garland 2014). Alexander "the Great" moved east, expanding Hellenist culture—so say western historians. Those looking from the east would see a sizeable army Persianized (this term is missing in western dictionaries). People along the routes of Macedonian and Persian armies (composed of men from many cultures) probably experienced the soldiers' advance as crisis, perhaps as deadly. Historical maps of the Roman Empire depicted and still depict an ever-expanding territory with, supposedly, well-functioning imperial institutions. In fact, soldiers—only at the beginning recruited in the Apennine Peninsula—aggressively annexed settled spaces, creating crises among peoples over whom they moved. In Gallia, they annihilated much of the population, in Judea the local elite quickly turncoated to the occupiers' structures while the already crisis-ridden rural people experienced a deep material as well as spiritual crisis. In Jewish faith, land was in the hand of (their) God, but their powerful took it from them. On the other hand, once conquest and concurrent destruction had been achieved, the new Roman rulers—all of migrant background—established a *pax romana* that prevented warfare between competing regional and local elites and permitted agricultural growth.

In detailed analysis by social group or stratum, the impact of in-migration on and the experience of crisis or accommodation by settled populations depended on whether the newcomers came in armed conquest of functioning, perhaps less complex, societies, or whether agrarian newcomers hoped to share relatively thinly settled expanses. Any conquest was crisis for the subjugated, any meeting with other migrating groups could result in mutual support and, perhaps, fusion. It could also mean assessing the relative strength of the "others" and, perhaps, the changing direction of migration. Or it could result in armed struggle. Such assessment of potential options and policies has, in contrast, neither been undertaken by those with power to establish contemporary master discourses and to fix terminologies nor by their followers who established one-way historical memories. The memories-to-be were first set *down* and thus fixed by contemporary victors; later—in this case western—scholars neutralized such partisan accounts as "sources of the time." They perpetuated narrations of the powerful and their scribes and expunged experiences of crisis from triumphant memory.

Ancient Mass Migrations and the Perception of Crises

Three "crises" between the second and eighth centuries will serve to demonstrate and analyze the next phase of inscribing one-sided or self-serving stories of migration into—seemingly smooth and convincing—master narratives in Western Europe and China. The questions remain the same: who experienced migration as crises, who memorized them at the time, who created "a usable past" for whom?

In the region of the Baltic Sea, a change of climate (historians still debate the initial impetus) induced people—in the sense of men, women, and children and not of "peoples"—to move south—or eastward from the second century CE: A *natural* crisis placed people in critical *economic* and *social* circumstances. Experiencing deteriorating living conditions, large sworn groups decided to diffuse the crisis by moving to sustaining environments. Those living along the routes chosen, in contrast, perceived advancing masses, mouths to be fed, and the migrants' weaponry: This meant crisis for their usually not easy lives. Upon further southward advance of the groups of thousands, several thousand, even tens of thousands, the leaders of the circum-Mediterranean many-cultured (Roman) Empire took note of the threat to imperial borders and borderlands. They diffused this perceived crisis by offering *foederati* [federated] status, and thus both incorporated the migrants as well as established distance: *Foederati* did not become citizens but were a cheap mobile soldiery to keep other peoples in place and out. These latter, in turn, may have perceived the double crisis *diffusion* upon the migrants' departure and their arrival in an imperial border zone as *crisis-prone* to themselves (Heather 2009; Pohl 2005).

The issue of what is normal and what is critical in these migrations has haunted memory-creating historiographic narratives ever since. Depending on conviction or perspective, the mobility has been named "peoples," "barbarian," or, neutrally, "great" migrations. The label "barbarian" was affixed by self-narrating civilized Roman elite to the migrants. The label "peoples" (folk, *Völker*) was a nineteenth-century national, nationalizing term that nationalist historians attached. Empirically, men and women of Baltic cultures had formed groups with fealty to or sworn armed service to under a ruling warrior elite to migrate off of. The ruling core's self-assigned or Roman-ascribed name—Goths, Vandals, Herulians, Langobards, Bavarians—nineteenth-century admirers of Roman grandeur constructed as names of genetically uniform peoples or nations. This construction is still deeply inscribed in historical belief systems: Maps in historical atlases, with arrows, indicate criss-crossing armed groups in the fixed and stable Roman-imperial territory from east and north moving on to the Italian and Iberian segments and finally to northern Africa. "Intrusions" of Slavic-speaking people—barbarians of another language family—occurred, say historians, into settled Germanic territories. Those mobile threatened fixed contiguous realms and established institutions of "the Romans" and, subsequently of "the" Carolingians (who had moved the label "Roman Empire" to their own sphere of power north of the Alps). Up to the present, no arrows indicate advancing imperial legions and Frankish soldiery or the refugee migrations they caused (Lohse 2014).

Juxtaposing the fixed-in-borders of the Roman empire and the aggressive mobility of Central Asian ("Huns") and German-language *Wandergenossenschaften* and positing each "people's" genetic unity as a given, the nineteenth-century historians of the emerging British, French and German empires agreed on a "crisis": the "fall" of the Roman Empire in the face of migrant hordes. Empirically, the "Gothic" elites, establishing themselves in the city of Rome, already were adopted and adapted members of the top Roman military; "Rome" was no longer a capital, the imperial government at that point residing in Constantinople; the seat of the Latin, also labelled "Roman" Church had been relocated to Ravenna and Milano. Whether those inhabitants remaining in the city of Rome experienced the newcomers as a crisis-inducing threat or as delivery from warring-throne pretenders in the "crisis of the third century" remains an open question. The 20,000 Gothic soldier families, about 100,000 in all, were settled in the countryside without opposition. Probably the preceding pretender-caused war crises had emptied peasant plots as well as *latifundia* (Demandt 1984). "Crisis" requires differentiated sociological analysis: Migrants might diffuse crises, add to them, pass by, or induce migrations of others. Results were often unintended and unforeseeable: Oncoming long-beards, originally from the Baltic and recomposed in the Pannonian Plain where they had tarried and were labeled "Langobards" by onlookers, appeared as threat to people living in the Veneto plain north of the Adriatic Sea. They fled to coastal islands, realized the trading opportunities, stayed and built a city called "Venice"—from crisis to constructive development. To backward-looking historians, both Langobards and Venetians became genetically defined peoples.

The third, East Asian, case-process involves different crises and population mobility. The Chinese Empire's core space from the Han to the T'ang dynasties (second century BCE to eighth century CE) was the Yellow River region. Three types of crisis changed sustainable living conditions to precarious ones: fourth-century incursions from northern mobile groups (again, not "peoples"); deteriorating climate conditions; and soil exhaustion and erosion due to—positively perceived—population growth. In order to diffuse the multiple crises, people decided to move southward to the attractive soils and rainfalls in the Yangtze River valley. The migrant families, culturally labeled "Han," crossed the climatic and topographic border zone between wheat and rice cultivation on their way and had to relearn skills and lifestyles. Once they had settled available lands in the plains, further generations moved westbound. "Advance" might involve conflict with and "retreat" of settled farming families—both terms involve discursive value judgments. By the end of the T'ang period, border posts—later styled the

"Great Wall"—could not stem further incursions of mobile northern people. *Métissage* followed but the "Han"-concept remained fixed.

The resulting imperial historians' master narrative did shape historical memory on a large scale: China's population amounted to one-third of the world's total by 900. Imperial authors emphasized the northern intruders' aggressiveness and consequent refugee-generating disruptions. Several of the armed, power-wielding incursions did involve destruction but, over a few generations, led to cohabitation or even rule of the newcomers. Whether and when "crisis" or "accommodation" predominated needs to be established by generation, by urban or rural life, by gender. The narrators noted interactive dual societal and political structures but created a long-prevalent discourse about "foreigners" and "Chinese." Even contemporary analysts questioned the constructed Sinitic hegemony or purity: The T'ang elite had emerged from *métissage* of Han and Northerners and was receptive to outside influences. The empire as unit incorporated many ethnocultural groups. However, the master-narrators juxtaposed non-Han "peoples" with "the Han" and this trope determines master narrative and master policies in the present. The population of the People's Republic of China is said to consist of Chinese, "Hakka" of migrant ancestors, and officially recognized "minorities." This classification places those minoritized in critical or precarious conditions and, in the present, has induced a crisis between self-reaffirming Uighur people and central police forces (Abramson 2008; Barfield 1989).

Forced Labor Mass Migrations: Slaveries

Over the same centuries and, depending on macro-regional economic regimes, a sequence of forced labor—or slave—migration systems emerged from greed of African and European slavers and labor needs of slave-users. These migrations seemed "normal" to those profiting from the—processually—enslaved. As cases, the European slavery regime from fifth-century Francia and Gallia and from eighth-century Varangian Kievan rule, both lasting to about 1500, as well as the Atlantic-American slavery regime, lasting from the mid-fifteenth to the late-nineteenth century, will be discussed. These forced migrations were economic-regime-induced, but historical accounts reflect mentalities of the raiders-buyers. Empirically, long-lasting regimes engaged in continuous crisis-generation: Each raid caused havoc in communities and families, and placed captured individuals in life-course crises.

In northwestern Europe, advancing armed bands of "Franks" imposed post-Roman slavery on resident populations from northern Francia to southern Gallia. In eastern Europe, Varangian men's penetration from the Baltic Sea's northern shores into the Lake Ladoga region (founding of Now-gorod, new city) and down the Dnieper River (founding of Kiev) involved enslavement of resident Slavic-speaking men and women.

Both aggressor-migrations caused major crises in lifeways of the subjugated rural families. In the West, the wars of expansion of Carolingian rulers into Slavic-, Frisian-, and Saxon-language regions was financed, in part, by sale of those subjugated into slavery, with Regensburg and Prague as major eastern markets and Metz (Lorraine) as transit node for sale into Muslim-ruled Iberia or, via Venice and other Mediterranean ports, to the Umayyad, Abbasid, and Fatimid caliphates (*c.* 660 to 1170) and to the Roman Empire-Constantinople. Demand increased massively when the 6th- and 7th-century plagues caused a crisis, neutrally phrased, in population levels or—phrased according to the elites' point of view—in availability of able-bodied male and female servants and workers.

Varangian and steppe societies' raiders supplied slaves of Slavic-language cultures down the Dnieper River and of Central-Asian-language speakers through Black Sea seaports with Constantinople and Cairo as markets. Historical memory, committed to writing in the receiving "high" cultures, has focused on the growing polities, Kievan, East Roman and Abbasid. Memory of resulting crises in the macro-regions of enslavement is absent from written accounts. The power- and finance-induced crises were exacerbated by natural food crises in years of poor harvests. Famine-stricken people had to opt for self-sale or parents for sale of children into slavery to ensure survival. This regime, called "Mediterranean slavery" in southern Europe, lasted towards the turn of the fifteenth/sixteenth centuries. To the present, "western" historical memorizing narrates sale to Muslim countries and hardly mentions slavery in Christian countries, notwithstanding early studies (Heers 1981; Verlinden 1955, 1977). Charlemagne's military raids greatly increased supply. Through Venice's slave-market probably more than three million enslaved men and women were sold and exported from 1204 to 1509. The story of raids and of the enslaved's forced migrations might be told in terms of crises in catchment regions and in human lives. The hegemonic historical discourse was developed by scholars in the Carolingian Empire and the burgeoning Venetian one.

The subsequent so-called "African" slavery may, at its inception, be considered an extension of Mediterranean slavery and of West and Central African debt-mandated rights-in-persons bondage. In the latter the proceeds of the labor but not the person belonged to the creditor. In the 1440s, armed Portuguese crown-sent trading vessels bought or captured West African "Gold Coast" men and women and imported them to Iberian societies, originally as bound but not enslaved persons. The subsequent commodification of the enslaved as "chattel" was neither "African" nor "Atlantic" slavery as master discourse has it. It was American slavery of African captives transported across the Atlantic. In the cases of personal slavery at African courts, slavery in Arab societies, and in Mediterranean Africa and Europe, historians may look at regimes functioning with unfree members or they may focus on the crises in communities used as catchment reservoirs.

Fast-growing Portuguese and, soon, other European powers' demand for enslaved bodies as well as warfare between competing "kingdoms" (the European term) like Benin, Kongo, and others resulted in regional crises of political organization and economies. Craft production, agricultural surplus, interregional exchange suffered. Agents of slavery were both small numbers of well-armed European migrant men and supportive African slave-raiding warrior states. The withdrawal of human and social capital disrupted West and Central African societies as a whole; in the lasting powerful-human-made crisis about twelve million men and women were force-migrated to the Americas before the 1870s. Havoc in African societies was exacerbated by the raids' high loss of human lives, destroyed villages, ruptured social relations, starved elderly, and children left behind. These crises were personal, familiar, and micro- and meso-regional. The slave trade limited population growth in West Africa up to 1750, caused population decline from 1750 to 1850, and kept the population stagnant thereafter. Some historians argue considerably higher damage: Depletion of the population of those in the best working and childbearing age caused a lasting demographic crisis: collapsing economies and massively reduced reproduction rates. Subsequently, European colonizers' territorial armed acquisitions made the last third of the nineteenth century the bloodiest period in African history (Klein 1987; Manning 1990). To the 1980s, historical research and public historical memory adhered to the "achievement" (or material goods) perspective: The plantation regimes achieved exports which supplied Europe (and North America) with sugar, tropical fruit, and, from the US slave economy, cotton. Only specialists in African history have looked at the "crisis side."

Migrations in the Atlantic, Indian Ocean, and North China Systems: Self-Decided under Crises Conditions

The end of the slave trade to the Americas, proclaimed in 1807–1808, came in the 1870s; the abolition of slavery as late as 1863–1865 in the United States and the 1880s in Brazil and Spanish-colonized Cuba. In the British colonized macro-region, parallel to abolition in the 1830s, imperial administrators organized a substitute system, indentured servitude or "second slavery" (Tinker 1974). Mainly Indian and Chinese working men and women had to work off debts over five years. Since debtors available did not meet demand for labor, British government and private merchant capital in the 1840s forced opium sales onto Chinese consumers in contravention to Chinese imperial rules. The newly addicted incurred debts and, apprehended, had to sign peonage "contracts." Potential employers and governmental administrators created an addiction crisis to reduce what they considered a critical shortage of workers. In this "Indian Ocean migration system"—which extended to South China, Caribbean plantations, and South American Pacific mines—far more self-paying so-called "passenger" migrants moved. The routes connected regions of options—jobs, trade, investment—with regions of "surplus" population: southern Chinese workers to Malaysian tin mines, Indian traders to East African societies, and others.

Three further large migration systems "developed" in the nineteenth century—correctly speaking, no system developed itself but potential migrants made decisions about their options "at home", inhospitable homes, comparing them to options in different spaces about which they had substantial information. The sum of millions of decisions in micro-regional socioeconomic frames to move toward similar wage-work—(or arable land)—that provided destinations added up to macro-regional "migration systems": (a) segments-of-Europe-to-the-Americas, mainly North America since 1815, involving some 50 million men and women (Hoerder 1985); (b) a European Russia-southern Siberia system since the 1860s involving some 10 to 15 million with some heading for new cities in Pacific Russia (Treadgold 1957); and (c) a Shandong-to-Manchuria system since the 1880s, involving tens of millions (McKeown 1999, 2008). Neither out-migration, nor trajectory, nor settlement in a specific micro-region has been associated with "crisis." All built societies—the United States, Manchuria, Argentina, and others. Historical memory deindividualizes migrants and merges them into generic "immigrants." In the "immigrant" society of Argentina, for example, only entrepreneurs, investors, and statesmen (of immigrant background) are remembered as individuals (Moya 1997).

A comprehensive approach, however, does discern crises. First, all three systems involved migration of peasant families searching for land and who are remembered as colonizers of "virgin" soils—a though-provoking terminology of domination. However, in each region of arrival resident Native people or First Peoples were displaced. In historical memory the crisis of displacement has no place—historiography of evictors as victors. After long struggles by descendants of the dispossessed some governments have recognized the injustices.

Second, national and nationalist historians in the push societies have, in general, asked no questions about causes for emigration. By emphasizing "their" migrants' role in building new societies, they could propound contribution histories. Reasons for departure were many: population growth beyond agricultural carrying capacity under existing technologies and tilling methods; cultivation of marginal, difficult-to-till lands distant from markets; shift from rural to urban production with too few factory jobs in relation to labor supply; social and political regimes that discouraged economic development either in a state as a whole or in specific regions, for example those inhabited by cultural groups (labeled "minorities") different from the majority (self-defined "national") group; oppressive stratification, often involving exploitation of tenant farmers or agricultural day laborers by *latifundia* owners; and poorly paid, demeaning working conditions in new industries. In addition to malnourishment or undernourishment many rural families experienced a "cash crisis" when home production of clothing by women lost any value because factory-produced cheap clothing became available—with no cash available in the subsistence households. Crises there were, all deliberately left out of view by nationalized historiography.

The crises-driven "generic" emigrants from rural and urban laboring classes in Europe and northern China became, in the vast majority, "unskilled" industrial or mining workers upon arrival. They did have skills, having earned their meager living before departure. In the economies of arrival, however, the skills were not marketable. They had to retool themselves while others labeled them as lacking skills. Europe has not been visualized by master narrators as composed of more disaster zones than wage-providing labor markets, even though internal migration involved more millions than the transatlantic one.

Mass outmigration in the three systems began at different times. In Europe, the steep rise in mobility has usually—and correctly—been related to the end of the revolutionary-Napoleonic-reactionary wars, 1789–1815. However, new global approaches and climate research emphasize a natural crisis, the Tambora volcano's eruption in Indonesia, 1815. Global ash clouds resulted in food crises, particularly cold winters and "missing" summers as far as Europe. In Russia, where serfdom was abolished in 1861 but landlord-imposed living conditions remained, millions of peasant families moved to the fertile and climatically suitable southern Siberian lands. More millions migrated seasonally from villages to urban jobs—thus reducing the impact of family cash-crises. In China in the 1880s, rural poverty in Shandong and neighboring provinces was even more pronounced than elsewhere while, in Manchuria, agriculture, mining, and industry were being developed, albeit from the mid-1890s, by investors from Russia and, more so, from militarizing Japan. The migrants achieved their goal—sustainable lives—but were denigrated as inferior race by the colonizing powers.

The macro-regional "critical" or "crisis-prone" circumstances were aggravated since the mid-1880s by a worldwide "agrarian crisis", well-studied in agricultural history (Bath 1963) but not in national or migration history. Peasant families departing from small plots and marginal lands had, upon arrival, cultivated the North American, South Russian, Argentine, and Australian easy-to-till plains. Mechanization of plowing and harvesting decreased production cost from the 1880s. Resulting mass production brought a crash of grain prices in world markets. Cultivation of family plots on hillsides and in marshy lands became unsustainable, millions more had to move in overproduction-crisis-induced migrations. Since industry, plantations, and mines still required large numbers of workers in North America, Argentina, and Brazil as well as in Manchuria, migration had a balancing effect between regions with a surplus of "labor," both men and women, and regions with a shortage of "labor." Or, in the view of potential migrants, between old homes with an undersupply of jobs and options and new homes with more options. In life-writings, migrants of the late-nineteenth and early-twentieth centuries remembered hard work but achievement of better standards of living compared to regions and regimes of departure (Hoerder 1997).

In the United States of the 1880s, high demand for immigrant labor notwithstanding, ideologues pushed new non-economic crises-perceptions: Self-assigned "whiteness" and skin-color-schemes imposed on "Others" threatened "the passing of the great [white] race" as author Madison Grant labeled his apocalyptic views in 1916. Whiteness advocates—or: racists—saw migrants from Asia as "yellow peril," while (colonized) Irish from Europe, Catholic and uncouth, could, like Jews from Russia, not be white "by definition" or by preconception. The mass arrival of eastern and southern European men and women led to extension of the color-coding: they were labeled "dark," "olive," or "swarthy." This "crisis"-propaganda was an important factor in the United States' closing of its doors from 1917 (Gabaccia 2005).

One further aspect, seemingly not associated with crises, demands attention. In both scholarship and public historical perception, Europeans' transatlantic migrations are remembered as "free" migrations in contrast to unfree slave and, later, "Asian" indentured workers' migrations. In view of the color-coding, this implies that white (Europeans) migrate "free" while black (Africans) and opium-den-bound yellow "Chinamen" are incapable of agency. Such racist ascriptions caused crises in life-projects and in income levels of all those thus segregated. In all three systems, but not in forced migration regimes, potential migrants themselves took the decisions to depart, usually in contexts of family interests and of information flows about conditions at preferred destinations. Only in this respect were they "free" to decide. In the crises conditions of their inhospitable home societies, they decided under extreme economic constraints.

Conclusion: Present-Day Discourses

Migrations under constraint or because of actual danger of death have been analyzed in terms of "crises" when causes were natural—such as famine, volcanoes, or floods—but not when crises were manmade, like war: The conventions of hegemonic language usage have "wars erupt" to absolve warmongering and declaring elites free from responsibility for crises. Invasions as well as large-scale warring among elites caused mass refugee migrations in China as well as in Europe during the trans-European wars of Thirty Years, 1618–1648, and the wars about regime change or retention of the old order from 1789 ro 1815. In Africa and Southeast Asia both internal wars and colonizer aggressions enforced mass flight. War may be analyzed as systemic political crises, as aggressions by powerful ruling men or ideologues of superiority, as motivated by economic expansion, or as intending to achieve liberation from foreign rule. For any person, family, or group dislocated it involves a crisis in intended life-courses with flight-migration as one option, often the only option.

The mass arrival of refugees in Eastern Mediterranean (since 2012) as well as North African and European societies (since 2015) has been—and, at the time of this writing, is—caused by warfare from Syria to Afghanistan, a macro-region that imperial Great Britain, France, and Russia have been attempting to instrumentalize for their interests since the 1830s. People leave this and other crisis-zones, trying to find a space in which to reconstruct their lives, but often arrive in societies unwilling or incapable to deal with newcomers. In the present, the migration-policy-crisis (European Union) or lack of means (North Africa) has led to reception crises. Unwilling to analyze their own systemic crises, many European talking heads and politicians, whether of specific states or in unison, label the newcomers, who lack access to public discourse and the power of definition, as crisis.

Relationships between crises and migrations are empirically traceable throughout history. Labor migrations from long-term economic disaster zones and from constraining work and agricultural regimes to more dynamic (i.e., sustenance-providing) regions and less restrictive regimes have been, and are a consequence of, uneven development. They require analyses of capital flows, colonialism, and neoimperialism. Similarly, fears about or rejection of in-migrants require analysis of internal uneven development: People left behind, living in regions that are marginalized, often express higher levels of fear of impending economic and cultural crisis imagined to be caused by the arriving "Others" than people secure in their standard of living, self-identifications, and views of diversity.

Historians as gatekeepers of public memory have often followed or even generated regime-supporting discourses about crises and migrations. They have thus contributed to the development of cliché-ridden imagery. Scholars as analysts undertake comprehensive economic analyses of departure and receiving regions, sociological analyses of groups moving or staying, and of who benefits or may be hurt by in-migration. Research requires an inclusive and analytical historical narrative as a basis for socialization into ways of thinking about migrations.

Note

1. This terminology has its own limitations: "settlement migration" implies fixed settling down and deemphasizes the labor involved; "labor migration" often connotes continuous mobility between jobs.

References

Abramson, M. S. 2008. *Ethnic Identity in Tang China*. Philadelphia: University of Pennsylvania Press.

Abu-Lughod, J. L. 1989. *Before European Hegemony: The World System A.D. 1250–1350*. New York: Oxford Univrsity Press.

Appadurai, A. 1991. "Global Ethnoscapes: Notes and Queries for a Transnational Anthropology." In *Recapturing Anthropology: Working in the Present*, edited by R. Fox, 191–210. Santa Fe, NM: School of American Research Press.

Appadurai, A. 2000. "Grassroots Globalization and the Research Imagination." *Public Culture* 12, no. 1: 1–19.

Barfield, T. J. 1989. *The Perilous Frontier: Nomadic Empires and China*. Cambridge, UK: Cambridge University Press.

Bath, S. van [B. H. Slicher]. 1963. *The Agrarian History of Western Europe, AD 500–1850*. Translated by Olive Ordish. New York: Edward Arnold.

Demandt, A. 1984. *Der Fall Roms: die Auflösung des römischen Reiches im Urteil der Nachwelt*. Munich: Beck Verlag.

Gabaccia, D. R. 2005. "The 'Yellow Peril' and the 'Chinese of Europe': Global Perspectives on Race and Labor, 1815–1930." In *Migration, Migration History, History: Old Paradigms and New Perspectives*, edited by J. Lucassen and L. Lucassen, 177–196. Bern, Switzerland: Campus.

Garland, R. 2014. *Wandering Greeks: The Ancient Greek Diaspora from the Age of Homer to the Death of Alexander the Great*. Princeton, NJ: Princeton University Press.

Heather, P. 2009. *Empires and Barbarians: Migration, Development and the Birth of Europe*. London: Oxford University Press.

Heers, J. 1981. *Esclaves et domestiques au moyen-âge dans le monde méditerranéen*. Paris: Pluriel.

Hoerder, D. 1997. "Segmented Macrosystems and Networking Individuals: The Balancing Functions of Migration Processes." In *Migration, Migration History, History: Old Paradigms and New Perspectives*, edited by J. Lucassen and L. Lucassen, 73–84. Bern, Switzerland: Campus.

Hoerder, D., ed. 1985. *Labor Migration in the Atlantic Economies*. Westport, CT: Greenwood.

Klein, M. 1987. "The Demography of Slavery in Western Sudan: The Late Nineteenth Century." In *African Population and Capitalism: Historic Perspectives*, edited by D. Cordell and J. Gregory, 50–61. Madison: University of Wisconsin Press.

Lefèbvre, H. 1991. *The Production of Space*. London: Blackwell.

Lohse, T. 2014. "Die Völkerwanderungskarte als europäischer Erinnerungsort. Ein Blick in die Geschichtsatlanten und—schulbücher des 18. bis 21. Jahrhunderts." In *Europa in der Welt des Mittelalters: Ein Colloquium für und mit Michael Borgolte*, edited by T. Lohse and B. Scheller, 33–98. Berlin: De Gruyter.

Manning, P. 1990. *Slavery and African Life: Occidental, Oriental and African Slave Trades*. Cambridge, UK: Cambridge University Press.

McKeown, Adam. 1999. "Conceptualizing Chinese Diasporas, 1842–1949." *Journal of Asian Studies* 58, no. 2: 306–337.

McKeown, Adam. 2008. *Melancholy Order: Asian Migration and the Globalization of Borders*. New York: Columbia University Press.

Moya, J. C. 1997. *Cousins and Strangers. Spanish Immigrants in Buenos Aires, 1850–1930*. Berkeley: University of California Press.

Pohl, W. 2005. *Die Völkerwanderung*. Stuttgart: Kohlhammer.

Roberts, A. F. 2006. "La 'Géographie Processuelle': Un nouveau paradigme pour les aires culturelles." *Lendemains* 31, no. 122–123: 41–61.

Tinker, H. 1974. *A New System of Slavery: The Export of Indian Labour Overseas 1830–1920*. London: Oxford University Press.

Treadgold, D. W. 1957. *The Great Siberian Migration: Government and Peasant in Resettlement from Emancipation to the First World War*. Princeton, NJ: Princeton University Press.

Verlinden, C. 1955, 1977. *L'esclavage dans l'Europe médiévale*. 2 vols. Bruges, Belgium: Rijksuniversiteit to Gent.

Wallerstein, I. M. 1974–1988. *The Modern World-System*. 3 vols. New York: Academic Press.

CHAPTER 2

MIGRANTS IN CRISIS IN NINETEENTH-CENTURY BRITAIN

ERIC RICHARDS

Crises Inducing Migration

"Crises" in nineteenth-century Britain were episodes of political turmoil and social turbulence which disturbed the equanimity of the political establishment and they sometimes coincided with movements of migrants. Communal crises were usually precipitated by economic, industrial, or sectarian circumstances which recurrently reverberated through parts of Victorian Britain, and were often associated with food shortages, industrial breakdown, or political tensions. They attracted the attention of journalists and were sometimes investigated by parliamentary enquiries, whose findings mainly served the narrowly defined political nation. Similarly, some of the consequences of instability in Europe, including the effects of revolution and deprivation, were also transmitted into Britain, creating another sense of crisis. Such episodes, at home and abroad, often reflected underlying shifts and conflicts in the structures of society; the dimensions of each crisis were determined in part by the reactions of authority and its capacity to contain the consequences.

These crises, internal and external, often induced episodes of migration, of people under duress seeking relocation or asylum either within Britain or by emigration. Such crises, derived for instance from food emergencies or industrial downturns, were not of their own making: migrants entangled in these episodes were governed and directed by structural forces at work in the Victorian world.

But migrants also came to be perceived and defined in themselves as crisis-ridden, either as carriers of crisis or the actual causes and conveyers of crisis. Thus local authorities, landlords, and working communities often construed people on the move and in extremis as harbingers of social breakdown, or of crime, of imported poverty and destitution, being people who undermined living standards and demanded humanitarian support from already overburdened receiving communities. Such migrants became the face of crisis, the source of fear and hostility as well as objects of humane compassion, depending on the scale of the migrant flow and the duration of the critical episode. Thus branded, the migrants necessarily entered the receiving society at a depressed and lowly point of entry.

Industrializing Britain in the nineteenth century witnessed a continuous stream of internal migration, the conventional and volitional readjustment of the population, which accounted for most Victorian mobility. But there were also recurrent episodes of migration under acute pressure, when people were extruded from certain parts of the industrial sector, victims of economic vicissitude or technological change, sometimes pushed outwards, even seeking refuge overseas. Concurrently, in rural Britain, many people were leaving the land, sometimes compelled by agrarian reconstruction, sometimes under the direct compulsion of eviction. In extreme times, notably in recurring famine in Ireland and parts of Scotland, hunger and deprivation caused by the collapse of food production, and the inability of the home society to provide relief for their swollen numbers, created critical emergencies and induced sudden migration. The treatment of migrants, within, into, and out of Britain, was a barometer of the capacity and willingness of the Victorians to handle what they deemed "crises" in their midst.

Mobile Britons

Within the British Isles, and also across the globe, the British were highly mobile in the great "Age of Migration." Mass international migration was pioneered from the British Isles, most notably in the identifiable discontinuity in the 1820s, and then in the surge in the 1840s which was further sustained throughout the rest of the century (Richards 2018). Emigration fluctuated but did not diminish despite rising living standards and the cumulative industrialization of the mature economy during Victorian times, reaching toward unprecedented peaks of exodus just before the First World War. Most of this emigration was ordinarily betterment migration. Thus while Britain continued its astonishing industrialization British people also departed in very large numbers, populating other continents despite Britain's own swelling appetite for labor. (Richards 2004)

This paradox was reinforced by the curious reality that Britain was both an emigrant and an immigrant country—large intakes and departures occurring simultaneously, rendering the statistical story at all times unreliable. It was a sender and a receiver and Britain experienced "crises" in both capacities.

Immigrants were arriving in substantial numbers throughout most decades of the 19th century, and there were sudden upsurges which caused anxieties in the home population. These immigrants complicated an already confusing story because many of the foreigners or in-comers or both were temporary populations, some sojourners, other transient people *en route* for further destinations, mostly from Europe to North

America. British ports were funnels for hundreds of thousands of migrants in transit, through Hull, London, Liverpool, and Southampton, stages along the much longer journey to the New Worlds.

The very definition of migration was further complicated by the very large internal migration. After 1750 there was an ongoing relocation of great numbers of people in Britain, the shift from rural to urban life which had changed the face of England and Scotland by 1850 and continued thereafter. And within this re-sorting of the British population, most of the movements were relatively short distance, usually less than twenty miles for a single generation within a family. Some of these internal movements were of longer distance and more turbulent in their impact on the public mind. Most of all, the movement of people out of Ireland into the rest of Britain, amounting to hundreds of thousands over many decades, constituted a migration akin to the great oceanic emigrations of the day. But the narrative is muddied by the fact that the Irish (like others within the British Isles, especially the Scottish Highlanders) included many temporary migrants, often seasonal workers vital in British industry and agriculture, and vital also for their home economies by way of remittances. Moreover many of the Irish reached English ports intent on stretching much further to America and Australia. The Irish were a large part of the turnover and swirling of the population. Poverty, food scarcity and population pressure were components of this migratory spectrum. Curiously a recent survey of present-day "Forced Migration" contains neither "famine" nor "demography" in its index. (Fiddian-Qasminyeh et al 2014, 317).

Nevertheless, in 19th-century Britain there were many instances in which people living through emergencies sought escape by emigration. At the same time Britain was also the haven for crisis-ridden foreigners who arrived sporadically in substantial numbers and thereby created a further sense of imported crisis for the British. Migrants in crisis were one category among many varieties of emigration in the great Age of Migration.

Structural Pressures

Most of the millions of people departing the British Isles in the 19th century fit into conventional understandings of "normal emigration"—people moving freely in pursuit of betterment, classic economic migrants in a time which was almost uniquely favorable and welcoming to the British emigrant. The absence of restraint on emigration by the state, and the welcoming arms of colonies in the Empire and, even more, the United States, constituted a special historical context. Similarly, immigrants were free to enter Britain, unconstrained by passport or citizenship requirements. The political context was extraordinarily favorable to inward and outward migration.

The liberal environment of migration, of course, obscures the myriad tensions that attended the decision and the logistics of virtually all migration. There were always degrees of pressure or inducement surrounding decisions to emigrate, and the anxiety was proportional to the distance and alienation involved. The pressure was intensified during times of "crisis." Yet more often there was a gradual build-up of adverse conditions over the long term—as opposed to the concentrated moment of emergency generated by, for instance, war, genocide, or famine. Thus the process of industrialization was itself the source of a great crisis in British society, a vast dislocation identified in the censuses and observed by alarmed social commentators. The structural reshaping of the economy forced the reorganization of the entire population, an almost total relocation over less than four generations. Migration was a function of this grand crisis, setting imperatives upon the population which were eventually irresistible. The readjustments pressed upon the population were manifested across the country, usually over a long run but sometimes in the form a sudden critical episode (such as evictions) which were recognizable as a "crisis," of which several are documented in this chapter. There were certainly instances of mass human displacement which undoubtedly fed the migrant trails. Such crises were sometimes associated with the phenomenon of communal "frenzy"—of an emotional state which attended the sudden clamor to find exit.

There was also a measure of "crisis mentality" among the people who were actually emigrating or immigrating. Terms such as "fever," "panic," and "hysteria" are often associated with waves of emigrants and the social history of the subject is full of such assertions. Colin Pooley and Jean Turnbull drew attention to personal crises which precipitated mobility in Britain and they identified seven sets of such events: these included illness in a family, redundancy or bankruptcy, the death of partner, or divorce or separation. The range of personal circumstances associated with emigration was almost infinite and could include also the death of a parent, or the need to provide care in old age; more often perhaps was leaving home after a bad family dispute (Pooley and Turnbull 1998).

Crisis emigration, in principle, might best be measured by the degree of structural pressure propelling the migration. The most obvious examples involved sudden influxes of immigrants, which raised alarm among the receiving communities and the government. Emigration from Britain was less excitable in terms of the public reception and rarely caused government to take much notice. Nevertheless emigration from Britain was associated with numerous local crises in Britain and exposed serious problems in the social fabric. The Irish dominated the headlines in the early nineeenth century; later Germans, Jews, and other Europeans caused alarmed responses across the country.

Migrants from Europe

Britain was mostly the last resort of refugees but was generally liberal in its reception of such people (Porter 2003). Colin Holmes has declared that there had been no major inflow of immigrants into Britain for two centuries following the well-known Huguenot influx in 1685, no large intake of refugees until the influx of émigrés fleeing the French Revolution in 1789 and 40,000 refugees during the Napoleonic Wars. (Holmes 1988,

8). Political refugees, at the time of the 1848 revolutions, were relatively few in number and not a serious threat to public order, but the arrival of a new surge of refugees in the aftermath of the 1871 Paris Commune aroused unaccustomed anxieties in the British government.

A larger flow of economic migrants might have been expected to reach Britain in its years of rapid industrialization. One of the key consequences of Britain's early start in industrialization was the gap it opened up between itself and other economies and countries—Britain became sensationally more productive and wealthy by mid-century—its competitive prowess all-conquering. Britain led the world until the United States and Germany eventually began to follow its footsteps and catch up. Consequently a differential in income and economic prospects was opened up which, *ceteris paribus*, would naturally generate a flow of immigrants seeking betterment in the new economy. In any event this was a relatively small phenomenon in the nineteenth century and was more usually an internal movement within the British Isles. Relatively few Europeans entered the country—probably because the continent was not activated by its own internal transformation until the 1850s and after. And when the urbanization of European labor began it was mainly absorbed internally or diverted to North America (though much of it passed through Britain *en route*, and some stayed on). But the essential point was that Europe did not flood industrializing Britain with economic immigrants during the critical decades. (Porter 2003, 18)

The European context shifted in the late 19th century – when the newly mobilized or ejected elements from as far away as Russia and Italy (and even Romania) began their westward march, substantial numbers terminating in Britain itself, though more were surging to the Atlantic ports for American destinations. Of these new inflows the component of "crisis" in their origins remains debatable.

Most of the incoming economic migrants into Britain were people drawn by the expanding industrial economy which offered higher incomes than available in the in-comers' homelands. As part of the same equation such people contributed to the economy in a predictable and beneficial fashion. This normal influx was subject to random intakes of people more obviously crisis-driven, refugees in an identifiable way, mainly elements in the mix of humanity on the move in late-19th-century Europe. Of European nationals in Britain the largest group until the 1880s was German in origin—32,823 in 1871 in England and Wales (out of a total of 89,829 from all European countries) and included a significant proportion of German clerks, probably well-educated types evading military conscription in Germany, though many were also simply attracted by the higher income levels prevailing in Britain. Other small groups ended up in Britain, some more obviously extruded by crisis-type forces—gypsies, for example, hounded out of the Balkans, Germany, and France and part of forced movements propelled by "a long-standing hostility toward gypsies." (Porter 2003, 25).

The scale of arrivals changed in the 1880s "when the arrival of thousands of Jews fleeing from pogroms in Russia and eastern Europe transformed the refugee problem." (Porter, 1979, 12–18). They were distinguished from Jews of earlier generations, who were well established and often prosperous. The new waves came from eastern Europe—especially from the late 1860s, most of all in the 1880s and then in the following thirty years—as part of the massive intake of migrants. They were part of the two million Jews who left Russia in 1880-1914—and many were also from Austria-Hungary and Romania—2.75 million in the years 1881–1914. (Porter 1979, 240) In Britain they mostly settled together in established districts of Jewish settlement—and were often associated with great generosity and religious solidarity (Holmes 1997, 319–320).

In 1880 there were 60,000 Jews in Britain but their number rose to 300,000 by 1914 (Holmes 1988, 25) much reinforced by the number of Russian Poles whose numbers in 1901 reached 82,844 and 95,540 by 1911 and they were significantly concentrated in London (68,420 in 1991), most notably in Stepney which took 80 percent of London's Russian and Polish Jews, though there were also concentrations in Leeds and Manchester. (Holmes 1988, 25). The East End of London received waves of immigrants and they were concentrated in textile industries though this concentration eventually diminished and dispersed. (Feldman 2011, 337–339).

The propellants were not so clear. General economic pressure in Russia certainly created conditions for escape—the Jewish population had grown very rapidly within the confined territory of the Pale. In these circumstances labor was transferred from eastern Europe toward the most advanced economies of the West. In effect Polish and Russian Jews were caught up in the demographic and economic transformation affecting European populations in general. But added to this context was the impact of Tsarist repression—"the unremitting persecution which prevailed between 1881 and 1914" with special severity upon the Jews, pressing them toward asylum in Britain, France, Argentina, South Africa, and the United States most of all. (Holmes 1988, 27). But Russian Jewish emigration was not simply the result of pogroms, though it rose in times of persecution. It was highly selective and included large numbers of relatively highly skilled craftsmen. Heavy Jewish migration derived also from Austria-Hungary—even though there they had possessed almost equal civil rights. Political persecution was merely one of the causes. Commercial specialization in agriculture was a more likely general cause, dislocating local communities and setting them on the road as migrants: emigration was one of the solutions to problems in European agriculture (Bouston 2007).

The sudden increase in "alien immigration" in Britain was associated with problems of overcrowding and the sweated trades. General antialien attitudes were ascendant at the turn of the century and there were attacks on Jewish workers in 1903–1904 in Wales and Ireland, but mostly the antagonism was centered in London where half of the European immigrants were located. The immigrants were entangled with the problems in "Outcast London" and part of the great poverty of the times. (Porter 1995, 301–303; White 2004, 154ff). There was rising xenophobia across the country. It became a major issue in British politics and eventually led to the Aliens Act of 1905—the first serious restriction on the right of entry into Britain. (Holmes 1997, 321–324; Pollins 1982, 130). Antagonism in England was vociferous—a handbook of 1909 talked of Britain being the "asylum for criminality and vagrant paupers—the scum of every foreign slum, the refuse of Europe." (Pollins 1982, 136). It was also an intellectual crisis for those who believed that freedom of movement was a crucial tenet of Britain's liberal philosophy.

Did the arrival of these groups constitute a "crisis" for Britain, the receiving society? Sporadic outbreaks of hostility to immigrants affected many groups—there was a long record of fear of foreigners and often their disfavoring—most obviously with incoming Jews and Irish over several centuries (George 1965, ch. 3). The sequence was repeated through the 19th century. (Holmes 1988, ch. 1; Winder, 2004). But until 1905 there were no controls over the entry of foreigners or refugees. (Holmes 1988, 57) The Irish received the greatest attention proportional to their numbers, but other groups attracted equally negative responses—usually associated with claims that they undermined their British counterparts, for instance the German clerks who worked for lower wages, producing some stereotyping and general criticisms, amounting to a broadly based paranoia by the turn of the century. Anti-Semitism was a recurring passion but the antipathy was magnified by their greatly augmented numbers, their competitive skills, and their concentration in London which gave them especially high visibility, heightened further by their alleged resistance to assimilation into the host community.(Holmes 1988, 68–69). Fear and distaste bubbled up and there were sporadic episodes of collective violence, though it hardly amounted to a "national crisis" (Holmes 1988, 71).

The Aliens Act of 1905 required immigrants to prove that they could keep themselves decently and would not become a burden on the state. (Garrard 1971). There had already been official action against in-comers, of whom some 32,000 had been sent out of the country since 1880. (Holmes 1988, 35). Most of the hostility was against proletarian migrants who were said to be competing for accommodation and jobs; there was also a general exaggeration of cultural differences; the state reacted and led some of this hostility against the immigrants.

In reality there were many categories of aliens seeking betterment and freedom in Britain—by 1914 there were 4,000 Lithuanians in England, 7,000 in Scotland; Italians were arriving also—5,000 in 1871, up to 20,389 by 1911 and mainly achieved by chain migration from particular districts in the north of Italy and from many different trades; there were also small groups of Asians and Caribbeans. (Holmes 1988) Clearly, among this array of foreigners entering Britain in the 19th century, some were refugees fleeing crisis in their homelands, mostly however they were economic migrants seeking betterment. (Winder 2004, chs. 10–16).

Famine and Migration

Overwhelming all other candidates in its scale and horror, universally recognised as such, was the Irish Famine migration crisis of the mid-century. This was an emergency of both emigration and immigration and caused political, economic, and demographic repercussions of massive proportions. The ultimate causes of the Irish crisis, apart from the disastrous disease in the potato crop, remain highly contentious. Some historians deny that Ireland in 1845 was overpopulated; one analyst claimed that "the British simply abandoned the Irish and let them perish," and that Britain had made it impossible for Ireland to industrialize and then refused to help when Ireland starved. (Mokyr 1983, 291)

The Famine was a severe emergency which generated great waves of emigration which were extremely unusual in the annals of famine in world history. This was a vast crisis in Ireland, but it also became a crisis in the receiving places, most of all in Britain itself. Famine and its connection to "crisis migration" is usually problematic because people affected by famine are almost always too poor and afflicted to emigrate, caught in an iron grip of deprivation which prevents their escape, thus exacerbating the fatal impact of famine. Famine victims are usually stranded and normally unable to evacuate out of their emergency unless special aid is available and the chance of some type of haven. The Irish case, however, was crucially different because it gave rise to "a larger permanent exodus than any other major famine in history." (Donnelly Jr. 2001, 178).

Migration in famine conditions is normally internal and unavailing for many—and there were certainly instances of this in Ireland. But, in the event, an astonishing number of Irish were able to escape out of Ireland and, though not widely welcomed, had several places to go to. They developed remarkably improvised means of evacuation from their own resources, mainly variations on the theme of chain migration. As early as 1847 there was already desperate emigration and, according to MacDonagh, it was less an emigration than "a headlong flight of refugees" which "bore all the marks of panic and hysteria." (Miller 1985, 292). The evacuation continued through the famine years and beyond.

The failure of the potato crop was a natural disaster visited upon a population in great peril. The structural problems derived from population overload and land shortages. Landlords and local authorities attempted to alleviate the crisis in different ways but were overwhelmed by the scale of the disaster. Emigration was one of several responses and many landlords subsidized and pressured their poor tenants to leave. This was not the normal volitional migration; it was migration under severe pressure and it continued for many decades. In terms of the structural transformations at work there were deep shifts in the foundations of Irish rural society which eventually caused the absolute reduction of the population: mass emigration was a vital component of the restructuring of Irish society.

The Irish case of famine emigration therefore ran against normal expectations because so many of the Irish actually emigrated out of the famine—which has, of course, to be set against the fact that a very large number of the famine victims did not escape and the mortality rate rose massively. Emigration increased spectacularly and was unquestionably driven by famine, but mass emigration had predated the famine, and the Irish continued to emigrate in great numbers in the decades after the famine. Ongoing Irish emigration was, according to Kerby Miller, generated by more "mundane reasons." (Miller 1986, 339.)

The Irish famine of the late 1840s was Europe's greatest natural disaster of the 19th century, claimed Cormac Ó Gráda (Crowley, Smyth, and Murphy, 2012, 170). It was also converted into "crisis migration" by the mass movement of famine refugees in all directions, many seeking to get to America or Australia. But mostly they first reached England, via Liverpool, which was sufficient indeed for the British of virtually all classes to regard it as an imported crisis of very large proportions. The percentage of Irish in England and Wales rose rapidly in the 1840s and 1850s and even more so in Scotland. The numbers in the emergency were comparable to modern examples of mass movements of desperate people who create alarm in receiving countries.

At the start of the Irish famine crisis England was in economic turmoil and Australia was not booming (Checkland 1964, 35–38); consequently the attraction of America was much enhanced and eventually the Irish headed most of all across the Atlantic. The process was helped by the lowered cost of the passage—in some cases as little as £2 and though some suffered extreme discomfort the actual shipboard mortality rates were less than 2 percent. Of the 2 million or so who left Ireland by 1851 1 million went to the United States in 1851, ¾ million to Britain, 1/4 million to Canada and 70,000 to Australia. Only a very small proportion of the emigration, possibly 3 percent or 4 percent, was assisted by the state or subsidized by landlords and this was the cause of severe denunciation at the time, widely regarded as an inadequate response by authority during the crisis. (Ó Gráda 1999, 55) Philanthropy was similarly restricted and many projects foundered for lack of funds. The evacuation of famine-ridden Ireland was therefore essentially self-helped—it was "a miracle of private ingenuity and determination," according to David Fitzpatrick—achieved from savings, loans, gifts, and remittance tickets. In 1849 it was said that three-quarters of all Irish emigration was paid for by money returned from America. It was the "enforced generosity" of expatriated Irish people confronting the imperatives of famine. (Fitzpatrick 1995, 175, 178–180).

The much enhanced emigration of the famine years continued for at least three generations beyond the famine but, as Fitzpatrick puts it, there was a transition from "a panic-stricken expulsion to a calculated pursuit of economic betterment" in a long continuum which had indeed preceded the famine. (Fitzpatrick 1995). Even before 1841 Britain had been receiving 50,000 Irish per annum and Britain was the main destination of tens of thousands of seasonal migrants from Ireland. The rate of emigration from Ireland much more than doubled in the years of the famine and continued into the 1850s. (Donnelly 2001, 178.). Ó Gráda calculates that 5 million left Ireland between 1852 and 1913, substantially more than the official statistics of the day represented. (Donnelly 2001, 179; Ó Gráda 1999, 55)

According to Ireland's leading historian of emigration, "The scale of the flight [from the Famine] was unprecedented in the history of international migration." (Fitzpatrick 1995). One million left between 1846 and 1850 and more in the following four years. Much of it was panic emigration. The reach of the famine extended the net of emigration, now encompassing the far western districts of the country, especially toward the southwest. The famine emigrants included, predictably, many of the better classes of farmers. But they included much higher proportions of paupers and the unemployed who took the very cheap passages from Dublin to Liverpool, in the cattle boats, hoping eventually to get to America—which involved picking up work, accommodation, and savings in England before being able to find a passage across the Atlantic. It was a severe episode in crisis emigration but became a national achievement, by way of highly articulated chains of remittance homewards, to supplement the family economy and fund cycles of emigration, generation upon generation. The outflow was increasingly composed of single males and especially single young women who became a distinctive element in Irish emigration in the late 19th century.

Famine was an accelerant and a climax of the outflow of the Irish, which had a career from at least 1825 to 1914. As Ó Gráda puts it, emigration was the saving of large number of Irish people: "in the absence of long-distance emigration as an outlet, many more would have perished, whether in Ireland, or in Great Britain"; emigration was therefore "a form of disaster relief." (Ó Gráda 1999, 106–107).This is what made the Irish crisis different from the common famine context and outcome. Emigration was a successful response to the calamity of the famine, even though it did not reach those in the greatest risk of dying. (Ó Gráda 1999, 111).

The immediate point of impact in the rest of Britain was Liverpool, the great conduit of inward-coming Irish, and the funnel for outgoing emigrants from all of the British Isles and many from Europe. In eleven months of 1847, according to a Liverpool magistrate, almost 300,000 Irish landed in Liverpool, more than a third of them "half naked and starving"—clearly in great distress, yet their reception was less than sympathetic. According to Rushton, the magistrate, they were "paupers, vagrants and thieves." (Belchem 2007, 34.) Evidently the crisis conditions in Liverpool stretched the resources and pressed down on the local population, not least upon its wages rates. The financial cost on Liverpool grew greatly and there was great resentment and rising sectarianism. (Twomey and Nugent, 505–506). Donnelly declares that Liverpool "was so overwhelmed by the Irish inundation of 1847, and so ravaged by epidemics of disease that thousands of would-be emigrants either perished there or were deprived of the financial means to get overseas." The very poorest were getting out by means of remittances. (Donnelly 2001, 181–184.)

There was an "increase in anti-Irish feeling, already intense, in host countries" (Donnelly 2001, 178). Medical officers, in for instance Liverpool in 1847, were the closest observers of the desperation of the immigrants and their reports defined some of the dimensions of the crisis. (Coleman 1972, 131–133.). And there were increased levels of mortality in England, probably connected to the ingress of many poor Irish: the rise of death rates in England in the 1840s probably stemmed in part from Irish immigration. (Donnelly 2001, 179; Ó Gráda 1999, 111) The politician Poulett Scrope had wanted to stop "the poisonous and fatal influx" of Irish paupers into England. (Griffiths 1987, 127.) The *Liverpool Times* in 1846 defined them as either "emigrants of hope" or "emigrants of despair," the latter being paupers who could not get to America. The local press voiced the great fear of their impact on local wages and poor rates and the spread of cholera and typhoid. The Irish were widely "oppressed, alienated, suspected and discriminated against," though this was neither universal nor comprehensive. British perceptions of the crisis, according to Graham Davis, passed "through a cultural filter that mirrors the values of the host nation without fully reflecting the variety of Irish emigrant experience." (Davis 2000, 19, 26, 28.)

The intensity and scale of the crisis was thus in part transmitted to Britain which had already received swelling numbers of Irish in the two decades before the famine and did so during the many decades that followed. The crisis in Britain was registered across the country: though the numbers are not easily counted we know that the Irish population in Britain rose from 415,000 in 1841 to 806,000 in 1851—but these were only those actually born in Ireland. By 1901 the number had fallen to 632,000. In Warrington in 1847–1848 out of 17,000 who passed through its workhouse, 12,000 of them were Irish: "hunger and need turned great numbers from that country into refugees" (Leeson 1980, 172). The fear in Britain had many faces—most of all that of its depressive effect on wages and the poor rates. The concentration of Irish in certain locations heightened the fear of urban crisis which was already present before the Famine and local attitudes to the incoming Irish were exacerbated by their assumed association with crime, disease, disorder, and unwanted Catholicism.

The 1851 census showed that the Irish were 22.3 percent of the Liverpool population, 18.9 percent of Dundee, 4.6 percent of London and 18.2 percent of Glasgow. Conditions among the Irish had already appalled Engels and distressed Carlyle. Even so the Irish met "sustained antagonism" and were denounced as alien in race and inferior in culture. They flooded the casual labor market. "The huge famine influx of Irish brought fear and resentment to fever pitch"—in towns flooded by the impoverished and disease-ridden Irish. During cholera epidemics the Irish became the scapegoats, producing a "hysterical response" in both England and Scotland. The Irish generally sustained their cultural differences, their group solidarity and there was little intermarriage with the host population until later (O'Tuathaigh 1981, 152, 159, 160, 162, 163, 167)

The Irish share in the British labor force rose from 3.4 percent in 1821 to 8.8 percent in 1861. The destitute Irish, it was thought, "would take the jobs and lower the standards of the decent English and Scottish working class." Moreover the general reputation was dominated by details of strikebreakers and slum conditions, sectarian riots, "poor Paddy" on the railway, and sporadic incidents of political violence, for example in Oldham in 1861 (Foster 1974, 236). There was less evidence of sanctuary and sympathy for the large invasion, yet eventually the Irish were mainly accommodated, the social fabric survived, and the nation grew more prosperous than ever. The American economist Williamson has indeed argued that the accommodation of the Irish in Britain demonstrated "the impressive absorptive capacity of the British economy." (Davis 2000, 24–28; Williamson 1986, 693–721). But according to Fitzpatrick, the Irish in Britain remained for several decades a "restless, transient people" facing exclusion and disadvantage—and mostly confined to the most menial, casual and impermanent sector of manual employment. (Fitzpatrick 1995, 198). Although the Irish in Britain were not ghettoized they clustered, neither integrated nor self-sustaining as a community. (Mulkern 1996, 119–136). Their accommodation to Britain was gradual but eventually achieved.

Landlords and the government regarded the efflux of emigrants from Ireland as preordained. (Moran 2004). The process was invested with a dimension of racial inevitability: the notion that the Celts were an inferior and declining race, relegated to service roles in cities and colonies across the Anglo-world. In April 1852 the *Illustrated London News* reported "The exodus of the Celtic Races": it described it as "... the flux of the emigrational tide toward the shore of the New World. The quays of Dublin, Cork and Liverpool are crowded with Irish emigrants," and they were often embittered.

> Year after year the efflux continues. . . .the very life-blood of the nation [is lost] . . . to that great kindred nation of America, which is destined in due time to overshadow the world with its power and glory, leave our shores in countless multitudes.

The greater the number emigrating in any one year, the larger the amount of funds received in Ireland in the next, to enable friends and relatives to follow to the land of plenty and independence. The same report declared that "The potato failure is working a mighty revolution." It had caused land to change hands and had "driven the very flower of the Celtic race across the Atlantic" and "This mighty emigration pays for itself. It seeks no aid from the public purse, but... establishes itself in regions that owe no fealty to the Crown of England." (Killen 1995, 257)

Sir Charles Trevelyan said that the evacuation of Ireland by way of emigration was the "natives' solution" to the national problem; *The Times* predicted that "In a few years a Celtic Irishman will be as rare in Connemara as a Red Indian on the shores of Manhattan." (Whelan 1995, 32). Gladstone himself was deeply disturbed, even ashamed, at the processes at work in Ireland.

Emigration became the most obvious choice for at least three generations of young Irish people. After the famine emigration became normal and expected. But it was always contentious—for instance, Horace Plunkett referred to the post-Famine exoduses as these "vast unaided emigrations"—for which he blamed the English. (Gault 2011, 174.) J. S. Mill took the view that "The land of Ireland, the land of every country, belongs to the people of that country" and he regarded Irish emigration as a forced expatriation and a denial of the rights of the Irish people.(O'Brien 1975, 344)

On the question of the effect of Irish immigration on England, the classical economists were unable to agree. Some of them asserted that their "defects of character—idleness, dissipation, improvidence, inefficiency, recklessness, cruelty, violence, vindictiveness and ignorance" made the Irish a negative force. Others feared that they would contaminate the English workforce. Nassau Senior did not agree and thought everybody benefited (Coats 1992, 167), a view echoed by modern economists if not by Irish nationalists. At the time, despite the hostility that often confronted the Irish emigrants in Britain, America, and Australia, there was a recognition that the Irish were vital in the construction of the new economies arising in all the receiving countries. One of the Irish landlords, Lord Clanricarde, an advocate of sponsored emigration, pointed out that, in prosperous times, cheap Irish labor had been of "great benefit in building up the great towns of England." (Conwell 2003, 50).

Crises across Industrializing Britain

Emigration from the British Isles over more than two centuries was frequently invoked as an answer to national and local crises. In the 1690s Scotland had wagered much of its national wealth and pride on a prospective new colony in Darien (in modern Panama) to rescue its place in European colonization and expand its horizons—it had appalling results for its nation and its credulous emigrants. (Richards 2015, 26–46). In the following century the British government sponsored several emigration schemes to settle demobbed soldiers along its imperial frontiers as a buttress against insurgents—especially in its North American territories. In the postwar turbulence in the British economy after Waterloo there were further efforts to employ emigration schemes to relieve poverty and avert radical disturbances—notably the schemes to establish a substantial colony at the Cape of Good Hope—which was highly oversubscribed by eager prospective emigrants seeking better opportunities beyond. These were schemes which entailed several thousand people; but, in national terms, they barely made a scratch on the "crises" they addressed, and incurred heavy and politically unsustainable expenditures by government. (See Johnston 1972; Tosh 2017)

Coerced emigration, in the form of transportation, was a means of disposing of British and Irish criminals and political prisoners and possessed a long history—some 60,000 were dispatched to the American colonies. American independence in the 1780s coincided with a mounting "crisis" in the level of crime in England and Ireland and this led to a frantic search for new locations for criminals who overflowed British gaols. The answer was the founding of the first Australian colonies in 1788, a forced emigration arising from a domestic emergency, and an example of institutionalized crisis emigration, eventually disposing of 160,000 convicts to the distant colonies of Australia. This was crisis emigration as both safety valve and social solution. It was the precursor of other efforts to "shovel out paupers" and social misfits to the colonies, to export British problems by emigration, each "crisis" defined as such by beleaguered local authorities, landowners, and employers.

In every domestic crisis there were repeated pleas for schemes of emigration to ameliorate the suffering of sections of the population. The plight of very large numbers handloom weavers, damaged by the changeover to power weaving, was severe. In the 1820s they were already destined for industrial oblivion—and their predicament prompted recommendations for emigration schemes to relieve the situation. But this was heavily resisted by local and national authority on the grounds of cost and also that it was amoral—that it offended the sacred principle that "every man born in England had a right to live in England." This was the basis for the idea that such people should instead be encouraged to return to the land, to take up waste lands. Neither emigration nor land settlement produced much traction. (Bythell 1969, 75, 158, 174fn, 212).

Almost always the government displayed rigorous resistance to any such involvement, mainly on the grounds of expense. There were however numerous episodes when serious efforts were employed to use emigration to mitigate domestic emergencies. An agrarian crisis in southern Ireland in the early 1820s generated such a scheme. This was known as the "Captain Rock" emergency, an outburst of protest involving social breakdown and violence targeted at the landlord establishment. It began in west Limerick and then spread to six counties during an intense economic depression across southwest Ireland. There was extreme alarm among landowners and government, and the terror induced a group of landowners to take a concerted interest in organizing a substantial scheme of assisted emigration to Canada, the idea being to rid their estates of the worst troublemakers. The third Earl of Kingston informed Lord Bathurst at the Colonial Office:

> "I think you may help us at very small expense to the government if you will send out a few families to Canada and provision for them for one year on land given to them by the government."
>
> (Donnelly 2009, 327).

An emigration scheme would diminish "Captain Rock's army." The plan emerged in the schemes of Peter Robinson in the years 1823 to 1825 which were expected to start a continuing flow of emigration from the troubled region. The Home Office found £10,000 for the project to take settlers from County Cork to Upper Canada where they would be provided with seventy acres per family and provisions for twelve months. Robinson began his plans in Cork in May 1823 where he found that the gentry "were unanimously of opinion that I should take as many persons as possible from the disturbed baronies in the county of Cork, which were at that time in a very distracted state." The first sailings from Cork carried 568 emigrants in July 1823. In the following year Robinson announced further sailings and he was besieged by about 50,000 applicants This provided evidence of pent-up demand for emigration in the Irish context (Donnelly, 2009, 323–336, 331). In the end Robinson took only about two thousand—in nine ships—but it was the biggest single group to cross the Atlantic at that stage. The results were not happy—the emigrants were beset with disease and general sickness and high rates of mortality. The emigrants then encountered difficult terrain though in the long run they did quite well. The entire project, an exercise in state-assisted emigration, eventually cost £52,000. Emigration soon proved to be too expensive to solve Irish problems.

The emigration experiments at the Cape of Good Hope and in Canada were not clear successes and were exceedingly expensive to a government anxious to avoid budgetary disturbance. Nevertheless during the continuing turbulence of the postwar years, into the 1820s (with fears of social breakdown, high unemployment, rising poor rates, and very fast population growth), many commentators were prompted to regard emigration as the obvious solution to the national crisis. The most vocal and repetitive advocate was Wilmot Horton at the Colonial Office who pressed the case for a grand national effort by government to mobilize and fund large-scale emigration. Horton's enthusiasm for assisted emigration was almost boundless, and he frightened all those who regarded the government's proper role as strictly limited. In 1825 Horton envisaged the emigration of up to 500,000 on the pattern of the Robinson schemes (Donnelly 2009, 431 fn) and he hatched even bigger plans in 1827 to spend £1,140,000 to remove 950,000. But Horton's plans were politically anathema and the idea collapsed: Horton was packed off to Ceylon into political exile.

Horton's grandiose plans, though they were clearly directed to solve crisis conditions in Britain (essentially from the fear of unemployment, overpopulation, and radicalism), foundered for several reasons: first, they were vastly too expensive to be contemplated by the British government; second, any benefit would have taken far too long to reach fruition; third, his plans were confronted by the skepticism of economic and political theorists of the day who decried the claimed benefits; conspicuous among these was Malthus who argued that emigration could produce no permanent benefits by way of population relief because the "vacuum" left by the departing emigrants would always be refilled by a resurgence of the birth rate to fill the void. (He allowed that the emigrants themselves would benefit, but that was hardly the issue). (Richards 2013, 42–60.)

Consequently government aid to promote emigration was denied—and this became a sticking point throughout the century—a doctrinaire resistance by the state to the idea of employing emigration to relieve emergencies. Emigration was revived as a form of social engineering in a radically different mode by the so-called "systematic colonizers," led by Edward Gibbon Wakefield who successfully persuaded colonial governments to employ their own revenues (from land sales in particular) to subsidize their immigrants. This however was not crisis emigration, merely a form of colonial engineering to fulfill rational and growing colonial requirements.

But this did not quite exhaust the uses of emigration to meet the sporadic crises in Britain during the rest of the century. For instance substantial philanthropic bodies emerged to assist the emigration of "problem" groups in the population and their activities often opened windows into the state of certain parts of the economy attracting such assistance. Thus young unmarried women came to be regarded as "surplus" who might make better lives, and become more useful, in the colonies. Similarly the problem of orphans and street children and unemployable youth led to schemes for their assisted emigration—designed to diminish and indeed export such social problems, those defined as such by urban authorities at the time. There were substantial schemes and the aggregated numbers—as though "shoveled-out"—were impressive, but nevertheless minor elements in the much greater flows of ordinary migration. (Peters 2000; Ruiz 2017).

Nottingham Lacemakers

The strange career of the Nottingham lacemakers in the 1830s and 1840s exemplifies the sporadic recourse to emigration to relieve particular difficulties in the economy. Under the impact of technical change, three thousand Nottingham lacemakers migrated with their work to Calais in the late 1830s. In 1848 however the English community in Calais was caught in the peripheral disturbances related to the 1848 Revolution. It was reported that "the greatest hostility . . . everywhere has been displayed by the populace against English workmen . . . and the consequence is that their masters were obliged to dismiss them. In many places they had to fly for their lives, and returned to England wholly destitute." The lacemakers were terrified by this eruption of anglophobia and their dire distress reached the notice of the British newspapers. The people involved and their sympathizers regarded the situation as a "crisis." They petitioned the British consul, pleading to escape persecution.

An inquiry instituted by the government reported that, though the lacemakers had exaggerated their danger in Calais, it confirmed that they were indeed suffering seriously from the economic depression in their trade. A charitable body, "the Committee of Noblemen and Gentlemen for the Relief of British workmen, Refugees from France," with royal support, took up their cause. Soon a plan emerged to seek free passages for the lacemakers to emigrate to Australia; a public subscription was raised for their aid to cover the high incidental expenses associated with the assisted voyage. Eventually the Colonial Emigration Commissioners relaxed their regulations regarding size of families, and, with the understanding that the lacemakers could turn their hands to agriculture, they provided assistance to Australia.

This was a somewhat exotic body of long-term double-emigrants and several hundred of the lacemakers arrived in the distant colonies in 1849. But they had emigrated out of one crisis and into another—on arrival they found the local economy in Adelaide in recession and unemployment rife; they were soon writing adverse letters back to Nottingham. They faced an overstocked labor market in the colony and much unemployment: "we found plenty out of work as well as ourselves," said one of them. Some were employed minding sheep in the outback; the accommodation they found was worse than the mud cabins of Old Ireland. They declared that they wished they had never left England. This was the typical situation of immigrants who had the misfortune to arrive at a time of recession: the lacemakers were doubly ill-fated crisis emigrants. (Irish University Press 1969; *Nottingham Review* 1848; Webster 1982; Webster 1985). During recessions immigrants were usually the first target of complaint in any receiving society.

An Industrial Crisis

The definition of "crisis" was, of course, elastic and often referred simply to ongoing readjustments in the economy—some of which were certainly painful and the cause of great distress. "Crisis" tends to refer to short-term emergencies but can also relate to long-term shifts which take on characteristics of a "General Crisis"—often derived from the buildup of certain conditions which accumulate eventually into a total turbulence across society, growing pressures which induce structural transformations. This had been the case across most of rural Britain for many decades into the nineteenth century—in effect the widespread disengagement of labor from the land which was expressed not so much in a sudden crisis but in generalized adversity and heightened outward mobilization, with increasing numbers of rural folk heading for the towns and for overseas through emigration. These tens of thousands were not recognizably refugees, but they were products of "general crisis," an ongoing transformation of the society.

The widespread decline of rural labor needs in Britain's agricultural sector was a long-lasting crisis which eventually rallied union solidarity to reinforce better wages and conditions. One stratagem employed by the agricultural unions was to encourage rural laborers to emigrate—a device designed to reduce labor availability and generate an upward pressure on wages rates. Hence several schemes emerged for such migration to New Zealand, Canada, and even Brazil (Kelly 1998; Richards 2004). This was a rational response, but peripheral in its impact.

A better-known instance of crisis emigration, in another sector, concerned the Lancashire cotton operatives in the early 1860s, an emergency greatly exacerbated by the curtailment of cotton supplies during the Civil War in the United States, commonly referred to as "the Cotton Famine." In 1860 cotton textiles had accounted for 38 percent of British exports—it then, following a great boom in the 1850s, plunged into decline in the most severe depression the industry had ever experienced. (Farnie 1979, 135ff.).

In January 1863 there had been 586,001 operatives in employment but by December 1864 their numbers had fallen to 440,801: the scale of the unemployment and distress was alarming. The emigration remedy was immediately advocated and it was said that "if means had been supplied, a very large proportion of the operatives would doubtless have left the country." But many of the Lancashire employers were resistant, thinking that if the cotton operatives emigrated, when the revival occurred they would have to recruit labor from the countryside, which would then upset the rural interest. In parliamentary debates, Ferrand declared that the government should appropriate £1.5million to aid emigration in the sector. He accused the manufacturers of "opposing emigration for selfish purpose, and complained that some of the richest men have not given even a sixpence to the relief fund." (Farnie 1979, 318–319).

Nevertheless committees were set up to aid emigration though their funds were limited. The "Emigrants' Aid Society" eventually funded the outfits of 836 adults and aided the passages of 385 of these. Queensland took 1,170 cotton operatives in 1863, much assisted by colonial funding and money raised in England. (Oxley Library 1863–1884). Meantime it was reported that migration agents had come from the "United States during the crisis and sought our hands for weaving and spinning, and having made engagements with them, paid their passage fees to America." Larger numbers went to the colonies. (Watts 1866, 213–217)

The Laissez-Faire Context

Emigration from the British Isles amounted to about ten million in the nineteenth century. Most emigration occurred unrestrainedly in a context of *laissez faire* and was directed to the Anglo-World—to the expanding Empire, though even more to the United States. Mostly British emigration flowed freely and without controversy and without government intervention (except for the regulation of conditions aboard the emigrant ships). The government had little involvement in the exodus and had little chance to influence the flows.

The narrative was punctuated with a number of episodes which aroused national alarm and which caused consternation across the nation. At the start there was anxiety about the loss of British people and attempts were made to impede and reverse the outflows. After 1825 this attitude quickly reversed. Thereafter there were recurrent and uncoordinated attempts to promote emigration as a solution to national problems.

People leaving Britain in the nineteenth century rarely caused much stir in political circles. Newspapers and charities aroused sympathy for poor tenantries being "shoveled out" of the country and for peasantries being evicted. Conditions aboard emigrant ships also attracted much opprobrium and eventual governmental intervention. Emigration was recurrently advocated as a solution to certain problems but it was limited in its role as a safety valve for people seeking a haven from their distress, out of adversity.

More crisis-laden responses attended sudden large-scale incursions which generated a degree of moral panic. The reception of large numbers of Irish caused alarm and hostility but, in the long term, they were well-absorbed into the expansive economy of Victorian Britain. The people who left the British Isles in large numbers were unlike modern economic migrants because they were generally welcomed on arrival and enjoyed a choice of destinations, mobile in the spectacularly liberal world of the day. The crises of British migration in the nineteenth century were contained in a context decidedly less fraught than many of those in the twenty-first century.

References

Belchem, J. 2007. *Irish, Catholic, and Scouse*. Liverpool, UK: Liverpool University Press.

Bouston, L. P. 2007. "Were Jews Political Refugees or Economic Migrants? Assessing the Persecution Theory of Jewish Emigration 1881-1914." In *The New Comparative Economic History*, edited by Timothy J. Hatton, 267–290. Cambridge, Mass.: MIT Press.

Bythell, D. 1969. *The Handloom Weavers*. London: Cambridge University Press.

Checkland, S. G. 1964. *The Rise of Industrial Society in England, 1815–1885*. London: Longmans.

Coats, A.W. Bob. 1992. *On the History of Economic Thought*. London: Routledge.

Coleman, T. 1972. *Passage to America: A history of Emigrants from Great Britain and Ireland to America in the Mid-nineteenth Century*. London: Hutchinson.

Conwell, J. J. 2003. *A Galway Landlord during the Great Famine*. Dublin: Four Courts.

Crowley, J., W.J. Smyth, and M Murphy, eds. 2012. *Atlas of the Great Irish Famine, 1845–52*. New York: New York University Press.

Davis, G. 2000. "The Irish in Britain, 1815–1939." In *The Irish Diaspora*, edited by Andy Bielenberg, 19–36. Harlow, UK: Longman.

Donnelly, J. S., Jr. 2001. *The Great Irish Potato Famine*. Stroud, UK: Sutton.

Donnelly, J. S., Jr. 2009. *Captain Rock: The Irish Agrarian Rebellion of 1821–1824*. Cork, UK: Collins.

"English Workmen at Calais". *Nottingham Review*7 April 1848: 2.

Farnie, D.A. 1979. *The English Cotton Industry in the World Market, 1815–1896*. Oxford: Clarendon.

Fiddian-Qasminyeh, E. et al., eds. 2014. *The Oxford Handbook of Refugee and Forced Migration Studies*. Oxford: Oxford University Press.

Feldman, D. 2011. "Eastern European Jews in London since the Late Nineteenth Century." In *Encyclopaedia of Migration and Minorities in Europe*, edited by K.J. Bade et al., 337–339. Cambridge, UK: Cambridge University Press.

Fitzpatrick, D. 1995. " Flight from Famine." In *The Great Irish Famine*, edited by Cathal Póirtéir, 174–184. Cork, Ireland: Mercier.

Foster, J. 1974. *Class Struggle and the Industrial Revolution*. London: Weidenfeld and Nicolson.

Garrard, J. A. 1971. *The English and Immigration, 1880–1910*. London: Oxford University Press for the Institute of Race Relations.

Gault, H. 2011. *The Quirky Dr. Fay*. Cambridge, UK: Gretton.

George, M. D. 1965[1925]. *London Life in the Eighteenth Century*. New York: Harper & Row.

Griffiths, A.R.G. 1987. *The Irish Board of Works, 1831–1878*. New York: Garland.

Holmes, C. 1988. *John Bull's Island*. Basingstoke, UK: Macmillan.

Holmes, C. 1997. "Hostile Images of Immigrants and Refugees in Nineteenth- and Twentieth-Century Britain." In *Migration, Migration History, History: Old Paradigms and New Perspectives*, edited by Jan and Leo Lucassen, 317–334. Bern: Peter Lang.

Irish University Press, ed. 1969. "Ninth General Report of the Colonial Land and Emigration Commissioners: May 1849: 4–6, 14." In *Irish University Press Series of British Parliamentary Papers*. Emigration 11. Shannon: Irish University Press.

Johnston, H. J. M. 1972. *British Emigration Policy, 1815–1830*. Oxford: Clarendon Press.

Kelly, G. 1998. *Well Suited to the Colony*. Queanbeyan: Australian Society of the Lace-Makers of Calais.

Killen, J., ed. 1995. *The Famine Decade: Contemporary Accounts, 1841–1851*. Belfast, Ireland: Blackstaff.

Leeson, R.A. 1980. *Travelling Brothers*. London: Allen & Unwin.

Letters from Emigrants to Queensland, 1863–1884. Facsimile. Brisbane, Australia: John Oxley Library, Brisbane.

Miller, K. 1985. *Emigrants and Exiles*. New York: Oxford University Press.

Miller, K. A. 1986. "Emigration as Exile: Cultural Hegemony in Post-Famine Ireland." In *A Century of European Migrations, 1830–1930*, edited by Rudolph J. Vecoli and Suzanne M. Sinke, 339–363. Urbana: University of Illinois Press.

Mokyr, J. 1983. *Why Ireland Starved*. London: Allen & Unwin.

Moran, G. 2004. *Sending out Ireland's Poor: Assisted Emigration to North America in the Nineteenth Century*. Dublin: Four Courts.

Mulkern, P. 1996. "Irish Immigrants and Public Disorder in in Coventry, 1845–1875." *Midland History* 21:119–135.

O'Brien, D.P. 1975. *The Classical Economists Revisited*. Princeton, NJ: Princeton University Press.

Ó'Gráda, C. 1999. *Black 47 and Beyond*. Princeton, NJ: Princeton University Press.

O'Tuathaigh, M. A. G. 1981. "The Irish in Nineteenth-Century Britain: Problems of Integration." *Transactions of the Royal Historical Society* 5th series, 31:149–173.

Peters, L. 2000. *Orphan Texts: Victorian Orphans, Culture and Empire*. Manchester, UK: Manchester University Press.

Pollins, H. 1982. *Economic History of the Jews in England*. Rutherford, NJ: Fairleigh Dickinson University Press.

Pooley, C., and J. Turnbull. 1998. *Migration and Mobility in Britain since the Eighteenth Century*. London: UCL.

Porter, B. 1979. *The Refugee Question in mid-Victorian Politics*. Cambridge, UK: Cambridge University Press.

Porter, B. 2003. "The Asylum of Nations: Britain and the Refugees of 1848." In *Exiles from European Revolutions: Refugees in Mid-Victorian England*, edited by S. Freitag, 43–56. New York: Berghahn.

Porter, R. 1995. *London: A Social History*. Cambridge, MA: Harvard University Press.

Richards, E. 2004. *Britannia's Children: Emigration from England, Scotland, Wales, and Ireland since 1600*. London: Hambledon and London.

Richards, E. 2013. "Malthus and the Uses of British Emigration." In *Empire, Migration and Identity in the British World*, edited by Kent Fedorowich and Andrew S. Thompson, 42–59. Manchester, UK: Manchester University Press.

Richards, E. 2015. "Darien and the Psychology of Scottish Adventurism in the 1690s." In *Imperial Expectations and Realities: El Dorados, Utopias, and Dystopias*, edited by A. Varnava, 26–46. Manchester, UK: Manchester University Press.

Richards, E. 2018. *The Genesis of International Mass Migration*. Manchester, UK: Manchester University Press.

Ruiz, M. 2017. *British Female Emigration Societies and the New World, 1860–1914*. Cham, Switzerland: Palgrave Macmillan.

Tosh, J. 2017. "From the Cape of Despair to the Cape of Good Hope: The Emigrant Poor in Early Nineteenth-century England." *Social History* 42, no. 4: 480–500.

Watts, J. 1866. *The Facts of the Cotton Famine*. London: Simpkin, Marshall and Co.

Webster, D. B. 1982. "A Migrant Lacemaker." *Descent* 12 (September 1982): 119–128.

Webster, D. B., ed. 1985. *The Binda Connection: Stories of Four Families*. Hackett, Australian Capital Territory: D. B. Webster.

Whelan, K. 1995. "Pre and Post-Famine Landscape Change". In *The Great Irish Famine*, edited by Cathal Póirtéir, 19–33. Cork, Ireland: Mercier.

White, J. 2004. *London in the Nineteenth Century*. London: Jonathan Cape.

Williamson, J. G. 1986. "The Impactof the Irish on the British Labor Markets during the Industrial Revolution." *Journal of Economic History* 46, no. 3: 693–720.

Winder, R. 2004. *Bloody Foreigners: The Story of Immigration to Britain*. London: Little, Brown and Co.

CHAPTER 3

MEMORIES OF A FRENCH MIGRATION CRISIS

The Harkis

LAURA JEANNE SIMS

IN 1962, the French state created a migration crisis through the way it managed the arrival and installation of the Harkis and their families in France. The Harkis are Algerians of North African origin who supported the French army during the Algerian War of Independence (1954–1962). Following Algerian independence at the conclusion of the war, the Harkis, along with their wives and children, faced reprisal violence at the hands of victorious Algerian nationalists. Between 10,000 and 150,000 were killed, while many more experienced the threat of violence. From 1962 to 1964, as many as 88,000 Harkis and their dependants were forced to migrate quickly and under duress to metropolitan France. Upon their arrival, the state placed nearly 25,000 in transit and internment camps. While most were resettled within the first two years, hundreds of families remained until the camps were closed in 1975.

This period of disruption and violence, which posed a serious threat to the welfare and security of the Harkis and their families, was transformed into a crisis by French policy responses. Anna Lindley has defined a crisis as an event that implies "some form of marked discontinuity" and "entail[s] a severe threat or damage to important human needs and goals" (2014, 2). The physical, material, and psychological welfare of the Harkis was endangered both before and after their migration to France. This migration was triggered by an extreme event, but the migration crisis was caused by specific French policies that were rooted in discriminatory, colonial logic. The state left the Harkis unarmed and vulnerable in Algeria, actively prevented the Harkis and their families from settling in France, and was responsible for the suffering of many of those who managed to migrate, due to the conditions in the camps.

French responses were the product of structural racism in France. Structural racism constitutes a "system in which public policies, institutional practices, cultural representations, and other norms work in various, often reinforcing ways to perpetuate racial group inequity" (The Aspen Institute 2018). Comparing the state's treatment of the Harkis with that of the Pieds-Noirs, the descendants of European settlers in Algeria, who likewise fled to mainland France following Algerian independence, reveals the existence and implications of this system. The migration of nearly one million Pieds-Noirs, most of whom passed through the city of Marseille, initially strained financial and administrative resources and provoked tensions with local inhabitants (Baussant 2012, 95). The Pieds-Noirs also inspired animosity among the French in the metropole as remnants of France's now shameful colonial past. However, the French state believed this population would ultimately be able to integrate into French society and their policies reflected this conviction. Government officials did not place similar restrictions on the arrival of these migrants as they did for the Harkis, priority was given to finding them housing, and they never experienced the indignity of life in the camps. In short, the state did not construct the same conditions of crisis for the Pieds-Noirs that the Harkis experienced. Perhaps unsurprisingly, today the Pieds-Noirs face the rare challenge of trying to resist complete assimilation in France. Indeed, scholars have argued that they will "soon vanish as a subgroup in French society" and that "any sense of *pied-noir* distinctiveness is now generated from within their community," whereas the Harkis continue to struggle for inclusion (Smith 2013, 67; Barclay 2014, 13).

The media and government leaders presented the arrival of the Harkis as a "problem" that the state was managing, rather than as a crisis it had created. They attempted to normalize French policy responses, making them appear natural and even benevolent. Ultimately, political actors sought to downplay the extent of the threat to the Harkis' welfare. Lindley has observed that when migrants are seen as posing "a challenge to the cohesion of national political communities," states may "promulgate a 'business-as-usual' or non-crisis discourse, seeking to deny or minimise empirical experiences and objective indicators of severe threat and discontinuity" (Lindley 2014, p. 6, 9). The French national community was particularly fragile in the aftermath of the Algerian War. This conflict constituted not only a war of decolonization, but also a civil war for France. The loss of French Algeria in 1962 challenged the very foundations of French national identity. It highlighted the contradictions between France's republican, universalist ideology and its status as a major colonial power.

The Harkis appeared particularly problematic on a symbolic level because their existence had been framed as evidence of indigenous support for French Algeria during the war. After Algerian independence, they served as inconvenient reminders of France's disgraced colonial policy. This may also explain why, despite being officially categorized as repatriates (*rapatriés*) like the Pieds-Noirs, they were essentially considered and treated as refugees. Whereas repatriates are defined as individuals returning to their country of birth, origin, or citizenship, refugees are individuals who have been forced to leave their country in order to escape war, persecution, or natural disaster. Technically both the Pieds-Noirs and the Harkis were migrating to their country of citizenship. In the French imagination, however, Harkis were not returning home to the metropole, but rather fleeing the place where they belonged. Furthermore, while the Secretariat of State for Repatriates was charged with handling the installation of the Harkis in France, they were always treated as a separate category from the other repatriates. The Pieds-Noirs, who included the Jewish population of Algeria, were considered European Repatriates from Algeria (*Européens rapatriés d'Algérie*), while the Harkis were classified first as French Muslim Repatriates (*Français musulmans rapatriés*), then French Repatriates of Islamic faith (Français rapatriés de confession islamique), and finally as Repatriates of North African Origin (*Rapatriés d'origine nord-africaine*). Thus, the state maintained a formal distinction among the repatriates based on religion and/or ethnicity, which echoed the administrative divisions that existed in colonial Algeria.

This chapter examines the different ways in which the Harki migration crisis was constructed and then framed in public discourse. It begins by examining the Harkis' lived experiences of migration, which reveal how their movement constituted a crisis for individuals, families, and the community at large. This approach also shows the extent to which the crisis was the result of French policy responses. The next section analyzes how Harki migration was presented in the media. In particular, it demonstrates that the state was described as resolving the crisis, rather than as having caused it. The chapter then exposes the structural racism underlying French policy decisions by comparing the Harkis' situation with that of the Pieds-Noirs and by analyzing the language used to describe the Harkis as refugees, as opposed to repatriates. Finally, it explores how Harkis, and especially their children, have constructed collective memories of this crisis. Whereas the first generation was silenced by the traumas of migration, the second-generation has focused on holding the French state responsible for its actions.

Construction of a Personal Crisis

On March 19, 1962, the Evian Accords, which marked the end of the Algerian War and signaled Algerian independence, went into effect. Article X of the Accords offered provisions for the Harkis, stipulating that they would not face reprisals for their support of France during the war. The following day, the French passed a decree stating the Harkis were to be offered three options: they could decide to enlist in the French army, return to civilian life with a bonus, or sign a six-month provisional contract as part of the local forces that were being formed. Most chose the second option, in part because they were encouraged to do so by their officers, and also because even during the war, they were only informally attached to the army (Crapanzano 2011, 86). The Harkis had retained their civilian status throughout the conflict and if they were injured in combat, their compensation fell under the category of a "work accident" (Besnaci-Lancou and Moumen 2008, 14, 16; Hamoumou 1993, 116). Some auxiliaries signed contracts with the army on a day-to-day basis and several Harkis have explained that they in fact saw themselves as laborers, rather than soldiers (Cohen 2006, 165).

The Harkis may also have overwhelmingly chosen to return to civilian life because they likely did not understand the risk they would face in doing so (Morelle 2004). Indeed, there are indications that the Algerian government reassured the Harkis that they would not be harmed (Besnaci-Lancou and Moumen 2008, 37). It quickly became apparent, however, that many Harkis were in serious danger and since the French army had disarmed the Harkis before leaving, they were entirely vulnerable to reprisal attacks from individuals and groups seeking vengeance for acts committed by the French during the war (Besnaci-Lancou and Moumen 2008, 45). It is also possible either that they may not have fully understood the options they were given or that the three choices were never proposed to some Harkis (Crapanzano 2011, 87). Several Harkis have testified to waking up one morning and being shocked to find that the barracks were empty and that French troops had departed with all of their weapons.

Historians have been unable to calculate how many people were targeted for their status as Harkis or for their association to a Harki, since we do not know exactly how many auxiliaries fought for France. Moreover, anyone who supported the French in a civil capacity or who was related to a Harki constituted a potential victim. We likewise cannot determine how many Harkis and their families were killed. Indeed, this may be the most uncertain figure in the history of the Algerian War (Pervillé, 2004, 486). While estimates range from 10,000 to 150,000, historians generally agree that the number is likely closer to 75,000 (Manceron 2011, 86).

Facing the significant threat of violence, then, tens of thousands of Harkis and their families sought to flee to France. Most Harkis and their wives have remained silent about their experiences of violence and migration, both in the public and private spheres. Their silence is due to many factors, including trauma, fear, a lack of outlets for expression, and a desire to integrate into French society. Many did not wish to draw attention to their presence in France, which they had been made to understand was both undesirable and problematic. The exceptions include Saïd Ferdi and Brahim Sadouni, who published memoirs in the 1980s, and two other Harkis, Messaoud Kafi and Abdallah Krouk, who did the same in 2009 and 2010. In 2006, one Harki daughter, Fatima Besnaci-Lancou, published collections of narratives by other Harkis, entitled *Treize chibanis harkis*, and their wives, entitled *Nos mères, paroles blessées*. In these accounts, not all report having witnessed acts of brutality, but many relate having at least heard rumours of horrific acts committed against Harkis. They have indicated that it was fear of a similar fate that prompted them to attempt to leave Algeria, their families, livelihoods, and communities. In Sadouni's memoir, he described a secondhand account of an incident in which a Harki was dragged behind a car and another in which a Harki's war medals were stuck into his skin before he was killed (1985, 5, 156). He explained that the constant danger, instability, and a specific threat against his safety prompted him to seek refuge in France. In *Nos mères, paroles blessées*, one Harki wife explained that she was "five months pregnant when she followed her husband to the nearest barracks, where other Harki families had taken refuge to go into exile and thus escape death" (Besnaci-Lancou 2006a, p. 23). Another described how her husband had been tortured after Algerian independence and that "we were obliged to leave our country in order to remain alive" (Besnaci-Lancou 2006a, 27). The failure of the army to properly plan for and execute the evacuation of the Harkis and their families created the conditions for these individual crises to occur.

Indeed, this period of extreme distress was exacerbated by the French state, which discouraged the Harkis' migration, even when leaders understood the threat and the extent of the violence that they were experiencing. Like the Harkis themselves, French authorities may have initially underestimated the risk the Harkis faced by remaining in Algeria (Besnaci-Lancou and Moumen 2008, 19). They perhaps expected, in all good faith, that Article X of the Evian Accords would be enforced (Besnaci-Lancou and Moumen 2008, 29). Yet when Pierre Messmer, the Secretary of the Army, Roger Frey, Minister of the Interior, and Louis Joxe, in charge of Algerian Affairs, became aware of the extent of the reprisal violence, they did not alter their policy. On May 12, 1962, Messmer sent a telegram sanctioning officers who had taken it upon themselves to evacuate groups of Harkis to France. That same day, Joxe ordered "any auxiliaries who arrived outside the general repatriation plan" to be sent back to Algeria (Besnaci-Lancou and Moumen 2008, 33). Three days later, Roger Frey declared that he believed some Harkis had taken it upon themselves to cross the Mediterranean without having been directly threatened with violence in Algeria. On May 25, *Le Figaro* reported that over one hundred Harkis and their families had been turned away when they landed in Marseille (Besnaci-Lancou and Moumen 2008, 33). Repeated restrictions and expulsions indicate that authorities sought to prevent the arrival of many Harkis and their relatives in France, thereby producing a humanitarian crisis and resulting in greater loss of life.

For those who managed to escape, through the limited official channels, with the assistance of sympathetic military officers, or on their own, their journey has often been described in terms of fear, confusion, and loss. In short, for many of the Harkis and their families, it constituted a personal crisis. This voyage appeared especially difficult for wives who were following their husbands because they were often not involved either in the decision to support France or to leave Algeria. One Harki wife explained how she left Algeria without having time to visit her mother and how she was "thrown into great distress" (Besnaci-Lancou 2006a, 44). Others recounted similar sorrow and anxiety at suddenly leaving their homes and their families. One woman described how she comforted the women who were crying on the boat and also helped a woman who gave birth in the ship's hold during the crossing. She explained that the baby died before arriving in France, but that the mother did not alert anyone out of fear that the military officers would throw his body in the sea (Besnaci-Lancou 2006a, 76).

Of the 60,000 to 88,000 Harkis and their families who fled to France, approximately 25,000 arrived through government repatriation plans (Cohen 2006, 169). Most of those who migrated through official channels were placed in transit camps in southern France. Many of these camps, the largest of which were Larzac, Bourg-Lastic, Rivesaltes, La Rye-Le Vigeant, and Bias, had previously detained other populations that did not fit neatly into the national community. The Rivesaltes camp, for example, was established as a solution for managing "undesirable foreigners" in 1939 and had housed refugees from the Spanish Civil War and French Jews during World War II, as well as suspected members of the FLN captured in France before the Harkis arrived in 1962 (Miller 2013, 21–22).[1]

Living conditions in the Harki camps were often atrocious, due in part to the fact that the number of arrivals far exceeded the state's expectations and preparations. Most of the camps were not equipped to meet the needs of the Harkis and their families who were interned there. The former military camp, Bourg-Lastic, for example, was turned into a "tent village" when there was no longer sufficient room in the barracks. This was still the case heading into the winter of 1962–1963, which was described as particularly harsh. Harkis and their wives who experienced this winter have told stories of children and the elderly who froze to death in the tents (Besnaci-Lancou 2006b, 43). When barracks were available, they have been described as dirty, humid, and full of cockroaches (Besnaci-Lancou 2006a, p. 34; Besnaci-Lancou 2006b, 50).

The well-being of the Harkis in the camps was also compromised by the fact that the camps were only minimally adapted for the Harkis and in many ways still functioned as military or prison camps. Harki families were interned behind barbed wire, subject to a military lifestyle with strict discipline, and prevented from leaving without permission (Besnaci-Lancou and Moumen 2008, 57). Many felt that they were essentially imprisoned, for which they suffered psychologically. A Harki wife described how, at Rivesaltes, "The windows were high so as not to be seen from outside. It seemed like a prison." Another explained, "Bias was a dreadful place and we found ourselves isolated and shut away like animals. No one got out of there unscathed. A shock for me and for all of us, some friends committed suicide and fathers became alcoholics" (Besnaci-Lancou 2006a, 92). One Harki evoked "the misery of the Harkis" and declared, "No one can live in such a place for long without losing some of their sanity there" (Besnaci-Lancou 2006b, 50).

Abderahmen Moumen and other Harki historians have argued that a colonial dynamic was recreated in the camps, some of which were run by Pieds-Noirs, who were thought to be familiar with Muslim culture and who might have spoken Arabic (2008, p. 73). Second-generation Harkis who experienced the camps have shared stories of being infantilized, mocked, and humiliated by these camp officers (Gladieu and Kerchouche 2003, p. 96). In the film, *Harkis*, based on a novel by the daughter of a Harki, entitled *Leïla: avoir dix-sept ans dans un camp de Harkis* [Leïla: Seventeen Years Old in a Harki Camp], the main antagonist was the head of the camp, who committed numerous injustices against the Harkis (Kerchouche 2006; Tasma 2007). When Leïla's uncle wrote a letter to a local official to complain about conditions in the camp, the head of the camp sent him to a special wing in a psychiatric institution set up specifically for "mentally ill" Harkis. When her uncle returned, he was mute and unresponsive, and the family was devastated. Abuses of power by camp officials thus appeared to aggravate the already precarious situation of the Harkis.

The camps were framed by officials and the media as a temporary measure for managing the installation of the Harkis and their families. Yet they remained open much longer than expected and even if most Harkis had been transferred out by 1964, they continued to be used for members of the Harki population who could not easily be resettled (*reclassé*) elsewhere. Bias, in particular, was employed as a solution for handling Harkis who were ill, infirm, or, "lost causes," as an article in *Le Monde* explained in

1963 (Legris). Hundreds of Harkis and their families stayed in Bias and similar camps until 1975, when protests by second-generation Harkis prompted the French state to close them. Since they had been isolated from the French population for over a decade, after leaving the camps many of these Harki families found it difficult to integrate into French society. Tom Charbit has observed that the children of Harkis who grew up in the camps have had great difficulty finding employment, due to serious educational delays and a near-total lack of professional qualifications (2008, 172). Karim Brazi, the son of a Harki, wrote a novel comparing the fates of a Harki son who grew up confined in a camp with one who escaped that fate and was therefore able to integrate more easily into French society. In Brazi's text, the Harki son living in the camps recalled "the harsh isolation of successive camps where he and those like him were assembled (*concentrés*). He told of how permanent mental slavery secluded and conditioned his community, how hard it was to mingle with the local population" (2007, 57). While he "just wanted to be normal, like everyone else, just a young Frenchman," the girl he was pursuing was chastised for hanging around with "those people" (Brazi 2007, 59). The integration process often posed particular challenges for Harki wives who did not work outside the home or attend school and therefore had fewer occasions to interact with other members of French society than their husbands or children. One Harki wife has written, "Many women and friends from the camp are no longer really living. Psychologically destroyed, they try to somehow forge ahead for the future of their children and move forward with these traumas" (Besnaci-Lancou 2006a, 92).

Perceptions of Crisis in the Media

A series of articles in the French newspaper *Le Monde*, published between May and November of 1962, appeared to normalize the French state's treatment of the Harkis. Indeed, these articles reveal that the paper did not find the fact that the Harkis, who had supported the French army during the Algerian War, were placed with their families in camps to be ethically or ideologically problematic. The authors drew a careful distinction between the Algerian nationalists who had been "detained" in some of the camps during the Algerian War and the Harki families who would now "dwell" there ("Sept cent cinquante détenus" 1962; "Quatre-vingts familles" 1962). As explained on June 1, 1962, "Finally, the Larzac internment camp, having been entirely evacuated, can be used as an accommodation centre" ("Montpellier"). In September of 1962, this former internment camp was now referred to as the "Larzac Centre," where a large number of Harkis were "welcomed" ("Les harkis du Larzac").

The paper's main source of concern regarding the camps appeared to be logistical. Several of its articles conveyed awareness that large numbers of Harki arrivals were overwhelming resources. In October of 1962, *Le Monde* reported that the camp facilities at Rivesaltes "are in such a state of disrepair that we cannot consider lodging women and children there for the time being" (Denuzière 1962). The following month, the newspaper disclosed that "Whereas the camp management staff are currently being lodged in old barracks that have been hastily renovated, the Harkis are living under tents and it is certain that most of them will spend the winter there" ("Des harkis réfugiés" 1962).

In general, however, the paper struck a reassuring tone. Several articles in the summer and fall of 1962 highlighted the temporary nature of the Harkis' situation and described plans that were underway to "promote their integration into the national economy" ("Les supplétifs musulmans" 1962). In particular, they explained that after "a rather brief stay in the camps," some Harkis would participate in professional training programs and others would be employed in logging operations ("Des supplétifs musulmans" 1962). Another article indicated that the integration process was being helped along by the fact that the Harkis "seemed to accept the idea" that they would need to find work in order to support their families (Legris 1962). Ostensibly, this observation was meant to reassure the public that the Harkis did not intend to strain public resources indefinitely and it in fact reflected an enduring stereotype from the colonial era that North African men were lazy and did not like to work.

The articles that appeared on the Harkis in 1963 continued to convey assurance to the general public and explained on several occasions that "the problem" was being resolved, without ever identifying what exactly that problem was or acknowledging the role the state had played in creating it. They suggested that resettling the Harkis was not an easy process, but that officials were making progress as best they could. An article published on the anniversary of the end of the war proclaimed "The resettlement of the repatriates, who, it must be noted, have received a warm welcome in the region, is already largely underway, and it is thought that in a year from now, the problem will be, if not resolved, at least on the right track ("Depuis juillet dernier" 1963). The article identified the Harkis as a subset of this group of repatriates who were being positively received and taken care of. Throughout 1963, *Le Monde* published a number of updates on the Harki resettlement process, each communicating that the issue was being satisfactorily handled. One June 19 of that year, one article explained that "The resettlement of the Harkis and the *moghaznis* who, with their families, sought refuge in France after Algerian independence, is advancing slowly, but is advancing" (Legris 1963).[2] The article notes that the Bias camp, which housed "lost causes," would be taken over by the Ministry of Health. "The problem," it declared, "thus seems to be in the process of being solved."

Structural Roots of the Crisis

The orders given by Pierre Messmer and Louis Joxe on May 12, 1962 constitute the most notable evidence that French military and political leaders actively attempted to restrict the arrival of the Harkis and their families in France, but other traces of their efforts exist as well. In June of 1962, Joxe was confronted by a representative in the National Assembly about a note he had sent on May 25. This document reiterated that "the auxiliary soldiers who landed in mainland France outside the general repatriation plan will, essentially, be sent back to Algeria" ('Le gouvernement expose" 1962).[3] It added, "Anyone who aids in or promotes premature repatriations will be subject to appropriate sanctions." Joxe went on to suggest in the note "It would be best to avoid publicizing this policy in any way." This reflection indicates a conscious attempt to limit public awareness of the crisis facing the Harkis, as well as of how the state was managing it.

Several months later, in November of 1962, Messmer denied an allegation that he had instructed officers in Algeria to no longer accept Harkis into French military camps and to no longer send to France any Harkis who were under the protection of the army. Yet his defence revealed a strikingly cavalier attitude towards the situation. Messmer asserted that the sole precaution he recommended taking to the general commander in Algeria was "to avoid having the army's assistance in turn diverted to benefit beggars who never had any connection to it, and who were attracted only by the lure of the aid being given and by a free trip to mainland France" ("32 000 harkis" 1962). This concern that Algerians posing as Harkis would take advantage of the situation to gain a complimentary voyage to France seems largely out of touch with reality, given the humanitarian crisis that the Harkis were facing.

The restrictions put on the Harkis and their placement in the camps must be understood in the context of the legal status of the Algerian population at the end of the Algerian War. For most of the colonial period, the majority of Muslims in French Algeria were categorized as subjects, rather than as citizens. In an attempt to maintain control of French Algeria in the face of growing demands for independence among the native population, the Fifth Republic extended political rights to this group. Thus, by 1958, the entire Algerian population had been awarded French citizenship. Yet, as Todd Shepard has explained, "in 1962 the Algerians were French in law (*droit*), but, in all other domains, the vast majority of them were treated and represented differently and worse than their co-citizens. In the case of the Harkis, this tension between the 'legal' and the 'real' was particularly accentuated" (2011, 56). The state's behavior toward the Harkis and their families after the war confirms that despite their official status, and despite the state's insistence for 130 years that Algeria was French, the population of North African origin was never fully understood or accepted as such.

The fact that this exclusion was based on racial and religious difference is revealed through a comparison of how the Pieds-Noirs were regarded after the war. Whereas French citizenship was automatically confirmed for this population, the Harkis, their wives, and their children were obliged to declare their French nationality in front of a judge (Besnaci-Lancou and Moumen 2008, 66). For those who had previously accepted the official rhetoric of inclusion, and had thus believed they were already French nationals, this requirement was unexpected and offensive.

In December of 1962, *Le Monde* reported that the majority of Harki refugees would choose to have French nationality ("Les harkis réfugiés" 1962a, 1962b). The semantic slippage between the terms "repatriate" and "refugee," which occurred in multiple articles that the paper published between 1962 and 1963, is very telling. Even though the Harkis were officially considered repatriates, their reception in France suggests that they were instead imagined as refugees. As Mohand Hamoumou has observed, the Harkis were treated as if they were fleeing their Algerian homeland, rather than returning to France (1987). Again, a comparison with the case of the Pieds-Noirs is pertinent here. The strikingly different conditions of arrival for the repatriates of North African origin versus those of the repatriates of European origin reveal a "hierarchization of populations" (Besnaci-Lancou and Moumen 2008, 62). The state prioritized finding and constructing housing for Pieds-Noirs, who were considered easier to integrate into French society (Besnaci-Lancou and Moumen 2008, 54). The Harkis, in turn, were confined in camps, an established practice for accommodating refugee populations. Indeed, over the course of the 20th century, which Denis Peschanski has called the "century of camps," France had established a pattern of using camps to handle populations it did not know how to assimilate into the national community (2002, 15). While the media and state emphasized the temporary nature of the camps as a solution to the Harki "problem," this was not how they were experienced by hundreds of Harki families. Moreover, their geographic exclusion reveals how the French state regarded this population of migrants.

Collective Memories of the Migration Crisis

For many children of Harkis, the combination of paternal silence about their family's past and institutional silence in France about the history of the Harkis provoked a form of identity crisis. Second-generation Harkis have written about the difficulty of growing up not knowing why their family had come to France and why they experienced a sense of rejection from other members of French society. In response to these challenges, the children of Harkis have created a collective identity around which they could rally and enact social change. Today the Harkis and their descendants understand themselves as victims of France's failed responsibilities: the way the nation created a crisis through its mismanagement of the migration and integration processes. Many of their collective memory practices are focused on holding the French state accountable for its treatment of the Harkis and their families in the aftermath of the Algerian War.

In 1975, second-generation Harkis began to break the silence that pervaded the public sphere about the Harkis and what they had experienced. They organized protests to draw attention to the plight of the Harkis, particularly those families still living in the camps, which led the state to finally close them down. Another round of demonstrations followed in 1991 to denounce the lack of employment opportunities for the children of Harkis. Through this activism, second-generation Harkis organized themselves around a collective identity of "*les oubliés de l'histoire*," history's forgotten people (Moumen 2003, 17). Leaders of the protests framed their demonstrations as "the Harkis' emergence from oblivion" and claimed, "We broke the wall of silence [surrounding the

Harkis]" (Crapanzano 2011, 143, 146). In 2006, another second-generation Harki activist, Boussad Azni, asserted the continuing relevance of the term, declaring "the appellation of '*oubliés de l'histoire*' sadly remains accurate. This psychological dimension is the foundation of our community's identity."

The 1991 protest slogan, "After betrayal, abandonment; after abandonment, exile; after exile, oblivion," reveals how second-generation Harkis framed "oblivion" as a new form of mistreatment (Eldridge 2009, 89).[4] The realm of memory, then, constituted yet another place where the French had forsaken the Harkis and describing themselves as "*les oubliés de l'histoire*" fit neatly into a narrative of France's failed obligations to the Harkis. At the same time, it has offered a way for Harkis and their descendants to reclaim control of their position in France. Whereas the first generation was betrayed by and subjected to the will of the state, second-generation Harkis have exercised agency by "breaking" France's silence. Claire Eldridge has explained, "Tired of being *les oubliés de l'histoire*, the children of the Harkis were determined to gain recognition on behalf of their parents for the sacrifices they had made for France and the suffering they had endured as a consequence" (2009, 89). Abderahmen Moumen has likewise asserted, "The big exploits undertaken by the French Muslims, at that time '*les oubliés de l'histoire*,', brought them to the forefront of the national stage" (2003, 17). It has also allowed them to make demands, including for reparation, from the French state (Pierret 2001, 181).

In September 2001, nine first- and second-generation Harkis, supported by a coalition of fifty Harki associations, filed a case against the French state for crimes against humanity (Moumen 2011, p. 166). Their case was intended to hold France accountable for its role in the reprisal violence that ensued after the Algerian War as well as to position the Harkis as the nation's victims. The plaintiffs accused the French state of having abandoned the defenceless Harkis in Algeria, prevented their escape to France with their families, and refused to intervene to protect their former auxiliaries, despite being aware of the extent of the violence they faced. A visit to France by Algerian President and veteran of the Algerian War, Abdelaziz Bouteflika, in June of 2001 appeared to have prompted these Harkis to bring the case against France. During his trip, Bouteflika was asked whether he would grant the Harkis the right to return to Algeria, as he had invited Pieds-Noirs to do. Bouteflika responded by drawing a comparison between the Harkis and Vichy collaborators during WWII. He declared, "It is exactly as if" [. . .] "one were to ask a French resistance fighter to shake the hand of a collaborator." This insult signaled for the Harkis that they had been symbolically banished from Algeria (Pierret 2001, 97). It also prompted them to assert their attachment to France. Vincent Crapanzano has explained that after Bouteflika's comments, "The Harkis were furious at the Algerian president and, if one can compare levels of fury, even more so at the French president [Jacques Chirac] for not having responded immediately to Bouteflika's insult—'an insult addressed to French citizens,' several of the Harkis said. [. . .] Chirac's failure seemed to be a replay of their abandonment by France" (2011, 172–173). Indeed it is significant that in pursuing the case against France for crimes against humanity, Harki children were not demanding retribution from Algerians, the actual perpetrators of the post-independence violence, but rather from the French (Manceron 2011, 88). They seemed more concerned with France's failings than with those of the FLN government in Algeria. The case was ultimately unsuccessful, but it demonstrated how descendants of Harkis understood themselves, how they had been treated, and their place in French society.

In addition to their struggle against "oblivion" and their efforts in the legal system, Harkis have also developed a shared sense of injustice over the existence of the internment camps. This outrage has become a defining feature in their collective memories. The majority of Harkis and their children never lived in the camps and those who did had vastly different experiences, depending on the length of their stay and the conditions they faced (Besnaci-Lancou and Moumen, 2008, 60). Still, the Harki camps remain central to their shared narrative of victimhood and serve as a prime example of France's failed moral obligations to the Harkis. The term "camps" is compelling, since it allows the Harkis to draw connections to other persecuted populations, and elicits compassion for their past. Second-generation Harkis referred to them as "concentration camps" or "ghettos" in their protests during the 1970s and 1990s in order to accentuate this parallel (Miller 2013, 37). Harki associations now organize visits to the locations of former camps, which have become important sites of memory (*lieux de mémoire*) for their community (Moumen 2010, 139). In 2015 the French state unveiled a memorial at the site of the former Rivesaltes camp to acknowledge and commemorate the experiences of the Harkis and other populations that had been interned there.

Finally, associations of Harkis and their children have begun commemorating May 12, the day when Messmer and Joxe sent orders to prevent Harkis from entering France, as the "Day of the Harki Abandonment" (Besnaci-Lancou and Moumen 2008, 33). In 2013, this date was marked by a march of approximately 150 Harkis and their families in Paris, demanding official French recognition of the role the French played in the violence that followed by disarming the Harkis and preventing their departure to France. They also called attention to a campaign promise that then-President François Hollande had made in 2012, in which he vowed to acknowledge French culpability. Former President Nicolas Sarkozy had made a similar promise during his campaign in 2007, which remained unfulfilled while he was in office. Harki descendants began drawing parallels between what they saw as a betrayal in 1962 and the contemporary deceptions of the French government toward them. On September 25, 2016, Hollande finally fulfilled this commitment, recognizing "the responsibility of French governments in abandoning the Harkis, the massacres of those remaining in Algeria, and the inhuman conditions for those transferred to France." This long-awaited symbolic gesture appeared to bring great satisfaction to the Harki community.

Conclusion

The Algerian War of Independence was an extreme event that triggered the migration of two populations, the Harkis and the Pieds-Noirs. For both communities, the journey to mainland France and the resettlement process were periods of distress, upheaval, and loss. Yet the French responses to these two groups were significantly different; these differences reflected institutional racism that had existed during the colonial period and persisted in postcolonial France. Whereas the Pieds-Noirs were considered to be repatriates, French men and women who were returning home, the Harkis were imagined as refugees who posed a threat to the national community. As Karen O'Reilly has observed, "Migration cuts to the heart of who 'we' and 'they' are, and to notions of identity, home, and belonging" (2012, 1). The French state's attempts to prevent the migration of the Harkis and its use of camps to geographically isolate the Harkis clearly designated them as an "Other" and excluded them from French society.

As a result, these policies produced a crisis that threatened the welfare of the Harkis and their families. These migrants experienced physical and psychological suffering due to the lack of structures in place to support them. The media and political actors then attempted to normalize the state's actions, suggesting it was responding to the inherent "problem" caused by the movement of the Harkis to the metropole. The children of the Harkis, particularly those who were subjected to life in the internment camps, are the ones who have challenged this narrative. Since 2001, they have centered their collective memory practices on holding the state responsible for the construction of the migration crisis that they and their families had experienced.

Author Note

All English translations are my own, unless otherwise noted.

Notes

1. The Front de libération nationale (FLN) was the main nationalist group during the Algerian War of Independence.
2. The *moghaznis*, like the Harkis, were a specific group of civil combatants who performed various tasks for the French army during the Algerian War. Since the end of the war, they have often been labeled "Harki" as well.
3. This term encompasses the Harkis, *moghaznis*, and other groups of civil combatants who supported the French army during the Algerian War.
4. Translated by Eldridge.

References

"32 000 harkis et membres de leurs familles ont été transférés en France déclare M. Messmer." 1962. *Le Monde*, November 17.

The Aspen Institute. "Glossary for Understanding the Dismantling Structural Racism/Promoting Racial Equity Analysis." 2018. https://assets.aspeninstitute.org/content/uploads/files/content/docs/rcc/RCC-Structural-Racism-Glossary.pdf. Accessed January 24, 2018.

Azni, B. 2006. "Discours de clôture." Presented at the Etats Généraux de la Communauté Harkie, FIAP Salle Jean Monnet (Paris), November 18. http://www.blogg.org/blog-54218-date-2006-11.html.

Barclay, F. 2014. "Reporting on 1962: The Evolution of Pied-Noir Identity across 50 Years of Print Media." In"Media, Memory and Nostalgia in Contemporary France," eds. H. Dauncey and C, Tinker, special issue, *Modern & Contemporary France* 23, no. 2: 1–15. https://doi.org/10.1080/09639489.2014.971720.

Baussant, M. 2012. "Caught between Two Worlds: The Europeans of Algeria in France after 1962." In *History, Memory and Migration: Perceptions of the Past and the Politics of Incorporation*, edited by Irial Glynn and J. Olaf Kleist, 87–105. New York: Palgrave Macmillan.

Besnaci-Lancou, F. 2006a. *Nos mères, paroles blessées: Une autre histoire de harkis*. Léchelle, France: Emina Soleil.

Besnaci-Lancou, F. 2006b. *Treize chibanis harkis*. Paris: Tirésias.

Besnaci-Lancou, F., and A. Moumen. 2008. *Les harkis*. Idées reçues. Editions Le Cavalier Bleu.

Brazi, K. 2007. *Le vilain petit berbère*. Paris: Société des Ecrivains.

Charbit, T. 2008. "Les harkis de la 'deuxième génération.'" In *Les harkis dans la colonisation et ses suites*, edited by Fatima Besnaci-Lancou and Gilles Manceron, 169–172. Ivry-sur-Seine: Editions de l'Atelier.

Cohen, W. B. 2006. "The Harkis: History and Memory." In *Algeria & France, 1800–2000: Identity, Memory, Nostalgia*, edited by Patricia M. E. Lorcin, 164–180. Syracuse, NY: Syracuse University Press.

Crapanzano, V. 2011. *The Harkis: The Wound That Never Heals*. Chicago: University of Chicago Press.

Denuzière, M. 1962. "Des milliers d'anciens harkis se préparent avec leurs familles à passer l'hiver sous les tentes du camp de Rivesaltes." *Le Monde*, October 8.

"Depuis juillet dernier 11 850 rapatriés ont été accueillis." 1963. *Le Monde*, March 19.

"Des supplétifs musulmans arrivent en métropole." 1962. *Le Monde*, June 14.

Eldridge, C. 2009. "'We've Never Had a Voice': Memory Construction and the Children of the Harkis (1962–1991)." *French History* 23, no. 1: 88–107.

Ferdi, S. 1981. *Un enfant dans la guerre*. Paris: Seuil.

Gladieu, S., and D. Kerchouche. 2003. *Destins de harkis*. Paris:Autrement.

Hamoumou, M. 1987. "Les français-musulmans: rapatriés ou réfugiés?" *AWR-Bulletin* 4: 115–174.

Hamoumou, M. 1993. *Et ils sont devenus harkis*. Paris: Fayard.

Kafi, M. 2009. *De berger à harki*. Édité à compte d'auteur.

Kerchouche, D. 2006. *Leïla: Avoir dix-sept ans dans un camp de harkis*. Paris: Seuil.

Krouk, A. 2010. *Harki*. Edition de l'Ixcéa.

"Le gouvernement expose les dispositions prises en faveur des harkis et de leurs familles.» 1962. *Le Monde*, July 2.

Legris, M. 1962. "Une intégration 'miniature.'" *Le Monde*, July 12.

Legris, M. 1963. 'Une intéressante expérience de promotion sociale et professionnelle a été entreprise'. *Le Monde*, June 19.

"Les harkis du Larzac seront répartis dans de nouveaux camps.» 1962. *Le Monde*, September 5.

"Les harkis réfugiés choisiront pour la plupart la nationalité française.» 1962a. *Le Monde*, December 31.

"Les harkis réfugiés en France passeront l'hiver sous la tente.» 1962b. *Le Monde*, November 19.

"Les supplétifs musulmans de Larzac et de Bourg-Lastic vont être transférés à Rivesaltes et à Lascours.» 1962. *Le Monde*, September 7.

Lindley, A., ed. 2014. *Crisis and Migration: Critical Perspectives*. 1st ed. London and New York: Routledge.

Manceron, G. 2011. "Un abandon et des massacres aux responsabilités multiples." In *Harkis 1962–2012: Les mythes et les faits*, edited by Claude Lanzmann, 65–89. Les Temps Modernes 666. Paris: Gallimard.

Miller, J. E. 2013. "A Camp for Foreigners and 'Aliens': The Harkis' Exile at the Rivesaltes Camp (1962–1964)." *French Politics, Culture & Society* 31, no. 3: 21–44.

"Montpellier: Des familles de harkis installées sur les Causses.» 1962. *Le Monde*, June 1.

Morelle, C. 2004. "Les pouvoirs publics français et le rapatriement des harkis en 1961–1962." *Vingtième siècle. Revue d'histoire* 83, no. 3: 109–119.

Moumen, A. 2003. *Les français musulmans en Vaucluse: 1932–1991*. Paris: Editions l'Harmattan.

Moumen, A. 2010. "Les lieux de mémoire du groupe social 'harkis': Inventaire, enjeux et evolution." In *Les harkis: histoire, memoire, transmission*, edited by F. Besnaci-Lancou and B. Falaize, 135–146. Paris: Editions de l'Atelier.

Moumen, A. 2011. "De l'absence aux nouveaux porte-parole: Évolution du mouvement associatif harki (1962–2011)." In *Harkis 1962–2012: Les mythes et les faits*, edited by Claude Lanzmann, 159–169. Les Temps Modernes 666. Paris: Gallimard.

O'Reilly, K. 2012. *International Migration and Social Theory*. New York: Palgrave Macmillan.

Pervillé, G. 2004. "La guerre d'Algérie: combien de morts?" In *La guerre d'Algérie: La fin de l'amnésie*, edited by Mohammed Harbi and Benjamin Stora, 477–493. Paris: Robert Laffont.

Peschanski, D. 2002. *La France des camps: L'internement, 1938–1946*. Paris: Gallimard.

Pierret, R. 2001. *Les filles et fils de harkis: Entre double rejet et triple appartenance*. Paris: L'Harmattan.

"Quatre-vingts familles de harkis hébergées au camp de Larzac vont être installées à Largentière.» 1962. *Le Monde*, August 4.

Sadouni, Brahim. 1985. *Français sans patrie: Premier témoignage écrit par un harki*. Grand-Couronne, France: B. Sadouni.

"Sept cent cinquante détenus algériens sont libérés du camp de Larzac.» 1962. *Le Monde*, March 30.

Shepard, T. 2011. "La république face aux harkis: Questions aux historiens." In *Harkis 1962-2012: Les mythes et les faits*, edited by Claude Lanzmann 53–64. Les Temps Modernes 666. Paris: Gallimard.

Smith, Andrea. 2013. "Settler Sites of Memory and the Work of Mourning." *French Politics, Culture & Society* 31, no. 3: 65–92.

Tasma, Alain, dir. 2007. *Harkis*. France 2: France Télévisions Distribution, DVD.

CHAPTER 4

DECOLONIZATION, NATION BUILDING, AND MIGRATION CRISES IN SOUTHEAST ASIA

ULBE BOSMA

As in many other places of the world, for centuries Southeast Asian people have massively fled from violence, from slave-raiding armies to pirates preying on their coasts (Hugo and Chan 1990, 22). Whereas colonial empires had established some peace after their military conquests or annexations, decolonization was attended by innumerable forced migrations. In general one can say that what happened in the Third World in the aftermath of decolonization was prefigured in the expulsion of Iberian Jews and the French Huguenots, the contraction of the Ottoman Empire, the breakup of the Austrian-Hungarian Empire, and the Russian Revolution. Even more than these European empires, colonial societies in Southeast Asia were plural societies, in Furnivall's definition, in which minorities such as the Chinese were found in trade and the Europeans occupied the commanding positions in administration and plantation enterprise. The decolonization process often entailed the reorganization of these plural societies.

Our understanding of what refugee or migration crises are, meanwhile, has been shaped by the intertwined effects of the wars of the twentieth century and the emergence of the international state system. Whereas the First World War, the Russian Revolution and the collapse of the Ottoman Empire caused the displacement of already 1 percent of the global population, the Second World War produced the horrendous figure of 7.6 percent, involving 90 million people for China alone (Gatrell 2013, 3). It was in this context that the "refugee regime" was born, in which the refugees were identified as people in well-founded fear of persecution. The notion of "refugee regime" implied the acceptance of the fact that the governments of the persecuting states could not be removed or changed but that other states should share the responsibility for the resettlement of the refugees. The notion that states had certain obligations toward displaced people emerged on a rather ad hoc basis after the First World War, in the wake of the Russian Revolution, and became institutionalized thanks to the work of Fridtjof Nansen, who introduced the "Nansen Passport" for displaced people. The formation of the United Nations High Commissioner for Refugees (UNHCR) in 1950 was of course a further major accomplishment in creating a global refugee regime. The refugee problem was defined as an international problem of people who, if not legally stateless, at least did not enjoy protection as state citizens and were castaways in the state system. This regime prescribed refugee organizations' adherence to strict impartiality and to observe the principle of noninterference as well as to uphold the notion that refugees were distinguishable from other categories of migrants (Hugo 2006). Obviously, this refugee regime, born in the aftermaths of the two World Wars, also had its Eurocentric bias. Prior to 1962, the UNHCR had only one office outside Europe, namely in Hong Kong a city that was flooded by Chinese refugees (Keeley 2001, 304, 307).

The concept of the "refugee regime" helps us to explain why population movements that are caused by social conflict are only selectively recognized as refugee or migration crises by international conventions. It also explains why Graeme Hugo observed thirty years ago that forced migrations in Southeast Asia were a neglected area among social scientists (Hugo 1987, 249). This despite the fact that the refugee flows that attended the process of decolonization in Southeast Asia had so many traits similar to the disappearance of the empires in Europe after the First World War. International conventions also fail to address how refugee migrations may have resulted in or are linked to other migrations and migration systems including human trafficking. Refugees are not just seeking safety but also a future. Extensive movements from the countryside to the cities in many regions of Southeast Asia, for example, were both caused by a push of rural unsafety and the pull of urban economic promise. Migrations are, moreover, often not confined to a single movement, but part of a chain of migrations. Today's condition of Southeast Asia as a massive emigration area is to no small extent related to earlier histories of displacement. Many of the 2.6 million Vietnamese refugees of the late 1970s would not stay in the country of the first arrival, and many among the almost one million who left Hong Kong in the fifteen years after the signing of the Sino-British Treaty of 1984 had been immigrants seeking safety and a future in this British Crown Colony.[1]

As I will explain in the following sections, the end of colonial empires initially led to waves of rural-urban migrations. The subsequent phase of economic nationalism and reshaping of plural economies brought about expulsions of minorities, as will be detailed in the next two sections, one of which will focus on the Sino-Indonesians and Indo-Europeans in Indonesia. This will be followed by a discussion of the similarities of the diasporas originating from Southeast Asia that often included repeated migrations. Finally, internal displacement became part of the policies of dispossession in the context of economic nationalism or just because of the greed of ruling elites.

The End of Colonial Empires and Urban Migrations

The dissolution of colonialism in Southeast Asia forged ahead with political drama and armed violence, but the drama for millions of people was also that it marked the end of an era of relatively open borders. Over the course of the nineteenth century Southeast Asia had become a massive producer of commodities for the industrial world. In the century preceding the Second World War, an estimated 15 million Indians went to Burma, 4 million to Malaysia, and hundreds of thousands to other countries in Southeast Asia. Further, 8 million Chinese went to the Malay Peninsula, 4 million to Indonesia, 4 million to Thailand and 2 to 3 million to Indochina (McKeown 2004, 158). The Great Depression that followed the Wall Street Crash of 1929 shattered the economic foundations of this extensive mobility. Borders were closed and migrant workers who were laid off returned (Amrith 2011). Chinese labor migrants starving in the streets of Straits Settlements were sent back with government sponsored shipping, for example. Of the 440,000 Chinese returning to China in the early 1930s 75,000 had their passage funded by the government of Malaya, which also paid for the repatriation of 200,000 Tamils (Ee 1961, 43–44; Huff 2001, 290, 309, 310, 315, 319).

When the postwar governments of Southeast Asia started to figure out who belonged where and to what state, many of their questions had already been answered by the colonial administrations, who had begun the work of engineering migration, of containing migration flows, and of the construction of citizen regimes. In general, the colonial governments of Southeast Asia were not keen to have immigrant laborers as settlers—the only exception was the presence of Indonesians in British Malaya, who were considered by the British administration to pose an ethnic-Malay counterweight to growing Chinese and Tamil presence. The immigration of Chinese in Southeast Asia, to mention the largest immigrant population, was on the one hand heavily pulled by the existence of the commodity-producing frontiers but on the other ruled by restrictive immigration regimes. The most restrictive rules were imposed by the American administration of the Philippines that simply extended the application of the Chinese Exclusion Act (1882) from the United States to its colonial dependency and as a result the Chinese newcomer population in this extensive archipelago numbered a mere 100,000 at the end of colonial rule. Meanwhile, any official references that would have suggested a Philippine plural society were erased: the large Mestizo Chinese population, about 10 percent of the total population, was consciously not counted as a separate category in the American census statistics of the early twentieth century. (Census of the Philippines 1903, vol. 2, 42; Purcell, 573–574, 581)

In other countries, however, the Chinese were considered indispensable as migrant workers and this pertained to Malaysia and the Netherlands Indies in particular. Its colonial administrations developed legal pluralism to protect the rights of the native population. Labor migrants were considered to be temporary residents.

Millions of Chinese workers came to the Netherlands Indies in the decades around 1900, but the first generation Chinese immigrants in the Netherlands-Indies numbered a modest 433,842 among a total Chinese population of 1,190,014 by 1930. Chinese immigration was actually discouraged among other things by imposing a head-tax on every Chinese entering the Netherlands Indies (Purcell 1951, 543). Less restrictive was British Malaya, where1931 258,523 Chinese were born in British Malaya and 916,254 elsewhere. For Indians British Malaya the numbers are 58,695 and 412,971 respectively. But this was as long as plantations exerted an insatiable demand for labor. By 1928 the government of Malaysia set the first restrictions on Chinese immigration, followed by a quota system for male Chinese immigrants in 1930 (Vlieland 1932, 42–43; Ee 1961, 42–43).

In mainland Southeast Asia settlement was also modest compared to the large migration flows. In Burma, which experienced 15 million immigrations from India, the total Indian population amounted to just a million among a total population of 16.9 million in 1941 (Furnivall, 1956, 186). Despite the 4 million migrants who entered Thailand the number of China-born Chinese residents stayed at 349,000 and together with the locally born 557,000 the entire ethnic Chinese population amounted to 9.8 percent of the country's population according to the reconstruction by Skinner by 1917 (Skinner 1957, 79). The government of this country issued a range of measures, including raising the cost of an entrance permit in the 1930s, to stem the additional influx of Chinese refugees from the Japanese invasion of China (Vatikiotis 1999, 221).

Many of the postcolonial discriminatory policies against Chinese minorities, particularly those against members who were engaged in retail trade, have their roots in colonial days. And these policies were in part a response to the Chinese nationality law of 1909 that was based upon the principle of *ius sanguinis*, which meant that the overseas Chinese offspring had Chinese nationality. This policy was countered in the Netherlands Indies by adopting the *ius solis* in 1910, making everyone born on the soil of the Netherlands Indies a Dutch subject and all persons recognized by a European father as their child a Dutch citizen. As a result ethnic Chinese born in the Netherlands Indies had a dual nationality (Purcell 1951, 515). What they shared with Europeans, moreover, was that they were not entitled to own land.

The colonial legal boundaries were shored up during the Japanese Occupation (1942–1945) of much of Southeast Asia. In the Netherlands Indies 110,000 Europeans, overwhelmingly with no Asian roots, were interned in camps, whereas the Indo-Europeans became more or less confined to rapidly narrowing urban spaces. The Japanese had tried to lure the Indo-Europeans or Métis on their side in Indonesia and Vietnam respectively. They failed to do so because in Indonesia the Indo-Europeans prided their Dutch citizenship, and in Vietnam the Métis were effectively drawn into the European camp by the Vichy administration (Pomfret 2009, 341; Thompson 1952, 49). An entirely different type of separation took place in Burma, where the Japanese Occupiers drove half a million Indians out of this country in 1942. Seventy thousand were evacuated by sea, another 4,000 or so by air, but over 400,000 had to walk back, in what became according to Hugh Tinker the forgotten "Long March" (Tinker 1975, 3–4). It was an exodus that followed upon a British defeat without any heroism; the refugees simply left on their own and Tinker himself was witness of the refugees' desperate conditions with only a "skeleton" of a refugee organization left. At least one in eight did not survive this ordeal (Tinker 1975, 10). It became an almost forgotten migration crisis.

Throughout Southeast Asia, the countryside became a particularly unsafe place to be in these years. The impact of Japan's "Greater East Asia Co-Prosperity Sphere" severely upset the rural economies. As a result severe famines in the final months of the War struck Indonesia, Vietnam, Malaysia, and parts of the Philippines.[2] In Indonesia there was the additional suffering of millions who had been enlisted in forced labor projects and about 270,000 Indonesians were sent to the Southeast Asian mainland as *romusha*—to be put to work at the notorious Burma railroad—of whom only 50,000 survived. Against this backdrop of hunger, destruction, and rural unrest, Sukarno proclaimed the Republic of Indonesia on August 17 and Ho Chi Minh established the Democratic Republic of Vietnam a few weeks later on September 2. They were immediately rebuffed by the colonial powers who sent in their troops and inflicted years of colonial war on their countries. In British Malaya a variant of this scenario developed. The Malaysian Communist Party had been the leading factor in the resistance against the Japanese Occupation and it found itself in a strong position when the British returned, but not strong enough, because it hardly appealed to other Malaysians as it advocated dual citizenship for Chinese in Malaya. A ten-year communist guerrilla war against British rule started in 1947. In the Philippines, the guerrilla movement against the Japanese occupation, the Huk Balahap, channeled its resistance in the postwar years against deeply unjust agrarian relations, which culminated in an outright rebellion against the Philippine government. Rural unsafe conditions made many people flee from the countryside.

The early years after Japanese capitulation in Malaysia, the Philippines, and Indonesia were years of extensive coerced or at least violence-induced migrations, but since this concerned predominantly movements from the countryside to the city most of these displacements were not identified as crises. The same happened with displacements during the wars of independence that continued during the early years of the new nations. An armed resistance movement against the Republic of Sukarno led in West Java to a massive flight from the countryside to the region's capital Bandung, which doubled in size in the 1950s to over a million residents (Hugo 2006, 73; McNicoll 1968, 44). Indeed, urbanization was another consequence of the War and the chaotic years of early independence. In Indonesia the many insurrections and constant violence—in Aceh, Tapanuli, West Java, East Java, and various parts of Sulawesi—in the first fifteen years of the Republic's existence made the countryside particularly unsafe, causing massive flows of displaced persons (Hugo 2006; McNicoll 1968, 43–48). Most of the refugee flows caused by rebellions against the government in Jakarta were either temporary as in Aceh or led to permanent settlement in the cities, leading to rapid growth for cities such as Banjarmasin in South Kalimantan and Makassar (Ujung Pandang), Pare-Pare, and Watampone in West Sulawesi (Hugo 2006, 76; McNicoll 1968, 48–50). Some refugee flows even crossed into other islands: about 10,000 residents of Sulawesi fled to Jambi (Sumatra) and another 5,000 settled along the coast of West Kalimantan.

Ethnic Chinese were disproportionally present among the refugees from the countryside. Malaysia saw a massive displacement and forced resettlement of mainly Chinese from 1949 to 1957, as part of the British response to the insurrection of the Malaysian Communist Party. About 573,000 people were resettled and the rural proportion of the Chinese population declined from 57 percent to 27 percent—for the average population it went from 74 percent to 58 percent—but one needs to recognize that the Chinese made up over a third of British Malaya's population at that time (Hirschman 1980, 118; Pryor 1979, 80, 82, 97). In Indonesia, the Sino-Indonesians were forced to move into the cities as well. Already an urbanized population in 1930, with 58.8 percent living in cities, by the late 1950s the figure stood at almost 80 percent (Coppel 1983, 7). The fact that so many Chinese had already left the countryside in Indonesia may have saved them from the worst of the 1965 killings during the suppression of the Communist party as a matter of fact (Coppel 1983, 59). Nonetheless, thousands of Chinese had to be evacuated from the Medan area in 1966. About 10,000 Chinese, who were not citizens of Indonesia, were driven out of Aceh by the order of the province's military commander (Coppel 1983, 69). The largest and gravest outburst of anti-Chinese riots took place in Kalimantan, where 5,000 Sino-Indonesians got killed and 45,000 expelled by the Dayaks in 1967. An estimated 60,000 fled to Pontianak and Sambas (Braithwaite 2010, 81; McNicoll 1968, 50). That this ethnic violence occurred between population groups that were highly intermarried can be explained by the fact that it was ignited from the outside. Sukarno in his confrontational politics towards Malaysia had sponsored Chinese guerrillas in adjacent Sarawak who had been left on their own after Indonesian appeasement of its neighbor. These fighters turned in 1966 against the Indonesian army but also attacked Dayak communities. It opened the gates of hell (Coppel 1983, 146).

Europeans and Chinese in Early Independent Indonesia

The migrations from the countryside to the cities and the evacuations almost seamlessly linked up to migrations out of the newly independent countries. Even though they concerned migrations that were the result of forced assimilation policies, they were not defined as crises. While for most Europeans their departure was for the obvious reason of the transfer of sovereignty, for many Eurasian or mestizo groups, who were emotionally firmly rooted in the former colonies but still visibly connected to the former rulers, the situation was far more complicated. This was particularly true for Indonesia, where the European upper crust had become very heavily creolized over the centuries. Although the Japanese occupiers had tried to lure the Indo-Europeans as "Asians" into their camp, only a few came over to their side, as the Indonesians were not only deeply attached to Indonesian soil but also thoroughly Dutch.

Immediately upon Japanese capitulation nationalist youth gangs (*pemuda*) turned violently against both white Europeans as their Indo-European offspring. Under these conditions, the elite, consisting of 70,000 Dutch, was quickly repatriated in 1945 to recover from their internment under Japanese occupation either as civilians or as prisoners of war. About 15 percent of these repatriated were academically trained and belonged to the upper crust of the colonial bureaucracy and colonial enterprise. The majority of the Indo-Europeans were not supposed to "repatriate" to the Netherlands. By late 1945, however, most of Java was under the control of the Republic of Indonesia proclaimed by Sukarno and about 65,000 Indo-Europeans were deported to protection camps, ostensibly to protect them against the *pemuda*, but actually to hold them as hostages.

In 1949, when the Europeans living in Indonesia had to choose between becoming either Dutch or Indonesian citizens, an unsurprisingly mere 10 percent opted for Indonesian citizenship. With the transfer of sovereignty many Europeans in government positions lost their jobs and about 50,000 persons left Indonesia. In private enterprise the management continued to stay in European hands, but the middle-ranking positions went to Indonesians. This Indonesianization condemned the Indo-Europeans who overwhelmingly had opted to keep their Dutch citizenship over poverty. Actually, in December 1957 all of the remaining Dutch citizens were declared persona non grata and all Dutch property was nationalized, which led to another exodus. In the following years, the Indo-Europeans who had opted for Indonesian citizenship desperately regretted their choice and thanks to intense mobilization of Dutch public opinion by repatriated colonial old hands the reluctant Dutch government was forced to organize their transfer to the Netherlands too. Only 5 percent of all Europeans who had lived in the Netherlands Indies stayed in Indonesia. In total, 330,000 Dutch citizens, 26,000 Moluccan colonial soldiers, and about 23,000 Indonesians (among whom were highly educated Chinese) came to the Netherlands between 1945 and 1967 (Beets et al. 2002, 56).

Whereas Dutch citizens had to make a difficult choice regarding their citizenship as part of the transfer of sovereignty, Chinese who were born in Indonesia automatically obtained dual citizenship. This was the upshot of two opposing legal principles. Whereas the Chinese law that followed the principle of *ius sanguinis* bestowed nationality on all Chinese descendants, the Indonesian legal principle of *ius solis* granted citizenship on the basis of birth on Indonesian soil. During late colonial society the ethnic Chinese had usually aligned themselves with the colonial status quo the way the Indo-Europeans and, to a certain extent, the Indonesian aristocracy had done. For obvious reasons, the Japanese had made no effort to appeal to the Chinese and during the Indonesian War of Independence (1945–1949), the latter usually took a neutral stand, to which they were ordered by the Kuo Ming Tang government in China (Purcell 1951, 561).

Suspicious about the very well-developed transnational bonds among ethnic Chinese, the Indonesian government pressed China to sign an agreement to end this automatic dual citizenship, which happened in the margins of the Bandung conference of 1955, and that went into force in 1960. This brought the Sino-Chinese into a situation comparable to where the Indo-Europeans of Indonesia had been since 1949. Since about a third of the Peranakan Chinese opted for Chinese citizenship and another third of the Chinese in Indonesia were born in China it resulted in the majority of ethnic Chinese in Indonesia becoming aliens. It was an uneasy situation because totok (China-born) Chinese continued to be highly influential in business and because Sino-Chinese and totok Chinese were highly intermingled through family bonds. This was the backdrop of Suharto's policy of making naturalization for totok Chinese easy and of exerting more than gentle pressure to assimilate on the entire ethnic Chinese population (Somers Heidhues 1999, 166).

Although their fate was not one of comprehensive expulsion as the Europeans had experienced, an ethnic Chinese Indonesia exodus did come about in the 1950s. Despite the fact that they had a powerful ally in the Communist party of Indonesia (PKI), their position became increasingly insecure with the ascendency to power of the military that had also led to the seizure of Dutch property (Somers Heidhues 1964, 17). At the orders of the military not only the schools for Dutch but also those for Sino-Indonesians were closed by late 1957 and early 1958. And while the Dutch were punished for the refusal of the Netherlands to hand New Guinea over to Indonesia, ethnic Chinese paid their price for the transnational assertiveness of both Kuo Ming Tang and PRC in Indonesia (Somers Heidhues 1964, 20–21). By the mid-1950s about 65 percent of the Chinese schools in Indonesia were PRC-minded and about 30 percent pro Kuo Ming Tang (Godley and Coppel 1990, 183–184). Although these children were firmly rooted in the country and spoke Bahasa or a local language, at school they were taught to speak and write Mandarin. Ethnic Chinese students who had completed secondary education had no university to go to in Indonesia, whereas China could boast of universities of world-class level in the 1950s (Godley and Coppel 1990, 180). The students who left for China did so abandoning their future option of becoming Indonesian again. Fingerprints were taken at the ports of embarkation and they were declared persona non grata, like the Dutch. In total about 50,000 higher-educated young Chinese went to China to pursue further education, out of idealism, and also to join the Maoist experiment.

For ethnic Chinese in Indonesia the situation worsened when in 1959 measures were taken against retail traders in the Indonesian countryside who were not citizens. The options for these Chinese shopkeepers were either to move to the city or to heed Chinese propaganda that they would find a warm welcome home as "patriots" (Tan 2010, 561). The Chinese government claimed that it could easily absorb half a million overseas Chinese and organized transport to "repatriate" 130,000 Chinese between 1959 and 1961 (Godley 1989, 335). These waves of students and economic refugees were followed by a third, and smaller, one in 1965 in the wake of the bloody repression of the Communist party, the PKI, by the Indonesian government.

The Forging of Nationhood and the Expulsion of Ethnic Chinese

What happened in Indonesia was part of a general trend in Southeast Asia, which we can define as a series of migration crises. Socialism and anticapitalism were often practically identical with creating a "pure" countryside cleansed from Chinese petty traders or, as was the case in Malaysia, from Communism. In the first fifteen years of Malaysia's independence half a million ethnic Chinese had been resettled to empty the pond, in which the Chinese communist guerrillas operated. After the resettlement, approximately 250,000 ethnic Chinese left the country, of whom 65,000 moved to Singapore, which had become a state separated from the Malaysian Federation in 1965 (Hirschman 1975, 42). In Cambodia, where the ethnic Chinese made up 10 percent of the population, few of them stayed after the US bombardments, the horrendous regime of Pol Pot, and ten years of Vietnamese occupation. From Laos also nearly the entire ethnic Chinese population of about 64,500 fled after the coup of Pathet Lao in 1975 (Ng Shui Meng 1999, 169–171). The military coup in Burma 1962, which declared the country a socialist state, propelled an exodus of 300,000 Indians and probably 100,000 ethnic Chinese. In 1967, violent anti-Chinese riots occurred leading to killings among ethnic Chinese (Lintner 1999, 140–143). To these figures came hundreds of thousands of internally displaced to whom I shall return later on.

In Vietnam, the ethnic Chinese, and the traders among them in particular, were one of the two important minorities who were threatened during the decolonization. The Catholic Vietnamese were the other minority consisting of 1.6 million people, or 8.5 percent of the Vietnamese population in 1945, who had immediately shown their allegiance to independence in September 1945 (Marr 2013, 428). With the implementation of the Geneva Accords between France and North Vietnam in 1954, 900,000 Vietnamese, 60 percent of whom Catholic, fled from North to South Vietnam and 140,000 Viethminh in the opposite direction. After the fall of the South Vietnamese regime in 1975, the refugee flows were relatively modest initially, but exploded in an exodus when Hanoi closed 30,000 shops in Cholon, the China town of Saigon (Ho Chi Minh City) home to one million ethnic Chinese (Osborne 1980, 41). It all happened under a barrage of government propaganda against yellow capitalism and about the Chinese holding 80 percent of the economy in South Vietnam (Van der Kroef 1979, 4). At that time China invaded North Vietnam. The threatened regime reacted at home by expropriation and massive internment of entrepreneurs and former South Vietnamese government officials. The first wave was followed by a broader exodus of farmers and fishermen who feared that the economic policies of the government in Hanoi would bring disaster (Van der Kroef 1979, 5–6).

From Repatriations to Migration Crises

The decolonization trajectories were attended by the repatriations of the colonial military, civil servants, and managers of private enterprise. In some countries where the higher echelons were already "Asianized," as was the case of the Philippines, this went rather smoothly; in other countries such as Indonesia and Korea where the colonial presence was deep and had led to the presence of large Dutch respectively Japanese populations, a painful exodus, a migration crisis, appeared to be unavoidable. Although the Netherlands and Japan were not particularly eager to "take back" their citizens who were often acculturated to the societies of their former colonies, they had little choice. Over 6 million Japanese were simply expelled from their former occupied territories and overseas possessions, including from Korea where they had been for a very long time. They were *hikiage*—literally lifted or pulled—from the colonies to Japan (Cohen 2012).

The Dutch government had tried to draw a line between the metropolitan-born or at least metropolitan-educated Dutch citizens in Indonesia and those who did not qualify as such and were in the government's gaze firmly rooted in Asian society. At this juncture the politicians and activists of the right, the colonial revanchists, stood firmly by the Indo-Europeans left behind in Indonesia, making the emotional plea that they should not be left at the mercy of an Indonesian president who had collaborated with the fascist Japanese occupier. Likewise, the willingness of the United States to take in Vietnamese refugees only emerged under the moral pressure of US veteran organizations pleading for their "comrades in arms." The first wave of these refugees were the civil servants, the better educated who in no way would find a place in the new regime. They were a group of about 80,000 people who were airlifted out of the chaotic collapse of the South Vietnamese regime in 1975. They had to be taken in by the United States, even though, according to a Gallup Poll held in 1975, about 54 percent of the American people were against admitting the Vietnamese refugees into their country (Hien 1996).

With respect to refugees who were closely affiliated with the colonial regimes the responsibilities were clear. The refugee wave from Indochina of 1979 took place in an entirely new context, however. Here we see the notion of international migration crises emerging. First of all, none of the countries in Southeast Asia that were receiving refugees from Indochina had been signatories of the 1951 Refugee Convention and hence they did not subscribe to the UNHCR definitions of refugees. Second, Hanoi clearly saw the refugee flow as a political leverage (Wain 1979, 160–161). Stories were circulating, and these seem to have been not entirely unfounded, that the government in Hanoi was involved in extorting money from the refugees and that high civil servants made in fact a business out of people fleeing their country (Van der Kroef 1979, 11). Many of the ethnic Chinese in Cholon, for example, were capable of buying their way out of the country, paying government officials (Hugo and Chan 1990, 24). For Singapore in 1980 this was an argument to become even more restrictive in allowing refugees in. The arrival of Vietnamese of Chinese descent arriving in Singapore could "upset the ethnic balance" and lead to tensions, the city state's government feared (Lavoie and Knock 1990, 49; Yuen 1990, 82–83).

The countries in Southeast Asia succeeded in negotiating a burden sharing by western countries with regard to resettling refugees from Indochina. Nonetheless Thailand, which had sheltered one million refugees since 1975, still housed 419,000 refugees in camps at the end of the Cambodian-Vietnamese war. These refugees had fled the heavy fighting near the Thai border (Chantavanich and Rabe 1990, 66). While Thailand became more generous in providing refuge in the 1980s, the western countries turned more restrictive and began to consider boat refugees as economically motivated migrants rather than refugees according the UNHCR definition (Chantavanich and Rabe, p. 71). With the colonial era further sinking into history, the West stepped back whereas the sense of responsibility among the ASEAN countries increased. From 1982 onwards a settlement fatigue became visible in western countries. All in all by 1988, half of the approximately 1.4 million refugees from Indochina who were resettled outside Southeast Asia lived in the United States, followed by China (284,000), Canada (121,182), Australia (117,997), and Hong Kong 68,000 (Hugo 1990, 186). For the United States it has been reported that many of the refugees were second-time migrants who had fled from North to South Vietnam in 1954 (Kelly 1986, 141; Osborne 1980, 47).

Refugee Diasporas

The reception of the refugees of decolonization varied widely, but some important similarities can be singled out. The first waves integrated relatively easily and—as often is the case with refugees—we can discern a selectivity here: it was the younger and more highly educated who tend to migrate first to escape from oppression. They often already had relatives overseas. Vietnamese students, for example, had gone to France and Canada for their studies in the early 1950s and stayed there (Chan and Dorais 1998, 294–297). When there were no relatives around, people were more likely to resettle. That happened, for example, with the ethnic Chinese and Europeans of Indonesia, many of whom ended up in Hong Kong respectively California. It is important to underline that 60 percent of the Europeans who were repatriated were of mixed Indonesian-European descent, had few relatives in the Netherlands, and were dispersed over the country. They experienced their new country as cold both in terms of physical climate as well as mentally. About 50,000 Indo-Europeans, particularly those who were born in the colonial Indonesia, eventually did not settle in the Netherlands but migrated again—half to the United States, others to Australia, Canada, New Zealand, Brazil, the Dutch Antilles, and Spain. Like the Indo-Europeans in the Netherlands, the Vietnamesee refugees who were went to the United States were dispersed over the country and had to accept low-paid jobs regardless of their training, as their certificates were simply not recognized (Hien 1996). Downward occupational mobility was the rule for the Vietnamese, particularly because a lack of language skills, but it also was the rule for Europeans who were repatriated during the Indonesian decolonization (Kelly 1986, 146).

But this downward social mobility was nothing compared to what Chinese from Indonesia experienced in China. The newly arrived were shocked to see the poverty and lack of sanitation; this was particularly shocking to the middle-class Chinese who arrived in China during the years of the Great Leap (Godley and Coppel, 1990, 187–188). The immigrants from Indonesia suffered from a complete lack of recognition of their own cultural needs. The Chinese who had been repatriated in 1960–1961 were overwhelmingly settled at Hainan Island or in separate communities and continued to speak Bahasa among themselves (the Indonesian national language) as they spoke many different Chinese languages, which severely hampered their integration into Chinese society. The Indo-Chinese students by contrast stayed closer to their relatives and integrated more easily into Chinese society, although they suffered severe mistreatment during the Cultural Revolution because of their "bourgeois" background. The other Sino-Indonesians fared hardly any better though, as they were always recognized as different even if they were not of mixed Indonesian-Chinese descent. Many "returnees" from Indonesia found their way toward Hong Kong and Macau, where they usually occupied the lowest societal strata. By 1976, 300,000 overseas Chinese, mostly from Indonesia, had left China, 250,000 to Hong Kong and 25,000 to Macao. According to a recent estimate about 350,000 "repatriated" Chinese from Southeast Asia are living in Hong Kong (Godley 1989, 349). In some quarters of Hong Kong one can hear local Indonesian languages mixed with Cantonese or Mandarin. Many of these residents were pupils of the Chinese-language high schools in Indonesia in the late 1950s (Godley and Coppel 1990, 103, 105).

Internal Displacements

The refugee diasporas are so to speak the tip of the iceberg of much larger displacements, which remained in the region and even within national boundaries. The largest single group of refugees in Southeast Asia who were registered as internally displaced were probably the 1,328,000 displaced in South Vietnam by 1968 (Gatrell 2013, 207). Internal displacement, and even mass killings, attracted little international public attention and geopolitical interests stood in the way of condemning responsible governments for causing migration crises. Four examples stand out here: first, the Indonesian occupation of East Timor; second, Papua New Guinea or Irian Jaya; third the conflict in the Muslim territories of the Philippines; and fourth the minorities in Burma and the Rohingyas in particular. In all these cases geopolitical interests severely diminished international recognition of the migration crises and even mass killings.

In the wake of the Carnation Revolution of Portugal in 1974, East Timor was on its way to become an independent nation under the leadership of the left-wing Fretelin, when Indonesia felt encouraged by anticommunist fears in the West, and the United

States in particular, to invade this country. From 1975 onwards, the Indonesian occupation forces fought a cruel war; after a few years half of the population was internally displaced. From 1975 until 1999, when the United Nations became the interim ruler, a third of the population lost their lives. About 20,000 managed to escape to Australia and 10,000 to Portugal (Wise 2004, 152). Noam Chomsky censured in 1979 the immense hypocrisy of the West that denounced Vietnam for causing the boat refugee problem, while staying silent about the butchering of the people of East Timor or adding insult to injury by delegitimatizing Fretilin (Chomsky 1979).

Chomsky's ire could have pertained to the situation in Irian Jaya as well. The Netherlands had been forced by the United States to hand over New Guinea—its official name at that time—to Indonesia in 1962. Resistance of the local population against this annexation had already cost 30,000 of the 900,000 Papuans their lives by the late 1970s (Van der Kroef 1978, 125). Probably tens of thousands of Papuans of Irian Jaya had fled to the eastern part of the island into Papua New Guinea. With the transmigration programme of Indonesia, bringing an influx of 250,000 Javanese and concomitant business interests in the 1980s, resistance gained new momentum and the result was a new exodus of intelligentsia and another 10,000 refugees heading Papua New Guinea.[3] It was not enough to mobilize international pressure to force the Indonesian government to soften its policies, although it was enough for the World Bank and other sponsors to discontinue their support for the Indonesian transmigration programme.

A third case concerns Mindanao, the southern Philippines. By 1960, the influx of 1.2 million Christian immigrants had turned this once sparsely populated territory into the home of 19 percent of the Philippine population (Feranil 1998, 12; Wernstedt and Simkins 1965, 95; Wernstedt and Spencer 1967, 138–139). It was a migration that would only accelerate as almost three million Christians were said to have settled in Mindanao between 1966 and 1976, as smallholders but also as self-employed artisanal gold miners in the Compostela Valley (Ahmad 1982, 9).[4] Meanwhile, plantation corporations committed extensive land grabbing, causing destruction and violence that attended the colonization of what once was the Islamic south of the Philippines. The Moros rebellion in the 1970s, a new depressing chapter in four hundred years of conflict, was crushed by an indiscriminate bombing of the cities of Jolo and Zamboanga, probably making half a million people homeless. It only came to be settled in 1976 after the involvement of Muammar Gadhafi—the leader of Libya and sponsor of the Moro uprising—as a mediator to negotiate autonomy of the Muslim populated areas in the southern Philippines (Algado 1992, 168). Since then the conflict has not abated at all and in 2016, the number of displaced people in Mindanao numbered almost 300,000 according the UNHCR (UNHCR 2018).

The fourth case is Myanmar, ruled by a regime that knows that the country is strategically located and that China, the United States, and ASEAN are keen to prevent one of the two others from gaining too much influence over the country. According to the Internal Displacement Monitoring Center (IDMC) there were 642,000 internally displaced people in this country as a consequence of violence by August 2017. Among them are the Christian Karen and the peoples, such as the Shahn, living in the border states with China, which is a true frontier infested with war lords, narcotics, and Chinese plantation and mining enterprises (IDMC 2017). Since then massive expulsions of Rohingya have taken place and 688,000 new refugees arrived in Cox's Bazar in Bangladesh between August 2017 and January 2018 (UNOCHA)[5] The current ordeal for the Rohingyas is the culmination of a history of oppression and displacement that harks back to the first days of the independence of Burma in 1948. Its new government denied citizenship to this large Muslim minority, who lived in the coastal stretch, which borders south of Bangladesh and where once the kingdom of Arakan was located. The exclusion was aggravated after the military coup of 1962, when the generals were looking for scapegoats for their failed socialist economic policies. A denial of citizenship for the Rohingyas was reiterated in the 1980s by the leader of the Burmese junta Ne Win, on the grounds that it concerned refugees from Bangladesh, a falsehood created to withhold their citizen's rights. Actually, Rohingyas have been shifted back and forth along the Bengal-Burmese border. A heightened level of communal violence against the Rohingyas has led to the displacement of 150,000 people between 2012 and 2014. Many of them tried to find a safer place abroad either over sea or over land, which has led to an extensive human trafficking network. In some of these networks that have made a business out of helping members of oppressed minorities out of the country Burmese and Thai generals have been collaborating, which came to light when mass graves were found of starved refugees who had been held for ransom before smuggling them into Malaysia (Human Rights Watch 2015; *Al Jazeera* 2017). However tragic this is, for the Myanmar government it is attractive to see international attention directed to human trafficking, as it deflects the public gaze from the underlying political drama and migration crisis (Ibrahim 2016, 93–95).

All four of the above cases underline to the point that it was only by the end of the Cold War that the issue of the internal displacements became more prominent in international organizations. In 1992, the UN appointed its first Special Rapporteur on the Human Rights of Internally Displaced Persons (Cohen 1998, 4). It was the sight of the Kurdish refugees relentlessly persecuted by Saddam Hussein seeking shelter at the border with Turkey that gave convincing proof to the fact that huge internal displacements were threats to international stability as well. In 1998, Roberta Cohen published *Masses in Flight*, with a preface by Secretary General of UN Kofi Annan, stating that the internally displaced, at that time an estimated 25 million people, were in worse conditions than international refugees, deprived as they were of medical facilities, proper food and housing.

The number of internally displaced in Southeast Asia during decolonization widely exceeds the number of international refugees, a barely noticed fact. This can first of all be explained by the fact that the internal displacement predominantly has been one from the countryside to the city. This is a well-recorded fact for Indonesia, but to a certain extent true for Malaysia, the Philippines, and Vietnam as well. It can also be explained by the fact that many internally displaced return to their homes after a while and last but not least by the sad fact that many internally displaced may not survive the violence attending their displacement.

Conclusion

The dissolution of the colonial regimes and economies in Southeast Asia brought about massive migration crises, which share a number of important characteristics with those of Europe at the time of the victory of the nation state model in the early twentieth century. But unlike in Europe the plural societies in Southeast Asia were part of economic globalization, a trend that was reversed by the 1930s. The decomposition of colonial empires and the economic nationalism of postcolonial governments, including their aggressive frontier policies, brought the large-scale displacements, most of which were not identified as migration crises. It was however a long chain of coerced migrations of ethnic minorities who did fit the nation building projects of the newly independent states. The parallel with Europe after the First World War has been obscured because of the long time span of this decolonization, covering more than thirty years since the Second World War, and the geopolitical interests that muted international indignation. Moreover, most of these displacements were internal. In the 1990s the international organizations began to take a different view of internal displacement partly because of the wider repercussions and because of the intermingling of oppression, refugee problems, and human trafficking. In that respect we are living in a world fundamentally different from the one a century ago, when the "refugee regime" came into existence.

Notes

1. For Vietnamese figures see Chan and Dorais 1998, 286.
2. The food shortages in Vietnam and Indonesia are well-known. For the food shortages in British Malaya see Kratoska 1988.
3. By the late 1970s, there were already 10,000 refugees in Papua New Guinea; in addition to this number a new flow of refugees came in the mid-1980s. For the 1970s see Nyamekye and Premdas 1979, 933; Bell, Feith and Hatley 1986, 541.
4. In the mining sector, artisanal gold mining grew massive in Mindanao, involving an estimated 125,000 to 500,000 workers. See Verbrugge 2015.
5. UNOCHA. http://www.businessinsider.com/rohingya-refugee-camps-myanmar-images-2017-12?international=true&r=US&IR=T

References

Ahmad, A. 1982. "Class and Colony in Mindanao. Colonization Destroyed the Basis of Moros Society." *Southeast Asia Chronicle* 82:4–10.

Algado, D. T. 1992. "The Political Economy of International Labor Migration from the Philippines." PhD diss., University of Hawaii.

Al Jazeera. 2017. "Guilty Verdicts for Rohingya Trafficking Deaths." http://www.aljazeera.com/news/2017/07/thai-court-deliver-verdict-people-smuggling-case-170719024750630.html. Accessed August 18, 2017.

Amrith, S. 2011. "Reconstructing the 'Plural Society': Asian Migration Between Empire and Nation, 1940–1948." *Past and Present* 210, supp 6: 237–257.

Beets, G., C. Huisman, E. van Imhoff, S. Koesoebjono, et al. 2002. *De Demografische Geschiedenis van de Indische Nederlanders*. The Hague: NIDI.

Bell, I., H. Feith, and R. Hatley. 1986. "The West Papuan Challenge to Indonesian Authority in Irian Jaya: Old Problems, New Possiblities." *Asian Survey* 26, no. 5: 539–556.

Braithwaite, J. 2010. *Anomie and Violence. Non-Truth and Reconciliation in Indonesian Peacebuilding*. Acton, Australia: ANU Press.

Census of the Philippine Islands, Taken under the Direction of the Philippine Commission in the Year 1903, in Four Volumes. 1905. Authored by Joseph Prentiss Sanger, Henry Gannett, Victor H. Olmsted. Bureau of the Census United States/Philippine Commission (1900–1916). Washington, DC: Government Printing Office. https://archive.org/details/censusphilippino1ganngoog. Accessed May 4, 2018.

Chan, K. B., and Louis-Jacques Dorais. 1998. "Family, Identity, and the Vietnamese Diaspora: The Quebec Experience." *Sojourn: Journal of Social Issues in Southeast Asia* 13, no. 2 (1998): 285–308.

Chantavanich S., and P. Rabe. 1990. "Thailand and the Indochinese Refugees: Fifteen Years of Compromise and Uncertainty." *Southeast Asian Journal of Social Science* 18, no. 1: 66–80.

Chomsky, Noam. 1979. "The Plight of East Timor." *The Australian Quarterly* 51, no. 1: 47–61.

Cohen, N. L. 2012. "Return of the Natives. Children of Empire in Post-Imperial Japan." In *Postcolonial Migrants and Identity Politics. Europe, Russia, Japan and the United States in Comparison*, edited by U. Bosma, J. Lucassen and G. Oostindie, 157–179. New York: Berghahn.

Cohen, R. 1998. *Masses in Flight: People Under Assault in Their Own Countries*. St. Louis, MO: Center for International Studies, University of Missouri.

Coppel, C. A. 1983. *Indonesian Chinese in Crisis*. Kuala Lumpur: Oxford University Press, 1983.

Ee, J. 1961. "Chinese Migration to Singapore, 1896–1941." *Journal of Southeast Asian History* 2, no. 1: 33–51.

Feranil, S. 1998. *The Philippine Banana Industry: Confronting the Challenge of Agrarian Reform*. Quezon City: Philippine Peasant Institute.

Furnivall, J. S. *Colonial Policy and Practice. A Comparative Study of Burma and Netherlands India*. New York: New York University Press, 1956.

Gatrell, P. 2013. *The Making of the Modern Refugee*. Oxford: Oxford University Press.

Godley, M. R. 1989. "The Sojourners: Returned Overseas Chinese in the People's Republic of China." *Pacific Affairs* 62, no. 3: 330–352.

Godley M. R., and C. A.Coppel. 1990. "The Pied Piper and the Prodigal Children. A Report on the Indonesian-Chinese Students who went to Mao's China." *Archipel* 39:179–198.

Hien, D. H. 1996. "The New Migrants from Asia: Vietnamese in the United States." 1996. *OAH Magazine of History* 10, no. 4: 61–66.

Hirschman, C. 1975. "Net External Migration from Peninsular Malaysia, 1957–1970." *Malayan Economic Review* 20:38–54.

Hirschman, C. 1980. "Demographic Trends in Peninsular Malaysia, 1947–1975." *Population and Development Review* 6, no. 1: 103–125.

Huff, W. G. 2001. "Entitlements, Destitution, and Emigration in the 1930s Singapore Great Depression." *The Economic History Review* 54, no. 2: 290–323.

Hugo, G. 1987. "Postwar Refugee Migration in Southeast Asia: Patterns, Problems and Policies." In *Refugees: A Third World Dilemma*, edited by John R. Rogge, 237–252. New Jersey: Rowman & Littlefield.

Hugo, Graeme. 1990. "Adaptation of Vietnamese in Australia: An Assessment Based on 1986 Census Results." *Southeast Asian Journal of Social Science* 18, no. 1: 182–210.

Hugo, G. 2006. "Forced Migration in Indonesia: Historical Perspectives." *Asian and Pacific Migration Journal* 15, no. 1: 53–92.

Hugo, G., and C. K. Bun. 1990. "Conceptualizing and Defining Refugee and Forced Migrations in Asia." *Southeast Asian Journal of Social Science* 18, no. 1: 19–42.

Human Rights Watch. 2015. "Mass Graves of Rohingya Found in Trafficking Camp." May 1. https://www.hrw.org/news/2015/05/01/thailand-mass-graves-rohingya-found-trafficking-camp. Accessed August 18, 2017.

Ibrahim, A. 2016. *The Rohingyas: Inside Myanmar's Hidden Genocide*. London: C. Hurst.

IDMC. "Myanmar: Mid-Year Update." 2017. http://www.internal-displacement.org/countries/myanmar/. Accessed August 20, 2017.

Keeley, C. B. 2001. "The International Refugee Regime(s): The End of the Cold War Matters." *The International Migration Review* 35, no. 1: 303–314.

Kelly, G. P. 1986. "Coping with America: Refugees from Vietnam, Cambodia, and Laos in the 1970s and 1980s." *The Annals of the American Academy of Political and Social Science* 487:138–149.

Kratoska, P. H. 1988. "The Post-1945 Food Shortage in British Malaya." *Journal of Southeast Asian Studies*, 19, no. 1: 27–47.

Lavoie, C., and R. B. Knock. 1990. "The ASEAN and International Response to the Southeast Asian Refugee Crisis: A Canadian Perspective." *Southeast Asian Journal of Social Science* 18, no. 1: 43–65.

Lintner, B. 1999. "Burma (Myanmar)." In *The Encyclopedia of the Chinese Overseas*, edited by Lynn Pan, 140–143. Richmond, VA: Curzon.

Marr, D. G. *Vietnam, State War and Revolution (1945–1946)*. Berkeley: University of California Press, 2013.

McKeown, A. 2004. "Global Migration, 1846–1940." *Journal of World History* 15, no. 2: 155–189.

McNicoll, G. 1968. "Internal Migration in Indonesia: Descriptive Notes." *Indonesia* 5:29–92.

Ng Shui Meng. 1999. "Laos." In *The Encyclopedia of the Chinese Overseas*, edited by Lynn Pan, 169–171. Richmond: Curzon.

Nyamekye K., and R. R. Premdas. 1979. "Papua New Guinea-Indonesian Relations over Irian Jaya." *Asian Survey* 19, no. 10: 927–945.

Osborne, M. 1980. "The Indochinese Refugees: Cause and Effects." *International Affairs (Royal Institute of International Affairs)* 56, no. 1: 37–53.

Pomfret, D. M. 2009. "Raising Eurasia: Race, Class, and Age in French and British Colonies." *Comparative Studies in Society and History* 51, no. 2: 314–343.

Pryor, R. J. 1979. "Malaysia. Patterns of Population Movement to 1970." In *Migration and Development in Southeast Asia: A Demographic Perspective*, edited by Robin J. Pryor, 79–97. Kuala Lumpur, Malaysia: Oxford University Press.

Purcell, V. 1951. *The Chinese in Southeast Asia*. London: Oxford University Press.

Skinner, G. 1957. *Chinese Society in Thailand: An Analytical History*. Ithaca, NY: Cornell University Press.

Somers Heidhues, M. 1964. *Peranakan Chinese Politics in Indonesia*. Modern Indonesia Project. Ithaca, NY: Cornell University Press.

Somers Heidhues, M. 1999. "Indonesia." In *The Encyclopedia of the Chinese Overseas*, edited by Lynn Pan, 166. Richmond, VA: Curzon.

Tan, C–B., 2010. "Reterritorialization of a Balinese Chinese Community in Quanzhou, Fujian." *Modern Asian Studies* 44, no. 3: 547–566.
Thompson, V. 1952. "The Vietnamese Community in France." *Pacific Affairs* 25, no. 1: 49–58.
Tinker, H. 1975. "A Forgotten Long March: The Indian Exodus from Burma, 1942." *Journal of Southeast Asian Studies* 6, no. 1: 1–15.
UNHCR, Phillipines. 2018. https://donate.unhcr.ph/#_ga=2.1
UNOCHA. https://www.unocha.org/rohingya-refugee-crisis; http://www.businessinsider.com/rohingya-refugee-camps-myanmar-images-2017-12?international=true&r=US&IR=T
Van der Kroef, J. M. 1978. "Irian Jaya: The Intractable Conflict." *Asian Affairs* 6, no. 2: 119–133.
Van der Kroef, J. M. 1979. "The Vietnamese Refugee Problem." *World Affairs* 142, no. 1: 3–16.
Vatikiotis, M. R. J. 1999. "Thailand." In *The Encyclopedia of the Chinese Overseas*, edited by Lynn Pan, 218–227. Richmond, VA: Curzon.
Verbrugge, B. 2015. "The Economic Logic of Persistent Informality: Artisanal and Small-Scale Mining in the Southern Philippines." *Development and Change* 46, no. 5: 1023–1046.
Vlieland, C. A. 1932. *British Malaya. A Report on the 1931 Census and on Certain Problems of Vital Statistics*. London: Office of the Crown, and The Malayan Information Agency.
Wain, B. 1979. "The Indochina Refugee Crisis." *Foreign Affairs*, 58, no. 1: 160–180.
Wernstedt, F. L., and J. E. Spencer. 1967. *The Philippine Island World: A Physical, Cultural, and Regional Geography*. Berkeley: University of California Press.
Wernstedt, F. L., and P. D. Simkins. 1965. "Migrations and the Settlement of Mindanao." *The Journal of Asian Studies* 25, no. 1: 83–103.
Wise, Amanda. 2004. "Nation, Transnation, Diaspora: Locating East Timorese Long-distance Nationalism." *Sojourn: Journal of Social Issues in Southeast Asia* 19, no. 2: 151–180.
Yuen, M. 1990. "Vietnamese Refugees and Singapore's Policy." *Southeast Asian Journal of Social Science* 18, no. 1: 81–93.

PART II

CONSTRUCTIONS OF CRISES

CHAPTER 5

MIGRATION CRISIS AND "BREXIT"

WILLIAM OUTHWAITE

A UK insurance company used for a time the slogan "We won't make a drama out of a crisis." When the UK voted by a narrow majority in the June 2016 referendum in favor of leaving the European Union after over forty years of membership, this result was substantially due to a campaign which came to be focused on a *perceived* migration crisis over the previous years.[1] This chapter suggests that, although there had indeed been a large migration flow, resulting in additional pressure on run-down public services in some parts of the UK, the perception that this was a crisis and that it could be resolved by recovering "control" over migration through leaving the EU was a deliberately fostered delusion. Over a year later, public opinion had largely recognized the necessity of much of this migration, while continuing to accept the government's mantra that "control" was worth pursuing, even at the cost of exclusion from the EU's Single Market which accounts for nearly half of UK trade.[2] Behind the migration issue is a broader background of indifference and hostility to EU membership and of social conservatism and xenophobia which coexists with a reality in which the UK is closely connected with the rest of Europe and more cosmopolitan than many other member states. This chapter traces the way in which the themes of migration, "free movement" inside the EU, and European citizenship played out in the UK and elsewhere in the EU.

The issue of migration bridges the divide between short-term and long-term explanations of Brexit. To put it briefly, short-term explanations stress the drift toward a referendum in British political competition (Westlake 2017), the opportunistic miscalculation by David Cameron, and the manipulation of the referendum vote by a grotesquely biased press and some of the same conspiratorial forces in Russia and elsewhere which helped to secure Trump's election. Longer-term explanations point to historical differences between the UK and (the rest of) Europe (Simms 2016); the fact that the UK escaped defeat and occupation in World War Two; the distinctive legal system shared by England, Wales and Northern Ireland (though not Scotland); and the UK's majoritarian political culture. (The absence of legal or formal constitutional checks on the activities of Parliament, which in practice means the executive, has led many commentators to speak of the UK as an electoral dictatorship.)

Migration and Brexit

Migration came to be a defining issue in the Leave campaign, giving a sharper focus to the slogan of "taking back control" and opposition to EU law and European human rights law, both giving rights to "foreigners" which were deemed unacceptable by many Conservatives as well as those further to the right. On the latter issue, in April 2016, the then Home Secretary (interior minister), Theresa May, declared that Britain should withdraw from the European convention on human rights (ECHR) irrespective of the EU referendum result. It was the convention and the court, rather than the EU, that had caused the extradition to the United States for terrorism offences of the extremist imam Abu Hamza to be delayed for years (on the reasonable grounds that he might be subjected to inhumane and degrading treatment) and had held up for a time the deportation to Jordan of another extremist cleric, Abu Qatada.

> The ECHR can bind the hands of parliament, adds nothing to our prosperity, makes us less secure by preventing the deportation of dangerous foreign nationals—and does nothing to change the attitudes of governments like Russia's when it comes to human rights . . . it isn't the EU we should leave but the ECHR and the jurisdiction of its court.
>
> (Gov.UK 2016)

Opposed and even derided by many of her Conservative colleagues,[3] May withdrew this suggestion just after the Referendum in June, as she launched her campaign to lead her party, only to revive it as Prime Minister as a prospective theme for the election which was scheduled for 2020 but overtaken by the 2017 election (Hope 2016; Asthana and Mason, 2016)[4]

It was *free movement* within the EU, however, which became, and has remained, the key issue in relation to Brexit. The refugee crisis had already created the image of a Union unable to handle the situation, and Leave campaigners raised the spectre of up to eighty million Turks joining the EU and enjoying the right of free movement. As Gurminder K. Bhambra (2017) has suggested, the campaign blurred the distinction between recent movement from Eastern Europe into the UK, the (very small) number of refugees also allowed to enter, and the earlier migrations from the Caribbean and South Asia.[5] In the UK, as elsewhere in Europe, those who opposed migration generally did not distinguish between different categories of migrants, making no exception for refugees.[6] It was common to hear prospective Leave voters justifying their preference by claiming that there were too many people in Britain from Pakistan and Afghanistan; I suspect there was a spillover in which this hostility extended to Eastern Europeans.

"Migration" in this context tended to be understood as relatively permanent immigration, rather than shorter-term or seasonal mobility from elsewhere in the EU or from elsewhere; the often deliberate failure by the UK political establishment to draw this distinction was politically very significant.

This hostility ran together things that had happened in the remote past (Commonwealth immigration), things that were increasingly unlikely to happen (Turkey's accession and the prospect of uncontrolled refugee movement), and things about which little could be done (the dependence of the UK on unskilled and poorly paid labor and the attraction of the UK as an English-speaking country with a relatively open but also poorly regulated and in some domains highly criminalized labor market).[7]

It is part of the definition of crises that they bring together independent elements into a larger whole. In this case, however, the UK—as so often in relation to EU affairs—was agitated about developments from which it was largely protected. The pound sterling, the increasingly fragile currency which remains a symbol for UKIP, the United Kingdom Independence Party, had been guaranteed survival in the UK for as long as it wished to retain it. More relevant in this context, the UK had been allowed to remain outside the Schengen area of border-free travel, dragging Ireland into the same peripheral state. This meant that, despite the tragic scenes in the "jungle" at Calais (an impromptu camp close to the UK border control point located on the French coast as part of a bilateral Anglo-French agreement), there was no prospect of refugees or other migrants flooding into the UK in an uncontrolled manner from the rest of the Union.

The UK and Ireland were also, along with Sweden, the only EU countries to allow free movement to citizens of states joining in the 2004 enlargement. This resulted in substantial migration from Poland, followed in 2014 by smaller numbers from Bulgaria and Romania after the ending of restrictions on the two states admitted in the 2007 enlargement. While the real impact of the UK's 2004 decision has been largely positive in economic terms, at least for the UK, if not for the northeastern accession states (Poland and the Baltic States, substantially drained of skilled labor) this may be seen as the beginning of a "migration crisis" in which the Polish delicatessen joined the mosque as, for some, a symbol of unwelcome change and diversity. A substantial proportion of this migration turned out to be short-term, but in the case of intra-EU movement, which made up around half the total, there was no requirement for it to be, and this fed a narrative of a "loss of control." More importantly, much of the migration from other parts of the EU was to areas such as the agricultural regions of eastern England, which had not previously experienced it except on a seasonal basis.

There was a further twist to the UK's *exceptionalism*. Similar to other member states, it could implement the habitual residence test that required EEA citizens (including UK citizens who had lived abroad for a substantial period) to demonstrate their entitlement to state benefits. In any case, as a Commission press release noted in 2014, " . . . economically non-active EU mobile citizens account for a very small share of beneficiaries and . . . the budgetary impact of such claims on national welfare budgets is very low"(European Commission 2013). A peculiarity of the UK is, however, that benefits paid to those in work but poorly paid have become an increasingly important proportion of household incomes, as wage rates stagnated after the 2008 crisis. As James Ferguson (2016) wrote:

> [T]he real story . . . is not about immigration per se, but about benefits more generally—especially in-work benefits, which are mostly paid to those with low-skilled, part-time jobs . . . The cost of the benefits system has gone up by 50% in inflation-adjusted terms per head since 2000 (from £2,200 to more than £3,300 by 2014).[8]

The underlying issue, then, is not the increase in immigration into the UK. This has indeed risen, from a gross figure (excluding emigration) of 2.7 million in the twenty years from 1975 to 1995 up to 8.7 million between 1995 and 2015. The population increase over this period is balanced by a reduction in fertility levels from around three children in 1965 to less than two over the past forty years (still, incidentally, a relatively high figure by European standards). This east-west movement was in fact part of a general European pattern. Across the EU as a whole, the enlargements of 2004 and 2007 roughly tripled immigration into the old member states (EU-15) (Holland et al. 2011; Portes 2016). In the UK, and specifically in England outside London, anti-immigration propaganda was able to seize *both* on a broader hostility to benefits claimants which has driven the drastic cuts implemented from 2016 onwards *and* on the resentment of those deprived of access to housing or timely medical services in areas which had experienced high numbers of new residents.

Migration and Free Movement

The old canards about immigrants taking "our" jobs and depressing wage levels have little, if any, substance.[9] Vince Cable, a Liberal Democrat cabinet minister in the coalition government of 2010–2015, has recently confirmed that they received a succession of reports demonstrating this, but that these were suppressed by Mrs. May at the Home Office. A Bank of England study by Stephen Nickell and Jumana Salaheen in 2008 and 2016 found that "a ten percentage point rise in the proportion of immigrants working in semi/unskilled services led to a 5.2 percent (2008) to 1.9 percent (2016) reduction in pay," and UK unemployment has been relatively low, though much of its employment is part-time and increasingly casualised—hence the astonishing size of the government subsidy to employers in the form of benefits paid to low-paid workers. This was exceeded only by payments to pensioners and was nearly ten times the figure for the UK's extremely meagre unemployment benefits.

It has also become increasingly clear, though not yet fully to mainstream public opinion in the UK, that there is no realistic way of reducing the UK's dependence on nonnative workers—at least until a remote future when the bulk of jobs in (what remains of) manufacturing and in transport are robotized. The inevitable economic decline resulting from Brexit (assuming it happens) will help, but even a 30 percent fall in GDP such as that inflicted on Greece might not suffice, and most current estimates put the likely fall closer to 10 percent(which I personally think is a serious underestimate)[10]. Admittedly, the UK might replace workers from the rest of the EU with even more easily exploitable ones from poorer parts of the world, but it is hard to see this placating those who voted to leave the EU, since a substantial proportion are racist as well as xenophobic. The partisans of Brexit conjured up a dangerous fantasy of an ethnically cleansed England perhaps even less realistic than that of a *judenrein* Europe; hence the question asked on the streets only days after the referendum: "We voted; why are you still here?"

We should, in any case, not be using the term immigrant to refer to European Union free movers. This misuse of language goes along with the use of the term to refer to any non-whites, as in the ridiculous term "third-generation immigrant."[11] (This way of thinking has a mirror image in the UK's deliberately racist formulation of "patriality," which gives a right of abode to someone with a British grandparent.) The UK's suspicion of the principle of free movement, no less than the prospect of using the absence of a land border with the rest of the EU as a way of controlling entry, drove its successful pursuit of an opt-out from Schengen. Antje Wiener (1999, 447), in a detailed analysis of UK policy at that time, noted the distinctive conceptions of identity and normative conceptions "which does not allow the government to easily opt in favour of European norms." It was this, rather than just the UK's geographical position or its border control practices, which drove the demand for an opt-out, facilitated by the fact that Schengen was originally established on an intergovernmental rather than community basis.[12] As Wiener noted, " . . . it is not sufficient to observe the strategic steps of decision-making. *Where* a decision is being made is crucial. This position is defined by a time axis, as well as by the location within the multilevel governance structure of the EU" (Wiener 1999, 457).[13]

Even now, recent surveys suggest that around two-thirds of UK voters want customs checks and for "immigrants" from the EU to be treated in the same way as non-EU migrants. (This, along with May's obstinacy and the irreconcilable conflicts in her party, is probably what will finally kill off the UK's membership of its only viable trading and political alliance.) Opinion remains divided on whether free movement should be allowed in exchange for freedom of trade, with a very small shift in favour of the proposition between September 2016 and February 2017 (Curtice 2017b; see also Curtice 2017a). Overall, at the time of writing, much UK opinion continues to embrace the fantasy that it might be possible to trade freely while closing the border to free movement. As Curtice (2017a, 13) notes, Remain and Leave voters differ most sharply on this issue, with 74 percent of Remainers opting for free trade as against 36 percent of Leavers.

As so often, however, the running sore of the UK is an indicator of a more fundamental problem in the EU as a whole. Free movement is, after all, also migration, and no less able to stir up anxieties in the receiving population. Welsh people may resent English "settlers", Danes the flow of Germans into Jutland, and so on. In Denmark, foreigners can only buy property as their permanent residence or place of business;

there are also some restrictions in Finland, Malta and Croatia (http://eur-lex.europa.eu/legal-content/EN/TXT/?uri=URISERV%3Al24404). The reference to EU law makes the point that, at least since the Treaty of European Union of 1993, free movement has been clearly distinguished from other forms of migration which are largely subject to the discretion of member states (Kostakopoulou 2014, 2).

The Union has, however, soft-pedaled on this issue, as on the related one of European Union citizenship, which remains tied to that of a member state, despite initiatives such as those by the Parliament in 1989 and again at the special summit at Tampere in 1999. Granting European citizenship to long-term residents would have alleviated many of the disadvantages suffered by "third country nationals," their numbers likely to be swelled if the UK's secession goes ahead. Again, it is the European Parliament, in the form of its Brexit negotiator, Guy Verhofstadt, who has reacted favorably to the suggestion that British residents elsewhere in the Union deprived of their European citizenship might be able to retain citizen rights in a modified form.

Even before the Brexit vote, however, free movement rights had been seriously weakened, in tandem with the erosion of EU citizenship and what Charlotte O'Brien (2016, 937–938) calls "welfare nationalism."

> EU citizenship has never been much help when it comes to claiming social assistance within Member States. However, recent ECJ rulings hollow out citizenship at EU level, and endorse nationality-based discrimination, creating a moral vacuum within the free movement framework.
>
> This ethical empty space has been exploited by Member States, whose interpretation of the free movement provisions can be sometimes narrow and exclusionary . . .

Here again one can see a perverse effect of the EU's historical emphasis on free movement in relation to *work*. In a context of increasing precarity of employment, this opens up the possibility for member states to exclude workers perceived as marginal from free movement rights. The TEU theme of "citizenship," which looked as if it might be the basis of a broader conception of free movement, has become more and more attenuated.

Jo Shaw (2015, 255) cites a media commentator, Dan Hodges (2014) who, before the theme of "post-truth" became established, suggested that UK politicians were

> trapped between absolute and political truth . . . They know that migrant labour, at all levels of the economy, is vital to Britain's prosperity . . . [but] . . . negative perceptions of the social, cultural, and economic impact of migration are so embedded as to make any attempt to reverse them political folly.

This is more a UK problem than one affecting the rest of the EU, where free movement is more respected, notably in the Visegrád countries and other parts of postcommunist Europe whose citizens have made substantial use of it, but also the progressive states of northern Europe (Shaw 2015, 252, notes 22 and 23). Nevertheless, widespread fears about immigration have created "a perfect storm in which free movement rights come to be seen as part of the problem (of a loss of sovereignty) rather than an element of the solution (through a pooling of sovereignty to combat challenges collectively rather than individually)." (Shaw 2015, 253)

I shall not attempt here to cover the refugee crisisand the broader issue of the relation between migration and crisis (Lindley 2014), except to make the obvious point that, whereas any advanced medium-sized state can more or less police its borders (the GDR did this quite successfully, if brutally, from 1961 to 1989), any collective approach will require complicated processes of coordination, and states may be tempted to simply seal their borders.[14] The issue of free movement, however, does raise fundamental issues about the self-understanding of the EU, the relation between EU and member state law, as well as the political allegiance of EU citizens.[15]

Membership and Citizenship

First, there is the Union's unwillingness to admit that free movement is also about migration, paralleled in the external domain by its claim that FRONTEX, the hopelessly underresourced external border service, is only about border control and not also about migration (Kasparek 2010, 119). Member states, of course, address issues of internal migration, such as migration flows from south to north Italy or from northern to southern England. The EU's architecture of FRONTEX and Schengen and its insistence on a sharp distinction between migration controlled by member states and its own free movement regime fall foul of member states (or quasi-members like Switzerland), which simply count "foreigners."

This conflict between EU legal principles and those of member states and quasi-members raise two further related points. One is the weakness of the concept of European citizenship, as mentioned earlier. This means, as Maurice Roche (1997, 3) pointed out, that "we are all denizens rather than citizens in Europe":

> 'Denizenship' rather than citizenship in Europe stems from the long-standing . . . imbalances between i) economic and social integration, and more generally between ii) economic integration on the one hand and constitutional (civil-political and socioeconomic) reform and institution-building on the other (Roche 1997, 19).[16]

It is worth briefly reviewing the history of European citizenship in the treaties of Maastricht (1992), Amsterdam (1997) and Lisbon (2007) and developments since then. Freedom of movement had already been established as a principle governing labor migration in the Rome Treaty, and a landmark court case in 1989 (*Cowan*) upheld the right to French criminal injury compensation for a British *tourist* attacked in Paris, thus establishing a free movement right independent of economic activity.[17] As Pietro Costa (2004, 222) wrote, "[i]t is clear why freedom of movement and residence is identified in the Maastricht Treaty as a central element of European citizenship, given the symbolic role of this principle of liberty."

Like many EU innovations, however, European citizenship had a lengthy and difficult gestation and birth, followed, more seriously, by stunted growth. As Alex Warleigh (2001, 26) put it, European citizenship was created both to improve the operation of the single market and to counteract the democratic deficit (which had been a topic of concern from the beginning of the 1980s). "This dual rationale has given European citizenship a schizophrenic nature . . ." The Amsterdam Treaty, he noted, "marked a return from citizenship proper to 'people issues'—those supposed to resonate with the concerns of the various national publics, such as freedom of movement". (Warleigh 2001, 28) Amsterdam also " . . . included immigration and asylum issues in the normal EU law-making fold." (Dell'Olio 2005, 62)—something which in retrospect has proved more controversial than it was no doubt expected to.

Jo Shaw (2007) traced some of the inconsistencies in the development of European citizenship, focusing particularly on political rights but also touching on issues of movement and migration. Reflecting on the movement of new EU citizens from postcommunist Europe (initially to the UK, Ireland, and Sweden, and later to the rest of the EU-15 states), she suggested that "in the longer term" this might become more like the western pattern of substantially skilled workers moving between equivalent jobs. (Shaw 2007, 28–29; see also Krieger and Fernandez 2006) In the event, and despite the EU's designation of 2006 as the "European Year of Workers' Mobility," the following decade saw a growing "moral panic" about migration in the UK and some other member states, as well as in Switzerland, also bound by free movement rules.

Mobilization against immigration takes many forms, from the elite MigrationWatch UK, founded in 2001 by a retired ambassador and an academic, to the more recent and much more demotic PEGIDA (*Patriotische Europäer gegen die Islamisierung des Abendlandes*) [*Patriotic Europeans against the Islamisation of the West*], founded in eastern Germany but with branches or allies in over a dozen other European states and also Australia.[18] As for political parties, it is hard to distinguish anti-immigrant parties (Fennema 1997) from the overlapping category of the extreme right. Here, there is the further tension between economic liberalism and nationalism (Betz 2001; Kitschelt 1995; McGann and Kitschelt 2005) and between an anti-statist ideology and social conservatism. In relation to migration, there is the particularly interesting twist in which movements and parties attack Muslim and other minorities for their conservatism in relation to issues of gender and sexuality. This "new racism" focuses on culture rather than biology and stigmatizes those who are perceived not to conform to the allegedly dominant culture (*Leitkultur* in the vocabulary of the German right).[19]

In the UK, UKIP was able to differentiate itself from the rest of the extreme right and attract a much wider base of support, including former Labour voters, by combining opposition to the EU with an anti-immigration agenda. The competition between UKIP and the Conservative Party, where these two motifs were also strong, led directly to Cameron's referendum promise in 2013, which his unexpected victory in the 2015 election more or less obliged him to keep. (Westlake 2017) In Switzerland, the redirection of the conservative Swiss People's Party (SVP) in an anti-EU direction also attracted working-class support.[20] As McGann and Kitschelt (2005, 161) put it, in their comparison of the SVP and the Austrian FPÖ, "It should not surprise us that the EU issue is a vital catalyst for the right in the Alps." The SVP's poster for its 2007 referendum initiative in favour of deporting criminal immigrants neatly linked the security theme with a gesture towards a broader racism.[21]

In Switzerland and also in Germany, discussion has been dominated by the concept of *Überfremdung*, a term difficult to translate into English ("overforeignisation") or, more relevant in the Swiss context, into French or Italian, but pointing to an alleged excess of foreign immigration. The term seems to have its origin in German anti-Semitism from the later nineteenth century and became an important motif in Nazism, with Goebbels in 1933 condemning the "overforeignization of German cultural life (*Geistesleben*) by Jewry." This history discredited it for some time in postwar West Germany, but by 1989 it was a key election theme for the extreme right *Republikaner* party, illustrated by an image of a future Berlin inhabited only by Turks. In Switzerland the term was less controversial and figured even in the legislation governing applications for naturalization, requiring attention to "cultural and economic interests, the degree of *Überfremdung* and the state of the labour market"; this was replaced more recently by the blander formulation of 'taking account of the demographic, social and societal development of Switzerland."[22]

I have discussed the Swiss context elsewhere (Outhwaite 2019), but the UK has recently caught up, lacking only an equivalent for the term *Überfremdung*. Opposition to immigration is a longstanding theme of British politics, focused initially on Irish and then on Caribbean and South Asian immigrants. A Conservative election campaign in 1964 had featured the slogan "If you want a nigger for a neighbour, vote Labour." The maverick Conservative politician Enoch Powell is remembered for a notorious speech in 1968 forecasting "rivers of blood," though he was rapidly expelled and forced to recycle himself in the more congenial Ulster Unionist party. MigrationWatch, as noted earlier, has been around since the beginning of the century, but it was the post-2004 migration which came to attract the most attention. The British public, with its very limited knowledge of the EU (only Latvia scored lower in Simon Hix's 2015 analysis of *Eurobarometer* data), did not differentiate between free movement and (other) migration, nor seemingly between a Polish doctor and a Syrian refugee (who might of course also be a doctor). Although the more lurid racist tropes could not easily be attached to migrants from the rest of the EU, there seems to have been a process akin to Freud's concept of screen memory, in which antipathy to the new arrivals concealed and merged with older hatreds and anxieties. (Bhambra 2017) Migration surged as an issue in the later stages of the referendum campaign, with an influential Leave poster featuring a queue of refugees who had entered Slovenia from Croatia (Pringle 2016).

Survey evidence reveals that nearly three quarters of people concerned about immigration voted Leave, as against just over a third of those who did not cite it as a major concern. (Curtice, 2017b, 9–10) As Curtice points out, however, concern about immigration is also a indicator of a wider pattern of social conservatism and authoritarianism.

Dividing respondents into "authoritarian" and "libertarian" groups revealed that "No less than 72 percent of the most 'authoritarian' group voted to leave, while just 21 percent of the most 'libertarian' group did so." (Those in between matched the overall referendum result, with 53 percent for Leave.) "How people voted in the referendum thus not only exposed a big social divide between graduates and those with few, if any, educational qualifications, but also a major cultural divide between those who prefer a relatively homogeneous society and those who are content with a more diverse one." (Curtice 2017, 9–10) It is significant that the street attacks which increased dramatically after the referendum were motivated by homophobia as well as xenophobia.

After the referendum, it became clear that there was little if any prospect of the EU allowing the UK to remain in the Single Market if it rejected the principle of free movement, though the government pretended for a time that this was a possibility. Just under a year later, public opinion seemed to be shifting towards prioritizing single market membership over immigration control, 49 percent to 41 percent in an Ipsos-MORI survey in mid-July 2017, as against a 44/42 split in January, though with a clear majority seeing immigration control as important. A recent survey (September 2017) has a bare majority (39 to 34) agreeing with the preservation of free movement. "Support increases to 47 percent of 18–24s and 50 percent of people who voted for the first time in the 2017 General Election. But most people want to find a compromise . . . [between this and ending immigration from the EU]" (Katwala et al. 2017, 25) The compromise urged in the British Future report, and for which it records substantial levels of support, is a rosy scenario in which the UK is able to restrict the mobility of unskilled workers while encouraging skilled immigration. It is hard to see how the EU would allow single market access on this basis, as Switzerland has discovered.

In the UK, European citizenship means even less than it does in other member states, with "Euroscepticism rising further since the referendum of 2016" (Curtice 2017b). More fundamentally, the UK has not internalized the idea of membership of a transnational political community equipped with what is essentially a federal supreme court.[23] It is now drifting into a self-destructive secession,[24] driven by an exaggerated anxiety about a pattern of migration which occurred for good reasons and (despite bottlenecks where mediocre and run-down local services have been overburdened) has been largely beneficial. The term "migration panic" is perhaps inappropriate in a situation in which the vast bulk of the public does not expect much reduction in immigration, at least within five years (Katwala et al 2017, 68), yet remains willing to risk massive economic damage for the sake of this chimera of control.[25] The referendum which, as David Cameron put it, was intended to lance a boil in British politics (and, he might have added, particularly in his own party), has instead spread a cancerous hatred across what had been a relatively cosmopolitan and welcoming member state.

The UK's apparently terminal state is part of a wider pattern. Switzerland remains threatened by calls for a less dramatic but also self-destructive policy of restrictions on free movement which would deprive it of the advantages of Single Market access and participation in EU scientific and cultural programs. In France, the Netherlands, and elsewhere, the combination of xenophobia and anti-EU propaganda is a powerful one, and the broader social conservative backlash documented by Inglehart and Norris (2016) seems likely to persist until it is weakened by demographic succession.[26] If sixteen-to eighteen-year-olds had been able to vote in the referendum, as they were in the Scottish referendum of 2014, along with long-time British residents in other EU countries and EU citizens resident in the UK (who can vote in local and European elections but not, unless they are Irish or Commonwealth citizens, in national ones), the UK might have escaped the Brexit catastrophe. But by the time the older generations die out,[27] the damage will have been done.

Acknowledgments

I am extremely grateful for helpful comments on earlier versions of this chapter by Adrian Favell and Simon Susen.

Notes

1. As Georgie Wemyss (2015, 187) noted, "The spectacle of the widely publicised televised dawn raid on multiply-occupied living spaces by border enforcement officers accompanied by politicians and media punctuate the British electoral cycle." See Castells 2018 on "Europe's Crises," esp. chs. 10 (refugees) and 17 (Brexit).
2. This is essentially the difference between what has come to be called a "soft" and a "hard" Brexit: the former (Norwegian) model which retains membership of the Single Market (and in the UK's case possibly also the EU's Customs Union) and the latter, in which there is either no agreement (the so-called "cliff edge") or at best a trade agreement such as that negotiated after many years between the EU and Canada.
3. David Davis pointed out that, "[i]f we pulled out of the ECHR, for which we would get much opprobrium, and stay in the EU, all that would happen is the European Court of Justice will do exactly what the ECHR did before but with more force, because the charter of fundamental rights is the European convention plus, not minus. Logically, it does not stand up."
4. Since her reelection to the head of a minority government propped up by a spectacularly xenophobic and homophobic party from Northern Ireland, she has returned to the theme: see "Theresa May's attacks on human rights laws are gifts for despots – UN" https://www.theguardian.com/law/2017/jun/26/theresa-may-attacks-human-rights-laws-despots-united-nations-commissioner).
5. It is interesting however to note that, in the UK's first referendum on membership, in 1975, called to confirm its entry in 1973 (and also to fix an internal party problem, though that time in the Labour Party), people who thought there was too much immigration into the UK were slightly *more* likely to vote in favour of continued membership of the Communities (Evans 2016: 270; Portes 2016, 14). See also, for recent surveys of opinion in Britain and the rest of the EU, Katwala, Rutter, and Ballinger 2017; "Fear and Hope 2017: An Overview." http://hopenothate.org.uk/fear-hope-2017-overview/; I. Pawel Karolewski and R. Benedikter, "The Migration Question: A Highly Politicized Issue Threatening to Split the European Union." *Global Policy*. http://www.globalpolicyjournal.com/blog/29/08/2017/migration-question-highly-politicized-issue-threatening-split-european-union

6. This had already been noted by Lauren McLaren (2001, 101–102); see also McLaren 2015. The distinction drawn (though not always consistently) by elites between external and intra-EU migration had not filtered through to the public, since "most citizens in EU countries view external and internal migration identically." As early as 2000, so long before the Eastern Enlargements, a clear majority of British and German respondents wanted restrictions on intra-EU mobility (Recchi and Favell 2009, 113). See also the Pew survey in June 2017, esp. p. 15, in which a large majority of respondents from nine countries wanted decisions over both EU and non-EU migration to be taken by their country rather than the EU. See Pew Research Center. "Post-Brexit, Europeans More Favorable Toward EU," http://www.pewglobal.org/2017/06/15/post-brexit-europeans-more-favorable-toward-eu/
7. For a fuller and more positive assessment of the UK's relative openness both as a labour market and as a culture, see Favell 2014, 2017; Favell and Barbulescu 2018; also Delhey 2016 on the way in which the Europeanization of attitudes diverges from that of practices.
8. See J. Ferguson, "Does Immigration Make Britain Richer or Poorer?" *MoneyWeek*, http://moneyweek.com/does-immigration-make-britain-richer-or-poorer/; see also M. Webb, "Why Productivity in the UK Is So Low: In-Work Benefits." *MoneyWeek*. http://moneyweek.com/merryns-blog/why-productivity-in-the-uk-is-so-low-in-work-benefits/ Also Kahunec and Zimmermann 2016
9. The last Labour Prime Minister, Gordon Brown, called in a speech in 2007 for "British jobs for British workers," a slogan from the neo-Nazi right. For comprehensive overviews of the background to free movement, see, for instance: O'Leary 1997, 2008; Condinanzi et al. 2008; Groenendijk 2014; Bauloz 2016, O'Brien 2015 and Delivet 2017. The history of the principle of free movement goes back to the ECSC, though then it was restricted to workers in the coal and steel industries. (Recchi and Favell 2009, 5).
10. The Mayor of London commissioned a study in which the "worst-case scenario" (which at the time of writing seems all too likely) would result in a loss of half a million jobs and £50 billion of investment by 2030. See Mayor of London, "Mayor Warns Hard Brexit Could Lead to 'Lost Decade' of Growth And Employment," https://www.london.gov.uk/city-hall-blog/mayor-warns-hard-brexit-could-lead-lost-decade-growth-and-employment (Accessed December 1, 2018).
11. More nuanced formulations such as "immigrant background", "*issu de l'immigration*" or "*mit Migrationshintergrund*" also tend to be racialized, even if they point to an important difference between Europe and North America or Australasia. (See Favell 2016).
12. A witness at the House of Lords Committee noted the following: "There are other European countries like, for instance, Germany and the Netherlands who have long relied on strict controls at the external borders and few controls inside while, for instance, Belgium and France have a long tradition of not so strict controls at the borders but more controls inside the country . . . Britain is not so typical [*sc.* untypical] in its reliance on strong external border controls, that is not a typical British tradition only" (cited by Wiener 1999, 447). Pehrson et al (2009) have stressed the importance of context in the relationship between "national identification and anti-immigrant prejudice."
13. Kenneth Armstrong (2017) rightly stresses the theme of time.
14. For the Norwegian hard right, for example, "[t]he refugee crisis was like a vitamin injection" (Anders Jupskas, of the Center for Research on Extremism, University of Oslo, quoted in Milne 2017.) More recently, the success of the AfD in the September 2017 Bundestag election reflects (or at least closely resembles) voters' views of the parties' relative competence in migration and integration policy. The CDU easily out-performed the SPD in

one survey published on September 17th, a week before the vote, with over 26 percent as against 16.5 percent, but so did the AfD, with 19%. See "Bundestagswahl Spezial!" *CIVEY*. https://civey.com/umfragen/bundestagswahl-spezial-wichtigste-themen-wahlkampf

15. On the relation between law and political science in this context, see for example Joerges and Kreuder-Sonnen 2017.
16. See also Shaw 2007, 26; Condinanzi et al. 2008, Colliot-Thélène 2017.
17. See, for example, Downes 2001, 97–98, and n. 4.
18. PEGIDA UK was substantially driven by recruits from the far-right English Defence League.
19. As Schinkel (2017, 135) puts it, "culturism is a functional equivalent of racism." See also Schrover and Schinkel 2014.
20. The party is generally referred to by its German name, though it is known in the other language areas of the country as the Union Démocratique du Centre, Unione Democratica di Centro and Partida populara Svizra.
21. On the context of the sheep poster, see Michel 2015.
22. The term *Überfremdung* has tended to be avoided except in the discourse of the extreme right. (Riedener 2017).
23. On the interplay of politics and law in this context, see again Joerges and Kreuder-Sonnen 2017.
24. On the neglected issue of the causes of secession and the question of its legitimacy, see Diez Medrano 2017 and Lord 2017, respectively; also Requejo and Nagel 2017.
25. Another response, which at worst may reflect panic, but probably more often is a rational response to the collapse of the pound and the poor economic prospects and increasingly threatening political situation in the UK, is the nine-year high level of emigration (122,000) by EU citizens, their numbers evenly divided between "old" and "new" member states; see Office of National Statistics figures for March 2016–2017.
26. One should note, however, that, although UKIP had little appeal for younger voters, this is not true of some other hard-right parties in Europe.
27. See Ian McEwan's speech in May 1027: Dan Roberts, "Death of '1.5m Oldsters' Could Swing Second Brexit Vote, Says Ian McEwan." *The Guardian*, May 12, 2017. https://www.theguardian.com/politics/2017/may/12/15m-oldsters-in-their-graves-could-swing-second-eu-vote-says-ian-mcewan

References

Armstrong, K. 2017. *Brexit Time: Leaving the EU—Why, How and When?* Cambridge: Cambridge University Press.

Asthana, A., and R. Mason. "UK Must Leave European Convention on Human Rights, Says Theresa May." *The Guardian*, April 25, 2016. https://www.theguardian.com/politics/2016/apr/25/uk-must-leave-european-convention-on-human-rights-theresa-may-eu-referendum

Bauloz, C. 2016. *"Blurred Lines: Migration and Mobility in EU Law and Policy." NCCR*. Working Paper #4. Neuchatel, Switzerland. February 2016. http://nccr-onthemove.ch/publications/blurred-lines-migration-and-mobility-in-eu-law-and-policy/

Betz, H. -G.. 2001. "Radikaler Rechtspopulismus im Spannungsfeld zwischen neoliberalistischen Wirtschaftskonzepten und antiliberaler autoritärer Ideologie." In

Schattenseiten der Globalisierung, edited by Dietmar Loch and Wilhelm Heitmeyer, 167–185. Frankfurt: Suhrkamp.

Bhambra, G. K. 2017. "Locating Brexit in the Pragmatics of Race, Citizenship and Empire." In *Brexit. Sociological Responses*, edited by William Outhwaite, 91–99. London: Anthem.

Castells, M., O. Bouin, J. Caraça, G. Cardoso, J. Thompson, and M. Wieviorka. (Eds.). 2018. *Europe's Crises*. Cambridge, UK: Polity.

Colliot-Thélène, C. 2017. "What Europe Does to Citizenship." In *The End of the Eurocrats' Dream: Adjusting to European Diversity*, edited by D. Chalmers, M. Jachtenfuchs and C. Joerges, pp. 127–145. Cambridge, UK: Cambridge University Press.

Condinanzi, M., A. Lang, and B. Nascimbene. 2008. *Citizenship of the Union and Free Movement of Persons*. Boston: Brill.

Costa, P. 2004. "From National to European Citizenship. A Historical Comparison." In *Lineages of European Citizenship*, edited by R. Bellamy, D. Castiglione and E. Santoro, pp. 207–226. Basingstoke, UK: Palgrave.

Curtice, J. 2017a. "Hard—But Not Too Hard: Much More On What Voters Want From Brexit." NatCen Report. https://whatukthinks.org/eu/wp-content/uploads/2017/03/Hard-but-not-too-hard.-Much-more-on-what-voters-want-from-Brexit.pdf

Curtice, J. 2017b. "Brexit. Litmus Test or Lightning Rod?" British Social Attitudes Report No. 34. http://www.bsa.natcen.ac.uk/latest-report/british-social-attitudes-34/brexit.aspx?gclid=EAIaIQobChMIjsyz7bO61QIVzp3tCh2GGA2xEAAYBCAAEgLsz_D_BwE

Delhey, J., and E. Deutschmann. 2016. "Zur Europäisierung der Handlungs—und Einstellungshorizonte: Ein makrosoziologischer Vergleich der EU-Staaten." *Berliner Journal für Soziologie* 26:7–33.

Delivet, P. 2017. "The Free Movement of People: Principle, Stakes and Challenges." *European Issues* 419 (January): 1–10.

Dell'Olio, F. 2005. *The Europeanization of Citizenship*. Aldershot, UK: Ashgate.

European Commission. 2013. European Commission Upholds Free Movement of People. http://europa.eu/rapid/press-release_MEMO-13-1041_en.htm

Diez Medrano, J. 2017. "Secessionism Revisited: Unequal Market Insertion and its Relevance for the Analysis of Brexit," Euborders Working Papers Series 03, http://www.euborders.com/download/WorkingPaper_03_Diez.pdf

Evans, G. 2016. "The People Are Perceptive: Immigration and the EU." In *More Sex, Lies, and the Ballot Box: Another 50 Things You Need to Know about Elections*, edited by Philip Cowley and Robert Ford. 269–273. London: Biteback.

Favell, A. 2014. "The Fourth Freedom: Theories of Migration and Mobilities in 'Neo-Liberal' Europe." *European Journal of Social Theory*, 17 (3): 275–289.

Favell, A. 2016. "Just Like the USA? Critical Notes on Alba and Foner's Cross-Atlantic Research Agenda." *Ethnic and Regional Studies*, 39 (1): 2352–2360.

Favell, A. 2017. "European Union versus European Society: Sociologists on 'Brexit' and the 'Failure' of Europeanism." In *Brexit: Sociological Responses*, edited by William Outhwaite, 193–199. London: Anthem.

Favell, A., and R. Barbulescu. 2018. "Brexit, 'Immigration,' and Anti-Discrimination." In *The Routledge Handbook of the Politics of Brexit*, edited by P. Diamond, P. Nedergaard, and B. Rosamond. London: Routledge.

Fennema, M. 1997. "Some Conceptual Issues and Problems in the Comparison of Anti-Immigrant Parties in Western Europe." *Party Politics*, 3 (4): 473–492.

Ferguson, J. 2016. "Does Immigration Make Britain Richer or Poorer?" *MoneyWeek*, http://moneyweek.com/does-immigration-make-britain-richer-or-poorer/

Gov.UK. 2016. https://www.gov.uk/government/speeches/home-secretarys-speech-on-the-uk-eu-and-our-place-in-the-world. 2016. Accessed January 25, 2017.

Groenendijk, K. 2014. "Recent Developments in EU Law on Migration: The Legislative Patchwork and the Court's Approach." *European Journal of Migration and Law*, 16 (3): 313–335.

Hodges, D. 2014. "Britons Have Become Scared of the Wider World." *Daily Telegraph*, August 5. https://www.unexplained-mysteries.com/forum/topic/270376-britons-have-become-scared-of-the-wider-world/

Holland, D., T. Fic, A. Rincon-Aznar, L. Stokes, P. Paluchowski. 2011. Labour Mobility Within the EU—The Impact Of Enlargement and the Functioning of the Transitional Arrangements. Final Report. London: National Institute of Economic and Social Research.

Hope, C. 2016. "Theresa May to Fight 2020 Election on Plans to Take Britain out of European Convention on Human Rights after Brexit is Completed." *Daily Telegraph*, December 28, 2016. http://www.telegraph.co.uk/news/2016/12/28/theresa-may-fight-2020-election-plans-take-britain-european/

Inglehart, R., and P. Norris. 2016. *"Trump, Brexit, and the Rise of Populism: Economic Have-Nots and Cultural Backlash."* Harvard Kennedy School, RWP 16-026. https://research.hks.harvard.edu/publications/getFile.aspx?Id=1401

Joerges, C., and C. Kreuder-Sonnen. 2017. "European Studies and the European Crisis: Legal and Political Science between Critique and Complacency." *European Law Journal*, 23 (1–2): 118–139.

Kahunec, M., and K. F. Zimmermann, eds. 2016. *Labor Migration, EU Enlargement, and the Great Recession*. Berlin: Springer.

Kasparek, B. 2010. "Borders and Populations in Flux: Frontex's Place in the European Union's Migration Management." In *The Politics of International Migration Management*, edited by Martin Geiger and Antoine Pécoud, 119–140. Basingstoke, UK: Palgrave Macmillan.

Katwala, S., J. Rutter, and S. Ballinger. 2017. "Time to Get It Right: Finding Consensus on Britain's Future Immigration Policy." *British Future*, September 2017. http://www.britishfuture.org/wp-content/uploads/2017/09/Time-to-get-it-right-.pdf

Kitschelt, H. 1995. *Radical Right in Western Europe: A Comparative Analysis*. Ann Arbor: University of Michigan Press.

Kostakopoulou, T. 2014. "Mobility, Citizenship and Migration in a Post-Crisis Europe." *Imagining Europe*, 9 (June): 1–27.

Krieger, H. and E. Fernandez. 2006. *"Too Much or Too Little Mobility in Europe? EU Policies to Promote and Restrict Mobility."* Dublin: European Foundation for the Improvement of Living and Working Conditions. https://www.eurofound.europa.eu/sites/default/files/ef_files/docs/areas/populationandsociety/mobility4paper2006.pdf

Lindley, A. (ed.). 2014. Crisis and Migration: Critical Perspectives. Abingdon: Routledge.

Lord, C. 2017. "The Legitimacy of Exits from the European Union." *Journal of European Integration*, 39(5): 499–513.

McGann, A, J., and H. Kitschelt. 2005. "The Radical Right in the Alps: Evolution of Support for the Swiss SVP and Austrian FPÖ." *Party Politics*, 11 (2): 147–171.

McLaren, L. M. 2001. "Immigration and the New Politics of Inclusion and Exclusion in the European Union: The Effect of Elites and the EU on Individual-Level Opinions Regarding European and Non-European Immigrants." *European Journal of Political Research*, 39: 81–108.

McLaren, L. 2015. *Immigration and Perceptions of National Political Systems in Europe*. Oxford: Oxford University Press.

Michel, N. 2015. "Sheepology: The Postcolonial Politics of Raceless Racism in Switzerland." *Postcolonial Studies*, 18 (4): 410–426.

Milne, S. 2017. "The Burden of Power." *Financial Times*, November 8, 2017, p. 7.

O'Brien, C. 2015. "The Pillory, the Precipice and the Slippery Slope: The Profound Effects of the UK's Legal Reform Programme Targeting EU Migrants." *Journal of Social Welfare and Family Law*, 37 (1): 111–136.

O'Brien, C. 2016. "Civis Capitalist Sum: Class as the New Guiding Principle of EU Free Movement Rights." *Common Market Law Review*, 53: 937–978.

O'Leary, S. 1997. *The Evolving Concept of Community Citizenship, From the Free Movement of Persons to Union Citizenship*. Boston: Kluwer Law International.

O'Leary, S. 2008. "Developing an Ever Closer Union between the Peoples of Europe?: A Reappraisal of the Case Law of the Court of Justice on the Free Movement of Persons and EU Citizenship." *Yearbook of European Law*, 27 (1): 167–193.

Outhwaite, W. 2019. "'Auf Wiedersehen, Pets.' Rejecting a European Identity?" In *Battlefield European Identity: New Challenges for Social Theory*, edited by Gallina Tasheva and Frank Welz. London: Routledge, forthcoming.

Pehrson, S., V. L. Vignoles, and R. Brown. 2009. "National Identification and Anti-Immigrant Prejudice: Individual and Contextual Effects of National Definitions." *Social Psychology Quarterly*, 72 (1): 24–38.

Portes, J. 2016. "Immigration, Free Movement and the EU Referendum." *National Institute Economic Review*, 236 (1): 14–22.

Pringle, B. 2016. "The UK Has Failed Us All." *Breaking Point*. June 20, 2016. https://politicaladvertising.co.uk/2016/06/20/breaking-point/

Recchi, E., and A. Favell, eds. 2009. *Pioneers of European Integration: Citizenship and Mobility in the EU*. Cheltenham, UK: Edward Elgar.

Requejo, F., and K. -J. Nagel. 2017. "Democracy and Borders: External and Internal Secession in the EU." Euborders Working Paper 14. http://www.euborders.com/download/WorkingPaper_14_Requejo_Nagel.pdf

Roberts, Dan. 2017. "Death of '1.5m Oldsters' Could Swing Second Brexit Vote, Says Ian McEwan." *The Guardian*, May 12, 2017. https://www.theguardian.com/politics/2017/may/12/15m-oldsters-in-their-graves-could-swing-second-eu-vote-says-ian-mcewan

Roche, M. 1997. "Citizenship and Exclusion: Reconstructing the European Union." In *European Citizenship and Social Exclusion*, edited by Maurice Roche and Rik van Berkel, 3–22. Aldershot, UK: Ashgate.

Riedener, C. 2017. "Die Schweiz und die 'Überfremdung.'" *Saiten*, 20. März. https://www.saiten.ch/die-schweiz-und-die-ueberfremdung/

Schinkel. W. 2017. *Imagined Societies*. Cambridge, UK: Cambridge University Press.

Schrover, M., and W. Schinkel, eds. 2014. *The Language of Inclusion and Exclusion in Immigration and Integration*. London and New York: Routledge. Also published as a Special Issue of *Ethnic and Racial Studies* 36 (7), July 2013.

Shaw, J. 2007. *The Transformation of Citizenship in the European Union: Electoral Rights and the Restructuring of Political Space*. Cambridge, UK: Cambridge University Press.

Shaw, J. 2015. "Between Law and Political Truth? Member State Preferences, EU Free Movement Rules and National Immigration Law." *Cambridge Yearbook of European Studies*, 17: 247–286.

Simms, B. 2016. *Britain's Europe: A Thousand Years of Conflict and Cooperation*. London: Allen Lane.

Warleigh, A. 2001. "Peaceful Opportunists? EU Institutions and the Struggle over European Citizenship." In *Citizenship and Governance in the European Union*, edited by Richard Bellamy and Alex Warleigh, 19–40. London: Continuum.

Wemyss, G. 2015. "Everyday Bordering and Raids Every Day: The Invisible Empire and Metropolitan Borderscapes." In *Borderscaping: Imaginations and Practices of Border Making*, edited by C. Brambilla, J. Laine, J. W. Scott and G. Bocchi, 187–196. Farnham, UK: Ashgate.

Westlake, M. 2017. "The Growing Inevitability of *That* Referendum." In *Brexit: Sociological Responses*, edited by William Outhwaite, 3–17. London: Anthem.

CHAPTER 6

REFUGEE AND ROMANI IMMIGRANT POPULATIONS IN BARCELONA

XAVIER CASADEMONT FALGUERA, ÒSCAR PRIETO-FLORES, AND JORDI FEU GELIS

In this chapter, we critically examine how the arrival of immigrants and refugees is constructed as a crisis, and how different actors influence the hegemonic definition of migratory crisis as well as the answers that they provide. Specifically, we analyze the responses of public institutions, the media, and social movements to the arrival of refugees and the immigrant Roma population in Catalonia over the last ten years (2007–2017).

The expression "migratory crisis," often used by the media and politicians, is controversial in that it is usually presented in a broad, vague and abstract way, often related to the capacity of societies to integrate various groups of immigrants (Lindley 2016; Scholten and Van Nispen 2015). In this sense, migrations and crisis are two concepts that are mostly perceived negatively, both in political and media discourse and in public opinion. These two terms are usually associated with exceptional phenomena that are neither desirable nor wanted, and which pose threats to the nation state, national identities, welfare, or social cohesion (Boin 2004).

The constructs of migratory crises originate from different perspectives and dimensions. In this process, it is important to identify the role of certain agents of socialization in the proliferation of discriminatory attitudes and practices. Thus, it is necessary to analyze how elite racism (van Dijk 1993) is subtly expressed through political parties as well as through socializing agents including family, school, and the media. Parallel to this, the identification of frames (Lakoff 2004) used in the social construction of migration crises is also relevant. For example, it is necessary to identify the use that is made of water metaphors (such as wave, avalanche, or container) to illustrate migrations in different European countries. As has been shown, these discursive frames often generate a defensive reaction among the population and are easily employed by far-right political parties that use immigration as an electoral weapon. However, they can also be used in a positive sense, emphasizing the need for immigration to maintain the current pension system and slow the aging of the population (Charteris-Black 2006).

Preparing public opinion by generating a certain political climate and narrative can be extremely useful for those in power trying to legitimize unpopular policies, such as the curtailment of civil rights and liberties in the wake of terrorist attacks (Bigo 2002). Similarly, certain groups, often marginalized or minority, may be accused and stigmatized for causing certain social problems. Identifying alleged perpetrators—for example, Muslim terrorists or invading refugees—achieves social support in the face of practices that may in fact be affecting fundamental rights and freedoms. This would be the case with immigrants, refugees, or ethnic minorities. Faced with these discourses, however, voices may appear that either reinforce or struggle to avoid a certain narrative, but their success depends on their ability to influence large segments of the population. This is the case, for example, of social movements, which seek to condition and pressure the different actors based, in most cases, on the defense of human rights.

In recent years, Europe has been experiencing the effects of the construction of several major migratory crises with different variants, depending on the reference state. Looking at the case of the Roma, in 2010 the European Parliament issued an instant resolution, mainly aimed at France and Italy, respecting human rights and fundamental freedoms by halting mass expulsions of Romani immigrants from their territories (European Parliament 2010). Prior to these expulsions, the media, political parties, and extreme right movements in both countries had created a context that legitimized the violation of fundamental rights and created the social construct of Roma people as "undesirables" (Sigona 2010).

Another more recent migratory crisis is the so-called Syrian refugee crisis. The war in Syria has caused the emigration of more than five million people in search of political asylum, a great number of them in Europe. The image of Syrian refugees in exile seeking refuge was widely disseminated by media outlets. On the one hand, they highlighted the humanitarian crisis and the need to welcome refugees. However, at the same time, they also emphasized that the so-called Islamic State terrorists who carried out the Bataclan attacks in Paris in 2015 had supposedly entered France following the path of Syrian and Iraqi refugees (Lendaro 2016). In this context, most governments took the opportunity to increase police controls at borders and place new barriers and restrictions on the immigrant and refugee population.

The Social Construction of Migration Crisis in Spain, Catalonia and Barcelona

Spain, together with Italy, Portugal, and to a lesser extent Greece, constitutes a singular case among all migration-sending-and-receiving countries: They have quickly gone from being emigrant to immigrant countries. In the specific case of Spain, between the first third of the 20th century and the 1970s it was clearly a country of emigration mainly due to political and economic reasons. From the 1980s onwards, Spain became a country of immigration, with the first decade of the 2000s being the most relevant. In 2015, 4,729,644 foreigners were accounted for, representing 10.17 percent of the population as a whole (INE 2017). As in many places in Europe, this immigration is concentrated in large cities. The case of Barcelona, the capital of Catalonia, is no exception. In 2015, the city had 262,459 foreign residents, equivalent to 16.76 percent of the whole population (IDESCAT 2015). In the Catalan context, migrations have been presented as a possible solution to the country's traditional low birth rates and aging population. At the same time, as in other contexts, immigration is also presented as the cause of the worsening of the labor conditions of the local population and of provoking the "collapse" of the welfare state, under the hypothetical argument that immigrants make intensive use of social services without contributing to their financing (Casademont, Cortada, and Prieto-Flores 2018).

Romanians make up the largest group of foreigners in Spain. Considering that the Romani population represents approximately 8.6 percent of the Romanian population (Council of Europe 2017), we could estimate that in Spain some 35,000 Romanian Roma people have settled in the metropolitan areas of Barcelona and Madrid as well as in other areas of the country. According to Matache and Mark (2014), the main reasons for the migration of the Romani population are socioeconomic factors, the discrimination and stigmatization they experience in their country of origin, lack of work because of their ethnic status, and the dream of being successful in Western Europe.

The relationship between the immigrant and national populations and the public authorities in Catalonia is polyhedral, not easily definable, and subject to the avatars of economic and political dynamics. While there has been economic growth and prospects for improvement, the business class has clearly benefited in every way. Even so, racism and the rejection of immigration are present in the Catalan public sphere, sometimes fuelled by sectors of the media and certain political parties. In the political spectrum, although in the early years of immigration there was a tacit agreement between the different political parties not to use this electorally, over time this pact has come apart and some political parties aligned on the right have used immigration for electoral benefit. In Catalonia, without looking any further, in 2002 a clearly xenophobic political party emerged (Plataforma per Catalunya) that, though seeming to have a certain presence in the municipal sphere, with 67 councilors in 2011, did not ultimately obtain representation in the Catalan Parliament. It remains to be seen what will happen in the future.

With regard to refugees, in view of the data provided by various international organizations and independent NGOs (CEAR 2016) we cannot say that Spain is, at the institutional level, a state sensitive to the reception of refugees. Specifically, between 2015 and 2017 the Spanish government committed to receive 17,000 refugees but had only relocated 1,299 people as of May 2017. This lack of sensitivity contrasts with the initiatives carried out in Catalonia by some local governments (Barcelona among others) that, together with civil society, have pressured the government of the State to obtain competencies to manage reception processes. Political leadership, through the adoption of reception policies and programs, as well as with public discourse and stance, is important in creating a favorable attitude toward approving support measures for refugees (Triandafyllidou 2000; Charteris-Black 2013). This policy shows the commitment of some administrations in favor of the reception of refugees, in a context in which, especially in Europe, ambivalent and porous policies abound because of the growing political support for extreme right-wing groups. We should point out that the hegemonic discourse in the media between September 2015 and March 2017 also revolved around the humanitarian crisis suffered by refugees, emphasizing the need to receive the Syrian population being held in refugee camps, mainly in Greece.

However, it should also be noted that although with some groups a symbolic reception process can be promoted, with others, such as the Romani immigrant population, the opposite occurs. In the cases shown below, we can observe how different agents of socialization create different political and media responses in terms of reception and expulsion in two specific cases.

The Role of Some Agents of Socialization in Creating Discourses of Welcoming or Expulsion

> Eastern European Roma are regarded as an inferior political, social, and economic ethnicity. They are virtually excluded from normal life, the life of whites. Refugees from the Middle East, Africa, or Central Asia are the *New Roma*, treated by the police and the army as if they were inert matter, and by the white population with indifference.
>
> (Gaspar Miklós Tamás, quoted in Tulbure 2015)

This quote from Tamás seeks to equate the experience of refugees who arrived [primarily] in Hungary during 2016 with the treatment received by the Roma population in the countries of Central and Eastern Europe. However, it is also worth mentioning that the creation of a migratory crisis can vary significantly from one context to another, depending on the social group to which it refers. It is also necessary to take into account the role of regional governments and other actors in this process (Weiner 1995). It is for this reason that in the case of Barcelona in particular, and Catalonia in general, the synchronicity Tamás emphasizes in both groups does not occur. Although the discourses around the refugee population are geared toward welcoming and presenting a public image of refugees as victims of war and the need to create solidarity ties, in the case of the Romani immigrant population the situation is rather the opposite.

Next, we analyze how mass media, political parties, and social movements have an influence in creating the hegemonic discourse around welcome and expulsion in both cases (refugee and Romani immigrant populations).

The Role of Mass Media in Generating Welcome or Expulsion Discourses

The role of the media in shaping perceptions and attitudes toward the refugee crisis (Castells 2009; Crawley 2005; McCombs 2014) is worthy of note. In some countries, such as the United Kingdom, the exaggeration of news relating to refugees, as well as links to terrorism, insecurity, and rising crime affect the perceptions of the population and contribute to generate a stereotyped and distorted image of reality (Blinder and Allen 2016).

In the case of Catalonia (also Spain), the public media have played a proactive role in explaining the causes of refugee flight, as well as the conditions suffered during their journey or in refugee camps. In addition, many activists on the ground, especially those involved in humanitarian tasks on Mediterranean coasts or in refugee camps, have used social networks to disseminate texts, images, testimonials and reports, which have favoured greater citizen mobilization. Previous analysis on anti-immigrant sentiments and media in Spain show the role of mass media in generating negative immigration-related news reports that impact natives' perceived group threat (Schlueter and Davidov 2013). However, while most of these analyses coincide with migration flows during the 2000s and immigrants in general, most recent analysis focused on the refugee crisis in the main Spanish tabloids diverges. For example, Seoane Pérez (2017) argues that, contrary to what is expected, refugees and the civic organizations that provide them with support have a voice in the two main Spanish tabloids (*El País* and *El Mundo*) and refugees are presented more as victims rather than perpetrators. The refugee case then appears to be an exception in the Spanish media tradition in dealing with diversity and immigration. Generally speaking, the Spanish (and Catalan) media have been critical of the position of the European Union and have stressed the need to support the refugee crisis without implying an open call for a more generous and open immigration and refugee policy (United Nations High Commissioner for Refugees 2016). This does not detract from the fact that there have been news reports that present the refugee population in a negative way, but greater emphasis has been placed on the need to welcome the refugee population and to raise awareness of the populace in the face of this humanitarian crisis.

Considering what we have just said, mass media in Catalonia have also played a part in the issue that we are discussing here. While some private television networks have tended to reify the concept of migratory crisis, presenting immigration and refugee reception as a problem for the general public, specifically the public television and radio of Catalonia (TV3 and Catalunya Ràdio) have, in general terms, treated the issue more responsibly, with some specific programs even trying to reverse this construct. Even so, the media that have promoted the need to receive refugees are not free of criticism when discussing their treatment of diversity in general. For example, some specific programs have received comments and criticisms for not making the cultural and religious diversity of the country visible and for stigmatizing certain groups. For instance, the director of a program on TV3 acknowledged the awkwardness of news reports when, on several occasions, they inappropriately nominalized or adjectivized immigration:

> . . . we find an abundance of words like avalanche, massive, assault, tsunami, sub-Saharan, invasion, illegal immigrants or illegal immigration, and other terms that refer to violence such as force, attack, violent . . . In all these cases, the intentionality of the media is clear: to link immigration to insecurity, irregularity and problems.
>
> (Solà 2014)

In the case of the Roma, the media played a central role in promoting, in general, a negative image of the Roma population of Eastern Europe when they began to arrive in Catalonia, specifically in the metropolitan area of Barcelona, at the beginning of the 2000s. It is also important to note that while in Catalan society there are signs of building a positive image of the Romani immigrant population (in certain political parties and media), hegemonic discourse is still one of not taking a stance or of attributing to an entire group attitudes with negative moral connotations.

The mass media was quick to echo the arrival of the Romani immigrant population as a collective that lives marginalized from society and survives through illegal activities, some of them related to crime (López Catalán 2014). During the first months of 2007, a hostile image was created of the Roma population from Eastern Europe similar to that created in the United Kingdom in the late 1990s (Clark and Campbell 2000), being a clear example of anti-Roma racism portraying Romani immigrants as "undesirables," which also ended up having political repercussions. This demonization of the other, disseminated by the media, has been identified by Cohen ([1972] 2011) as the generation of social problems through the spread of moral panic and the creation of media monsters (*folk devils*), who must be eradicated to solve the problem. Unfortunately, this media treatment did not favor visibility of the diversity of the Romanian Roma population. For example, it did not show the Romanian Roma with university degrees, although there are some, or others who are actively employed in the labor market, which could be the majority (Prieto-Flores, Puigvert, and Santa Cruz 2012).

Specifically, some of the media during 2007 and 2008 addressed the arrival of the Romani immigrant population from the complaints of a group of neighbors who demonstrated with a banner reading, "Romanians go home, no to incivility, we are not racists". Several media outlets disseminated the existence of these neighborhood mobilizations. Most of the news from the written press associated Roma people with negative stereotypes, using terms such as criminals, antisocial people, or squatters, which have traditionally accompanied the Roma population throughout history. They also played a key role in highlighting statements by neighbors or other people with discriminatory and racist overtones, magnifying these declarations while not giving Roma people of Romanian origin the opportunity to make their own statements. While in the case of refugees, statements by the protagonists were very present—even emphasizing the role of people with university studies or people similar to us—in the case of the Eastern European Roma, their voice had very little presence and this identification "with us" was non-existent.

This media coverage gave rise to new protests by neighbors. The same media returned a few days later to cover the news, again reinforcing the stereotype. Some examples are the following: "They say that they are dirty, anti-social and that they brought cockroaches here with them" (*La Vanguardia* 2007), or "Squatter families picked up their belongings and left hastily . . . behind them, they left a bleak spectacle: an abundance of scrap metal and junk in the yard, blackened walls, trash bags, ruined furniture, an unbearable stench" (*La Vanguardia* 2007). The news reports of these incidents were among the first to enjoy wide media coverage about the Roma population from Eastern Europe.

The Role of Local Governments and Political Parties in Generating Welcome or Expulsion Discourses and Practices

In Catalonia, the City Council of Barcelona took the lead in designing a strategy to accommodate refugees, as well as pronouncing a favorable political discourse on their reception. Specifically, the mayor of Barcelona, Ada Colau,[1] along with the mayors of Paris, Lesbos and Lampedusa, among others, promoted a manifest (*Colau, Hidalgo and Nicolini*, 2015) in 2015 to put pressure on European institutions to relocate refugees in cities that have explicitly expressed their desire to receive. Similarly, the mayor sent a letter to the president of the Spanish government in which she urged him to offer political solutions, to take advantage of the display of solidarity that had emerged in Europe and to engage in the funding of basic services, instead of promoting security measures (*Alcaldessa de Barcelona*, 2015).

All these measures demonstrated the tensions inherent in multilevel governance of global phenomena, in which cities become increasingly relevant political actors (Barber 2014; Harvey 2012; Sassen 2001), and apply pressure at the state and supranational levels to adopt measures that allow them to improve the daily life of their citizens.[2] "The states are deciding on asylum, but it is the cities that give shelter and that guarantee the daily coexistence of different ideas, cultures and religions. We are doing this every day on a small scale and we can do it on a larger scale. All that is required is the political will to do so (*Barcelona Ciutat Refugi, 2015*).

The strategy of Barcelona entitled "Barcelona, Refuge City" is a municipal plan approved in late 2015 that aims to create its own permanent model of reception that would prepare the city to receive refugees with the necessary services to guarantee human rights. The plan was developed in four areas of work: the reception of refugees; care of the refugees who are already in Barcelona; citizen participation and information; and external action, especially coordination with other cities. This plan is managed in a coordinated way with social entities, as well as with the collaboration of volunteers. It also has an initial budget of 10.5 million Euros, a provision that is hardly negligible given the situation of economic crisis that has affected Catalonia and Barcelona since 2008.

For its part, the Generalitat [Government of Catalonia] approved the International Protection Plan of Catalonia in January 2014. Later, in 2017, the Catalan Refugee Programme was presented, which aims to cover basic subsistence needs, as well as providing access to other public services. The refugee agrees to participate in a training program, which includes language courses, job training, and knowledge of their new environment. In addition, the program includes the participation of volunteers who agree to act as mentors from two to four hours a week during one year. The program received good public acceptance, as more than 2,700 people registered as mentors[3]. Another of the important actions promoted by the Generalitat was the launching of a website (*Guia de Benvinguda*, 2018) that welcomes and provides useful information for newcomers, as well as showing various resources that are being offered and information of interest on the causes that lead to the arrival of refugees. This website was disseminated through an institutional advertising campaign that once again showed the population the political commitment of Catalonia to welcome refugees, while avoiding ambiguous attitudes involving electoral costs for the government. In addition, in this case, this program has been launched in conjunction with organizations working on issues related to asylum and refugees.

With regard to the Romani immigrant population, various comprehensive political plans for their social inclusion have been put into effect since 2006 in Catalonia. In particular, the comprehensive plan for the Roma population (2009–2013) is the first that aims to specifically promote the participation of Roma citizens from Eastern Europe in social, economic and political life and facilitate their access to services and resources on an equal basis (Generalitat of Catalonia 2009, 2014). Even so, and although it should be emphasized that the intentionality of the plan is good—bringing together different departments to improve the living conditions of the Roma population and encourage their voice in decision-making processes—there have been some situations in the implementation of the plan that contradict this declaration of good intentions. Specifically, the expulsion of Roma immigrant families from Catalan territory has been implicitly promoted in some cases. Although Catalonia does not have competence in migration matters regarding expulsion and deportation of people, forced mobility mechanisms can be generated through the child protection system. Some examples occur, for instance, when social services workers, driven by the image that appears in the mass media of Roma immigrants as antisocial or "incapacitated" to protect and take care of their children, take custody of their children away from them and make their recovery conditional on their "voluntary" return to their country of origin (Vrăbiescu, 2017).

At the local level, some politicians have attempted to seize the opportunity of media coverage of the Romani immigrant population for political advantage. To this end, the leader of the Popular Party (right-wing conservative party in Spain) in the municipality of Badalona, Xavier García Albiol, attended demonstrations to support residents and demand that the City Council expel the Romanian Roma from the city. During the following three years, the insistence of discourses relating crime with immigration in general and more specifically with the immigrant Roma population continued. In 2011, the municipal electoral campaign was conditioned by the distribution of a leaflet with the words "Insecurity, Delinquency, Incivility, Uncleanliness" with photographs of the previously described mobilizations of neighbors against the Romanian Roma population, as well as photographs of Romanian Roma begging on the street.

In one of the main rallies of the electoral campaign, Garcia Albiol referred to the situation in some cities of the Metropolitan Area of Barcelona with the following statement:

> Here we do not have Roma camps like in France; here the situation is even worse. They are spread across several districts of the city making life miserable for residents and moreover, when we complain, we are attacked and branded as racist.
>
> (*El País*, July 25, 2015)

Garcia Albiol appealed to the notion of territoriality to emphasize how the situation in France was better since they were confined in camps and segregated from the general population. Picker (2017) emphasizes that this type of policy of racial segregation, especially present with the Roma population in France and the United Kingdom, has its origins in the assumption of ensuring hygiene and public order through policies that reproduce racial segregation. In this regard, the main motto of his election campaign was "Cleaning Badalona." Garcia Albiol's purpose was to "cleanse" the city through the use of police order and the expulsion of Roma. In this case, we can also see how Romaphobia occurs through prejudice rooted in the traditional European notion of territoriality (McGarry 2017)—in short, in not accepting the Roma population because they do not belong to our imaginary. While in other European contexts, as in the case of France, the persecution of the Roma population has been taken on by the State and its security forces (Balch, Balabonova, and Trandafoiu 2014), in the specific case of Spain and Catalonia this responsibility has been given to the local administrations, where local politicians and police forces seek to ensure the safety of the rest of the citizens while attempting to monitor and expel the Roma population from the city.

With this type of discourse, Albiol won the municipal elections of 2011 and was proclaimed mayor. This case exemplifies how criminalizing a group generates a social problem through the media and how certain political parties try to gain political advantage from this situation. This situation did not occur in isolation in the Metropolitan Area of Barcelona, but was also present in other European contexts. The case of Italy, for example, Sigona (2010) emphasizes how anti-Roma sentiment was also a relevant component in the political battle over security during the campaign in the 2008 national elections.

a) *The role of social movements in generating welcome or expulsion discourses and practices*

The cases of Barcelona and Catalonia illustrate a link and a certain feedback between the political leadership and the action of pressure from social movements in the case of refugees. In spite of everything, the involvement of civil society and citizens in the face of the refugee situation has yielded surprising results, which did not occur, for example, years ago with the arrival of numerous contingents of immigrants in Catalonia, mainly for economic reasons. Yet recently different social movements have emerged that fight and denounce situations that affect immigrants already residing in Catalonia. In this direction, of particular interest is the fight to close the Foreigners Internment Centre (CIE) in the Zona Franca of Barcelona,[4] or the work of entities such as *SOS Racisme*, which year after year denounces cases of racism and discrimination towards immigrants, as well as other mobilizations for more distant realities, such as human rights violations on the southern border (Melilla), and the tragedy of people dying in the Mediterranean. The sum of these mobilizations has created a favorable climate to encourage social involvement with the refugee crisis.

The main actor seeking to raise awareness about migrations and refugees is the organization Casa Nostra, Casa Vostra [Our Home, Your Home], formed in mid-2016 by activists and social entities. Their demands not only focus on refugees, but also on people who are already living in Catalonia and have difficulties developing themselves in dignity. Their campaign, strongly driven through social networks, began with the drafting of a manifesto, which has obtained more than 120,000 signatures. Thanks to the collaboration of volunteers, different awareness-raising activities were organized throughout the territory. The peak points were a concert in Barcelona, attended by more than 25,000 people, with the selfless participation of musicians and artists and that served to raise funds for various entities, and a demonstration with 500,000 people in the streets of Barcelona. After these two events, the Parliament of Catalonia unanimously approved a motion on reception policies in Catalonia,[5] as well as approving a government agreement to reinforce the commitment to the reception policies.[6] In spite of this, this entity has denounced what they consider the lack of a response from both state and autonomous administrations[7].

Despite the efforts and mobilizations to promote policy changes, as of mid-2017 Spain had only received 7.5 percent of the 17,387 refugees they had promised to accept. For this reason, a new campaign, called Veniu Ja! [Come Now!], has begun, which is attempting to focus attention on the degree of noncompliance with the commitments of the Spanish government. Thus a website was created with a counter that records the time left for the State to comply with its commitments, the number of people that have arrived so far, and those that arrive every day.

Apart from the advocacy efforts directed at political actors, we must not lose sight of the role of entities in raising awareness of the citizenry as a whole, as well as in intervention on the ground in helping refugees. One of the best-known cases in Catalonia is the Proactive Open Arms NGO, founded in 2015, with the aim of rescuing people at sea fleeing wars and trying to reach Europe via the central Mediterranean and Aegean Sea. Their lifesaving task has earned them multiple recognitions, both international and national, as well as a prominent media presence, which has allowed, as discussed above, the refugee crisis to be placed in the spotlight of Catalan society.

During the Badalona incidents described earlier, the mobilization of local and regional Roma civic organizations was important in order to try to mediate and stop the image being propagated by the media about the immigrant Roma population. Roma associations felt attacked as some media and politicians used the same stereotypes and historical prejudices that had been attributed to the nonimmigrant Roma population (Prieto-Flores and Sordé 2011). In this regard, several organizations carried out awareness campaigns to denounce the discrimination suffered by the Roma population in general and Roma immigrants in particular, which can be found in their annual reports on discrimination. These documents denounce the racism suffered by the Roma population and the image disseminated by the media, reiterating the need for them to be more careful in the language they use. For example, the 2014 report highlights the need to openly combat existing anti-Roma racism in Spain by using the example of Albiol's case and calls for the existence of an independent body that would promote equal treatment and nondiscrimination (Fundación Secretariado Gitano 2015). Lastly, some Roma organizations, such as FAGIC (Federation of Romani Associations of Catalonia), initially added their voice to the complaint filed by SOS Racisme and the Public Prosecutor against Albiol for inciting hatred and violence in the case described above.

Looking further, there are not many initiatives that this type of organization undertakes to improve the ties between the immigrant and nonimmigrant Roma population. In this area, we can highlight the role of organizations such as the Roma women's association Drom Kotar Mestipen, which has carried out grassroots actions to create bonds of sisterhood through promoting joint work among Romani women of different origins (immigrant and nonimmigrant), weaving networks of solidarity and overcoming the racialized discourses prominent in the public sphere (Sordé et al. 2014).

Conclusion

In this chapter, we analyze how similar phenomena, the arrival of immigrants whether economically or politically motivated, give rise to political, social, and media responses that differ considerably. Thus, while in some cases an explicit message of welcome and reception of refugees is promoted, in others, a less empathetic view occurs. In this sense, not all migration crises are created in the same way for all groups, nor do they receive the same responses. Rather, we must examine contextual and historical elements and the image that is disseminated in the media, social movements, and the political class regarding each one of the groups referred to.

The case of Catalonia and Barcelona shows how, in spite of certain divergences, political, social and media actors have promoted an explicit action in favour of receiving refugees. The mobilization of civil society has been especially praiseworthy, putting the problem on the political agenda and directly addressing the responsible institutions. Thus the City Council of Barcelona and the Generalitat, despite not having direct competencies in key areas for welcome and reception, have planned reception policies and have put pressure on the central government and European institutions to attend to their requests.

On the contrary, however, the treatment received by other collectives, traditionally victims of exclusion and discrimination, such as the Romani immigrant population, has been markedly different. On the one hand, this is due to less involvement or indifference on the part of state and local public institutions that have historically discriminated against the Roma population, and on the other, to the active role of some media and local political agents in promoting the crisis and expulsion of the population from the territory. In this regard, it should be noted that while cities and regions can generate their own political frameworks in response to local needs, sometimes having an orientation that diverges from the policy of the state (Penninx et al. 2004; Zapata-Barrero, Caponio and Scholten 2017), it should be clarified that these may also diverge in their approach (reception or expulsion) depending on the reference group and the socio-historical moment we live in.

Translated from the Catalan by Michael Weiss

Notes

1. Ada Colau became the mayor of Barcelona in May 2015, leading a candidacy formed by a coalition of different political organizations and social movements that emerged from the 15M movement. Previously, she was a prominent activist, especially in the area of housing rights and the fight against evictions, through the Platform of People Affected by Mortgages.
2. This issue has been a constant since then, with several symbolic actions in which Barcelona aims to take the initiative to collaborate with other cities in supporting refugees, in light of what it considers the inoperability of the European Union and States. In this regard, Barcelona has signed agreements with Lampedusa and Lesbos to collaborate with specialized technicians, or with Athens to relocate refugees, as well as delivering an address at the United Nations headquarters on behalf of cities, in 2016.
3. Source: Secretary of Equality, Migrations and Citizenship. Consulted: 05/04/2017

4. CIEs are centers where people who have committed an administrative fault (they are in an irregular situation) are interned pending an order of expulsion from the country. Despite being defined as temporary and nonpenitentiary centers, they have received numerous allegations of human rights violations, including the death of Idrissa Diallo at the CIE in Barcelona, as well as criticism of the opacity with which the administration manages this center.
5. Motion 102/XI of the Parliament of Catalonia on reception policies in Catalonia.
6. Government agreement that reaffirms the Government's commitment to Catalan society for the reception of refugees (Government Session, February 21, 2017):. http://presidencia.gencat.cat/web/.content/departament/transparencia/acords_govern/2017/2017_02_21/SIG17TSF0138.pdf. Accessed January 10, 2018.
7. As this chapter was being finished, however, the City Council of Barcelona presented the approval of a *city identification card*, which will serve to guarantee universal access to municipal services (a government measure to promote access to regularity and prevent irregularities from occurring).

References

Alcadessa de Barcelona. 2015. Carta de l'alcaldessa de Barcelona al President del Govern de 5 de setembre de 2015. http://ajuntament.barcelona.cat/premsa/wp-content/uploads/2015/09/CartaRajoyCiutatRefugi_DEF.pdf. Accessed April 29, 2018.

Balch, A., E. Balabanova, and R. Trandafoiu. 2014. "A Europe of Rights and Values? Public Debates on Sarkozy's Roma Affair in France, Bulgaria and Romania." *Journal of Ethnic and Migration Studies* 40, no. 8: 1154–1174. doi: 10.1080/1369183X.2013.854691

Barber, B. 2014. *If Mayors Ruled The World: Dysfunctional Nations, Rising Cities*. New Haven, CT: Yale University Press.

Barcelona Ciutat Refugi. N.a., 2015. http://ciutatrefugi.barcelona/ca/el-pla. Accessed April 29, 2018.

Bigo, D. 2002. "Security and Immigration: Toward a Critique of the Governmentality of Unease." *Alternatives* 27, no. 1: 63–92. doi: 10.1177/03043754020270S105

Blinder, S., and W. L. Allen. 2016. "Constructing Immigrants: Portrayals of Migrant Groups in British National Newspapers, 2010–2012." *International Migration Review* 50, no. 1: 3–40. doi: 10.1111/imre.12206

Boin, A. 2004. "Lessons from Crisis Research." *International Studies Review* 6, no. 1: 165–194. doi: 10.1111/j.1521-9488.2004.393_2.x

Casademont, X., P. Cortada, and Ò. Prieto-Flores. 2018. "Citizenship and Immigrant Anti-Rumour Strategies: A Critical Outlook from the Barcelona Case." *Citizenship Studies* 22, no. 1: 37–52.

Castells, M. 2009. *Communication Power*. Oxford: Oxford University Press.

CEAR. 2016. *Informe 2016: Las persones refugiades en España y Europa*. Madrid: Comisión Española de Ayuda al Refugiado. http://www.ccar.cat/wp-content/uploads/2016/06/Informe-2016.pdf

Charteris-Black, J. 2013. *Analysing Political Speeches: Rhetoric, Discourse and Metaphor*. Basingstoke, UK: Palgrave Macmillan.

Charteris-Black, J. 2006. "Britain as a Container: Immigration Metaphors in the 2005 Election Campaign." *Discourse & Society* 17, no. 5: 563–581.

Clark, C., and E. Campbell. 2000. "'Gypsy Invasion': A Critical Analysis of Newspaper Reaction to Czech and Slovak Romani Asylum-Seekers in Britain, 1997." *Romani Studies*: 10, no. 1: 23–47. doi: 10.3828/rs.2000.2

Cohen, S. [1972] 2011. *Folks, Devils, and Moral Panics. The Creation of the Mods and Rockers*. London: Routledge.

Colau, A., A. Hidalgo, and G. Nicolini. 2015. " Nosotros, las ciudades de Europa." *El Pais*, September 12. http://politica.elpais.com/politica/2015/09/12/actualidad/1442074231_219516.html?ref=rss&format=simple&link=link. Accessed April 29, 2018.

Council of Europe. 2017. *Estimates on Roma Population in European Countries: Document Prepared by the Support Team of the Special Representative of the Secretary General of the Council of Europe for Roma Issues*. http://www.coe.int/en/web/portal/roma. Accessed June 6, 2017.

Crawley, H. 2005. *Evidence on Attitudes to Asylum and Immigration: What We Know, Don't Know and Need to Know*. Working Paper Series 23. Oxford: COMPAS, University of Oxford.

European Parliament. 2010. *European Parliament Resolution of 9 September 2010 on the Situation of Roma and on Freedom of Movement in the European Union*. P7_TA(2010)0312. Brussels: European Parliament. http://www.europarl.europa.eu/sides/getDoc.do?pubRef=-//EP//TEXT+TA+P7-TA-2010-0312+0+DOC+XML+V0//EN. Accessed May 5, 2017.

Fundación Secretariado Gitano. 2015. *Discriminación y Comunidad Gitana. Informe anual 2014*. Madrid: Fundación Secretariado Gitano. https://www.gitanos.org/centro_documentacion/publicaciones/fichas/109822.html.es

Generalitat de Catalunya. 2014. *Pla integral del poble gitano de Catalunya 2014–2016*. Barcelona: Departament de Benestar Social i Família. http://treballiaferssocials.gencat.cat/web/.content/03ambits_tematics/18_accio_comunitaria_i_voluntariat/01_accio_comunitaria/04_pla_integral_poble_gitano/pipg2014.pdf

Generalitat de Catalunya. 2009. *Pla integral del poble gitano de Catalunya 2009-2013*. Barcelona: Departament de Benestar Social i Família.

Guia de benvinguda per a les persones refugiades que arriben a Catalunya, n.a., 2018. http://refugee.cat/ca/home-ca/. Accessed April 29, 2018.

Harvey, D. 2012. *Rebel Cities: From the Right to the City to the Urban Revolution*. London: Verso.

IDESCAT. 2015. *Evolució de la població total i estrangera*. Barcelona: Institut d'Estadística de Catalunya. https://www.idescat.cat/poblacioestrangera/?b=0&nac=d341.

INE. 2017. *Número de personas extranjeras según país de nacimiento*. Madrid: Instituto Nacional de Estadística. http://www.ine.es/prensa/cp_2017_p.pdf. Accessed April 30, 2018.

La Vanguardia. 2007. *Las protestas por los pisos patera se extienden por Badalona*. February 10. Suplemento Vivir, p. 5.

Lakoff, G. 2004. *Don't Think of an Elephant! Know Your Values and Frame the Debate*. White River Junction, VT: Chelsea Green.

Lendaro, A. 2016. "A 'European Migrant Crisis'? Some Thoughts on Mediterranean Borders." *Studies in Ethnicity and Nationalism* 16, no. 1: 148–157. doi: 10.1111/sena.12169

Lindley, A. 2016. *Crisis and Migration: Critical Perspectives*. London: Routledge.

López Catalán, Ó. 2014. "Piedra, Papel y Tijera. Vivienda y Gestión del Asentamiento de la Población Rrom/Gitana Rumana en el Área Metropolitana de Barcelona (2006–2014)." *Revista Andaluza de Antropología* 7: 102–129.

Matache, M., and D. Mark. 2014. "Confined by Narrow Choices: The Stories of Roma Adolescents" In *Human Rights and Adolescence*, edited by Jacqueline Bhabha, 270–292. Philadelphia: University of Pennsylvania Press.

McCombs, M. 2014. *Setting the Agenda: The Mass Media and Public Opinion*. Cambridge, UK: Polity.

McGarry, A. 2017. *Romaphobia: The Last Acceptable Form of Racism*. London: Zed.

Penninx, R., K. Kraal, M. Martiniello, and S. Vertovec. 2004. *Citizenship in European Cities: Immigrants, Local Politics and Integration Policies*. London: Routledge.

Picker, G. 2017. *Racial Cities: Governance and the Segregation of Romani People in Urban Europe*. London: Routledge.

Prieto-Flores, Ò., L. Puigvert, and I. Santa Cruz. 2012. "Overcoming the Odds: Constricted Ethnicity in Middle-Class Romà." *Identities, Global Studies in Culture and Power* 19, no. 2: 191–209. doi:10.1080/1070289X.2012.672856

Prieto-Flores, Ò., and T. Sordé. 2011. "The Institutionalization of Panethnicity from the Grassroots Standpoint in a European Context: The Case of Gitanos and Roma Immigrants in Barcelona." *Ethnicities* 11, no. 2: 202–217.

Sassen, S. 2001. *The Global City: New York, London, Tokyo*. Princeton, NJ: Princeton University Press.

Schlueter, E., and E. Davidov. 2013. Contextual Sources of Perceived Group Threat: Negative Immigration-Related News Reports, Immigrant Group Size, and Their Interaction, Spain 1996–2007. *European Sociological Review* 29, no. 2: 179–191.

Scholten, P., and F. van Nispen. 2015. "Policy Analysis and the 'Migration Crisis': Introduction." *Journal of Comparative Policy Analysis: Research and Practice* 17, no. 1: 1–9. doi:10.1080/13876988.2015.1006408

Seoane Pérez, F. 2017. Framing of the Syrian Refugee Crisis in the Spanish Press. In *The Migrant Crisis: European Perspectives and National Discourses*, edited by M. Barlai, B. Fähnrich, C. Griessler, and M. Rhomberg, 267–282. Zürich, Switzerland: LIT Verlag.

Sigona, N. 2010. "Gypsies out of Italy! Social Exclusion and Racial Discrimination of Roma and Sinti in Italy." In *Italy Today: The Sick Man of Europe*, edited by Andrea Mamone and Giuseppe A. Veltri, 143–157. London: Routledge.

Solà, C. 2014. *En la cobertura de les migracions es fan errors que en alters temes no es permeten*. https://www.media.cat/2012/06/20/"en-la-cobertura-de-les-migracions-es-fan-errors-que-en-altres-temes-no-es-permeten"/. Accessed November 19, 2017.

Sordé, T., O. Serradell, L. Puigvert, and A. Munté. 2014. "Solidarity Networks That Challenge Racialized Discourses: The Case of Romani Immigrant Women in Spain." *European Journal of Women's Studies* 21, no. 1: 87–102. doi: 10.1177/1350506813510425

Triandafyllidou, A. 2000. "The Political Discourse on Immigration in Southern Europe: A Critical Analysis." *Journal of Community & Applied Social Psychology* 10, no. 5: 373–389.

Tulubre, C. 2015. "Gaspar Miklós Tamás: 'Los refugiados son los nuevos gitanos.'" *Público*, Oct. 15. http://www.publico.es/internacional/gaspar-miklos-tamas-hungria-refugiados.html. Accessed April 29, 2018.

United Nations High Commissioner for Refugees. 2016. *Press Coverage of the Refugee and Migrant Crisis in the EU: A Content Analysis of Five European Countries*. http://www.unhcr.org/protection/operations/56bb5a876/press-coverage-refugee-migrant-crisis-eu-content-analysis-five-european.html. Accessed November 18, 2017.

van Dijk, T. A. 1993. *Elite Discourse and Racism*. New York: SAGE.

Vrăbiescu, I. 2017. "Roma Migrant Children in Catalonia: Between the Politics of Benevolence and the Normalization of Violence." *Ethnic and Racial Studies* 40, no. 10: 1663–1680. doi:10.1080/01419870.2016.1229491

Weiner, M. 1995. *The Global Migration Crisis. Challenge to States and to Human Rights.* New York: Harper Collins College Publishers.

Zapata-Barrero, R., T. Caponio, and P. Scholten. 2017. "Theorizing the 'Local Turn' in a Multi-Level Governance Framework of Analysis: A Case Study in Immigrant Policies." *International Review of Administrative Sciences* 83, no. 2: 241–246. doi:10.1177/0020852316688426

CHAPTER 7

THE MYTH OF A MIGRATION CRISIS IN FRANCE

Transformations of Public Actions and Solidarist Actions

ISABELLE RIGONI

France has a long tradition of receiving foreign populations, especially since the second half of the nineteenth century (Green and Poinsot 2008; Noiriel 1988). Until the second half of the twentieth century, it was the country in Europe with the highest immigration rate, the second in the world after the United States. Initially a border migration (German, Belgian, Swiss), this diversified in the late nineteenth century (Italian, Spanish), and even more after the First World War, to meet the needs of the country's reconstruction. As early as the nineteenth century, immigration from the colonies also began; around 1895, immigrants from North Africa numbered a few hundred. Likewise, despite the Dreyfus affair, France remained very attractive for Jews in Central and Eastern Europe who were still subject to persecution and discrimination. During the First World War, France appealed to "foreign labor" for the munitions needs of its army. Thus the Ministry of Armament recruited Belgians, Swiss, and Italians, but also Kabyles, or more generally subjects from North African colonies, as well as Indochinese (Annamese and Tonkinese) and 35,000 Chinese for hazardous work. The country also mobilized 600,000 "Senegalese riflemen" from the colonies to fight for France. Forced recruitment did not only serve military needs: in September 1939, the governor general of Indochina was charged with recruiting voluntarily or forcibly 20,000 Indochinese workers. They were disembarked at the Baumettes prison in Marseille and sent mainly to the Camargue to develop rice growing. In the aftermath of the Second World War, the migratory landscape diversified and Italian immigration was replaced by Spanish, Portuguese, Yugoslav, Turkish, Tunisian, and Moroccan immigration and finally immigration from sub-Saharan countries. Practices used in the colonies were imported into mainland France. An administrative commission set up a surveillance system, and built migrant workers' hostels, most of which housed Kabyles from North Africa. Many of the hostel directors were from the military and colonial administration, and were supposed to have gained experience in managing this "high risk" population. So this social housing policy responded in particular to a logic of social control.

Yet colonial and postcolonial France has been slow to recognize itself as a country of immigration, and its policy has been marked by permanent hesitations between an interventionist policy and a liberal policy, between opening and closing borders. In domestic politics, the assimilationist model predominated in the years 1880–1960, with the idea that communitarianism is generally dangerous for national cohesion. Then postcolonial France adopted the integrationist model, based on major public institutions; in particular, French-style integration for immigrants and their descendants is traditionally and historically constructed by schools (Schnapper 1992) and by the army (Bertossi and Wihtol de Wenden 2005).

From the 2000s, the security context produced a new stage in migration and asylum policies. As in other European states, there is a tendency towards more restrictive discourses around security and identity. Public discourse and policy directions in the "fight againt terrorism" reflect a concern or even an anxiety about the issues of migration, Islam, "social cohesion," and the very future of the nation-state. Despite very different historical traditions regarding the role of immigration and minorities in European countries, a common concern over national identity has emerged (Smith 1991; Noiriel 2007). Although this debate reappears after every important period of migration and at times of economic crisis, in this case it was reinforced by major political events whose paroxysmal point was represented by the attacks of September 11, 2001 in the United States and those which followed in Spain, Britain, France, and Germany. The tragic and traumatic nature of these events has legitimized the strengthening of national security laws, fueled more conservative attitudes regarding cultural and ethnic diversity, and fed into debates on communitarianism, multiculturalism, and universalism.

Despite the rise of political tensions on migration issues, the French Jacobin centralist system is the subject of fierce debate, and policies relating to the integration of ethnic minorities and immigrants have begun to be accused of blindness to diversity (Blanchard, Bancel, and Lemaire 2005). Also, in spite of competition between parties in each successive election as to which can appear the toughest on security and the relative success of the vote for the extreme right-wing party Front National, a section of public opinion has mobilized to defend the rights of immigrants, such as movements in support of undocumented migrants in the second half of the 1990s (Siméant 1998) and asylum seeker solidarity movements in recent years.

While migration issues were put on the political agenda on a recurring basis throughout the 20th century, a turning point has occurred recently with the intensive use of the term "crisis." This chapter first discusses how migratory dynamics have been constructed into a crisis in contemporary France, then focuses on the various initiatives of civil society toward what politics and media consider a migration or refugee crisis: a wide range of positions and practices, conventional and unconventional, hospitable and unhospitable. Finally, this chapter will look at the modes of action used by the various actors, social and institutional, in this context of an imagined migration crisis.

The Context of an Imagined Migration Crisis

The term "migratory crisis" has become commonplace both in the media and in scientific publications. Similarly political discourse is focused on an immigration described as rampant, which would justify the need for adequate measures to reduce or even stop the "flows." The migratory crisis in Europe refers to the increase in the number of migrants arriving in the European Union from Africa, the Middle East, and South Asia in the 2010s via the Mediterranean Sea or the Balkans.

Within public opinion, the growing media coverage of deaths in the Mediterranean has had a psychological effect on the supposed existence of a migration crisis. Several tragedies have been widely relayed by the mainstream media, from the sinking of a boat containing about 500 migrants on October 3, 2013 near the Italian island of Lampedusa to the death by drowning of young Alan Kurdî on September 2, 2015 off the Turkish city of Bodrum. These two emblematic media events have led to a positive awareness of public opinion about the reality of migration issues, showing the urgent need for an appropriate political response. Nevertheless, part of public opinion has been confronted with an impression of "submersion" in complete agreement with the terminology used too often by political and media actors when they describe migrations as "flows" and "waves."

The Myth of an Unprecedented Increase in Migratory "Flows"

Eurostat statistics focusing only on applications from citizens of nonmember states show a gradual increase in the number of asylum applications within the EU-27 and later the EU-28 until 2012, after which the number of asylum seekers rose at a more rapid pace, with 431,000 applications in 2013, 627,000 in 2014, and around 1.3 million in both 2015 and 2016. As such, the number of asylum applications within the EU-28 in 2015 and 2016 was approximately double the number recorded within the EU-15 during the previous relative peak of 1992 (Eurostat 2017a). In 2016, 85,244 asylum applications were registered by France, of which 36,233 were granted refugee status (OFPRA 2017).

The reasons given by politicians and the media for qualifying the current period as a migration crisis are based on the statistical increase in these arrivals. Yet the idea of an unprecedented increase in migratory flows is based on a myth. The current population movements do not constitute a historical break. Migrations from the Middle East to

Europe are in continuity with older episodes. The war in Syria since 2011 is not the first to push civilians to the borders of Europe: before it came the civil war in Lebanon from 1975 to 1989, the conflicts in the former Yugoslavia during the 1990s, the civil war in Algeria in the early 1990s, and the wars that affected Iraq from 1980 onwards. Of course, the population movements that followed the Arab Spring are massive and have affected four million people. But migrants have been mainly internally displaced or in neighboring countries (Thiollet 2013), so that migration is almost exclusively circumscribed within the Arab world, in countries where refugee status is very often nonexistent and where the living conditions of migrants remain precarious.

Of the 4.7 million immigrants in the EU in 2015, 2.4 million come from third countries. Political conflicts in the Middle East and on the African continent, and of course the war in Syria, pushed many people to flee, of whom more than one million arrived in Western Europe by land in 2015 (Turkey, then Eastern and Central Europe) or by sea (Turkey via the Aegean Sea and Libya via the Mediterranean Sea). However, these arrivals from third countries account for barely more than half of the migratory flows to Europe. Moreover, in the same year, 2.8 million people left the territory of the EU, thus contributing to a reduction in net migration.

However, the fear of massive arrivals has nevertheless led the EU member states, including France, to lock their territories a little more and to restrict their asylum policies. The economic downturn had already contributed to the generalization of policies to limit immigration, under the influence of increasingly hostile public opinion. This fear of a migratory overflow with the massive arrival of supposedly dangerous populations is a recurring phenomenon in the history of immigration in France. Thus, Armenians fleeing the 1915 genocide and arriving in Marseilles were sorted by the French authorities on the island of Friuli, and were the subject to health control. The authorities spoke then of a "formidable current of immigration of the peoples of the East [. . .] smallpox, typhus, plague are coming to us"[1] (Témime and Attard-Maraninchi 1990). In 1923, a Health Commission even proposed evacuating Armenian refugees to Morocco, to reduce the fear of a migration crisis coupled with a health crisis. At the same time, the arrival of migrant populations from colonies also provoked reactions linking the hypothetical migration crisis and the security crisis, which also show the interweaving of migration policies and colonial policies: in 1925 the Prefecture of Police of Paris created the Department of North African Indigenous Affairs to supervise immigration, considered potentially "dangerous," at the initiative of the municipal councilor Pierre Godin, a former colonial administrator. In the interwar period, many of the officials in charge of managing immigrant populations, whether at the North African Affairs Brigade, the Home Office, or the Ministry of Social Affairs, came from the colonial administration.

In the twenty-first century, migration from Arab or Muslim countries, most of them former colonies, is also perceived through the prism of security concerns related to Islamist terrorism. In this context of an immigration described by some as potentially massive and uncontrolled, France has experienced in recent times a legislative frenzy, each new government inspiring a new law on migration. In 1995, the French government created the "offence of hospitality" (*délit d'hospitalité*), threatening every person helping foreigners in an irregular situation (Le Blanc and Brugère 2017). Thus, the number of newcomers continues to decline, with 363,900 immigrants in 2015, more than four times less than Germany and almost half than in the United Kingdom (Eurostat 2017b). Collective regularizations have been abolished, targets have been set for the number of deportations, and the result is a current but also cyclical national suspicion of migrants and ethnic and religious minorities.

Local Contexts Favorable to the Emergence of the Concept of Migration Crisis

Since the 2010's and the new cycle of arrival of migrants to Europe, tensions are palpable everywhere. In France, these are crystallized particularly around two major areas: the Calais region, with its passage points to England, and the Roya valley, which connects Italy and France via the Ventimiglia-Menton/Nice route or through the mountains.

In a context marked by the arrival of people fleeing their country for political or war-related reasons, France differs from other Western European countries in its low absorption rate of asylum seekers.[2] Political power, under different governments, has implicitly accepted the decay of the social and migration climate in the Calais region since the closure of the Red Cross's shelter and reception center in Sangatte in 2002 and the subsequent springing up of multiple camps (Djigo 2016; Lequette and Le Vergos 2016). While most migrants arrive in France by their own means, others are sent by Greece or Italy, in line with the European program of "relocation" validated in the summer of 2015, which provides that France welcomes 30,000 refugees over a total European target of 160,000 relocated in two years. The French authorities see this as an opportunity to justify a policy of dispersing asylum seekers throughout French territory. This dispersal had already begun several years ago but has been accentuated by the dismantling of the Calais jungle, which occurred gradually in 2015, and finally altogether in October–November 2016, but which is being formed again in 2017 following the destruction of the Grande-Synthe camp in April and the dismantling of the La Chapelle camp in Paris in May. This allocation policy also applies to unaccompanied foreign minors who were either randomly dispersed from Calais at the beginning of November 2016 or are subject to the policy of equalization, which has the direct consequence of sending them from one local administrative entity (*département*) to another as well as the perverse effects of extending the procedural timeframe, multiplying age estimates, and sometimes even leading to situations of students being removed from the school system only to be put back in again.

These political decisions and their implementation have contributed to the multiplication of reception mechanisms as well as the actors involved in the field of migration and asylum (such as institutional, service providers, social workers, voluntary associations, and activists). The policy of "sheltering," which led to the creation in 2015 and 2016 of nearly four hundred reception and orientation centers (see CAO, *centres d'accueil et d'orientation*, and CAOMIE, for unaccompanied foreign minors) throughout the country (outside Paris and its suburbs, and Corsica) (Statistics from the French Interior Ministry 2017) to accommodate 12,000 migrants particularly favored the emergence of local dynamics, in rural as well as in urban areas, whether helping or on the contrary resistant to the reception of migrants. These new configurations have made the relationships between a multiplicity of actors with different objectives, means, and strategies more complex. Social reactions reflect the already widely divisive political spectrum on the migration issue, ranging from anti-immigrant positions acting on insecurity and vigilantism to actions of solidarity toward migrants or to naïve questions by inhabitants. These different types of social actors are developing relationships on an unprecedented scale with asylum professionals.

Institutional and Associative Initiatives

The policy recently adopted by successive governments aims to dismantle migrant gatherings by creating new reception structures throughout France to respond to the "migration crisis." This has had the unintended effect of duplicating solidarity initiatives: The organization Sursaut citoyen identifies more than 1000 self- reported initiatives, set up locally by associations and collectives (Sursaut Citoyen. 2017). These initiatives for migrants, involving volunteers of all ages and conditions, who are not always familiar with migration issues, have led to the emergence of complex and protean social relations with the social field's historical actors and migrants and refugees right activists as well as with institutional actors.

Complementarity and Tensions between Various Actors

Since 2015, the public authorities have relied on the idea of a migration crisis to justify a policy of dispersal of migrants, both adults and unaccompanied foreign minors, throughout France. To prevent migratory flows from congregating in certain regions or conurbations, the French State has set up a dispersal policy that forces most local authorities to accept a number of asylum seekers or unaccompanied foreign minors in proportion to their total population. This distribution policy goes hand in hand with the new law of July 29, 2015, which defines the conditions of asylum. This has led to the introduction of various mechanisms. At the institutional level, new structures have been added to existing ones, such as the CAO and the Emergency Accommodation for Asylum Seekers (HUDA, *Hébergement d'Urgence pour Demandeurs d'Asile*), which compensate for the congestion of the existing Centers for Asylum Seekers (CADA, *Centres d'Accueil pour les Demandeurs d'Asile*). Other structures replace the existing ones, such as the Single administrative desk for Asylum Seekers (GUDA, *Guichet Unique d'accueil des Demandeurs d'Asile*), which brings together in one place the services of the prefecture and those of the French Office of Immigration and Integration (OFII), or the Hosting Program for Asylum Seekers (PRAHDA, *Programme d'Accueil et d'Hébergement des Demandeurs d'Asile*), principally dedicated to people affected by the Dublin procedure.[3] The dispersal policy forced each area to take its share of migrants, and has the collateral effect of favoring the creation of many migrant-friendly initiatives by civil society. On the other hand, the regular transition from one structure to another, in sometimes very arbitrary conditions, sometimes from one area to another, contributes to disorienting asylum seekers and breaking any links they might have created with social workers, volunteers, or residents. The case of unaccompanied foreign minors is even more worrying, some even being taken out of school to be sent to other local authorities where their underage status is again checked and where they are sometimes not educated for several months. This proactive policy of administrative dispersal has a heavy impact on the social and psychological disorientation of migrants. It is underpinned by the political goal of ending the so-called pull factor dear to supporters of a so-called migration crisis.

As the structures diversify so the actors correspondingly multiply, interacting sometimes in a complementary way, sometimes in a conflicting way. The issue of migration and asylum now passes through all institutional strata. At the regional level, prefectures are more exposed to the networks of citizens and associations: The dismantling of the Calais Jungle and the implementation of CAOs forces prefects to organize information meetings at municipal level, exposing them to criticism by organizations that are favorable to or, on the contrary, opposed to immigration policy. These meetings are also an opportunity for associative actors to solicit directly and in an exceptional way the prefectural bodies on particular situations. The local authorities are also directly solicited regarding their central role in the protection of unaccompanied foreign minors through the social welfare service for childhood (ASE, *Aide Sociale à l'Enfance*). They are solicited not only by historic organizations such as the Without Borders Education Network (RESF, *Réseau Éducation Sans Frontière*) but also by associations specializing in the learning of French and emergency housing for unaccompanied foreign minors or both, which ASE is no longer able to provide. Associations regularly ask the departmental council (*conseil départemental*) to denounce the systematic practices of reassessment of the age of unaccompanied foreign minors sent by other departments within the framework of the equalization scheme, as well as requesting a more rapid treatment of their social care by ASE, particularly with regard to housing and schooling. Finally, municipalities, some of which have never received migrants on their territory, particularly in rural areas, are obliged, on the orders of prefects, to open a CAO and hence to organize the reception of migrants in cooperation with all stakeholders (elected members of the opposition, social structures, managers of migrant centers, associations, citizens). In some municipalities, tensions are palpable, and some municipal councils have voted against the project of welcoming migrants in their territory. In other municipalities, on the contrary, the principle of solidarity has prevailed, with municipal councils voting motions in favor of the reception of migrants and refugees.

The most recent structures for migrants are mainly managed by the historic actors of social housing. However, some others are also managed by secular or religious associations, sometimes more specialized in emergency aid than specifically focused in on migrants and the question of asylum. In the absence of official data, those collected from field informants and disseminated by the Plateforme de Service aux Migrants (CAO Octobre 2016) show that the major CAO operators are large national structures such as ADOMA and COALLIA.[4] Also, to a lesser extent, there are training centers (such as those of the Association for the Training of Adults—AFPA) or holiday centers (such as those of EDF), secular (France Terre d'Asile (FtdA), Forum Refugiés) and religious organizations (Emmaüs), as well as local associations and even town halls in small localities. The main management networks are also ADOMA and COALLIA, followed by FTdA or Catholic (Society of Saint Vincent de Paul) and Protestants (Diaconate) organizations.

Even though some of these managers were already working with migrants, they were criticized for having been regulated by the state. Tensions are all the more exacerbated when managers are associations recognized for their commitment to the most deprived people, especially migrants. Thus, during the dismantling of the Calais shantytown, the triage of migrants, in particular minors, carried out by FTdA was strongly criticized not only by activists from the various associations intervening on the spot but also by the NGO Médecins Sans Frontières, which left the Calais camp on October 25, 2016 in protest at these methods of triage of migrants. The same tensions are taking place at the Humanitarian Center for Refugees located at La Chapelle in Paris, also dedicated to the triage of migrants. Emmaüs Solidarités is under criticism by activists in view of its management of the site. The association Utopia 56, partner of Emmaüs in the project and mandated by the mayor of Paris, is also accused of playing the role of the State and its restrictive immigration policy; it withdrew from the Humanitarian Center in September 2017.[5] In the field, when they take part in an institutional approach by managing triage or reception centers, the management organizations are opposed by their counterparts who have not signed any agreements with the state and, more frequently, by pro-asylum activists. The organizations to which the state has entrusted missions for the management of reception and orientation centers or camps (Jules Ferry in Calais, Grande Synthe, and Porte de la Chapelle) are denounced by other associations providing assistance to migrants outside any mandate granted by the public authorities. Tensions are all the greater because these nonmandated associations are undergoing institutional and police repression attempts since the dismantling of the main sites in Calais and in Paris to prevent a migrant crowd from gathering again (including banning the installation of showers for migrants as well as food distribution, and police harassment of activists and migrants).

Beyond this associative divide, which mainly concerns migrant settlement and encampment sites, pro-migrant nonprofit organizations are emerging throughout France, as is also the situation in Germany after the dispersal of migrants in the Länder. As a result of the relocation and equalization policy, solidarity-based citizens gather locally for the purpose of welcoming and accompanying migrants to access to care, rights, leisure and learning the French language. In the absence of official data, the Info CAO Platform, set up by the Auberge des Migrants and Utopia 56, counts 155 local initiatives around the CAO, CAOMIE, and CAOFIE (CAO for foreign isolated women) (Infocao 2017). Nevertheless, the number of such initiatives is underestimated, as verified in the field when taking into account highly active but non-registered groups, sometimes specialized, especially on unaccompanied minors. These organizations are often spontaneous, created on the occasion of the implementation of CAO or the arrival of unaccompanied minors. They rely on networks of acquaintances, succeeding in bringing together simultaneously activists from well-known nationwide organizations and some local residents wanting to offer aid and comfort to refugees from a humanitarian perspective. They become operational quickly because they are structured in the urgency of the reception. These local initiatives are distinguished from NGOs and professional associations (Pette 2016), as well as from the No Border-type militant group which since 1999 has been bringing together anti-border activists (Walters 2016) who are in favor of regularizing migrants, the closure of administrative detention centers, and the stopping of deportations, situating their struggle within those of anarchist-libertarian networks.

Border crossing points are also an indicator of citizen mobilization. At such crossings, the most emblematic actions are those carried out in the Alpes-Maritimes department (06) where the Roya valley (border with Italy) is located; the association Roya citoyenne and the Comité de soutien aux citoyens solidaires du 06 includes mediated figures such as Pierre-Alain Mannoni (an engineering researcher at the CNRS, prosecuted for having taken migrants in his car); Félix Croft (worker and fisherman, also prosecuted for having taken migrants in his car); and Cédric Herrou (farmer, prosecuted for helping foreigners in an irregular situation).

Faced with these "hospitable" mobilizations, there are "inhospitable" mobilizations emanating from people anxious about the proximity of (male) migrants in their neighborhood. These "inhospitable" mobilizations are sometimes also instrumentalized or even orchestrated by organizations of the radical right and the identitarian movement. Among these activists, there are representatives of the Bloc Identitaire, a radical right-wing group, classified to the right of the Front National, at the initiative of the network "*Citoyens en colère*" (Angry Citizens).

In addition to the ideological competition between organizations supporting migrants and refugees and those opposed to reception and asylum, the multiplicity of actors involved in the field of migration has had the effect of increasing the complexity of relations of power and of interdependence between institutional actors at every local scale, including the organizations managing reception centers and structures that are activist or simply welcoming. The same applies to relations among migration and asylum control officers, social workers, and voluntary and NGO activists. Complementarity is essential on the ground for the implementation of different types of support (social, legal, health, learning, and leisure). Nevertheless, tensions are constant between the public authorities; guarantors of immigration and asylum policies; social workers caught between their professional ethics and respect for administrative directives; and educational, social, and NGO actors working for the right to asylum and, for minors, the rights of the child and the right to schooling. Each of these actors is caught up in particular logics, and they have different strategies, modes of action, and repertoires of mobilization that sometimes complement each other, but often collide, only sometimes leading to a discourse on migration crisis.

The Effects of the Migration Crisis Discourse on the Mobilization and Action Repertories by Social and Political Actors

The types of intervention that can be used by the various actors involved in the migration and asylum field are manifold and make a rereading of the literature on the repertoires of mobilization and action necessary. The observation of the sociopolitical contexts of "sheltering," the functioning of "sheltering" structures, and the multiplicity of actors around them invite us to reexamine the literature of the evolution of the repertoires of action in the early 2000s. In the context of a supposed migration crisis, the study of contemporary social movements leads to questioning about a "transnational and solidarist" orientation (Cohen and Rai 2000), also interpreted as based on "internationalism" and "expertise" (Neveu 2002).

Social Actors, between Protest and Non-Protest Actions

Traditionally, the repertoires of solidarist mobilization and action are carried by associations whose members often practice a variety of commitments. (Pette and Eloire 2016). Since the diversification of solidarity initiatives in favor of migrants and refugees, profiles are more varied: there are both nonaffiliated volunteers but also sympathizers and activists from various national organizations with solid knowhow concerning asylum. Some repertoires of action are partly linked to a local dynamic of mutual assistance (such as moments of conviviality, workshops, cultural and sporting meetings), while others are inspired by those systematized at national level, benefiting from the support of lawyers (information and assistance to administrative appeals procedures) and activists trained by their struggles for freedom of movement and settlements (such as gatherings and petitions relayed by social networks). In some areas in tension, this proximity between volunteers and activists is the subject of violent controversy, as in Calais, where NGO and trade union officials denounce the authorities' focus on the No Border network: "One would have to believe that (during the incidents of 2015–2016 in Calais) the criminals are some activists who try to shed light on an untenable situation for six thousand migrants. It is incomprehensible and unacceptable. The responsibility is that of the government."[6]

In this context, social workers employed in "shelter" centers or working in the child welfare sector for the protection of unaccompanied foreign minors are sometimes caught between two contradictory dynamics: on the one hand, their professional ethics, which imply the accompaniment of individuals in precarious situations and, on the other hand, compliance with the prefectural and governmental directives which require the application of the Dublin procedures and the return to the first transit country for adults and which also discourage the recognition and care of unaccompanied foreign minors. Some social workers make explicit reference to this difficulty, which has led some to cease their activity of social worker (Le Berre 2017) and others to circumvent the impossible equation by entrusting the researcher with information and soliciting assistance of NGO volunteers under cover of absolute anonymity. The crossing of boundaries between mobilization and action and the meeting between volunteers, sympathizers, NGO activists, and social workers seem to validate the existence of a continuum suggested by Michel Offerlé (1998, 2008) between antiestablishment repertories of action expressed by visible mobilizations (supported by NGOs) and nonprotesting action repertoires, expressed in more discrete arenas, or even in the form of silent mobilizations (carried by some social workers, bounded by both professional secrecy and the fear of losing their job).

Conventional Public Actions: Administrative and Legal Tools

For their part, the state and its representatives use a range of repertoires of action equally rich but strained by objectives related to the security and control myth of a migration crisis. The gradual tightening of migration policies over several decades has led to the implementation of conventional public actions, in particular an arsenal of legislative measures to limit incoming migratory movements (Akoka 2013; Fischer and Hamidi 2016; Spire 2016). At the local level, politicians use these tools to discourage arrivals and settlement. The work of humanitarian organizations, migrant support associations, and volunteers is thus hampered by local political decisions that encourage police practices on the margins of legality and which lead to lengthy legal battles. For example, in the Calais region, in the middle of winter, associations were prevented, by prefectoral order, from distributing food and hot drinks to migrants. In Calais, several municipal by-laws passed in February and March 2017 prohibited the distribution of meals to migrants. At the same time, the nonprofit organization L'Auberge des Migrants received an injunction from the Pas-de-Calais prefecture to raise its kitchen to the same standards of hygiene as catering professionals, under penalty of closure. In June, law enforcement agencies prevented the distribution of water to migrants by local associations. Similarly, Secours Catholique/Caritas has been often worried about installing modular units equipped with showers for migrants who have been wandering in Calais since the dismantling ladder, of a huge dumpster in front of the entrance to the site to prevent any delivery, and police controls allowed by a requisition of the state prosecutor).

In the other border area of the Roya valley, migrant relief associations denounce the "crime of solidarity." This expression, which appeared in 1995 when the Immigrant Support and Information Group (Gisti) initiated a "manifesto of solidarity offenders," refers to Article L 622-1 of the Code of Entry, Foreigners' Residence and the Right of Asylum (Ceseda), which provides that "any person who, by direct or indirect assistance, facilitates or attempts to facilitate the entry, movement or illegal stay of a foreigner in France" risks up to five years of imprisonment and a fine of 30,000 euros. The policy of the Ministry of Immigration and National Identity led by Eric Besson under the presidency of Nicolas Sarkozy had again led the undocumented migrants associations to denounce the increasing use of this article against their members or other citizens assisting migrants. At the beginning of January 2017, within a week, the highly publicized cases of Pierre-Alain Mannoni and Cédric Herrou reopened the debate on help provided by volunteers to migrants, particularly at border crossings.

Institutional actors thus use a variety of conventional repertoires of action in order to discourage new arrivals and perpetuate the fantasy of a migratory crisis. These modes of action, aimed at both the migrant-friendly volunteers and the migrants themselves, are carried out within a legal framework, without questioning the legitimacy of the system, since their main mode of operation is based on administrative and legal tools. Nevertheless, field observations and the identification of legal remedies by NGO actors and assisting citizens show how tenuous the boundary between conventional and nonconventional public actions is. Many administrative or judicial appeals result in decisions supporting the actions of migrant-friendly volunteers, recognizing the illegality of some local political practices. Thus, the Correctional Court of Nice acquitted Pierre-André Mannoni, who was sentenced in November 2016 to six months' suspended imprisonment for "assistance for stay and movement" after having taken migrants from Italy into his car. The judge hearing the application for interim measures of the Administrative Court of Lille suspended several decisions of the Mayor of Calais to prevent the distribution of meals (Tribunal Administratif de Lille 2017). The administrative court of Lille condemned the city council of Calais for having prevented the Secours Catholique from installing on its land a container equipped with showers intended for migrants, the judge considering that "the mayor of Calais has inflicted a serious and clearly illegal violation of the right to private property". The Administrative Court of Nice condemned in March 2017 the prefect of the Alpes-Maritimes for "serious and manifestly unlawful attack on the right of asylum" following the impediment of an Eritrean family seeking asylum, and several humanitarian associations had found repeated violations of law enforcement authorities in the Code of Foreigners and the European Convention on the Rights of the Child.

Late but not least, in its decision 2018-717 / 718 given on July 6, 2018 the French Constitutional Council considered that the assistance to the stay and the circulation of a person in an irregular situation, when it was made for humanitarian and disinterested reasons, could not be considered as delictual. Putting into practice the principle of fraternity, one of the three pillars of the Republic with equality and freedom, does not make citizens criminals or smugglers. However, the offense of hospitality is not abolished with regard to aid for entry into the territory.

Nonconventional Public Actions: From the Register of Trust to Intimidation

Above all, the increasing polarization of the political debate on migration issues gives rise to the use by institutions, notably at local level, of political actions, this time unconventional, which are on the margins or even in breach of legality and which are based on two main styles: trust and intimidation. The register of confidence has been used by the State to play the appeasement card and evacuate the shantytown of Calais between October 2015 and November 2016, the Home Secretary Bernard Cazeneuve promising orally to not apply the Dublin procedure for the voluntary migrants going in CAOs. However, most of the prefectures have not respected this promise once the migrants have been dispersed over the territory and have filed their asylum application. The institutional discourse here is misleading: on the one hand, promises are made to migrants and associations to not proceed to Dublin expulsions; on the other hand, circulars and instructions are sent to the prefects asking them to carry them out.[7] The common practice is to put Dublin migrants to be deported under house arrest outside their CAO, or even to lock them into an administrative detention center once their CAOs are closed. The practices of the prefectures differ on that point, and the issue is the subject of complex relations between associations and the administration.[8]

A register of trust is also mobilized with unaccompanied foreign minors, whether at the time of the departures organized from the Calais area or during the national policy of dispersal. When the approximately 1,900 unaccompanied foreign minors from the Calais camps were dispatched to shelters in different regions, it was also promised that their situation would be examined and in particular, in collaboration with the British authorities, there would be taken into consideration applications for family reunification of young Afghans who claim to have family in the United Kingdom, under European regulations and the humanitarian provision of the Immigration Act adopted by the British Parliament in 2016 dealing with unaccompanied minors, known as the Dubs Amendment. In total, only two hundred of these unaccompanied foreign minors have been accepted by the United Kingdom, while the others have remained in shelters, most of whom have rapidly fled. The lack of care afforded to these young migrants is repeatedly denounced by humanitarian organizations such as Human Rights Watch, as well as by activists and even employees of these shelters.

This same register of trust is used by the local actors of the national dispersal policy, which is based on the law of 14 March 2016 on the protection of the child, giving a legal basis for the distribution of unaccompanied foreign minors between departments. By decision of the judge and in view of a clear concern of balance between administrative territories, unaccompanied foreign minors are transferred from one department to another after assessment of their age. Some of them are thus desocialized and taken out of school to be sent to another department where their care, at best, takes several months to be implemented by local authorities. The noneducation of unaccompanied foreign minors was also denounced in the 2016 annual report of the Defender of Rights focusing on the Rights of the Child: "The Defender of Rights reminds the departmental councils of their obligation to ensure effective access to schooling or to vocational training, to all unaccompanied minors under their care, including when they are over 16 years of age."[9] Beyond stances of protest, volunteers and some social workers who are involved with these unaccompanied foreign minors denounce these administrative practices by calling into question the psychological and social consequences of the use and misuse of trust.

Finally, some public actions are based on a repertory traditionally attributed to protest groups questioning the legitimacy of the system but which in this case becomes an institutional strategy based on a register of intimidation and the fear generated by the system. Thus, in certain areas where there is an influx of migrants, as in the Calais area or Paris, the use of public violence, physical or psychological, supersedes the principle of the right of asylum. Residents and associations testify to weeks of police "harassment" on the streets of Paris during the winter of 2017 to remove blankets from migrants sleeping in the street.[10] On many occasions, encampments have been dispersed without proposals for shelter being formulated. On the outskirts of the humanitarian center of La Chapelle in Paris, the public authorities have deposited blocks of stones to prevent any new settlement of migrants while the center is full.

As in every era and in every social movement, the repertory of political action is not fixed and informs us about the convergences and divergences of all the actors involved, as well as the social and political climate. However, the use of nonconventional means of action, traditionally used by social actors in order to influence decisions taken by elected representatives, is appropriate by institutional actors here, thus constituting a break both operationally and conceptually. This disturbance in the genre of the repertoires of political action hits many NGO actors engaged in solidarity actions, but, even more, tests social workers, caught in a sometimes unsustainable tension between respect for the ethical requirements of their profession and the injunctions of the institutional actors not to "welcome all the misery of the world."

Conclusion

The issue of the migration crisis appears in a context of economic crisis and political uncertainty as to the reception of migrant populations, as has been the case at other times in history. The recurrence of the use of vocabulary of crisis, applied both to the economic situation and to population movements, says a lot about the interweaving of the two phenomena in the political and media imaginary—an imaginary which is itself not without influence on common sense. It is therefore useful to consider whether it would be more appropriate to discuss a *humanitarian* crisis to describe the low priority given to the migration issue by the host countries.

Moreover, the setting up of mechanisms for the sorting and selection of migrants has contributed to exacerbating tensions between institutional actors, the professional associations managing the reception and accommodation centers, and their staff, as well as the nonprofit pro-migrant organizations. Twenty years after *Les lois de l'inhospitalité* (Fassin, Morice, and Quiminal 1997) and *L'injustifiable* (Chemillier-Gendreau 1998) regarding immigration policies after attempts to end immigration, asylum policies are steadily increasing, practices of control and deportation are intensifying, and legislators are solicited both by associations helping migrants and by the state, the two parties engaging each other in local legal battles. Analysis of the mobilization tools used by public authorities and by volunteers and NGO activists reflects a mixing of genres between conventional and unconventional repertories of action used by the different parties.

Finally, proponents of the theory of the migration crisis, fearing the arrival of massive human flows, contribute to imprisoning the migrant or foreigner in a pariah category. Therefore, to be "from here" is not only to build a border but to build permanently the idea of truth on this side of Europe and error outside Europe (Le Blanc and Brugère 2017). This essentialization of migrants is not unrelated to a certain idea of the greatness of Western civilization, which was one of the foundations of colonialism.

Acknowledgments

The author is indebted to Daniel Gordon, Senior Lecturer in European history at Edge Hill University, for his careful reading of this paper for corrections in English usage.

Notes

1. Original version: "Un redoutable courant d'immigration des peuples d'Orient [. . .] la variole, le typhus, la peste sont en route vers chez nous".
2. France ranks 14th in Europe for the reception of asylum seekers per inhabitants in 2015 and 25th (out of 32 countries) for the acceptance rate of asylum applications (27% in first instance), according to Eurostat. In the third quarter of 2016, 360,000 asylum applications were made in Europe, of which 237,000 in Germany and only 20,000 in France.
3. The Dublin III regulation is used to determine the European country responsible for an asylum application, most often the country of entry into the European Union, the presence of fingerprints in the Eurodac database being a proof.
4. ADOMA is the former National Society for the Construction of Workers' Housing (Sonacotra), which is responsible for building and managing a large number of social housing (migrant workers' homes, social residences, shelters, centers for asylum seekers, areas for Travelers, etc.). COALLIA is formerly known as Aftam which, since 1962, helped nationals of former colonies to live in safe housing and to access care (and whose first president was Stéphane Hessel), and is an association for aid and social accompaniment for social housing, social promotion and medical and social care for marginalized populations, excluded from the labor market, without resources or without housing.
5. Utopia 56 also managed the Grande-Synthe humanitarian camp during the first two months of the opening, from 7 March to 7 May 2016, and supervised 10,000 days of volunteer work.
6. "On voudrait faire croire que [lors des incidents de 2015-16 à Calais] les criminels, ce sont quelques militants qui essaient de mettre la lumière sur une situation intenable pour six mille migrants. C'est incompréhensible et inacceptable. La responsabilité, c'est le gouvernement qui la porte." Words of Thierry Kuhn, president of Emmaüs France, quoted by Enora Ollivier, « *Calais: les « No Border », une poignée de militants décriés* », *Le Monde*, 5 février 2016. See also Sylvain Mouillard, « *A Calais, la tension monte entre police et migrants* », *Libération*, 11 novembre 2015.

7. See Circular of the Ministry of Housing, Equality of Territories and Rurality, 9 novembre 2015, https://passeursdhospitalites.files.wordpress.com/2015/11/151120-circ-centre-mise-abri-calais-1.pdf; Circular of the Home Office (Directorate General of Foreigners in France) and of the Ministry of Housing, Equality of Territories and Rurality (Directorate General of Social Cohesion), 7 décembre 2015, https://passeursdhospitalites.files.wordpress.com/2015/12/2015-12-07_circulaire-mi-cao.pdf; Instruction of 29 June 2016 on the creation of new places for reception and orientation centers for migrants, Ministry of Housing and Sustainable Housing, https://passeursdhospitalites.files.wordpress.com/2016/07/intk1615585j.pdf.
8. Under the law of 7 March 2016 on the right of foreigners, which has passed relatively unnoticed during the debates in Parliament, prefectures are given the possibility of assigning residence to "Dublin" migrants (L 742-2 du code de l'entrée et du séjour des étrangers et du droit d'asile). https://www.legifrance.gouv.fr/affichCode.do;jsessionid=5EA174901865BDCF336A4CBF83AAC615.tpdila15v_2?idSectionTA=LEGISCTA000030957657&cidTexte=LEGITEXT000006070158&dateTexte=20161221
9. « Le Défenseur des droits rappelle aux conseils départementaux leur obligation d'assurer un accès effectif à une scolarité ou à une formation professionnelle, à tous les mineurs non accompagnés dont ils ont la charge, y compris lorsqu'ils sont âgés de plus de 16 ans. » Défenseur des droits, *Droit fondamental à l'éducation: une école pour tous, un droit pour chacun*, Rapport droits de l'enfant 2016.
10. See "MSF Dénonce Un 'Harcèlement' Policier Contre Des Migrants", *20 Minutes: Fr.*, September 1, 2017, http://www.20minutes.fr/paris/1992263-20170109-paris-msf-denonce-harcelement-policier-contre-migrants, in which Médecins Sans Frontières (MSF) denounces the "systematization of police violence targeting hundreds of Parisian migrants wandering in the capital.

References

Akoka, K. 2013. "Pour une histoire sociale de l'asile politique en France." *Pouvoirs, Dossier Les Réfugiés* 1, no. 144: 67–77.

Blanchard, P., N. Bancel, and S. Lemaire, eds. 2005. *La fracture coloniale: La société française au prisme de l'héritage colonial.* Paris: La Découverte.

Bertossi, C., and C. W. de Wenden. 2005. *Les militaires français issus de l'immigration*, Paris: Les documents du C2SD.

CAO Octobre. 2016. https://drive.google.com/file/d/0ByMEwaoeDDkBdlJOVnpJRnBoTUR2dFgxTFJFbWo3ZoE4LTU4/view

Chemillier-Gendreau, M. 1998. *L'injustifiable: Les politiques françaises de l'immigration.* Paris: Du Centurion.

Cohen, R., and S. Rai, eds. 2000. *Global Social Movements.* London: Athlone.

Djigo, S. 2016. *Les migrants de Calais.* Marseille, France: Agone.

Eurostat. 2017a. "Asylum Statistics." http://ec.europa.eu/eurostat/statistics-explained/index.php/Asylum_statistics. Accessed on September 26, 2017.

Eurostat. 2017b. "Migration and Migrant Population Statistics." http://ec.europa.eu/eurostat/statistics-explained/index.php/Migration_and_migrant_population_statistics. Accessed on September 26, 2017.

Fassin, D., A. Morice, and C. Quiminal, eds. 1997. *Les lois de l'inhospitalité.* Paris: La Découverte.

Fischer, N., and C. Hamidi. 2016. *Les politiques migratoires*. Repères coll. Paris: La Découverte.
Green, N., and M. Poinsot. 2008. *Histoire de l'immigration et question coloniale en France*. Paris: La Documentation française.
Infocao. 2017. "Suite à l'incendie de Grande-Synthe." April 13. http://www.infocao.net
Le Berre, R. 2017. *De rêves et de papiers: 547 jours avec les mineurs isolés étrangers*, Paris: La Découverte.
Le Blanc, G., and F. Brugère. 2017. *La fin de l'hospitalité: Lampedusa, Lesbos, Calais. . . jusqu'où irons-nous?* Paris: Flammarion.
Lequette, S. and D. Le Vergos, eds. 2016. *Décamper*. Paris: La Découverte.
Neveu, E. 2002. *Sociologie des mouvements sociaux*. 3rd Edition. Paris: La Découverte.
Noiriel, G. 1988. *Le creuset français: Histoire de l'immigration—XIXe-XXe siècles*. Paris: Seuil.
Noiriel, G. 2007. *A quoi sert l'identité nationale*, Paris: Agone.
Offerlé, M. 1998. *Sociologie des groupes d'intérêt*, Paris: Montchrestien.
Offerlé, M. 2008. "Retour critique sur les répertoires de l'action collective (XVIIIe-XXIe siècles)." *Politix*, 81: 181–202.
OFPRA. 2017. "Chiffres de l'asile en France en 2016." https://ofpra.gouv.fr/fr/l-ofpra/actualites/premiers-chiffres-de-l-asile-en-o. Accessed on September 26, 2017.
Pette, M. 2016. "Venir en aide aux migrants dans le Calaisis. Entre action associative locale et crise migratoire international." *Savoir/Agir* 36, no. 2: 47–52.
Pette, M., and F. Eloire. 2016. "Pôles d'organisation et engagement dans l'espace de la cause des étrangers. L'apport de l'analyse des réseaux sociaux." *Sociétés contemporaines* 1, no. 101: 5–35.
Schnapper, D. 1992. *L'Europe des immigrés: Essai sur les politiques d'immigration*. Paris: Bourin.
Siméant, J. 1998. *La cause des sans-papiers*. Paris: Presses de Sciences Po.
Smith, A. 1991. *National Identity*. London: Penguin.
Spire. 2016. "La politique des guichets au service de la police des étrangers." *Savoir/Agir, Dossier Accueillir les migrants* 2, no. 36: 27–31.
Statistics from the French Interior Ministry. 2017. https://etat-a-calais.fr/laccueil-en-france/ Accessed on April 11, 2017.
Sursaut Citoyen. 2017. "1 000 initiatives citoyennes de solidarité avec les migrants." https://sursaut-citoyen.org
Témime, É., and M. -F. Attard-Maraninchi, eds. 1990. *Histoire des migrations à Marseille*. Aix-en-Provence France: Edisud.
Thiollet, H. 2013. "Migrations, exils et printemps arabes." In *Afrique du Nord Moyen-Orient: La double recomposition*, edited by F. Charillon and A. Dieckhoff, 133–146. Paris: La Documentation française.
Tribunal Administratif de Lille. 2017. "Distribution de Repas ux Migrants à Calais." http://lille.tribunal-administratif.fr/Actualites/Communiques/Distribution-de-repas-aux-migrants-a-Calais Accessed on April 11, 2017.
Walters, W. 2016. "No Border: Games With(out) Frontiers." *Social Justice* 33, no. 1: 21–39.

CHAPTER 8

THE MANUFACTURING OF THE US-MEXICO BORDER CRISIS

MARIA CRISTINA MORALES

LOCATED at the geographic, demographic, economic, and political margins of the US nation state, the US-Mexico border has historically and contemporarily been subjected to public officials' depictions as a region in crises. The subjugation of the southern border in the United States is in part attributed to it being the site of clandestine border crossing and being occupied by society's unwanted—brown and impoverished immigrant communities (Morales and Bejarano 2009). In the present chapter, I argue that the manufacturing of the southern border crisis is in part rooted in subjugation of place, along with criminalized perceptions of its inhabitants and border crossers, which in turn create US public policies that put the mechanisms in place to exacerbate actual crises.

Northern Mexico and the southwest United States, also referred to as the US-Mexico border or as the Southwestern North American (SWNA) region, is considered an artificially bifurcated region (Vélez-Ibáñez and Heyman 2017). Gloria Anzaldúa (1987) famously claimed, "The U.S-Mexican border *es una herida abierta* [an open wound] where the Third World grates against the first and bleeds. And before a scab forms it hemorrhages again, the lifeblood of two worlds merging to form a third country—a border culture." While some scholars accentuate the deterritorialization of culture given migratory flows in this globalized era (e.g., Chavez 2001, 49), scholarship on the US-Mexico border is centered on territory or place (e.g., Bejarano et al. 2012; Macías-Rojas 2016; Payan 2016; Vélez-Ibáñez and Heyman 2017). This chapter, is grounded on the US-Mexico borderlands, where place is at the core of its geopolitical existence.

Ambivalence and contradictions are what sustain the manufacturing of the US-Mexico border crisis. The contemporary marginalization of the southern border and the criminalization of Latina/os occurred under public policies implemented for national security.

The attacks on September 11, 2001 are the impetus for the current national security effects at the US-Mexico border although this region had little to do with 9/11 (Payan 2016). The Border Network for Human Rights, a nonprofit advocacy organization, has passionately proclaimed how national security policies stand in sharp contrast to community security (Sáenz and Morales 2015). Specifically, the increases in border security after 9/ 11 exacerbated the following militaristic measures: increases in border patrol agents, at least 700 miles of border fencing (so far), National Guard deployment, fixed watch towers, fixed remote video surveillance systems, mobile surveillance systems, ground sensors, thermal and night vision goggles, VADER radar systems, UH-1N helicopters, AS-350 light enforcement helicopters, Blackhawk Helicopters, marine vessels, and drones (Sáenz and Morales 2015). While the surveillance of immigrants and Latina/os have extended to the interior of the United States (Leerkes et al. 2013), there is still no other region in the United States where residents are subjected to warlike conditions as in the borderlands (Sáenz and Morales 2015). Indeed, in addition to the pseudo-war like conditions described above, the southern border is also marked by border patrol presence in schools (Dunn 2010) and universities, a border wall that is a constant reminder that Latina/os are not wanted in the United States, and the bodies of migrants that are a tragic feature of the border terrain. This brings into question the civil and human rights of seven million border residents from San Diego, California to Brownsville, Texas (Sáenz and Morales 2015). Moreover, the Border Immigration Council (2017)—consisting of private attorneys, legal service providers, and advocacy organizations in the border city of El Paso—has argued that in contrast to serving border communities and national interests, the decisions of US Customs and Border Protections (CBP) and US Immigration and Customs Enforcement (ICE) officials undermine the US values of justice, fairness, and democracy.

Vignette

The concept of the "sister cities" is commonly used to describe cities located on the US side of the border and its adjacent city to the south in Mexico. An example of sister cities is El Paso-Cuidad Juárez where from El Paso not only can one see the hustle and bustle of Juárez with its 1,332,131 inhabitants but you can hear Juárez. The inhabitants in sister cities are referred to as *fronterizos* or borderlanders that are joined by culture and family ties but are separated by a political boundary marked by multiple layers of border fences. This is the region that was home to 15-year-old Sergio Adrian Hernández Güereca, who was unarmed and outside of his home in Juárez, Mexico when he was shot and killed by a US border patrol agent.

While one might wonder how a US federal agent ends up shooting an unarmed Mexican teen in Mexican territory while on the job, geographically speaking, one can find residents living right up to the border fence along the Rio Grande in the United States and Mexico, typically the most impoverished in each respective community. On the afternoon of June 7, 2010, 15-year-old Sergio was along the levee of the Rio Grande on the Mexican side of the border by his home. Simultaneously on the US side of the border, a US Border Patrol Agent was detaining someone when allegedly someone started throwing rocks from Juárez. The agent took out his gun and started shooting—killing Sergio.

The US Justice Department declined to press any charges against the agent claiming he was trying to stop "smugglers attempting an illegal border crossing" (Wagner 2017). This tragic incident raised a lot of questions. Is this incident in part attributed to public officials' depiction of the southern border as lawless and its people as smugglers, terrorists, and "illegals"? Why is throwing rocks a justified use of deadly force? Also, what would be the US reaction if a US citizen would be shot by a Mexican law enforcement official while in American soil? Thus Sergio's case is a contemporary example of how border patrol practices extend beyond its territorial boundary to threaten the collective safety of Mexican *fronterizos* and border crossers.

While it is still to be determined by US courts, Sergio and his family's rights are questionable given his body was in Mexico and because he was depicted as a smuggler/criminal. Agents on the ground make daily determinations about whether immigrants are criminals or right-bearing individuals (Macías-Rojas 2016).

Hernandez's parents sued the agent and the courts are to determine if Fourth Amendment protections against unjustified use of deadly force extend beyond the country's borders. This case was recently heard by the US Supreme Court who then sent it back to a lower court in June 2017. The outcome of this case has important implications for the rights of residents on both sides of the southern border—a region, which, as of now, represents a "black hole" in terms of legal protections according to one of the lawyers for the Hernandez family (Sanchez 2016).

This is not an isolated incident. As rocks were hurled from Nogales, Mexico, a border patrol agent shot and killed sixteen-year-old José Antonio Elena Rodríquez in his own neighborhood (Santos 2013). José Antonio was shot eleven times, seven of which were from behind (Santos 2013). José Antonio was also unarmed, only carried a cellphone, and appeared to be an innocent bystander (Binelli 2016). Armed agents operating in the backyards of children's and youth's homes searching for suspected smugglers and terrorists has become *normalized violence* or adaptation to everyday violence (Bourgois 2001) at the borderlands. From January 2010 to October 2012 US Customs and Border Protection (2013) documented sixty-seven events of use of deadly force: twenty-five cases involved shots fired by agents who had been victims of rock attacks while on land and four cases involved agents on boats.

These incidents are in part a result of the manufacturing of the border crisis that created a surveillance society at the borderlands. Public officials' framing of the border crisis is among the root causes for the policing of the borderland region that subjects border residents and crossers, including youth, to "state-sanctioned violence"—where state policies and initiatives legitimize violent measures against vulnerable people. Equating undocumented immigrants and border residents with drug and human smugglers and terrorists is the impetus behind the excessive use of force and warlike border security measures that not only result in the hypersurveillance along the border, but exacerbate uses of deadly force.

Historical Overview of the Border Militarization

The role of the state at the US-Mexico border has evolved throughout history as the United States gained hegemonic power over the region through war, and where today militaristic border security policies continue to control the borderlands. Historically, the Mexican-American War (1846–1848) powered American imperialism, adding what is today Arizona, California, Colorado, New Mexico, Nevada, Texas, Utah, and Wyoming (Gómez 2007). The physical boundary of the US-Mexico border was established with the Treaty of Guadalupe Hidalgo in February 1848 and finalized in 1853 with the Gadsden Purchase (see Payan 2016). While in the late-nineteenth and early-twentieth centuries the US-Mexico border evolved to being more symbolic, where both Mexicans and Americans crossed it without any difficulty (Gómez 2007), today the US-Mexico border is a paramilitarized region.

Even before 9/11 the US-Mexico border legacy of conquest surfaced through various border operations or administrative regulations aimed at "showing force" to all border crossers and border communities. Tim Dunn (1996) was among the first to characterized the border as militarized where he argued that immigration and drug enforcement efforts along the US-Mexico border during 1978–1992 period reflected low-intensity conflict. Yet, the militarization of the borderlands can be traced back even further.

The inspiration for border operations can be traced back to 1950, when border patrol inspector Albert Quillin of South Texas launched a new strategy to curtail undocumented migration (Hernández 2006; Sáenz and Morales 2015). Specifically, Quillin set up a detail of twelve border patrol agents with two buses, one plane, one truck, and nine automobiles along the Texas-Mexico border as a miniature immigration station with instructions to apprehend as many undocumented migrants as possible (Hernández 2006; Sáenz and Morales 2015). Quillin's strategy resulted in the apprehension of over one thousand undocumented migrants in four days (Hernández 2006; Sáenz and Morales 2015).

Quillin's model was the inspiration behind "Operation Wetback" launched in 1954 (Hernández 2006; Sáenz and Morales 2015). The pseudo-warlike responses to concerns over undocumented migration continued when President Eisenhower selected retired Army general Joseph Swing as the commissioner of Immigration and Naturalization Service (INS) to lead the operation (see Hernández 2006; Sáenz and Morales, 2015). Placing a high ranked military general in charge and naming this border security strategy as "operation" illustrates the pseudo-war-like approached to immigrant apprehensions. "Operation Wetback" terminated at the end of the Eisenhower administration and accounted for approximately 1.3 million apprehensions (Sáenz and Morales 2015).

In the early 1990s we witnessed a resurgence of border operations under the Clinton administration. In 1993 INS initiated Operation Blockade, later becoming Operation Hold the Line in El Paso, Texas (Sáenz and Morales 2015). Under the leadership of former congressman Silvestre Reyes, Operation Hold the Line expanded the pseudo-warlike border strategy right out of military manuals (Payan 2016). In 1994, INS launched Operation Gatekeeper in San Diego and soon after Operation Safeguard in Nogales, Arizona (Sáenz and Morales 2015). In 1997, Operation Rio Grande was launched in the southern Texas border (Sáenz and Morales 2015). Such border operations did not simply respond to the alleged crisis of "illegal" immigration but helped to create it through the expansion of enforcement (see Nevins 2002). As argued by Nevins (2002), Gatekeeper's greatest significance entailed its role in nation-state-building and in the creation of "illegal" migrants.

Although the model for the militarization of the border had been in place since the 1950s, most contemporary discussions on warlike tactics used for border security center on the aftermath of 9/11. Following the attacks President George W. Bush established the Department of Homeland Security (DHS) that includes Immigration and Naturalization Service (INS), among twenty-one other federal departments, and signed the USA PATRIOT (Uniting and Strengthening America by Providing Appropriate Tools Required to Intercept and Obstruct Terrorism) Act of 2001 (Douglas and Sáenz 2013). This resulted in budget increases for immigration enforcement, tripled the number of border patrol agents, expanded the government's ability to detain and deport terrorists, and instituted a "Special Registration" program that required men aged 16 to 45 from Arab and Muslim countries in residence in the United States to register with the DHS and answer questions [this program ended in May 2003] (Douglas and Sáenz 2013).

In the aftermath of 9/11 policy and public perceptions of immigrants, particularly undocumented border crossers, started to be framed in terms of possible terrorism (Andreas and Nadelmann 2006; Bejarano et al. 2012; Macías-Rojas 2016; Payan 2016). While daily border patrol operations in the Southwest have not involved intercepting terrorism or chemical weapons or apprehending migrants from "state sponsors of terrorism" (Macías-Rojas 2016), national security policies' framing of the terrorist crises resulted in an increase in the criminalization of Latina/o immigrants and exacerbating community insecurity at the southern border. In line with manufacturing the border crisis, Macías-Rojas (2016, 8) argued that "Although 9/11 linked immigration and national security, this link occurred more in the national imagination than in practice" and agents are yet to apprehend a noncitizen on national security charges along the US-Mexico border.

It is necessary to emphasize that national security efforts are overwhelmingly focused on the southern border, which is a Latina/o immigrant route and is occupied by communities that are overwhelmingly brown and poor, in contrast to the northern border. This ideology of a dangerous southern border stands in sharp contrast to these borderlands that are also among the safest regions in the country (Borunda 2013Macías-Rojas

2016). Yet the hypervigilance in the southern border is even documented in a 9/11 Commission Report that accentuated the lack of balance in patrolling the southern vs. the northern border and attributed this disproportionate show of force to Congress's concentration on undocumented migration and the lack of priority in securing the northern border despite evidence that terrorists had entered the United States from Canada (Haddal 2010).

Almost two decades since 9/11, border security continues to be concentrated in the southern border. Figure 8.1 illustrates Customs and Border Protection (CBP) data on total and Southwestern apprehensions from 2006 to 2015. As we can see, the number of apprehensions in the southern border represent almost the total number of apprehensions from 2006–2015 (Figure 8.1). The increases in border security, legitimized under national security concerns, continue to focus on the US-Mexico border although agents are yet to apprehend noncitizens on national security charges (see Macías-Rojas 2016).

In the post 9/11 era, framing immigrants as criminals not only equated them with terrorists but promoted the profit-making "immigration industrial complex" focused on detention and deportation of migrants (Diaz 2012; Douglas and Sáenz 2013; Golash-Boza, 2009). Immigrant detention has drastically increased resulting in daily averages climbing from 6,785 in 1994 to 33,330 in 2011 (Douglas and Sáenz 2013; Sáenz and Morales 2015; Siskin 2012). The criminalization of migration or the "crimmigration crisis" (Stumpf 2006) transformed detention and deportation in ways that merged the immigration and criminal justice systems. Expanding upon the "immigration industrial complex" the Border Immigration Council (2017) documented systemic failures in detention and asylum procedures that are indicative of a "border security complex" where an overlapping web of agencies and individuals, detention centers and courts, and enforcement priority mechanisms denies justice to immigrants, mixed status families, children, and those that come to the United States seeking asylum.

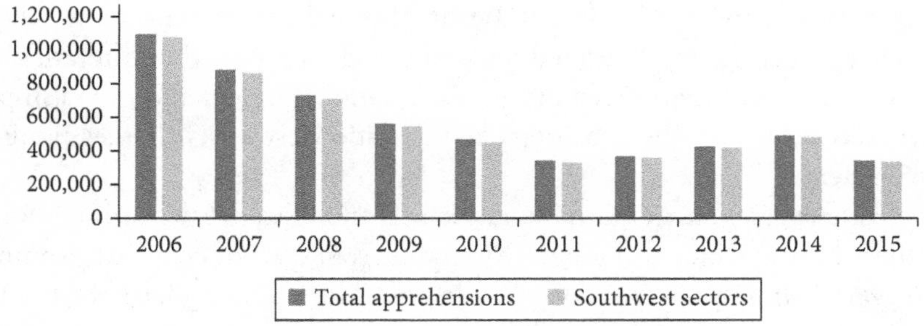

FIGURE 8.1 Total Apprehensions and Border Patrol Southwest Sector, 2006–2015.

Source: Compiled from CBP data.

Border Security and Immigration Enforcement Public Policy and Depictions of the US-Mexico Border

In line with the history of militarization of the southern border, discussed above, President Trump continues the legacy of border militarization at the southern in contrast to the northern border, under the premise that flows of lawbreakers are entering the United States. In this section I provide a critical discourse analysis to examine public policy provisions outlined in the Executive Order: Border Security and Immigration Enforcement Improvements set in motion by the Donald Trump presidency on January 2017 (Trump 2017) that continues to shape the border crisis.

From the onset, the Executive Order stated that "Aliens who illegally enter the United States without inspection or admission present a significant threat to national security and public safety" (Trump 2017, 2). As a continuation of post 9/11 federal policies during the Bush and Obama eras (see Andreas and Nadelmann 2006; Bejarano et al. 2012; Dunn 1996; Macías-Rojas 2016; Payan 2016; Sáenz and Morales 2015) the bureaucratization of border security under Trump conflates the issues of terrorism with undocumented immigration. These policy constructions that make undocumented status synonymous with criminality have been in place since the 1980s and enforced in 1996 through the Illegal Immigration Reform and Immigrant Responsibility Act and Antiterrorism (IIRIRA) and Effective Death Penalty Act (Abrego et al. 2017; Ewing, Martínez, and Rumbaut 2015) and continue to be used to intensify border surveillance.

Additionally, the Order sought legitimacy for increased militarization based on erroneous assumptions of out-of-control flows of undocumented migrants at the US-Mexico border. Indeed, the Order stressed the presence of a "recent surge of illegal immigration at the southern border with Mexico" (Trump 2017, 2), but this statement even stands in contrast to federal data on border patrol apprehensions. Figure 8.1, shown previously, in addition to illustrating the concentration on securing the southern vs the northern border, also displays the drastic decline in total apprehensions from 2006 to 2011 (data incidents of apprehensions and not individuals). While the decrease in apprehensions of undocumented migrants may in part be attributed to increases in border enforcement, it is also strongly connected to the economic conditions in the United States after the 2008 financial crisis and to Mexico's demographic statistics (Payan 2016). Despite such declines, the border patrol is staffed better than any time in history with more than 21,000 border agents, mostly in the Southwest border (US Customs and Border Protection (n. d.)), and an additional 5,000 agents proposed in Section 8 of the Executive Order (Trump 2017).

The Executive Order also follows through Donald Trump's campaign promise to build the border wall. In Section 2 the order stated to "secure the southern border of the United States through the immediate construction of a physical wall on the southern border, monitored and supported by adequate personnel so as to prevent illegal immigration, drug and human trafficking, and acts of terrorism" (Trump 2017, 2). Again, this is not new. Indeed, in accordance with the Secure Fence Act and IIRIRA there already is about seven hundred miles of fencing, mostly in the urbanized regions of the US-Mexico border. Although not specified in the Executive Order, Trump proposed in his campaign to extended the wall along the entire 1,989-mile-long US-Mexico border. Yet, in contrast to his presidential campaign, where Donald Trump suggested passing the cost of the wall to Mexico directly or indirectly through NAFTA, the Order does propose to allocate federal funds for the planning, designing, and construction of the physical wall. As of December 2017, President Trump's national security strategy still entails the construction of a wall on the southern border as an effort to defend the homeland (Trump 2017b).

The expansion of the border wall is particularly devastating for border communities. Figure 8.2 shows a picture of the expansion of the border in Sunland Park, New Mexico. It is particularly hurtful to extend the border fence/wall in this location being that it has become the site where residents on both sides of the border join for special events such as religious celebrations and activism. For instance, the Bishops and priests from the borderplex (El Paso, Las Cruces, and Juarez) hold a yearly mass here to remember the deceased migrants around the world and to promote justice. In another event, "Hugs not Walls," the Border Network for Human Rights gathered along the fence/wall to reunite approximately four hundred families separated by deportation. In these events at

FIGURE 8.2 Construction of US-Mexico Border Wall and Domestic and Federal Law Enforcement at the Sunland Park, NM and Cd. Juárez, Chihuahua, Mexico.

the fence/wall people on both side of the border not only get to see each other but join hands and pass messages through letters and signs. Currently, the space where a significant portion of events are held is inaccessible as it is occupied by construction equipment, border patrol, and even local police focusing on keeping the community out as the border wall is enforced and extended upward (Figure 8.2).

The Executive Order also plans to extend what scholars refer to as the "immigration prison industrial complex" (Diaz 2012; Douglas and Sáenz 2013; Golash-Boza 2009) by ending what is perceived as abuses to parole and asylum practices, expanding the construction of detention centers, and terminating "catch and release" protocol. Specifically, Section 11 of the Executive Order called for an "end of the abuse of parole and asylum provisions currently used to prevent the lawful removal of removable aliens" (Trump 2017, 6). An in-depth study in the El Paso Sector (El Paso and New Mexico) by the Borderland Immigration Council (2017), Customs and Border Protection (CBP), and US Immigration and Customs Enforcement (ICE) practices deter asylum-seekers at all the points in the asylum process. Indeed, asylum seekers are frequently turned away, leading to their deportation, and often sending them back to extremely dangerous situations. Also detrimental to asylum claims and to the well-being of families is the practice of family separation whereby minors are torn from their parents and caregivers, especially male family members, forcing children into state custody (Border Immigration Council 2017).

Detention practices are also being expanded. Section 5 states that "The Secretary shall take all appropriate action and allocate all legally available resources to immediately construct, operate, control, or establish contracts to construct, operate, or control facilities to detain aliens at or near the land border with Mexico" (Trump 2017, 4). Such efforts not only subject border crossers to prison-like conditions in detention centers in the United States but the undocumented population already present in the United States (see Donato & Armenta 2011; Gonzales and Chavez 2012; Hagan et al. 2011; Menjívar and Abrego 2012) and even US legal permanent residents (Douglas and Sáenz 2013; Golash-Boza and Hondagneu-Sotelo 2013) creating a climate of fear. Simultaneously increased efforts to fill those detention beds are also outlined in the Executive Order as it calls for the "termination of the practice commonly known as 'catch and release,' whereby aliens are routinely released in the United States shortly after their apprehension for violations of immigration law" (Trump 2017, 4). Prior to the Executive Order, the border patrol used its discretion to release migrants who are pending immigration court proceedings into US society. Terminating this practice puts in place the mechanisms to fill the detention beds by requiring all who are pending immigration court proceedings to detention centers. Also, expanding the need for detention centers, BIC's (2017) study found arbitrary denials of parole of those held in detention even among those with established family ties and community sponsors in the United States, those with family members needing urgent medical care, and parents of minor children. This pattern deviates from previous leadership.

Moreover, illustrating what Menjívar (2014) described as the multilayer enforcement regime consisting of federal, state, and local laws and ordinances that act simultaneously to enforce immigration, the Executive Order fortified partnerships across various levels of government for immigration enforcement. The Order on border security stated that it is the policy of the Executive Branch to: "cooperate fully with States and local law enforcement in enacting Federal-State partnerships to enforce Federal immigration priorities, as well as State monitoring and detention programs that are consistent with Federal law and do not undermine Federal immigration priorities" (Trump 2017, 3). Such partnerships are solidified through the reinstatement of 287(g) agreements that facilitate partnerships between state and local law enforcement agencies to enforce federal immigration law (for discussions on 287[g] see Armenta 2016; Provine et al. 2016). Although 287(g) increased immigrants' fear and distrust of law enforcement (Nguyen and Gill 2016) and it was consequently phased out by President Obama due to its costs and civil rights violations (see Abrego et al. 2017; Provine et al. 2016), the Trump administration reinstated it in January 2017 (also see Abrego et al. 2017). Indeed, the Order strengthens 287(g) by requiring the Secretary of Homeland Security to persuade Governors of State, as well as local officials, to enter into 287(g) agreements. The policing of federal immigration laws legalized the hypersurveillance and racial profiling of Latina/os, causing more criminal arrests and detentions of Latina/os by state and local police (Golash- Boza 2012; Heyman 2010) and weakening American identity and decreasing psychological well-being across racial and ethnic groups, including whites (Santos and Menjívar 2013).

The security regime outlined in the Executive Order also furthers the myth that migrants are draining societal resources; this time it is not by utilizing social services but by posing economic pressures to sustain the bureaucratization of border security. Specifically, the Order states that "The recent surge of illegal immigration at the southern border with Mexico has placed a significant strain on Federal resources and overwhelmed agencies charged with border security and immigration enforcement, as well as the local communities into which many of the aliens are placed" (Trump 2017, 2). While the economic strain of creating a surveillance society on federal, state, and local levels may be true, it is the politically charged social constructions of the "surge" of illegal activities—clandestine border crossings, smuggling activities, and terrorism—that are the root cause of the economic strain. Moreover, the federal government has passed down some of the costs of border security to local communities, who are already the among the poorest in country. Currently in Texas several counties including Austin, El Paso, El Cenizo, Houston, Maverick, and San Antonio are in ongoing court battles to sue the state over SB4, an anti-sanctuary bill forcing local governments to enforce federal immigration laws (Aguilar 2017). Some of the concerns over SB4 and other state-level initiatives to enforce federal immigration laws include violations to the US Constitution, lack of funding to absorb potential civil rights lawsuits, and attaching federal duties to local law enforcement departments that are already resource-strapped.

This examination of the Executive Order: Border Security and Immigration Enforcement Improvements set in motion by the Donald Trump presidency on January 2017 helps us to understand the patterns of power relations between the federal government and geopolitical southern border and its inhabitants and border crossers. These federal governmental directives that create community insecurity under the guise of national security are based on social constructions of immigrant illegality and a dangerous border. Indeed, the Executive Order allows for abuses toward immigrants (Abrego et al. 2017) and it does not mention any legal mechanisms for the protection of civil and human rights.

Border-Crossing-Related Deaths

As a result of the manufacturing of the border crisis and the lack of human rights protections there has been an escalation in border-related-deaths. While scholars have established the role of border security policies that rerouted migrants to more dangerous terrain to increases in migrant fatalities along the US-Mexico border (Cornelius 2001; Eschbach et al. 1999; Payan 2016; Rubio-Goldsmith et al. 2006), some political rhetoric also uses migrant deaths to justify the militarization of the southern border. For instance, political rhetoric surrounding the tragedy in San Antonio, Texas where dozens of migrants—men, women, and children—were trapped inside a tractor-trailer with no water and no air, resulting in ten fatalities, is used for political gain and to legitimize anti-immigrant policies (Sáenz 2017). Rogelio Sáenz (2017) pointed to the irony where conservative political commentator Ann Coulter tweeted how migrants in the San Antonio tragedy would still be alive if Trump's wall were in place. Similarly, Lt. Gov. Dan Patrick (TX) used this same tragedy to legitimize the recent passage of SB4, an antisanctuary bill, and reasoned that undocumented migrants keep coming to the United States for safety and protection in sanctuary cities (Sáenz 2017).

The US Customs and Border Protection (CBP) collected data on migrant deaths at the southwest border from 1998 to 2016. Elsewhere, the International Organization for Migration (IOM), UN Migration Agency, initiated the Missing Migrant Project to globally track migrant deaths and those gone missing along migration routes. Figure 8.3 illustrates the number of migrant fatalities at the US-Mexico border from 2014–2016

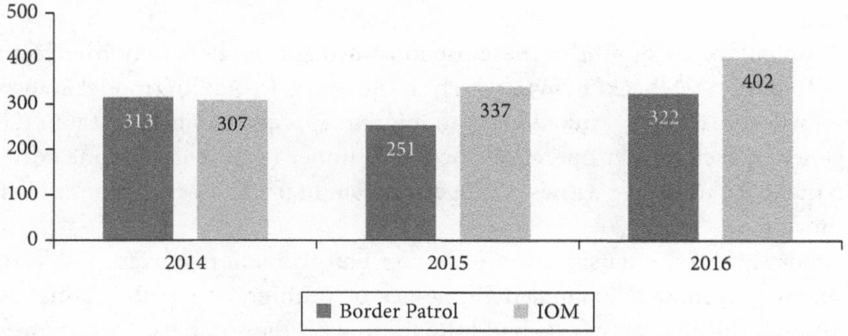

FIGURE 8.3 Migrant Fatalities at the US-Mexico Border, 2014–2016.

Source: Data complied from IOM; Missing Migrant Project, 2017; and U.S. Border Patrol, 2017.

based on both CBP and IOM data. Note, IOM data is only available from 2014 to the present.

Two things are evident in Figure 8.3: 1) migrant deaths are on the rise, and 2) IOM estimates are generally higher than CBP. In 2014, migrant deaths along the US-Mexico border ranged between 307 (IOM) to 313 (CBP) to slightly over 400 (IOM) in 2016 (Figure 8.3). Moreover, despite what appears to be fewer migrant crossings at the US-Mexico border in 2017 (Figure 8.1), more people are dying (Black 2017). Specifically, from January to July 2017 there are 240 migrant deaths so far, a 17 percent increase from the same period in 2016 (Black 2017).

Missing from the data in Figure 8.3 are the deaths of migrants en route to the United States. According to IOM estimates, from 2014 to July 2017, 442 migrants lost their lives in Central American and Mexico (see Missing Migrants Project 2018) probably en route to the United States. Therefore, between 2014 and July, 31, 2017 approximately 1,568 to 1,728 migrants died in the US Southwest, Central America, and Mexico. While these deaths represent a humanitarian crisis, ironically, they are partly a result of national security rhetoric of a lawless and porous border (also see Sáenz 2017) or of manufacturing of the border crisis.

Conclusion

In this chapter, I have described some of the public policies that exacerbate the manufacturing of the US-Mexico border crisis as a threat to national security which in turn creates community insecurity for southern border crossers and *fronterizos*/borderlanders. The vignette provided an example of how policy constructions of Latina/o and migrant criminality exacerbated "state-sanctioned violence," particularly towards the most vulnerable. The deaths of the unarmed Mexican youths fatally shot by the US border patrol while in their own neighborhoods in Mexico are tragic examples of how pseudo warlike border security tactics and perceptions of Latina/o criminality extend beyond US soil and exacerbate state-sanctioned violence against US-Mexico border residents.

The contemporary origins of these pseudo-warlike responses to border security include "Operation Wetback" in 1954, which can be traced to Quillin's model in 1950 where a show-of-force strategy resulted in 1,000 migrant apprehensions in just four days. The resurgence of such border operations occurred under President Clinton's administration in the 1990s where we witness a range of paramilitary border operations from Texas to California.

Another shift and intensification of border enforcement occurred post-9/11 where the federal government entangled the issues of immigration and national security. Even though the attacks on 9/11 had little to do with the southern border (see Payan, 2016), border enforcement efforts aimed to deter terrorism continue to be almost exclusively at the southern versus the northern border (Figure 8.1). Yet, the depictions of the border crisis are also evident in other regions through the "border security complex" where systemic failures in detention and asylum procedures and enforcement priority mechanisms deny justice to immigrants, mixed status families, children, and those that come to the United States seeking asylum (Border Immigration Council 2017).

The overview of border militarization highlights the origins of border security policy that continue to shape today's southern border crisis under the Trump presidency. The Executive Order: Border Security and Immigration Enforcement Improvements set in motion on January 2017 by President Trump heightened a sense of alarm about the US-Mexico border, not in terms of the structural conditions that have created vulnerabilities for border residents and migrants, but about terrorism, trafficking, and Mexico. The Executive Order exacerbates perceptions of the border crisis via continuing dehumanizing constructions of undocumented migrants as "illegals" that arose in the 1980s (Abrego et al. 2017; Ewing, Martínez, and Rumbaut 2015) and continuing to falsify connections between terrorism and undocumented migration (see Andreas and Nadelmann 2006; Bejarano et al. 2012; Dunn 1996; Macías-Rojas 2016; Payan 2016; Sáenz and Morales 2015). The Order also depicts a surge in illegal border-crossing activity that stands in contrast to federal CBP data showing drastic declines in apprehensions from 2006 to 2015 (Figure 8.1).

Trump's Executive Order also expands the immigration prison industrial complex (Diaz 2012; Douglas and Sáenz 2013; Fernandez 2007; Golash-Boza 2009) by adding 5,000 border agents, expanding the border wall, increasing the number of detention centers, and terminating "catch and release" protocol. Ironically, the Order also uses "blaming the victim" rhetoric by accusing undocumented migrants of causing a federal economic strain to finance this security regime, while failing to acknowledge how the costs of border security is being transferred to state and local governments through the expansion of 287(g) programs and similar initiatives.

Lastly, I highlighted how the border crisis exacerbates border-crossing-related deaths and how these tragedies are used to legitimize the border security regime. It is well established that border security policies rerouted migrants to more dangerous terrain, causing increases in migrant deaths along the US-Mexico border (Cornelius 2001; Eschbach et al. 1999; Payan 2016; Rubio-Goldsmith et al. 2006). While CBP data show almost an over 50 percent decline in apprehensions from 2006 to 2015 (Figure 8.1), border-crossing-related deaths are on the rise (Figure 8.3). Moreover, missing from US policy discussion and CBP data are the fatalities of migrants in route to the United States but who never made it. When considering migrant deaths in Central America and Mexico, in addition to the US Southwest, estimated border-crossing-related deaths increased from 1,568 in 2014 to 1,728 in July 2017. Also concerning is the political rhetoric surrounding migrant deaths. In San Antonio, for example, after the tragic death of ten migrants in a truck trailer, rather than acknowledging the incident as a humanitarian crisis, political rhetoric used blaming the victim depictions and even used the tragedy to legitimized immigration enforcement (Sáenz 2017).

In sum, this chapter highlights how political rhetoric of a southern border crisis produces the subjugation of the US-Mexico border that puts in place the mechanisms to exacerbate actual crises for *fronterizos/borderlanders* and migrants. Included in this security regime are border operations and contemporary paramilitary strategies implemented for national security that stand in sharp contrast to the failure of community security where border residents and migrant crossers are exposed to violence. Such bureaucratization of border security measures at the southern border, in contrast to the northern border, continue although very few apprehensions pose high security risks.

References

Abrego, L. J., M. Coleman, D. E. Martínez, C. Menjívar, and J. Slack. 2017. "Making Immigrants into Criminals: Legal Processes of Criminalization in the Post-IIRIRA Era." *Journal on Migration and Human Security* 5, no. 3: 694–715.

Aguilar, J. 2017. "Judge Dismisses Paxton Lawsuit Over 'Sanctuary Cities' Law." *Texas Tribune*, August 9, 2017. https://www.texastribune.org/2017/08/09/judge-dismisses-paxton-sb4-lawsuit/. Accessed September 10, 2017.

Andreas, P., and E. Nadelmann. 2006. *Policing the Globe*. Oxford: Oxford University Press.

Anzaldúa, G. 1987. *Borderlands—La Frontera: The New Mestiza*. Vol. 3. San Francisco: Aunt Lute.

Armenta, A. 2016. "Between Public Service and Social Control: Policing Dilemmas in the Era of Immigration Enforcement." *Social Problems* 63:11–126.

Bejarano, C., M. C. Morales, and S. Saddiki. 2012. "A Comparative Analysis of the Mexico-U.S. and Moroccan-Spanish Regions: Understanding Conquest through a Border Lens" In *Beyond Walls and Cages*, edited by Jenna M. Loyd, 27–41. Tucson, AZ: University of Arizona Press.

Borderland Immigration Council. 2017. "Discretion to Deny: Family Separation, Prolonged Detention, and Deterrence of Asylum Seekers at the Hands of Immigration Authorities along the U.S.-Mexico Border." https://docs.wixstatic.com/ugd/e07ba9_56ec955564434a63a49071f76005c26d.pdf. Accessed February 2017.

Binelli, M. 2016. "10 Shots Across the Border." *The New York Times Magazine*, March 3, 2016. https://www.nytimes.com/2016/03/06/magazine/10-shots-across-the-border.html. Accessed July 2017.

Black, J. 2017. "Migrant Deaths on the U.S.-Mexico Border." *Missing Migrant Project, International Organization for Migration*. https://missingmigrants.iom.int/migrant-deaths-us-mexico-border.

Borunda, D. 2013. "El Paso Ranked Safest Large City in U.S. for 3rd Straight Year." *El Paso Times*, February 6, 2013. https://archive.li/GZBE8. Accessed April 30, 2018.

Bourgois, P. 2001. "The Power of Violence in War and Peace: Post-Cold War Lessons from El Salvador." *Ethnography* 2, no. 1: 5–34.

Chavez, L. R. 2001. *Covering Immigration: Popular Images and the Politics of the Nation*. Berekely, CA: University of California Press.

Cornelius, W. A. 2001. "Death at the Border: Efficacy and Unintended Consequences of USImmigration Control Policy." *Population and development review* 27, no. 4: 661–685.

Diaz, J., Jr. 2012. "Prison and Immigration Industrial Complexes: The Ethnodistillation of People of color and Immigrants as Economic, Political, and Demographic Threats to theUS Hegemony." *International Journal of Criminology and Sociology* 1:2653–2684.

Douglas, K. M., and R. Sáenz. 2013. "The Criminalization of Immigrants and the Immigration-Industrial Complex." *Daedalus* 142, no. 3: 199–227.

Donato, K. M, and A. Armenta. 2011. "What We Know about Unauthorized Migration." *Annual Review of Sociology* 37:529–543.

Dunn, T. 1996. *The Militarization of the US–Mexico Border, 1978–1992*. Austin: Center for Mexican American Studies, University of Texas.

Dunn, T. J. 2010. *Blockading the Border and Human Rights: The El Paso Operation that Remade Immigration Enforcement*. Austin: University of Texas Press.

Eschbach, K., J. Hagan, N. Rodriguez, R. Hernandez-Leon, and S. Bailey. 1999. "Death at the Border." *International Migration Review* 33, no. 2: 430–454.

Ewing, W. A., D. E. Martínez, and R. G. Rumbaut. 2015. "The criminalization of immigration in the United States." Special Report, July 15, 2015, American Immigrant Council. https://static1.squarespace.com/static/54704f60e4b0b3e05f68476d/t/55c115e9e4b07af739792746/1438717417405/Immigrants+and+Crime.pdf. Accessed June 13, 2018.

Golash-Boza, T. 2009. "The Immigration-Industrial Complex: Why We Enforce Immigration Policies Destined to Fail." *Sociology Compass* 3, no. 2: 295–309.

Golash-Boza, T. 2012. *Due Process Denied: Detentions and Deportations in the United States*. New York: Routledge.

Golash-Boza, T., and P. Hondagneu-Sotelo. 2013. "Latino Immigrant Men and the Deportation Crisis: A Gendered Racial Removal Program." *Latino Studies* 11, no. 3: 271–292.

Gómez, L. E., 2007. *Manifest Destinies: The Making of the Mexican American Race*. NYU Press.

Gonzales, R. G. and L. R. Chavez. 2012. "'Awakening to a Nightmare' Abjectivity and Illegality in the Lives of Undocumented 1.5-Generation Latino Immigrants in the United States." *Current Anthropology* 53, no. 3: 255–281.

Haddal, C. C. 2010. "Border Security: The Role of the U.S. Border Patrol. Congressional Research Service Report for Congress." Congressional Research Service. August 11, 2010. https://fas.org/sgp/crs/homesec/RL32562.pdf. Accessed June 30, 2017.

Hagan, J. M., N. Rodriguez, and B. Castro. 2011. "Social Effects of Mass Deportations by the United States Government, 2000–2010." *Ethnic and Racial Studies* 34, no. 8: 1374–1391.

Hernández, K. L. 2006. "The Crimes and Consequences of Illegal Immigration: A Cross-Border Examination of Operation Wetback, 1943 to 1954." *Western Historical Quarterly* 37:421–444.

Heyman, J. 2010. "Arizona's Immigration Law—S.B.1070." *News: A Publication for the Society of Applied Anthropology* 21, no. 3:23–26.

Leerkes, A., J. D. Bachmeier, and M. A. Leach. 2013. "When the Border is 'Everywhere': State-Level Variation in Migration Control and Changing Settlement Patterns of the Unauthorized Immigrant Population in the United States." *International Migration Review* 47, no. 4: 910–943.

Macías-Rojas, P. 2016. *From Deportation to Prison: The Politics of Immigration Enforcement in Post-Civil Rights America*. New York: NYU Press.

Menjívar, Cecilia. 2014. "The 'Poli-Migra': Multilayered Legislation, Enforcement Practices, and What We Can Learn About and From Today's Approaches." *American Behavioral Scientist* 58, no. 13: 1805–1819.

Menjívar, C., and Abrego, L. 2012. "Legal Violence: Immigration Law and the Lives of Central American Immigrants." *American Journal of Sociology*, *117*(5): 1380-1421.

Missing Migrants Project. http://missingmigrants.iom.int. Accessed April 29, 2018.

Morales, M. C., and C. Bejarano. 2009. "Transnational Sexual and Gendered Violence at the Borderlands: An Application of Border Sexual Conquest." *Global Networks: A Journal of Transnational Affairs* 9:420–439.

Nevins, J. 2002. *Operation Gatekeeper: The Rise of the" Illegal Alien" and the Making of the US-Mexico Boundary*. Routledge: New York.

Nguyen, M. T., and H. Gill. 2016. "Interior Immigration Enforcement: The Impacts of Expanding Local Law Enforcement Authority." *Urban Studies* 53: 302–323.

Payan, T. *The Three US-Mexico Border Wars: Drugs, Immigration, and Homeland Security*. ABC-CLIO, 2016.

Provine, D. M., M. W.Varsanyi, P. G. Lewis, and S. H. Decker. 2016. *Policing Immigrants: Local Law Enforcement on the Front Lines*. Chicago: The University of Chicago Press.

Rubio-Goldsmith, R., M. M. McCormick, D. Martinez, and I. M. Duarte. 2006. "*The 'Funnel Effect' and Recovered Bodies of Unauthorized Migrants Processed by the Pima County of the Medical Examiner, 1990–2005*." Report Submitted to Pima County. Binational Migration Institute. University of Arizona. https://papers.ssrn.com/sol3/papers.cfm?abstract_id=3040107. Accessed June 13, 2018.

Sáenz, R. 2017. "Sáenz: Trailer Tragedy Arouses Absurd Logic." *Houston Chronicle*, July 28, 2017. http://www.houstonchronicle.com/opinion/outlook/article/S-enz-Trailer-tragedy-arouses-absurd-logic-11656404.php. Accessed July 27, 2017.

Sáenz, R., and M. C. Morales. 2015. *Latinos in the United States: Diversity and Change*. Cambridge, UK: Polity.

Sanchez, S. 2016. "Supreme Court Action in Shooting Case Could Have Broad Implications." *El Paso Times*, October 17, 2016. http://www.elpasotimes.com/story/news/national/2016/10/15/us-supreme-court-decision-shooting-case-could-have-far-reaching-implications/92098318/. Accessed June 1, 2017.

Santos, F. 2013. "Shootings by Agents Increase Border Tensions." *New York Times* June 10, 2013. http://www.nytimes.com/2013/06/11/us/shootings-by-agents-increase-border-tensions.html?mcubz=0. Accessed June 30, 2017.

Santos, C., and C. Menjivar. 2013. "Youths' Perspective on Senate Bill 1070 in Arizona: The Socio-Emotional Effects of Immigration Policy." *Association of Mexican American Educators Journal* 7, no. 2: 2–17.

Siskin, A. 2012. "*Immigration-Related Detention: Current Legislative Issues*." Congressional Research Service Report for Congress. Order Code RL 32369. Washington, DC: Congressional Research Service. http://www.fas.org/irp/crs/RL32369.pdf. Accessed April 22, 2014.

Stumpf, J. P. 2006. "The Crimmigration Crisis: Immigrants, Crime, and Sovereign Power." *American University Law Review* 56:367.

Trump, D. J. 2017. *Executive Order: Border Security and Immigration Enforcement Improvements. The White House, Office of the Press Secretary.* Januray 25, 2017. https://www.whitehouse.gov/the-press-office/2017/01/25/executive-order-border-security-and-immigration-enforcement-improvements. Accessed May 1, 2017.

Trump, D. J. 2017. 2017b. "Remarks by President Trump on the Administration's National Security Strategy." *The White House*. https://www.whitehouse.gov/briefings-statements/remarks-president-trump-administrations-national-security-strategy/ Accessed January 1, 2018.

US Customs and Border Protection. (n. d.) "Border Patrol Overview." https://www.cbp.gov/border-security/along-us-borders/overview. Accessed April 29, 2018.

Vélez-Ibáñez, C. G., and J. Heyman, eds. 2017. *The US-Mexico Transborder Region: Cultural Dynamics and Historical Interactions*. Tucson: University of Arizona Press.

Wagner, M. 2017. "Supreme Court to Hear Case of Mexican Teen Killed by U.S. Border Agent." *Tribune Media Wire, Fox40*, February 21, 2017. http://fox40.com/2017/02/21/supreme-court-to-hear-case-of-mexican-teen-killed-by-u-s-border-agent-tmwsp/. Accessed May 25, 2015.

CHAPTER 9

REFUGEES IN THE UNITED STATES AND THE POLITICS OF CRISIS

STEPHANIE J. NAWYN

THE phrase "refugee crisis" frequently gets thrown around, and more often than not we take for granted that we know what it means. But do we? The label "crisis" connotes numerous types of potential threats to safety and stability, and many of these threats have particular gendered consequences that are not immediately obvious. In the context of migration to the United States, where the face of a dangerous migrant is usually a brown-skinned man and the face of a dependent migrant is often a brown-skinned woman with children, using the term "refugee crisis" to describe a particular migration flows is not an apolitical act. Rather, it is a way of framing a migration situation in such a way that it garners an emotional reaction, either one of compassion, fear, or even anger. But it often obscures the real nature of the migration, the challenges and possibilities it presents, and while "crisis" can motivate quick action, it does not always facilitate action that is thoughtful and effective.

When the term "crisis" is used to refer to refugees entering, attempting to enter, or even just potentially entering the United States, it is worthwhile to ask some key questions:

1. What makes this situation a crisis? Is it concerns about the number of people entering the United States, the speed at which they are entering, who they are or where they are coming from, or the ability of the United States government or civil society to process, accommodate, or otherwise integrate them?
2. For whom is this a crisis? Is it a crisis for the US government, the government of the sending country, the migrants themselves, or the people currently living in the United States (or a particular subset of those people)? What are the different options for responding to the crisis that different parties have? Are some parties' options more limited than others?

3. What are the consequences of using the language of crisis? Who benefits and who is harmed by such language?

Additionally, it is key for understanding the particular problem at hand, and the nature of migration more broadly, to delineate between "crisis" and "challenge." Migration of all kinds tends to introduce challenges, because change is challenging and migration is inherently about change. What differentiates between a challenge and a crisis is the response; challenges do not always evolve into crises unless the challenges are not sufficiently addressed. In this chapter, I will critique the imprecise and sometimes reckless use of the term "crisis" in the context of refugees coming to the United States, interrogate what people might mean when they refer to a refugee "crisis," and describe what the data indicate about the reality of admission and integration of refugees into US society. Using the recent case of Central American asylum seekers coming to the United States, I will illustrate how assumptions surrounding the term "crisis" fuel wrongheaded policies that do not solve the problems presented by refugee migrations and cause harm to refugees themselves.

What Does "Crisis" Really Mean?

When people refer to the "refugee crisis," they are expressing a concern or fear about the situation of a given refugee migration. Some aspect of that situation presents challenges that people deem to be threatening, either to themselves or to others, including the refugees involved. Perhaps most often the use of the label "crisis" emerges from a perceived threat *from* rather than *to* refugees, that the particular refugee migration presents challenges that require repelling, isolating, or even detaining or imprisoning the refugees. So what threats does the American public perceive in current day refugee migrations? These usually fall into one of four categories: refugees are security threats, there are too many refugees and they will drain resources, the people coming are not true refugees and thus not deserving of protection, and the refugees cannot or will not assimilate and therefore will be a long-term burden to the United States.

Refugees present a security threat: This concern has become more acute as the refugees resettled in the United States have increasingly come from Muslim-dominant countries, particularly since September 11, 2001. Gendered and racial politics are embedded in these discourses of refugees as a source of threat. Muslim men's masculinity is constructed as dangerous and foreign (Kimmel 2003), framing any male refugee from a Muslim-majority country as too dangerous to resettle in the United States, rather than someone who is fleeing danger and thus in need of protection. This discourse has emerged not from any evidence of danger in the United States but rather in response to terrorist attacks overseas. Pending legislation such as the Security Against Foreign Enemies (SAFE) Act, which was passed by the US House of Representatives in November 2015 but has not moved forward since, was created in response to a recent terrorist attack in Paris committed by French nationals (not refugees), and required an additional background check for refugees originating from Iraq or Syria. The additional background check described was actually less thorough than what had been instituted as part of the refugee resettlement system following 9/11, making the legislation seem more like a political statement than something that would address a real security issue with resettling refugees (and may have been written by legislators or their aides that were unfamiliar with the security checks already in place). The current system requires screenings conducted by the US Department of State, the Department of Homeland Security, the Federal Bureau of Investigations, and the Bureau of Counterterrorism, and involves DNA and biometric data to ensure that the applicant is not already on a terror watch list. For countries like Syria, in which individuals likely had direct contact with government agents or insurgent fighters, the screening process often goes much longer than the two-year average advertised by the Department of State because each moment of contact with a persecuting regime requires a battery of questions. The process is now so vigorous that, short of better information sharing that might identify low-level combatants that would not be eligible for resettlement, it is difficult to imagine the procedures being any stricter without eliminating resettlement entirely.

There have been complete halts of refugee resettlement, in efforts to assess the system for national security weaknesses. Following 9/11, all resettlement was stopped for three months while the US government assessed the existing security procedures (it was after this time that procedures were strengthened). After three months the resettlement of certain groups considered to be lower security risks were restarted (mainly those fleeing communist regimes like Uzbekistan), but other groups that were considered higher risk (and tend to be criminalized more broadly, such as African refugees) had their resettlement delayed much longer. The Trump administration's so-called "Muslim Ban" (referred to this way because of Donald Trump's campaign promise of a "total and complete shutdown of Muslims entering the United States"; see Johnson 2015) is another example of a policy that targeted many refugee- sending countries (Saudi Arabia, for example, was not on the banned list) under the auspices of security concerns about refugees. Given that no person has been found to have entered the United States on a refugee visa with the intent of committing a terrorist act (unlike what has happened with student and business visas), the focus on refugees as a security threat is misplaced, and contributes to the marginalization of already marginalized migrants.

It also is a misplaced concern for the kinds of refugee migrations that usually come to the United States, a country whose geographic location limits any unmanaged refugee migration. Unlike the top refugee hosting countries of Turkey or Pakistan, the United States does not share any land borders with major refugee-sending countries, and is bounded on the east and west by large oceans that limit which migrants can make their way to US shores. So even the challenges for Greece, which during parts of 2015 was receiving over one thousand asylum seekers every day, are not challenges for the United States. The Greek government, while they could have anticipated the influx, did not have the proper resources allocated to border enforcement to process the large numbers of migrants who were coming to their country. By contrast, the

United States almost never receives such large numbers of refugees or asylum seekers unexpectedly; in recent times only the migration of Central American asylum seekers come close, and even the number of border apprehensions is much smaller than what the United States managed during high migration periods of unauthorized migrations from Mexico. This fact emerges from a particular history of colonialism and global economic development; it is not an inevitable result of natural history. Thus, it is subject to change through the unfolding of history. But given current conditions, there is nothing that would warrant the fear of mass refugee flows into the United States that appears to be fueling present-day anti-refugee sentiment and reactive migration policies.

While the security measures have been increased substantially in the past sixteen years, it is another question whether or not such enhanced security is even necessary. The current conception of refugees as security threats is particularly directed at refugees coming from Muslim-majority countries,[1] with the stereotypes of Muslim men as terrorists part of a broader fearmongering about Arab and Middle Eastern masculinity being inherently dangerous. When not treated as terrorists, Muslim men are assumed to be rapists that pose a threat to native-born women (Rettberg and Gajjala 2016), an assumption that is connected to a larger moral crusade that has justified US and Western intervention in the Middle East in the interests of saving Muslim women from Muslim men (Abu-Lughod 2013). These assumptions are not born out by evidence, as research consistently shows that immigrants to the United States generally are less likely to commit crimes than US native-borns (Chavez and Griffiths 2009; Martinez and Lee 2000; Rumbaut et al. 2006), and the claims that Muslim immigrant men present an acute sexual danger to non-Muslim women has not been supported by data (Dagistanli and Grewal 2012).

There Are Too Many Refugees; We Do Not Have the Resources to Support Them

Resource allocation is always a contentious debate, and when it comes to resources that might go to noncitizens it is usually followed up with the phrase "we need to help our own people." Embedded in this concern are two issues; how much resources refugees might require, and their worthiness to receive those resources (or any resources at all).

When considering whether the current number of refugees entering the United States is a problem of crisis proportions, it is worth comparing those numbers to other countries. The United States has long been the top resettlement country in the world; in most years about half of all refugees resettled come to the United States. But less than 1 percent of the world's refugees are resettled, so those that are resettled are already a very small proportion of the total population. *Hosting* countries, those that have refugees enter their country usually as a country of first asylum, crossing over directly from the country from which they are fleeing, bear a much larger burden than *resettlement* countries.

Below is Figure 9.1 from the Migration Policy Institute showing the historical trajectory of refugee admissions to the United States, both the annual ceilings (or upper limits) that Congress set and how many refugees were actually admitted. It begins in 1980, which marked the passage of the Refugee Act, the legislation that regularized refugee admissions to the United States and created the resettlement program that we have in place today.

This graph demonstrates that the ceilings for admissions over the past fifteen years is at historical lows, with actual admissions since 2001 being among the lowest since the passage of the Refugee Act. Considering that the United States admitted far more refugees through most of the 1980s and 1990s when the United States population was lower and the economy smaller, it stands to reason that the current resources we have to resettle refugees is not necessarily insufficient. This is especially true given that in real dollars much less is spent on resettlement than it was in the past. Rather, this figure indicates that the United States has sufficient resources to resettle far more refugees than it currently does, and that the problem is more of a lack of priority for resettling refugees.

The claim that there are too many refugees for the United States to protect may emerge from a conflation of a refugee "crisis" in the United States with what is happening in hosting countries and regions with large numbers of asylum seekers like Europe: the state of refugee migrations worldwide tends to shape how we perceive refugee migrations into the United States. When large numbers of refugees (mostly from Syria and Afghanistan but also northern Africa) were entering EU countries in 2015, that sense of invasion that dominated European discourses trickled into the public debates in the United States, and some people referenced the problems that EU countries had

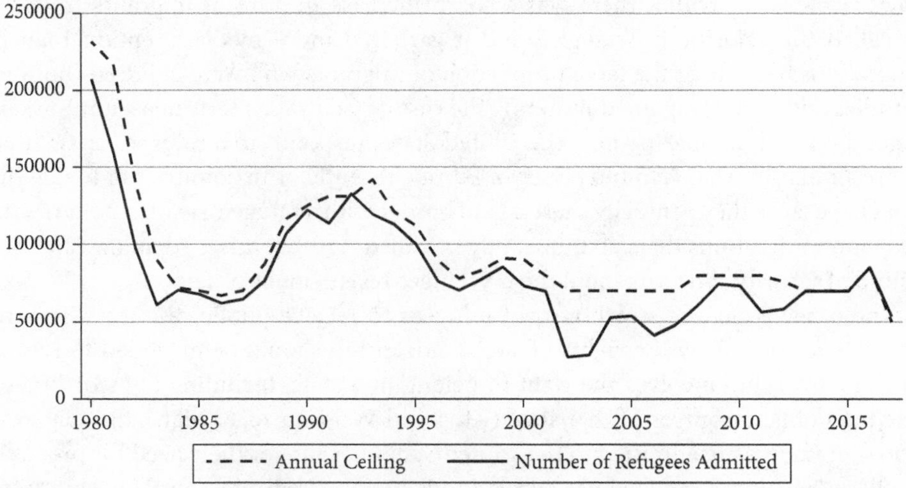

FIGURE 9.1 U.S. Annual Refugee Resettlement Ceilings and Number of Refugees Admitted, Fiscal Years 1980–2017.

Source: Data from Migration Policy Institute (MPI). Available at https://www.migrationpolicy.org/programs/data-hub/charts/us-annual-refugee-resettlement-ceilings-and-number-refugees-admitted-united

processing large numbers of asylum seekers that they were not prepared to handle with the very different challenges that refugee migrations presented to the United States. Unlike Greece and Italy, the United States is not located near a country currently sending refugees. So refugee migrations into the United States have always been far more orderly than the recent migrations into Europe, and overall numbers are far lower than countries like Turkey, Pakistan, and Jordan which have received millions of asylum seekers and have far fewer resources to allocate (United Nations High Commissioner for Refugees 2016a). So the term "global refugee crisis" is exceptionally misleading; it is more accurate to say that large-scale refugee migrations are reaching a crisis level in certain countries or regions, but the vast majority of countries are only indirectly affected if at all.

Similar to the discourses about dangerous Muslim men, the discourses in Europe were often around the threats that culturally "backwards" refugee men posed to the liberal democratic values of Europe. These discourses were mobilized with great effect in the Brexit campaign, in which large billboards showing a seemingly endless stream of mostly brown-skinned men were used to influence Brits to vote in favor of exiting the European Union. Again, these migration flows were not coming directly into the UK; the photos were taken in southern Europe where states like Greece and Bulgaria were receiving the sudden influx of asylum seekers. But the specter of these migrants eventually making their way to the UK was enough to sway many Brits to vote in favor of Brexit (Dobiles 2017).

The possible exception to the United States's isolation from large-scale influxes of refugees and asylum seekers has been the migrants originating from Central America (specifically El Salvador, Honduras, and Guatemala) and entering from Mexico. While small in number compared to asylum seekers entering Europe through the Mediterranean corridor, there was a sharp increase in 2014 of migrants from what is called the "Northern Triangle," and it garnered more media attention than past migrations because of the large proportion of migrants who were children (both with families and unaccompanied minors). The case of Central American asylum seekers is a good one for comparing how the United States responds to a refugee "crisis" that is more similar to what is found either in Europe recently or in countries of first asylum, which, because they generally share a land border with a refugee-sending country, must respond to situations that can more aptly be called "refugee crises" than the largely unfounded security concerns about the US refugee resettlement system.

The other issue, the worthiness of refugees to receive public resources, is part of the debate about how the rights of social citizenship should be extended to refugees. Social citizenship involves the right to belong in a state, including the worthiness to use the public resources of that state (King and Waldron 1988; Marshall 1964; Powell 2002). Refugees are admitted to the United States because of their need for protection, unlike other immigrants whose admission is mostly predicated on their ability to be self-sufficient, or supported by family members already in the United States, or in other ways being "productive." Refugees are admitted regardless of their potential to be economically dependent on the state, and this has made them worthier of state resources, at least within the hierarchy of non-citizens. In the popular American imagination, the involuntary nature of their migration positions refugees as "deserving" poor who are worthier of social welfare benefits than other migrants (Fujiwara 2005).

However, with the expansion of neoliberalism the benefits of social citizenship are deteriorating, leading to greater privatization of resources that had formally been the responsibility of the state. Somers (2008) refers to this as "market fundamentalism" and Brodie (1997) calls it "market citizenship." Market citizenship defines state membership based on a person's economic productivity, so rather than being worthy of state resources because of legal citizenship or legal presence in a state territory, worthiness is constructed based on how much an individual can contribute economically (Brodie 1997, 2000). The neoliberal move towards market citizenship has presented a particular burden on refugees, who are often limited in their ability to contribute economically through a number of barriers ranging from a lack of wealth, insufficient linguistic skills, lack of social networks, and educational and literacy levels that do not give them access to living wage jobs (Nawyn 2011, 2013). Gender and family dynamics also come into play, with refugee households that include a larger ratio of healthy adults to dependents having an easier time achieving self-sufficiency while single mothers face both the inability to bring in enough money for their households to survive and the stigma that American culture attaches to dependency (Grace, Nawyn, and Okwako 2018). Given the wealth and economic power of the United States, claims that the United States does not have enough resources to help refugees is really a claim that refugees are not worthy of state resources, or that under neoliberalism the resources of the state are no longer available to people based on economic need.

These Refugees Will Never Assimilate or Acculturate; They Will Change the Culture or Demographics of the United States: Concerns about the potential of different immigrant groups to assimilate is long-standing, and it has shaped many of the restrictionist policies in the United States. During the early period of migration management, we had the Chinese Exclusion Act (limiting Chinese immigration), the Gentleman's Act (limiting Japanese immigration), and the Emergency Quota Act (setting national quotas that limited nonwhite immigration broadly), all based on the premise that these migrant groups would never become "American." It is fair to expect that immigration will change the demographics of the United States; we have new racial and ethnic categories for Americans because of immigration, and the US Census Bureau projects that people of Anglo-European descent will become the majority-minority group in the United States by 2044 (Colby and Ortman 2015). However, it is also fair to interrogate the categorization of that as a "concern" or "problem" and examine the white supremacist underpinnings that construct racial and ethnic demographic shifts as inherently bad.

Compared to many countries outside of the Americas, the United States has a long history of integrating immigrants into its society, albeit not without conflict but not with the level of conflict seen in some European countries or less developed countries elsewhere. For refugees in particular, integration takes time but we see similar rates of naturalization for the same refugee groups between Canada and the United States, despite disparities in naturalization rates for nonrefugee groups (Bloemraad 2006). A study by the Pew Research Center (2011) found that Muslim Americans widely adopted mainstream American values.

Immediately following resettlement it is typical for refugees to be underemployed, and for highly educated refugees to experience downward mobility compared to their occupational status in their home country. But over time, with greater experience in the US labor market, improved language skills, and extended social networks, most refugees improve markedly. Although still underemployed compared to their premigration skills, most Vietnamese refugees who arrived in the 1970s acquired basic fluency within twenty-seven months (Stein 1979). Economic integration now takes longer, as newer cohorts of refugees tend to start at a greater earnings disadvantage (Capps et al. 2015). But with greater English fluency and social networks with established coethnics and white Americans, they still experience positive economic improvements (Mamgain and Collins 2003; Nawyn et al. 2012).

It is worth noting that integration is a two-way street. Refugees benefit from having higher levels of human and social capital, and they need to make a concerted effort to advance in US society following resettlement. But social structures that exclude and marginalized refugees make successful integration less likely to happen (Phillimore and Goodson 2006). The United States has a better track record than many European countries in terms of creating economic structures of opportunities for refugees, in part because the singular focus on economic self-sufficiency does not just open opportunities to enter paid employment for refugees, but requires it. The "jobs first" focus has historically led to better outcomes than other resettlement regimes that tend to isolate refugees more over concerns that they crowd out citizens from the labor market (Peisker and Tilbury 2003). However, the time during which resettlement cash assistance is available to refugees has shrunk from five years in the 1980s (Rumbaut 1989) to between one and three months currently in most states (Nawyn 2011). This may lead to an erosion of integration, or an increase in the time required for refugees to achieve some modicum of self-sufficiency or feeling of belonging in the United States.

Rather than conceptualizing integration as an individual-level process that is based on the choices that migrants make (i.e., to put in time and effort to learn the dominant language versus spending time in the ethnic community rather than interacting with the host society), integration is better understood as an interaction between individual-level characteristics, community characteristics, and receiving society institutions and systems. Much scholarship on immigrant integration demonstrates that access to rights is foundational to successful integration. Ager and Strang (2008) argue that citizenship and rights provide a foundation that supports the learning of language and cultural knowledge, achieving stability and safety in the receiving society, and the development of social capital in which migrants expand their social networks beyond their ethnic community to host society residents.

Ager and Strang (2008) and others also note the importance of understanding integration as multifaceted. The refugee resettlement program in the United States focuses primarily and almost exclusively on facilitating the entry of refugees in the paid labor market (Nawyn 2011). The United States government defines the acquisition of paid employment as achieving economic self-sufficiency, even though the employment may not be (and often isn't at first) sufficient for supporting an entire household. The focus on the integration of individual refugees rather than households and the needs of households that may have many dependents and few able-bodied adults of working age tends to make this gap in "employment-self-sufficiency" invisible in resettlement metrics (Grace, Nawyn, and Okwako 2018).

There is also no consideration for the gendered needs of refugees that, when not met, might inhibit holistic integration. The problem of refugee women who experienced sexual violence prior to resettlement (a common experience for refugees fleeing certain situations) is not explicitly addressed by the "jobs first" approach of US resettlement, and absent any treatment threatens to leave those women feeling anxious, vulnerable, and poorly equipped to engage with their new communities (Wachter et al. 2016). Gendered stereotypes also shape the institutional resources available to refugee women, with assistance organizations facilitating refugee women's entry into gendered occupations that are often low-paid but easier for refugee women to access (Nawyn 2010). But refugee women also interact with these institutions in ways that reinvent gender relations (Koyama 2014). Ultimately, there is no stagnant culture or social system to which refugees are integrating; over time most successfully become part of US society and their local communities in ways that preserve some aspects of culture but also contribute to its inevitable evolution.

People Claiming Refugee Status Are Not Really Refugees: This concern is more commonly expressed in Europe, as exemplified by Slovak prime minister Robert Fico when he declared that "95% of these people [migrants entering Europe in the summer of 2015] are economic migrants" (Vasagar, Byrne, and Barker 2015). Refugee and asylum seekers represent a larger proportion of the total migrant population in Europe, and more often involve asylum seekers who have yet to be vetted, compared to refugees who are resettled in the United States after a lengthy vetting process. But it also happens in the United Stares, calling into question the obligation of the United States to provide protection to certain groups. As Hathaway (2002) argues, refugee law is not immigration law, and involves a different balance between international obligations and national sovereignty. If migrants are legitimate refugees, states have greater international responsibilities to them. This is why states have at times kept asylum seekers from entering their territory, as Hathaway describes in the case of Australia refusing to allow rescued refugees to dock at an Australian port (2002). It is also why states and other actors attempt to delegitimate refugees, which moves them from the category of state responsibility to deportable subjects.

While most refugees who enter the United States do so through resettlement and have been recognized as refugees by the US government, Central American migrants who have been coming to the United States seeking asylum for decades have not been frequently granted that same recognition. Refugee adjudication is a political process that is shaped by political circumstances, and in the United States the status determination of Central American asylum seekers has been strongly influenced by the Cold War in which asylum seekers fleeing communist regimes were granted protection but asylum seekers fleeing similar situations from other regimes were not (Coutin 2011). Hamlin (2012) argues that during the Cold War the US government created the category of "refugee" and "asylum seeker" separately from that of "migrant," with an explicitly politicized conception that reflected fears about the spread of Communism. Further, during the 1960s and 1970s the number of asylum seekers was relatively small, which kept pressure on the asylum adjudication process to a minimum. Hence, the asylum policy was linked with refugee policy (which was regularized by the 1980 Refugee Act) and international politics, and was relatively insulated from domestic policy and migration controls. The end of the Cold War coincided with a surge of asylum seekers globally. This precipitated a shift in asylum adjudication that still privileged asylum seekers fleeing communist regimes (who, like in the case of Cubans, could be categorized as "special entrants"), but tied asylum to the increasing attempts to protect the US southern border from unauthorized crossings.

It was within this historical context of residual anticommunism and much greater focus on border enforcement that the numbers of Central Amerian asylum seekers increased. Many Central American asylum seekers coming to the United States were granted Temporary Protected Status (TPS), rather than asylum which would give them the opportunity to apply for legal permanent residency. TPS is granted for a particular period of time, and can be extended but also discontinued, leaving migrants in a state of liminal legality (Menjívar 2006a) in which their legal limbo negatively affects all aspects of their lives (Menjívar 2011). This includes family life, as TPS recipients cannot sponsor family members to come to the United States, often leading to family separation (Menjívar 2006b, Menjívar 2012). TPS in no way replicates the protection of asylum, and the refusal of the US government to recognize certain Central Americans as legitimate refugees while granting asylum to other Central Americans who have had similar experiences of persecution, has devastating effects on individuals, families, and communities.

These four claims construct refugees as the source of crisis, rather than people suffering under crisis conditions. To claim that a person seeking protection is not a legitimate refugee is to claim that there is no crisis to begin with, except that the said person is attempting to enter the United States under false pretenses. To make the other claims is to acknowledge the legitimacy of the person's flight but to absolve the United States of any responsibility to respond except to protect citizens from the refugee's presence. Thus, the crisis becomes the presence of refugees and asylum seekers that the United States cannot or should not take in. These dynamics have played out in the case of Central American asylum seekers coming to the United States.

Refugee Crisis in the United States: Central American Asylum Seekers

While most refugee migrations to the United States have been predictable and regularized, the migration of Central American asylum seekers is a recent exception. The US-Mexico border has for decades been a contentious geopolitical space where national security and sovereignty, transnationalism, and global capitalism have intersected. The focus had been almost entirely on the porousness (or lack thereof) of capital, drugs, and Mexican migrants, with both US and Mexican policies focused on how to maximize the economic partnership between the two countries while still limiting the movement of illicit materials (both drugs and guns) and enacting Janus-faced agendas that in some cases encouraged and in others discouraged human migration. But starting in the early 2000s increasing violence in El Salvador, Guatemala, and especially Honduras led to increased displacement of people from those countries and drew them to the United States where long-standing migration ties with their home countries, relative political stability, and a regularized asylum adjudication process existed. In 2014 there was a large spike in the number of apprehensions of Central Americans at the US-Mexico border, although "apprehensions" is a bit misleading; these were migrants who did not have authorization to enter the United States but most submitted themselves to authorities quickly and requested asylum. The numbers dropped in 2015, then jumped back up in 2016 (Musalo and Lee 2017).

The increase made news headlines for a couple reasons. The first was the rise in Central American asylum seekers proportionate to total apprehensions. Overall the number of apprehensions was small compared to previous years. Total border apprehensions dropped, and the number of Central Americans apprehended, while larger than previous years, was not as dramatic a change as one might think. But because the number of Mexican migrants apprehended dropped precipitously, Central American apprehensions became more visible than they had in previous years. The second reason was that the migrants being apprehended included many more children than had been seen before, both coming with families and as unaccompanied minors. The greater presence of children highlighted the desperate situation of the migrants (i.e., that the situation in the sending countries had grown bad enough that people would risk sending their children through Mexico to the United States, sometimes unaccompanied), and presented new challenges for housing child migrants and processing their asylum claims.

This situation was labeled a crisis for a couple of reasons. First, the number of asylum claims from the Northern Triangle increased in several countries, including Costa Rica and Belize as well as Mexico and the United States. The United Nations High Commissioner for Refugees (UNHCR) released a press briefing stating that there was an asylum claim increase of 176 percent in Costa Rica and ten-fold increase in Belize, and there was insufficient capacity in the asylum adjudication apparatuses to efficiently respond to the claims (United Nations High Commissioner for Refugees 2016b). So across Central America and the southern portion of North America, asylum claims increased beyond the current capacity to process them (although capacities can be increased, and in the United States they were).

Second, the fact that so many asylum seekers were families and unaccompanied children required a different response from state and supra-governmental agencies tasked with protecting migrant rights. Unaccompanied migrant children cannot be released to their own guardianship the way that adult asylum seekers can, and detention facilities (where asylum seekers increasingly end up) designed for adults cannot appropriately accommodate children. While some of these children were put into foster care while their asylum cases were being considered, many ended up in detention facilities. The US federal government commissioned the construction of two new family detention facilities, paying a $1 billion contract to Corrections Corporation of America to house women and children specifically (Harlan 2016), so that children would not be detained in facilities designed for adults. But the conditions in some detention facilities are abhorrent; Riva (2017) argues that these detention facilities are intended to be carceral rather than protective, and that they are spaces in which the categories of asylum seeker, unwanted immigrant, and criminal are intermingled. In addition to inhumane physical conditions (with extremely cold cells and dog kennel-like quarters), women asylum seekers are commonly treated with violence from detention guards. Riva calls for greater scrutiny of how these facilities act as part of a deterrence strategy, in which harsh practices which are banned by official policy are nevertheless enacted as a way to discourage future asylum seekers from coming to the United States.

The limited rights afforded to adult asylum seekers, if not on paper than certainly in practice, took on heightened importance when unaccompanied children were involved. Asylum hearings are civil cases, not criminal, and thus the migrant who is seeking asylum does not have a right to an attorney the way an accused person in a criminal case would be. In a deposition filed for JEFM v. Lynch (2017), Judge Jack H. Weil argued that 3- and 4-year olds could be taught immigration law sufficiently so that they could represent themselves in immigration court. While that assertion has been challenged by numerous legal experts and the US Justice Department, it is not unusual for children to go through asylum procedures without legal representation (Bhabha and Schmidt 2008; Ataiants et al. 2017). While most immigration scholars have critiqued this practice as a source of crisis, in popular discourse it is the presence of the children itself that is constructed as a crisis, not how they are treated by the state.

The treatment of asylum seekers has arguably constituted human rights violations (Musalo and Lee 2017). For women and children in particular, the physical and sexual violence that many experienced en route to the United States demonstrates the desperate conditions that led them to seek asylum in the first place (Schmidt and Buechler 2017), and compounds the gravity of their treatment upon arrival. From the perspective of these asylum seekers, the violence they experience in their home country, throughout Mexico, and that which is enacted by the US state arguably constitutes a crisis.

But the response of the US government demonstrates a different understanding of crisis, positioning the presence of asylum seekers as the source of the problem. Although the Obama administration instituted the Central American Minors (CAM) program that allowed children to request asylum before leaving their home country (and thus avoid both a more dangerous journey to the United States without authorization and the challenges the state faced processing them after their arrival), the Trump administration plans to phase out CAM in fiscal year 2018 (Rosenberg and Torbati 2017).[2] Gender and racial politics in the United States in late 2017 (as of this writing) are such that most immigrants are defined in public discourse as unwanted, and brown-skinned male migrants embody danger while brown-skinned female migrants embody dependence and cultural genocide. In this context, the presence of immigrants alone constitutes crisis. While refugees, especially those that are women or children, traditionally have been depicted as pitiable and worthy of empathy and assistance, increasingly the discourses of threat, resource drain, and cultural and demographic change have converged to create a hostile reception for even the most vulnerable refugees and asylum seekers.

Conclusion

The comparison of challenges posed by refugee migrations to the United States and other Global North countries to those experienced by countries in the Global South provide a window into how the term "crisis" gets defined in political ways that do not correspond to material situations. Countries of first asylum, such as Turkey (which hosts as of this writing over three million Syrians) or Pakistan (which hosts approximately 1.45 million, almost all Afghanis) face much more challenging conditions emerging from the movement of refugees across their borders. In addition to the much larger numbers, these migrations are less controlled; large numbers of people may show up at border crossings suddenly without time to process everyone, they may be in danger and not able to wait at or near the border before crossing, and people may arrive with many injuries and few material resources.

Conversely, refugees most often come to the United States with the benefit of preplanning, and those entering through the resettlement program receive medical screenings, orientations, and sometimes even minimal English instruction before they arrive. With the exception of surges of asylum seekers (which are still numerically much smaller than the large movements of refugees managed by Global South countries), refugee migrations to the United States are far more predictable, and resources can be allocated based on expectations of need that can be anticipated with reasonably accuracy. Additionally, since passage of the Refugee Act, the United States has developed an intricate system of civil society organizations that are equipped with the knowledge of how best to integrate refugees into American society. While their programs aimed at achieving fast employment sometimes recreate existing gendered and racialized hierarchies in the labor market, they also have the flexibility to respond to the gendered integration needs of refugees.

Thus, the term "crisis" has very different meanings in the Global South compared to the Global North. While the source of the crisis in the Global South is often one of insufficient resources to deal with somewhat unexpected and sudden demands, in the Global North it might better be understood as insufficient political will to allocate resources towards the protection and integration of refugees. As nationalist populism expands globally, the benefits of crisis language appear to be accrued by those who maintain political power by stoking xenophobic and racist fears of refugees, constructing them as sources of danger and degradation of national culture and identity. And while crisis language can also motivate quick action and additional resources for refugees, in the current climate refugees are the losers in crisis language, as it has motivated hardened borders rather than compassionate assistance and protection.

Notes

1. Refugees coming from Muslim-majority countries are commonly treated in popular discourse through the lens of Islamophobic tropes, whether or not the refugees themselves are Muslim. For example, many Iraqi refugees that come to the United States are Chaldean Christians, yet they often suffer the same Islamophobic stereotypes as Muslim Iraqis.
2. The CAM program had only limited success. Applications took a long time to process, making it untenable for minors who needed to escape immediate danger and the available slots were limited (Hipsman and Meissner 2015; Menjivar and Perreira, forthcoming).

References

Abu-Lughod, L. 2013. *Do Muslim Women Need Saving?* Cambridge, MA: Harvard University Press.

Ager, A. and Strang, A. 2008. "Understanding Integration: A Conceptual Framework." *Journal of Refugee Studies* 21, no. 2: 166–191.

Ataiants, J., C. Cohen, A. H. Riley, J. T. Lieberman, M. C. Reidy, and M. Chilton 2017. "Unaccompanied Children at the United States Border: A Human Rights Crisis That Can Be Addressed with Policy Change." *Journal of Immigrant and Minority Health*, doi: 10.1007/s10903-017-0577-5.

Bhabha, J. and S. Schmidt. 2008. "Seeking Asylum Alone: Unaccompanied and Separated Children and Refugee Protection in the US. *The Journal of the History of Childhood and Youth* 1, no. 1: 126–138.

Bloemraad, I. 2006. *Becoming a Citizen: Incorporating Immigrants and Refugees in the United States and Canada.* Berkeley: University of California Press.

Brodie, J. 1997. "Meso-discourses, State Forms and the Gendering of Liberal-Democratic Citizenship." *Citizenship Studies* 1, no. 2: 223–242.

Brodie, J. 2000. Imagining Democratic Urban Citizenship. In *Democracy, citizenship and the global city*, ed. I. F. Isin, 110–128. London: Routledge.

Capps, R., K. Newland, S. Fratzke et al. 2015. "Integrating Refugees in the United States: The Successes and Challenges of Resettlement in a Global Context." *Statistical Journal of the IAOS* 31, no. 3: 341–367.

Chavez, J. M., and E. Griffiths. 2009. "Neighborhood Dynamics of Urban Violence: Understanding the Immigration Connection." *Homicide Studies* 13, no. 3: 261–273.

Colby, S. L., and J. M. Ortman. 2015. "Projections of the Size and Composition of the U.S. Population: 2015 to 2060." *U.S. Census Bureau*, March 3, 2015. https://www.census.gov/library/publications/2015/demo/p25-1143.html.

Coutin, S. B. 2011. "Falling Outside: Excavating the History of Central American Asylum Seekers." *Law & Social Inquiry* 36, no. 3: 569–596.

Dagistanli, S. and K. Grewal. 2012. "Perverse Muslim Masculinities in Contemporary Orientalist Discourse: The Vagaries of Muslim Immigration in the West." In *Global Islamophobia: Muslims and Moral Panic in the West*, edited by G. Morgan and S. Poynting, 119–142. Aldershot, England: Ashgate.

Dobiles, K.M. 2017. "*The Imagery of Migrants in the British Media and its Impact on the Brexit Vote in the Midlands.*" Master's thesis, University of Washington.

Fujiwara, L. H. 2005. "Immigrant Rights are Human Rights: The Reframing of Immigrant Entitlement and Welfare." *Social Problems* 52:79–101.

Grace, B., S. J. Nawyn, and B. Okwako. (2018). "The Right To Belong (If You Can Afford It): Market-Based Restrictions on Social Citizenship in the United States." *Journal of Refugee Studies* 31, no. 1: 46–62.

Hamlin, R. 2012. "Illegal Refugees: Competing Policy Ideas and the Rise of the Regime of Deterrence in American Asylum Politics." *Refugee Survey Quarterly* 31, no. 2: 33–53.

Harlan, C. 2016. "Inside the Administration's $1 Billion Deal To Detain Central American Asylum Seekers." *The Washington Post*, August 14, 2016. https://www.washingtonpost.com/business/economy/inside-the-administrations-1-billion-deal-to-detain-central-american-asylum-seekers/2016/08/14/e47f1960-5819-11e6-9aee-8075993d73a2_story.html?utm_term=.f946b32957c5.

Hathaway, J. C. 2002. "Refugee Law is not Immigration Law." *University of Michigan Law School Scholarship Repository*. http://repository.law.umich.edu/cgi/viewcontent.cgi?article=2724&context=articles.

Hipsman, F. and D. Meissner. (2015). "*In-country Refugee Processing in Central America: A Piece of the Puzzle.*" Washington, DC: Migration Policy Institute. https://www.migrationpolicy.org/research/country-processing-central-america-piece-puzzle

JEFM v. Lynch (2017). 873 F.3d 1026 (9th Circuit).

Johnson, Jenna. 2015. "Trump calls for a'total and complete shutdown of Muslims entering the United States'" *Washington Post*, December 7. https://www.washingtonpost.com/news/post-politics/wp/2015/12/07/donald-trump-calls-for-total-and-complete-shutdown-of-muslims-entering-the-united-states/?noredirect=on&utm_term=.38bf5a735bae.

Kimmel, M.S. 2003. "Globalization and Its Mal(e)Contents: The Gendered Moral and Political Economy of Terrorism." *International Sociology* 18, no. 3: 603–620.

King, D. S. and J. Waldron. 1988. "Citizenship, Social Citizenship and the Defence of Welfare Provision." *British Journal of Political Science* 18:415–433.

Koyama, J. 2014. "Constructing Gender: Refugee Women Working in the United States." *Journal of Refugee Studies* 28, no. 2: 258–275.

Mamgain, V. and K. Collins. 2003. "Off the Boat, Now Off to Work: Refugees in the Labour Market in Portland, Maine." *Journal of Refugee Studies* 16, no. 2: 113–146.

Marshall, T. H. 1964. *Citizenship and Social Class: Essays*. Garden City, NY: Doubleday.

Martinez, R., Jr., and M. T. Lee. 2000. "Comparing the Context of Immigrant Homicides in Miami: Haitians, Jamaicans and Mariels." *International Migration Review* 34, no. 3: 794–812.

Menjívar, C. 2006a. "Liminal Legality: Salvadoran and Guatemalan Immigrants' Lives in the United States." *American Journal of Sociology* 111, no. 4: 999–1037.

Menjívar, C. 2006b. "Family Reorganization in a Context of Legal Uncertainty: Guatemalan and Salvadoran Immigrants in the United States." *International Journal of Sociology of the Family* 32, no. 2: .223–245.

Menjívar, C. 2011. "The Power of the Law: Central Americans' Legality And Everyday Life in Phoenix, Arizona." *Latino Studies* 9, no. 4: 377–395.

Menjívar, C. 2012. "Transnational Parenting and Immigration Law: Central Americans in the United States." *Journal of Ethnic and Migration Studies* 38, no. 2: 301–322.

Menjívar, C. and K. M. Perreira. Forthcoming. "Undocumented and Unaccompanied: Children Of Migration in the European Union and the United States." *Journal of Ethnic and Migration Studies*. doi:10.1080/1369183X.2017.1404255.

Musalo, K. and E. Lee. 2017. "Seeking a Rational Approach to a Regional Refugee Crisis: Lessons from the Summer 2014 'Surge' of Central American Women and Children at the US-Mexico Border." *Journal on Migration and Human Security* 5, no. 1: 137–179.

Nawyn, S. J. 2010. "Institutional Structures of Opportunity in Refugee Resettlement: Gender, Race/Ethnicity, and Refugee NGOs." *Journal of Sociology and Social Welfare* 37, no. 1: 149.

Nawyn, S. J. 2011. "'I have so many successful stories'": Framing Social Citizenship for Refugees. *Citizenship Studies* 15, no. 6–7: 679–693.

Nawyn, S. J. 2013. "Refugee Resettlement Policies and Pathways to Integration." In *Routledge International Handbook of Migration Studies*, edited by S. J. Gold and S. J. Nawyn, 107–117. New York: Routledge.

Nawyn, S. J., L. Gjokaj, D. L. Agbényiga, and B. Grace. 2012. "Linguistic Isolation, Social Capital, and Immigrant Belonging." *Journal of Contemporary Ethnography* 41, no. 3: 255–282.

Peisker, V. C. and F. Tilbury. 2003. "'Active' and 'Passive' Resettlement: The Influence of Support Services and Refugees' Own Resources on Resettlement Style." *International Migration* 41, no. 5: 61–91.

Pew Research Center. (2011). "Muslim Americans: No signs in Growth of Alienation or Support for Extremism." August 11, 2011. http://www.people-press.org/2011/08/30/muslim-americans-no-signs-of-growth-in-alienation-or-support-for-extremism/.

Phillimore, J. and L. Goodson. 2006. "Problem or Opportunity? Asylum Seekers, Refugees, Employment and Social Exclusion in Deprived Urban Areas." *Urban Studies* 43, no. 10: 1715–1736.

Powell, M. 2002. "The Hidden History of Social Citizenship." *Citizenship Studies* 6:229–244.

Rettberg, J. W., and R. Gajjala. 2016. "Terrorists or Cowards: Negative Portrayals of Male Syrian Refugees in Social Media." *Feminist Media Studies* 16, no. 1: 178–181.

Riva, S. 2017. "Across the Border and Into the Cold: Hieleras and the Punishment of Asylum-Seeking Central American Women in the United States." *Citizenship Studies* 21, no. 3: 309–326.

Rosenberg, M., and Y. Torbati. 2017. "U.S. will Phase Out Program for Central American Child Refugees." *Reuters*, September 27. https://www.reuters.com/article/us-usa-immigration-minors/u-s-will-phase-out-program-for-central-american-child-refugees-idUSKCN1C234G.

Rumbaut, R. 1989. "The Structure of Refuge." *International Review of Comparative Public Policy* 1: 97–129.

Rumbaut, R.G., R. G. Gonzales, G. Komaie, and C.V. Morgan. 2006. "Debunking the Myth of Immigrant Criminality: Imprisonment Among First- and Second-Generation Young Men." *Migration Information Source*. https://www.migrationpolicy.org/article/debunking-myth-immigrant-criminality-imprisonment-among-first-and-second-generation-young

Schmidt, L. A., and S. Buechler. 2017. "'I risk everything because I have already lost everything'": Central American Female Migrants Speak Out on the Migrant Trail in Oaxaca, Mexico." *Journal of Latin American Geography* 16, no. 1: 139–164.

Somers, M. 2008. *Genealogies of Citizenship: Markets, Statelessness, and the Right to Have Rights*. Cambridge, UK: Cambridge University Press.

Stein, B. N. (1979). "Occupational Adjustment of Refugees: The Vietnamese in the United States." *International Migration Review* 13, no. 1: 25–45.

United Nations High Commissioner for Refugees. 2016a. "Mid-Year Trends 2016." http://www.unhcr.org/statistics/unhcrstats/58aa8f247/mid-year-trends-june-2016.html.

United Nations High Commissioner for Refugees. 2016b. "Action Urgently Needed as Central American Asylum Claims Soar." UNHCR Spokesperson Adrian Edwards Press Briefing. http://www.unhcr.org/news/briefing/2016/4/570379fa9/action-urgently-needed-central-america-asylum-claims-soar.html.

Vasagar, J., A. Byrne, and A. Barker. (2015). "East-West Tensions Break Out over Call to Share Migrant Burden." *Financial Times*, August 31, 2015. https://www.ft.com/content/ef5179bc-4ff7-11e5-8642-453585f2cfcd#axzz3kSi3wjWA.

Wachter, K., L. C. Heffron, S. Snyder, M. B. Nsonwu, and N. B. Busch-Armendariz. 2016. "Unsettled Integration: Pre-and Post-migration Factors in Congolese Refugee Women's Resettlement Experiences in the United States." *International Social Work* 59, no. 6: 875–889.

CHAPTER 10

THE POLITICS OF THE REFUGEE CRISIS IN HUNGARY

Bordering and Ordering the Nation and Its Others

CÉLINE CANTAT AND PREM KUMAR RAJARAM

THIS chapter explores the production of a migration crisis in Hungary and the politics it authorizes, working with the premise that discourses of crises are performative: they produce representations of the politically normal and desirable that fulfill particular functions. It is therefore necessary to explore not only the way in which a migration crisis has been constructed, but also the implications this has had both for migrants and citizens in the country. In particular, this chapter argues that the notion of a migration crisis has been used to engage in practices of bordering and ordering of a Hungarian national body.

The representation of crisis works inward as well as outward. Inward, it establishes a dominant regulating norm of the politically desirable and of acceptable political subjects that allows for the othering and marginalization of those deemed as undesirable and unacceptable. This in turn justifies internal inequalities and varying access to rights. Outwardly, the framing of migrant movement as crisis creates an abstracted understanding of complex situations that allows for policymakers and commentators to treat migration as exceptional "events," distinct from the political norms and in need of rectification through (often brutal) interventions. Since 2015, the idea that Hungary is experiencing a migration crisis has become a key aspect of public and political discourse. Migrants have been the subject of racist representations, underpinned by a broad range of mechanisms such as show trials, antimigrant billboard campaigns, and "national consultations" on migration. The government has also developed a rhetoric that affirms a link between migration and terrorism, or the destabilization of public order.

These mechanisms have presented migrants as threats to Hungarian and European culture, "way of life," and security. Laws have passed to limit migrant incorporation into Hungarian society and have rendered a number of brutal practices toward migrants "banal." All this helps to define a desirable Hungarian public, a valuable entity that must be protected. In the midst of fierce campaigning in the lead-up to a general election, in the Spring of 2018, citizens have been invited by the ruling party, Fidesz, to join "residents' forums" to discuss how to "defend the nation." Prime Minister Viktor Orbán has also on numerous occasions compared the threat represented by migrants to other dangers facing the Hungarian public, most prominently Roma citizens of the country. This is reminiscent of Charles Tilly's memorable description of the state's protection racket, defining a danger or threat that strengthens its hold over territory (Rajaram 2015; Tilly 1982).

The aim of this chapter is to describe the production of a migrant crisis in Hungary and to parse out its effects. It first provides further context into the way a discourse of crisis was produced and utilized in the Hungarian situation. A recent addition to Hungarian politicians' lexicon, the notion of a migration crisis has nonetheless become central to the political life of the country since 2015. The chapter then moves on to reflect on the spectacularization practices that have been deployed in order to justify the continuous use of the idea of crisis in a country where a limited number of people have entered or received international protection over the last two years. Mechanisms are illustrated through which the discourse and representation of crisis are kept alive and performed, and the chapter also shows how discourses of crisis work in a number of ways to restrict the social, political, and economic space afforded to migrants. The crisis enables a politics of depoliticization, where migrants are made hypervisible threats which helps to authorize their social and economic neglect. Finally, by connecting discourses of the threatening migrant to processes of marginalization and othering that have affected other social groups in the country, most particularly Roma, the chapter examines the association between narratives of migration crisis and other economic and political processes that have shaped Hungary since the end of state socialism. In particular, we observe how the adoption of capitalist modes of development have led to new moral economies that rely on and necessitate the production of various "others." Ultimately, this chapter shows how discourses about migrants in Hungary emerge from a specific historico-political juncture.

Contextualizing Hungary: The "Hungarian Solution" to Migration

Discourses and politics of migration and crisis entered Hungarian public and political life in 2015, when over 220,000 migrants transited through the country on their way to Western and Northern European countries. At the time, it was generally accepted that the whole of Europe was experiencing a "migration crisis." The notion of Europe's migration crisis emerged in April 2015, following a series of shipwrecks in the Central Mediterranean leading to a combined death toll of over four hundred. A series of measures was subsequently adopted in order to "tackle" the crisis, including proposals to deploy military forces against smuggling networks operating in Libya and additional border control to prevent unauthorized departures from North African coasts. This led to a mass reorientation of migratory movement. Over the summer of 2015, the so-called Western Balkan route—which in fact starts in Turkey, and transits through Greece and Macedonia and then from Serbia into Hungary and onwards towards Western Europe—became a critical juncture of the so-called crisis.

Hungary occupies a key position within the Western Balkan route, both as a corridor between Serbia and Austria and as the southernmost Schengen and Dublin state in southeast Europe since Greece's *de facto* withdrawal from the Dublin system in 2011 (Kasparek and Speer 2015). It thus found itself at the heart of the unfolding "crisis." Though representing events as amounting to a crisis presumes their exceptionality and out-of-the-ordinary nature, many countries in the European Union (EU) have long been deemed to experience migration crises. The southern borders of the Schengen Area, places such as Lampedusa or Ceuta and Melilla, seem to be permanent crisis sites, while Calais in northern France has been experiencing a migration emergency since the late 1990s. In Hungary however, the notion of migration crisis was a newcomer to the public discourse. Yet the Hungarian government was quick to adopt and utilize the discourse. As will be seen in more detail in the next section, in the name of "stopping the crisis," a series of repressive measures was swiftly adopted with the aim of preventing or reverting migrant movement.

A key tension regarding the way discourses of migration crisis were activated in Hungary concerns representations of Europe and the country's place within the European project. This tension was expressed in two key ways. On the one hand, European governments severely criticized Hungary by declaring that Hungarian authorities did not respect European values in their reception of migrants. To the xenophobic practices of Central and Eastern European countries, they opposed the progressive response of Western member states of the EU trying to find collective solutions to migration. French Foreign Affairs Minister Laurent Fabius claimed that Eastern European countries "did not respect Europe's common values" (Euractiv 2015). This is a striking statement considering that a country like Hungary, which shares borders with the EU's external borders, has been strongly encouraged to reinforce its capacity in terms of border control and migrant detention since its entry into the EU (Cantat 2016).

It is precisely this contradiction that was picked up on by Prime Minister Viktor Orbán to articulate Hungary's discourse of migration crisis with issues related to the position of the country within Europe. Indeed, the second way in which issues of crisis and Europe intersected in Hungary was through Orbán's insistence that Hungary was performing his role as protector of Europe against mass immigration. The bordering practices enacted over the summer 2015 by Hungarian authorities have been in large part justified precisely in the name of Europe and of the preservation of "Europeaness" (Cantat 2016). Orbán has repeatedly stated that Hungary was defending "Hungarian and European culture" against "an invasion of outsiders" (Hungarian Free Press 2015). Of interest here is the distinction made by Orbán between Europe, whose identity and culture he claims are based on its Christian roots, and the EU, which he stated was in "the grip of madness" over immigration (*The Guardian* 2015). The near-systematic stopping, detention and returning of migrants is what Orban calls the "Hungarian solution" to the "migration crisis." This approach, Orban has claimed, is what Europe needs and will soon adopt (Rajaram 2016). In a February 2016 press conference, Orbán declared that the "Hungarian solution" had now become common sense:

> [N]ow for the first time the European Union has accepted the Hungarian solution . . . we have prioritized border protection and the stopping of the migrant masses. . . . We have to stop them; our external borders must be protected and the Schengen Accord must be upheld 100 per cent by everyone. . . . [T]he Balkan route countries and Austria have finally taken the path of common sense.. . . [W]hat the countries along the Balkan route and Austria are doing is in reality the Hungarian solution. They have built fences, even if they don't call them fences; they have stopped migrants and have returned migrants. This was always the Hungarian stand. I am certain that the protection of Europe's southern borders is impossible by any other instruments.
>
> (Orbán 2016)

By stating its responsibility to protect Europe, Orbán successfully reshuffles the position of Hungary in European hierarchies, and presents the country as Europe's vanguard. This rhetorical maneuver is not unlike previous speeches by Orbán in which he attempted to justify a number of repressive or authoritarian measures through claims regarding the nature and culture of Hungary.

In 2014, in a speech at a youth camp in a Hungarian community in Romania, Orbán outlined his vision of an "illiberal democracy." Orbán said that in order to make the state more competitive, an "illiberal" mode of political organization was needed. The work of civil society and NGOs, Orbán continued, obstructed this vision (*EUObserver* 2014). Authority to govern moved from society to the state. Winning a two-thirds majority in the 2010 elections enabled the Fidesz government to rewrite the Constitution. The Constitution, Hungary's Fundamental Law, begins with a prelude on the Christian tradition noting "[w]e recognize the role of Christianity in preserving nationhood" and "[w]e are proud that our people has over the centuries defended Europe in a series of struggles and enriched Europe's common values with its talent and diligence" (cited by Uitz 2015).

The Fundamental Law enabled the passing of so-called "cardinal laws" that can only be changed by a two-thirds majority. These cover a number of areas, ranging from family law (where marriage is stipulated as the union of a man and a woman) to the rights of individual and collective minorities to fiscal policy (Brodsky, n.d.). By effectively removing questions about family, individual and collective rights and economic justice from political and public discussion, Fidesz intends a seachange in the nation's culture: these complex issues and the difficult social questions that underpin them are resolved so that a particular ideological take on these issues becomes an unchanging backdrop to politics and the life of the nation. The illiberalism of Viktor Orbán distils a specific idea of European culture which emphasizes Christian values and capitalist competitiveness. By categorizing contentious issues as "cultural" the scope for tolerance or acceptance of other positions becomes increasingly limited: disagreement is not simply political but a cultural opposition to a Hungarian way of life.

This illiberalism relies on the continuous identification of the boundaries of the legitimate political community, affirmed through the production of its "others"—those who do not belong. This requires the ongoing fabrication and visibilization of otherness: the discourse of a "migration crisis" threatening the country is a central device for the performance of this ideology. The next section focuses on the mechanisms that Hungarian authorities have employed in order to perform a crisis situation. As will be shown, in spite of the limited numbers of people seeking and receiving asylum in the country, the figure of the "illegal" migrant has become central to Hungarian public and political life.

Bordering the Nation: Mechanisms of Performing Crisis

In order to continuously produce representations of the country as facing a migration crisis, the Hungarian government has deployed a number of mechanisms aimed at spectacularizing migratory events and border control. One of the most visible devices of bordering used by Hungarian authorities was the building of razor wire fences at its borders with Serbia and Croatia. Arguing that the EU was "too slow to act" in the face of the crisis represented by migratory movement to and through Hungary (*The Telegraph* 2015), in June 2015 Prime Minister Viktor Orbán ordered the building of what became a 175-kilometer long fence along the Serbian border. In October of the same year, Hungary constructed barriers on sections of the Croatian border. The fences led to an immediate reduction in numbers of people entering the country, as migrants now had to pass through transit zones located at the borders, and in which only a dozen of people would be admitted daily.

The building of the fences came after the deployment of a billboard campaign by the Hungarian government in June 2015. The posters featured messages such as: "If you come to Hungary, don't take the jobs of Hungarians" or "If you come to Hungary, you have to keep our laws." Although the messages displayed on the billboards seemed to be addressing migrants, they were written in Hungarian. It thus seems that their primary audience was, rather, the Hungarian public. The billboards and advertisements were in fact part of the government's campaign to raise awareness about what it called a "national consultation on immigration and terrorism" that was run between May and July 2015. As part of the consultation, virtually all Hungarian households received a questionnaire featuring leading questions of a xenophobic and anti-EU nature. Questions included in the consultation included: "Do you agree with the Hungarian government that instead of supporting immigrants, the support of Hungarian families and future babies is needed?" and "Would you support the Hungarian government in the introduction of stricter immigration laws as opposed to the permissive policies of Brussels?" (Migszol 2015).

With the building of the fences in the Fall of 2015, the number of people entering Hungarian territory dramatically decreased. Yet in March 2016 the Hungarian government declared a national state of emergency in the name of the "crisis" and countering potential terror threats. A few months later, in June of the same year, a counterterrorism legislative package was adopted. The package amended the Constitution and included changes to the laws governing the police, national security services, and defense forces. It granted additional powers to the executive—including increased competencies in terms of surveillance, and established a new Counterterrorism Intelligence and Criminal Analysis Center tasked with collecting and analyzing data on public security threats. A key focus of these new counterterrorism measures concerned border security.

Since then, in order to implement its securitizing agenda and to maintain the issue of migration in the public debate, the Hungarian government has continued devising mechanisms that produce the idea of a migration crisis and assert a connection between migration and the destabilization of public order. An important aspect of this strategy was the 2 October 2016 referendum calling for people to vote against the EU's proposed mechanism of refugee relocation. The campaign leading up to the referendum was overwhelmingly focused on affirming a link between migration and terrorism. The government printed and displayed a new series of posters and newspaper advertisements, displaying messages such as "Did you know that the Paris attacks were carried out by migrants?" It also distributed a booklet to over four million Hungarian households containing sentences such as "illegal immigration increases the threat of terror." The referendum put the following question to Hungarian citizens: "Do you want the European Union to be able to mandate the obligatory resettlement of non-Hungarian citizens into Hungary even without the approval of the National Assembly?" With only 40.4 percent valid ballots, the referendum fell short of the 50 percent participation that is constitutionally required under Hungarian law for a referendum to be valid and binding. In spite of this apparent failure, Prime Minister Viktor Orbán presented the referendum as a victory for his government, on the basis that ballots casted were in his favour (BBC 2016).

In spite of the extremely low number of refugees in the country, with only 1216 people being granted international protection in 2017 the focus on the threat represented by migrants remains at the heart of Hungarian political life (Hungarian Helsinki Committee 2018a). In the lead-up to the April 2018 general election, through which the ruling party Fidesz aimed to regain the two-thirds majority in parliament required to make constitutional changes which it narrowly lost in a 2015 by-election, migration and security were again key campaign themes. Prime Minister Orbán stated in a speech that the "number one issue" was whether "security and European culture and way of life" could be protected (*Daily News Hungary* 2018). Orbán insisted on the need to fight all external forces and international powers supporting "mass immigration" and attempted to turn Hungary into an "immigrant country." A key figure among these putative "external" agents has been Jewish Hungarian-American financier George Soros, against whom the Hungarian government launched the "Stop Soros" campaign in January 2018, right during the build-up to the election. The campaign accused George Soros of working "to settle millions from Africa and the Middle East" in Europe (*Hir Magazin* 2018). It included a draft legislative package targeting a range of migrants' rights and human rights organizations in the country and penalizing a set of activities such as providing legal and material support to asylum-seekers.

Beyond this series of spectacular antimigrant discourses, the Hungarian government has also engaged in practices aimed at demonstrating its power to discipline and exclude those it deems undesirable. A key example of this mechanism was the trial of eleven people arrested at the Hungarian-Serbian border on 16 September 2015, the day after the border fence was completed. On that day, hundreds of people who had for the most part been traveling along the then-existing "Balkan corridor" in an attempt to reach western and northern European countries, found themselves stuck at the Röszke/Horgoš border crossing between Serbia and Hungary. Many attempted to break through the new border fence, to which Hungarian police responded with tear gas and water cannons. One Syrian man in particular, known as Ahmed H., tried to intervene by seizing a megaphone and attempting to negotiate between the police and the refugees. As Hungarian forces continued their brutal efforts to contain people, the situation led to some clashes between travelers and the police.

Following these events, Ahmed H. and ten other people were arrested and either placed under house arrest in asylum centers or detained. In the summer of 2016, ten of the defendants were charged with "illegal entry," a criminal offense introduced into Hungarian law in September 2015, and "participation in a mass riot." The fact that these people aimed to enter European territory in order to claim asylum, which under international conventions related to refugee protection should protect them from charges of "illegal entry," testifies to the Hungarian government's disqualification of all border crossers as "illegal" migrants. Ahmed H., because he was seen using a megaphone by witnesses in the trial (who happened to all be policemen), was charged with much more serious offenses: he was accused of illegal entry and terrorism. At the end of November 2016, in the Hungarian city of Szeged, Ahmed H. received a ten-year prison sentence. After appealing, his sentence was reduced to seven years in March 2018.

These trials, and particularly Ahmed H.'s, have been deemed "show trials" by human and migrants' rights groups. Beside numerous issues with the procedure (mistranslation of defendants' statements, only taking into accounts police witnesses, among others), it also seems that a key aim of these trials was to make a spectacle of migrants as criminals in order to further their othering and marginalization. They were used as hypervisible illustrations of the Hungarian government's discourse of crisis and threat, and as confirmation of its power to enforce exclusion, thereby affirming its ability to provide "safety" to the Hungarian public against the "migrant menace." These spectacular exercises in controlling the "crisis" and establishing the borders of the Hungarian nation have far-reaching implications. They translate into and make legitimate a range of "banal" antimigrant practices that have consequences for the social, political, and economic space afforded to migrants in the country (Cantat 2017).

Examples of antimigrant acts that have become banalized through the spectacularization of a "migration crisis" are numerous in the Hungarian context. Besides the hypervisibilised posters, billboards, advertisements, and speeches targeting migrants, a series of measures have been taken that authorize various forms of physical and symbolic violence towards migrants and their bodies. In early 2016, the Hungarian government drastically reduced support to asylum-seekers (who are simultaneously prevented from working) and cut all benefits specific to refugees on the ground that there should be no differential treatment compared to the Hungarian people. That same year, in the heart of particularly cold winter, the authorities closed one of the oldest reception centers in the country, located in the city of Bicske, closed to Budapest. Bicske reception centre had relatively decent facilities and buildings, and its geographical location meant that its residents could commute to the city, where most migrants' rights groups in the country are based, and where they could develop crucial connections to prepare for a future life in Hungary. Instead, the government moved Bicske's residents to extremely insalubrious tents and containers in smaller camps located close to the borders of the country. This move is a striking example of an attempt at pushing migrants as far away as possible from places where they may build new socialities: it amounts to a thought-through strategy of marginalization on the part of the Hungarian government, that relies heavily of processes of invisibilization of migrants. A few months later, in April 2017, the Hungarian government decided to stop providing food to asylum-seekers detained in one of the reception camps, which hosts primarily people going through an asylum appeal process (*Budapest Beacon* 2017).

Narratives of migration crisis in Hungary have thus had important consequences since 2015. In spite of the limited numbers of people claiming asylum in the country, a series of initiatives by the government has kept the idea of a crisis alive: this has amounted to a complete rearticulation of Hungarian political and public life, now fully centered around migration, and the assertion of a link between migrants and terrorism. Controlling borders and separating those "who belong" from those who don't have become central aspects of the government's discourses and practices. In turn, this has justified the adoption of a series of laws that work towards the securitization of the country. It has also translated into a series of neglectful and often brutal antimigrant measures which have further marginalized and isolated migrants in the country.

Ordering the Nation: Refugees and Roma

As we have argued, policies, and discourses that border the nation produce migrants as deviant or dangerous others. This production of others signifies a desirable Hungarian public as virtuous and worthy of protection. This is a biopolitical regime that centres on distinguishing between valuable populations and subject positions while also denoting pouplations and subjects to be neglected as 'others' with a tangential belonging to the national community (Foucault 2008). The discourses and practices of othering that we have explored are also, therefore, connected to citizenship regimes. Which is to say that there is a biopolitical function of this othering: a public that can be governed and is worthy of government is continuously reproduced through the discourses and practices of othering migrants. A state-led biopolitics closes the gaps that may exist between a people and a territory. The biopolitics of the Hungarian state at this time reasserts the primary role of the state in recognizing, protecting and giving meaning to individual and collective identity in Hungary. The discourse of migration crisis heighten this process of ordering a nation and perhaps adds new twists as it emphasizes a condition of emergency where it is ever more necessary for a virtuous public to fall in behind the state.

This section will explore how discourses of crisis enable the ordering of a specific idea of the nation and desirable public and their connections to each other. It will argue that the othering of migrants is connected to the othering of other domestic populations in Hungary, primarily the Roma. This othering stems from the instantiation of a new moral economy after the socialist period where economic systems became geared to the reproduction and affirmation of specific subjectivities and the dialectic production of a population that could be justifiably neglected. An important consequence of what may be called the culturalization of economic systems is the connection of economic participation and productivity with social value and right to participation in a public sphere. Roma in post-socialist Hungary see their room for political, social, and economic participation under threat. This enables their instrumentalization as dangerous to public security, as a way of denoting a desirable Hungarian public and nation. The discourse of crisis and the othering of migrants are inflected by this political process in Hungary and are inscribed into a dominant moral economy that the current Fidesz government has been adept at exploiting for political gain.

These discourses and practices did not, then, emerge in Hungary out of the blue. A process of distancing Roma from the political norm has been a present feature of Hungarian politics for a number of years. At the beginning of the 1990s, with the collapse of the socialist economy and the transition to capitalism, poverty came to be racialized. Policies, and state discourses, classified poverty as a distinct *cultural* phenomenon disassociated from the inequalities of social relations of capitalist modes of production. One important consequence of this was the rise of a discourse, soon backed up by policies, that read the capacity for effective and productive economic participation in culturalist terms. Groups were poor not because of the inequalities and uneven development of the new capitalism, but because of their cultural traits. Racialization, and the creation of otherness, arose then through efforts from a privileged class to keep themselves out of the category "poor." Those who were "poor" were blamed for their condition, their poverty was due to cultural traits, or even biological difference (Emigh et al. 2001).

The moral economies of the new capitalist system then instantiated a specific idea of virtue and right. Economic positions became connected to social status. The transformation of the economic system established a specific idea of who had prior right to belong, whose subjectivities and ways of living should be fostered by the economy and whose could be left in conditions of neglect. This is biopolitical: forms of desirable living were distinguished from those that were to be either disciplined or neglected.

To the extent that socialist economies fostered full employment, people identified as Roma were guaranteed employment and cash income, though often in the most marginal of positions as factory workers in heavy industry. With the collapse of this heavy industry by the early 1990s in Hungary, many members of the Roma population no longer had an economic role; they became a surplus population. The new moral economies of capitalism, in particular its association of economic productivity with social status, meant that people in positions of surplus could be blamed for their position because of cultural traits and, importantly, they fell out of the regimes of value, thus enabling their instrumentalization for political purposes. By this we refer to the consequences of the loss of social value, which is largely related to changes in moral economy, meaning that Roma in Hungary became increasingly subjects of political action, rather than political subjects with a secure right of political and social participation.

One tangible result of the promotion of capitalist modes of development has been the further affirming of a specific Hungarian subjectivity from which Roma are marginalized. This is apparent in gentrification of Budapest neighborhoods. In one much discussed example, the transformation of the iconic and historic Corvin quarter in Budapest's 8th district replaced social housing with a shopping mall and other markers of consumerism advertised as opening the area to a new Hungarian middle class. The 8th district has long been a "Roma neighborhood" and people living in the district's social housing are disproportionately Roma. The gentrification of the Corvin quarter impacted hardest on those in social housing, who were moved to outlying areas of the district (Czirfusz et al. 2015). Gentrification in the 8th district transformed neighborhoods from being spaces of social reproduction to spaces where capital is reproduced. At its core then is perhaps the articulation of a new citizenship regime where a consumer citizen is produced and given priority. This consumer citizen has prior right of belonging in social space creating conditions of marginalization that hit hardest on Roma populations.

The transition to capitalism in Hungary, as elsewhere in Central and Eastern Europe, saw the development of a moral economy that privileged particular subjectivities. The current Fidesz government in Hungary was and is adept at playing on this. Fidesz saw first with the Roma population, and then with migrants, an opportunity to build on an increasingly culturalist sense of belonging that was promoted and strengthened by the new capitalism. The lack of social voice, of authority to participate socially and politically that became connected to economic participation, enabled the instrumentalization of populations and the direction of the new culturalist senses of belonging towards Fidesz and its ideas of the nation. Policies such as work for welfare programs became means of controlling and disciplining a Roma population (Szoke 2015). Up to 45 percent of Roma children are in segregated schools. Following a European Union challenge to this, the Hungarian government insisted that the channeling of Roma children to special schools was not discrimination but an inevitable consequence of their poverty (Rorke 2016). In the midst of clearing of "slums" in the northeastern city in Miskolc, residents of an overwhelmingly Roma neighborhood are to be given compensation for the loss of their property only if they use that compensation to buy or rent property outside the city and not return for five years. A public security argument was deployed, justifying the destruction of homes and banishment of Roma due to their criminality (OSCE 2016).

In March 2018, in the midst of electoral campaigning, Viktor Orban gave a speech in Miskolc linking Roma and migrants and the public security threat they pose:

> I don't want to talk about this at length because I don't have to talk about this much in Miskolc, where people know what immigration is. There was a time in Miskolc when masses came into the city from outside the city. They witnessed what happened. The people of Miskolc experienced what happened then. And the people who came to Miskolc came from inside the territory of Hungary. Now just imagine when a people with a completely different culture, habits, and a view of life come here from outside our borders. And the people of Miskolc should know that migrants always go to the big cities — that's where the ghettos will be established, the no-go zones, parallel societies. That is where the difficulties of coexistence and the deterioration of public safety will occur
>
> (*Budapest Beacon* 2018).

There has by now been a steady stream of slippages between discourses about the public security threat posed by migrants and by Roma. Most explicitly in 2015 Orban spoke against a proposed quota system for settling refugees across Europe:

> Hungary's historical given is that we live together with a few hundred thousands of Roma. This was decided by someone, somewhere. This is what we inherited. This is our situation, this is our predetermined condition . . . We are the ones who have to live with this, but we don't demand from anyone, especially not in the direction of the west, that they should live together with a large Roma minority
>
> (cited by Rorke 2015).

The spectacularization of both Roma and migrants in Hungary establishes a situation where their hypervisibility as potential public danger enables a specific ordering of a desirable public. It is in this sense that the encounter—a staged encounter—with dangerous Roma or migrants constitutes a citizenship regime. Particular subject positions with a privileged belongingness are authorized in relation to the perceived threat of others and perhaps center on the production of a consumer citizen where economic participation becomes conjoined with cultural privilege. This discourse has material impact. Roma populations' right to housing and to education become tangential, their hold on these is dependent on how they relate to and potentially impact on the right of Hungarian citizens to these. As we have noted, people with refugee status in Hungary have had welfare benefits and help with settling into the country withdrawn: there is no government assistance in learning the language, finding housing, educating children, or finding jobs.

As nongovernmental organizations scramble to fill this gap, the Hungarian government passed legislation in the summer of 2018 that will impose a 25 percent tax on foreign donations and make it possible for people to ban individuals under investigation for assisting "illegal immigration" from entering an 8 km zone around the country's non-Schengen borders (Hungarian Helsinki Committee 2018b). It is here that, in times of "crisis," the role of the other takes on a sharp new twist. Not simply to be left in conditions of neglect, migrants are to be actively crowded out and support for them becomes intolerable.

A consequence of othering is the b/ordering of the nation that gives privileged economic, social, and political participation to a specific Hungarian public and therefore a limited or tangential participation to other residents in Hungary, citizens or otherwise. This chapter has argued that the culturalization of economic positions—where poverty is isolated as an outcome of culture—enables the ongoing production of groups of people who do not belong. As people who do not belong, Roma and migrants are subject to political instrumentalisation (i.e., the deployment of discourses where a perceived threat is made hypervisible as a means of ensuring political authority).

The discourse of migration crisis appears to be connected to and to arise from this process of producing "others." Which is to say, it is not an isolated phenomenon but stems from a key consequence of economic restructuring in postsocialist Hungary where economic participation and productivity came to be connected to cultural and racialized positions. The blaming of the poor for their poverty enhanced a lack of political and social voice and enabled their instrumental use for the cohering and ordering of a specific idea of a nation. The discourse of migrant threat is instrumentalized, in the same way that the public security threat of Roma are, for political gain. In the midst of a crumbling health and education system and endemic public corruption, the 2018 election campaign which was focused on "stopping migrants" and the threat they pose to Hungarian culture, values, and security, is a striking example of this process.

Conclusion

This chapter has argued that the politics of refugee crisis in Hungary centers on the performative production of those who belong and those who don't. A number of mechanisms that spectacularize the border and the migrant as sources of hypervisible threat entrench the otherness and illegitimacy of migrants in Hungarian economic, political, and social space. This results in authorizing neglect—migrants have welfare benefits and help with social inclusion removed—as well as punitive action to defend, variously, Christian values, Europe, and a Hungarian public.

Lacking social and political voice, migrants actions and subjectivities may be used for political gain. We have noted how Ahmed H.'s actions at the border were blown up into terrorist threats and how this was enabled in part by irregularities in court that were not recognized as important. The ruling Fidesz party evidences a frightening contempt for migrants and their lives, and has shown a readiness to fudge reality for political gain.

Discourses of migration crisis in Hungary are, at root, cynical ploys that do not reflect social or political reality.

The readiness to instrumentalize migrants for party political purposes may be connected to the illiberalism of the Fidesz government. Changes in the Fundamental Law and the introduction of durable, hard-to-change cardinal laws describes the country in terms of a nationalistic and jingoistic Christian vision where Hungary is spoken about as protector of Europe. This chapter has argued also that the readiness to pillory migrants as others may be connected to the culturalization of economic arrangements, and thus to the othering of Roma who are cast as poor and blamed for being poor. A consequence is the erosion of their claim to social belonging and the consequent rise of policies of neglect and of active marginalization. These themes are repeated in the discourses and policies that performatively reproduce a migration crisis.

Discourses of migration crisis in Hungary show the consequence of a territorial regime that actively figures migrants as potential threats to ways of life. This chapter has noted that Hungarian policies are not in contradiction to European policy or discourse, despite protestations about their noncompliance with "progressive" Western European nations. While Hungary may appear as an extraordinary example not in keeping with European norms or practice, it is more apt—and more discomfiting—to note that the Hungarian illiberal discourse against migrants emerges from a history of attempts to exclude migrants central to the very imagination of a European Union.

References

BBC News. 2016. "Hungary PM Claims EU Migrant Quota Referendum Victory." October 3, 2016. https://www.bbc.com/news/world-europe-37528325.

Brodsky, Clava (n.d.). "Hungary's Dangerous Constitution." *Columbia Journal of Transnational Law—Bulletin*. http://jtl.columbia.edu/hungarys-dangerous-constitution/

Budapest Beacon. 2017. "Hungary Will Cease Providing Kiskunhalas Asylum-Seekers with Food by End of April." April 20. https://budapestbeacon.com/hungary-will-cease-providing-kiskunhalas-asylum-seekers-food-end-april

Budapest Beacon. 2018. "Orbán Says Migrants Are Like Gypsies, but Migrants Are Worse because They Come from Outside Hungary." March 2, 2018. https://budapestbeacon.com/orban-says-migrants-like-gypsies-migrants-worse-come-outside-hungary/. Accessed 30 March 2018.

Cantat, C. 2016. "The Ideology of Europeanism and Europe's Migrant Other." *International Socialism* 152. http://isj.org.uk/the-ideology-of-europeanism-and-europes-migrant-other/

Cantat, C. 2017. "The Hungarian Border Spectacle; Migration, Repression and Solidarity in Two Hungarian Border Towns." *CPS Working Paper Series*, 2017/3. https://cps.ceu.edu/sites/cps.ceu.edu/files/attachment/publication/2900/cps-working-paper-hungarian-border-spectacle-2017.pdf.

Czirfusz, M., M. Horvath, C. Jelinek, Z. Posfai, and M. Szabo. 2015. "Gentrification and Rescaling Urban Governance in Budapest-Józsefváros." *Intersections: East European Journal of Society and Politics* 1, no. 4: 55–77.

Daily News Hungary 2018. *Orbán: Migration Number One Issue*, March 26. https://dailynewshungary.com/election-2018-Orban-migration-number-one-issue/

Emigh, R. J., E. Fodor, and I. Szelenyi. 2001. "The Racialization and Feminization of Poverty?" In *Poverty, Ethnicity and Gender in Eastern Europe During the Market Transition*, edited by R. J. Emigh and I. Szelenyi, 1–32. Westport, CT: Praeger.

EUObserver. 2014. "Orban Wants To Build 'Illiberal State'." July 28. https://euobserver.com/political/125128

Euractiv. 2015. "Fabius calls Eastern Europe's reluctance to receive migrants 'scandalous'." August 31, 2015. https://www.euractiv.com/section/justice-home-affairs/news/fabius-calls-eastern-europe-s-reluctance-to-receive-migrants-scandalous/. Accessed 30 March 2018.

Foucault, M. 2008. *The Birth of Biopolitics: Lectures at the College de France, 1978-79*. Basingstoke: Palgrave Macmillan.

Hir Magazin. 2018. "A STOP Soros visszavonását követeli a Helsinki Bizottság." February 9. https://www.hirmagazin.eu/a-stop-soros-visszavonasat-koveteli-a-helsinki-bizottsag

Hungarian Free Press. 2015. "Viktor Orbán on Defending Europeans and 'the Invasion of the Outsiders'." November 18. http://hungarianfreepress.com/2015/11/18/viktor-orban-on-defending-europeans-and-the-invasion-of-the-outsiders/. Accessed 30 March 2018.

Hungarian Helsinki Committee. 2018a. "Hungary: Key Asylum Figures for 2017." https://www.helsinki.hu/wp-content/uploads/HHC-Hungary-asylum-figures-1-January-2018.pdf. Accessed 8 August 2018.

Migszol. 2015. "Fidesz's National Consultation is No Consultation at All. It is a Shameless Piece of Propaganda". *Migszol Blog*. http://www.migszol.com/blog/fideszs-national-consultation-is-no-consultation-at-all-it-is-a-shameless-piece-of-propaganda-a-migszol-commentary. Accessed 8 August 2018.

Nolan, D. 2015. "Hungary Orders 100-Mile Serbia Border Fence To Keep Out Migrants." *The Telegraph*, June 17. https://www.telegraph.co.uk/news/worldnews/europe/hungary/11680840/Hungary-orders-100-mile-Serbia-border-fence-to-keep-out-migrants.html

Orbán, V. 2016. "Orbán Viktor sajtótájékoztatója az Európai Tanács ülését követően" (Viktor Orbán's Press Conference following the European Council's meeting), Government of Hungary, February 21. www.kormany.hu/hu/a-miniszterelnok/beszedek-publikaciok-interjuk/orban-viktor-sajtotajekoztatoja

OSCE. 2016. "The Housing Rights of Roma in Miskolc, Hungary." *Report on the ODIHR Field Assessment Visit to Hungary, 29 June–1 July 2015*. Warsaw: OSCE. https://www.osce.org/odihr/262026?download=true

Rajaram, P. K. 2015. "Beyond Crisis: Rethinking the Population Movements at Europe's Border." *FocaalBlog*, October 19. www.focaalblog.com/2015/10/19/prem-kumar-rajaram-beyond-crisis.

Rajaram, P. K. 2016. "Europe's 'Hungarian solution'," *Radical Philosophy* 197, Series 1. https://www.radicalphilosophy.com/commentary/europes-hungarian-solution.

Rorke, B. 2015. "The End of a Decade: What Happened to Roma Inclusion?" *Open Democracy*, September 29. https://www.opendemocracy.net/can-europe-make-it/bernard-rorke/end-of-decade-what-happened-to-roma-inclusion. Accessed 30 March 2018.

Rorke, B. 2016. "Segregation in Hungary: The Long Road to Infringement." *European Roma Rights Centre Blog*, May 30. http://www.errc.org/blog/segregation-in-hungary-the-long-road-to-infringement/106. Accessed 30 March 2018.

Szöke, A. 2015. "A 'Road to Work'? The Reworking Of Deservedness, Social Citizenship and Public Work Programmes in Rural Hungary." *Citizenship Studies* 19, no. 6–7: 734–750.

Tilly, C. 1982. "Warmaking and Statemaking as Organised Crime." *CROS Working Paper*, February, No 256. https://deepblue.lib.umich.edu/bitstream/handle/2027.42/51028/256.pdf.

Traynor, I. 2015. "Migration Crisis: Hungary PM says Europe in Grip of Madness." *The Guardian*, September 3. http://www.theguardian.com/world/2015/sep/03/migration-crisis-hungary-pm-victor-orban-europe-response-madness

Uitz, R. 2015. "Can You Tell When an Illiberal Democracy Is in the Making? An Appeal to Comparative Constitutional Scholarship from Hungary." *International Journal of Constitutional Law* 13, no. 1: 279–300.

CHAPTER 11

EAST ASIAN EXCEPTIONALISM TO WESTERN POPULISM AND MIGRATION CRISIS

JOHN LIE

In the late 2010s, erudite analysts would be forgiven for thinking that they live in the age of populism and migration crisis. Political mobilization across the European Union frequently feature strong nativist and anti-immigration sentiments. The same can be said about the rejuvenation of right-wing nationalism, with clear echoes of the fascist past, in France, Italy, Austria, Hungary, Poland, and elsewhere. Islamophobia in particular and xenophobia in general, especially against people from the Global South, dominate the airwaves and cyberspaces of the West. Indeed, as voiced by political leaders in France, Germany, and the United Kingdom—some of the wealthiest and most progressive of European polities—there is a widespread sentiment that multiculturalism seems to be failing, if not moribund (Chin 2017). In the United States, the rise of the Tea Party was followed by the unexpected ascension of Donald Trump. "Build the Wall" and "Make America Great Again"—the most oft-repeated slogans of the 2016 Trump presidential campaign—clearly pointed to the salience of a major migration crisis and an attempt to roll back the post-racial politics of the Obama era in the United States. Not surprisingly, social scientists have written scores of books on the rise of populism and the looming migration crisis (e.g., Bhabha 2018; Delsol 2015; Müller 2016). Political movements and intellectual discourses converge on the ostensibly global character of the migration crisis and the reactionary political drift.

From the perspective of East Asia—Northeast Asia (or China, Taiwan, North Korea, South Korea, and Japan) to be more accurate geographically (Lie 2018)—the specter of migration crisis in particular and that of populism in general is largely a Western—European and North American (primarily the United States)—affair. Beyond demonstrating Northeast Asian deviance from the Western norm in matters of migration and populist politics, this chapter will analyze the principal causes of the divergence and the potential for convergence in the near future.

Presence of Absence, or Absence of Presence

Common sense is remarkably difficult to demonstrate and prove. What is clear to *everyone*—or so it seems to the majority of the population in a given area—requires neither extended commentary nor even a statement of the obvious. The same set of common sense propositions remains, however, opaque to outsiders (showing thereby that those not in the know are outsiders). At the same time, it is much more challenging—indeed, impossible—to prove absence than presence.

Nevertheless, it is fair to say that—based on conversations, observations, and readings—problems of migration or refugees rank low on the issues that affect or concern Northeast Asians. The Pew Research Center's survey of global attitudes confirms my assertion (Poushter and Marevich 2017). Whether the threat is ISIS- or Islam-inspired terrorism or the topic is migrants or minorities that rankle Europeans and North Americans, Northeast Asians remain relatively unfazed. Moreover, there are no major political parties in Northeast Asia that focus on migration or refugee problems or even present themselves as overtly populist. It is not surprising that to the extent that there are books on populism or migration crisis they are about what is happening in the West (e.g., Miyajima 2016). It is not that educated Japanese or Chinese people are oblivious to the potential threat of Islam-inspired terrorism or upheavals around the world that generate refugees and asylum-seekers, but these issues are news and problems from elsewhere: the proverbial fire across the river. In short, it would take a heroic stretch of the political imagination to insist that the same sort of populist politics and migration concerns that embroil much of the West is salient in Northeast Asia.

Needless to say, political issues are matters of contested definition, which renders objective and neutral assertions or conclusions well nigh impossible. The word "populism"—imported as a Western political vocabulary and simply transliterated (that is, not even translated into native idiom)—does appear from time to time in analyses of East Asian politics. The Japanese political scientist Ōtake Hideo (2006), for example, described Prime Minister Koizumi Jun'ichirō's popularity in the first decade of the twenty-first century in terms of populism (see for Asia in general Phongpaichit and Mizuno 2009). Yet Koizumi's political rhetoric or appeal—in particular, his political demonology or the purported enemies of him and Japan—hardly matches or approaches those of the UK Independence Party, Front National, Alternative für Deutschland, or other contemporary Western populist parties. Whereas the European populists often highlight the threat or undesirability of long-standing minority groups or recent immigrants, Koizumi had virtually nothing to say about either. Neither did his political vision depict a golden past that Western populists are often so eager to recover. Koizumi was more popular than populist, at least from the vantage point of contemporary Western populism.

It seems axiomatic that contemporary Western populism revolves around the axis of "us" against "them," or "insiders" against "outsiders," and the effort to contain, if not expel, "them" and "outsiders" from the body politic in order to restore the status quo ante. The populist articulation of the analytic is in effect to tell the putative others to "go back to where you came from" so that "we have our country back" (cf. Bremmer 2018; Polakow-Suransky 2017). As presciently analyzed by Ulrich Beck (1986), the insider-outsider dichotomy begins to supersede the classic class-based divisions of the post–World War II era, which in turn was fueled by the supranational division of the Cold War in the postindustrial era. To be sure, the shift from "vertical" class-based politics to "horizontal" identity-based politics occludes the salience of the very definition of the "people" as at once against the elite and the others. One might rephrase August Bebel's quip that "populism (or anti-immigrant sentiments) is the socialism of fools," replacing the class enemy with the ethnoracial others (Bebel 1906). The reactionary tenor of Western populism stems from the desire to recover a past (usually, and implicitly, the Golden Age of post-World War II economic growth in the 1950s and 1960s) when the people flourished and the others hadn't arrived to spoil the purity of the nation. Be that as it may, the contemporary Western dynamic of populism usually targets ethnoracial and religious others, exemplified in the stock characters that have arrived recently: immigrants and refugees. The inevitable correlation between decline and impurity gives considerable emotional resonance to the populist appeal. It is precisely this dynamic and demonology that is not as salient in Northeast Asia as it is in the West in the early twenty-first century.

This essay is focused on the contemporary reality of Northeast Asia. The general situation in Southeast Asia—though one should be careful to generalize about such a vast and diverse region—is distinct from that of the West and Northeast Asia. As postcolonial and relatively poor countries, Southeast Asian states have achieved limited national integration. Nevertheless, there is a widespread sense that populism is on the rise in Southeast Asia (Case 2017), such as in Indonesia, Malaysia, and the Philippines (see, respectively, Heydarian 2018; Mietzner 2015; and Munro-Kua 2017). These instances, however, are far from approaching the Western norm of populist politics. The political demonology of the migration crisis that is central to Western populism is absent in Southeast Asia. All these countries with purported populist surges in Southeast Asia, after all, tend to send, rather than receive, international immigrants. Colonial experience—they were colonized, rather than colonizers—also skews their perspective on international politics. Rather than contemporary Western populism, the current Southeast Asian brand of populism champions a strong leader who can protect and promote the people against foreign and domestic elites. We should not confuse the rise of strong leaders in Southeast Asia with the rise of Western-style populism in the region.

To declare that populist politics or migration crisis is a global phenomenon is a product of ethnocentrism, usually but mistakenly called Eurocentrism (in the case of the US-based scholars, the more proper term would be Americacentrism or US-centrism). At least as of the late 2010s, we cannot talk at any length about a migration crisis or a surge of anti-immigration populist politics in Northeast Asia.

Tempting though it would be to finish this essay here, it is necessary to embark on two lines of thinking. First, why is it that there isn't anything approximating a migration crisis—or, for that matter, political populism—in contemporary Northeast Asia? Secondly, and necessarily more speculatively, is it possible that Northeast Asia will face in the near future something approaching a crisis over migration or something like populism that dominates the contemporary Western political landscape?

Nationalist Political Economy

One of the enduring political myths of modernity is the ideology of the nation-state (Lie, 2004). Widely regarded as the modal political form and the building block of international society (the United Nations is a society of societies or nation-states in popular reckoning), nowhere in the West is there a polity that comes close to approximating the ideal type of the nation-state (one nation, one ethnicity: not coincidentally the ideal of contemporary Western populists). After all, many Western polities were imperialist or colonial-settler societies in which the population was at once heterogeneous and hierarchical. For example, France colonized portions of Africa and Asia, and rendered the colonized subjects French in some sense but inferior to the metropolitan or homeland French people. The United States subjugated a native population and imported slaves from Africa and the Caribbean, along with workers from Europe and Asia. Even smaller European polities arose out of the feudal past as a conglomeration of distinct communities, as exemplified by Switzerland and its four official languages. It is indeed the case that modernity is largely coeval with nation making that included the formation of a standard national language and a sense of common peoplehood. Yet however powerful the call of patriotism and the pull of nationalism, Western polities nowhere came close to achieving a condition of ethnoracial homogeneity in the past or the present. Put another way, the purported ideal of contemporary Western populists is a mirage. It is only the recognition of recent arrivals, such as immigrants or refugees; or the amnesia of past arrivals, such as what we would today call Italians or Spanish today into France; or historical differences, such as the pervasive reality of regional distinction, that sustain the political myth of contemporary Western populism. That is, populists seek to restore a past that never was.

If we should turn our gaze to Northeast Asia, then what is striking is that the Western ideal of nationalism and its concept of the nation-state became not only normative but also came much closer to realization than in their birthplace. In part it is a product of the fervor of the converted and that Northeast Asian political elites were good students of Western political philosophy, but it is also in part the centrality of the state in forging industrial and infrastructural development in Northeast Asia. Later industrializing countries, as Alexander Gerschenkron (1962) influentially argued, rely more on the state, and less on individuals or corporations, in launching and sustaining economic development. Greater surveillance within the polity and at national borders reinforces the possibility of not only a nationalist labor market but also more effective control over population movements.

The political economy of Northeast Asian industrialization relied almost exclusively on domestic labor. Occurring after the end of Western imperial expansion and the carve-up of the non-Western world, with the exception of pre–World War II Japan, Northeast Asian polities had no extranational areas to colonize or extranational populations to exploit. Indeed, industrialization is largely a post–World War II phenomenon in Northeast Asia, again with the exception of Japan. Rapid and compressed industrialization spurts in post–World War II Japan were followed by South Korea and Taiwan from the 1960s and China from the 1980s. In each case, unlike the post–World War II experience in many European countries, such as France and Germany, domestic labor supply sufficed and obviated the need for foreign sources of labor. Domestic farmers or peasants became workers. The plentiful and inexpensive source of labor did not generate noticeable demands for foreign migrant workers. Nationalist political economy entailed a national labor market in East Asia.

A major consequence of the absence of Western-style colonialism is the relative absence of ex-colonials in Northeast Asia or a large flux of foreign workers or slaves, with the partial exception of Japan. There is no disputing the fact that contemporary Northeast Asia has relatively few ex-colonial or ex-migrant populations. Even the exception of Japan has come to prove the rule in Northeast Asia. After 1945, Japanese development relied almost exclusively on domestic labor. The combination of post–World War II nationalist economic experience and the distinct trajectories of ex-colonial identity formation has vitiated challenges to the idea of monoethnic Japan (Lie 2001). Okinawans, for example, have become ideologically assimilated to the majority Japanese population. Ethnic Koreans, the largest of the ex-colonial population, constitute perhaps 1 percent of the total Japanese population. In spite of considerable prejudice and discrimination against them by the dominant ethnic Japanese population, they are much more culturally and linguistically assimilated to the dominant Japanese norm than the largely post–World War II populations of European ex-colonial populations (Lie 2008). Beyond their small numbers, they have been relatively silent and invisible to the ethnic Japanese majority (Lie 2001). China and Taiwan or the two Koreas neither colonized another population nor relied on external sources of labor and therefore we don't find any notable ex-colonial population. Indeed, Northeast Asia was, at least until recently, more a region that sent emigrants rather than one that received immigrants. Consequently, there is hardly a backlash against—and sometimes even recognition of—ex- or postcolonial populations among native populations in Northeast Asia.

Thus industrialization process and state (and nation) making created a Northeast Asia in which its major nation-states approached the Western ideal of the nation-state much more closely than did their Western counterparts. The state as the focal point of identity construction, whether through the military or the school system, generates a powerful common identity qua national subjects or citizens (Lie 2004). Put simply, the role of the state was much more pervasive in modern Northeast Asian development than in modern European history. Not surprisingly, then, we find greater unification of language and schooling in Northeast Asia than in the West. Few Japanese, Koreans (North and South), or Chinese (or Taiwanese) deny the dominance of a majority ethnic group in the constitution of their country; they believe they live in a relatively ethnically homogeneous nation-state. Nationalist historiography in turn burnishes this mindset. Political and cultural nationalism became the base assumption of China (and Taiwan) and the two Koreas—however inconvenient that one nation should be divided into two polities—as well as Japan. The dominance of Han, Korean, and Japanese (Yamato) ethnicity within China (and Taiwan), the Koreas, and Japan, respectively, came to be taken for granted, which at times generated a belief in the existence of an ethnically homogeneous polity (for Japan, Lie 2001; for South Korea, Lie 2015; for North Korea, Myers 2010; for China, Carrico 2017). The pervasive belief in the nationalist constitution of the polity forged a nationalist policy mindset, including intermittent xenophobic practice and attitude. To be sure, the ineluctable reality of ethnic and linguistic diversity in China, as well as fealty to residual communist universalism, projected China as a multiethnic polity (Mullaney 2010). Imperial Japan was perforce multiethnic and post–World War II Japan remained multiethnic (Lie 2001). Nevertheless, by the latter decades of the twentieth century, all the polities shared the presumption that each Northeast Asian nation was a nation-state, and a relatively homogenous one to boot.

The answer to the first question I posed is that Northeast Asian political-economic development was nationalist in character and relied minimally on foreign migrant workers. There is no Western-style migration crisis in Northeast Asia because there are very few ex-colonials and a paucity of foreign migrant workers in contemporary Northeast Asia. As Sartre famously suggested, there don't need to be Jews in order to generate anti-Semitism, but the relatively small populations of foreign migrant workers have not led to strong anti-immigration discourses or movements in contemporary Northeast Asia.

Needless to say, there are other factors at work. Consider only the distinct experiential universes of modal Europeans and Northeast Asians. ISIS, Islam-inspired terrorism, and Islamophobia central to Western populism are largely absent in Northeast Asia, with the partial exception of China (which has a large Muslim population, especially in Xinjiang). As of the late 2010s, terrorist incidents are part of Western life; the same cannot be said of Northeast Asia. The major sources of the contemporary refugee crisis in West Asia and Africa are close to Europe but very far from Northeast Asia. As Syrians or Sudanese seek to escape their war-ravaged homeland, they strive largely to go to Europe and not to Northeast Asia (in part because of relative proximity but also because of existing conational populations and the relatively liberal asylum and refugee policy in some European polities). To be sure, nationalist ideology and policy have not opened doors readily for foreigners into Northeast Asia. In the mid 2010s, the total number of refugees in Japan was 21,941 and in China 317,927, whereas the figure for Germany was 1,268,885 and for France 368,887 (UNHCR 2017). Given the larger population size of

Northeast Asian nation-states, refugee and asylum intakes in Northeast Asian polities are mere fractions of those of their European counterparts (the German intake per capita is roughly seventy times that of China). Experientially, almost every German citizen would encounter a refugee or asylum-seeker in everyday life; the same cannot be said for her counterpart in Northeast Asia. As noted previously, the purported populist Prime Minister Koizumi was not ranting and raving against Filipino migrant workers or Muslim Indonesians in Japan. The political imaginaries of Northeast Asia are largely bereft of the sort of enemies and demons that populate the minds of Western populists.

In summary, there is nothing approaching a Western-style migration crisis in East Asia because the political, economic, and everyday reality in Northeast Asia—however diverse the character of each country—diverges from that in the West—again, however varied the experience of each polity. Not surprisingly, therefore, Western-style populist politics, which gains support from its anti-immigration, anti-minority, and anti-Islam stance, generates nary a ripple in Northeast Asia. The nature of political-economic development and the contingencies of geography and geopolitics explain the critical divergence between the West and Northeast Asia in the matter of anti-immigration and populist politics.

Beneath and Behind the Divergence

Appearance can be deceptive. Although there is nothing approaching Western populist parties or movements, it's not that there aren't rumblings similar in form and content to those in the West in Northeast Asia. Furthermore, nationalist rhetoric masks the discontents generated by massive rural exodus and intranational migration: internal or domestic immigrants face rhetoric and hostility similar in form and content to Western anti-immigrant rhetoric. That is, there are functional equivalents to Western populism and the migration crisis in Northeast Asia.

First, populism. In contemporary Japan, for instance, a particularly noxious source of nationalist and xenophobic discourse (and occasionally public demonstrations) is the internet-based right wing groups (*netto uyoku*). Operating under the cover of anonymity, bloggers and trolls lambaste liberal and left-wing figures, non–ethnic Japanese, and others deemed inimical to their image of nationalist Japan (Yasuda 2012). In the name of patriotism and protecting their country, they mercilessly attack purported enemies of Japan. Their particular ire is directed against ethnic Koreans in Japan—usually called Zainichi, largely an ex-colonial population—for their putative privileges. Needless to say, Zainichi have been subjected to considerable discrimination and do not enjoy special advantages in Japanese society today, but they serve as the racial other, akin to blacks or Muslims in the West (Lie 2008). The rhetoric of *netto uyoku* echoes right-wing nationalists and populists in the West who yearn for a nation devoid of racial or religious others and to return to the glories of the pristine nation that never was. In South Korea, internet trolls pillory neighboring Japanese and Chinese, immigrants, and non-Korean residents in South Korea, and express obscene misogyny (Dunn 2017). Similarly, in contemporary China there are the so-called Little Pinks (*xiao fenghong*), who canvass the full range of the contemporary social media to attack those deemed inimical to Chinese nationalist interest (Ruan 2016). Devoid of ex-colonial minority groups or Islam-inspired terrorists, they nevertheless target enemies of China. Popular targets include Japan, the erstwhile aggressor in the last major war, and racial and religious others, including those Chinese who are deemed insufficiently "Chinese" or patriotic. Although no one has conducted a systematic study, it is clear that the majority of internet trolls and US-style alt-right or right wing populist figures are younger men who rely primarily on the internet to air their grievances and exude their hatred (cf. Scheff and Schorr 2017). They evince more than a family resemblance to the political demonology of Western populists, seeking national functional equivalents or enemies of the nation to vent their venom.

Thus, closer and deeper scrutiny reveals nascent forms of Western-style populism across Northeast Asia. In the name of patriotism and the nation, would-be populists cast aspersions on those who defile or deviate from their image of the nation. Given the absence of viable political parties to represent or organize them, however, they have remained fringe figures that rely disproportionately on the internet to propagate their odious messages. For the reasons articulated in the previous section, they have so far failed to capture the political imagination of a significant slice of the population. The existence of proto-populist and anti-immigration voices in Northeast Asia should not be mistaken for their far-reaching influence. No Western-style populist is running for parliaments or commanding mass-media audiences. They remain, at least as of 2018, largely subterranean and marginal.

Secondly, the migration crisis. As I said, there are no major public concerns about immigration in contemporary Northeast Asia. However, this does not mean that there aren't serious social issues that impinge on migration. In the case of China, it is not an exaggeration to argue that its rapid economic development in the past three decades has rested on the shoulders of migrant workers: an instance of perhaps the largest and most compressed movement of human beings in history (cf. Miller 2012). The scale of intranational migration in China is staggering, involving roughly the entire population of the United States in the past four decades (International Organization for Migration 2018). Nationalist framing of immigration studies misses the indelible reality that internal migration was tantamount to being international migration, whether calibrated in terms of sheer physical distance traveled or cultural hurdles faced, such as the existence of distinct languages (linguistic diversity in China is greater than that in Europe, according to Ramsey 1987). What is indisputable is the magnitude of migration and attendant human suffering (Loyalka 2013). Yet class division and economic exploitation have not generated populist anger from below (Whyte 2010), but rather a growing and explicit disdain toward migrant workers expressed by the urban middle class (cf. Zavoretti 2016). Especially in large, littoral cities, there is a burgeoning sense that immigrants are overwhelming the city, which has contributed to their marginalization and even efforts at their removal (Haas 2017). Put differently, once we jettison the distinction between international and intranational migration, there is something approaching a migration problem in China, including open expressions of anti-immigrant sentiments. Nevertheless, we should be mindful that China is *not* a democratic polity. Any mass movement is under suspicion and surveillance, if not suppressed outright, by the Communist Party and the state. It is not a fertile ground for populism, unless mobilized from above, especially when the Communist Party seeks to elicit popular support.

In Japan, the situation, however functionally similar, is different. Rather than worrying about domestic migration—though it has occurred on a large scale in the past century—the concern is rather on the potential rise of foreign migrant workers. Indeed, Japan has had at least two prior instances of a near moral panic over immigration in the past half-century. In the early 1970s and in the late 1980s, there was great public attention on the rising number of foreign workers (Lie 2001). Ensuing economic downturn—the first the result of the oil crisis and the second the bursting of the property-speculation bubble—ended the potential panic. Although Japan is not experiencing a massive economic upsurge in the late 2010s, the declining youth population has led to a labor shortage. From convenience stores to elderly care facilities, the availability of relatively low-waged workers is a manifest labor-market shortage problem. In spite of serious efforts toward automation and robotics, Japan has faced an almost inevitable choice of loosening its restrictive international labor and migration policy. In the absence of explicit policy shift, there has in fact been de facto liberalization. The proportion of foreigners among the employed population in Japan has been growing steadily and is over 2 percent of the total employed population in the late 2010s. Not surprisingly, then, there are occasional, Western-style populist tirades about the dangerous encroachment of foreigners (e.g., Mitsuhashi 2017). The potential for the third immigration crisis in the post–World War II period is rife. However it does not exist, except, as emphasized before, largely in the world of cyberspace.

In the case of South Korea, the labor shortage in the past two decades has been met mostly by factory automation and the influx of ethnic Koreans from China. In spite of its nationalist tenor, the state has pursued globalization policies, including a relatively open policy toward marriage and even labor migrants (Lie 2015). The proportion of foreigners among South Koreans is over 3 percent, but the preponderance of co-ethnics has occluded the increasing heterogeneity of the labor force. In spite of the state effort to promote multicultural policy, there are significant problems for non-native South Koreans in adapting or assimilating to South Korea (Lie 2015). The patriotic and nationalist tenor of mainline South Korean politicians and indeed people contributes at times to xenophobic utterances that are not so distinct from right-wing nationalists and populists in the West. Cyberspace, not unlike in Japan, is replete with rabid anti-foreign utterances, especially against Japan and China.

What about the rest of Northeast Asia? North Korea is infamous for its closed, hermetic polity. To be sure, there were moments of openness in the 1950s and 1960s, true to its universalistic, communist origins and because of its patrons, including the Soviet Union and China. Nevertheless, its autarkic policy and persistent poverty have made the country unattractive to foreign migrant workers. Given the severe restrictions on freedom, including the internet, by the central government, it is difficult to detect any overt signs of populism or anti-immigration sentiments. North Korea lives at odds with capitalist globalization and has remained relatively free of its problems (as well as its benefits). What is clear is that North Korea's patriotic nationalist ideology has drummed insistently on the perfidies of other, especially neighboring, governments. The strength of nationalism, however, does not necessarily lead to a powerful expression of Western-style populism. In striking contrast, Taiwan has pursued a relatively open and liberal policy since its democratization in the 1980s. Its relative independence from mainland China is matched by its recognition of indigenous and minority populations on the island (Brown 2004; Yu and Li 2012). There is, in addition, considerable labor immigration. To be sure, one would be remiss to bypass small but insistent voices that articulate a Taiwanese permutation of populist, anti-immigration expressions: racism, sexism, and xenophobia. Yet it would be misleading to exaggerate the impact of the largely internet-based expressions of hatred in Taiwan.

In short, if we look especially to cyberspace, it is possible to find expressions of populism and anti-immigration discourse that, save for proper nouns in the gallery of enemies, reveal a family resemblance to those that are stridently expressed in the West. Stentorian though individual posts and blogs may be in Northeast Asia, it would be misleading to classify them as more than a marginal phenomenon at the present. After all, almost no major public organizations—political parties, religious groups, media outlets, and so on—espouse Western-style populism or highlight the threat of immigration. Whatever the orientation of the state toward international immigrants or anti-immigrant sentiments, the topic of migration hardly registers as a major problem, much less a crisis. Functional equivalents of Western populism and anti-immigration rhetoric exist, but there are no major organizations or movements that have significant consequences for national policy or public opinion in Northeast Asia to generate Western-style populism or migration crisis.

Migration Crisis in the Making?

Give the existence of proto-populist discourses and movements in Northeast Asia, might it be the case that a crisis is looming? In other words, is it just a matter of time before Northeast Asia will be awash with populist politics and the sort of migration crisis that has afflicted much of the West in the past decade?

A nationalist mindset, forged by decades of nationalist policy, is liable to contribute to populism but it has in fact tampered the influx of foreigners within Northeast Asian national borders. In this regard, factory automation, foreign investment, and outsourcing have been the primary tools of Japanese and South Korean corporations in the past several decades. In other words, there hasn't been much of an effort to encourage the influx of low-paid workers from abroad. Similarly, outside of manufacturing, Japanese state policy has steadfastly encouraged automation, including robotics, and other means that do not rely on the influx of foreign workers in care work. China, in contrast, continues to have a large supply of domestic labor. Unless there is a massive crisis or a major economic growth spurt, then, it is unlikely that Northeast Asia will see a significant increase in the influx of foreign migrant workers. Certainly, few domestic workers express concern about employment competition from foreign migrant workers in contemporary Northeast Asia. There are minority groups that bear the burden of the dominant ethnic group's ire and are often cast as black sheep of the nation. Yet precisely because only Japan had an empire, neither China (and Taiwan) nor the two Koreas have any substantial body of people to whom the would-be populist can inveigh to "go back to where you came from." As noted, Japan, for instance in the case of Zainichi, is a partial exception.

It is clear that a migration crisis isn't born just from the presence of ethnic others or migrant workers. Yet the major vectors of East Asian politics remain inimical to the efflorescence of Western-style populism. ISIS and kindred Islamic-related terrorist organizations rarely target East Asia. Neither are Northeast Asians avid supporters of radical Islam's enemies, such as Israel, nor are they believed to be anti-Arab or anti-Islam by the Arab and Muslim world. Furthermore, nowhere in Northeast Asia is an ethnic minority group a serious political force. As I have noted, ethnoracial others remain largely invisible and silent to the vast majority of the dominant ethnic group in each nation-state. Instead what provokes Northeast Asians tends to be the perfidies of neighboring polities and peoples. Internet-based youths often engage in aggressive rhetoric against neighboring polities and peoples. Although intra-Asian enmity remains rife and at times kindles major conflagrations, the general trend is toward mutual accommodation and acceptance (Lie 2018).

More importantly, Northeast Asian domestic politics remain oriented in such a way as to lessen the likelihood of populist politics that focus on the problem of migration (see in general Lie 2018). In China, the fundamental gravity of politics centers on the Communist Party. That is, politics in China is all about whether one supports the Party or critical of it. The centrality of the Communist Party makes nearly all major political issues matters of Party affairs and policies, whether corruption or pollution, economic inequality or press freedom. In South Korea, the politics of the left and the right, based on Cold War divisions, remains the basic grammar of politics. That is, the division that became crystallized during the 1970s and 1980s—between supporters of conservative, growth-oriented political economy and those against—continues to inform and energize South Korean politics. In this context, there is a curious convergence between the left and the right on the generally pro-globalization and pro-multiculturalist policies of the past two decades in South Korea. In Japan, the predominance of the Liberal Democratic Party ensures the continuation of the status quo ante, albeit with considerable disagreements and discontent. Given the prevailing presumption of a relatively ethnically homogenous polity, the very idea that ethnicity or immigration is a major social issue is alien to the dominant Japanese mindset. In all three cases, then, the basic issues in politics are insistently involuted and domestic in orientation. Thus, the valorization of a foreign threat, such as the way Islamic radicalism operates in Europe, or a threat within, such as foreign migrant workers, is marginal and unlikely to mobilize the populace. Put differently, populist politic is likely to remain a sideshow in Northeast Asia because dominant concerns and assumptions bypass the politics of migration or minority policy.

Politics in the West has tended to rely less on class-based divisions and conflicts (and international politics on the Cold War division), and increasingly more on subnational concerns and divisions, especially those that differentiate insiders from outsiders. Yet we should not ignore the background of class-based politics—against the premodern aristocracy or the modern capitalists—that in part fuels the contemporary populist rage. There is, as I said, a widespread nostalgia for the Golden Age: post-World War II economic growth that not only enriched many but also occurred in the context of postwar recovery, stability, and imagined homogeneity. More recently, the influx of foreign migrant workers and the postcolonial arrival of ex-colonial immigrants have accentuated the rift between "us" and "them," overlaid as it is by ethnoracial, religious, and other differences. The situation in Northeast Asia is different. Precisely because national integration is more complete and there are relatively few ex-colonial or foreign migrant workers, the main focus of Northeast Asian polities tends to be insistently domestic in orientation. Yet Northeast Asia is not only largely devoid of ex-colonial migrant populations but also class enemies, whether premodern nobles or modern capitalists. The weakness of class politics occurs in the context where the idea of progress remains potent. Put simply, with the partial exception of Japan, very few people in Northeast Asia are looking fondly back on the golden past but rather striving for a wealthier, better future. There is very little room for populist-style nostalgia in Northeast Asia. As I have stressed, to the extent that external threat is mooted, it is usually all about its immediate neighbors.

Needless to say, the future is perforce uncertain. It may very well be that Japan and South Korea will experience a surge in foreign migrant workers, which in turn may generate populist anti-immigration politics. Minority movements in China may escalate and generate counterminority discourse among the majority Han population. Who knows what sort of havoc a major economic or environmental crisis will wreak on Northeast Asia and cause in turn unfathomable consequences? Yet, at least in the coming decade or so, it is unlikely that populist politics or anti-immigration discourse will become significant in Northeast Asian polities.

References

Bebel, A. 1906 [1893]. *Antisemitismus und Sozialdemokratie*. Berlin: Buchhandlung Vorwärts.
Beck, U. 1986. *Risikogesellschaft*. Frankfurt am Main: Suhrkamp.
Bhabha, J. 2018. *Can We Solve the Migration Crisis?* Cambridge, UK: Polity.
Bremmer, Ian. 2018. *Us vs. Them*. New York: Portfolio.
Brown, M. J. 2004. *Is Taiwan Chinese?* Berkeley: University of California Press.
Carrico, K. 2017. *The Great Han*. Oakland: University of California Press.

Case, W. 2017. *Populist Threats and Democracy's Fate in Southeast Asia*. Abingdon, UK: Routledge.

Chin, R. 2017. *The Crisis of Multiculturalism in Europe*. Princeton, NJ: Princeton University Press.

Delsol, C. 2015. *Populisme*. Paris: Rocher.

Dunn, M. 2017. "South Korea's Alt-Right." *The Chronicle*, September 25. https://www.thechronicle.com.au/news/south-koreas-alt-right-trolls-extremists-and-paedo/3227662/

Gerschenkron, A. 1962. *Economic Backwardness in Historical Perspective*. Cambridge, US: Harvard University Press.

Haas, B. 2017. "China's 'Ruthless' Campaign To Evict Beijing's Migrant Workers Condemned." *The Guardian*, November 26. https://www.theguardian.com/world/2017/nov/27/china-ruthless-campaign-evict-beijings-migrant-workers-condemned

Heydarian, R. J. 2018. *The Rise of Duterte*. Singapore: Palgrave Macmillan.

International Organization for Migration. 2018. *World Migration Report 2018*. http://www.iom.int/wmr/world-migration-report-2018

Lie, J. 2001. *Multiethnic Japan*. Cambridge, US: Harvard University Press.

Lie, J. 2004. *Modern Peoplehood*. Cambridge, US: Harvard University Press.

Lie, J. 2018. *The Dream of East Asia*. Ann Arbor, MI: Association for Asian Studies.

Lie, J., ed. 2015. *Multiethnic (South) Korea?* Berkeley: Institute of East Asian Studies, University of California, Berkeley.

Loyalka, M. D. 2013. *Eating Bitterness*. Berkeley: University of California Press.

Mietzner, M. 2015. *Reinventing Asian Populism*. Honolulu: East-West Center.

Miller, T. 2012. *China's Urban Billion*. London: Zed.

Mitsuhashi, T. 2017. *Imaya sekai 5i*. Tokyo: Tokuma Shoten.

Miyajima T. 2016. *Gendai Yōroppa to imin mondai no genten*. Tokyo: Akashi Shoten.

Mullaney, T. S. 2010. *Coming to Terms with the Nation*. Berkeley: University of California Press.

Müller, J- W. 2016. *Was Ist Populismus?* Frankfurt am Main: Suhrkamp.

Munro-Kua, A. 2017. *Authoritarian Populism in Malaysia*. Selangor, Malaysia: SUARAM.

Myers, B. R. 2010. *The Cleanest Race*. Brooklyn, NY: Melville House.

Ōtake, H. 2006. *Koizumi Jun'ichirō popyurizumu no kenkyū*. Tokyo: Tōyō Keizai Shinpōsha.

Phongpaichit, P., and K. Mizuno, eds. 2009. *Populism in Asia*. Kyoto: Kyoto University Press.

Polakow-Suransky, S. 2017. *Go Back to Where You Came From*. London: Hurst.

Poushter, J., and D. Marevich. 2017. "Globally, People Point to ISIS and Climate Change as Leading Security Threats." Pew Research Center, August 1. http://www.pewglobal.org/2017/08/01/globally-people-point-to-isis-and-climate-change-as-leading-security-threats/.

Ramsey, S. R. 1987. *The Languages of China*. Princeton, NJ: Princeton University Press.

Ruan, L. 2016. "The New Face of Chinese Nationalism." *Foreign Policy*, August 21. http://foreignpolicy.com/2016/08/25/the-new-face-of-chinese-nationalism/.

Scheff, S., and M. Schorr. 2017. *Shame Nation*. Naperville, IL: Source Books.

UNHCR. 2017. *Statistical Yearbook 2016*. http://www.unhcr.org/en-us/statistics/country/5a8ee0387/unhcr-statistical-yearbook-2016-16th-edition.html.

Whyte, M. K. 2010. *Myth of the Social Volcano*. Stanford, CA: Stanford University Press.

Yasuda, K. 2012. *Netto to aikoku*. Tokyo: Kōdansha.

Yu, G., and L. Li, eds. 2012. *Taiwan shao shu min zu*. Fuzhou, China: Fujian renmin chubanshe.

Zavoretti, R. 2016. *Rural Origins, City Lives*. Seattle: University of Washington Press.

PART III

CONTEXTS OF PROTRACTED CONFLICTS: PRODUCING CRISES

CHAPTER 12

CENTRAL AMERICAN REFUGEES REVEAL THE CRISIS OF THE STATE

LEISY J. ABREGO

On August 10, 2016, twenty-two Central American women detained at the Berks County Residential Center in Pennsylvania penned an open letter directed at then Secretary of Homeland Security, Jeh Johnson: "The reason for this letter is to inform you that since Monday, August 8, we have begun a hunger strike to protest our indefinite detention . . ."[1] Among other things, their letter contained details about their suffering and their children's suicidal thoughts borne of confinement. Just over two years prior to their hunger strike, President Obama had referred to people like them as constituting an "urgent humanitarian situation." He qualified the "significant rise in apprehensions and processing of minors and individuals from Central America" as a "humanitarian crisis" that required the United States to take "aggressive steps" to "deter both adults and children from this dangerous journey, increase capacity for enforcement and removal proceedings, and quickly return unlawful migrants to their home countries."

This chapter analyzes President Obama's and his Administration's language of "crisis" to establish migrants as the problem while simultaneously erasing the role of US policies in the region that make migration necessary. The true "crisis" is rooted in historical and contemporary US intervention in Central America that, along with elite accomplices in the region, ensures widespread poverty, insecurity, and human rights abuses. It is what allows crime to be so pervasive and deadly in El Salvador, Guatemala, and Honduras. That true crisis is the foundation of all of the involved states—the countries of birth, transit, and desired destination—that repeatedly fail to protect human rights.

These states have perpetually not enforced international human rights protections for some of the most vulnerable populations, thereby leaving individuals with no option but to use their own bodies to respond to and make visible these crises of the state. It is in this context that Central Americans, including poor women and children, are leaving everything behind in their home countries to cross international borders in search of safety and stability. Later, for those who are able to reach the United States, human rights abuses in detention force them once again to use their own bodies to denounce injustice.

The Language of Crisis

At the level of organizations and in the realm of international relations, among other things, a situation is considered a crisis when it threatens some of the most important values of an organization and is unanticipated (Farah and Meacham 2015, 64). A crisis, moreover, requires action and change at a moment of extreme behavior and even if there are insufficient resources (Farah and Meacham 2015). In the case of the Central American refugees and asylum-seekers, President Obama loosely labeled the rise in border apprehensions as a "humanitarian situation"(White House 2014).[2] As it is listed in the White House digital archives for the Obama Presidency, even the title of that first letter to congressional leaders on June 30, 2014 includes the term, "humanitarian situation." The text of the letter went on to use this phrase three more times. Toward the bottom of the letter, as Obama neared the section in which he proposed next steps, he used the more definitive term, "humanitarian *crisis*" (White House 2014).[3] To match the language of "humanitarian" situation and crisis, the President ended the letter by proposing solutions geared toward what he qualified as "*humanitarian standards* for detention of adults with children" (White House 2014).[4]

At the outset of the letter, President Obama requested Congress' support for "new tools and resources . . . to implement a unified, comprehensive Federal Government response" to this "urgent humanitarian situation." He went on to state that while migration in general was at historically low levels, the isolated problem now was specifically confined to the "Rio Grande Valley area of the Southwest border." It is there, he noted, that children and individuals from Central America were crossing into the United States. The crux of the crisis, as he identified it in this letter, was that migrants "who embark upon this perilous journey are subject to violent crime, abuse, and extortion as they rely on dangerous human smuggling networks to transport them through Central America and Mexico" (White House 2014). The various forms of violence and criminal activities he associated with this particular group of migrants (even if he portrayed them in that instance as the targets rather than as the perpetrators of these acts) were what threatened the United States' purported humanitarian values.

The text may also be interpreted to suggest implicitly that within the United States, the government was doing its job competently to limit migration levels to historic lows. This particular group of people, then, was now bringing in and causing the "crisis" in an unanticipated way. That is, their very presence and the associated problems of violence were what constituted the crisis. Had they not entered the country, there would not now be an urgent need to consider solutions, as the letter suggested that the violence that happened to them took place in the distant and distinct spaces of Central America and

Mexico—places that the border clearly and efficiently demarcates and detaches from the United States.

As is typical of other instances of crises, the decontextualized language of crisis in this case suggests that the phenomenon is new, unexpected, unpredictable, and therefore something that no one could have prepared for in advance. In Obama's letter, the fact that he juxtaposed the increase in Central American migration with historic lows of overall migration implies that the United States was successfully controlling migration otherwise and could not have foreseen the present "crisis." In reality, however, the migration of Central Americans traveling by land through Mexico to the United States was not new. Children and adults had moved through this Mexican route to the United States since at least the 1980s (Jonas and Rodríguez 2015). More recently, since 2009 the United Nations High Commissioner on Refugees (UNHCR 2014, 2015) had been tracking a steady rise in the number of migrant adults and children from Central America to the United States, documenting the perils and extensively explaining the immediate reasons propelling increased migration.

The decontextualized language of crisis in Obama's approach did not recognize the reality of a steady increase in migration from Central America. Instead, as is true in most crises, his language suggested a need to act quickly, even if haphazardly to respond. He reassured congressional leaders that the quick response would be informed by "humanitarian standards." This rhetorical approach underscored the need for leniency from leaders and the public as the Administration presented itself as working hard to quickly and thoughtfully solve the problem, guided by humanitarian standards that are purportedly a core value of the United States.

Crisis as Opportunity

The erroneously framed crisis permitted questionable logic that ushered in problematic policies and practices of enforcement. Although he described the dangerous conditions of migration as the source of the problem, in the letter President Obama went on to propose policy solutions aimed almost entirely at deterrence and enforcement. The crisis, as he had laid it out, now served to justify a call for a "surge of resources" for the Department of Justice (DOJ) and the Department of Homeland Security (DHS) where "[p]art of this surge will include detention of adults traveling with children." And even at the earliest moments of ascertaining the situation, President Obama relayed that DHS was already "working to secure additional space that satisfies applicable legal and humanitarian standards for detention of adults with children."

Indeed, at every step of delineating the problem and proposing solutions, Obama circled around to family detention as a central response. He claimed that his goal was to establish forms of deterrence to prevent the victimization of migrants in transit, but in what can only be described as dubious logic, proposed mainly the use and expansion of detention centers. Completely disregarding the well-being of migrants whose insecurity and victimization he had explicitly acknowledged, he suggested that detention was necessary as it allowed authorities to weed out those who should legally be protected from those who should be promptly removed. After portraying the violence against migrants in transit as the crux of the crisis, he proposed a more institutionalized form of continued violence, through the deprivation of freedom for adults and children. Indeed, Obama would go on to deceptively use this crisis as an opportunity to vastly expand the practice of family detention (Hernández 2015; Lovato 2016). Today this deterrence approach continues to guide both the United States and Mexico's policies toward Central American refugees and asylum-seekers (Correa-Cabrera and Clark 2016; Kovic and Kelly 2017).[5]

Beyond the expansion of family detention, Obama also proposed increased funding for law enforcement domestically and abroad. As he justified, a US response needed "to attack the criminal organizations and smuggling rings that are exploiting these individuals," even if in practice it was at the expense of the migrants' safety in their home countries, in transit, and in the United States. Setting aside the dire economic and insecurity situation refugees were fleeing in their homelands, Obama's response focused solely on "surging law enforcement task forces . . . with a focus on stepped-up interdiction and prosecution."

In the entirety of Obama's letter, there was no mention of the ways the United States was significantly to blame for the mass exodus from Central America. The letter suggested that in this sudden and unexpected context of crisis, the United States was forced to better fund regional law enforcement efforts when, in fact, it had spent years funding and supporting similar programs in the region. The Obama Administration's speeches and most publicized actions willfully omitted the long history of the United States' role in propping up and defending the very policies that were arguably at the root of rising migration.

The Crisis of US Intervention

One way to ascertain the role of the US government in propelling Central American migration is to consider its history of intervention through foreign assistance. According to a 2012 report by the Congressional Research Service, a congressional think tank that conducts nonpartisan legal and policy research and analysis for members of the congress, "[f]oreign assistance is one of the tools the United States employs to advance US interests in Latin America and the Caribbean, and the focus and funding levels of aid programs change along with broader US policy goals" (Hornbeck 2012, 2). Due to its geographic proximity, the United States has often understood Latin America to constitute something akin to its backyard. Motivated by a desire to establish and maintain profitable conditions for US interests, the United States has used various means to control the economic and political landscapes of the region: from helping Panama gain independence from Colombia with the sole purpose of building an interoceanic canal

(Greene 2009), to staging numerous coups d'état and propping up puppet governments throughout the region (Booth et al. 2015). As the Congressional Research Service corroborates, US governments have pursued different strategies to protect US economic and security interests in the region, depending on changing conditions globally and in Central America:

> U.S. assistance to the region spiked in the early 1960s following the introduction of President John F. Kennedy's Alliance for Progress, an antipoverty initiative that sought to counter Soviet and Cuban influence in the aftermath of Fidel Castro's 1959 seizure of power in Cuba. After a period of decline, U.S. assistance to the region increased again following the 1979 assumption of power by the leftist Sandinistas in Nicaragua. Throughout the 1980s, the United States provided considerable support to Central American governments battling leftist insurgencies to prevent potential Soviet allies from establishing political or military footholds in the region. US aid flows declined in the mid-1990s following the dissolution of the Soviet Union and the end of the Central American conflicts.
>
> (Hornbeck 2012, 2–3)

The "considerable support" of the United States in the 1980s funded military efforts in Guatemala's civil war where they sponsored genocide against Mayan communities who suffered the majority of the estimated 200,000 murders (McAllister and Nelson 2013).[6] In neighboring El Salvador, US funding provided military training and equipment for a civil war that ended with 75,000 deaths and tens of thousands disappeared (Booth et al. 2015). In each case, neighboring Honduras was the training base from which the US government could closely keep an eye on the operations it supported nearby, with harmful geopolitical consequences for the country (Portillo Villeda 2011). In all cases, natural and human resources, as well as infrastructure, were vastly destroyed.

Following its heavy military investment in the region, rather than increasing assistance to facilitate a robust stabilization process in the critical postwar years, the United States moved instead to quickly divest. Having ensured that its enemy, the Soviet Union, would not have much influence in the region, US interest in the region waned. Already devastated and now without US aid, El Salvador, Guatemala, and Honduras could do little to rebuild their infrastructure. Unable to strengthen social institutions, the region only saw worsening conditions. The consequences have been dire, as partially documented by the Congressional Research Service:

> A legacy of conflict and authoritarian rule has inhibited the development of democratic institutions and respect for the rule of law in many countries. Protracted armed conflicts also resulted in the widespread proliferation of illicit firearms in the region, as well as a cultural tendency to resort to violence as a means of settling disputes. Some former combatants have put the skills they acquired during their countries' armed conflicts to use in the service of criminal groups. In El Salvador, for example, illicit networks that smuggled arms and other supplies to

> both sides involved in the armed conflict have been converted into transnational criminal networks that smuggle drugs, people, illicit proceeds, weapons, and other stolen goods.
>
> (Meyer and Seelke 2015, 5)

The "legacy of conflict and authoritarian rule" is not natural to the region, but rather placed there through uneven US intervention that funds destabilization and wanes when support is needed for reconstruction. Indeed, US intervention has "inhibited the development of democratic institutions"; every time there has been a democratically elected leader in the region who sought to improve the life chances of their people, the United States moved decisively to protect their economic interests, often violently replacing leaders (Booth et al. 2015). As a result, what the report labels a "cultural tendency to resort to violence as a means of settling disputes" was borne of impossible social, political, and economic contexts imposed through US intervention. In fact, it was US military training that provided former combatants with the "skills" (including torture techniques and scorched earth tactics) that they must now "use in the service of criminal groups" because their countries have not recovered from the devastation of "protracted armed conflicts." Moreover, the necessary infrastructure that would allow them to live dignified lives does not exist (McAllister and Nelson 2013; Moodie 2010).

Without assistance from the United States, the end of armed conflicts brought about greater societal problems. Along with widespread poverty, trauma from war, and physical devastation, as the Congressional Research Service asserts, "[t]he failure to fully implement post-conflict institutional reforms that were initiated in several countries in the 1990s has left police, prisons, and judicial systems weak and susceptible to corruption" (Meyer and Seelke 2015, i). Without fair and well-funded resolutions, it is no coincidence, therefore, that today these countries are among the poorest and most dangerous in the world, expelling their children and families in mass numbers. US intervention, through uneven foreign assistance, played a crucial role in the long-term destabilization of the region.

Free Trade and Security

Years later, in what could arguably be considered a move to maintain their capitalist interests (The Mesoamerican Working Group 2013; Osuna 2015), following the sharp decline in aid to the region in the post-conflict 1990s, US intervention was evident once again through assistance that "remained on a generally upward trajectory through the first decade of this century" (Hornbeck 2012, i). Under the guise of battling the international Drug War, the United States moved to closely monitor the region to protect conditions for profitable free trade ventures by funding law enforcement efforts.

Given its geographic proximity, Central America was once again of interest to the United States in the mid 2000s. In July 2005, under the George W. Bush Administration, Congress passed the Dominican Republic-Central America-United States Free Trade Agreement (CAFTA-DR). Central American countries ratified it on a rolling basis from 2006 through 2009. Although the United States expected only marginal financial gains, it established CAFTA-DR to take advantage of the "differences in wages, skills, and productivity" across the region (Hornbeck 2005, 4). In 2012, the Congressional Research Service explained the United States' continued interest in free trade in Central America:

> By removing regional barriers to trade, CAFTA-DR encouraged the development of specialized coproduction in assembly manufacturing between the United States and CAFTA-DR countries based on comparative advantage and economies of scale. . . .Firm competitiveness rests on value-added supply chain relationships, particularly in the area of apparel manufacturing, later extended to automobile parts, medical equipment, integrated circuits, and other products. Tariff preferences under CAFTA-DR . . . have helped [US] firms remain marginally competitive with Asian and other low-cost global producers.
>
> (Hornbeck 2012, 2)

US firms, therefore, are able to take advantage of cheap labor and no tariffs to compete in manufacturing with economic competitor nations in other parts of the world. It is on the backs of Central American labor, while ensuring their poor working conditions and poverty wages, that US corporations gain a slight competitive edge in the global market.

One of the central features of free trade is the ability to move goods quickly across borders. In the apparel industry, for example, a steady and endless progression of fashion trends is most profitable when large orders are met almost instantaneously (Canizales 2015). Products must be made, transported, and stocked in retail stores to sell to zealous consumers immediately. In that process, the proximity between the United States and Central America can make a difference in helping US companies beat out other "low-cost global producers" only if the goods can move quickly without unnecessary delays across borders. Free trade agreements ensure speedy border crossings for such goods.

To optimize corporate profits, conditions for workers and their families must worsen. CAFTA-DR brought in agricultural competition that devastated rural livelihoods (Behrens 2009). This increased the availability of cheap and flexible labor as workers were forced to turn to maquiladoras—one of the few areas of job growth in their countries—for survival. But maquiladoras also pay poverty wages (CISPES 2017). Unable to thrive in such poor working conditions and under poverty wages leads to other problems for workers. In such a dearth of opportunities, for example, the drug trade becomes an option for financial stability. The growth in this trade, in turn, leads to greater violence and insecurity. Migration, therefore, also becomes more likely as financial and physical instability trickles down to shape every aspect of daily life (Menjívar 2011; Moodie 2010).

In conjunction with free trade, the US government must also implement security measures to protect profits and facilitate border crossings for goods while blocking the path for potential migrants (Behrens 2009).[7] Shortly after CAFTA was ratified by the countries of the so-called Northern Triangle of Central America, in 2007 the Bush Administration implemented the Mérida Initiative, a bilateral partnership with Mexico focused among other things on "(1) disrupting organized criminal groups, (2) institutionalizing the rule of law, (3) [and] creating a 21st -century border" (Seelke and Finklea 2017, i). To protect US interests through the North American Free Trade Agreement (NAFTA), the program provided funding mostly for Mexico but shaped the experiences of Central Americans, as well. Besides also providing limited funding to Central America, the Mérida Initiative's goal to create a "21st-century border" helped to militarize Mexico's southern border with Guatemala, leading to increased risks for Central American migrants on that journey (Behrens 2009).

Most of the $1.6 billion of US assistance to Mexico through the Mérida Initiative to date is earmarked for "security and public safety" (Seelke and Finklea 2017, i). Funding has enabled:

> the purchase of equipment to support the efforts of federal security forces (military and police). That equipment included $590.5 million worth of aircraft and helicopters. US assistance focused on (1) counternarcotics, border security, and counterterrorism; (2) public security and law enforcement; and (3) institution building and the rule of law.
>
> (Seelke and Finklea 2017, 9)

Prior to the Cold War, US aid to Latin America, even when it was mostly focused on supporting the military, also supported, at least to a small degree, social programs to help alleviate poverty. As is evident in this breakdown in the report of the Congressional Research Service, however, since the Cold War, money has been more exclusively geared toward militarization, security, and law enforcement. In the case of the Mérida Initiative, it was only when "US Congressional leaders complained about the secrecy of negotiations . . . and the absence of human rights guarantees" that they were able to include the comparatively small sum of $1 million (out of over $1 billion) in the package to support human rights groups in Mexico (Behrens 2009).

The Mérida Initiative, which provided counterdrug and anticrime assistance mainly to Mexico, also granted limited funding to Central America. In 2010, shortly after all the nations of the region had ratified CAFTA-DR, "the Obama Administration re-launched the Central America portion of the Mérida Initiative as the Central America Regional Security Initiative (CARSI)" (Meyer and Seelke 2015, 1). CARSI was designed to address a broad array of "security concerns." Since 2008, the US government had, through the Mérida Initiative and through CARSI, been providing Central American nations:

> with equipment, training, and technical assistance to support immediate law enforcement operations. CARSI is also designed to strengthen the long-term capacities

> of Central American governments to address security challenges and the underlying social and political factors that contribute to them. Since FY2008, Congress has appropriated nearly $1.2 billion for Central America through CARSI.
>
> (Meyer and Seelke 2015, ii)

Well before the inaccurately depicted "crisis" of Central American migrants in the summer of 2014, then, the United States was aware of and purportedly invested in fixing the deep security problems of the region.

Assistance for military and law enforcement efforts to protect free trade-based profits had been in place since at least 2008, yet insecurity continued unabated, establishing the conditions that forced people to migrate in search of survival. On May 4, 2013, for example, a year before the "crisis" had caught the attention of mainstream media, Obama's Administration released a Fact Sheet declaring some forms of ongoing US support in the region (White House Press Secretary 2013). Titled, "FACT SHEET: United States Support for Central American Citizen Security," this document provided a list of eight US priorities in the region, seven of which were law-enforcement-centered. Only one of the eight areas of priority mentioned services, including vocational training and life skills development for youth in high-risk communities. Even after years of US assistance for law enforcement, the unauthorized movement across international borders of tens of thousands of people in the coming years would reveal the depth of the failure of these nation-states to protect the human rights of the most vulnerable in these societies.

"Root Causes" of Migration

Just a year later, soon after mainstream media released images of young children in overcrowded holding cells near the US southern border in June 2014 (*PBS* 2014), President Obama dubiously identified a new crisis. In response, he proposed to "stem the flow of migrants taking the dangerous trip to the United States" (White House 2014), by pursuing an agenda that in fact merely ramped up the failed law enforcement efforts his Administration (and several previous presidential administrations before him) had been investing in for years. In a White House Fact Sheet released on June 20, 2014, the administration laid out its proposed budget of assistance to deal with "root causes" of migration from Central America (White House Press Secretary 2014). Funding allocation suggests that the Obama administration understood root causes as applying mainly to security issues—the very same security issues that were created largely through uneven US intervention. For example, In Honduras, under CARSI, they proposed to "provide $18.5 million to support community policing and law enforcement efforts to confront gangs and other sources of crime" (White House Press Secretary 2014). Illogically, though perhaps unsurprisingly, what they deem to be solutions to this "crisis" of migration are more of the same: funding law enforcement, increasing the budget for policing, targeting gangs, and generally taking a crime and violence approach.

Another central "solution" that received a surge of resources under Obama's leadership was the expansion of detention practices in the United States. His immediate proposal in the face of the "crisis" consisted of seven points, the first five of which were exclusively related to enforcement. He called for more authority for the DHS Secretary; increased penalties for smugglers; an "aggressive" strategy for the removal of and repatriation of recent border crossers; sustained border security and enhanced domestic enforcement; and an increased number of immigration judges. It was only in the sixth point that Obama mentioned, embedded within a list of various efforts in the home countries, the need to address "root causes." He then ended the list with a call for "the resources necessary to appropriately detain, process, and care for children and adults."

The targets for this expanded system of detention were the incoming refugees. In fiscal year 2014, over 66,000 children and another 66,000 families arrived to the United States (UNHCR 2015). The numbers increased the following year. When asked why they were fleeing their homelands, refugees cited brutal domestic violence as well as "pervasive and systemic levels of violence" from gangs, criminal armed groups, and authorities (UNHCR 2015, 15). In the minds of refugees, the root causes of their flight were the direct violence they witnessed and survived, as well as their lack of trust in what they perceived as corrupt or inept governments. For example, in many cases, refugees gave testimony that state authorities were direct perpetrators, especially against women, or that they worked in conjunction with armed criminals, such as gangs (UNHCR 2015, 23). Children, similarly, flee violence in their neighborhoods and in their homes, though many also migrate to reunite with parents (UNHCR 2014, 7). Like all of the violent symptoms that migrants cite as reasons for fleeing, family separation through migration is also a consequence of various forms of US intervention in Central America (Abrego 2014).

Speaking to the details of each Central American state's failure to protect its citizens, a 2015 report from the bipartisan policy-focused think tank, Center for Strategic & International Studies, notes that:

> Although the United States allocated $642 million for the Central America Regional Security Initiative (CARSI) from 2008–2013, the region's security conditions have continued to deteriorate. The most dramatic demonstration of the security situation's sharp downward spiral was the 2014 mass exodus of tens of thousands of unaccompanied minors from the Northern Triangle across the U.S. border. The crisis of governance is currently seen in the mass protests, the most widespread and persistent in decades in the region, demanding an end to the pervasive corruption that touches every aspect of life and the impunity that allows the corruption to flourish.
>
> (Farah and Meacham 2015, vi)

Indeed, the regional security crisis (stated as a "crisis of governance" in this piece) is a problem that has been well funded yet woefully unimproved—if not deeply exacerbated—by the United States for years. In El Salvador, for example, people were fleeing and dying at the same rate in 2016 as they did during the country's civil war (Lakhani 2016). Without support from authorities or protection from the state, refugees can do little more than remove themselves from the situation through unauthorized migration (UNHCR 2015).

Many of those fleeing and later being detained in Mexico and the United States are women. Women in Central America are especially vulnerable as femicide rates in El Salvador, Guatemala, and Honduras are among the highest in the world (Walsh and Menjívar 2016). Even when rights for women are inscribed in the law, they are not upheld in practice. Widespread impunity speaks volumes as the state's inaction to prosecute victimizers serves to normalize violence against women (Menjívar 2011). Women understand the message and many have no option but to leave.

Leaving does not guarantee safety, however. Mexico's Southern Border Program (Plan Frontera Sur) was launched in July of 2014 to detain and deport Central Americans before they could reach the United States (Kovic and Kelly 2017). The militarization of Mexico's southern border, much of it achieved with US funding, pushes Central American refugees through more dangerous routes as they occupy "liminal spaces" that place their lives in grave danger between their home and desired destination countries (Izcara Palacios 2016). Even though migrants understand the dangers they will face while in transit, the lack of protection at home propels them to leave (Hiskey et al. 2016). During their journey, as many as six in ten migrant women are raped, some will be abducted, and others trafficked into sex work. The same level of impunity and corruption that expelled them from their homelands makes them vulnerable while in transit through Mexico (Schmidt and Buechler 2017). Those who are later detained in the United States only experience further trauma in detention centers. Conditions in detention are so unbearable that even "children have considered committing suicide, made desperate from confinement" (Madres De Berks 2016).

Migrants as Embodiment of Crisis

When migrants flee, they are risking their lives yet again in search of safety in a far away place. Those who make it to the US border may turn themselves in or be apprehended by Border Patrol. In those cases, many women with children are incarcerated in the euphemistically named, "family residential centers." These practices take place in small out-of-the-way towns that are difficult to access and even more difficult to imagine. But as details of the various forms of abuse carried out against refugees and asylum applicants in detention were reported in the media, different sectors, including "immigration attorneys, NGOs, the ACLU, scholars, faith leaders, and even a federal court order" demanded the release of detainees.

On August 3, 2016, in the face of growing public outcry against the prolonged detention of families, the Department of Homeland Security (DHS) Chief, Jeh Johnson, defended the practice of family detention. He sanitized the description of conditions, and stated publicly that the DHS was ensuring that "the average length of stay at these facilities is 20 days or less" (Lillis 2013). The 22 detained mothers who conducted a hunger strike a week later penned a letter in which they underscored that they had, in fact, been detained between 270 and 365 days (Madres De Berks 2016). By putting their bodies on the line, they made visible the lies of the administration.

The refugee hunger strikers used the open letter to provide a glimpse into their situation. They explained that, "We left our homes in Central America to escape violence, threats and corruption" (Madres De Berks 2016). The conditions that were established in some eras of US intervention and abandoned or exacerbated in other eras are what forced these women to embody their resistance and desire for survival by moving physically across borders. "We risked our own lives and those of our children so we could arrive on safe ground" (Madres De Berks 2016). Cognizant of their home country government's inability or unwillingness to protect them in the face of direct violence, either from criminal organizations or from prolonged domestic abuse, they fled with their children, risking their lives in search of safety and stability. Their move across national territories placed their bodies at greater risk but the masses of people in the same situation together drew attention to the crisis of state failure to protect human rights in the region.

Aware that they have little power in the face of the US security machine, they turn once again to their bodies to draw the world's attention to their plight: "We decided to begin this hunger strike, hoping that our voices will be heard and that we will obtain the liberty from detention that we need so much." When they have been detained for such long periods of time, they take matters into their own hands and collectively use their bodies to risk their health and their lives in a hunger strike. "We thought this country would help us, but now we are locked up with our children in a place where we feel threatened, including by some of the medical personnel, leaving us with no one to trust." Knowing that state representatives in the detention centers will not help them, the only way to be in control and to take their message to a broader public is to embody their resistance exposing the true crisis through the endangerment of their own bodies.

The women end the letter by stating: "We are desperate, and we have decided that we will get out dead or alive." Through their embodied actions, they have made more widely visible the crises they have endured in multiple nation-states. Across national contexts, the only thing that persists for these migrants is insecurity and vulnerability: to gang members, partners, organized crime, corruption, state lack of protection, detention, and state violence. Migrants, who are blamed and identified as the "crisis," live the consequences of these crises in embodied ways. "While here, our children have told us they sometimes consider suicide, made desperate from confinement" (Madres De Berks 2016). It is telling that even at their most vulnerable while in detention, they must use their bodies, in this case as hunger strikers and potential suicidal subjects, to demand rights. In a sense, they are using their bodies and the media to create a different kind of crisis for the state, one that requires the state to have to explain why even though the government's rhetoric is about "moral obligations" and "humane" treatment, they are enacting violence on refugees' bodies, forcing them to recognize publicly that the true crisis is the various states' failure to protect human beings.

Conclusion

Central America has often been associated with crisis. Only mentioned during peak moments of civil war and violence, the region has come to represent crisis writ large. Since the spike in migration in 2014, President Obama, while he labeled it a "humanitarian crisis," moved quickly to implement an "aggressive deterrence strategy" that involved detaining mothers with their children for prolonged periods of time or fast-tracking their deportations to their home countries. This chapter argues that the real crisis is the lack of protections and fulfillment of rights across the region's nation-states: in the home, transit, and destination countries that fail to protect migrants' human rights.

The migration crisis is actually a crisis of the state—of those Central American states that cannot or are unwilling to protect their citizens, and of the Mexican state that refuses to recognize the human rights of people in transit, that takes US money to do the dirty work of impeding migration. The crisis is in the United States that always protects profits over human beings. These crises, so well hidden in policies and foreign assistance categories, are only made visible to the public when those most vulnerable use their bodies to protest. Central American migrants are not the crisis, they merely reflect to us the crises that nation states do not want us to see.

Notes

1. These detention centers for mothers and children are euphemistically officially called, "residential centers" or "family residential centers" (see, for example, US Immigration and Customs Enforcement, Berks Family Residential Center, https://www.ice.gov/detention-facility/berks-family-residential-center). Because the buildings are former prisons; because the same for-profit corporations that run prisons manage them; and because the lived experiences of the people in them are akin to criminal imprisonment, detainees and activists refer to them as simply prisons or baby jails. See also Madres De Berks, "Mothers to Homeland Security: We Won't Eat Until We Are Released," *NY Times*, "On The Ground." August 12, 2016. https://kristof.blogs.nytimes.com/2016/08/12/mothers-to-homeland-security-we-wont-eat-until-we-have-asylum/?smid=tw-share
2. The Obama Administration referred to this set of migrants as "unlawful immigrants" and "illegal immigrants." This chapter refers to them as refugees and asylum-seekers because Article 31 of the 1951 Refugee Convention states that refugees may need to flee their countries and enter another country without authorization (see L. J. Abrego, *Sacrificing Families: Navigating Laws, Labor, and Love Across Borders*, Stanford, CA, Stanford

University Press, 2014; see also http://www.huffingtonpost.com/leisy-j-abrego/president-obama-deception_b_7314656.html).

3. I have italicized for emphasis. "Crisis" is not italicized in the original letter.
4. I have italicized for emphasis. "Humanitarian standards" is not italicized in the original letter.
5. Indeed, the Trump Administration has picked up where the Obama Administration left off by investing in the construction of new detention centers, with plans to detain even more immigrants in a scheme that will greatly profit private prison corporations. See Meredith Hoffman, "Immigrant Center to Be Built in Texas for $110M," *USNews*, April 13, 2017, https://www.usnews.com/news/best-states/texas/articles/2017-04-13/texas-getting-first-immigrant-lockup-built-under-trump
6. In 1999, President Bill Clinton publicly recognized the US government's role in the genocide when he offered an apology to the people of Guatemala for US support (John M. Broder, "Clinton Offers His Apologies To Guatemala," *NYTimes*, March 11, 1999, http://www.nytimes.com/1999/03/11/world/clinton-offers-his-apologies-to-guatemala.html
7. These are precisely the goals that appear to inform the allocation of aid in the region (see Hornbeck 2012 for details).

References

Abrego, L. J. 2014. *Sacrificing Families: Navigating Laws, Labor, and Love Across Borders*, Stanford, CA: Stanford University Press.

Behrens, S. F. 2009. Plan Mexico and Central American Migration. *North American Congress on Latin America*. January 12, 2009. http://nacla.org/node/5406

Booth, J. A., C. J. Wade, and T. W. Walker. 2014. *Understanding Central America: Global Forces, Rebellion, and Change*, Boulder, CO, Westview.

Canizales, S. 2015. "Fast Fashion, Slow Integration: Guatemalan Youth Navigate Life and Labor in Los Angeles." *Youth Circulations*, September 6. http://www.youthcirculations.com/blog/2015/9/9/fast-fashion-slow-integration-guatemalan-youth-navigate-life-and-labor-in-los-angeles.

CISPES. 2017. "Victory for Salvadoran Garment Workers!" October 12. http://cispes.org/article/victory-salvadoran-garment-workers

Correa-Cabrera, G., and J. B. Clark. 2016. "Re-Victimizing Trafficked Migrant Women: The Southern Border Plan and Mexico's Anti-Trafficking Legislation." *Eurasia Border Review* 7: 55–70.

Farah, D., and C. Meacham. 2015. *Alternative Governance in the Northern Triangle and Implications for U.S. Foreign Policy: Finding Logic within Chaos*. Washington, DC: Center for Strategic & International Studies.

Greene, J. 2009. *The Canal Builders: Making America's Empire at the Panama Canal*, New York: Penguin.

Hernández, D. M. 2015. "Unaccompanied Child Migrants in "Crisis": New Surge or Case of Arrested Development?" *Harvard Journal of Hispanic Policy* 27: 11–17.

Hiskey, J. T., A. Córdova, D. Orcés, and M. F. Malone. 2016. *Understanding the Central American Refugee Crisis: Why They Are Fleeing and How U.S. Policies Are Failing to Deter Them*. Washington, DC: American Immigration Council.

Hornbeck, J. F. 2005. *The Dominican Republic-Central America-United States Free Trade Agreement (DR-CAFTA)*. Washington, DC: Congressional Research Service.

Hornbeck, J. F. 2012. *The Dominican Republic-Central America-United States Free Trade Agreement (CAFTA-DR): Developments in Trade and Investment*. Washington, DC: Congressional Research Service.

Izcara Palacios, S. P. 2016. "Violencia postestructural: Migrantes centroamericanos y cárteles de la droga en México." *Revista de Estudios Sociales* 56: 12–25.

Jonas, S., and N. Rodríguez. 2015. *Guatemala–U.S. Migration: Transforming Regions*, Austin: University of Texas Press.

Kovic, C., and P. Kelly. 2017. "Migrant Bodies as Targets of Security Policies: Central Americans Crossing Mexico's Vertical Border." *Dialectic Anthropology* 41: 1–11.

Lakhani, N. 2016. "Central America's Rampant Violence Fuels an Invisible Refugee Crisis." *The Guardian*, October 13. https://www.theguardian.com/world/2016/oct/13/central-america-violence-refugee-crisis-gangs-murder

Lillis, M. 2013. "DHS Chief Defends Child Detention." *TheHill*, August 10. http://thehill.com/policy/national-security/290316-dhs-chief-defends-child-detention-practices

Lovato, R. 2016. "Mapping the New Solidarity." *NACLA Report on the Americas* 48, no. 1: 28–35.

Madres De Berks. 2016. "Mothers to Homeland Security: We Won't Eat Until We Are Released." *NY Times*, "On The Ground." August 12. https://kristof.blogs.nytimes.com/2016/08/12/mothers-to-homeland-security-we-wont-eat-until-we-have-asylum/?smid=tw-share

McAllister, C. and D. M. Nelson, eds. 2013. *War By Other Means: Aftermath in Post-Genocide Guatemala*, Durham, NC: Duke University Press.

Menjívar, C. 2011. *Enduring Violence: Ladina Women's Lives in Guatemala*. Berkeley, University of California Press.

Mesoamerican Working Group. 2013. "Rethinking the Drug War in Central America and Mexico: Analysis and Recommendations for Legislators." November 2013. Washington, DC: MAWG. http://www.ghrc-usa.org/wp-content/uploads/2013/12/Mesoamerica-Working-Group_Rethinking-Drug-War-Web-Version.pdf

Meyer, P. J., and C. R. Seelke. 2015. *Central American Regional Security Initiative: Background and Policy Issues for Congress*. Washington, DC: Congressional Research Service.

Moodie, E. 2010. *El Salvador in the Aftermath of Peace: Crime, Uncertainty, and the Transition to Democracy*, Philadelphia, University of Pennsylvania Press.

Osuna, S. 2015. "Policing the Wretched: Transnational Apparatuses of Social Control in the Early 21st Century." PhD diss., University of California, Santa Barbara.

PBS NewsHour. 2014. "No Country For Lost Kids." June 20. http://www.pbs.org/newshour/updates/country-lost-kids/

Portillo Villeda, S. 2011. "Honduran Immigrants." Pp. 933–968 in *An Encyclopedia of the Newest Americans*, edited by R. H. Bayor, Santa Barbara, CA: Greenwood.

Schmidt, L., and S. Buechler. 2017. "'I risk everything because I have already lost everything': Central American Female Migrants Speak Out on the Migrant Trail in Oaxaca, Mexico." *Journal of Latin American Geography* 16, no. 1: 139–164.

Seelke, C. R., and K. Finklea. 2017. *U.S.-Mexican Security Cooperation: The Mérida Initiative and Beyond*. Washington, DC: Congressional Research Service.

UNHCR. 2014. *Children on the Run: Unaccompanied Children Leaving Central America and Mexico and the Need for International Protection*. Washington, DC: United Nations High Commissioner for Refugees.

UNHCR. 2015. *Women on the Run: First-Hand Accounts of Refugees Fleeing El Salvador, Guatemala, Honduras, and Mexico.* Washington, DC: United Nations High Commissioner for Refugees.

Walsh, S. D., and C. Menjívar. 2016. "Impunity and Multisided Violence in the Lives of Latin American Women: El Salvador in Comparative Perspective." *Current Sociology* 64, no. 4: 586–602.

White House. 2014. "Letter from the President—Efforts to Address the Humanitarian Situation in the Rio Grande Valley Areas of Our Nation's Southwest Border." *The White House.* https://obamawhitehouse.archives.gov/the-press-office/2014/06/30/letter-president-efforts-address-humanitarian-situation-rio-grande-valle

White House Press Secretary. 2013. "Fact Sheet: United States Support for Central American Citizen Security." *The White House.* May 4. https://obamawhitehouse.archives.gov/the-press-office/2013/05/04/fact-sheet-united-states-support-central-american-citizen-security

White House Press Secretary. 2014. "Fact Sheet: Unaccompanied Children from Central America." June 20. https://obamawhitehouse.archives.gov/the-press-office/2014/06/20/fact-sheet-unaccompanied-children-central-america

CHAPTER 13

CONFLICTING PERSPECTIVES ON THE "MIGRANT CRISIS" IN THE HORN OF AFRICA

JOHN R. CAMPBELL

In 2014 the media, in response to statements by the European Union (EU) and certain European states that Europe was overwhelmed by the arrival of 300,000 refugees and "migrants," began to carry reports about a "migrant crisis." These reports were given further impetus by the arrival of more migrants in 2015, a situation made worse by the refusal of EU member states to agree on a common EU policy for assessing, settling, and integrating refugees and migrants and their failure to agree on the "external dimension" of EU asylum policy (Faure, Gavas, and Knoll 2015). In the wake of this policy failure, and facing the prospect of yet of more "migrants" arriving, the EU Commission committed significant political and economic resources to support specific policy initiatives aimed at preventing "migrants" from reaching Europe.

Thus in 2015 the EU initiated a €3 billion deal with Turkey to stop the flow of "migrants"—the use of the term "migrant" by European states and the EU is highly problematic because it subsumes many individuals who have a valid claim to refugee status—entering southern Europe (Collett 2016). At roughly the same time the EU hosted the Valletta Summit where it linked its concerns about migration to the Africa-wide Khartoum Process (IOM 2017). In 2015 the EU also created "The EU-Horn of Africa Action Plan" which sought to create a co-ordinated inter-continental policy response aimed at "managing" migration and facilitating the return of African migrants back to their country of origin.[1] To date this strategy has funded 118 projects across the continent and it has established migration "partnerships" with countries situated on the principal migration routes to Europe. This policy dialogue is supported by funding from a variety of different EU initiatives which include the EU's Common Security and Defence Policy and €1.8 billion from the "EU Trust Fund" for the period 2015–2020.[2] The Trust Fund is aimed, in large part, at building "the capacity of governments to manage migration more efficiently." Additional bilateral funding for related initiatives has been provided by EU states desperate to stem the flow of migrants and reduce political pressure in the runup to general elections (Mason 2017; Wintour 2017).

The policy initiative adopted in the Khartoum Process has been defined by the EU as a problem specific to Africa, one which can be regionally contained by enhancing the capacity of regional states to manage their borders (i.e., entrenched political problems are rendered and transformed into technical and bureaucratic practices by policy discourse; see Apthorpe 2003). The policy language employed by the EU seeks to persuade rather than inform the public about the nature of a specific problem; it also uses "key words" (migration partnerships) and makes selective use of data and facts to arrive at a specific policy prescription, namely that enhanced border control will stop "illegal migration" which is caused by human traffickers and smugglers. This policy message, which seeks to persuade the public that the EU understands and can successfully address the key "drivers" of illegal migration, is based on a gross simplification of a complex set of social, political, and economic processes. As will become clear, policy "success" is contingent on the willingness and ability of African states to support EU objectives.

Except for the scale of what is being pursued, the thinking behind the initiative is not new. Andersson (2014, 2016) reminds us that the EU's "fight against irregular migration" began with the introduction of the Schengen agreement on free movement in the EU in the mid-1990s which led to a massive economic investment in the EU's external borders. As part of its enforcement activities the EU initiated a succession of policy initiatives—the European Neighbourhood Policy with African states, Operation Hera in West Africa, Operation Sophia in the central Mediterranean, and the EU "Hotspot Policy" in the Eastern Mediterranean—which were rolled out to deal with successive migration "crises." The 2015–2016 "crisis" is the most recent and the most ambitious attempt to link EU concerns about the "migrant crisis" to aid negotiations with African states.

Against a background in which the EU has "managed" successive migration crises by investing massively in the "illegality industry" (Andersson 2014), this chapter focuses on three issues. The first section examines the structural processes which generate migration in the Horn of Africa (which includes Ethiopia, Eritrea, Somalia [including Puntland and Mudug], Sudan and South Sudan). The second section examines EU initiatives aimed at stemming migration to Europe and how regional states have responded to the initiative. Given that migration is a logical social response to poverty and conflict, the chapter concludes by considering whether regional and EU migration policies are likely to succeed and, if not, whether it is time to rethink security-oriented approaches to political, developmental, and humanitarian problems?

Understanding Population Movement in the Horn of Africa

What do we know about the individuals transiting toward Europe from the Horn? First they constitute a small percentage of the total number of individuals in the Horn who reside outside their country of origin. Individuals fleeing persecution initially seek refuge in refugee camps located just outside their country of origin. However these camps have become increasingly large and insecure places where individuals are warehoused. In theory encamped refugees should have three options available to them. First registered refugees should be able to apply for resettlement to a third country (they wait in the camps pending a decision). However the number of individuals accepted for resettlement has rapidly declined. Second, host countries can offer refugees the choice of local integration. However none of the states in the Horn currently grant status to refugees which means that there is no possibility for refugees to legally settle in a host country. A final but equally limited possibility arises if conflict in a refugee's country of origin abates. When this happens UNHCR initiates a program of voluntary repatriation to send refugees home. The only repatriation programme currently in operation is for Somali refugees in Kenya who are being repatriated to Sudan.[3] The situation in the region's refugee camps is therefore precarious: the camps have become very large, insecure, and unsafe; food supplies have been drastically cut; and residents are experiencing hopelessness and despair. The situation in the camps has led increasing numbers of individuals to avoid or leave the camps.

To understand what propels individuals to leave the region we need to reject the simplistic policy-based distinction between forced and voluntary migration which depends on making assumptions about the "motives" of migrants (Turton 2003). Instead we need to look at the complex factors which influence migration including the politics of governance; political economy (poverty, inequality etc.); geography, social networks, and what happens to migrants/refugees while they are in transit.

Economic factors have been important in spurring migration. Poverty is clearly one factor behind rural-urban migration, but equally important are ecological problems, landlessness, and unsustainable rural livelihoods (IOM 2006; Markos Ezra 2003). Since the 1950s differential levels of development across the region has led individuals to migrate to find work and access higher education. It is partly for these reasons that Eritreans migrated to Ethiopia and Sudan in the 1960s, northern Sudanese migrated to Egypt and the Middle East, Ethiopians migrated to Yemen and Saudi Arabia, and Somalis migrated to the Gulf. Subsequent population movement has been spurred by civil war, economic recession, and conflict, which has resulted in growing levels of migration to Europe, the Middle East, and North America.

Migration over the past decade is increasingly dominated by youth, especially young men from Eritrea, Somalia and Ethiopia and it seems to be shaped by new political-economic factors and new sensibilities.[4] For instance poor migrants target regional labor markets and, at least initially, have little intention of moving outside the region. At the same time increasing numbers of young, fairly well-educated youth are leaving (in groups) for Europe (Triulzi 2013).

The principal factors driving young people to migrate are concerns about the limited value of their education, peer pressure (many friends are leaving), an awareness that Diaspora nationals with better qualifications monopolize the best jobs, and because "there is nothing to do" at home (Kuschminder et al 2012; Nimo-Ilhan Ali 2016; van Heelsum 2016). Better-educated migrants from better-off households with better social networks tend to target Europe; whereas poor migrants with limited social networks seek work in regional labor markets. Regardless of the motivations or the economic status of migrants, most encounter violence, extortion, and death on the transit routes.

The decision to migrate is shaped by many factors. First youth believe that they can achieve more by leaving rather than staying home. Second while individuals do assess the potential costs and problems of migration, their assessment of the risks is outweighed by the expected benefits of reaching Europe. Third their assessment of the costs—which includes knowledge about smugglers, demands for ransom, and possible death—are assuaged by the development of "leave now—pay later" schemes which are negotiated directly with "smugglers" in their communities. These schemes substantially lower the initial cost of transiting to Europe by placing the financial burden on family and kin after an individual has left. Finally the decision about where to migrate to—within the region or Europe—is partly determined by the existence of an extended social network in the Diaspora. An extended network allows individuals to call on their kin to pay the costs of migration which are substantially higher if the destination is Europe (i.e., to get money to bribe smugglers and officials to release them from captivity or detention, to pay multiple demands for ransom, and to secure transport and food [Belloni 2016]).

The low level of development across the Horn of Africa is caused by periodic drought and recurrent political conflict which has created high levels of population displacement and has exacerbated poverty. Nicholson's (2014, 78) examination of data on drought in the Horn for the period 1998–2012 indicates that while drought tended to follow a 10–12 year cycle in the period prior to 1984, it has recurred in 1998, 2000, 2005–2006, 2007, 2008, 2009, and 2011. Indeed the 2016–2017 drought is estimated to affect 20 million people. Historically the impact of drought has been exacerbated by: (a) the absence of reliable data on rainfall, food crops, and regional markets (which allows authorities to anticipate food shortages, strategically position relief supplies, and request emergency assistance in a timely manner); (b) the absence of a viable economic infrastructure which allows relief supplies to be moved and positioned where they are needed; (c) the absence of credible civil administrative systems that can be trusted to respect human rights and manage and deliver development assistance, food aid, etc.; and (d) ongoing political conflict.

The region has a long history of political instability which has given rise to *coup d'états* in every state, which in turn has led to a dismantling and reconstruction of state administrations, including famine early warning systems, and to population displacement and growing poverty (de Wall 2015). The resultant failure of regional states to create the conditions for peace and economic development has made it difficult for donors to respond with adequate assistance.

Regional states also have a poor human rights record. Al Shabaab—an Al Qaeda-inspired political movement—operates in Somalia where, in addition to its terrorist activities, it is responsible for population displacement and for preventing the distribution of relief to victims of drought and conflict. Despite recent elections and the formation of a national government, the frailty of political authority in Somalia is underwritten by international peace keeping forces under the umbrella of AMISOM (AMISOM 2018).

In Sudan it was hoped that conflict would end following the independence of the Republic of South Sudan in 2010. However Sudan has continued its efforts to undermine South Sudan and, at the same time, rival ethnic-based political parties in South Sudan are attacking each other and the civilian population, causing massive population displacement, food shortages and famine. In 2011 a UN mission was established with the aim of protecting civilians, human rights monitoring, and supporting the delivery of humanitarian assistance and for the implementation of the Cessation of Hostilities Agreement (UN Peacekeeping 2017). The Republic of Sudan has been run by a military junta since 1989 which, in addition to destabilizing South Sudan, has pursued an indiscriminate war in Darfur and with Chad and Libya. In 1997 the complex political situation in Sudan led to UN intervention (Ulich 2017; United Nations Peacekeeping 2017), which has seen its mandate expand to include South Sudan, Abyei, and Darfur.

In 1991 a liberation front seized power in Ethiopia which facilitated the creation of the state of Eritrea. However in 1998 Eritrea and Ethiopia engaged in a bitter two-year border war that resulted in widespread death, the displacement of over one million people, and the flight of several hundred thousand individuals from the region (Campbell 2014). War set back development in the region by a decade. Subsequently Ethiopia, supported by the international community, has seen significant improvements in the country's economic infrastructure, a significant decline in the level of poverty, but also rising expectations for a better standard of life. Even so persistent drought, water, and food shortages, extreme climate events and ongoing conflict has caused internal population displacement and a steady flow of refugees. In Eritrea the ruling party has suspended the constitution, refused to hold elections, established indefinite military conscription, and overseen a deterioration of the economy and the exodus of its population. At the other extreme is Somaliland which, while not recognized as a state by the international community, has managed to create a relative island of political and economic stability as a result of investment by its Diaspora.

Box 1 (below) indicates the scale of the development challenge in the Horn. The region covers a huge geographic area, has a very limited economic infrastructure, a large and geographically dispersed population, high levels of poverty and inequality, and high levels of population displacement (i.e. Internally Displaced Persons or IDPs).

The region also hosts and produces large numbers of refugees. Disparities in development and protracted conflict contribute to extensive population displacement and migration. A sense of the scale of the refugee problem is provided by Verwimp and Maystadt (2015, 7). Their data, indicates that refugee numbers have never dropped below two million; numbers peaked in the early 1990s at 4.5 million, began to decline in the late 1990s, but are once again rising.

By the late 1990s increasing numbers of refugees and migrants began to move out of the region in mixed migration flows along one of four routes (Campbell 2009, 2014; Horwood 2009; Soucy 2011). There are two principal routes out of the Horn which came into being in the 1960s.[5] The first route, along which as many as 50,000 individuals moved each year, was to Puntland (northern Somalia) and across the Straits of Hormuz to Yemen. Yemen recognized the asylum claims of Somali nationals and provided them with access to refugee camps; however the Yemeni authorities saw Ethiopians as economic migrants who were subject to arrest and deportation. Even so thousands of Ethiopians used smugglers to make their way north to Saudi Arabia while others moved to Turkey and to Europe.[6] However this route became increasingly dangerous in 2011 when Saudi Arabia built a border wall. The situation confronting illegal immigrants in Saudi Arabia worsened in recent years when the authorities imposed a "Saudization" policy which led to the arrest and deportation of hundreds of thousands of migrants back to their country of origin. The number of people moving along this route appears to have substantially dwindled.

The second major route out of the region was to Egypt or Libya via Khartoum: individuals were either trafficked northwest from Khartoum to Kufra (Libya) or north to Cairo (some individuals who travelled to Cairo entered Israel where they are incarcerated; see Campbell et al. 2013). The number of individuals moving on these routes has varied. For instance when difficulties were encountered in Egypt making further movement difficult (e.g., due to the arrest of migrants by the Egyptian authorities or Israel's construction of its border barriers in 2010) migrant flows were rerouted from Khartoum to Libya.

The principal embarkation point to Europe has been the Central Mediterranean route from Khartoum to Libya along which an estimated 673,000 persons entered Europe between 2011 and mid-2017.[7] Data on the nationality of individuals using this route (see Table 13.2) show that between 2014 and 2106 the number of individuals arriving in

Table 13.1 Profile of Regional Development

Country	Population (million)	Human Development Index	Territory (square kilometres)	Poverty rate	Per capita income (US$)	IDPs (million)	Displaced to other countries
Somalia	10.8	n/a	637,657	73%	$284	1.1	1.1m
Eritrea	6.3	0.351	125,000	69%	$531	nil	363,000
Sudan	34	0.414	1,886,000	46.5%	$1,270	3.1	666,000
Ethiopia	90	0.435	1,104,000	29.6%	$1,523	298,000	87,000
South Sudan	12.3	0.418	619,745	65.9%	$1,630	2.0	1.75m

Note: IDPs are Internally Displaced Persons.

Source: Data from Mixed Migration Hub (MHUB), 2017.

Table 13.2 Individuals Entering Europe via Libya (by Percent)

	Year			
Country	2014	2105	2016	2017
Eritrea	23%	27%	12%	6%
Somalia	3%	4%	4%	–
Sudan	1.7%	6%	5%	5%
West Africa	9.4%	18%	56%	52%
Other countries	62.9%	45%	23%	37%
Total	138,796	154,000	181,000	116,000

Note: 2017 data is for the first 10 months of 2017

Source: Sahan (2016, 12); UNHCR 2017; ESI 2017; IOM 2016; and European Commission 2017.

Europe from the Horn has substantially decreased.[8] The fluctuation in the number and the nationality of individuals travelling this route illustrates that EU-African strategies to contain or prevent migration do not work: a blockade imposed on one route results in individuals being rerouted through a different and potentially more risky route.[9] Research clearly indicates that conflict and poverty are the main reasons why people initially leave their country of origin and that large numbers of "migrants" become immobile/stuck in transit (MEDMIG 2016) as a direct result of actions by state and non-state actors involved in extortion, torture, and holding individuals for ransom (e.g., see Healey and Forin 2017). By the end of 2016 the growing risks on this route saw migrants from the Horn being rerouted back toward Cairo (Frontex 2016; Malakooti 2016). (see Table 13.2).

Regional Policy Initiatives

The movement of individuals out of the Horn toward Europe, which contributed to a sense of "crisis" Europe, is in sharp contrast to the views of most governments in the Horn who view the situation with indifference. To understand why this situation exists requires an examination of how the EU has responded to the "migration crisis" and how states in the Horn have responded to EU initiatives.

The EU has targeted the Horn because it is seen as a major source of irregular or illegal migrants or both and because it is a transit route to Europe. The EU has pursued its antimigration agenda via two distinct policies. First in 2007 it initiated and funded the Joint Africa-EU Strategy Roadmap (JAES) which sought to expand cooperation with the African Union in eight policy areas including "migration, mobility and employment."

The EU has invested heavily in this process.[10] More recently the EU has focused its resources on the agenda set out in the Joint Valetta Action Plan which identified five "priority domains" which have been picked up in the Khartoum Process.[11] It is not possible to summarize all the discussions and projects pursued by the Khartoum Process in this chapter. Nevertheless it is clear that the EU is attempting to steer consultations in ways that prioritize its concerns. This conclusion becomes clear by looking at the allocation of expenditure committed to different policy/priority domains and it is reflected in the language of the "analysis report" and documents which summarize the efforts made in 2017 (Khartoum Process 2017).[12] The principal planning document submitted to Senior Officials in February 2017 makes it clear that there are tensions between African states and the EU regarding the focus of policy dialogue (it also documents the lack of progress on the ground) and the fact that EU funding is driving the process (many African states have failed to finance national and regional initiatives).

European Commission documents suggest that African states are concerned about the failure of the EU to facilitate access to visas to enter the EU and they are unwilling to support a "returns policy" to speed up the return of "migrants" back to their country of origin.[13] However even if the EU facilitates the entry of highly skilled Africans into the EU the large number of young and unskilled migrants transiting toward Europe will be excluded. The exclusion of migrants arriving in Europe, not to mention those in transit, raises questions about how they are to be "returned" to the region, a subject that has received insufficient attention and funding. In the absence of evaluations and reports on the numerous projects overseen by the Khartoum Process, we are left to read between the lines of official communiques which contrast a call for further consultations on key policy issues with the need to secure clear agreements that will facilitate efficient border management and prevent "migrants" entering Europe. The urgency to prevent "migrants" from reaching Europe is reflected in the political calculations of certain EU states who are keen to seen by their electorates as being tough on migration.[14]

The EU's attempt to create a strategic partnership with Africa via the Khartoum Process is fraught with contradictions. First, policy dialogue reflects a fundamental asymmetry of power in which the EU identifies priorities and decides how funding will be allocated: this strategy is very familiar to its African "partners." Second the "priority domains" identified by the EU do not address the structural causes of migration and population displacement. Third while the EU is investing considerable sums of money in this initiative, its investment is disbursed across the continent in a variety of projects which may have a limited impact unless they can be effectively coordinated. Fourth a narrow focus on migration fails to address other important policy issues which confront the continent, namely how to contain and manage ongoing regional conflict and the need to create a more diversified economy with highly skilled jobs that will be attractive to educated nationals (60 percent of the continent's population is under the age of 30). Finally, the failure of EU member states to fund this initiative has led the European Commission draw on other, more limited sources of funding.[15]

If we look at regional migration initiatives pursued in the Horn it becomes clear just how wide the policy gap is between the EU and its "partners." African states are expected to guarantee and protect the human rights of migrants; however historically they have made little effort to protect their nationals from exploitation or risk once they are outside their country of origin (e.g., with regard to the large number of migrant deaths involved in crossing the Straits of Hormuz and the failure to create policies to allow for the free movement of nationals within the region). The policy situation began to change in 2012 when, under pressure from the EU, regional states signed international conventions. Nevertheless a careful look at regional migration policies shows that they primarily reflect concerns with national security (Majidi and Oucho 2015). Regional states have criminalized migration rather than offered protection to vulnerable migrants. While formally complying with EU expectations regarding enhanced border management, policy implementation is creating new threats to migrants and new opportunities to smugglers and traffickers who collude with officials to exploit migrants. This situation prevails because there are no legal migration channels within the region or between the region and Europe (MHUB 2015).

In 2007 Ethiopia signed the *Convention against Organized Transnational Crime* and in 2012 it signed the *UN Protocol against the Smuggling of Migrants by Land, Sea and Air.*[16] In 2012 it established the Council against Human Trafficking and Smuggling, which is chaired by the Deputy Prime Minister (Sahan Foundation 2016, 32-f). The Council established four working groups supported by law enforcement and has set up "community-based task forces" in 400 localities. During this period the Federal police "intercepted" more than 30,000 individuals believed to be vulnerable to trafficking along the Sudan-Ethiopian border and convicted 640 "human traffickers."

In 2014 Sudan ratified the Palermo Protocol "to Prevent, Suppress and Punish Trafficking in Persons," joined the Joint Africa-EU Strategy to enhance EU-African cooperation, and created the Asylum Regulation Act (2014).[17] In 2014 Sudan also established the National Committee for Combating Human Trafficking and adopted the Combating of Trafficking Act (2014) which set out maximum prison sentences of ten and twenty years for smuggling and for smugglers who cause the death of migrants. Worryingly, in 2013 a former warlord commanding irregular troops drawn from Darfur was given the task of policing the border with Ethiopia, Eritrea, Egypt, and Libya. This "Rapid Support Force" has been given immunity from prosecution "for all acts committed in the course of its work" (AI 2016; Ali 2017). In 2015 Sudan established joint border patrols with Ethiopia which focused on the Gedaref/Kassala and the Humera/Metema regions. Twenty-one operations were reportedly conducted between 2014 and 2015 which led to the "release" of 850 victims of trafficking. However trafficking was rerouted rather than stopped, and the Sudanese authorities continue to arrest, mistreat, and *refoulé* individuals back to Eritrea and Ethiopia (United States 2017).[18]

Despite ratifying international conventions and creating new legislation, migrants, refugees, and asylum seekers in Sudan remain vulnerable to sex trafficking and forced labor. Indeed individuals without legal status find themselves in a situation in which corruption, lack of access to justice, and a criminal justice system characterized by arbitrary arrest, torture, and detention pushes individuals to move onward toward Europe (Oette and Abdesalam Babiker 2017). Indeed Khartoum continues to function as the central hub for individuals going to Libya, Egypt, and Turkey (Frontex 2016). There is considerable scepticism regarding the intention of the government to implement any of the conventions and laws to protect vulnerable migrants and refugees; this concern is underlined by a deliberate policy of transforming tens of thousands of nationals of South Sudan resident in the Republic into stateless persons.

Eritrean policies include imposing strict controls on movement within the country, arbitrary security sweeps, mass arrests, and a policy of shooting individuals attempting to leave (MHUB 2015, 53–54). Indeed Ethiopia has repeatedly argued that Eritrea should be excluded from access to the EU-Horn of Africa Trust Fund because it is "the main driver" of refugees in the Horn, because it has repeatedly refused to respond to previous EU initiatives, and because it is a "serious threat to peace in the region." The Ethiopian argument is reinforced by Eritrea's occupation of a disputed area along its border with Djibouti in June 2017. In sharp contrast, Puntland and Somalia have no resources to create border controls.

Looking across the region it is clear that states do not share a common political agenda on migration. Indeed the evidence suggests that while they are willing to accept funding from the EU for specific projects (for equipment, training, or institutional capacity support) they lack the capacity to coordinate policies between key ministries/departments (IGAD 2016, 6-f) and they are unwilling to sign up to the EU agenda (Ali 2017, 45-f; EC 2017, 12-15).

Conclusion

The picture which emerges regarding the "migration crisis" in the Horn of Africa is complex and fluid. First it should be clear that Europe's concern about "migrants" is driven by anti-immigrant sentiment which had fed into electoral politics in the UK, Italy, Greece, Germany, and new accession states (Hungary, Austria, Czechoslovakia). The EU is promoting short-term managerial solutions to a problem defined as emanating from the Horn of Africa by imposing legal and technical solutions (i.e., capacity building). This narrow policy focus defines the problem as African in origin and it fails to address the structural factors causing migration. Furthermore EU policy does not take into account the deep-seated problems of governance reflected in the failure of its African "partners" to protect the human rights of citizens and migrants.

In sharp contrast to the EU, states in the Horn of Africa do not buy into the notion of a "migration crisis"; high levels of migration and displacement are normal and it is not a priority in the region. In all probability it will be difficult for the EU, through the Khartoum Process and other multi- and bilateral development initiatives, to establish effective border management in the Horn of Africa that will prevent "migrants" reaching Europe.

Within the region there is abundant evidence that conflict is unmanageable. Regional states have proved to be unable or unwilling to negotiate an end to conflict and, without extensive international assistance, they are unable to support the growing number of IDPs and refugees. This situation has occurred despite the presence of four ongoing UN interventions in the region, and it reflects the unaccountable nature of elite politics across the region. Without peace there can be no development, and without development population displacement and migration will continue.

A notable feature of the Khartoum Process is the extent to which African development needs are sidelined by the EU's focus on migration. Not only has the EU failed to address key structural factors responsible for population movement and migration—factors which differ by country and region—it is negotiating from a perceived position of strength based on the belief that Europe holds all the bargaining chips, namely access to a huge export market, to finance, and to development assistance. This view fails to recognize that a migration policy based on deterrence will fail because it displaces rather than prevents migration and because it incentivizes states and international firms to deceive the EU in an attempt to secure funding or recognition or both in exchange for a promise to control migration. The continued pursuit of such policies indicates that the EU has not learned from earlier policy failures in West and North Africa which attempted to prevent irregular migration into Europe.

The Khartoum process represents a much more fragile political basis for preventing irregular migration than the EU is prepared to admit. Negotiations are underpinned by the transfer of huge amounts of EU and EU member state funding to a multiplicity of state and nonstate actors who are linked together by a variety of formal and informal agreements. These actors have very different interests in the outcome of the process. Indeed many actors to whom responsibility for migration control has been delegated cannot be held to account for human rights violations they commit in the name of managing migration or for failing to implement agreements. This lack of accountability extends well beyond states in the Horn of Africa and includes local police, military, and paramilitary organizations, as well as European-based organizations such as Frontex and international firms funded by the EU to build border fences, construct and manage immigration detention centers, deport failed asylum seekers, and provide increasingly sophisticated forms of border surveillance paid for by European citizens.

Notes

1. See: http://www.consilium.europa.eu/en/press/press-releases/2015/10/26/fac-conclusions-horn-africa/ (accessed 7 July 2017)
2. See: "EU Missions and Operations 2017," https://eeas.europa.eu/sites/eeas/files/csdp_missions_and_operations_factsheet.pdf, and "EU Emergency Trust Fund for Africa" at http://ec.europa.eu/europeaid/regions/africa/eu-emergency-trust-fund/horn-africa_en. Funding from this source excludes other EU and EU member-state funding mechanisms.
3. However implementation of this program is facing serious difficulties. See European Commission. "European Civil Protection and Humanitarian Aid Operations," http://ec.europa.eu/echo/files/aid/countries/factsheets/factsheet_kenya_april_17_rio_co.pdf

4. I am indebted to Mesgina Tedla and Hyab Yohannes for talking to me about their research and their experience of transiting from Eritrea to Europe. While Eritrean youth are clearly leaving in order to avoid indefinite military service, in other ways their motivations differ little from their counterparts in Ethiopia and Somalia.
5. The other routes, which are not discussed here, are: (a) flying direct to the Middle East ostensibly on pilgrimage or to work as domestic labor; (b) through the southern Africa corridor to South Africa and out; and (c) by flying to Europe, North America and elsewhere.
6. Tens of thousands of Ethiopians have illegally migrated to the Middle East allegedly to practice the Haj and have stayed—in Saudi Arabia, Kuwait, and Lebanon—to work, including large numbers of young and poorly educated women who work as domestic labor. The Ethiopian government has only recently attempted to control the large number of "labour recruiters" in Addis Ababa who are involved in recruiting women to work in the Middle East.
7. See: EPSC, "Irregular Migration via the Central Mediterranean," February 2, 2017, https://ec.europa.eu/epsc/publications/strategic-notes/irregular-migration-central-mediterranean_en and IOM, "Mediterranean Migrant Arrivals Approach 43,000 in 2017; Deaths: 962," April 21, 2017, https://www.iom.int/news/mediterranean-migrant-arrivals-approach-43000-2017-deaths-962 In 2016–2017, an estimated 2,225 individuals drowned in an attempt to reach Europe on this route.
8. The statistics clearly indicate that the majority of individuals entering Europe on this route are from West Africa, though an increasing number are from Bangladesh. For an overall view see Declan Butler, "What the Numbers Say about Refugees," *Nature* 543, no. 7643, http://www.nature.com/news/what-the-numbers-say-about-refugees-1.21548
9. In 2017 increasing numbers of migrants were diverted away from Libya and attempted to take boats from Tunisia and Algeria.
10. The EU committed €845 million to the 2014-2017 JAES program. The EU also underwrites 80 percent of African Union programs and has committed about €18 billion per year in development assistance to sub-Saharan Africa (EU 2014: 10). See also Africa and Europe in Partnership. "Action Plan," 2014, http://www.africa-eu-partnership.org/sites/default/files/documents/action_plan_mmd.pdf.
11. For information on these discussions and to understand how it is funded, see Khartoum Process, "Joint Valletta Action Plan, Senior Officials' meeting (SOM) in Malta 8-9 February 2017," http://www.khartoumprocess.net/news-and-events/news/42-joint-valletta-action-plan-senior-officials-meeting-som-in-malta-8-9-february-2017
12. See the 2017 reports at European Commission, "EU Emergency Trust Fund for Africa," https://ec.europa.eu/europeaid/regions/africa/eu-emergency-trust-fund-africa_en and on EU migration compacts at their "Press Release Database," http://europa.eu/rapid/press-release_IP-17-1595_en.htm.
13. Apparently they fear that if the "diaspora" is forcibly returned there will be a significant decline in remittances which constitutes the largest flow of foreign exchange into Africa (EC 2017, 14).
14. See the "Joint Statement Addressing the Challenge of Migration and Asylum," Paris, August 28, 2017 between France, Germany. Italy, Spain, the EU and Niger, Chad and Libya at: https://m.bundesregierung.de/Content/DE/_Anlagen/2017/08/2017-08-28-statement-refugee-migration-english.pdf?__blob=publicationFile&v=1.
15. See Jennifer Rankin, "EU 'Running Out of Money' to Stop Migrants Travelling from Africa," *The Guardian*, October 20, 2017, https://www.theguardian.com/world/2017/oct/20/eu-running-out-of-money-stop-migrants-travelling-africa

16. See: UNODC, United Nations Convention Against Transnational Organized Crime And The Protocols Thereto, https://www.unodc.org/documents/middleeastandnorthafrica/organised-crime/UNITED_NATIONS_CONVENTION_AGAINST_TRANSNATIONAL_ORGANIZED_CRIME_AND_THE_PROTOCOLS_THERETO.pdf, and UN, Protocol Against the Smuggling Of Migrants By Land, Sea and Air, Supplementing the United Nations Convention against Transnational Organized Crime, 2000, https://www.unodc.org/documents/southeastasiaandpacific/2011/04/som-indonesia/convention_smug_eng.pdf
17. See The Asylum Regulation Act 2014, www.pclrs.com/downloads/asylum-act-2014.doc.
18. See: Arthur Neslen, "EU Urged to End Cooperation with Sudan after Refugees Whipped and Deported," *The Guardian*, February 27, 2017, https://www.theguardian.com/global-development/2017/feb/27/eu-urged-to-end-cooperation-with-sudan-after-refugees-whipped-and-deported, and "Sudan: Hundreds Deported to Likely Abuse," *Human Rights Watch*, May 30, 2016, https://www.hrw.org/news/2016/05/30/sudan-hundreds-deported-likely-abuse.

References

Ali, H. A. 2017. *Human Smuggling and Trafficking in Eastern Sudan*. Sudan Report 2. C. Michelsen Institute & EDGE. Khartoum. https://reliefweb.int/sites/reliefweb.int/files/resources/6325-human-smuggling-and-trafficking-in-eastern-sudan.pdf

AMISOM. 2018. http://amisom-au.org/

Amnesty International (AI). 2016. *Human Rights Impacts and Risks Associated with the Khartoum Process*. Submitted to All Party Parliamentary Group for Sudan and South Sudan. October. London. https://www.amnesty.org/en/documents/afr54/5337/2016/en/

Andersson, R. 2014. *Illegality Inc: Clandestine Migration and the Business of Bordering Europe*. Oakland: University of California Press.

Andersson, R. 2016. "Europe's Failed 'Fight' against Irregular Migration: Ethnographic Notes on a Counterproductive Industry." *Journal of Ethnic & Migration Studies* 42, no. 7: 1055–1075.

Apthorpe, R. 2003. "Writing Development Policy and Policy Analysis Plain or Clear: On Language, Genre and Power." In *Anthropology of Policy*, edited by C. Shore and S. Wright, 43–58. Oxford: Routledge.

Belloni, M. 2016. "'My uncle cannot say 'no' if I reach Libya': Unpacking the Social Dynamics of Border-Crossing among Eritreans Heading for Europe." *Human Geography* 9, no. 2: 47–56.

Campbell, J. 2009. "Caught between the Ideology and Realities of Development: Transiting from the Horn of Africa to Europe." *Migration Studies Unit Working Papers* no. 2009/01. LSE. http://eprints.soas.ac.uk/6373/1/Isolation_and_Identity_-_MSU_Working_Paper_2009.pdf

Campbell, J. 2014. *Nationalism, Law and Statelessness: Grand Illusions in the Horn of Africa*. Oxford: Routledge.

Campbell, J., H. Yaron, and Nurit Hashimshony-Yaffe. 2013. "'Infiltrators' or Refugees? An Analysis of Israel's Policies toward African Asylum-Seekers." *International Migration* 51, no. 4: 144–157

Collett, E. 2016. "The Paradox of the EU-Turkey Refugee Deal." Migration Policy Institute. http://www.migrationpolicy.org/news/paradox-eu-turkey-refugee-deal

De Wall, A. 2015. *The Real Politics of the Horn of Africa: Money, War and the Business of Power*. Cambridge, UK: Polity.

European Commission. 2017. "Joint Communication to The European Parliament, the European Council and the Council. Migration on the Central Mediterranean Route: Managing Flows, Saving Lives." Brussels. https://eur-lex.europa.eu/legal-content/EN/TXT/?uri=CELEX%3A52017JC0004

ESI (European Stabilization Initiative). 2017. "The Refugee Crisis through Statistics." Berlin. https://www.esiweb.org/pdf/ESI%20-%20The%20refugee%20crisis%20through%20statistics%20-%2030%20Jan%202017.pdf

Faure, R., M. Gavas, and A. Knoll. 2015. *Challenges to a Comprehensive EU Migration and Asylum Policy*. London: Overseas Development Institute.

Frontex. 2016. "Africa: Frontex Intelligence Community Joint Report." Warsaw: Frontex. https://frontex.europa.eu/assets/Publications/Risk_Analysis/AFIC/AFIC_2016.pdf

Healey, C., and F. Forin. 2017. "What Are the Protection Concerns for Migrants and Refugees in Libya?" ICMPD Policy Brief. Vienna, November. https://gmdac.iom.int/research-database/sites/default/files/documents/ICMPD%20Policy%20Brief.pdf

Horwood, C. 2009. *In Pursuit of the Southern Dream: Victims of Necessity: Assessment of the Irregular Movement of Men from East Africa and the Horn to South Africa*. Geneva, Switzerland: IOM.

Inter-Governmental Authority on Development (IGAD). 2016. *4th Meeting of the IGAD Regional Migration Coordination Committee: Migration Governance in the IGAD Region*. Summary Report, 16th–17th May. Khartoum, Sudan. http://migration.igad.int/4th%20IGAD%20RMCC%20Report.pdf

International Organization for Migration. 2006. "Field Mission Report: Stranded Ethiopian Migrants in Bossasso, North Eastern Somalia/Puntland." Nairobi, Kenya: IOM. https://reliefweb.int/report/ethiopia/field-mission-report-stranded-ethiopian-migrants-bossasso-north-east-somaliapuntland.

International Organization for Migration (IOM). 2016. "Mixed Migration Flows in the Mediterranean and Beyond." http://migration.iom.int/docs/2016_Flows_to_Europe_Overview.pdf

Khartoum Process. 2017. "Analysis Report of the Khartoum Process in preparation for the Senior Officials Meeting (SOM) of 8 and 9 February 2017." http://www.khartoumprocess.net/news-and-events/news/42-joint-valletta-action-plan-senior-officials-meeting-som-in-malta-8-9-february-2017

Kuschminder, K., L. Andersson, and M. Siegel. 2012. "Profiling Ethiopian Migration: A Comparison of Characteristics of Ethiopian Migrants to Africa, the Middle East, and The North." In *Crossing African Borders: Migration and Mobility*, edited by Centre of African Studies, 28–43. Lisbon, Portugal: University Institute of Lisbon.

Majidi, N., and L. Oucho. 2015. "East Africa." Altai Consulting. In *Migration Trends across the Mediterranean*, edited by Altai Consulting, 55–84. Geneva: IOM.

Malakooti, A. 2016. "The Dynamics of Migrant Smuggling in North Africa: Focus on the Central Mediterranean Route." In *IE Mediterranean Yearbook*, 104–108. Dossier: Mobility and Refugee Crisis in the Mediterranean.

Markos, E. 2003. "Environmental Vulnerability, Rural Poverty, and Migration in Ethiopia: A Contextual Analysis." *Genus* 59, no. 2: 63–91

Mason, R. 2017. "Britain Sends £9 Million to Libya to Fight Terror Threat and Migration Crisis." *The Guardian*, August 23. https://www.theguardian.com/politics/2017/aug/23/britain-sends-9m-aid-package-libya-fight-terror-threat-migrant-crisis-boris-johnson.

MEDMIG. 2016. "Destination Europe? Understanding the Dynamics and Drivers of Mediterranean Migration in 2015." Final Report: November. http://www.medmig.info/wp-content/uploads/2016/12/research-brief-destination-europe.pdf

MHUB. 2015. "Conditions and Risks of Mixed Migration in Northeast Africa." Study 2. Regional Mixed Migration Secretariat, UNHCR, Danish Refugee Council, IOM.

MHUB. 2017. "Monthly Trend Bulletin." http://www.mixedmigrationhub.org/monthly-trend-bulletins/

Nicholson, S. 2014. "A Detailed Look at the Recent Drought Situation in the Greater Horn of Africa." *Journal of Arid Environments* 103: 71–79

Nimo-Ilhan Ali. 2016. "Going on Tahriib: The Causes and Consequences of Somali Youth Migration to Europe." Rift Valley Institute Research Paper 5. London & Nairobi. http://www.refworld.org/docid/57e92d114.html.

Oette, L., and M. Abdelsalam Babiker. 2017. "Migration Control a la Khartoum: EU External Engagement and Human Rights Protection in the Horn of Africa." *Refugee Survey Quarterly* 36, no. 4: 64–89. doi:10.1093/rsq/hdx013

Sahan Foundation. 2016. "Human Trafficking and Smuggling on the Horn of Africa—Central Mediterranean Route." IGAD. February. https://igad.int/attachments/1284_ISSP%20Sahan%20HST%20Report%20%2018ii2016%20FINAL%20FINAL.pdf

Soucy, A. 2011. *Mixed Migration from the Horn of Africa to Yemen. Protection Risks and Challenges*. Danish Refugee Council. Denmark.

Triulzi, A. 2013. "'Like a plate of spaghetti': Migrant Narratives from the Libya-Lampedusa Route." In *Long Journeys: African Migrants on the Road*, edited by A. Triulzi and R. McKenzie, 218–232. Leiden, The Netherlands: Brill.

Turton, D. 2003. "Refugees, Forced Re-Settlers And 'Other Forced Migrants': Towards a Unitary Study of Forced Migration." New Issues in Refugee Research Working Paper no. 94. UNHCR. http://www.unhcr.org/research/RESEARCH/3f818a4d4.pdf

Ulich, Oliver. 2017. "The UN Security Council's Response to Darfur: A Humanitarian Perspective." HPN, June 2005. https://odihpn.org/magazine/the-un-security-councils-response-to-darfur-a-humanitarian-perspective/

UNHCR. 2017. "Mediterranean Situation." Operational Portal Refugee Situation. October, 2017. http://data2.unhcr.org/en/situations/mediterranean/location/5205

United Nations Peacekeeping. 2017. http://www.un.org/en/peacekeeping/missions/unmiss/

United States. "2017 Trafficking in Persons Report." Washington, DC: Department of State, 2017. https://www.state.gov/j/tip/rls/tiprpt/

van Heelsum, A. 2016. "Why Migration Will Continue: Aspirations and Capabilities of Syrians and Ethiopians with Different Educational Backgrounds." *Ethnic and Racial Studies* 39, no. 8 (2016): 1301–1309

Verwimp, P., and J. –F. Maystadt. 2015. "Forced Displacement and Refugees in Sub-Saharan Africa. An Economic Inquiry." Policy Research Working Paper 7517. World Bank Group: Africa Region, Chief Economists Office, December 2015. http://documents.worldbank.org/curated/en/546181468194940969/pdf/WPS7517.pdf.

Wintour, Patrick. 2017. "Italy's Deal to Stem Flow of People from Libya In Danger of Collapse." *The Guardian*, March 10. https://www.theguardian.com/world/2017/oct/03/italys-deal-to-stem-flow-of-people-from-libya-in-danger-of-collapse

CHAPTER 14

PRECARIOUS MOBILITY IN CENTRAL AMERICA AND SOUTHERN MEXICO

Crises and the Struggle to Survive

MARTHA LUZ ROJAS WIESNER
AND AILSA WINTON

Whose Crisis?

While debates look set to continue over the so-called global migration crisis, and Central America experiences a prolonged spike in displacement linked to a surge in organized criminal violence and a complicated deterioration in human security, Mexico has carried on business as usual, in continuing to deal with migration in this historically extremely mobile region in terms of contention.[1] The Mexican government—keen to assuage its powerful neighbors to the north—seeks to control what has been termed the US's "third border" (Grayson 2006) between Mexico and Guatemala/Belize, attempting to reduce the number of people able to cross Mexico and reach the US border from Central America.[2] Border extension and political pressure in this area from the United States has grown more acute since the "crisis" stemming from the arrival and containment of an unprecedented number of unaccompanied Central American children at the US border in 2014–2015 (Serrano and Jaramillo 2017). An overriding interest in controlling the migration of Central Americans through Mexico has meant neither the United States nor Mexico is willing to recognize the scale of violence-based displacement in and from Central America and the associated need for protection. While in the last century Mexico was recognized as a country of refuge and asylum during the armed conflict in neighboring Guatemala, this is not the case in the present day. It has been suggested that the asylum process is complicated in Mexico given the historic migration flows in the region (Cobo and Fuerte 2012). Yet it seems the government is also reluctant to recognize criminal violence as grounds for asylum *per se*, perhaps in part because it would tacitly mean that displacement within Mexico linked to criminal violence would also have to be acknowledged, something that has been strongly resisted by the State (see Rubio Díaz-Leal and Albuja 2014). In any case, the system is highly discretional, and the number of asylum applications granted in Mexico is dwarfed by its deportation figures.[3]

This speaks to the seemingly contradictory dual function of national borders: as sites of humanitarian need or engagement or both (based on a logic of *universal* human rights which while individual, still have to be enacted in a national territory), and as key sites of national security enactment (protection of sovereignty at the same national scale) (Winton 2017). This apparent paradox is in fact two sides of the same geopolitical coin: the very fact that some borders are "becoming spaces of humanitarian engagement is only because border crossing has been made, for certain segments of the world's migratory population, into a matter of life and death" (Walters 2011, 147). A stark example of this was the recent so-called crisis of unaccompanied minors arriving at the Mexico-US border. While this "crisis" was labeled a humanitarian one by then President Obama, he was in fact referring specifically to the high numbers of children "stuck" at the US border during 2014–2015 (see Heyman et al., forthcoming). As the crisis was constructed not as the children fleeing per se, but rather as the fact they were *stuck*, the problem was addressed through swift and massive deportations of children, many of whom were fleeing violence (see Orozco and Yansura 2015), and a vague commitment to tackling the causes of displacement. Borders create (rather than resolve) humanitarian crises (Walters 2011), and moreover "contention promotes attention, thus promoting the crisis discourse, and in turn the crisis discourse raises the level of excitement and engagement in contention" (Heyman et al., forthcoming).

Mexico appears to play out this tension not just at its borders, but deeply within them. Physically and politically wedged between what non-state actors have repeatedly called a humanitarian crisis in Central America to its south (crisis as a *cause* of displacement), and the panic-inducing migration "crisis" to its north at the US border (displacement or migration itself constituting crisis), Mexico could in fact be seen as a country that acts as one big border.

This push-back from Mexico's southern border has been described as an "elastic border" (Ángeles 2003), and as a "vertical border" (Rigoni 2007) that reaches right through national territory. The control routes established throughout the country by migration authorities in turn have given rise to an "unofficial vertical border" of criminal groups, or the "bastard industry" of migration control (Basok et al. 2015), which operates as a direct result of migrants being pushed into new territories controlled by criminal gangs. The line between official and criminal migration controls is blurred since state agents sometimes collude with criminal groups (Yee and Torre 2016). The heightened dangers for people forced to move clandestinely and often with illegal assistance in Mexico-as-border as a result of increased official and unofficial controls is well-documented (e.g., REDODEM 2017). In this nation-border, humanitarianism barely reaches the "minimalist biopolitics" (Redfield 2005) of simply keeping people alive; rather it serves as a handy discourse to justify detention and expulsion strategies, evidenced by the official discourse of the "rescue" of irregular migrants, who are really detained and deported (see Isacson et al. 2017), back to what for many are hostile and often highly dangerous situations. Humanitarianism thus morphs perversely into the (further) criminalization of migration as trafficking.

In sum, in political terms migration and border control in Mexico are linked to the construction of crisis inasmuch as the US border crisis has extended south through Mexico. The migration controls demanded of Mexico by the United States amidst growing violence-based displacement from Central America, require denial of the scale and significance of this deterioration of security in Central America, sparking in turn what civil society groups have called a humanitarian crisis. Yet amid the growing body of work analyzing the political construction of such migration and humanitarian crises (that is, manufactured crises of control and care), there is much less attention given to the experiences of those directly involved. Through recent work carried out in the region by the authors which has sought to understand migration and displacement as embodied, material experiences, the chapter explores the relationship between protracted crisis, displacement, and precarity, in which crisis is seen first through the personal lens, as a condition of perpetual uncertainty (see Lindley 2014). Yet we also engage with this political/personal binary in thinking through how "crisis" as both political and personal is inseparable from marginality. We posit that a critical understanding of *crisis as marginality* (personal) and *marginality as crisis* (political) could help to unpack and question preconceptions about migration and borders.

From Crisis Migration to Precarious Mobility

> Both [crisis and migration] are often viewed as threatening: crisis as jeopardising social systems and human welfare; migration as undermining the integrity of the nation-state and bounded identities. At the same time, both are often described as characteristic of the contemporary world.
>
> (Lindley 2014, 1)

Despite this heavy discursive baggage, the notion of crisis migration has gained currency in recent years, as part of an effort to rethink migration and mobility in the context of the many large-scale, complex (chronic and acute) threats to human security that have driven significant population movements in recent years. The emerging literature on crisis migration has directly and productively exposed its own caveats (for example, Lindley 2014; McAdams 2014; see introduction of this volume), but particularly pertinent here is Lindley's (2014, 6) observation that while at times the construction of crises is politically expedient, at others it may be more convenient to promulgate a non-crisis discourse even in the face of objective, empirical indicators of severe threat or discontinuity (particularly when this threat is faced disproportionately by marginalized groups such as irregular migrants): thus crisis and non-crisis are political, not empirical, categories.

Humanitarian crisis may be framed through a rhetoric of emergency, with its connotation of exceptionality and drama beyond "normal" border management (Campesi 2012). Yet even if is explained that crisis is as much about the situation of immediate danger as people's individual and collective capacity to deal with it (Betts 2010), and that exceptionality is not the same as crisis (exceptional circumstances may not equate to crisis, just as some "crises" are not exceptional [McAdam 2014]), this very relativism means that the notion of crisis has no objective empirical significance. Moreover, it is argued here that if large-scale situations of extreme personal threat coexist with "non-crisis" political discourse and praxis, such as in the current context, crisis does not exist independently of marginality.

In terms of *mobility* crises, marginality—particularly as determined by class (see Castles 2011) and race (see de Genova 2013)—is central to political border and migration crises, as these are constructed to contain and repel the unwanted. In the personal sphere, mobility crises are lived through the intractable relationship between displacement and marginality. In this way, mobility becomes a problem—politically or personally—when it is associated with marginality (the rich are not displaced, rather they relocate). We are concerned here with exploring this relationship between crisis, marginality, and mobility particularly in terms of protracted, complicated, multi-scale spatial and social displacement.

Such an approach speaks to a particular, critical understanding of mobility, which feeds into an increasingly established field of work on mobilities that is concerned not only with physical movement, but also potential movement, blocked movement, immobilization, and forms of dwelling and placemaking (Sheller 2011). Moving through space brings out differences between a subject and their surroundings: mobility is impinged by inequality, and associated with justice and injustice (see Cresswell 2006), but at the same time it may be a crucial resource for many types of escape (Winton 2015). Rather than focusing on the fact of movement itself, this approach is broadly concerned with the *production, practice*, and *representation* of mobilities, considering "how particular modes of mobility are enabled, given licence, encouraged and facilitated while others are, conversely, forbidden, regulated, policed and prevented" (Cresswell 2006, 735).

Work that bridges critical mobilities and migration research has highlighted in particular how legal frameworks that facilitate some mobilities while restricting others are themselves inseparably bound up with the embodied politics of difference (Blunt 2007; see for example Basok et al. 2015 on Mexico), and thus how it is that some mobilities are constructed as crises, while others are not. Similarly, others have explored how some movements are imposed upon populations that long for stillness, such that mobility—far from universally emancipatory—may itself may play a part in subjugating populations (Gill et al., 2011). This body of work has disrupted linear (neocolonial, heterosexist, etc.) assumptions about safety and mobility. Extending feminist and postcolonial perspectives on spatiality and subjectivity, mobility scholarship has highlighted the importance of movement in the lives of those who are "out of place," such that mobility produces a new sense of self precisely through experiences of anonymity, temporariness, and displacement (see Waitt and Gorman-Murray 2011 on heterosexism and mobility). At the same time, the self can be *consciously remade* as a way of confronting precarious mobility (Basok et al. 2015).

Similarly, for Doná (2010) the supposition that geographical dislocation (being "in") is equated with psychological and social displacement (being "of") does not capture the experiences or needs of forced migrants. In practical terms, she argues, there is nothing in the experience of territorial dislocation *per se* that makes a person healthy or unhealthy. When displacement is framed in terms of processes, geographical dislocation becomes a life event like any other. It is the way in which negotiations with this life event evolve that affects well-being (Doná, 2010), such that policy should deal with being "of" (social processes that influence well-being), rather than simply being "in" (country of "refuge").

Viewed this way, it is easier to see the everyday, unjust, social world-making aspects of mobility. Life happens through movement; the fact of migration is not remarkable, but what is of concern here as we reflect on the situation in Mexico is how personal-political mobility regimes are related to precarity and damage. Moreover, the time and space of mobility morph and bend as conditions fluctuate. This means, as Schapendonk (2012) notes, that migrants may become stuck, stranded, or settled; trajectories turn into processes of shifting destinations, whereby periods of mobility may easily change into moments of immobility and vice versa. Developing new conceptual frameworks along these lines is not a mere academic exercise: dismantling rigid understandings of migration—both in terms of who moves (migrant or refugee) and how (origin, transit, destination, or return)—and with them damaging mobility regimes is an urgent task in Mexico and beyond.

This chapter draws from this emerging body of work as it seeks to sketch out some additional conceptual bridges. Mobility is approached here through the broad lens of precarity, whereby marginality is lived (as embodied and material) through dynamic (spatial and temporal) mobility. As is conceptually and empirically explored below, mobility is not just related to precarity as a cause or effect, but rather it is enacted through mobility.

Precarity as a concept in its broadest sense is similar in many ways to vulnerability: while there is no clear consensus on specific definitions, both deal with how structurally reproduced disadvantage is expressed and experienced. Butler (2009, ii), for example, posits precarity as:

> a politically induced condition in which certain populations suffer from failing social and economic networks of support and become differentially exposed to injury, violence, and death. Such populations are at heightened risk of disease, poverty, starvation, displacement, and of exposure to violence without protection [...].

Alternatively, the terms have been used to explain different aspects of structural disadvantage, as conditions (precarity) and outcome (vulnerability) (see Rojas 2017).

Building on the notion of mobility regimes (Glick-Schiller and Salazar 2013; Shamir 2005), we suggest that the notion of precarity—as distinct from vulnerability—is especially useful in thinking through the pernicious aspects of these regimes in that it incorporates instability and uncertainty (Anderson 2010): temporal aspects that are crucial to the experience of precarious mobility, and which have been given growing yet still relatively little attention in the literature on migration and mobility (for example Çağlar 2016; Griffiths 2014; Pascucci 2016). This field of work has as produced such evocative notions as "permanent temporariness" (Bailey et al. 2002), the simultaneous experience of "imminent change and endless waiting" (Griffiths 2014), and "time-suspension" (Conlon 2011).

This chapter examines these insights in relation to lived, precarious mobility regimes. As Anderson (2010) has noted, precarity *prevents people from anticipating the future*; as a concept it alludes to instability, flux, and uncertainty associated with damaging mobility regimes. Temporality is also a crucial dimension of resistance and resilience, be that through migrants practicing forms of "irregular," "makeshift" citizenship in the here and now; through "self-*un*making of citizenship" (as opposed to citizenship-as-future) (Nyers 2013, cited in Pascucci 2016); or through explicitly temporal (mobile) self-making. It is argued here that time is therefore not only a key dimension of the control and management of movement, but is by definition a crucial aspect of precarious mobility. The remainder of the chapter explores these broad ideas through two personal accounts of mobility and survival in Central America-Mexico, highlighting the continuities and ruptures associated with mobility as people navigate situations of acute and chronic threat.

Unsettling Stories

The factors underlying migration and displacement more broadly in the Central America-Mexico region have been amply documented and discussed: economic marginalization, a lack of labor market opportunities, food insecurity, continuing political instability, and widespread insecurity and myriad forms of violence (Alba and Castillo 2012; Albuja 2014; ; Castillo and Toussaint 2010; Orozco and Yansura 2015; Programa Estado de la Nación 2016; Rojas and Ángeles 2008). Recently, the effects of climate change and other environmental phenomena (flooding, landslides, drought, hurricanes) are seen as increasingly relevant particularly for their effect on subsistence farming in the region[4] (CEPAL 2010; Programa Estado de la Nacion 2016; WFP et al. 2017). Seen another way, and for the purposes of this chapter, these are part of the broad contexts of individual mobility regimes (and at once, some of the structural aspects of precarity). As such, movement is not a break with some sedentary norm, nor is it a fleeting moment. The stories told here crisscross over some common ground, but each highlights particular, often prolonged struggles enacted through different mobilities. The backdrop of migration and border policy is subsumed in complex personal stories of ongoing displacement and persistent precarity.

"One of us has to leave and see what else is out there"

Now 40, Teresa grew up in Sonsonate, a municipality in the west of El Salvador. She recounted her story when she again found herself in Tapachula, Mexico in September 2012, attempting to embark on yet another journey north.[5]

Teresa first left El Salvador in 1993, when she was twenty-two years old. At that time, she had an 8-month-old daughter and a 5-year-old son. When her older brother (the eldest of her nine siblings), who was living in Miami, found out she was being abused by her husband, he paid for her to be brought across Mexico and over the border. The clandestine journey took almost two months. After a year of work, she sent money home for her children to come, but her mother only sent her son. Frustrated after years of being in legal limbo, in 2009 she tried to go with her son to Canada, but they were detained on the way and deported to El Salvador.

Arriving back in El Salvador was traumatic for both Teresa and her son. For more than two years (2009–2011) she tried to settle there, but she became "desperate, depressed, because [. . .] I didn't adapt to life back in El Salvador". Her son also became depressed because of all the problems they were facing. They had no money and were moving from house to house. Teresa had been sending money back for a house to be built for her, but when they arrived it was being lived in. She felt "like a beggar, asking my sister, my father, anyone to take in me and my children." The tension grew between her and her family. Confronted with this critical situation, she asked her sister to take care of her daughter, while she and her son tried to get to the United States, by now in 2011. But they were caught by the migration authorities in Mexico, about 300 km north of the Mexico-Guatemala border.

After being deported again to El Salvador, Teresa was finally able to take possession of her home, but their economic situation deteriorated further, which was made worse when the local gang started to demand "rent" from her son. Despite attempts by Teresa's mother to diffuse the problem with the gangs, the harassment did not stop. Teresa went to the human rights commission but was told they could not help as her son was not physically hurt, and also because their situation was so common: "If I help you, I would have to help so many families who are going through the same thing."

Faced with a dire lack of money, Teresa decided to set up a stall outside her house to sell things, but the gangs started to demand money. Feeling trapped by the constant harassment and threats, she decided to try and go back to the United States:

> I said to my son, "I don't know how I'm going to do it, but one of us has to leave and see what else is out there, see if we can't survive somehow," I said, "because here, you will end up dead, I will end up dead, and I can't have that."

She set off in August 2012. She took two days to reach Tapachula, but by the time of this interview she had been in there for eleven days, trying to get enough money to continue her journey. She had stayed at first in the migrant shelter for the maximum stay of three days; the rest of the time she slept in different places, and did not know where she would sleep in the coming days; she ate only sporadically. During the day, she went with another migrant to look for work.

Teresa was worried about her son who had stayed behind in El Salvador. She asked her brother and his wife to help her get him out of the country:

> [T]hat's all I asked of them, I don't care if I stay where I am, I said, but just help me get my son out, the gangs are really hassling him; he can't go out on his own, he spends all his time shut up indoors, and he's become depressed. Sometimes he says to me that it's my fault he's suffering. And I tell him, "even if I die on this journey, I'm going to do everything I can to get you out of there" [. . .]. But he's still annoyed, and he says "no mum, not any more. Let's just accept that we're going to die here." I said "no! I'm not going to give up. I'm going to see how I can help you to get out of there."

She hoped to make her way gradually up to the US border, working along the way to subsist and keep moving. She was determined to carry on, and was hopeful that she would get there without being sent back: "this time they're not going to deport me. I pray they won't; I pray it won't happen again [. . .]. They say, "third time lucky," and I'm at that third time now [. . .]. Even if I take a year to get there, god willing, I think I will make it."

Teresa's narrative is permeated by shifting but persistent insecurity, uncertainty, and unease. Both she and her son feel trapped by their circumstances, by a long series of personal crises, each of which is a tipping point for yet another move or shift, when difficult circumstances become intolerable. These crises—which are at once economic, personal, and political—are revealed as such in the emotional experience of this precarious mobility, of frustration, desperation, determination. Teresa and her son have little familial, social, or state support with which to confront the hostile circumstances in their "homeland," which are marked by dislocation and economic and personal insecurity.

Teresa's protracted, precarious mobility in many ways seems to embody the notion of "permanent temporariness" mentioned by Bailey et al. (2002); in her case, this is not about extended periods of waiting, but rather a kind of continuous and deeply frustrating unsettling: she is unable to find a place to make her own. So, hers is also a story of the shifting otherness that accompanies and *drives* movement, here under the gaze of society at large when away from home, and then in turn under that of her own family as she tries to slip back into a space that no longer fits her. Precarious mobility is often about the inability to stay (see Winton 2018). Her story moreover is not just about her many trips North, but also a very local kind of imposed wandering. These scales of mobility are deeply emotional for Teresa, inextricably tied up not just with the future of her children but also a reluctant and frustrated homecoming whose emotional effects seem more pronounced than the much longer, arduous movement North and back. Her displacement is both a consequence and cause of the crises she has had to overcome, and while her survival is fragile, her resolve to keep moving until she finds her destination is unshakable.

"Overnight I had nothing"

An ex-police officer, and refugee in Mexico since 2011, Susana was living in Tapachula, Mexico with her aunt and three children at the time of this interview in September 2015. Her relatively stable life was interrupted in 1996 when her sister was killed, after which point changes in her circumstances and the decisions she has to make would set her on course for a much more precarious life:

> I was a housewife then, but when [my sister was killed] I joined the police academy. I knew who had killed my sister, and some colleagues and I went after them. They were arrested and put in prison, they got 30 years but in 2010 their sentence was reduced, and they were released. [. . .] It was her killers who were threatening me, harassing me, with extortions, doing all kinds of things. I had to move house four times, to different towns. I was all over the place, and they kept on at me: "we're watching you," "we know where you are." I couldn't cope with the threats any more, couldn't cope. I wasn't free to go out of the door. There were bags of blood by the front door, and a note that said "how would you like your head?" I couldn't stand it. It was a real crisis for me, a terrible psychosis [. . .]. The police chief himself said to me "look, if you don't go, whatever happens they're going to kill you."
>
> So, I started to look up about asylum on the internet, how I could ask for asylum in another country and I saw about COMAR [. . .]. I decided to leave my daughters [. . .] with their father, as I really didn't have any money, and didn't know what to expect. So just me and my aunt left.

After being robbed and extorted at the Guatemala-Mexico border, they crossed over to Mexico with nothing.

> I was now desperate, and went into the Catholic church that was there. The priest stared at us, and I explained what was happening to us, and he said "don't worry, let me try and speak to someone in Tapachula, If she's there, I can take you there right now." Well, he spoke to this person, and he told us "we're just going to pray that Migration don't catch us, because that would be the end of it." And so it was, the priest took us to the migrant shelter in Tapachula, and we were there almost a month while we applied for asylum and everything [. . .].
>
> We left there and went to work for a woman who took us from the shelter to work at her *botanero*.[6] We had to get up at 5am to start preparing everything, [and worked] right up to 10, 11, 12 o'clock at night, all for 50 pesos.[7] And she would humiliate us [. . .]. She used to say to me "if you open your mouth, things will go badly for you." So, I was scared, I didn't say anything [. . .].

After a few months, her now ex-husband brought her daughters to her in Tapachula, but her older son had stayed behind alone:

> The *maras* were making him pay "rent," and saying that if he didn't pay he would have to sell drugs instead, or they would kill him. So, I was sending him money to pay them off for about a year and a half, until he was 18 and could migrate on his own [. . .]. So, then he came here to apply for asylum too. My heart rejoiced when I saw him, to have him with me, but at the same time it made me sad because we were living in even worse conditions than we are now. [. . .][8]
>
> I would have had no need to emigrate; my whole life changed, it was a terrible shock because I had it all, a house, a bed, food. A middle-class life, and overnight I had nothing, I was in another country, where you arrive and know nobody, where you don't even know where to go to ask for a glass of water, I mean, it's really dreadful. I just wanted a safe place where I could protect my life and the lives of my children, so it's really hard because even though we've been here almost five years, we still suffer shortages of the most basic things [. . .].
>
> I don't have a steady job. Right now, I'm working handing out flyers, I get a bit of commission depending on how many I give out. But I'm basically on my own in this, I have to see that we have money to eat and pay the rent, and it's really hard with the two girls in school. [. . .] But in the end, we do have the peace that people in El Salvador don't, and that we certainly didn't have. My mother [in El Salvador] has had to move house about seven times. So, I say thank God, I was accepted as a refugee, and I've been allowed to stay here, no? Believe me, the discrimination in Mexico is awful, and I've had some nasty things happen to me because of that, but I'm getting there.

Similar to Teresa, a sense of ongoing precarity permeates Susana's experience, but here there was a clear "tipping point," a moment of crisis that meant Susana had no choice but to flee. Yet, it was not the murder of her sister *per se*, or indeed her subsequent decisions that brought her to that point, but rather a stark lack of state protection: first, she was impelled to *become the law* to bring her sisters killers to justice, and then forced to flee in the face of threats from criminal groups from which she had no protection. How this violence-based displacement is experienced depends very much the amount and kind of resources available to those moving. Susana was living a relatively comfortable life in El Salvador, but fleeing home not only has an emotional cost, but also a very real material one. For those who get by economically—that is, maintain a reasonable standard of living, but without significant capital—the resources they have available are often place-based (local family and social ties, emergency support networks, local sources of income). Leaving that place without the economic, social, or political capital needed to prosper in another country exposes them to a new crisis: one of acute precarity that is associated not with further displacement, but rather stuckedness (Hage 2009), and of being "in" without being "of" place (Doná 2010).

So the nature of Susana's struggle has shifted as she passed through different moments in her displacement: leaving (fleeing direct threats of violence and associated trauma), arriving (managing to cross the border and reach Tapachula), and staying (providing for her family, and negotiating confounding bureaucracy to obtain papers for her and her children). The continuous nature of her struggle is alluded to in the tense of her experiences: she recounts arriving in Mexico and telling the priest not what *had* happened to them (why they were fleeing), but rather what *was happening* to them, which was an ongoing and far more pressing predicament). Susana is one of the "lucky" very few of those fleeing violence in Central America who has some legal protection in the form of refugee status in Mexico, but this has given her little terms of creating conditions necessary for her to be able to rebuild her life. She is simply unable to get back on her feet, and is stuck. The tipping point for Susana was when she could not stand the threats against her life anymore. She left to save her life, but at the cost of her stability. Time and circumstances will tell if in the future she once again feels she has more to lose by staying than by moving on from her precarious existence in Tapachula.

Final Reflections

This chapter has been an attempt to critically engage with the notion of crisis as this relates to migration and displacement in the Central America-Mexico region. Politically, Mexico is caught up in a migration "crisis" not strictly its own, but which certainly is a convenient means for the government to carry on business as usual in the continued containment and increasing criminalization of Central American migration, despite serious deterioration of security in that region and important increases in national and international violence-based displacement. Asylum policy in Mexico is a tokenistic minimum through which the government complies with international "humanitarian" commitments, but which in no way fits the scale of the need for protection in the region, nor with the needs of the people themselves.

In this context, the chapter has explored the notion of crisis in relation to mobility and particularly displacement, not in terms of how a "crisis" is discursively constructed and materially enacted as migration and border policy, but rather looking at the complex experiences of those caught up in this damaging geopolitical game; mobility is both a political and personal problem when it is associated with marginality. Moreover, it has been important to remember and demonstrate that these personal experiences do not begin and end at borders, nor do they suddenly emerge alongside a political crisis. While as Kaiser (2014) rightly observes, crisis is not just about mobility, likewise mobility is not just about crisis; we argue that in the personal sphere, mobility "crises" are lived as part of the ongoing and shifting but intractable relationship between displacement and marginality.

The stories shared come from different periods of the recent past, in order to show that what are contemporary concerns about displacement, violence, and control in the region are not new phenomena, and really are not a break from a non-crisis "norm." It goes without saying that the stories recounted here do not tell *the* story about migration and mobility in the region. For every person who seeks asylum, there are many more who flee into Mexico unnoticed by everyone except those who prey on them, and many more who are detained and deported back to the country they are fleeing from. For all those who find some safety in Mexico, there are many who have to keep running from the same gangs or from precarity itself. For everyone who has to stay put even in the face of imminent danger, and who manages to keep a low profile and survive, there are others for whom the price of staying is their forced cooperation with the local gang and possibly their life. Yet the stories portray something of how complicated and intractable the relationship between mobility, marginality, and survival is, and how the very fact of this association has such profound effects on increasingly precarious lives. Furthermore, it is important to stress that mere survival is too often achieved in spite of government action in Central America, Mexico and the United States, both in terms of a lack of adequate protection, and excessive, selective repression.

The narratives shared are unsettling not just in an immediate sense for the conditions and hardships they describe, but also in the sense that they open up alternative ways of reading "crises" as part of protracted struggles for survival. Lived mobility is a deeply historical, personal, and conditioned process, in which the self—at the center of a complex web of shifting opportunities and oppressions—is itself in flux, at the apex of damage and possibility. Precarious mobility is peppered with moments of crisis or rupture: tipping points at which crucial decisions are made. These ruptures—which are economic, personal, and political at their core—are lived as emotional experiences, of frustration, uncertainty, desperation, and of resolve. As political crises are created to contain and repel perceived threats (objectively, regional or global-level solutions to any sudden population movement are relatively straightforward), the harm associated with the protracted struggles to survive of many people on the move is going largely unnoticed.

Notes

1. This increase can be partially inferred from emigration census data: between 2000 and 2015, the total number of international emigrants from the seven Central American countries increased from 2.2 to 4.1 million (Canales and Rojas 2017). Over the past two decades, northern Central American countries (Guatemala, Honduras, and El Salvador) have consistently represented around 95 percent of all migrants moving through Mexico to the United States (see data at SEGOB, Boletines Estadísticos, http://www.politicamigratoria.gob.mx/es_mx/SEGOB/Boletines_Estadisticos).
2. Much has been made of the increase in deportations as a result of the implementation of the Integral Southern Border Program in 2014, in particular as this has been associated with a sharp increase in migration control measures (see Isacson et al. 2017). Deportations from Mexico (of which a steady 95 percent are from northern Central America) have increased gradually but they are nothing new. In the 1990s the average number of deportations carried out by Mexican authorities each year was 115,000, increasing in the 2000s to a yearly average of 147,000 deportations, and increasing again between 2000 and 2016 with an average of 180,000 deportations each year (see SEGOB, http://www.politicamigratoria.gob.mx/es_mx/SEGOB/Boletines_Estadisticos).

3. Official statistics relating to deportations from Mexico are available at: SEGOB, http://www.politicamigratoria.gob.mx/es_mx/SEGOB/Boletines_Estadisticos
4. In 2014 for example, in an area called the "dry corridor" that stretches across all countries in the region, drought had a serious impact on subsistence farming, particularly in coffee-producing areas that had already been affected by *roya* (coffee rust) disease: while the drought lasted, 512,000 families suffered losses in production, in their ability to feed their families, and in their access to safe water, all of which generated water-based conflicts and increased emigration (Programa Estado de la Nación 2016, 208).
5. The two interviews cited here were conducted as part of two projects: "Mobility in Transnational Zones of Precarity: A View from the Guatemala-Mexico Border," funded by the Social Sciences and Humanities Research Council of Canada and coordinated by Tanya Basok and Danièle Bélanger, in which Martha Luz Rojas Wiesner was co-researcher (see Basok et al., 2015). Researchers participating in this project have given their consent for the use of material presented here; "The Mobility 'Crisis' in Central America and Mexico," coordinated by Ailsa Winton, funded by IOM and carried out in collaboration with UNHCR Mexico. The chapter was written in the context of the multidisciplinary project "Perspectives on Vulnerability in the Southeast of Mexico: Megadiversity and Alternative Practices for Wellbeing" funded by ECOSUR.
6. A kind of restaurant/bar that serves alcoholic drinks and bar snacks.
7. Just under $3 USD.
8. A particular kind of youth gang with presence throughout the region, and one of the main violent criminal groups whose actions are causing continued displacement (see Winton 2018).

References

Alba, F., and M. A. Castillo. 2012. *New Approaches to Migration Management in Mexico and Central America*. Washington, DC: Migration Police Institute.

Albuja, S. 2014. "Criminal Violence, Displacement, and Migration in Mexico and Central America." In *Migration and Humanitarian Crisis: Causes, Consequences and Responses*, edited by Susan F. Martin, Sanjula Weerasinghe, and Abbie Taylor, 113–137. New York: Routledge.

Anderson, B. 2010. "Migration, Immigration Controls and the Fashioning of Precarious Workers." *Work, Employment and Society* 24, no. 2: 300–317. doi: 10.1177/0950017010362141.

Ángeles Cruz, H. 2003. "La Migración Internacional a través de la Frontera Sur. La Dimensión de las Estadísticas para el Soconusco." *Ecofronteras* 19: 5–8.

Bailey, A. J., R. A. Wright, A. Mountz, and I. M. Miyares. 2002. "(Re) producing Salvadoran Transnational Geographies." *Annals of the Association of American Geographers* 92, no. 1: 125–144. doi: 10.1111/1467-8306.00283.

Basok, T., D. Bélanger, M. L. Rojas Wiesner, and G. Candiz. 2015. *Rethinking Transit Migration: Precarity, Mobility, and Self-making in Mexico*. Basingstoke, UK: Palgrave Macmillan.

Betts, A. 2010. "Survival Migration: A New Protection Framework." *Global Governance: A Review of Multilateralism and International Organizations* 16, no. 3: 361–382.

Blunt, A. 2007. "Cultural Geographies of Migration: Mobility, Transnationality and Diaspora." *Progress in Human Geography* 31, no. 5: 684–694. doi: 10.1177/0309132507078945.

Butler, J. 2009. "Performativity, Precarity and Sexual Politics." *AIBR. Revista de Antropología Iberoamericana* 4, no. 3: i–xiii.

Çağlar, A. 2016. " Still 'Migrants' after All Those Years: Foundational Mobilities, Temporal Frames and Emplacement of Migrants." *Journal of Ethnic and Migration Studies* no. 6: 952–969. doi: 10.1080/1369183X.2015.1126085.

Campesi, G. 2012. "Migraciones, seguridad y confines en la teoría social contemporánea." *Revista Crítica Penal y Poder* 3: 1–20.

Canales, A., and M. L. Rojas Wiesner. 2017. *Panorama de la migración internacional en México y Centroamérica.* Informe presentado en la Reunión Regional Latinoamericanay Caribeña de Expertas y Expertos en Migración Internacional preparatoria del Pacto Mundial para una Migración Segura, Ordenada y Regular, 30 y 31 de agosto, Santiago de Chile: Comisión Económica para América Latina y el Caribe. https://refugeesmigrants.un.org/sites/default/files/eclac_mexico_y_centroamerica_resumen_ejecutivo.pdf

Castillo, M. A., and M. Toussaint. 2010. "Seguridad y migración en la frontera sur." In *Seguridad nacional y seguridad interior, vol. 15, Los Grandes Problemas de México*, coordinated by Arturo Alvarado, and Mónica Serrano, 269–300. Mexico City: El Colegio de México.

Castles, S. 2011. "Migration, Crisis, and the Global Labour Market." *Globalizations* 8, no. 3: 311–324. doi: 10.1080/14747731.2011.576847.

CEPAL (Comisión Económica para América Latina y el Caribe). 2010. *La economía del cambio climático en Centroamérica. Síntesis 2010*, Naciones Unidas. https://www.cepal.org/es/publicaciones/35228-la-economia-cambio-climatico-centroamerica-sintesis-2010.

Cobo, S., and P. Fuerte. 2012. *Refugiados en México: Perfiles sociodemográficos eintegración social.* Mexico City: ACNUR, Centro de Estudios Migratorios, Instituto Nacional de Migración, and Comisión Mexicana de Ayuda al Refugiado.

Conlon, D. 2011. "Waiting: Feminist Perspectives on the Spacings Timings of Migrant (Im) Mobility." *Gender, Place & Culture* 18, no. 3: 353–360. doi: 10.1080/0966369X.2011.566320.

Cresswell, T. 2006. "The Right to Mobility: The Production of Mobility in the Courtroom." *Antipode* 38, no. 4: 735–754. doi: 10.1111/j.1467-8330.2006.00474.x/full.

De Genova, N. 2013. "Spectacles of Migrant 'Illegality': The Scene of Exclusion, The Obscene of Inclusion." *Ethnic and Racial Studies* 36, no. 7: 180–1198. doi: 10.1080/01419870.2013.783710.

Doná, G. 2010. "Rethinking Well-Being: from Contexts to Processes." *International Journal of Migration, Health and Social Care* 6: 3–14. doi:10.5042/ijmhsc.2010.0606.

Gill, N., J. Caletrío, and V. Mason. 2011. "Introduction: Mobilities and Forced Migration." *Mobilities* 6, no. 3: 301–316. doi: 10.1080/17450101.2011.590032.

Grayson, G. W. 2006. "Mexico's Southern Flank: The "Third" U.S. Border." *Orbis* 50, no. 1: 53–69. doi: 10.1016/j.orbis.2005.10.005.

Glick Schiller, N., and N. B. Salazar. 2013. "Regimes of Mobility across the Globe." *Journal of Ethnic and Migration Studies* 39, no. 2: 183–200. doi: 10.1080/1369183X.2013.723253.

Griffiths, M. B. E. 2014. "Out of Time: The Temporal Uncertainties of Refused Asylum Seekers and Immigration Detainees." *Journal of Ethnic and Migration Studies* 40, no. 1: 1991–2009. doi: 10.1080/1369183X.2014.907737.

Hage, G. 2009. "Waiting out the Crisis: On Stuckedness and Governmentality." In *Waiting*, edited by Vic Carlton, 97–106. Melbourne, Australia: Melbourne University Press.

Heyman, J., J. Slack, and E. Guerra. Forthcoming. "Bordering a 'Crisis': Central American Asylum Seekers and the Reproduction of Dominant Border Enforcement Practices." *Journal of the Southwest.*

Isacson, A., M. Meyer, and H. Smith. 2017. *La frontera sur de México: Seguridad, migración centroamericana y políticas estadounidenses*, WOLA, June 2017. https://www.wola.org/wp-content/uploads/2017/06/WOLA-Frontera-sur-de-Mexico-2017.pdf

Kaiser, T. 2014. "Crisis? Which Crisis? Families and Forced Migration." In *Crisis and Migration: Critical Perspectives*, edited by Anna Lindley, 181–202. New York: Routledge.

Lindley, A. 2014. "Exploring Crisis and Migration: Concepts and Issues." In *Crisis and Migration: Critical Perspectives*, edited by Anna Lindley, pp. 1–23. New York: Routledge.

McAdam, J. 2014. "Conceptualizing Crisis Migration." In *Migration and Humanitarian Crisis: Causes, Consequences and Responses*, edited by S. F. Martin, S. Weerasinghe, and A.Taylor, 28–50. New York: Routledge.

Nyers, P. 2013. "Liberating irregularity: no borders, temporality, citizenship." In *Citizenship and Security: The Constitution of Political Being*, edited by X. Guillaume, and J. Huysmans, 49–64. New York: Routledge.

Orozco, M., and J. Yansura. 2015. *Centroamérica en la mira: La migración en su relación con el desarrollo y las oportunidades para el cambio*. Buenos Aires: Teseo.

Pascucci, E. 2016. "Transnational Disruptions: Materialities and Temporalities of Transnational Citizenship among Somali Refugees in Cairo." *Global Networks* 16, no. 3: 326–343. doi: 10.1111/glob.12115.

Programa Estado de la Nación. 2016. *Quinto Informe Estado de la Región en Desarrollo Humano Sostenible*. San José, Costa Rica: Programa Estado de la Nación.

Redfield, P. 2005. "Doctors, Borders, and Life in Crisis." *Cultural Anthropology* 20, no. 3: 328–361. doi: 10.1525/can.2005.20.3.328

REDODEM (Red de Documentación de las Organizaciones Defensoras de Migrantes). 2017. *Migrantes en México: Recorriendo un camino de violencia. Informe 2016*. Mexico City: REDODEM. http://www.fm4pasolibre.org/pdfs/informe_redodem_2016_17.pdf

Rigoni, F. M. 2007. "La última frontera del crimen: El secuestro del migrante indocumentado." *Migrantes. Revista de Información y Pastoral Migratoria* 13, no. 3: 3.

Rojas Wiesner, M. L. 2017. "Precariedades y vulnerabilidades en la migración. Notas para el análisis de la situación de mujeres centroamericanas en México." *Astrolabio: Revista Internacional de Filosofia*. 19: 218–230.

Rojas Wiesner, M. L., and H. Ángeles Cruz. 2008. "Gendered Migrations in the Americas: Mexico as Country of Origin, Destination and Transit." In *New Perspectives on Gender and Migration: Livelihood, Rights and Entitlements*, edited by Nicola Piper, 189–245. New York: Routledge.

Rubio Díaz-Leal, L., and S. Albuja. 2014. "Criminal Violence and Displacement in Mexico." In *Crisis and Migration: Critical Perspectives*, edited by Anna Lindley, 73–92. New York: Routledge.

Schapendonk, J. 2012. "Migrants' In/Mobilities on their Way to the EU: Lost in Transit?" *Tijdschrift voor economische en sociale geografie* 103, no. 5: 577–583. doi: 10.1111/j.1467-9663.2012.00735.x.

Serrano Herrera, C., and M. Jaramillo Benítez. 2017. *Anuario de migración y remesas: México 2017*. Mexico City: Fundación BBVA Bancomer / Consejo Nacional de Población.

Shamir, R. 2005. "Without Borders? Notes on Globalization as a Mobility Regime." *Sociological Theory* 23, no. 2: 197–217. doi: 10.1111/j.0735-2751.2005.00250.x.

Sheller, M. 2011. "Mobility." *Sociopedia.isa*. http://www.sagepub.net/isa/resources/pdf/mobility.pdf

Waitt, G., and A. Gorman-Murray. 2011. " 'It's About Time You Came Out': Sexualities, Mobility and Home." *Antipode* 43, no. 4: 1380–1403. doi: 10.1111/j.1467-8330.2011.00876.x.

Walters, W. 2011. "Foucault and Frontiers: Notes on the Birth of the Humanitarian Border." In *Governmentality: Current Issues and Future Challenges*, edited by U. Bröckling, S. Krasmann, and T. Lemke, 138–164. New York: Routledge.

Winton, A. 2015. "Violence, Borders and Boundaries: Reframing Young People´s Mobility." In *Movement, Mobilities and Journeys*, edited by C. Ni Laoire, A, White, and T. Skelton, 131–149. Geographies of Children and Children and Young People 6. Singapore: Springer. doi: 10.1007/978-981-4585-93-4_4-1.

Winton, A. 2017. "Cuerpos disidentes en movimiento: Miradas sobre movilidad transgénero desde la frontera sur de México." *El Cotidiano* 202: 115–126.

Winton, A. 2018. *Desplazamiento por violencia en el Norte de Centroamérica: Historias de supervivencia, Report 23, Observatorio Iberoamericano sobre Movilidad Humana, Migraciones y Desarrollo, Universidad Pontificia Comillas, Madrid.* https://www.comillas.edu/images/OBIMID/boletines_e_informes/Informe_OBIMID_FEBRERO2018.pdf.

WFP (World Food Programme), IADB (Inter-American Development Bank), IFAD (International Fund for Agricultural Development), OAS (Organization of American States), and IOM (International Organization for Migration). 2017. *Food Security and Emigration. Why People Flee and the Impact on Family Members Left Behind in El Salvador, Guatemala, and Honduras. Research Report.* https://docs.wfp.org/api/documents/WFP-0000019629/download/.

Yee Quintero, J. C., and E. Torre Cantalapiedra. 2016. "Lidiando con la frontera vertical: estrategias migratorias de los hondureños en tránsito por México." *Revista Interdisciplinar da Mobilidade Humana* 24, no. 47: 97–114.

CHAPTER 15

MIGRATION, CRISES, AND SOCIAL TRANSFORMATION IN INDIA SINCE THE 1990S

SMRITI RAO AND VAMSI VAKULABHARANAM

THIS paper looks at the close tension and relationship in India between recent social transformations and migration crises.[1] It focusses on two specific transformations—accelerated urbanization, and deeper penetration of a neoliberal kind of capitalism over the last two to three decades in rural and urban India. The current Indian urbanization, along with Chinese urbanization since 1980s, should be seen as a globe-transforming phenomenon, as about a tenth of the world's population are changing their status from rural to urban, primarily through internal migration (but also through extended urbanization). Simultaneously, these economies have increasingly come under the logic of neoliberal capitalism, greatly increasing the spread of capitalism over the past three to four decades. This chapter argues that internal migration in India is mainly a reordering of productive and reproductive labor that signifies a deep transformation of society. It is accentuated by three overlapping crises (in practice) that we present below.

The first two of these three crises are widely acknowledged: an *agrarian crisis* marked by low agricultural growth rates, a livelihoods crisis for small farmers, and reduced wage employment in agriculture; and an *employment crisis* where nonagricultural employment (in urban and rural areas) is inadequate in quantity and quality to compensate for the decline in agricultural employment. The first crisis pushes large numbers of rural residents to seek employment outside of agriculture, which means moving to urban areas for jobs in construction and low-skill services. The second (employment) crisis accentuates the phenomenon of urban precarity and informality, and makes migration transient, with migrants returning to rural homes once a particular spell of employment is completed, only to start a new journey later. The migration process in India thus challenges boundaries of urban and rural and raises the question of what this phenomenon of increased migration signifies, something explored in the subsequent sections.

The third overlapping crisis that shapes migration patterns is a social reproduction crisis in which a lack of social provisioning by the state, and declining access to the rural and urban commons, have expanded rather than compressed the temporal and spatial disconnect between productive and reproductive work, making it more difficult for workers to bridge this divide. This background of social reproductive crisis helps explain why family migration is relatively common in India. Although there are significant streams of single male migration, particularly in North-Central India, many temporary migrants move as couples, often with their children. This may be due to relatively rigid gender divisions of labor when it comes to productive labor in industries such as construction. However, studies of urban labor also point out the impossibility of ensuring basic biological reproduction on very low wages without substantial reliance upon unpaid labor, whether it is to generate food, access unreliable and distant sources of water, or to ensure that children are clothed and fed.

In presenting these overlapping crises this chapter examines patterns that go back at least two decades. The term "crisis" suggests something that is contained in time and space (and can alternate with moments and places of non-crisis), and neither of these appears to be the case in India today. These are also not crises that are bringing the system to a halt, or even causing political or economic upheaval. Instead, each of these elements appears to be accepted as part of the social fabric, to be worked around and within, to be *normal* in fact. Thus this paper theorizes the *new normal* of Indian development as something that is defined by a state of continuous movement of labor (both of the productive and reproductive kinds) across the rural and urban divide, that is precarious and informal in nature, and that allows for capital to more easily extract surplus.

In this sense, the three interrelated crises are not crises for capital (they actually facilitate easier accumulation), but are crises for a sustained and rooted reproduction of the majority of working people. These crises transform themselves into transient movement and migration (not a paralysis of labor), with an ameliorating role (with respect to the crises) played by gender relations that ensure that reproductive labor absorbs the uncertainty and precarity of this movement. Therefore, migration can be understood as the transformation of the overall division of social labor, resulting from the three overlapping crises presented above.

Migration to Urban India

The literature analyzes migration to urban India across two main temporal-spatial axes: permanent versus temporary, and rural–urban versus urban–urban, to which we add interstate versus intrastate. The absence of reliable national level data on temporary migration means that the analyses of temporary migration are often qualitative rather than quantitative, with the reverse being true for permanent migration. Despite the data limitations however, two important trends emerge from these studies. First, migration to urban India has increased in quantity over the last two decades. Second, this increase is driven by both temporary, circular employment migration of the "footloose" kind (Breman 2010) and permanent marriage migration, even as permanent economic migration remains stagnant. It is not a coincidence that these changes have occurred at the same time as the intensification of the three kinds of crises discussed in this paper. These crises have transformed the way that the majority of Indians earn a livelihood, forcing them to seek work wherever they can find it, including in the city. The burden of these crises is borne in gendered way, however, requiring an intensification of women's work, without which even this extremely precarious means of existence would not be viable.

Temporal Categories: Permanent Migration

Permanent migration in India is defined by the decennial Indian Census, as well as the Indian National Sample Survey (NSS) as a move to a new "usual place of residence" for a year or more. According to the Census, the share of Indians engaged in permanent migration has been relatively stagnant, with about 30 percent of the population reporting themselves as permanent migrants over the last several decades. The NSS data indicates an increase from 23 percent to 28 percent between 1983 and 2007–2008 (Table 15.1). While both the Census and the NSS provide us with data on migration, due to the greater degree of detail in the NSS, it merits greater focus.

According to the NSS data, the share of urban migrants within all permanent migrants has risen slightly after 1988, indicating an urbanization of permanent migration. The increase in the overall share of permanent migrants is, however, driven by the migration of women who move to their marital homes after marriage.

The NSS divides permanent migrants into migrants for "economic" reasons, migrants for studies, "follower" migrants (who accompany a primary earner), and marriage migrants. Among working age male migrants, the first category is the largest, but relatively unchanged. Among working age women, on the other hand, while the first and second categories are falling, the share of marriage migrants has grown. Between 1983 and 2008, marriage migration increased across most parts of India (Mazumdar et al. 2013; Rao and Finnoff 2015). In almost every state in the northern, central, eastern, and western regions, 60 percent or more of working age women reported being marriage migrants in 2008, with the highest concentration of marriage migrants in the relatively poor "Hindi heartland" states. Thus female marriage migrants constitute the largest and fastest growing group of permanent migrants in India (Tables 15.1 and 15.2). Due to the ubiquity of patrilocal marriage for women, Indian girls are effectively raised as migrants in the making, constantly reminded that their home will eventually be elsewhere.

The profile of male, mostly economic, permanent migrants and that of female, mostly marriage migrants differs in one important way. Permanent male urban migrants tend to have higher levels of education and skill, and tend to experience upward mobility in the destination area, with urban-urban migrants being the best off. Thus male permanent migration tends to accentuate rural–urban inequality through a "brain drain" of sorts (Vakulabharanam and Thakurata 2014). Not surprisingly, female follower

Table 15.1 Permanent Migrants as a Share of the Population

	1983	1988	1999	2008
All permanent migrants	23	25	26	28
Economic migrants	3	3	3	3
Marriage migrants	13	16	17	19
Percent of migrants who are women	74	76	78	81
Percents of migrants to urban areas	32	29	32	33

Source: Authors' calculations based on NSS survey data

Table 15.2 Characteristics of Working Age Urban Permanent Migrants by Gender (in Percentages)

Women	1983	1988	1999	2008
Marriage migrants	58	61	64	65
Economic migrants	5	4	3	3
Follower migrants	31	27	26	26
Urban–urban migrants	40	40	41	41
Men	**1983**	**1988**	**1999**	**2008**
Marriage migrants	1	2	2	1
Economic migrants	63	63	61	64
Follower migrants	19	18	19	18
Urban–urban migrants	40	40	39	38

Source: Authors' calculations based on NSS survey data

migrants share the relatively better off socioeconomic profile of male permanent economic migrants (Rao 2017). However, female urban marriage migrants have education levels below the average for urban nonmigrant women, and most rural–urban marriage migrants appear to enter the households of relatively poor urban men. Rao and Finnoff (2015) see this as a result of rising rural–urban inequality in combination with the employment crisis. They argue that even poorer urban households become desirable as marriage alliances for rural households, since the jobs crisis in urban India makes the marriage market a more feasible way to gain an urban foothold than the labor market. It is unclear whether the women thus married into the urban precariat are left better off, but control over the bodies of women thus becomes one way that rural families are able to access an exclusionary urban economy.

Temporal Categories: Temporary Migration

The data on temporary and circular migrants is a great deal less reliable. Neither the Census nor the NSS is able to capture these forms of migration with much accuracy, although the 2007–2008 NSS survey does make a more serious attempt to do so. The NSS defines migration for durations of more than one month but less than six months as "temporary". As Table 15.3 shows, by this definition in 2007–2008 almost 14 million Indians were engaged in temporary migration, double the number in 1999–2000. However, this data also indicates a decrease in temporary migration to urban areas in this period (Vakulabharanam and Thakurata 2014). There is almost universal agreement that this is an underestimation. As squatters and pavement dwellers, temporary urban migrants do not have a fixed residence in urban areas and are therefore not captured by the Census or NSS surveyors (Breman 2010; Roy 2007).

Field studies from across the country (Breman 2010; Garikipati 2008; Guérin et al. 2007; Mosse et al. 2002; Pattenden 2016; Picherit 2018; Rogaly and Rafique 2003; Roy 2007; Shah 2006) show that temporary migration has become an integral part of the livelihood portfolio for most rural Indians. There is evidence from this literature that the scale of such temporary migration increased in the 2000s partly as a consequence of the agrarian crisis that began in the 1990s. Deshingkar and Start (2003) estimate that there might be up to 100 million temporary migrants in India today.

These field studies, as well as an analysis of the NSS data on temporary migration (Keshri and Bhagat 2012) show that temporary migration is a strategy pursued by those who are relatively poor, have little or no land, are low-skilled or semi-skilled, and are lower caste. Temporary migrants also rely upon (and are drawn into relations of debt dependence upon) labor contractors and brokers in ways that permanent migrants are less likely to. The least well off of these migrants tend to move with at least some members of

Table 15.3 Temporary Migration: NSS Data (in millions)

	1999		2008	
	Total	Urban	Total	Urban
Male	6.9	1.5	11.6	0.9
Female	4	0.9	2	0.2

Source: Vakulabharanam and Thakurata (2014)

their families, so that the share of women temporary migrants, while hard to pin down exactly, does seem to be higher than the NSS estimate (Guérin et al 2015; Lahiri-Dutt 2008; Pattenden 2012; Virk 2004). However, not all of these women may perform paid work in the urban destination, for reasons discussed later.

Many of these migrants work in seasonal industries such as construction, the brickmaking industry, small and artisan mining, and assorted low-skill services in urban areas (Agnihotri and Mazumdar 2009; Lahiri-Dutt 2008). Due to the sex-segregated nature of labor in both construction and brickmaking work in India, workers are hired as "jodis," or couples, encouraging the migration of families, and providing employment to some low-skill migrant women as well as men. For women, an additional important source of employment is domestic work in urban households, which has expanded with the increase in the number of urban professional workers and double-earner households (Mazumdar et al 2013). Domestic workers labor alone, doing work that is highly stigmatized, in the "private" space of a home. They are therefore routinely subjected to economic exploitation, sexual abuse, and various kinds of social humiliation, but have little ability to protect themselves against such abuse or to seek recourse when abuse occurs (Coelho et al 2013). For both men and women who migrate, therefore, the employment opportunities that are available are "indecent" along multiple axes.

What is known about the lives of urban migrants suggests that the term "temporary" migration is misleading in two ways. The primary sources on this kind of migration show that while some temporary migrants do indeed move for less than a year, others do so for several years at a time, but to spaces that escape official efforts to enumerate them. Furthermore, as Breman (2010) famously argued in proposing the term "footloose labor," temporary migrants engage in multiple moves across a migrant's lifetime, not always to the same destination. They eventually return to homesteads in rural areas, in part because exclusionary urban development denies them the possibility of an urban space of their own. A particular migratory trip may thus be bounded by time, but migration is a much more permanent condition of existence for such migrants than for "permanent" one-time migrants.

Spatial Categories: Rural–Urban and Urban–Urban Migration

The NSS data on urban permanent migrants summarized in Table 15.2 suggests that among both men and women, rural–urban migration is the larger stream (rural–rural remains the largest, but is not the subject of the chapter) and, among male migrants, growing faster than urban-urban migration. As mentioned above, urban–urban migrants among both women and men also appear to be significantly better off than nonmigrants both before and after migration (Vakulabharanam and Thakurata 2014).

Among temporary migrants as well, rural–urban may be the larger category and growing faster than urban–urban migration, contributing to the process of urbanization discussed below. However, empirical reality may have overtaken traditional classifications, with many temporary migrants being footloose labor: moving sometime from village to city, at others from one city to another, and at yet other times from one village to another (Breman 2010). While there are well established migratory paths in some parts of the country (Bihar to Delhi and Punjab, Mahbubnagar to Mumbai and Hyderabad), new ones appear to be rapidly emerging, and as suggested earlier, rigid divisions between rural and urban destinations may no longer be as useful to understand this world of insecurity and impermanence.

Spatial Categories: Interstate versus Intrastate

Substantial inequalities between Indian states have developed over time, with Indian states in the center and east falling behind others in the west, south, and northwest. One question is thus whether interstate migration has played a role in reducing or increasing these inequalities. As far as permanent migration goes, almost 85 percent of marriage migration is still intrastate as a result of cultural and linguistic commonalities. Interstate migration accounted for 41 percent of all permanent economic migration in 2008, according to the NSS (Table 15.4). However, an early study by Cashin and Sahay (1996) argued that at least until 1990s, interstate economic migration was unable to create convergence between regions. Although Table 15.4 shows an increase in the share of interstate migration within the overall stagnant shares of permanent economic migration over the 2000s, the small numbers of relatively privileged migrants involved suggests that this stream is inequality reinforcing rather than inequality reducing (Vakulabharanam and Motiram 2016).

With temporary migration, in the absence of data we must once again rely upon microstudies. These do seem to suggest the expansion of interstate migration routes. The growth of the southern cities of Bengaluru and Hyderabad mean that workers from Odisha, Bihar, and the Northeast are now finding their way southward. The most documented streams of temporary migration are from relatively poor states such as Bihar, UP, Madhya Pradesh, and Odisha to Delhi and the other metropolitan cities, for construction and brick kiln work. There is also evidence of temporary migration from and within states like Tamil Nadu and Gujarat, which have much higher living standards

Table 15.4 Interstate Permanent Migration to Urban Areas

	1983	1988	1999	2008
As a share of urban economic migrants	32	31	31	41
As a share of urban marriage migrants	16	15	14	15

Source: Authors' calculations based on NSS survey data

on average, but also have relatively high levels of inequality. Deshingkar et al (2008) trace the increasing rates of migration among villages in Madhya Pradesh, with villagers traveling to new destinations in Gujarat and Delhi. In this case the authors do see increases in "accumulative" migration that improves the economic conditions of migrants, thus possibly reducing inequality between origin and destination (see also Rodgers and Rodgers 2011). But this study is countered by several others that conclude that temporary migration remains distress migration that results in little long term improvement in living conditions (Breman 2010; Mosse et al. 2005; Roy 2007). Most studies indicate that even when temporary migrants do bring back some savings, they are unable to invest them in assets in rural areas, usually spending them on health needs or the repayment of debt (Pattenden 2012). However, migration to urban areas may still enable challenges to caste-based hierarchies of power in the home village, even as it makes workers more vulnerable to capitalist exploitation (Guérin et al. 2007; Picherit 2018).

The second interesting aspect of interstate migration is the degree to which language, clothing, caste-composition, and cultural norms vary between Indian states. One implication of this has been mentioned earlier—marriage migration remains mostly intrastate. The second implication is that interstate migration is a risk-laden and potentially alienating experience in India in a way that is more than just a function of the greater distance traveled. Making the connections that lead to jobs, or housing, or a rich community life is much more complicated when language, clothes, and food change. Migrants from out of state are often cast as "outsiders" in periodic political mobilizations that target their real or perceived economic gains as at the expense of "insiders." Interstate migration may thus create pools of migrant labor even easier to monitor and discipline.

The Three Overlapping Crises and Migration: Agrarian Crisis

Starting in the mid-1990s, India's society and economy has witnessed an agrarian crisis that has spread unevenly across the country. One startling manifestation of this crisis is that more than 300,000 farmers have committed suicide, according to official estimates from National Crime Records Bureau in India (Sainath 2015). This suicide phenomenon started in the mid-1990s, when India embarked on a drive to liberalize its agriculture. Liberalization, in the Indian context, meant connecting the Indian agriculture to the larger world economy, as well as dismantling multiple support structures that Indian farmers had won from the Indian state through their movements. The rest of this chapter describes the main features of this crisis.

While the agrarian crisis in India coincides with the introduction of market-oriented reforms in agriculture, the reforms are not solely responsible for the crisis, although they constitute the most important causal factor (Vakulabharanam and Motiram 2011). The soil and groundwater-eroding effects of the Green Revolution experiment of the 1960s have also been critically important to the slowdown of productivity improvements across the country by the 1990s. While the Green Revolution had been introduced in a few pockets of grain production in the late 1960s in India, its technologies spread to other parts of the country and to the cultivation of non-grain crops (a phenomenon termed as a "Lagged Green Revolution") by the 1980s (Vakulabharanam 2004). In the last decade or so, there have been three additional explanations for the increasing agrarian distress. First, through processes of "accumulation by dispossession" the advancing urban spaces as well as industry (through the creation of special economic zones) have begun to displace large numbers of farmers from their farmlands and livelihoods (Jenkins et. al. 2014). Second, it has been suggested in recent research that climate change may be closely linked to the distress and the suicide phenomenon (Carleton 2017). Third, there has also been an increase in the presence of corporate capital through arrangements like contract farming and corporate farming (Motiram and Vakulabharanam 2007). All these different factors have converged in creating and deepening a widespread and spatially uneven distress phenomenon in Indian agriculture (slowing agricultural growth rates is one of many manifestations of this).

Many researchers have identified agricultural liberalization as the main contributing cause for the agrarian crisis (for an edited volume that covers multiple aspects of the crisis, see Reddy and Mishra 2010). Especially in the period 1995 to 2006, integrating Indian agriculture with the world markets coincided with a global agricultural recession that pushed the Indian agricultural prices downward relative to other sectors in the economy. Domestic liberalization measures such as reducing subsidies, and cutting down formal (relatively cheaper) state-supported agricultural credit meant that farmers faced higher costs. A lot of farmers were pushed to borrowing from informal moneylenders at astronomical interest rates (ranging from 24 percent per annum to 60 percent per annum). This created a "double squeeze" of the Indian farmers (Vakulabharanam 2004). Alongside other factors mentioned above (and the social reproductive crisis discussed below), this has created a sense of insecurity about deriving a stable livelihood from agriculture. Although agricultural growth rates at the national level have picked up after 2006, several pockets of Indian agriculture have remained distress-prone.

This has created a massive impetus to migrate over the last two decades in India. In the mid-1990s, about 70 percent of the Indian population was still directly or indirectly dependent on agriculture while the fastest growing sectors in India were services and manufacturing, mainly in urban spaces. Not all migration from rural areas is distress-induced. There is a class distinction in the way migration has progressed. On the one hand, the better-off farmers have tended to move their capital to urban areas or pursue the route of higher education in order to integrate into the higher echelons of the neoliberal class configuration (Damodaran 2008). On the other hand, the vast majority of farmers and agricultural workers (in those areas where the distress phenomenon has been rampant) have tended to integrate into the informal and precarious domains of the urban economy. However, as described in the next subsection, the out-migration of the majority of the agricultural population has not been matched by growing organized employment in manufacturing (as happened in the East Asian countries, including the recent experience of China). The impetus to migrate has been met with a deep employment crisis in the otherwise fast-growing urban spaces. What this has meant is that migration remains transient, footloose, and uncertain. The migrants have to choose from a portfolio of laboring options in agricultural and nonagricultural sectors to eke out a precarious livelihood.

The Three Overlapping Crises and Migration: Employment Crisis

This section briefly presents the main contours of the employment crisis over the last three decades. If the economy is divided into two parts, agricultural and non-agricultural sectors, the main narrative of employment can be laid out clearly. The first point is about the volume of employment. According to the Indian national sample survey employment and unemployment rounds, between 1983 and 2011–2012, the overall labor force has risen from 305 million people to about 473 million. Of this increase of about 170 million jobs, only about 20 million new jobs have been created in agriculture, and about 150 millions in the nonagricultural sector. In 2011–2012, agriculture contributed to about 225 million jobs and the nonagricultural sector contributed the remaining 248 million jobs. However, if we look at the recent period (after 2004), there has been negative addition to the agricultural jobs (about –33 million), while nonagricultural employment has risen by about 50 million jobs. In terms of employment growth during this entire period, the fastest growth was experienced in the period 1983–2005, while growth rates have slowed considerably after this period (Thomas 2014).

If we further analyze the growth in nonagricultural employment, several interesting features can be found. First, the major increases in nonagricultural employment are in the construction industry (Thomas 2014). These jobs are temporary, precarious, and informal in nature. These jobs also require low skills, so they are suitable for a transient, migrant workforce (Shrivastava 2012). Second, urban males have largely captured the higher quality employment (a relatively small proportion of employment). This is in sectors such as information technology, finance, insurance, and real estate (Thomas 2014). Third, according to these official data, both in rural as well as urban areas, women constitute a small proportion of the total employment in nonagricultural sector (about a fifth of the total employment).

In terms of the nature of employment, self-employment and casual labor dominate predominantly in rural areas (about 70 percent of the total) in 2004–2005. In urban areas, self-employment and casual labor contribute about 60 percent of the total employment in 2004–2005 (Shrivastava 2012). The informal sector contributes about 92 percent of the total employment in the Indian economy in 2011–2012 (ILO 2016).

Several important inferences can be made from the above statistics. First, agricultural is an overall shrinking sector in terms of employment, so there is a clear reordering of productive labor away from agriculture. Second, since high quality and regular formal jobs (with contracts) are not forthcoming, labor has moved into informal occupations (i.e., informal enterprises, self-employment, and informal jobs in formal corporations). In other words, labor has become increasingly flexible, even as workers have performed increasingly precarious and transient work. Third, in conjunction with the agrarian crisis described above and from various micro-studies on Indian labor, this signifies the proliferation of insecure labor (i.e. workers now perform highly seasonal and fragmented labor). It is labor that is constantly on the move between urban and rural, between agriculture and nonagriculture, and for women, it is also a more complex combination of productive and reproductive labor in multiple locations in any extended period. This latter phenomenon is what we turn to in the next sub-section.

The Three Overlapping Crises and Migration: Crisis of Social Reproduction

Social reproduction, or the production and maintenance of human life itself, requires not just the act of biological reproduction, but also the provisioning of basic needs (through the production of goods and services such as cooking, cleaning, fetching water), and care work (the care of children, the elderly, the sick, etc.) (Razavi 2007). The labor required to perform these tasks, referred to as reproductive labor here, has traditionally been assigned to women (Elson 2010).

One important aspect of reproductive labor is that it serves as space-connecting and time-connecting labor (Massey 2013). And while time and space compression may be a hallmark of many capitalist processes in India, migration being one possible example of such compression, there are several ways in which the spatial and temporal disconnect between productive and reproductive labor has grown quite significantly in both rural and urban India.

First, the decline in agricultural employment, particularly agricultural wage employment for rural women, has meant a decline in work that is geographically closer to home (Narain and Nischal 2007). Second, there has been a significant privatization of rural and urban common property resources, particularly in the postliberalization era (Gidwani and Baviskar 2011; Maringanti et al 2012). This has meant an increase in the time needed to collect the basic raw materials of social reproduction. The lack of access to these raw materials could possibly serve as an additional "push" factor that leads to temporary migration. In Roy's study of migrants in Kolkotta (Roy 2007), one woman interviewee reported commuting to the city to collect twigs and paper that she could use as firewood back in her village. In her village, she explained, she did not have access to even that much.

Third, the increase in temporary, circular migration destabilizes any existing patterns of access to these raw materials. With every move, sources of water and fuel must be sourced anew, and, as has now been widely documented, these basic elements of social reproduction are extremely difficult to access in the slums and squatter settlements, and on the city pavements where the majority of urban migrants live (Coelho et al. 2013; Truelove 2011). As an example, Mosse et al (2005) cite data that urban migrants resort to burning plastic and tires as fuel for cooking. To the extent that urban migrants are also less likely to be part of social networks of other women who can share some of the burdens of care work, these contradictions only intensify further (Coelho et al. 2013).

These pressures can be resolved by abandoning paid work when it cannot be easily combined with reproductive labor (Banerjee and Raju 2009). In India's urban slums, the hours required to collect water alone can reduce women's ability to engage in full-time paid work (Coelho et al. 2013; Truelove 2011). The pressures of social reproduction can also result in the abandonment of certain forms of reproductive labor, particularly the care of children or the elderly. In both urban and rural India, the very young, the very old, and the sick are left to fend for themselves during the work day, or, in the case of some migrant families, for much longer periods of time as the spatial disconnect between productive and reproductive labor becomes impossible to bridge (Mosse et al. 2002; Pattenden 2012).

Last but certainly not least, these pressures can be partially accommodated by increases in the work day of women who bear this double burden. There is a large literature that explores how increases in reproductive labor can help mitigate the effects of capitalist crises by acting as a "shock absorber" (Elson 2010). This is the crux of this chapter's argument. The intensification of women's work and of women's responsibilities props up this system of precarious and fragmented livelihoods as increases in unpaid labor are used to fulfill basic needs and allow workers to survive what would otherwise be an unsustainable destruction of livelihoods (Naidu and Rao 2018). As Roy (2007) vividly describes in the context of urban squatters in Calcutta, in conjunction with the employment crisis and rigid gender divisions of labor, this can lead to the phenomenon of underemployed men, living with, and off, overworked women. Thus capitalist crises get displaced into the sphere of social reproduction and on to the (malnourished) bodies of women and children.

This last dynamic is especially important since it does not appear that most migrants expect to solve their problems of lack of access to water, fuel or even lack of time for care work through migration. Other than in Roy's work (2007), there are no references to expectations among unskilled workers that the raw materials of social reproduction would be easier to find in the city (it may be a different matter for skilled migrants with access to taps and electricity). One possible implication is a decrease in the likelihood that women will migrate at all. Garikipati (2008) argues that awareness of the substandard living conditions and lack of sanitation at migration destinations, along with the inflexibility of women's care obligations toward children and the elderly, reduced their willingness and ability to migrate with their spouses, leading to majority male migrant streams in the villages she studied.

On the other hand, as discussed earlier, family migration is a significant form of temporary migration in India, and the fraught conditions of social reproduction at both origin and destination of temporary migrants help us to understand why. Mosse et al. (2005) point out that family migration (including children) is more likely among poorer, unskilled distress migrants, and it is relatively skilled young men who can earn high wages who are able to "opportunistically" migrate alone. Pattenden (2012) found that family migration dominated among unskilled workers. Guérin et al. (2007) found that family migration was more likely the greater the debt dependence of the migrants, and that family migration had increased among resurveyed migrants (Guérin et al. 2015). For such migrants, the difficulty of securing the conditions of social reproduction even after migration makes the "subsidy" provided by the unpaid reproductive labor of women critically important.

Migration as Social Transformation

As discussed above, according to the Indian census, in 2016 (based on projections from the last census in 2011), the Indian urban population was about 33 percent of the total population. This is, most likely, a gross underestimation of the urban population in India. Urbanization in India is progressing rapidly in India along two lines. The first one is along the axis of extended urbanization, wherein urban areas envelop and annex villages in their growth. Second, there is increased migration from rural to urban areas. As mentioned above, this is both the permanent migration as well as short-term migration. Both these axes are not carefully captured in the Indian census. Several villages that now have lost their rural character (like the dominance of agricultural occupation) around cities are still governed by village panchayats (village-level administrative bodies) and much of the short-term migration is not counted as urban. In the latter case, because the migrants have one foot in rural areas, and another in the urban, they do not get counted in the urban. However, in this urban-rural sense, the boundaries have become much more fluid than what a clearly demarcated rural–urban axis would illuminate. The increasing dominance of the urban in the national economy and society is the first structural transformation in India (i.e., rapid urbanization).

Migration crises (of the three overlapping kinds discussed above) have played a key role in determining the character of this first transformation. Some of the permanent migrants who have access to some land and wealth have been able to use either capital or education to integrate into the upper echelons (professionals and skilled members) of the working class, while a vast majority either permanently or temporarily join the informal, precarious, and low-paying urban occupations. Spatially, many of these migrants are either housed in the inner-city slums or in the new squatter settlements that come up on the fringes of the Indian cities. Many villages that are integrating into urban areas also provide a temporary residential space for the migrants. Many of the migrants also engage in various occupations that are premised on self-employment given the employment crisis in the organized and formal sector. This produces city spaces that are highly unequal, and enclave-like, with the rich and the better-off professionals occupying certain preferred locations, while the low-skilled and temporary migrants live on the fringes or in densely populated slums. The logic of social reproduction (as described previously) in cities plays a key role in the survival of these vast majorities of workers, who survive without decent work and housing.

The second major transformation that migration crises signify is the deeper penetration of Indian capitalism over the last two to three decades across the rural–urban divide. There have been two major processes at work in this second transformation. The first process involves the privatization of public properties (such as public sector units, as well as the capture of government lands for private use), privatization and erosion of commons, and the increased dispossession of the productive assets of petty commodity producers. These subprocesses heighten the agrarian and social reproductive crises. This, then, results in the strengthening of private capital but also in a releasing a lot of new labor into the precarious labor market that was not at the command of private capital in a direct way. The second process through which Indian capitalism has deepened is through the use of this newly available labor (on top of the previously available labor in urban spaces). There are many ways in which this newly available labor is integrated into Indian capitalism.

One of the ways in which migrants are integrated into the labor market becomes clear by following the field studies of interstate migrant communities. Interstate migration is often associated with greater reliance on middlemen and debt dependence upon them. Mosse et al. (2005) report that workers often do not know which employer they have worked for during the migratory stint, their relationship being entirely with the broker. While in some cases brokers merely facilitate migration, paying workers on a daily or weekly basis at the migration work site, in other cases brokers pay workers upfront, extending a loan that the worker pays off with his or her labor. Guérin et al. (2015) point out that the forms of debt bondage that result from the latter practice are now widespread, if temporary, arguing that this is one example of the way that capitalism may effectively harness so-called noncapitalist relations of dependence.

The NSS employment-unemployment surveys show a perceptible increase in the phenomenon of self-employment and casual labor in urban areas, and more broadly nonagricultural work. A lot of this increase in self-employment is the result of the increased work in putting out systems that are characterized as subcontracting processes (Shrivastava 2012). A significant part of the increase in self-employment is nothing but the outsourcing of work that happened in larger organizations to the poorer migrant households that do not, therefore, have to be covered by labor legislation or any welfare legislations. The increase in casual labor is a much more direct integration into the labor market of the migrants and the previously poor urban residents. This integration is into the realm of precarious and informal work built on the imagined infinite elasticity of women and children as shock-absorbers in this fast-paced transformation of the Indian economy into a rapidly growing capitalist one with multiple labor arrangements that involve different degrees of freedom and servitude.

What is the nature of this capitalism? It is clearly not a story of workers achieving "double freedom" in the sense Marx meant it. Workers may be largely free of their means of production but they do not always enter the institution of free wage labor. For women workers we may actually see falling shares of both self-employment as well as wage labor as burdens of reproductive labor intensify. However, whatever the nature of the labor arrangement and the servitude associated with it, capital has found a way to access the newly available labor through subcontracting processes or through complicated debt peonage structures. The distinction Banaji (2013) makes between two levels of analysis (i.e. forms of labor exploitation, and the larger social relations) is apposite in this context. Purely analyzing the labor exploitation modes, one would conclude that free wage labor as an arrangement is not as widely prevalent. However, if we take out the teleological implications of the expression "formal subsumption of labor," the Indian economy has become more deeply capitalist (of a neoliberal kind) through this episode of massive migration that will only continue in the coming decades.

Conclusion

The overall conclusion of this short paper is that the Indian economy over the last two to three decades has been witnessing two interrelated phenomena. On the one hand, a majority of rural residents have been hit by an unevenly spread-out agrarian crisis, an employment crisis, and a social reproductive crisis that creates the impetus to migrate to urban spaces. On the other hand, the absence of decent forthcoming employment in urban areas means that the workers migrate into low-paying informal and precarious occupations, and live in a permanent state of movement and mobility between the rural and urban areas. These phenomena basically facilitate the yanking of labor (both of the productive and reproductive kinds) from its rooted locations, creating labor-in-general or abstract labor (in Marx's terminology) that is increasingly more available to capital to appropriate cheaply, and more directly. This manifests as a rapidly growing Indian economy with growth rates of over 7 percent since the 1990s. Many observers see this growth process as driven by the urban growth engine, which in our view is a reordering of productive and reproductive labor on a massive spatial scale. While crises contribute to this migration phenomenon, they represent, in our view, the other side of the deep transformation of the overall society. It is a transformation that has already instituted new forms of inequality and precarity of livelihoods for the vast majority, while affording new opportunities of wealth making for the chosen few—the owners, managers, and a small privileged group of the working class, the professionals.

Note

1. The crises we discuss here are those that induce migration and challenge the ability of Indian households to ensure stable, rooted, social reproduction. The term "migration crises" is not used to imply that migration itself is a crisis, nor do we think that what is being witnessed is a crisis for capitalist accumulation itself.

References

Agnihotri, I. and I. Mazumdar. 2009. "Dusty Trails and Unsettled Lives: Women's Labor Migration in Rural India." *Indian Journal of Gender Studies* 6, no. 3: 375–399.

Banaji, J. 2013. *Theory as History: Essays on Modes of Production and Exploitation*. Delhi: Aakar.

Banerjee, A. and S. Raju. 2009. "Gendered Mobility: Women Migrants and Work in Urban India." *Economic and Political Weekly* 44, no. 28: 115–123.

Breman, J. 2010. *Outcast Labour in Asia: Circulation and Informalization of the Workforce at the Bottom of the Economy*. Oxford: Oxford University Press.

Carleton T. A. 2017. "Crop-Damaging Temperatures Increase Suicide Rates in India." *Proceedings of the National Academy of Sciences* 114, no. 33: 8746–8751.

Cashin, P. and R. Sahay. 1996. "Internal Migration, Center-State Grants, and Economic Growth in the States of India." *Staff Papers* 43, no. 1: 123–171.

Coelho, K., T. Venkat, and R. Chandrika. 2013. "Housing, Homes and Domestic Work." *Economic and Political Weekly* 4, no. 43: 39–46.

Damodaran, H. 2008. *India's New Capitalists: Caste, Business, and Industry in a Modern Nation*. London: Palgrave Macmillan.

Deshingkar, P., and D. Start. 2003. *Seasonal Migration for Livelihoods in India: Coping, Accumulation and Exclusion*. London: Overseas Development Institute.

Deshingkar, P., P. Sharma, S. Kumar, S. Akter, and J. Farrington. 2008. "Circular Migration in Madhya Pradesh: Changing Patterns and Social Protection Needs." *The European Journal of Development Research* 20, no. 4: 612–628.

Elson, D. 2010. "Gender and the Global Economic Crisis in Developing Countries: A Framework for Analysis." *Gender & Development*, 1, no. 2: 201–212.

Garikipati, S. 2008. "Agricultural Wage Work, Seasonal Migration and the Widening Gender Gap: Evidence from a Semi-Arid Region of Andhra Pradesh." *The European Journal of Development Research* 20, no. 4: 629–648.

Gidwani, V. and A. Baviskar. 2011. "Urban Commons." *Economic and Political Weekly* 46, no. 50: 42–43.

Guérin, I., B. Augendra, Parthasarthy, and G. Venkatasubramanian. 2007. "Labor in Brick Kilns: A Case Study in Chennai." *Economic and Political Weekly* 42, no. 7: 599–606.

Guérin, I., G. Venkatasubramanian, and S. Kumar. 2015. "Debt Bondage and the Tricks of Capital." *Economic and Political Weekly* 50: 26–27.

ILO. *Indian Labor Market Update*. ILO Country Office of India (July 2016). http://www.ilo.org/wcmsp5/groups/public/---asia/---ro-bangkok/---sro-new_delhi/documents/publication/wcms_496510.pdf

Jenkins, R., L. Kennedy, and P. Mukhopadhyay. 2014. *Power, Policy and Protest: The Politics of India's Special Economic Zones*, New Delhi: Oxford University Press.

Keshri, K. and R. B. Bhagat. 2012. "Temporary and Seasonal Migration: Regional Pattern, Characteristics, and Associated Factors." *Economic and Political Weekly* 47, no. 4: 81–88.

Lahiri-Dutt, K. 2008. "Digging to Survive: Women's Livelihoods in South Asia's Small Mines and Quarries." *South Asian Survey* 15, no. 2: 217–244.

Maringanti, A., V. Vakulabharanam, S. Motiram, and S. Surepally. 2012. "Tragedy of the Commons Revisited (i)." *Economic and Political Weekly* 47: 10–13.

Massey, D. 2013. *Space, Place and Gender*. London: John Wiley & Sons.

Mazumdar, I., N. Neetha, and I. Agnihotri. 2013. "Migration and Gender in India." *Economic and Political Weekly* 48, no. 10: 54–64.

Mosse, D., S. Gupta, M. Mehta et al. 2002. "Brokered Livelihoods: Debt, Labour Migration and Development in Tribal Western India." *Journal of Development Studies* 38, no. 5: 59–88.

Mosse, D., S. Gupta, and V. Shah. 2005. "On the Margins in the City: Adivasi Seasonal Labour Migration in Western India." *Economic and Political Weekly* 40, no. 28: 3025–3038.

Motiram, S., and V. Vakulabharanam. 2007. "Corporate and Cooperative Solutions for the Agrarian Crisis in Developing Countries." *Review of Radical Political Economics*, 39, no. 3: 360–367.

Naidu, S., and S. Rao. 2018. "Reproductive Labor and Female Labor Force Participation In Rural India." Political Economy Research Institute, Amherst, Working Paper no. 458. https://www.peri.umass.edu/component/k2/item/1070-reproductive-work-and-female-labor-force-participation-in-rural-india

Narain, V., and S. Nischal. 2007. "The Peri-Urban Interface in Shahpur Khurd and Karnera, India." *Environment and Urbanization* 19, no. 1: 261–273.

Pattenden, J. 2012. "Migrating between Rural Raichur and Boomtown Bangalore: Class Relations and the Circulation of Labour in South India." *Global Labour Journal* 3, no. 1: 163–190. doi:10.15173/glj.v3i1.1117

Pattenden, J. 2016. *Labor, State and Society In Rural India: A Class-Relational Approach*. Oxford: Oxford University Press.

Picherit, D. 2018. "Rural Youth and Circulating Labour in South India: The Tortuous Paths Towards Respect for Madigas." *Journal of Agrarian Change* 18, no. 1. doi:10.1111/joac.12196.

Rao, S. 2017. "Women and the Urban Economy in India: Insights from the Data on Migration." In *Gender and Time Use in a Global Context*, edited by E. Kongar and R. Connelly, 231–257. New York: Palgrave Macmillan.

Rao, S., and Finnoff, K. 2015. "Marriage Migration and Inequality in India, 1983–2008." *Population and Development Review* 41, no. 3: 485–505.

Razavi, S. 2007. "The Political and Social Economy of Care in a Development Context: Conceptual Issues, Research Questions and Policy Options." United Nations Research Institute for Social Development, Working Paper 3. June. http://www.unrisd.org/80256B3C005BCCF9/%28httpAuxPages%29/2DBE6A93350A7783C12573240036D5A0/$file/Razavi-paper.pdf

Reddy, D. N., and S. Mishra. 2010. *Agrarian Crisis in India*, Delhi: Oxford University Press.

Rodgers, G. and J. Rodgers. 2011. "Inclusive Development? Migration, Governance and Social Change in Rural Bihar." *Economic and Political Weekly* 46, no. 23: 43–50.

Rogaly, B., and A. Rafique. 2003. "Struggling to Save Cash: Seasonal Migration and Vulnerability in West Bengal, India." *Development and Change*, 34, no. 4: 659–681.

Roy, A. 2007. *Calcutta Requiem: Gender and the Politics of Poverty*. Minneapolis: University of Minnesota Press.

Sainath, P. 2017. "The Slaughter of Suicide Data." *People's Archive of Rural India (PARI)*, April. https://psainath.org/the-slaughter-of-suicide-data/

Shah, A. 2006. "The Labor of Love: Seasonal Migration from Jharkhand to the Brick Kilns of Other States in India." *Contributions to Indian Sociology* 40, no. 1: 91–118.

Shrivastava, R. 2012. "Changing Employment Conditions of the Indian Work Force and Implications for Decent Work." *Global Labour Journal* 3, no. 1: 63–90.

Thomas, J. J. 2014. "The Demographic Challenge and Employment Growth in India." *Economic and Political Weekly* 49, no. 6: 15–17.

Truelove, Y. 2011. "(Re-) Conceptualizing Water Inequality in Delhi, India through a Feminist Political Ecology Framework." *Geoforum* 42, no. 2: 143–152.

Vakulabharanam, V. 2004. "Immiserizing Growth: Globalization and Agrarian Change in Telangana, South India between 1985 and 2000." Ph.D. diss., University of Massachusetts, Amherst.

Vakulabharanam, V., and S. Motiram. 2011. "Political Economy of Agrarian Distress Since 1990s." In *Understanding India's Political Economy: A Great Transformation*, edited by S. Corbridge, J. Harriss, S. Reddy, and S. Ruparelia, 101–126. New York: Routledge.

Vakulabharanam, V., and S. G. Thakurata. 2014. "Why Do Migrants Do Better Than Non-Migrants At Destination? Migration, Class and Inequality Dynamics in India." *The Singapore Economic Review* 59, no. 1: 1450003. doi:10.1142/S0217590814500039

Vakulabharanam, V., and S. Motiram. 2016. "Mobility and Inequality in Neoliberal India." *Contemporary South Asia* 24, no. 3: 257–270.

Virk, R. 2004. "Women Construction Workers in Amritsar City." In *Distressed Migrant Labour in India: Key Human Rights Issues*, edited by K Gopal Iyer, 162–177. New Delhi: Kanishka Publishers.

CHAPTER 16

SYRIAN REFUGEES AND TURKEY

Whose "Crisis"?

CENK SARAÇOĞLU AND DANIÈLE BÉLANGER

The first argument of this chapter is that the unprecedented exile of Syrians in Turkey is not the source but rather a symptom of a crisis unfolding in Turkey's foreign policy with its Middle Eastern neighbors and the EU. This political crisis requires an analysis of the Turkish government's Islamist-nationalist project and neo-Ottomanist vision, as well as its contentious relationship with the EU regarding Turkey's accession to the union. Instead of depicting and representing the flow of Syrian refugees into Turkey as the source of a demographic and humanitarian crisis, we emphasize the role of Turkish foreign policy both in the exodus of Syrians from their country and their "containment" on Turkish soil.

The second argument of this chapter is that xenophobic sentiments against refugees in Turkey are not simply the consequence of the large presence of Syrians. Based on literature and original fieldwork conducted in Izmir, this chapter argues that prevalent anti-Syrian sentiments in Turkey is a symptom of the ideological crisis of the ruling government. More specifically, it shows that secularists, Alevi, and Kurdish populations interpret the government's refugee policy as threatening their own fragile cultural or class current positions in the country and that this anxiety fuels anti-Syrian xenophobia. Depicting the Syrian inflow as a "crisis" does not provide adequate grounds for future policies that could secure livelihoods and status for Syrians and promote peaceful relations with host communities. Before developing these arguments, the chapter provides a summary of the context and the ways in which the existing discourses has laid the ground for the idea of a "Syrian refugee crisis" in Turkey.

CONTEXT

To be sure, the recent Syrian refugee migration to Turkey is of an unprecedented scale. While the country has been one of transit and destination for more than a decade (Kirisci 2007), it has never hosted such a large immigrant population. As of 2018, the Syrian population is estimated to be 4 million. This number includes 3.5 million registered refugees under temporary protection (Ministry of Interior 2018) and 500,000 to 700,000 unregistered persons (ICG 2018).[1] Syrian refugees thus represent 5 percent of Turkey's population. The war-related Syrian refugee migration in Turkey began in 2011 with the settlement of a few temporary camps near the border. The initial open border policy, which referred to refugees as "guests," was put in place under the assumption that Syrians would stay only temporarily in Turkey. Figure 16.1 indicates the increase in Syrians registered under the temporary protection regime and shows that the influx of asylum-seekers accelerated in 2013, which corresponded to a period of intensification of warfare. As the numbers increased, Turkey established various policies and structures to deal with the newcomers.[2]

The vast majority of Syrians in Turkey reside in cities and only 6 percent live in camps (Ministry of Interior 2018). Map 16.1 shows a key feature of this migration: Syrian refugees registered under temporary protection live in every province of the country. While Syrians initially enjoyed a period of "free movement,"since 2016 they are required

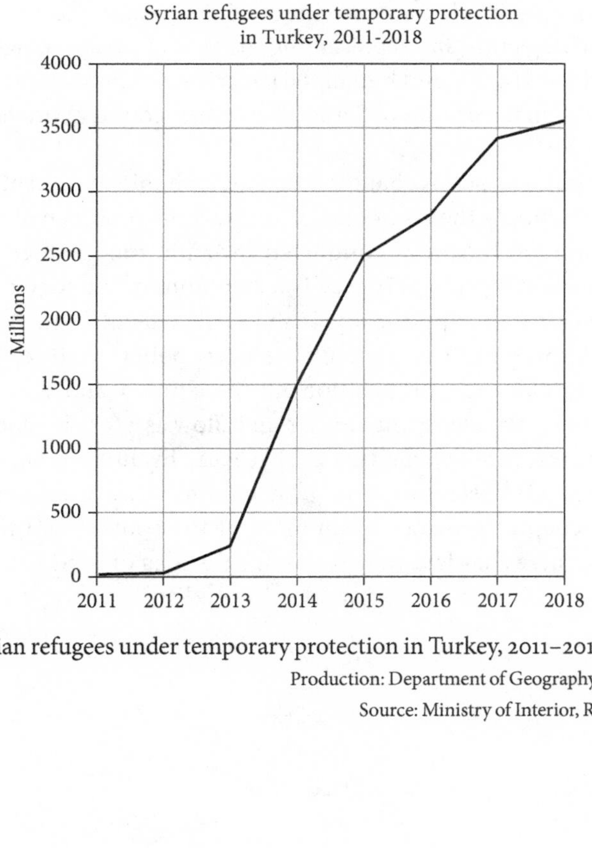

FIGURE 16.1 Syrian refugees under temporary protection in Turkey, 2011–2018.

Production: Department of Geography, Laval University, 2018

Source: Ministry of Interior, Republic of Turkey, 2018

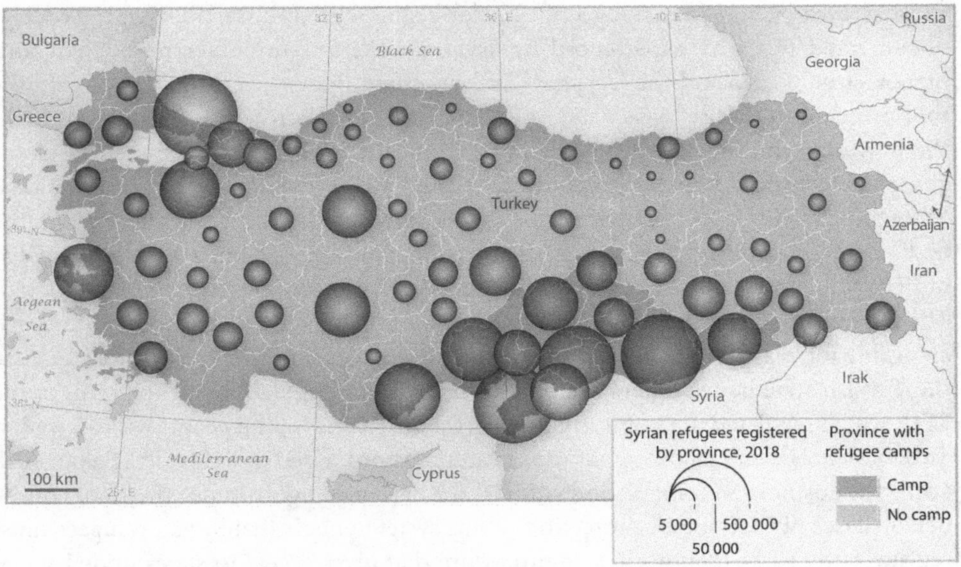

MAP 16.1 Syrian refugees registered by province 2018.

Production: Department of Geography, Laval University, 2018
Source: Ministry of Interior, Republic of Turkey, 2018

to seek authorization to move to another city and social services can only be accessed in the city where one is registered.

The largest concentration of refugees (half a million) is found in Istanbul, while more than 200,000 live in the provinces of Sanliurfa, Hatay, Gaziantep, and Mersin. Five other provinces (Adana, Bursa, Izmir, Kilis, and Konya) are home to over 100,000 refugees. In terms of percentages, over 95 percent of the border town of Kilis is Syrian (105,000 in camps and 130,000 in the city). Other provinces with the highest proportions of Syrians (relative to host community) include Sanliurfa (24 percent), Hatay (28 percent) and Gaziantep (19 percent). Prior to the Syrian conflict, locals in border cities had extensive contact with Syrians who used to come to Hatay, Gaziantep, or Sanliurfa for business or as tourists. Hatay is a unique case given its local Arabic-speaking population and large Alevi population. Very specific interethnic and political relations unfold in this area (Can 2017). Moreover, Syrian Kurds were hosted in Kurdish neighborhoods of various cities, including Istanbul, where the original feelings of solidarity have gradually given way to antagonisms due to changing economic and spatial relationships in these neighborhoods (Kilicaslan 2016). Besides geographic proximity to the Syrian border; ethnic, personal, and family networks; and regionalization policies, opportunity for labor incorporation is another key factor in settlement. Gaziantep and Izmir, for instance, both cities with a large industrial and service sector, incorporate large numbers of Syrian workers. Many Syrian families also engage in internal migration in pursuit of agricultural work in various areas of the country (Kavak 2016).

Most research on Syrian refugees in Turkey begins with the assertion that the widely-documented precarity experienced by asylum-seekers is the outcome of their ambiguous legal status and the fact that Turkey ratified the Geneva Convention and the 1961 protocol so that refugee status would be applied to European applicants only. As the flow of asylum seekers from the regions in Turkey's vicinity continued to intensify, the Turkish parliament passed in 2013 the Law on Foreigners and International Protection (LFIP) which provided for the asylum seekers from outside Europe the first legal framework and the status of "conditional refugee" in line with the standards of EU and international conventions. The same law also precipitated the foundation of The Directorate General of Migration Management (DGMM) that is deemed to be responsible for registering and providing services to those needing protection. In 2014 the Turkish state issued a new "Temporary Protection Regulation" on the basis of the LFIP, which regulated the status, rights and responsibilities of the people who arrived in Turkey *en masse* and whose applications cannot be processed individually (Baban et al. 2016, 7). This new 2014 regulation situated the Syrian refugees under the status of the beneficiaries of "temporary protection" . This system entails that Syrian refugees must register with Turkish authorities, a procedure that gives access to state-funded social services, including education and health care, in the place of registration only. Another important step was achieved in January 2016, when Syrians under temporary protection obtained the legal right to a work permit under strictly defined conditions (Memisoglu and Ilgit 2016, 8). Research, however, unanimously indicates that Syrians face serious difficulties in benefiting from these rights due to Turkish institutions' lack of sufficient capacity to manage such a large and sudden refugee inflow (Icduygu 2015; Kaya 2016; Koca 2016; Yildiz and Uzgören 2016).

Research on Syrian refugees in Turkey in general often approached within the "crisis" framework, discusses three main themes. First, research examines the impact of the Syrian migration on market relations. Syrian refugees have been incorporated into Turkish real estate market as the "providers of rent" and into the labor market as the "providers of cheap labor." Landlords charge higher rents to Syrian refugees than to local residents (Baban et al. 2016; Montabone 2016). This situation drives prices upward, which negatively impacts both refugees and Turkish low-income earners (Baban et al. 2016, 10). As for the labor market, despite laws and regulations that are supposed to strictly limit the inclusion of Syrian workers into the formal Turkish labor market, the state developed an ad hoc leniency toward the informal low-wage employment of Syrian migrants (Baban et al 2016, 9). This situation has led to the formation of a domain of informal labor relations in which Syrian migrants lack social and legal protection against the free market that operates in an unfettered manner (Bélanger and Saracoglu 2018; Canefe 2016; Erol et al. 2017). One of the outcomes of this situation has been the emergence of new Turkish and Syrian informal economic interest groups who take advantage of the precarious conditions of Syrians. With respect to work permits, only 15,000 had been issued as of January 2018, a very small number considering that at close to 1 million would be on the labor market (ICG 2018). The inclusion of Syrians in the informal labor market has implications for the host community, including reduced wages, displacement, and increased unemployment.[3] Observers further note the high incidence of child labor among Syrian children and new patterns of internal migration among Turk nationals, especially Kurds, impacted by the changing labor market.

Second, in the field of social care, the state, along with national and international nongovernmental organizations, carries out certain programs and activities that provide temporary financial assistance in the form of modest monthly cash stipends, temporary relief through food or basic items distribution, and legal counsel to Syrians. This is a field where there is competition among various actors, including the state's official government institutions, domestic and international not-for-profit organizations (including the UN agencies), Islamist-oriented philanthropic organizations, and religious-oriented informal networks, as well as unofficial networks and organizations formed by the Syrians themselves (Erder 2016, 127). These actors are directed by different principles, ideological visions, political positions, and cultural perspectives that often collide with each other (Erden 2016, 11). Furthermore, research on health tends to problematize Syrians as a new public health concern or documents the difficulty in accessing adequate health care services despite the official policy granting them free access. Shortage of interpreters and providers, refugees' lack of knowledge about their rights, and negative attitude among health care staff have been documented by research (Samari 2017; Torun et al. 2018).

Third, in the realm of education, Syrian children and youth may attend public schools run by the Turkish state or temporary education centers supported and administered by private initiators from Syria and Turkey. As of 2017, 40 percent of over 1 million Syrian children at school-age were not receiving any form of schooling (UNHCR 2017). In public schools, where the language of instruction is Turkish, the specific educational needs of Syrians are not adequately met, which compromises the quality of education (Aydin and Kaya 2017). Those attending temporary education centers, which have been initiated on the basis of the prediction that the presence of the Syrians in Turkey would be rather short-term and set up to address the unmet need for education, are subject to different standards determined by the social actors running these institutions. Hence, the social vision and religious and cultural tendencies of private initiators and sponsors shape the content and pedagogical approaches (Aras and Yasun 2016, 8; Sert 2016, 282). Some actors, for instance, may provide curriculum promoting gender segregation and religiosity, while others may situate their teaching in a secular and gender equalitarian paradigm. Having recognized the fact that the Syrian refugee presence in Turkey would be long-lasting than expected, the Ministry of Education announced that all temporary education centers will be phased out in 2019 and all school-age Syrian children will be integrated into public school system.

In sum, most studies conducted to date provide vivid accounts and thorough analyses of the precarious lives of Syrian refugees in Turkey (Baban et al. 2016; Kivilcim 2016; Korkut 2016; Rygiel et al. 2016; Senses 2016) and emphasize precariousness as the outcome of Syrians' ambiguous legal status, as well as the limited access to social rights, work permits, education, and health care services. Many scholars call for a different legal framework that would recognize Syrians as refugees, provide a secure status, and make available more resources. These facts form the basis for representations and understandings of the "refugee crisis" in most public discussions.

Unpacking Turkey's Crises

The scholarly treatment of the Syrian inflow into Turkey typically reflects the general tendency to "link migration with crisis" in a negative fashion (Lindley 2014, 1). In many academic articles, op-ed pieces and research reports published on Syrian refugees in Turkey since the beginning of the war in Syria, the situation has generally been portrayed as yet another "refugee crisis" or a "migration crisis" that the international community and the Turkish state must manage efficiently. In contrast, in mainstream media, social media, and in the discourse of some political opponents of the government's "Syrian policy," the influx of Syrian refugees in Turkey has been presented as a threat to the security and well-being of Turkish society (Doganay and Kenes 2016). Both the liberal-humanitarian perspective of experts and the nationalist and exclusionary popular discourse have in common the tendency to construct an image of a crisis created from the very presence of Syrian refugees within Turkish national borders. But this tendency is problematic in so far as labeling Syrians as a source of crisis (explicitly or implicitly) conceals the role played by social and political processes on the global and regional levels. Given that the word "crisis" implies a "suspension of normal social processes" (Lindley 2014, 5), the phrase "Syrian refugee crisis" suggests that Turkey's conditions prior to the Syrian inflow were characterized by an absence of crisis. The term must be refocused and pluralized to shed light on the larger social and political processes that instigated the exodus from Syria and that continue to shape refugees' social positions and living conditions in Turkey.

The Crisis of Neo-Ottomanist Foreign Policy

In the existing literature on Syrian refugees in Turkey the notion of "crisis" is associated with the Syrian presence and Turkey is represented as a country that has been exposed to an unexpected humanitarian crisis. In this interpretation, the position of the Turkish state vis a vis the exodus of millions of Syrians from their country is reduced to that of host to a sudden and large influx of people forced to flee from a neighboring country. As such, what is typically scrutinized or problematized are the policies and practices of the Turkish state and its legal framework and institutional structure designed to regulate the living conditions of the Syrians within Turkish borders. The problems that Syrians face in Turkey are thus attributed to the deficiencies and loopholes in the institutional architecture, legal framework, and refugee management strategies of the Turkish state.

By reducing Turkey to a passive recipient of refugees, this depiction neglects Turkey's and other international actors' role in influencing the course of the Syrian civil war. International and regional actors' role is not limited to the post-migration process; rather, it concerns the very preliminary conditions that instigated the exodus from Syria in the first place. This role must be factored into an analysis of the so-called refugee crisis in Turkey.

During the Cold War, Turkey and Syria's diplomatic relationships were tumultuous and tense. The countries were opposed, with Turkey being a member of NATO and Syria aligning itself with the USSR. Since that time, the relationship has continued to be contentious over issues concerning each country's relationship with Iraq, Iran, Israel, the United States, and the EU, as well as concerning water shares of the Euphrates River and the Kurdish movement alongside the Syrian-Turkish border. Between the late 1990s and 2011, Syrian-Turkish relations entered a period of "normalization," during which time visa-free travel was established, bilateral agreements were signed, and commercial relations flourished. Previous antagonism resurfaced in 2011 when Turkey took an active role in the Syrian war by giving its political and military support to various opposition groups against the Syrian regime. It is essential to analyze Turkey's bold intervention in Syria as emerging not only from past relations located in complex regional and international geopolitical dynamics, but also as an outcome of the ruling party AKP's (Justice and Development Party's) neo-Ottomanist foreign policy and its concomitant Islamist-nationalist conception of the Middle East.

The neo-Ottomanism of the AKP, as opposed to the conventional Kemalist framework, declares the former Ottoman territories a "geocultural basin" to which the Turkish state seeks to extend its influence. In 2013 Ahmet Davutoğlu, the former ministry of foreign affairs and architect of the AKP's neo-Ottomanist foreign policy, stated:

> The other states say to us, "do not engage in adventures in foreign policy, do not follow an active politics." And we keep saying "Turkey has always been a subject, can never be objectified. We have always been a subject, and no one can make this nation an object. Today, could anyone, particularly Palestine, oppose anything in the Middle East without the presence of Turkey? We should do what our history necessitates. This nation has always been a subject of history and will continue to be so."[4]

As a former Ottoman territory, Syria is perceived by the ruling government as a space in which the Turkish state's interests can be proactively and legitimately pursued. The Syrian uprising of 2011 became the AKP government's golden opportunity to pursue and validate these ideological and territorial ambitions. It was expected that post-Assad Syria would represent the cultural values and aspirations of the Sunni majority that were expected to fully embrace the neo-Ottoman vision promoted by the government. It was based on this ideological vision and strategic calculations that the AKP, with the encouragement of the United States in the initial stages of the conflict, supported anti-Assad opposition groups on both political and military grounds (Cop and Zihnioglu 2017, 35). In sum, the Syrian conflict was a springboard for the validation of the government's neo-Ottomanist vision of the Middle East and its Islamist-nationalist conception of foreign policy.

In this respect, Turkey's refugee policy has not been simply a reaction to an unexpected and particularly large refugee migration across the Turkish borders. Rather, it has been an integral part of its neo-Ottomanist calculations in the Syrian conflict. Turkey's foreign policy strategy in Syria was, from the outset, embedded in the formation and implementation of its refugee policy. The disorderly incorporation of Syrian refugees in Turkey does not only reflect the limitations of Turkey's domestic institutional and legal structures but it also marks the crisis of Turkey's over-optimistic foreign policy in Syria that expected the swift fall of the Assad regime. In this way, the government's neo-Ottomanist vision must be taken into account when trying to understand Turkey's widely criticized refugee policy, the government's logic and rhetoric toward refugees, and the resulting precariousness faced by nearly four million Syrians in Turkey.

The unfolding of Turkey's policy and discourse toward Syrians reveals this agenda. In the initial stages of the war, Turkey maintained an "open-border policy" that allowed Syrian refugees, as well as opposition fighters from various groups, to cross the border and find safety in Turkey. As mentioned previously, the underlying rationale behind this open-door policy was the expectation that the Assad regime would fall in a short time period with the support provided by Turkey and its then international allies (the United States, Saudi Arabia, and Qatar) and that the refugees would consequently return to Syria (Oktav and Celikaksoy 2015, 411). It is in this context that the government set up exemplary camps near the border and initially refused international assistance in dealing with the situation. In the media, the government presented its open-door policy to the international public as the fulfillment of a humanitarian responsibility and thereby "branded itself as the voice of conscience and benevolence, thus a leader of the underrepresented nations" (Cevik and Sevin 2017, 402). To the Turkish public, this policy was presented as an expression of the Turkish state's solidarity with the oppressed Muslim people of Syria. The label "guests" used by the government to designate the status of Syrian refugees was also reflective of this vision. Underlying the discourse of humanitarian responsibility and the imperative duty to host Syrians as temporary guests was also a political motivation. As an active supporter of the opposition groups and the protector of the repressed opponents of the Syrian government, the Turkish government hoped to be a legitimate and leading actor in the reconstruction of post-Assad Syria, while safe-guarding its opportunity to deploy and materialize its neo-Ottomanist vision in Syria (Serbos and Baxevanis 2016, 402). In other words, the policy of welcoming displaced Syrians was an integral part of an overoptimistic foreign policy strategy that not only expected but also actively participated in a swift regime change in Syria.

New dynamics changed the balance of power in Syria, such as the expansion of ISIL in Syria and Iraq and the Russian intervention in support of the Syrian state. As the war became protracted, the optimism about the fall of the Syrian government began to fade away along with Ankara's neo-Ottomanist politics. As the war in Syria escalated and expanded further, the number of Syrians seeking asylum in Turkey increased to an unprecedented level, while the expectation that most refugees would return to their home country vanished.

In short, what is referred to as a "refugee supply shock" in the literature (Icduygu and Diker 2017, 29) was not simply an unexpected event that the Turkish government was passively exposed to and was caught unprepared to deal with. Rather, it was an outcome of the strategic calculation made by governments that fought the Assad government and expected its quick fall. The so-called refugee crisis in Turkey is in fact a symptom of the crisis of Turkish foreign policy. This set of problems is an outcome of the contradiction between the refugee management strategies designed in accordance with the expectations of Turkish foreign policy and the realities of the Syrian war that did not comply with these expectations.

The Crisis of EU–Turkey Relations

Rather ironically, the Turkish state has used the Syrian refugee inflow to manage its gradually exacerbated relations with the European Union. Having been in the accession negotiation process with the EU since 2005, Turkey was expected to fulfill certain standards on various issues for the completion of full membership. This brought about EU supervision over Turkish legal and political institutions and critiques regarding the extent to which democratic standards designated by the Copenhagen Criteria were being fulfilled. Over the last decade, this gave birth to serious frictions between the EU and the Turkish government as the latter felt restricted by the EU's regular allegations regarding the deterioration of democratic rights and freedoms under its rule. Political tensions escalated to such an extent that the European parliament voted in November 2016 to approve a *nonbinding* decision to suspend negotiations with Turkey.

The AKP government was not deterred by this decision nor did it recognize the EU as the legitimate authority to interfere its domestic affairs. Still, the EU did not suspend negotiations or abandon their efforts to normalize relations with Turkey. One of the factors that gave broad room for maneuver to the AKP was the EU's fear that damaging its diplomatic relations with the AKP government would increase the flow of refugees from Turkey into its borders. In the wake of right-wing populism and anti-Muslim political parties and movements, a possible refugee influx into EU borders became the greatest anxiety of European political elites (Serbos and Baxevanis 2016, 394). EU politicians deployed all their energy and resources to make sure the 2015 "migration crisis" would not happen again and this project required the absolute cooperation of Turkey in containing the "flow." Aware of this, Turkey's President Erdoğan threatened the European countries in November of 2016, "to open Turkey's borders and allow masses of refugees to flow into Europe" if the EU were to actually freeze talks on Turkey's membership accession (Hintz and Feehan 2017).

The irregular crossings of a minority of all Syrian refugees in Turkey to the EU since 2011, and especially since 2016, has shown that the prevention of such migration is reliant upon Turkey's willingness to retain refugees within its borders and tighten border controls to obstruct passages. It was under these circumstances that the EU and Turkey signed a deal in March 2016 stipulating that every person arriving irregularly on European soil (Greece) will be returned to Turkey. The EU also committed to take one Syrian for each Syrian returned from Greece to Turkey. In exchange for preventing the departure of asylum-seekers, Turkey would receive 6 billion euros in refugee assistance and Turkish citizens would be granted visa-free entry to EU countries. The latter promise has not been fulfilled. Both sides thus used refugees as a bargaining chip in an unethical political game, neglecting the lives of millions of people expelled from their homeland (Bryant 2016). This deal appeased European anxieties about a possible refugee influx but it consequently crippled on political, ideological, and moral grounds the EU's capacity and legitimacy to exert pressure over Turkey's compliance with the EU's standards regarding human rights and democracy. On political grounds, the EU prioritized the sustainability of the deal as an actual criterion for shaping its relations with Turkey. The EU's decision aimed at avoiding any additional sharing of the burden of the humanitarian catastrophe that the EU itself contributed to. On moral and ethical grounds, this political orientation further entrenched and severely weakened the EU's already questionable legitimacy to supervise Turkey's human rights performance. Overall, it was by means of the presence of Syrian refugees that Turkey could claim a moral superiority vis-a-vis the European Union and manage its foreign policy crisis with this political body. Thus the rapid and unprecedented migration of Syrian asylum-seekers in Turkey, which has been depicted as a refugee crisis, is in fact another manifestation of a crisis of the EU project itself and of EU's relations with Turkey.

Turkey's Ideological Crisis

As the number of Syrian refugees in Turkey increased and as it became more apparent that their stay was not likely to be temporary, a rise in anti-Syrian sentiments began to be documented in Turkish cities (Erdoğan 2014; ICG 2016, 12; ICG 2018, 30, 33; Şenoğuz 2017, 9; WFP Report 2018, 9).[5] Survey-based academic articles and reports reveal that a large number of people in cities no longer view Syrians "as the victims of a horrible civil war, but as people who disturbed the peace and harmony of communities and (are) taking advantage of the Turkish government" (Nielsen 2016, 102). This research provides important information about the attitudinal patterns among people sharing xenophobic feelings against Syrians. This chapter's ethnographic fieldwork, which was conducted between 2016 and 2018 in the city of İzmir, explores the complex relationship between anti-Syrian sentiments and the government's political orientation. In a city hosting 130,000 Syrian refugees, these xenophobic sentiments were not simply a spontaneous reaction of Turkish society toward a sudden inflow of nonnationals (often referred to as "Arabs" by locals). Similarly, our research refutes the ideas that the anti-Syrian position can be reduced to economic competition between the members of host communities and the newcomers in local labor markets. Common to both of these explanations is an implicit assumption that it is the inflow of the Syrian refugees that has triggered anti-Syrian attitudes and that increasing xenophobia is thus another pathology associated with the Syrian refugee crisis. From this perspective, the demographic shock caused by a sudden migration flow gives rise to xenophobia by locals who feel invaded by foreigners who were originally supposed to be temporary guests but are now embedding themselves economically and culturally into the life of the city. Consequently, violent altercations between locals and newcomers, frustrations and anger on the part of Turkish citizens, and Syrians' experiences of exclusions are seen as the natural consequence of demographic and economic tensions resulting from the rapid inflow of refugees. Yet our research suggests that this logic is insufficient because it ignores preexisting relations and tensions between various social, ethnic, and religious groups, on the one hand, and the role of the ideological orientation and the policies of the ruling government on the other.

It can be demonstrated that anti-Syrian sentiments reflect a deep and longstanding ideological crisis in Turkey. Our ethnographic observations and in-depth interviews, conducted with seventy-eight informants in Ankara, Gaziantep, Hatay, and Izmir between 2016 and 2018, indicated that anti-Syrian sentiments in Turkey are replete with and colored by discursive positions, convictions, and anxieties stemming from the contradictions of AKP's Islamist-nationalist ideological project that preceded the inflow of Syrian refugees into Turkey. As such, anti-Syrian xenophobia must be analyzed against the backdrop of the ideological crisis in Turkey, rather than simply as an outcome of the Syrian refugee movement.

The Islamist nationalism of the AKP is a hegemonic project that redefines the boundaries, symbolic content, and historical genesis of the "nation" based primarily on common Islamic values. It aims to reconstruct the hegemonic links between the population, the state, and the existing economic order on the basis of a new ideological foundation. At the core of this ideological project, is the designation of "Muslimhood" defined along the lines of Sunni-İslamic interpretation as the overarching identity that supposedly unites different ethnic or linguistic groups (including the Kurds) under a single nation (Saracoglu and Demirkol 2015). The project included an ambitious and far-reaching reorganization of the educational system, art, and cultural domains, as well as everyday life along the lines of Islamic values.

As the AKP continues to take further steps to shape the state's official discourse and transform the state's ideological apparatus in accordance with the necessities of this project, some elements of Turkish society are critical of this agenda. Among the diverse mix of those voicing anger and discontent are the secularists, who are attached to Kemalist modernism and secularism and see the government's project as a political and cultural threat to the foundations of the Turkish Republic. The Alevis too show concern, as they comprise almost 15 percent of the entire population, have a distinct belief system, and are thus invested in maintaining secular republicanism. The new imagined nation (Hintz 2016, 346), with its systemic prioritization of coservative Islamic values signifies exclusion and marginalization for this group. Those sections of the Kurdish population that support the Kurdish movement (and hence give priority to Kurdishness over Muslimhood) interpret the government's project as yet another attempt to assimilate the Kurds under a new ideological framework and to eradicate the political influence of the Kurdish national movement. Furthermore, large sections of youth and women see a potential for oppression in the Islamic conservatism of the government.

As a result, as the AKP gradually secured its power and increased its control over the state institutions, the government's Islamic nationalist project led to sharp divides in Turkish society between the supporters of this party, on the one hand, and those who felt threatened and alienated by this project, on the other. The fact that this divide is manifested in all controversial political issues in Turkey points to an ongoing ideological crisis: Despite the fact the government spent huge efforts to mobilize the ideological apparatus of the state, including the media, to popularize the main premises and symbols of its new conception of the nation, Islamist nationalism has not been successful in developing into a common and all-encompassing hegemonic framework for Turkish society.

Throughout Izmir's neighborhoods, anti-Syrian sentiments take many discursive forms, are rationalized in different ways, and reflect existing political polarization. In some cases, these sentiments respond directly to the AKP's Islamic conservative and nationalist vision to justify to the Turkish public its deep involvement in the Syrian war and its references to "Islamic brotherhood" to explain the major tenets of its refugee policy and define the status of Syrian refugees in Turkey (Korkut 2016). As stated previously, in the government's discourse, Syrian refugees share common religious bonds with people in Turkey and are inhabitants of a former Ottoman territory. For these reasons, the Turkish government presents interventions in Syria and its refugee policy as part of the Turkish state's responsibility to protect Syrians. Islamic words, such as *ensar*, have been occasionally used to define Turkey's open-door policy and protective discourses toward the Syrians.[6] This Islamic framework is also manifested in the realm of nongovernmental activities. Research indicates that secular organizations and citizen-based initiatives that endeavor to provide aid to refugees from a universalist and secularist perspective face difficulties in acquiring permissions from official authorities. Meanwhile, more conservative and Islamic associations operate more freely and effectively (ICG 2018, 20). As such, the management of Syrian lives in Turkey has become yet another domain in which the major premises of Islamic nationalism are reproduced.

In interviews conducted in İzmir, Turkish informants' exclusionary discourses about the Syrians go beyond a reaction to an "outsider community" but are rather inseparably combined with their position toward the AKP's Islamist-nationalist project and its neo-Ottomanist vision. Among the Alevis and secularists in the Izmir City and Province neighborhoods of Konak, Limontepe, and Torbali, the Syrian inflow and the earlier open door policy was conceived as an AKP agenda for the Islamization of urban social life. The tendency to identify all Syrians with Islamist militants was prevalent among these respondents. Existing political and ideological contentions in Turkey also shape the perspectives of some of our Kurdish interviewees. Among Kurdish workers in the industrial zone of Işıkkent and activists in Torbali, the AKP's support for the Free Syrian Army in Syria was seen as part of the Turkish state's strategy of curbing the increasing influence of the Kurdish movement in the Middle East in general and Turkey in particular. Based on this political conviction, they conceive the Sunni Arab refugees as supporters of Islamic militant groups such as ISIL and the Turkey-backed Free Syrian Army who fight against the Kurdish PYD in Syria. In the discourse of some urban Kurds, specific political concerns go hand in hand with commonsense stereotypes of Syrians that widely circulate in urban life; namely, that Syrians are deprived of traits necessary to integrate into Turkey's public life and that they are opportunistic and lazy.

Existing surveys and this chapter's ethnographic research suggest that the government's Islamist-nationalist narrative depicting Syrian refugees as Muslim guests from a former Ottoman land has failed to hold ideological appeal to large sections of society. On the contrary, it is the categorical rejection of the neo-Ottomanist vision that has, among certain sections of society, prepared the ground for certain forms of anti-Syrian sentiments. In this respect, the increasing anti-Syrian sentiments in Turkish society could be seen as another symptom of the ongoing ideological crisis in Turkey that is characterized by the Islamist nationalism's inability to generate an encompassing political and moral reference point for a country deeply divided along religious, ethnic, and sectarian lines.

Conclusion

Undoubtedly, the precarious living conditions of a very large population of Syrian refugees require careful attention and comprehensive solutions. However, a thorough examination of this situation should be informed by an analysis of the social and political context of the so-called "refugee crisis." The first step to doing so is to understand how the term "crisis" might be better applied to the larger social and political dynamics that induced the forced migration from Syria and continue to shape the conditions of the Syrian refugees in Turkey today. As such, we assert that the presence and conditions of the Syrian refugees in Turkey today is an epitome of the crisis of Turkey's foreign policy in the Middle East, a symptom of the crisis of the ideals and principles of the European Union, and a reflection of the ongoing ideological crisis in Turkey. This analysis points out that such crises pose a structural obstacle to the development of a coherent and sustainable program to successfully manage and incorporate Syrians in Turkey. The first step to reducing insecure and precarious conditions and to minimizing xenophobic reactions against Syrian refugees is to recognize that both of these problems are not the natural outcome of the inflow of Syrians but rather a symptom and manifestation of the political and ideological crises of Turkey and international institutions such as the European Union.

Notes

1. In addition, Turkey has close to a half-million refugees from other countries, mostly from Iraq, Afghanistan, and Iran. The UNHCR registers these refugees and identifies cases eligible for resettlement to a third country. Syrian refugees are managed by the Turkish government; UNHCR is only involved in small numbers of cases of resettlement.
2. For thorough reviews of how the policy framework evolved and its impacts on refugees see the 2016 special issue of *New Perspectives on Turkey* edited by Eder and Özkul (2016).
3. Economic analyses indicate the absence or very negligible impact of Syrian refugees on the formal labour market but increasing impact on the informal one (see Ceritoglu et al. 2017; Duruel 2017; Lordoglu and Aslan 2016; Tumen 2016, 457).
4. *Ihlas News Agency*, March 3, 2013.
5. In addition to incidences of violence and widepread discrimination, social media also relay xenophobic sentiments. For example, in July 2017, the racist hashtags #suriyelilerevinedonsun (Syrians should go home), #suriyelilersinirdisiedilsin (Syrians should be deported) and #suriyeliistemiyoruz (We do not want Syrians) went viral on Twitter in Turkey for nearly a week (Atac et al. 2017).
6. *Ensar* refers to the support and care of Medina people to the prophet Muhammad when he migrated from Makkah to this city.

References

Aras, B., and S. Yasun. 2016. "The Educational Opportunities and Challenges of Syrian Refugee Students in Turkey: Temporary Education Centers and Beyond." Istanbul: Istanbul Policy Center Policy Brief. http://research.sabanciuniv.edu/29697/1/syrianrefugees.pdf

Ataç, I., G. Heck, S. Hess, Z. Kaşlı, P. Ratfisch, C. Soykan et al. 2017. "Contested B/Orders. Turkey's Changing Migration Regime. An Introduction." *Movements. Journal for Critical Migration and Border Regime Studies*, 3, no. 2: 9–21.

Aydin, H., and Y. Kaya. 2017. "The Educational Needs of and Barriers Faced by Syrian Refugee Students in Turkey: a Qualitative Case Study." *Intercultural Education*, 28, no. 5: 456–473. doi:10.1080/14675986.2017.1336373

Baban, F., S. Ilcan, and K. Rygiel. 2016. "Syrian Refugees in Turkey: Pathways to Precarity, Differential Inclusion, and Negotiated Citizenship Rights." *Journal of Ethnic and Migration Studies* 43, no. 1: 41–57. doi:10.1080/1369183X.2016.1192996.

Bélanger, D., and C. Saracoglu. 2018. "The Governance of Syrian Refugees in Turkey: The State-capital Nexus and Its Discontents." *Mediterranean Politics*. doi: 10.1080/13629395.2018.1549785

Bryant, R. 2016. "Bargaining Bodies: The Eu's Deal with Turkey Has Sacrificed Europe's Principles to Appease Domestic Politics." LSE European Politics and Policy (EUROPP) Blog. http://eprints.lse.ac.uk/70643/

Can, S. 2017. "The Syrian Civil War, Sectarianism and Political Change at the Turkish–Syrian Border." *Social Anthropology* 25, no. 2: 174–189. doi:0.1111/1469-8676.12413.

Canefe, N. 2016. "Management of Irregular Migration: Syrians in Turkey as Paradigm Shifters for Forced Migration Studies." *New Perspectives on Turkey* 54, no. 1: 9–32.

Ceritoglu, E., H. B. Gurcihan Yunculer, H. Torun, and S. Tumen. 2017. "The Impact of Syrian Refugees on Natives' Labor Market Outcomes in Turkey: Evidence from a Quasi-experimental Design." *IZA Journal of Labor Policy* 6, no. 1: 1–28.

Cevik, S., and E. Sevin. 2017. "A Quest for Soft Power: Turkey and The Syrian Refugee Crisis." *Journal of Communication Management* 21, no. 4: 399–410. doi:10.1108/JCOM-04-2017-0042.

Cop, B., and Ö. Zihnioglu. 2017. "Turkish Foreign Policy under AKP Rule: Making Sense of the Turbulence." *Political Studies Review* 15, no. 1: 28–38. doi:10.1111/1478-9302.12088.

Doganay, Ü., and H. C. Kenes. 2016. "Yazılı Basında Suriyeli 'Mülteciler': AyrımcıSöylemlerin Rasyonel ve Duygusal Gerekçelerinin İnşası." *Mülkiye Dergisi* 40, no. 1: 143–184.

Duruel, M. 2017. "Suriyeli Sığınmacıların Türk Emek Piyasasına Etkileri Fırsatlar ve Tehditler", *Uluslararası Ekonomik Araştırmalar Dergisi* 3, no. 2: 207–222.

Eder, M., and D. Özkul, D., eds. 2016. "Editors' introduction: Precarious Lives and Syrian Refugees in Turkey." Special issue, *New Perspectives on Turkey*, 54, no. 1: 1–8.

Erden, O. 2016. "Building Bridges for Refugee Empowerment." *Journal of International Migration and Integration* 18, no. 1: 1–17. doi:10.1007/s12134-016-0476-y.

Erder, S. 2016. "Preliminary Thoughts on the Syrian Refugee Movement." *New Perspectives on Turkey* 54, no. 1: 119–130. doi:10.1017/npt.2016.10.

Erdogan, M. Murat. 2014. "Perceptions of Syrians in Turkey." *Insight Turkey* 16, no. 4: 65–75.

Erol, E. et al. 2017. *Suriyeli Sığınmacıların Türkiye'de Emek Piyasasına Dahil Olma Süreçleri ve Etkileri: İstanbul Tekstil Sektörü Örneği*. Istanbul: Birleşik Metal-İş Yayınları.

Hintz, L. 2016. " 'Take it Outside!' National Identity Contestation in the Foreign Policy Arena." *European Journal of International Relations* 22, no. 2: 335–361. doi:10.1177/1354066115588205

Hintz, L., and C. Feehan. 2017. "Burden or Boon? Turkey's Tactical Treatment of the Syrian Refugee Crisis." Middle East Institute, January 10. http://www.mei.edu/content/map/burden-or-boon-turkey-s-tactical-treatment-syrian-refugee-crisis.

Icduygu, A. 2015. *Syrian Refugees in Turkey: The Long Road Ahead*. Washington, DC: Migration Policy Institute.

Icduygu, A., and E. Diker. 2017. "Labor Market Integration of Syrian Refugees in Turkey: From Refugees to Settlers." *The Journal of Migration Studies* 3, no. 1: 12–35.

ICG (International Crisis Group). 2016. *Turkey's Refugee Crisis: The Politics of Permanence*. Europe Report 241, November 30. https://www.crisisgroup.org/europe-central-asia/western-europemediterranean/turkey/turkey-s-refugee-crisis-politics-permanence.

ICG (International Crisis Group). 2018. *Turkey's Syrian Refugees: Defusing Metropolitan Tensions*. Europe Report 248, January 29. https://www.crisisgroup.org/europe-central-asia/western-europemediterranean/turkey/248-turkeys-syrian-refugees-defusing-metropolitan-tensions.

Ihlas News Agency. 2013. "Davutoğlu: Biz Tarihin Yazımında Hep Özne Olduk", http://www.iha.com.tr/haber-davutoglu-biz-tarihin-yaziminda-hep-ozne-olduk-265944.

Kavak, S. 2016. "Syrian Refugees in Seasonal Agricultural Work: A Case of Adverse Incorporation in Turkey." *New Perspectives on Turkey* 54, no. 10:33–53. doi:10.1017/npt.2016.7

Kaya, A. 2016. "Syrian Refugees and Cultural Intimacy in Istanbul: 'I Feel Safe Here!'" SSRN. Istanbul, Turkey: Robert Schuman Centre for Advanced Studies Research Paper No. RSCAS 2016/59.

Kilicaslan, G. 2016. "Forced Migration, Citizenship, and Space: The Case of Syrian Kurdish Refugees in İstanbul." *New Perspectives on Turkey* 54, no. 10: 77–95. doi:10.1017/npt.2016.8.

Kirisci, K. 2007. "Turkey: A Country of Transition from Emigration to Immigration." *Mediterranean Politics* 12, no. 1, 91–97.

Kivilcim, Z. 2016. "Legal Violence Against Syrian Female Refugees in Turkey." *Feminist Legal Studies* 24, no. 2: 193–214. doi:10.1007/s10691-016-9323-y.

Koca, B. T. 2016. "Syrian Refugees in Turkey: From 'Guests' to 'Enemies'?" *New Perspectives on Turkey* 54, no. 1: 55–75. doi:10.1017/npt.2016.4.

Korkut, U. 2016. "Pragmatism, Moral Responsibility or Policy Change: The Syrian Refugee Crisis and Selective Humanitarianism in the Turkish Refugee Regime." *Comparative Migration Studies* 4, no. 2: 1–20. doi:10.1186/s40878-015-0020-9.

Lindley, A. 2014. "Exploring Crisis and Migration: Concepts and Issues." In *Crisis and Migration*, edited by Anna Lindley, 13–35. London: Routledge.

Lordoglu, K. & M. Aslan. 2016. "En Fazla Suriyeli Göçmen Alan Beş Kentin Emek Piyasalarında Değişimi: 2011-2014.", *Çalışma ve Toplum* 49, no. 2: 789–808.

Memisoglu, F., and A. Ilgit. 2016. "Syrian Refugees in Turkey: Multifaceted Challenges, Diverse Players, and Ambiguous Policies." *Mediterranean Politics* 22, no. 3: 317–338. doi:10.1080/13629395.2016.1189479.

Ministry of Interior, Republic of Turkey. 2018. "Relocation of Syrians for the Third Countries within 2014–2018." http://www.goc.gov.tr/icerik6/temporary-protection_915_1024_4748_icerik.

Montabone, B. 2016. "The Wartime Emergence of a Transnational Region between Turkey and Syria (2008–2015)." In *The Transnational Middle East, People, Places, Borders*, edited by Leila Vignal, 181–198. New York: Routledge.

Nielsen, S. Y. 2016. "Perceptions between Syrian Refugees and their Host Community." *Turkish Policy Quarterly* 15, no. 3: 99–106.

Oktav, O. Z., and A. Celikaksoy. 2015. "The Syrian Refugee Challenge and Turkey's Quest for Normative Power in the Middle East." *International Journal: Canada's Journal of Global Policy Analysis* 70, no. 3: 408–420. doi:10.1177/0020702015584305.

Rygiel, K., F. Baban, and S. Ilcan. 2016. "The Syrian Refugee Crisis: The EU-Turkey 'Deal'and Temporary Protection." *Global Social Policy* 16, no. 3: 315–320. doi:0.1177/1468018116666153.

Samari, G. 2017. "Syrian Refugee Women's Health in Lebanon, Turkey, and Jordan and Recommendations for Improved Practice." *World Medical & Health Policy* 9, no. 2: 255–274.

Saracoglu, C., and Ö. Demirkol. 2015. "Nationalism and Foreign Policy Discourse in Turkey under the AKP Rule: Geography, History and National Identity." *British Journal of Middle Eastern Studies* 42, no. 3: 301–319.

Şenoğuz, H. P. 2017. "Border Contestations, Syrian Refugees and Violence in the Southeastern Margins of Turkey." *Movements: Journal for Critical Migration and Border Regime Studies*, 3, no. 2: 165–178.

Senses, N. 2016. "Rethinking Migration in the Context of Precarity: The Case of Turkey." *Critical Sociology* 42, no. 7–8: 975–987. doi:10.1177/0896920515606503.

Serbos, S., and C. Baxevanis. 2016. "Aligning Europe: The Syrian Refugee Crisis and the Geopolitics of the Region." *International Relations* 4, no. 6: 390–406.

Sert, D. 2016. "The Oxymoron of Perpetual Temporary Protection: Syrians in Turkey." *Migraciones Internacionales* 8, no. 4: 279–284.

Torun, P., et al. 2018. "Health and Health Care Access for Syrian Refugees Living in İstanbul." *International Journal of Public Health* 63, no. 5: 6011–6088. doi:10.1007/s00038-018-1096-4

Tumen, S. 2016. "The Economic Impact of Syrian Refugees on Host Countries: Quasi-Experimental Evidence from Turkey." *American Economic Review* 106, no. 5: 456–460.

UNHCR (The UN Refugee Agency). 2017. *Turkey: Education External Update*. https://data2.unhcr.org/en/documents/download/53953.

WFP (World Food Programme). 2018. *Social Cohesion in Turkey: Refugee and Host Community Online Survey*. https://reliefweb.int/report/turkey/social-cohesion-turkey-refugee-and-host-community-online-survey-round-1-december-2017.

Yildiz, A., and E. Uzgören. 2016f. "Limits to Temporary Protection: Non-Camp Syrian Refugees in İzmir, Turkey." *Southeast European and Black Sea Studies* 16, no. 2: 195–211. doi:10.1080/14683857.2016.1165492.

PART IV

CLIMATE AND ENVIRONMENT

CHAPTER 17

CLIMATE-MIGRATION RESPONSES IN THE PACIFIC REGION

CELIA MCMICHAEL, CAROL FARBOTKO, AND KAREN E. MCNAMARA

CLIMATE change impacts—such as sea-level rise, desertification, shifting rainfall patterns and increasing temperatures, and extreme weather events—are expected to shape human migration and mobility. Low-lying communities, atoll populations, and island nations have often been the focus of global attention, particularly in relation to the threat of sea-level rise. The Pacific islands region has a high profile as an iconic site of climate change impacts and subsequent climate migration risk. Migration, displacement, and relocation are widely positioned as foregone and inevitable responses to climate change for many Pacific communities (see Bedford and Bedford 2010; Locke 2009). Yet in low-lying Pacific islands such as Tuvalu, Kiribati, and the Carteret Islands (Papua New Guinea) where the phenomenon of climate migration is generally well understood and might be expected to have traction, studies have identified that climate change impacts (anticipated or current) have limited influence on contemporary migration decision making (Connell 2016; Farbotko et al. 2016; Mortreux and Barnett 2009). Furthermore, many Pacific peoples including politicians, leaders, and activists refute the idea that they will become "climate refugees" (Farbotko and Lazrus 2012; McNamara and Gibson 2009).

For inhabitants of low-lying communities and islands in the Pacific, there is increasing awareness of the scientific forecasts around environmental change, local observation of changing environmental conditions, and growing acceptance that climate change impacts require adaptation and policy response. Furthermore, Pacific Islanders have long histories of mobility and migration through seafaring, family and social networks, and job opportunities, and narratives of mobility are central to oral histories, identities, and cultures (Hau'ofa 1994). Nonetheless, highly publicized scenarios in which people are forcibly displaced as communities and islands become uninhabitable remain, for some, almost existentially untenable (Farbotko 2018). While migration and relocation might be part of a suite of adaptive responses to an environmental future in which communities and countries are severely impacted by climate change threats, including sea-level rise, *in situ* adaptive options are often preferred by the communities and national governments concerned (see Barnett and McMichael 2018; McNamara and Gibson 2009). Despite multitudes of claims in the global media and by civil society groups that the Pacific has generated the first "climate refugees," it remains difficult to identify migration in the Pacific that is attributable entirely to the impacts of climate change. Yet the emergence of policies dealing with climate-related mobility raises the imperative of moving beyond the question of whether climate change amplifies and generates migration to examine how people caught up in the complex sociopolitical field of "migration as adaptation" are responding to changing policy, social, and biophysical domains associated with climate-related migration.

The chapter begins with a brief summary of the relationships between climate change and migration. It then highlights the framing of climate migrants and implications of this discursive production, arguing that the idea of "migration as adaptation" can provide a hopeful pathway toward climate resilience, yet, less positively, can also position at-risk populations as agents who bear responsibility for adapting to climate change impacts, despite their often limited contribution to the creation of the problem itself. The chapter next discusses three case studies that focus on the phenomenon of climate-related migration in the Pacific: Fiji where relocation of low-lying coastal villages is planned and implemented in response to coastal erosion and flooding; Tuvalu where people resist projections of future displacement from their homes and homeland under scenarios of inundation and submerged islands; and Kiribati where the previous government developed a policy of "migration with dignity," while also calling for industrialized countries to reduce greenhouse gas emissions to prevent loss and exodus. In the final discussion, the chapter provides a brief reference to international, regional, and national adaptation policies and frameworks that focus on climate-related migration, displacement, and relocation, and concludes with a discussion of how people in these Pacific countries respond to the dynamic discursive, policy, social, and biophysical domains of "migration as climate change adaptation."

Climate-Related Migration

Climate change–related migration is predominantly forecast, anticipated, and expected rather than a phenomenon observable in, for example, international migration statistics (Baldwin et al. 2014; Bettini 2017). Since 1990, when the Intergovernmental Panel on Climate Change noted that human migration could be the most significant impact of climate change, there have been multiple attempts to quantify its potential scale and to predict future numbers of migrants (Kothari 2014). Predictions of climate migrant numbers should be handled with caution, and estimated numbers of climate migrants are much debated (IPCC 2014). Reports of predictions of large numbers of climate migrants have been widely discredited, given methodological flaws that included calculations based on assumptions that place-based adaptation would not occur, as well as significant data gaps (Betts and Pilath 2016; Gemenne 2011). As Gemenne notes, "despite their flaws and biases, predictions and estimates [of climate migrant numbers] made a lasting impact in both policy and scholarly debates: they are now often quoted as scientific truth, without any questioning of the methodology used" (2011, s46). Critical analyses highlight that environmental and climatic changes influence and interact with other drivers of human mobility including political, demographic, social, and economic factors. In most cases it is impossible to isolate environmental and climatic change as the sole cause of migration. Most climate-related migration will occur within countries, and will be temporary (Foresight 2011; Massey et al. 2010). Furthermore, the influence of changing climatic and environmental conditions on mobility will often be region- or place-specific (Gray and Wise 2016). Nonetheless, there is broad consensus that climate change is influencing, to varying degrees, migration patterns globally.

Climate change-related mobility encompasses migration, forced displacement, and planned relocation (Foresight 2011). Forced displacement refers to situations where people leave their place of residence, typically where a sudden-onset environmental disaster or risk is a primary driver of mobility; those already facing poverty and other vulnerabilities are most likely to be temporarily displaced. Migration as adaptation refers to orderly, governed migration that builds on social networks, mobilizes human capital, diversifies livelihoods, and reduces exposure to environmental risk; migration (e.g., seasonal or circular migration or rural-urban migration) is positioned as a positive adaptive or anticipatory response to climate stress (Bettini 2017). Forced displacement and voluntary adaptive migration are often considered distinct categories (e.g., with forced migrants displaced by sudden-onset environmental disaster, and voluntary migrants choosing to migrate in response to slower-onset changes) but the two categories are potentially overlapping along the mobility spectrum; for many, both external forces and personal choice shape migration decisions. Planned relocation usually takes place within national borders, and is proposed as a strategy to avoid displacement and loss where other adaptation is unsuccessful or unfeasible. It is typically instigated and carried out by the state—ideally with the consent and support of the community—with the aim of reducing environmental risk, and it should entail restoration of community and socioeconomic conditions (ODI 2016). Furthermore, climate change impacts and environmental stressors may limit people's capacity to move, thereby contributing to reduced mobility (Black et al. 2011; Foresight 2011). The Foresight Report on Migration and Global Environmental Change (Foresight 2011) notably developed projections of global economic, environmental, and demographic futures to examine the consequences for human migration. It highlighted the notion of "trapped populations" and included a focus on reduced mobility and immobility associated with climate impacts. As this report and others have noted, the populations with most vulnerabilities to climate change impacts will include those who are immobile or even trapped in place (Black et al. 2013; Gray and Wise 2016).

Framing Climate-Related Migration

Debates on climate migration have generated alarmist accounts of floods of so-called "climate refugees." This framing provides a conceptual tool via which to convey and understand climate-related migrants as "victims", acting as a form of meta-communication that contains "between-the-lines" information and that links climate-related mobility to the refugee context (see Van Gorp 2007); it has been somewhat influential in academic scholarship (see Biermann and Boas 2010; Myers 2002; Stern 2007; Westra 2009), in advocacy that seeks to protect so-called "climate refugees" (Christian Aid 2007; Environmental Justice Foundation 2009; Friends of the Earth 2007) and in some policy arenas (Council of the European Union 2008; WBGU 2008). Within the media, the figure of "climate refugee" has been mobilized to provide a human face to dangerous climate change.

Claims are frequently made about national or geopolitical security implications of increased migration associated with climate change (e.g., Bawden 2014; Schwartz and Randall 2003), such as escalating scarcity of natural resources resulting in violent conflict (Homer-Dixon 1999). Such links and assertions, however, have been extensively critiqued on the basis of methodology, theory, and lack of evidence to support them. Barnett (2003, 12) has made the case that due to broader political and institutional forces at play, the influx of migrants into new places due to climate change impacts, "can be a significant factor in violent conflict . . . [but] by no means all, indeed very few, large scale migrations end in conflict" (Barnett 2003, 12). Migration associated with climate change is therefore, at best, a highly contested risk to national security (Betts and Pilath 2016; Gemenne et al. 2014; Hartmann 2010; Ransan-Cooper et al. 2015; Reuveny 2007). It is, however, widely agreed within the research community that human security is significantly undermined and at risk as a result of anthropogenic climate change (Barnett and Adger 2007; IPCC 2014; Tacoli 2009).

In the Pacific, there has, in some arenas, been a normalization of loss of low-lying communities and nations, including through popular media in which the Pacific represents the "ground zero" of climate change (Farbotko 2005; Farbotko and Lazrus 2012). Imagery circulates of "drowning islands" and "sinking states"; media headlines include "Refuge from the Sinking Islands" and "Global Warming: Thousands Flee Pacific Islands on Front Line of Climate Change." The idea of the so-called 'climate refugee' has, since the late 1980s, had significant news value, but it is typically foreign journalists, researchers, and activists who use the term; it is widely rejected among island populations. Furthermore, it is often either the crossing of international borders, or migration as "proof" of climate change impacts, that is frequently at the heart of the newsworthiness of stories about migration associated with climate change, rather than the plight of displaced people themselves (Farbotko 2012).

Policy, however, particularly at the international level, has progressed beyond the crisis-and-victims narrative, and there is now an established and widely accepted understanding of climate-related migration as an issue of human security, to be addressed in broader development agendas (McNamara et al. 2016). Many agencies and organizations—such as the International Organization for Migration (IOM), the UN High Commissioner for Refugees (UNHCR), and the United Nations Framework Convention on Climate Change (UNFCCC)—understand migration to be an adaptive response to emerging and realized climate threats. There are explicit policy and program connections with disaster risk reduction, resilience, and development. Governed and forward-looking migration is seen to represent a strategy of risk management and adaptation whereby environmental risks are avoided, human capital is mobilized, labor migration is supported, and remittance flows offer a buffer to environmental stress (ADB 2012; Bettini 2017). In this framing, migration is not a crisis; it represents a positive adaptive response to climate stress. As Tacoli has written:

> . . . mobility and migration are key responses to environmental and nonenvironmental transformations and pressures. They should therefore be a central element of strategies of adaptation to climate change. This requires a radical change in policymakers' perceptions of migration as a problem and a better understanding of the role of local and national institutions in supporting and accommodating mobility.
>
> (2009, 513)

Yet critics warn that the idea of migration as adaptation "aims at disciplining labor mobility, with circular and temporary migration presented as the most virtuous forms. The goal is to produce remittance flows financing self-adaptation, offering surrogate insurance to the noninsurable" (Bettini 2017, 35–36). The concept of migration as adaptation positions vulnerable populations—who are at the margins of the capitalist system and patterns of high consumption, and who have made limited contributions to greenhouse gas emissions—as adaptive agents who should migrate in response to local impacts of climate change. Yet there will be those who are unable or unwilling to migrate, perhaps because of indigenous bonds to place, or who experience "maladaptive" migration if they move to areas with different and increased environmental risks (e.g., low-lying urban-poor settlements). Other concerns raised by scholars about "migration as adaptation" include the movement of people into sites of environmental vulnerability such as urban informal settlements, or the potential deemphasis on international action to reduce greenhouse gas emissions or a lessening of *in situ* adaptation efforts if migration is pitched as the adaptation solution to climate change (Felli 2012; McNamara 2007).

Case Studies

In the following three case studies—Fiji[1], Tuvalu and Kiribati[2]—we explore how people in these countries variously respond to current or anticipated climate change impacts and the discursive, policy, and social domains of "migration as climate change adaptation." These countries are among the first globally to respond to current or anticipated climate change impacts through development and (in the case of Fiji) implementation of migration and relocation policies. Despite commonalities, particularly the threat of sea-level rise, local experiences and responses are diverse.

Relocation in Fiji

The Republic of Fiji is in the South Pacific region and is made up of over three hundred islands. Fiji's National Climate Change Policy indicates that while Fiji makes insignificant contributions to greenhouse gas emissions, and thereby climate change, the country is very vulnerable to its impacts. Climate change is expected to lead to accelerated sea-level rise, contribute to increases in the intensity of extreme events such as droughts and cyclones, and threaten marine and terrestrial ecosystems (via, for example, coral bleaching, coastal erosion, and salt water intrusion in low-lying coastal areas) (Republic of Fiji 2012).

Across Fiji, villagers in low-lying communities report experiences of sea-level rise, higher tides, coastal flooding, salt-water intrusion, storm surges, and coastal erosion. Many *in situ* adaptation measures, such as mangrove planting and sea-wall construction, have been undertaken to address problems including coastal erosion and flooding but these have had limited sustained success with faltering sea-walls and mangrove shoots that have washed away (McMichael and Katonivualiku, under review). Integrated vulnerability assessments, primarily of iTaukei (Indigenous Fijian) villages, have been conducted by the Fiji Government Climate Change Unit to assess impacts and resilience to climate change and natural disasters and to inform the Fiji government on village adaptation responses that may include relocating inland. The Government has estimated that many villages may require relocation in the next five to ten years (*Fiji Times* 2016), with 81 communities/areas specifically identified for "potential relocation" in Fiji's second national communication report to the UNFCCC (Republic of Fiji 2014). While the relative contributions of climate-related sea-level rise, tectonic changes, tidal and storm surges, cyclones, and human modifications to coastal flooding and shoreline erosion in Fiji are uncertain, villagers in low-lying areas, government officials and national policy documents all refer to relocation initiatives as an adaptive response to climate change impacts.

In 2014, villagers from Vunidogoloa in the Province of Cakaudrove relocated to higher land because of coastal erosion, saltwater intrusion, and increased flooding. One older woman explained how experiences of flooding led to her supporting the relocation:

> I supported the move. I experienced it, and I was scared because of the river and the sea and the other side there is a river and when there is a big rain it flooded. It is an experience I had. From down there, when it is heavy rain it came inside the village. It came from the sea and the river as well. My house was flooded.
>
> (Vunidogoloa village, Cakaudrove Province; interview with older woman)

The old village (*koro makawa*) was located close to the foreshore and had a population of approximately 140 people living in 26 houses. Earlier efforts to adapt to erosion and flooding included short-distance retreat of houses and construction of two sea-walls. In 2006, Vunidogoloa's residents approached the Government seeking assistance for relocation. Vunidogoloa became the first village in Fiji to receive government support for relocation away from a site of environmental vulnerability. Many government Ministries and development agencies were involved in planning, implementation, and funding; strong village leadership was central to building consensus, understanding, and support. A new site was identified 2km inland, importantly, still within *mataqali* [customary] land. Community members designed the village layout and thirty weatherboard houses were constructed, each with solar-powered lighting, toilet, shower, and laundry; external kitchens have been self-constructed. The new village has four fish ponds, pineapple and banana plantations, and a copra drier that provide income generation. The total project cost was FJD 978,228 (approx. USD 472,789). Vunidogoloa's residents consider relocation to be a success in terms of reduced environmental risk, proximity to roads and transport, improved access to services, and increased livelihood opportunities. However, they await a second project phase to further improve livelihoods and complete infrastructure works.

In other low-lying villages in Fiji, relocation is anticipated as a response to sea-level rise. In Tokou, a low-lying coastal village in Lomaiviti Province, villagers consider relocation likely—whether in a few years or few decades—particularly in light of Vunidogoloa's experience. There was also widespread awareness of emerging national relocation planning and policy in Fiji, and this lent persuasive power to the idea of relocation as an adaptive response to environmental change. With relocation increasingly accepted as likely, some people in Tokou explained they were reluctant to invest in their homes and villages. As one man explained, "I was thinking about renovating the house, but what's the point? In five years' time if could be filled with sea water. We need to move to higher land. It's a wise move" (Tokou village, Lomaiviti Province; interview). Beyond villagers' lived experience of environmental change and anticipated environmental futures, the global moral dimensions were noted whereby villagers bear responsibility for adapting to environmental change through relocation, despite their limited contribution to greenhouse gas emissions. As one older man explained, "other big countries caused the problem. And the small countries suffer" (Vunisavisavi village, Cakaudrove Province; interview). Relocation entails much more than geographic repositioning of people and material assets; it is a complex sociopolitical process. Fiji is among the first countries globally to plan for and implement climate-related relocation.

Voluntary Immobility in Tuvalu

Tuvalu is an island nation in the Pacific consisting of nine scattered low-lying atolls. The elevation of the country does not exceed three meters above mean sea level, and land area in total is 26 square kilometers. Tuvalu is considered extremely vulnerable to the climate change impacts. Rising sea levels and extreme weather events contribute to inundation, saltwater intrusion, and coastal erosion (Government of Tuvalu 2012a). Yet in Tuvalu, there is arguably a rejection of climate change as a crisis of mobility. This is not to say, however, that the crisis is not framed in other ways. Indeed, what seems clear from both the national policy position and from informal articulations of the climate change threat to Tuvalu, is that there is a preference among many Tuvaluans to remain indefinitely on indigenous lands for cultural and spiritual reasons, even in the face of significant deterioration in health and livelihoods associated with climate change impacts. The Tuvalu Climate Change Policy states that the Tuvalu Government intends to guarantee the security of the people of Tuvalu from the impacts of climate change and maintain national sovereignty. A key stated policy issue is the "fear of losing Tuvalu's identity and culture" (Government of Tuvalu 2012b, 25). Climate change migration and resettlement planning are officially deemed as an option only for the worst-case scenario. The government policy position does extend to recommending securing international migration schemes (such as the Special Pacific Access Category for Tuvaluans) and establishing professional training programs to facilitate employment in neighboring countries if climate change migration becomes necessary (Government of Tuvalu 2012a). Nevertheless, it is *in situ* adaptation that is prioritized at the national level, and migration is positioned as an individual choice.

Climate change is not often cited as a driver of migration among people in Funafuti, Tuvalu's capital (Mortreux and Barnett 2009). Climate change is strongly felt, however, to be presenting risks to indigenous rights to self-determination (Farbotko et al. 2016). In some cases, Tuvaluan people express preparedness to die on traditional territory rather than relocate. Climate change is being articulated as an existential threat to culture, identity, and connections to land and sea: a crisis of indigeneity. For many Tuvaluan people, climate-related migration is associated with suffering and with loss of identity and home: "climate change has prompted a shying away from mobile histories and geographies, and an elevation of the importance of rootedness" (Farbotko et al. 2016, 8).

Such voluntary immobility can be interpreted as an important indigenous adaptation strategy, helping to strengthen political agency and cultural resilience among those facing a lost homeland. Moreover, voluntary immobility in a changing climate is an opportunity, and arguably presents an obligation, for development organizations and donors to engage in more culturally meaningful integration of development, mobility, (including relocation) and adaptation to climate change with governments, civil society groups, and communities in at-risk places such as Tuvalu.

"Migration with Dignity" in Kiribati

The Republic of Kiribati is made up of 33 atolls and one raised coral atoll spread over 3.5 million km^2. Making up only 810 km^2 in land area, the majority of atolls are less than two to three meters above sea level and only a few hundred meters wide. Kiribati, with a population of just over 100,000 people, is highly vulnerable to the adverse impacts of climate change. Inundation and coastal erosion destroy land, and storm surges contaminate the fresh groundwater lens (Republic of Kiribati 2007). Consequently, both arable land and potable water are limited throughout the country. In response to the degradation of critical livelihood resources by sea-level rise and salt water intrusion, among other impacts, the previous government (led by Anote Tong) developed a policy of "migration with dignity," which seeks to negotiate entry and resettlement of the people of Kiribati (known as "i-Kiribati") in neighboring states including Fiji (Klepp and Herbeck 2017). This policy is part of the Kiribati Adaptation Program (KAP), developed over three phases between 2003 and 2016, which aimed to: promote mitigation of greenhouse gases; adapt to climate change impacts (e.g., via water supply management and coastal management protection); and prepare for the future by planning for population settlement and relocation (i.e., "migration with dignity"). In exploring relocation options, former President Tong prepared for the failure of mitigation and adaptation, indicating that he would "rather plan for the worst and hope for the best" (in Barnett 2017, 6).

While rural-urban migration (to Kiribati's capital, Tarawa) has been occurring rapidly over the last decade or more, there is no sustainable, long-term internal migration strategy for Kiribati due to limited higher ground and narrow width of most atolls. The "migration with dignity" policy has been established as part of Kiribati's long-term nationwide relocation strategy (Office of Te Beretitenti 2015). The policy contains a number of key aims and components. The first is to establish opportunities for i-Kiribati to migrate abroad now, or in the near future, if they wish to. It is hoped that expatriate communities in various receiving countries, such as Australia and New Zealand, would be set up to support other migrants in the future to help alleviate difficulties associated with relocation, enhance opportunities for remittances to be sent back to Kiribati, and attempt to maintain i-Kiribati culture outside of Kiribati. The numerous international labor schemes, such as those involving seasonal workers in the fruit-picking and horticulture industries in Australia and New Zealand and seafarers working for international shipping companies in North America and Europe, are examples of this component of the policy. A second key part of the policy relates to enhancing the levels of qualifications (educational and vocational) for i-Kiribati so they are more "migration-ready" for destination job markets. The Kiribati Institute of Technology is located in Tarawa and provides technical and vocational training with the costs being largely subsidized by the government. This upskilling helps i-Kiribati to migrate abroad "with dignity." The last component of the policy relates to the purchase of 6,000 acres of land by the Kiribati Government in Fiji (on Vanua Levu). While former President Tong indicated that the land is for food security, it is unclear if there will be plans for possible relocation in the longer-term. Overall, the policy is highly pragmatic, as put by Barnett: "This is the politics of pragmatism; accepting that loss is possible and planning for it by sensitising the population to its possibility, and through skills training for nurses and seafarers so that a larger number of i-Kiribati can work elsewhere, and through purchases of land in Fiji" (2017, 6).

However, the policy does not reach nor protect all i-Kiribati—it speaks to a limited number: those who are ready to migrate and those with the capabilities to do so (McNamara 2015). For instance, it does not "speak to" those with limited literacy skills, those whose livelihoods are largely subsistent, or those that do not wish to (voluntarily immobile populations) or cannot (trapped populations) leave their homeland. Furthermore, while part of the policy is attempting to "move" culture from one place to another, which is encouraging, the loss of traditional lifestyles that are connected to place could never be entirely replicated elsewhere. Putting these limitations and challenges aside, the Kiribati Government is constrained in its options to protect the livelihoods of its people, but it also appears to be steering clear of a victim narrative. The policy is about providing agency and options for i-Kiribati. In this way, it has been argued that such a policy (that is responding, similarly to the Tuvaluan Government previously, as an "option of last resort") is indeed a visionary policy given the nascent legal and political practices and opportunities that it creates (Klepp and Herbeck 2017).

Discussion

Human mobility and migration are—and will be—possible and, in some cases, necessary responses to climatic and environmental changes. There are policies and frameworks around climate-related migration, urgent global imperatives of greenhouse gas mitigation and climate justice, and emerging initiatives related to "loss and damage" as a pathway to highlight exposure to climate impacts and generate climate action.

Climate-Related Migration Policy and Frameworks: Global, Regional, and National

In 2010, signatories to the UNFCCC agreed at the Cancún Conference of Parties (COP) that adaption and mitigation of greenhouse gas emissions should receive equal attention and effort; signatory nations were encouraged to formulate National Adaptation Plans. The Cancún Adaptation Framework recognized migration, displacement and planned relocation as central to climate change adaptation (UNFCCC 2010). Subsequent to the Cancún meeting, international and regional initiatives have engaged in developing policy and legal instruments around climate-related migration, displacement, and relocation.[3] Key examples include the Peninsula Principles on Internal Displacement and the Nansen Initiative on Cross-Border Climate-Induced Displacement. The Marrakesh COP advocated for more substantial engagement with displacement in the UNFCCC context. These international frameworks seek to support and accommodate migration where it is necessary or judicious.

Within the Pacific, there are many regional and national efforts to develop strategies and address climate change rather than relying on externally devised frameworks. The

Framework for Resilient Development in the Pacific: An Integrated Approach to Address Climate Change and Disaster Risk Management 2017–2030 has been developed (to replace the *Pacific Disaster Risk Reduction and Disaster Management Framework for Action 2005–2015*) (SPC et al. 2016). Within these voluntary guidelines, there are specific sections with a focus on migration, relocation, and displacement. They call for "National and Subnational Governments and Administrations" to:

> Integrate human mobility aspects, where appropriate, including strengthening the capacity of governments and administrations to protect individuals and communities that are vulnerable to climate change and disaster displacement and migration, through targeted national policies and actions, including relocation and labour migration policies.
>
> (SPC et al. 2016, 15)

The *Pacific Islands Framework for Action on Climate Change 2006–2015* has been guiding regional activities (SPC et al. 2013). A few Pacific-nation National Adaptation Programmes of Action (NAPAs) and National Adaptation Plans (NAPs) refer to migration, including ways to support planned relocation as an adaptation strategy, particularly in the context of rising sea levels (Martin, 2009). For example, in the Pacific, the Solomon Islands referred to relocation of at-risk coastal populations, and—as discussed—Tuvalu has outlined steps for determining the need for and supporting migration and resettlement for each island in view of climate change impacts worst case scenarios (McDowell 2013; Warner et al. 2014).

Climate-related migration and mobility need not be a "crises" if they are supported and addressed through well-designed adaptation policies. As the example of the relocation of Vunidogoloa in Fiji illustrates, carefully planned and participatory decision making can support good migration or relocation processes, experiences, and outcomes. Yet while there is value in the idea of "climate migration as adaption" (rather than "climate migration as crisis"), it is far from unproblematic. Where there is disproportionate focus on the likelihood and urgency of climate-related migration, this obscures the potential for other adaptive measures that might prevent or reduce out-migration from communities and countries. This is important, as migration does not represent a hopeful future and is not the preferred option for many. As the Tuvalu case study illustrates, local people prefer to adapt *in situ*, and widely resist tropes of climate-related displacement from homes and homelands. Furthermore, if migration as adaptation is assumed, there is the risk of lack of investment in sites of climatic vulnerability. This risk was evident in Tokou, Fiji, where local villagers were reluctant to invest in maintenance and development of their homes and villages given the threat of sea-level rise. Beyond local decision making, there is also the risk that governments and donors will not invest in the development in "vulnerable" sites.

Greenhouse Gas Mitigation: An Urgent Global Task

The idea of "migration as adaptation" seemingly offers an adaptive solution to climate change impacts, thereby reducing the imperative for deep cuts in greenhouse gas emissions.

Yet climate change impacts are a global crisis: mitigation remains an urgent global task. This point is aptly made in the Kiribati case study that highlights their nation's call for high-emission countries to take responsibility for deep cuts in greenhouse gas emissions, even while planning for "migration with dignity." The 2015 Paris Climate Agreement aims to limit global average warming to 2°C above preindustrial levels, and emphasizes that the international community should pursue efforts to limit it to 1.5°C. About two thirds of the total carbon dioxide "budget" for limiting global average warming to below 2°C has already been emitted. Even if every country were to meet their post-2020 emission reductions targets (i.e. Intended Nationally Determined Contributions), there will still be global average warming of 2.6–3.1°C above preindustrial levels by the end of this century. Given the current greenhouse gas emissions trajectory, higher rates of warming are likely (Rogelj et al. 2016).

This seemingly unavoidable level of climate change threatens all societies, and particularly the social and ecological systems of low-lying island communities, nations, and territories (Barnett 2017). This threat is particularly unjust given that different countries have different levels of contribution and vulnerability to climate change. As is frequently stated, anthropogenic climatic change is largely the result of greenhouse gas emissions produced through capitalist enterprise, carbon-intensive economies, and overconsumption in high- and middle-income countries. Meanwhile, those communities least responsible for causing climate change—including Pacific island nations—typically face the greatest exposures and risks. Their immediate environments, lives, and futures are compromised by climatic changes created by activities of those in other countries (see Connell 2016; Lazrus 2012).

Loss and Damage

The UNFCCC now positions displacement and mobility within the Warsaw International Mechanism on Loss and Damage, as established at the 19th COP in November 2013. Small island states have been a driving force behind the "loss and damage" initiative, as it represents another pathway via which to highlight their exposure to adverse climate change impacts and—ideally—generate climate action (Barnett 2017). While there is no commonly accepted definition, "loss and damage" has been defined as the "negative effects of climate variability and climate change that people have not been able to cope with or adapt to" (Warner et al. 2012, 20). This definition includes inability to respond to climate threats (i.e., inaction) and the costs and losses associated with coping and adaptive strategies (i.e., migration). There is an embedded understanding within the "loss and damage" initiative that current mitigation efforts cannot sufficiently stabilize greenhouse gas emissions so as to prevent climate change impacts (Roberts and Huq 2015). Many perspectives limit the loss and damage agenda to a matter of determining liability and seeking financial compensation; while this is important (for reasons that include global funding and aid for adaptation in Pacific Island countries being significantly less than the estimates of funding and aid required), it reduces the complexity of problems. Financial compensation may provide a normative solution to loss and damage experienced by vulnerable countries, but it does not mean that all needs are addressed. It is critical to understand and address loss and damage beyond quantifiable economic impacts that are measured in terms of physical assets or gross domestic product and consider broader social loss and damage.

The intersections between "loss and damage" and human migration are twofold. First, migration can be understood as the result of local loss and damage due to climate impacts, including loss of ecosystems, habitable land, and livelihoods; second, migration can be understood as an adaptive strategy which itself can then embody experiences of loss and damage, including erosion of place attachment, economic costs, adverse health impacts, and disrupted social structures (McMichael 2016; McNamara et al. 2016). People and policymakers in sites of climatic vulnerability face difficult decisions about when to support migration and relocation as a response to unavoidable losses and damages, and how to support migration so as to avoid further loss and damages associated with the process itself. "Loss and damage" will likely become an increasingly important aspect of the climate-related migration discourse, funding and approach in coming years and decades.

Conclusion

For now, climate-related human mobility in Pacific communities, countries, and territories is predominantly an anticipated phenomenon and an area of policy development, rather than a reality of people on the move. Pacific countries are forging policy and programmatic response without the benefit of learning from the experiences and responses of others. There is, however, some emerging preemptive and responsive human migration in the Pacific in the face of climate impacts, including in Fiji. While this migration affords an adaptive response to climate change impacts, it positions vulnerable populations who have made limited contributions to global warming—such as low-lying communities and countries in the Pacific—as necessarily bearing the burden of response to local impacts of climate change.

"Migration as adaptation" must not be uncritically assumed and assigned to Pacific countries and territories. Climate-related migration remains something that could be potentially avoided, or at least ameliorated, through global greenhouse gas emission reductions and expanded approaches to adaptation. Furthermore, while there is substantial scientific evidence indicating that sea levels will rise, coastal erosion and flooding will occur, and some atolls and coastal areas may become uninhabitable, there remains lack of certainty as to whether, when, how, and to what extent migration and relocation may be necessary. It is critical that the notion of climate migration in the Pacific is not normalized as an emerging crisis or a foregone adaptive response, but rather that diverse adaptation efforts are supported. Third, while deep cuts in greenhouse gas emissions remain critically important, and diverse adaptive responses to existing and future climate chance impacts are required, climate change does present dire risks to Pacific which will contribute to migration and displacement: decision making and planning for climate-related migration should be led by Pacific islanders with support from external agents—including necessary aid and financial support—so that local people can plan for their futures, and consider and accommodate human mobility as a response to climate impacts.

Notes

1. This case study reports the findings of qualitative fieldwork conducted in low-lying iTaukei (indigenous) villages in Fiji in 2015 and 2016.
2. This case study refers to interviews (n=13) undertaken with representatives from government ministries, intergovernmental organizations, and international and local nongovernmental organizations in 2014.
3. See Nansen Principles and Nansen Initiative Protection Agenda, which has been endorsed by 109 government delegations (Bettini 2017; NRC 2011); UNHCR's document Protection and Planned Relocations in the Context of Climate Change (see Ferris 2012); The Peninsula Principles on Climate Displacement within States (see Displacement Solutions 2013); the Guiding Principles on Climigration (see Bronen 2011); and the Disaster Displacement Platform which is a high-level initiative targeting international displacement in the context of disasters and climate change (as follow-up to the Nansen Initiative).

References

Asian Development Bank (ADB). 2012. *Addressing Climate Change and Migration in Asia and the Pacific*. Mandaluyong City, Philippines: Asian Development Bank. https://www.adb.org/publications/addressing-climate-change-and-migration-asia-and-pacific

Baldwin, A., C. Methmann, and D. Rothe. 2014. "Securitizing "Climate Refugees": The Futurology of Climate-induced Migration." *Critical Studies on Security* 2, no. 2: 121–130.

Bawden, T. 2014. "Official Prophecy of Doom: Global Warming Will Cause Widespread Conflict, Displace Millions of People and Devastate the Global Economy." *The Independent*, March 18, http://goo.gl/fMbCJA

Barnett, J. 2003. "Security and Climate Change." *Global Environmental Change* 13, no. 1: 7–17.

Barnett, J. 2017. "The Dilemmas of Normalising Losses from Climate Change: Towards Hope for Pacific Atoll Countries." *Asia Pacific Viewpoint* 58, no. 1: 3–13.

Barnett, J., and W. N. Adger. 2007. "Climate Change, Human Security and Violent Conflict." *Political Geography* 26, no. 6: 639–655.

Barnett, J., and C. McMichael. 2018. "The effects of climate change on the geography and timing of human mobility." *Population and Environment* 39, no.4: 339–356.

Bedford, R. and C. Bedford. 2010. "International Migration and Climate Change: A Post-Copenhagen Perspective on Options for Kiribati and Tuvalu." In *Climate Change and Migration: South Pacific Perspectives*, edited by B. Burson, 89–134. Wellington, NZ: Institute of Policy Studies.

Bettini, G. 2017. "Where Next? Climate Change, Migration, and the (Bio)politics of Adaptation." *Global Policy* 8, no. 1: 33–39.

Betts, A. and A. Pilath. 2016. "The Politics of Causal Claims: The Case of Environmental Migration." *Journal of International Relations and Development* 20, no. 4: 1–23. https://doi.org/10.1057/s41268-016-0003-y

Biermann, F., and I. Boas. 2010. "Preparing for a Warmer World: Towards a Global Governance System to Protect Climate Refugees." *Global Environmental Politics* 10, no. 1: 60–88.

Black, R., W. N. Adger, N. W. Arnell, S. Dercon, A. Geddes, and D. Thomas. 2011. "The Effect of Environmental Change on Human Migration." *Global Environmental Change* 21, supp. 1: s3–s11.

Black, R., N. W. Arnell, W. N. Adger, D. Thomas, and A. Geddes. 2013. "Migration, Immobility and Displacement Outcomes Following Extreme Events." *Environmental Science & Policy* 27, supp. 1: s32–s43.

Bronen, R. 2011. "Climate-Induced Community Relocations: Creating an Adaptive Governance Framework Based in Human Rights Doctrine." *N.Y.U. Review of Law and Social Change* 35, no. 2: 101–148.

Christian Aid. 2007. *Human Tide: The Real Migration Crisis*. London: Christian Aid.

Connell, J. 2016. "Last Days in the Carteret Islands? Climate Change, Livelihoods and Migration on Coral Atolls." *Asia Pacific Viewpoint* 57, no. 1: 3–15.

Council of the European Union. 2008. *Climate Change and International Security—Report from the Commission and the Secretary-General/High Representative to the European Council*. Brussels, March 14, 2008. http://www.consilium.europa.eu/ueDocs/cms_Data/docs/pressData/en/reports/99387.pdf)

Displacement Solutions. 2013. *The Peninsula Principles on Climate Displacement within States*. Geneva: Displacement Solutions.

Environmental Justice Foundation. 2009. *No Place Like Home—Where Next for Climate Refugees?* London: Environmental Justice Foundation. https://ejfoundation.org/reports/no-place-like-home-where-next-for-climate-refugees

Farbotko, C. 2005. "Tuvalu and Climate Change: Constructions of Environmental Displacement in the *Sydney Morning Herald*." *Geografiska Annaler* 87 B, no. 4: 279–293.

Farbotko, C. 2018. "Voluntary Immobility: Indigenous Voices in the Pacific." *Forced Migration Review* 57. http://www.fmreview.org/syria2018/farbotko.html.

Farbotko, C. and H. Lazrus. 2012. "The First Climate Refugees? Contesting Global Narratives of Climate Change in Tuvalu." *Global Environmental Change* 22, no. 2: 382–390.

Farbotko, C., E. Stratford, and H. Lazrus. 2016. "Climate Migrants and New Identities? The Geopolitics of Embracing or Rejecting Mobility." *Social & Cultural Geography* 17, no. 4: 533–552.

Felli, R. 2012. "Managing Climate Insecurity by Ensuring Continuous Capital Accumulation: "Climate Refugees" and "Climate Migrants"." *New Political Economy* 18, no. 3: 337–363.

Ferris, E. 2012. *Protection and Planned Relocations in the Context of Climate Change*. Geneva: United Nations High Commissioner for Refugees.

Fiji Times. 2016. "64 Villages in Fiji To Be Relocated due to Climate Change." *Fiji Times*, August 4, 2016. https://www.postguam.com/news/pacific/villages-in-fiji-to-be-relocated-due-to-climate-change/article_0d4239c8-597c-11e6-a463-63e44c267cf2.html

Foresight. 2011. *Final Project Report—Foresight: Migration and Global Environmental Change*. London: The Government Office for Science. *Gov.UK*. https://www.gov.uk/government/publications/migration-and-global-environmental-change-future-challenges-and-opportunities

Friends of the Earth. 2007. *A Citizen's Guide to Climate Refugees*. Melbourne, Australia: Friends of the Earth.

Gray, C. and E. Wise. 2016. "Country-specific Effects of Climate Variability on Human Migration." *Climatic Change* 135, no. 5: 555–568.

Gemenne, F. 2011. "Why the Numbers Don't Add Up: A Review of Estimates and Predictions of People Displaced by Environmental Changes." *Global Environmental Change* 21: s41–s49.

Gemenne, F., J. Barnett, W. N. Adger, and G. D. Dabelko. 2014. "Climate and Security: Evidence, Emerging Risks, and a New Agenda." *Climatic Change* 123, no. 1: 1–9.

Government of Tuvalu. 2012a. "Tuvalu National Strategic Action Plan for Climate Change and Disaster Risk Management: 2012–2016." Available at: https://www.pacificclimatechange.net/sites/default/files/documents/NSAP%20Eng%20new%20web.pdf

Government of Tuvalu. 2012b. "Te Kaniva: Tuvalu National Climate Change Policy 2012–2021." http://reliefweb.int/sites/reliefweb.int/files/resources/TUV_2012_Te_Kaniva_CCpolicy.pdf

Hartmann, B. 2010. "Rethinking Climate Refugees and Climate Conflict: Rhetoric, Reality and the Politics of Policy Discourse." *Journal of International Development* 22, no. 2: 233–246.

Hau'ofa, E. 1994. "Our Sea of Islands." *The Contemporary Pacific* 6, no. 1: 148–161.

Homer-Dixon, T. 1999. *Environmental Scarcity and Violence*. Princeton, NJ: Princeton University Press.

IPCC. 2014. *Climate Change 2014: Synthesis Report. Contribution of Working Groups I, II and III to the Fifth Assessment Report of the Intergovernmental Panel on Climate Change*. Edited by R.K. Pachauri and L.A. Meyer. Geneva, Switzerland: IPCC. https://www.ipcc.ch/pdf/assessment-report/ar5/syr/AR5_SYR_FINAL_SPM.pdf

Klepp, S., and J. Herbeck. 2017. "Politicising Climate Change Adaptation: Negotiating Environmental Migration in the European Union and the Pacific." In *Climate Change, Migration and Human Rights: Law and Policy Perspectives*, edited by D. Manou, D. Cubie, A. Baldwin, A. Mihr, and T. Thorp, 169–188. Abingdon, UK: Routledge-Earthscan.

Kothari, U. 2014. "Political Discourses of Climate Change and Migration: Resettlement Policies in the Maldives." *The Geographical Journal* 180, no. 2: 130–140.

Lazrus, H. 2012. "Sea Change: Island Communities and Climate Change." *Annual Review of Anthropology* 41: 285–301.

Locke, J. T. 2009. "Climate Change-Induced Migration in the Pacific Region: Sudden Crisis and Long-Term Developments." *The Geographical Journal* 175, no. 3: 171.

Martin, S. F. 2009. "Managing Environmentally Induced Migration." In *Migration, Environment and Climate Change: Assessing the Evidence*, edited by F. Laczko, and C. Aghazarm, 353–384., Geneva: IOM.

Massey, D.S., W. G. Axinn, and D. J. Ghimire. 2010. "Environmental Change and Out-Migration: Evidence from Nepal." *Population and Environment* 32, no. 2: 109–136.

McDowell, C. 2013. "Climate Change Adaptation and Mitigation: Implications for Land Acquisition and Population Relocation." *Development Policy Review* 31, no. 6: 677–695.

McMichael, C. 2016. "Winds of Change: Climate Change, Migration and Health." In *Handbook of Migration and Health*, edited by F. Thomas, 277–295. Cheltenham, UK: Edward Elgar.

McMichael, C., and M. Katonivualiku. Under review. "Navigating Rising Seas: Planned Relocation in Fiji." *The Geographical Journal*.

McNamara, K.E., R. Bronen, N. Fernando, and S. Klepp. 2016. "The Complex Decision-Making of Climate-Induced Relocation: Adaptation and Loss and Damage." *Climate Policy* 18, no. 1: 111–117. doi.org/10.1080/14693062.2016.1248886

McNamara, K. E. 2007. "Conceptualizing Discourses on Environmental Refugees at the United Nations." *Population and Environment: A Journal of Interdisciplinary Studies* 29, no. 1: 12–24.

McNamara, K. E. 2015. "Cross-Border 'Migration with Dignity' in Kiribati." *Forced Migration Review* 49: 62.

McNamara, K. and C. Gibson. 2009. "'We do not want to leave our land': Pacific Ambassadors at the United Nations Resist the Category of 'Climate Refugees.'" *Geoforum* 40: 475–483.

Mortreux, C. and J. Barnett. 2009. "Climate Change, Migration and Adaptation in Funafuti, Tuvalu." *Global Environmental Change* 19, no. 1: 105–112.

Myers, N. 2002. "Environmental Refugees: A Growing Phenomenon of the 21st Century." *Philosophical Transactions: Biological Sciences* 357, no. 1420: 609–613.

NRC. 2011. *The Nansen Conference: Climate Change and Displacement in the 21st Century*. Norwegian Refugee Council. Oslo, Norway, June 5–7. http://www.unhcr.org/4ea969729.pdf

ODI. 2016. *Climate-Induced Migration and Displacement: Closing the Policy Gap*. London: Overseas Development Institute.

Office of Te Beretitenti. 2015. *Relocation*. Kirbati Climate Change. http://www.climate.gov.ki/category/action/relocation

Ransan-Cooper, H., C. Farbotko, K. McNamara, F. Thornton, and E. Chevalier. 2015. "Being(s) Framed: The Means and Ends of Framing Environmental Migrants." *Global Environmental Change* 35: 106–115.

Republic of Fiji. 2012. *National Climate Change Policy*. Suva, Fiji: Secretariat of the Pacific Community. https://www.preventionweb.net/files/Fiji%20National%20Climate%20Change%20policy.pdf

Republic of Fiji. 2014. *Second National Communication to the United Nations Framework Convention on Climate Change*. Suva, Fiji: Ministry of Foreign Affairs. https://unfccc.int/resource/docs/natc/phlnc2.pdf

Republic of Kiribati. 2007. *National Adaptation Program of Action*. Tarawa: Government of Kiribati. http://unfccc.int/resource/docs/napa/kir01.pdf

Reuveny, R. 2007. "Climate Change–Induced Migration and Violent Conflict." *Political Geography* 26, no. 6: 656–673.

Roberts, E., and S. Huq. 2015. "Coming Full Circle: The History Of Loss And Damage under the UNFCCC." *International Journal of Global Warming* 8, no. 2: 141–157.

Rogelj, J., M. den Elzen, N. Höhne, T. Fransen et al. 2016. "Paris Agreement Climate Proposals Need a Boost to Keep Warming Well below 2°C." *Nature* 534, no. 7609: 631–639.

Schwartz, P. and D. Randall. 2003. "An Abrupt Climate Change Scenario and its Implications for United States National Security." October 2003. http://www.futurebrief.com/dod-climate.pdf

SPC, UNISDR, and SPREP. 2013. *Roadmap Toward an Integrated Regional Strategy for Disaster Risk Management and Climate Change in the Pacific by 2015*. Secretariat of the Pacific Community, The United Nations Office for Disaster Risk Reduction, and the Secretariat of the Pacific Regional Environment Programme. https://reliefweb.int/report/world/roadmap-towards-integrated-regional-strategy-disaster-risk-management-and-climate

SPC, SPREP, PIFS, UNDP, UNISDR and USP. 2016. *Framework for Resilient Development in the Pacific: An Integrated Approach to Address Climate Change and Disaster Risk Management 2017—2030*. Secretariat of the Pacific Community et al. http://www.pacificdisaster.net/dox/FRDP_2016_Resilient_Dev_pacific.pdf

Stern, N. 2007. *The Economics of Climate Change: The Stern Review*. Cambridge, UK: Cambridge University Press.

Tacoli, C. 2009. "Crisis or Adaptation? Migration and Climate Change in a Context of High Mobility." *Environment and Urbanization* 21, no. 2: 513–525.

UNFCCC. 2010. "The Cancun Agreements: Outcome of the work of the Ad-Hoc Working Group on Long-term Cooperative Action under the Convention." March 15, 2011. http://unfccc.int/resource/docs/2010/cop16/eng/07a01.pdf

Van Gorp, B. 2007. "The Constructionist Approach to Framing: Bringing Culture Back In." *Journal of Communication* 57: 60–78.

Warner, K., W. Kälin, S. Martin et al. 2014. *Integrating Human Mobility Issues within National Adaptation Plans.* UNU-EHS Publication Series, Policy Brief No. 9. Environmental Migration Portal. https://environmentalmigration.iom.int/integrating-human-mobility-issues-within-national-adaptation-plans

Warner, K., K. van der Geest, S. Kreft et al. 2012. *Evidence from the Frontlines of Climate Change: Loss and Damage to Communities despite Coping and Adaptation: Loss and Damage in Vulnerable Countries Initiative. Policy Report. Report No. 9.* Bonn: United Nations University Institute for Environment and Human Security (UNU-EHS). http://www.ciesin.org/binaries/web/global/news/2013/cdkn-report.pdf

WBGU. 2008. *World in Transition: Climate Change as a Security Risk.* London: Earthscan.

Westra, L. 2009. *Environmental Justice and the Rights of Ecological Refugees.* London: Earthscan.

CHAPTER 18

MIGRATION AND ENVIRONMENTAL CRISES IN AFRICA

AYOKUNLE OLUMUYIWA OMOBOWALE, OLAYINKA AKANLE, OLUGBENGA SAMUEL FALASE, AND MOFEYISARA OLUWATOYIN OMOBOWALE

SINCE the 1980s, Africa has emerged as a region of primary discourse in migration studies. Africa is largely constructed as the continent of crises in both scholarly literature and the mass media, and international migration is a plausible norm for most Africans. This chapter discusses the migration of Africans within the context of environmental crises. As used here, these entail those challenges traditionally deemed as environmental crises such as desertification and natural disasters, as well as related crises due to social action such as economic crises, armed conflict, and health challenges which make the African environment backward compared to other continents. Africans are globally noted for international economic migration and asylum claims (Whitaker 2017). Social constructions about the 'peculiarity' of negative socioeconomic environments and disasters have catalyzed both international and internal migration in Africa. Also Liberia, Sierra Leone, Congo, Uganda, Sudan, Rwanda, and Burundi, among others, have passed through periods of civil war in the recent past while Somalia has been under the stranglehold of warlords since 1991 (Ahmad 2015). Religious, ethnic, and class conflicts reverberate across Africa and the subsistence-level socioeconomic environment puts more than 70 percent of Africans below the poverty line (Buhaug, Cederman, and Gleditsch 2014; World Bank 2017a). Again, livelihood needs are largely inaccessible to the poor and thus, life expectancy at birth, though has improved from 48.1 years in 1980 to 58.9 years in 2015, remains comparatively the worst in the world (World Bank 2017b). Sub-Saharan Africa's over 1 billion population exist in a precarious environment—that is, though blessed with natural and human resources, they are incapacitated by corruption, capital flight, inefficiency, and low social esteem, which precipitate internal and international migration.

The physical and social contexts in African countries make international migration a preferred alternative for many who are 'entrapped' in the continent's crises. African migrants take every possible means, legal or illegal, to move to Europe and North America especially. The trans-Saharan route is a major migration pathway for many illegal African migrants. The trans-Saharan route has a network of traffickers who convey migrants through the desert up to the coast of Morocco and Libya from where migrants make the dangerous sea journey to Spain and Italy in rickety and crowded boats (Barbara et al. 2017). Few migrants make it to Europe through this route; many also lose their lives in the desert and the high seas. This chapter discusses the context and realities of migration in Africa. The developed world is constructed as the 'promised land' with 'green pasture' that could provide succor from economic crises, disasters, maternal and child mortality, and the challenges of climate change.

An in-depth scrutiny of the African social environment provides a profound explanation of why many Africans prefer migration from the continent. Since the period of colonization, the West has been constructed as the land of great opportunities (Omobowale 2013). Anglophone indirect rule, as well as Francophone and Lusophone assimilation policies, institutionalized the process of making the West and its civilization the ideal (Ndlovu-Gatsheni 2015). Both educational and religious epistemologies constructed Africa as the disadvantaged (educational) and cursed (religious) land (Omobowale 2015). The colonial and postcolonial social structure internalizes in the individual the value of Western spatial and cultural superiority and of course, a preferred space for social existence and migration (Omobowale 2013). Irrespective of the assumptions about migration predisposing factors in Africa, many Africans emigrate to the West because of the internalization of values, which construct and present Europe and North America as the lands that solve all challenges. According to the United Nations (2016), out of the 244 million international migrants globally, 34 million were Africans, and the major destinations of African migrants are Europe (25 percent), Asia (10 percent) and North America (5 percent). It is important to note that whereas Europe and North America are the preferred destinations, Asia is receiving an increasing number of migrants because it presents a plausible alternative to individuals emigrating from Africa at all costs with the hope of reaching the West someday. Hence, an average successful emigrant assumes the status of a 'star'. Once again, this chapter discusses migration and environmental crises in Africa. The first section provides the background; the second section discusses economic crises and migration, because hardly could migration crises in Africa be discussed without a focus or link to the economic context, which provides a critical foundation to the construction of migration crises on the continent. The third, fourth, and fifth sections examine disaster and migration, migration and maternal and child health and climate change, and migration respectively, while the last section concludes the chapter.

Economic Crises and Migration

A foundational construction of migration crises in Africa has an economic context. Since contact with European explorers and subsequent colonization, migration to the West has been culturally classified as progress and of strategic economic benefit (Imoagene 2017; Omobowale 2013). Lindley (2014) examines the structural context of migration and submits that migration is a major feature of capitalist development and a consequence of capitalist primitive acquisition. The global migratory labor force is thus a product of capitalism serving the interest of the bourgeois class, at the expense of the integration of the global working class. For Lindley, crisis and migration are connected, and they are embedded in wider patterns of social change and transformation. Migration is not merely a consequence of crisis, but it is integral to the explanation of how populations experience crises.

The link between economic crisis and migration is important in understanding the migratory flow that occurs in African countries. Within sub-Saharan Africa, Ghana and Cote d'Ivoire became major destinations of African economic migrants in the late 1960s (Adepoju 1995). In 1969, Ghana expelled a large number of foreigners under the Aliens Compliance Order, but by late 1970s, economic problems in the country made many Ghanaians migrate to other African countries in search of better opportunities. During this period, Nigeria experienced economic prosperity as a result of the oil boom and became a major attraction to neighboring countries including Ghanaians. By 1983, about 2 million Ghanaians were working in diverse sectors of the Nigerian economy as artisans and professionals. Most of these Ghanaians were described as illegal migrants and were deported in 1983 and 1984 (Adebayo 1985). The deportees mostly parked their luggage in cheap 'weightless' luggage, which is euphemistically called 'Ghana Must Go' even in contemporary times. 'Ghana Must Go' luggage has since become preferred cheap but durable carriage bags for travel and household loads, and it is used as well for storage among Nigerians.

By the mid-1980s, the implementation of the Structural Adjustment Policy (SAP) negatively affected African economies, leading to mass pauperization. The SAP entailed the withdrawal of government from fiscal administration, commercialization, and privatization of government enterprises to ensure competitiveness and profit, as well as commercialization of social services, embargos on employment and salary increases, and the adoption of laissez faire principles (Olutayo and Omobowale 2007). The World Bank and the International Monetary Fund proposed SAP as a policy for economic recovery. Unfortunately, SAP led instead to the dumping of foreign goods, the collapse of industries, loss of jobs, poverty, and a decreased standard of living. Nigeria hence experienced a sudden reverse immigration status from being a major destination country in Africa to a major migrants supply nation.

Migration of Africans within and outside the continent is a response to economic depression and consequent social reconstruction of the West as the land of enormous opportunities for any person who could move there, legally or illegally, whether it was safe or risky. With the poor state of the economy of most African countries, especially following SAP, people find every possible means to move to Europe, North America, and lately Asia to improve their standards of living. In this regard, Africans mostly migrate for economic purposes. Opportunity differentials are responsible for this process of migration. As Banulescu-Bogdan and Fratzke (2015) noted, the process of migration signifies a chance to regain and realize a standard life that has been ruptured by political and economic turmoil, conflict, or persecution. Africa has the fastest growing and most youthful population in the world, with over 40 percent under the age of 15 and 20 percent between the ages of 15 and 24 (Williams 2012). For most within the productive age group, economic opportunities are bleak. In most African countries, rural infrastructure and economy are derelict. Facing lifelong economic deprivation, the rural young are compelled to move to urban areas or emigrate internationally. These migrants are mostly vibrantly energetic but unskilled married and unmarried men and women who move to care for their families. Migrants usually leave their spouses and children behind with the hope of chain-migrating left-behind families, or of return migration to the loving hands of family and friends (Akanle and Olutayo 2012; Whitaker 2017). Adepoju (1995) also notes a strategic division of labor among African migrants whereby husbands migrate for wage and employment while wives maintain home and farms. It is important to point out that with female education and professionalization, skilled women (usually nurses and other health and social service professionals) migrate to wealthy nations. Such rich countries include Saudi Arabia, Oman, Kuwait, and the United Arab Emirates (the Middle East/Asia); Great Britain, France, Netherlands, and Germany (Europe); and the United States and Canada (North America).

Despite migrants' popular preference for Europe and North America, most African migrants move within Africa due to travel limitations bordering on visa restrictions and costs. While some countries such as South Africa and Nigeria simultaneously serve as origin, transit, and destination nations, most other sub-Saharan African countries principally serve as source countries due to economic depression and poor socioeconomic conditions. Nigeria mostly attracts periodic migrant working-class labor, farmhands, and beggars from neighboring West African countries such as Benin, Chad, Niger, and Mali (Fayehun and Salami 2014; Salami and Olugbayo 2013). Local gifting and *zakat* culture in many communities in Nigeria accommodate both domestic and migrant beggars as a vulnerable population that should be catered for through voluntary gifting. The end of apartheid as well as a relatively improved economy over the years regarding advanced infrastructure, economic opportunities, and abundant natural resources have attracted migrants from sub-Saharan Africa to South Africa. For example, Crush (2008) reported that 81 percent, 29 percent, and 23 percent of Lesotho's, Mozambique's, and Zimbabwe's adult population respectively live in South Africa. In fact, African migrants are a huge population of South Africa's professionals, especially in the academic and health sectors (Dube and Rukema 2013). However, as the working-class economy of South Africa continues to be dominated by migrants, xenophobic hostilities regularly occur against African migrants in South Africa. The South African black population constructs black migrants as the cause of South Africa's social problems, especially drug trafficking, heists, and armed robbery. Successful African migrants are seen as either illicit businessmen and businesswomen, con-men, or people whose earnings are suspect and must be edged out to allow black South Africans to be economically active (Hickel 2014). Kumolu (2017) reported that since the 1990s, no fewer than two hundred foreign nationals (mostly Africans) had been maimed or killed in xenophobic attacks in South Africa.

African emigrants to Europe and North America appear to be wealthier and more educated than those to other African countries (Shaw 2007). Excellent infrastructure, good security, and efficient economy serve as pull factors that draw migrants. This process of migration is predicated on the historical and linguistic trails of colonialism, which makes Britain (and other Anglophone Western countries) and France the preferred countries for most migrants from the former British and French colonies.

Zeleza (2002) emphasized that the economic processes of international migration are intertwined and that African migrations are part of the complex variety of transnational cultural flows as they are of labor and other economic flows. Also, the continuous interaction among countries due to globalization, as well as the various patterns and directions of migration, have influenced the social, economic, and political development of countries involved. As these interactions increase, some migration flows are considered crises, while others are viewed as non-crises. The education and professional labor migrations that may advance economic development in the destination countries, and contribute to the countries of origin through remittances, are hardly considered as crises (see Akanle and Adesina 2017a; Capps, McCabe, and Fix 2012). Africans migrate outside the continent mostly to have economic advantages in destination countries. While some migrants fulfil their dreams many others become poor, jobless, and economically deprived in destination countries they hitherto viewed as greener pastures (Biney 2011).

Disasters and Migration

Disasters are some of the leading causes of migration in Africa. More often than not, disasters that have caused migration in Africa are socially constructed through human inefficiency, structural default, poor infrastructure, corruption, and avoidable conflicts among human-influenced actions. Hence, common disasters in Africa such as drought and other famine; flood; and violent environmental conflicts such as the Niger Delta conflict in Nigeria and the diamond-induced wars in Liberia, Sierra Leone, and Congo have severe devastating effects on the affected populations, because prevention mechanisms and immediate relief are poor or unavailable. Drought affects 50 percent of the population across West Africa (particularly Senegal, Mauritania, Mali, Chad, Burkina Faso, and Nigeria); East Africa (especially Somalia, Djibouti, Ethiopia, and Kenya); and Southern Africa (particularly South Africa, Madagascar, Malawi, and Mozambique. and

Lesotho) (Morris, Cervigni, Guo, and Koo 2016). Most of the affected populations are farmers and pastoralists; they represent a significant rung of the poor and vulnerable, their situation is worsened by drought, and drought negates development efforts and interventions in affected countries.

Drought areas are usually vast, in the outlands, and far from the center of political and economic activities, often neglected by central governments and prone to conflict over limited resources. Drought exacerbates both permanent and circular migration. Permanent migration is defined as when migrants relocate for more than six months with little or no intention of return, while circular migration refers to short-term movement (two to six months) to cities or wetlands for productivity and survival with the intention to return (Findley 1994; Gray and Mueller 2012). Despite the harsh conditions in arid regions, the embedded social structure somewhat attaches normative and identity values that support short-term migration and return for the sustenance of the area. For example, the research of Gray and Mueller (2012) confirms circular mobility in rural Ethiopia while Findley's (1994) study reveals a short-term migration to close destinations in rural Mali. Children in particular migrated to more affluent areas under the care of foster parents while men and women migrated for economic reasons. Nevertheless, migrants return to contribute to family welfare. The case is similar to African pastoralists, constantly on the move to find green pasture for their livestock. Pastoral movements, especially in West and East Africa, often lead to conflict with farmers due to the destruction of crops (Raleigh and Kniveton 2012). The pastoral movements and conflicts transcend international borders and are becoming increasingly complicated with the use of sophisticated weapons and destruction of livestock and farms by conflicting parties, leading to further population displacement and migration.

Flood remains a major environmental challenge in Africa. Flood plains attract both poor and rich. The wealthy reside in exclusive neighborhoods along flood plains, while the poor live in overpopulated wetland slums, with poor infrastructure and drainages as well as depleted mangrove areas due to human activities. Hence, the poor are most affected by flood and by the economic devastation caused by flood. With little options, the poor and vulnerable may migrate out of flood plains only for short periods, only to return to same flood-prone environments. The rich and the poor face different flood realities. While the rich reside in flood plains and close to waters as a reflection of their wealth and elitist statuses, the vulnerable reside in slum sections with damaged and nonfunctional infrastructure and drainages due to poverty. The wealthy replace damaged property and return to their exclusive areas in satisfaction of elitist values, while the poor face more stringent challenges and are internally displaced, but eventually return to flood plains because that is all they can afford. For the poor, the social relations of poverty normalize flood plains as conducive, view periodic movement due to flood as expected, and take human and material loss due to flood as inevitable consequence of their economic impairment. Thus the poor eagerly return to flood plains without adequate physical and social structures to mitigate the effects of flood.

Africa is resource rich, with enormous deposits of crude oil, gold, diamond, copper, bauxite, cobalt, uranium, and silver among other resources, but these resources have contributed little to Africa's development (Asiedu 2006). Investment and exploration of Africa's natural resources have also resulted in environmental degradation and resource conflict (Okeke 2008). Countries such as Angola, Liberia, Democratic Republic of Congo (DR Congo), and Sierra Leone have experienced diamond fueled civil wars while conflicts and civil wars have occurred in Nigeria, Sudan, and South Sudan because of oil (Koubi, Spilker, Böhmelt, and Bernauer 2014; Wegenast and Schneider 2017).

Campbell (2002) detailed the activities of the Foday Sankoh–led Revolutionary United Front (RUF), a rebel movement, which invaded Sierra Leone from Liberia in the early 1990s. The RUF financed its war machinery through illegal diamond exports, brutalized villagers, and spread its terror by amputating victims' hands and limbs. The RUF's diamond-influenced brutalities have been couched in the blood diamond discourse (Balestri and Maggioni 2014). Again, the story of DR Congo from independence is fraught with conflict, mismanagement, and lately civil wars (Omobowale 2009a; Ross 2004). As of the late 1990s, DR Congo has witnessed the emergence of numerous rebel groups that are propelled by the prospects of diamonds. The conflicts in DR Congo have been difficult to effectively put to an end, due to the blood diamond influence; the blood diamonds of Congo and Sierra Leone have been illegally traded through a network of rebels, government soldiers, customs agents, middlemen, and international merchants who ensure a continual flow of illicit diamonds from Africa through the black market.

Sudan was embroiled in a long-drawn civil war between the Sudanese government and the Sudanese Peoples Liberation Movement (SPLM) under the leadership of John Garang from 1983 to 2005, following the discovery of a large deposit of oil in Southern Sudan in 1978 (Deng 2010). Following a peace treaty, John Garang, SPLM and South Sudan leader, joined the government of Sudan as vice president in July 2005. Garang, unfortunately, died in a plane crash in August 2005. South Sudan became an autonomous region in October 2005, and its war with Sudan over the oil rich Abyei region continued intermittently from 2006 to 2009, when South Sudan accepted the ruling of the Hague arbitration court. The Hague ruling delineated Abyei between North and South Sudan and placed the main oil field in Northern Sudan (Daase 2013). South Sudan secured its independence in 2011. Unfortunately, South Sudan has subsequently been engulfed in oil-propelled civil war since its independence (De Waal 2014).

The Niger Delta is Nigeria's greatest oil-producing region, which produces Nigeria's wealth but is also one of Nigeria's poorest regions. Basic infrastructure is dilapidated and air, land, and water are eroded by oil pollution. The region gains little or nothing from oil and protests by oil activists were brutally put down, while Ken Saro Wiwa, an award winning playwright and oil activist, was executed under the government of General Sani Abacha in November 1995 (Brittain 2015; Omobowale 2009b). Unfortunately, systemic corruption has also resulted in little gain from special allocation to the region while specially constituted development boards—particularly the Oil Mineral Producing Areas Development Commission (OMPADEC) and the Niger Delta Development Commission (NDDC)—failed to provide succor (Agbiboa

2015). Between 1995 and 2007, the Niger Delta regressed into insurgency, with multiple warlords and militias engaging in attacks of government infrastructure and oil facility, kidnapping of oil workers, oil bunkering, and piracy. The government of Nigeria initially responded with limited military action, but then, under President Umaru Musa Yaradua, implemented an amnesty program in 2009, which subsequently brought relative peace in the Niger Delta (Udoh 2013). Nevertheless the Niger Delta remains volatile, environmental pollution remains a debilitating challenge, and militants still engage in the bursting of pipelines, illegal and unsafe oil refining, and kidnapping for ransom. As Nigeria's Niger Delta has again only seen relative peace, the environmental crises which propel migration are still very much embedded in the social structure of the region.

Migration and Maternal and Child Health

Both voluntary and forced migrations entail a change of social and physical environment with direct and indirect effects on maternal and child health and well-being. About 12 million people cross borders in West and Central Africa in search of either economic opportunities or fleeing from conflict (Flahaux and De Hass 2016; UNICEF 2017). Many of these migrants are mothers and children, and in the course of their migration, they face enormous health challenges, which negatively impact maternal and child morbidity and mortality in Africa. Furthermore, migration makes mothers and children vulnerable to diseases and violent attacks. The UNICEF (2017) posits that globally about 65 million children are on the move, while hundreds of thousands of these children are moving unaccompanied. Many African mothers and children who are subject to forced migration are vulnerable, disadvantaged, and subject to ill health socially, physically, or psychologically (Avogo and Agadjanian 2010, Perreira 2008).

Within Africa, urban–rural migration also affects maternal and child health sometimes positively, and many times negatively. Migration is positive when it involves relocation to the urban center; mothers can access better and more efficient antenatal and postnatal care and adequate child immunization, and up-to-date maternal and child health information that results in improved child survival. Migration to the urban center may improve the economic status of parents, which will enable them to attend promptly to health needs of their children. For instance, availability of antenatal, postnatal, and pediatric care in urban areas enhances mother-and-child survival in urban areas unlike in the rural areas where the only existing health center may be several kilometers away from their reach or inaccessible. When such primary health centers are accessible, they are ill-equipped to handle maternal and child care. Also, maternal migration may pose negative challenges because it could result in a disruptive process for the maternal economic well-being and may, therefore, lead to poor health-seeking behavior. However, when mothers and children finally settle down in the new environment, they may adapt and create new social networks (Smith-Greenaway and Madhavan 2015)

Furthermore, following the introduction of the Structural Adjustment Programme in the 1980s, many African countries experienced a brain drain of health professionals who migrated to developed countries for greener pastures and enhanced skill acquisition (Asampong et al. 2013). The mass movement of health professionals out of many African countries resulted in the deterioration of modern health care systems, with dire consequences to the health of African mothers and children, while quacks gained wide popularity among the poor in providing maternal and child healthcare (Ugwa and Ashimi 2015). During this period, infant mortality rates in Nigeria for instance rose from 104 deaths per 1000 live births in 1988 to 114 deaths per 1000 live births in 1992, while child mortality also increased from 174/1000 live births to 191/1000 live births around the same period (Orubuloye and Oni 1996).

The dismal statistics on infant mortality reveal a precarious health system in Nigeria in particular and Africa in general. The affluent opt for expensive private healthcare while some go all the way for medical tourism to the West, especially to the United States, Great Britain, and France. Accessing prenatal and postnatal care, as well as gynecological and pediatric care, in developed countries affords temporary medical migrants some of the best care available. However, for many, the main attraction is usually status symbolism and the potentiality of child citizenship or residency, which could afford future opportunities for the newborn.

Remittances are also a strategic context in migration, and maternal and child health in Africa (Omobowale, Omobowale, and Ajani 2010). The World Bank (2017c) estimates indicate that sub-Saharan Africa received US$33 billion worth of remittances in 2016. Remittances potentially present families that have their members in the developed world with material advantages, which could positively impact maternal and child health. Remittances may help erase social inequality and provide economic resources to access improved antenatal and postnatal care as well as pediatric care and access to unsubsidized immunization for children.

Climate Change and Migration

One of the most controversial issues in global polities and economies is climate change. Of critical importance is its impact on Africa, even though Africa contributes very little to causes of climate change. Climate change has been constructed as crises in scholarship and national and international policymaking. The incidence of global warming and its consequent impact on natural processes are engendering impacts in Africa which continually make emigration a survival option. This can be seen from the experiences of the Horn of Africa—Eritrea, Somalia, and even Ethiopia—and Libya, Nigeria, and sub-Saharan Africa generally. While it is common to categorize many African migrants as economic migrants, climate change somewhat plays an increasing role in driving migrations of Africans, as it determines the population of migrants, as well as their strategies and destinations.

Just as climate change plays an increasing role in contemporary migrations it will play a determining role in future migrations if current situations continue. Consequences of climate change that propel migrations include environmentally induced conflicts and crises, heavy rainfalls, aggravated droughts, heat waves, and shrinking socioeconomic (agricultural) and culture-related bodies of water (Forster and Fraser 2016). Under the category of nutrition, problems include poor crop productivity and negative impacts on livestock. Environmental changes also induce diseases, vulnerabilities, environmental degradation and stressed water resources (Allen and Ober 2008). These climate change–induced environmental changes have affected harvests and human relations so negatively that many Africans have been forced to migrate in droves. Unfortunately, Africa lacks emergency response preparedness and human and technological capabilities to cope with consequences of climate change on the continent, thereby forcing these migrations. Climate change is a real threat to African countries, and its effects are very noticeable in increasing food insecurity and increasing vulnerabilities, especially in poorer African countries like Somalia, Sudan, and South Sudan.

Even when migrations are usually multicausal (an interplay of socioeconomic, political, and environmental causes) and those causes are often controversial and inconclusive, there is a link between climate change and migrations of Africans. Climate change certainly has some significant effects on migrations of Africans and generalized human displacements. A good case in point is that of Malawi experience where people migrated due to climate change–induced poor harvests which threatened survival within local environments (Forster and Fraser 2016). Threats to human survival due to climate change precipitate migration because the local population constructs their immediate environment as cursed and crisis-ridden and then visualizes destination environments as panacea to all the challenges they face locally. Climate change usually has the double impacts of both enabling migrations, as people are forced to move, and disabling migrations, as people may lack resources to move. However, the youths, the ambitious, and the healthy are usually compelled to move.

A key issue in climate change and migration discourses in Africa is how to frame the migrants. A major challenge is (a) how to separate those displaced by climate change from those who are displaced by Africa's economic underdevelopment and (b) how to classify those displaced by climate issues based on existential realities regarding migration. Most migrants from Africa are usually economic migrants. This is because many African countries experienced reversed development from the 1980s, as governments implemented the Structural Adjustment Programme that rolled back the state and stifled private growth as discussed previously. Unfortunately, while most movements at this time were mainly economic and aggressive to the West, destination countries also tightened border controls and broadly classified migrants from Africa as economic migrants—*migrants escaping economic problems at home.* This blanket categorization of Africans as economic migrants exists to this day and sometimes influences policies, responses, and interventions even when real climate change–induced migrations are involved. A note to sound here is that while many migrants of African origin are economic migrants, not all migrants from the continent are indeed economic. This is important for border and citizenship profiling and critical in responses to climate change and migrations from Africa.

There is also a need to engage "climate migrants" or "climate refugees" or both. These two broad classifications are related in the sense that unlike in the case of economic migrants, both refer to people who move based on genuine climate challenges (Intergovernmental Panel on Climate Change [IPCC] 2007). An interesting twist, however, is that many other migrants also take the label of climate migrants or climate refugees to legitimize migration for benefits optimization. Causes and courses of migration, origin of migrants, and painstaking efforts of officials and careful policies are therefore key in this regard. Surveillance is also crucial to avoid the confusion and opportunistic infiltrations. Sometimes, climate migrants and climate refugees are used interchangeably in policy documents, but the real point is that both refer to genuine climate change–induced migrants. Since no consensus exists on how best to define the main actors and agencies on the issue of climate-induced migration and displacement, the two concepts are often resorted to interchangeably, but the key issue is climate inducement of human movement from its origin. It is important to note that paying attention to the classification of migrants within migration and climate change systems is critical for effective prevention, intervention, and optimization. Classification, profiling, and operationalization along these three lines is therefore not academic but policy-related, legal, operational, and programmatic. Understanding categories in climate change and migration systems will help intergovernmental agencies, states, border officials, environmental actors, migrants themselves, legal officials, and civil societies to productively and effectively navigate climate change and migration corridors for the benefits of all.

It is common for policy and advocacy documents to favor and adopt the term climate change refugees against climate change migrants. This is for strategic reasons rather than derogatory ones. The term "refugees" easily attracts intervention efforts and creates a sense of urgency needed from key stakeholders to rally and intervene in usually emergency climate change and migration situations, especially in climate change–induced emergency or natural disaster situations or both. The term "climate refugees" has also achieved prominence in the media, intergovernmental and civil societies' global narratives, and reports to draw attention to the impacts of climate change on Africans who contribute less than 10 percent to the climate change problems. There is thus a sense of global justice to redress the plight of climate refugees. This is however not to suggest that the term "climate refugee" is only for advocacy and programs as *refugee* has a long legal and effective history that can be adapted in climate change and migration narratives—particularly under the 1951 Refugee Convention. The term "climate refugees" also gives legal cover against persecution compared to the economic migrants who are sometimes seen as irregular and parasitic in the host countries.

Climate change migrants and refugees from Africa are from poor African countries and often have had their livelihood destroyed before their migration. Many have their lives under threat at home and can never return. This must be factored into policies and interventions, and all states and other actors must appreciate the need to safely accommodate and account for climate change–induced migrations from Africa. Climate change and migrations are real problems in Africa, and the nexus is critical. All stakeholders must, therefore, step up efforts to save this threatened category of migrants who are even often ill-prepared for the migrations they embark upon, and thus also become economic migrants, with plans and hope for personal, family, and community investment and development (Akanle and Adesina 2017a, 2017b).

Conclusion

Migration is a social reality in Africa. It is a constructed reality, informed by the continent's colonial and postcolonial relations with the developed world. Africa's social reality describes industrialized countries as the centers of privileges for the redress of all challenges and for socioeconomic advancement and strategic placement in the elitist class. Irrespective of the supposed primary causes of migration, the environmental social and economic strains in migrant countries of origin are major factors. Socioeconomic considerations are the underlying factors in deciding whether to move, where to move to, and the course of moving. Issues of economic crises, disasters, maternal and child health and climate change are strategic for the understanding migration crises in Africa. However, it is important to note that the construction of the developed world as the panacea for local challenges and possible socio-economic advancement of successful migrants and their families in home countries propels migration in Africa.

References

Adebayo, A. 1985. "Brain Drain within the ECOWAS Region." *African Issues: A Journal of Opinion* 14: 37–38.

Adepoju, A. 1995. "Migration in Africa: An Overview." In *The Migration Experience in Africa*, edited by Jonathan Baker and Tade Akin Aina, 87–108. Uppsala, Sweden: GOTAB.

Agbiboa, D. 2015. "Transformational Strategy or Gilded Pacification? Four Years On: The Niger Delta Armed Conflict and the DDR Process of the Nigerian Amnesty Programme." *Journal of Asian and African Studies*. 50 no. 4. doi:10.1177/0021909614530082

Ahmad, A. 2015. "The Security Bazaar: Business Interests And Islamist Power In Civil War Somalia." *International Security* 39, no. 3: 89–117.

Akanle, O., and J. O. Adesina. 2017a. "International Migrants' Remittances and Kinship Networks in Nigeria: The Flip-Side Consequences." *Journal of Anthropological Research* 73, no. 1: 66–91. doi:10.1086/690609

Akanle, O., and J. O. Adesina. 2017b. "Remittances and Household Welfare in Nigeria." *African Population Studies* 31, no. 7: 3194–3211.

Akanle, O. and A. O. Olutayo. 2012. "Ethnography of Kinship Constructions among International Returnees in Nigeria: Proverbs as the Horses of Words." *Journal of Anthropological Research* 68, no. 2: 249–271.

Allen, K. and K. Ober. 2008. "Desertification and Sea-Level Rise: New Trends Causing Environmental Refugees in the Twenty-First Century." *Scribd*. American University. https://www.scribd.com/document/15631856/Desertification-and-Sea-Level-Rise-New-Trends-Causing-Environmental-Refugees-in-the-Twenty-First-Century.

Asampong, E., J. A. Harrison, L. Yarney, K. Opoku-Mensah, A. Karim, and J. Fobil. 2013. "Back to My Roots: A Study of 'Returning' Emigrated Health Professionals in the Greater Accra Region of Ghana." *Africa Today* 59 no. 4: 118–130.

Asiedu, E. 2006. "Foreign Direct Investment in Africa: The Role of Natural Resources, Market Size, Government Policy, Institutions and Political Instability." *The World Economy* 29, no. 1: 63–77.

Avogo, W. A. and V. Agadjanian. 2010. "Forced Migration and Child Health and Mortality in Angola." *Social Science & Medicine* 70, no. 1: 53–60.

Balestri, S. and M. A. Maggioni. 2014. "Blood Diamonds, Dirty Gold and Spatial Spill-Overs Measuring Conflict Dynamics in West Africa." *Peace Economics, Peace Science and Public Policy* 20, no. 4: 551–564.

Banulescu-Bogdan, N., S. Fratzke. 2015. *Europe's Migration Crisis in Context: Why Now and What Next?* Migration Policy Institute, September 24. www.migrationpolicy.org/article/europe-migration-crisis-context-why-now-and-what-next

Barbara, G., F. Collini, C. Cattaneo et al. 2017. "Sexual Violence and Unwanted Pregnancies In Migrant Women." *The Lancet Global Health* 5, no. 4: e396–e397.

Biney, M. O. 2011. *From Africa to America: Religion and Adaptation among Ghanaian Immigrants in New York*. New York: New York University Press.

Brittain, V. 2015. "Ken Saro-Wiwa: A Hero for Our Times." *Race and Class* 56, no. 3: 5–17.

Buhaug, H., L. E. Cederman, and K. S. Gleditsch. 2014. "Square Pegs in Round Holes: Inequalities, Grievances, And Civil War." *International Studies Quarterly* 58, no. 2: 418–431.

Campbell, G. 2002. *Blood Diamonds: Tracing the Deadly Path of the World's Most Precious Stones*. New York: Westview.

Capps, R., K. McCabe, and M. Fix. 2012. *Diverse Streams: African Migration to the U.S.* Washington, DC: Migration Policy Institute.

Crush, J. 2008. *South Africa: Policy in the Face of Xenophobia*. Migration Policy Institute. July 28. http://www.migrationpolicy.org/article/south-africa-policy-face-xenophobia/

Daase, C. 2013. "Peace Agreements between State and Non-State Parties and International Arbitration: Lessons Learned from the Abyei Arbitration." *Verfassung Und Recht in Übersee / Law and Politics in Africa, Asia and Latin America* 46, no. 2: 152–173.

De Waal, A. 2014. "When Kleptocracy Becomes Insolvent: Brute Causes of the Civil War in South Sudan." *African Affairs* 113, no. 452: 347–369.

Deng, L. 2010. "Social Capital and Civil War: The Dinka Communities In Sudan's Civil War." *African Affairs* 109, no. 435: 231–250.

Dube, G., and J. Rukema. 2013. "Intracontinental Brain Drain and African Migrant Social Science Scholars in South Africa." *International Journal of Sociology* 43, no. 1: 68–78.

Fayehun, O. A., and K. K. Salami. 2014. "Older Persons and Malaria Treatment in Nigeria." *African Population Studies: Etude de la Population Africaine* 27, no. 2: 424.

Findley, S. E. 1994. "Does Drought Increase Migration? A Study of Migration from Rural Mali during the 1983-1985 Drought." *The International Migration Review* 28, no. 3: 539–553.

Flahaux, M., and H. De Hass. 2016. "African Migration: Trends, Patterns, Drivers." *Comparative Migration Studies* 4, no. 1: 1–25.
Forster, P., and E. Fraser. 2016. "How Climate Change Could Affect African Migration Patterns." *The Conversation*. June 7. http://theconversation.com/how-climate-change-could-affect-african-migration-patterns-60466
Gray, C., and V. Mueller. 2012. "Drought and Population Mobility in Rural Ethiopia." *World Development*, 40, no. 1: 134–145.
Hickel, J. 2014. "'Xenophobia' in South Africa: Order, Chaos, and the Moral Economy of Witchcraft." *Cultural Anthropology* 29, no. 1 (2014): 103–127.
Imoagene, O. 2017. "Affecting Lives: How Winning the US Diversity Visa Lottery Impacts DV Migrants Pre—and Post-Migration." *International Migration* 55, no. 6. doi:10.1111/imig.12359
Intergovernmental Panel on Climate Change (IPCC). 2007. *Climate Change 2007: Impact, Adaptation, and Vulnerability*. Working Group II Contribution to the Intergovernmental Panel on Climate Change Fourth Assessment Report UNEP. https://www.ipcc.ch/publications_and_data/publications_ipcc_fourth_assessment_report_wg2_report_impacts_adaptation_and_vulnerability.htm
Koubi, V., G. Spilker, T. Böhmelt, and T. Bernauer. 2014. "Do Natural Resources Matter for Interstate and Intrastate Armed Conflict?" *Journal of Peace Research*, 51, no. 2: 227–243.
Kumolu, C. 2017. "S/AFRICA Xenophobic Attacks: 200 Foreigners Killed, Maimed Since 1994—Investigation". *Vanguard*, February 26. https://www.vanguardngr.com/2017/02/safrica-xenophobic-attacks-200-foreigners-killed-maimed-since-1994-investigation/
Lindley, A. 2014. *Crisis and Migration: Critical Perspective*. New York: Routledge.
Morris, M., R. Cervigni, Z. Guo, and J. Koo. 2016. "The Central Role of Drylands in Africa's Development Challenge." In *Confronting Drought in Africa's Drylands: Opportunities for Enhancing Resilience*, edited by R. Cervigni and M. Morris, 29–36. Washington: The World Bank.
Ndlovu-Gatsheni, S. 2015. "Genealogies of Coloniality and Implications for Africa's Development." *Africa Development / Afrique Et Développement* 40, no. 3: 13–40.
Okeke, C. 2008. "The Second Scramble for Africa's Oil and Mineral Resources: Blessing or Curse?" *The International Lawyer* 42, no. 1: 193–209.
Olutayo, A.O., and A. O. Omobowale. 2007. "Capitalism, Globalization and the Underdevelopment Process in Africa: History in Perpetuity." *Africa Development* 32, no. 2: 97–112.
Omobowale, A. O. 2009a. "Lumumba, Patrice (1925–1961)." In *International Encyclopedia of Revolution and Protest*, edited by I. Ness, 2137–2139. Oxford: Wiley-Blackwell.
Omobowale, A. O. 2009b. "Oil and Nigeria's Niger-Delta." In *State and Civil Society Relations in Nigeria*, edited by O. A. Olutayo, I. S. Ogundiya, and J. Amzat, 391–404. Ibadan, Nigeria: Hope Publication.
Omobowale, A. O. 2013. *The Tokunbo Phenomenon and the Secondhand Economy in Nigeria* Oxford: Peter Lang.
Omobowale, A. O. 2015. "Stories of the 'Dark' Continent: Crude Constructions, Diasporic Identity, and International Aid to Africa." *International Sociology Reviews* 30, no. 2: 108–118.
Omobowale, A.O., M. O. Omobowale, and O. O. Ajani. 2010. "Emigration and the Social Value of Remittances in Nigeria." In *Across the Atlantic: Immigrants in the United States*, edited by E. Yewah and D. R.Togunde. Illinois: Common Ground.
Orubuloye, I. O., and J. B. Oni, J. B. 1996. "Health Transition Research in Nigeria in the Era of the Structural Adjustment Programme." *Health Transition Review* 6: 301–324.

Perreira, K. M. 2008. "Migration and Health Behaviour during Pregnancy." *BMJ: British Medical Journal*, 336, no. 7652: 1027–1028.

Raleigh, C., and D. Kniveton. 2012. "Come Rain or Shine: An Analysis of Conflict and Climate Variability in East Africa." *Journal of Peace Research* 49: 51–64.

Ross, M. 2004. "What Do We Know about Natural Resources and Civil War?" *Journal of Peace Research*, 41, no. 3: 337–356.

Salami, K. K., and A. O. Olugbayo. 2013. "Health-Seeking Behavior of Migrant Beggars in Ibadan, Southwestern Nigeria." *Health* 5, no. 4: 792.

Shaw, W. 2007. *Migration in Africa: A Review of the Economic Literature on International Migration in 10 Countries*. Washington, DC: The World Bank.

Smith-Greenaway, E., and S. Madhavan, S. 2015. "Maternal Migration and Child Health: An Analysis of Disruption and Adaptation Processes in Benin." *Social Science Research* 54: 146–158.

Udoh, I. 2013. "A Qualitative Review of the Militancy, Amnesty, and Peacebuilding in Nigeria's Niger Delta." *Peace Research* 45, no. 2: 63–93.

Ugwa, E. A. and A. Ashimi. 2015. "An Assessment of Stillbirths in a Tertiary Hospital in Northern Nigeria." *The Journal of Maternal-Fetal and Neonatal Medicine* 28, no. 13: 1585–1588.

UNICEF. 2017. *In Search of Opportunities: Voices of Children on the Move in West and Central Africa*. https://www.unicef.org/emergencies/childrenonthemove/uprooted/

United Nations. 2016. *International Migration Report 2015*. New York: United Nations. http://www.un.org/en/development/desa/population/migration/publications/migrationreport/docs/MigrationReport2015_Highlights.pdf

Wegenast, T., and G. Schneider. 2017. "Ownership Matters: Natural Resources Property Rights and Social Conflict in Sub-Saharan Africa." *Political Geography* 61: 110–122.

Whitaker, B. 2017. "Migration within Africa and Beyond." *African Studies Review*, 60, no. 2: 209–220.

Williams, S. 2012. "Africa's Youth: The African Development Bank and the Demographic Dividend." *African Development Bank*. https://www.afdb.org/fileadmin/uploads/afdb/Documents/Generic-Documents/AFDB%20youth%20doc.pdf

World Bank. 2017a. *Poverty & Equity: Sub-Saharan Africa*. Washington, DC: The World Bank. http://povertydata.worldbank.org/poverty/region/SSA

World Bank. 2017b. *Sub-Saharan Africa*. Washington, DC: The World Bank. http://data.worldbank.org/region/sub-saharan-africa

World Bank. 2017c. "Remittances to Developing Countries Decline for Second Consecutive Year." April 22, 2017. Washington, DC: The World Bank. http://www.worldbank.org/en/news/press-release/2017/04/21/remittances-to-developing-countries-decline-for-second-consecutive-year

Zeleza, P. T. 2002. "Contemporary African Migrations in a Global Context." *African Issues* 30, no. 1: 9–14.

CHAPTER 19

EFFECTS OF CLIMATE CHANGE ON MIGRATION CRISES IN OCEANIA

CHRISTIANE FRÖHLICH AND SILJA KLEPP

LARGE migration movements, regardless of their causes, have frequently been presented as a threat to national and international security, particularly when the movement is from the Global South to the Global North (Adamson 2006; Alexseev 2006; Ceccorulli and Labanca 2014; Huysmans 2000). Since large numbers of people have been predicted to be displaced by climate change, so-called "climate migration" has often been considered to be one of the main security risks of global warming (Brown 2008; Myers 2005). In its first assessment report, for instance, the Intergovernmental Panel on Climate Change (IPCC) warned in 1990: "the gravest effects of climate change may be those on human migration as millions are displaced by shoreline erosion, coastal flooding and severe drought" (IPCC 1990, 20). This was the basis for predictions of major conflict in receiving regions both within countries suffering from climate change and internationally.

At the core of such predictions is the conviction that climate change will engender or exacerbate resource scarcities, which in turn might drive migration as well as conflict. Climate migration has thus been presented as a phenomenon causing a multitude of crises on different levels, in the worst case leading to political instability and violence. However, there are few systematic studies researching this causality (Raleigh and Jordan 2010; Reuveny 2008). On the contrary, academic research into the links between climate change, migration and (violent) conflict—as the ultimate form of crisis—has predominantly been critical about such predictions (Brzoska and Fröhlich 2016), as empirical studies show that migration due to environmental factors is always a complex phenomenon. These studies also demonstrate counterintuitive results: populations under environmental pressure might get too poor to move in the future ("trapped populations," see Foresight 2011), and internal displacement is often much more probable than South-North migration.

The goal of this chapter is to outline how global warming impacts migration crises in Oceania, with a focus on securitization tendencies and critically inquiring into who defines what a crisis is. Regarding climate change migration today, climate scenarios for Small Island Developing States (SIDS) have led to powerful discourses and an active negotiation process on climate change and migration in the Pacific region. Various activities are planned and are already going on, including the development of the "migrate with dignity"-strategy and a land-buy in Fiji by Kiribati, the relocation of villages in Fiji and Papua New Guinea, as well as different court cases in Australia and New Zealand. Pacific Islanders are actively asking for climate justice in various forums and on various levels, and parts of the debate are asking for new kinds of citizenship and solidarity (Klepp and Herbeck 2016). This very active regional negotiation process in Oceania can also be seen as contrary to a policy stalemate and a legal gap regarding the protection of climate migrants on a global level (Klepp and Herbeck 2016). Nonetheless, the vast majority of debates are pointing to the future and it is not clear yet if the climate crisis will also become a migration crisis. This will depend on the global community and on our capacity to react to the challenges of global warming with innovative and flexible solutions in law and decision-making processes (Burkett 2011, Klepp forthcoming).

This chapter will first define the relevant terminology. It will then outline our overall approach and research questions before addressing them to the Pacific region. Finally, the chapter formulates alternative ways of framing the relationship between global warming and human mobility in the Pacific by addressing climate change as an " 'imaginative resource' (. . .) for our collective futures" (Klepp 2017, 3) in order to find "emancipative, migration-friendly" solutions which also take climate justice aspects into account (Klepp 2017).

Securitizing (Climate) Migration

We understand a *crisis* to be a critical event which, if not handled appropriately and in a timely manner, or if not handled at all, may turn into a disaster or catastrophe. Thus, a crisis can also be seen as a potential *tipping point* (Gladwell 2001), the handling of which decides about a potentially disastrous, and, importantly, irreversible outcome. The term *migration crisis* thus, for the purposes of this chapter, denotes the movement of a group of people from one place to another (within a state or beyond it), which threatens to generate conflict on different societal scales with potentially disastrous outcomes.

Central to the understanding of and response to a crisis is the degree of *securitization* of the critical event at the time the crisis occurs. Securitization is the presentation of an object or process as an existential threat to a particular audience which, if accepted by the targeted audience, allows for extraordinary political responses to the securitized object (Buzan et al. 1998). Securitization processes or moves point to the centrality of perceptions, underlying power structures and positionality for the interpretation of a crisis as existential or minor, thereby deciding about the range of possible responses.

For instance, South to South migration movements (from the Democratic Republic of Congo to Uganda, for instance) are not usually presented as existential threats in Western discourses, whereas South to North migration is successfully being securitized in Europe today, with the securitization opening up space for political measures commonly outside of the European political toolbox, like *refoulement* of migrants or border violence (Pallister-Wilkins 2017). Importantly, securitization processes are embedded in sociopolitical contexts, which are characterized by different understandings of security, affecting both the issues which are likely to be securitized as well as the audiences addressed by such securitizing moves. In other words, it makes a difference if the subject to be secured from a perceived existential threat is a national population, the international community, the human individual, or an ecosystem (McDonald 2013; Fröhlich 2016). In the context of climate change, different authors have observed a tendency for securitization, especially with regard to migration (Bettini 2013; Oels 2012). Historical and cultural differences as well as the complexity of migration movements are often neglected in such securitizing moves. Oels (2012) even speaks of a "climatization" of the security sector; according to her, this "climatization" of the security and defense sector contributes to the "securitization" of migration generally (Oels 2012, 199). For the diffuse idea of protecting the environment, racist discourses and fears of "millions of climate refugees" are fueled by a variety of actors, including environmentalists (see, e.g., Kolmannskog 2008, 9)

One important tool for constructing climate migration as "critical" is the concept of *vulnerability* (see Brzoska and Fröhlich 2016 for the following). Vulnerability is usually measured by the ratio between an entity's individual adaptive capacity to and the potential impact of climate change (Fay, Block, and Ebinger 2010). Thus vulnerability should rise when the impacts of global warming—like sea-level rise, weather extremes, desertification, floods, and land degradation—are negatively influencing the natural resource base, and when such environmental challenges are not met with effective governance structures and integrated planning for adaptation. Is that the case, then assumptions about decreasing sociopolitical stability, for instance in the form of political unrest, insurgencies, or state fragility, are only one further step away.

The main pathways of securitization of climate migration through the concept of vulnerability are two different paradigms that have developed in the field of environmental crisis research, including the study of climate-related human mobility (Black et al. 2013). The behavioralist paradigm assumes that natural disasters can be traced back to a lack of effective planning of responses and a general lack of preparedness, whereas the structuralist paradigm focuses on deeply ingrained societal structures that determine who is vulnerable to climate change, when, and to what extent, with a focus on power and resource distribution, wealth inequalities, and resulting interdependencies.

Both paradigms rely on the concept of *adaptation* for establishing the link between climate change impacts, human mobility, and crisis. Adaptation refers to activities designed to cope with negative consequences of climate change. However, adaptation is not usually used as a neutral term; instead, it explicitly or implicitly connotes which types of adaptation activities are considered better than others, such as infrastructural investments, technological or social innovation, or capacity building (Kumamoto and Mills 2012). Here we would like to point to Hein de Haas (2012), who highlighted that the celebration of migration in the context of global warming as a "self-help tool" of sorts is often driven by neoliberal ideologies which take the focus away from structural development constraints and hence diminish the responsibility of migrant-sending states to pursue political and economic reform.

Generally speaking, human mobility in the context of climate change needs to be understood as happening within a continuum of (in)voluntariness and (im)permanence, which is also affected by individual levels of vulnerability and adaptive capacity, leading to what Castles (2002) has termed "conceptual fuzziness." In order to understand the underlying logic of climate change securitization in the field of human mobility, it is necessary to uncover relevant power structures which determine a) who defines what can be considered a (migration) crisis, b) how human mobility challenges preestablished ideas of citizenship, belonging, and national identity, and c) how climate change figures in these topical fields and political processes.

Which Migration Crises? (Climate) Migration Scenarios in the Pacific Region

Climate change impacts are already affecting and are expected to increasingly influence the habitability of different geographical spaces (IPCC 2014), including in the Pacific region. Depending on the relative adaptive capacities and vulnerabilities to a range of slow- and fast-onset climate impacts, the likelihood or requirement of migration may rise (Brzoska and Fröhlich 2016; Tacoli 2011; Warner and Afifi 2014). Thus the Pacific region is a good example for the actual or expected impact of climate change on human mobility. With its low-elevation island nations, it is considered particularly vulnerable to environmental changes. Locke (2009), for instance, predicted the Pacific region to be among those that will feel the negative effects of global environmental change most acutely.

All regional states are expected to suffer from effects of climate change, but the small atoll countries of Kiribati, the Marshall Islands, Tokelau, and Tuvalu are considered particularly vulnerable. By no means does this mean that the other, bigger states are not also significantly vulnerable; heavily populated areas in the capitals of Fiji, Solomon Islands, Papua New Guinea, and Vanuatu are only the most obvious areas vulnerable to long-term climatic changes, and by no means the only ones. Many inhabitants of these countries live in coastal areas, and critical infrastructures such as ports, roads, and airports are also located on the coasts. Compared to the smaller atoll states, however, these bigger states have the invaluable advantage of possessing higher altitude territories to which people can move if necessary. In larger islands in particular, most migrations are therefore expected to be temporary and internal, rural to urban and from lower, coastal, to higher altitudes (Tabucanon 2013), especially when environmental events are short-term (Campbell and Bedford 2012). Longer-term and potentially irreversible processes like sea level rise or the destruction of fresh water resources through salinization, however, require long-term solutions, which seem to require at least some extent of international resettlement.

Under an optimistic climate scenario, Small Island Developing States (SIDS), especially atoll islands like Tuvalu and Kiribati, will become partly inhabitable; in a pessimistic one, they will vanish completely due to rising sea levels, thereby threatening to displace their entire population (see Barnett and Adger 2003; 65 million people are living on all SIDS together). As Campbell (2014, 4–5) has written, the SIDS as human habitats are threatened in three ways: a) with regard to physical availability of land (land security), b) with regard to food production and commercial activities (livelihood security), and c) with regard to health risks and general habitability of remaining land masses (habitat security). A further aspect here is the social meaning of land for identity and place-making processes as well as for genealogies and notions of belonging. Land, home, and the land of the ancestors are central to the identity of people in Oceania, so that land loss can cause a deep sense of alienation for Pacific Islanders (Kempf and Hermann 2014; Stratford et al. 2013; Teaiwa 2005). These identity and place-making processes are "marked by rootedness as well as migration" (Burkett 2011, 360) and have a deeply transnational character.

Why Migration Crises? A Historical Perspective

It has been established above that climate change impacts, in particular sea level rise, pose a very real threat to livelihoods in the Pacific region. This has resulted in a perpetual language of "crisis," which sees current and expected migration movements as "critical" per se (Hartmann 2010; McNamara and Gibson 2009). This is not the only possible perspective, however; local and regional voices in particular have repeatedly pointed out that migration is in no way a new practice in Oceania. Looking back to precolonial times, Epeli Hau'ofa (1993) has described Oceania as a "sea of islands" where people moved frequently and created social networks, traded and exchanged goods, and found new friends, enemies, or partners. As sea people, islanders were skillfully voyaging extensive spaces for new settlements, as attested in oral tradition and in archeological findings (McCall 2006, 32).

Looking at the more recent history as well as the present, a similar picture arises: Many people in the region have transnational lifestyles, and relationships are kept alive through remittances, major festivities, as well as, more recently, through social media. Of course, some members of the diaspora can never afford to go home, but their heritage islands are still central to them regarding spiritual as well as social life. This underlines the fact that historically, environmental migration has always been an important adaptation measure (see also McNamara et al. 2016), and that generally, migration is a normal societal process and not an exception. On the contrary: Migration with the overall goal of improving or generating livelihood or of improving educational and employment opportunities is an integral part of human history (de Haan 2000).

This is, however, contrary to the "Western" perspective, which during colonial times and even today underlines the vastness of the Pacific and the isolation of islands spread across it (Lee 2009, 7). What is more, the "Western" idea of the Westphalian state, which has developed into the dominant model of societal organization over centuries, regards migration as an "outlier," as an "exception," and therefore at least potentially as "critical" (Bretell 2015; critically de Haas 2012; Hollifield 2012; Massey et al. 1998; Portes and Celaya 2013; Sassen 1996; Weiner 1995). Human mobility fundamentally challenges both the territoriality inherent in the Westphalian state model as well as societal values such as cultural pluralism and tolerance and collective rights (Bordoni 2013); from this point of view, people on the move cross territorial (nation) state borders, they often defy legal and political categories—for instance, between refugees and migrants—and they blur the boundaries of national belonging and citizenship. The migrant thus becomes the object of colonial, white "Western" worry about the North's ability to control order and disorder in its dominion and about its borders' permeability (Fröhlich 2017, Fröhlich 2018). This perspective diffuses into international relations as well as global debates on (climate) migration.

Hastrup et al. therefore highlight that the study of environmental migration today is based on a very "sedentary understanding of human society" (Hastrup and Fog Olwig 2012, 12; see also Bakewell 2008), which is contrary to historical experience, but points toward the power structures underlying the decision as to whether a particular migration movement is considered "critical" or not. In order to uncover and deconstruct such power structures, we suggest the application of a post/de-colonial lens, as the political, legal, and academic discussions and depictions of human mobility have been and are heavily influenced by colonial decision-making processes (i.e., interpretations by hegemonic decision makers) and structures. Both the transatlantic slave trade originating in former colonies and the far-reaching forced migration movements during and after liberation movements to end colonial rule illustrate the latter's impact on human mobility.

In the Pacific, patterns of mobility during colonial times were dominated by labor migration and forced relocations by the colonial government. Labor mobility led to a distinct demographic reconfiguration of many Pacific Island societies in the mid-19th century (Weber 2015). Blackbirding (i.e., the kidnapping of Pacific islanders from their home islands mainly to work on plantations) was a widespread practice and can be seen as the first migration crisis in the Pacific. Conservative numbers claim that almost one million Pacific Islanders and a further half million Asians have been involved in the Pacific labor trade between the 1860s and 1939 (Weber 2015). Men were recruited for whaling and for copra, cotton, and sugar-cane plantation development; many of them never saw their island again.

In terms of forced relocation, Glibertese (today Kiribati) were brought to the Solomons and Fiji, and Samoans and Solomon Islanders to Fiji (McCall 2006, 33).

A large number of Islanders, up to 60,000, were working in the sugar-cane fields in Australia until 1901, when they were deported back to their homelands (McCall 2006, 34). Another example of forced relocation is the case of Banaba. Banaba, a part of Kiribati, was mined for phosphate from 1900 until 1980. Today, the center of the formerly fertile island has lost all fertile soil and is uninhabitable. The population of Banaba was displaced to camps in Naurua, Kosrae, and Tarawa by Japanese forces in 1942 and was then relocated to Rabi Island, Fiji, by the colonial government in 1945 (Teaiwa 2005, 178).

The twentieth century saw mass migration of Pacific islanders. New Zealand has accepted large numbers of labor migrants from the Cook Islands and Samoa. The United States took over the territories that were administered by Japan prior to World War II, leading to larger communities of people from Guam, the Northern Mariana Islands, and American Samoa living in the United States today. Only 15,000 Cook Islanders still live on their islands, while more than the same number now lives around the Pacific Rim, mainly in New Zealand. While 190,000 people still live in Samoa, another 120,000 Samoans moved overseas, mainly to New Zealand (World Bank 2011). Other examples could be added here and, as mentioned previously, many of these migrants lead transnational lifestyles. Furthermore, the most common migration movements in the region today are from rural areas and Outer Islands to metropolitan zones; this is mostly for reasons of education and health. Maribel Casas-Cortes et al. highlight the discrepancy between a geography of migration which was created by colonial expansion and imperial histories, and which continues to impact contemporary politics and international relations until today, and modern capitalism, which is structurally connected to labor mobility, but has been confronted with the problem of controlling it since its nascence (see Casas-Cortes et al. 2015, 61).

Another issue to be analyzed within this context is the current Australian refugee regime and migration policies. The prelude to an establishment of an extraterritorial Australian refugee regime, known as the so-called "Pacific solution," began in August 2001 in international waters. A Norwegian cargo ship, the MS Tampa, had rescued 439 Afghans from distress following a rescue call from the Australian Navy. As usual in this case, the captain headed to the Australian Christmas Island as the next safe haven (place of safety) to debark the rescued refugees. However, the Australian government refused to allow MS Tampa to enter its coastal waters, leading to a serious diplomatic conflict between Norway and Australia. Finally, the refugees were transferred from the MS Tampa to an Australian Navy ship four nautical miles away from Christmas Island. On the controversial legal basis of the Australian Border Protection Bill 2001, which was brought into being overnight, they were disembarked on the Pacific island nation of Nauru (Giannacopoulos 2005, 32). Ever since then, Australia has established a varying number of offshore processing centers. Currently, it maintains one such center on the Pacific island nation of Nauru, but had to close one on Manus Island in Papua New Guinea (PNG). Papua New Guinea's Supreme Court ruled in 2016 that restricting the movement of asylum seekers who have committed no crime was unconstitutional.

Since 2013, asylum seekers are not allowed to be settled in Australia, even if they are recognized as refugees. They may be settled in Nauru or Papua New Guinea, and four were settled in Cambodia. Australia pays high sums of money to the receiving countries and to the countries that have established camps. Rights groups say, however, that Nauru, among the other islands where camps were established, is not equipped to receive refugees. Nauru has an area of just 21 sq. km, much of which is uninhabitable due to phosphate mining during colonial times and afterwards, leading to significant environmental degradation. Conditions in the PNG and Nauru camps are inadequate, including poor hygiene; cramped conditions for children, women and men; unbearable heat; and a lack of facilities. Holding asylum seekers in indefinite detention has caused widespread psychological harm, and exposed them to dangers including physical and sexual assaults (Amnesty International 2016).

This so-called "Pacific solution" is one reason why Pacific Islanders are aware of very low standards for refugees globally and especially regionally. It is also the main reason why it is inacceptable to islanders to become "climate refugees," as people in Kiribati, for instance, have underlined repeatedly (Klepp and Herbeck 2016). Furthermore, critics speak of an inacceptable reconfiguration of colonial politics versus Pacific island states through the establishment of such extraterritorial camps, not to mention the severe human rights violations for the detained refugees.

It is in the light of such historical and recent political analysis that so-called climate change-related migration should be analyzed and understood. The "Pacific solution" stands in harsh contrast to human mobility that has been and is a common practice to diversify livelihoods in Oceania. In Oceania, mobility is not seen as predominantly critical, but as normal. So what does this mean for future migration movements in the region, regardless of their causes? What does the continuing securitization of migration tell us about the asymmetries and divergent interests in the international system and about the far-reaching consequences of colonial times (or the "on-going colonial present" as Bhabha called it [1994, 183])? According to philosopher Etienne Balibar, it is precisely the ideas and practices of inclusion and exclusion, which are particularly evident in migration and refugee regimes, that turn borders and migration regimes into touchstones for civil rights and civility (Balibar 2005, 9). Research into the processes of negotiating climate migration, crises, and refugee regimes sheds light on social processes and orders that can be influenced and redesigned through these negotiating processes. How does such a perspective change potential models of addressing and solving the so-called "migration crises" in the context of global warming in Oceania?

The Way Forward: Migration-Friendly Solutions

Regarding so-called "climate migration," different climate scenarios for the SIDS have led to proactive plans of resettlement for affected populations, like the government of

Kiribati purchasing 2,282 ha of land in Vanua Levu Island, Fiji, in order to support agricultural as well as fisheries development (Campbell and Bedford 2012), but with the (albeit more vague) option of using the land for resettlement of Kiribati's population. Other examples include Vunidogoloa village in Fiji, the residents of which chose to relocate in early 2014 in order to reduce their vulnerability to encroaching sea level and floods (McNamara and Des Combes 2015), and the so far futile attempts of Carteret Islands inhabitants to resettle on another Pacific atoll, namely Bougainville Island.

But the climate migration strategy developed by the former government of Kiribati and President Anote Tong (2003–2016) is probably the most concrete thus far. The motto and strategy of Tong's government, "migrate with dignity," has been articulated in many international and regional negotiations and gained a lot of attention by the media as well as by academics. This strategy, which includes regional migration programs, plans for community relocation to Fiji, and an education campaign, was discussed under the motto "migrate with dignity" by the former government of Kiribati (Klepp and Herbeck 2016). The program aims to promote a self-determined, culturally sensitive and solidarity-expressing way of coping with the current and future effects of climate change, and tries to avoid a scenario where the people of Kiribati (the *I-Kiribati*) become refugees. Based mostly on arguments from climate justice, this approach exceeds those debates in the Global North which characterize climate change impacts on migration as being a security threat or as a purely humanitarian issue. In search of solutions for affected people in the region, legal and political measures are being discussed with various state and nonstate actors (Klepp and Herbeck 2016). It is certainly safe to say that "migrate with dignity" has gained momentum during Tong's presidency and is still widely discussed in the Pacific region and beyond as an innovative climate migration strategy that could avoid a future "migration crisis."

Despite (or because) of alarmist debates regarding climate change and migration in the Pacific, many Islanders, together with scholars and activists, are arguing against the (mis-)use of Oceania as an iconographic "warning symbol" for the effects of climate change, as well as a field of experiments for Western researchers, journalists, and actors of international cooperation. They all create a distorted image of victimization for the Pacific area, as well as a scandalizing image of the effects of climate change (Barnett and Campbell 2010, 177; Farbotko 2010; Farbotko and Lazrus 2012; Lazrus 2012). In the debates on natural scientific predictions about the assumed devastating consequences of climate change that have shaped media and academic discourses in recent years, very little attention is being paid to island inhabitants' own interpretations of climate change, to their agency, and to their potential strategies for responding to it (Barnett and Campbell 2010, 21). The island states are pictured as isolated, vulnerable, and in need of development, as well as small, poor, and not equipped for economic growth (Kempf 2009; Lazrus 2009, 248; Rubow 2009, 89).

These constructions are an expression of constellations of knowledge and power which have formed during colonial times and which have been reconfigured and revitalized in the context of climate change (Fröhlich 2017, Fröhlich 2018). Tools of othering, used as tools of power during the colonial period, have gained new meaning.

In this context, Carol Farbotko explains that such othering practices change the political agency of and create a new "eco-colonial" perspective on these island states (2010, 58). Above all, the atoll island states of Kiribati and Tuvalu are characterized as "Titanic States" (Barnett and Campbell 2010, 168). Headlines such as "Sinking islands cling to Kyoto lifebuoy," "Rising sea level forcing evacuation of island country," or "will Tuvalu disappear beneath the sea [. . .]" (quoted in McNamara and Gibson 2009, 479) dominate media discussions and reinforce the discourse of victimization and othering. Even more importantly, these discourses impede both an active search for migration-friendly solutions as well as the development of emancipative solutions for the future of SIDS outside of alarmist "vanishing islands" debates and narrow citizenship-centered approaches.

McNamara and Gibson (2009) state that most Pacific island states reject the role of the victim or supplicant on the international stage, and instead demand a stronger reduction in greenhouse gases. Carol Farbotko (2010) emphasizes the position of increased moral power of countries such as Tuvalu and Kiribati, which play an increasingly important role in UNFCCC negotiations. Various alliances have been created in order to bind together the efforts of small island states in these negotiations. The international organizations *Alliance of Small Island States* (AOSIS) and *Small Island Developing States* (SIDS) are central in this regard.

The Alliance of Small Island States (AOSIS) came out of the organization of Small Island Developing States (SIDS). AOSIS is an alliance of island and coastal states, almost all of which are vulnerable to climate change. AOSIS is the negotiating voice for the Small Island Developing States (SIDS) at the United Nations. The group currently has forty-four members from the Pacific Ocean, Africa, the Caribbean, the Indian Ocean, and the South China Sea. At the UNFCCC negotiations, the AOSIS representatives are among the tireless advocates calling for effective climate protection policies and for climate justice. From the SIDS, the "Malé Declaration on Global Warming and Sea Level Rise" is a pioneer that was brought into being in 1989 and was recreated by SIDS in 2007 as the "Malé Declaration on the Human Dimension of Global Climate Change." The declarations of SIDS and AOSIS express that their member countries have made relatively little contributions to climate change in terms of CO_2 emissions, but are nevertheless strongly affected by its consequences. They demand to be provided with the necessary tools and resources to self-determinedly deal with the effects of climate change.

In addition, several religious institutions and actors are active in the debate around climate justice in the Pacific area. In 2009, representatives of Christian churches, which are organized in the *Pacific Conference of Churches* (PCC) with headquarters in Suva, Fiji, published the "Moana-Declaration," which calls for climate justice and contains conventions for environmental migrants as well as solutions for their resettlement and migration projects. The call is aimed explicitly at the countries of the Pacific Islands Forum, whose members include Australia and New Zealand. Pacific countries are also involved in a large number of campaigns for climate justice which are initiated by NGOs. This has doubtlessly promoted the debates around climate justice and the vulnerability of Pacific Island states. NGOs such as *Many Strong Voices* (MSV), contrary to some NGOs' tendency to describe the islanders exclusively as victims of climate change, play an important, empowering role. MSV, a coalition between the Small Island Developing States and the coastal arctic inhabitants, which was founded in order to fight climate change and its side effects, focuses on self-determination. Various actors of civil society and government are brought together, and experiences around climate change adaptation and political fights around climate justice are exchanged. The network *Climate Justice Now!* was created in the framework of the UNFCCC negotiations in 2007 in Bali by more than 30 NGOs and grassroots organizations. Similar movements joined at the People's Summit Klimaforum09 in Copenhagen in 2009, including *Climate Justice Now!* During the *People's Conference on Climate Change and the Rights of Mother Earth* in April 2010 in Bolivia, the Bolivian government also initiated a large movement for climate justice. Similar to the aforementioned organizations and forums, it aimed to create a counter-discourse against the UNFCCC negotiations that does not focus on a reduction in greenhouse gases and a solution for climate change through a "greening" economy, but rather demands a radical system change. *The People's Agreement*, created at the congress in Bolivia, demands far-reaching rights of self-determination, such as access to water, land rights, and food production, "through forms of production that are in harmony with Mother Earth and appropriate to local cultural contexts" (People's Agreement 2010).

Such activities and movements point the way to alternative ways of framing the relationship between global warming and human mobility in the Pacific by addressing climate change as an "imaginative resource" (Hastrup and Fog Olwig 2012, 2). In order to achieve such a discursive reframing, a repoliticization of the debate is necessary that questions the victimizing, passive image of the "drowning" climate-change migrant, and that criticizes the continuing securitization of climate change and related human mobility. It is necessary to develop and implement "migration-friendly" policies which focus on the human rights and the dignity of the citizens of affected states, which allow for self-determination of migrants, and which do not include labeling them as "refugees"—or their movement as "crisis" (Bedford and Bedford 2010; Boncour and Burson 2010; Campbell 2010; Klepp and Herbeck 2016).

References

Adamson, F. B. 2006. "Crossing Borders: International Migration and National Security." *International Security* 31: 165–199.

Alexseev, M. A. 2006. *Immigration Phobia and the Security Dilemma.* Cambridge, UK: Cambridge University Press.

Amnesty International. 2016. "Island of Despair. Australia's 'Processing' of Refugees on Nauru." Amnesty International. https://www.amnesty.org/en/documents/asa12/4934/2016/en/

Bakewell, O. 2008. "Keeping Them in Their Place: The Ambivalent Relationship between Development and Migration in Africa." *Third World Quarterly* 29: 1341–1358.

Balibar, E. 2005. *Sind wir Bürger Europas?* Bonn, Germany: Bundeszentrale für politische Bildung.

Barnett, J. and W.N. Adger. 2003. *Climate Dangers and Atoll Countries. Climatic Change* 61, no. 3: 321–337.

Barnett, J., and J. Campbell. 2010. *Climate Change and Small Island States: Power, Knowledge and the South Pacific*. London: Earthscan.

Bedford, R., and C. Bedford. 2010. "International Migration and Climate Change: A Post-Copenhagen Perspective on Options for Kiribati and Tuvalu." In *Climate Change and Migration—South Pacific Perspectives*, edited by B. Burson, 89–134. Wellington, New Zealand: Institute of Policy Studies.

Bettini, G. 2013. "Climate Barbarians at the Gate? A Critique of Apocalyptic Narratives on Climate Refugees." *Geoforum* 45: 63–72.

Bhabha, Homi K. 1994. *The Location of Culture*. London: Routledge.

Black, R., N. W. Arnell, W. N. Adger, D. Thomas, and A. Geddes. 2013. "Migration, Immobility and Displacement Outcomes Following Extreme Events." *Environmental Science and Policy* 27S: 32–43.

Boncour, P., and B. Burson. 2010. "Climate Change and Migration in the South Pacific Region: Policy Perspectives." In *Climate Change and Migration—South Pacific Perspectives*, edited by B. Burson, 5–29. Wellington: Institute of Policy Studies.

Bordoni, C. 2013. "A Crisis Of The State? The End Of The Post-Westphalian Model." *Social Europe*, February 12. https://www.socialeurope.eu/a-crisis-of-the-state-the-end-of-post-westphalian-model

Bretell, C. B. 2015. "Theorizing Migration in Anthropology." In *Migration Theory: Talking Across Disciplines*, edited by C. B. Betrell and J. F. Hollifield, 113–159. New York: Psychology Press.

Brown, O. 2008. *Migration and Climate Change*. Geneva: International Organization for Migration.

Brzoska, M., and C. Fröhlich. 2016. "Climate Change, Migration and Violent Conflict: Vulnerabilities, Pathways and Adaptation Strategies." *Migration and Development* 5, no. 2: 190–210.

Burkett, Maxine. 2011. "The Nation Ex-Situ: On Climate Change, Deterritorialized Nationhood And The Post-Climate Era." *Climate Law* 2: 345–374.

Buzan, B., O. Waever, and J. de Wilde. 1998. *Security: A New Framework for Analysis*. Boulder, CO: Lynne Riener.

Campbell, J. 2010. "Climate Change and Population Movement in Pacific Island Countries." In *Climate Change and Migration—South Pacific Perspectives*, edited by B. Burson, 29–51. Wellington: Institute of Policy Studies.

Campbell, J. 2014. "Climate-Change Migration in the Pacific." *The Contemporary Pacific* 26, no. 1: 1–28

Campbell, J., and R. Bedford. 2012. "Migration and Climate Change in Oceania." In *People on the Move in a Changing Climate: Comparing the Impact of Environmental Change on Different Regions of the World*, edited by E. Piguet and R. Laczko, 177–204. Dordrecht, The Netherlands: Springer.

Casas-Cortes, M., Cobarrubias, S., De Genova, N., Garelli, G., and Grappi, N. 2015. "New Keywords: Migration and Borders." *Cultural Studies* 29, no. 1: 55–87.

Castles, S. 2002. "Environmental Change and Forced Migration: Making Sense of the Debate." New Issues in Refugee Research. Working Paper 70. Geneva: UNHCR. http://www.unhcr.org/research/RESEARCH/3de344fd9.pdf

Ceccorulli, M., and N. Labanca. 2014. *The EU, Migration, and the Politics of Administrative Detention*. Routledge Advances in European Politics. NY: Routledge.

de Haan, A. 2000. *Migrants, Livelihoods And Rights: The Relevance of Migration in Development Policies*. Social Development Working Paper no. 4. London: DFID (Department for International Development).

De Haas, H. 2012. "The Migration and Development Pendulum: A Critical View on Research and Policy." *International Migration* 50, no. 3: 8–25.

Farbotko, C. 2010. "Wishful Sinking: Disappearing Islands, Climate Refugees and Cosmopolitan Experimentation." *Asia Pacific Viewpoint* 51: 47–60.

Farbotko, C., and H. Lazrus. 2012. "The First Climate Refugees? Contesting Global Narratives of Climate Change in Tuvalu." *Global Environmental Change* 22: 382–390.

Fay, M., R. Block, and J. Ebinger. 2010. *Adapting to Climate Change in Eastern Europe and Central Asia*. Washington, DC: World Bank Publications.

Foresight. 2011. "Migration and Global Environmental Change. Final Project Report." London: The Government Office for Science. https://www.gov.uk/government/publications/migration-and-global-environmental-change-future-challenges-and-opportunities

Fröhlich, C. 2016. "Menschliche Mobilität im Kontext ökologischer und politischer Krisen. Das Beispiel Syrien." In *Friedensgutachten 2016*, edited by M. Johannsen, B. Schoch, M. Mutschler et al. (eds.), 89–100. Münster, Germany: LIT.

Fröhlich, C. 2017. "A Critical View on Human Mobility in Times of Crisis." *Global Policy* 8, supp. S1: 5–11.

Fröhlich, C. 2018. "Flucht als Herausforderung neokolonialer Herrschaftsstrategien". *Zeitschrift für Friedens- und Konfliktforschung* 2, Special Issue De- und Postkoloniale Perspektiven in der Friedens- und Konfliktforschung, edited by Cordula Dittmer, 99–124.

Giannacopoulos, M. 2005. "Tampa: Violence at the Border." *Social Semiotics* 15, no. 2: 29–42.

Gladwell, Malcolm. 2001. *The Tipping Point: How Little Things Can Make a Big Difference*. New York: Little, Brown and Company.

Hartmann, B. 2010. "Rethinking Climate Refugees and Climate Conflict: Rhetoric, Reality and the Politics of Policy Discourse." *Journal of International Development* 22: 233–246.

Hastrup, K., and K. F. Olwig, eds. 2012. *Climate Change and Mobility. Global Challenges to the Social Sciences*. Cambridge, UK: Cambridge University Press.

Hau'ofa, Epeli. 1993. "Our Sea of Islands." In *A New Oceania: Rediscovering our Sea of Islands*, edited by V. Naidu and E. Waddell, 2–17. Suva, Fiji: University of the South Pacific.

Hollifield, J. 2012. "Migration and International Relations." In *The Oxford Handbook of the Politics of International Migration*, edited by D. Tichenor and M. Rosenblum. Oxford: Oxford University Press.

Huysmans, J. 2000. "The European Union and the Securitization of Migration." *Journal of Common Market Studies* 38: 751–777.

IPCC. 1990. *First Assessment Report: Climate Change*. Working Group II. Geneva. http://ipcc.ch/publications_and_data/publications_ipcc_first_assessment_1990_wg2.shtml

IPCC. 2014. *Summary for Policymakers. Climate Change 2014: Impacts, Adaptation, and Vulnerabilities*. Cambridge, UK: Cambridge University Press.

Kempf, Wolfgang. 2009. "A Sea of Environmental Refugees? Oceania in an Age of Climate Change." In *Form, Macht, Differenz: Motive und Felder Ethnologischen Forschens*, edited by E. Hermann, K. Klenke, and M. Dickhardt, 191–205. Göttingen, Germany: Universitätsverlag Göttingen.

Kempf, W., and E. Hermann. 2014. “Uncertain Futures of Belonging. Consequences of Climate Change and Sea Level Rise in Oceania.” In *Belonging in Oceania: Movement, Place-Making and Multiple Identifications*, edited by E. Hermann, W. Kempf, T. van Meijl, 189-214. New York: Berghahn.

Klepp, S. Forthcoming. “Framing Climate Change Adaptation from a Pacific Island Perspective—The Anthropology of Emerging Legal Orders.” *Sociologus*, Special issue: Climate Change as Travelling Idea.

Klepp, S. 2017. “Climate Change and Migration.” Oxford Research Encyclopedia of Climate Science, April. http://climatescience.oxfordre.com/view/10.1093/acrefore/9780190228620.001.0001/acrefore-9780190228620-e-42

Klepp, S., and J. Herbeck. 2016. “The Politics of Environmental Migration and Climate Justice in the Pacific Region.” *Journal of Human Rights and the Environment* 7: 54–73.

Kolmannskog, V. 2008. *Climate Changed: People Displaced*. Oslo: Norwegian Refugee Council.

Kumamoto, M., and A. Mills. 2012. “What African Countries Perceive To Be Adaptation Priorities: Results From 20 Countries in the Africa Adaptation Programme.” *Climate and Development* 4: 265–274.

Lazrus, H. 2009. “The Governance of Vulnerability: Climate Change and Agency in Tuvalu, South Pacific.” In *Anthropology and Climate Change: From Encounters to Actions*, edited by S. Crate and M. Nuttal, 240-249. Walnut Creek, CA: Left Coast Press.

Lazrus, H. 2012. “Sea Change: Island Communities and Climate Change.” *Annual Review of Anthropology* 41: 285–301.

Lee, H. 2009. “Pacific Migration and Transnationalism: Historic Perspectives.” In *Migration and Transnationalism*, edited by H. Lee and S. Tupai Francis, 7–43. Pacific Perspectives. Canberra, Australia: ANU ePress.

Locke, J. 2009. “Climate Change-Induced Migration in the Pacific Region: Sudden Crisis and Long-Term Developments.” *The Geographical Journal* 175: 171–180.

Massey, D. S., J. Arango, G. Hugo, A. Kouaouci, A. Pellegrino, and J. E. Taylor. 1998. *Worlds in Motion, Understanding International Migration at the End of the Millenium*. Oxford: Clarendon.

McCall, G. 2006. “Migration in Oceania: A Quick Overview of the Settlement and Continuing Occupation of an Aquatic Continent.” In *Migration Happens: Reasons, Effects and Opportunities of Migration in the South Pacific*, edited by K. Ferro and M. Wallner, 29–43. Vienna: LIT Verlag.

McDonald, M. 2013. “Discourses of Climate Security.” *Political Geography* 33: 43–51.

McNamara, K., R. Bronen, N. Fernando, and S. Klepp. 2016. “The Complex Decision-Making of Climate-Induced Relocation: Adaptation and Loss and Damage.” *Climate Policy* 18, no. 1: 111–117.

McNamara, K. E., and C. Gibson. 2009. “We do not want to leave our land”: Pacific Ambassadors at the United Nations Resist the Category of ‘Climate Refugees.’” *Geoforum* 40: 475–483.

McNamara, K. E., and H. J. Des Combes. 2015. “Planning for Community Relocations Due to Climate Change in Fiji.” *International Journal for Disaster Risk Science* 6: 315–319.

Myers, N. 2005. *Environmental Refugees: An Emergent Security Issue*. Vienna: Organization for Security and Co-operation in Europe.

Oels, A. 2012. “From ‘Securitization’ of Climate Change to ‘Climatization’ of the Security Field.” In *Climate Change, Human Security and Violent Conflict. Challenges for Societal Stability*, edited by J. Scheffran, M. Brzoska, H. G. Brauch, P. M. Link, and J. Schilling, 185–207. London and New York: Springer.

Pallister-Wilkins, P. 2017. "Humanitarian Rescue/Sovereign Capture and the Policing of Possible Responses to Violent Borders." *Global Policy* 8, no. 1: 19–24.

People's Agreement. 2010. "People's Agreement of Cochabamba." World People's Conference onf Climate Change and the Rights of Mother Earth. April 22. https://pwccc.wordpress.com/2010/04/24/peoples-agreement/.

Portes, A., and A. Celaya. 2013. "Modernization for Emigration: Determinants and Consequences of the Brain Drain." *Daedalus* 142, no. 3: 170–184.

Raleigh, C., and L. Jordan. 2010. "Climate Change and Migration: Emerging Patterns in the Developing World." In *Social Dimensions of Climate Change*, edited by R. Mearns and A. Norton, 103–131. Washington, DC: World Bank.

Reuveny, R. 2008. "Ecomigration and Violent Conflict: Case Studies and Public Policy Implications." *Human Ecology* 36: 1–13.

Rubow, C. 2009. "Metaphysical Aspects of Resilience: South Pacific Responses to Climate Change." In *The Question of Resilience: Social Responses of Climate Change*, edited by K. Hastrup, 88–114. Copenhagen: The Royal Danish Academy of Sciences and Letters.

Sassen, S. 1996. *Losing Control? Sovereignty in an Age of Globalization*. New York: Columbia University Press.

Stratford, E., C. Farbotko, and H. Lazrus. 2013. "Tuvalu, Sovereignty and Climate Change: Considering Fenua, the Archipelago and Emigration." *Island Studies Journal* 8, no. 1: 67–83.

Teaiwa, K. M. 2005. "Our Sea of Phosphate: The Diaspora of Ocean Island." In *Indigenous Diasporas and Dislocations*, edited by G. Hravey and C. D. Thompson Jr., 169–191. Aldershot, UK: Ashgate.

Tabucanon, G. M. P. 2013. "ASEAN and Pacific Environmental Migration." *Cosmopolitan Civil Societies Journal* 5, no. 1: 19–38.

Tacoli, C. 2011. "Not Only Climate Change: Mobility, Vulnerability and Socio-Economic Transformations In Environmentally Fragile Areas Of Bolivia, Senegal and Tanzania." Human Settlements Working Paper Series—Rural-Urban Interactions and Livelihood Strategies, IIED, Vol. 28. http://pubs.iied.org/10590IIED/

Warner, K., and T. Afifi. 2014. "Where the Rain Falls: Evidence from 8 Countries on How Vulnerable Households Use Migration To Manage the Risk of Rainfall Variability and Food Insecurity." *Climate and Development* 6: 1–17.

Weber, E. 2015. "Envisioning South-South Relations in the Fields of Environmental Change and Migration in the Pacific Islands—Past, Present and Futures." *Journal of the Global South* 2, no. 6: 1–21.

Weiner, M. 1995. *The Global Migration Crisis*. New York: Harper Collins.

World Bank. 2011. *Migration and Remittances Factbook* 2011. 2nd ed. Washington, DC: World Bank.

CHAPTER 20

CLIMATE CHANGE AND MIGRATION CRISIS IN AFRICA

CAROLINE ZICKGRAF

The Climate Change–Migration Nexus

Climate change presents one of the greatest global challenges of the 21st century. Yet, even though climate change constitutes a global crisis, its impacts are not distributed equally. The great "double injustice" of climate change is generational and geographical: the generations, countries, and populations that are largely responsible for greenhouse gas emissions are not those that will bear its burden (cf. Gough 2011). The poorest, most destitute, and socially vulnerable populations of developing countries suffer the most, with migration from these countries constructed as a major international threat by the very countries culpable. In fact, migrants and displaced people have come to embody the face of global warming, its most visible victims (Gemenne 2011a). Climate change has been widely and repeatedly linked to migration crisis in the media and in political arenas. The migration crisis takes shape through oversimplified narratives that assume deterministic and monocausal links between environmental change and population movements. Its purveyors warn of millions, or hundreds of millions, of climate refugees that will arrive in desperate masses in the Global North, threatening national sovereignty and international security while also posing monumental humanitarian challenges for destination countries (Christian Aid 2007; Myers 2002; Myers and Kent 1995). This discourse of future European and Western borders awash with floods of climate refugees continues to permeate social consciousness around climate change, playing on existing humanitarian and security concerns most commonly associated with those flows coming from Africa and Asia (Zickgraf 2016).

These grim future scenarios, based more on speculation than scientifically rigorous evidence, rarely recognize that human mobility in its various forms is already underway in many developing countries across the world in response to climate change. Any simplistic, direct causal linkages, however, are difficult to establish (Black 2001). The patterns of migration within and out of areas affected by climate change are rather the result of multicausal chains of impact that are far from linear or deterministic (Dasgupta et al. 2014). Migration responses range widely even if we isolate a single hazard or extreme event or continent. Climate change does not occur in a vacuum: social, political, economic, demographic, and other environmental forms of degradation (apart from climate change) collide to push, or prevent, human migration. Several scholars have therefore debunked the idea that we can isolate climate change as a migration driver (Black et al. 2011a; Black et al. 2011b).

This chapter, reflective of the academic community at large, emphasizes climate change as it contributes to population movements in Africa, while also recognizing its interaction with other forces at play. Importantly, climate change strikes populations that are firstly geographically exposed to risk, but that also have preexisting vulnerabilities that make them susceptible to its impacts. On the African continent, regions and countries vary greatly in terms of geographical exposure and topographical diversity as well as heterogeneous social, economic, political, and demographic conditions. Developing countries, emerging economies, and fragile states marked by poverty, poor governance, natural resource dependence, conflict, and humanitarian crises, for example, are more vulnerable to the impacts of climate change, and thus distress migration. It should be no surprise then that the great diversity of the African continent's experiences of climate change and migration cannot be simply stated or summarized, despite the overwhelming public tendency to singularly frame migration as crisis.

What is sure is that Africa is currently one of the most vulnerable global regions to climate change and that, concomitantly, its populations are also among the most mobile in the world. Not only are many of its countries facing increasing frequency and intensity of extreme, sudden-onset events and more progressive climate impacts, but it also contains within it some of the other areas identified as the most vulnerable to climate change: deltas and low-lying islands (Nicholls et al. 2007). As climate change manifests in a variety of forms across the African content, and even within subregions, so too does climate change result in a variety of temporal, spatial, and geopolitical migration patterns (Zickgraf et al. 2016). Considering the wide diversity of the impacts of climate change and migration dynamics, and the sheer size of the continent, this contribution aims to give an overview of certain coexisting patterns rather than an exhaustive overview. Moreover, a major impediment in comprehensively assessing these patterns and trends remains the dire lack of data, particularly on internal migration flows and stocks. Undoubtedly, the insights and evidence presented here will not hold true across all African countries or regions, geographies, or populations.

Climate Change and the Construction of Migration as Crisis

In 1990, the IPCC warned, "One of the gravest effects of climate change could be on human migration" (1990, 20). This and other early reports helped lay the foundation for an eventual explosion in interest on the topic.[1] Journalists, private research institutions, nongovernmental organizations, and environmental activists were and remain among the key sources of dramatic predictions of "climate refugees" desperately fleeing drought, sea-level rise, and famine, and flooding the shores of Europe should climate change continue unchecked (Bettini 2013; Zickgraf 2016). Migrants offered a means with which environmentalist groups and other interested actors could create public and political awareness about climate change and promote climate action. Assisting in the construction of an impending migration crisis, massive displacement projections of hundreds of millions typically accompany this apocalyptic imagery (Farbotko and Lazrus 2012). Environmentalist Norman Myers first predicted 150 million people, then 200 million people would be displaced by 2050, with Christian Aid upping the figure to 300 million (Christian Aid 2007; Myers 1993, 2002). These estimates and predictions have been instrumental in constructing the climate change-migration crisis—despite extensive scientific critique and dismissal—by emphasizing the unprecedented magnitude of migration flows (Gemenne 2011b; Kolmannskog 2008).

The very countries that are largely responsible for climate change are also those that fear its migratory impacts the most. The migration crisis narrative thus gains the most traction in the Global North, even though current evidence suggests that international migration to Europe in response to climate change will pale in comparison to that within Africa and other countries of the Global South. Nonetheless, a crisis narrative plays off of, and into, European and North American xenophobia about migration, on one hand, and fears of conflict and instability brought by mass forced migration, particularly in Africa, on the other. Climate change and environmental advocates, seeking climate action more often than targeted migration policies, have framed such migration as both a security threat as well as a humanitarian cause.[2] For example, a 2007 report by Christian Aid, entitled "Human Tide: The Real Migration Crisis," warned, "The danger is that this new forced migration will fuel existing conflicts and generate new ones in the areas of the world—the poorest—where resources are most scarce. Movement on this scale has the potential to destabilize whole regions where increasingly desperate populations compete for dwindling food and water" (Christian Aid 2007, 2). More recently, those perpetuating doom-and-gloom narratives caution that the current European migration crisis represents only a taste of what the future holds in a world ravaged by climate change. With sub-Saharan Africa projected to be the area most affected by climate change, along with small island states and coastal and deltaic regions (Gemenne 2011a), it is no wonder that African migrations are often at the center of such securitarian discourses. In a 2017 piece by the Environmental Justice Foundation, and promoted by the Guardian, retired US military corps brigadier general Stephen Cheney warned: "If Europe thinks they have a problem with migration today . . . wait 20 years [. . .] See what happens when climate change drives people out of Africa—the Sahel [sub-Saharan area] especially—and we're talking now not just one or two million, but 10 or 20 [million]. They are not going to South Africa, they are going across the Mediterranean" (Taylor 2017).[3]

While "futurology" dominates many climate-migration media and official reports, other international organisations and scholars assert that existing realities and protection gaps already qualify as crisis.[4] In a joint article, the UN Secretary General's Special Representative for Disaster Risk Reduction and the head of the UN Office for Disaster Risk Reduction, Professor Robert Glasser, and the Director General of the International Organization for Migration, William Lacy Swing, declared, "Climate change migration is reaching crisis proportions. Over the last 18 months, some 20 countries have declared drought emergencies forcing millions off their land. Often not for the first time and, for many, it may likely be the last time as they turn their backs on the countryside and try to make a life in urban slums and informal settlements" (Glasser and Swing 2017). Indeed, massive displacement in the wake of environmental disasters, natural or manmade, requires emergency responses and urgent humanitarian action consistent with crisis. The migration and displacement challenges faced by countries struggling with the impacts of climate change (yet again not those that caused them) undoubtedly warrant thorough scholarly and public attention. Yet, as this chapter will show in the case of the African continent, the complexity of these challenges belies any simple, singular crisis framing or response.

Climate Change and Vulnerability in Africa

The Intergovernmental Panel on Climate Change (IPCC) deemed the African continent the most vulnerable in the world to climate change impacts (Boko et al. 2007). In its 2014 assessment, the IPCC noted that temperatures could rise by 3°C to 6°C in some parts of Africa, including the Sahel, by 2100, and are likely to be accompanied by a significant increase in natural disasters (Niang et al. 2014). African regions are expected to be the most affected by climate changes and climate vulnerability, including hotter and drier conditions, rainfall variability, and extreme events such as floods, as well as more gradual environmental changes including sea-level rise, land degradation, and desertification. Sub-regionally, weather pattern projections vary over the twenty-first century including an increase in drought and heavy rainfall in southern and east Africa, more intense precipitation in west Africa, and more frequent heat waves in north Africa (Niang et al. 2014).

However, it is not merely geographical exposure to hazards or climate variability that make Africa vulnerable: in 2014, the Draft African Union Strategy on Climate Change declared, "Africa is the most vulnerable continent to climate variability and change, a situation that is aggravated by the interaction of 'multiple stresses', including high dependence on rainfed agriculture, widespread poverty, and weak adaptive capacity" (African Union 2014). Hence, the crisis of climate change aggravates, and is aggravated by, existing development challenges such as poverty, conflict, and humanitarian crises, weak infrastructure, governance failures, limited access to various forms of capital, livelihood fragility, and deteriorating food security (Rain et al. 2011). Importantly, the World Bank lists twenty of the continent's fifty-four countries as fragile and conflict-affected situations (World Bank 2017). Climate change and climate variability have the potential to exacerbate or multiply existing threats to human security including food, health, and economic insecurity in Africa: the same threats known to drive conflict (Niang et al. 2014).[5] On top of this, demographically speaking, sub-Saharan Africa's current and expected population growth, population density, and "youth bulge" also interact with the impacts of climate change, exacerbating socioeconomic pressures to migrate in search of better opportunities and livelihoods and increasing disaster risk in overpopulated megacities.[6] Climate change, rather than producing these issues, acts as a threat multiplier amplifying migration pressures on top of preexisting vulnerabilities.

Climate change is expected to increase the occurrence of several major hazards in Africa, including sudden-onset events and more gradual disasters like drought, sea-level rise, and coastal erosion. Drought has been particularly devastating in Africa, with particular countries and regions taking the greatest hits: between 1980 and 2014, droughts affected over 363 million people in sub-Saharan Africa, of whom 203 million were in eastern Africa, followed by southern Africa with 86 million, western Africa with 74 million and central Africa with less than one million (FAO 2015b). These effects are highly subregional—a mere five countries accounted for nearly half of all drought-affected populations: Ethiopia, Kenya, Malawi, the Niger, and South Africa (FAO 2015b). These agricultural impacts of drought and other climate-related extreme events threaten livelihoods, but also the human security of millions in east and southern Africa. The devastating 2015–2016 El Niño increased food insecurity and malnutrition in these regions by exacerbating drought. By August 2016, close to 24 million people in the Horn of Africa region were facing critical and emergency food insecurity levels, twice the number compared to August 2015. In Ethiopia alone, 9.7 million people required emergency food assistance to meet their basic food needs (OCHA 2016).

However, the occurrence of a hazard does not necessarily result in disaster unless human communities are adversely affected.[7] A major factor in African vulnerability to climate change is the continent's dependence on natural resources for livelihoods and local, national, and regional economies. The agricultural population in Africa stands at 530 million people according to recent estimates and is expected to exceed 580 million by 2020. Those relying on agricultural livelihoods accounts for 48 percent of the total population, with East Africa reaching rates of almost 70 percent (NEPAD 2013). This contributes to overall vulnerability, and particularly to livelihood migration, considering that the IPCC stated with high confidence that "climate change will interact with non-climate drivers and stressors to exacerbate vulnerability of agricultural systems, particularly in semiarid areas" of Africa (Niang et al. 2014, 1202). Across a range of climate change scenarios, significant impacts on the agricultural sector, dominated by smallholder farming and typically rainfed, are expected, with the very likely result of an overall negative effect on cereal crop yields (Collier et al. 2008; Dasgupta et al. 2014; Hassan 2010). As much as 84 percent of the economic impact of drought falls on agriculture: the sector accounted for US$11.4 billion of a total US$13.6 billion in loss and damage caused by drought in Kenya (2008–2011), Djibouti (2008–2011), and Uganda (2010–2011) (FAO 2015b). According to climate scenarios, losses in maize production from a one-in-twenty-five-year drought in Malawi could be 23 percent higher in the years 2016 to 2035 than they were from 1981 to 2010. Given that agriculture contributes 30 percent to Malawi's GDP, this could push the country over a resilience threshold in terms of the national economy and poverty, exacerbating migration pressures (UNISDR 2015).[8]

In addition to farm-based agriculture, the role of small-scale fisheries in Africa plays an important role in sustaining local livelihoods and national economies. The value added by the fisheries sector as a whole in 2011 was estimated at more than US$24 billion, 1.26 percent of the GDP of all African countries. The fisheries sector as a whole employs 12.3 million people as full-time fishers or full-time and part-time processors, representing 2.1 percent of Africa's population of between 15 and 64 years old (de Graaf and Garibaldi 2014). What's more, the sector has been traditionally underrecorded and unrecognized in most parts of the continent, though both inland and coastal fishery resources are substantial and have had a long history of use and impact, with long-established patterns of fishing and seasonal migration of fishers (FAO 2008–2017). Fisheries are also affected by drought, as well as the depletion of maritime fish stocks and biodiversity often caused by overfishing by foreign trawlers, and further eroded by climate change's maritime impacts, destabilizing millions of livelihoods.

The Climate Change-Migration Nexus in Africa

In multiplying cumulated, existing vulnerabilities, climate change contributes to the shape, size, and characteristics of population dynamics in Africa. In the IPCC's Fourth assessment report, Niang et al. (2014, 1204) noted, "many of the interacting social, demographic, and economic drivers of observed urbanization and migration in Africa are sensitive to climate change impacts." However, just as climate change does not occur in a vacuum, migration is a long-established hallmark of African societies. Migration for a variety of reasons is common within the continent and out of it. Sensationalist portrayals fundamentally mischaracterize African migration as predominantly characterized by misery (Flahaux and de Haas 2016). While indeed conflict and disaster displacement occur at higher rates compared to some continents, organized, regular migration is a major and routine part of many African people's lives. West Africa is, in fact, the most mobile region in the world. According to the bilateral migration matrix, developed by the World Bank, over 58 percent of migration flows in West Africa take place within the sub-region.[9] If we compare this to other African regions, East African rates reach 30.9 percent, central Africa 21 percent, North Africa 1.8 percent, and 24.8 percent in the southern Africa. With some 8.4 million people, West Africa also has the largest stock of migrants of any subregion in the world (UN DESA 2013).

Similar to broader migration patterns, population movements stemming from environmental changes, scarcity, or abundance are nothing new. Regions like the Sahel and the Horn of Africa have long histories of cross-border transhumance mobility linked to seasonal variability that are affected but not singularly produced by climate change (Vigil 2017). However, in acknowledging the fundamentally mobile characteristics of African societies, distress migration related to environmental and climate change should not be underestimated. Arguably, the most frequent humanitarian association made is with displacement caused by famine stemming from droughts in the Horn of Africa. Droughts are slow-onset disasters that accumulate to influence migration through various pathways. Rural outmigration is indeed a common humanitarian and economic repercussion of rainfall variability and land degradation considering the importance for rainfed agriculture, livelihoods, and socioeconomic conditions (Henry et al. 2004). These human security issues understandably contribute to outmigration from affected areas, yet evidence linking drought and migration is contradictory across the continent. Distress migration associated to drought is well documented in the Sahel and East Africa, but there are also studies that challenge any deterministic linear link (cf Kniveton et al. 2008). Findley (1994) found mixed results in assessing the impacts of droughts in rural Mali (1983–1985). On one hand, short-distance circular movements increased, while on the other hand overall migration rates did not dramatically increase, with long-distance, international migration of men to France in fact decreasing during drought periods. These findings were supported by studies in Ghana and Burkina Faso, with severe droughts inhibiting migration through impacts on people's resources and financial assets (Henry et al. 2004; van der Geest 2009). A broader review of African case studies found that a lack facilitating networks also placed constraints on people's migration during drought (Jónsson 2010).

Drought is far from the only hazard associated to climate change that influences migration in Africa. In terms of rapidly occurring events, floods account for 90 percent of disaster displacement on the continent (IDMC 2016). Flooding affected approximately 44 million people from 2000 to 2015 (CRED 2016), displacing more than 14 million people in Africa between 2009 and 2015, or an average of 5,000 people per day (IDMC 2016). Looking to West Africa, the number of people affected by floods has grown steadily since 1980 and are one of the most visible drivers of human displacement. In Nigeria, floods in September and October of 2012 caused the displacement of over six million people, or 3.6 percent of the Nigerian population (IDMC 2013). In Benin, at least

20,000 people were displaced by floods in 2009 and 2010, with a total of 150,000 people losing their homes (Ferris and Stark 2012).

Intertwined with flooding in driving migration is the impact of sea-level rise as its mobility impacts are often inseparable in coastal areas. Due to the permanent, irreversible nature of sea-level rise, it is more likely to induce permanent migration (Gemenne et al. forthcoming). According to UNESCO estimates, the number of people threatened by coastal flooding will dramatically increase along the Gulf of Guinea and the Senegalese and Gambian coasts (UNESCO 2012). Studies have shown that among African port cities most exposed to rising sea levels, six are in West Africa (Lagos, Abidjan, Lomé, Conakry, Dakar, Accra) (Nicholls et al. 2008). This rise in sea level can also cause soil salinization and thus damage land, agricultural productivity and food security, driving distress migration alongside more voluntary forms of migration, where local livelihoods are increasingly difficult to sustain (Zickgraf et al., 2016; Zickgraf and Gemenne 2015).

Patterns of Migration in Response to Climate Change

A lack of data and cross-country studies hamper an attempt to accurately portray current migratory responses to climate change in Africa, or to hypothesize future scenarios of climate change migration links. Nonetheless, existent literature clearly favors a nuanced portrayal that conveys complexity and differentiated volume dynamics, geographical and geopolitical characteristics, and temporal patterns.

One misconception about African migration, amplified by a security framing of impending floods of "climate refugees" to European countries, is that it is, or will be, international and intercontinental in nature. Although some sub-Saharan Africans crossing North Africa and the Mediterranean Sea in hopes of reaching Europe experienced environmental stress in their home region, the majority of migration flows observed in response to environmental change take place within Africa, and, even more so, within country boundaries, reflecting the broader nature of African mobility trends (Jäger et al. 2009). However, quantifying internal migration of this nature, particularly in slow-onset contexts, represents a major challenge due to a lack of available, reliable data. The threat to agricultural production posed by climate change, especially in terms of precipitation, has been identified as potentially increasing migration out of rural areas toward urban areas in sub-Saharan Africa (cf. Barrios et al. 2006). Africa has witnessed massive amounts of urban growth in the past decades, but currently rural dwellers represent nearly 60 percent of the total population, of which more than 50 percent are agriculture-based (FAO 2015a; UN DESA 2013). Despite the importance of rural–urban migration, case studies from Africa have also demonstrated the importance of rural–rural migration, as in the case of Senegal where farmers from rain-dependent zones move seasonally to better-irrigated areas in the North to engage in farming during the dry season (Zickgraf et al. 2016). Afifi et al. (2016) found that in response to rainfall variability in Tanzania, the majority of migrants appeared to move to other rural areas with more favorable weather conditions, where they could engage in familiar livelihoods of farming and livestock-keeping activities or to find work as laborers. Similarly, the same research found that in situations "leaning toward more poverty, vulnerability, and food insecurity" human mobility favored rural–rural trajectories.[10] In Ghana, they highlight, many rural populations facing rainfall variability appeared to move to mining areas in search of employment. Therefore, rather than assuming *a priori* urbanization linked to climate change, we must also investigate the conditions that lead to rural–rural migration.

Despite the importance of internal migration in response to sudden and slow-onset environmental events, studies have also shown that African populations also cross international borders, especially where borders are more permeable such as the Sahel (Findley 1994; Seck 1996), and in borderland areas where international migration remains a short-distance movement (Zickgraf 2018b). For example, the drought that ravaged the Sahelian region in 2012, combined with the political instability and conflict occurring in the north of Mali, displaced hundreds of thousands of people to the drought-affected communities in the south and in neighboring countries. Naudé (2009), using a dynamic panel data model, found that natural disasters do have a positive correlation with international migration from sub-Saharan Africa. Importantly, migration is not necessarily an either-or situation. It can be involved across the spectrum of agency and simultaneously include internal and international movements: for example, in Senegal, sea-level rise and coastal erosion combine with overfishing and the impacts of climate change on maritime fisheries to drive both displacement and relocation away from coastal risk alongside labor migration of local fishers to Mauritania (Zickgraf 2018b).

Similarly, it varies as to whether migration is permanent or temporary in response to the impacts of climate change. Seasonal migration characterizes much of migration amongst fishers, reflecting traditional livelihood responses to seasonal variation in fish stocks and reproductive seasons. However, evidence from Senegal demonstrates that the impacts of climate change and other environmental disruptions caused by overfishing lead to longer migration periods in comparison to historical patterns (Zickgraf et al. 2016; Zickgraf 2018b). Sea-level rise and coastal erosion effect more permanent migration forms, due to their irreversibility and the uninhabitability of coastal zones claimed by the sea. Even sudden-onset disaster-induced displacement varies in its migratory responses. While some populations are able to return home after a flood, storm, or other catastrophe occurs, protracted displacement (longer than one year) is an increasingly common phenomenon. Moreover, initial disaster displacement can transform into long-term or permanent migration depending on the devastation and the prospects for future risks and livelihood sustainability (Black et al. 2013).

Additionally, volume of migration, again difficult to quantify, overwhelmingly assumes that migration will increase because of the impacts of climate change. While Europe struggles with the so-called "migration crisis," some proclaim that this is merely a small-scale rehearsal for what's to come as the impacts of climate change envelop developing countries in Africa (and Asia), presumably forcing millions of people to flee their homes in the future. It has become commonplace to assert that climate change will increase human migration. While it is true that weather-related disaster displacement is on the rise (IDMC 2017), it is far from a universal, or continental, truth that increased migration is an inevitable outcome of the impacts of climate change (Black and Collyer 2014). In fact, we may be facing a world in which *fewer* people are able to move as a result of climate change (Foresight 2011; Zickgraf 2018a). The evidence is far from consensual on the impacts that climate change will have on human migration: some say substantial impacts will occur (ADB 2011), others minor (Tacoli 2011). Although increasing exposure to risks and cumulated vulnerabilities may increase migration among some African populations, it may be just as likely that more people will be stuck in place, at risk of displacement or death, because of the erosion of their resources resulting from climate change, land degradation, and water mismanagement, or because governments are keen to prevent migration, particularly to overcrowded coastal megacities. Assuming migration occurs and increases because of proliferating impacts of climate change underestimates the role of peoples' actual abilities to migrate. Without some level of resources the possibility to move even across relatively short distances is drastically hindered. Crucially, those left behind may be equally if not more vulnerable than the people who are able to leave areas affected by climate change, becoming what has been termed "trapped populations" (Foresight 2011). Certainly on a long-distance, international scale, migration requires resources that are simply unavailable to the most destitute, who are often those who are characterized by social, economic, and political marginalization (Flahaux and de Haas 2016; Zickgraf 2018a). For example, while relatively poor Senegalese fishers are able to engage in migration because of private labor recruitment schemes to Mauritania, the debt accrued in this process and the lower earning potential mean that only the wealthiest of fishers can afford to build homes away from coastal erosion within their home region (Zickgraf et al. 2016; Zickgraf 2018b). In northern Mozambique, where drought collided with conflict, cross-border migration increased among men whereas women were less able to engage in traditional mobility responses to drought due to the dangers of conflict occurring in the area (Lubkemann 2008).

Lastly, in assessing any of these dynamics currently or in the future, a far too often overlooked aspect is the importance of perceptions of climate change among affected populations. There exists an assumption that populations move based on externally observed climate data and trends; yet evidence from African case studies shows that climate data does not always align with the perceived environmental changes and risks. Based on an analysis of AMMA survey data, Zickgraf and colleagues (2016) found that in Burkina Faso perceptions of climate trends regarding rainfall events and seasons did not always align with climate data from rainfall stations.[11] This is as an important finding considering that migration decisions and intentions are based on perceived vulnerabilities rather than external assessments, especially when there are few efforts to inform local populations about climatic risks in disaster and climate change-affected

African countries. Migration may therefore occur before a climate tipping point is reached, or displacement can occur when populations do not perceive a risk to their security far in advance to evacuate or move preemptively.

Assessing the Impacts of Migration on Areas Affected by Climate Change

Assessing the linkages between the crisis of climate change and migration across the African continent requires more than determining the dynamics of migration flows. To better inform policy and scholarship, we must also address the impacts of these population movements. Whether the movement is internal, international, or intercontinental, temporary or long-term, short- or long-distance, forced or relatively voluntary, or movement is inhibited, the evidence from Africa is mixed. Case studies in African countries connecting migration specifically to its impacts on adaptive capacity to climate change are lacking. Forced relocation or displacement is often by nature a negative experience for those affected, who lose homes, assets, livelihoods, social status, and networks, among the many reasons forced migration should be avoided whenever possible, including health risks. Moreover, displaced persons and migrants often move into other areas of environmental risk. The assumption prevails that migrants move from an unsafe departure point to a safe point of arrival. Unfortunately, that is not always the case. Rural to urban migration away from drought or land degradation, for example, frequently results in migration to flood risk zones on African coastlines, where megacities lack the infrastructure and capacity to provide for further population increases on top of weak or nonexistent disaster risk reduction strategies such as early warning systems or evacuation procedures. Alongside the aforementioned examples of precarious and dangerous migration from rural areas to urban African megacities, a specific threat to certain populations is the competition over natural resources that climate change can exacerbate partially, but not entirely, through migration. In northern Benin, tensions have been reported between native populations and incoming pastoralists from drought-prone Niger over grazing lands for livestock.[12] While these were small-scale tensions, conflict can result from increased competition over resources that stems from the impacts of climate change and resulting in-migration to fragile ecosystems, which are sometimes amplified by ethnic tensions in parts of the continent already marred by political instability (c.f. Reuveny 2007).

However, there is evidence that migration, regardless of the drivers, also has the potential to build resilience and decrease vulnerability in origin communities and to support local adaptation and mitigation efforts. For example, in sub-Saharan Africa, Naudé and Bezuidenhout (2014) found that remittances will increase after a natural disaster even in the presence of controls—independently of incomes, exchange rates, or the banking sector—and that the stability of remittances can be counted on to support household incomes and consumption in times of natural disaster. In Senegal, Zickgraf et al. (2016) found that labor migration by male fishermen to Mauritania generated financial and social remittances including commuter practices that enabled household relocation away from coastal erosion. Remittances have also demonstrated their potential in financing innovation and intensification of farming in Africa (Tacoli 2009; Tiffen 2003); however, most migrant-generated remittances will be prioritized for meeting basic household needs such as food, clothing, and shelter before investment in longer-term needs or community-wide adaptation or mitigation efforts (Zickgraf and Gemenne, forthcoming).

Food security in African rural households is in fact heavily reliant on the benefits of international and internal migration. The Southern African Migration Programme (SAMP) conducted household surveys in several countries on food expenditures in migrant-sending households (Crush 2013; Dodson 2008). A regional study of 4,276 international migrant-sending households found that cash remittances were the most important source of household income; 74 percent of reporting households received remittances, with as many as 95 percent in Lesotho and 83 percent in Zimbabwe. Moreover, 37 percent of households received remittances in kind. The vast majority of households (93 percent) purchased food and other groceries with their income. In contrast, only 15 percent spent income on agricultural inputs (mainly in Swaziland). Remittances are therefore a critical component of food security for origin households that have the potential to increase adaptive capacity to the impacts of climate change across the continent.

Conclusion

Climate change is a global crisis, but its effects, including on human mobility, are largely felt in developing countries and regions. Migration across the African continent is caused by a variety of factors such as economic crises, armed conflict, generalized violence, violations of human rights, large-scale development projects, and natural disasters, alongside more normalized, less problematic motivations of labor, family, and education. No singular crisis narrative surrounding the climate change-migration nexus can accurately portray the complexity of human migration in Africa regarding its causes, patterns, or impacts. Much of future migratory responses to the global climate change will be determined by political responses to climate change and other underlying vulnerability factors. Whether migration is a forced movement or adaptation strategy will depend on a number of factors such as the type of climate shock; the characteristics of the affected population; and the capacity of institutions (local, national, and international) to prevent the effects adverse climatic shocks (Coniglio and Pesce 2011). As just one example, inappropriate and ad hoc political responses to climate change can further drive migration and displacement (Gemenne et al., forthcoming). Local, national, and international political responses must therefore take into account the growing threat of climate change but also the heterogeneity of its effects on human migration in Africa. Fearmongering about future migration crises and unsubstantiated predictions of mass international movement do little to protect those currently in harm's way, nor do they do justice to the agency and adaptive capacity of many African migrants, families, and societies.

Notes

1. Cf. El-Hinnawi 1985; Jacobson 1988.
2. Although it is true that many entities and organizations in recent years have pushed for protection instruments for those displaced by climate change.
3. This is despite the fact that most scholars recognize that migration and forced displacement remains largely internal (cf. Methman and Oels 2015).
4. Baldwin, Methmann and Rothe (2014) call this tendency to look at future scenarios and projections rather than realities in climate-migration studies "futurology"
5. However the link between climate change and violent conflict is a tenuous one (like migration) because of the interaction of a number of context-specific factors (Niang et al. 2014).
6. For more on Africa's demographic transition, see Canning, Raja and Yazbeck 2015.
7. For more on defining disasters, see United Nations Office for Disaster Risk Reduction terminology (UNISDR). "Terminology." https://www.unisdr.org/we/inform/terminology
8. Regional variability is, however, anticipated: in the Rift Valley in Kenya and in Niger, where agriculture generates 30 percent and 38 percent of GDP (respectively), the losses would actually decline in the same climate change scenario (GAR 2015).
9. The importance of intraregional migration in West Africa can be partly explained by the creation in the late 1970s of an area of free movement of people within the Economic Community of African States West (ECOWAS). In fact, migration between West African countries are mostly from neighboring countries. It is the only region of Africa where intraregional migration is greater than outward migration (34.5 percent, mainly to Europe) (Ndiaye and Robin 2010; World Bank 2011).
10. Of their eight case studies, they include here Bangladesh, India, Guatemala, Ghana, and Tanzania.
11. This particular analysis was performed by Florence de Longueville.
12. Incidents were reported during a consultation organized by the International Center for Migration Policy Development (ICMPD) for the MIEUX 2 Project on the implementation of the Nansen Initiative Protection Agenda.

References

Afifi, T., A. Milan, B. Etzold, B. Schraven, C. Rademacher-Schultz, P. Sakdapolrak et al. 2016. "Human Mobility in Response to Rainfall Variability: Opportunities for Migration as a Successful Adaptation Strategy in Eight Case Studies." *Migration and Development* 5, no. 2: 254–274. https://doi.org/10.1080/21632324.2015.1022974.

African Union. 2014. "Draft African Union Strategy on Climate Change." http://www.un.org/en/africa/osaa/pdf/au/cap_draft_auclimatestrategy_2015.pdf

Asian Development Bank (ADB). 2011. *Climate Change and Migration in Asia and the Pacific*. Manila, Philippines: Asian Development Bank.

Baldwin, A., C. Methmann, and D. Rothe. 2014. "Securitizing 'Climate Refugees': The Futurology of Climate-Induced Migration." *Critical Studies on Security* 2, no. 2: 121–130. https://doi.org/10.1080/21624887.2014.943570.

Barrios, S., L. Bertinelli, and E. Strobl. 2006. "Climatic Change and Rural–Urban Migration: The Case of Sub-Saharan Africa." *Journal of Urban Economics* 60, no. 3: 357–371. https://doi.org/10.1016/j.jue.2006.04.005.

Bettini, G. 2013. "Climate Barbarians at the Gate? A Critique of Apocalyptic Narratives on 'Climate Refugees.'" *Risky Natures, Natures of Risk* 45 (March): 63–72. https://doi.org/10.1016/j.geoforum.2012.09.009.

Black, Richard. 2001. "Environmental Refugees: Myth or Reality?" New Issues in Refugee Research, Working Paper 34. Geneva: UNHCR. http://www.unhcr.org/en-us/research/working/3ae6a0d00/environmental-refugees-myth-reality-richard-black.html

Black, R., W. Neil Adger, N. W. Arnell, S. Dercon, A. Geddes, and D. Thomas. 2011a. "Migration and Global Environmental Change." *Global Environmental Change* 21, supp. 1: S1–2. https://doi.org/10.1016/j.gloenvcha.2011.10.005.

Black, R., W. Neil Adger, N. W. Arnell, S. Dercon, A. Geddes, and D. Thomas . 2011b. "The Effect of Environmental Change on Human Migration." *Migration and Global Environmental Change—Review of Drivers of Migration* 21 (supp. 1): S3–11. https://doi.org/10.1016/j.gloenvcha.2011.10.001.

Black, R., W. Neil Adger, N. W. Arnell, A. Geddes, and D. Thomas. 2013. "Migration, Immobility and Displacement Outcomes Following Extreme Events." *Environmental Science & Policy* 27, supp. 1: S32–43. https://doi.org/10.1016/j.envsci.2012.09.001.

Black, R., and M. Collyer. 2014. "Populations 'Trapped' at Times of Crisis." *Forced Migration Review* 45:52–56.

Boko, M., I. Niang, A. Nyong, C. Vogel, A. Githeko, M. Medany et al. 2007. "Africa." In *Climate Change 2007: Impacts, Adaptation and Vulnerability. Contribution of Working Group II to the Fourth Assessment Report of the Intergovernmental Panel on Climate Change*, edited by O.F. Canziani, M.L. Parry, J. P. Palutikof, P. J. van der Linden, and C.E. Hanson, 433–467. Cambridge, UK: Cambridge University Press.

Canning, D., S. Raja, and A. S Yazbeck. 2015. *Africa's Demographic Transition: Dividend or Disaster?* Washington, DC: World Bank Publications.

Christian Aid. 2007. "Human Tide: The Real Migration Crisis." London: Christian Aid. https://www.christianaid.org.uk/sites/default/files/2017-08/human-tide-the-real-migration-crisis-may-2007.pdf

Collier, P., G. Conway, and T. Venables. 2008. "Climate Change and Africa." *Oxford Review of Economic Policy* 24, no. 2: 337–353. https://doi.org/10.1093/oxrep/grn019.

Coniglio, N., and G. Pesce. 2011. "Climate Variability, Extreme Weather Events and International Migration." COMCAD Arbeitspapiere-Working Papers No 92. Paper presented at the ESF-UniBi-ZiF research conference on "Environmental Change and Migration: From Vulnerabilities to Capabilities," Bad Salzuflen, Germany, December 5–9. http://www.unibi.de/tdrc/ag_comcad/downloads/Coniglio-Pesce_Climate-Variability-Extreme-Weather-Events-International-Migration.pdf.

CRED. 2016. "EM-DAT: The International Disaster Database." Centre for Research on the Epidemiology of Disasters (CRED). http://www.emdat.be/database.

Crush, Jonathan. 2013. "Linking Food Security, Migration and Development." *International Migration* 51, no. 5: 61–75.

Dasgupta, P., J. F. Morton, D. Dodman, B. Karapınar, F. Meza, M. G. Rivera-Ferre et al. 2014. "Rural Areas." In *Climate Change 2014: Impacts, Adaptation, and Vulnerability. Part A: Global and Sectoral Aspects. Contribution of Working Group II to the Fifth Assessment Report of the Intergovernmental Panel of Climate Change*, edited by C. B. Field, V. R. Barros, D. J. Dokken, K. J. Mach, M. D. Mastrandrea, T. E. Bilir, et al. Cambridge, UK: Cambridge University Press.

de Graaf, G., and L. Garibaldi. 2014. "The Value of African Fisheries." FAO Fisheries and Aquaculture Circular No. 1093, NEPAD. Rome: Food and Agricultural Organization of the United Nations. http://www.fao.org/3/a-i3917e.pdf

Dodson, B. 2008. "Gender, Migration and Remittances in Southern Africa." SAMP Migration Policy Series No. 49. Cape Town: The Southern African Migration Project. http://samponline.org/wp-content/uploads/2016/10/Acrobat49.pdf.

El-Hinnawi, Essam. 1985. "Environmental Refugees." Nairobi: United Nations Environmental Programme. http://wedocs.unep.org/handle/20.500.11822/2651

Environmental Justice Foundation (EJF). 2017. "Beyond Borders: Our Changing Climate, Its Role in Conflict and Displacement." London: Environmental Justice Foundation. https://reliefweb.int/report/world/beyond-borders-our-changing-climate-its-role-conflict-and-displacement

FAO. 2015a. FAOSTAT database: http://www.fao.org/faostat/en/ Accessed 21/12/2015.

FAO. 2015b. "The Impacts of Disasters on Agriculture and Food Security." Rome: Food and Agricultural Organization of the United Nations. http://www.fao.org/3/a-i5128e.pdf.

FAO. 2008–2017. Small-scale Fisheries—Africa. FI Institutional Websites. Food and Agriculture Organization of the United Nations. November 10, 2017. http://www.fao.org/fishery/

Farbotko, C., and H. Lazrus. 2012. "The First Climate Refugees? Contesting Global Narratives of Climate Change in Tuvalu." *Global Environmental Change* 22, no. 2: 382–390.

Ferris, E., and C. Stark. 2012. "Internal Displacement in West Africa: A Snapshot." Washington, D.C.: Brookings Institute.

Findley, S. E. 1994. "Does Drought Increase Migration? A Study of Migration from Rural Mali during the 1983-1985 Drought." *International Migration Review* 28, no. 3: 539–553.

Flahaux, M-L., and H. De Haas. 2016. "African Migration: Trends, Patterns, Drivers." *Comparative Migration Studies* 4, no. 1:. doi:10.1186/s40878-015-0015-6

Foresight. 2011. "Foresight: Migration and Global Environmental Change Final Project Report." Final Project Report. London: The Government Office for Science.

Gemenne, F. 2011a. "How They Became the Human Face of Climate Change. Research and Policy Interactions in the Birth of the 'Environmental Migration' Concept." In *Migration and Climate Change*, edited by A. Pecoud and P. P. E. De Guchteneire, 225–259. Cambridge and Paris: Cambridge University Press/UNESCO.

Gemenne, F. 2011b. "Climate-Induced Population Displacements in a 4°C+ World." *Philosophical Transactions of the Royal Society of London A: Mathematical, Physical and Engineering Sciences* 369, no. 1934: 182–195. https://doi.org/10.1098/rsta.2010.0287.

Gemenne, F., S. Vigil, and C. Zickgraf. Forthcoming. "Desk Review on Climate Change and Migration." Rome: Food and Agricultural Organization of the United Nations.

Glasser, R and W. L. Swing. 2017. "Climate Change and the Migration Crisis." *Huffington Post*, October 6. https://www.huffingtonpost.com/entry/59de7e34e4b069e5b833b201.

Gough, I. 2011. "Climate Change, Double Injustice and Social Policy: A Case Study of the United Kingdom." UNRISD Occasional Paper: Social Dimensions of Green

Economy and Sustainable Development. http://www.unrisd.org/80256B3C005BCCF9/(httpPublications)/2C2C37BEB8A50F08C125797B00651177

Hassan, R. M. 2010. "Implications of Climate Change for Agricultural Sector Performance in Africa: Policy Challenges and Research Agenda." *Journal of African Economies* 19 (supp 2):ii77–ii105. https://doi.org/10.1093/jae/ejp026.

Henry, S., B. Schoumaker, and C. Beauchemin. 2004. "The Impact of Rainfall on the First Out-Migration: A Multi-Level Event-History Analysis in Burkina Faso." *Population and Environment* 25, no. 5: 423–460. https://doi.org/10.1023/B:POEN.0000036928.17696.e8.

IDMC. 2013. "Global Estimates 2012: People Displaced by Disasters." Geneva: Internal Displacement Monitoring Centre (IDMC). http://www.internal-displacement.org/publications/global-estimates-2012-people-displaced-by-disasters

IDMC. 2016. "Africa Report on Internal Displacement." Geneva: Internal Displacement Monitoring Centre (IDMC). https://reliefweb.int/report/world/2016-africa-report-internal-displacement

IDMC. 2017. "2017 Global Report on Internal Displacement." Geneva: Internal Displacement Monitoring Centre (IDMC). http://www.internal-displacement.org/global-report/grid2017/

IPCC. 1990. "Policymakers' Summary of the Potential Impacts of Climate Change. Report from Working Group II to IPCC." Commonwealth of Australia: Intergovernmental Panel on Climate Change. https://digitallibrary.un.org/record/763957

Jacobson, J. 1988. "Environmental Refugees: A Yardstick of Habitability." World Watch Papers 86. Washington, DC: World Watch Institute.

Jäger, J., J. Frühmann, S. Günberger, and A. Vag. 2009. "Environmental Change and Forced Migration Scenarios (EACH-FOR) Project Synthesis Report."

Jónsson, G. 2010. "The Environmental Factor in Migration Dynamics—a Review of African Case Studies." *IMI Working Papers* 21.

Kolmannskog, V. O. 2008. "Future Floods of Refugees: A Comment on Climate Change, Conflict and Forced Migration." Oslo: Norwegian Refugee Council. https://www.nrc.no/resources/reports/future-floods-of-refugees/

Kniveton, D., K. Schmidt-Verkerk, C. Smith, and R. Black. 2008. "Climate Change and Migration: Improving Methodologies to Estimate Flows." IOM Migration Research Series 33. Geneva: IOM. http://www.iom.cz/files/Climate_Change_and_Migration_MRS_331.pdf

Lubkemann, S. C. 2008. "Involuntary Immobility: On a Theoretical Invisibility in Forced Migration Studies." *Journal of Refugee Studies* 21, no. 4: 454–475.

Methmann, C., and A. Oels. 2015. "From 'fearing' to 'empowering' Climate Refugees: Governing Climate-Induced Migration in the Name of Resilience." *Security Dialogue* 46, no. 1: 51–68. https://doi.org/10.1177/0967010614552548

Myers, N. 1993. "Environmental Refugees in a Globally Warmed World." *BioScience* 43, no. 11: 752–761. https://doi.org/10.2307/1312319.

Myers, N. 2002. "Environmental Refugees: A Growing Phenomenon of the 21st Century." *Philosophical Transactions of the Royal Society of London. Series B: Biological Sciences* 357, no. 1420: 609–613.

Myers, N., and J. Kent. 1995. "Environmental Exodus: An Emergent Crisis in the Global Arena." Climate Institute. http://climate.org/archive/PDF/Environmental%20Exodus.pdf

Naudé, W. A. 2009. "Natural Disasters and International Migration from Sub-Saharan Africa." *Migration Letters* 6, no. 2: 165–176.

Naudé, W. A., and H. Bezuidenhout. 2014. "Migrant Remittances Provide Resilience Against Disasters in Africa." *Atlantic Economic Journal* 42, no. 1: 79–90. https://doi.org/10.1007/s11293-014-9403-9.

Ndiaye, M., and N. Robin. 2010. "Les Migrations Internationales En Afrique de l'Ouest: Une Dynamique de Régionalisation Articulée À La Mondialisation." *International Migration Institute (IMI) Working Papers* 23.

NEPAD. 2013. "African Agriculture, Transformation and Outlook." http://www.un.org/en/africa/osaa/pdf/pubs/2013africanagricultures.pdf

Niang, I., O. C. Ruppel, M. A. Abdrabo, A. Essel, C. Lennard, J. Padgham et al. 2014. "Africa." In *Climate Change 2014: Impacts, Adaptation, and Vulnerability. Part B: Regional Aspects. Contribution of Working Group II to the Fifth Assessment Report of the Intergovernmental Panel of Climate Change*, edited by V. R. Barros, C. B. Field, D. J. Dokken, M. D. Mastrandrea, K. J. Mach, T. E. Bilir et al. Cambridge, UK: Cambridge University Press.

Nicholls, R. J, S. Hanson, C. Herweijer, N. Patmore, S. Hallegatte, J. Corfee-Morlot et al. 2008. "Ranking Port Cities with High Exposure and Vulnerability to Climate Extremes." OECD Environment Working Papers. Paris: OECD. https://www.oecd-ilibrary.org/docserver/011766488208.pdf?expires=1530801831&id=id&accname=guest&checksum=04DD3EC93D90454FD1A114FBA75A1F37

Nicholls, R. J., P. P. Wong, V. Burkett, J. Codignotto, J. Hay, R. McLean et al. 2007. "Coastal Systems and Low-Lying Areas. Climate Change 2007: Impacts, Adaptation and Vulnerability." In *Contribution of Working Group II to the Fourth Assessment Report of the Intergovernmental Panel on Climate Change*, edited by M. L. Parry, O. F. Canziani, J. P. Palutikof, P. J. van der Linden, and C. E. Hanson, 315–356. Cambridge, UK: Cambridge University Press.

OCHA. 2016. *El Niño: Overview of Impact, Projected Humanitarian Needs, and Response*. New York/Geneva: OCHA (United Nations Office for the Coordination of Humanitarian Affairs). https://reliefweb.int/report/world/el-ni-o-overview-impact-projected-humanitarian-needs-and-response-16-august-2016

Rain, D., R. Engstrom, L. Christiana, and S. Antos. 2011. "Accra Ghana: A City Vulnerable to Flooding and Drought-Induced Migration." In *UN-Habitat, Global Report on Human Settlements: Cities and Climate Change, 2010/2011*. https://unhabitat.org/wp-content/uploads/2012/06/GRHS2011CaseStudyChapter04Accra.pdf

Reuveny, R. 2007. "Climate Change-Induced Migration and Violent Conflict." *Political Geography* 26, no. 6: 656–673. https://doi.org/10.1016/j.polgeo.2007.05.001.

Seck, E. S. 1996. "Désertification: Effets, Lutte et Convention." Dakar: ENDA-TM.

Tacoli, C. 2009. "Crisis or Adaptation? Migration and Climate Change in a Context of High Mobility." *Environment and Urbanization* 21, no, 2: 513–525.

Tacoli, C. 2011. *Not Only Climate Change: Mobility, Vulnerability and Socio-Economic Transformations in Environmentally Fragile Areas in Bolivia, Senegal and Tanzania*. Vol. 28. Rural-Urban Interactions and Livelihood Strategies. Human Settlements Working Paper Series. IIED

Taylor, M. 2017. "Climate Change 'Will Create World's Biggest Refugee Crisis.'" *The Guardian*. November 2. https://www.theguardian.com/environment/2017/nov/02/climate-change-will-create-worlds-biggest-refugee-crisis

Tiffen, M. 2003. "Transition in Sub-Saharan Africa: Agriculture, Urbanization and Income Growth." *World Development* 31, no. 8: 1343–1366. https://doi.org/10.1016/S0305-750X(03)00088-3.

UNDESA. 2013. "2013: World Population Prospects: The 2012 Revision, Highlights and Advance Tables." United Nations, Department of Economic and Social Affairs (UN DESA) Population Division Working Paper No. ESA/P/WP.228. New York: UN DESA Population Division. https://esa.un.org/unpd/wpp/publications/Files/WPP2012_HIGHLIGHTS.pdf

UNESCO. 2012. "Adapting to Climate Change in Coastal Areas of West Africa." Dakar: United Nations Educational, Scientific and Cultural Organization (UNESCO). http://www.unesco.org/new/en/dakar/about-this-office/single-view/news/adapting_to_climate_change_in_coastal_areas_of_west_africa/

UNISDR. 2015. "Making Development Sustainable: The Future of Disaster Risk Management. Global Assessment Report on Disaster Risk Reduction." Geneva, Switzerland: United Nations office for disaster risk reduction. https://www.preventionweb.net/english/hyogo/gar/2015/en/home/GAR_2015/GAR_2015_1.html.

Van der Geest, K. 2009. "Migration and Natural Resources Scarcity in Ghana." Case Study Report for the Environmental Change and Forced Migration Scenarios Project. Brussels: EACH-FOR Project, European Commission. https://dare.uva.nl/search?identifier=9f47737c-0d25-43f5-a231-7b887b7e10f7

Vigil, Sara. 2017. "Climate Change and Migration: Insights from the Sahel." In *Out of Africa: Why People Migrate*, edited by G. Carbone, 51–72. Milan: Ledizioni.

World Bank. 2011. Global Bilateral Migration Database. Washington DC: World Bank Group. http://data.worldbank.org/data-catalog/migration-andremittances , accessed 10/05/2014.

Zickgraf, C. 2016. "International Migrants Day: The 'Story' of Water Migration." Delft: UN-IHE Institute for Water Education. https://www.un-ihe.org/news/international-migrants-day-%E2%80%98story%E2%80%99-water-migration.

Zickgraf, C. 2018a. "Immobility." In *Routledge Handbook on Environmental Displacement and Migration*, edited by F. Gemenne and R. McLeman. London: Routledge.

Zickgraf, C. 2018b. "'The Fish Migrate and so Must We': The Relationship between International and Internal Environmental Mobility in a Senegalese Fishing Community." *Journal Medzinarodne Vztahy* 16, no. 1: 5–21.

Zickgraf, C., and F. Gemenne. 2015. "Background Paper on Migration, Climate Change and Environment in West Africa: With a Focus on Benin, Togo and Guinea-Bissau." Brussels: International Centre for Migration Policy Development (ICMPD).

Zickgraf, C., and F. Gemenne. Forthcoming. "How Remittances Address Poverty and Resilience in the Context of Climate Change: Synthesis of the Existing Evidence." Washington, DC: World Bank Group.

Zickgraf, C., S. V. D. Telenti, F. De Longueville, P. Ozer, and F. Gemenne. 2016. "The Impact of Vulnerability and Resilience to Environmental Changes on Mobility Patterns in West Africa." *Global Knowledge Partnership on Migration and Development (KNOMAD) Series*. https://www.knomad.org/publication/impact-vulnerability-and-resilience-environmental-changes-mobility-patterns-west-africa

PART V

MIGRATION CORRIDORS AND TRANSIT COUNTRIES

CHAPTER 21

"REFUGEE CRISIS" IN THE SOUTHEASTERN EUROPEAN COUNTRIES

The Rise and Fall of the Balkan Corridor

DRAGO ŽUPARIĆ-ILJIĆ AND MARKO VALENTA

THIS chapter focuses on the asylum policies and measures in the southeastern European countries that formed an essential part of the migration corridor during the recent mass-arrivals of refugees and other migrants traveling toward Germany, Sweden and other countries in Western Europe. It is argued that an important aspect of how transit countries dealt with the influx of migrants was shaped by a concern to avoid becoming a migrant hotspot. This seemed more important to the authorities than concerns about refugees' access to protection systems and integration into local communities. Such notions have been especially fostered within the area commonly referred to as the Balkan corridor, which emerged as a semi-formalized route of safe passage for the massive transit of refugees and migrants, which lasted from summer 2015 to spring 2016. The idiosyncratic posturing of the countries in the region enabled more than one million people to trespass on Balkan sovereign states in a swift and, at times, overtly controlled and organized manner.

However, data and statistics concerning the numbers of refugees and migrants in transit over southeastern Europe has been imprecise due to the massive numbers involved in terms of migrant movements, and the ill-prepared state actors responsible for the management of official statistical facilities. There were frequent instances of omitting the migrants' registration deliberately. Yet, in spite of the lack of rigor applied, in terms of the reliability of the statistics, it is abundantly clear that the majority of asylum seekers that applied for asylum in Europe, during the abovementioned period, did travel through the Western Balkan area.[1]

In the following pages, several research questions are discussed, namely: a) What were the responses at state level in the Balkan countries regarding recent migratory movements? b) What were the structural frames that influenced the responses and the local constructions of "the crisis"? c) How were the mass-migrations interpreted and constructed at the local and the regional levels? d) What kind of relationships were established between local authorities, NGOs, and civic society in the process of accommodating, assisting, and organizing further transit?

This chapter is divided into several interrelated parts. In the first part, we contextualize the emergence of the corridor and discuss how various countries in the region responded to the mass arrivals. Thereafter, we analyze the local constructions of "the crisis" and the relationships between the authorities and the NGOs. Here, we focus primarily on the Croatian experience. Finally, we examine the closure of the corridor and further securitization measures that followed. Discussion is based on the findings of a research project, conducted over a three-year period (2014–2017). In 2014 and 2015, the focus was on conducting in-depth interviews with asylum seekers and refugees in Croatia, investigating their agency, and the reasons why they chose Croatia as a country of transit, and yet avoided it as the final destination country (see Valenta, Zuparic-Iljic, and Vidovic 2015). Later on, during 2016 and 2017, the research focus shifted to that of examining the institutional responses of relevant authorities and NGOs in the region to mass-arrivals of refugees. This research was conducted by means of expert interviews and documenting participant observations, as experienced within the transit reception center camps and at border points along Croatia, Serbia, and Slovenia.

Responses on the Mass Arrivals along the Balkan Corridor

In forced migration literature, a specific framing of "migration as crisis" ("migration crisis") refers to situations of:

> [C]omplex, often large-scale migration movements caused by a crisis which, typically, involves significant attendant vulnerabilities for affected individuals and communities. A migration crisis may be i) sudden or of slow-onset, ii) have natural or manmade causes, iii) take place internally or across borders.
>
> (IOM 2012, 1)

Therefore, "migration crisis," as such, is understood as a consequence of "a crisis," rather than its cause. Likewise, to conceptualize "crisis migration" requires a term which is politically, administratively, and socioculturally constructed. Jane McAdam (2014, 29–31) understands "crisis migration" as mobility related to any crisis situation, whereby such circumstances, defined as exceptional and extraordinary, seek immediate measures and emergency solutions. Several of the previously mentioned elements have characterized the mass arrivals of migrants in Balkan countries in 2015–2016. However, some authors understand the events of the Balkan corridor not as a refugee and migration crisis *per se*, but as a specific type of politically and socioculturally constructed, conveyed, and perpetuated discourse on crisis (de Genova and Tazzioli 2016, 15–21).

In order to contextualize the discussion on responses and constructions of the crisis, we also need to stress some of the relevant historical and socioeconomic factors that have framed the responses to a recent mass migration occurrence in the region. Firstly, it is important to remember that several countries in the region experienced recent armed conflict and refugee movements of their own populations. Displacement of more than four million people, as a result of war atrocities following the dissolution of Yugoslavia in the 1990s, created multiple local and regional solutions for protracted refugee and internal-displacement status in the Balkans.

The disintegration of Yugoslavia and the wars that followed resulted in large refugee movements from the region to the receiving countries in Europe (Black and Koser 1999; Valenta and Strabac 2013). During the 1990s, the largest receiving countries outside the region were Germany, Austria, and Sweden.[2] In addition, several West Balkan countries received large numbers of internally displaced people. Most countries in the region were also destinations for hundreds of thousands migrants and refugees from other Yugoslavian republics (Ramet and Valenta 2016). Serbia received Serbian forced migrants and refugees from Croatia, Bosnia, and Kosovo, while Croatia received the Croatian displaced population and refugees from Bosnia and Northern Serbia.[3] Croatia alone had, in 1992, 800.000 refugees and IDPs. Therefore, providing shelter, humanitarian aid, and repatriation support to IDPs and refugees has, for a number of years, remained one of the crucial humanitarian and sociopolitical tasks for Croatia, as well as for several other countries in southeastern Europe, primarily, Serbia, Kosovo, and Bosnia and Herzegovina (Lukić and Nikitović 2004; Mesić and Bagić 2011; Ramet and Valenta 2016; Valenta and Ramet 2011). Thus, experiences of displacement, both for local authorities and local populations, should be taken into consideration when we discuss the reactions of local people to the recent mass arrivals that took place in 2015 and 2016. Throughout the whole region, the responses of the local populations and NGOs were often related to their own experiences of conflict and displacement and, also, of dealing with refugee populations back in the 1990s. In Croatia, some of the most affected areas during the conflict, which also generated the largest refugee movements, were the same areas that experienced mass arrivals of transit migrants in 2015 and 2016.

Secondly, individual countries' policy positions in the EU, and their relations with the EU, should be taken into consideration. Greece, Hungary, and Slovenia are all part of the Schengen zone, and also part of the Dublin system of cooperation. In the case of EU countries Croatia and Bulgaria, they have also adopted the Dublin Regulation, but they are not part of the Schengen zone. Yet other countries in the region (such as Macedonia and Serbia) are not in the EU and, thus, are not part of the same cooperation dynamics. Nevertheless, the dynamics of developing their own asylum, migration, and border management systems in most Balkan countries were driven mainly by their progression toward trying to achieve EU accession (Lalić Novak 2016; Stojić Mitrović 2014). Croatia became a member in July 2013, while accession progress for Serbia, Macedonia, and Bosnia and Herzegovina are hindered by various political and administrative impediments.

A third factor relates to the arrival of catastrophic floods in Croatia, Serbia, and Bosnia during May 2014. The resultant huge material damage brought about a sort of "crisis migration" response where relevant authorities and NGOs were rapidly mobilized into helping temporarily displaced populations (Župarić-Iljić 2017). During and after this natural disaster, the crisis management response was one of evacuate, shelter, and return of affected populations. Later, when the mass migrations from Syria and other countries started to arrive in the previously mentioned countries in 2015, some of the recent experiences and tools, which had been utilized during the earlier floods, were promptly deployed to manage the mass arrivals of migrants.

Finally, we should take into account the fact that, without exception, the southeast European states have weak economies and suffer from high levels of unemployment which, for a number of years, have generated substantial emigration movements, primarily to Western Europe. For example, Serbia in particular, is a state whose citizens form a sizable share of asylum seekers in EU countries (Grupković et al. 2016, 16–20). In the case of Croatia, tens of thousands of its citizens became labor migrants in other EU countries. Joining the EU gave Croatians access to its labor markets. The economic recession and high unemployment levels in Croatia generated the largest single out-migration toward Western Europe since the armed conflicts of the 1990s (Jutarnji List 2017). Within this context, it is not surprising that the West Balkan countries—and refugees and migrants in transit—were in tacit agreement that such countries could not be regarded as destination countries. Indeed, the analysis of the mass arrivals in 2015–2016 should also take into account migrants' agency and how they position themselves vis-à-vis the European migration system and its different subelements. In this system, the EU countries at the southeastern borders of the EU are usually considered as transit countries and a least desired final destination for migrants making their way toward large asylum destination countries in the Schengen area, with more developed reception conditions and better integration opportunities.

Several of the aforementioned structural factors need to be taken in account in any analysis of the local constructions of crisis and how West-Balkan countries responded to the mass-migrations in 2015–2016, which also resulted in the rise and fall of Balkan corridor.[4]

The Rise of the Balkan Corridor

The disintegration of Yugoslavia, the wars and the migrations, within and from the region, have attracted much attention, from both politicians and researchers (Black and Koser 1999; Lukić and Nikitović 2004; Mesić and Bagić 2011; Valenta and Strabac 2013). Yet, transit migrations in the region that took place in the post-conflict period attracted little attention (Lukić 2016; Papadopoulou 2004; Valenta et al 2015). In the last decade, irregular migrations to Europe have, primarily, been associated with the transit migrations via Libya and the central Mediterranean region.[5] However, the topic of transit migrations, via Libya and the central Mediterranean region, was not at the forefront of debate in 2015 as the focus of media and politicians changed with the rise of the Balkan corridor. In 2015, the vast majority of migrants entering Europe went through the Balkan corridor, and the sufferings of those migrants, stranded at the borders, or transiting the region, started to dominate the debates.

These separate and unrelated outbreaks of political and social upheaval, leading to mass migrations, were fused together under the same shorthand label of "the refugee crisis" in Europe. The situation escalated in the summer of 2015 with mass arrivals of migrants from Turkey to the Greek islands. Thereafter, hundreds of thousands of those migrants continued further onward, toward Western Europe via Macedonia, Serbia, Hungary, Croatia, and Slovenia. It is maintained that this phenomenon was the product of a combination of different push-forces, such as political instability and wars in Syria, and elsewhere, such as in Iraq, Afghanistan, Eritrea (Fargues and Fandrich 2012; Heisbourg 2015). But it is also clear that an important factor shaping "the crisis" was the array of various idiosyncratic responses from both transit and receiving countries in Europe. Prior to the mass arrivals in 2015, countries bordering the Union had applied, for many years, a set of established externalizing asylum policies, border protection, and deterrence measures in order to reduce numbers of irregular migrants and asylum seekers. Several states in the southern and southeastern regions of Europe have, for some years, engaged in cooperation with their neighbors regarding the prevention of irregular migrations, before migrants in transit can reach their borders, while also serving as "buffer-zones" for the rest of the core EU countries (Boswell 2003). Another part of the externalization of border control and asylum policy has been the readmission agreements between the EU and its neighbors, such as, the Western Balkans, Turkey, Ukraine, Belarus, and Moldova. Countries lying on the borders of the Union have also, at times, reached bilateral readmission agreements such as those between Greece and Turkey, Spain and Morocco and Italy and Libya. In addition to these measures, several countries bordering EU territories have, at times, prevented migrants and refugees from reaching their destination country, either by intercepting them at sea or by various deterrence and pushback practices (Triandafyllidou and Dimitriadi 2014).

However, in 2015, the Balkan countries unexpectedly stopped serving as "buffer-zones" for the rest of the core EU countries, complying with the fact that Germany and Sweden had previously declared they would grant protection to Syrian asylum seekers reaching these two countries (DW 2015). The Balkan countries also maintained that they were not "wished for" final destinations, while Germany, Sweden, and other West European countries were wanted destinations by refugees themselves. Consequently, the Balkan territories defined themselves as transit countries, while, at the same time, engaging in the zero-sum game where each country along the Balkan corridor, overtly or covertly, avoided becoming a long-term receiver of asylum seekers. This was the main practice, with different countries reacting in different ways to the growing arrival of migrants, some opening their borders with a focus on short-term humanitarian aid, but with the overall aim of securitized and swift transit to the next country in the migration chain. Additionally, other countries also attempted to deflect migrants from their territories by building wire barriers and razor-fences, and sending a military presence to protect their borders (i.e., Bulgaria, Macedonia, and Hungary).

Hungary was the most sought after as transit country since it was part of the Schengen Zone (FRONTEX 2015). Migrants who managed to evade Hungarian border patrols and cross the border between Serbia and Hungary undetected were able to continue to their target destination countries in the EU without facing new border controls. In early 2015, the major response to the mass arrivals in the region was to allow and tolerate nonassisted transit through their countries, such as in case of Serbia and Macedonia (Beznec, Speer, and Stojić Mitrović 2016). In the first stages of arrivals, Hungary and most countries in the region oscillated between closing and reopening the borders, indeterminately tolerating transit to the West. When Hungary completed the construction of a barbed wire fence in September 2015 and closed the international border crossings with Serbia, refugees and other forced migrants turned toward Croatia, trying to enter the Schengen Zone via Croatia through Hungary and later on through Slovenia. The response of Slovenia was to erect barbed wire fencing along its border with Croatia. In order to deflect migrants transiting via Greece, Macedonia also militarized its border with Greece and erected a barbed wire fence.

In autumn 2015, regular reception centers for accommodation of asylum seekers soon became very full. In response, Serbian, Croatian, and Slovenian governments opened several "transit reception centers" along the corridor, hosting thousands of people in transit. Croatia and Slovenia continued with overtly assisted transit of migrants through their territories, regulating the pace of their movement by halting them in reception centers in which short-term accommodation and assistance was provided (Greider 2017; Kogovšek Šalamon 2016; Šelo Šabić 2017).

The situation in southern parts of the corridor, which received the largest percentage of transiting migrants, was far worse. It resulted in overcrowded and poor conditions in reception camps and centers on Greek islands, and in centers close to the Greek-Macedonian and the Macedonian-Serbian borders. Due to insufficient state assistance, thousands of migrants were faced with inhumane living conditions—surviving in makeshift shanty towns that sprang up on the outskirts of the big cities (Lukić 2016). However, the majority of people stayed there only for short periods of time as the hasty transit of refugees was tolerated by the local authorities and carried out either in a self-organized or smuggling-assisted manner, as in Macedonia and in part Serbia, or by means of state-controlled and assisted ways, as in Croatia and Slovenia. This tolerated and overtly secured transit had reduced the sufferings of migrants along the Balkan corridor. It also lowered the human and economic costs of migration, but increased the pressure on the destination countries in the Western Europe.

In sum, initial responses by all countries along the Balkan corridor in 2015 shared several similar features. Firstly, they were characterized by the application of *ad hoc* solutions in response to specific situations or perceived problems arising from developments on the ground. They formed part of an emergency and exceptional measures response, manifested through over displays of surveillance measures and physical deterrents. Another similarity that all countries along the Balkan corridor shared, when compared with receiving countries in Western Europe, was that they met arriving migrants with insufficient protection systems characterized by low and inadequate reception standards, high rejection rates for claimants, and few integration opportunities for refugees who were granted protection (Coleridge 2013; Greider 2017; Porobić and Župarić-Iljić 2017; Valenta et al. 2015). Even so, evident differences have been identified between the countries' positioning in regard to "crisis management" strategies. In Macedonia and Serbia, authorities issued 72-hour temporary permits and tolerated transit through their countries, but refugees, after exiting registration and reception centers, were left to find their own ways and means of how best to travel across the country to the next border. In the case of Croatia and Slovenia, state budgets had been purchased as a matter of formal policy so that strict control could be exercised in terms of their entering and transiting through countries. At the same time, refugees' minimal stay in transit reception centers, in both countries, has mainly been carried out in a highly excluding, isolating, and segregating manner.

Rhetoric and the social constructions of the crisis also diverged at the peak of the mass arrivals. Probably the major difference was that Serbian and Croatian authorities alike promoted a quite different approach to mass arrivals in comparison with other West Balkan countries. According to Šelo Šabić and Borić, who provided an extensive overview of the local responses to the migrant influx in the region, the views of participants in Serbian public debates were predominantly empathetic toward migrants, with particular reference to human solidarity, the humanitarian aspect of the migrations, and Serbians own experiences of displacement from the wars in former Yugoslavia. The authors also argued that among all the Western Balkan countries explored in their report, "the Serbian government has conveyed the most positive discourse on the arriving migrants" (Šelo Šabić and Borić 2016, 10).[6]

Both Serbian and Croatian authorities maintained that their responses were humane and humanitarian, and in strong opposition to the strategies of those countries that decided to "defend" their borders with walls and razor-fences (i.e. Macedonia, Bulgaria, Slovenia, and Hungary).[7] In contrast, the Hungarian rightist government, headed by Viktor Orban, took the harshest stance against arriving migrants. Compared with Croatia and Serbia, Hungarian political elites used overtly xenophobic rhetoric. Also, in Slovenia, political elites were more concerned to close off the borders and, to this end, decided to build fences. The Slovenian government placed a constant emphasis on their role as protector of Schengen's external borders and related security aspects, which resulted in growing public fear and discomfort (Kogovšek Šalamon and Bajt 2016). These kinds of attitudes and resort to rhetoric in Hungary, Slovenia, and subsequently also in several other countries in the region, led to further securitization of state responses in the form of "state of emergency" and "state of exception" measures. This consequently led to further militarization and securitization of asylum, migration, and border management policies, as well as the criminalization and irregularization of forced migrants' movements.

Constructions of "the Crisis" in Croatia: "You are welcome, but travel on."

At the very peak of mass arrivals in in the fall of 2015 came the best opportunity to closely follow the public discourse and responses of authorities in Croatia. Indeed, Croatian society accepted the massive arrivals of refugees by expressing largely positive, humanitarian attitudes, both at the level of the Government's representatives representing the public and of civil organisations. A welcoming atmosphere on the part of the public has been clearly noted among local citizens living in the Croatian postwar areas where refugees entered the country and where, later on, the first transit reception center was located. On the other hand, placing people in closed facilities of transit reception camps, and then executing a highly controlled and managed transportation to the next border, in reality removed any possibility for the majority of the local population to come into direct contact with the refugees, as opposed to seeing them featured in media reporting. Those extraordinary reception centers were organized as short-term humanitarian camps, and run jointly by police forces, local and international humanitarian actors, volunteers, and refugee-rights civil actors, utilizing intertwined humanitarian and securitarian "crisis management" practices.

Several factors might have influenced the official responses and discourses—inter alia, how they have been shaped and reshaped by Croatian political turmoil in the parliamentary preelection time and, secondly, through episodes of friction with neighboring states that were affected by the Croatian authorities' balancing between the national political and economic interests and pressures from the European Commission. Until November 2015, the main focus was on practical challenges such as to organize reception for some 5,000 people who arrived daily at few entry spots at borders. After their brief retention in the transit reception centers, the next task was to execute further state-sponsored and organized transfer to Schengen borders. In the fall of 2015, the arrival numbers of refugees were not lessening. Additionally, Croatia aggravated the process further in its transfer of refugees from the borders of Serbia to Hungary and, later, to the Slovenian border. Knowing that it would be unfeasible to control the possible attenuation of the Balkan route through Bosnia and Herzegovina to Croatia, the Croatian government did not close Croatian borders with Serbia, but instead, decided to facilitate a highly controlled "few-hours" reception and then hasten transit toward Hungary and Slovenia. Such strategy increased tension between Croatia and the previously mentioned countries. On the other hand, the state response of offering free transportation across Croatian territory significantly reduced the risk and incidence of smuggling, trafficking, and exploitation (Šelo Šabić, 2017). Although it should be stressed that Croatia's positive, welcoming, humanitarian stance must be viewed in terms of an overtly proclaimed aim—namely, to ensure that arriving migrants were being welcomed into the country on a temporary basis only.

In Croatia during that time the Social Democratic government framed "the crisis" as the need to take a humane and humanitarian approach, as well as to protect national (security) interests. The rightist opposition strongly criticized the government for occasional bouts of friction and disputes with neighboring Slovenia and Hungary; even after agreeing upon a joint solution (i.e., the corridor). Šelo Šabić and Borić pointed out that the previous left-centrist government

> needed to show that it was capable of controlling the crisis . . . [and that] Croatia would contribute to the orderly and humane transit of migrants across its territory, but would not allow itself to become a haven for migrants, a prospect feared and vociferously criticized by the opposition.
>
> (Šelo Šabić and Borić 2016, 13)

This being so, the priority was to organize, control, and execute the most effective way to achieve the swift transit of people along the Balkan corridor, with an emphasis on "responsibility, capability and humanity" of all actors in their handling of humanitarian challenges, and providing at the very least temporary shelter, food, clothes, and medicine in the Croatian transit reception camps. Such a stance has been summarized, in the words of the former prime minister, thus: "You are welcome in Croatia and you can pass through Croatia. But, go on. Not because we don't like you, but because this is not your final destination."[8]

Laid bare, the state's "public-face" strategy of advocating human(itarian) approaches was, in practice, restricted to enabling a more humane "transit" process rather than one of aiding "longer-term solutions" such as assured residence status and local integration into Croatian society. Nonetheless, migrants personally did wish for trajectories following that line, because a huge majority of them did want to leave Croatia and head further West.[9]

Parliamentary elections in Croatia, in November 2015, also influenced the ways in which the political, media and public discourse toward the movement of people was shaped and presented as a situation of, firstly, "refugee arrivals" and then, later, as one of "refugee and migration crisis." This reconceptualization coincides with the start of more serious securitization practices of ethnic profiling of "*genuine* refugees" (Syrian, Iraqi, and Afghani nationals) as opposed to "other" migrant nationalities being contained at borders. In first days of people arriving and "trespassing" through Croatia, media reporting on refugees was, in the main, mostly positive. The media promoted personal stories of people, exemplifying their suffering, gratitude of acceptance in Croatia, and overall sympathetic treatment by police officers and other civil servants working with them. A level of annoyance at the way in which they were treated in Greece, Macedonia, Serbia, and Hungary was visibly evident. One aspect was a focus on the stories of the local population from the easternmost Croatian counties, who recalled their own experience of displacement and solidarity during the war in the 1990s.

Following parliamentary elections in November 2015 the new government—a political coalition dominated by rightist parties—has adopted a similar discourse of responsibility and humanity in their handling of the migrations.[10] However, the new government's focus, gradually over time, and especially after Paris the terrorist attacks and Köln harassments, has shifted more and more toward convergence with Slovenian, Hungarian, and the Visegrad group's securitization discourse on preventing irregular migration, fighting smuggling networks, handling the forcible returns, and defending borders and presumed national interests.

Similarly, other countries along the Balkan corridor also expanded gradually in a direction of securitization of asylum issues and deterioration of refugee and migrant rights. When mass arrivals started, the Macedonian government allowed the transit of migrants to Serbia. However, later on, push-back practices were implemented—enforced by the police, army patrols, and the use of tear gas at borders—in order to deflect people back to Greece. This approach served only to further intensify already existing tensions between the two states. Similarly, Vezovnik (2017, 25) stresses how, in order to protect state borders from irregular movements, both Croatian and Slovenian authorities in 2016 delegated some of the border police tasks to the armed forces, should the security situation merit such intervention.

Relations between the Stakeholders in Handling "the Crisis"

In all countries along the Balkan corridor, international and local NGOs provided considerable humanitarian aid to arriving migrants. Here, we can distinguish between, at least, four types of interrelated efforts of the NGOs: a) the mobilization and organization of large numbers of local and foreign volunteers who provided immediate assistance to newcomers at borders and in transit reception camps; b) citizen donations of various necessities to migrants, where such actions were often initiated and organized by NGOs, which also distributed the donated items to the migrants; c) NGOs providing relevant information to the migrants and volunteers and the local population, with part of this endeavor focused on fighting prejudices and xenophobia; d) last, but not least, several NGOs taking on the role of watchdog by providing information, appraisals, and warnings about human rights violations that occurred along the corridor (Šelo Šabić and Borić 2016). However, several of the NGO-coordinated efforts were combined with and controlled by the authorities' own endeavours to manage the transit migrations.

Deployment of emergency crisis measures shape what Rajaram (2015) calls "acceptable forms of mobilities" as solely those which are organized and controlled by states. This control was particularly evident during the overtly securitized, highly controlled and effective swift reception and transit of refugees within the Croatian territory.

The transit system in Croatia consisted of two reception camps. The first mass arrivals were managed via the reception camp close to the Serbian border in Opatovac. At the beginning of November 2015, the new Winter Reception Transit Centre in Slavonski Brod opened. People were transported by train to this new camp from the Serbian border under police escort. Services in the camps for refugees included basic reception and accommodation in a large UNHCR-provided warehouse of heated tents, with an area for single men and separate facilities for families and vulnerable groups. Also provided was emergency medical care, and food and clothing services. There was also a child-friendly place opened by UNICEF, and a support service to help with family tracing and reunification. In addition, the specific needs of pregnant women and mothers with babies was also addressed. The Red Cross was mandated by the Croatian Government to coordinate the humanitarian assistance work of the NGOs operating within the camp (Hameršak and Pleše 2017).

In the report of Larsen et al. (2016) the authors concluded that, within the reception transit camps, mutually cooperative and coordinated action was evident. The report posits that the involvement of local authorities and communities was based on their responses during the humanitarian crises generated by war in 1990s and a natural disaster in 2014 (Larsen et al. 2016, 5). It involved an extensive number of international, national, and local stakeholders that provided fast and appropriate responses to meet people's needs. At the same time, one arguably "beneficial consequence" of this level of effectiveness was that authorities could more easily achieve their particular aims—namely, to ensure the rapid mobility of migrants through and out of the country and thus out of their remit of responsibility.

Analyzing how the state and society reacted to mass arrivals of refugees at Keleti train station in Budapest, in the summer of 2015, Kallius et al. describe how:

> [m]igrants both challenge and confirm the vertical politics of state power, whether that power is expressed through the state's immobilisation strategies or through volunteers' humanitarian intervention.
>
> (Kallius et al. 2016, 10)

At the same time, new forms of "horizontal solidarities" originated from dialectics of *ad hoc* coalitions among different stakeholders (such as various activists, volunteers, humanitarians, and service providers) who were helping refugees. Similar tendencies were observed in the Croatian context. For example, humanitarian organizations' ability to operate in the state-led transit centers always had to be approved by the vertical, hierarchical power structure, embedded in the Ministry of the Interior. "The crisis"-coordinating body that was set up during the floods in Croatia was the same organizational structure mobilized by the "National Crisis Headquarters for the Migrant Crisis," which included several ministries, the National Protection and Rescue Directorate, and the Croatian Red Cross. However, several representatives we met, from various NGOs, had stressed that the institutional capacity to manage large-scale movements of people was also shaped by the strategy of controlled and organized transit through the country rather than by unambiguously expressed solidarity toward refugees' concerns. And it seems that in achieving that aim many of the basic humanitarian and human rights' standards were called into question.[11]

Local NGOs played an important role as indirect or direct facilitators of transit migrations through the country, very often following the same humanitarian-securitization logic. However, the authorities' aim of swift transit, and the security concerns of the police, stood in conflict with rights-based and direct solidarity approaches of humanitarian actors in assisting refugees in terms of meeting their daily needs within the camps. Different old and new refugee rights, human rights, and humanitarian organizations, associations, initiatives, and networks were involved in humanitarian work. They participated, more or less in a formal capacity, in immediate aid and assistance practices, responding to needs of people, working at border crossing points and in reception centers. Few of them were religious and faith-based groups while others were more or less professional, secular, and civil initiatives and networks.

Some of them chose to participate only in humanitarian help, yet indirectly they were also party to aiding the securitization practices laid down by the authorities. The activities of the NGOs within the camps were also closely monitored by the state. Thus, until its closure in April 2016, the camp in Slavonski Brod had remained a highly securitized place where involvement of various actors was defined and restricted by the state apparatus. Within this framework, the activities and roles of humanitarian- and solidarity-based organizations became undermined. Within such a context there were few opportunities for political engagement in terms of challenging and opposing such a rigid state security regime. However, some of the NGOs were more skeptical than others in terms of how the authorities were constructing and dealing with "the crisis." These actors remained critically oriented in their reflections on the securitization practices of the state bodies: in particular, those that most directly interfered with their everyday activities in the camp, and the rights of refugees (for example, unreasonable detention of refugees and prohibiting volunteers' specific activities across the various sectors).

Some civil organizations and individuals started the "Refugees Welcome Initiative," as a kind of humanitarian platform, advocacy initiative, and a network for organizing volunteers. Other citizens interested to help started the "Are you Syrious?" network, which has become the largest grass-roots citizens' initiative all along the Balkan corridor. They expanded their network of volunteers and activities helping along the Syrian-Turkish border, at Idomeni and other camps in Greece, all the way to Calais. Both initiatives took on a more antagonistic stance toward the authorities, some of them taking on a "watchdog" role and becoming increasingly critical to the work of the authorities fostering transnational and transborder solidarity and cooperation while disobeying and challenging the dominant official discourses of the crisis and securitization. Their similar humanitarian and solidarity practices also connected them with other regional and international humanitarian and refugee rights actors along and across the Balkan corridor, through activities such as information sharing, institutional and informal networking, and political framing of solidarity, as well as advocating welcoming, inclusive attitudes and more open, fair, and humane EU policies and protection systems.

Fall of the Balkan Corridor and the Deterrent Measures

At the beginning of 2016, Austria restricted the number of refugee arrivals by introducing restrictive limits on the number of asylum claims permitted. The drastic measure of reducing asylum applications to 80 per day came into force, with 3,200 refugees being transported into Germany on a daily basis. In mid-February 2016, the heads of police forces in the countries of Macedonia, Serbia, Croatia, Slovenia, and Austria came together to hold a meeting in the Croatian capital, Zagreb. At this meeting, they agreed on reducing "the refugee movement" (now conceptualized as "migrants' movement") through the joint adoption of a standardized migrant registration system, supporting the FRONTEX activities, and selecting and profiling migrants on the basis of their nationality. In effect, this meant the gradual ending of the Balkan corridor as a safe passageway for refugees. The aim of reducing the refugee movement was taken seriously by those countries in the region. In 2016, we witnessed several new deterrent measures being implemented. In Hungary, Slovenia, and Macedonia authorities decided to reinforce the barbed wire fence and boosted the presence of army and police forces along their borders. In addition, Serbia formed joint police and military units for the purpose of patrolling its borders with Macedonia and Bulgaria. And in Croatia, the government proposed military measures in which the Croatian national army would be allowed to support the police in armed protection of the borders.[12] Such securitization and deterrent measures were combined in most countries in the region with harsher treatment meted out to arriving migrants. These measures supplemented the EU-Turkey agreement which directly contributed to ending of the Western Balkan corridor.

The EU-Turkey Summit and agreement was signed on March 7, 2016.[13] On the following day, Slovenia closed its border, announcing its full compliance with the Schengen Border Code and, consequently, the same was done by Croatia, Serbia, and Macedonia. In the following days it became apparent that tens of thousands of refugees and other forced migrants were trapped at Idomeni on the Greek-Macedonian border. Several reports made by NGOs emphasized that non-Syrian-Iraqi-Afghani (non-SIA) nationals had been denied access to the protection system, let alone denied access to the desired territories of Schengen EU. Thus the basic provisions of international refugee law, skewed by German politics (i.e., allowing access to Germany as a "desired territory", regardless of Dublin Regulations), were removed and in few months it became unattainable for asylum seekers previously passing through the Balkan corridor to reach intended destinations in Europe.

After the Balkan corridor was, to a great extent, closed off, there was increased resentment against migrants and increased interest by the authorities in many of the securitization practices that remained potentially valid in a "post-emergency setting." This referred not only to direct detention, readmission, and pushbacks on the very borders of Schengen, but also to high rejection rates and resistance to relocation and resettlement quotas. Indeed in several countries these proposals were openly rejected by governments. Of those who are now being forcibly returned to countries in southeastern Europe, via the Dublin Regulations, readmission arrangements result in an increasing number of rejected, stranded asylum seekers. Throughout the region, there is a clear lack of workable policies and programs of assistance for these people. Also some of those who got protection and refugee status experience absence of proper integration opportunities and assistance. This includes an absence of language-learning facilities, a lack of education opportunities, inadequate welfare provision, and exclusion from the labor market and civic participation. In this way, asylum seekers and refugees are kept in a situation of protracted stress and trauma.

Furthermore, changes in national asylum and migration policies of several countries in the region have resulted in provisions which tend to criminalize certain solidarity practices of direct help and support to migrants, thus pushing the debate further into the scope of irregularity and illegality. It is repeatedly noted in various reports that these restrictive developments in the legal framework also include implementation of highly problematic, institutional obstacles for refugee arrivals. For example, the BCHR et al. (2017) report indicated that asylum seekers have, regularly, been arbitrarily expelled across the region, from one country to another, very often with the use of brute force, intimidation, and devious tactics by state authorities, denying them access to asylum procedure. In this way, even the two basic pillars enshrined in the international refugee protection standards, access to territory and access to procedures for applying for international protection, are obstructed and restricted.[14]

Conclusion

In this chapter, here has been a contextualization and analysis of the local responses on transit migrations over the Balkan corridor during the recent massive arrivals of refugees in Europe in 2015–2016. Most of asylum seekers who arrived in southeastern Europe were not eager to apply for asylum in countries in this region. Inadequate reception conditions and lack of integration opportunities, along with extremely high rejection rates, have been some of the major factors that have deterred asylum seekers from the region.[15] Hence, only a small, insignificant number have decided to apply for a status that acknowledges the Balkans as a transit area they needed to traverse in order to reach anticipated destinations in Western Europe. However, the European asylum system has developed several lines of deterrence, which are intended to prevent asylum seekers from reaching these wished-for destinations.[16] In order to apply for asylum and get refugee protection, it is necessary to first arrive in Europe, which is aggravated in many ways. Several physical and juridical obstacles, designed to prevent such migrations, must first be overcome. These impediments have had a clear and marked effect on asylum migrations. The externalization measures, the Schengen/Dublin cooperation, readmissions, pushbacks, and other deterrent measures have, for years, contributed to reducing the numbers of asylum seekers reaching the core of the EU.

However, the deterring tools of the European migration system malfunctioned during the summer of 2015 when the (Western) Balkan corridor gradually emerged as a semi-institutionalized passage for the swift transit of Syrian and other refugees and migrants via Turkey to Western Europe. It was a corridor that lasted until the spring of 2016. Indeed, with a rise of the Balkan corridor, many migration obstacles were put aside for a short period of time, and the existence of the corridor came to be a unique, controlled, and state-managed passage for the massive transient movement of populations to desired destinations in Germany and other Western Europe countries. This recent mass arrival of migrants will be remembered for being the impetus of several unexpected changes in positioning of countries at the southeastern frontier of the EU. These countries, politically and administratively, constructed this phenomenon as one of refugee transit, and, later on, linked as one of "migrant crisis." One that seeks exceptional and immediate emergency relief measures in a situation of mass arrivals of people. Encountering thousands of migrants along their shores and borders, countries abandoned their usual standard responses. The ordinary measures of deterrence were put aside. Instead, Balkan countries formally defined themselves as transit countries, opening their borders, and allowing, even facilitating their further journey onto the next country through the corridor, into the core of the EU.

Indeed, at the peak of mass arrivals, the national governments along the corridor prioritized a fast, controlled, and accelerated transit over Dublin registrations and detainments. Moreover, this stance was supported by local NGOs as they saw that the corridor reduced the human costs of migration to the West. Thus, they cooperated with authorities by providing various forms of humanitarian help to transiting migrants. At the dawn of the Balkan corridor, security discourses were again more and more prominent in the official responses, media representations, and public opinion, while measures of deterrence were reestablished and reinforced. With these measures, criticisms of the authorities' policy also increased among the civil organizations, which resulted in the cooperation between the authorities and the local humanitarian actors becoming soured.

During the existence of the Balkan corridor, different approaches of humanitarianism and securitization intertwined and interplayed together, balancing from humanitarian aid, assistance, and solidarity with refugees—to that of detainment, forcible returns, pushbacks, and other securitization practices.[17] The welcoming politics of transit assistance gradually diminished over restrictive solutions, embodied in the closure of the corridor, and reintroduction of rigid border regimes with interception at borders, readmission, and deportation measures. In the post-corridor period, the SEE countries are no longer transiting areas for large numbers of migrants as they were in 2015 and 2016. Yet hundreds of migrants are still trying to cross the region on a daily basis. In the post-corridor period, the costs of migration through the region have increased, since they are not assisted by the authorities as they were during the existence of the corridor. In the current situation, they have to trespass unnoticed on their journeys further north in the migration system, in order to avoid detention, registration, and pushback. Those who end up as asylum seekers in the region have often been characterized as reluctant or stranded asylum seekers. They remain there against their will and, due to the Dublin Regulations, are denied the power to apply for asylum in intended destination countries.[18]

It seems that initial responses to the situation of mass arrivals of more than a million refugees—and the unfolding of a potential "humanitarian crisis"—actually stem from the challenges of finding common and effective institutional solutions in order to facilitate burden-sharing and reception of newcomers. Rejecting the responsibility of sharing in a form of relocation and resettlement quotas, the EU member states failed to provide mutual trust and contingency in terms of their basic values—achieving solidarity among member states, within the common asylum system. Indeed, the way the Union dealt with the recent mass events has revealed deep weaknesses in the EU cooperation structure. The aim of Brussels to deal with the mass arrivals through common, collective action—based on a responsibility-sharing principle—with cooperation and solidarity between the countries—has not been achieved. But what may be said about the particularities of the West Balkan countries' responses? Have they achieved their aims?

In the post-corridor period, there are still sizable numbers of asylum seekers in the region. Balkan countries have never been popular destination countries for asylum seekers. During the mass arrivals in 2015 and 2016, they were popular transit countries, but due to recently deployed deterrent policies and tools in the region, they are not popular in that sense neither. However, at the time of writing of this chapter (summer 2017) it seems that the strategy of aided transit further on in the system used by Croatia and most of the countries in the region in 2015 and 2016 has succeeded. The aim of the local authorities was to avoid becoming the hub or hotspot for large numbers of refugees and, indeed, most of the countries along the corridor that admitted hundreds of thousands of migrants in 2015 and 2016 did not end up as large hubs for asylum seekers, as was the case with Germany and Sweden. But the previously mentioned strategy of aided transit has provoked many reactions in the EU. In terms of the Dublin Regulations, EU countries bordering the Balkan corridor, such as Croatia, are currently being pressed by other EU countries to readmit some numbers of asylum seekers that were transiting the Balkans during 2015 and 2016. The local authorities fiercely oppose these claims. It remains to be seen whether Croatia and other countries in the region will be forced to accept massive returns of asylum seekers from other EU countries.[19] It is unclear who will win this dispute, but, on the other hand, it is absolutely clear that the local authorities in the region do not have adequate reception and resettlement facilities as well as efficient integration programs to offer to large groups of persons seeking or enjoying international refugee protection. In these circumstances different sociopolitical, administrative, and humanitarian challenges may unfold even with smaller numbers of refugees than those we have witnessed trespassing during the corridor phase, one that was defined and contested as "the refugee/migration crisis."

NOTES

1. However, due to the large numbers of arriving refugees, some "EU official statistics" may, in some cases, have inadvertently, misrepresented the numbers of arrivals. Sigona (2015) pointed to the fact that FRONTEX, in its statistical exercise, counted multiple entries for migrants, by including each border they had crossed or attempted to cross, into the territories of EU member states. Thus, a transit of an individual person may be somewhat multiplied which, retroactively, influenced the media's portrayal of the "mass arrivals," which was framed—by political rhetoric—as the "crisis of the EU (Schengen) border protection" or the "crisis of the Common European Asylum System," among other constructions of "crisis" (see de Genova and Tazzioli 2016, 7–15).
2. Large numbers of these migrants and refugees resided permanently in Austria and Sweden and other destination countries in Western Europe. Others were expelled or they returned voluntarily after the war ended in their countries. Large numbers of Kosovars were returned and majority of Bosnian refugees who in early 1990s got temporary reception in Germany were returned after the war in the country ended (Black and Koser 1999; Valenta and Ramet 2011).
3. In addition, in the early 1990s, Slovenia received tens of thousands of refugees from Bosnia while, in the late 1990s, Macedonia received several hundred thousand refugees from Kosovo (Donev, Onceva and Gligorov 2002; Valenta and Ramet 2011).
4. There are several other factors that may influence the responses of the countries in the region such as differences in the political orientations of local political elites. For example, in Croatia, the Social Democrats were in power during the time of the mass arrivals. In contrast, Hungary had a right-wing-oriented government led by Viktor Orban. This difference in political orientation influenced the way in which each country dealt with the influx of migrants. Furthermore, a lack of willingness to provide more permanent protection to the migrants may also be related to general attitudes toward immigrants within the regions.
5. Such a large interest in the transit migrations via Libya and the central Mediterranean region may be related to at least two factors. First, prior to 2015, transit migrations via Libya and the central Mediterranean route were, indeed, of a considerably larger scale than those that went through the Balkans. Second, transit migrations through Libya and the central Mediterranean region raised large media attention, as this route was, by far, the most dangerous migrant route into Europe. As a result, the debates on irregular migrations into Europe were dominated by media images of drownings in the Mediterranean Sea and reports on trafficking, exploitative practices, and quasi-slavery experiences of migrants who transited through Libya and its neighboring countries.
6. Šelo Šabić and Borić (2016) link the positive stance of the Serbian authorities with Serbia's negotiations with the EU, and Serbia's candidate status regarding future EU membership. Accordingly, Serbia's authorities did their best to appear as a responsible, constructive key partner to the EU.
7. On the official daily reports on arrivals, reception, accommodation and transit of refugees in Croatia, see MoI (2015) and MoI (2016). Also, for the initial response of the Croatian state and civil actors to the massive arrivals of refugees see Čapo (2015) and Šelo Šabić and Borić (2016).
8. See Weaver (2015) in *The Guardian*.

9. Out of 660,000 counts of migrants, only a small fraction of them (some twenty-four) lodged asylum applications during the corridor phase in Croatia (Ombudsman 2016, 152).
10. Ultimately, the left-centrist government lost in the parliamentary elections, but more because of perceived poor economic performance and social politics, rather than the issue of migration management.
11. This was also emphasized in the report of Larsen et al. (2016, 5).
12. In March 2016, the Croatian Act on State Border control, was amended with a series of provisions under which the army was given the right to "provide assistance to border police for protection of national borders in the event of security or humanitarian needs" (RoC 2016).
13. The EU-Turkey agreement included several important elements that contributed to the reduction of migrant outflows from Turkey. For further details, see EC (2016) and CoEU (2016).
14. For example, the Hungarian authorities introduced in June 2016 "deep border control," which allows police to deport migrants who were detected within eight kilometers from the border.
15. See also Baričević 2013; Brekke and Brochmann 2015; Coleridge 2013; Porobić and Županić-Iljić 2017; and Valenta et al. 2015.
16. For more see Boswell 2003 and Triandafyllidou and Dimitriadi 2014.
17. See Banich, Gerbig and Homberger 2016 and Županić-Iljić and Valenta, 2019.
18. See Brekke and Brochmann 2015 and Valenta et al. 2015.
19. In July 2017, by the judgment of the Court of Justice of the European Union, and calling on Dublin III Regulation, the Republic of Croatia is regarded as responsible for all those who crossed its border irregularly in the mass arrivals of 2015–2016. It is yet to be seen how this decision will reshape the Croatian protection system in practice. For more see CJEU (2017).

References

Banich, S., L. Gerbig, and A. Homberger. 2016. *Report on Systemic Police Violence and Push-Backs against Non-SIA People Conducted by Croatian Authorities.* Moving Europe Project, Belgrade, January 28. http://moving-europe.org/wp-content/uploads/2016/01/28.01.2016_Report-Police-Violence-and-Push-Backs.pdf

Baričević, V. 2013. "Europeanization of Asylum System and Refugee Protection: Croatian Asylum and Migration Policies." PhD diss., Ljubljana University.

BCHR, MYLA, and OXFAM (Belgrade Centre for Human Rights, Macedonian Young Lawyers Association and Oxfam). 2017. *A Dangerous 'Game': The Pushback of Migrants, Including Refugees, At Europe's Borders.* April 2017. Oxfam International https://www.oxfam.org/sites/www.oxfam.org/files/file_attachments/bp-dangerous-game-pushback-migrants-refugees-060417-en_0.pdf

Beznec, B., M. Speer, and M. Stojić Mitrović. 2016. *Governing the Balkan Route. Macedonia, Serbia and European Border Regime.* Belgrade, Serbia: December 2016. Rosa Luxemburg Stiftung Southeast Europe. https://www.rosalux.de/fileadmin/rls_uploads/pdfs/engl/Governing_the_Balkan_Route.pdf

Boswell, C. 2003. "The 'External Dimension' of EU Immigration and Asylum Policy." *International Affairs* 79, no. 3: 619–638. doi:10.1111/1468-2346.00326

Brekke, J. -P., and G. Brochmann. 2015. "Stuck in Transit: Secondary Migration of Asylum Seekers in Europe, National Differences, and the Dublin Regulation." *Journal of Refugee Studies* 28, no. 2: 145–162. doi:10.1093/jrs/feu028

CoEU (Council of the European Union). 2016. *Statement of the EU Heads of State or Government*. March 7. http://www.consilium.europa.eu/en/press/press-releases/2016/03/08/eu-turkey-meeting-statement/

CJEU (Court of Justice of the European Union). 2017. *Croatia is Responsible for Examining Applications for International Protection by Persons Who Crossed Its Border En Masse during the 2015–2016 Migration Crisis*. Press Release No 86/17. Luxembourg, July 26. Judgment in Cases C-490/16, A.S. v Slovenian Republic and C-646/16 Khadija Jafari and Zainab Jafar. https://curia.europa.eu/jcms/upload/docs/application/pdf/2017-07/cp170086en.pdf

Čapo, J. 2015. "The Security-scape and the (In)Visibility of Refugees: Managing Refugee Flow through Croatia." *Migracijske i etničke teme* 31, no. 3: 387–406. doi:10.11567/met.31.3.3

Coleridge, B. 2013. *From Back Door to Front Door: Forced Migration Routes Through Macedonia to Croatia*. Brussels: Jesuit Refugee Service Europe. http://www.refworld.org/docid/52453e7e4.html

De Genova, N., and M. Tazzioli. 2016. "Europe / Crisis: New Keywords of "the Crisis" in and of "Europe." *New Keywords Collective*. http://nearfuturesonline.org/wp-content/uploads/2016/01/New-Keywords-Collective_11.pdf

Donev, D., S. Ončeva, and I. Gligorov. 2002. "Refugee Crisis in Macedonia during the Kosovo Conflict in 1999." *Croatian Medical Journal* 43, no. 2: 184–189. http://neuron.mefst.hr/docs/CMJ/issues/2002/43/2/11885045.pdf

DW (Deutsche Welle). 2015. *Germany Suspends 'Dublin Rules' for Syrians*. August 25. http://www.dw.com/en/germany-suspends-dublin-rules-for-syrians/a-18671698

EC (European Commission). 2016. *European Commission—Fact Sheet / EU-Turkey Statement: Questions and Answers*. Brussels, March 19. http://europa.eu/rapid/press-release_MEMO-16-963_en.htm

Fargues, P., and C. Fandrich. 2012. *The European Response to the Syrian Refugee Crisis—What Next?*. MPC RR 2012/14, Robert Schuman Centre for Advanced Studies, San Domenico di Fiesole. (FI): European University Institute, http://cadmus.eui.eu/handle/1814/24836

FRONTEX. 2015. *Annual Risk Analysis 2015*. Warsaw: European Agency for the Management of Operational Cooperation at the External Borders of the Member States of the European Union. Warsaw: April. http://frontex.europa.eu/assets/Publications/Risk_Analysis/Annual_Risk_Analysis_2015.pdf

Greider, A. 2017. "Outsourcing Migration Management: The Role of the Western Balkans in the European Refugee Crisis." *Migration Policy Institute*, August 17. https://www.migrationpolicy.org/article/outsourcing-migration-management-western-balkans-europes-refugee-crisis

Grupković, B., M. J. Kojić, and V. Petronijević. 2016. *Serbia on the Refugee Route—The Humanitarian Response and Legal Adjustments*. Belgrade, Serbia: Fridrih Ebert Stiftung and European Movement in Serbia, Forum for International Relations. February. http://library.fes.de/pdf-files/bueros/belgrad/12942.pdf.

Hameršak, M., and I. Pleše. 2017. "Winter Reception and Transit Center in the Republic of Croatia: An Ethnographic View of the Slavonski Brod Refugee Camp." *Narodna umjetnost* 54, no. 1: 101–127. doi:10.15176/vol54no106

Heisbourg, F. 2015. "The Strategic Implications of the Syrian Refugee Crisis." *Survival* 57, no. 6: 7–20. doi:10.1080/00396338.2015.1116144

International Organization for Migration (IOM). 2012. *IOM Assistance and Protection to Migrants Caught in Crisis Situations.* Geneva, Switzerland, October, http://www.iom.int/files/live/sites/iom/files/What-We-Do/docs/Assisting-migrants-caught-in-crisis-IOM-activities-2012.pdf

Jutarnji List. 2017. *Uznemirujuća istina o egzodusu Hrvata: Od ulaska u Europsku uniju iseljavanje je eksplodiralo, samo je u Njemačku odselilo 180.000 naših građana.* Kristina Turčin. February 18. http://www.jutarnji.hr/vijesti/hrvatska/uznemirujuca-istina-o-egzodusu-hrvata-od-ulaska-u-europsku-uniju-iseljavanje-je-eksplodiralo-samo-je-u-njemacku-odselilo-180000-nasih-gradana/5650383/

Kallius, A., D. Monterescu, and P. K. Rajaram. 2016. "Immobilizing Mobility: Border Ethnography, Illiberal Democracy, and the Politics of the 'Refugee Crisis' in Hungary". *American Ethnologist* 43, no. 1: 25–37. doi:10.1111/amet.12260

Koser, K., and R. Black. 1999. "Limits to Harmonisation: The 'Temporary Protection' of Refugees in the European Union." *International Migration* 37, no. 3: 522–543. doi:10.1111/1468-2435.00082

Kogovšek Šalamon, N. 2016. "Asylum Systems in the Western Balkan Countries: Current Issues." *International Migration* 54, no. 6: 151–163. doi:10.1111/imig.12273

Kogovšek Šalamon, N., and V. Bajt, eds. 2016. *Razor-Wired: Reflections on Migration Movements through Slovenia in 2015.* Ljubljana, Slovenia: Peace Institute. http://www.mirovni-institut.si/wp-content/uploads/2016/03/Razor_wired_publikacija_web.pdf

Lalić Novak, G. 2016. *Azil: pravni i institucionalni aspekti* [Asylum: Legal and Institutional Aspects]. Zagreb, Croatia: Pravni fakultet Sveučilišta u Zagrebu, Studijski centar za javnu upravu i javne financije. doi:10.11567/met.33.1.5

Larsen, M., E. Demir, and M. Horvat. 2016. *Humanitarian Responses by Local Actors: Lessons Learned from Managing the Transit of Migrants and Refugees through Croatia.* IIED Working Paper. August. London: International Institute for Environment and Development. http://pubs.iied.org/pdfs/10795IIED.pdf

Lukić, V. 2016. "Understanding Transit Asylum Migration: Evidence from Serbia." *International Migration* 54, no. 4: 31–43.

Lukić, V., and V. Nikitović. 2004. "Refugees from Bosnia and Herzegovina in Serbia: A Study of Refugee Selectivity." *International Migration* 42, no. 4: 85–110. doi:10.1111/j.0020-7985.2004.00296.x

McAdam, J. 2014. "Conceptualizing 'Crisis Migration': A Theoretical Perspective." In *Humanitarian Crises and Migration: Causes, Consequences and Responses,* edited by S. F. Martin, S. Weerasinghe, and A. Taylor, 28–49. New York: Routledge.

Mesić, M., and D. Bagić. 2011. *Minority Return to Croatia—Study of an Open Process.* UNHCR, Croatia. http://www.refworld.org/docid/553a08424.html

Ombudsman. 2016. *Izvješće Pučke Pravobraniteljice za 2015. Godinu* [Ombudsman's Report for 2015]. March 31. http://ombudsman.hr/hr/component/jdownloads/send/67-2015/745-izvjesce-pp-2015-pdf

Papadopoulou, A. 2004. "Smuggling into Europe: Transit Migrants in Greece." *Journal of Refugee Studies* 17, no. 2: 169–186. doi:10.1093/jrs/17.2.167

Porobić, S., and D. Župarić-Iljić. 2017. "Access to Asylum and Reception Conditions in Western Balkans: Focus on Bosnia and Herzegovina and Croatia." In *States, the Law, and Access to Refugee Protection: Fortresses and Fairness*, edited by M. O'Sullivan and D. Stevens, 191–221. Oxford: Hart.

Rajaram, P. K. 2015. "Beyond Crisis: Rethinking the Population Movements at Europe's Border." *FocaalBlog*. October 19. http://www.focaalblog.com/2015/10/19/prem-kumar-rajaram-beyond-crisis

Ramet, S. P., and M. Valenta, eds. 2016. *Ethnic Minorities and Politics in Post-Socialist Southeastern Europe*. Cambridge, UK: Cambridge University Press.

Republic of Croatia MoI (Ministry of Interior). 2016. *Archive 2015: Reception and Accommodation of Migrants*. http://stari.mup.hr/main.aspx?id=225851

Republic of Croatia. MoI (Ministry of Interior). *Reception and accommodation of migrants*. http://stari.mup.hr/219696.aspx

Republic of Croatia. 2016. Zakon o dopuni zakona o nadzoru državne granice [Amendments to the Law on State Border Control], *Narodne novine* 83/2013, 27/2016. https://narodne-novine.nn.hr/clanci/sluzbeni/2016_03_27_784.html

Sigona, N. 2015. "Seeing Double? How the EU Miscounts Migrants Arriving at its Borders." *The Conversation*. October 16. https://theconversation.com/seeing-double-how-the-eu-miscounts-migrants-arriving-at-its-borders-49242

Stojić Mitrović, M. 2014. "Serbian Migration Policy Concerning Irregular Migration and Asylum in the Context of the EU Integration Process." *Issues in Ethnology and Anthropology* 9, no. 4:1105–1120. https://www.eap-iea.org/index.php/eap/article/view/96/88

Šelo Šabić, S., and S. Borić. 2016. *At the Gate of Europe: A Report on Refugees on the Western Balkan Route*. Zagreb, Croatia: Friedrich Ebert Stiftung. http://library.fes.de/pdf-files/bueros/kroatien/13059.pdf

Šelo Šabić, S. 2017. "Humanitarianism and its Limits: The Refugee Crisis Response in Croatia." In *The Migrant Crisis: European Perspectives and National Discourses*, edited by M. Barlai, B. Fähnrich, C. Griessler, M. Rhomberg, 93–106. Münster, Germany: LIT Verlag.

Triandafyllidou, A., and A. Dimitriadi. 2014. "Deterrence and Protection in the EU's Migration Policy." *The International Spectator* 49, no. 4: 146–162. doi:10.1080/03932729.2014.956280

Valenta, M., and S. P. Ramet, eds. 2011. *The Bosnian Diaspora: Integration in Transnational Communties*. Farnham, UK: Ashgate.

Valenta, M., and Z. Strabac. 2013. "The Dynamics of Bosnian Refugee Migrations in the 1990s, Current Migration Trends and Future Prospects." *Refugee Survey Quarterly* 32, no. 1: 1–22. doi:10.1093/rsq/hdt013

Valenta, M., D. Zuparic-Iljic, and T. Vidovic. 2015. "The Reluctant Asylum-Seekers: Migrants at the Southeastern Frontiers of the European Migration System." *Refugee Survey Quarterly* 34, no. 3: 95–113. doi:10.1093/rsq/hdv009

Vezovnik, A. 2017. "Securitizing Migration in Slovenia: A Discourse Analysis of the Slovenian Refugee Situation." *Journal of Immigrant & Refugee Studies* 16, no. 1–2: 1–18. doi:10.1080/15562948.2017.1282576

Weaver, M., and Agencies. 2015. "Croatia 'Will Not Become a Migrant Hotspot' Says Prime Minister." *The Guardian*, September 18. www.theguardian.com/world/2015/sep/18/croatia-refugees-zoran-milanovic-migrant-hotspot

Župarić-Iljić, D. 2017. "Environmental Change and Involuntary Migration: Environmental Vulnerability and Displacement Caused by the 2014 Flooding in South-Eastern Europe."

In *Ecology and Justice: Contributions From the Margins*, edited by M. Domazet, 137–164. Zagreb, Croatia: Institute for Political Ecology. http://ipe.hr/wp-content/uploads/2017/06/Ecology-and-Justice-WEB.pdf

Župarić-Iljić, D., and M. Valenta. 2019. "Opportunistic Humanitarianism and Securitization Discomfort along the Balkan Corridor: The Croatian Experience." In *Refugee Protection and Civil Society in Europe*, edited by M. Feischmidt, L. Pries, and C. Cantat, 129–160. New York: Palgrave Macmillan.

CHAPTER 22

WARS AND MIGRATION CRISES IN CENTRAL AMERICA

On Missing Persons during Armed Conflict and International Migration

NINNA NYBERG SØRENSEN

THE relationship between war and migration is complex and complicated by the fact that neither of them is a monolithic phenomenon (Knudsen, Strand, and Paasche 2013). Armed conflicts, whether within or between states, produce migration, as well as containment and involuntary immobility (Carling 2002; Lubkeman 2008). Postwar political economies produce sustained pressures to migrate that often divide families between different countries and produce the physical absences of loved ones that may invoke memories of wartime losses. Apart from being a mere economic option, international migration may become the "social project of a postwar generation," a project that in times of enhanced border control may demand "as much ingenuity as joining a revolutionary movement must have required" in earlier generations (McAllister and Nelson 2013, 33). How much those mobilized by war or dispossession become internally displaced, asylum seekers, or immigrants in third countries generally depends as much on the global migration regime as on the so-called root causes of these phenomena, as does the construction of particular migration flows as a crisis (Zolberg 2001).

The *Merriam Webster Dictionary* defines a crisis as "an unstable or crucial time of state of affairs in which a decisive change is impending, one with the distinct possibility of a highly undesirable outcome." "Crisis," the *Oxford English Dictionary* adds, is moreover "a time of intense difficulty and danger" during which "difficult or important decisions must be made." A crisis involves a turning point that might lead to either recovery or catastrophe. Thus, crises are understood as temporary. However, for a great number of people, they are endemic rather than episodic. War may turn into an aftermath or post-conflict situation without altering the social inequalities that led to it in the first place, grievances merely being displaced to other sectors. For those struggling to make ends meet by migrating without permission, a sense of crisis may become a chronic and constant background, not a decisive moment of opportunity, but a condition (Vigh 2008).

Crisis is a central concept in migration research. Scholars, and often the migrants themselves, explain migration as reaction to a crisis. Generally, crises have tended to be thought of in economic terms in conventional labor migration studies. Forced migration and refugee studies have tended to emphasize the political and security aspects of crisis situations (Stepputat and Sørensen 2014). However, economic and political factors cannot easily be disentangled when trying to understand migration trajectories in Central America (Morrison and May 1994). Rather, what emerges is a complex mobility system consisting of internal, regional, and international migration, mobilized by shifting structural conditions over time. Simultaneously, different trajectories tend to converge and coexist according to the relationship between economic and political instabilities in the country of origin and the hope for better livelihood opportunities, security, or family reunification in *el Norte*.

Meanwhile, irregularity, together with references to "alarming numbers" or "chaotic forms of arrival," habitually develop into crises, as happened in 2014, when an "unprecedented" number of Central American children and young people crossed the Mexico-US border just as the race for the US presidential elections was beginning. Staging irregular migration in general and child migration in particular as a migration crisis, Trump declared "war on migration." This war and its solution, envisaged as "a beautiful wall," should be seen as the culmination of stricter and increasingly militarized border enforcement policies. However, framing migration as a crisis without regard to its underlying realities has resulted in a reshuffling of the meanings of irregular, undocumented, or unauthorized migration, which is now to be thought of as "illegal," "criminal" and a risk to national identity and security (Massey, Duran, and Pren 2016). When such discursive moves are made, migration ceases to be understood as a reaction to a crisis and becomes the crisis itself.

From the perspective of Central American migrants, the relationship between war and migration emerges in different forms and evokes different memories in those affected. Some may compare the risk of fleeing armed conflicts to the risk of dying along the migration trail, while others may draw parallels between forced displacement and deportation. To the extent that historical experiences of political violence and its consequences continue to inform contemporary migration experiences, the legal violence encountered upon arrival can be compared equally to the violence suffered during the armed conflicts at the place of origin. Some migrants may experience similarities between the militarization of life in Central America and the immigration enforcement strategies of the United States, while others find parallels between the disappearance of the politically targeted in Latin America and deportations from the United States (Menjivar 2013, 231). For Central American children who migrated with their parents and who for various reasons continue to live in a tenuous legality, being "exiled home" (deported) and having to go through yet another displacement trauma (Coutin 2016) spells crisis in capital letters.

The focus of this paper is on the tangled histories of war and postconflict migration and the missing persons that both produce. The chapter uses forced disappearances during Guatemala's thirty-six years of armed conflict and clandestine postwar migration experiences as the empirical basis for the analysis. Despite experiences that are particular to the Guatemalan context, most notably the genocide against the Mayan people, the analysis applies to Central America in general.

Two interlinked concepts are used to capture the phenomenon of disappearances: "missing person" and "forced disappearance." While the term "missing person" foregrounds the loss and uneasy position of the relatives and communities left behind, the term "forced disappearance" directs attention to the intentionality of state actions directed at establishing order through terror, and as such turns our attention to the perpetrators. Following Parr and Fyfe's (2012) call for a conceptual reassessment of disruptive human mobilities, the chapter highligths differences and continuities in the crises provoked by disappearances in families and communities, as well as in the forms of politics that disappearances give rise to.

Global concern for missing people is predominantly cast as responses to war, armed conflict, terrorism, and natural disasters, or, when involving migrants, to trafficking, and is then framed largely in terms of right-to-know legislation for those reporting the disappearance (Parr and Fyfe 2012, 620). As the significance of forced disappearances lies in the "power it has to induce collective anguish that can be exploited for social and political ends" (Robins 2016, 308), the interest in juxtaposing them stems from the observation that both situations seem to involve disciplinary effects.

Trespassing Concepts: Theorizing Missing Persons during Armed Conflict and Migration

"Missing persons" and "forced disappearance" are two legal categories introduced to politics and policies around bodies that cannot be accounted for. These terms have different histories and foreground questions of suffering and accountability in different ways.

Missing persons are defined as "all those whose whereabouts are unknown to their families or, based on reliable information, who are reported missing as a consequence of armed conflict, internal violence or internal disturbances".[1] This definition points to a need to address the uncertainty of the prolonged absence of particular people from their families and social surroundings, but it does not refer to the possibility of intentionality or force having been behind their disappearance.

The need to define a missing person arises from the practical problems faced by relatives of the missing. When a person goes missing, the legal position of other family members may be disturbed, as many rights and duties are regulated through family position. Large international organizations, such as the International Committee of the Red Cross (ICRC) and the International Commission of Missing Persons (ICMP), advocate "missing person" as an administrative and legal category situated between the living and the dead. Beyond practical matters in need of a solution (inheritance, child custody rights, remarriage, to name but a few), the notion of the missing person is additionally tied to psychological models of trauma, mourning and healing, as well as to discourses of human rights. The families left behind arguably possess "the right to know," a right that, in the aftermath of war, has often extended to political processes of reconciliation.[2]

Obviously not all missing persons wish to be found, provoking the questions "missing for whom" and "whose right to be found?" In the Central American context, some may be fleeing abusive family relations or escaping threats from or recruitment into deadly gangs. Others prefer to conceal their whereabouts from relatives because of "failed migration projects" or to avoid unfulfillable pressures to send back remittances. Yet others, often those who suffer fatal injury during the undocumented voyage, may wish to stay "missing" to relieve poor relatives from yet another burden (Sørensen 2013). The disappearance of many others, however, may be due to injuries and deaths occurring as an effect of the global migration system.

The category of *forced disappearances* evolved in the latter part of the twentieth century, when Latin America became associated with the state-sponsored practice of abducting student leaders, trade unionists, human rights activists, and others considered political dissidents or subversives, who were taken to secret places, where they were never heard from again. The Latin American legacy is engraved in the very term "disappearance," which is a translation of the Spanish word *desaparecido*.[3]

Forced disappearance was established as a crime against humanity in the Inter-American Convention on the Forced Disappearance of Persons, adopted by the Organization of American States (OAS) in 1994 and entering into force in 1996.[4] The OAS convention preceded the International Convention for the Protection of All Persons from Enforced Disappearance (ICPPED), adopted by the United Nations General Assembly in December 2006, and entering into force on December 23, 2010.[5] The two conventions essentially contain the same elements. They establish a definition of forced disappearance as the arrest, detention, and other forms of deprivation of freedom, by or with the acquiescence of agents of the state, followed by a refusal to acknowledge the deprivation of liberty, concealment of the fate, or whereabouts of the disappeared person, and denying that person recourse to legal remedies and protection of the law (Frey 2009).

State practices of forced disappearances take the form of secret or hidden actions that conceal evidence and distort the assigning of accountability. However, the secrecy of these actions is contradicted by the fact that disappearances are not only a question of getting rid of unwanted persons with impunity, but are also intended as a warning to the family and community of the disappeared. The enforced disappearance of persons is not just a state practice of the past, Ralph Rozema (2011) argues, but has become linked to specific processes of globalization in which dehumanizing images of victims coalesce and interact with a variety of actors in specific localities. This is certainly the case for migration experiences in contemporary Central America. Although several recent studies confirm that stricter border enforcement practices are the principal cause of the growing number of injuries, deaths and disappearances of those who travel irregularly through Mexico and along the Mexican-US border (Massey, Durand, and Pren 2016; Sanchez 2015), it remains a contested issue whether missing persons should be included among the forcibly disappeared.

Prevention through Deterrence

Much of the analysis of forced disappearance has taken the Italian philosopher Giorgio Agamben's (2005) notion of a "state of exception" as a point of departure for understanding the deployment of this extreme form of violent practice by states and state-like actors. The state of exception denotes the augmentation of government powers during times of crisis, often perceived or represented as situations in which sovereignty is under threat. It materializes in the authorization of an unusual extension of power, presented as a provisional measure that legalizes the suspension of the normal legal order and strips individuals of their rights and even legal identities. A central part of Agamben's argument is that the state of exception has tended to become a normal or normalized technique of governing during the twentieth century, a rule rather than an exception.

Given the mounting evidence that states prevalently resort to practices of forced disappearance, it may be difficult to sustain the argument that such disappearances are exceptional phenomena. However, if the term "exceptional" is taken to indicate the conditions under which emergency legislation is used to suspend constitutional protections or the (inter)national rule of law, disappearances, like other forms of state violence, can be interpreted as exceptional phenomena. This interpretation also reveals that the state of exception not is a special kind of law, but rather a de facto suspension of the judicial order itself, in which instances of extralegal sovereign violence become routinized (Banu Barger 2014).

Since the early 1990s there has been a general tendency to increase the barriers against unwanted migration, suggesting a broad commitment to border enforcement as the primary instrument of immigration control (Andersson 2014; Cornelius and Salehyan 2007). A side effect of making effective border control the principal activity has been a "reassemblage of the politics of containment and migrant movement" and an "intertwinement of military and humanitarian interventions" (Tazzioli 2016, 2). In order to mobilize our gaze beyond the notion of "migration as crisis" and to approach the "human security crises" produced by border politics, Tazzioli suggests that we view the humanitarian frontier in terms of mechanisms of the capture, selection, and apprehension of migrants' lives, as well on the increases in the costs and risks associated with crossing borders, including the growing number of border deaths and disappearances among unauthorized travelers.

Much of the analysis of border militarization and enforcement along the Mexico-US border has centered around the "prevention through deterrence strategy" adopted by the US Border Police in 1994 as an operational strategy for securing this border. The strategy consists in the strengthening of enforcement at well-established urban crossing points (such as Tijuana-San Diego and Ciudad Juarez-El Paso) and the consequent pushing of people into remote and dangerous border zones (Slack et al. 2016). The approach has been rolled out in stages and implemented in different sectors at different times (Massey, Durand, and Pren 2016). An indisputable consequence of concentrated border enforcement operations is the spatial dispersal of irregular attempts at entry and a rechanneling of migration paths into remote and treacherous areas of the border (Doty 2011). In addition to rechanneling, prevention through deterrence significantly increases the costs and physical risks associated with irregular border crossing and has led to an increase in migrant apprehensions and deaths. Observing the shifts in the political geography of migration policy in ever more deadly directions, Roxanne Lynn Doty suggests that contemporary migration policies turn irregular migrants into "bare life" whose deaths are deemed of little importance. Spaces of exception are created in dangerous border areas in which "bare life can be taken without apology, classified as neither homicide nor sacrifice" (Doty 2011, 601). Such spaces function to provide a moral alibi for any responsibility for the death of traveling migrants and asylum-seekers on the part of the states involved.

Reporting from the Mexico-US borderlands, Jason De León suggests that forced disappearances experienced by Central American migrants are "neither random, nor senseless, but rather are part of a federal plan that rarely has been publicly illuminated and exposed for what it is: a killing machine that simultaneously uses and hides behind the viciousness of the Sonoran Desert" (De León 2015, 3). To the extent that the strategy is used explicitly to demonstrate that migrants crossing through remote, uninhabited expanses of land along the border can find themselves in mortal danger, it could be argued that violence, not security objectives, is what guides border enforcement strategies, through a militarized logic and strategic plan for enforcement that emphasizes pain, suffering, and trauma as deterrents to undocumented migration (Slack et al. 2016, 8). It is easy to draw parallels between this situation and the warning effects of forced disappearances during times of war.

Other parallels can be drawn as the destruction of bodies scattered to the winds has similar political implications. Left in remote locations, the destruction of clothes, personal effects, and bones creates an actual undercounting of migrant deaths. In effect, the destruction of corpses both erases evidence of the human costs of state practices and sends a strong message to the families of missing migrants, who cannot be sure whether their traveling relatives are dead or alive: "Don't go, you may die! Or, if you go and end up dying, it's your own fault!" In drawing parallels between historical disappearances during periods of political conflict in Latin America and the migrants currently being "swallowed up by the desert and never heard from again," De Leon further pinpoints how the bodies left in the desert reveal the physical boundaries of sovereignty and the symbolic edge of humanity (De León 2015, 84).

Looking at migrant disappearances through the prism of "disruptive human mobilities" further enables analysis of the "missing" as an active category. A range of people, offices and techniques are involved in defining the "missing" person and seeking explanations and closure through a range of practices. Who is missing and for what reasons is thus a political project, in which being missing is always partial, "cast in the shadow of unacknowledged ungrievable lives," and certain subgroups of any population are likely to remain unreported. The unreported missing should remind us that "absence is a political ascription" and that the "recognition of diverse powers of erasure is fundamental to a project which seeks to understand missing geographies" (Parr and Fyfe 2012, 618).

Los desaparecidos: Guatemala's Missing

> If one day I don't appear or they kidnap me or something happens to me, don't go looking for me, because you'll never find me.
>
> (Jorge Humberto Ganados Hernández)[6]

Since 2010, August 30 has marked the International Day of Enforced Disappearances. The proposal to commemorate the forcibly disappeared was put forward by the Latin American Federation of the Detained-Disappeared (FEDEFAM), a regional organization dedicated to assisting associations of relatives and human rights bodies in the investigation of *all cases* of forced disappearances and the judgment and sanctioning of those responsible for such crimes. That the initiative came from Latin America can be seen in light of the fact that more than 150,000 people were forcibly disappeared during the violent dictatorships and armed conflicts that haunted most of the region during the 1970s and 1980s.[7] As Kirsten Weld emphasizes, the estimates are "necessarily imprecise because the crime itself is designed to produce uncertainty, leaving no corpses, no traces, no explanations, and hence, no accountability" (Weld 2013, 8).

Guatemala's Armed Conflict

Guatemala experienced Central America's longest and most violent armed conflict, which lasted from 1960 to 1996, when peace accords were finally reached. During these years, state-sponsored campaigns of terror and mass killings left a death toll of between 150,000 and 200,000 civilians, rupturing the country's social fabric. Some 440 villages were razed to the ground (Sanford 2003). Only 6,159 enforced disappearances were registered during the conflict, many of those who were taken never making it into the official records. It is estimated that the total number of forcibly disappeared Guatemalans is closer to 50,000, including around 5,000 children who were separated from their families, murdered, put up for adoption after their parents were murdered, or escaped to the refugee camps where they were taken care of by other families (International Commission of Jurists 2015). The conflict also displaced as many as 1.5 million Guatemalan nationals, of whom an estimated 200,000 fled to Mexico and fewer to other Central American countries, the United States, and Canada, while the rest remained internally displaced within Guatemala's borders (Sørensen 2015). According to testimonies and other sources collected by the Commission for Historical Clarification (CEH 1999), the military and other state-sanctioned entities such as the state police and the auto-defense civil patrols (PACs) were responsible for 93 percent of the human rights violations and acts of violence conducted during the conflict. Only three percent of the atrocities were attributed to the guerrilla forces, responsibility for the remaining four percent never being established. The Project to Recover Historical Memory (REMHI 1998), commissioned by the Catholic Church, attributed just under 80 percent of the violations to the army and just under 10 percent to the guerrillas. Both reports, however, determine significant state involvement in the more than 600 massacres and acts of genocide against the Mayan population. The massacres peaked during the early to mid-1980s when the military carried out scorched earth campaigns in rural areas, literally wiping out hundreds of indigenous villages (Sanford 2003; Schirmer 1998; Stepputat 1999).[8]

Additional forced disappearances took place in urban areas. Testimonies given to human rights defenders by family members established the modus operandi: usually a group of armed individuals dressed as civilians snatched targeted individuals from the streets in pure daylight, forced them into cars with polarized windows, and took them to interrogation centers, where information was extracted through torture. Others were taken from their homes during the night. Relatives and friends of the abducted were never officially notified and usually never ascertained whether their relatives were dead or alive. Very few of the forcibly disappeared ever reappeared alive, being disposed of instead in secret mass graves in local cemeteries or clandestine graves on the grounds of military bases.

Efforts to End Impunity and Recognize the Victims

Demands by family members and other actions carried out by nonstate actors such as the National Coordinating Committee of Guatemalan Widows (CONAVIGUA), the Mutual Assistance Group (GAM), and the Association of Families of Detained and Disappeared Persons in Guatemala (FAMDEGUA) have been crucial in claiming justice. Another important player in establishing truth and accountability is the Guatemalan Forensic Anthropology Foundation (FAFG). From its foundation in 1997 to the present, FAFG has exhumed more than 1,650 gravesites, discovered the remains of over 7,000 victims, helped identify missing family members, and provided crucial testimony in trials in Guatemala and Spain, all aimed at holding the intellectual authors and perpetrators to account and winning justice for surviving family members. The

Guatemalan state, however, has a long way to go in complying with its obligation to find the missing.

Contrary to the experiences reported elsewhere in Latin America, where it is possible to talk about a time before, during, and after dictatorships and armed conflicts, forced disappearances remain a current threat to the Guatemalan population, as does impunity for the crime of forcibly making people disappear. Most of the disappearances that take place within Guatemala's borders are perpetrated by powerful parallel or hidden structures, including drugs and human trafficking networks, or until recently illegal adoption networks, in which state officials have been repeatedly proven to be implicated (Reyes Aragón/Impunity Watch 2013). Contemporary cases of forced disappearances are often neglected by the Guatemalan authorities, who insist on labeling them acts of organized crime without political motives. That political motives remain operative is evidenced by reports of social leaders involved in protests against, for example, mega-mining projects being kidnapped and later being found dead with bodies showing signs of torture.[9]

Convictions of Forced Disappearance, Perpetrators, and the Guatemalan State

In 1999 the first efforts to hold the intellectual masterminds behind the Guatemalan genocide to account began in Spain, based on a criminal complaint against former president Ríos Montt and other senior officials filed by the Rigoberta Menchú Foundation. The legal proceedings in Spain helped construct a court case in Guatemala, which in 2012 indicted Ríos Montt on accusations of torture, genocide, forced disappearances, state terrorism, and crimes against humanity. The trial resulted in Ríos Montt's conviction and a sentence of eighty years in prison and was the first time that a former head of state had been convicted of genocide by a national court. However, a few weeks later, the judgment was overturned. A retrial was ordered but suspended in a ruling in May 2016. Almost a year later, on March 31, 2017, the court ruled that Rios Montt could stand trial for genocide in the *Dos Erres Massacre*, in which more than two hundred civilians were killed. At the time of writing, the case is still pending.[10]

The crime of forced disappearance was included in the Guatemalan penal code in 1996. In 2008, the Constitutional Court accepted the continuous character of the crime. To date, however, only eight cases have reached the courts, and of these two are still pending. The first, the *Chotalum* or *Cusanero* case, concerns at least five men and one woman who were subjected to forcible disappearance during 1982–1984; it led to the conviction of a military commissioner in 2009. Later that year, two military commissioners and one colonel were sentenced to fifty-three years in prison for the forced disappearances of eight men in *el Jute*. In this case, the court declared open the criminal proceedings against the National Ministry of Defense, the Chief of Staff of National Defense, and the Commander of Military Reserves of the department of

Chiquimula. The third and fourth cases both concern the forced disappearance of university student Edgar Fernando Garcia, who was arrested by the National Police in 1984. On October 10, 2010, two agents of the National Police were sentenced to forty years in prison. For the first time, evidence was provided from the Historical Archive of the National Police (discovered in 2005), as well as the documents known as the "Military Diary." These documents were given probative value, since they give credence to the coercive and violent measures that the government of the time used to attack those it declared internal enemies. Three years later, the same case resulted in forty-year prison sentences being handed down to the former director of the National Police and his deputy, after it was established that the National Police had served as an instrument of the Guatemalan army in capturing and forcing "subversive elements" to disappear. The fifth case, that of Paredes Cheguen, also concerns a student who was arrested by the security forces in 1982. The case was first lost in 2011 but appealed and won almost two years later. The final case resulting in a prison sentence concerns the forced capture, torture, and later forced disappearance of Edgar Enrique Sáenz Calito. In two of these cases, the lawsuit was presented by the Human Rights Law Office (BDH) together with the Association of Families of the Detained-Disappeared in Guatemala (FAMDEGUA). The remaining cases were prepared by the Group of Mutual Assistance (GAM) and/or the Human Rights Ombudsman's Office (PDH).[11]

For over ten years, victims' groups have worked tirelessly for the passage of legislation to establish a National Commission to Search for Victims of Enforced Disappearance and other forms of Disappearance (Law 35-90), recommended by both CEH and REHMI. The law was introduced in 1996, but has not yet been passed by Congress.

Guatemalan Mobilities and Disappearances

> Back then the Guatemalan army disappeared people. Today people disappear along the migrant trail. *La migra* and the US police have become the new authority.
>
> (Personal interview, 2012)[12]

The author had the luck to live and work in Guatemala from 2005 to 2009. During these years, the official attitude toward the ordinary Guatemalan migrant of poorer, rural, and often indigenous descent changed from celebrating the "remittance-sending migrant hero" to a somewhat more indifferent attitude toward "the deportee trash" (Sørensen 2011). Toward the end of the 1990s, the numbers of undocumented Guatemalan migrants forcibly returned from Mexico or the United States steadily increased, and the special office of the Human Rights Ombudsman's Office for the Uprooted and Migrants (the Defensoría de población desarraigada y migrante) began to receive reports of migrants going missing.

But what is the history of Guatemalan migration, and how is it connected with war? Due to the high profile of refugees during the civil war, early Guatemalan labor migrations have received little scholarly attention (Jonas 2013). However, until the 1970s, such involvement was generally regional and temporal in character, its purpose being to sustain local livelihoods (Morales Gamboa et al. 2011). The civil war (1960–1996) changed this pattern by causing massive forced displacements, primarily during the second half of the 1970s and throughout the 1980s. When the Peace Accords were finally agreed, an estimated 43,000 refugees were officially repatriated to Guatemala (Stepputat 1999). Others returned under their own steam. The bulk of the approximately 120,000 asylum applications handed in by Guatemalans in the United States were routinely rejected without necessarily leading to a return. Of those remaining without documentation in the United States, some were able to legalize their status later, while many, maybe up to two-thirds, remained undocumented. Whatever their legal status, Guatemalans living and working in the United States provided information and social network links for family members, who, due to a mixture of poverty, a lack of public policies, and increasing local insecurity, continued to leave the country (Hagan 2008).

During the armed conflict, Guatemalan government officials claimed that many of the disappeared were in reality individuals who had left for the United States as economic migrants without telling their families. Today both Mexican and United States state officials attribute the disappearances of irregularly travelling Guatemalan migrants to human smugglers, traffickers, and organized criminal networks, which they define as unscrupulous, greedy, and violent. In these accounts, disappearances are naturally attributed to either the migrant or nonstate actors alone, thus downplaying the social contexts that shape these journeys and make reliance on smugglers necessary in the first place (Sanchez 2017) and denying the responsibility of human-made policies and practices of exercising force.

Ironically, President Otto Peréz Molina—a former Guatemalan army general and intelligence chief accused of involvement in civil war atrocities in 2013 and jailed on accusations of involvement in a multimillion customs fraud case in September 2014—wrote a comment for the British newspaper *The Guardian* in which he blamed the United States for quickly forgetting US cold war involvement in Central America and the war on drugs as structural factors behind the "child migrants crisis." His own involvement was of course left unmentioned.[13]

Body Counts

Until recently, Guatemala did not keep records of the kidnapping, disappearance, or killing of Guatemalan nationals on Mexican territory. However, the discovery of mass graves containing irregular Central American migrants in Tamaulipas in 2010 and San Fernando in 2011 raised national awareness of the problem. During 2011, approximately a hundred reports of the disappearance of a family member were filed with the Foreign Ministry or the Human Rights Ombudsman's Office (Sørensen 2015). Eight percent of the identifiable bodies found between 2001 and 2014 in southern Arizona were Guatemalan.[14] During 2014 and 2015 the Foreign Ministry of Guatemala (MINEX) received reports of 82 adults and four children having disappeared without a trace after leaving for the United States. But few cases are reported to MINEX, as the process is complicated. Before filing a complaint, family members must present themselves to the Ministry of Justice and obtain a certificate proving a complaint has been made. They are then sent to the Office for Victim Attention, which then sends the cases to particular prosecutors, such as the Prosecutor of Crimes against Life or the Prosecutor of Organized Crime. Due to a lack of funding, no special Prosecutor for Attention to Migration Issues has so far been established, and the family members of disappeared migrants basically depend on how MINEX, through its understaffed consular offices, manages each case before the Mexican or US governments. Apart from complicated processes, many are afraid to report a family member missing due to the fact that they left clandestinely: As there relatives travelled irregularly, they do not think that they have the right to be looked for. Human Rights groups report that the family members of disappeared migrants suffer from traumas comparable to those suffered by the families of victims of forced disappearances, including physical and psychological illness due to a lack of closure.[15]

A joint analysis conducted by the Mexican Institute for Studies and Dissemination on Migration (INEDIM) and the Guatemala-based Central American Institute for Social and Development Studies (INCEDES) points to restrictive border control policies as the main factor behind the disappearances of Guatemalan migrants while in transit in Mexico (INEDIM 2011). Interestingly, social organization around the issue of migrant disappearances uses the powerful symbol of missing persons developed by civil society and victim or survivor groups or both to address the issue of forced disappearances by making themselves publicly visible with a picture, often a worn and faded one, of their lost family member. They also use the political demand developed during the war: "Alive you took them, alive we want them back."

The Central American Migration Movement and the *Caravanas* established by Central American mothers, who over the past sixteen years have gone searching for disappeared migrants along the migration trails, insist that current migration from the region not is irregular labor migration, but rather a case of forced displacement.[16] Central American migrants flee from extreme violence and the risk of imminent death caused by death threats, extortion, or the assassination of a close relative by criminal gangs or "the narcos," who operate with impunity in the region. They build their argument around various estimates of the abduction of more than 20,000 migrants on Mexican territory every year, of between 72,000 and 120,000 migrants who went missing between 2006 and 2016, of 24,000 bodies buried in unmarked graves in municipal cemeteries, of 40,000 unidentified bodies brought to public morgues, and of 174 mass graves that have so far been acknowledged and keep appearing throughout Mexico. The ample evidence of the complicity of government officials with organized crime and human smuggling networks legally qualifies these disappearances as forced.[17] Evidence produced by international organizations such as Medecins Sans Frontières confirms that current migration from Central America's Northern Triangle constitutes a human(itarian) security crisis, in which people are running for their lives (MSF 2017).

In response to the crisis of migrant disappearances, FAFG has diversified its traditional activities in the area of transitional justice to include disappearances related to migration, citizen security, and natural disasters. In those cases in which people have disappeared during migration, FAFG focuses on their identification by taking DNA samples from family members that can be matched later with unidentified migrants in mass graves or morgues in Mexico and elsewhere.[18] In times of donor withdrawal from sectors related to the peace process and postconflict restructuring this is probably a wise move, and a move that fits the present situation in Guatemala well. However, as the Guatemalan state's provision of justice to the victims of forced disappearances is still an open battlefield, a recent proposal from a multilateral donor to include migrant disappearances in its work against forced disappearances has received mixed reactions from the group of organizations behind Law 35-90.[19] A few hardliners may find wartime disappearances of revolutionaries more honorable than the disappearance of poor migrants. Others are afraid that joining forces with victims of contemporary disappearances could weaken the cause of the many, still unresolved, historical cases.

Conclusion

When contextualized historically, forced disappearances can only be regarded as a constant threat to Guatemalan lives. During the armed conflict, the Guatemalan state systematically used forced disappearances to stabilize state power through terror and to produce "national" communities purified of unwanted (but national) political subjects. In the postwar period, Guatemalan citizens remain subject to forced disappearances in various situations, most notably (but not exclusively) when attempting to cross state borders without authorization. In the latter case, forced disappearances move from the national to the transnational arena. Whereas the missing persons produced during instances of armed conflict generally are nationals, and state responsibility therefore more easily can be placed on a particular nation state, disappearances along the migration trajectory mostly affect nonnationals, whose mobility increasingly is deemed a criminal activity for which the migrants themselves therefore tend to be held personally responsible, or, as is perhaps more often the case, their disappearance can be attributed to the workings of a criminal human smuggling and trafficking industry.

The logic behind this reasoning somehow resembles the tendency within migration studies to rank migrants along a continuum of choice, ranging from free (voluntary) and thus proactive migration at one end to unfree (forced) and thus reactive migration in response to living situations encompassing various aspects of threat at the other (Khosravi 2010). Only the latter deserves a humanitarian response.

However, writing on Post-Gatekeeper US-Latina fiction and nonfictional accounts written on the theme of border deaths, Marta Caminero-Santangelo (2010) turns our attention to the ways in which dead migrant bodies become a focal point for critiques of border policy. By turning exactly to the trope of the absent body of one who is lost during times of political repression and often invoking the United States in respect of the political situation in the home country, transnational causes behind the disappearances come into focus. The question of what migrant disappearances do to a sense of collective and individual identity, Caminero-Santangelo argues, is related to the history of political disappearances in Latin America. In both instances, the instability of identity is underscored not by the materiality of found bodies but by the absence of bodies to even attempt to identify (Camineroro-Santangelo 2010). Despite similarities, the family members of those who have disappeared due to the actions of repressive state forces generally know who the perpetrators are and may subsequently be able to attribute responsibility to them. Border disappearances, on the other hand, render causes and explanatory factors more uncertain and may in fact therefore be more disruptive of family structures: Has a father disappeared, or has he abandoned his wife and children? Has a young woman disappeared through force, or did she choose to vanish without a trace in order to escape family violence, or other forms of repression capable of being extended transnationally when migrant social networks connect localities scattered over great distances?

In the case of Central America, recognizing migrants as subject to forced disappearances has gone through a process in which "disappearance" was first acknowledged without adding to it the adjective "forced," as the participation of state agents was not determined at the outset. After violent conflicts, formal bodies are often established to deal with victims and perpetrators, such as truth commissions and prosecutorial bodies, whose rulings determine who can be considered a victim. The families of missing migrants have no access to such processes, creating ambiguity in the very notion of forced disappearance. However, by calling the disappearances of migrants forced and by pointing to the involvement of state agents in such disappearances (thereby underscoring the state of impunity that surrounds such acts), the ground is prepared for converting the notion of "migration crises" from a question of unwanted flows in need of military responses to a human crisis produced exactly by the militarization of the global migration regime.

Notes

1. See passage on "Guiding Principles/Model Law on the Missing" in ICRC, "The Domestic Implementation of International Humanitarian Law: A Manual, Annex IV," https://www.icrc.org/eng/resources/documents/publication/pdvd40.htm
2. See ICMP, "The Missing," https://www.icmp.int/the-missing/
3. Disappearance is attributed to the characteristic tactics of abduction and secret execution used by Guatemalan death squads during the armed conflict from 1960 to 1996 (Frey 2009). Similar tactics were used by other military dictatorships in South America in the 1970s and 1980s (Chile, Argentina, Paraguay, and Uruguay); during the armed struggle in Peru during the 1980s; and throughout the more than fifty years of internal conflict in Colombia (Fingscheidt 2007). Additionally, numerous forced disappearances occurred during El Salvador's civil war, as well as during the period of the US-backed Honduran regime of the 1980s.

4. As of December 2016, sixteen of the thirty-four American states have signed the convention and fifteen have ratified it.
5. At the moment of writing, ninety-six states have signed the ICPPED and fifty-three have ratified it.
6. Quote by Jorge Humberto Ganados Hernández, a Guatemalan human rights and social justice activist taken by the police in early 1984. Amnesty International, 2012. City of the Disappeared – Three Decades of Searching for Guatemala's Missing. https://www.amnesty.org/en/latest/news/2012/11/city-disappeared-three-decades-searching-guatemalas-missing/
7. Reported enforced disappearances in the region include as many as 30,000 in Argentina, 60,000 in Colombia, 15,000 in Peru, 3,200 in Chile, 423 in Paraguay, 300 in Uruguay, 8,000 in El Salvador, 5,000 in Nicaragua, 200 in Honduras, and 45,000 in Guatemala.
8. During the 1960s, the United States was intimately involved in equipping and training the Guatemalan security forces. *Operación Limpieza* (Operation Cleanup) in 1966 aimed to crush all forms of political dissent and targeted at least thirty members of the Communist Party, who were rounded up, tortured, and dropped by plane into the Pacific Ocean, from where some of their remains were later washed ashore. Soon afterwards, similar techniques were implemented by the dictatorships of the Southern cone, not least through Operation Condor, the plan of systematic extermination coordinated by Argentina, Bolivia, Brazil, Chile, Paraguay, and Uruguay, and supported technically by the United States. Declassified US intelligence documents show that the CIA retained close ties to the Guatemalan army throughout the 1980s, meaning that US officials were aware of the killings and disappearances following from the army's scorched earth massacres in the countryside and police roundups in the cities. See the unclassified secret US Reports in US Department of State, http://nsarchive.gwu.edu/NSAEBB/NSAEBB15/08-01.htm
9. 2013 interview with Director of Impunity Watch Guatemala, Wilson de los Reyes Aragón; see Emma Buckhout, "Until We Find Them, Part 3." *Latin American Working Group*, March 18, 2013, www.lawg.org/action-center/lawg-blog/69-general/1172-until-we-find-them-part-3-the-disappeared-in-guatemala
10. See the Center for Justice and Accountability (CJA), "Genocide of Mayan Ixil Community," http://cja.org/what-we-do/litigation/the-guatemala-genocide-case/
11. See "Desaparición Forzada," *Bufete Juridico de Derechos Humanos*, http://bdh.org.gt/index.php?id=desaparicion-forzada
12. Postville deportee interviewed by author in Guatemala, June 2012.
13. See *The Guardian*, "Guatemalan President Accused of Involvement in Civil War Atrocities," April 5, 2013, https://www.theguardian.com/world/2013/apr/05/guatemalan-president-accused-civil-war
14. See Nigel Dara, "Why Border Crossings Are Down but Deaths Are Up in Brutal Arizona Desert," *LA Times*, October 27, 2015, http://www.latimes.com/nation/la-na-ff-immigrant-border-deaths-20151021-story.html
15. Interview with PDH conducted by the author in 2011.
16. The activism of the Central American mothers of missing family members began in Honduras in 1999 with the establishment of the Committee of Relatives of Migrants from El Progreso (COFAMIPRO), which in 2000 embarked on the first caravan from Honduras to Tecún Umán, the northwestern Guatemalan border town connected with Tapachula in the Mexican state of Chiapas. Since 2008, the Central American Migration Movement (MMM) has been the main organizer of the search caravan throughout Mexico, and from 2012, women from the Central American countries of

El Salvador, Guatemala, Honduras, and Nicaragua have made the trip together and linked up with a number of Human Rights NGOs, including some of those established in search of war-time disappearances.

17. See *Movimento Migrante Mesoamericano*, https://movimientomigrantemesoamericano.org/2016/07/13/central-american-migration/
18. See Fundación de Anthropología Forense de Guatemala (FAFG). Conectando Vidas. https://fafg.org/
19. Interviews conducted in Guatemala in 2017 by the author.

References

Agamben, G. 2005. *The State of Exception*. Chicago: The University of Chicago Press.

Andersson, R. 2014. *Illegality Inc.: Clandestine Migration and the Business of Bordering Europe*. Oakland: University of California Press.

Caminero-Santangelo, M. 2010. "The Lost Ones: Post-Gatekeeper US-Latina Fiction and the Construction of Cultural Trauma." *Latino Studies* 8, no. 3: 304–327.

Carling, J. 2002. "Migration in the Age of Involuntary Immobility: Theoretical Reflections and Cape Verdean Experiences." *Journal of Ethnic and Migration Studies* 28, no, 1: 5–42.

Cornelius, W. A., and I. Salehyan. 2007. "Does Border Enforcement Deter Unauthorized Immigration? The Case of Mexican Migration to the United States of America." *Regulation & Governance* 1, no. 2: 139–153.

Coutin, S. B. 2016. *Exiled Home: Salvadoran Transnational Youth in the Aftermath of Violence*. Durham, NC: Duke University Press.

De León, J. 2015. *The Land of Open Graves: Living and Dying on the Migrants Trail*. Oakland: University of California Press.

Doty, R. L. 2011. "Bare Life: Border-Crossing Death and Spaces of Moral Alibi." *Environment and Planning D: Society and Space* 29: 599–612.

Fingscheidt, A. 2007. "Tracing Patterns of Disappearances in Latin America." *Asian Federation against Involuntary Disappearances*. http://www.afad-online.org/voice/aug_07/latinamerica.htm

Frey, B. A. 2009. "*Los Desaparecidos*: The Latin American Experience as a Narrative Framework for the International Norm against Forced Disappearances." Hispanic Issues Series. *Hispanic Issues On Line* 5, no. 1: 52–72. https://conservancy.umn.edu/bitstream/handle/11299/182852/hiol_05_04_frey_los_desaparecidos_1.pdf?sequence=1&isAllowed=y

Hagan, J. 2008. *Migration Miracle: Faith, Hope, and Meaning on the Undocumented Journey*. Cambridge, MA: Harvard University Press.

Historical Clarification Commission (CEH). 1999. *Guatemala: Memory of Silence*. Guatemala City, CEH. https://www.aaas.org/sites/default/files/migrate/uploads/mos_en.pdf

Instituto de Estudios y Divulgación sobre Migración, A.C. (INEDIM). 2011. *Construcción de Espacios y Estrategias de Diálogo y Comunicación en torno a la Problemática de Migración y Seguridad en Centroamérica y México*. Mexico, D.F.. http://www.estudiosdemigracion.org/inedim2013/documentosypub/publicaciones/construccionISBNdic2011.pdf

International Commission of Jurists. 2015. "Enforced Disappearance and extrajudicial execution: Investigation and Sanction." *A Practioners Guide*. Geneva. https://www.icj.org/wp-content/uploads/2015/12/Universal-Enforced-Disappearance-and-Extrajudicial-Execution-PGN09-Publications-Practitioners-guide-series-2015-ENG.pdf

Jonas, S. 2013. "Guatemalan Migration in Times of Civil War and Post-War Challenges." Migration Information Source. *Migration Policy Institute*. March 27. http://www.migrationpolicy.org/article/guatemalan-migration-times-civil-war-and-post-war-challenges

Khosravi, S. 2010. *Illegal Traveler: An Auto-Ethnography of Borders*. Basingstoke, UK: Palgrave MacMillan.

Knudsen, A. J., A. Strand, and E. Paasche. 2013. "War and Migration." In *Encyclopedia of Global Human Migration*, 111–127. Edited by Peter Ballwood and Immanuel Ness, Oxford: Blackwell.

Lubkemann, S. 2008. "Involuntary Immobility: On a Theoretical Invisibility in Forced Migration Studies." *Journal of Refugee Studies* 21, no. 4: 454–475.

Massey, D. S., J. Durand, and K. A. Pren. 2016. "Why Border Enforcement Backfired." *American Journal of Sociology* 121, no. 5: 1557–1600.

McAllister, C., and D. M. Nelson. 2013. "Aftermath: Harvest of Violence and Histories of the Future." In *War by Other Means: Aftermath in Post-Genocide Guatemala*, edited by C. McAllister and D. M. Nelson, 1–45. Durham, NC: Duke University Press.

Menjivar, C. 2013. "Central American Immigrant Workers and Legal Violence in Phoenix, Arizona." *Latino Studies* 11, no. 2: 228–252.

Medecins Sans Frontières (MSF). 2017. *Forced to Flee Central America's Northern Triangle: A Neglected Humanitarian Crisis*. Mexico City, New York, Rio de Janeiro, Barcelona. May 2017. https://www.msf.org/sites/msf.org/files/msf_forced-to-flee-central-americas-northern-triangle_e.pdf

Morales Gamboa, A. 2011. "Precentación y Introducción." In *Territorios locales e integración regional en Centroamérica: Migración de Relevo*, edited by A. Morales Gamboa, 7–17. San José, CA: Facultad Latinoamericano de Ciencias Sociales (FLACSO).

Morrison, A. R., and R. A. May. 1994. "Escape from Terror: Violence and Migration in Post-Revolutionary Guatemala." *Latin American Research Review* 29, no. 2: 111–132.

Parr, H., and N. Fyfe. 2012. "Missing Geographies." *Progress in Human Geography* 37, no. 5: 615–638.

Recuperación de la Memoria Histórica (REMHI). 1998. *Nunca Más*. 4 vols. Guatemala, the Human Rights Office of the Archdiocese of Guatemala (ODHAG). http://www.odhag.org.gt/html/Default.htm

Robins, S. 2016. "Discursive Approaches to Ambiguous Loss: Theorizing Community-Based Therapy After Enforced Disappearance." *Journal of Family Theory and Review* 8, no. 3: 308–323.

Rozema, R. 2011. "Forced Disappearance in an Era of Globalization: Biopolitics, Shadow Networks, and Imagined Worlds." *American Anthropologist* 113, no. 4: 582–593.

Sanchez, G. E. 2015. *Human Smuggling and Border Crossings*. Abingdon, UK: Routledge.

Sanchez, G. E. 2017. "Critical Perspectives on Clandestine Migration Facilitation: An Overview of Migrant Smuggling Research." *Journal of Migration and Human Security* 5, no. 1: 9–27.

Sanford, V. 2003. *Buried Secrets: Truth and Human Rights in Guatemala*. New York: Palgrave MacMillan.

Schirmer, J. 1998. *The Guatemalan Military Project: A Violence Called Democracy*. Philadelphia: University of Pennsylvania Press.

Slack, J., D. Martinez, A. E. Lee, and S. Whiteford. 2016. "The Geography of Border Militarization: Violence, Death and Health in Mexico and the United States." *Journal of Latin American Geography*, 15, no. 1: 7–32.

Sørensen, N. N. 2013. "Migration between Social and Criminal Networks: Jumping the Remains of the Honduran Migration Train." In *The Migration Industry and the Commercialization of International Migration*, edited by T. Gammeltoft-Hansen and N. N. Sørensen, 238–261. London: Routledge.

Sørensen, N. N. 2015. "Homeland Security? The Effects of Border Enforcement in Guatemala." In *Mobility and Migration Choices: Thresholds to Crossing Borders*, edited by M. Van der Velde and T. Van Naerssen, 153–165. Farnham, UK: Ashgate.

Sørensen, N. N. 2011. "The Rise and Fall of the Migrant Superhero and the new Deportee Trash: Contemporary Strain on Mobile Livelihoods in the Central American region." *Borderlines: Journal of the Latino Research Center*. 5: 90–120.

Stepputat, F. 1999. "Politics of Displacement in Guatemala." *Journal of Historical Sociology* 12, no. 1: 54–80.

Stepputat, F., and N. N. Sørensen. 2014. "Sociology and Forced Migration." In *Oxford Handbook of Refugee and Forced Migration Studies*, edited by E. Fiddian-Qasmiyeh, G. Loescher, K. Long, and N. Sigona, 86–98. Oxford: Oxford University Press.

Tazzioli, M. 2016. "Concentric Cages: The Hotspots of Lesvos after the EU-Turkey Agreement." *Open Democracy*, May 20, 2016. https://www.opendemocracy.net/mediterranean-journeys-in-hope/martina-tazzioli/concentric-cages-hotspots-of-lesvos-after-eu-turkey-

Vigh, H. 2008. "Crisis and Chronicity: Anthropological Perspectives on Continuous Conflict and Decline." *Ethnos* 73, no. 1: 5–24.

Weld, K. 2013. "Because They Were Taken Alive: Forced Disappearance in Latin America." *ReVista, Harvard Review of Latin America* 13, no. 1: 8–11.

Zolberg, A. R. 2001. "Introduction: Beyond the Crisis." In *Global Migrants, Global Refugees: Problems and Solutions*, edited by Aristide R. Zolberg and Peter M. Benda, 1–16. New York and Oxford: Berghahn.

CHAPTER 23

AFGHAN EXPERIENCES OF DISPLACEMENT

RUCHIRA GANGULY-SCRASE

GLOBALLY there has been a significant shift in conceptualizing refugees as a problem: from worthy categories of persons needing protection to a security threat. Pakistan is no exception. This chapter focuses on research among internally displaced Afghan communities who had fled to Pakistan over the protracted periods of conflict, returning in periods of relative calm. However, they were unable to return to their homes and were currently living in temporary accommodation. While some hoped that they would be able to return home in the future, others were planning to migrate elsewhere. Over the last three decades Pakistan's complex geopolitical involvement has meant that it has received several millions of documented and undocumented migrants from Afghanistan. Despite the diverse and complex status of those fleeing a war-torn country Afghans were portrayed as heroic fighters deserving refuge. Now they are being demonized as Islamic militants. At the time of writing millions of "unregistered" Afghan refugees were facing forced repatriation. For many young people of Afghan origin they have known no other abode.

Interviews were carried out over a period of several months with those living in Kabul and Jalalabad. Most respondents were drawn from minority ethnic groups of Balouchis, Hazaras, and Tajiks. This is in marked contrast to the dominant Pashtun groups of documented and undocumented migrants living in Pakistan. The latter's historically shared cultural identity brings into question the "refugeehood" of a people who have continually traveled across this region. Given that neither Pakistan nor Afghanistan recognizes the official border consisting of the Durand line drawn up by the British during colonial rule, cross-border movements of "forced" migrants of Pashtun ethnicity is an anomaly. This is not to deny the ongoing maligning of Afghan refugees in Pakistan as Islamic militants or as a financial burden. Pakistan is an interesting case in point. On the one hand it is not a signatory to the UN Convention on Refugees. On the other it must be considered that as a developing country it has hosted one of the largest human exoduses from its neighbor. Arguably, the so-called refugee crisis in Pakistan today is to a great extent an outcome of its own making (Ghufran 2011; Steadman and Tanners 2003)[1] Therefore, this chapter does not seek to examine the discourses of refugees as a crisis in Pakistan. Instead it highlights the perspectives of those labeled as minority other, who remain as the target of Pakistan's anger toward an indeterminable refugee crisis. Put another way, the current simultaneous paradoxical situation affecting the displaced constitutes a "real" crisis and an ideological construct.

Furthermore, by exploring the perspectives of the internally displaced this chapter can shed some light on the decision-making processes of asylum-seekers, thereby highlighting the agency of the victim. Once again some caution needs to be exercised between those who are being forced to flee in an instance and those who face a prolonged interment in an area not of their choosing, whether it is within their nation-state or in another country. Some of the respondents fled to neighboring Iran, a country which in recent years has reversed its previously warm attitudes toward Afghan migrants who now face both formal and popular xenophobia. Adelkhah and Olszewska (2007) show the history of Afghan migration to Iran to be longstanding. The nineteenth-century pastoral nomadism, coupled with labor migration in the 1960s and 1970s, was followed by the granting of refugee status of *mohajerin* (141). According to Dimitriadi (2018) *mohajerin* are "religious migrants" accorded a particular system of protection, which is considered honorary. To this she adds that in Pakistan under the *Pashtunwali* code, an ethical principle which affords asylum between Pashtuns, " . . . has always regarded its hospitality to Afghans as a religious and humanitarian duty" (Turton and Marsden 2002, 14, cited in Dimitriadi 2018, 47)

This chapter follows Crawley's (2010) UK Refugee Council research recommendation of the importance of producing data that is based on the perspectives of the displaced by drawing attention to role of human agency and decision making. It concurs with Zimmermann's (2010, 201) view based on fine-grained micro-level analysis for the need "to contribute to an understandings of forced migration in order to help to produce effective solutions which help to avert the prevailing fears, antagonism, and distrust about asylum movements." This enables deeper understanding of the context of the decision-making by involuntary migrants in their point of origin, as they contemplate to set off for different parts of the world. The narratives and the life-stories of the forced migrants help researchers to draw a vivid picture of the entire process of migration. The ensuing accounts inform the national and international migration debate with insights drawn from reliable data collection and analysis rather than public speculation, as is currently the case. For instance, two decades ago Koser's (1997) significant study in OECD countries supported the view that the reactive model of asylum in place is no longer sustainable and that the artificial separation of economic, political, and social aspects of refugee migration is of limited utility for yielding explanations of refugee flight. Furthermore, as Agier (2002, 363) stresses it is of utmost importance to understand the precise context of refugees' situations, given the diversity of the places, histories, and trajectories of their lives.

Writing in more optimistic times, the German political philosopher Otto Kirchheimer (1959) situated the institution of asylum "at the crossroads of national and international law, compassion and self-interest, raison d'état and human capacity for shame" (Kirchheimer 1959, 986–987). The most recent tragedies involving deaths of asylum-seekers traveling by boats in the Horn of Africa toward Europe, brutal exploitation of Rohinga refugees, and most significantly the threat of expulsion awaiting Afghan refugees in Pakistan underscore the need for asylum policies that extend greater generosity and compassion to the displaced, while recognizing the legitimate concerns of nation-states. As Battersby (2008, 16) argues, "were governments to focus on the reasons why people risk all to escape war and its consequences, they might create broader public support for more effective and more expensive forms of intervention."

Such perspectives dovetail with the truth of Long and Crisp's (2010) assertion that:

> . . . anti-mobility strategies are unequal to the task of providing a serious answer to the increasingly complex challenges faced by those seeking to provide effective international protection to those in need. These challenges . . . are all symptomatic of a serious imbalance between international responses to forced displacement and the socioeconomic protection needs of those who are displaced.
>
> (2010, 56)

As Papastergiadis (2010, 354) contends, "it is therefore more appropriate to consider the way migrants plot their journeys and utilize extensive networks of information as part of the normal and conscientious efforts by which people dignify their lives." Consequently, the need for research that addresses the intentionality of individual forced migrants in the context in which asylum decisions are in the process of formation is of paramount importance. Havinga and Böcker (1999, 59) argue that, " . . . no single or even restricted number of factors can explain the patterns of origin and destination for asylum-seekers. Some factors are generally not important but may nevertheless be very important for asylum-seekers from a particular country of origin going to a particular country of destination at a particular time." As Robinson and Segrott (2002, 7) explain, "adopting such a view of decision-making does not totally individualize all decision making or deny the possibility of generalizing about decision making since people who live in the same historical, political, and cultural setting will share elements of their biographies." However, we need to caution against narratives privileging refugees over migrants; instead the emphasis should lie in examining the political economic maneuvers shaping the constructions of a migration "crisis" in order to understand the experience of the displaced (Crawley and Skleparis 2018). Border ethnographies reveal that migration crises are the discursive formations reflecting the anomalies and deeper malaise of the contemporary global order (Holmes and Casteneda, 2016; Kallius et al, 2016).

Globalization and the Ambivalence of Nation-States

In the globalized world of the twenty-first century, material and symbolic goods travel relatively freely across national borders. At the same time, movements of people, or at least particular categories of people, are becoming increasingly understood as a problem in need of control (Briskman and Cemlyn 2005; de Haas 2007; Turner 2010). Migration has become "one of the most controversial areas of policy and practice facing virtually all countries" (Crawley 2006, 25). Perceptions of porous boundaries and unlimited opportunities coexist in the public imaginary with hardened attitudes toward desperate humans who seek to cross national borders without authorization by receiving states.

Throughout the Global North, humanitarian ideals of social justice toward asylum seekers have given way to a preoccupation with national security and border control (Innes 2010; Stalker, 2001) and the consequent criminalization of migrants who arrive "onshore" without authorization (De Giorgi 2010; Fekete and Webber 2010; Hörnqvist 2004; Welch and Schuster 2005). When formalized in law, these take the form of increasingly restrictive immigration laws and regulations, intensified border controls, carrier sanctions, deterrent policies, and return migration policies (de Haas 2007, 823–824). While Fassin and d'Halluin (2007, 308) point out that "there has never been a Golden Age for refugees" and that "(a)lways, in practice, asylum has come second to nations' economies and securities," the hardening of global attitudes toward asylum seekers is reaching unprecedented levels in popular and institutional discourses. Even previously generous European states are seeking to reduce their intake of asylum-seekers. Such heightened levels of paranoia against asylum-seekers comes at a time when UNHCR reports an increase in new conflict zones which has displaced millions in the past five consecutive years; currently there are 65.5 million forcibly displaced people worldwide (UNHCR 2016).

Asylum-seekers embody "the contradiction between the national logic of migration control and the transnational logic of international migration" (Castles 2007, 31), and are thus disruptive to visions of a "national order of things" (Blommaert 2009; Limbu 2009; Turner, 2004). According to Tazreiter (2008) "the arrival of persons without a legal right to stay in a nation-state is often seen as a challenge to the sovereignty of that state." As a consequence, the governments of receiving states strive to contain and repel those whose life trajectories belie the salience of nation-states under conditions of globalization. While the specific policies of states in the Global North vary, they can be seen to share a common aim: "to ensure that refugees and asylum-seekers have minimal access to the protection regimes of the receiving state." In defiance of international treaties to which they themselves have been signatories, governments around the world are adopting legislation designed to restrict citizenship, secure national borders, and send a strong message of deterrence to those contemplating unauthorized migration. These include stressful assessment procedures, detention under inhumane conditions, denial of the opportunity to work and to participate in civic life, and barriers to family reunion, social security support, and a range of health services (Rees and Silove 2006). Paradoxically, these same states have recognized, via international treaties, that failure to provide asylum to refugees is not only reprehensible on humanitarian grounds, but renders the international order less stable. Such inconsistencies point to the "multiple and often contradictory interests and identities of the modern nation-state" (Watson 2009, 1).

Evidently, the situation of the receiving country discussed in this chapter is vastly different from the countries of the industrialized North. However, there are some commonalities in the ways in which refugees are now perceived as a burden and a threat. Pakistan's distinctiveness, as noted previously, is that it is not signatory to the UN Refugee Convention. Yet, its adherence to the social and cultural constructions embodied in the Pashtunwali code of hospitality coupled with the Cold War politics of the 1980s meant that it granted asylum to millions of its neighboring Afghans. Similarly another neighboring state, Iran, where many Afghans fled to, upholds the perspective of *mohajerin* and subsequently granted them asylum. Transformations in global political economy have led to a reversal of these policies, which deeply affects the plight of many Afghans in these countries.

The Malignant Positioning of Asylum-Seekers

While there may be some justifiable concern over possible illegal activities of undocumented migrants in the current global and regional political climate within South Asia, there appears to be an overreporting of the potential risks, while elsewhere in most industrialized countries there is a simultaneous underreporting of the final determination of undocumented migrants who apply for asylum and are indeed finally recognized as refugees. For example, an Australian study by The ERC (2001) reports that among the Afghan unauthorized arrivals 93 percent of asylum-seekers were recognized as legitimate refugees. Asylum-seekers come from a variety of social backgrounds, ranging from an African teenager documented by Williksen (2004), who had never seen an identity card or passport and had no idea that these were needed to get into a country, to the range of professionals interviewed by Taylor (2009, cited in Bloom 2010). As O'Doherty and Lecouteur (2007, 2) observe, "(e)ven referring to them as a social group is problematic because the nationalities, political status, legal status, and alleged intentions, as well as many of the features of this aggregation of people, appear to vary considerably." However, these disparate individuals are routinely and collectively disparaged in popular and political discourses in terms that deny their individuality and suggest that they are morally less than human. Classification systems routinely order human experience, "embodying moral and aesthetic choices that in turn craft people's identities, aspirations, and dignity" (Bowker and Star 2000, 4). As a result one attributes images or terms or both to certain categories of people even if there has been no direct contact with them. Diversity among refugees coupled with the shifting classifications of Afghan refugees in Pakistan was the primary reason in this chapter for choosing specific groups.

Sabat (2003) terms the categorization of human subjects as nonpersons "malignant positioning," in recognition of the negative effects not only on the way the individual so positioned is thought of and treated by others, but for his or her own self-perception. In the receiving countries within the Global North, asylum-seekers are represented as an "out-of-control, agentless, unwanted natural disaster." (Wodak et al. 2008, 287) A common trope employed by politicians and journalists alike to convey images of nonpersonhood is the liquid metaphor (Bleasdale, 2008), which discursively transforms asylum-seekers into a mindless, overwhelming, and potentially unstoppable mass. In this regard, the groundbreaking work of Daniel and Knudsen (1995) is noteworthy; it shows how a new vocabulary in the German language has arisen. German, which has a marked propensity for compound words, has begun to give combined expression to hydrophobic and xenophobic preoccupations. This includes -the terms "Asylschwemme" (asylum flood), "Lawine" (asylum avalanche), "Zeitbombe" (asylum time bomb), "Asylschnorrer" (asylum parasite) and "Erschleicher" (asylum black marketer) (Daniel and Knudsen 1995, 116).

In contemporary refugee discourse the notion of personhood is rarely present. Instead the emphasis lies on the primacy of the state, which is represented by an enduring metaphor of a container of limited capacity (Hart 2008). When asylum-seekers are imagined as formless water, it becomes difficult to "see" the humanity located within any single individual. As "tides" (Hatton 2009), "flows" (Turner 2010), "floods," "waves," and even "tsunamis," very small numbers of asylum-seekers are feared to carry the potential to engulf nation-state containers that are "already full," and justify the implementation of restrictive immigration policy in order to stop the perilous flow of water (Hart 2008, 101). When embedded in such metaphors, the word "refugee" "does not swell with a sense of warmth, safety, succour, or welcome but seethes with menace and foreboding" (Daniel 2002, ch.14).

While typically endowed with limited material resources due to the disruption of their lives, forced migrants regularly draw on personal strengths of courage, resilience, and initiative, as well as strengths embodied in social networks. As Muecke (1992, 520) observes, "refugees present perhaps the maximum example of the human capacity to survive despite the greatest of losses and assaults on human identity and dignity."

Attending to the Perspectives of Forced Migrants

Across the globe research studies on refugee camps, mental sufferings, discrimination, and problems faced by displaced people, refugee coping mechanisms after resettlement and second-generation refugee perspectives are abundant. There is also a strong focus on the dilemmas that grapple nation-states as they remain entangled in the debates between the right of imperiled people to seek refuge and the right of a nation to safeguard its citizens and resources. But knowledge about real experiences that *generate* the idea of leaving everything behind for a new location and a new future is scant. Typically, and often with benign intent, public representations serve to obscure the intentionality of forced migrants. Academic discourses, for example, tend to focus on the macro-political causes of refugee flight. But the micro-perspectives and accounts based on ethnographic field work are perfunctory. Some notable exceptions include Glastra and Vedder's (2010) study of learning strategies of highly educated refugees in The Netherlands; Halleh Ghorashi's (2007) work on Iranian refugee women who have settled in the United States and H.H. Askland's (2007) study of young East Timorese asylum seekers in Australia. They have used the method of documenting the narratives and life-stories to get a deeper understanding of the refugee situation. However these studies focus on the groups that are already settled in a new country. Therefore there is a pressing need to document the narratives and life stories of forced migrants who are about to flee or are in transit.

In their focus on the suffering and trauma experienced by refugees, humanitarian discourses can also homogenize the refugee experience, drawing on powerful categorizations such as women and children in order to engage the sympathies of ever more skeptical western donors (see Malkki 1995). However, it is the "malignant positioning" of asylum-seekers in popular and political discourses that is of greatest concern, since, rather than overlooking or subordinating the intentionality of asylum-seekers, it instead misrepresents and misattributes that intentionality in terms of greed and wilful deception. "In this context, the right to asylum has become increasingly restricted, and the connotation of the term "refugee" has changed. The "refugee" becomes increasingly suspect—suspected of secrecy and lies, of being a "false refugee". He or she becomes a paradigm of the false" (Sinapi 2008, 534).

Attention to the intentionality of individual asylum-seekers can forestall dangerous "category errors" (Clarkson 2003) such as the confusion of people with water, which are born of confusion, misinformation, and ideological contamination. For most people, the arrival of asylum-seekers in their home country is what Boudon (1989, cited in Rydgren 2009) terms a "black box" situation, in which people encounter new situations that present them with cognitive processing dilemmas.

In order to understand better the complexities of asylum-seeking, there is a pressing need to prioritize the voices, experiences, expectations, and explanations of those at the center of the debate –asylum-seekers themselves (Dwyer 2008; Zimmermann 2010). Attending to the voices of asylum-seekers can then challenge the dominant perspectives that inform the creation of policy (Zimmermann 2010, 204). When the voices of forced migrants themselves are rendered audible through grounded qualitative research, the stories they tell reveal intentions and circumstances that differ markedly from the representations outlined previously. Above all, they confirm the forcibly displaced as active agents rather than passive and helpless victims, who, as Moore and Shellman (2007, 812) note, are "making choices under highly constrained circumstances."

In studies in which the lived experiences of the displaced seeking refuge have been actively sought and recounted, a very different picture has emerged from that represented in public discourses. Moreover, forced migrants are not a category apart in relation to the rest of humanity. Rather, they are "ordinary people who have had extraordinary experiences" (O'Neil and Spybey 2003, 8), "fully fledged actors in the life-drama; people, like all of us, endowed with motives that reach beyond the instinct of survival and purposes that transcend the breadline, and who engage in interaction or decline interaction, weave networks of social bonds or tear them apart" (Bauman 2002, 344).

Popular and political discourses routinely condemn asylum-seekers for not adhering to rules of law or of "fair play." However such notions imply the presence of a neat and methodical structure for decision making which is far from the chaotic conditions experienced by many forced migrants. Refugee camps and other spaces occupied by forced migrants are "typically defined by social chaos and subversive economies where affected populations experience a profound sense of confusion and disorientation" (Rodgers 2004, 48). As Silove (2002) argues, often there will be no opportunity to access sites of regularized authority and the chances of a positive outcome may be slight.

One option that is relatively freely available to asylum-seekers and other migrants with the financial means is the use of people smugglers (termed "agents" by Robinson and Segrott 2002). The services of smugglers become more valuable when receiving states limit access to their protection and opportunities (Loescher and Milner 2003), and people smuggling is on the rise around the world (Antonopoulos and Winterdyk 2006). Whereas official channels may be nonexistent in particular localities or may be perceived to be inappropriate or too dangerous to access, people smugglers are often highly visible and easy to contact directly or through social networks (Koser and Pinkerton 2002). Specific services performed by agents included providing travel documents, facilitating journeys (sometimes accompanying refugees and reclaiming false documentation at the destination point), and channeling individuals toward or away from particular countries (Robinson and Segrott 2002).

Cashmore (2006) recounts the story of a young Afghan asylum-seeker whose only chance of escaping abduction by the Taliban had lain with a people smuggler known to a contact of his father. From such a powerless position, many asylum-seekers are compelled to cede control over logistical decision making, with some not knowing where they were going until after they arive. Robinson and Segrott (2002) report that in some instances, only one destination was on offer by smugglers and asylum-seekers needed to seize that opportunity or risk further persecution or deportation if they remained.

Poor Outset Conditions

Since flight is a basic mechanism of human survival, it is "natural" and predictable that people in peril will go to extreme lengths to seek safety for themselves and their children. However forsaking valued homelands, families, and possessions in exchange for an unknown future is not undertaken other than for the most compelling reasons; even under conditions of danger, most refugees avoid this option for as long as possible (Silove 2002, 290–291). However when conditions are considered unendurable, Hayenhjelm (2006, 194) argues, "refraining from taking any action is also a kind of risk taking."

Existing empirical studies attest to a single, overriding motivation for the flight of asylum-seekers—the fear of persecution, torture, or death. Robinson and Segrott (2002) identify the primary factor diving refugee flight as immediate peril in asylum seekers' countries of origin. When people have reached this stage, the lure of particular Western countries is not a particularly salient issue. Moore and Shellman (2007, 812) note that forced migrants do not unthinkingly respond to a persecution threat by fleeing to the nearest safe haven. Rather, they are people making choices under *highly constrained circumstances* (emphasis in original). Nevertheless, as Zimmermann (2010) emphasizes what people need and seek as refugees is far more important than where they go—a finding also supported by Robinson and Segrott (2002).

Having contextualized some of the key concerns surrounding the situation of forced migrants the forgoing discussion considers findings based on the case study of Afghans who fled to Pakistan and (to a lesser extent) Iran, only to return temporarily to decide on their future prospects.

Afghan Experiences of Displacement: Findings

Interviews were carried out over a period of several months in 2010–2011 among Afghans in Kabul and Jalalabad. The findings show that most people fled to neighboring countries; over the protracted period of conflict, most Afghans had been in Pakistan—only to return in periods of relative calm. It is generally assumed asylum-seekers plan to undertake unauthorized travel to a Western country to seek asylum, yet, a number of Afghan respondents expressed the desire to settle in nearby countries that they had previously traveled to. This is in part due to their diverse socioeconomic and cultural backgrounds, ranging from wealthy businessmen, who had fallen on hard times, to professionals, to petty traders. The dominant discourse surrounding Afghan refugees focuses on those from poorer, working-class backgrounds; among them many also had relatives in Western countries and, thus, were prepared to risk the journey. Although different classes have been affected by civil wars resulting in displacement, the causes and manifestations of conflicts are distinctive. Therefore, this chapter focuses on the responses of middle-class participants.

Increases in violent encounters at home were the primary motivation for fleeing. As noted previously the discussion focuses primarily on the internally displaced, drawing particular attention to the fact that most had lived temporarily in Pakistan. Upon return they were compelled to relocate to another, relatively safer, part of Afghanistan. Living in a country with many different cultural groups and differing political affiliations, participants found circumstances in their communities changed quickly, as well as frequently, during conflict. People escaped when their cultural identity or past affiliations meant that they were perceived to be allied with the "then" enemy of that community. The enemy, rather than being one group consistently, shifted and changed with different facets of the war and the dominance of one or another cultural group in a region.

A 32-year-old female college professor from a Tajik community fled when her father was murdered for unknown motives. A Hazara man in his late 40s was forced out of his community when he was suspected of being a spy for the Taliban; in his words: "First my father was killed at the hands of Mujahideen and then my nephew was killed by Taliban. We would have met the same fate if we did not migrate."

On the other side of the conflict, a middle-aged Baluchi male was harassed by the Taliban:

> They threatened to blast my shop as well as target my family. Honestly, I have no political affiliation with any party or any connection with army. One day, they fired in the air in front of our house which frightened us a lot. We had only one option to migrate to some safer place. I left my home along with my elderly mother, three kids, and a wife. Now I am living in extreme poverty.

A nurse in her early 30s also suffered a Taliban attack: "Many girls including me were made victims of sexual harassment that night. It was very hard to bear such humiliation and mental torture." Businessman Mr. Askari was at risk as running his business required political alliances and the family became increasingly unpopular among different groups but, finally, he said, "in the last days of 2002, my brother was killed. . . . It was the time of high uncertainty for us and we had no idea of our destination."

A 52-year-old poetry-loving Tajik male, appropriately named Omar Khayyam, was living in the Gardez district, a relatively peaceful area until the Taliban stepped up attacks. Another Tajik male, Dr Ahmed, from Surkhi Parsa district also a relatively peaceful region, had left just before crisis point:

> [W]hen we were leaving, Taliban had almost reached our area. Afterward, our people also took up arms against Taliban because there was no other option left except to face them. One of my relatives has lost their two sons at the time of their migration.

It goes without saying that the displacement experiences were chaotic and traumatic. The decision to leave was quick and people only left at the point they feared for their lives. In general, there was no migration plan; instead, they were fleeing without a clear destination or fleeing to family or trusted friends, who would then assist with relatively safe passage across the border.

A woman informant explained that she escaped without considering a destination or help:

> It was not possible to ask for anybody's help. The whole area was engulfed in a war. Saving one's own life than [that of] others was the top priority of every one at that time. Neither we had time to ask for somebody's help nor did any one extend it.

Shahram, a Tajik man from Parwan province, stated similarly: "Asking help from those who are also passing through the same situation seems quite ridiculous. Nobody has enough time to think of other."

Others felt entirely reliant on family or friends. Kalsoom left her home in Farah province with her mother and sisters first for a small village in Anar Dara. Since she had some contacts in Iran she would go there for a while, until it would be safe to return to Kabul, whereas Gul Sher, from Fayzabad traveled to Kabul, but this was worse than home. So he wanted to seek refuge among his relatives in Qandahar, but was trapped when he realized that he was now an enemy of a different cultural group who had aligned themselves with the United States forces in Qandahar. Gul Sher reflected on the importance of kinship support:

> We would have vanished long before had we not been supported by relatives and friends. In Afghanistan we have strong bonds of relationships and friendships. Many others like us were supported by relatives and friends.

Samiaullah from Nimroz province when narrating his experiences about taking refuge with relatives in a nearby village pointed out that it being a Pashtun-dominated area, the Taliban's visits were frequent. Subsequently, the local people began to suspect them. At first the family was considered to be friends of Russia and now loyal to the United States. As a result, he said, "we had to leave that place also after a brief stay there and came to Nanghar in a very miserable condition." Ahmad recalled the chaos in the following words:

> [T]he situation had worsened beyond imagination. It was before the US attack on al Qaeda or Afghanistan. I am not sure but one of the groups either Hizb-e-Islami or Taliban was after us. We had a very huge business and it was really very difficult for us to leave all at once. Moreover, a big chunk of our money was still tied up in the market. But when life is in danger, money has little importance.

Most people perceived that their current location was only marginally safer than their own villages and towns. A common explanation was: "Here in Kabul, the conditions are not very favorable, but comparatively better than languishing in Pakistan." It was implied that this would be a temporary measure until returning home. While most did not aspire to immigrate, when considering this option, they preferred Uzbekistan, Kazakhstan, and Tajikistan as destinations as these countries were perceived to be culturally suitable and more liberal than neighboring Pakistan or Iran. "They are near to us. We are also familiar with their cultures," was a common saying. Additionally, Faiz, a Hazara, explained, "in the past, we had migrated to these countries," while Shaihak, a Baluchi, would select Uzbekistan as an option because "they still respect us." Omar, a Tajik added: "I have been to Uzbekistan, Kazakhstan, and Tajikistan. They are really very friendly and open-hearted people. We do not consider ourselves strangers there."

The respondents had regarded their sojourn in Pakistan or Iran to be temporary. The reasons were twofold. First, they noted that although there were many successful

Afghans living in Pakistan they were predominantly Pashtun; as minorities their chances were limited. Second, they felt both Iran and Pakistan had handled the burden of various waves of migrations during different wars in the region and, economically, could not be expected to bear the burden without further support from the international community. For example, a Hazara taxi driver stated:

> Even though Hazaras are traditionally respected in Iran, giving shelter to someone for a whole thirty years is indeed a difficult job. I have heard that Iran and Pakistan are already on the way to expel the migrants. It will be quite unfair to expect too much from these countries as they are already burdened by their own problems.

Moreover, neighboring countries were becoming less of a migration option because, as some respondents with a cosmopolitan outlook explained, in the past, they had the opportunity to go to Central Asian states for higher education or employment. However, migrating to these states became progressively difficult due to certain activities of militants. Subsequently, the Afghans were labeled as either extremists or terrorists. "We faced the same kind of situation in Iran and Pakistan now," noted Gulzaar. Many participants considered this to be the current broader problem since they were afraid that the reception in these countries would be no longer positive, particularly for a minority community among Afghans. According to a middle-aged man:

> [W]e have very few friends or sympathizers in other countries. In my experience, these countries accepted and received us with open hearts at the beginning but now things have changed. These countries are suspicious and a bit scared of us.

This unfair treatment was considered to be the underlying reason for many Afghan refugees in Pakistan returning home. In analyzing their situation, the well-educated participants looked further abroad toward Western countries. Ahmad felt that he had reasonable chances of settlement abroad and would seek political asylum if appropriate business opportunities became available in France.

Suleman, a businessman would also select a Western country if given the option:

> My kids were used to a luxurious life and were insisting on shifting to America. Actually, the issue of my kids' education was compelling me to think over the option of taking refuge in some foreign country. We wanted to leave our area and move to the United States by hook or by crook because, I had heard that many of my friends who had left earlier than us were still struggling to survive in other areas [of Afghanistan].

However, even for the educated authorized migration as a refugee was not perceived to be easily achievable. Despite the difficulties in obtaining authorized migration, no interviewee was currently considering unauthorized travel. This stands in stark contrast to the dominant perspective, which has drawn attention to the Afghan asylum-seekers' growing frustration over refugee resettlement processes and subsequent attempts by numerous people risking unauthorized travel. Subsequently, numbers seeking unauthorized travel to Europe have increased. Yet according to the internally displaced persons (IDPs) interviewees, the human traffickers required to facilitate this migration were perceived as untrustworthy. The following remark sums up the overall sentiments of my respondents:

> [T]hey are fraudsters. They have cheated many people. Many people have made it to Europe, the United States, and Central Asian states by paying hefty amounts to these agents. But personally, I don't trust these agents. These agents are only good at hoodwinking helpless people like us.

Moreover, participants feared criminalization. This was exemplified by drawing attention to the story of a family who hired a human trafficker who had promised to take them to Germany or Norway, but the agent disappeared in Peshawar. The Pakistani authorities arrested the family and sent them to jail to serve a sentence of seven months. Most people were aware of the consequences of paying people smugglers. It would lead to either arrest or loss of money, and, more seriously, they knew that once a person is arrested then he or she would be banned from that country. All respondents pointed to numerous cases of people being held in detention for many years instead of securing political asylum in Western countries.

Kalsoom Nazoo perceived that a peaceful and orderly life would not be achieved by breaking rules to reach that safer destination: "I will respect their law because I myself am fed up with lawlessness here. I can only travel with proper documents." Clearly, for many people the financial resources required were beyond their reach. One informant explained:

> I am a head of nine family members and they ask about 5 million for the whole family, which is beyond my affordability. Secondly, these agents do not give you any guarantee whether I will get settled abroad or not. This is only possible when it is done on a state level. And I see no hope of that.

Although some respondents felt that theoretically the only secure option was the internationally coordinated legal migration, they were thoroughly skeptical of it coming to fruition. Suffice to say my findings from Afghanistan challenge the conventional understanding of authorized migration coordinated by the international community as the safest and best option, since participants repeatedly emphasized that they were not hopeful that the international community would step in to aid their safety. Firoza, a teacher lamented:

> The international community turned a blind eye to the problems of peaceful Afghans like us. They left us at the mercy of these ignorant people. We had many hopes from the international community but they were only after their vested interests due to which our country is at the verge of destruction.

In some cases people felt that international intervention had destabilized Afghanistan in the first place, leading to the continual conflict and the displacement they experience today. This was a strongly held view with comments, such as, "Foreign interference is the root of all evil," and "If foreign interference is ended today, peace will return to this unfortunate land in days not in months." Nousafarin was emphatic: "We were living happily and peacefully with one another for centuries but when foreign powers started interference the situation deteriorated beyond imagination." The respondent added that peace and safety in Afghanistan would only be achieved if "the people of Afghanistan realize that we have to build this country on our own and not with the help of some foreign power which has its own vested interests." Haamein, on the other hand, felt that the international community could facilitate peace, but with appropriate solutions, not merely sending aid: "I ask one favor from the international community to please bring peace to our country, instead of useless funds."

Against popular misconceptions about motivations of asylum-seekers, it is interesting to note that some Afghans did not want to go anywhere; rather they had the overwhelming desire for conditions to return to a state of normalcy and security. "Migrations are no solution. I ask one thing from the powers that be. I appeal to them to come and work sincerely for the rebuilding of our beloved country," implored Kalsoom. Some were passionate about their homeland and said: "I will never leave Afghanistan. It is my mother country and very beautiful." Golzaar reflected on the futile nature of migrating from place to place: "Sometimes, it seems as if our whole life would be wasted in shifting from one place to another." Ghulam summed it up succinctly when he said: "it is indeed very disheartening to leave one's own land." Yet they all recognized that it was still too violent to return home.

Overall, the internally displaced Afghans in my study felt helpless about their personal circumstances and did not demonstrate a sense of empowerment regarding their future. Ideally, they hoped for a return to home if peace prevailed, and felt that finding peace in a foreign country was an extremely difficult goal to attain—particularly when there was little logistical support on the ground. Their focus was on day-to-day survival. For those for whom migration might be an option, they would like it to be safe and have the desire to return home once stability is achieved. These accounts also dispel the popular myth prevailing in the Global North that asylum-seekers are inherently economic migrants seeking a better lifestyle.

Conclusion

This chapter has drawn attention to the need for interviewing in the place and time that decisions are being formulated by potential asylum-seekers. Such an approach enables the researcher to address the temporal and spatial aspects of decision-making and issues and contexts specific to particular groups and to recognize emergent patterns.

Perceptions of time within the context of particular lives affect larger macro-political processes, by shaping the assessment and intentions of social actors. If a situation is thought to be temporary or to last indefinitely, this will affect the willingness of actors to bear the strain (Aminzade 1992) of dismal protracted situations such as waiting in camps. When potential asylum seekers are considering flight options, their temporal orientation is toward the future. As Brown and Michael (2003, 4) observe, there is a "need for scholarship to engage with the future as an analytical object, and not simply a neutral temporal space into which objective expectations can be projected." In particular, they highlight "the need to shift the analytical angle from *looking into* the future to *looking at* the future, or how the future is mobilized in real time to marshal resources, coordinate activities, and manage uncertainty."

Conducting research at the same time that forced migrants are considering their situation also enables avoidance of some of the drawbacks of analyzing retrospective accounts of refugee flight. After resettlement, "migrants may be far removed in both time and space from their experiences of departure so that their reasons for leaving no longer have the relevance that they once did (Collyer 2010, 279). While studies undertaken after settlement have provided useful data, asylum claimants are likely to emphasize reasons that they believe the decision makers want to hear when arguing their case after arrival in the host country (see Barsky 1995). Furthermore, this means Koser and Pinkerton's (2002) cautionary remark—that people who have reached a country of potential asylum are inclined to focus on positive experiences or to misrepresent their experiences—assumes critical significance.

In the final analysis, I have shown the diversity of experiences among the displaced in Afghanistan. Despite the reality of widespread forced migrations, current discourses of "crises" remain limited in contributing to the understanding of their involuntary mobility since such narratives have been artificially constructed in response to specific political and economic agendas of the given states. Undoubtedly the agency responsible for managing the crisis, the UNHCR, did not assume a neutral role during the proxy war led by the United States in Afghanistan as the United States was the largest donor to its refugee relief programs. The politicization of the refugee phenomena in Pakistan has further complicated their situation. As negotiations over the plight of Afghans proceed locally and globally forced migrants will continue to strategically manoeuvre the direction of their mobility in their own limited ways.

Note

1. Pakistan used refugees as a strategic asset for its own political purposes by drawing on international humanitarian aid to support differing warring groups.

References

Adelkhah, F., and Z. Olszewska. 2007. "The Iranian Afghans." *Iranian Studies* 40, no. 2: 137–165. doi:10.1080/00210860701269519

Agier, M. 2002. "Still Stuck between War and City: A Response to Bauman and Malkki." *Ethnography* 3, no. 3: 361–366 doi:10.1177/146613802401092805

Aminzade, R. 1992. "Historical Sociology and Time." *Sociological Methods and Research* 20, no. 4 (1992): 456–480. doi:10.1177/0049124192020004003

Antonopoulos, G. A., and J. Winterdyk. 2006. "The Smuggling of Migrants in Greece: An Examination of its Social Organization." *European Journal of Criminology* 3, no. 4 (2006): 439–461. doi:10.1177/1477370806067912

Askland, H. H. 2007. "Habitus, Practice and Agency of Young East Timorese Asylum-Seekers in Australia." *The Asia Pacific Journal of Anthropology* 8, no. 3: 235–249. doi:10.1080/14442210701516561

Barsky, R. F. 1995. "Arguing the American dream à la Canada: Former Soviet Citizens' Justification for Their Choice of Host Country." *Journal of Refugee Studies* 8, no. 2: 125–141. doi:10.1093/jrs/8.2.125

Battersby, P. 2008. "A World Turned Upside Down: Risk, Refugees and Global Security in the 21st Century." In *Asylum-Seekers: International Perspectives on Interdiction and Deterrence*, edited by A. Babacan and L. Briskman, 10–27. Newcastle, UK: Cambridge Scholars Publishing.

Bauman, Z. 2002. "In the Lowly Nowherevilles of Liquid Modernity: Comments on and around Agier." *Ethnography* 3, no. 3 (2002): 343–349. doi:10.1177/146613802401092788

Bleasdale, L. 2008. "Under Attack: The Metaphoric Threat of Asylum Seekers in Public-Political Discourses." *Web Journal of Current Legal Issues* 1. http://webjcli.ncl.ac.uk/2008/issue1/bleasdale1.html

Blommaert, J. 2009. "Language, Asylum, and the National Order [with comments]." *Current Anthropology* 50, no. 4 (2009): 415–441. doi:10.1086/600131

Bloom, T. 2010. "Asylum-Seekers: Subjects or Objects of Research?" *The American Journal of Bioethics* 10, no. 2: 59–60. doi:10.1080/15265160903506426

Bowker, G. C., and S. L. Star. 2000. *Sorting Things Out: Classification and Its Consequences.* Cambridge, MA: MIT Press.

Briskman, L., and S. Cemlyn. 2005. "Reclaiming Humanity for Asylum-Seekers: A Social Work Response." *International Social Work* 48, no. 6: 714-724. doi:10.1177/0020872805056989

Brown, N., and M. Michael. 2003. "A Sociology of Expectations: Retrospecting Prospects and Prospecting Retrospects." *Technology Analysis & Strategic Management* 15, no.1: 3–18. doi:10.1080/0953732032000046024

Cashmore, J. "Yasser." In *Fenced Out Fenced In: Border Protection, Asylum and Detention in Australia*, edited by N. Bolzan, M. Darcy, and J. Mason, 9–12. Melbourne, Australia: Common Ground.

Castles, S. 2007. "The Factors That Make and Unmake Migration Policies." In *Rethinking Migration: New Theoretical and Empirical Perspectives*, edited by Alejandro Portes and Josh DeWind, 29–61. New York: Berghahn.

Clarkson, P. 2003. "War; Bystanding and Hate—Why Category Errors Are Dangerous." *Psychotherapy and Politics International* 1, no. 2: 117–132. doi:10.1002/ppi.59

Collyer, M. 2010. "Stranded Migrants and the fragmented journey." *Journal of Refugee Studies* 23, no. 3: 276–293. doi:10.1093/jrs/feq026

Crawley, H. 2006. "Forced Migration and the Politics of Asylum: The Missing Pieces Of The International Migration Puzzle?" *International Migration* 44, no. 1: 21–26. doi:10.1111/j.1468-2435.2006.00352.x

Crawley, H. 2010. *Chance or Choice?: Understanding Why Asylum Seekers Come to the UK.* London: British Refugee Council.

Crawley, H., and D. Skleparis. 2018. "Refugees, Migrants, Neither, Both: Categorical Fetishism and the Politics of Bounding in Europe's 'Migration Crisis.'" *Journal of Ethnic and Migration Studies* 44, no. 1: 48–64 doi:10.1080/1369183X.2017.1348224

Daniel, E. V. 2002. "The Refugee: A Discourse on Displacement." In *Exotic No More: Anthropology on the Front Lines*, edited by Jeremy MacClancy, 270–286. Chicago: University of Chicago Press.

Daniel, E. V, and J. C. Knudsen. 1995. *Mistrusting Refugees*. Berkeley: University of California Press.

Dimitriadi, A. 2018. *Irregular Afghan Migration to Europe: At the Margins, Looking In*. London: Palgrave Macmillan.

De Giorgi, A. 2010. "Immigration Control, Post-Fordism, and Less Eligibility: A Materialist Critique of the Criminalization of Immigration across Europe." *Punishment and Society* 12, no. 2: 147–167. doi:10.1177/1462474509357378

de Haas, H. 2007. "Turning the Tide? Why Development Will Not Stop Migration." *Development and Change* 38, no. 5: 819–841. doi:10.1111/j.1467-7660.2007.00435.x

Dwyer, P. 2008. "Meeting Basic Needs? Exploring the Survival Strategies of Forced Migrants." Project Report, Economic & Social Research Council. United Kingdom. http://usir.salford.ac.uk/id/eprint/12815

ERC (Edmund Rice Centre for Justice and Community Education). 2001. "Debunking the Myths about Asylum-Seekers," https://d3n8a8pro7vhmx.cloudfront.net/erc/pages/107/attachments/original/1460519416/Debunking_myths_combo.pdf?1460519416

Fassin, D., and E. D'Halluin. 2007. "Critical Evidence: The Politics of Trauma in French Asylum Policies." *Ethos* 35, no. 3: 300–329 doi:10.1525/eth.2007.35.3.300

Fekete, L., and F. Webber. 2010. "Foreign Nationals, Enemy Penology and the Criminal Justice System." *Race and Class* 51, no. 4: 1–25. doi:10.1177/0306396810362868

Ghorashi, H. 2007. "Giving Silence a Chance: The Importance of Life Stories for Research on Refugees." *Journal of Refugee Studies* 21, no. 1: 117–132. doi:10.1093/jrs/fem033

Ghufran, N. 2011. "The Role of UNHCR and Afghan Refugees in Pakistan." *Strategic Analysis* 35, no. 2 (2011): 945–954.

Glastra, F., and P. Vedder. 2010. "Learning Strategies of Highly Educated Refugees in the Netherlands: Habitus or Calculation?" *International Migration* 48, no. 1: 80–105. doi:10.1111/j.1468-2435.2009.00532.x

Hart, C. 2008. "Critical Discourse Analysis and Metaphor: Toward a Theoretical Framework." *Critical Discourse Studies* 5, no. 2 (2008): 91–106 doi:10.1080/17405900801990058

Havinga, T., and A. Böcker. 1999. "Country of Asylum by Choice or by Chance: Asylum-Seekers in Belgium, the Netherlands and the UK." *Journal of Ethnic and Migration Studies* 25, no. 1: 43–61. doi:10.1080/1369183X.1999.9976671

Hatton, T. J. 2009. "The Rise and Fall of Asylum: What Happened and Why?" *The Economic Journal* 119, 535: F183–F213. doi:10.1111/j.1468-0297.2008.02228.x

Hayenhjelm, M. 2006. "Out of the Ashes: Hope and Vulnerability as Explanatory Factors in Individual Risk Taking." *Journal of Risk Research* 9, no. 3: 189–204. doi:10.1080/13669870500419537

Holmes, S., and H. Castaneda. 2016. "Representing the 'European Refugee Crisis' in Germany and beyond: Deservingness and difference, Life and Death."*American Ethnologist*, 43, no 1: 12–24. doi:10.1111/amet.12259

Hörnqvist, M. 2004. "The Birth of Public Order Policy." *Race and Class* 46, no. 1: 30–52. doi:10.1177/0306396804045513

Innes, A. J. 2010. "When the Threatened Become the Threat: The Construction of Asylum Seekers in British Media Narratives" *International Relations*, 24, no 4: 456–477. doi:10.1177/0047117810385882

Kallius, A., D. Monterescu, and P. K. Rajaram. 2016. "Immobilizing obility: Border Ethnography, Illiberal Democracy, and the Politics of the 'Refugee Crisis' in Hungary". *American Ethnologist*, 43, no. 1: 25–37. doi:10.1111/amet.12260

Kirchheimer, O. 1959. "Asylum." *The American Political Science Review* 53, no. 4: 985–1016.

Koser, K. 1997. "Social Networks and the Asylum Cycle: The Case of Iranians in the Netherlands." *International Migration Review* 31, no. 3: 591–611.

Koser, K., and C. Pinkerton. 2002. *The Social Networks of Asylum-Seekers and the Dissemination of Information about Countries of Asylum*. Migration Research Office. University of London: Home Office, Research, Development and Statistics Directorate. http://www.urbanlab.org/articles/Koser_2002_SocialNetworksOfAsylumSeekers.pdf

Limbu, B. 2009. "Illegible Humanity: The Refugee, Human Rights, and the Question of Representation." *Journal of Refugee Studies* 22, no. 3: 257–282. doi:10.1093/jrs/fep021

Loescher, G., and J. Milner. 2003. "The Missing Link: The Need for Comprehensive Engagement in Regions of Refugee Origin." *International Affairs* 79, no. 3: 583–617. doi:10.1111/1468-2346.00325

Long, K., and J. Crisp. 2010. "Migration, Mobility and Solutions: An Evolving Perspective." *Forced Migration Review* 35:56–57. http://www.fmreview.org/disability-and-displacement/katy-long-and-jeff-crisp.html

Malkki, L. H. *Purity and Exile: Violence, Memory, and National Cosmology among Hutu Refugees in Tanzania*. Chicago: University of Chicago Press. 1995.

Moore, W. H., and S. M. Shellman 2007. "Whither Will They Go? A Global Study of Refugees' Destinations, 1965–1995." *International Studies Quarterly* 51, no. 4: 811–834. doi:10.1111/j.1468-2478.2007.00478.x

Muecke, M. A. 1992. "New Paradigms for Refugee Health Problems." *Social Science and Medicine* 35, no. 4: 515–523. doi:10.1016/0277-9536(92)90344-P

O'Doherty, K., and A. Lecouteur. 2007. "'Asylum-seekers,' 'boat people,' and 'illegal immigrants': Social Categorisation in the Media." *Australian Journal of Psychology* 59, no. 1: 1–12. doi:10.1080/00049530600941685

O'Neill, M., and T. Spybey. 2003. "Global Refugees, Exile, Displacement and Belonging." *Sociology* 37, no. 1: 7–12. doi:10.1177/0038038503037001385

Papastergiadis, N. "Wars of Mobility." *European Journal of Social Theory* 13, no. 3: 343–361. doi:10.1177/1368431010371756

Rees, S., and D. Silove. 2006. "Rights and Advocacy in Research with East Timorese Asylum Seekers in Australia." *Journal of Immigrant & Refugee Studies* 4, no. 2: 49–68. doi:10.1300/J500v04n02_03

Robinson, V., and J. Segrott. 2002. *Understanding the Decision-Making of Asylum-Seekers*. Home Office Research Study 243. Migration Unit, University of Wales. http://citeseerx.ist.psu.edu/viewdoc/download?doi=10.1.1.473.3461&rep=rep1&type=pdf

Rodgers, G. 2004. "'Hanging Out' with Forced Migrants: Methodological and Ethical Challenges." *Forced Migration Review*, 21: 48–49. http://www.fmreview.org/return-reintegration/rodgers.html

Rydgren, J. 2009. "Beliefs." In *The Oxford Handbook of Analytical Sociology*, edited by P. Hedström and P. Bearman, 72–93. Oxford: Oxford University Press.

Sabat, S. R. 2003. "Malignant Positioning and the Predicament of the Person with Alzheimer's Disease." In *The Self and Others: Positioning Individuals and Groups in Personal, Political, and Cultural Contexts,* edited by R. Harré and F. Moghaddam, 85–98. Westport, CT: Greenwood.

Silove, D. 2002. "The Asylum Debacle in Australia: A Challenge for Psychiatry." *Australian and New Zealand Journal of Psychiatry* 36, no. 3: 290–296. doi:10.1046/j.1440-1614.2002.01036.x

Sinapi, M. 2008. "The Displacements of the 'Shadow Line.'" *Social Science Information* 47, no. 4: 529–539. doi:10.1177/0539018408096445

Stalker, P. 2001. *The No-Nonsense Guide to International Migration.* Oxford: New Internationalist Publications.

Steadman, S.J, and F. Tanners, eds. 2003. *Refugee Manipulation: War, Politics and the Abuse of Human Suffering.* Washington, DC: Brookings Institution Press.

Taylor, D. 2009. *Underground Lives: An Investigation into the Living Conditions and Survival Strategies of Destitute Asylum Seekers in the UK,* Leeds: PAFRAS - Positive Action for Refugees and Asylum Seekers. http://www.iraqiassociation.org/pdf/Underground_Lives.pdf

Tazreiter, C. 2008. "Asylum." In *Encyclopedia of Race, Ethnicity, and Society,* edited by Richard T. Schaefer. London: Sage.

Turner, S. 2004. "Under the Gaze of the 'Big Nations': Refugees, Rumours and the International Community in Tanzania." *African Affairs* 103, no. 411: 227–247. doi:10.1093/afraf/adh006

Turner, B. 2010. "Enclosures, Enclaves, and Entrapment." *Sociological Inquiry* 80, no. 2: 241–260. doi:10.1111/j.1475-682X.2010.00329.x

Turton, D., and P. Marsden. 2002. *Taking Refugees for a Ride? The politics of refugee return to Afghanistan,* Issues Paper Series, The Afghanistan Research and Evaluation Unit (AREU), December. http://www.refworld.org/pdfid/47c3f3cb1a.pdf

UNHCR. 2016. *Global Trends: Forced Displacement in 2016,* UNHCR, The UN Refugee Agency. http://www.unhcr.org/5943e8a34.pdf

Watson, S. D. 2009. *The Securitization of Humanitarian Migration: Digging Moats and Sinking Boats.* Abington, UK: Routledge.

Welch, M., and L. Schuster. 2005. "Detention of Asylum-Seekers in the US, UK, France, Germany, and Italy: A Critical View of the Globalizing Culture of Control." *Criminal Justice* 5, no. 4: 331–355. doi:10.1177/1466802505057715

Williksen, S. 2004. "On the Run: The Narrative of an Asylum-Seeker." *Anthropology and Humanism* 29, no. 2: 117–132. doi:10.1525/ahu.2004.29.2.117

Wodak, R., P. Baker, C. Gabrielatos, M. KhosraviNik, M. Krzyzanowski, and T. McEnery. 2008. "A Useful Methodological Synergy? Combining Critical Discourse Analysis and Corpus Linguistics to Examine Discourses of Refugees and Asylum- Seekers in the UK Press." *Discourse and Society* 19, no. 3: 273–306. doi:10.1177/0957926508088962

Zimmermann, S. "Why Seek Asylum? The Roles of Integration and Financial Support." *International Migration* 48, no.1: 199–231. doi:10.1111/j.1468-2435.2009.00552.x

CHAPTER 24

MIGRATION CRISES IN TURKEY

ZEYNEP KIVILCIM

According to the UNHCR, Turkey is the country that hosts highest number of refugees in the world (UNHCR 2016; UNHCR 2017). The vast majority of the individuals who are named as "refugees" in UNHCR's statistics and hosted in Turkey are non-European asylum-seekers (IOM 2017), whereas Turkey's legislation accords refugee status to the asylum-seekers only if they originate from European countries.[1] The definition of "migrant" in the Turkish legislation is also highly specific. The Settlement Law provides that migrants are persons of Turkish descent and culture who immigrated to Turkey[2]. The important differences between the essential categories of international law of migration and Turkey's legislation are not due to the normative difficulties of distinction of "refugees" and "migrants" in the current refugee flows within the UN Refugee Convention's criteria, but rather to Turkish state's politics of legality in the field of migration.

This chapter aims to study the dynamics of migration policies in Turkey and the self-interest of Turkish state as a motivating factor to its legal responses to refugee "crises." It maintains that the figures of refugees are referential and affirmative resources for states' sovereign practices and that the rhetoric of "crisis" provides larger opportunities for this practice.

The paradigm of crisis nurtures and sustains legislation and policies in the field of migration and asylum in Turkey. The Turkish state's migration legislation consists mainly of the subsequent codifications of its practice relating to different crises constructed around the mass influxes of migrants into its territory. This context of crisis determines not only the scope and content of the legislative and political measures but also shapes the structures of the institutions in the field of immigration. Besides the paradigm of "Europeanization," materializes in the effort for the alignment of the national legislation with the legal regimes governing migrants in Europe.

The Paradigm of Crisis Motivates and Shapes Immigration Policy and Legislation

Turkey's policies in the field of migration followed the main shifts in the global politics developed around the category of "refugee" during and after the Cold War. During the Cold War the legal articulation of the refugee category evolved around the ideological opposition between two camps. Receiving countries could make use of population flows to discredit the government and the ideological system in the country of origin (Haddad 2008, 88–140). After the end of Cold War this ideological basis of asylum disappeared. The refugee no longer has the same ideological or political value. The post–Cold War legal paradigm demonstrates a move from protection to physical and legal containment of people in "holding zones" or "holding legal regimes" of temporary protection (Goodwin-Gill 2008; Mertus 1998). The governments invest interest on means and modalities of forced containment of refugees as well as the new flexibilities for their fast return to their countries of origin.

During the last decades, the impact of national security discourse has increased in the field of refugee law. In response to major armed attacks in the United States and Europe, lawmakers believed that more safeguards were needed to prevent the use of international refugee protection as a safe haven by "foreign terrorists" (Bhat 2013; De Genova 2017, 10–15; Greenhill 2016, 323–324). The application of the exclusion grounds in the Refugee Convention were what was needed and sufficient. But states made changes to national refugee protection legislation in which "terrorist activities" were defined so broadly as to leave the administrative authorities a great deal of discretion to determine which organizations were considered to be terrorist ones and according to what evidence a link could be established between such organizations and migrants. This shift is crucial for asylum-seekers because they are frequently engaged in opposition movements against repressive governments. The global politics of legality in the field of migration have impacted on Turkey's migration policy, which is nurtured by the crisis paradigm and oriented by the interests of the Turkish state.

Constructing and Governing the Migration Crises According to Changing Political Interests

During the Cold War, Turkey received mass influxes from the ex-Soviet bloc countries of the Balkan region, as well as from eastern Turkestan and Afghanistan. These migration flows are not officially named as "crisis" and not managed under the "crisis" rhetoric. The arriving migrants were legally qualified as "persons who are of Turkish origin and belonging to Turkish culture" and received privileged treatment. The favorable treatment accorded to these individuals is attributed to their ethnic or linguistic links to Turkey. But it has also its ideological reasons in Turkey's anticommunist policies during the Cold War for sheltering the ones fleeing from "communist persecution" (Kirişçi 1996). Being of Turkish origin and culture always implied and still implies social and legal advantages. Persons of Turkish descent and culture who immigrated to Turkey are authorized to reside in Turkey upon their arrival; they are also eligible for citizenship according to a simplified naturalization procedure.[3] The International Workforce Law provides that foreigners "declared by Ministry of Interior or Ministry of Foreign Affairs as of Turkish origin" may be granted exceptional work permits (International Workforce Law 2016).

The flows that are constructed by Turkish governments as "migration crises" are essentially the influxes of asylum-seekers who fled Iraq and Syria searching for refuge in Turkey. Turkey did not have a migration law until 2014. Before the entry into force of the Law on Foreigners and International Protection in 2014, Turkey's asylum regime had been regulated by the 1994 Asylum Regulation and the 2006 Implementation Directive.[4]

The Asylum Regulation is motivated and framed by Turkey's experience of the 1988 and 1991 Iraqi refugee "crisis." When in 1988 the Iraqi Kurds fled Iraqi military forces and came to Turkey's borders, the Turkish government opened the border only after domestic and international pressure (Ihlamur-Öner and Suna Gülfer 2013, 195). The Kurdish Iraqi families are housed in temporary shelter centers close to Iraqi border. They are expected to leave Turkey as soon as possible and are considered as "temporary guests" rather than asylum seekers. Turkey did not grant refugee status to them because of its geographical limitation to the Geneva Convention. The UNHCR was not allowed to approach them to give assistance and protection (Içduygu 2000).

In 1991, a bigger influx of Iraqi Kurdish refugees came to Turkey. The influx was stopped on the border, the border was closed, and the Turkish security forces moved into the Iraqi side of the border to keep Kurdish refugees out of the Turkey's territory (Frelick 1997, 26–27). The border was opened only following the UN Security Council Resolution and the refugees were temporarily settled in a camp. [5]

The 1994 Asylum Regulation was the codification of the governments' practices relating to Iraqi Kurdish influxes and it enabled them to govern the mass arrivals according to the political considerations. The regulation provided that the mass movement of refugees should be stopped at the border, and that asylum-seekers should be prevented from crossing into Turkey unless "no political decisions are taken to the contrary."[6] The Asylum Regulation aimed to determine the rules governing asylum-seekers coming from non-European countries with an enhanced control of Turkish authorities over the immigration, residence, and resettlement procedures. But it was not successful in reaching its objectives. It established an asylum regime that neither responded to government's aims to control the migration flows nor to the country's international legal obligations under human rights treaties. It has been modified several times, mainly for responding to international critics and in particular following the decisions of the European Court of Human Rights condemning Turkey's legislation and practices.

Turkey's second legislative attempt for regulating migration and asylum was generated simultaneous to the construction of another migration "crisis." The Law on Foreigners and International Protection and the Temporary Protection Regulation was drafted and adopted during the influxes of Syrian refugees into Turkey that began in 2011.[7] The Law and the Regulation both entered into force in 2014.

The global post–Cold War legal paradigm of physical and legal containment of people in "holding zones" or "holding legal regimes" is visible in the 1994 Asylum Regulation, which also shapes the Law on Foreigners and International Protection. The vast majority of the refugees in Turkey are not physically contained in camps.[8] However, the law ensures their legal containment in different legal categories and prevents their access to international protection.

Turkey maintains its geographical limitation to the UN Refugee Convention and the Law on Foreigners and International Protection accords refugee status to European asylum-seekers. Because of that limitation, there are very few (approximately one hundred) people with refugee status in Turkey (Skribeland 2016, 13). The individuals who have not become refugees as a result of events occurring in Europe and who enter Turkey due to a well-founded fear of persecution can be granted a "conditional refugee status" after a determination procedure and an evaluation of their application. The law provides also a "subsidiary protection" status for those protection-seekers who are not considered to be refugees or conditional refugees but would face a risk of the death penalty, torture, inhuman or degrading treatment, or serious threat of violence in situations of international or nationwide armed conflict at the country of origin. The "humanitarian residence permit holders" are predominantly Iraqi nationals (IOM 2017). The beneficiaries of the status of conditional refugee, subsidiary protection, or holders of humanitarian residence permits receive a lesser set of rights and entitlements as compared to "refugee" status-holders.

Turkish legislation does not provide a real option for integration or naturalization. The European refugees, non-European conditional refugees, persons under subsidiary protection, or holders of humanitarian residence permits and persons under temporary protection cannot apply for long-term residence permits.[9] The Migrant Integration Policy Index (MIPEX) Report, ranked Turkey last place out of thirty-eight countries studied (Migrant Integration Policy Index 2015), because the country's legislation and practice fails according to almost all 167 indicators used in the study.[10] The study indicates that the adoption and implementation of the Law on Foreigners and International Protection did not make any significant change but generally formalized existing practices.

Besides Turkey's geographical limitation to the UN Refugee Convention, the second and most important barrier that hinders non-European asylum seekers in Turkey in attaining international protection is their legal containment in the Temporary Protection Regime. Turkey's temporary protection regime deserves scrutiny, not only because it is the legal regime that governs the world's biggest refugee population, but also because, according to the EU-Turkey Refugee Deal of 2016, this regime is endorsed by the European Union as the only safe solution to the so called "refugee crisis."

The Turkish Temporary Protection Regulation provides a temporary protection regime conceived for responding the mass influxes of migrants. It states that temporary protection shall be granted to foreigners who were forced to leave their countries and are unable to return to the countries they left and who arrived at or crossed Turkey's borders in masses to seek urgent and temporary protection and, finally, whose international protection requests cannot be taken under individual assessment.[11] The Regulation indicates that "persons benefiting from temporary protection shall not be deemed as having been directly acquired one of the international protection statuses as defined in the Law."[12] The Regulation prevents the persons under temporary protection to apply for international protection.[13] After the termination of the temporary protection, the Council of Ministers can allow some groups of persons to apply for international protection. Otherwise "exits of persons benefiting from temporary protection following the Council of Ministers' decision on the termination of temporary protection shall be essential."[14]

The Temporary Protection Regulation clearly demonstrates that the temporary protection regime is operated discretionally by the Council of Ministers. According to the Regulation, the temporary protection decision is taken by the Council of Ministers and the Council of Ministers is also solely authorized to determine who will be covered under temporary protection; the effective date of temporary protection and its duration if considered necessary; the conditions for extending and ending temporary protection; and whether or not temporary protection will be implemented countrywide or in a specific region.[15]

Additionally, Temporary Protection Regulation's provisions are implemented deliberately in a selective way; parts of the Regulation can be de facto suspended and can be revitalized afterwards at an unforeseen moment if implemented discretionally by changing operational actors (Baklacıoğlu and Kivilcim 2015). Lack of transparency is another important concern. Implementation of the Law on Foreigners and International Protection as well as the Temporary Protection are shaped by various governmental and administrative decisions, orders, or circulars that are not made publicly available (Skribeland 2016, 18).[16]

Ninety percent of asylum-seekers in Turkey are Syrians who fled from the civil war ravaging the country since 2011. Temporary Protection Regulation provides that persons coming from Syria due to events that have taken place in the country since April 28, 2011 shall be covered under temporary protection, even if they have filed an application for international protection. The Article urges that their individual applications for international protection shall not be processed during the implementation of temporary protection.[17] As such, 3.5 million Syrian asylum-seekers are kept in an exceptional legal regime with no legal possibility of obtaining international protection. The keeping of Syrians in the temporary protection regime for an indefinite period should be interpreted as a political strategy by the government of Turkey, given that it is openly involved in the Syrian conflict. Syrians are detained in the temporary protection regime and are forced to accept its conditions given that their stay in Turkey's territory depends on the sole discretion of the government.

The discretion of the executive is extremely extensive after the declaration of the state of emergency in July 2016. The state of emergency regime entitles the Turkish Council of Ministers to issue emergency decrees with the force of law, which can restrict the fundamental rights of individuals—citizens and noncitizens alike. These emergency decrees are not subject to review by the Turkish Constitutional Court. The government makes use of the decrees for modifying the immigration regulations.[18]

Economically Useful "Crisis": The Exploitation of Unfree Syrian Labor

Ensuring and increasing the flexibility of the labor market is one of the primary goals declared in Turkey's National Economic Development Plan (Republic of Turkey Ministry of Development 2014) as well as in the National Employment Strategy (Republic of Turkey Ministry of Labour and Social Security 2014). As Calavita points out, economies with an emphasis on flexibility derive substantial benefits from marginalized immigrants and refugees: "law is a pivotal factor in shoring up the economic flexibility that is a welcome by-product of the marginalization" of refugees (Calavita 1998). The refugee crisis paradigm and the keeping of Syrian refugees in a separate and impermeable regime of temporary protection provide for the Turkish government the opportunities for the exploitation of this new workforce under specific legal conditions.

The concept of "unfree labor" is used to describe migrant workers who are not free to circulate in the country or between sectors in the labor market. The Temporary Protection Regulation indicates that the procedures and principles concerning the work of persons under temporary protection will be determined by the Ministry of Labor and Social Security after the proposal by the Council of Ministers, with specific restrictions based on geography and sector.[19] The Regulation on Work Permit of Refugees Under Temporary Protection was issued on January 15, 2016. It covers Syrians who have completed their registration procedure and it provides that they will be able to apply for a work permit six months after they obtain a temporary protection status, but the work permit is not required in part-time seasonal jobs in agriculture. The Regulation imposes a quota; the number of refugees holding a work permit must not exceed 10 percent of the total number of employees at any workplace.[20] The regulation stipulates that the persons under temporary protection will not be paid below the minimum wage.

It is expected that the new Regulation will lead to a rise of supply in the number of Syrian refugees working in seasonal agricultural production in coming years. However some reports estimate that the Regulation risks impacting negatively on Syrian refugees. It is noted that there is a room for employers to take advantage of struggling Syrians by demanding unofficial fees for employment applications, or by underpaying Syrians who are desperate enough not to complain about the violation of the Regulation (Refugee International 2016). Another report points out that the Regulation's piecemeal approach to regularizing Syrian workers without the formalization of entire sectors or the regularization of all migrant workers cannot benefit Syrian refugees, but it risks increasing the unemployment of Syrians in low-wage and in informal sectors as other, cheaper workers of different nationalities are hired (Shadow Report 2016).

There are particular concerns that the Regulation would not have any positive impact for Syrian refugees employed in small enterprises. It is noted that small enterprises will be less able to offer the work permit sponsorship and may well continue to rely upon informal workers, including Syrians (Refugee International 2016). According to the Regulation, Syrian refugees can be employed only within the province they are registered. This restriction complicates the legal employment of refugees since they are generally registered at the border towns following their entry into Turkish territory, but have to move to larger cities for finding a job.

The entry of the Syrian workers into labor market under these conditions resulted in a segment of native workforce losing employment, yet they also enabled others to transition from the informal to the formal labor market. The results of the researches indicate the gendered impact of the Syrian refugees' arrival on the Turkish labor market and emphasize that low-skilled native female workers were affected worst by refugee influx (Del Carpio and Wagner 2015; Erol et al. 2017,100).

Exploitative conditions of work in informal sector, including long working hours and wages lower that the Turkish coworkers, are reported in many field researches. Almost half of the Syrian children under temporary protection are out of school; many refugee children are working instead of attending school because of their parents' inability to cover their family costs with their parents' wages alone (Refugee International 2016, 7). Efforts by the Turkish government to formalize employment, particularly for Syrians under temporary protection through the Regulation on the Work Permits for Foreigners under Temporary Protection, have been largely ineffective. The Turkish government issued 14,000 work permits to persons under temporary protection since the adoption of the concerned Regulation (Refugee International 2017). Commentators argue that the economic and sectoral realities, widespread disregard for formalized labor in Turkey, the stratified structure of the labor markets, and discrimination compounded with the restrictions provided in the legislation makes it unlikely to reach the goal of formal employment among Syrian refugees in the future. (Observatory for Human Rights and Forced Migrants in Turkey 2017).

The Challenge of Europeanization: Alignment with Two Contradicting European Regimes of Migration

The second paradigm governing Turkish migration policies is the "Europeanization" of migration legislation and institutions. The jurisprudence of the European Court of Human Rights (ECtHR) and the European Union's regulations in the field of migration are two main external factors having extensive impact on reframing of migration and asylum institutions and policies. However, while the ECtHR decisions constituted a defining factor in the further improvement of the migrants' rights, the EU constituted a legitimizing factor for further strengthening of the border security. The EU-Turkey Refugee Deal that was agreed between Turkey and the heads of the EU member states was presented as the necessary legal tool for managing the constructed European refugee crisis of 2015.

European Union Policy Transfer to Turkey: Deflecting the Arrival of Asylum-Seekers and Deterring Their Access to International Protection

The impact of the EU immigration policy and regulations on Turkey occurs under two different processes. In the first place, the Turkish legislative, administrative, and political system in the field of immigration is transformed as part of the 'externalization' of the EU migration control towards its neighboring countries. The conditionality for EU membership frames the second process through which Turkey's regulations and institutions are transformed. As a candidate state Turkey has accepted the transformation of its political and legal system within the adoption of the EU *acquis communitaire* and this is achieved through legislation and policy harmonization in its pre-accession process. This process of alignment with the EU *acquis* generates an important catalyst of the EU policy transfer to Turkey similar to other candidate countries. The adoption of the EU *acquis* and the harmonization of immigration legislation, in some respects, is encouraging a decline in protection of refugee rights.

Since the beginning of the EU accession process in 2003, the EU conditionality has risen as an important imperative in the further adoption and implementation of the EU *acquis* and has had an impact on the institutional building and legislative efforts in the field of immigration. The Turkish National Action Plan on Asylum and Migration adopted in 2005 and the National Action Plan on Integrated Border Management enacted the following year were the cornerstones of Europeanization of Turkey's asylum policy. Ensuring border security, fighting irregular migration, and organized crime are raised as the primary areas of action under the Turkey's Harmonization Program to the EU *Acquis*.[21] Legal developments since 2003 within the frame of the harmonization of Turkish legislation on migration and asylum with the EU *acquis* provided the gradual securitization of the immigration field and the transformation of Turkey to a buffer zone at the edge of EU. These developments included the ratification of the UN Convention against transnational organized crime and its additional protocol against the smuggling of migrants by land, sea and air; the adoption of the national action plan on combating human trafficking as well as the adoption of the national action plan for the implementation of integrated border management strategy in 2006; and the drafting of the Law on border security and the adoption of the Directive on Removal centers in 2014.

The externalization of the EU's asylum policy demonstrates a strong tendency to deter refugees from seeking asylum in the territories of its member states. Through the legal modifications required within the asylum *acquis*, the EU tries to keep refugees in transit countries, including Turkey, which is encouraged to improve its conditions for access to asylum process for being qualified as 'first country of asylum' (Yıldız 2016).

The influence of the EU on Turkey persisted even after the negative context of EU-Turkey relations and the severe hardship in the accession negotiations after 2006. This continuity is explained by the policy conditionally articulated by the EU through the short term and relatively more obtainable goal of visa liberalization. The 2013 Readmission Agreement between EU and Turkey is adopted thanks to the introduction of the visa liberalization road map that will enable Turkish citizens' visa-free travel to the EU member states.[22] The readmission agreements are an important tool of the EU's 'migration management'. They allow for the readmission by states into their territory of both their own nationals and nationals of other states who have found in an illegal situation in the territory of the EU. In return, the concerned state receives some benefits adjusted according to the regional political dynamics or the state's bargaining power vis-à-vis to the EU (Wolff 2014). The EU-Turkey Readmission agreement establishes for Turkey the obligation to readmit the migrants who hold a residence permit issued by Turkey or who entered the territory of the EU member states after having stayed on, or transited through, the territory of Turkey.

The EU readmission agreements are criticized because of the lack of guarantee for the individual and fair identification procedure for migrants. There are also concerns because these agreements give rise to chain readmissions. Turkey is an example in this respect. Turkish Ministry of Foreign Affairs declares that Turkey has readmission agreement with fifteen countries (Greece, Russian Federation, Yemen, Nigeria, Bosnia Herzegovina, Kyrgyzstan, Pakistan, Romania, Syria, Ukraine, Belarus, Montenegro, Moldova, Kosovo, and Norway).[23] In addition to Iran and Iraq, Turkey has proposed Afghanistan, Algeria, Bangladesh, Cameroon, Eritrea, Morocco, Ghana, Myanmar, the Republic of Congo, Somali, Sudan, and Tunisia to conclude readmission agreements (Kart 2016). These networks of readmission work for the return of individuals fleeing from persecution to their country of origin.

The literature acknowledges the EU and the objective of the adoption of EU *acquis* in the field of immigration as the most important external factor that influenced the Turkish Law on Foreigners and International Protection (Bürgin and Aşıkoğlu 2017; Demiryontar 2016). The Turkish Law of Foreigners and International Protection has incorporated the EU's externalization policy and includes the concepts of "first country of asylum" and "safe third country" as well as accelerated procedures.[24] The EU-Turkey Refugee Deal that was agreed to in 2016 is one of the most important examples of the externalization of the EU migration control to neighboring countries and the legal tool for managing the constructed refugee crisis of 2015.[25]

In 2015, the influx of migrants to Europe taking the dangerous or even deadly sea crossing from Turkey to Greek islands and the increase in the numbers of people applying for asylum in Europe was framed as a 'crisis' by politicians as well as by the media in Europe. What was experienced in 2015 were the consequences of the EU's regulations that prevent refugees from traveling legally to the EU, the inability for Syrian refugees to establish an acceptable form of subsistence in the region, and the lack of possibility for resettlement in third countries.

The EU-Turkey Refugee Deal was presented as the "only possible solution" to this constructed refugee "crisis" and it was designed to reduce the number of migrants crossing into Europe from Turkey. The rationale behind the Deal is that 'we face a crisis' and that it is impossible to manage this "crisis" through application of the already existing EU regulations. This rationale is questionable for two reasons. First, Europe appears to feel so surrounded by and fearful of the refugee influx but from the perspective of absolute numbers such a reaction seems overwrought. According to UNHCR statistics, the overwhelming majority, more than 90 percent of Syrians who fled the country, remain in the region.[26] Europe, by contrast, has given refuge to around a million Syrians— that is, less than 0.2 percent of its population. The Europe's refugee "crisis" seems almost virtual or even hypocritical regarding the numbers of arrivals and Europe's own history of migrations.[27]

The arguments according to which EU has no preexisting legislation applicable for dealing with the refugee influx of 2015 are also questionable because the EU has a Directive that deals specifically with mass influxes of migrants: The Temporary Protection Directive of 2001.[28] This directive was elaborated following the former refugee "crisis" that the EU faced at the end of the 1990s because of the conflicts in the former Yugoslavia, but never activated since its adoption. The 2015 refugee influx could have been the opportunity for the first implementation of that Directive. But EU member states decided that it was not convenient for them and a deal with Turkey was considered and presented as the only possible option. The Turkish Temporary Protection Regulation that governs Syrians refugees in Turkey was drafted following the model of the EU Temporary Protection Directive. The EU considered the EU Directive as inappropriate for dealing with the Syrian refugee influx but it returned these refugees to Turkey where the legal frame set up according to this Directive was implemented.

The EU-Turkey Deal and the way it is implemented are in explicit breach with EU member states' and Turkey's obligations under international refugee law and international human rights law. It constitutes an important precedent of an international outlaw refugee regime. Openly setting back the principle of respect for human rights, the deal evidences a new politics of legality in the field of immigration. The United Nations High Commissioner for Refugees (UNHCR) expressed strong concerns about the Deal, warned the Deal presents a real risk of overlooking EU's human rights law obligations, and urged the EU to implement practical recommendations made by UN and other international organizations (UN Human Rights Office of High Commissioner 2016a). The UN Special Rapporteur on the human rights of migrants stated that it appeared EU member states considered human rights and the rule of law to be dispensable as regard migrants under the circumstances (UN Human Rights Office of High Commissioner 2016b). At the first anniversary of the Deal, UNICEF warned that after the Deal refugee and migrant children face greater risks of deportation, detention, exploitation, and deprivation (UNICEF 2017). Amnesty International described the deal as "a historic blow to rights" and a "shameful stain on the collective conscience of Europe" (Amnesty International 2017). Human Rights Watch reported that the Deal that "traps people in abuse and denies them refuge" "has set a dangerous precedent by putting at risk the very principle of the right to seek refuge" (HRW 2017)

The Impact of the European Court of Human Rights' Jurisprudence and the Improvement of Asylum-Seekers' Rights

The European Court of Human Rights (ECtHR) is the second international actor that shows extensive impact on the legislative and institutional transition of the asylum system in Turkey. The Court's decisions influence Turkish asylum regulations, policies, and practices by different ways. First, several ECHR decisions have given raise to regulative changes. Although these punctual revisions were not part of a holistic legislative reform but consist of eclectic reactive changes to each of ECtHR's decisions, they had crucial importance for the improvement of asylum-seekers' rights in Turkey (Kivilcim 2014, 160).

The short-term period for submitting an asylum application provided in the Turkish Asylum Regulation has been increased and the right to appeal has been provided to asylum-seekers whose application have been refused.[29] Asylum-seekers in the so-called "guest houses" are given access to UNHCR, to refugee status determination (RSD) procedure, and to a lawyer.[30] Prohibition of long-term detention of irregular migrants in police stations as well as the guarantee of *non-refoulement* for rejected asylum-seekers to their home countries before the risks that he/she faces are assessed in the framework of European Convention of Human Rights are all changes introduced following the decisions of the ECtHR condemning regulations and administrative practices of Turkey in the field.[31]

The ECtHR's jurisprudence related to refugees and asylum-seekers human rights was taken into consideration while drafting the Law on Foreigners and International Protection.[32] Reflecting the ECtHR jurisprudence, the Law grants certain procedural guarantees to asylum-seekers during the application process such as free legal aid by bar associations, access to interpretation services, and the right to stay at reception and accommodation centers during the asylum process.[33] It guarantees the UNHCR's access to asylum-seekers and special assistance and priority to unaccompanied minors and persons with special needs.[34]

The ECtHR interim measure procedure constitutes for asylum-seekers and refugees in Turkey, just like in other European countries, the only prompt and effective measure for preventing their removal to the territories where they risk torture and ill treatment.[35] Because of the failure of the member states to assure the proper assessment of risks which operate with respect for human rights and to provide national remedies with suspensive effect in deportation cases, the European Court of Human Rights assumes, in many cases, the role of the immigration appeals tribunal of Europe.

Conclusion

Shaped by the paradigm of crisis, Turkey's migration regulations and institutions govern the world's biggest refugee population. While these regulations were gradually 'Europeanized,' the nationalist paradigm continues to frame the legislation and determine migrants' legal status according to their presumed affiliation to Turkish culture and language. The fragmental legal landscape governing the migrants and refugees' status in Turkey mainly demonstrates the Turkish state's politics of legality in the field of migration. It provides flexibility for discretionary governance in order to define who deserves protection and what kind of protection according to Turkey's changing political and economical interests.

Migrants and refugees emerge as the site of human rights. The existing human rights norms and their implementation by the ECtHR limit the discretion of the Turkish state for the full instrumentalization of migration movements according to its self-interest.

On the other hand, adoption of the EU *acquis* and the externalization of the EU's migration control deflects the arrival of asylum-seekers and prevents their access to international protection in Turkey. The EU-Turkey Refugee Deal, presented as the 'only possible solution' to the constructed European refugee 'crisis,' masks the incredible failure of European migration policies and also destroys the very principle of the human right to seek refuge.

Notes

1. 90 per cent of the foreign nationals present on Turkey's territory who seek international protection are Syrians. In addition, there are more than 380,000 asylum-seekers and refugees consisting of different nationalities, but mainly coming from Afghanistan, Iraq, Iran, and Somalia reside in Turkey (IOM 2017). Turkey is one of the few countries that maintain the geographical limitation pursuant to Article 1B of the 1951 Convention. Thus, the application of the 1951 Convention is limited "to persons who have become refugees as a result of events occurring in Europe." In this context, Turkey defines Europe as all members of the Council of Europe, including Russia and ex-Soviet states west of the Urals (including the Caucasus).
2. Settlement Law, Sept. 19, 2006, Article 3. See also the Regulation on the Implementation of the Turkish Citizenship Law, April 6, 2010, Article 3 (g).
3. Settlement Law, Articles 5-8, Citizenship Law Article 12 (d).
4. See Regulation No. 1994/6169 on the Procedures and Principles related to Possible Population Movements and Aliens Arriving in Turkey either as Individuals or in Groups Wishing to Seek Asylum either from Turkey or Requesting Residence Permission in order to Seek

Asylum from Another Country, No. 1994/6169, 19 January 1994. See also Implementation Directive, Ministry of the Interior, 22 June 2006 (No: B.05.1.EGM.0.13.03.02/16147 71810–12/Gnl.D.6-6, Directive NO: 57).

5. Security Council resolution adopted on 5 April 1991, S/RES/688 (1991).
6. Article 8 of the Asylum Regulation.
7. Temporary Protection Regulation, 22 October 2014. The English translation of the text of the Regulation is available at http://www.refworld.org/docid/56572fd74.html. Turkey: Law No. 6458 of 2013 on Foreigners and International Protection, 4 April 2013. The English translation of the text of the Law is available at http://www.refworld.org/docid/5167fbb20.html.
8. More than 90 percent of the asylum seekers, including Syrians live in urban areas (DGMM 2016).
9. Article 42 (2) of the Law on Foreigners and International Protection.
10. Immigrant workers and their families have restricted rights and little-to-no state support. The policies are unfavorable for labour market mobility, education, and political participation. Turkey has the weakest protections against discrimination, and settled immigrants face not only a slightly unfavorable path to citizenship but also one of the least favorable paths to simply a long-term residence permit.
11. Article 7 (1). Following the adoption of the EU-Turkey Refugee Deal in 2016, an amendment to the Regulation provided that those Syrians who have irregularly transited through Turkey to Greece and are returned by Greece after 20th of March 2016 may upon request be provided with temporary protection under the Regulation.
12. Article 7 (3) of the Temporary Protection Regulation.
13. Article 16 of the Temporary Protection Regulation.
14. Article 14 of the Temporary Protection Regulation.
15. Article 9 and 10 of the Temporary Protection Regulation.
16. There is also restriction on research on Syrian refugees. The conduct of the research by academics as well as national or international institutions on Syrian refugees was subjected to the prior approval of concerned ministries during most of 2015. In a directive dated April 10 and classified as "secret," the Higher Education Council (YOK) informed the administration of all universities in the country about this restriction, justifying it by respect for refugees' privacy. Following intense critics, the restriction is lifted in December 2015.
17. The provisional Article 1 of the Temporary Regulation, which prevents categorically all Syrians from applying for international protection for unlimited time, is in conflict with Turkey's international legal obligations under the UN Refugee Convention and is therefore in breach with Turkey's Constitution. Article 16 of Turkey's Constitution provides that "the fundamental rights and freedoms in respect to aliens may be restricted by law compatible with international law." State of Emergency Decree-Law 676 of 29.10.2016 made significant amendments concerning the deportation of asylum-seekers and refugees and removed significant safeguards against *non-refoulement*.
18. A state of emergency decree-law promulgated on 29th of October 2016 amended three articles of the Law of Foreigners and International Protection. Accordingly, asylum-seekers and fully recognized refugees can be deported at any point if they are recognized as a member of terrorist organization. The provision does not require a court decision or formal procedure for declaring a foreign national to be a member of a terrorist organization.
19. Article 29 of the Temporary Protection Regulation.

20. The Ministry of Interior can establish geographical limitations; in the provinces notified by the Interior Ministry as objectionable for public order and security or public health reasons, the Labour Ministry will cease to issue work permits to Syrian refugees.
21. Immigration and asylum issues are part of Chapter 24 (Justice, Freedom and Security) of the European Union *acquis*.
22. Agreement between the European Union and the Republic of Turkey on the Readmission of Persons Residing without Authorisation, Signed on 16/12/2013; Official Journal of the European Union, 7.5.2014, L 134/3.
23. Republic of Turkey Ministry of Foreign Affairs, Turkey on Irregular Migration, http://www.mfa.gov.tr/turkey-on-irregular-migration.en.mfa.
24. The Law provides that the applications of persons coming from a first country of asylum or safe third country will be refused (Article 72). Applications of asylum-seekers who have used forged documents or mislead the authorities, who have been placed under administrative detention pending removal, or who pose a public order or public security threat shall be evaluated under accelerated procedure. Under the accelerated procedure, the assessment of the application shall be finalized no later than five days after the interview. The accelerated procedure limits the rights of the applicant for the judicial review of the decision. The decision of the administrative court on the assessment of the application will be final, and the applicants are prevented from appeal in higher instances. (Article 79). For further details see (Soykan 2017).
25. The legal nature of the text is uncertain. It is named as 'Statement', 'Deal' or 'Agreement'. European Council, EU-Turkey Statement, Press release, 144/16, 18 March 2016.
26. Turkey hosts 3.5 million Syrian refugees, Lebanon hosts one million and another 650,000 have found refuge in Jordan. See UNHCR, Syria Regional Refugee Response, http://data.unhcr.org/syrianrefugees/regional.php.
27. UNHCR, Europe: Syrian Asylum Applications, http://data.unhcr.org/syrianrefugees/asylum.php
28. See Council Directive 2001/55/EC of 20 July 2001 on minimum standards for giving temporary protection in the event of a mass influx of displaced persons and on measures promoting a balance of efforts between Member States in receiving such persons and bearing the consequences thereof
29. The concerned amendments to the 1994 Asylum Regulation are introduced following the decision of European Court of Human Rights (ECtHR) in the case of Jabari. (See ECtHR. 2000, Fourth Section, Case of Jabari v. Turkey (Application no. 40035/98) Judgment, 11 July 2000, Final, 11/10/2000.
30. These regulative changes are done by the two circulars of the Ministry of Interior introduced as a response to ECtHR decisions concerning the ECtHR. 2010, Case of Abdolkhani and Karimnia v. Turkey (Application no. 50213/08), Judgment, 27 July 2010 and the ECtHR. 2011, Case Mogaddas Moghaddas v. Turkey, (Application no. 46134/08), Judgment 15 February 2011. The Circular 2010/18 provided that the immigrants held in the 'repatriation centers' will be given access to UNHCR upon their request. They can also access a lawyer, providing that they cover the charges. The Circular 2010/19 provides that asylum-seekers who have been arrested after having entered Turkey illegally, during the period that they are awaiting for their expulsion, will by all means be given access to refugee status determination (RSD) procedure.
31. Following the deportation of two detained Uzbek asylum-seekers to Uzbekistan in April 1999 in contradiction to the European Court of Human Rights interim decision, The

Court ruled that a failure by a contracting state to comply with interim measures is to be regarded as preventing the Court from effectively examining the applicant's complaint and that consequently Turkey is in breach of its obligations under Article 34 of the Convention (see ECtHR. 2005, Mamatkulov and Askarov v. Turkey, Applications nos. 46827/99 and 46951/99) Judgement, 4 February 2005). The following year, the Ministry of Interior issued a Circular that indicated that the rejected asylum-seeker would not be returned to his/her home country before the risks that he/she faces are assessed in the framework of European Convention of Human Rights.

32. Turkey Grand National Assembly, Reports of the Human Rights Commission and Commission of Internal Affairs on the Draft Law of Foreigners and International Protection, 24/2, No: 310, 1/619. https://www.tbmm.gov.tr/sirasayi/donem24/yil01/ss310.pdf.
33. Article 81 and 95.
34. Article 92, 66, and 67.
35. The European Court of Human Rights may, under Rule 39 of its Rules of Court, "indicate interim measures to any State party to the European Convention on Human Rights. Interim measures are urgent measures which, according to the Court's well-established practice, apply only where there is an imminent risk of irreparable harm". With regard to asylum-seekers, the Court would order the concerned State to stay the execution of their removal to their country of origin or another country.

References

Agreement between the European Union and the Republic of Turkey on the Readmission of Persons Residing without Authorisation. 2013. Signed on 16/12/2013, Official Journal of the European Union, 7.5.2014, L 134/3. https://eur-lex.europa.eu/legal-content/en/TXT/?uri=CELEX%3A22014A0507%2801%29

Amnesty International. 2017. "A Blueprint for Despair. Human Rights Impact of the EU-Turkey Deal." January 2017, https://www.amnesty.org/en/documents/eur25/5664/2017/en

Baklacıoğlu, N. Ö., and Z. Kıvılcım. 2015. *Sürgünde Toplumsal Cinsiyet: İstanbul'da Suriyeli Kadın ve LGBTI Mülteciler.* Istanbul: Der Yayınları.

Bhat, N. 2013. "My Name is Khan and I Am Not a Terrorist: Intersections of Counter Terrorism Measures and the International Framework for Refugee Protection." *San Diego International Law Journal* 15: 299.

Bürgin, A., and D. Aşıkoğlu. 2017. "Turkey's New Asylum Law: A Case of EU Influence." *Journal of Balkan and Near Eastern Studies* 19, no. 2: 121–135.

Calavita, K. 1998. "Immigration, Law and Marginalization in a Global Economy: Notes from Spain." *Law and Society Review* 32: 529–566.

Council Directive 2001/55/EC of 20 July 2001 on Minimum Standards for Giving Temporary Protection in the Event of a Mass Influx of Displaced Persons and on Measures Promoting a Balance ff Efforts between Member States in Receiving Such Persons and Bearing the Consequences Thereof. https://eur-lex.europa.eu/legal-content/EN/TXT/?uri=celex:32001L0055

De Genova, N. 2017. "The 'Migrant Crisis' As Racial Crisis: Do Black lives Matter in Europe?" In Special Issue: Race and Crisis. *Ethnic and Racial Studies* 41, no. 10: 10–15.

Del Carpio, X.V. and M. C. Wagner. 2015. "The Impact of Syrian Refugees on the Turkish Labor Market". World Bank Policy Research Working Paper No. 7402. Washington,

DC: World Bank. http://documents.worldbank.org/curated/en/505471468194980180/The-impact-of-Syrians-refugees-on-the-Turkish-labor-market

Demiryontar, B. 2016. "European Union and Turkish Migration Policy Reform: From Accession to Policy Conditionality." *In Turkish Migration Policy*, edited by İ. Sirkeci and B. Pusch, chapter 4. London: Transnational Press.

ECtHR. 2000. Fourth Section, Case of Jabari v. Turkey (Application no. 40035/98) Judgment, 11 July 2000, Final, 11/10/2000). http://www.asylumlawdatabase.eu/en/content/ecthr-jabari-v-turkey-application-no-4003598-11-july-2000

ECtHR. 2005. Mamatkulov and Askarov v. Turkey, Applications nos. 46827/99 and 46951/99. Judgement, 4 February 2005. http://www.asylumlawdatabase.eu/sites/www.asylumlawdatabase.eu/files/aldfiles/Mamatkulov%20and%20Askarov.pdf

ECtHR. 2010. Second Section Case of Abdolkhani and Karimnia v. Turkey, Application no. 50213/08, Judgement 27 July 2010.

ECtHR. 2011. Mogaddas Moghaddas v. Turkey, Application no. 46134/08, Judgment 15 February 2011. http://www.refworld.org/pdfid/4d5a969fd.pdf

Erol, A., P. Salman, M. Gümüşcan, and M. Kahveci. 2017. *Suriyeli Göçmen Emeği: İstanbul Tekstil Sektörü Araştırması*. Istanbul: Birleşik Metal-Iş Yayınları.

Frelick, B. 1997. "Barriers to Protection: Turkey's Asylum Regulations", *International Journal of Refugee Law* 9, no. 1: 26–27.

Goodwin-Gill, G. S. 2008. "The Politics of Refugee Protection." *Refugee Survey Quarterly*" 27, no. 1: 8–23.

Greenhill, K. M. 2016. "Open Arms behind Barred Doors: Fear, Hypocrisy Ad Policy of Schizophrenia in the European Migration Crisis." *European Law Journal* 22, no. 3. https://doi.org/10.1111/eulj.12179

Haddad, E. 2008. *The Refugee in International Society: Between Sovereigns*. Cambridge, UK: Cambridge University Press.

HRW Greece. 2017. "A Year of Suffering for Asylum Seekers: EU-Turkey Deal Traps People in Abuse and Denies Them Refuge," March 15. https://www.hrw.org/news/2017/03/15/greece-year-suffering-asylum-seekers

Içduygu, A. 2000. "The Politics of International Migratory Regimes: Transit Migration Flows in Turkey." *International Social Science Journal* 52, no. 165: 357–367.

Ihlamur-Öner, S. G. 2013. "Turkey's Refugee Regime Stretched to the Limit? The Case of Iraqi and Syrian Refugee Flows." *Perceptions* 18, no. 3: 191.

International Workforce Law. 2016. No. 6735, Issued in the Official Gazette on 13 August 2016, No. 29800. Turkish Labor Law. https://turkishlaborlaw.com/international-workforce-law/420-international-translation-of-international-workforce-law-is-in-our-website

IOM. 2017. *Annual Report, DTM Turkey: Migrant Presence Monitoring Overview of the Situation with Migrants*. http://migration.iom.int/docs/Sitrep_Turkey_Annual_2017.pdf

Kart E. 2016. "Turkey Seeks Readmission Deals with Iraq, Iran." *Hurriyet Dailynews*, April 12. http://www.hurriyetdailynews.com/turkey-seeks-readmission-deals-with-iraq-iran-97699

Kirisci, K. 1996. "Is Turkey Lifting the Geographical Limitation-The November 1994 Regulation on Asylum in Turkey". *International Journal of Refugee Law* 8:293.

Kıvılcım, Z. 2014. "Human rights, Asylum and Migration in Turkey." In *Migration, Asylum, and Refugees in Turkey: Studies in the Control of Population at the Southeastern Borders of the EU*, edited by N. Özgür Baklacıoğlu and Y. Özer Edwin. Edgar Melen Press.

Law No. 6458 of 2013 on Foreigners and International Protection, 4 April 2013. http://www.refworld.org/docid/5167fbb20.html.

Mertus, J. 1998. "The State and the Post-Cold War Refugee Regime: New Models, New Questions." *International Journal of Refugee Law* 10, no. 3: 321–348.

Migrant Integration Policy Index. 2015. Huddleston, Thomas; Bilgili, Ozge; Joki, Anne-Linde and Vankova, Zvezda. http://www.mipex.eu/what-is-mipex.

Observatory for Human Rights and Forced Migrants in Turkey. 2017. "A Year of Impunity: A One-Year Visual Database of Migration-Related Human Rights Abuses." Final Report. doi:10.13140/RG.2.2.36222.69448

Refugees International. 2016. "Planting the Seeds of Success?: Turkey's New Refugee Work Permits." http://www.refworld.org/pdfid/573591274.pdf

Refugees International. 2017. "'I am only looking for my rights': Legal Employment Still Inaccessible for Refugees in Turkey." Regulation No. 1994/6169 on the Procedures and Principles related to Possible Population Movements and Aliens Arriving in Turkey either as Individuals or in Groups Wishing to Seek Asylum either from Turkey or Requesting Residence Permission in order to Seek Asylum from Another Country, No. 1994/6169, 19 January 1994. http://www.refworld.org/docid/49746cc62.html

Regulation on the Implementation of the Turkish Citizenship Law. 2010. April 6. http://www.resmigazete.gov.tr/eskiler/2010/04/20100406-9.htm

Republic of Turkey Ministry of Development. 2014. *Tenth Economic Plan (2014–2018).* http://www.mod.gov.tr/Lists/RecentPublications/Attachments/75/The%20Tenth%20Development%20Plan%20(2014-2018).pdf.

Republic of Turkey Ministry of Foreign Affairs. 2016. *Turkey on Irregular Migration.* http://www.mfa.gov.tr/turkey-on-irregular-migration.en.mfa

Republic of Turkey Ministry of Labour and Social Security. 2014. *National employment strategy (2014–2023).* http://www.uis.gov.tr/Media/Books/UIS-en.pdf.

Shadow Report. 2016. *Report on Turkey to the UN Committee on the Protection of the Rights of All Migrant Workers and Members of Their Families.* 24th Session. http://tbinternet.ohchr.org/Treaties/CMW/Shared%20Documents/TUR/INT_CMW_NGO_TUR_23327_E.pdf

Skribeland, O. G. 2016. *A Critical Review of Turkey's Asylum Law and Practices: Seeking Asylum in Turkey.* Norwegian Organization for Asylum Seekers (NOAS). https://www.noas.no/wp-content/uploads/2017/07/Seeking-asylum-in-Turkey_2016.pdf

Soykan. C. 2017. "Access to International Protection–Border Issues in Turkey." In *States, the Law and Access to Refugee Protection. Fortresses and Fairness,* edited by M. O'Sullivan and D. Stevens, chapter 4. New York: Oxford University Press.

Temporary Protection Regulation. 2014. *National Legislative Bodies/National Authorities,* October 22. http://www.refworld.org/docid/56572fd74.html.

Turkey Grand National Assembly. 2012. *Reports of the Human Rights Commission and Commission of Internal Affairs on the Draft Law of Foreigners and International Protection, 24/2, No: 310, 1/619.* https://www.tbmm.gov.tr/sirasayi/donem24/yil01/ss310.pdf

UNHCR. 2018. Europe: Syrian Asylum Applications. http://data.unhcr.org/syrianrefugees/asylum.php

UNHCR. 2016. Global Trends: Forced Displacement in 2016. http://www.unhcr.org/5943e8a34.pdf

UNHCR. 2018. Syria Regional Refugee Response. http://data.unhcr.org/syrianrefugees/regional.php

UN Human Rights Office of High Commissioner. 2016a "UN Rights Chief Expresses Serious Concerns over EU-Turkey Agreement." http://www.ohchr.org/EN/NewsEvents/Pages/DisplayNews.aspx?NewsID=18531&LangID=E

UN Human Rights Office of High Commissioner. 2016b. "UN Special Rapporteur on the Human Rights of Migrants Concludes His Follow-Up Country Visit to Greece." http://www.ohchr.org/EN/NewsEvents/Pages/DisplayNews.aspx?NewsID=19972&LangID

UNHCR Turkey Factsheet—October 2017. https://reliefweb.int/report/turkey/unhcr-turkey-factsheet-october-2017

UNICEF. 2017. "One Year On after EU-Turkey Statement the Human Cost to Refugee and Migrant Children Mounts Up." Press Release, March 17. https://www.unicef.org/media/media_95185.html

Wolff, S. 2014. "The Politics of Negotiating EU Readmission Agreements: Insights from Morocco and Turkey." *European Journal of Migration and Law* 16, no. 1: 69–95.

Yıldız, A. G. 2016. *The European Union's Immigration Policy: Managing Migration in Turkey and Morocco*. New York: Springer.

CHAPTER 25

MANAGING THE "REFUGEE CRISIS" ALONG THE BALKAN ROUTE

Field Notes from Serbia

CLAUDIO MINCA, DANICA ŠANTIĆ, AND DRAGAN UMEK

ON one freezing day in January 2017, the authors of this article visited the asylum center of Krnjača, in the periphery of Belgrade. This camp had served for a long time as a hospitality center for Serbian refugees during and after the period of conflict that provoked the dissolution of former Yugoslavia. It was opened in fact in 1993, one year after the *Commissariat for Refugees*[1] was created in order to coordinate and provide humanitarian support to thousands of Serbs fleeing from their homes to seek protection (Commissariat for Refugees and Migration, 2018).[2] Today the center is largely populated by asylum-seekers coming from many different parts of the world, all somehow stranded in Serbia after the borders between this country and Hungary and Croatia have been formally closed to the passages of "irregular migrants" (see, among others, Santer and Wriedt 2017). Belgrade is the capital of Serbia, but perhaps also the informal capital of the refugee Balkan Route (see Figure 25.1), a route that has become so important in the past few years for thousands of individuals coming from the war zones of the middle east (Syria and Iraq) and from central Asia (mainly Afghanistan and Pakistan) and trying to enter the European Union over land (Šantić et al. 2017). This was the authors' third visit to this camp. The atmosphere was relaxed despite the precarious personal conditions of all the guests. Some of the "registered guests" at Krnjača had spent already several months there and seemed to have created a new kind of social spatiality within the camp, a sort of ordinary life in suspended spatiotemporal conditions (see Jansen 2018). When interviewed, they all repeated the same narrative made of a mix of regret for their condition of immobility, recognition of the humanitarian support on the part of the Serbian

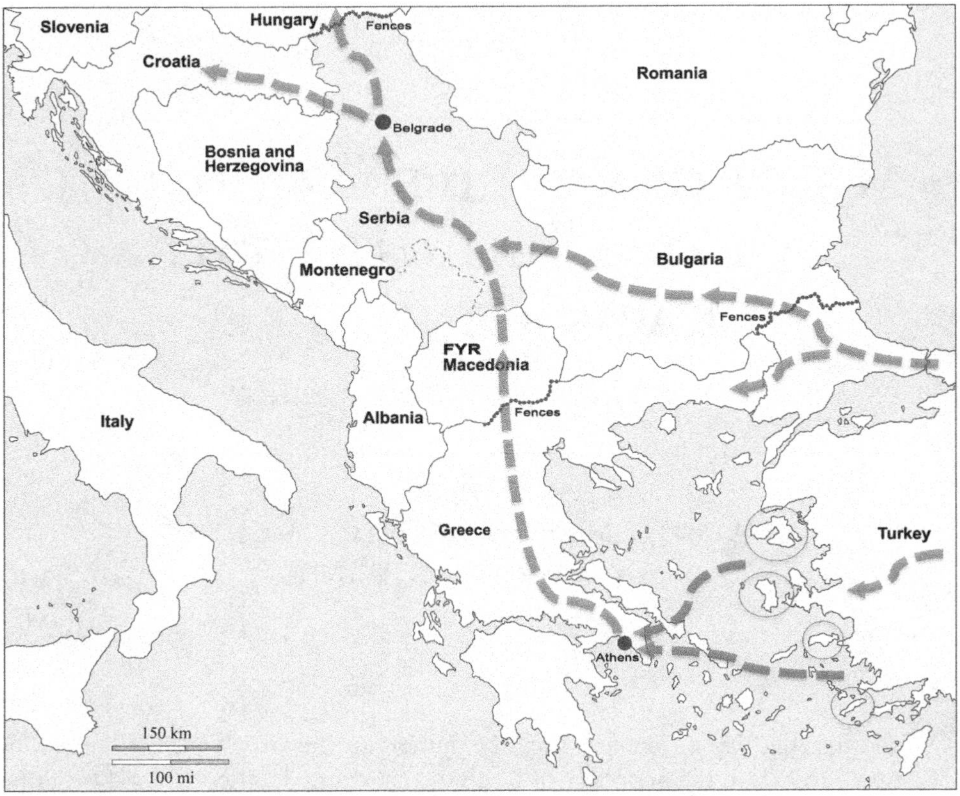

FIGURE 25.1 The Balkan Route through Serbia

Source: http://d-maps.com/carte.php?num_car=4982&lang=en, modified by D. Umek, 2018.

authorities, tales of horrific travel experiences along the route prior to their arrival in Belgrade, and plans to reach Germany or another western European country when that opportunity will be given. They were aware of who the authors were, and from their stories what often transpired was a clear broader sense of victimhood declined in terms of humanitarian grand narrative (for a similar case see Altin and Minca 2017).

The representatives of the Commissariat in charge of the camp were extremely welcoming and keen to engage with the interviews, from those related to the daily living conditions of the refugees—the everyday life in the camp—to issues concerning the role of Serbia along the Balkan Route and the relations with the bordering countries. They all seemed to accept the fact that the refugees, including those who have applied for asylum, will not stay and that it was only a matter of time before they left the country to go north. They also explained that, while the residential hosts are registered and often spend several months in the camp, food and shelter is provided also to those (unregistered) migrants who pass by with no intention to remain since directed north in their (undeclared) attempts to cross the border irregularly (authors' field notes, January 2018).

The reason this essay opens with these asylum-seekers and their hospitality camp is directly linked to its main argument: the so called "refugee crisis" in the Balkan region is not a crisis anymore, and the paradoxical "normality" of the life in this and many other refugee camps visited during fieldwork in 2016, 2017, and 2018 shows that the presence of asylum-seekers in Serbia is not perceived (and not managed) by the authorities as an emergency, but rather conceived as a structural element in the informal mobility of irregular migrants who decided to engage with the Balkan Route to reach their final destinations. What is more, the role of buffer state played by Serbia in the new European geographies of such informal mobility, a role accentuated by the establishment of tougher controls at its western and northern borders with the EU, has produced a situation in which a variable (but somewhat stable) population of stranded migrants resides in Serbia, while at the same time a thriving smuggling industry is organized in order to respond to the increasing demand of irregular journeys across the borders coming from the stranded refugees (on the ambivalent role of the smuggling networks see the special issues edited by Zhang et al. that appeared in *the Annals* in 2018).

This chapter thus reflects on the management of the "refugee crisis" along the Balkan Route on the part of the Serbian authorities by highlighting how, with the exception of the dramatic months of the second part of 2015, when, according to the UNHCR, over 800,000 refugees crossed with largely no opposition the entire region to reach the rest of Europe, the presence of refugees in Serbia and their related mobility have been somehow normalized, despite the media occasionally recalling the existence of such a situation in that country and capitalizing on the idea of a present crisis.[3] Serbia has been long prepared to provide humanitarian support to the refugees using the informal Balkan Route, since their presence is not considered contingent but rather constitutive of the mutated European geographies of irregular migrations. The "refugee crisis" also puts Serbia under a positive light internationally compared to some of the neighboring countries thanks to the relatively unconditional humanitarian support that guides its policy toward these families and individuals on the move (Beznec et al. 2016). While this may place Serbia in a stronger position when negotiating its present and future relationship with the European Union (see Umek et al. 2018), this study has also revealed that the permanent presence of the refugees and of the related network of hospitality camps is also important for the impact that they have on some local economies and for the streams of funding coming from the rest of Europe. It thus problematizes the idea of a permanent "refugee crisis" along the Balkan Route and in Serbia in particular, and at the same time it emphasizes how the role of Serbia in the new European geographies of humanitarian management of displaced people is increasingly important for its integration into the broader economic and political geographies of the continent (see European Parliament 2016; Kilibarda 2016; Minca et al. 2018).

A Geography of Crisis?

According to Alison Mountz not only "relationships among nations and borders materialize bodily most obviously for the displaced person or migrant," but states often tend to be "reorganized geographically and discursively through the production of migrant identities" (Mountz 2010, 119). What is often represented as a crisis and a related threat for the integrity of a specific state can thus be seen also as a strategic way for governments to popularize and, accordingly, implement their specific policies concerning people's mobility and, at the same time, give their apparatuses more capacity of intervention on all possible practices of bordering and border making (see, among others, Balibar 2009; Silberman et al. 2012; Till et al. 2013; Van Houtum and Pijpers 2007). As noted by Louise Amoore (2006), the border is today often literally inscribed on the body of the migrant. The management of displaced populations and irregular migrants has become in many cases a key element in the ways in which governments and other state institutions represent themselves (Brown 2017; Vallet 2014). These representations are accordingly crucial in order to endorse their policy. The idea of a permanent "refugee crisis" in Europe has thus contributed in the past few years to change the political landscape of the continent, as well as the popularity of related powerful narratives associated to ideas of weak and permeable borders in need of constant reinforcement and of a potential invasion of alien populations (Stevens and Tonkin 2015). For some countries in the Balkan region, the visual and practical management of state borders has thus become key in fueling a sense of fear and vulnerability in their broader public and in legitimizing ever-new proclaimed interventions to block the refugees and other migrants outside their respective frontiers. The idea of a "refugee crisis" out of control, again, is central to these strategies (see, among others, Korac-Sanderson 2017). The figure of the refugee, especially when objectified and popularized by the media, thus becomes literally a site where the battle over the present and future identity of some countries in the region and their international role is engaged. The management and scripting of bodies, in our case of real-and-imagined migrant bodies, has become key to the production and the *visualization of the body politic*, to the building of the "body corporeal geographies of the nation-state" (see Mountz 2010, 119).

This is why it is important to critically reflect on the idea of "refugee crisis" in the Balkan region and along the Balkan Route. Inspired by Mountz's (2010) work on the interplay between refugee mobilities, invisible geographies of smuggling, and practices of state bureaucracies, the idea of a permanent "refugee crisis" in Serbia and along the Balkan Route should be problematized. The analysis presented in this article is the result of almost two years of fieldwork in the country, including visits to most of the institutional refugee camps and several makeshift camps and the opportunity to interview not only registered and unregistered migrants, but also volunteers and staff of the Commissariat involved in the humanitarian management of these populations-on-the-move. Despite the often superficial but nonetheless highly effective representations of the "refugee crisis" on the part of the media, the work in the field has revealed that the embodied experience of the migrants and of the people working with them in Serbia has become a constitutive and relatively ordinary element of the geopolitical role played by this country in Europe, but also of the established presence of a network of invisible smugglers which has become part of the very same geographies of irregular migration (see Tinti and Reitano 2016). Serbia in fact is not confronted with a crisis generated by a situation of emergency—something limited to a few months in 2015 and 2016—but rather with a consolidated political geography of irregular migrations made of basic humanitarian management of the fleeing populations, but also of camps, corridors, routes, borders, fences, holes in those very fences, bureaucratic procedures, new jobs for social workers, funding from the rest of Europe, (moderate) police intervention, thriving local economies around the presence of a refugee camp, makeshift encampments, Twitter and Facebook spaces of communication, and, largely, the indifference of the media and of the European broader public (see, again, Minca et al. 2018; see also, Kasparek 2016).

As noted previously, during the second part of 2015, about 800,000 migrants were allowed to cross the region using all possible means of transportation and not being checked at state borders (Šantić et al 2017). This exceptional situation was related to the humanitarian emergency caused by the war escalation in the Middle East and the millions of refugees fleeing their homes to find protection elsewhere. While the majority of these refugees found shelter in the neighboring countries, a significant contingent decided to reach central and northern Europe via Greece, FYR Macedonia, or Bulgaria, Serbia, Hungary or Croatia, and Slovenia. In those days, the media were populated by shocking images of long lines of individuals walking in the fields of southeast Europe with little more than a bag, or of family desperately trying to board on a train in Belgrade or Budapest, or of buses loading exhausted refugees to take them to a camp or to the next city or country. Anyone driving in that part of Europe, as happened on several occasions to the authors of this article, could be confronted with the sight of random migrants walking along the highway with their plastic bags. A share sense of being in the presence of a true humanitarian crisis was soon accompanied, however, in the accounts of some media and in the rhetoric of some state leaders, by narratives around the possibility of a biblical exodus and of loss of control over state borders (The Visegrad Group 2016).

The view of thousands of men and women freely roaming the European cities and fields thus provided powerful support to the implementation of tighter border controls and to a nationalist (and often even racist) rhetoric of protection of the national territory from these alien bodies and their unknown intentions (for an overview, see BBC News 2016) The corporeal geographies of some nation states in the Balkan region were thus directly produced on the bodies on random refugees often via alarmistic media representations and the erection of fences and walls along the borders (Minca and Rijke 2017). The humanitarian crisis was therefore often presented as a political crisis of the institutions (the European Union *in primis*) unable to protect the integrity of the respective states and their borders, and the need of urgent interventions to prevent further arrivals and passages. Already in the Fall of 2015 the Hungarian government inaugurated the first part of the double fence erected along the border with Serbia and announced the end of that stage of the "refugee crisis" (Šantić et al 2017). This was followed by similar interventions on the part of other governments in the region: in March 2016 several countries, including FYR Macedonia, Croatia, and Slovenia, declared the Balkan Route officially closed. No refugee was allowed to enter their territories unchecked anymore. The "refugee crisis," while remaining present in the overall rhetoric of a permanent emergency on the part of these countries, was thus translated into new border politics and in the refusal to host and provide humanitarian support to irregular migrants (see Weaver and Siddique, 2017).

What happened in the following months is possibly well known to most readers since it took central stage in the news for some time: the closure of the Route caught thousands of refugees along their way, with the formation in Idomeni, on the border between Greece and FYR Macedonia, of the larger makeshift camp in Europe that, until its dismantlement on the part of the Greek authorities, hosted at its peak over 15,000 refugees (see Anastasiadou et al 2017; also Amnesty International 2015 and UNHCR 2016). More refugees were stranded in Serbia, the only country along the Route that decided not to close its borders and to continue providing humanitarian support (see Tomić 2016). After the erection of the Hungarian wall, the Route took a deflection for a brief period, with the refugees entering Croatia and then Slovenia. But in the Spring 2016 also this branch of the Route was closed with virtually no refugee admitted from that moment onwards (Smith 2016). At the same time, the majority of the refugees arriving from the war zones in the Middle East were forced to remain in camps in Turkey as the result of the agreement reached in the same period between that country and the European Union (Bialasiewicz and Maessen 2018; Council of the European Union 2016). The crisis was only virtually over, in the sense that most of the refugees coming from Syria and Iraq were now stranded in Turkey, a few thousands deported to Greek camps, and many others on the loose in the fields and the forests of the Balkan region. The official number of arrivals in that part of Europe suddenly declined and those in favor of the closure of the borders soon announced that their policy had succeeded. However, the potential return of the refugees and the urge to remind the electorate of the need to protect the nation body politic from the consequences of new future crises have remained at the core of many political agendas, with the rise of populist and nationalist parties in most countries of the region and, partially, in the rest of Europe as well (BBC News 2016).

But how much of a "refugee crisis" is faced today by a country like Serbia that has decided to adopt an alternative political agenda and to play the humanitarian card as a geopolitical priority in such a European context? While during the peak of the crisis in 2015 the media attention on this phenomenon was extraordinary, after the official closure of the Route and the dismantlement of the Idomeni makeshift camp the interest for the situation of the stranded refugees in Serbia and in the Balkan region rapidly evaporated. Only in January 2017 would the international press rediscovered the existence of a presumed "refugee crisis" in Serbia by reporting the dire living conditions of about two thousand refugees who had occupied the so-called warehouses makeshift camp in the core of Belgrade (see *The Guardian* 2017 and Specia 2017). Again, shocking images of freezing and poorly dressed young men lining up for some food relief traveled globally leading many to denounce the Serbian authorities for their indifference and to build untenable parallels with archival pictures of 1943 portraying German prisoners in Stalingrad (*The Daily Mail* 2017). After that sudden noise, and the reaction of the Serbian authorities promising to close the warehouses and accommodate the refugees in hospitality camps (something that indeed happened a few months later), the crisis in the Balkan region was forgotten once again by the global media. However, the crisis was not forgotten by some key actors in the production of the present geographies of irregular migrations along the Balkan Route: in the first place, the Hungarian government, now distilling the entrance of asylum-seekers by selecting about ten individuals every week from an informal list that circulated between the two countries (Council of the European Union 2017, 11); secondly, the Serbian authorities, eager to provide a buffer zone for the irregular migrations coming from the Balkan Route and blocked by the Schengen countries, but also eager to benefit from the financial support and the recognition of various European institutions; thirdly, the NGOs and other volunteer organizations, whose presence and intervention (and the related jobs) in Serbia was necessarily associated with the existence of a presumed humanitarian crisis in that country; fourthly, the refugees stranded in Serbia and those who are still arriving and are convinced that they will be able to cross the borders to go north, no matter at what cost; and finally, the smuggling organizations, which are prone to take advantage of the official closure of the route and the related need for the refugees to find different ways to reach their desired destination.

Camps, Routes, Buffer Zones, Geographies of Irregular Migrations

When, in January 2018, the authors visited one of the largest camps in Obrenovac (30 km away from Belgrade), they were informally told that, while in May 2017 this camp was originally opened to host a large part of the refugees dwelling in the warehouses makeshift camp in Belgrade, since then the population of the camp had changed almost entirely (field notes, January 11, 2018). This means that the original hosts are now elsewhere, and that the camp is arguably populated by new arrivals. The "refugee crisis" in Serbia is thus the reflection of a broader development in the management of refugees and irregular migrants in that part of Europe, possibly in line with what Mountz has described as the tendency on the part of many state authorities to "regionalize" the management of refugees: "nation states are increasingly practicing enforcement in transnational, dispersed fashion. Part of this dispersion involves the creation and exploitation of geographically and legally ambiguous sites . . . characterized by both the presence and the absence of the nation states" (Mountz 2010, 123). This is in many ways happening also along the Balkan Route. Despite having been declared officially closed, the Balkan

Route is still used by a significant number of refugees. While the number of arrivals in Serbia has dramatically dropped after the closure, at the same time a flow of people continues to enter the country and is accommodated in the hospitality camps.

Serbia responded to the emergency of the peak period, when the Balkan Route was open, by providing emergency humanitarian support to the thousands of migrants moving north and allowing them to move freely in the country in order to reach their next destinations. In those months, the one stop center of Preševo, for example, located in the extreme south of the country near the border with FYR Macedonia, was accepting and offering immediate relief to thousands of people every week, at times even thousands in one single day (field notes, August 22, 2016). At the same time, the migrants were moving north across the Serbian territory via all possible travel arrangements: by bus, taxi, train, but also, many, on foot. Belgrade, in those days, was an overcrowded transportation hub marked by the development of a congested local economy that benefited from the provision of food, accommodation and different forms of mobility to the refugees. The so-called Afghan Park, a square where the refugees used to meet in order to organize their travel north, turned into a sort of iconic place in the geographical imaginations of the Balkan Route. Once a migrant had reached Afghan Park in Belgrade, her or his chances of crossing the border to enter the EU at that point was very high (interviews with Commissariat representatives, January 2017 and January 2018). During that period, Serbia activated a number of other refugee camps along the route, at times using existing asylum-seekers' centers, like Krnjača, other times converting former motels, military barracks, or holiday camps into refugee camps with different characteristics and capacities, but all aimed at providing humanitarian support for the refugees (in those days largely Syrians and Iraqis, including many families and unaccompanied minors).

After the closure of the route in the Spring 2016, the situation rapidly changed for a country faced with a significant number of stranded refugees. Since then the number of stranded refugees officially hosted in the archipelago of Serbia camps has shifted from between four thousand and seven thousand (Commissariat 2017; IOM 2017, 2018), while the number of non-registered presences has remained largely unknown. In fact, since the route has become an entirely informal path for irregular migrants, the country has experienced the appearance of a series of makeshift camps: the most important ones being the previously mentioned warehouse camps in the core of the capital with a peak of about two thousand refugees at the beginning of 2017 (see Figure 25.2) and a number of other precarious and improvised settlements in the regions near the Hungarian border and, more recently, near the Croatian border. The position on the authorities toward these improvised dwellings has been conspicuously ambivalent: at times, adopting a policy of nonintervention, as it has been the case for several months with the warehouses in Belgrade and with a couple of abandoned factories in the north occupied by irregular migrants; other times, under the pressure of the international media (in the case of the warehouse camps), or of the local population (in the north), intervening to dismantle such precarious living arrangements (that will reappear elsewhere). The authors found no evidence, however, of direct violence being used against the refugees during these operations.

FIGURE 25.2 Signs on a building of the warehouse makeshift camp in Belgrade
Source: Photo by D. Umek, 25 January 2018.

As mentioned several times, the Serbian territory has now become a sort of buffer zone in the new geographies of the informal migrations in Europe. The border with Croatia is virtually closed, while the informal passages continue, something confirmed by interviewees, but also by the persistence of local informal economies in the Šid area that seem to thrive thanks to the organization of these unofficial passages (field notes, January 10, 2018). The Hungarian border, marked by the well-known double fence, remains officially open to about ten asylum-seekers per week. These passages are arguably organized on the basis of a list, again, mentioned by all our interviewees, a list that defines who has the right to be considered for asylum by the Hungarian authorities and when. However, it was not possible to get more details on how this list was formed and according to which criteria. The about four thousand registered migrants hosted in the seventeen Serbian refugee camps (five asylum centers and twelve hospitality centers) in the first months of 2018 were technically either waiting to apply for asylum in this country (it is enough to declare such intention to be accepted in the camps) or virtually waiting to be included in the list. This means that there is an outstanding population of migrants who are officially waiting to go to Hungary or to be granted asylum protection in Serbia. De facto, however, as it clearly emerged during our interviews, all these migrants-in-waiting are hoping to go north via irregular means. This population of registered migrants is complemented by the unregistered migrants who are either on the move—virtually invisible to the statistics—or in the makeshift dwellings near the border.

What we would like to argue here is that this ambivalent geography made of official and unofficial mobilities, sealed but still partially porous borders, hospitality camps, and asylum camps but no real asylum-seekers willing to stay in Serbia (!), is not the result of a crisis or a situation of emergency but rather the reflection of a structural way of managing the presence of irregular migrants and the related border politics in the broader region. The interplay between regular and official processes and unofficial and informal spatialities is thus constitutive of a broader politics of migrations aimed at, to refer again to Mountz, rendering migrants stateless by geographical design: "I use the term 'stateless by geographical design' to signify extraterritorial locations that are neither entirely inside nor outside of sovereign territory, but that subject migrants to graduated degrees of statelessness by introducing ambiguity into their legal status . . . the contradictions of border policies come to the fore" (Mountz 2010, 121). The next section thus turns to this geographical design in the context of the Balkan Route, a context made of partially extraterritorial locations and contradictory border politics in which the role of Serbia, with its humanitarian geopolitical agenda, is somewhat complementary to the tough border policies applied by neighboring countries and by Hungary and Croatia in particular. If the rise of massive state apparatuses controlling population movements between states appears to Mountz (2010, 122) as "the most striking development of new global geographies of irregular mobility," Serbia, in the geographies of irregular mobility of the Balkan Route, plays an important role in supporting the irregular migrants but also in appearing as a reliable partner for other major European countries and the EU authorities as a whole. It is therefore time to return to the Route and reflect on how it is somehow informally kept open and how its very existence is arguably essential for the reproduction of set of specific (geo)political arrangements of that region and, perhaps of the whole continent. The "refugee crisis" along the Balkan Route, again, is not a humanitarian-emergency-generated-crisis anymore; rather, it has become a structural element of the broader political geographies of the Balkan region. The provocative suggestion is that the complete disappearance of irregular migrants would in fact open a (problematic) empty space in those political geographies made of border enforcement, nationalist rhetoric, humanitarian management, and human smuggling economies.

The Humanitarian Management Imperative

In November 2016, the Serbian government formally forbade the NGOs operating in the country to distribute food and clothes to those refugees who are outside the network of institutional camps (although, according to interviewees, they continued to do so, at least, in part).[4] The reason behind this somehow controversial decision had to do with the government's declared intention to incorporate all the migrants arrived in Serbia in the official structures of hospitality, but also to limit the appearance of makeshift camps and spontaneous precarious dwellings on the parts of migrants-on-the-loose, often found in the fields of rural areas along the northern borders, or around transportation hubs in the cities along the Balkan Route (field notes, January 2018). The result of this decision was a growing tension between some of these NGOs and their operators, on the one hand, and the Commissariat, on the other, together with the emergence of a series of grey areas in the actual structure of hospitality. At present, there are numerous NGOs operating in Serbia in collaboration with the Commissariat, including some of the major international humanitarian organizations like Caritas, Save the Children, Médecins Sans Frontières (MSF), the Red Cross, Danish Refugee Council (DRC), but also several national ones like SOS Children Villages Serbia, NGO Atina, Divac Foundation, Belgrade Centre for Human Rights, Asylum Protection Centre (APC), and a plethora of others. Most of these organizations argue that the state's structure of humanitarian support is not capable of proving accommodation and humanitarian aid to all the migrants present in the country, and that therefore their intervention outside the camps will not be entirely canceled by the present restrictions, since many migrants continue to roam around some urban areas seeking for help and especially trying to arrange ways to go north without being incorporated by the camp system and its bureaucratic procedures (interviews with NGO representatives, November 5, 2016 and January 25, 2017). The NGOs and the volunteer organizations therefore denounce the existence of a permanent state of emergency that requires their presence and the support to those in need of basic humanitarian relief. What is more—they claim—the police authorities in some periods apparently refuse to register all the new arrivals, with the exception of the families and women accompanied by minors (Council of the European Union 2017). The police also normally ignore the presence of makeshift dwellings or of loose migrants, and intervene only when requested, for example in the few cases in which the local residents complained about the hygienic conditions of the areas where irregular migrants were roaming or even sleeping outdoors in the absence of portable toilettes. This is the space in which the humanitarian organizations intervene and where they try to compensate for the deliberate lack of support on the part of the state authorities. The authorities, however, explain that the refugees should enter the camps and receive only the official humanitarian aid, and that the NGOs with their interventions outside the camps indirectly facilitate the emergence of makeshift dwellings and unprotected grey areas in which the migrants become more vulnerable and are deprived of any comprehensive humanitarian support (Interviews with Commissariat representatives, November 2016 and January 2018). What we have here is an ambivalent political geography of irregular migrations made of official and unofficial interventions, but also of endlessly mutable intersections of institutional and makeshift refugee and humanitarian spatialities. The ambivalent nature of these geographies is arguably what allows many to claim that Serbia is permanently facing a "refugee crisis." In the final part of the chapter this claim is problematized.

To summarize the present situation, this ambivalent geography of irregular mobilities is actively supported by the system of camps managed by the Commissariat to provide hospitality and humanitarian aid to both registered and unregistered migrants (about four thousand people as we write). Such geography is also supported by the interventions of the humanitarian organizations previously described, in the camps but also outside of the networks of hospitality established by the state authorities; the latter strategically alternate intervention and nonintervention in the grey areas where makeshift camps appear and where the informal border crossings are arranged. One example out of many illustrating this kind of interplay was the decision on the part of the Serbian police not to intervene for months to relocate the migrants squatting in the warehouses close to the railway station in the center of Belgrade (Interview with Info Park volunteers, Belgrade, November 5, 2016). At the same time, no humanitarian organization was allowed to support the refugees with food or any other provisions. De facto, food was distributed, and some very basic humanitarian support provided by MSF and other local organizations.

Arguably, this interplay of formal and informal geographies is complemented by the presence of an active network of smugglers who have become de facto the only actors capable of taking the migrants further north, since no legal way to cross the borders exists for the migrants, with the exception of the restricted and uncertain procedure to enter Hungary based on "the list." The intersection of all these interventions with the actual mobilities of the irregular migrants is what keeps the Balkan Route informally open, despite all the proclaims on the part of some governments that wish to capitalize on the presumed closure of the route and the sealing of the national borders. These geographies are not geographies of a crisis generated by an endless condition of emergency. Not only has the Route now become a consolidated overland path toward "Europe" made of a network of hospitality camps; formal and informal provision of services including transportation, accommodation and others forms of support; and irregular and only partially visible individual mobilities, but the very presence of the migrants and of the smuggling enterprises in the Balkan region have become essential elements in justifying the tough language of border protection and security used by the governments of most countries in the Balkan region—with the exception of Serbia, which has strategically decided to play an entire different but somewhat complementary role in this geopolitical narrative concerning the threat of an invasion of the respective national territories on the part of uncontained waves of migrants (see Beznec et al. 2016; also Timur and Nordland 2016; The Visegrad Group 2018).

What has emerged in the fieldwork is that the sustained presence of irregular migrants and the related need for a true archipelago of camps and a network of humanitarian aid in Serbia has had a positive impact on some local economies but also, nationally, on some key sectors involved in the provision of goods and services to the migrants and to the large contingent of operators involved in their "humanitarian management" (on the economic potential of refugee flows see Bianchini et al. 2017). During the months of the refugee emergency in 2015, the actual possibility of moving north legally and the need to cross the Serbian territory as rapidly as possible stimulated in particular the growth of an improvised transportation complex made of regular bus companies and taxis, but also private cars and vans willing to capitalize on the urge on the part of the migrants to go north. However, in those months many other activities in the center of

Belgrade, but also in other locations along the Route, experienced an extraordinary increase in the demand of all sorts of products and services: from basic accommodation, to food and personal products, to any imaginable form of support in the preparation of the next step of their journey. After the closure of the route in March 2016, these same activities were impacted by the sudden reduction of arrivals but also by the now irregular presence of the refugees along the route internationally. This is when the international smuggling organizations began to thrive in the region, often supported by a dense network of local mediators facilitating the "delivery" of the promised services (see Tinti and Reitano 2016, x, and the section on the Balkan Route), as it will be discussed in the conclusion. While the days when thousands of new migrants would stop by along the Route are over, at the same time, the persistence and consolidation of a population of stranded refugees waiting to go north via irregular means has generated in some areas of the country, mostly around the presence of refugee camps, or near the transportation hubs in Belgrade, or even in some border towns in the north (Šid being a noticeable case with three refugee camps in the surroundings and the proximity of Croatian border), a consistent and sustained demand for low-cost services, with small local companies thriving thanks to the presence of the migrants and their demands: grilled meat kiosks, phone and sim cards shops, groceries shops and bakeries, small restaurants and bars, money transfer providers and currency exchange offices, among many others services (field notes August 2017 and January 2018).

After two-and-a-half years of fieldwork the authors remain under the impression that, with few exceptions, the Serbian population has reacted relatively well to the presence of the migrants, despite the conflicting messages from the media: on the one hand, the media close to the government's positions (see, among others, *Politika*, September 20, 2016; *Novosti*, December 6, 2017) tend to minimize if not even ignore the presence of the refugees, and therefore the existence of any situation of crisis; on the other, the local tabloids tend to emphasize all the possible negative perceptions of these "aliens bodies" in the streets of the Serbian cities, including the alleged possibility of violence, disease, dirt, disorder, but also illegal activities related to the presence of mobile "random individuals" (often young men from Afghanistan and Pakistan, who have largely replaced the Syrians and the Iraqis along the Route after its closure and after the EU-Turkey agreement concerning the retention of mainly Syrian refugees—see, among others, *Kurir*, May 24, 2017; *Alo!*, April 8, 2017; *Blic*, March 24, 2017). One possible explanation for the relative lack of tension with the local population, according to some of interviewees, is that Serbia has been hosting refugees since 1990s as a consequence of the violent implosion of former Yugoslavia; also, many Serbs, now integrated into the broader society, have directly experienced the condition of being a refugee, of which they keep clear memories. Another explanation that was provided by some representatives of the Commissariat is that the Serbian public overall supports the government's decision to put the humanitarian imperative as the first priority of their policy toward irregular migrations and the related positive image of the country among the refugees but also among the other European partners. Having said that, like in many other corners of Europe, even in Serbia a few moments of tension among components of the local population and the refugees have emerged: from episodes of intolerance, to complaints on the part of residents about the degradation of public spaces due to the continued presence of migrants on the loose, or about the presence of illegal activities (and their perpetrators) related to such presence. Concerns were also expressed among the general public for the sustainability of such a situation in the long run considering the fragility of the Serbian economy. At the same time, visits to the camps made clear how the management of refugees has represented and continues to represent an important source of employment for many young Serbs and, indirectly, for those busy in the previously mentioned activities of formal and informal support to the refugees (Interviews with Commissariat staff in Obrenovac, January 12, 2018).

Overall, while the humanitarian policy applied by the Serbian authorities toward the refugees must be praised, especially when compared to what happens in other parts of the region, at the same time it must be recognized that its humanitarian management "machine" is an integrated part of a broader political geography which has relevant implications internally but also internationally (e.g., on Europe's border geopolitics—see, among many others, Janković 2017 and Vaughan-Williams 2015). There is no "refugee crisis" in Serbia at present. Rather, the presence of stranded refugees in this country is perceived and managed as a situation that will possibly consolidate in the future, with all the related implications, the most important of which is the fact that the Balkan Route will remain open, just in a different form, and that Serbia's humanitarian imperative will be related to the border policy and politics employed by Hungary and Croatia and the related development of flourishing smuggling networks.

Conclusion

This chapter concludes highlighting how the concept and, to some extent, the reproduction of a "refugee crisis" in Serbia is key to understand the workings of two areas of interventions related to broader questions of irregular migrations in this important region: the smuggling organizations and the humanitarian sector. Tinti and Reitano (2016, 4), in analyzing the growing importance of the smuggling networks globally, argue that "the actualization of the [refugee] crisis is enabled and actively encouraged by an increasingly professional set of criminal groups and opportunistic individuals that is generating profits in the billions." This situation, they insist, is facilitated by erection of walls and fences and by the increasing restrictions on the acceptance of asylum-seekers on the part of many governments: "In lieu of safe, legal paths to seeking refuge and opportunity, new barriers are forcing migrants to pursue more dangerous journeys and seek the services of more established mafias and criminal organizations" (2016, 5). This seems to be the case also of the Balkan region after the official closure of the Route. As we write, there is no legal possibility for asylum-seekers to enter the EU along this Route, the only exception being "the list" allowing ten applicants per week across the Hungarian border via a dedicated "gate." All the other migrants waiting in the formal and informal camps of Serbia will try to cross the border by other means. Despite the fact that some may initiate this journey independently, the large majority will rely on some form of support on the part of the smuggling organizations. Again, for Tinti and Reitano (2016, 6), "the consolidation and codification of these networks also means that smuggling networks now seek to create contexts in which demand for their services will thrive. They have become a vector for global migration, quick to identify loopholes, exploit new areas of insecurity, and target vulnerable populations whom they see as prospective clients. They no longer simply respond to demand for smuggler services: they actively generate it." Is this the case in Serbia and along the Balkan Route? While due to the sensitive and secretive nature of such activities, it was impossible to collect solid data to inform our analysis, at the same time, what the authors' interviews and field notes seem to show is the existence of an active geography of irregular mobilities, whose presence is broadly acknowledged in the sector, and whose consolidation is the response to the official closure of the Route. The condition of crisis, real or perceived, seems to be an essential element for the coexistence of these irregular mobilities and humanitarian aid, especially when provided by nongovernmental organizations. And this brings us to the second point, concerning the putative role of what Michel Agier defines as "humanitarian exceptionalism" in responding but also in reproducing the conditions of a perpetuated (refugee) crisis.

For Agier, who is well known for his criticism toward the international system of humanitarian management of displaced people, ". . . today's humanitarian organization shave made a specialty for themselves of 'managing' these spaces and population apart . . . humanitarian action today is always deeply ambiguous. It has a power of life and death in the space assigned to it, but also and above all a major role in the transformation of individual lives, of social and cultural models, in the places where it operates" (2011, 4–5). What is particular interesting in Agier's analysis is the idea that humanitarianism management is "rather than a 'system' proceeding unconsciously by itself, [. . .] an unstable arrangement made up of networks, leaderships, and values" (2011, 5). These unstable arrangements are what the authors have witnessed in visits to the camps in Serbia, especially where their workings were related by the operators and by the refugees themselves to a situation of (alleged) permanent crisis. What is more, in the Serbian context, like in many other similar contexts defined by a "refugee crisis," ". . . the categories of 'temporary', 'humanitarian' or 'subsidiary' asylum and assistance make it possible to remove the individual thus designated from the international legal framework, and give more room to manoeuvre to national or intergovernmental policies [. . .] regarding the duration attaching to this category [. . .] and the scope of rights accorded" (2011, 22). This may explain the "light" formalization of the presence of irregular migrants after their arrival in Serbia and when they enter a camp: they are "registered" but no identification process is implemented, with many cases in which they simply roam around the country without being clearly identified while trying to go north.

The previously mentioned "list" to enter Hungary also plays an important role in the production of specific vague and unstable conditions in the management of humanitarian aid for the migrants: on the one hand, some individuals declare that they wish to apply for asylum in Serbia—although they normally never do apply; others merely declare that they are waiting to be included in "the list"; others simply wait for the opportunity to go through irregularly. Also in this respect the Serbia situation of crisis responds, at least in part, to Agier's observation that, as part of the humanitarian management of displaced people, we often "see a proliferation of categories that makes the management of flows of people more complex, and the real figures more opaque, as well as the conditions of life of all those who come under these categories." (2011, 22). What we are trying to say is that the idea of a *permanent crisis* is also at the origin of a specific set of arrangements that assign different but somewhat complementary roles to the humanitarian machine and the smuggling networks in the overall support of irregular migrations. The relative or potential porosity of the borders (the hypothetical "holes in the fence" mentioned by many migrants as a possibility to go north) is what makes these arrangements effective and, arguably, they represent the structural elements in the reproduction of the conditions of a permanent (refugee) crisis. The migrants that have been interviewed seem to be all aware of the rules of the game (they literally call it "the game") and fully appreciate the importance of adapting their strategies to go north to the previously described conditions of crisis.

While it is uncertain whether the Serbian situation can be generalized, perhaps one lesson can be learned from this unique constellation of humanitarian, geopolitical, and legal circumstances. The concept of "refugee crisis" is certainly essential in describing moments in which, like the late months of 2015, an extraordinary amount of people engaged the Balkan Route to escape the war zones of the Middle East. However, in other cases it may become a way of describing and managing a relatively established situation in which irregular mobilities are supported in the name of the humanitarian imperative, but also as a form of political technology able to reproduce, indefinitely, conditions of precariousness and illegality for the migrants, while at the same time securing the presence and the proliferation of activities related to ever-increasing border control enforcement, humanitarian management of displaced individuals, and smuggling services. The "refugee crisis" in Serbia is thus a sort permanent arrangement among the different actors described and around a sustained flow of people who, despite all the limitations and the new border policies, will possibly continue to (irregularly) travel along the Balkan Route.

Notes

1. The Commissariat for Refugees was established in 1992 ("RS Official Gazette," No. 18/92); in 2012, with the adoption of the new Law on Migration Management ("RS Official Gazette," No. 107/2012), it was renamed as the Commissariat for Refugees and Migration (hereinafter Commissariat).
2. The Krnjača refugee camp was originally built as a village for workers of the Ivan Milutinović-PIM, a national engineering and construction company that during the socialist period manufactured waterways and harbour infrastructures. In 1993, it was converted into one of the several centers set up by the Government to shelter Serbian refugees and IDPs forced to leave their home in Croatia, Bosnia and Kosovo.

3. More precisely, the UNHCR counted 815,000 passages. However, the European Parliament estimated that about 596,000 migrants used the Route in 2015, while for the IOM they amounted to 639,152. According to FRONTEX, 885,000 illegal border crossings were conducted in the same period.
4. In depth interviews with Commissariat representatives in Krnjača and NGOs operators in Belgrade took place in November 2016, January 2017 and January 2018, and in Obrenovac in January 2018.

References

Agier, M. 2011. *Managing the Undesirables*. London: Polity.

Agier, M. 2016. *Borderlands*. London: Polity.

Alo! 2017. "Horror in Šid. Migrant has robbed two eleven year old girls." http://www.alo.rs/vesti/hronika/migrant-sa-sekirom-opljackao-dve-jedanaestogodisnjakinje-video/102449/vest

Altin, R., and C. Minca. 2017. "The Ambivalent Camp." In *Carceral Mobilities, Interrogating Movement in Incarceration*, edited by Jennifer Turner and Kimberley Peters, 30–44. London: Routledge.

Amoore, L. 2006. "Biometric Borders: Governing Mobilities in the War on Terror." *Political Geography* 25, no. 3: 336–351.

Anastasiadou M., M. Athanasios, M. Panagiota, and M. Speer. 2017. "*From Transit Hub to Dead End. A Chronicle of Idomeni." Supported by Rosa-Luxemburg-Stiftung with funds from the German Federal Foreign Office*. Bordermonitoring.eu, Munich. http://bordermonitoring.eu/berichte/2017-idomeni/

Balibar E. 2009. "Europe as Borderland." *Environment and Planning D: Society and Space* 27, no. 2: 190–215.

BBC News. 2016. "Guide to Nationalist Parties Challenging Europe." June 5. http://www.bbc.com/news/world-europe-36130006

Beznec, B., M. Speer, and M. Stojić-Mitrović. 2016. "Governing the Balkan Route: Macedonia, Serbia and the European Border Regime." Belgrade: Research Paper Series of Rosa Luxemburg Stiftung South East Europe 5. Bordermonitoring.eu. http://bordermonitoring.eu/analyse/2017/01/governing-the-balkan-route-macedonia-serbia-and-the-european-border-regime/

Bialasiewicz, L., and E. Maessen. 2018. "Scaling Rights: The 'Turkey Deal' and the Divided Geographies of European Responsibility." Patterns of Prejudice 52, no. 2–3: 210–230. doi:10.1080/0031322X.2018.1433009

Bianchini, S., M. Borraccetti, M. Zoppi and P. Cavanna. 2017. "Territorial and Urban Potentials Connected to Migration and Refugee Flows—Inception Report." European Territorial Observatory Network (ESPON) - European Grouping for Territorial Cooperation (EGTC).

Blic News. 2017. "Migrant Robbed the House in Batrovci." https://www.blic.rs/vesti/hronika/u-batrovcima-migranti-uhvaceni-u-kradi-piva/sx6n1rh

Brown, W. 2017. Border Barriers as Sovereign Swords: Rethinking Walled States in Light of the EU Migrant and Fiscal Crises. In "*Interventions on the State of Sovereignty at the Border*," edited by R. Jones, C. Johnson, W. Brown, G. Popescu, P. Pallister-Wilkins, A. Mountz et al. *Political Geography* 59:1–10.

Commissariat for Refugees and Migration (KIRS). 2017. "Overview of the Activities Undertaken during the Increased Influx of Migrants." http://www.kirs.gov.rs/articles/navigate.php?type1=3&lang=ENG&id=2330&date=0.

Commissariat for Refugees and Migration (KIRS). 2018. "About Us." http://www.kirs.gov.rs/articles/aboutus.php?lang=ENG.

Council of the European Union. 2016. "EU-Turkey Statement, 18 March 2016." Press release, 144/16, 18.03.2016. http://www.consilium.europa.eu/en/press/press-releases/2016/03/18-eu-turkey-statement

Council of the European Union. 2017. *Report of the Fact-Finding Mission by Ambassador Tomáš Boček, Special Representative of the Secretary General on Migration and Refugees to Serbia and Two Transit Zones in Hungary. Information Documents SG/Inf* 33, October 19, 1–43. http://ungarn.bordermonitoring.eu/2017/10/19/report-of-the-fact-finding-mission-by-ambassador-tomas-bocek-special-representative-of-the-secretary-general-on-migration-and-refugees-to-serbia-and-two-transit-zones-in-hungary-12-16-june-2017/

The Daily Mail. 2017. "Belgrade Migrants Wait: Food Pictures Similar to Second World War." http://www.dailymail.co.uk/news/article-4107102/Belgrade-migrants-wait-food-pictures-similar-Second-World-War

European Parliament. 2016. "Serbia's Role in Dealing with the Migration Crisis." Briefing, October 2016. http://www.europarl.europa.eu/thinktank/es/document.

International Organization for Migration (IOM). 2017. "Mixed Migration Flows in the Mediterranean. Compilation of Available Data and Information June 2017." http://migration.iom.int/europe/Monthly Flows Compilation Report July 2017.pdf

International Organization for Migration (IOM). 2018. "Mixed Migration Flows in the Mediterranean. Compilation of Available Data and Information January 2018." http://migration.iom.int/europe/Monthly Flows Compilation Report January 2018.

Janković, S. 2017. "Stuck In-Between: Exploring the Liminality inside the Migratory Transfer to Europe." In *Towards Understanding of Contemporary Migration: Causes, Consequences, Policies, Reflections*, edited by Mirjana Bobić and Stefan Janković, 241–267. Belgrade: Institute for Sociological Research.

Jansen, B. 2018. *Kakuma Refugee Camp: Humanitarian Urbanism in Kenya's Accidental City*. London: Verso.

Jones, S. 2015. "Lockdown at the Macedonian Border—Illegal Pushbacks of Refugees to Greece." Amnesty International, December 17. https://www.amnesty.org/en/latest/news/2015/12/lockdown-at-the-macedonian-border/

Kasparek, B. 2016. "Routes, Corridors, and Spaces of Exception: Governing Migration and Europe." *Near Futures Online 1: Europe at a Crossroads* (March 2016): Zone Books. http://nearfuturesonline.org/routes-corridors-and-spaces-of-exception-governing-migration-and-europe/.

Kilibarda, P. 2016. "Serbia Facing the Refugee and Migrant Crisis." *Mitteilungen Zeitschrift der Südosteuropa-Gesellschaft* 56, no 2: 32–45.

Korac-Sanderson, M. 2017. "Bordering and Rebordering Security: Causes and Consequences of Framing Refugees as a 'Threat' to Europe." In *Towards Understanding of Contemporary Migration. Causes, Consequences, Policies, Reflections*, edited by Mirjana Bobić and Stefan Janković, 25–40. Belgrade: Institute for Sociological Research.

Kurir News. 2017. "Migrants Steal Goods from a Store in Šid." https://www.kurir.rs/vesti/drustvo/2433543/ceo-sid-u-strahu-gradani-se-zale-da-ih-migranti-terorisu-policija-nemocna.

MacDowall, A., and E. Graham-Harrison. 2017. "Influx of Refugees Leaves Belgrade at Risk of Becoming 'New Calais.'" *The Guardian*, January 14. https://www.theguardian.com/world/2017/jan/14/influx-of-refugees-means-belgrade-risks-becoming-new-calais.

Minca, C., and A. Rijke. 2017. "Walls! Walls! Walls!" Society and Space 4 (April 2017). https://societyandspace.org/2017/04/18/walls-walls-walls/.

Minca C., D. Šantić, and D. Umek. 2018. "Walking the Balkan Route." In *The Camp Reconsidered*, edited by Irit Katz, Diana Martin and Claudio Minca, 35–39. Boulder, CO: Rowman & Littlefield.

Mountz, A. 2010. *Seeking Asylum*. Minneapolis: Minnesota University Press.

Novosti. 2017. "Humanitarian Aid because of the Migrant Crises: Reliable Water Supply Is Provided in Preševo." https://www.novosti.rs/.../srbija.73.html%3A699758-POMOC-ZBOG-MIGRANTSKE-KRIZE-Obezbedjeno-pouzdano-vodosnabdeva...

Official Gazette of the Republic of Serbia. 2012. Law on Migration Management of the Republic of Serbia, 107/2012.

Politika. 2016. "Migration Crisis is the Future of Europe." http://www.politika.rs/sr/clanak/Стефановић-Мигрантска-криза-је-будућност-Европе

Santer, K., and V. Wriedt. 2017. "(De-)Constructing Borders. Contestations in and around the Balkan Corridor in 2015/16." *Journal for Critical Migration and Border Regime Studies* 3, no 1: 141–150.

Šantić, D., C. Minca, and D. Umek. 2017. "The Balkan Migration Route: Reflections from a Serbian Observatory." In *Towards Understanding of Contemporary Migration. Causes, Consequences, Policies, Reflections*, edited by Mirjana Bobić and Stefan Janković, 221–240. Belgrade: Institute for Sociological Research.

Silberman, M., K. E. Till, and J. Ward, eds. 2012. *Walls, Borders, Boundaries: Spatial and Cultural Practices in Europe*. New York/Oxford: Berghahn Books.

Smith, H. 2016. "Macedonia Forcibly Returns Thousands of Refugees to Greece." *The Guardian*, March 15. https://www.theguardian.com/world/2016/mar/15/macedonia-forcibly-returns-refugees-greece-idomeni

Specia, Megan. 2017. "The Desperate Conditions Inside a Serbian Migrant Camp." *The New York Times*, January 24.

Stevens, J. and Tonkin, S. 2015. "We Have Lost Control of Borders, Says EU Chief: Warning Hours before Summit Comes as Britain Faces £150m Bill To Support Other Nations Despite Not Taking Part in Resettlement Programme." *The Daily Mail*, September 24.

Till, Karen, et al. 2013. "Interventions in the Political Geographies of Walls." *Political Geography* 33: 52–62.

Timur, S. and R. Nordland. 2016. "Erdogan Threatens to Let Migrant Flood into Europe Resume." *The New York Times*, November 25. https://www.nytimes.com/2016/11/25/world/europe/turkey-recep-tayyip-erdogan-migrants-european-union.html

Tinti, P., and T. Reitano. 2016. *Migrant, Refugee, Smuggler, Saviour*. London: Hurst.

Tomić, L. 2016. "Migrants Stranded in Serbian No-Man's Land." *Deutsche Welle*, July 28. https://www.dw.com/en/migrants-stranded-in-serbian-no-mans-land/a-19429213

Umek, D., C. Minca, and D. Šantić. 2018. "The Refugee Camp as Geopolitics: The Case of Preševo, Serbia." In *Mediterranean Mobilities* edited by Maria Paradiso, 37–53. London: Springer.

UNHCR. 2016. "Greece: Idomeni Refugee Site Transfers." May 27. http://www.unhcr.org/news/videos/2016/5/5748522e4/greece-idomeni-refugee-site-transfers.html

Vallet, E., ed. 2014. *Borders, Fences and Walls: State of Insecurity?* Burlington, VT: Ashgate.

Van Houtum, H. and R. Pijpers. 2007. "The European Union as a Gated Community: The Two-faced Border and Immigration Regime of the EU." *Antipode* 39, no. 2: 291–309.

Vaughan-Williams, Nick. 2015. *Europe's Border Crisis: Biopolitical Security and Beyond.* Oxford: Oxford University Press.

The Visegrad Group. 2016. Joint Statement on Migration. June 28. www.visegradgroup.eu/calendar/2016/joint-statement-on

The Visegrad Group. 2018. Joint Statement on The Future of Europe. www.visegradgroup.eu

Weaver, M., and H. Siddique. 2017. "Refugee Crisis: Hungary Uses Teargas and Water Cannon at Serbia Border—As It Happened." *Twhe Guardian*, September 16, updated April 8, 2017. https://www.theguardian.com/world/live/2015/sep/16/first-refugees-head-for-croatia-after-hungarys-border-crackdown-live-updates.

Zhang, S. X., G. E. Sanchez, and L. Achilli, eds. 2018. Special Issue: "Migrant Smuggling as a Collective Strategy and Insurance Policy: Views from the Margins." *The Annals*, 676, no. 1.

PART VI

POLICY RESPONSES: CRIMINALIZATION, CONTROL, AND DETENTION

CHAPTER 26

THE CRIMINALIZATION OF MIGRATION IN CANADA AND ITS UNINTENDED POLICY CONSEQUENCES

IDIL ATAK

OVER the past years, several sudden or large movements of migrants crossing irregular international borders have been witnessed in different parts of the world. The notion of "crisis" has been a popular way of describing these movements as well as states' responses (Ansems de Vries et al. 2016). The most prominent example is the so-called "European refugee crisis" in 2015 when the majority of the European Union Member States reacted to the spontaneous arrival of more than one million forced migrants, mostly from war-torn Syria, by closing their borders and erecting fences. In a global context where anti-refugee discourse and policies are on the rise, Canada has enjoyed praise for its humanitarian commitment to forced migrants and its global leadership in the resettlement of refugees. Indeed, the Liberal government of Prime Minister Justin Trudeau resettled more than 40,000 Syrian refugees in 2016 with notable thanks to a successful private sponsorship program (Government of Canada n.d., #*Welcome Refugees*). This compares to a total of 189,300 refugees admitted for resettlement globally during the same period (UNHCR 2017).

But the success of Canada's refugee resettlement program belies the criminalizing policy and practices toward in-land asylum seekers (i.e. individuals who claim refugee status from within Canada).[1] In fact, the Conservative government of Stephen Harper (2006–2015) introduced exceptionally harsh refugee policies following the arrival, in June 2009, of *MV Ocean Lady*, a cargo boat which carried 76 Tamil asylum seekers from Sri Lanka on the west coast of Canada, followed one year later by another boat *MV Sun Sea* with 493 asylum seekers aboard. The Protecting Canada's Immigration System Act (PCISA 2012) and the Balanced Refugee Reform Act (BRRA 2010) amended the Immigration and Refugee Protection Act (IRPA 2001) and include: creation of new classes of refugee claimants, expedited refugee claim hearings, reduced procedural guarantees, growing use of socioeconomic deterrents, and increased immigration detention.

A crisis-led policy model was followed by the previous government as a response to these boat arrivals. The notion of "crisis" has two distinctive features: 1) it denotes a condition of disruption, instability, or a danger affecting an individual, group, community, or whole society; 2) it leads to a decisive change. Indeed, the imminence of disruption or danger points to a need for immediate action and triggers fundamental transformation (Koselleck and Richter 2006). De Genova and Tazzioli discuss how in Europe, alarmist reactions to the unauthorized movements of people have largely served to justify the necessity of new "emergency" policies and the deployment of new means of control (2016, 8). This chapter argues that a similar process has been at play in Canada. The Conservative government resorted to a crisis narrative to justify the major overhaul of Canada's refugee status determination system in 2012. The irregular arrivals of asylum seekers in 2009 and 2010 were portrayed as an existential threat to Canada's security and to the integrity of its refugee system (Molnar Diop 2014). This chapter also contends that this crisis-led management has been counterproductive as it arguably rationalized policies that contributed to the criminalization of the refugee status determination system.

The criminalization of migration can be defined as the merging of criminal law and immigration law. It involves an increased reliance on the criminal law to enforce immigration statutes, thereby fundamentally changing the nature of the immigration law. Enhanced by a crisis narrative, the process ensures that violations of immigration law carry greater criminal consequences than ever before—without the implementation of procedural protections applicable to criminal law within immigration law settings (Guild 2010; Provera 2015; Stumpf 2006). In addition, the criminalization allows the expansion of law enforcement and correctional powers with immigration enforcement increasingly resembling criminal law enforcement (Stumpf 2006, 381). Hence, the process reinforces the government's discretion to decide who may be excluded from the territory and from membership in the society.

Against this backdrop, this chapter examines the criminalization of Canada's refugee policy and its unanticipated consequences with a special focus on the human rights of asylum seekers. It particularly deals with the Designated Foreign National (DFN) policy, created by the PCISA (2012), and the increased role of the Canada Border Services Agency (CBSA) as they exemplify the crisis-led management of the aforementioned boat arrivals.

The chapter draws on the findings of a field research that was conducted between October 2015 and May 2017 in three major provinces (Quebec, Ontario, and British Columbia) that host the majority of asylum seekers in Canada. The research included 64 research participants from Toronto, Ottawa, Montreal, Victoria, and Vancouver. It involved 58 semi-structured interviews (one-on-one or in-group) with stakeholders from various governmental and nongovernmental professional perspectives and profiles including: civil servants (14), elected members of the local and Federal governments (2), practitioners (19), intergovernmental organization representatives (2), and nongovernmental service provider organizations working with migrants and refugees (22) as well as academics and researchers in Canada (5).[2]

The first part discusses how the DFN policy, supported by a strong discourse delegitimizing the protection needs of asylum seekers, altered the substance of refugee law and curtailed procedural guarantees available. The second part examines the increased law enforcement by the CBSA, which has been a prominent feature of the criminalization of irregular migrants and asylum seekers in Canada, especially since 2012.

The DFN: The Crisis Narrative and the Criminalization of Asylum Seekers

The DFN policy allows the Minister of Public Safety to "designate as an irregular arrival the arrival in Canada of a group of persons if he or she

(a) is of the opinion that examinations of the persons in the group, particularly for the purpose of establishing identity or determining inadmissibility—and any investigations concerning persons in the group—cannot be conducted in a timely manner; or
(b) has reasonable grounds to suspect that, in relation to the arrival in Canada of the group, there has been, or will be, a contravention of subsection 117(1) for profit, or for the benefit of, at the direction of or in association with a criminal organization or terrorist group" (IRPA s. 20.1 [1]).[3]

The new policy targets those asylum seekers who arrive to Canada irregularly, in a group and with the help of a migrant smuggler.[4] It mandates the arrest and detention of DFNs aged 16 and over (IRPA s. 55(3.1)). Other features are:

- DFNs should prepare the hearing, before the Refugee Protection Division (RPD) of the Immigration and Refugee Board (IRB), within 45 days of being found eligible; compared with 60 days for non-designated claimants and 18 months in the previous system;
- DFNs are ineligible to apply for a work permit until their claim is approved by the IRB, or until their claim has been in the system for more than 180 days and no decision has been made (IRPA, s. 24(5));
- DFNs whose refugee claims are rejected by the RPD of the IRB are denied a right of appeal to the Refugee Appeal Division (RAD) (IRPA, s. 110(2)(a)) and face immediate deportation;

- DFNs do not have the right to an automatic stay of removal upon applying for leave and for judicial review to the Federal Court, and can therefore be deported during their application;
- Finally, even when they obtain refugee status or the status of a "person in need of protection," DFNs are required to wait five years before applying for permanent residence and before they can sponsor their family members. By contrast, foreign nationals who obtain the status of "refugee" or "protected person" can apply for permanent residence after 180 days have passed, and sponsor family members once they gain permanent residence (IRPA, s. 11(1.2)).

Given the potentially anticonstitutional nature of these measures, it is not a surprise that the policy was used only once since its entry into force on December 15, 2012. The previous government designated retroactively 85 individuals, including 35 children, who illegally crossed the Canada-U.S. border into the province of Quebec between February and October 2012 (Public Safety 2012). According to the figures provided by the IRB, Immigration Division has heard eleven of these cases since January 2013, leading to nine Romanian citizens being removed from Canada and two released. Despite being seldom used, the DFN class is undoubtedly the best illustration of Canada's move toward the criminalization of its asylum system. Negative narratives targeting refugee claimants were part of this process together with the marked changes in both substantive and procedural refugee law.

Policy Rationale: The Role of the Political Discourse in the Criminalization of Asylum Seekers

The DFN policy, which is defined by one immigration lawyer as amounting to "the demonization of refugees" (Participant 7, Toronto), illustrates how criminalization is, first and foremost, a political discourse aiming to deter certain behavior. The first iteration of the proposed law entitled the *Preventing Human Smugglers from Abusing Canada's Immigration System Act* is a telling example. Moreover, it was initially suggested that designated foreigners, including children, would not have any judicial review of their mandatory detention, for up to twelve months. The government had to drop some of the most controversial features of the draft law after having faced strong resistance by the opposition parties and refugee advocates.

The crisis narrative deployed by the Conservative government indicates a number of policy rationales. First, it heavily focused on the security threat allegedly represented by the boat arrivals in Victoria, B.C. in 2009 and 2010. One interviewee who witnessed these arrivals, noted:

> [C]BSA's concern was given the gender, that they were all male, and they were all relatively young, that, and I think a number of them had scars of battle; they figured

> these were all Tamil Tiger warriors, who were fleeing, at a time when the civil war was coming to an end. . . . And the second boat was clearly political. They wanted to send a very, very strong message, to would-be refugee claimants overseas: "Don't come because you're not going to get a positive reception."
>
> (Participant 59, Vancouver)

Indeed the Federal government's rhetoric suggested that asylum claimants on board of the two boats may be supporters of or potential contributors to terrorist activities (Bradimore and Bauder 2011; Kaushal and Dauvergne 2011). Then Parliamentary Secretary to the Minister of Citizenship and Immigration held that "the *MV Sun Sea* . . . was not a CRUISE ship. (. . .) On board many of these ships are criminals and terrorists from a country and the human smugglers themselves who, unbeknownst to others, are dressed as if they are also in a position to claim refugee status in our country" (House of Commons Debates, Dykstra, 2012).

The political discourse also conflated asylum seekers with migrant smugglers. Then Minister of Immigration stated:

> We need to include deterrents in the bill for the potential clients of the smugglers. That is why we are proposing a five-year temporary residence period instead of permanent residence for immigrants who arrive here illegally and who are recognized as protected persons. We have to have deterrents for the clients in order to reduce the human smuggling market.
>
> (House of Commons Debates, Kenney 2012; Neylon 2015, 304)

Such stereotypical representations enhanced what Bigo describes as the establishment of "an (in)security continuum transferring the illegitimacy of crime and terrorism to migrants"(1996, 263). They thereby criminalized a population who was not involved in any criminal activity. This process justified the need for harsh refugee policies to deal with the presumptive dangers to Canadians and to the life of the nation. Rehaag and Grant explain how the CBSA went into crisis management mode, issuing a strategic internal memorandum to its employees. Amongst other instructions, the memo provided that the CBSA will be aggressive in building evidence and arguing for inadmissibility. It also stated that the CBSA will take maximum advantage of detention as an effective tool against those who circumvent immigration processes (2015).

Security reasons were not the only policy rationale behind the DFN policy and other repressive measures adopted following the boat arrivals. As a High Official within the Federal government put it, the government's response also meant to protect Canada's economic interests by keeping the borders open while reassuring the United States of their safety:

> [I]t was the balance. To the extent that we can make sure that criminals don't use loopholes in our system, to enter our countries, then hopefully we can avoid having that land border thickened with, or securitized or militarized. The countries, we've

> been allies for too long. There's too much of our livelihood that depends on cross border traffic, cross border trade, even just families and cultural ties. There's so many thousands and thousands of crossings a day, that it's important for the Canadian people, for the Canadian government to keep that border flowing smoothly.
>
> (Participant 27, Ottawa)

Another policy rationale was the need to restore the refugee system's integrity and efficiency by streamlining the refugee status determination process, filtering out fraudulent asylum claims, and deporting swiftly those who are rejected. Indeed, the Conservative government's anxiety over asylum seekers hid an ongoing preoccupation over irregular migration and the control of the Canadian borders. As an interviewee put it:

> [I]t was all about the number of claims . . . how do you control that number. . . . The concern was that too many fraudulent refugees would come to Canada, bogus refugees, that whole line of thinking . . . that was the fixation; it was about volume. It wasn't about security. . . . the big change of course, was September 11th, 2001. . . . They never gave up on the issue of volume and too many refugees. . . . And the whole issue of fraud, which was linked to that. . . . They often talked about it in terms of security, but often, that was their smoke screen, for what, in actuality, was trying to suppress numbers.
>
> (Participant 22, Ottawa)

Finally, fostering the administrative and fiscal efficiency of the Canadian refugee system appears to be an important policy rationale. Several provisions pertaining to the DFN regime can be considered key tools to make the system faster and reduce the cost of the refugee status determination process. By accelerating processing timelines, the government strived for reducing refugee backlogs at the IRB, which had reached a high of 62,000 claims by 2009. Further, between 2010 and 2012, it took an average of twenty-one months to receive a positive decision from the RPD and an average of twenty-four months to exhaust all remedies. According to the government, the situation created a considerable pressure on the system, which had come to be viewed as "inefficient," "costly," and "slow" (IRCC 2016a, iv and v). It was presumed that part of the systemic strain was attributable to persons who "abused" the system. Then Canadian Citizenship, Immigration and Multiculturalism Minister claimed that "quick removal of failed claimants would help discourage individuals from using the asylum system to try to jump the immigration queue to enter Canada. . . . By shortening the time failed claimants remain in Canada, we could reduce the costs faced by provincial and territorial governments" (CIC 2012).

Hence, the new claims processing timelines appear as a deterrent which makes the system less attractive and sends a message to Canadians that the government kept the refugee policy and spending under control. Overall, the DFN policy can be considered as an attempt to "manage" the number of asylum seekers. It includes provisions the purpose of which is to deter asylum claimants and to make their stay in Canada less attractive. Take as an example the temporary denial of a work permit or the five-year bar which prevents DFNs who obtain refugee status from applying for permanent residence and from sponsoring their family members (IRPA s. 11[1.2]).[5] The use of this type of socioeconomic deterrents, which impede several human rights (in particular, the right to family reunification) is described in the literature as "attrition through enforcement." The aim is to marginalize and disempower migrants to the point of making their life unlivable with the goal of deterring them or spurring self-deportations (Vaughan 2006). In a landmark decision regarding the healthcare cuts, Justice Mactavish of the Federal Court noted that:

> The executive branch of the Canadian government has intentionally set out to make the lives of these disadvantaged individuals even more difficult than they already are. It has done this in an effort to force those who have sought the protection of this country to leave Canada more quickly, and to deter others from coming here to seek protection.
>
> (*Canadian Doctors* et al. 2014, FC 149)

The case concerned, among others, claimants from "designated countries of origin" (DCO), another new class of claimants who, like DFNs, face shorter processing timelines than non-DCO/non-DFN asylum seekers and a host of limitations.

These various rationales put forward by the government both denote a condition of danger and prescribe fundamental changes to deal with the presumptive danger. It is noteworthy that, in the past, similar arguments proved to be baseless. In fact, over the past decades, the judiciary in Canada questioned the administrative and fiscal efficiency argument (i.e., saving tax payer money and using resources efficiently by processing claims and deporting refused asylum seekers swiftly). The argument has been contested by courts on the grounds that restrictive policies put asylum claimants' lives at risk and perpetuate negative stereotypes, all while failing to adhere to the principles of natural justice and procedural fairness (SCC *Singh* 1985; *Canadian Doctors* et al. 2014 FC 149).

It is noteworthy that thanks to its relative geographical isolation, Canada does not receive as many asylum claims as some other destination countries, such as the United States and Western European States. Canada is also better protected from irregular migration than most comparable countries. Indeed, irregular boat arrivals are rather an exception in Canada. As noted by Neve and Russell, over the past thirty years, there have been eight arrivals of ships carrying approximately 1,500 people in total to Canada, taking a ballpark estimate of 25,000 refugee arrivals per year in Canada over the past three decades—the 1,500 who have arrived on these eight ships reflect just over 0.2 percent of the total (2011, 40). These figures illustrate the gap between the demonstrated facts and the perceived threat. However such narratives justified the passage of repressive legislation that altered Canada's refugee system.

The DFN and the Impact of the Criminalization on the Human Rights of Asylum Seekers

Using the DFN as a case study, this section discusses how the criminalization affects both refugee law and the human rights of asylum seekers in Canada. As previously stated, the policy creates a new class of claimants with weaker substantive and procedural rights than non-DFNs, with a focus, in particular, on two measures: truncated processing timelines and mandatory detention.

DFNs have less time (forty-five days) to prepare the hearing before the RPD of the IRB than nodesignated asylum seekers (sixty days). Claimants are also required to submit all evidence ten days before the hearing. The average timeline was eighteen months in the previous system. Accelerated timelines have had a number of negative systemic and human rights consequences for all streams of claimants. One can reasonably argue that these issues, some of which are outlined subsequently, are even more pressing in the case of DFNs. Refugee lawyers and community service representatives invariably thought that the new timelines typically do not give claimants enough time to navigate the system and to prepare their claims, including to hire a counsel, to apply for legal aid and an interpreter, and to compile the evidence and expert reports they need. As a representative of a community organization put it:

> [W]here it might be detrimental is the speed at which claims are being heard now, and the pressure to get a decent lawyer, when you don't know the network and you don't know who's trustworthy or responsible as an advocate and communicating back home, trying to get documents that are just difficult to get and the pressure that comes with that, . . . it's the shortness of time that contributes to distress then . . . Even just mobilizing your internal resources to get the things you need, when all you want to do is curl up in a corner, or where you're disoriented and you're having trouble focusing. And all of those things contribute to making it even more difficult to get your status. That difficulty then compounds the stress, because you're not doing well in preparing for the hearing.
>
> (Participant 42, Montreal)

A refugee lawyer in Vancouver explained how the timelines form a major obstacle in the preparation of the cases where medical or other expert reports are needed:

> [s]o, with the client this morning, I've never met her before. And it takes time to develop rapport, and I need her to double check what this medical nurse that did the examinations after the sexual assault can testify to. But we don't have time to wait, [be]cause the person's in Sri Lanka. That would add, like, a day or two, and it's little things like that that really, even if the claim has a lot of merits, really chips away at the

> credibility (*sic*), and that's unfair, because it's just a timing issue. If I had two weeks extra, we would deal with all this in due course.
>
> (Participant 59, Vancouver)

As this quote illustrates it, accelerated timelines affect even more vulnerable claimants, such as those with mental health issues, LGBTQ, torture victims, or human trafficking victims, who usually experience considerable difficulties providing formal legal and factual materials to prove the credibility of their claims.

Some participants argued that restrictive time frames can lead to a rise in the number of unrepresented claimants or aggravate the risk of inferior legal representation and incentivize volume-based practices by some counsels or consultants. Overall there is a heightened risk for legitimate applications being rejected and individuals deported from Canada without a thorough analysis of their claims' merits. This in turn would amount to a violation of the principle of *non-refoulement* (i.e., the prohibition of deportation of individuals to places where they may face persecution or the substantial risk of torture or similar abuse [Article 33(1) of the *Convention relating to the Status of Refugees* (Refugee Convention); Article 3 of the UN *Convention against Torture*; IRPA s. 115]).

The challenges relating to timelines may become insurmountable for DFNs who are subjected to mandatory detention upon arrival. Several participants expressed concern on how the new timelines work against detained claimants. The issues outlined previously are exacerbated by the obstacles that many counsels and frontline support agencies face in gaining access to detention facilities in a timely manner (Bates et al. 2016, 65). Thus lengthy mandatory detention is another example that illustrates the substantive and procedural law changes in Canada's refugee system. In other words, immigration law has become punitive with a view to deterring unwanted migrants, without providing DFNs with adequate procedural guarantees that normally accompany such punitive measures.

As an illustration, the policy subjects DFNs, including of 16- and 17-year-old children, to such detention, but lacks the legal safeguards allowing a prompt review of the detention's lawfulness. An officer *must* detain DFNs, on their entry into Canada (IRPA s. 55 (3.1)) whereas the decision to detain non-DFNs is always made on a discretionary (case-by-case) basis, which means that the special circumstances of each case are among factors taken into consideration. As well, the detention of DFNs is reviewed only after fourteen days, followed by another review after six months and then every six months. In comparison, initial detention review of non-DFNs takes place within forty-eight hours, followed by a review within seven days, and then every thirty days from the previous review (IRPA s. 57). The DFN detention provisions constitute a violation of not only the United Nations *Convention on the Rights of the Child* to which Canada is a signatory, but also the right to a prompt review of detention under s. 10 (c) of the *Canadian Charter of Rights and Freedoms* (the Charter).[6] The lack of such review makes the detention arbitrary (SCC, *Charkaoui* 2007, par. 91; *Chaudhary* 2015 ONCA 700). In fact, immigration detention has become a prominent feature of the criminalization of migrants in Canada. Immigration officers have the power to arrest and detain a foreigner without a warrant where there are "reasonable grounds to suspect" that the individual is "inadmissible on grounds of security" (IRPA s. 55[3][(b]). By contrast, the normal level of evidence for preventive detention and detention for investigative purposes in criminal matters is that the officer must "believe on reasonable grounds" that a criminal activity will be committed or that an individual is implicated in the criminal activity under investigation (*R v. Mann* 2004, SCC 52). Hence, the criminalization allows a low standard of evidential proof and other procedural rights when immigration rules are enforced (Provera 2015). As noted by Stumpf, the convergence of immigration and criminal law brings to bear the harshest elements of each area of law (2006, 378). As well, Sklansky contends that the criminal law is used instrumentally and selectively because of its effectiveness in securing immigration enforcement objectives when noncriminal law measures are not as advantageous to states—rather than its normative underpinning or because the action is inherently "wrong" (2012, 50). This process can also be observed in DFNs being denied the procedural rights which are, with some exceptions, normally available to asylum claimants in Canada, such as the right to appeal to the RAD of the IRB and the right to an automatic stay of removal pending such appeals.

Moreover, the DFN regime penalizes refugees in violation of Article 31 of the Refugee Convention that enjoins states not to impose penalties on refugees, on account of their illegal entry or presence, provided they present themselves without delay to the authorities and show good cause for their illegal entry or presence (see also Section 133 of IRPA). In 2015, the Federal Court ruled that the differential treatment of claimants from DCOs in comparison with those from nondesignated countries amounts to a violation of Section 15 (Equality Rights) of the Charter. The decision states that such treatment "puts [claimant's] lives at risk and perpetuates the stereotypical view that they are cheats, that their refugee claims are 'bogus', and that they have come to Canada to abuse the generosity of Canadians" (*Canadian Doctors* et al. 2014 FC 149, par. 851).

Although the decision did not concern the DFNs, one can conclude that discrimination based on the mode of arrival would raise similar concerns as a differentiated treatment on grounds of nationality. Chances are high that a court of law reaches a comparable verdict, should a DFN case be filed.[7] This is all the more true as in *Appulonappa* (2015), the Supreme Court of Canada stated that refugee claimants should not be punished solely on the basis of their irregular arrival with the help of smugglers:

> Art. 31(1) of the *Refugee Convention* seeks to provide immunity for genuine refugees who enter illegally in order to seek refuge. For that protection to be effective, the law must recognize that persons often seek refuge in groups and work together to enter a country illegally. To comply with art. 31(1), a state cannot impose a criminal sanction on refugees solely because they have aided others to enter illegally in their collective flight to safety.
>
> (*Appulonappa*, para. 43)

Similarly in *B010*, another landmark decision, the Supreme Court ruled that a migrant who aids in his own illegal entry or the illegal entry of other asylum seekers in their collective flight to safety should not be excluded from refugee status (B010 v. Canada 2015). The Court emphasized that acts of humanitarian and mutual aid (including aid between family members) do not constitute people smuggling under the IRPA (2015).

These judgments challenge the use of criminal sanctions against asylum seekers who have not committed any crime. They also question the main premises of the DFN regime which presume the criminality of asylum seekers who arrive irregularly in Canada and contest the genuineness of those claimants who use the services of migrant smugglers. It is noteworthy that the criminalization has little effect on migrant smuggling which is a flourishing business (MPI 2015), but it penalizes smuggled asylum seekers whose access to international protection is considerably constrained. Macklin refers to the "erosion of the idea that people who seek asylum may actually be refugees"—in part a result of Canadian policies of deterrence which force asylum seekers to cross borders illegally—means that real refugees are discursively erased and replaced by "illegals" (Macklin 2005).

The DFN policy can therefore be considered as a tool of deterrence which aims to reassure audiences such as the Conservative electorate and the United States that Canada's borders are well guarded and the abuse of the refugee system would not be tolerated. In her analysis of similar political moves in the United Kingdom, Aliverti highlights how the criminal law is used symbolically "as an attempt to appease a sector of the electorate, the media and the opposition about the 'immigration problem' to bring immigration under control. The invocation of criminal law in cases of immigration offences serves mostly as a threat rather than to actually prevent the offense or persecute the offender" (2012, 434).

The DFN regime had come at the expense of the principles pertaining to refugee protection in Canada. While the criminalization process rendered the substantive refugee law more punitive, alarmingly, this move has been accompanied by an overall weakening of procedural rights available to refugee claimants. It seems unlikely that the current Liberal government will make use of it any time soon, despite the intensification of irregular border crossings from the United States following the election of Donald Trump in November 2016 (IRCC 2018). As a refugee lawyer stated: "it's one of those provisions that are there. If another boat comes, they'll use it. It's sort of in their back pocket kind of thing." Several interviewees called for the government to rescind the policy which is contrary to the Charter and Canada's international obligations under the Refugee Convention. As of October 2018, the Liberal government of Justin Trudeau has not responded to such calls. In a statement issued to mark the fifth anniversary of the changes to Canada's refugee determination system, the Canadian Council for Refugees, a national nonprofit umbrella organization representing over 180 organizations across Canada, expressed concern about the fact that the DFN regime remains in place, even though the government's own evaluation found it counterproductive (CCR 2017).

The Role of Law Enforcement in the Criminalization of Asylum Seekers

One of the principal features of the criminalization is the increased similarity between immigration enforcement and criminal law enforcement, a process which offers immigration officers leverage to enforce compliance with restrictive rules (Stumpf 2006, 387). These two types of enforcements in Canada have become similar with the creation of the CBSA, a part of the Public Safety Portfolio, in the aftermath of the September 11, 2001 terrorist attacks in the United States. Over the years, the CBSA has been granted a wide range of punitive investigative powers such as the collection and sharing of information with police and intelligence agencies for preventing illegal entries at ports of entry and overseeing the detention of migrants in correctional institutions and deporting them (CARL 2016, 31).

The changes in the refugee system in 2012 have been accompanied by a considerable increase in law enforcement and correctional mandate and capacity of the CBSA, including wide discretionary powers in immigration detention. Indeed the CBSA's mandate and activities have become almost indistinguishable from that of a criminal law enforcement organization. CBSA agents are empowered to conduct surveillance and raids. The Agency enjoys wide discretion when they deal with asylum seekers at the border. For instance, according to an interviewee, CBSA agents in British Columbia require claimants who irregularly cross the border to fill out refugee claim forms within only seven to eight days, although the legal timeline is fifteen days. This type of punitive discretionary decision, which goes unchecked, reflects CBSA agents' perception of such claimants as bogus refugees and more generally the negative political narrative that led to restrictive policies in 2012.

Another area where wide discretionary power is exercised by CBSA officers, with little scrutiny, is detention and removal decisions. Immigration detention has become more frequent and systematic since 2012. Recent data from the CCR (2016) show that 4,258 detained foreign nationals spent an average of 55 days in detention in 2015, whereas detained migrants spent an average of 20 days in detention in 2012-13 (CBSA n.d.). Vulnerable people, including children, are detained in prisons or in centers that resemble prisons based on concerns regarding their identity, their flight risk, or the potential danger they allegedly pose to society. In 2013, nearly one-third of migrants were detained by the CBSA in provincial prisons intended for the criminal population. Some detainees have no past criminal record, but are detained on the basis that they are a flight risk or because their identity cannot be confirmed (Gros and van Groll 2015).

In addition, the previous Conservative government pledged to accelerate the removal of refused asylum seekers and set the target for the CBSA to get 80 percent of removals to be completed within twelve months of an IRB decision (IRCC 2016b). To that end, Section 48 of the IRPA about removal timelines was amended to enable CBSA to remove a noncitizen *as soon as possible*, as opposed to *as soon as was practicable*, which was upheld in the former legislation. The result was an increase in lengthy administrative detention of refused asylum claimants whose identity cannot be established. A refugee lawyer noted how such practices are deemed to be illegal under criminal law:

> They're (the CBSA) using detention as a mechanism to coerce cooperation. And that is not an appropriate use of administrative detention. . . .If you're not complying with your obligations under the income tax act. . . . Like, if I don't file my taxes, there may be administrative penalties, but the administrative penalties are fines . . . ultimately, what you're trying to do is to enforce compliance, which is criminal law. And it's a criminal law power that's being exercised through an administrative process.
>
> (Participant 61, Vancouver)

The detention of noncriminal foreign nationals in prisons forces them to commingle with incarcerated convicts and reinforces public perception that they are criminals (Molnar Diop and Silverman 2016). Research has documented the detrimental impact of detention policy, including attempted suicide, self-harm, depression, and PTSD among those under custody (Gros and van Groll 2015; Kronick and Rousseau 2015).

In this context, the Agency is considered by several interviewees as having a distinct institutional security-oriented culture within the federal immigration and refugee policy field. Nongovernmental interviewees tend to see the CBSA as strongly embedded in its enhanced law enforcement mandate and as neglecting other key policy objectives, such as upholding Canada's humanitarian approach and international human rights obligations. A refugee lawyer remarked: "I don't see how you make significant changes to a bureaucracy that is focused solely on enforcement and doesn't see that it has any function to look at any kind of humanitarian and compassionate considerations, or common sense" (Participant 65, Victoria).

Some interviewees pointed out that with increased powers, the CBSA maintains a culture of fear targeting racialized asylum seekers. Some see detention as a tool to intimidate or exert power over them. The CBSA's enforcement mandate is seen as unsympathetic to the Canadian values, such as the protection of the best interest of the child. A refugee lawyer maintained that:

> [t]he CBSA almost never looks at the best interests of the child. When the *MV Sun Sea* came, there were 49 children who were detained, some for over six or eight months. They were in an actual detention centre. They were in the Burnaby Youth Detention Centre, in Burnaby B.C. Young people should not be detained under any circumstances, let alone when they haven't committed a crime. And being a refugee is not a crime.
>
> (Participant 7, Toronto)

Similarly, several lawyers and service providers have brought up the CBSA's general lack of willingness or ability to consider the special needs of vulnerable individuals, including migrants with mental health issues. Some interviewees pointed out to the lack of proper training of CBSA officers and highlighted that there needs to be an independent oversight mechanism to hold agents accountable for misconduct and human rights violations. An immigration and refugee lawyer noted that "one of the biggest problems with the border services agencies is, Canada Border Services, the CBSA, it is a huge police force now . . . without any controls, without any kind of monitoring or surveillance, without a history of how police operate" (Participant 2, Toronto). Another participant concurred by stating that it is "ludicrous and unacceptable" that CBSA as one of the "largest paramilitary organizations in the country has no independent oversight" (Participant 65, Vancouver). The CBSA's expanded law enforcement mandate can be considered as a policy response to the "crisis" created by the two boat arrivals in 2009 and 2010. It reflects the presumption that exceptional measures are needed to deal with the threat and take back the control of borders. Nevertheless, such developments have created institutions and resulted in practices that conflict with the rule of law.

Conclusion

Canada prides itself on being "open, accepting, and generous—qualities that should be reflected in Canada's immigration policies and in our approach to welcoming those seeking refuge from conflict and war" (Office of the Prime Minister, Mandate Letter 2016). Indeed, one of the objectives of its refugee policy is "to grant, as a fundamental expression of Canada's humanitarian ideals, fair consideration to those who come to Canada claiming persecution" (IRPA s. 3[2][c]). However over the past decades, a crisis-led management of in-land asylum claims has been at play. Successive governments have been preoccupied with controlling the number of asylum seekers who spontaneously arrive in Canada. The criminalization of Canada's refugee system has been a policy response. This chapter examined how the irregular boat arrivals of Tamil asylum seekers in 2009 and 2010 served as a catalyst for the Conservative government to implement a crisis-led policy model. The arrivals were depicted as a danger affecting Canada's safety and the integrity of its refugee policy. Further, they were presented as evidence that Canadian policy was prone to be abused by "bogus refugees" and a decisive change was needed to deal with the presumptive threat. The result was a major overhaul of Canada's refugee status determination system. This chapter aimed to demonstrate that one of the features and consequences of the crisis-led policies is the criminalization of the refugee system. The measures discussed exemplify this process and include the use of a negative rhetoric against asylum seekers, the transformation of substantive law, and the elimination or weakening of procedural guarantees, as well as increased law enforcement. The new policies are meant to deter potential asylum seekers and to demonstrate to the public that the government has migration under control (Düvell 2011, 293–294). The creation of DFN, a new class of refugee claimants with limited access to refugee protection and restricted rights, shows how some measures have a purely discursive meaning. Indeed several provisions of the DFN scheme are blatantly unconstitutional and would not pass a Charter challenge. That is arguably why it has been used only once, by the government, since December 2012. Hence the DFN illustrates how the invocation of criminal law in cases of immigration offences serves mostly as a deterrent rather than to actually prevent the offence or prosecute the offender. It is also based on the erroneous assumption that if only deterrents are made severe enough, people will change their behavior (Aliverti 2012). Strikingly, this controversial policy and many others are still in force despite the pledge of the Liberal government to review and either amend or remove unsound measures, and generally to restore humanitarian commitment and respect for international human rights as a pillar of our immigration and refugee system (Office of the Prime Minister 2016). While the Liberal government kept its promises in terms of the resettlement of Syrian refugees, it has not made any noticeable improvements to Canada's refugee system. This points to the continuity in policy among Canadian governments irrespective of political ideology. The policy is still decidedly focused on advancing Canada's economic interests and preserving its safety, through notably controlling the volume of asylum seekers.

The Canadian experience also illuminates the reasons why a crisis-led refugee policy is likely to be inefficient and counterproductive. Despite the acceleration of the refugee claims' processing timelines and the reduction of some procedural guarantees for all refugee claimants, the government has fallen short of processing refugee claims and appeals in accordance with regulated time limits (IRB 2016, 17). In addition, the target for the swift removal of failed asylum seekers was not met (IRCC 2016, iv-v). In fact, major changes have been introduced in the refugee system in 2012 without a thorough assessment of their feasibility, their consistency with the Charter, and their long-term consequences. It should not come as a surprise that these changes have engendered a number of negative unintended results. The vast majority of the participants in our research agreed that many of the new measures violate the rights of refugee claimants in Canada. Sanctions for irregular border crossings and systematic detention criminalize refugee claimants. The measures carry implications for the ability of refugee claimants to access to justice as they seek protection in Canada (Bates et al. 2016, 71–72). They ultimately create systemic conditions and various barriers that heighten the risk of erroneous decisions, therefore, of *refoulement*. Several participants felt that the government's approach has shifted from humanitarianism and protecting refugees to control through punitive policies. More particularly, they raised concerns regarding the lack of fairness of the new system and its discriminatory impact for specific groups. Courts have on several occasions agreed that some recent measures against asylum seekers contravene the *Charter* and are not justified by the principles and purposes of the IRPA. The government should take the opportunity to repeal the most controversial measures, such as the DFN regime, and take the necessary steps to provide equal access to and protection within the asylum system.

Notes

1. Persons can claim refugee status from within Canada either to the CBSA at a port of entry, or to an inland office operated by IRCC or the CBSA. Eligible claims are referred to the Refugee Protection Division (RPD) of the Immigration and Refugee Board (IRB), which is in charge of determining whether the claimant is a "*Convention* refugee" (IRPA s. 96) or a "Person in need of protection" (IRPA s. 97[1]).
2. The preliminary findings of the research project were published in I. Atak, G. Hudson, and D. Nakache. "Making Canada's Refugee System Faster and Fairer: Reviewing the Stated Goals and Unintended Consequences of the 2012 Refugee Reform." *CARFMS Working Paper* No. 2017/3, Toronto. http://carfms.org/wp-content/uploads/2017/05/CARFMS-WPS-No11-Idil-Atak.pdf see also: I. Atak, G. Hudson, and D. Nakache. "The Securitization of Canada's Refugee System: Reviewing the Unintended Policy Consequences." Refugee Survey Quarterly 37, no. 1: 1–24.
3. IRPA s. 117 prohibits human smuggling and outlines penalties for those who contravene the prohibition.
4. The Act does not define the term "group." The arrival of two or more individuals can arguably constitute a group.
5. In comparison, non-DFN claimants' work permits are issued for twelve months from the date of their claims' referral to the IRB.
6. Article 37 (b) of the Convention states that "No child shall be deprived of his or her liberty unlawfully or arbitrarily. The arrest, detention or imprisonment of a child shall be in conformity with the law and shall be used only as a measure of last resort and for the shortest appropriate period of time."
7. Neylon 2015 discusses the possibility for the DFN refugee to dispute her designation and the subsequent limitation of her rights as a discriminatory practice under section 15 of the Charter.

References

Aliverti, A. 2012. "Making People Criminal: The Role of the Criminal Law in Immigration Enforcement." *Theoretical Criminology* 16: 417–434.

Ansems De Vries, L., S. Carrera, and E. Guild. 2016. "Documenting the Migration Crisis in the Mediterranean." *CEPS Paper in Liberty and Security in Europe* 94, no. 1: 1–8.

Atak, I, G. Hudson, and D. Nakache. 2017. "Making Canada's Refugee System Faster and Fairer: Reviewing the Stated Goals and Unintended Consequences of the 2012 Refugee Reform." *CARFMS Working Paper* 3, no. 1: 1–48.

B010 v. Canada (Citizenship and Immigration). 2015. SCC 58, [2015] 3 S.C.R. 704.

BRRA. 2010. *Balanced Refugee Reform Act*, S.C. 2010, c. 8.

Bates, E., J. Bond, and D. Wiseman. 2016. "Troubling Signs: Mapping Access to Justice in Canada's Refugee System Reform." *Ottawa Law Review* 47, no. 1: 1–72.

Bigo, D. 1996. "Polices en réseaux, l'expérience européenne." *Presses de la Fondation Nationale des sciences politiques* 47, no. 2: 227–232.

Bradimore, A., and H. Bauder. 2011. "Mystery Ships and Risky Boat People: Tamil Refugee Migration in the Newsprint Media." *Canadian Journal of Communication* 36, no. 4: 637–661.

CARL (Canadian Association of Refugee Lawyers). 2016. *Reform Proposals for Canada's Inland Refugee Determination System and Other Aspects of the Immigration System*. July 2016. http://www.carl-acaadr.ca/articles/137

CBSA (Canada Border Services Agency). n.d. "Annual Detention Statistics." https://www.cbsa-asfc.gc.ca/security-securite/detent/stat-2012-2017-eng.html

CCR (Canadian Council for Refugees). 2017. "Five Years Later, Refugees Are Suffering the Consequences of Unfair and Inefficient Changes to the Refugee System." December 14. http://ccrweb.ca/en/media/five-years-later-refugee-system

CCR (Canadian Council for Refugees). 2016. *Immigration Detention Statistics 2015*. http://ccrweb.ca/sites/ccrweb.ca/files/immigration-detention-statistics-2015.pdf

Canadian Doctors for Refugee Care et al. v. Canada (Attorney general), 2014 FC 651.

Charkaoui v. Canada (Citizenship and Immigration), [2007] 1 SCR 350, 2007 SCC 9.

Chaudhary v. Canada (Public Safety and Emergency Preparedness), 2015 ONCA 700.

CIC (Citizenship and Immigration Canada). 2012. "Making Canada's Asylum System Faster and Fairer." Ottawa, November 30.

De Genova, N., and Tazzioli, M., eds. 2016. "Europe/Crisis: New Keywords of 'the Crisis' in and of 'Europe.'" New Keywords Collective. *Near Futures Online 1*, no. 1: 1–45.

Düvell, F. 2011. "Paths into Irregularity: The Legal and Political Construction of Irregular Migration." *European Journal of Migration and Law* 13, no. 3: 275–295.

Government of Canada. (n.d.). *#Welcome Refugees: Key Figures*. http://www.IRCC.gc.ca/english/refugees/welcome/milestones.asp

Gros, H., and P. van Groll. 2015. "'We Have No Rights': Arbitrary Imprisonment and Cruel Treatment of Migrants with Mental Health Issues in Canada." International Human Rights Program: University of Toronto, Faculty of Law. https://ihrp.law.utoronto.ca/We_Have_No_Rights

Guild, E. 2010. "Criminalization of Immigration in Europe: Human Rights Implications." *Commissioner of Human Rights, Council of Europe*.

House of Commons Debates, 41st Parl, 1st Sess, No 108, (April 23, 2012) at 7048 (Jason Kenney).

House of Commons Debates, 41st Parl, Bill C- 31 2nd Reading, (June 8, 2012) (Rick Dykstra, Parliamentary Secretary to the Minister of Citizenship and Immigration).

IRB. (Immigration and Refugee Board of Canada). 2016. *Executive Evaluation Report of the Refugee Determination System of the Immigration and Refugee Board of Canada: Policy, Planning and Corporate Affairs Branch*. http://www.irb-cisr.gc.ca/Eng/transp/ReviewEval/Pages/ExecEvalRep2016.aspx

Immigration and Refugee Protection Act (IRPA), S.C. 2001, c. 27.

IRCC. (Immigration, Refugees and Citizenship Canada). 2018. *Members of the Ad Hoc Intergovernmental Task Force on Irregular Migration Maintain Collective Efforts to Address the Asylum Claimant Situation*. Ottawa. https://www.canada.ca/en/immigration-refugees-citizenship/news/2018/08/members-of-the-ad-hoc-intergovernmental-task-force-on-irregular-migration-maintain-collective-efforts-to-address-the-asylumclaimant-situation.html

IRCC (Immigration, Refugees and Citizenship Canada). 2016a. *2016 Annual Report to Parliament on Immigration*. Ottawa. http://www.canada.ca/en/immigration-refugees-citizenship/corporate/publications-manuals/annual-report-parliament-immigration-2016.html

IRCC (Immigration, Refugees and Citizenship Canada). 2016b. *Evaluation of the In-Canada Asylum System Reforms*. Ottawa. April 2016. https://www.canada.ca/en/immigration

-refugees-citizenship/corporate/reports-statistics/evaluations/canada-asylum-system-reforms.html

Kaushal, A., and C. Dauvergne. 2011. "The Growing Culture of Exclusion: Trends in Canadian Refugee Exclusions." *International Journal of Refugee Law* 23, no. 1: 54–92.

Koselleck, R. and M. Richter. 2006. "Crisis." *Journal of the History of Ideas* 67, no. 2: 357–400.

Kronick, R. and C. Rousseau. 2015. "Rights, Compassion and Invisible Children: A Critical Discourse Analysis of the Parliamentary Debates on the Mandatory Detention of Migrant Children in Canada." *Journal of Refugee Studies* 28, no. 4: 544–569.

Macklin, A. 2005. "Disappearing Refugees: Reflections on the Canada–US Safe Third Country Agreement." *Columbia Human Rights Law Review* 36: 365–426.

Migration Policy Institute (MPI). 2015. *Big Business of Smuggling Enables Mass Movement of People for Enormous Profit*. December 15. http://www.migrationpolicy.org/article/top-10-2015-%E2%80%93-issue-4-big-business-smuggling-enables-mass-movement-people-enormous-profits

Molnar Diop, P. 2014. "The 'Bogus' Refugee: Roma Asylum Claimants and Discourses of Fraud in Canada's Bill C-31." *Refuge: Canada's Journal on Refugees* 30, no. 1: 67–80.

Molnar Diop, P., and S. Silverman. 2016. "Cracks Where the Light Gets In: Recent Legal Breakthroughs in Detention and Crimmigration in Canada." MetroPolitics.eu: December 6. http://www.metropolitiques.eu/Cracks-Where-the-Light-Gets-in.html.

Neve, A. and T. Russell. 2011. "Hysteria and Discrimination: Canada's Harsh Response to Refugees and Migrants Who Arrive by Sea." *University of New Brunswick Law Journal* 62: 37–46.

Neylon, A. 2015. "Ensuring Precariousness: The Status of Designated Foreign National under the Protecting Canada's Immigration System Act 2012." *International Journal of Refugee Law* 27: 297–326.

Office of the Prime Minister, Minister of Immigration, Refugees and Citizenship Mandate Letter. 2016. http://pm.gc.ca/eng/minister-immigration-refugees-and-citizenship-mandate-letter

PCISA. 2012. *Protecting Canada's Immigration System Act*, S.C. 2012, c. 17.

Provera, M. 2015. "The Criminalisation of Irregular Migration In The European Union." *CEPS Paper in Liberty and Security 80*: 1–53.

Public Safety Canada. 2012. *Minister of Public Safety makes First Designation of Irregular Arrival under Protection Canada's Immigration System Act*. December 5. https://www.publicsafety.gc.ca/cnt/nws/nws-rlss/2012/20121205-en.aspx

Rehaag, S. and A. Gavin Grant. 2015. "Unappealing: An Assessment of the Limits On Appeal Rights in Canada's New Refugee Determination System." *Osgoode Legal Studies Research Paper Series* 132: 1-48.

R. v. Mann, [2014] 3 S.C.R. 59, 2004 SCC 52.

R. v. Appulonappa, 2015 SCC 59, [2015] 3 S.C.R. 754.

Singh v. Canada. Minister of Employment and Immigration. [1985] 1 S.C.R. 177.

Sklansky, D. A. 2012. "Crime, Immigration and Ad Hoc Instrumentalism." *New Criminal Law Review In International and Interdisciplinary Journal* 15, no. 2: 157–223.

Stumpf, J. P. 2006. "The Crimmigration Crisis: Immigrants, Crime, and Sovereign Power." *American University Law Review* 56: 367–419.

UNHCR. United Nations High Commissioner for Refugees 2017. *UNHCR Global Trends: Forced Displacement in 2016*. http://www.unhcr.org/globaltrends2016/

Vaughan, J. 2006. "Attrition through Enforcement: A Cost-Effective Strategy to Shrink the Illegal Population." Center for Immigration Studies. https://cis.org/Attrition-Through-Enforcement

CHAPTER 27

VIOLENCE AT THE US-MEXICO BORDER

MARÍA DOLORES PARÍS POMBO

SINCE the 1980s, successive Democratic and Republican administrations in the United States have declared multiple wars along the country's southwestern border. These are wars in which the named enemies are merchandises or abstractions. During the Reagan administration, the "war on drugs" was the legitimizing slogan for tightening border control. In the 1990s, this was also true of the fight against "illegal immigration." In the beginning of the twenty-first century, the enemy became an amalgam of terrorism, "radical Islamism," drugs, and "illegal aliens."

Unlike other wars undertaken by the United States, these involve very little loss of life by soldiers or security forces. An observer could ask, therefore, "What is the legitimate basis of a decades-long border war without armed conflict?" and, especially, "Why have migrants become the main victims of this war without battles?"

In Mexico, the "war on drugs" had little following among the political class or in the mass media until the presidential administration of Felipe Calderón (2006–2012). In January 2007, that president, dressed in an army uniform and flanked by his Secretary of Defense, declared war. From then on, the enemies have taken the form of drug-trafficking criminal organizations, and the human losses have been incalculable: police and military personnel, politicians, public officials, criminals, and many victims of "collateral damage" in civil society. Migrants have been among the main casualties of this war.

This chapter will not examine the combat between criminal organizations, military and police forces, or the long-standing territorial disputes over the routes for illegal trafficking between the two countries. Rather, it seeks to explain how the political discourses about the border war lead to multiple forms of violence against migrants—that is, the objective here is to delve behind the spectacular and discursive foreground to analyze the layers of violence that affect the life and death of migrants on both sides of the US-Mexico border. This involves analyzing the critical relationships among war, violence, and human mobility. War is here conceptualized as a nonnegotiable conflict or an extreme power relationship, which at the same time constitutes a substratum of all political relations and all institutions (Foucault 1997). Thus, this chapter examines violence as it is produced and structured by discourses and public policies, violence executed through security forces, state institutions, pressure groups, and organized crime.

The questions that will guide this chapter are the following: What are the consequences, for migrants, of the wars declared by the United States and Mexican governments along their common border? How is the violence structured within a given social space by the political-administrative boundary between the two nation-states and by the division between two very unequal economic systems? What are migrants' experiences of violence, as determined by their unauthorized border crossings and their frequent expulsions?

The chapter is divided into three parts. The first analyzes the creation of mechanisms of social control through declarations of war on the southwestern US border. This will include description of the processes of structuring violence through immigration policy and border control. The second part will examine the forms of institutional violence carried out against migrants by the agencies of border surveillance and immigration control, and will explain the relationship between such violence and the day-to-day verbal, physical, and sexual aggressions on the part of agents of the United States Border Patrol (USBP). The third part will describe some of the effects of the so-called "war against drugs" on the proliferation of criminal violence in northern Mexico, and will finally explain the repercussions of the commodification of migrants' bodies in the formation of chains of violence and exploitation: kidnappings, human trafficking, sexual violence, and massacres.

The concept of violence covers a broad semantic field of the social sciences. Studies of the sources and consequences of violence, physical aggression, and aggressiveness have been followed by theories of symbolic violence (Bourdieu 1980), structural violence, and institutional violence (Galtung 1975). Those theories analytically link the structures of domination and power relations to forms of direct and indirect aggression against individuals, social groups, or entire peoples. Similarly, they show how deep socioeconomic inequalities, legitimized by sexist, racist, or nativist ideologies, directly impact the physical or psychological integrity of broad social groups.

The concept of "structural violence" was originally proposed by Galtung (1975) in his theories regarding peace. The Norwegian sociologist attempted to demonstrate that even in situations in which no declared war exists, latent forms of indirect violence can cause serious damage to people's lives and integrity. But because such violence is inherent in economic and political structures, compiling a list of victims is impossible, as is pointing to an institution to be held responsible. Rather, institutional violence has been tied directly to the legal framework and the actions of institutional bureaucracies, both public and private (Galtung 1975).

According to Bourdieu (1980), structures of domination produce and reproduce a symbolic violence that is daily, internalized, legitimated, and experienced as natural. The role of the social scientist is to expose or denaturalize this violence—that is, to demonstrate the interests that guide the structuring of violence and power.

This chapter will have recourse to these theories for the purpose of analyzing the continuities among distinct forms of power and violence that provoke the social suffering of migrants in the US-Mexico border area. The principal goal is thus to study the strategies of the United States enforcement agencies, and the strategies of Mexican government in the war against drugs, to understand the political and institutional construction of this violence.

War on the Southwestern Border of the United States

From a sociological perspective, the border is a social construction involving multiple actors such as government agencies, immigrants, politicians, and academics (Rodríguez 1997). Historical processes of cultural and commercial exchange, and of transborder family and social relations, have created historical ties that on some occasions erase the border and on others render it impenetrable. From a distance, for the elites and the national media, the border is a collective imaginary through which notions of belonging and difference, identity and otherness, are configured.

From a geopolitical point of view, the border is constructed along the discursive axis of war. This historical-political discourse has material and performative consequences. The materiality is evident in the enormous military apparatus installed at the boundary of the two countries. The performative aspect consists of practices of surveillance, control, and coercion. The constitutive elements of this discourse of war were created by politicians and enforcement agencies throughout the twentieth century and the early twenty-first. The discourse has designated a series of successive and overlapping enemies, which shift in accord with the relations of national and international forces. These have been drugs, "illegal immigrants," terrorists, and "radical Islamists."

War generates a punitive legal framework—or a form of legalized violence (Menjívar and Abrego 2012) against migrants—with the justification of protecting sovereignty, national security, and territorial (or racial) integrity. As Foucault (1997) argued, war does not end where law begins, but rather law is born out of conflict and power relations. The laws relative to migration and border control can be justified only by a state of war. The legal framework gives rise to state of exception along the border: a territory where the legislative and judicial powers are subsumed by the executive power, and where individual freedoms are suspended. The border is thus the continuation of war or the permanent demonstration of victory (Foucault 1997).

In this sense, the border means much more than just the boundary between the two nation-states. It is a broad geographical belt which must function to protect the nation by means of surveillance, containment, detention, and the expulsion of "threatening elements"; it includes extensive networks of migrant detention facilities, roundups along the highways, and inspection of identity documents in the streets. Throughout regions up to 100 miles from the border, surveillance by authorities pervades all social spaces (Heyman 2014). The inhabitants, always suspected of being "illegal aliens"—particularly if they are Hispanic—must be sure to carry their documents on their person at all times. To maintain this state of exception, the institutions must harp on the continual threat from the enemy. This explains the repetition of alarming discourses on "migration crisis," and on "the border out of control."

In 1986, very near the end of the Cold War, when communist regimes were on the point of collapse and thus the primary enemy of the Cold War period was evaporating, the Reagan administration characterized "drugs" as a threat to national security and declared a new war in which they were the enemy. It defined the southern border as a major front in that war (Andreas 2000; Dunn 1996). In the mid-1990s, the changes in surveillance and control strategies were justified through a redefinition of the enemy: not just drugs but also "illegal immigration." Security and police agencies had ideological recourse to the concept of "illegality" and associated it with the southwestern border (Heyman 2014; Rodriguez and Paredes 2014). This notion blended the two discursive elements (drugs and immigration) in the semantic frame that currently legitimizes institutional violence against migrants.[1]

The peak period of the border war arrived after the terrorist attacks of September 11, 2001. That security crisis led to the propagation of new fears and to sharper images of the enemy and of the lines dividing "us" from "the others" in cultural, religious, political, and military terms (Paasi 2011). In this atmosphere of anxiety, President George W. Bush declared a war on terrorism. In the name of security, the Homeland Security Act of 2002 compromised the liberties of US citizens themselves. The newly created Department of Homeland Security took over border control and the fight against various forms of terrorism, drug trafficking, and "illegal immigration."

The militarization of the border involved two basic aspects linked to the notions of national security put forward from Washington: an increase in the number of military personnel in the southwest and the militarization of the border and immigration control agencies themselves. Thus the USBP went through important institutional changes. With the dissolution of the Immigration and Naturalization Services, which had been under the institutional umbrella of the Department of Justice (DOJ), the USBP became a sub-agency of Customs and Border Protection (CBP), which fell within the Department of Homeland Security (DHS). The new homeland security perspective implied the militarization of its equipment and strategies. Still, we must realize that militarization of the border has been a long-term process. That is, the perspective of national security was part of the work of border surveillance and control before the creation of DHS.

The most visible aspect of the war has been rapid growth of both military infrastructure and staffing levels of the multiple security agencies stationed on the border. Since the 1990s, the institutions dedicated to "protecting the border" have benefited from an extraordinary growth in their budgets, staff, and political power. For example, the number of USBP agents quintupled between 1992 and 2014, while the agency's budget multiplied tenfold.[2] In addition to CBP, the ten other federal agencies belonging to DHS, DOJ, and Defense Department that guard the southwest border also continually increase their staff in the region and compete among themselves to "protect the border" (Isacson and Meyer 2012).

Making a comparison to the wars carried out in Central America during the 1980s, some authors (Dunn 1996; Heyman 2014) use the term "low-intensity warfare" to describe the work carried out by these security agencies. That work includes intense collaboration among units of the army, navy, USBP, and police for the purpose of permanent surveillance of the "targeted population" and repeated acts of coercion or cooptation of the population living in the region. However, the wars in El Salvador and Guatemala were carried out against an armed enemy (the guerrilla fronts) and eventually led to losses in the regular armies of those counties or among US military personnel; the war in Nicaragua likewise confronted an armed enemy (the Sandinista government) and led to losses among the US proxy force (*the contras*). By contrast, in the border war, no armed confrontations are visible, nor have the army and navy reported any human losses.[3] Nevertheless, the "collateral damage" has been considerable. Besides low standards in relation to constitutional guarantees, human rights and academic organizations have reported the deaths of people trying to cross the border without authorization.

Structuring Institutional Violence

As various researchers have pointed out, while the security apparatus on the border has grown steadily since the 1990s, so have the supply of drugs. Undocumented immigration has tripled between 1990 and 2014, from 3.5 million to 11.1 million, despite a slight decline during the economic crisis (2007–2009) and leveling off thereafter (Pew Research Center 2016). In that sense, the strategies of border control and deportations have been spectacular failures. However, if we observe the political-electoral achievements linked to the discourse of border war, as well as the sizable economic benefits that have accrued to the detention-deportation industry, we have to recognize that the war has been productive. The discourse of fear, the warnings on migration crisis, the demonization of the immigrant—or even of the Mexican—and the references to a southwestern US border that is "out of control" have all become defining elements of electoral campaigns, as we could see in the presidential election of 2016. The military strategy has also been very beneficial from the economic point of view for a booming private industrial and commercial sector that participates, through government contracts, in the use of coercion against migrants.

For the migrants, the tightening of surveillance and adoption of punitive laws and policies have meant an increase in social suffering. The need to evade border patrols and border fences has led them to follow much longer routes that cross through very risky terrain, with treacherous mountain topology and climatic extremes (Eschbach et al. 1999). Many migrants suffer dehydration, lack of food, and injury or death from falls. The deaths of migrants trying to cross the border have been attributed to strategies of border control (Massey 2007).

Nonetheless, there is no mechanically causal connection between the authorities' control strategies and the migrants' deaths. The number of bodies found by the USBP and by immigrant defense organizations varies from year to year in accord with multiple factors including USBP containment strategies, climatic variations, and actions to aid and seek lost migrants carried out by the Border Patrol itself and by social organizations.[4] This wide spectrum of causes allows the bureaucrats to evade their responsibility for the implementation of social policies that threaten migrants' lives (Rodríguez 2012).

Faced with the deaths during unauthorized border crossings and the enormous power imbalance between the two countries, some authors resort to the concept of "structural violence" (Nevins 2008). But this concept can hide institutions' political and ethical responsibility. For example, in a report for the International Organization for Migrations (IOM), Brian and Laczko (2014) suggest that the deaths of migrants in the southwest US border can be explained by structural violence, while deaths during their crossing through Mexico are due mainly to direct physical violence from criminal gangs. In the case of deaths provoked by exposure to environmental dangers, it would be difficult—according to these authors—to identify a victim and a perpetrator. The causal factors would have to be found in analysis of socioeconomic structures and legal frameworks established over the long term.

If we accept this explanation, the effect is to dilute the notion of institutional responsibility. The mass media and US government immigration authorities frequently suggest that the smugglers of migrants are the ones responsible for their deaths. Some even blame the migrants themselves for attempting such dangerous journeys and putting their lives at risk. But the decisions made by individuals—such as the choice to migrate and the selection of a route—fall within a framework of public policies designed, implemented, and evaluated by institutional actors. The deaths of migrants do not occur only under the passive observation of the government. There is often an express choice to let migrants die as a dissuasive check on human mobility.[5]

Dehumanizing the migrants and viewing their deaths as "collateral damage" form part of an ideology that permeates coercive bureaucracies not only in their large-scale strategies around immigration and border control but also in their day-to-day interactions with the migrants (Rodríguez and Paredes 2014). Thus there is a continuity between the violence contained in the security strategies and apparatus, and other, everyday forms of physical, verbal, and psychological violence committed by institutional agents against the migrants. In other words, to understand the processes of structuring violence it is important to analyze the relationships between the macropolitical context determined by the declarations of war, the institutional violence, and what Scheper-Hughes and Bourgois (2004) call "the everyday small atrocities." These range from threats, multiple forms of humiliation, and verbal devaluation of the migrants to sexual abuse, rape physical aggression, and murder.[6] Far from indicating an intrinsic evil in USBP agents, the actions of the individuals are embedded in violent institutional practices whose objective is to inflict social suffering. This institutional violence is, simultaneously, informed by the militarization of the border and the discourses of war.

The military and national security discourse is also based on notions of masculinity that explain not only the fact the USBP is ninety-five percent male, but also the repeated reports of sexual abuse and rape of migrants and even of the few female agents (Maril 2016; Staudt 2009). As feminist academics have pointed out on many occasions, sexual violence is not about sex but rather about power (Falcón 2001). Sexual violence should be explained, therefore, as a gendered effect of military ideology. It is a result of the extreme power imbalance between agents and migrants and the discretional power of the former.

The institutional structures provoke systematic processes of disempowerment of migrants connected to detention, processing, and expulsion. The conditions in CBP detention centers entail physical and emotional stress. After being apprehended, migrants may spend hours or days in overcrowded conditions. The detention centers are kept at such low temperatures that the detainees refer to them as *hieleras* (coolers). As many studies have pointed out, the migrant detainees are not given sufficient food and water and are frequently denied basic services of hygiene and health care.

In the immigration courts along the border, particularly since the beginning of Operation Streamline (2005), trials for "illegal entry" seem like a mockery of judicial proceedings, involving the systemic violation of due process. Migrants without any criminal history, and sometimes without any previous history of migration, are processed *en masse* in front of immigration judges in what appears to be simply a staged exercise in humiliation. Handcuffed, in leg shackles, and with chains around their waists, dozens of accused persons are paraded all at once before a single judge, without lawyers or with very minimal defense. Almost all of them plead guilty, one by one, without having time or conditions to understand what the accusation means. In spite of suits against Operation Streamline filed in federal court by civil rights organizations, DOJ and DHS have modified only minimal aspects of the show, like the number of migrants presented simultaneously before the judge (Lydgate 2010).

The collective humiliation that results from these processes comes close to psychological torture, as it is called in testimony by migrants and reports of human rights groups.[7] The conditions of detention, processing, and expulsion thus intentionally create disempowerment, an effect defined as diminution or elimination of the capacity of agency or resistance.

It is in this context of institutional violence that other common aggressions carried out by USBP should be understood. For example, using data from the Migrant Border Crossing Study (MBCS), Slack et al (2016) find that at least 20 percent of migrants detained by US immigration authorities were insulted while in custody, and at least 10 percent were physically attacked. Furthermore, the verbal abuse is significantly more frequent for women than for men. Other important data found by the MBCS researchers are the systematic denial of food (44.5 percent), and denial of medical attention when the migrants declare they need it (37.3 percent). The findings show that use of physical and verbal violence is systematic and is an intrinsic part of the strategy of social control.

The War on Drugs, the expansion of Criminal Organizations, and the Commodification of Migrants

The fundamental differences between the military apparatus and security strategies on the two sides of the border show that the effects of the discourse of war depend very much on the legal and political context from which that discourse emerges. In Mexico, the phrases "illegal immigration" and "migration crisis" did not resonate within the political institutions. Likewise, the "war against drugs" had little capacity to mobilize or convoke the political class, at least until 2007. It was a discourse utilized primarily in the international sphere, with the goal of obtaining economic or political benefits in relation to the United States.

Since the 1980s, through speeches, formal accords, and direct forms of collaboration between enforcement agencies of the two countries, every Mexican administration has committed itself to the US fight against drugs. Also, every Mexican president has defined drug trafficking as a risk to national security. Nonetheless, in domestic politics, the Mexican emphasis was on sovereignty, understood as territorial integrity in the face of possible interference by the United States. Calderón was the first president not only to abandon this discourse of concern about US interference, but also to demand greater US government involvement in the war on drugs in Mexico (Fondevila and Quintana-Navarrete 2015).

Thus in March 2007, two months after his declaration of war on the drug trafficking organizations, Calderón began negotiations in Mérida (Yucatán) with the administration of then-president George W. Bush, leading to the signing of what became known as the Mérida Initiative. This initiative implied much closer collaboration and massive US government financing of Mexican government security agencies, including the National Migration Institute (Spanish initials INM). Calderón carried out military operations in cities along the northern border, but extensive rural areas near the borderline remained unchanged insofar as security apparatus is concerned.

Vast territories near the borderline have limited communication systems; across thousands of square miles of northern Mexico, transportation routes are limited to dirt roads on which state agents are rarely seen. In the regions where unauthorized border crossings are common, the criminal organization or gangs of assailants tend to patrol the border so as to extort money both from the smugglers and from the Mexican or Central American migrants trying to cross without papers.

The security operations of the Mexican war on drugs take place mostly in certain cities along the northern border and in narcotics-producing regions in west and south. The majority of migration control operations are carried out in the southern part of the country. However, it is worth noting that some roadblocks set up by the INM and the Mexican army are situated close to the country's northern border in order to control the movement of merchandise and people from south to north, as Mexican authorities want to prevent them from "abandoning" the country.[8] This "emigration" control could signify intense collaboration between migration authorities in Mexico and the United States, or the active participation of the Mexican authorities in the criminal extortion systems.

Given the existence of such roadblocks and detention centers through Mexico, some human rights and academic organizations speak of a "vertical border" (Ruiz 2006), meaning one that traverses the country on a north-south axis. As revealed by interviews with migrants who reach Mexico's northern cities, those who have sufficient economic resources to undertake the journey eventually succeed in crossing this vertical border by paying bribes at the roadblocks. It can also happen that they are detained and deported in spite of paying the so-called "quota."[9]

Many highway roadblocks have double or triple institutional representation (federal police, armed forces, and migration control agents). Others have been installed by the criminal organizations with the goal of detecting, extorting, or kidnapping migrants. That is, the system of surveillance and control seems to be shared between illegal private corporations and public security institutions.

One consequence of the military strategy has been an extraordinary rise in homicides tied to organized crime. During the Calderón administration, the "war" cost more than 120,000 lives (Guerrero Gutierrez 2015). Under Peña Nieto (since December 2012) it has continued as endemic violence, a normalized everyday phenomenon. At the beginning of this war, the areas most affected by the violence were the cities on the northern border. In particular, Ciudad Juárez (in the state of Chihuahua) accounted for more than half of all homicides tied to organized crime between 2006 and 2011. It became the most dangerous city in the world, reaching 216 homicides per 100,000 inhabitants in 2010 (Ríos 2013).

Forced disappearances, kidnappings, and sexual violence against migrants have remained hidden underneath this wave of death. Considered non-citizens, lacking in political value, the kidnapped, raped, and murdered migrants went practically unnoticed until the massacre at San Fernando (Tamaulipas state) in August 2010, in spite of several previous reports about such massive violations of human rights.

A form of violence inherent in militarization and war has been gender-based violence, particular sexual violence and femicide. Since the 1990s, Ciudad Juárez has been famous for its hundreds of murders of young women and even girls, sexually tortured before being killed and dropped in vacant lots. As feminist analyses have shown, systematic sexual torture and murder became part of the narratives of power and impunity in Mexico (Segato 2013; Wright 2011). In a detailed discourse analysis of the statements of government officials and the justice system, statements issued with the goal of devaluing the victims as "loose women," Melissa Wright demonstrates that "the gendering of public space as a principal mechanism of necropolitics" is at the heart of the war against drugs (Wright 2011, 719).

Often, gender-based violence is the main factor pushing migrant women and LGBTIQ people out of their places of origin. Subsequently, these forms of violence accompany them throughout their journeys, particularly in border regions. The United Nations High Commissioner for Refugees (UNHCR 2015) reports, for instance, the systematic practice of migrant women being held for days or weeks by *coyotes* (smugglers) in border cities, where they suffer a variety of forms of sexual abuse or violence.

Violence against migrants and, at the extreme, rapes, murders, and massacres, can be analyzed as "collateral damage" in the combat between security agencies and criminal organizations, or within their ranks, over control of the routes of traffic in illicit merchandise and migrants. Territorial control allows for systems of extortion that yield enormous benefits to public and private agents. Controlling the routes of transport and the border crossing, criminal organizations and security agencies can require smugglers to pay them large sums of money, and can regulate the frequency and route of crossing and the number of migrants who can travel in a group. When the smugglers fail to pay the extortion or break any of the rules, or when they leave a group of migrants to their fate, the migrants may be kidnapped and turned over to the networks of human trafficking, or they may be massacred (Martínez 2014). Thus, the earnings extracted from unauthorized migration are based not only on extortion, but also on a whole chain of exploitation that includes robbery, assault, sexual violation, kidnapping, detention in safe houses, and trafficking for purposes of sexual exploitation or forced labor for criminal organizations.

Such commercial exploitation of human mobility by corporations or by the migrants' states of origin, transit, and destination is not new. Studies of the "migration industry" have already described them in depth (Castles and Miller 1998; Hernández-León 2013). According to these scholars, this industry is a heterogeneous economic field of legal and illegal activities that facilitate or simply profit from human mobility. The field is made up of very diverse actors, including the emigrants themselves. Many services can occasionally be offered without monetary cost through migratory networks; that is, is they depend on the social capital that the migrants have.

Without denying that these services continue to be offered in Mexico—although under much more restrictive political conditions than in the past—the extreme violence in the chains of exploitation requires thinking about the emergence of a criminal market parallel to the migration industry. The actors in this market do not only profit from human mobility but from the commercialization or commodification of the migrants themselves, of their sexuality and their potential labor power.

Since 2008, human rights organizations have denounced thousands of large-scale kidnappings of migrants by organization such as the Gulf Cartel and the Zetas, with frequent participation by police (CNDH 2009). Sometimes the collaboration of security agencies is direct, while at other times the police take care of surveilling the territory and protecting the criminals. In some municipalities of northeastern Mexico, the criminal organizations function in association with local police departments, such that there is a sort of embeddedness between institutional power and criminal power.[10]

The massacres of migrants in northern Mexico reveal the disposable nature of the migrant, the extreme of his or her reification. The first massacre to become public took place in August 2010 in San Fernando (Tamaulipas), eighty-five miles from the border.[11]

The next year, forty-seven common graves containing 193 bodies were found in the same municipality. Other such massacres followed, much less publicized in the Mexican media and practically ignored internationally. In May 2012, forty-nine migrants were massacred and dismembered in Cadereyta (Nuevo León), fifty-four miles from the border; in June 2015, an unknown number of Central Americans were pursued and killed by a heavily armed group in Caborca (Sonora), forty-three miles from the border.[12] These extreme aggressions against migrants appear to conflict with functional and structural interpretation of violence as a source of profit. Felbab Brown (2014, 12) describes this criminal market as "not a particularly effective business model, but one that is, again, characteristic of the 'disintegration' of Mexico's criminal market toward greater violence and 'chaos.'" However, the data produced by human rights organizations in Mexico seem to show, on the contrary, that this criminal business model has been particularly profitable in economic terms. For example, in their Special Report on Kidnappings of Migrants in 2011, the National Human Rights Commission (a Mexican government body, Spanish initial CNDH) estimated that the annual abduction of 20,000 migrants, with an average ransom price of $3000 each, implied annual revenue of $60 million for criminal organizations (CNDH 2011).

All violence, even that where the instrumental function is dominant—like extortion, kidnapping, and trafficking in human bodies—includes an expressive dimension (Segato 2013). Underneath the surface of this extortionist or destructive violence can be found a violence that constructs power relations and institutions. Massacres, gang rapes, and mutilation can be analyzed in terms of the construction of power relations, masculinities, complicities, and forms of oppression. In analyzing the multiple killings of women in Ciudad Juárez and their sexual connotations, Rita Segato (2013, 25) states that "the victim is the refuse of the process, a disposable piece," while the privileged conversationalists in those acts of extreme violence are other powerful men, the peer group of the murderers. The massacre of migrants could also be decoded as messages between criminal organizations, written on the land.

Conclusion

On the American/Mexican border, several forms of violence coexist and are reinforced. There is political or legal violence, directed specifically and intentionally against migrants who cross the border without authorization. In a context in which migration law and criminal law coincide, enforcement of the former leads to processes of criminalization that result in subjection, humiliation, and exclusion of migrants (Menjívar and Abrego 2012). The absence of individual guarantees in detention centers, and the mass trials of migrants led in chains before a judge and required to plead guilty, demonstrate the transformation of the "illegal immigrant" into the main enemy of the border war. The enormous military infrastructure on the southwestern border of the United State reinforces this legal violence.

On the other side of the boundary, daily physical and psychological violence carried out by state agents against the migrants, or the serious and generalized violation of human rights in northern Mexico, should be seen in the framework of impunity guaranteed and legitimized by the discourse of war. In this context, human security is subordinated to or subsumed within the notion of national security. The systemization and impunity with which the aggressions occur—including that of sexual assault—seem to indicate that they form part of institutional strategies of coercive control. That is, they cannot be analyzed simply as "defects in the system," but rather constitute a mechanism of coercion used deliberately to maintain an extremely unequal power relationship.

Factors of gender intervene in the violence suffered by migrants in a crucial way. Feminists have analyzed sexual violence as a weapon of war in situations of conflict and extensive militarization (Falcón 2001). For criminal organizations or for state agencies, sexual violation and aggression are ways of demonstrating their territorial control through control of bodies. At the same time, gang rape or more subtle and everyday forms of abuse are instruments to demoralize or humiliate groups of migrants.[13]

On the Mexican side of the border, the migrants are booty for state agencies and criminal bands. In a historical process of embeddedness between the state and organized crime, migrants' bodies have become lucrative merchandise among the many commodities that circulate legally or illegally along the routes controlled by criminal organizations. Thus migrants' vulnerability derives from a combination of restrictive migration policies and territorial control on the part of state agencies and criminal networks. The commodification of migrants' bodies should also be understood in the context of a neoliberal ethic—that is, of social elites' broad justification and acceptance of profit at all costs, the penetration of mercantile logic into every social crevice.

In spite of the fences, the security apparatus, and the multiple forms of violence looming over potential migrants, hundreds of thousands of people cross the border without authorization each year. Many of them succeed in entering their intended destination, the United States, thanks largely to their networks of trust and mutual aid, or to structural support from the migration industry. On the one hand, these migrants find themselves subject to high-vigilance, security-obsessed systems that carry out institutional violence. On the other hand, through their own social networks and collective practices, the migrants carry out multiple forms of resistance and reconfigure the territories of migration.

Although this chapter has focused on the political forces that construct and institutionalize the violence, migrants as social agents generate forms of adaptation or strategies of resistance; mobilize family, social, and community resources in order to enter labor markets; reproduce collective identities and defend their rights. If we have analyzed here the geopolitical and military context that constrains their mobility or increases the risks of migration, we still need to analyze the creative processes and the constant reinvention of the means and methods of movement and settlement.

Translated from the Spanish by Dick Cluster

Notes

1. The book edited by Cecilia Menjívar and Daniel Kanstroom (2014) on the construction of illegality allows us to understand the diversity of meanings and the historical-political construction of the notion of "illegal immigration."
2. The number of agents grew from the 3,555 in 1992 to 18,611 in 2014, while the budget rose from $326 million to $3.642 billion. www.cbp.gov.
3. The border patrol reports thirty-one deaths "in the line of duty" in the past ten years. See US Customs and Border Protection, last published March 26, 2018. www.cbp.gov/about/in-memoriam/memoriam-those-who-died-line-duty
4. For example, in one particularly hot year in southern Texas (2012), the total reached 471 bodies, and the level stayed high at 451 in 2013. Yet the total in 2014 was 251. See USBP (2017) https://www.cbp.gov/sites/default/files/assets/documents/2017-Dec/BP%20Southwest%20Border%20Sector%20Deaths%20FY1998%20-%20FY2017.pdf
5. In the case of deaths in the Mediterranean—which reached more that 5000 in 2015 and again in 2016—some European governments have expressly refused to cooperate with rescue missions, arguing that these incite other migrants to undertake the journey (De Lucas 2015).
6. According to former Border Patrol's head of internal affairs, James F. Tomsheck, between 2010 and August 2014 twenty-eight unarmed migrants have died at the hands of US Customs and Border Protection, and not one agent has faced criminal charges in the killings. (Bogado 2014)

   Three important cases are those of Anastasio Hernández, murdered in San Ysidro in 2010, Sergio Hernández in Ciudad Juárez in 2010, and José Antonio Elena in Nogales in 2012. The first was brutally attacked by several border patrol agents in San Ysidro during the deportation process. The agents continued beating him and tasering him, even when he was lying motionless on the ground. Sergio and José Antonio, both minors, were murdered by border patrol agents from US territory even when they were in Mexican soil. Neither of the two was armed or presented any threat.
7. The 1984 United Nations convention against torture defines it as "severe pain or suffering, whether physical or mental," inflicted intentionally by agents of public order.
8. For instance, near the city of Reynosa (just across the border from McAllen) a Colef study (París et al. 2015) found two INM roadblocks devoted to extortion or detention of Central American migrants headed for the United States.
9. Fieldwork by the author in Ciudad Juárez, Nogales, Mexicali, and Tijuana, 2015–2016.
10. Some studies estimate that seven out of every ten kidnappings involve the participation of police (Felbab-Brown 2014).
11. Investigations by journalists and human rights organizations have revealed that some of the direct perpetrators were municipal police. See Más de 72, www.masde72.periodistasdeapie.org.mx
12. In this last case, Mexican authorities seem to have outdone their capacity for looking the other way. Testimony by some surviving migrants gave clear indications of another massacre. These survivors told how the group took off running and some of its members fell under a hail of bullets, though the survivors, as they fled, could not see how many died. On June 9, CNDH began an investigation into "the probable execution of three Central American migrants" in Caborca and interviewed the thirteen survivors detained in the migration-control station in Hermosillo, Sonora (CNDH 2015). Meanwhile, a group of social

organizations demanded further investigation of the events and protection for the victims. In spite of this, authorities deported the thirteen survivors to their countries of origin.

13. Many testimonies show that, when whole groups of migrants are attacked, the assailants often require the women to undress.

References

Andreas, P. 2000. *Border Games: Policing the U.S.-Mexico Divide.* Ithaca, NY: Cornell University Press.

Bogado, A. 2014. "Ousted High-Ranking Official: Border Patrol Has Become a 'Paramilitary Force.'" *Colorlines*, August 28, 2014. https://www.colorlines.com/articles/ousted-high-ranking-official-border-patrol-has-become-paramilitary-force

Bourdieu, P. 1980. *Le sens pratique.* Paris: Éditions de Minuit.

Brian, T., and F. Laczko. 2014. *Tracking Lives Lost during Migration.* Geneva: International Organization for Migration (IOM).

Castles, S., and M. Miller. 1998. *The age of Migration. International Population Movements in the Modern World.* London: MacMillan Press LTD.

Comisión Nacional de los Derechos Humanos (CNDH). 2009. "Informe Especial sobre los casos de secuestro en contra de migrantes." June 15. http://www.cndh.org.mx/sites/all/doc/Informes/Especiales/2009_migra.pdf

Comisión Nacional de los Derechos Humanos (CNDH). 2011. "Informe Especial sobre secuestro de migrantes en México." February 22. http://www.cndh.org.mx/sites/all/doc/Informes/Especiales/2011_secmigrantes.pdf

Comisión Nacional de los Derechos Humanos (CNDH). 2015. "Investiga la CNDH la probable ejecución de tres migrantes centroamericanos, cuyos cuerpos fueron hallados en Caborca, Sonora." June 9, 2015. www.cndh.org.mx/comunicados

Customs and Border Protection (CBP). 2018. "In Memoriam to Those Who Died in the Line of Duty." https://www.cbp.gov/about/in-memoriam/memoriam-those-who-died-line-duty

De Lucas, J. 2015. "Muertes en el Mediterráneo." *Quaderns de la Mediterrània* 22: 272–277

Dunn, T. J. 1996. *The Militarization of the U.S.-Mexico Border, 1978–1992: Low-Intensity Conflict Doctrine Comes Home.* Austin: CMAS, University of Texas at Austin.

Eschbach, K., J. Hagan, and N. Rodriguez, Nestor. 1999. "Death at the Border." *International Migration Review* 33, no. 2: 430–454.

Falcón, S. 2001. "Rape as a Weapon of War: Advancing Human Rights for Women at the U.S.-Mexico Border." *Social Justice* 28, no. 2: 31–50.

Felbab-Brown, V. 2014. *Changing the Game or Dropping the Ball? Mexico's Security and Anti-Crime Strategy under President Enrique Peña Nieto.* Washington, DC: Latin America Initiative, Foreign Policy at Brookings.

Fondevila, G., and M. Quintana-Navarrete. 2015. "War Hypotheses: Drug Trafficking, Sovereignty and the Armed Forces in Mexico." *Bulletin of Latin American Research* 34, no. 4: 1–17. DOI:10.1111/blar.12328

Foucault, M. 1997. *Il faut défendre la société: Cours au Collège de France, 1976.* Paris: Seuil.

Galtung, J. 1975. *Peace: Research. Education. Action. Essays in Peace Research.* Vol. 1. Copenhagen: Christian Ejlers.

Guerrero Gutierrez, E. 2015. "¿Bajó la violencia?" *Nexos*, February. http://www.nexos.com.mx/?p=24035.

Hernández-León, R. 2013. "Conceptualizing the Migration Industry." In *The Migration industry and the Commercialization of International Migration*, edited by Thomas Gammeltoft and Ninna Nyberg, 24–44. New York: Routledge.

Heyman, J. 2014. " 'Illegality' and the U.S.-Mexico Border: How It Is Produced and Resisted." In *Constructing Immigrant 'Illegality': Critiques, Experiences, and Responses*, edited by Cecilia Menjívar and Daniel Kanstroom, 11–135. Cambridge, UK: Cambridge University Press.

Isacson, A., and M. Meyer, eds. 2012. *Beyond the Border Buildup Security and Migrants Along the U.S.-Mexico Border*. Washington, DC: Washington Office on Latin America (WOLA).

Lydgate, J. 2010. "Assembly-Line Justice: A Review of Operation Streamline." Policy Brief: The Chief Justice Earl Warren Institute on Race, Ethnicity & Diversity. University of California, Berkeley Law School. January. https://www.law.berkeley.edu/files/Operation_Streamline_Policy_Brief.pdf

Maril, L. 2016. "The Border Patrol Needs to Hire, Retain, Mentor, Promote More Female Agents." *The Fence. Lee Marill*. October 24. https://leemaril.com/2016/10/24/the-border-patrol-needs-to-hire-retain-mentor-promote-more-female-agents/

Martínez, Óscar. 2014. "Los coyotes domados." *El Faro*. March 24. http://www.salanegra.elfaro.net/es/201403/cronicas/15101/

Más de 72. http://www.masde72.periodistasdeapie.org.mx

Massey, D. S. 2007. "Understanding America's Immigration 'Crisis.'" *Proceedings of the American Philosophical Society* 151, no. 3: 309–327.

Menjívar, C., and Abrego, L. J. 2012. "Legal Violence: Immigration Law and the Lives of Central American Immigrants." *American Journal of Sociology* 117, no. 5: 1380–1421.

Nevins, J. 2008. *Dying to Live: A Story of U.S. Immigration in an Age of Global Apartheid*. San Francisco: City Lights.

Paasi, A. 2011. "A Border Theory: An Unattainable of Realistic Aim for Border Scholars?" In *The Ashgate Research Companion to Border Studies*, edited by D. Wastl-Walter, 11–31. Farham, UK: Ashgate.

Pew Research Center. 2016. "U.S. Unauthorized Immigration Population Estimates." November 3. http://www.pewhispanic.org/interactives/unauthorized-immigrants/

Ríos, V. 2013. "Why Did Mexico Become So Violent? A Self-Reinforcing Violent Equilibrium Caused by Competition and Enforcement." *Trends in Organized Crime* 16, no. 2: 138–155. doi: 10.1007/s12117-012-9175-z

Rodríguez, N., and C. Paredes. 2014. "Coercive Immigration Enforcement and Bureaucratic Ideology." In *Constructing Immigrant "Illegality": Critiques, Experiences, and Responses*, edited by C. Menjívar and D. Kanstroom, 63–84. Cambridge, UK: Cambridge University Press.

Rodríguez, N. 1997. "The Social Construction of the U.S.-Mexico Border." In *Immigrants Out! The new Nativism and Anti-immigrant Impulse in the United States*, edited by J.F. Perea, 223–243. New York: New York University Press.

Rodríguez, N. 2012. "Contrôle des frontières. Questions de droits humains et d'éthique sur une stratégie états-unienne." *Hommes et Migrations* 1296: 54–63. doi:10.4000/hommesmigrations.1506.

Ruiz, O. 2006. "Migración y fronteras: retos actuales y futuros." In *México 2006–2012: Neoliberalismo, movimientos sociales, y política electoral*, edited by J. Rus and M. Tinker, 57–66. México: Universidad Autónoma de Zacatecas y M. A. Porrúa.

Segato, R. 2013. *La escritura en el cuerpo de las mujeres asesinadas en Ciudad Juárez*. Buenos Aires: Tinta Limón.

Scheper-Hughes, N., and P. Bourgois. 2004. “Introduction: Making Sense of Violence.” In *Violence in War and Peace: An Anthology*, edited by Nancy Sheper-Hughes and Philippe Bourgois, 1–31. Oxford: Blackwell.

Slack, M., A. Lee, and S. Whiteford. 2016. “The Geography of Border Militarization: Violence, Death, Health in Mexico and the United States.” *Journal of Latin American Geography* 15, no. 1: 7–32.

Staudt, Kathleen. 2009. “Violence against Women at the Border: Unpacking Institutions.” In *Human Rights along the U.S.-Mexico Border: Gendered Violence and Insecurity.* Edited by Kathleen Staudt, Tony Payan and Antony Kruszewski, 107–124. Tucson: University of Arizona Press.

United Nations High Commissioner for Refugees (UNHCR). 2015. “Women on the Run. First Hand Accounts of Refugees Fleeing El Salvador, Guatemala, Honduras, and Mexico.” http://www.unhcr.org/publications/operations/5630f24c6/women-run.html

United States Border Patrol (USBP). 2017. “Southwest Border Sectors. Southwest Border Deaths By Fiscal Year (Oct. 1st through Sept. 30th).” Washington DC, Department of Homeland Security. https://www.cbp.gov/sites/default/files/assets/documents/2017-Dec/BP%20Southwest%20Border%20Sector%20Deaths%20FY1998%20-%20FY2017.pdf

Wright, M. W. 2011. “Necropolitics, Narcopolitics, and Femicide: Gendered Violence on the Mexico-U.S. Border.” *Signs* 36, no. 3: 707–731

Further Reading

Menjívar, C., and D. Kanstroom, eds. 2014. *Constructing Immigrant 'Illegality': Critiques, Experiences, and Responses*. Cambridge, UK: Cambridge University Press.

Staudt, K., T. Payan, and A. Kruszewski, eds. 2009. *Human Rights along the US-Mexico Border*. Tucson: University of Arizona Press.

CHAPTER 28

REGIONAL MIGRATION AND ARGENTINA'S "HOSPITALITY" IN CRISIS

TANYA BASOK

On Jan 27, 2017, the President of Argentina Macri issued a Necessity and Urgency Decree (*Decreto de Necesidad y Urgencia* or DNU) that reformed the 2004 Immigration Law # 25,871. In contrast to Law # 25,871, widely recognized as one of the most liberal immigration laws in the world, DNU 70/2017 denies entry or residence to some migrants, namely those who have any criminal record, regardless of the gravity of their offense. It also sets in motion a process of expeditious expulsions of migrants deemed deportable. The President justified this decree by alluding to a public safety "crisis" that exceptional measures, outlined in the decree, would alleviate.

In public discourses, migration is often associated with images of a crisis, understood as "a condition of sudden change that causes alarm" (Mountz and Hiemstra 2014, 383), that precipitates an adoption of certain practices of exceptionalism (Agamben 2005; Albahari 2015, 13–14). Harsh measures to contain migration "crises" have been adopted in many European countries, the United States, and elsewhere in the world (e.g., Mountz and Hiemstra 2014; De Genova et al. 2016). However, what is remarkable in the case of Argentina is that the crisis discourses and the corresponding policy reforms have occurred in a country that prides itself on its openness to immigration and commitment to migrant rights and integration. Yet, as I will argue in this chapter, the crisis mentality with respect to migrants who are poor and racialized is deeply rooted in Argentina, and it has coexisted with liberal immigration policies.

The analysis presented in this chapter is based on speeches and arguments articulated by some public officials, deputies, and civil society critics during the hearings at the Inter-American Human Rights Committee (IAHRC) (youtube.com/watch?v=yMPoCo3fn7o) and the Bicameral Congress Committee on Decree 70/2017 (youtube.com/watch?v=Yb3O7kKXtsY); media coverage of recent (November 2016–March 2017) events; and such documents as DNU 70/2017, Immigration Law

#26,871(Government of Argentina 2014), and Argentina's Constitution, as well as secondary literature.[1] This chapter begins by discussing liberal immigration trends in Argentina and other South American migrants. The section that follows will focus on DNU 70/2017 (Government of Argentina 2017), its provisions and the social construction of the "crisis" that was used as a justification by the Argentina's executive power officials for this decree. The chapter then turns attention to the counterarguments presented by civil society activists who argued that the evidence of the "emergency" used to justify the decree had been fabricated and who insisted that this decree was indicative of the legal, political, and social solidarity crises in Argentina. And finally, the chapter will outline continuities between the depiction of migrants in DNU 70/2017 and the assiduous imaginaries of Argentina as a "white country," inconsistent with the presence of migrants of indigenous or mixed descent.

Toward a Human Rights Approach to Migration in South America

Reversing the anti-migrant rhetoric, policies, and practices of the earlier decades, in the first decade of the twenty-first century South America became a region that claimed to welcome migrants, promote human rights approaches to migration, and extend protections and benefits to all migrants, including migrants in irregular migratory conditions. Affirming that all migrants are subjects of rights and that free circulation is a right inherent to all persons, the South American Conference on Migration, comprising all South American countries, has been meeting annually to discuss the facilitation of status regularization, laws, and public policies to foster the exercise of migrant rights, joint action against human trafficking, and other initiatives to advance migrant rights (see, SACM 2016, for instance).

Immigration Law #25,871 affirmed the right to migrate as essential and inalienable to the person (Article 4), as did the Ecuadorian Constitution that advocated "the principle of universal citizenship, the free movement of all inhabitants of the planet, and the progressive extinction of the status of alien or foreigner as an element to transform the unequal relations between countries, especially those between North and South" (Article 416). Over the years, populist political leaders such as Christina Kirchner of Argentina, Lula da Silva of Brazil, and Rafael Correa of Ecuador, critical of the treatment of their co-patriots in Northern countries, called for unconditional respect for the rights of migrants, including those in irregular conditions (Acosta and Freier 2015). In 2008, Correa removed visa requirements for all visitors, thus opening its borders to all and allowing foreign nationals to stay in Ecuador visa-free for as many as 90 days (Acosta and Freier 2015).

To address the needs of migrants in irregular migratory conditions, South American countries introduced policies to regularize their migratory status (Texidó and Gurrieri

2012). The Residency Agreement for Nationals of Mercosur Member States, signed on 6 December 2002 and ratified by all member states and associates by 2009, permits any national of a MERCOSUR or associate member state to reside and work for a period of two years in another member state, subject to criminal clearance. A temporary resident may then apply for a permanent status provided that he/she has sufficient resources to sustain himself or herself (Acosta and Freier 2015; Margheritis 2013).

Additionally, special status regularization programs have been launched in some countries, including Chile, Argentina, Venezuela, Brazil, Paraguay, Ecuador, and Colombia (Alfonso 2013; Texidó and Gurrieri 2012). The most ambitious status regularization program was launched in Argentina, the main magnet of the intraregional migration in South America in the last three decades (Margheritis 2013). Known as the Patria Grande, this program made it possible for the nationals of the MERCOSUR countries, Bolivia, Chile, and later Peru, Ecuador and Colombia, who had entered Argentina before April 17, 2006, to obtain legal residency documents (Acosta and Freier 2015; Basok et al. 2013; Domenech 2013).[2] The Patria Grande regularization program was framed in relation to migrant rights: it promised to reduce vulnerabilities of the migrants found in irregular migratory conditions such as labor and civil rights violations, and lack of access to healthcare and education (Basok et al. 2013; Domenech 2008). Finally, social rights have been extended to all migrants, including those in irregular conditions, in such countries as Argentina, Bolivia, and Uruguay, where migrants can access medical care, social security, education, and labor rights protections (Ceriani and Freier 2015).

In 2004 the Argentinean state replaced its repressive and restrictive 1981 immigration law, named Videla after the dictator who introduced it, by Law #25,871 that granted migrants social and legal rights, a change that was seen by policymakers and researchers as a "paradigm shift" from the policy rooted in national security to an approach proclaiming respect for human rights (see Domenech 2007 and Domenech and Pereira 2017 for an overview of the literature and critical discussion of this shift). This shift can be attributed to a combination of factors, including the inclusion of the human rights principles in the 1994 Argentine Constitution; a growing population of undocumented migrants in the country; a dynamic migrant rights advocacy network;[3] and litigation challenging the Videla Law at the Inter-American Commission on Human Rights (IACHR) (Hines 2010). Regional integration negotiated by Mercosur countries and the affiliated countries also played an important role in this process (Albarracin 2004; Margheritis 2015; Novick 2012). December 6, 2002 marks a day when an agreement on residence for nationals of the party states to the expanded Mercosur was signed. Under the agreement, Mercosur members stated their commitment to "strengthen and deepen the process of integration." Affirming that "[t]he implementation of a policy to ensure the free circulation of persons in the region is essential to achieving these aims," Mercosur members committed themselves to "resolve the migratory status of the nationals of the party states and members in the region in order to strengthen the links binding the regional community" (Novick 2012, 223). In December 2006, Argentina also signed the Internal Convention on the Rights of Migrant Workers and Members of their Families. Thus it appears that in South America in general, and Argentina in particular, both the rhetoric on migration and the corresponding policies have been more welcoming to migrants than elsewhere in the world. Within this context, DNU 70/2017, with its emphasis on the immigrants' criminality and the need for a more restrictive approach, seems to be a step back. As discussed in the section that follows, this urgent measure was justified as a way to contain the alleged public safety "crisis" for which poor and racialized migrants (those from Peru, Paraguay, and Bolivia) were held responsible.

DNU 70/2017: Protecting Argentina's Safety?

To construct social phenomena as a "crisis," certain discursive claims need to be advanced and popularized (Spector and Kitsuse 2001; Wienberg 2009). Electronic and printed media play in important role in this process of claim making, as is evident in Argentina's case. As a prelude to DNU 70/2017, in late 2016, Argentineans were subjected to anti-immigrant rhetoric in a series of media debates on the threat migrants pose to the nation's well-being. On November 1, 2016, in a televised interview on La Mirada on Channel 26, a senator and president of the Front for Victory party Miguel Ángel Pichetto questioned the "egalitarian culture" responsible for migrants' access to health care and education. "Receiving so many poor immigrants, how much misery can Argentina tolerate?" he asked. He went on to say: "We have to cease being so stupid. The problem is that we always solve social problems for Bolivia and criminal problems for Peru . . . Peru solved its security problems by sending away its drug traffickers; main shantytowns in Argentina are now taken over by the Peruvians." The senator's statements triggered media debates and discussions, and while many activists spoke against Pichetto's xenophobic sentiments, others chimed in with him to vilify Argentina's immigrants for "stealing" jobs from the nationals and engaging in criminal activities (see, for instance, ["Las polémicas declaraciones" 2016]).

Although immigration reforms had already been contemplated, one particular incident triggered the adoption of "urgent measures." On December 24, 2016, while fleeing from a robbery scene, a 15-year-old Peruvian-born delinquent Brian Joel shot and killed a 14-year-old boy Brian Aguinaco in Flores, a low-income neighborhood in Buenos Aires. Brian Joel had assumed that the car in which Brian Aguinaco was traveling was pursuing him. Captured in Chile, Brian Joel was returned to Argentina and subsequently, he and his family were deported to Peru (see, for instance, "Liberaron al chico" 2017). As was reported in the press, Brian Joel's parents were involved in drug trafficking, and his father had been convicted (see, for instance, "La familia del adolescente detenido" 2016). In an interview with *Clarín*, Brian Aguinaco's parents observed, "With our country's laws and the open-door policies, anyone can come here, and this is crazy" ("Así llegó a Perú" 2017). The connection between the country's generous immigration policy and crime, articulated by Brian Aguinaco's parents, was echoed in other discourses put forward by the media and policy-makers, such as the Minister of National Security Patricia Bullrich. According to the latter, 33 percent of inmates in federal prisons detained for drug trafficking were comprised of the immigrants. Furthermore, according to Bullrich, most immigrants from Peru, Paraguay, and Bolivia were involved in crime: "Peruvians citizens come here and end up murdering others in their fight for drug control . . . Paraguayan citizens come here and end up murdering others in their fight for drug control . . . And moreover, many Paraguayans, Bolivians, and Peruvians work as drivers and mules as part of the drug trafficking networks" ("Patricia Bullrich" 2017). Blaming the open-door immigration policy for this public safety "crisis," Bullrich called for a legal reform.

Three days later, on January 27, 2017, the President of Argentina Mauricio Macri issued DNU 20/2017 that proposed to reform the 2004 Immigration Law 25,871. Under Article 29 (c) of the Immigration Law #25,871, admission or residency is denied to those who have been convicted or were serving a sentence in Argentina or abroad, or have a history of trafficking in arms, persons, narcotics, money laundering, investments in illegal activities, or a crime punishable, according to Argentinean law, by a prison sentence of three (3) years or more. DNU 70/2017 proposed to remove the minimum three-year requirement, thus making deportable immigrants charged with even minor offences. To expedite expulsions, DNU 70/2017 also proposed to reform regulations outlined in Decree 616/2010 (Government of Argentina 2010).

Article 99, paragraph 3 of the Constitution of Argentina authorizes the Executive Power (that is, the President and the Cabinet) to issue decrees for reasons of necessity and urgency "only when exceptional circumstances make it impossible to follow the ordinary procedures foreseen by the Constitution" (*República de Argentina* 1994). Exceptional circumstances are defined by the Supreme Court of Justice of Argentina as those that pose "grave social risks" (Avalos 2012). For the Executive Power, such a "grave social risk" did exist. First, it was argued that the deportation process was prolonged and ineffective. It was pointed out that while officially it required approximately 400 days to be carried out, in fact, some expulsions never occurred or took up to seven years to be executed. It was asserted that by allowing migrants with a criminal record to remain in Argentina for such a prolonged time, the National Migration Directorate was failing in its duty to guarantee public safety.

Second, as specified in the Decree, the percentage of foreign nationals within federal prisons had increased in the last few years to 21 percent of the total prison population in 2016. Among the inmates imprisoned for drug trafficking, according to the Decree, the percentage had gone up to 33 percent. It was therefore concluded that in the country whose foreign-born population constitutes 4.5 percent, foreign-born inmates in federal prisons were vastly overrepresented. As the Decree avowed, "the national well-being suffers gravely as a consequence of such crimes as the smuggling of arms, humans, organs, tissues, and narcotics, money laundering, investments in illicit activities, human trafficking, genocide, war crimes, terrorist acts, crimes against humanity, and other acts recognized by the International Criminal Court" (Government of Argentina 2017). For the President and his Cabinet, this "crisis" justified the adoption of urgent measures that would expedite the expulsion of foreign nationals who are involved in criminal activities as well as those who have entered Argentina in a clandestine fashion, avoiding migratory control (although it was not clear why the latter group was also portrayed as a threat to public safety). By classifying the situation as a "crisis," the executive powers provided a justification for practices of exception. As De Genova et al. (2016) contend, "the 'crisis' itself operates as a critical moment that allows governments to push through controversial policies while citizens are too intellectually distracted, emotionally manipulated, or otherwise paralyzed by the border spectacle to organize any adequate or consequential form of resistance." Yet, not all Argentinean citizens were "intellectually distracted" or "emotionally manipulated," as the next section illustrates.

DNU 70/2017: Is There Necessity or Urgency?

Civil society organizations, such as Centre for Legal and Social Studies (Centro de Estudios Legales y Sociales or CELS); the Argentinean chapter of Amnesty International; Committee for Refugees and Migrants (Comisión Argentina para Refugiados y Migrantes or CAREF); the Argentinean Institute for Equality, Diversity, and Integration (IARPIDI); the National Network of Migrants and Refugees in Argentina; the Argentina's Migrant Front; and the Breaking Walls Civil Association were outraged by the Decree, as were many social scientists who articulated their objections to the decree in a letter addressed to the Chambers of Deputies and Senators, signed on February 28, 2017, by thirty-five directors of research centers and deans and close to a thousand faculty members and researchers. NGOs filed a complaint with the Inter-American Committee on Human Rights, and representatives from CELS, CAREF, IARPIDI, and the National Network of Migrants and Refugees were invited to a hearing held on March 10, 2017. Furthermore, most of them had an opportunity to voice their views at a hearing held by the Bicameral Congress Committee on Decree 70/2017 on February 16, 2017.

Opponents contended that there was no urgency in existence to justify this decree. In the letter addressed to the Congress, social scientists questioned the statistics on overrepresentation of migrants in the penal system for drug-related and other offenses and found that the figures used the justify this decree were highly exaggerated. In their submissions, they maintained that, according to official data from the National System of Penal Execution Statistics (SNEEP), in 2015, foreigners detained nationwide for all types of crimes amounted to 4,449, representing 0.2% of the almost 2,000,000 immigrants residing in the country and approximately 6% of the total population in prison (71,500 people), and that there had been no major changes in the composition of the prison population with respect to the country of origin in the last 15 years. Similarly, drawing from the SNEEP data sources, Amnesty International reported that among the prisoners incarcerated for drug-related offenses throughout the country, 82 percent were from Argentina and only 18 percent or 1426 prisoners were foreigners. The latter constituted 0.07 percent of all migrants residing in Argentina. In a media interview, CELS activist Diego Morales explained how statistics had been manipulated to give the wrong impression about the link between Argentina's immigrants and criminality:

> The figures also conceal that it is generally expected that for a crime like drug trafficking, foreigners would always be overrepresented. It happens all over the world, because it is a crime that has a cross-border component. Between 40 and 50 percent of Argentinian prisoners abroad are arrested for drug trafficking. Would you say that there is a problem of Argentinian drug dealers around the world? I don't think so.
>
> (Ginzberg 2017)

Critics of DNU 70 also questioned whether it took as long to complete expulsion procedures under the 2004 Immigration Law, as the National Department of Immigration (DNM) claimed. Pablo Ceriani, a legal scholar from the National University of Lanús, commented in his presentation at the Bicameral Congress Committee on DNU 70/2017 hearing:

> It was mentioned that some administrative cases of expulsion lasted eight years. It would be interesting to have complete statistics. How many cases lasted eight years? One, ten, fifteen, twenty? Are we going to forge a state policy on the basis of a few cases? I believe, this is one case when there is a need for a serious, deep, democratic, participatory and legislative debate, as required by the Constitution. And we need to have real statistics to be able to construct state policies of central importance for our history and our present such as the migration policy.
>
> (transcribed and translated from youtube.com/watch?v=Yb3O7kKXtsY)

The Legal, Political, and Social Solidarity Crisis

While challenging the myth that migrants were responsible for the public safety "crisis," critics of DNU 70/2017 blamed the Argentinean executive powers for creating a legal and social solidarity "crisis." In the deposition given at the Bicameral Congressional Committee hearing, Ceriani contended:

> Rather than responding to an urgency or an emergency, the decree creates a social, political, and legal emergency. Social, because of the process of stigmatization of the entire migrant population and xenophobia against it. Somehow, the latent

> xenophobia that exists in our society is transformed into public policy, and this is profoundly troubling. Political emergency, because there is a whole series of policies that are affected by this decree, not only immigration policy, but also integration, social and criminal policies that will be harmed by this decree, among other things. Legal emergency with respect to all laws. Not only the immigration law, but also the rules on jurisdiction, administrative procedures law, the National Constitution, human rights treaties, such as the Convention on the Rights of the Child and Convention on the Protection of the Rights of All Migrant Workers, among others, are affected by this decree.
>
> (transcribed and translated from youtube.com/watch?v=Yb3O7kKXtsY)

Critics of DNU 70/2017 argued that it would disproportionately target vulnerable and poor migrants, and not drug traffickers since any offense, no matter how minor, would result in expulsion. Thus people detained for street vending, participation in a public demonstration, driving offenses, or for having entered the country without legal authorization would be subject to expulsion from Argentina. By contrast, as noted by a CELS activist Manual Tufro, mechanisms to expel those who commit most serious crimes had already been in place prior to the publication of DNU 70/2017 (Ginzberg 2017).

In fact, as civil society activists articulated in their depositions at the two hearings, DNU 70/2017 would be ineffective in combatting international drug trafficking. They pointed out that upon deportation, the Argentinean State would renounce criminal prosecution and investigation into the operation of international criminal networks, thus allowing their activities to continue. The activists also raised concerns that these expeditious expulsions for minor and arbitrary reasons, would result in forced separations of family members and produce hardships for children (including Argentinian-born offspring) of the expelled migrants.

Furthermore, according to the civil society critics, the proposed expeditious procedures would deny migrants their legal right to due process. Under this decree, a person may be expelled from Argentina or denied access even if he or she has not yet been found guilty of the crime for which he or she has been charged, thus violating the presumption of innocence. The expeditious expulsion procedures to be completed in three days would make it virtually impossible for migrants to gather evidence to prove their innocence prior to the expulsion, particularly if they are kept in detention without legal aid.

Furthermore, at both hearings and other events, civil society critics articulated their alarm that by linking immigration control to immigrants' criminality, DNU 70/2017 was igniting xenophobia in the Argentinian society. In their letter addressed to the Bicameral Congress Committee, social scientists wrote:

> This DNU will strengthen the xenophobic and racist conceptions that persist in our society. By unjustly and arbitrarily applying different and unequal punishments to persons who have allegedly done the same thing (complete judicial process for nationals vs. expulsion for foreigners), the logic of suspicion, segregation and

> prejudice are reinforced and legitimized. These practices are, without a doubt, a central element in the formation of a violent and unjust society.
>
> (transcribed and translated from youtube.com/watch?v=Yb3O7kKXtsY)

Addressing the Bicameral Congressional Committee, Iberth Mamani of the Front of Migrant Argentina supported the view that the anti-migrant sentiments that underlie the decree would reverberate among common people. He noted: "One of the consequences of this DNU is that it gives license to the police to stop and card us, and when we don't have documents, they detain us and take us to the police station where migrants are forced to pay a bribe to avoid expulsion."

In sum, this decree seems to contravene the principles of fairness to migrants that Argentina and other South American countries have entrenched in their national laws and policies in the last fifteen years. Yet rather than seeing DNU 70/2017 a reversal of the "liberal tide" (Acosta and Freier 2015), it's vital to explore whether this legal, political, and social solidarity "crisis" had been seeded in the previous times, including the "liberal" decade.

Plus Ça Change, Plus C'est La Même Chose

It is important not to overstate the "paradigmatic shift" in the South American states' immigration policies. As Margheritis (2015, 60) points out, liberal discussion on the Residency Agreement and the corresponding regional citizenship went hand-in-hand with measures aimed at reinforcing security and control considerations. She lists several Mercosur agreements that "reflect a persistent concern with controlling human mobility and preserving governments' capacities to decide selectively on the movement and settlement of people across borders." Argentina's seemingly hospitable migration policies affirm the vitality of the security and control undercurrents in the migration policies of this region. An important rationale behind the Patria Grande status regularization program was the desire to "manage migration," that is, to gather information on the migrant population found in irregular conditions, eradicate "irregularity," and create a population of residents who would pay taxes and contribute to social security. Unable to prevent the flow of "irregular" migrants, the Argentinian state chose to address what it perceived as a "problem" by making this population knowable (through the information gathered), countable (through statistics collected in the process), and thus manageable (Basok et al. 2013; Domenech 2007, 2008; Margheritis 2015). It is noteworthy that the 1984 and 1992 amnesties coincided with repression against migrants from neighboring countries, and they had more to do with the need to prevent the informalization of the economy than with the desire to attract immigrants from these countries (Albarracin 2004; Novick 2012), to say nothing of the migrants' "human rights."

For the proponents and advocates of Decree 70/2017, respect for human rights and migration control are two sides of the same coin. Public officials insisted that this Decree does not break with Argentina's human rights approach to migration and its respect for cultural pluralism. Addressing the Bicultural Congress Committee on Decree 70/2017, Horacio José García, the DNM Director, stated, "We constitute an institution of control, but it means that we are not divorced from the outlook that emphasizes integration and hospitality; we are profoundly hospitable." He went on to provide statistics on status regularization and contended, "We are fighting against migratory irregularity, and not against irregular migrants." Evoking the case of Brian Joel, mentioned above, he observed, "This decree is linked directly to the topic of security. It doesn't attack the immigration policy. The immigration policy is still as open as ever. But it is evident that we need to address public safety."

Claudio Avruj, Secretary of Human Rights and Cultural Pluralism, speaking at the Inter-American Commission on Human Rights, summarized Argentina's achievement in the promotion of respect for cultural diversity, interculturalism, and the fight against discrimination and xenophobia and concluded his presentation by saying: "Control, security, and human rights do not have to be contradictory. To control entry and residence of the migrants is also a way to protect their human rights."

Similar to most world countries, South American states rank migrant hopefuls from the least to most desirable and design programs and mechanisms to attract the migrants who are believed to strengthen their economy and enrich their social and cultural fabric, while preventing migrants presumed to be a drain on the economy and a threat to the country's safety, security, and integrity. It is no accident that only six months after Ecuador opened its borders to all travelers, visa requirements were reintroduced for Chinese citizens, and eighteen months later for citizens of Afghanistan, Bangladesh, Eritrea, Ethiopia, Kenya, Nepal, Nigeria, Pakistan, and Somalia. Furthermore, most migrants who arrived in Ecuador in 2008 without visas and stayed behind found themselves in irregular migratory conditions since status regularization procedures were nonexistent for these migrants (Acosta and Freier 2015).[4] The eviction and subsequent arrest and deportation of more than a hundred of Cubans camping out at a Quito park by the National Police (Gámez and Fernández 2016) is a vivid illustration of the illiberal practices that coincide with the open-door policies. In fact, in all South American countries, migrants from Asia, Africa, and the Caribbean have restricted opportunities to regularize their status (Acosta and Freier 2015; OAS 2016).

Since the late nineteenth century, Argentina has entrenched an immigration policy that has privileged certain groups of migrants over the others. The construction of the Argentinian identity as a white country composed of European descendants shaped the way regional migration was treated for most of the 19th and 20th century. As one of the major destination countries for European migrants, predominantly for Spain and Italy, certain strategies were put in place to encourage migration from some European countries (e.g. the UK and the Basque region of Spain) while tolerating the presence of the massive waves of immigrants from Italy and non-Basque regions of Spain. Except for labor activists, held responsible for the political unrest, for most of the twentieth century European immigrants were considered to be most beneficial for Argentina's economic development, especially in rural regions (Bastia and vom Hau 2014; Novick 2012). By contrast, throughout the twentieth century, regional migrants, particularly those born in Bolivia, Paraguay, and Peru—that is, countries, with a relatively high percentage of people of indigenous or mixed descent—were viewed as "useless" or even a threat to the persistent imaginary of Argentina as a "white" country (Bastia and vom Hau 2014). The repressive Videla regime immigration policy sanctioned measures to prevent migration from these countries. The policing and deportation of migrants increased as immigration authorities compelled ordinary citizens to denounce migrants found in irregular migratory conditions (Albarracin 2004; Bastia and vom Hau 2014; Novick 2012). Another decree, adopted in 1993, authorized the DNM to increase search and verification of immigrants' legal status and deport those without legal documents (Albarracin 2004; Novick 2012).

In the last two decades of the twentieth century, not only did the regional migration come to constitute 90 percent of the immigrant population in Argentina, but the ethnic composition also changed. While the proportion of Chilean and Uruguayan immigrants (most of whom are also of European ancestry) decreased, the proportion of Peruvians and Bolivians increased. Furthermore, whereas earlier in the century, regional migrants settled in the countryside, close to the borders of their countries of origin, in the 1980s and 1990s, the geographic distribution of regional migrants within Argentina changed, with most choosing to reside in the metropolitan area of Buenos Aires (Grimson 2006). According to the 2010 census, there were 1.8 million immigrants in Argentina, with a half million being from Paraguay and 350,000 from Bolivia. Peruvian immigrants, numbering 160,000, are the fourth largest immigrant group in Argentina (INDEC 2012). This new pattern of settlement, combined with the changing ethnic composition of the regional migration, made migrants much more visible, and politicians, media, organized labor, and the general population used them as easy scapegoats for the country's woes (Caggiano 2005; Grimson 2006; Halpern 2007). Predominantly poor, they were portrayed by the media as responsible for crime, unemployment, epidemics, and social tensions (Albarracin 2004; Grimson and Caggiano 2012; Ramos 2015).

In 1999, xenophobia against migrants was reaching its peak, with public officials, police, and politicians circulating exaggerated statistics on immigrants' criminality and unleashing a witch hunt against undocumented migrants (Grimson 2006; Halpern 2007). The government presented a bill to Congress calling for increased control and penalties against migrants who entered the country illegally, sanctions against companies that employed "illegal foreigners," streamlining of the expulsion procedures, and a mandate to be granted to the Executive Power to establish criteria and requirements to regulate the admission of foreigners (Grimson 2006). Surveyed by Grimson in the 1990s, many Bolivians reported being looked down upon by the general population and in public offices (Grimson 2006).

These attitudes persisted in the twenty-first century despite the fact that Argentina adopted an immigration policy that proclaims respect for migrant rights. Focusing on Bolivian migrants, Pacecca and Courtis (2009) report discrimination against them in both public and private spaces, whether they seek public services (in hospitals, public transportation, schools), apply for jobs, or interact with vendors, customers, or the general public. Testimonies from Bolivian immigrants collected by Pacecca and Courtis (2009) elucidate the image of a foreigner as a suspect, who is likely to be engaged in criminal, fraudulent, and illegitimate action. Bolivian women interviewed in another study (Basok et al. 2013) also reported being denied hospital services and being ridiculed, harassed, and looked down upon by employers, service providers, and others.

Media and public officials' reactions to the occupation of Parque Indoamericano, a large park situated between Villa Soldati and Villa Lugano, the most deprived shantytowns in Buenos Aires, provide a vivid illustration of the vitality of xenophobic attitudes against poor migrants in Argentina. Many of the Peruvian, Bolivian, and Paraguayan immigrants inhabit the capital's shantytowns (Gutiérrez 2016; Mera and Vaccotti 2013). In December of 2010, some 13,000 people, including both Argentineans and immigrants, particularly Bolivians and Paraguayans, occupied the 320-acre park to pressure the government to provide social housing to the shantytowns' residents (Hölzl 2015; Mera and Vaccotti 2013). In their coverage, mass media tended to focus selectively on Paraguayan and Bolivian protesters, thus projecting the image that immigrants were behind this unrest, and that immigration, and not the shortage of social housing, was its main cause (López 2012). In his press conference, Mauricio Macri, the current president of Argentina, and the Mayor of Buenos Aires at the time of the incident, was quick to blame immigrants for the park seizure and portray all immigrants as criminals, involved in the drug trade and responsible for the decline in public safety in Buenos Aires. Contending that immigration was "out of control" in Argentina, he called for strategies to protect the Argentinean society against the advance of drug trafficking and delinquency and to defend the rule of law (Macri 2010). In an interview given to the press before and after the Parque Indoamericano occupation, Macri asserted that immigrants from Peru, Paraguay, and Bolivia came to Argentina to take advantage of the country's health care and public education, something that he saw as a "catastrophe" for the host society (López 2012).

These xenophobic discourses echoed other transformations taking place in South America at the same time. Although the "liberal" immigration rhetoric never erased the preoccupation with migration "management," in the second decade of the twenty-first century, immigration control priorities have once again become prevalent. The changes were triggered by fluctuating global dynamics, such as the increase in the African, Asian, and Caribbean (predominantly Cuban and Haitian) migration toward South America (OAS 2016) and the "humanitarian crises" evolving at the borders between Columbia and Ecuador and Venezuela and Columbia, combined with the aftershocks of the 2008 world economic recession, and the growing anti-immigrant sentiments in Europe and USA (Domenech 2017). Between 2010 and 2016, the political and media discourses on migrants' "criminality" surfaced in the media, particularly during preelectoral campaigns, and in debates taking place in the Congress (Domenech 2017). It is noteworthy that the number of expulsion orders increased significantly during this time; whereas in 2004 there were only 232 expulsion orders issued by the DNM, by 2014 the number had risen to 1,615, and in the first six months of 2015, it was as high as 1,081 (DNM 2015). To exert control over the migrants with expulsion orders, on September 1, 2016, DNM opened a detention center in Buenos Aires (Rosende 2016).

The 2016–2017 wave of xenophobia and the criminalization of migrants from Peru, Bolivia, and Paraguay prevalent in the media, as well as DNU 70/2017, are consistent with previous trends, particularly the hardening of the anti-migrant discourse and migration control policies. The fact that there was a 2004 proclaimed commitment to migrants' human rights seems to have made little difference to the migrants who are still accused of being a burden on the Argentinian economy, suspected of drug trafficking, and portrayed as a menace to the nations' well-being. Thus, rather than breaking with the "liberal" values, DNU 70/2017 seems to illustrate that these "liberal" discourses can coexist with illiberal practices.

Conclusion

Real or imagined crises are often used by policymakers to justify the adoption of extreme measures to contain the situation. In the case of migration, unprecedented increases in the volume of migration by any particular group are often socially constructed as a crisis. But even when migration remains stable, under changing social, economic, or political circumstances such as economic recession or rising violence or crime, migrants are often assigned the blame for the declining security. Nativist political leaders manipulate public opinion to project the image of migrants being responsible for the country's calamities, as we have seen in the United States under Trump, in the UK among the Independence Party supporters, and in France among the followers of Marine Le Pen's National Front. Using such metaphors as a "swarm of people" (as did UK's former Prime Minister David Cameron), tougher measures are proposed to restrict migrants' flows and rid the country of those who, in the eyes of the politicians, do not belong.

Despite its stated commitment to the rights of *all* migrants, Argentina, similarly to other host societies, welcomes only some migrants (those of European ancestry) while taking measures, such as DNU 70/17, to restrict admission and deny permanent residency to those considered less deserving, such as poor immigrants and those of non-European ancestry. While supporting the principle of free circulation of people within South America, Argentina seems to be searching for ways to prevent some migrants from exercising this right.

DNU 70/17 was justified as a reasonable response to an emerging crisis in Argentina—that is, the rise of criminal activities among immigrants from Peru, Paraguay, and Bolivia, something that civil society activists dismissed as a myth. For many pro-migrant activists, DNU 70/17, with its authorization of such illiberal practices as the denial of due process, disrespect for the presumption of innocence, and the expansion of criteria for nonadmissibility, is representative of a reversal of Argentina's otherwise liberal policy towards migrants. Yet, as argued in this chapter, there is more continuity than discontinuity between DNU 70/17 and the "liberal" approaches toward regional migrants proclaimed at the turn of the century. Prejudices and discrimination against migrants from Peru, Paraguay, and Bolivia never abated in Argentina, nor did the desire to control and discipline them. Entrenching the right to dispose of the unwanted migrants expeditiously, the decree grants Argentinian authorities not only the power to deny residency to some migrants but to make all migrants deportable. As such, DNU 70/17 can be viewed as a *technique of discipline* to keep resident migrants in line and preclude them from any acts such as participation in a protest, resistance to authorities, or unauthorized economic activities, all of which may, under DNU 70/17, result in their incarceration and subsequent deportation. As a technique of discipline, and not merely as a strategy to dispose of some migrants who have a criminal record, DNU 70/17 has a far-reaching impact on the marginalized migrants in Argentina.

Acknowledgement

I would like to thank Eduardo Domenech for his generous and insightful comments and suggestions and assisting me in accessing some documents and publications.

Notes

1. The official Spanish-language name of the program is *Programa Nacional de Normalización Documentaria Migratoria*
2. In the 1990s, civil society organizations, and particularly CELS (Centre de Estudios Legales y Sociales or the Centre for Legal and Social Studies) called attention to the stigmatization, discrimination, labor rights abuses, and civil rights violations perpetrated against undocumented migrants by the police, employers, and public officials and called for status regularization. They also argued that a legal status would improve migrants' access to healthcare, education, police protection, and housing conditions (Basok et al. 2013).
3. In 2010, Ecuador launched two regularization programs that benefited approximately 400 Haitian and 650 Cuban migrants (see Alfonso 2013 and Acosta and Freier 2015).

References

Acosta A. D., and L. F. Freier. 2015. "Turning the Immigration Policy Paradox Upside Down? Populist Liberalism and Discursive Gaps in South America." *International Migration Review* 49, no. 3: 659–696. doi:10.1111/imre.12146.

Agamben, G. 2005. *State of Exception*. Chicago: University of Chicago Press.

Albahari, M. 2015. *Crimes of Peace: Mediterranean Migrations at the World's Deadliest Border*. Philadelphia: University of Pennsylvania Press.

Albarracin, J. 2004. "Selecting Immigration In Modern Argentina: Economic, Cultural, International and Institutional Factors." PhD diss., University of Florida.

Alfonso, A. 2013. *La experiencia de los países Suramericanos en materia de regularización migratoria* . Buenos Aires, Argentina: IOM.

"Así llegó a Perú el menor acusado de matar a Brian." *Clarín*, January 11, 2017. https://www.clarin.com/policiales/llego-peru-menor-acusado-matar-brian_0_S1anmiXIl.html

Avalos, E. 2012. "Los Decretos de Necesidad y Urgencia en Argentina: Desde 1853 hasta Nuestros Dias." *Revista de la Facultad* 3, no. 1, Nueva Serie 2: 147–157

Basok, T., N. Piper, and V. Simmons. 2013. "Disciplining Female Migration in Argentina: Human Rights in the Times of Migration Management." In *Disciplining the Transnational Mobility of People*, edited by M. Geiger and A. Pecaud, 162–184. New York: Palgrave Macmillan, 2013.

Bastia, T. and M. vom Hau. 2014. "Migration, Race and Nationhood in Argentina." *Journal of Ethnic and Migration Studies*, *40*, no. 3: 475–492. http://dx.doi.org/10.1080/1369183X.2013.782153

Boletin Oficial. 2017. Government of Argentina. Migraciones. Decreto 70. https://www.boletinoficial.gob.ar/#!DetalleNorma/158336/20170130

Boletin Oficial No 31.898. 2010. Government of Argentina. Decreto 616. http://www.migraciones.gov.ar/pdf_varios/residencias/Decreto_616_2010.pdf

Caggiano, S. 2005. *Lo que no entra en el cresol: Inmigración boliviana, comunicación y procesos identitarios*. Buenos Aires, Argentina: Prometeo.

Ceriani, P. and L. F. Freier. 2015. "Migration Policies and Policymaking in Latin America and The Caribbean: Lights and Shadows in a Region In Transition." In *A Liberal Tide? Immigration and Asylum Law and Policy in Latin America*, edited by D. J. Cantor, L. F. Freier, and J. -P. Gauci, 1–32. London: Institute of Latin American Studies, School of Advanced Study, University of London.

DNM (Dirección Nacional de Migraciones). 2015. "Estadistica de Expulsiones: Informe Actualizado al 1er Semestre 2015." Retrieved from http://www.migraciones.gov.ar/pdf_varios/estadisticas/estadistica_expulsiones_DNM_2009-2015_1er%20semestre.pdf

De Genova, N., E. Fontanari, F. Picozza, L. Soto Bermant, A. Spathopoulou, M. Stierl, et al. 2016. "Migrant Crisis/Refugee Crisis." New Keywords Collective. http://nearfuturesonline.org/europecrisis-new-keywords-of-crisis-in-and-of-europe-part-3/

Domenech, E. 2007. "La agenda politica sobre migraciones en América del Sur: El caso de la Argentina." *Revue Européenne des Migrations Internationales* 23, no. 1: 71–94.

Domenech, E. 2013. "'Las migraciones son como el agua': Hacia la instauración de políticas de 'control con rostro humano'. La gobernabilidad migratoria en la Argentina." *Polis: Revista Latinoamericana* 12, no. 35. https://polis.revues.org/9280

Domenech, E. 2017. "Inmigración, legislación y políticas en la Argentina actual: Escenas etnográficas de prácticas de control y vigilancia." In *Migración, Estado y políticas: Cambios y continuidades en América del Sur*, coordinated by J. Ramírez, 13–46. La Paz, Bolivia: Vicepresidencia del Estado Plurinacional de Bolivia/CELAG.

Domenech, E. and A. Pereira. 2017. "Estudios migratorios e investigación académica sobre las políticas de migraciones internacionales en Argentina." *Íconos. Revista de Ciencias Sociales* 58: 83–108.

Domenech, E. 2018. "Migraciones internacionales y Estado nacional en la Argentina reciente: De la retórica de la exclusión a la retórica de la inclusión. III Congreso Latinoamericano de Población." ALAP, Córdoba. https://myslide.org/the-philosophy-of-money.html?utm_source=migraciones-internacionales-y-estado-nacional-en-la-argentina-reciente-de-la-retorica-de-la-exclusion-a-la-retorica-de-la-inclusion

Gámez, T. N., and A. Fernández. 2016. "Cubans in Ecuador: Chronology of a Crisis." *Miami Herald*, July 14. Retrieved from http://www.miamiherald.com/news/nation-world/world/americas/cuba/article89618677.html

Ginzberg, V. 2017. "Hay una operación para asociar migración con delincuencia" *Página 12*, January 29. https://www.pagina12.com.ar/16865-hay-una-operacion-para-asociar-migracion-con-delincuencia

Grimson, A. 2006. "Nuevas xenofobias, nuevas políticas étnicas en la Argentina." In *Migraciones regionales hacia la Argentina: Diferencia, desigualdad y derechos*, edited by A. Grimson and E. Jelin, 69–99. Buenos Aires: Prometeo.

Grimson, A., and S. Caggiano. 2012. "Xenofobias descontroladas." In *Racismo, violencia y política: Pensar el Indoamericano, dos años después*. Los Polvorines, Argentina: Universidad Nacional de General Sarmiento.

Gutiérrez, F. 2016. "La xenofobia argentina en pleno auge." *El Observador*, December 4. http://www.elobservador.com.uy/la-xenofobia-argentina-pleno-auge-n1006398

Halpern, G. 2007. *Medios de comunicación y discriminación: Apuntes sobre la década del '90 y algo más*. Boletín de la Biblioteca del Congreso de la Nación 123. Buenos Aires: Biblioteca del Congreso de la Nación.

Hines, B. 2010. "The Right to Migrate as a Human Right: The Current Argentine Immigration Law." *Cornell International Law Journal* 43, no. 3: 472–511.

Hölzl, C. 2015. "The Occupation of the Parque Indoamericano in Buenos Aires Discourse Dynamics and Stakeholder Practices." *Latin American Perspectives*, *44*, no. 3: 113–134.

INDEC (Instituto Nacional de Estadística y Censos). 2012. Censo Nacional de Población, Hogares y Viviendas 2010 Censo del Bicentenario, Resultados Definitivos, Serie B, Número 2, Tomo 1. http://www.indec.gov.ar/ftp/cuadros/poblacion/censo2010_tomo1.pdf

"La familia del adolescente detenido por el crimen de Brian, en la mira." 2016. *TN*, December 30, https://tn.com.ar/policiales/la-familia-del-adolescente-detenido-por-el-crimen-de-brian-en-la-mira_763146

"Las polémicas declaraciones de Miguel Pichetto sobre los inmigrantes." 2016. *La Nación*, Nov 2. http://www.lanacion.com.ar/1952583-las-polemicas-declaraciones-de-miguel-pichetto-sobre-los-inmigrantes

"Liberaron al chico de 15 años acusado de matar a Brian y lo enviaron a Perú." 2017. *Clarín*, Jan 10. https://www.clarin.com/policiales/liberaron-chico-15-anos-acusado-matar-brian-enviaron-peru_0_S1jqZQ8g.html

Ley 25871. 2014. "Migraciones: Government of Argentina." http://www.migraciones.gov.ar/pdf_varios/residencias/ley_25871.pdf

López, M. 2012. "'Vos sos bienvenido' pero ellos no: Abordaje crítico de los discursos del Jefe de Gobierno de la Ciudad de Buenos Aires, Mauricio Macri, en el contexto de la "toma" del Parque Indoamericano." *Revista Isla Flotante* 4, no. 4: 35–56.

Macri, M. 2010. "Discurso y Conferencia de prensa ante la ocupación del parque Indoamericano." *PaperBlog: Revista Jurídico*. September 12. http://alonsojuliosantiago.blogspot.ca/2010/12/discurso-y-conferencia-de-prensa-ante.html

Margheritis, A. 2013. Piecemeal Regional Integration in The Post-Neoliberal Era: Negotiating Migration Policies within Mercosur." *Review of International Political Economy*, 20, no. 3: 541–575, doi:10.1080/09692290.2012.678762

Margheritis, A. 2015. "Mercosur's Post-Neoliberal Approach to Migration: From Workers' Mobility to Regional Citizenship." In *A Liberal Tide? Immigration and Asylum Law and Policy in Latin America*, edited by D. J. Cantor, L. F. Freier, and J. -P. Gauci, 57–79. London: Institute of Latin American Studies, School of Advanced Study, University of London.

Mera, G., and L. Vaccotti. 2013. "Migración y Déficit Habitacional en la Ciudad de Buenos Aires." *Argumentos* 15: 176–202

Mountz, A., and N. Hiemstra. 2014. "Chaos and Crisis: Dissecting the Spatiotemporal Logics of Contemporary Migrations and State Practices." *Annals of the Association of American Geographers, 104*, no. 2: 382–390.

Novick, S. 2012. "Transformation and Challenges of Argentine Immigration Policy in Relation to the International Context." *Revista Migraciones Internacionales*, 6 no. 22: 206–232, doi:10.17428/rmi.v6i22.744

OAS. 2016. *Flujos de Migrantes en Situación Migratoria Irregular Provenientes de África, Asia y el Caribe en las Américas.* Informe Regional. Washington, DC: OAS. http://rosanjose.iom.int/site/sites/default/files/Reporte%20OIM_OEA_030817web.pdf

Pacecca, M. I., and C. Courtis. 2009. "Con la cara que tenes, estas en en horno. . . . " Migracion boliviana y discriminacion." *Estudios Migratorios Latinoamericanos* 22–23, no. 67: 397–416.

"Patricia Bullrich: 'Acá vienen ciudadanos peruanos y paraguayos y se terminan matando por el control de la droga.'" 2017. *La Nación*, January 24. http://www.lanacion.com.ar/1978531-patricia-bullrich-aca-vienen-ciudadanos-peruanos-y-paraguayos-y-se-terminan-matando-por-el-control-de-la-droga

Ramos, V. 2015. *La Guerra de las Palabras*, Buenos Aires, Argentina: Instituto contra la discriminación, el racismo y la xenofobia (INADI).

Rosende, L. 2016. "El Gobierno creó un centro de detención de migrantes: Alarma entre organismos de DDHH." *Política Argentina*, August 26. http://www.politicargentina.com/notas/201608/16208-el-gobierno-creo-un-centro-de-detencion-de-migrantes-alarma-entre-organismos-de-ddhh.html

República de Argentina. 1994. *Constitución de la República de Argentina* http://servicios.infoleg.gob.ar/infolegInternet/anexos/0-4999/804/norma.htm

SACM. 2016. XVI South American Conference on Migration Declaration of Asuncion, Asuncion, Paraguay, Nov 3–4, retrieved from http://csm-osumi.org/sites/default/files/conferencias/2_declaracion_csm_ingles.pdf

Spector, M., and J. I. Kitsuse. 2001. *Constructing Social Problems.* New Brunswick, NJ: Transaction.

Texidó, E., and J. Gurrieri. 2012. *Panorama Migratorio del América del Sur 2012.* Buenos Aires, Argentina: IOM.

Wienberg, D. 2009. "On the Social Construction of Social Problems and Social Problems Theory: A Contribution to the Legacy of John Kitsuse." *American Sociologist* 40: 61–78.

CHAPTER 29

AUSTRALIA AND PEOPLE SEEKING ASYLUM WHO ARRIVE BY BOAT

CAROLINE FLEAY

PUBLIC officials and the media can play a major role in framing the movement of people fleeing persecution as a crisis and portraying negative representations of the people themselves. This includes in Australia where for forty years there have been examples of political leaders framing people seeking asylum and their arrival by boat in this way. This has been particularly evident over the past eight years and has continued in the aftermath of the Coalition's electoral successes since September 2013. For example, in September 2016 former Australian Prime Minister Tony Abbott told an audience of European conservatives that European governments were in the midst of a crisis and should adopt Australian policies in response to the arrival of people seeking asylum. He declared that: "This crisis can't be managed, it has to be resolved. That's what Australia did, under my government; we stopped illegal boats at sea and escorted them back to Indonesian waters" (Remeikis 2016). Despite no longer being a government minister since being deposed as Prime Minister by his party in September 2015, Abbott's statements continue to attract substantial media coverage in Australia, highlighting his capacity to draw attention to and reinforce the framing of people seeking asylum as those who must be stopped from entering the country.

While Australia's history over the past four decades includes the arrival of thousands of migrants each year, including some who arrive to Australia by plane on a valid visa and then lodge a refugee claim, it is the arrival of comparatively few people by boat to seek asylum that has attracted such claims of a crisis. Categorizing their arrival as a crisis may reflect the domestic political imperatives of those who make this claim, as well as Australia's history of colonization and its citizens' perceptions of themselves, the rest of the world, and their relationship with those who are "not from here." What categorizing people arriving by boat as a crisis does not reflect is the scale of the phenomenon.

This chapter explores how people seeking asylum who arrive in Australia by boat have been categorized by political leaders, and relayed via sections of the media, as illegal and their arrival a crisis, and the implications of these categorizations. Following Brubaker's observation that a category can be used as "both a category of analysis and a category of practice" (2012, 2), the use of the term crisis in relation to the arrival of people by boat to Australia is understood as both a category of analysis as well as practice. Similarly, the use of other more pejorative categories to describe people who are seeking safety outside their own country, such as queue jumpers, illegal, and economic refugees, are also understood as both categories of analysis and practice.

After discussing categories of practice and the dominant terms that have been used to categorize people seeking asylum who arrive by boat to Australia, the labeling and communication of the arrival of people by boats by key political leaders over the past forty years will be outlined. The implications of these categorizations will then be explored as well as an interrogation of the use of the term crisis in the Australian context.

Categories of Practice

The words used by political leaders and the media to describe or label people who flee their own countries and seek safety in another can have a significant impact on their reception in the host country. How people and their arrival are described can be understood as categories, the "intellectual boundaries" (Stone 1988, 307) used in order to make sense of someone or some phenomenon. The use of a category to refer to someone can result in their being primarily understood according to the category they are allocated to, with the consequence that they become associated with the qualities communicated by that category and their other qualities ignored. Categorization can also be a process of outlining the differences between a particular group of people and those who are considered to be members of the "in-group." In so doing, the process emerges from particular social and political contexts and structures (Rosenberger and Stöckl 2016, 3).

Categorization is a means of generating and reinforcing a particular understanding of particular people. In this regard, Brubaker's (2012) distinction between a category of analysis and a category of practice is useful. A category of analysis is the use of a term to denote how a particular person or group is defined or understood, with an emphasis on the category as a descripter (Rosenberger and Stöckl 2016, 3). Recognising that there are "actor" and "observer" categories (Benjamin and Kuusisto 2016), it is the latter that is of concern here—that is, the use of such terms by those who see themselves as distinct from who they are defining, and particularly those who have a position of authority from which they are able to categorize others and communicate this to a broader audience.

Understanding a category as a practice highlights that the use of a category to describe a person can serve to reinforce a representation of that person as primarily comprising the characteristics the category is or has become associated with. In other words, there is an emphasis here on how a meaning that may have become inherent in the category, and therefore not requiring further explicit articulation, can be reinforced through the category's use (Rosenberger and Stöckl 2016, 3). As such, the use and reuse of categories when referring to a particular person or group of people needs careful consideration. Indeed, "the heavy traffic between" categories of analysis and practice, "in both directions, means that we risk using pre-constructed categories of journalistic, political or religious common sense as our categories of analysis" (Brubaker 2012, 2). However, unlike Brubaker's focus on how a category of practice may impact on the "self-identification" of those so categorized, here we are concerned with "other-identification" (2012, 2).

This chapter will interrogate what have become the categories of practice that are communicated by political leaders in Australia about people seeking asylum who arrive by boat. This reflects that in "elite and public settings" there is a particular use of exclusionary constructions of people seeking asylum and that "discussions in these settings are routinely held to inform and shape broader understandings and policy" (Sambaraju and McVittie 2017, 100). Political leaders have the capacity to identify and categorize particular individuals and groups of people and effectively convey such categories to a broad audience given their access to the necessary resources and institutions to do so (Benjamin and Kuusisto 2016).

In particular, government ministers and agencies often have access to considerable resources to help them communicate their messages to the public. For example, Australia's Department of Immigration and Border Protection now spends "$1 million on media staff and another $7 million on public relations, media monitoring, and internal communications staff" each year. This includes twenty-two staff dedicated to "24/7 media operations" in addition to the Minister for Immigration and Border Protection employing three media officers (Gartrell 2016). Access to such resources provides political leaders with a potent capacity to convey their categorizations of people seeking asylum on a national scale.

As Doherty (2015) highlights in the Australian context, the mainstream media also tends to privilege the public statements of senior political leaders about the arrival of people seeking asylum. A significant proportion of media outlets will communicate these views uncritically, including media commentators who are sympathetic to the rhetoric used, as well as others, given there can be a reliance on media statements in constructing media reports. This may be due to journalists not being familiar with the terms and laws of refugee rights as well as the diminishing resources available for investigative journalism in many media outlets. In addition, in Australia journalists are often restricted in their access to people seeking asylum given the policy of mandatory detention and the precarious situations that many face once released into the community (Doherty 2015).

Recent categories used by the political leaders of the current Coalition Government include that people who arrive to Australia by boat to seek asylum are illegal maritime arrivals and their arrival is a crisis. These draw on the previous use of such categories by political leaders, as will be outlined in the next section, which have been consistently communicated to a broad audience over the past eight years.

Using the term crisis to refer to people who come to a country to seek asylum is to use the word as a category of practice that speaks *for* others and labels people collectively, diminishing their humanness. It also positions the site of ethical considerations about their arrival as being in the realm of how those in receiving countries are (or should be) experiencing the arrival of asylum seekers, rather than about what people seeking asylum are experiencing. In other words, categorizing the arrival of people seeking asylum as a crisis in countries such as Australia reinforces that "in general, it is those phenomena that global elites view as negative that become constructed as a crisis in public and political debate."[1] As such, there is a need to interrogate the use of this term as a category and to be attentive to the context within which something is called a crisis.

The use of terms such as queue jumpers, illegal, and economic refugees similarly is to speak *for* people arriving seeking asylum and categorize them as a collective. To identify someone seeking asylum as part of a group categorized in a pejorative sense serves to reinforce that the person is not desirable or worthy of settlement in the country of arrival. Thus these categories also need to be challenged. However, even if someone is categorized as a refugee or asylum seeker consistent with definitions in international law such as the United Nations Convention Relating to the Status of Refugees and its 1967 Protocol (UN Refugee Convention), but are then identified as part of a collective whose arrival is deemed a crisis, this still serves to reinforce that their arrival is somehow a threat to those living in that country.

In an attempt to be mindful of the impacts of how someone is categorized, in this chapter those arriving to Australia to seek asylum whose refugee status is yet to be determined will be referred to as people seeking asylum. This is consistent with recent advocacy efforts that seek to reinforce that those who arrive to Australia in boats to seek asylum are first and foremost people. The term refugee is understood here according to the definition provided by the UN Refugee Convention that outlines someone is a refugee if it is considered likely they would face persecution in their home country due to their race, religion, nationality, membership of a particular social group, or political opinion.

The term crisis can be understood in various ways, although, as Boin et al. observe, definitions usually "refer to some threat that must be urgently averted or addressed in order to avoid dire consequences" (2013, 6). In the context of how political leaders may use the term in relation to their national responsibilities and how they communicate them, crisis suggests a phenomenon that is "a perceived threat to the core values or life-sustaining systems of a society that must be urgently addressed under conditions of deep uncertainty" (Boin et al 2013, 6). Understanding something as a crisis conveys the view that a society or polity is facing a potentially profound challenge to its continued existence. In this vein, identifying such a threat leads to the conclusion that a justifiable and imperative response is to diminish or eradicate that threat. Communicating to a broader population that something is a crisis, therefore, is to outline that something must be done urgently to address the situation.

However, categorizing something as a crisis does not necessarily mean that those doing the labeling hold a deep conviction that such a threat *is* a profound challenge to the continued existence of a society. The use of the term could be for instrumental reasons, such as for political advantage through attempts to persuade the broader population that a crisis exists. Political leaders categorizing the arrival of people seeking asylum as a crisis can serve to exacerbate or create concerns within the broader population, which may lead to greater support for a political party that highlights that it is able to stem the cause of the crisis. As Dempster and Hargrave argue, "the language of 'crisis' used around recent movements of refugees and migrants into Europe may have projected a sense of vast scale and unmanageability" (2017, 20), which may not have been perceived on such a widespread scale if not for this construction. This argument is just as relevant in Australia. With the repeated use of terms such as crisis to describe the arrival of people seeking asylum in Australia, these categories of practice reinforce that this is how the arrival of people can and should be understood and that something must be done to stop their arrival.

Categorizations of People Seeking Asylum Arriving by Boat to Australia

Over the past forty years a range of political leaders in Australia have categorized the arrival of people by boat as, or something akin to, a crisis and that the people themselves are illegal, queue jumpers, or economic refugees. While there have been periods when such rhetoric has been much less salient, usually when there have been no people arriving by boat, over the past eight years (2010–2017) it has particularly escalated. An overview of the responses of political leaders to the arrival of people seeking asylum leading up to this point illustrates how the categories more recently practiced were first established and reinforced.

The use of negative rhetoric to describe people seeking asylum who arrive by boat to Australia by political leaders was first evident in the late 1970s in the aftermath of the Vietnam War. While the first boat of people identifying as refugees arrived to Australia in 1969 (a small boat of West Papuans), it was the small but increasing number of boatloads of Vietnamese that began to garner negative attention in Australia in late 1977 in the midst of a federal election campaign. Negative responses to their arrival began to be expressed by the Opposition Labor Party and considerable media attention was given to the issue. This generated increasing concerns within the Fraser Coalition Government about how to respond, given it had avoided using such negative rhetoric (Doherty 2015, 23; Neumann 2015, 251–270). Senior Opposition leaders and sections of the media labeled the people arriving by boat as boat people, illegal, and queue jumpers who were being unfair to those who waited in camps. The arrivals of boats were also labeled as "floods," suggesting that Australia was in danger of facing a crisis, illustrating a preoccupation with the perceived impact of people fleeing the violence in Vietnam on Australians, rather than the experiences of those fleeing the violence. As Neumann concludes, the "1977 federal election was the first in Australian history in which one of the major parties appealed to the public's unease about unauthorized boat arrivals," and thus the later "anti–'boat people' rhetoric to which Australians became accustomed . . . made its first appearance" (2015, 284).

Following the Coalition's re-election in 1977, and the continued use of the negative rhetoric by the Opposition and sections of the media, by the end of 1979 the Fraser Government's descriptions of the Vietnamese arriving by boat had hardened. When a further fifty people arrived in a boat in November, Immigration Minister Michael MacKellar described them as being "unfair to those in refugee camps who are prepared to wait for orderly processing" (see Doherty 2015).[2] However, rather than this rhetoric being for the government's "own policy purposes," it can be understood as "a rhetoric of defence, created by a government in response to a rising public opposition" (Doherty 2015, 25). Unlike more recent governments, the Fraser Government proceeded to help organize an international resettlement program that reduced the need for people to get on boats in the first place. By 1982 Australia had accepted 55,000 Vietnamese refugees through this program, in addition to 2,000 who had arrived by boat (Viviani 1996, 10). The Fraser Government had also put considerable effort into making the policy bipartisan and explaining it to the public. But the categorization of people arriving by boat as queue jumpers and illegal, and their arrival as something suggesting a crisis, had been introduced and would be drawn upon by various political leaders of both major parties, and sections of the media, in the following decades (Doherty 2015, 26).

It was not until November 1989, during the Hawke Labor Government's term in office, that significant numbers of people seeking asylum began to arrive by boat to Australia once again. This time most were fleeing war-torn Cambodia and by June 1995 more than 1,900 people had arrived by boat (Viviani 1996, 16). While Australia continued to accept some 50,000 Indochinese refugees from 1991 to 1996 through an extension of the resettlement program initiated by the Fraser Government (Jupp 2003, 188), official responses to those arriving by boat significantly hardened under the Hawke Labor Government (1983–1991) and the following Keating Labor Government (1991–1996).

This included the adoption of the mandatory detention policy, enshrined in legislation in 1992, that allowed for the detention of all people seeking asylum who arrived without a valid visa until their refugee claims could be assessed, for up to 273 days (McMaster 2001, 81–82). Upon introducing the bill to Parliament, Immigration Minister Gerry Hand argued that it would send "a clear signal . . . that migration to Australia may not be achieved by simply arriving in this country and expecting to be allowed into the community" (Hand 1992). The mandatory detention policy, since expanded upon to allow for indefinite detention, clearly differentiates between people seeking asylum based on their mode of arrival. Someone who arrives to Australia by plane with a valid visa and then claims asylum is not routinely detained, while someone who arrives by boat, generally without a valid visa, is detained. Mandatory detention thus serves to further entrench the categorization of someone arriving by boat to seek asylum as illegal.

By 1990 Prime Minister Bob Hawke was describing people arriving by boat from Cambodia as "economic refugees" and "queue jumpers" (McMaster 2001, 57). This was in response to media questions about his government's willing acceptance of thousands of Chinese students in Australia in the wake of the killings in Beijing in June 1989. From June 1989 to November 1993 some 40,000 Chinese students in Australia were allowed to apply for refugee status and, when most failed, the government allowed them to apply for a new visa category focused on educational qualifications (Viviani 1996, 20–21). None of the Chinese students were detained while their claims were processed. That Chinese students were willingly accepted by Australia while people seeking asylum from Cambodia were being detained and described using pejorative terms, reinforced the categorization of people seeking asylum according to whether they had arrived unauthorized or had been invited by the government.

By the time of the election of the Howard Coalition Government in 1996, people arriving by boat to seek asylum had already been categorized by various political leaders as queue jumpers and illegal, and their arrival indicative of a crisis. Perceptions of control over asylum seeker numbers had assumed increasing importance, with corresponding policy responses, despite little evidence that Australia was facing a "flood." This was soon reinforced by Pauline Hanson winning a seat at the 1996 election on a platform that included anti-Asian immigration sentiment, and her One Nation Party winning a million votes at the 1998 election. The Howard Government's responses to people seeking asylum over the following years appeared designed to appeal to this anti-immigration sentiment in the electorate (Fleay 2010, 105–121; Marr and Wilkinson 2003, 381), and its policies and the public statements of senior ministers illustrated a willingness to further reinforce the categorization of their arrival as both a crisis and illegal.

A pivotal moment was evident in August 2001, three months before a federal election and in the midst of dismal opinion polls for the Coalition, after the Norwegian vessel *MV Tampa* had rescued 433 people seeking asylum from a sinking boat. When the captain sailed his dangerously overcrowded boat towards the nearest Australian port, the Howard Government refused it permission to enter Australian territorial waters. Prime Minister John Howard declared: "I believe that it is in Australia's national interest that we draw a line on what is increasingly becoming an uncontrollable number of illegal arrivals in this country" (Howard 2001b).

In response to the captain's refusal to sail his vessel elsewhere, the government ordered the Special Air Services to board the ship and forcibly remove those on board who were seeking asylum. They were subsequently taken to a site of immigration detention on Nauru, which was soon followed by the introduction of the government's "Pacific solution," whereby people arriving on boats to seek asylum would no longer be allowed to reach Australian territory. Instead their boats would either be returned to Indonesia or they would be taken to the offshore locations of Nauru and Papua New Guinea's Manus Island and detained while their refugee claims were processed (Crock et al 2006, 116; Marr and Wilkinson 2003). Media portrayals of this unfolding drama called it the "Tampa crisis," further reinforcing the government's categorization of the arrival of people seeking asylum. Many media outlets also relayed the Howard Government's claims (later found to be false) that people seeking asylum on another boat had thrown their children overboard. For example, Melbourne's most popular newspaper reported

Prime Minister Howard's declaration that "I don't want people like that in Australia. Genuine refugees don't do that . . . They hang on to their children" (Marr and Wilkinson, 2003). After the terrorist attacks in the United States of America the following month, Prime Minister Howard linked many Australians' fears of terrorism with the arrival of people seeking asylum (Marr and Wilkinson 2003, 370). After mentioning the 9/11 attacks in a major election campaign speech, he declared that "a military response and wise diplomacy and a steady hand on the helm are needed to guide Australia through those very difficult circumstances" which includes "having an uncompromising view about the fundamental right of this country to protect its borders." He then famously declared: "we will decide who comes to this country and the circumstances in which they come" (Howard 2001a). Further policies subsequently implemented by the government included excising Australian islands surrounding the mainland for immigration purposes so that people arriving at those islands could not access Australia's refugee protection system. In addition, only temporary visas were granted to those found to be refugees who had arrived by boat and been able to access Australia's protection procedures (Crock et al 2006, 116–117).

The Howard Government's harsh border protection stance was an important factor in its reelection in November 2001, illustrating how much its rhetoric and policies resonated with the electorate at that time (McAllister 2003). The government continued to act to prevent and deter the arrival of people seeking asylum over the following years, and to categorize people arriving by boat as illegal and queue jumpers (Cameron 2013), even as numbers of boat arrivals significantly fell. While much of its rhetoric and policies had received Opposition support, the period following the 2004 election highlighted that there was also significant public and political opposition growing to the government's harsh responses (Fleay 2010, 116).

By the time of the 2007 election a collection of Australian and international nongovernment organizations, United Nations human rights agencies, quasi-government bodies, individual activists, academics, journalists, and people seeking asylum themselves had provided a rich source of arguments against restrictive government policies, including the impacts that policies were having on the people subjected to them. Many reports, research publications, and inquiries into the treatment of people seeking asylum in Australia highlighted the immense suffering and harm that the policies created. Mirroring this opposition was a group of Howard Government backbenchers who by 2006 had forced their Prime Minister to negotiate over the treatment of people seeking asylum. They ultimately raised awareness about the impacts of the government's policies and helped to bring about the release of women and children, and most long-term detainees, from immigration detention in 2006 (Fleay 2010, 121–126). In the midst of this period of no boat arrivals, the Labor Party too began to publicly oppose Australia's responses to people seeking asylum and included in its 2007 election platform that it would adopt "fair" asylum policies that included "humane" detention conditions as well as alternatives to detention (Australian Labor Party 2007).

After its electoral success in 2007, the Rudd Labor Government duly adopted several measures consistent with its platform, including closing the offshore sites of detention on Nauru and Manus Island and abolishing temporary protection visas (Briskman et al. 2008). Immigration Minister Chris Evans also announced that "detention in Immigration Detention Centres [would] be used as a last resort and for the shortest practicable time" and children would not be detained (Evans 2008). However, as increasing numbers of people seeking asylum began to arrive on boats once again, along with reports of people drowning on route, senior members of the Opposition publicly rebuked the government's asylum policies. In response, the Rudd Government's policies began to harden although, in contrast to the Opposition, it avoided using the terms illegal and queue jumper. Border protection remained the stated goal of the Rudd (2007–2010) and Gillard (2010–2013) governments but "people smugglers" became the deviants that needed to be stopped, principally because of the argument that it was their "trade" that was leading to the loss of lives at sea. The problem of people arriving by boat became framed as a transnational crime issue where there was a criminal enemy. Thus while the policies adopted were increasingly punitive to people seeking asylum, the people themselves were not being explicitly categorized as illegal or queue jumpers (Cameron 2013, 253).

The mandatory detention policy was maintained under both the Rudd and Gillard governments, and increasing numbers of people were held for lengthy periods of time in Australian immigration detention centers. Finally, at the end of 2011, the Immigration Minister began to exercise his discretion to allow most to be released from detention into the community, with the right to work, while they waited for their refugee claim to be finalized. But the numbers of boats arrivals continued to increase in 2012, along with the continued announcements by the Opposition decrying the government's inability to manage the so-called crisis. With the Labor minority in the Senate also making the passage of legislation difficult, the Gillard Government commissioned an Expert Panel on Asylum Seekers in an attempt to adopt policies that would convey that the government was "still in charge of Australia's borders" (Phillips and Boese 2013).

Following the release of the Panel's report and its recommendation that offshore processing be once again instituted on Nauru and Manus Island, sites of immigration detention were re-opened on both islands and the Gillard Government announced that anyone arriving by boat to Australia would be sent offshore. However, when more people arrived by boat than could be sent offshore, increasing numbers were held once again in Australian detention centers (Fleay and Hartley 2015). In November the Gillard Government adopted a further attempt at deterrence, declaring that all people who had arrived by boat since August 13, 2012 but had not yet been sent to a regional processing center could be released from Australian sites of detention into the community, but with limited entitlements and no right to work (Cullen 2012).

As numbers of boats continued to make it to Australian territory, so too did the Opposition's categorization of people seeking asylum as illegal and their arrival as a crisis. In July 2013, several months before the federal election and after more people seeking asylum had arrived by boat over the preceding twelve months than in any previous year (25,173; see Phillips 2017), the Leader of the Opposition Tony Abbott described their arrival and the deaths of hundreds at sea on route as "the crisis on our borders" and a "national emergency" (Laughland 2013). He announced that the Liberal Party would adopt a new policy, Operation Sovereign Borders, should it win the forthcoming election, which would comprise a militarized and coordinated response to the arrival of boats, headed by a three-star general reporting to the Minister for Immigration and Border Protection (2013). This announcement was widely reported by the Australian media and subsequently and frequently reinforced by the Opposition leader and other senior members of his party. Their repeated use of the phrase "Stop the Boats" served to powerfully reduce the complexity of the arrival of people seeking asylum to a three-word slogan. Coalition campaigning that drew on this slogan leading up to the 2013 election, and beyond, reinforced it as a categorization that while new in its wording was familiar in that it drew on understandings already established by previous political leaders (Abbott 2012).

After winning the 2013 election, the Abbott Coalition Government quickly began to operationalize elements of its Operation Sovereign Borders, including instructing the Royal Australian Navy to turn back boats of people seeking asylum to Indonesia and Sri Lanka. The categorization of people seeking asylum who arrived by boat as illegal was further strengthened through the introduction of the official term "illegal maritime arrivals."

Conditions worsened for some 26,000 people seeking asylum who were living in the community on a bridging visa without the right to work and with no indication of when their refugee claim would be processed. The Abbott Government denied most access to funded legal assistance to prepare their refugee claim application, and introduced legislation that significantly limits the capacity for independent review of claims decisions, introduces expedited claims processing, and only allows for temporary protection visas to be issued to those recognized as refugees (Refugee Council of Australia 2015). One of the few positive developments was an announcement in December 2014 that people seeking asylum on bridging visas would at least be granted the right to work, although the process was administratively difficult and it was many months before most were finally granted this right (Fleay and Hartley 2015). The other punitive policies have continued under the Coalition Government of Prime Minister Malcolm Turnbull, in office since September 2015.

Conditions have also worsened for those who remained on Nauru and Manus Island under the Abbott and Turnbull governments, with reports continuing of the terrible mental and physical health consequences for the more than 2,000 people still held on the islands. This includes people being subjected to acts of physical and sexual violence, frequent acts of self-harm, and the grossly inadequate access to healthcare (GetUp! and Human Rights Centre, 2017). There have also been eight deaths reported (Border Crossing Observatory, 2017). As at October 2017, 87 percent of those detained on Nauru and 74 percent on Manus Island had received positive decisions on their refugee claims (DIBP 2017). While the Australian deal agreed upon with the United States in 2016 to resettle some of those on the islands was reportedly still proceeding, only 54 had been resettled there by mid-October 2017 (Tlozek 2017).

Immigration Minister Peter Dutton has continued to declare that no one on Nauru and Manus Island would be resettled in Australia. In addition to making disparaging comments about refugees in Australia, the Minister recently categorized people who had been detained on Manus Island as "economic refugees" (AAP-SBS 2017). As outlined earlier, former Prime Minister Tony Abbott has also recently reiterated that the arrival of people seeking asylum is a crisis when referring to events in European countries over the past few years. After reportedly more than two years without any boats reaching Australian land (Phillips 2017), people seeking asylum continue to be categorized as illegal and their arrival as a crisis.

The Implications of these Categories of Practice

As outlined previously, people seeking asylum have long been categorized by political leaders in Australia as illegal as well as queue jumpers or economic refugees. Their arrival has also been categorized either explicitly as a crisis for Australia or as something akin to one. While there have been instances where some leaders have not drawn on the categories of illegal, queue jumpers, or economic refugees over the past forty years, such as senior ministers in the Fraser Government and the Rudd and Gillard governments, the policies they ultimately adopted in the face of growing opposition to the arrival of people by boat have served to reinforce an understanding that boat arrivals must be stopped.

Senior members of the Coalition have been particularly pronounced in their use of these categories, both during the time of the Howard Government and over the past eight years. Coalition leaders have repeatedly categorized people seeking asylum who arrive by boat as illegal and queue jumpers, and occasionally as economic refugees, and that their arrival is a crisis for Australia. The Coalition Government currently has significant resources to be able to convey these categories to a broad audience via a mainstream media that tends to privilege the statements of political leaders. These understandings of people seeking asylum and their arrival have been repeatedly reinforced to a broad audience and, given their previous use, the categories now require little justification or explanation.

Through this practice, the terms illegal and crisis in particular have become "pre-constructed categories" of analysis (Brubaker 2012, 2) that are too often used uncritically in the public and political sphere. Similar to Dahinden's common-sense categories, pre-constructed categories can be understood as being "anchored in the normalization discourse" and thus naturalized (2016, 2213). In other words, the categorization of the arrival of boats as a crisis has been reinforced and become naturalized by the continued practice or use of this term by political leaders, relayed via sections of the media. Categorizations that construct the people on the boats as illegal and, therefore, distinct from others in Australia, are also reinforced and become naturalized through their continued practice. Furthermore, they explicitly outline that people seeking asylum who arrive by boat are different to those refugees who wait in the "mythical queue" (Power 2017) for resettlement in another country. Categorizing someone as illegal conveys that they are not desirable for Australia.

It is also appears that the categorizations of people seeking asylum by political leaders have resonated with a significant proportion of the population in Australia given the extent that the punitive asylum policies of recent Australian governments have been supported. This in part reflects that this portrayal of people both draws on and perpetuates a long history of racism and xenophobia among the dominant white population. Australia's history since the beginning of European colonization is one of racism against and fear of those considered the "other" (Tazreiter 2010, 202). This includes the brutal displacement of the First Nations Peoples following the arrival of the colonizers in the eighteenth century and its ongoing impacts (Moreton-Robinson 2007). It also includes the White Australia immigration policy that sought to maintain the dominance of Australia's white population and, despite its official abandonment in 1973, its continuing legacy (McMaster 2001, 40–47).

More recently, religious prejudice and fears of the "Islamisation" of Australia have become a key contributor to negative attitudes about people seeking asylum (Muller 2016). Studies also argue that political discourse portraying people seeking asylum as "negative-others" can help to produce and reproduce prejudice and racism in the community (Pedersen and Hartley 2015). For example, Australian studies have found that people who were more prejudiced against people seeking asylum supported the negative-other representations, including queue jumpers and illegals, used in political discourse (for example, see Suhnan, Pedersen, and Hartley 2012).

The categories that have been repeatedly used by Coalition leaders for some eight years have also been reinforced by policies, legislation, and structures that have been implemented to prevent and deter the arrival of further people seeking asylum by boat. Some of these continue the responses of previous governments, such as mandatory detention and offshore sites of detention, while others are more recent. For example, throughout all of the Department of Immigration and Border Protection's materials, procedures, and practices, people seeking asylum who arrive by boat are now labeled and only referred to as illegal maritime arrivals. Such a system of classification further reinforces the Coalition Government's narrative about people seeking asylum. Through becoming "embedded" in such "material practices" (Mayblin 2016, 823), the categorizations of people seeking asylum as illegal, and that their arrival must be stopped, can become further entrenched.[3]

Whose Crisis is It?

Categorizing people arriving by boat to Australia as a crisis does not reflect the scale of the phenomenon. There have been relatively small numbers of people seeking asylum arriving in this way compared with those who have sought asylum in many other countries. For example, during the year 2012–2013 when numbers of people arriving by boat to seek asylum reached its highest, the figure was 25,173 (Phillips 2017). This was equivalent to 2.1 percent of the numbers of people seeking asylum worldwide for the calendar year 2013 (and this did not include the 50 million people already recognized as refugees or who were internally displaced at that time) (UNHCR 2013). The number arriving to Australia that year was also very small compared with the many people seeking asylum and refugees who continued, and continue, to reside in the countries that neighbor those they have fled. According to the United National High Commissioner for Refugees, by the end of 2013 there were 14.4 million or 86 percent of the world's refugees residing in countries neighboring their own (2013). In addition, Australian Department of Immigration and Border Protection (DIBP) figures on the refugee claims finalized at that time highlight that 88 percent of the refugee claims processed in 2012–2013 for those who came to Australia by boat resulted in protection visas being granted. During the previous three years, over 90 percent of these claims resulted in protection visas being granted (DIBP 2013). In other words, the vast majority of people arriving by boat were being found to be in need of Australia's protection.

The number of people arriving by boat to Australia in 2012–2013 was also equivalent to 0.1 percent of the country's population and 12 percent of the figure for the number of permanent residents accepted into Australia that year (Phillips and Simon-Davies 2017). Thus the relatively small number of people arriving to Australia by boat suggests that it is not a phenomenon that would threaten "the core values or life-sustaining systems of a society" (Boin et al 2013, 6), even if those numbers were to continue to arrive. But the construction of their arrival as a crisis is not about the comparative numbers, it is about how the arrival of anyone in this way has been categorized by political leaders in Australia, and consistently communicated to a broader population via sections of the media. It is also about how this categorization has resonated with enough within the broader Australian population that the Australian government's punitive asylum policies are at least tolerated if not supported.

It is vital that the categories used to convey an understanding of people seeking asylum who arrive to Australia by boat are both interrogated and challenged. The dominant categories outlined here clearly ignore the needs and experiences of people seeking asylum and frame the area of concern as the impacts their arrival may have on the Australian state and its citizens. Categorizing the arrival of people seeking asylum as a crisis for Australia obscures for who it really is a crisis—people who have fled persecution in their own country. Shifting the perspective of how their arrival is understood in Australia is vital in order to ensure their experiences are prioritized in how they are treated once they arrive.

Notes

1. This observation was made by Nicola Pratt in her presentation at European International Studies Association Conference, Barcelona, 13 September 2017.
2. "50 Vietnamese Boat People Arrive in WA," *The Canberra Times*, 11 November 11, 1979, p. 3; cited in Ben Doherty, *Call Me Illegal: The Semantic Struggle Over Seeking Asylum in Australia*, University of Oxford, 2015, p. 25.
3. This is drawn from Lucy Mayblin's argument that when a political narrative becomes "embedded in material practices", it can become entrenched as a hegemonic imaginery. Lucy Mayblin, "Complexity Reduction and Policy Consensus: Asylum Seekers, the Right to Work, and the 'Pull Factor' Thesis in the UK Context", *The British Journal of Politics and International Relations*, 18, no. 4 (2016): pp. 812–828, p. 823.

References

AAP-SBS Wires. 2017. "Dutton Describing Refugees as Armani-Clad 'Absurd Beyond Belief'." SBS News. September 28, 2017. http://www.sbs.com.au/news/article/2017/09/28/dutton-describing-refugees-armani-clad-absurd-beyond-belief

Abbott, T. 2012. "Landmark Speech: The Coalition's Plan for More Secure Borders." Address to the Institute of Public Affairs. Melbourne. April 27. http://parlinfo.aph.gov.au/parlInfo/search/display/display.w3p;query=Id%3A%22media%2Fpressrel%2F1603644%22 (last accessed 10 October 2017).

Australian Labor Party National Platform and Constitution. 2007. http://parlinfo.aph.gov.au/parlInfo/search/display/display.w3p;query=Id%3A%22library%2Fpartypol%2F1024541%22.

Benjamin, S. and A. Kuusisto. 2016. "Analytical and Methodological Considerations for the Use of Social Categories in Identity Research." *International Journal of Bias, Identity and Diversities in Education* 1, no. 1: 13–27.

Boin, A., M. Ekengren, and M. Rhinard. 2013. *The European Union as Crisis Manager: Patterns and Prospects*. Cambridge, UK: Cambridge University Press.

Border Crossing Observatory, "Australian Border Deaths Database." http://artsonline.monash.edu.au/thebordercrossingobservatory/publications/australian-border-deaths-database/

Briskman, L., S. Latham, and C. Goddard. 2008. *Human Rights Overboard: Seeking Asylum in Australia*. Carlton North, Australia: Scribe.

Brubaker, R. 2012. "Categories of Analysis and Categories of Practice: A Note on the Study of Muslims in European Countries of Immigration." *Ethnic and Racial Studies* 36, no. 1: 1–8. doi: /10.1080/01419870.2012.729674.

Cameron, M. 2013. "From 'Queue Jumpers' to 'Absolute Scum of the Earth': Refugees and Organised Criminal Deviance in Australian Asylum Policy." *Australian Journal of Politics and History* 59, no. 2: 241–259.

Crock, M., B. Saul, and A. Dastyari. 2006. *Future Seekers II: Refugees and Irregular Migration in Australia*. Leichhardt, Australia: Federation Press.

Cullen, S. 2012. "First Asylum Seekers Arrive on Manus Island." *ABC News*. November 21. http://www.abc.net.au/news/2012-11-21/first-asylum-seekers-arrive-on-manus-island/4383876

Dahinden, J. 2016. "A Plea for the 'De-migranticization' of Research on Migration and Integration." *Ethnic and Racial Studies* 39, no. 13: 2207–2225. doi: 10.1080/01419870.2015.1124129.

Dempster, H., and K. Hargrave. 2017. "Understanding Public Attitudes Towards Refugees and Migrants." Chatham House. Working Paper 512. June 2017. https://www.odi.org/sites/odi.org.uk/files/resource-documents/11600.pdf

DIBP (Department of Immigration and Border Protection). 2013. Australian Government. "Asylum Trends: 2012–2013." November. https://www.homeaffairs.gov.au/ReportsandPublications/Documents/statistics/asylum-trends-aus-2012-13.pdf

DIBP (Department of Immigration and Border Protection). 2017. "Operation Sovereign Borders Monthly Update: September 2017." October 10. http://newsroom.border.gov.au/channels/media-releases/releases/ecba2582-f774-46d7-b4ff-7e987056209c

Doherty, B. 2015. "Call Me Illegal: The Semantic Struggle Over Seeking Asylum in Australia." Reuters' Institute Fellows Paper, University of Oxford. https://reutersinstitute.politics.ox.ac.uk/our-research/call-me-illegal-semantic-struggle-over-seeking-asylum-australia

Evans, C. 2008. "New Directions in Detention—Restoring Integrity to Australia's Immigration System." *APO*. August 4. http://apo.org.au/node/3582

Fleay, C. 2010. *Australia and Human Rights: Situating the Howard Government*. Newcastle-upon-Tyne, UK: Cambridge Scholars Publishing.

Fleay, C., and L. Hartley. 2015. "'I Feel Like a Beggar': Asylum Seekers Living in the Australian Community Without the Right to Work." *Journal of International Migration and Integration* 17, no. 4: 1031–1048.

Gartrell, A. 2016. "Peter Dutton Spends $8 million on Spin Doctor Army." *Sydney Morning Herald*. September 1. http://www.smh.com.au/federal-politics/political-news/peter-dutton-spends-8-million-on-spin-doctor-army-20160901-gr60as.html

GetUp! and Human Rights Law Centre. 2017. "Four Years Too Many: Offshore Processing on Manus Island and Nauru." July 31. https://d68ej2dhhub09.cloudfront.net/2263-HR-Manus-Report-Print-Friendly.pdf

Hand, G. 1992. *House of Representatives Hansard*. May 5. 2371.

Howard, J. 2001a. "Australian Federal Election Speeches." October 28. https://electionspeeches.moadoph.gov.au/speeches/2001-john-howard

Howard, J. 2001b. "Interview on Radio 3AW, Melbourne, August 31." *PM Transcripts*. http://pmtranscripts.pmc.gov.au/release/transcript-12043

Jupp, J. 2003. *From White Australia to Woomera*. Cambridge, UK: Cambridge University Press.

Laughland, O. 2013. "Is the Asylum Problem a 'National Emergency,' as Tony Abbott Says?" *The Guardian*. July 26. https://www.theguardian.com/world/2013/jul/26/asylum-seekers-national-emergency-abbott

Marr, D., and M. Wilkinson. 2003. *Dark Victory*. Crows Nest, Australia: Allen & Unwin.

Mayblin, L. 2016. "Complexity Reduction and Policy Consensus: Asylum Seekers, the Right to Work, and the 'Pull Factor' Thesis in the UK Context." *The British Journal of Politics and International Relations* 18, no. 4: 812–828.

McAllister, I. 2003. "Border Protection, the 2001 Australian Election and the Coalition Victory." *Australian Journal of Political Science* 38, no. 3: 445–463.

McMaster, D. 2001. *Asylum Seekers: Australia's Response to Refugees*. Melbourne, Australia: Melbourne University Press.

Moreton-Robinson, A. 2007. *Sovereign Subjects: Indigenous Sovereignty Matters*. Sydney, Australia: A&U Academic.

Muller, D. 2016. "'Islamisation' and Other Anxieties: Voter Attitudes to Asylum Seekers." Centre for Advancing Journalism, University of Melbourne. February 15. http://socialequity.unimelb.edu.au/__data/assets/pdf_file/0009/1986201/MULLER-D-Islamisation-and-other-anxieties.pdf

Neumann, K. 2015. *Across the Seas: Australia's Response to Refugees: A History*. Melbourne, Australia: Schwartz.

Pedersen, A., and L.K. Hartley. 2015. "Can We Make a Difference? Prejudice Towards Asylum Seekers in Australia and the Effectiveness of Antiprejudice Interventions." *Journal of Pacific Rim Psychology*, 9: 1–14.

Phillips, J. 2017. "Boat Arrivals and Boat 'Turnbacks' in Australia Since 1976: A Quick Guide to the Statistics." Parliament of Australia. January 17. http://www.aph.gov.au/About_Parliament/Parliamentary_Departments/Parliamentary_Library/pubs/rp/rp1617/Quick_Guides/BoatTurnbacks

Phillips, J., and J. Simon-Davies. 2017. "Migration to Australia: A Quick Guide to the Statistics." Parliament of Australia. January 18. http://www.aph.gov.au/About_Parliament/Parliamentary_Departments/Parliamentary_Library/pubs/rp/rp1617/Quick_Guides/MigrationStatistics

Phillips, M., and M. Boese. 2013. "From White Australia to Stopping the Boats: Attitudes to Asylum Seekers." *The Conversation*. June 21. https://theconversation.com/from-white-australia-to-stopping-the-boats-attitudes-to-asylum-seekers-15244

Power, P. 2017. "Rebuilding Our Damaged Reputation: A Strategy for Australian Leadership on Refugee Protection." Bob Hawke Prime Ministerial Centre, University of South Australia. September 7. https://www.refugeecouncil.org.au/wp-content/uploads/2014/08/Rebuilding-damaged-reputation-170907.pdf

Refugee Council of Australia. 2015. "Migration and Maritime Powers Legislation Amendment (Resolving the Asylum Legacy Caseload) Act 2014: What it Means for Asylum Seekers." http://www.refugeecouncil.org.au/wp-content/uploads/2015/02/1502-Legacy-Caseload.pdf

Remeikis, A. 2016. "Tony Abbott Says European Migrant Crisis Has the 'Look of a Peaceful Invasion.'" *Sydney Morning Herald*. September 18, 2016. http://www.smh.com.au/federal-politics/political-news/tony-abbott-says-european-migrant-crisis-has-the-look-of-a-peaceful-invasion-20160918-grjole.html (last accessed 10 October 2017).

Rosenberger, S., and I. Stöckl. 2016. "The Politics of Categorization—Political Representatives with Immigrant Background Between 'The Other' and 'Standing For.'" *Politics, Groups, and Identities* 6, no. 2. doi:10.1080/21565503.2016.1194764.

Sambaraju, R., and C. McVittie. 2017. "The European Union and the Refugee 'Crisis': Inclusions, Challenges, and Responses." *Journal of Community & Applied Social Psychology* 27, no. 2: 99–104.

Stone, D. 1998. *Policy Paradox and Political Reason*. New York: Harper Collins.

Suhnan, A., A. Pedersen, and L. Hartley. 2012. "Reexamining Prejudice Against Asylum Seekers in Australia: The Role of People Smugglers, the Perception of Threat, and Acceptance of False Beliefs." *The Australian Community Psychologist* 24: 79–97.

Tazreiter, C. 2010. "Local to Global Activism: The Movement to Protect the Rights of Refugees and Asylum Seekers." *Social Movement Studies* 9, no. 2: 201–214.

Tlozek, E. 2017. "Manus and Nauru Refugees Told They'll Be Resettled in US, More Approvals Expected in Coming Months." *ABC News*, September 20. http://www.abc

.net.au/news/2017-09-20/manus-and-nauru-refugees-approved-for-us-resettlement/8962086

United Nations High Commissioner for Refugees. 2013. "War's Human Cost: UNHCR Global Trends 2013." http://www.unhcr.org/5399a14f9.html

Viviani, N. 1996. *The Indochinese in Australia 1975–1995: From Burnt Boats to Barbecues*. Oxford: Oxford University Press.

CHAPTER 30

THE CRISIS MENTALITY OF RUSSIAN MIGRATION MANAGEMENT

CARESS SCHENK

RUSSIA is in a constant state of crisis management as it deals with the world's second largest immigrant population.[1] Crises affect all political systems and come in many shapes and sizes, but are typically marked by "severe threat, time pressure, and high uncertainty" ('t Hart, Rosenthal, and Kouzmin 1993). In Russia, some crises related to migration are real, while others act as substitutes obscuring unrelated political problems, or are invented for populist purposes. Whether real or not, the government's response is the same: crisis management has become a mentality, whereby policymakers react to the most pressing problems of the day, while neglecting long-term solutions or policy programs.

A number of factors contribute to the crisis mentality of Russian officials. The country is in the midst of a long-standing demographic crisis, which is especially pronounced in the working age population, leading to a labor market crisis where as many as a million new migrants are needed each year to maintain economic growth. While a refugee crisis in Ukraine and social, political, and economic crises in the countries of post-Soviet Central Asia push many migrants to seek work and/or permanent residence in Russia, a national identity crisis manifested in displays of xenophobia often means that non-Slavic minorities will find an unwelcome reception. In this context, the government in Russia must manage competing policy interests in order to balance the needs of the economy and population growth with public opinion. Because competing policy interests are affected by the previously mentioned crises, the orientation of policymakers becomes a mentality of crisis management.

The current migration crisis in Russia, marked by these interlocking issues, is reflective of larger global trends and concepts of migration crises. Although Russia is a newer addition to the group of receiving states that urgently seek to manage migration amid challenges from all sides, some commentators have seen migration as a crisis globally for decades. Central to the current era of global politics is the political salience of the international migration crisis. Though the European refugee crisis has received the most attention in recent years, the broader migration crisis is made up of refugee flows from a variety of political crises (Syria, North Africa, Ukraine, etc.). Combined with politics in receiving countries that were already strained by integration problems from previous migration flows, migration pressures create a diabolical mix of circumstances that are easily sensationalized and mobilized in populist political projects. In most cases, however, the crisis does not originate from actual threats migrants may pose to security, the labor market, or culture and identity, but rather is a result of the way migration issues are framed by political elites and the media. Largely a political construction, migration is nonetheless framed as any other crisis, creating a sense of existential threat and uncertainty and evoking public pressure (even hysteria). In this sense, Russia is not an isolated or unique case.

Policymakers throughout the world apply a crisis-oriented mentality in their framing of migration and in the policy reform process, which serves to create the perception of crisis, respond with securitized policies that would not be otherwise justified, and obscure real crises that are longer-term in nature (e.g., Russia's demographic crisis). Similarly, the policy responses of many governments involve immediate resolute actions taken to solve the short-term consequences of crisis. What the Russian case highlights are the mechanisms by which a crisis mentality extends beyond official discourse and embeds itself into the political process. Over time, Russian policymakers have routinized crisis decision making through repeated reactionary moves that are institutionalized into law, creating continued crisis feedback loops.

Crisis decision making in the political context is most comprehensively addressed in the public policy (Boin 2009; Boin and 't Hart 2003), and foreign policy literatures (Allison 1969; Holsti 1989). These literatures address issues such as responses to recent financial crises, and crises or disasters of other types including terrorism, geopolitical conflict, epidemics, and natural disasters. Crises are often conceptualized as exogenous shocks, though recent research demonstrates that many modern crises have a "transboundary" nature that cannot be contained within geographic borders or other types of boundaries (between sectors of the economy, or a certain period of time, for example) (Boin 2009). Because of this unbounded aspect of crises in the modern period, some scholars argue there is an increased sense of risk and vulnerability among publics across the globe, which are often quite separate from real risks (Boin and 't Hart 2003). As a result, there is ample room for political leaders to interpret and frame crises in various ways, which become inherently political (Boin 2009).

Crisis framing can be used to paint a securitized picture of a given situation in order to create a window of opportunity for policy reform (Eriksson and Noreen 2002) or justify a preferred security-oriented response (Balzacq 2014). Security framing is compatible with the "politics of fear" that has become palpable in the current age of populism, which capitalizes on the sense of risk and vulnerability that comes in the modern age of unbounded crises (Wodak 2015). Populist politics often mobilize public fears around issues like migration for the sake of political (electoral or otherwise) gain. In securitized or populist discourses, migration is framed as a crisis because it is seen to threaten the security and identity of a host state and society (Huysmans 2000). These frames are then used to justify restrictive policies such as entry bans, border walls, increasingly restrictive entrance requirements such as exams and quotas, and visible enforcement mechanism such as migrant raids.

There are many instances of populist and securitized discourse accompanied by dramatic policy measures in the Russian case. One recent example occurred in 2013 when a brawl erupted in a street market in the capital of Moscow. The municipal government responded to the disorder with a crackdown on migrants, who are frequent denizens of these types of retail outlets. Mayor Sergei Sobyanin claimed ensuing migration raids were "absolutely normal . . . In any society, in any country, if an emergency situation happens, then the government and society begin to act more harshly" (Myers and Roth 2013). These words are a textbook example of securitization, showing that "the special nature of security threats justifies the use of extraordinary measures to handle them . . . by saying 'security', a state representative declares an emergency condition, thus claiming a right to use whatever means are necessary to block a threatening development" (Buzan, Wæver, and Wilde 1998). The Moscow city government's reaction to the events in the market focused on a security response, which they justified as a measure that would protect the public from crisis or threat. This response occurred in a larger context of increased mainstreaming of nationalist ideas by the government and an upsurge in antimigrant media rhetoric (Kolstø and Blakkisrud 2016; Tolz and Harding 2015).[2]

A number of experts have assessed the Russian leadership's responses to a range of crises though the lenses of shoring up political legitimacy (Bertrand 2013; Feklyunina and White 2011). Many of these characterizations argue that there is widespread bureaucratic incompetence in response to disasters, which is countered by the charismatic actions of President Vladimir Putin, who routinely interjects himself into disaster and crisis response to save the people from the failures of the state (Petrov, Lipman, and Hale 2013). The mobilization of public sentiment through crises is not unique to Russia, however, as many leaders take a personal and visible role in calming public fears and setting a course for recovery, as did Jimmy Carter in the midst of the Iran hostage crisis and George W. Bush following the September 11 terrorist attacks (Boin and 't Hart 2003). In fact, crises (whether real or created) demand a resolute response from the political leadership regardless of regime type ('t Hart, Rosenthal, and Kouzmin 1993). The Russian case can offer insight into how governments manage crisis in light of complex political situations and prioritize solutions that can be used for political gain.

Real Crises: Long-Term Solutions Bypassed by Short-Term Mentalities

The migration sphere in Russia is linked to a number of crises that are long-term in nature, demonstrating how modern crises are increasingly less time bound (Boin 2009).

The interaction of these crises creates challenges for prioritizing migration policies. The Russian case shows that long-term solutions are often bypassed in favor of policies that address short-term political threats. These are either unrelated to migration (substitute crises) or play to antimigrant sentiments for the sake of political gain (invented crises). The resulting policies are restrictive and reduce the possibility that labor and long-term migrants will be able to legalize their status and integrate permanently.

Russia's long-term crises are related to demography and the labor market, involving an aging and declining population with few solutions except increased migration (Vishnevsky 2013). Because demographic decline is especially acute among the working age population, it has important implications for the labor market, requiring upwards of a million migrants per year to maintain economic growth (Ioffe and Zayonchkovskaya 2010).

In response to these interdependent and ongoing crises, policymakers have created various "policy concept" documents, such as the *Concept of Demographic Policy* and *Concept of State Migration Policy*, which lay out long-term priorities, policy goals, and targets. According to these concepts, migration is not seen as the primary mechanism to produce permanent population growth. Rather, it is deemphasized in favor of policies that will encourage the birth rate and increase life expectancy. Any migration that is a part of long-term goals prioritizes permanent residence and citizenship, especially of return migrants and highly-skilled workers. While the government has developed programs for attracting return migrants, and for regulating highly-skilled workers, the numbers of participants in these programs pales in comparison to the millions of temporary low-skilled laborers that come to Russia each year. The selective focus of long-term priorities does not give sufficient weight to the demand for and regulation of low-skilled labor migrants, nor does it acknowledge the potential for these workers to integrate permanently.

The return migration program has been particularly criticized for producing lackluster results primarily because of the unattractive conditions it provides.[3] However, in the aftermath of war in Eastern Ukraine beginning in 2014, which sent a flood of refugees into Russia, the program was amended and refugees were given simplified access to permanent residence if they would participate (Myhre 2017). At first glance, the reform could be seen as an effort to ease entry and integrate migrants permanently, responding to a (real geopolitical) crisis with a policy that would help to solve the long-term demographic crisis. Yet underlying political goals overshadowed the potential of policy reforms.

Though there was indeed an increase in the number of participants in the return migration program from 34,000 in 2013 to 100,000 in 2014 and to nearly 200,000 in 2015, this number is outstripped by the number of Ukrainians seeking temporary legal status as labor migrants (via policies that did not offer preferential access to Ukrainian refugees).[4] In the end, the ability to integrate into the labor market or the permanent population was impeded by bureaucratic hurdles that left many refugees with undocumented status (Kuznetsova 2017; Myhre 2017). The largely symbolic effort to channel refugees into the previously criticized return migration program boosted the visibility of an ongoing pet project of president Vladimir Putin without creating truly reformed policies that would allow refugees easier access to long-term integration (Schenk 2016).

Contrast the generally ineffective policy approach toward long-term crises to the Russian government's crisis-oriented *mentality*. In the latter, major reforms are defined by immediate threats, urgency or pressure, and uncertainty, the main defining features of a crisis ('t Hart, Rosenthal, and Kouzmin 1993). The preceding example of Ukrainian refugees highlights this mentality in that the (real) urgent need to accommodate an influx of migrants created the impetus to reform migration policy, though in the end short-term political gains (legitimacy of a failed policy project) overshadowed long-term priorities (integrating immigrants permanently).

The migration policy reform mentality in Russia is frequently driven by short-term "crises" of a substitute or invented nature. Substitute crises use migration policies to solve unrelated political crises, while invented crises tap into populist politics that garner public support. Neither of these strategies meet the long-term needs of attracting legal labor and permanent migration, and often do not even meet the stated aims of policy except in a symbolic way. Resulting reforms are instituted into law as large-scale policy programs, which receive widespread media coverage, framing reforms as urgent solutions to migration-driven crises that justify and reinforce the need for restrictive, control-oriented mechanisms and enforcement. However, while policies may provide visible results in the official statistics that the government can use to measure success, enforcement remains largely symbolic in its ability to fulfill short-term policy aims and does little to reach long-term migration goals. In fact, most policies reduce the possibility for migrants to legalize and integrate, either temporarily or permanently.

Substitute Crises: Pursuing Non-Migration Goals

Emblematic of substitute crises is Russia's policy response to recent economic difficulties. Shortly after Putin's reelection in 2012, he passed a series of decrees outlining short- and medium-term economic targets. It quickly became apparent that the targets were unrealistic, and the pressure to find creative solutions to budget problems became urgent (Remington 2014). Sanctions and falling oil prices beginning in 2014 created a currency crisis, further exacerbating the economic situation. As a result, creating new sources of revenue became a driving factor in many areas including migration policy reform (Schenk 2018a). Linking migrant labor permits more concretely to tax payments became a way to alleviate budgetary pressures and is an example of how political goals unrelated to migration created an urgent sense of threat and pressure that could be addressed (at least in part) through migration policy. Purportedly simplified labor migration procedures were adopted with the stated goal of encouraging migrants to obtain legal documents. Yet increased fees and other restrictive measures ensured that immediate political goals (raising revenue) could be accomplished without truly easing migrants' entry or integration into the labor market.

Labor permits called patents were introduced in 2010 as a simplified fee-based system for migrants from Commonwealth of Independent States (CIS) countries working for private individuals (e.g. as a gardener or housekeeper).[5] In 2015, the patent system was expanded to cover all jobs and replaced other types of labor permits altogether for migrant workers from CIS countries. Monthly taxes were also increased as a part of the reform. The revenue brought in by the monthly payments nearly doubled from 2014 to 2015 (reaching 34 billion rubles) even though fewer patents were issued. Though in the first year of the new policy, revenue from patents made up a small portion of overall GDP (around 0.04 percent in 2015), in some regions (such as Moscow) it surpassed taxes collected from oil companies (Moscow Multifunctional Migration Center 2016). This fact was widely publicized in the media to demonstrate the money-making potential of patents and show the government's capacity to raise funds amid economic crisis.

To accommodate the number of patent-seeking migrants and streamline the issuing process, several regions opened state-affiliated migration centers to offer one-stop service for processing documents. These centers also became an important stream of revenue for the government, as the proceeds of all administrative fees are deposited directly into regional government budgets. In 2015, the newly created Moscow Multifunctional Migration Center brought in 1.6 billion rubles in service fees alone. Through both of these mechanisms, patents themselves with increased fees and the migration centers that administer them, the government has been able to use migration policy to address budgetary shortfalls during severe economic crisis.

Despite the claims that the patent reforms would simplify and streamline the documentation process, restrictive mechanisms accompanying the reforms have produced the opposite effect, legalizing fewer migrants. In 2014, prior to the new rules, Russia hosted 3.1 million legal labor migrants (2.1 million on patents and another 1 million on other types of work permits). In 2015, the number shrank to only 2 million migrants (1.8 million patents in addition to 200,000 work permits issued to migrants from non-CIS countries). Officials and the media were quick to frame the decrease as an effect of economic crisis, arguing that migrants who could not find work returned home.[6] While economic crises *can* lead migrants to to return home as workers see opportunities dry up, economic downturns can also lead to increased opportunity for migrants (especially illegal migrants) as employers seek cost saving measures (Koser 2010). Therefore a decrease in the number of legally documented labor migrants does not necessarily signal a decrease in the number of migrants actually living and working in Russia, but rather simply reflects a decrease in their ability to legalize their status. An alternative to the official explanation is that with the patent reform came an increased bureaucratization of the process that made patents more difficult to obtain than before.

Prior to 2015, obtaining a patent was relatively simple by presenting an application, tax payment, and identity documents to the migration services. When the system was reformed, several requirements were added. As of 2015, migrants are required to pass a language, cultural, and legal norms exam (a purported test of their integration potential), obtain medical clearance, and purchase a medical insurance policy within 30 days of arrival. In particular, the 30-day requirement, language exam, and increased patent fee became major barriers for migrants. These barriers are the likely causes of decreased numbers of legal migrants in 2015. While it is difficult to completely extract the proportion of decrease that could come from economic versus policy factors, a powerful indicator of the veracity of this alternative explanation is that in 2015 *more* migrants arrived to Moscow (the top immigration destination in Russia) signaling their intent to work when crossing the border than in 2014, yet the number of legal migrants decreased by two-thirds.[7]

This alternative interpretation demonstrates the substitute crisis nature of patent reform. The threat and urgency of economic crisis evoked resolute action, or a crisis response, on the part of the government. Migration policy was used not to increase access for migrants to legal status, but rather to contribute to the state budget in difficult economic times. In the end, the focus on solving short-term goals of raising revenues to compensate for economic crisis neglected the long-term need to liberalize migrants' access to the labor market.

Invented Crises: Symbol over Substance in Populist Policies

The need to legitimize high-level policy decisions (i.e., Putin's unrealistic economic targets) further demands that Russian policymakers frame policies (in this case the moneymaking potential of patents) in a way that will play well to the public. Contrary to tropes about the irrelevance of the public in authoritarian regimes, the role of public opinion and public support are crucial to the legitimacy of the Russian political system, giving anti-immigrant populism a key role in managing migration (Schenk 2018a).

Populist framings of immigration-highlighting threats, such as an increased risk of terrorism or other myths that migrants take local jobs, compromise national identity, pose public health risks, or are a threat to law and order by engaging in crime at various levels, are a means of managing public opinion and balancing disparate interests between social, economic, and political actors. Policy developments in Russia since 2012 demonstrate how political attention is given to populist causes, particularly amid election-year politics, inventing crises that will produce political capital. These policy developments demonstrate the government's crisis-oriented mentality as they play up (mythical) threats that migrants pose to security, culture, and economic welfare, and reinforce public pressure to create stricter policies. For example, in the wake of a new free labor zone among the countries of the Eurasian Economic Union, parallel policies that securitize and criminalize migration were also adopted. These restrictive policies have the added benefit of demonstrating muscular state efforts to control the migration sphere, especially when enforcement efforts are widely publicized.

Policies adopted since 2012 have increasingly criminalized migration, justified on the basis of reducing illegal immigration, and evoking the myth that migrants pose a security threat while at the same time offering solutions that can be framed as successful state management. The (invented) crisis of illegal immigration gained ground during Putin's reelection campaign in 2011–2012 and reached critical mass in 2013.[8] Though Putin's rhetoric can be characterized as very careful and tending toward technocratic on the topic of migration, it is also vague at times and when his speeches are quoted in the media, they can be framed in a way that supports anti-migrant views (Schenk 2018b). Therefore, when migration was a central theme of Putin's reelection campaign, it opened the door for a new phase of justifying more stringent migration policy in response to illegal immigration. Officials below the president are often much more inflammatory in their anti-migrant statements than the president and, along with a noted increase in anti-migrant media rhetoric beginning in 2012 (Tolz and Harding 2015), the invented crisis of illegal immigration became firmly established.

For example, during Putin's 2012 presidential campaign he promised to clean up "rubber apartments," or residences where numerous migrants either physically stayed or were registered.[9] After Putin's election, as the government was preparing legislation to criminalize rubber apartments, a number of sensational articles were run in the media telling of hundreds of migrants being registered in single apartments.[10] The issue also became a visible theme of several mayoral campaigns in 2013 before legislation criminalizing *false* registrations (registration in an apartment where a person is not physically staying) was passed in December of that year.[11]

A renewed focus on securitized migration policies came in response to the increasing focus on illegal immigration. In particular, policies that produce large measurable outcomes, such as numbers of those captured in migration raids or put on "blacklists," became a way for policymakers to demonstrate their commitment to fighting illegal immigration. However, these efforts are primarily a numbers game that produce symbolic gains rather than actual reductions of illegal immigration. As in the previous section, which argued that lower official numbers of labor migrants do not necessarily indicate an actual reduction of migration, seemingly dramatic enforcement statistics are not synonymous with lower numbers of illegal immigrants. Producing statistics that obscure the migration picture is a way to frame migration in a way that is politically favorable, yet in the end it does not serve long-term goals of attracting legal labor and long-term migration.

A policy innovation that demonstrates the dynamic of dramatic yet largely symbolic enforcement quite starkly is the increasing use of migrant "blacklists" or entry bans, preventing individual migrants from entering Russia. Since 2013, there has been increasing attention on migrant blacklists due to several legal changes as well as a significant increase in the use of existing legislation, which has produced a four- to sixfold increase in the yearly number of migrants blacklisted compared to 2012.[12] Entry bans have garnered significant attention from migrants, human rights activists, and scholars, and have become especially salient in the bilateral relations of Russia and major migrant sending countries such as Kyrgyzstan, increasing the crisis nature of the policy (and producing the unintended illusion that the policy is effective). In practice, many migrants have found themselves blocked from entering Russia for relatively minor administrative violations, or for reasons that cannot be determined (Kubal 2016). Yet despite the securitized thrust of blacklists and the rhetoric about its onerous nature, there are a number of points that uncover its largely symbolic nature.

First, the migration services publish two statistics related to the blacklist: "decisions about closed entry" and "actually closed entry."[13] Prior to 2013, only the number of decisions was reported, but in each subsequent year the two numbers are similar. Similar numbers make it seem that if a foreigner is put on the blacklist, they are in fact prevented from entering Russia. In reality, many migrants on the blacklist remain in Russia either because the migrants do not know they are on the list or because they avoid leaving out of fear they will not be able to return. Those whose entry is actually prevented could indeed be on the blacklist, or they may be denied entry due to unrelated problems at the border (i.e., problems with documents, violation of border crossing or customs rules, having a communicable disease or illness, etc.). Migrants who are prevented from entering Russia (whose entry is "actually closed"), therefore, do not necessarily correspond to migrants whose names are on the blacklist.

Second, while the migration services maintain a database that is supposed to contain information about foreigners from all government agencies in Russia, coordination between agencies has been poor and as a result the database is not comprehensive (Bahovadinova 2016). The blacklist created from information in the database is based on audits of records detailing administrative violations (Kubal 2016), thus deliberately gathering information about certain types of activities warranting an entry ban (i.e., administrative violations) while ignoring others. It is likely then, that the migration services have focused disproportionately on the new legal possibility of blacklisting migrants for administrative violations as an opportunity to create a visible pool of migrants to punish.

Third, a number of informal practices have arisen in response to the blacklists, both on the part of migrants and officials. Migrants may bribe officials to avoid the blacklist in the first place or send family members in their stead if they are prevented from entering Russia. If they prefer to return themselves, various strategies could assist them in their efforts, including getting a new passport under a different name, bribing border guards (which is easier at land borders than at airports), and crossing into Russia illegally. While these strategies aren't guaranteed to work, persistent migrants may find them worth the effort. The success of migrants' strategies often depends on the complicity of a corrupt official. Corruption of migration officials and police is widespread enough across Russia that it can be seen as a reliable solution to various problems, although different mechanisms are at play depending on, for example, the region, position of the official, or agency, requiring that migrants be savvy enough to know which opportunities are available to them.

Finally, the discourse surrounding migrant blacklists in Russia has dominated discussions of the migration arena, yet is often imprecise about legal mechanisms and statistical nuances as discussed previously. Not infrequently discussions of the blacklist will refer to deportation or being declared "undesirable," which are separate legal mechanisms.[14] While deportation and being declared "undesirable" often result in being placed on the blacklist, they are not the only reasons for being added to the list. Administrative expulsion and deportation can only be processed through the court system, while blacklisting a migrant can be done by a number of different government agencies, from the border services to the health ministry, all of whom can define their own additional criteria that justify decisions to ban foreigners' entry.[15] Nevertheless, increased attention to increasing rates of administrative expulsion and deportation in recent years has led to the current fervor over the related control mechanisms, their conflation, and their purported impact.

All of these factors should be considered when interpreting the overall numbers of migrants on the blacklist. According to the migration services, 1.8 million migrants were placed on the blacklist (cumulatively) between 2013 and 2016 (reflecting "decisions about closed entry"). As a percentage of foreigners in Russia at any given time (10–12 million) this number is significant but certainly not a majority. However, considering that in any given year 20–30 million foreigners enter Russia, the percentage of those not permitted to enter is actually quite low. Furthermore, the yearly figures of foreigners crossing the border have remained resilient since 2013 despite policy reforms and economic crisis, showing that the blacklists do not have a demonstrable effect on migration flows. Nevertheless, they have great populist appeal because they produce visible enforcement statistics that can be used to claim the government is cracking down on migration-related problems.

Though mechanisms like blacklists do not affect the majority of migrants in Russia, and thus are largely symbolic, they create a securitized atmosphere that both increases anxiety among migrants and reduces their willingness to engage the state. There is some irony in the fact that that policies aimed at controlling and restricting illegal migrants actually serve to increase the number and proportion of illegal migrants. Increasing the number of migrants on blacklists in recent years has also led to a situation where migrants who would otherwise travel to their home countries frequently (circular migrants) remain in Russia to avoid trouble upon reentry. This phenomenon of creating a more permanent stock of migrants is well documented in other contexts as well, showing that restrictive policies often backfire (Cornelius 2005; Doomernik and Jandl 2008; Lahav and Guiraudon 2006). Reducing illegal immigration is better accomplished by giving migrants *easier* access to legal status. But while liberalizing access to documents would solve long-term goals of attracting labor and permanent migrants, it is politically dangerous and does not produce the type of populist currency accomplished through securitized policies.

Discussion and Conclusion

Both substitute and invented crises demonstrate the mentality of the Russian government's policymaking approach. Their efforts create a perception of crisis, evoking an urgent threat, and justifying reform on the basis of public or political pressure. Yet these strategies themselves create uncertainty because of their short-term focus. This mentality tends to cause reactionary moves by the government, creating laws that institutionalize securitized or control-oriented policies, but do not address long-term priorities. The result is an ongoing cycle of policies that leave the migration sphere ripe for future crises.

Substitute crises use migration policy to solve other political goals, such as budget shortfalls, legitimizing favored policy programs, or as leverage in geopolitical feuds (Schenk 2016). In these cases, the government mobilizes support for a set of migration policies though migration-related goals are not the key measure of success. Invented crises of the populist sort focus on perceived threat migrants pose to security, the labor market, and culture. Public sentiment is easily mobilized, yet the policies remain more symbolic than substantive. Both types of crises detract from the long-term goals addressing ongoing crises in the demographic makeup and labor market of the country.

In order to solve long-term demographic and labor market problems, more temporary labor and permanent migrants are needed in Russia. However, migration policies most frequently focus on control-oriented mechanisms that make it difficult, if not impossible, for increasing numbers of migrants to legalize their status and integrate into society. In this sense, by focusing on short-term crises, the Russian government creates crisis feedback loops that ensure long-term goals will not be met. Focusing on short-term goals also creates a number of consequences, including increasing the proportion of illegal migrants in the country and making those illegal populations more permanent. Restrictive policies such as patent fees and language exams produce lower numbers of official migrants. The government can use these official numbers to give the impression that fewer migrants are coming to the country and working in the labor market. However, absent dramatic changes in the economy, if demand for labor is not reduced the likelihood that migrants will simply shift from the legal labor market to the shadow labor market is high.

The Russian case offers insights into migration management that extend to other migrant receiving countries. When policymakers approach migration as though it is a crisis, adopting securitized policies and populist strategies, long-term economic and demographic goals can suffer. If Russia, with its noncompetitive electoral system, employs these short-term strategies for the sake of political goals such as public legitimacy and electoral framing, how much more will these solutions be tempting for politicians in liberal electoral systems that force true competition for public support? In the Russian case these populist strategies are employed by the state itself and can therefore be more easily realized into policy. In countries where the most radical populism still finds itself outside electoral representation, the Russian case stands as a warning of how migration might be approached once populist strategies are implemented into mainstream politics. When populist strategies extend beyond discourse and are institutionalized into policy, as shown in the Russian case, the short-term focus creates self-reinforcing cycles of crisis decision making that solidify into policymaking mentalities.

Notes

1. Germany briefly displaced Russia as second among migrant receiving countries after accepting large numbers of Syrian refugees.
2. Russia's media is largely state-owned or state-allied, and while the media is not simply a mouthpiece for the government, there is a degree to which the influence of the media cannot be cleanly extracted from state-directed messages.
3. Namely, migrants are restricted to certain destinations (the most economically vibrant cities such as Moscow and St. Petersburg do not participate in the program) and must still go through the intermediate steps of applying for temporary and then permanent residence before accessing citizenship.
4. Figures of participants in the return migration program include those from all countries. Numbers of labor migrants from Ukraine increased from 167,000 in 2013 to 395,800 in 2014 and leveled to 210,000 in 2015.
5. Citizens of CIS countries have visa-free access to Russia and can obtain labor permits on arrival. Countries of the CIS include Armenia, Azerbaijan, Belarus, Moldova, Kazakhstan, Kyrgyzstan, Tajikistan, and Uzbekistan. Ukrainian citizens are also extended the same entry and work privileges, though Ukraine is not an official member of the CIS. Since 2015, citizens of the Eurasian Economic Union (Armenia, Belarus, Kazakhstan, and Kyrgyzstan) are not required to have labor permits to work in Russia.
6. This discourse was a risky choice in that it highlighted the effects of crisis on the labor market. The crisis was largely a political creation since sanctions from the West and countersanctions by Russia isolated the Russian economy for the sake of geopolitical goals. As a result, this strategy could have ended up focusing peoples' attention on the political elite's failures and led the public to blame the government. However, in this case the official line served to further a discourse that had been pushed in previous crises (i.e., the 2008 global financial crisis) that the goal of the government was to preserve domestic jobs and insulate domestic workers from labor market pressure, framing *any* decrease in migration (for any reason) as a positive outcome.
7. 1.7 million migrants arrived to Moscow in 2014 writing "work" as their purpose of visit on migration documents, compared to 2.4 million in 2015. Yet the same years saw a decrease in legally documented labor migrants from 1.5 million in 2014 to 500,000 in 2015.
8. Russia does indeed have a tremendous problem with illegal immigration, with estimates of illegal immigrants often exceeding those of legal immigrants. The invented nature of the crisis at hand is not the fact of illegal immigrants on the ground, but rather the characterization of why migrants are illegal, what potential dangers these illegal populations pose to society, and what mechanisms will reduce illegal migration.
9. Registration at a concrete location is required for citizens and foreigners alike in Russia.

10. While some rubber apartments indeed housed numerous migrants, others were simply covers for corruption schemes where a migration official would use an address (of either an unsuspecting person or someone complicit in the scheme) to register numerous migrants in exchange for a kickback.
11. In the end, there was no limit placed on the number of people who could be registered in a single apartment, only that those registered must by physically staying on premises.
12. The legal changes included a number of increased penalties for certain violations such as overstaying the period of legal stay in Russia or committing repeated administrative violations (which could be as routine as a simple traffic ticket or an unpaid mobile phone bill). These increased penalties added to a list of reasons migrants could be denied entry into Russia. The legal basis for preventing certain migrants from entering Russia, and mechanisms used to justify entry bans, are embedded in multiple layers of laws and government and ministerial orders, extending back to the 1990s.
13. "Closed entry" is not a legal category, leaving a gap between how the law defines migrants who are prevented from entering Russia and the statistics gathered that purportedly reflect these same foreigners.
14. A number of government agencies can declare a foreigner "undesirable" for various reasons defined by the particular agency. Penalties for being declared undesirable can include, but are not limited to, being added to the blacklist.
15. In most cases administrative expulsion and deportation are self-executed and do not physically ensure that a migrant will leave the country. This situation leads to the possibility that an increasing pool of deported (and thus blacklisted) migrants live in the shadows in Russia.

References

Allison, G. T. 1969. "Conceptual Models and the Cuban Missile Crisis." *American Political Science Review* 63, no. 3: 689–718.

Bahovadinova, M. 2016. "Tajikistan's Bureaucratic Management of Exclusion: Responses to the Russian Reentry Ban Database." *Central Asian Affairs* 3, no. 3: 226–248.

Balzacq T. 2014. "Legitimacy and the 'Logic' of Security." In *Contesting Security: Strategies and Logics*, edited by T. Balzacq, 1–9. New York: Routledge.

Bertrand, E. 2013. "Disaster, Communication and Legitimization of Power in Russia: The Case of the Forest Fires in Summer 2010." *The Soviet and Post-Soviet Review* 40, no. 2: 260–286.

Boin, A. 2009. "The New World of Crises and Crisis Management: Implications for Policymaking and Research." *Review of Policy Research* 26, no. 4: 367–377.

Boin, A., and P. 't Hart. 2003. "Public Leadership in Times of Crisis: Mission Impossible?" *Public Administration Review* 63, no.5. doi:10.1111/1540-6210.00318

Buzan, B., O. Wæver, and J. De Wilde. 1998. *Security: A New Framework for Analysis*. Boulder, CO: Lynne Rienner.

Cornelius, W. A. 2005. "Controlling 'Unwanted' Immigration: Lessons from the United States, 1993-2004." *Journal of Ethnic and Migration Studies* 31, no. 4: 775–794.

Doomernik, J., and M. Jandl. 2008. *Modes of Migration Regulation and Control in Europe*. Amsterdam: Amsterdam University Press.

Eriksson, J., and E. Noreen. 2002. *Setting the Agenda of Threats: An Explanatory Model*. Uppsala, Sweden: Department of Peace and Conflict Research, Uppsala University.

Feklyunina, V., and S. White. 2011. "Discourses of 'Krizis': Economic Crisis in Russia and Regime Legitimacy." *Journal of Communist Studies and Transition Politics* 27, no. 3–4: 385–406.

Holsti, O. R. 1989. "Crisis Decision Making." In *Behavior, Society and Nuclear War*, edited by P. E. Tetlock, J. L. Husbands, R. Jervis, P. C. Stern, and C. Tilly, 8–84. New York: Oxford University Press.

Huysmans, J. 2000. "The European Union and the Securitization of Migration." *Journal of Common Market Studies* 38, no. 5: 751–777.

Ioffe, G., and Z. Zayonchkovskaya. 2010. "Immigration to Russia: Why It Is Inevitable, and How Large It May Have to Be to Provide the Workforce Russia Needs." *NCEEER Working Paper*, Seattle, WA: The National Council for Eurasian and East European Research.

Kolstø, P., and H. Blakkisrud. 2016. *The New Russian Nationalism*. Edinburgh: Edinburgh University Press.

Koser, K. 2010. "The Impact of the Global Financial Crisis on International Migration." *The Whitehead Journal of Diplomacy & International Relations* 11: 13–20.

Kubal, A. 2016. "Entry Bar as Surreptitious Deportation? *Zapret na v'ezd* in Russian Immigration Law and Practice: A Comparative Perspective." *Law & Social Inquiry* 42, no. 3: 744–768.

Kuznetsova, I. 2017. "Dangerous and Unwanted: Policy and Everyday Discourses of Migrants in Russia." In *Migration and the Ukraine Crisis*, edited by A. Pikulicka-Wilczewska and G. Uehling, 149–163. Bristol, UK: E-International Relations.

Lahav, G., and Virginie Guiraudon. 2006. "Actors and Venues in Immigration Control: Closing the Gap Between Political Demands and Policy Outcomes." *West European Politics* 29, no. 2: 201–223.

Moscow Multifunctional Migration Center. 2016. "Sobyanin: Prodazha patentov migrantam prinosit v byudzhet bol'she dokhodov, chem neftyanye kompanii [Sobyanin: The sale of patents brought more income to the budget than oil companies]." *Press release*. February 2, 2016. https://mc.mos.ru/presscenter/news/detail/2483728.html.

Myers, S. L., and A. Roth. 2013. "Russia Steps Up Raids Against Migrants." *The New York Times*, August 12, 2013. http://www.nytimes.com/2013/08/13/world/europe/russia-steps-up-raids-against-migrants.html.

Myhre, M. H. 2017. "'Compatriot Refugees' from Ukraine: Accessing Legal Residency and Citizenship in the Russian Federation." *Conference paper presented at the Association for the Study of Nationalities, Columbia University, May*. https://docs.wixstatic.com/ugd/ff1dca_bcc7ec2e52494416b8e0810a6066c78e.pdf

Petrov, N., M. Lipman, and H. E. Hale. 2013. "Three Dilemmas of Hybrid Regime Governance: Russia from Putin to Putin." *Post-Soviet Affairs* 30, no. 1: 1–26.

Remington, T. F. 2014. *Presidential Decrees in Russia: A Comparative Perspective*. New York: Cambridge University Press.

Schenk, C. 2016. "Assessing Foreign Policy Commitment Through Migration Policy in Russia." Demokratizatsiya: *The Journal of Post-Soviet Democratization* 24, no. 4: 475–499.

Schenk, C. 2018a. *Why Control Immigration? Strategic Uses of Migration Management in Russia*. Toronto: University of Toronto Press.

Schenk, C. 2018b. "Anti-Migrant, but Not Nationalist: Pursuing Statist Legitimacy through Immigration Discourse and Policy." In *Russia Before and After Crimea: Nationalism and Identity, 2010–2017*, edited by P. Kolstø and H. Blakkisrud, 236–257. Edinburgh: Edinburgh University Press.

't Hart, Paul, U. Rosenthal, and A. Kouzmin. 1993. "Crisis Decision Making: The Centralization Thesis Revisited." Administration & Society 25, no. 1: 12–45.

Tolz, V., and S. -A. Harding. 2015. "From 'Compatriots' to 'Aliens': The Changing Coverage of Migration on Russian Television." *The Russian Review* 74: 452–477.

Vishnevsky, A. 2013. "The Impact of Migration on Russia's Demographic Development." In *Migration in Russia 2000–2013*, edited by Igor Ivanov, 194–208. Moscow: Russian International Affairs Council.

Wodak, R. 2015. *The Politics of Fear: What Right-Wing Populist Discourses Mean*. Los Angeles: Sage.

CHAPTER 31

THE UNITED STATES AND MIGRATION CRISES

Refugees in the Past and Present

PABLO S. BOSE

Migration and immigration have long been controversial topics, in the United States as in the rest of the world. Immigrants are often the bedrock upon which community and economic development is founded, providing low-wage labor, varied skills, and helping to diversify the population of cities, towns and entire regions. And yet immigrants and so-called "outsiders" have for an equally long history been targeted by xenophobic, racist, and bigoted rhetoric and practices in many of the countries into which they have settled. This is true especially (but not exclusively) in times of economic turmoil, cultural upheaval, and political conflict. In 2018, despite (or perhaps as a result of) several decades of sustained increases in the migration of bodies, capital, and labor through various forms of globalization, immigrants find themselves under assault in many parts of the world. Examples include the election of an unabashedly anti-immigrant President and administration in the United States, a referendum for Britain to leave the European Union that was largely a backlash against European immigrants in the UK, and rising right-wing anti-immigrant political movements in Germany, France, Hungary, South Africa, the Scandinavian countries, the Persian Gulf, and many other places besides. Such cases have led to the tightening of restrictions on visas and the movement of migrants, reduction or outright closure of refugee and asylum programs, and mass incarcerations and deportations of undocumented immigrants. The public discourse regarding immigrants has coarsened worldwide as well, with nativist sentiments and a rising tide of xenophobia seemingly dominating debates on migration. Such negative characterizations are not monolithic by any means; immigration continues to have many proponents as well as detractors across the globe. Yet this "hot-button" issue—which many would argue has *always* been controversial—appears especially prominent in the current moment.

This chapter focuses on the US response to a particular context in migration, that of refugees who have been displaced by conflict from their former homes and resettled in the US as a result. They are a very particular and relatively small part of the overall migration picture, both globally and within the United States. Only a very small proportion of those who are officially recognized as "legitimately" forced from their homes are then resettled in a "safe" third country—in 2017 for example, less than 200,000 of the estimated 65 million displaced persons worldwide were resettled in a third country (UNHCR 2018). And in the United States, approximately 3 million refugees have been resettled since the program began in 1980, out of a total immigrant population of nearly 45 million, far fewer than those entering the country as labor migrants, for education, or for family reunification (US Census Bureau 2018). Yet refugees are an interesting case to examine in the context of the current controversies—until recently, they were often venerated as "worthy" or "deserving" migrants due to the situations which they were fleeing (Steimel 2010). Additionally, refugees are much more directly supported and controlled by the US state, at least for their initial resettlement. It is the US state and its parastatal partners who determine where a refugee will be placed, and it is they who provide direct social services and benefits of a kind that most other immigrants do not have access to (Bose 2016).

This question of who and what a refugee is, and the values attached to such determinations is a crucial one. It is important to recognize, to begin with, that the different categories of migrants and how one does or does not fit under various labels are quite subjective. The conditions that "force" one to migrate might have considerable parallels in both causes *and* effects; that is to say that being displaced by the building of a dam, the effects of a civil war, the basis of one's sexual orientation, the impact of an earthquake, the lack of economic opportunity, or the fallout from crop failure due to drought might look quite similar (Lunstrum, Bose, and Zalik, 2016). Yet the determination of who is "legitimately" entitled to protection remains in the eye of the beholder—in this case, in the eyes of the international legal system and individual nation states. While the specific circumstances of each group and individual may differ, from a lived perspective there is very little to distinguish a refugee from civil war from a refugee from an earthquake or an asylum-seeker from political repression from a migrant fleeing the lack of economic opportunity. Legal definitions (and more importantly recognitions) are, however, another matter.

As mentioned previously, such legal recognition has not stopped officially "protected" refugees from being caught up in today's backlash against migration and immigrants. Many countries around the world and indeed the international community at large are currently grappling with a vexed question: what challenges and responsibilities do countries face when faced with an influx of refugees? How does the world at large deal with the consequences of the exodus of migrants from a particular region or country? Such situations are not new; large-scale population movements have existed for as long as there have been large scale populations. But questions about "what to do" regarding migrant "crises" need to be critically analyzed because at their heart they betray the great ambivalence that characterizes the treatment and image of refugees worldwide, both now and in the past. What is it about refugees that makes them seem such a threat that individual nations—or indeed entire continents—could be "swamped" by their arrival? What about their presence poses such a "burden" for other countries? Why does their movement within countries and across borders present various "crises" for the global community and for individual nations, even wealthy ones?

This chapter looks at the broader context of forced migration and national responses through a specific set of cases—the response of the United States to refugee situations, both in the past and in the current moment. First, it will explore the central question of what constitutes a "migration crisis" itself, following on from the recognition that this, like the "refugee" and "migrant," is a socially constructed category and phenomenon. Next the chapter will examine the global refugee regime to understand what systems are currently in place that help to structure national and international responses to such forced migration "crises." The chapter will conclude with an overview and analysis of US policy toward refugees since the post-WWII period in order to give context to contemporary practices and trends.

The Nature of a Crisis

The first question we have to ask ourselves when looking at the US and global responses to the current seemingly exponential growth in the numbers of forced migrants worldwide is how and why a crisis is defined as such in the first place—and indeed, who has the power to make and enforce such definitions. As Brubaker argues in a paper on the use of the word "Muslim" in the analysis of migration and integration of specific groups in Europe, we must be careful not to either conflate categories of analysis with categories of practice or to reify specific and narrow meanings in our use of terms. He suggests that:

> We may have no good alternative to using analytical categories that are heavily loaded and deeply contested categories of practice; but as scholars we can and should adopt a critical and self-reflexive stance toward our categories. This means, most obviously, emphasizing that 'Muslims' designates not a homogenous and solidary *group* but a heterogeneous *category*.
>
> (Brubaker 2013, 6)

In a similar fashion, before embarking upon a discussion of how the United States and the world responds to a "migrant crisis" it is important to acknowledge the constructed and contested notion of what such a term means—building on the earlier recognition that the different categories of migrants are themselves also constructed and contested. On the face of it, there appears much evidence that we are indeed in an unparalleled moment of forced migration crises. Between 2013 and 2018, the number of refugees worldwide has spiked to levels not seen in decades. Over 65 million people are now estimated to be displaced by war, conflict, and various forms of persecution (UNHCR 2018). Civil wars, ethnic conflicts, oppression of groups based on religion, ethnicity, gender, sexuality or other forms of identity, natural disasters, changing environmental conditions, and development projects are among the reasons that so many people are currently on the move, whether within their own countries or across a border (Edwards 2016). Not all of them are recognized or afforded protections by the international community—those displaced by the building of a dam or by rising sea levels, for example, are not recognized as official refugees (Penz, Drydyk, and Bose 2011). If we counted these other groups of forced migrants, potentially tens of millions more would be added to the lists of those in need. This does not even begin to account for the numbers who are displaced due to environmental conditions—loss of arable land, crop failures, severe climate events—or those driven by famine or economic insecurity out of their homelands. Yet even if we continue to limit our view of refugees only to those who have been affected by conflict and persecution, the trend toward a growing number of displaced is unlikely to abate any time soon. Even as the Syrian civil war that has driven so many from the country begins to wind down other conflicts—in South Sudan, the Democratic Republic of Congo, Yemen, and Myanmar to name just a few—threaten to spiral out of control (Doyle and Aleinikoff 2017). In just the fall of 2017 alone, some 600,000 Rohingya fled across the border from Myanmar into Bangladesh as a result of a sustained policy of what many critics have called ethnic cleansing by the national government and its allied ethnonationalist militias (Albert 2017).

However, while it is clear in this scenario that the forced displacement of so many poses a significant problem, in what way and to whom is a much less straightforward set of questions. For some, the crisis is for those who are forced to flee—how will they protect their bodies and their lives, how will they rebuild their communities and their culture, what will be the long and short-term impact upon them? For others the crisis is one of economic and political security—what will the influx of newcomers mean, how will they be integrated, what capacity is there to absorb them in host countries, how might their presence destabilize other societal dynamics? For yet others, the crisis is for the humanitarian agencies and workers, those overwhelmed by their practical and moral obligations to those they seek to help who have been caught up in conflicts, persecuted for who they are, or affected by natural disasters. In light of such a diversity of views of what the actual problem at hand is, it is thus important for us not to narrow our understanding of the "migration crisis"—it has and will continue to mean very different things to different groups. Depending on one's perspective and political leanings, the mere fact that a particular group shifts from one location to another can be seen—and responded to—in very different ways.

Does the presence of nearly eleven million undocumented immigrants in the United States in 2018 constitute a migration crisis? Many would agree that it does, but again from very different perspectives. The currently ascendant forces of xenophobia and nativism in the United States rail against immigrants for their impacts on jobs or the economy or for destabilizing culture—fears of "the other" that have scant evidence in reality. For pro-immigration advocates, on the other hand the crisis is one of millions of individuals forced to live in the shadows, faced with detention, deportation, loss of livelihoods, separation from families, and many other impacts that are much more concrete and real than the phantom fears of immigrants stoked for centuries in the United

States. When we consider US responses to "migrant crises" then, we must think critically about what the crisis is before examining any reaction to it.

If we look at the United States and its history with different types and waves of migration, we see this to be clearly evident (Portes and Rumbaut, 2014). The "crisis" of slavery led to a raft of racialized legislation and conflict whose legacy carries to the present day. The "crisis" of indigenous populations standing in the way of settler expansion led to their forced relocation to ever smaller reservations. The "crisis" of labor shortages and economic needs in multiple sectors has led to waves of recruitment of migrants both within and across borders and the response of legislative constraints and deportations when their presence was deemed less desirable. The influx of Mexican, Chinese, and Eastern and Southern European immigrants in the late nineteenth and early twentieth centuries constituted a "crisis" of racial and political identity in the United States and resulted in all manner of responses, from race riots to officially legislated immigration exclusions to deportations. The "crisis" of mass migration of African-Americans from the south to the north and west throughout the first half of the 20th century precipitated the response of "white flight" out of US cities to a newly forged suburbia and all manner of housing restrictions within the American urban landscape as a whole (Roediger 2005). We must thus be very careful when we look at the current situation of the global forced migration crisis and US responses to it in not examining this as a straightforward technical solution to a complex problem.

Forced Migration and the Global Context

When we speak of the challenges and responsibilities of dealing with such situations there are several distinctions we have to draw in terms of who is affected. First and foremost, we need to recognize that there is a global refugee resettlement system, one that is governed by the 1951 UN Refugee Convention—an agreement (or whose successor agreements) to which 145 countries in the world have agreed to (Loescher, Betts and Milner, 2008). These treaties build upon the 1948 UN Human Rights Agreement as a way of trying to protect forced migrants and arose out of the experience of the Second World War and the masses of displaced persons (primarily in Europe) caused by that conflict. They have at their core several central beliefs: that all people are deserving of protection under international law from harm, that they have the right to return to their homes once the conflict ends *but* equally that they should not be forced to return if the conditions that displaced them have not improved. There are different ways to enter the global refugee protection system—those who are able to can hopefully find shelter in a refugee camp and be granted official recognition and status. If conditions in their home countries improve, the hope is that they will be able to return and rebuild their lives. But for many such an outcome is unlikely, especially in situations where ethnic cleansing and the resulting demographic shift has occurred in their home countries. For them a protracted stay in the camp occurs—for many Bhutanese and Somali refugees, for example, entire generations have lived, died, and been born in foreign camps (Devictor and Do 2017). At this point the main solution is that of being resettled in a third country—which in the current global refugee system has meant primarily wealthier countries around the world such as the United States, Canada, Australia, and various parts of Europe.

The limitations of WWII-era refugee protections became increasingly clear throughout the second half of the twentieth century as new types of conflicts and persecution took shape, especially as decolonization, the Cold War, diverse insurgencies, and new social movements reshaped the ways in which nations, nationalism, and identity were understood by institutions and individuals alike. For example, while the original treaty was focused on those who had been forced to cross an international border in order to be counted as a refugee, today the category of "internally displaced persons" is in fact the major subgrouping recognized by the UNHCR. And while neither development nor environmental refugees are currently recognized internationally, a lively debate continues that they should be (Gemenne 2011; Steiner, Gibney, and Loescher, 2013).

Yet while refugees are given status by an international system, their most immediate impacts are felt locally, most often in the countries nearest to them. In the case of the Rohingya, for example, it is Bangladesh—already a relatively poor country subject to its own share of crises—that has been the overwhelming recipients of people fleeing atrocities. When an earthquake devastated Haiti in 2010, it was primarily wealthier hemispheric neighbors such as the United States and Canada that granted "temporary protected status" to the thousands that fled—protections that have progressively been withdrawn even though conditions in many cases have arguably not improved. Looking more closely at the Syrian refugee situation—the most significant forced migration crisis of the past half-decade—shows us a similar pattern and also highlights the complexities of challenges, responsibilities, and opportunities of these dynamics.

The exodus of so much of Syria's population is due to a number of factors including the civil war that has gripped the country since 2011. The country was severely destabilized by the US invasion of Iraq in 2003 and the subsequent rise of extremists in the region, especially the so-called Islamic State group. Syria was also one of several countries caught up in the Arab Spring, a series of popular uprisings against military rule, oppressive regimes, and dictatorships that led to the overthrow of governments in Egypt, Tunisia, and Libya and destabilized the region as a whole (Bayet 2017). In Syria, this uprising eventually morphed into a civil war, with the regime of Bashar al-Assad fighting initially against a number of secular and primarily Sunni Muslim rebel groups (Bakke and Kuypers 2016). Eventually a number of other countries and nonstate actors were drawn into the conflict, with Iran and Shiite militias such as Hezbollah supporting Assad's forces, and the United States and other Western powers, as well as, the Gulf countries and Islamist forces including Al Qaeda and ISIS supporting (or indeed comprising) the various rebel factions. The entrance of Russia into the fray on the side of the Assad regime and the focus of the United States and its allies on defeating ISIS in both Syria and Iraq decisively changed the conflict by 2016, moving into a new phase, and leaving a shattered country in its wake. By 2018 the conflict between Turkey and Syrian Kurds in the north of the country and the fall of the last rebel-held enclaves in other parts of Syria threatened to usher in yet more instability in the country. It is not surprising that in light of all of this violence—and especially the sectarian nature of the conflict, with mainly Sunnis on one side and a coalition of various other ethnic and religious groups on the other—that many millions have fled their homes, seeing little hope for a peaceful resolution. Over the many years of conflict, a significant proportion of Syria's population has been displaced, either internally or as refugees abroad. How has the international community responded to this situation, both near and from afar?

The answers are not of course the same. Geographic proximity can help determine both what one can—and what one must or is willing—to do. As in most cases of forced migration, those fleeing the conflict go to the closest safe haven—often a neighboring country. Many of these countries may themselves be poor or in the midst of their own problems—as we see with the Rohingya arriving in Bangladesh or Congolese in Rwanda and Burundi. Similarly, with the Syrian refugees, the countries that were most directly affected by the exodus were those in the immediate vicinity. Turkey has taken in more than three million refugees from Syria, while Lebanon has over two million and Jordan over one million (Culcasi 2017). Key issues for such countries include an initial verification challenge to establish that those who arrive are in fact in legitimate need of protection, the capacity to house and provide support for so many noncitizens arriving with little means to provide for themselves, often for extended periods of time, and an effect on their own local communities and politics. In the case of Turkey, for example, the country has long struggled with calls for self-determination and rights amongst its Kurdish minority—the arrival of Syrian Kurds amongst the refugees and ethnic solidarities with Turkish Kurds adds another dimension of complexity to the situation (Okyay 2017). The Turkish government has most recently launched a military offensive against Syrian Kurdish enclaves in Northern Syria, threatened by the possibility that these would provide a haven for Kurdish nationalist groups in Turkey (O'Connor 2018).

For many of the Syrian refugees the situation in neighboring countries seemed equally tenuous as staying at home, and with little seeming resolution on the horizon, many fled further afield. This led to a large-scale migration across dangerous routes, both by land and sea, as increasing numbers sought asylum in other countries. By 2015, European countries were in the grip of a full scale "crisis"—though the numbers of Syrians arriving in Europe were in the tens of thousands, not millions as in countries of the Middle East. The initial responses were primarily humanitarian in nature, as the world in general recoiled at the images of dead migrants—especially children—washing up on the shores of Italy and Greece (Doboš 2017). In Germany, over half a million Syrians were granted asylum, while the European Union agreed to take smaller numbers in other countries as well as to provide support to Turkey in exchange for lessening the flow of migrants through that country and into Europe. Such measures—in combination with the evolution of the actual conflict in Syria—have helped to abate the exodus from the country.

But 2015 also saw a significant shift in the discourse about and treatment of refugees worldwide. A growing number of terrorist attacks in cities in Europe and North

America—many of them falsely blamed upon or associated with Syrian refugees—created a backlash against their acceptance in Europe and elsewhere. In the United States, for example, the initial response to the crisis had been to accept Syrian refugees above and beyond existing resettlement quotas—the Obama administration had planned to accept an additional 10,000 Syrians in 2015 and nearly 30,000 in 2016 (Federal Register 2016). While nearly 15,000 Syrians were resettled over that two-year period, the backlash against Syrians in particular (and refugees in general) in the United States intensified during the 2016 presidential campaign and continued on into the first year of the Trump administration, with repeated attempts to block Syrians' entry into the country and successful caps on refugee admissions. Many governors and other politicians specifically sought to bar Syrians from resettling in their states (Kennedy 2016).

What caused this backlash against Syrian refugees in the United States? Some have pointed to a growing trend of Islamophobia and anti-immigrant sentiment in the United States (as has happened in liberal democracies across the world). Others have raised concerns regarding the screening and verification of Syrians and the attempts by extremists to infiltrate their migration routes. Others still suggest that the arrival of so many refugees at one time would overwhelm the capacity of host countries to properly integrate them—a somewhat dubious argument given the reality that millions of refugees have been successfully resettled for decades, especially in wealthier countries of the west. One issue in the United States has been the conflation of refugees (those who are vetted and processed through the global resettlement system while awaiting approval abroad) with asylum-seekers (those who arrive in a country and seek asylum). While many asylum seekers have arrived in European countries, the realities of geography dictate that a far fewer number could even make it to the shores of the United States—at which point existing federal policies make it highly unlikely that they would be granted sanctuary.

Asylum seekers have traditionally been a relatively small group in the United States, primarily because the US has always been highly selective and subjective when choosing those whom it deems "worthy" of protection. During the Cold War, for example, those fleeing the Soviet Union and the Iron Curtain or Cuba might find refuge in the United States, but those fleeing oppressive regimes in Central or South America—especially those from governments allied with the United States—would be hard pressed to find any safe harbor. Geopolitical considerations have always driven US refugee and asylum-seeker policies; in 2018, nativist fears in the federal government have led to the cancellation of a number of Temporary Protected Status programs that allowed some migrants to legally live and work in the United States and made the asylum claims of others yet more tenuous. Nevertheless, it remains unlikely that Syrian refugees who came to the United States would resemble in numbers or backgrounds those who showed up in Europe—yet many of the same anti-immigrant fears animating the backlash in Europe resonated amongst many in the US (Rettberg and Gajjala 2016).

Yet all of these realities bring us back to our central question—what is owed to Syrian refugees and by who? This discussion has primarily focused on the humanitarian concern—that populations under dire threats to their well-being deserve the protection of both the international community at large as well as individual nations. Yet it is also true that one can argue many of the individual countries where Syrians have sought refuge have an obligation to shelter them. Turkey, the largest recipient of these people, has played a significant role in the unrest in Syria, engaged in its own conflict with Kurds on both sides of the border, and provided aid for some of the combatants (O'Connor 2018). The United States in its invasion of Iraq in 2003 has played a direct role in creating the conditions that have destabilized the region and especially fomented the rise of Islamist groups like ISIS in both countries. Many other countries in Europe and the Gulf have similarly contributed to the violence in the region. It could thus be argued that the international community and individual countries have more than a humanitarian obligation to protect Syrian refugees; they owe it to the residents of a country that they have played a part in tearing apart to defend them from the forces of violence they have helped to unleash.

Perhaps the best example of the kind of response that *ought* to happen in these difficult circumstances is that of Canada. It too bears a responsibility for violence in the region, participating in international coalitions that have intervened in various conflicts. But unlike the United States—with which it has many geographic parallels in terms of proximity—Canada has accepted a large number of Syrian refugees (over 40,000) in a short period of time and is focused primarily on resettling and integrating them to the best of their ability (Carlier 2016). While the process has not been without its flaws, this may be the most productive way of thinking about the original question—yes, there are complex challenges in addressing the arrival of many refugees on one's doorstep, but this is not simply a choice that individual nations or the international community can choose to undertake or ignore. Instead, countries must face up to the obligations and responsibilities they have for their own actions and in the common interest of securing a peaceful and stable world protect and provide for refugees from conflicts, even if they occur halfway across the globe.

The United States and Refugee Resettlement

This final section returns more specifically to the US experience with refugee resettlement, both historically and in the current context. As described earlier, the previous decade has witnessed many upheavals in refugee resettlement patterns in the United States as well as globally. Refugee placements have been affected both by the worldwide forced migration "crisis"—with the highest numbers of displaced seen since the end of WWII—and by a serious backlash against refugees in many of the nations that have long served as a backbone for third-country resettlement. The current US administration has set as its FY2019 targets for refugee acceptance the lowest numbers seen since the inception of the modern program in 1980. But what do such figures mean historically in terms of established ceilings and admissions domestically and in relation to the specific circumstances that have driven displacement globally during the same time periods?

The US refugee program that is currently in place has its roots in the 1970s and 1980s. The modern global refugee regime is, as detailed in the previous section, a product of the post-WWII period. The United States was not an initial signatory to either the 1948 Human Rights Convention nor the 1951 UN Refugee Convention, but by the 1950s had admitted hundreds of thousands of displaced Europeans through a number of other mechanisms and through later international protocols. During the Cold War period tens of thousands of refugees from the Soviet Union and Communist bloc followed suit. Much of this resettlement was led by private ethnic and religious organizations, whose successors continue on in new forms in today's US resettlement agencies.

The most significant development in US refugee policy occurred in the 1970s. In the aftermath of the Vietnam War, hundreds of thousands of Vietnamese, Cambodians, and other Southeast Asians were accepted into the country through direct presidential action between 1975 and 1979 (Hein 2006; Miyares 1998). Recognizing the need for a more standardized system instead of the ad hoc manner in which refugee resettlement had functioned since the end of WWII and especially since the US withdrawal from Vietnam in 1975, Congress unanimously passed the Refugee Act of 1980, with President Carter signing it into law in early 1980. Between 1975 and 1979 an ad hoc Refugee Task Force worked to try and assist the hundreds of thousands attempting to flee Southeast Asia and this legislation was designed to regularize resettlement (Pho, Gerson, and Cowan 2007). The Act amended the Immigration and Nationality Act and the Migration and Refugee Assistance Act, and expanded asylum to all those fleeing their homes under "a well-founded fear of persecution" as standardized by the 1951 UN Geneva Convention (Betts and Loescher 2011). The system developed as a result of this legislation—the US Refugee Admissions Program (USRAP)—was a public-private partnership, with the federal government primarily responsible for choosing and vetting prospective refugees and its partner resettlement agencies—a collection of faith-based, ethnic, and humanitarian organizations—tasked with helping newcomers make the transition to their homes in the US (Mott 2010). The large-scale resettlements of this period up to and including 1980 reflected what has arguably always been as central to US refugee policy as any humanitarian motive—geopolitical considerations (Haines 2010).

This is not to say that there were no altruistic motives behind US resettlement during this period. The protection of human rights and responding to atrocities overseas strongly influenced public opinion in support of resettlement. Yet one might argue that a humanitarian agenda motivating refugee policy in the US was primarily driven by private actors—faith groups and ethnic communities—rather than by the US government, whose main goals were pursuing foreign policy objectives of destabilizing its international rivals and not antagonizing various allies and client states (Portes and Rumbaut 2014). This focus on US foreign policy interests became increasingly clear during the Reagan administration as the scope of whom the US would allow—and in what numbers—began to narrow (RPC 2018). Indeed, even though the number of refugees worldwide grew by nearly 400 percent between 1975 and 1985, the United States' annual ceiling steadily decreased until 1986, when it was capped at 67,000 (RPC 2018). For the Reagan administration, third party resettlement to the United States was not the ultimate goal in addressing displacement overseas. Instead, it repeatedly argued that resettlement was the least desirable option, and instead advocated for repatriation in the home country and resettlement within the sending region as the better courses of action (Bloemraad 2006).

Of those who were granted refugee status in the United States, admissions heavily favored those fleeing communist countries, such as Cuba, the Soviet Union and other countries of the Soviet bloc. At the same time, many forced migrants within the United States regional sphere of influence—such as those from US-allied regimes in El Salvador, Guatemala, and Honduras and other conflicts in Central and South America—had little chance of being granted status in the United States, and were instead labeled as economic migrants rather than as refugees or asylees. President Reagan also launched the so-called Private Sector Initiative during his second term, which brought a limited number of refugees (primarily Soviet Jews and Cubans) through private sponsorship—a total of approximately 16,000 during the eight years of the program (Bloemraad 2006).

Several decades of the Cold War-stalemate had led to relatively little population movement in Europe, but the collapse of the Soviet Union caused massive upheavals throughout the region. The Lautenberg Amendment of 1989 admitted Jews from the former Soviet Union without their having to demonstrate specific persecution (Bruno 2015). This law was later expanded to apply to other religious minorities worldwide and altogether contributed to the resettlement of hundreds of thousands. Additionally, the breakup of Yugoslavia and the subsequent Balkan Wars resulted in a tremendous exodus of refugees from the area, with over 2.5 million people displaced in the region, the largest displacement in Europe since WWII (Kandel 2014). This led to significant third-party resettlement in other countries, including the United States, which was to eventually resettle tens of thousands of refugees from the region. In 1993, the United States approved the acceptance of 142,000 refugees—the highest number since the program's first two years, even though the actual number admitted ended up being slightly higher in 1992 (RPC 2018). Toward the end of the 1990s, a second spike in resettlement approvals occurred, due to the conflict in Serbia over the struggle for independence in Kosovo. By the end of the decade, Balkan region refugees comprised the largest groups admitted into the United States, with admissions for African refugees also rising in response to the Rwandan genocide and other regional African conflicts (RPC 2018).

During this period, the United States increased its position as a global leader in third-party resettlement, certainly in absolute numbers if not in terms of per capita acceptance of refugees. In the 1980s, annual admission ceilings averaged 116,170—this includes 1980–1981, when the ceilings were greater than 200,000, while they averaged 110,400 throughout the 1990s. The actual number of refugees who were resettled in the US was slightly higher in the 1990s—1,009,885—compared to the 1980s—974,006 (RPC 2018). However, while those admitted during the 1980s were clearly related to US foreign policy objectives and conflicts overseas; during the 1990s, the United States increasingly became a key player in the global refugee regime including addressing international conflicts in which it did not have as direct or as obvious a stake, in both short-term and protracted situations. This role became especially important as the number of displaced persons worldwide grew due to a number of conflicts as well as expanding definitions for protection throughout the 1990s.

The shift in the US role and its direct relation to (some) refugee-producing conflicts meant that as the waves of displacement from the Balkans, former Soviet Union, and Southeast Asia began to wind down, the US resettlement program correspondingly began approving fewer refugees. This did not mean that there were fewer refugees in the world—as mentioned previously there continued to be many conflicts and expanding recognition of conditions for flight worldwide as the 2000s dawned (Betts and Loescher 2011). But rather than resettling large groups from just one or two countries, in the early 2000s, the USRAP began to adjust its scope by dividing the refugee intake among many smaller and more diverse cases. Refugees from nearly eighty countries were being resettled in the United States, some in large numbers and others in much smaller groups, with resettlement capacity dropping from an average of 90,000 individuals a year in 1990 to 80,000 in 2000, and actual resettlements averaging closer to 70,000 per year in both decades (RPC 2018). This led to a much more diverse refugee population and often considerable challenges in stretching resources across multiple locations while trying to address significantly different contexts—including languages, reasons for flight, security screenings, and integration capacities—for the various groups of refugees (Committee on Foreign Relations 2010; GAO 2012). By the beginning of 2001, African refugees surpassed Europeans as the largest forced migrant group being resettled in the US (RPC 2018).

The combination of shifting priorities and the challenge of resettling newer (and more diverse) groups meant that the number of admissions had slowed by the early 2000s, but the terrorist attack of September 11, 2001 resulted in wholesale changes to the program—and indeed immigration itself—across the United States and indeed much of the western world. Heightened screenings and the suspension of many visa programs—including a two-month freeze in the refugee resettlement program—meant a significant reduction in newcomers. Domestic fears that terrorist groups or dangerous individuals might exploit the USRAP to enter the United States led to a close and lengthy review of vetting that resulted in additional measures taken to heighten the security of the program and ensure the overall thoroughness of the admissions process. As a result, instead of the nearly 70,000 spaces for refugees originally allocated in 2002, just over 27,000 individuals were actually allowed into the country, the lowest on record since the passing of the Refugee Act of 1980 (RPC 2018). Globally, refugee acceptance numbers in third countries also fell sharply. Between 2001 and 2003, the USRAP was characterized by low admission numbers, reflecting these changes to the admissions process. Additionally, global instability in multiple regions meant that planned interviews were often put on hold and vetting of applicants in many places moved at a snail's pace. By 2004, however, new screening mechanisms and the focus on different groups meant that admissions began to recover as they rose to above 50,000 for 2004–2005. As former US State Department official Arthur E Dewey, Assistant Secretary for Population, Refugees, and Migration stated in 2003, "9/11 may have given us reason to be more vigilant about those who may threaten us, but it has not diminished our commitment to aiding and protecting the world's most vulnerable people" (Dewey, 2003).

The USRAP slowly increased admissions over the next few years; by 2009 the number of refugees approved for resettlement reached 70,000 again for the first time since 2000 (RPC, 2018). The annual ceiling never fell below 70,000 during the Obama administration, and each of the final four years saw admissions within 100 persons of the ceiling. Admissions dipped in FY2011 and 2012, but asylum figures for those years were slightly higher than usual.

Between FY2012 and FY2014 the USRAP was approving close to 75,000 refugees each year for admission to the United States. In response to the Syrian civil war and resulting migration crisis—especially in the huge increase in asylum-seekers from the Middle East and North Africa to Europe and other parts of the world—the Obama administration raised the annual ceiling in FY2016 to 85,000 (Federal Register, 2016) and unlike in previous years the actual number of refugees who arrived in the United States came close to matching those approved. For FY2017, the Obama administration planned on an even greater expansion, with an approval ceiling of 110,000 refugees—somewhat closer to the numbers in the USRAP's peak periods during the early 1980s and mid 1990s and the highest in over twenty years (Federal Register, 2017). For the Obama administration, this was a question of both need—by 2015 there were over 45 million refugees and displaced persons worldwide—and of the United States having the capacity to absorb more refugees.

Others, however, did not agree with this assessment. Refugee resettlement, which has always represented a fairly small part of the overall immigration landscape in the United States, became especially politicized due to a number of reasons. European anxieties regarding an influx of migrants, growing Islamophobia, and mass terrorist attacks carried out by Islamic extremists across the globe—often blamed on refugees and asylum-seekers but carried out for the most part by native-born or immigrant (but not refugee) individuals and groups—led to a significant backlash against refugees worldwide. In the United States, multiple state governors and a smaller number of cities announced in November 2015 (following the mass attacks in Paris) that they would no longer support refugee resettlement in their areas. The issue became a central feature of the Republican presidential primaries in 2015–2016, with eventual leading candidate Donald Trump taking a leading role in advocating against refugee resettlement, especially from Muslim-majority countries. In 2016 states like Texas and Maine officially withdrew from the USRAP, though refugees were still resettled in those states, especially Texas, which has the largest share of refugee arrivals in the United States (Kennedy 2016). And following his surprise election, the ascendance of Trump to the US presidency ushered in an era of uncertainty and anxiety for the USRAP.

Such fears, it seems, were not unfounded. In one of his first acts, President Trump instituted a ban on arrivals from several Muslim majority nations as well as an immediate suspension and review of the USRAP, all in the name of national security. While these so-called "travel bans" were challenged successfully in court in the months to follow, the resettlement program in particular was deeply affected (Pierce and Meissner 2017). Where the USRAP and the many government and nonprofit agencies that comprise the program had planned on expanding in 2017, in practice what occurred was the opposite. The program ended up settling little more than 50,000 people—far less than half of what the Obama Administration had planned, and more in line with what the original travel ban had threatened. In fall 2017, when the USRAP approval numbers for F2018 were released, the total admissions had been slashed drastically, to a record low of 45,000—by far the lowest since the inception of the program in 1980 (Federal Register, 2017). This is at a time when refugees and forced migrants around the world are at an all-time high—more than at any point in the past century including World War II, with nearly 66 million persons forced to flee to a refugee camp in a neighboring country, housed in an internally displaced persons camp, seeking asylum, or granted refugee status in a third country (UNHCR 2018).

There are those who argue that cutting refugee numbers is just "common sense" in terms of both security and in terms of focusing the United States' humanitarian efforts on its own citizens. And it is true that both of these concerns are real ones—the US government has a duty to protect its people and to provide services to those who need them. It is also true that the threat of extremism has only grown in recent years. But are refugees or the USRAP to blame for any of this? There is no evidence that they are. Indeed, contrary to the assertions of some politicians that refugees are not properly "vetted" or that we do not know who they are or what they believe, refugees are among the most heavily screened groups in the US. To be approved for resettlement in the United States one must go through an average of one thousand days of screenings. Of the over three million refugees resettled since the program's inception and nearly 900,000 since 9/11, only three have been convicted of terrorism-related charges, all of them for overseas activities (Newland 2015). Additionally, the argument that refugee resettlement is a drain on other programs has little evidence backing it; most serious scholarly research would suggest on the contrary that there is a substantial net economic benefit to refugee resettlement in the United States (Evans and Fitzgerald 2017). Refugees have also been resettled in many places outside of the traditional metropolitan gateway cities of the United States (Massey 2008; Singer and Wilson 2011). For many of these communities—often in the rustbelt or with declining or aging populations—refugees bring in much needed vitality, start new businesses, provide a more stable taxpayer base, and diversify schools and neighborhoods (Bose 2016).

While the United States has played a historically significant role—especially in the past three decades—in global refugee resettlement, the trends set by the current administration move the country in the opposite direction. Where the United States has at times accepted more than all other countries combined (though per capita the Scandinavian countries take more refugees), drastically cutting the program imperils the very delicate systems of protection that have emerged to help those in the greatest need. Moreover, by shrinking the USRAP and limiting the scope of its protections, the United States undermines its own moral leadership in the area of human rights, as well as weakening its geopolitical importance with allies and neighbors.

References

Albert, E. 2017. "The Rohingya Migrant Crisis." Council on Foreign Relations. September 13. https://www.cfr.org/backgrounder/rohingya-migrant-crisis

Bakke, P. C. and J. A. Kuypers. 2016. "The Syrian Civil War, International Outreach, and a Clash of Worldviews." *KB Journal* 11, no. 2: 1–3

Bayet, A. 2017. *Revolution without Revolutionaries: Making Sense of the Arab Spring*. Stanford, CA: Stanford University Press

Betts, A., and Loescher, G. 2011. *Refugees in International Relations*. Oxford: Oxford University Press.

Bloemraad, I. 2006. *Becoming a Citizen: Incorporating Immigrants and Refugees in the United States and Canada*. Berkeley: University of California Press.

Bose, P. S. 2016. "Challenging Homogeneity: Refugees in a Changing Vermont." In *After the Flight: The Dynamics of Refugee Settlement and Integration*, edited by M. Poteet and S. Nourpanah, 228–253. Newcastle-upon-Tyne, UK: Cambridge Scholars Publishing.

Brubaker, R. 2013. "Categories of Analysis and Categories of Practice: A Note on the Study of Muslims in European Countries of Immigration." *Ethnic and Racial Studies* 36, no. 1: 1–8.

Bruno, A. 2015. "Refugee Admissions and Resettlement Policy." *Current Politics and Economics of the United States, Canada, and Mexico* 17, no. 3: 485–500.

Carlier, M. 2016. "Explaining Differences in the Canadian and American Response to the Syrian Refugee Crisis." *Virginia Policy Review* 9, no. 2: 56–82

Committee on Foreign Relations. 2010. *Abandoned upon Arrival: Implications for Refugees and Local Communities Burdened by a U.S. Resettlement System That Is Not Working* (No. 9780160862458 0160862450). Washington: US Government Printing Office.

Culcasi, K. 2017. "Displacing Territory: Refugees in the Middle East." *International Journal of Middle East Studies* 49, no. 2: 323–326

Devictor, X., and Q-T Do. (2017) "How Many Years Have Refugees Been in Exile?" *Population and Development Review* 43, no. 2: 355–369

Dewey, A. 2003. "Immigration after 9/11: The View from the United States." Remarks to the American Society for International Law, Washington, DC, April 3, 2003. https://2001-2009.state.gov/g/prm/rls/2003/37906.html

Doboš, P. 2017. "Imaginative Geographies of Distant Suffering: Two Cases of the Syrian Civil War on Television" *Social & Cultural Geography* 9365:1–25

Doyle, M., and A. Aleinikoff. 2017. "Global Refugee Crisis" *Forced Migration Forum*. February 13. https://forcedmigrationforum.com/2017/02/13/global-refugee-crisis/

Edwards, A. 2016. "Global Forced Migration Hits Record High." *UNHCR*. June 20. http://www.unhcr.org/news/latest/2016/6/5763b65a4/global-forced-displacement-hits-record-high.html

Evans, W. and D. Fitzgerald, D. 2017. "The Economic and Social Outcomes of Refugees in the United States: Evidence from the ACS." National Bureau of Economic Research Working Paper No. 23498. June 2017.

Federal Register. 2016. Presidential Determination on Refugee Admissions for Fiscal Year 2017. 81 FR 70315. Executive Office of the President. No. 2016-13. September 28. https://www.federalregister.gov/documents/2016/10/11/2016-24736/presidential-determination-on-refugee-admissions-for-fiscal-year-2017

Federal Register. 2017. Presidential Determionation on Refugee Admissions for Fiscal Year 2018. 82 FR 49083. Executive Office of the President. No. 2017-23140.

September 29. https://www.federalregister.gov/documents/2017/10/23/2017-23140/presidential-determination-on-refugee-admissions-for-fiscal-year-2018

GAO. 2012. "Refugee Resettlement: Greater Consultation with Community Stakeholders Could Strengthen the Program." GAO-12-729. Washington: US Government Printing Office.

Gemenne, F. 2011. "How They Became the Human Face of Climate Change: Research and Policy Interactions in the Birth of the 'Environmental Migration' Concept." In *Migration and Climate Change*, edited by É Piguet, A. Pécoud, and P. de Guchteneire, 225–260. Cambridge, UK: Cambridge University Press:

Haines, D. W. 2010. *Safe Haven? A History Of Refugees in America*. Sterling, VA: Kumarian.

Hein, J. 2006. *Ethnic Origins: The Adaptation of Cambodian and Hmong Refugees in Four American Cities*. New York: Russell Sage.

Kandel, W. A. 2014. "Permanent Legal Immigration to the United States: Policy Overview" Congressional Research Service 7-5700. https://fas.org/sgp/crs/homesec/R42866.pdf.

Kennedy, M. (2016). "Texas Pulls Out Of Federal Refugee Resettlement Program." *NPR*. September 30. http://www.npr.org/sections/thetwo-way/2016/09/30/496098507/texas-pulls-out-of-federal-refugee-resettlement-program

Loescher, G., A. Betts, and J. Milner. 2008. *The United Nations High Commissioner for Refugees (UNHCR): The Politics and Practice of Refugee Protection into the 21st Century*. London: Routledge.

Lunstrum, E., P. S. Bose, A. Zalik. 2016. "Environmental Displacement: The Common Ground of Climate Change, Extraction and Conservation." *Area* 48, no. 2: 130–133.

Massey, D. S. 2008. *New Faces in New Places: The Changing Geography of American Immigration*. New York: Russell Sage Foundation.

Miyares, I. 1998. *The Hmong Refugees Experience in America: Crossing The River*. New York: Routledge.

Mott, T. E. 2010. "African Refugee Resettlement in the US: The Role and Significance of Voluntary Agencies." *Journal of Cultural Geography* 27, no. 1: 1–31.

Newland, K. 2015. "The US Record Shows that Refugees Are Not a Threat." Migration Policy Institute. https://www.migrationpolicy.org/news/us-record-shows-refugees-are-not-threat

O'Connor, T. 2018. "Turkey Is Launching the Next Middle East War with Attacks on Kurds in Iraq and Syria." *Newsweek*. March 21. http://www.newsweek.com/turkey-launching-next-middle-east-war-attacks-kurds-iraq-syria-855945

Okyay, A. 2017. "Turkey's Post-2011 Approach to Its Syrian Border and Its Implications for Domestic Politics." *International Affairs* 93, no. 4: 829–846

Penz, P., J. Drydyk, and P. Bose. 2011. *Displacement by Development: Ethics, Rights and Responsibilities*. Cambridge, UK: Cambridge University Press

Pho, T.-L., J. Gerson, and S. Cowan. 2007. *Southeast Asian Refugees and Immigrants in the Mill City: Changing Families, Communities, Institutions—Thirty Years Afterward*. Burlington, UK: University Press of New England.

Pierce, S. and D. Meissner. 2017. *Revised Trump Executive Order and Guidance on Refugee Resettlement and Travel Ban*. Washington, DC: Migration Policy Institute.

Portes, A. and R. Rumbaut. 2014. *Immigrant America: A Portrait*. Berkeley: University of California Press.

Rettberg, J. W., and R. Gajjala. 2016. "Terrorists or Cowards: Negative Portrayals of Male Syrian Refugees in Social Media." *Feminist Media Studies* 16, no. 1: 178–181.

Roediger, D. 2005. *Working toward Whiteness: How America's Immigrants Became White: The Strange Journey from Ellis Island to the Suburbs*. New York: Perseus.

RPC. 2018. "Admissions and Arrivals." http://www.wrapsnet.org/admissions-and-arrivals/

Singer, A., and J. H. Wilson. 2011. "From 'There to Here': Refugee Resettlement in Metropolitan America." In *Race, Ethnicity, and Place in a Changing America*, edited by J. Frazier, E. Tettey-Fio, N. Henry, 364–388. 2nd ed. Albany: State University of New York Press.

Steimel, S. 2010. "Refugees as People: The Portrayal of Refugees in American Human Interest Stories." *Journal of Refugee Studies* 23, no. 2: 219–237.

Steiner, N., M. Gibney, and G. Loescher, eds. 2013. *Problems of Protection: The UNHCR, Refugees, and Human Rights*. London: Routledge.

UNHCR. 2018. "Figures at a Glance: Forcibly Displaced People Worldwide." http://www.unhcr.org/figures-at-a-glance.html

US Census Bureau. 2018. "Foreign Born." https://www.census.gov/topics/population/foreign-born.html

CHAPTER 32

DEPORTATION, CRISIS, AND SOCIAL CHANGE

HEIKE DROTBOHM AND INES HASSELBERG

In contemporary migration policy and practice across the globe, migration has been so liberally and persistently linked to crisis that it has become hard to dissociate one from the other. In this context deportation has emerged as an apparently inevitable response to real, or otherwise perceived, migration crises. However, we share with others a skeptical attitude towards the analytic use of "crisis" in the context of migration and concentrate on the political genealogy of the term, which culminates in the justification of "emergency" policies and the implementation of new measures of control. Nonetheless—when states govern undocumented or unwanted residents through deportation and employ the notion of crisis for justifying irregular and often violent acts towards deportable subjects, a situation emerges that shares key characteristics with the definition of crisis: not only deportees, but also their families and other community members perceive the threat, the execution and the outcome of deportation as a radical disruption of the norm, a break of a situation considered normal, stable and healthy. In this chapter we will unpack the political uses of deportation vis-à-vis the logic of crisis. In doing so we wish to complicate popular and political notions of membership, security and mobility.

The notion of deportation includes all persons—typically foreign nationals—removed by a given state from its own territory. While the grounds of removal may vary, and will be discussed further down, those most affected by deportation policies tend to be failed asylum seekers, visa overstayers, regular migrants convicted of criminal offenses, and other undocumented migrants. Due to the constantly changing conditions of noncitizen residency, even so-called "permanent residents" cannot rely fully on the permanence of a territorial inclusion they had been granted before. It is not always easy however to determine whether a particular departure should be taken as deportation or not, as many forms of departure, while not officially marked as deportation may be, and are indeed, experienced as such for those forced to leave. During the last years, the distinction between assisted voluntary return schemes and self-deportation also gained prominence, the former simplifying (as well as accelerating) the return of rejected asylum seekers by providing return tickets or financial reintegration assistance upon return, the latter indicating a self-organized return prior to legal measures such as detention and the imposition of a ban on return. In both cases, the distinction between voluntariness and coercion is blurred, as both modes of return occur when the state has made clear its intention to enforce removal. Preventive measures such as pushback operations in the Mediterranean Sea and Australia´s detention in offshore centres in Manus Island, to name only two, have come to further complicate definitions of deportation, as migrants are removed before reaching the physical territory of the state that is excluding them. In this chapter we take deportation in its broader sense, except when stated otherwise.

It is even more complicated to quantify deportation, let alone provide cross-country comparative statistics. Not only do practices of forced return that qualify as deportation vary across jurisdictions, but also there is no immediately accessible compilation of such data worldwide.[1] And yet a quick look at national deportation annual figures for a number of countries across the world reveals an alarming situation that has not gone unnoticed. In 2016 the United States (US) removed 240,255 foreign-nationals from its territory, while the member-states of the European Union (EU) ordered over 500,000 non-EU citizens to leave its territory and forcibly removed an additional 230,000 people (Eurostat 2017).[2] Australia's figure may appear modest in comparison and yet it stands at 14,660 removals for 2016/17, with South Africa amounting to 23,004 deportations for the same period (Australian Government 2017, Republic of South Africa 2017). Over the past two decades a plethora of academic texts, policy briefs, institutional reports, and articles of investigative journalism have documented the devastating impacts of deportation and deportability in deporting countries as well as in the countries at the receiving end of such practices. The contemporary uses of deportation have been described and conceptualized as the deportation turn (Gibney 2008), deportation regime (Peutz and de Genova 2010), the age of deportation (Boehm 2016), the deportation crisis (Golash-Boza and Hondagneu-Sotelo 2013) and perhaps more vividly as a deportations delirium (Kanstroom and Lykes 2015), to name but a few. These terms point to the systematic and persistent nature of deportation enforcement in contemporary society. The word "delirium," in addition, supports the reality that deportation has become to a large segment of the foreign-national population in a large number of jurisdictions across the world, while simultaneously drawing our attention to an almost irrational undertext to it. In fact, despite its dubious effectiveness, and its well documented adverse impacts and legacies, deportation remains the preferred tool to deal with "unwanted" foreign-nationals. What was otherwise an exception has become a normalized tool of state power. In looking at its close links to the construction of crisis we will in the next section reveal the need to unpick the complicated relation between crisis and deportation. We will then focus critically on the specific modes of engagement between crisis and deportation. The parlance of crisis often implies a radical transformation separating the pre-crisis period from that of post-crisis (Lindley 2014b). Yet, we question to what extent are deportation crises transformative? And transformative for whom? In looking at the epistemological interconnections between deportation, crisis and social change we seek to explore such questions and pave the way for further questioning of the rationale of deportation in the context of crisis.

Mobility, Crisis, and Deportation

According to Narotzky and Besnier (2014), the notion of crisis can be understood as being part of a trope in which ordinary people reason about well-being and its achievement. "Crisis contrasts with forms of stability that enable the design of projects and that support the trust that existing configuration will enable the realiziation of those projects" (Narotzky and Besnier 2014, S7). At the same time, the labeling of particular events or circumstances as *crisis* is not an apolitical act. Quite on the contrary, it has been shown before how the logic of crisis persistently enables the management of undesirable events in ways that serve the political aims of a particular group (Roitman 2014). The notion of crisis is a powerful political instrument because it demarcates particular conditions or situations as unexpected, extraordinary, threatening, and potentially transformative. The way a problem is defined—and the very fact that a particular occurrence is defined as problem in the first place—will determine its solution. Crises thus allow for specific sets of policies to be put into practice, while providing an opportunity to veil the continuing structural inequality affecting particular segments of the population (Agamben 1998; Dauvergne 2016; Peutz and De Genova 2010).

When it comes to migration, the parlance of crisis has been used profusely, but prevalent assumptions in current public and political discourse connecting migration to crisis are nevertheless politically charged and demand unpacking. Holmes and Castañeda (2016, 12) see the construction of events as crisis as part of a "war of position," a political struggle over meaning, legitimization and the power of representations. Often the fruit of what remains a sedentarist mode of thought (Lindley 2014b), such connections take human mobility, and migration in particular, as both exceptional and menacing, much like crises themselves (Dauvergne 2016; Lindley 2014b; see also contributions in Lindley 2014a). Often, the "crisis frame" reflects both "regimes of power as well as fears and imaginations regarding the unknown future" (Holmes and Castañeda 2016, p. 29). Particular circumstances where the movement and circulation of people is heightened, or their mobility significantly restrained, are articulated as crisis by political actors when it "serves to justify, or reorient the dominant policy agenda in ways they deem desirable" (Lindley 2014b, 6). Most importantly, the parlance of crisis enables the adoption and enforcement of emergency practices that are otherwise exceptional (Agamben 2005, but also Jeandesboz and Pallister-Wilkins 2014). Such responses not only have the potential to mask underlying and ongoing marginalization and vulnerabilities, but they also "methodically procrastinate to a never attainable future the analysis of the conditions that enable them" (Albahari 2015, 13). "Emergencies do not last two decades," Albahari writes in the context of the Mediterranean cross-sea migration, "the political priorities, active policies, and structural negligence that perpetuate them as such do" (2015, 203). Focusing on what are perceived as temporary but urgent needs successfully moves the gaze away from root causes allowing states to sidestep questions of responsibility (Albahari 2015; Jeandesboz and Pallister-Wilkins 2014; Lindley 2014b).

And yet, what is taken—or constructed—as crisis by government bodies may not be experienced as such my migrants and their families. Bylander (2017) shows how this was the case when in 2014 there was a mass return exodus of Cambodian migrants from Thailand. Although depicted as an alarming crisis by the media and the political elites on both sides of the border, the events were experienced and understood by those returning to Cambodia, and their families, as just a "more extreme version of the everyday" (2017, 1) where the " most significant impacts of the exodus—financial loss, indebtedness, involuntary immobility, and fear of violence and deportations—have been, and continue to be regular features of the Cambodian-Thai migration system"(2017, p. 6). Bylander shows the continuities between the perceived stable and crisis times, and in doing so, she reveals everyday forms of control that have been developed over time (see Jeandesboz and Pallister-Wilkins 2014, 117) and that impact on and restrict the lives of irregularised migrants in Thailand. It points also to the normalcy—not exceptionality—of deportation in the everyday lives of vulnerable migrants. Comparable situations have been described in the context of Afghanistan (Khosravi 2016; Schuster and Majidi 2013), Zimbabwe (Galvin 2015) or the US (de León 2015), when deportees are pushed back or returned, sometimes frequently, from neighboring countries. These studies show that deportation can be so widespread as to become a routine and ordinary event, eventually perceived mainly as an annoying hazard (Schuster and Majidi 2013, 646).

As mentioned above, the logic of crisis assumes that some sort of stability has been breached by unusual events that consequently produce extraordinary consequences. In doing so it suggests that "precarity, vulnerability, and exclusion are produced through acute changes to, or crisis within, otherwise stable migration systems" (Bylander 2017, 3). It fails to see that such consequences may not be as extraordinary as they seem, rendering invisible the ongoing and normalized vulnerability and precariousness of certain groups of the population. Instead of using the logic of crisis, Bylander argues for the adoption of a framework that provides an understanding of the continuities across regular and extraordinary times and circumstances.

On the one hand, we can summarize that deportation today is hardly new, extraordinary, or unexpected. But, on the other, combining deportation and the notion of crisis may still be a useful framework as it allows us to question the articulation of such circumstances as crisis, and to take into consideration more nuanced understandings and experiences of those directly affected by it. Furthermore, in revealing continuities across pre-crisis and crisis times, such an approach has the potential to unveil the unfailing and tenacious vulnerability and precariousness of deportable and deported populations across the world. Yet, this is not to say that crises do not exist, or that only the political elites have the power to conjure them. Quite to the contrary, crises is an emic term, which proliferates in contemporary society and may be articulated as such also by those experiencing it or lobbying for change or both.

In the following sections, we will complicate the engagement between crisis and deportation by first looking at how deportation came to be articulated as the unavoidable way to respond to crisis. We will then move our gaze away from deportation as response and towards deportation as cause of crises revealing the transformative potential of deportation and related practices of detention and control.

Responding to Crisis

Financial crisis and their social impact on the lives of migrants has long been linked to voluntary and forced return. With regards to voluntary return, the tendency has been to assume that a given financial loss can encourage migrants to return to their countries of origin, in particular as demand for labor decreases. Yet studies have consistently challenged this assumption (Bylander 2017). Boccagni and Lagomarsino (2011) for instance, conducted research among Ecuadorian migrants in Spain at a time of global economic crisis. While both Spain and Ecuador developed programs to incentivize the exit or return of Ecuadorians, the authors found that economic crisis and unemployment were not enough motivations to leave Spain. This was so in particular when stable social relationships had been developed in Spain, investment in housing or business enterprises had been made, or where children were well settled. From migrants' point of view, return was thus "not contingent on economic factors only" (2011, 293) and most opted to wait out the crisis. Assumptions linking financial crisis with voluntary return thus tend to downplay how rooted migrants may already be in their countries of residence.

On the other hand, however, in times of financial crisis it is not uncommon that "states engage in strong migration restriction and deportation . . . in an attempt to mitigate the impact of crisis on the local population" (Lindley 2014b, 18). In fact, in the US context, the work of Tanya Golash-Boza and colleagues has been instrumental in revealing and analysing the correlations between global financial crises and periods of mass deportation (Golash-Boza 2016; Golash-Boza and Hondagneu-Sotelo 2013; Patler and Golash-Boza 2017). They show how mass deportation has become a tool of state repression in times of financial recession. In fact, the use of deportation in times of crisis is not successful only in allegedly alleviating the labor market by removing a "surplus" of work force. Most importantly, deportation policies comply with public expectations and electoral politics; they assure the voting public that the problem has been identified and is being addressed through state power (Bosworth 2008; Gibney and Hansen 2003; Hasselberg 2016a; Leerkes and Broeders 2010). In seeking to expel the unwanted, deportation reveals "citizenry as community of value as much as community of law," and this is where the symbolic and definitive power of deportation lies (Anderson et al. 2011, 548). History has shown that the tightening of immigration laws and the facilitated removal of aliens can be observed particularly in politically strained times, when populist movements employ symbolic actions for protecting the citizens of wealthy nations-states as well as imagined benefits, such as a "national culture," "social peace," and "security." Hence, deportation can be seen as a populist response to diffuse anxieties and feelings of insecurity (De Genova 2007; Drotbohm 2013; Gibney 2008; Walters 2002).

Furthermore, across the world deportation is increasingly employed as a disciplinary tool of social governance and control (Bloch and Schuster 2005; Gibney 2008; Kanstroom 2000). Again here we draw on the work of Tanya Golash-Boza, which reveals how "global economic restructuring has played out in gendered and racialized ways" (Golash-Boza 2016, 488). Deportations are unevenly distributed with a majority of deportees being male and black or latino (see also Griffiths 2015; Turnbull and Hasselberg 2017 for the British context). Black and Latino men in the United States are already a vulnerable and stigmatized group historically subjected to state control with recourse to mass incarceration and now too, for those lacking formal citizenship, through mass deportations (De Genova 2011). Again continuities in the structural marginalization of this group, flowing from ordinary to crisis times, are underlined. Much like mass incarceration, mass deportation of black and Latino males in the United States is justified by means of a "racialized and gendered politics of fear" (Golash-Boza 2016, 488; see also Bosworth 2012 and Griffiths 2017 for the British context).

Interestingly, the labeling of "crisis" of a certain situation or condition in countries of reception can go hand in hand with the construction of "security" and "stability" in countries of origin. In Germany and the UK, to name only two, governments have developed great efforts in attempting to designate countries like those of former Yugoslavia or Afghanistan as "safe third countries" as a way to reduce the scope for asylum claims and facilitate the deportation of irregularized migrants to world regions in which wars and political violence persist (Holmes and Castaneda 2016). Stierl (New Keywords Collective 2016) interprets these designations in the context of new techniques of EU-level border control, which impose new forms of coerced mobility and a politics of containment. The increasing merging of criminal justice and immigration enforcement (Stumpf 2006) across the globe, along with the securitization of borders in the wake of 9/11, has meant that larger numbers of foreign-nationals become liable to deportation and thus subjected to forms of state surveillance and control (Hasselberg 2014a and 2014b).

In the next section we discuss experiences of deportability and forced removal at the individual, family, and community levels. In doing so we seek to move beyond the policy level to how policies are experienced and understood by those directly affected by them, and how they have an impact on individual behavior, family strategies, and the social fabric of communities.

Creating Structural Predicaments: Deportability, Detention, and Forced Return

Of the US context Deborah Boehm writes:

> This age of deportation is marked both by order and disorder. Through calculated efforts, the US state deports hundreds of thousands of undocumented migrants each year. By expelling those it labels 'aliens', the state ostensibly aims to create stability. Yet this system of supposed order also depends on and results in—and may even intentionally create— disorder for millions of formal and informal residents of the nation.
>
> (Boehm 2016, 2)

In this section we bring to the discussion the notion of deportation crises as crises that are brought about by the expansion and reach of deportation regimes. We do so as way to underline the disruption and transformation arising from current deportation regimes, not just in altering the social makeup of deportable and deported communities but also in producing changes in behavior and sense of self.

Within migration scholarship it is now common-sense that the regimes that are imposed through immigration laws constitute an ubiquitous menace and a source of uncertainty for noncitizens, who can become "illegal" or "undocumented" and hence "deportable" through multiple ways. Not only illegal entry or a criminal conviction, but also losing one's residency status or leave to remain by overstaying its temporal limits, constitute typical reasons behind a change in residence status (i.e., from regular or even "permanent" into an "irregular," "undocumented" or "illegal" status) (Golash-Boza 2014). According to Nicolas de Genova (2002, 2007, 2011), the construction of immigrants' "unlawful presence" is part of disciplinary apprenticeships, which render them controllable, arrestable, detainable, and dis-placeable by state force. This state of legal vulnerability, he notices, serves the state's interest in the denial of fundamental rights, especially for the production of cheap, "disposable" labor. De Genova's approach has been taken on by others who work in different national contexts and explore the impact of this legal limbo on the everyday lives of migrants, whose modes of membership and belonging are eroded. In some national contexts, state benevolence, along with perceptions of migrants' deservingness, can constitute the grounds for the suspension of deportation (Castañeda 2010; Coutin 2003).

The insecurity and fear produced through the awareness of deportability can indeed be labeled as a "crisis," as it is perceived as the radical exception from an aspired and hoped-for normality (Thronson 2008). Sarah Willen (2007), working in Israel, showed how the social condition of deportability impacts deeply on African migrants' daily experience of time and space, for instance, when they hide themselves during certain hours for avoiding the contact with police or other state representatives. Against a similar background, Menjívar and Kanstroom (2014) have problematized how laws that render noncitizen residents "illegal," and hence, deportable, create a new subclass of individuals, shadow populations, who remain unprotected from the law and eventually internalize this subject position. Joana Dreby (2012) explores the condition of deportability among Mexican immigrants in the United States and highlights the emotional consequences for migrant families and children in particular. When immigrant children, US-born or not, live with constant fear and worries that their parents might be deported, they begin to conflate immigration with illegality.

In the UK (and elsewhere) foreign nationals whose status is being adjudicated are subjected to numerous forms of control. They may be taken to immigration removal centers where they are held in prison-like conditions and regimes for an undetermined amount of time. The experience of immigration detention bears many negative enduring impacts on detainees physical and mental health but also on their perceptions of justice as they find themselves incarcerated on account of their immigration status alone (i.e., no criminal action at stake). It also impacts greatly on detainees' sense of self as they are constantly made to feel untrustworthy, infantilized and dehumanized (Bosworth 2012; Hasselberg 2014a; Turnbull 2016). Although their actions are restrained, the detained exercise their agency and resistance, from protests and hunger strikes to other forms of less visible resistance (Fischer 2015; McGregor 2011). Once released from immigration detention, migrants remain subject to strict forms of surveillance and control through reporting requirements, home curfews, electronic monitoring, and other limits on their mobility and action (Hasselberg 2014a). Their lives are marked by the uncertainty of deportation and the constant possibility of being detained once again (Hasselberg 2016a; Reeves 2015). On the other hand, in some contexts, immigration controls and the general policing of public spaces outside of the workplace can become so frequent, that the sense of deportability can become normalized. Especially in places, where borders are crossed frequently or more easily than in other places or where legal frameworks constantly change, deportation can immediately lead to re-migration (Galvin 2015; Hagan et al. 2008; Wooding and Moseley-Williams 2004).

While the de facto procedure leading to removal can take different forms, in most cases it is experienced as a deeply confusing, depressing, and often shocking event (Hasselberg 2016a). Some deportees return after signing a removal order, others remain in detention until being heard, others return "voluntarily" (i.e., choose a form of deportation with different legal consequences after realizing that the encounter with state force can hardly be avoided). The technical mode of return also differs. Deportation can occur over land, as in the case of immediate push-backs on the US-Mexican borders, or without attracting much attention on regular commercial flights (Kleist 2017). In many cases, however, especially when it happens by air, deportees are escorted by security personnel, who use handcuffs or other forms of physical force upon their bodies (Walters 2016). Walters suggests examining the forces applied in airports and planes as a "political economy of violence," comparable to other practices by which territorial and citizenship borders are made (Walters 2016, 443). All in all, deportation is not only a political articulation, but a deeply corporeal and materialized act, which impacts on the senses and feelings of deported subjects. Indeed, the often horrific character of deportation is confirmed by reports documenting determined attempts of resistance, some of which even ending in the death of the targeted person (Ellermann 2010; Fischer 2015; McGregor 2011). While the enormous stress for deportees cannot be negated, the act of removal often also constitutes a heavy predicament for other actors involved. In his ethnography in the German asylum bureaucracy, Tobias Eule (2016) describes vividly the emotional stress and frustrations among caseworkers responsible for executing deportations. They forcibly enter migrants' homes, often at dawn, and have to cope with the panic among fathers or mothers who are separated from their partners, children, or friends. Due to their violent character, forced removals often generate opposition and acts of solidarity, not only from the deportees' immediate relatives and social environment, but also from human rights activists, community representatives, lawyers, doctors, or other engaged citizens (Kalir and Wissink 2015). Deportation binds together deportees with a large range of actors who accompany, witness, and observe the procedure (Rosenberger and Winkler 2014).

For avoiding a methodological nationalism and for connecting the crisis produced through deportability and de facto deportation in the Global North to the contemporary living conditions in the allged "home countries" (i.e., the receiving states) we have introduced elsewhere the notion of the "deportation corridor," which connects both ends of the deportation continuum between "here" and "there" (Drotbohm and Hasselberg 2015). The metaphor of the corridor refers to an outside space of in-betweenness that stands in opposition to rooms of clearer positionality, assignment, and representation. In contrast to the perception of deportation prior to the act itself, the de facto removal of an immigrant may seem to be an individualizing experience, as citizenship and immigration status are tied to individuals. However, the social outcome of deportation is likewise experienced by larger networks of people, and the lives of families, friends, classmates, or colleagues are likewise profoundly transformed (see contributions in Khosravi 2018 and Roberts et al. 2017). According to Drotbohm (2015) deportation can be understood as a "reverse migration," not only because the direction of migration is reversed but also because former achievements of transnational mobility and support capacities are negated. Deborah Boehm argues in the same direction, when she calls deportation a "family deunification" (i.e., as "the antithesis of family reunited, disrupting and even dismantling transnational families, separating and displacing members of kin networks" [2016, 91]).

Many deportees had previously managed to establish their lives, some had taken their entire family over, some were working in regular jobs and had secured material achievements. In many cases, families lose a key breadwinner through deportation and the households remaining behind may easily slip into poverty. Generally, as men are more frequently removed than women, deportation creates a large number of female-headed single-parent households, who become sole providers for their children. According to Joanna Dreby (2012), who carried out research among Mexican families in different locations in the United States, many of these women bear both the financial burden of their partner's forced return as well as the economic insecurity caused through their absences (see also Menjívar et al. 2016).

The difficulties generated through deportation are also documented by other scholars, who combined their analysis of economic constraints with the costs of physical and mental health consequences caused by family separation (Hagan et al. 2008; Kanstroom 2012). "Explicitly through state action," Boehm writes, "individuals and their families are dispossessed not only of material possessions but also of less quantifiable, more abstract things, including home, nation, and relationships with one another" (2016, p. 76). Through her interviews with US-born children who experienced the forced return of (at least) one of their parents, Dreby (2015) brings to light the psychological stress and anxieties as well as educational barriers and health problems brought into families whose lives involuntarily stretch over large distances and become precarious through state action. In line with this argument, Drotbohm pinpoints the counterproductivity of deportation, which generates both economic and psychological instability among immigrant populations, which then needs to be compensated by the deporting state (e.g. in form of therapeutic measures for children remaining behind [Drotbohm 2015]).

Evidently, the crisis produced through the act of deportation also accompanies those who return under unforeseen and unplanned circumstances. In her work on the perception of deportation in Cape Verdean transnational networks, Drotbohm (2012, 2017) shows that involuntary return disturbs the internal logics of transnational livelihoods and the moral expectations toward a regular return, which can serve as a means for articulating status hierarchies within transnational social fields. We now have numerous studies covering deportees' conditions of living and social reintegration after their state-initiated return (Coutin 2011; Plambech 2017a, 2017b; Turnbull 2018; Zilberg 2004). Especially in social contexts in which deportation challenges a shared understanding of transnational family arrangements (i.e., in societies that rely strongly on emigration as well as the financial dimension of cross-border support systems) deported migrants can experience a loss of status, which often goes along with the stereotype of criminality and stigmatization (Drotbohm 2012; Schuster and Majidi 2013).

Generally speaking, deportees often face difficulties in finding adequate employment for supporting their families back in the (former) destination country. In many contexts of involuntary return, fathers, sometimes also mothers, who are rendered unable to fulfil the financial responsibilities necessary to maintain their social obligations, are likely to lose touch with their families in the global north (Dreby 2015; Drotbohm 2015). This can result in their exclusion from families and communities in their countries of origin as well as an unforeseen dependency on their transnational kin networks (Menjívar et al. 2016). Seen in this light, deportation adds a connotation of "crisis" to the societal evaluation of return migration (Drotbohm 2017). For shaping our understanding of the radical transformation of livelihood conditions after an involuntary return, Nauja Kleist (2017) compares the situation of deportees with emergency returnees, who are also relocated against their will and also often return emptyhanded, having lost their belongings while being abroad. She identifies comparable characteristics and risks of post-return life, such as continuing precariousness and attempts of re-migration as well as, in some cases, social and economic regeneration. In many cases, the living conditions of involuntary returnees are worse than prior to migration, aggravated by debt and the absence of social integration (Kleist 2017, see also Menjívar et al 2016). Again, the stigma of forced return does not remain on the individual level, as entire families have to renegotiate the unanticipated shift in the directionality of their transborder lives. Especially when children, many of whom are legal citizens in the country of destination, accompany their deported parents back to the country of origin, they regularly have to cope with feelings of being uprooted and trapped in daily life, as their own prospects of transborder mobility are questioned and hence future imaginings have to be rearranged (Boehm 2016). Several scholars have shown that deportees often respond to this social stigma by re-migrating, at least whenever this is technically possible (Hagan et al. 2008; Hasselberg 2016b; Schuster & Majidi 2013).

In addition to stigma, destitution, and a change in societal values, deportation may bring about a crisis as it shakes long-term legal resident deportees' sense of self. Daniel Kanstroom argues that the United States has "undertaken a radical social experiment with massive deportation enforcement" (2012, ix) which has led to the development of a new American diaspora: "a forcibly uprooted population of people with deep and cohesive connections to each other and to the nation-state from which they were removed" (2012, xi). Being expelled from the country where they were raised and to which they were acculturated brings about a great sense of injustice and wrongdoing, but also has complex implications with regards to legal rights and moral claims of membership (Kanstroom 2012, see also Hasselberg 2016a for the British context).

Conclusion

In this chapter we sought to disentangle crisis from deportation by first unpicking their multiple engagements, and then seeking to bring them back together to show the impact that deportation bears on the lives of individual migrants, their families and communities. We have questioned the labeling of "migration crisis," and undermined assumptions that take deportation as the inevitable, and most effective, response to such crises. We then brought to the fore the notion of deportation crises as crises that are brought about by the expansion and reach of political regimes which fuse migration control with securitization. In many contexts, the threat of deportation not only brings anxieties to deportable or deported actors, but also deeply impacts on their social environment and members of the civil society, both in the deporting state as well as in the alleged "home countries," some of which are unknown territories for those who have migrated at an early age. In the end, state bureaucrats, the police, as well as employees of transport agencies are also confronted with the crises of deportation, when deportees question or resist the physical act of removal. While we are weary of using the term crisis in this context, we have done so here to emphasize not just the disruption brought about by deportation enforcement but also, and perhaps most importantly, its transformative power (Hasselberg 2018). We thus argue that deportation is bringing about social change, not just in altering the social makeup of deportable and deported communities but also in producing changes in behavior and sense of self. Thus, deportation, often employed on the political level for justifying "emergency" policies, contributes to the creation of a global crisis, not only on an imaginary, but on a very concrete level of social experience.

Acknowledgments

We are grateful to the editors of this volume for the opportunity to be a part of this important publication. Ines Hasselberg's work to this chapter was made possible through generous funding by both Mary Bosworth's European Research Council Starting Grant (2012–2017) no. 313362 and by Fundação para a Ciência e a Tecnologia (Postdoctoral Grant SFRH/BPD/118075/2016). Heike Drotbohm's continuing research on deportation was funded by a Heisenberg scholarship of the German Research Foundation (Deutsche Forschungsgemeinschaft, DFG).

Notes

1. But see the Deportation Global Information Project at http://postdeportation.org/ [last accessed on November 22, 2017], which compiles available data on deportation *to* (soon available *from*) different countries worldwide.
2. For total ICE Removals Fiscal Year 2016, see https://www.ice.gov/removal-statistics/2016 [last accessed on November 12, 2017]

References

Agamben, G. 1998. *Homo Sacer: Sovereign Power and Bare Life*. Stanford, CA: Stanford University Press.

Agamben, G. 2005. *State of Exception*. Chicago: University of Chicago Press

Albahari, M. 2015. *Crimes of Peace. Mediterranean Migration at the World's Deadliest Border*. Philadelphia: University of Pennsylvania Press.

Anderson, B., M. J. Gibney, and E. Paoletti. 2011. "Citizenship, Deportation and the Boundaries of Belonging." *Citizenship Studies* 15, no. 5: 547–563. doi: 10.1080/13621025.2011.583787.

Australian Government. 2017. Department of Immigration and Border Protection Annual Report 2016/17 https://www.border.gov.au/ReportsandPublications/Documents/annual-reports/complete-annual-report-2016-17.pdf [last accessed on November 12, 2017]

Bloch, A., and L. Schuster. 2005. "At the Extremes of Exclusion: Deportation, Detention and Dispersal." *Ethnic and Racial Studies* 28, no. 3: 491–512. doi: 10.1080/0141987042000337858.

Boccagni, P., and F. Lagomarsino. 2011. "Migration and the Global Crisis: New Prospects for Return? The Case of Ecuadorians in Europe." *Bulletin of Latin American Research* 30, no. 3: 282–297. doi: 10.1111/j.1470-9856.2010.00494.x.

Boehm, D. A. 2016. *Returned: Going and Coming in an Age of Deportation, California Series in Public Anthropology*. Oakland: University of California Press.

Bosworth, M. 2008. "Border Control and the Limits of the Sovereign State." *Social & Legal Studies* 17, no. 2: 199–215. doi: 10.1177/0964663908089611.

Bosworth, M. 2012. "Subjectivity and Identity in Detention: Punishment and Society in a Global Age." *Theoretical Criminology* 16, no. 2: 123–140.

Bylander, M. 2017. "Migration Disruption: Crisis and Continuity in the Cambodian Mass Returns." *International Migration Review*. doi: 10.1111/imre.12342.

Castañeda, H. 2010. "Deportation Deferred: 'Illegality,' Visibility, and Recognition in Contemporary Germany." In *The Deportation Regime: Sovereignty, Space and the Freedom of Movement*, edited by N. De Genova and N. Peutz, 245–261. Durham, NC: Duke University Press.

Coutin, S. B. 2003. "Suspension of Deportation Hearings and Measures of 'Americanness.'" *Journal of Latin American Anthropology*, 8, no. 2: 58–95.

Coutin, S. B. 2011. Legal Exclusion and Discolated Subjectivities: The Deportation of Salvadoran Youth from the United States. In *The Contested Politics of Mobility: Borderzones and Irregularity*, edited by V. Squire, 169–183. London, New York: Routledge

Dauvergne, C. 2016. *The New Politics of Immigration and the End of Settler Societies*. New York: Cambridge University Press.

De Genova, N. 2002. "Migrant 'Illegality' and 'Deportability' in Everyday Life." *Annual Review of Anthropology* 31: 419–447.

De Genova, N. 2007. "The Production of Culprits: From Deportability to Detainability in the Aftermath of 'Homeland Security.'" *Citizenship Studies*, 11, no. 5: 421–448.

De Genova, N. 2011. Alien Powers: Deportable Labour and the Spectacle of Security. In *The Contested Politics of Mobility: Borderzones and Irregularity*, edited by V. Squire, 91–116. London, New York: Routledge.

De León, J. 2015. *The Land of Open Graves: Living and Dying on the Migrant Trail*. Oakland, CA: University of California Press.

Dreby, J. 2012. "The Burden of Deportation on Children in Mexican Immigrant Families." *Journal of Marriage and Family* 74: 829–845.

Dreby, J. 2015. *Everyday Illegal: When Politics Undermine Immigrant Families*. Oakland: University of California Press.

Drotbohm, H. 2012. "'It's Like Belonging to a Place that has Never Been Yours': Deportees Negotiating Involuntary Immobility and Conditions of Return in Cape Verde." In *Migrations: Interdisciplinary Perspectives*, edited by R. Schröder and R. Wodak, 129–140. Vienna: Springer.

Drotbohm, H. 2013. "Deportation. An Overview." In *Encyclopedia of Global Human Migration*, edited by Immanuel Ness, 1182–1188. Oxford: Blackwell.

Drotbohm, H. 2015. "The Reversal of Migratory Family Lives: A Cape Verdean Perspective on Gender and Sociality Prior and Post Deportation." *Journal of Ethnic and Migration Studies* 41, no. 4: 653–670. doi:10.1080/1369183X.2014.961905.

Drotbohm, H. 2017. "Frozen Cosmopolitanism: Coping with Radical Deceleration in Cape Verdean Contexts of Forced Return Migration." In *Identity in an Overheated World*, edited by T. H. Eriksen and E. Schober, 42–58. London: Pluto.

Drotbohm, H., and I. Hasselberg. 2015. " Deportation, Anxiety, Justice: New Ethnographic Perspectives." *Journal of Ethnic and Migration Studies*, 41, no. 4: 551–562.

Ellermann, A. 2010. "Undocumented Migrants and Resistance in the Liberal State." *Politics & Society* 38, no. 3: 408–429.

Eule, T. 2016. *Inside Immigration Law. Migration Management and Policy Application in Germany*. London, New York: Routledge.

Eurostat. 2017. Statistics on Enforcement of Immigration Legislation http://ec.europa.eu/eurostat/statistics-explained/index.php/Statistics_on_enforcement_of_immigration_legislation [Accessed on November 12, 2017.]

Fischer, N. 2015. "The Management of Anxiety. An Ethnographical Outlook on Self-mutilations in a French Immigration Detention Centre." *Journal of Ethnic and Migration Studies*, 41, no. 4: 599–616. doi: 10.1080/1369183X.2014.960820.

Galvin, T. M. 2015. "'We Deport Them but They Keep Coming Back': The Normalcy of Deportation in the Daily Life of 'Undocumented' Zimbabwean Migrant Workers in Botswana." *Journal of Ethnic and Migration Studies* 41, no. 4: 617–634. doi:10.1080/1369183X.2014.957172.

Gibney, M. J. 2008. "Asylum and the Expansion of Deportation in the United Kingdom." *Government and Opposition* 43, no. 2: 146–167. doi:10.1111/j.1477-7053.2007.00249.x.

Gibney, M. J., and H. Hansen. 2003. "Deportation and the Liberal State: The Forcible Return of Asylum Seekers and Unlawful Migrants in Canada, Germany and the United Kingdom." *New Issues in Refugee Research Working Paper 77*. Geneva: UNHCR. http://www.unhcr.org/en-us/research/working/3e59de764/deportation-liberal-state-forcible-return-asylum-seekers-unlawful-migrants.html

Golash-Boza, T. 2014. "From Legal to 'Illegal': The Deportation of Legal Permanent Residents from the United States. In *Constructing Migrant "Illegality": Critiques, Experiences, and Responses*, edited by C. Menjívar and D. Kanstroom, 203–224. New York: Cambridge University Press.

Golash-Boza, T. 2016. "The Parallels between Mass Incarceration and Mass Deportation: An Intersectional Analysis of State Repression." *Journal of World-Systems Research* 22, no. 2: 484–509. doi:10.5195/jwsr.2016.616.

Golash-Boza, T., and P. Hondagneu-Sotelo. 2013. "Latino Immigrant Men and the Deportation Crisis: A Gendered Racial Removal Program." *Latino Studies* 11, no. 3: 271–292. doi:http://dx.doi.org/10.1057/lst.2013.14.

Griffiths, M. 2015. "'Here, Man Is Nothing!': Gender and Policy in an Asylum Context." *Men and Masculinities* 18, no. 4: 468–488. doi: 10.1177/1097184x15575111.

Griffiths, M. 2017. "Foreign, Criminal: A Doubly Damned Modern British Folk-Devil." *Citizenship Studies* 21, no. 5: 527–546. doi: 10.1080/13621025.2017.1328486.

Hagan, J., K. Eschbach, and N. Rodriguez. 2008. "U.S. Deportation Policy, Family Separation, and Circular Migration." *International Migration Review* 42, no. 1: 64–88. doi:10.1111/j.1747-7379.2007.00114.x.

Hasselberg, I. 2014a. "Coerced to Leave: Punishment and the Surveillance of Foreign-National Offenders in the UK." *Surveillance & Society* 12, no. 4: 471–484.

Hasselberg, I. 2014b. Whose Security? The Deportation of Foreign-National Offenders from the UK. In *The Anthropology of Security: Perspectives from the Frontline of Policing, Counter-Terrorism and Border Control*, edited by M. Maguire, N. Zurawski, and C. Frois., 139–157 London: Pluto.

Hasselberg, I. 2016a. *Enduring Uncertainty. Deportation, Punishment and Everyday Life, Dislocations*. Oxford and New York: Berghahn.

Hasselberg, I. 2016b. "Reshaping Possible Futures. Deportation, Home and the United Kingdom." *Anthropology Today* 32, no. 1: 19–21. doi: 10.1111/1467-8322.12226

Hasselberg, I. 2018. "Fieldnotes from Cape Verde: On Deported Youth, Research Methods and Social Change." In *After Deportation: Ethnographic Perspectives*. Edited by S. Khosravi,15–35. Basingstoke, UK: Palgrave Macmillan

Holmes, S., and H. Castaneda. 2016. "Representing the 'European Refugee Crisis' in Germany and Beyond: Deservingness and Difference, Life and Death." In *American Ethnologist* 42, no. 1: 12–24.

Jeandesboz, J., and P. Pallister-Wilkins. 2014. "Crisis, Enforcement and Control at the EU Borders." In *Crisis and Migration. Critical Perspectives*, edited by A. Lindley, 115–135. London and New York: Routledge.

Kalir, B. and L. Wissink. 2015. "The Deportation Continuum: Convergences between State Agents and NGO Workers in the Dutch Deportation Field," *Citizenship Studies* 20, no. 1: 34–49.

Kanstroom, D. 2000. "Deportation, Social Control and Punishment: Some Thoughts about Why Hard Laws Make Bad Cases," *Harvard Law Review* 113:1890–935.

Kanstroom, D. 2012. *Aftermath: Deportation Law and the New American Diaspora*. Oxford and New York: Oxford University Press.

Kanstroom, D., and M. Brinton Lykes, eds. 2015. *The New Deportations Delirium: Interdisciplinary Responses*. New York: New York University Press.

Khosravi, S, ed. 2018. *After Deportation: Ethnographic Perspectives*. Basingstoke, UK: Palgrave Macmillan.

Khosravi, S. 2016. "Deportation as a Way of Life for Young Afghan Men." In *Detaining the Immigrant Other. Global and Transnational Issues*, edited by R. Furman, D. Epps, and G. Lamphear, 169–181. Oxford: Oxford University Press.

Kleist, N. 2017. "Trajectories of Involuntary Return Migration to Ghana: Forced Relocation Processes and Post-Return Life." *Geoforum*. https://doi.org/10.1016/j.geoforum.2017.12.005

Leerkes, A., and D. Broeders. 2010. "A Case of Mixed Motives? Formal and Informal Functions of Administrative Immigration Detention." *British Journal of Criminology* 50, no. 5: 830–850. doi:10.1093/bjc/azq035.

Lindley, A., ed. 2014a. *Crisis and Migration: Critical Perspectives. Routledge Series in Development, Mobilities and Migration*. London and New York: Routledge.

Lindley, A. 2014b. "Exploring Crisis and Migration: Concepts and Issues." In *Crisis and Migration. Critical Perspectives*, edited by Anna Lindley, 1–23. London and New York: Routledge.

McGregor, J. 2011. "Contestations and Consequences of Deportability: Hunger Strikes and the Political Agency of Non-Citizens." *Citizenship Studies* 15, no. 5: 597–611.

Menjívar, C. and D. Kanstroom. 2014. "Introduction—Immigrant 'Illegality': Constructions and Critiques." In *Constructing Migrant "Illegality": Critiques, Experiences, and Responses*, edited by C. Menjívar and D. Kanstroom, 1–36. New York: Cambridge University Press,

Menjívar, C., L. J. Abrego, and L. C. Schmalzbauer. 2016. *Immigrant Families*. Cambridge, UK: Polity.

Narotzky, S., and N. Besnier. 2014. "Crisis, Value, and Hope: Rethinking the Economy: An Introduction to Supplement 9." *Current Anthropology*, 55, supp. 9: 4–16.

New Keywords Collective. 2016. "Europe / Crisis: New Keywords of 'the Crisis' in and of 'Europe.'" Near Futures Online 1 "Europe at a Crossroads." http://nearfuturesonline.org/europecrisis-new-keywords-of-crisis-in-and-of-europe/

Patler, C., and T. M. Golash-Boza. 2017. "The Fiscal and Human Costs of Immigrant Detention and Deportation in the United States." *Sociology Compass* 11:e12536-n/a. doi: 10.1111/soc4.12536.

Plambech, S. 2017a. "Sex, Deportation and Rescue: Economies of Migration among Nigerian Sex Workers." *Feminist Economics* 23, no. 3: 134–159. doi: 10.1080/13545701.2016.1181272.

Plambech, S. 2017b. "God Brought You Home: Deportation as Moral Governance in the Lives of Nigerian Sex Worker Migrants." *Journal of Ethnic and Migration Studies* 43, no. 13: 2211–2227. doi:10.1080/1369183X.2017.1280386

Peutz, N., and N. De Genova. 2010. "Introduction." In *The Deportation Regime: Sovereignty, State and the Freedom of Movement*, edited by N. De Genova and N. Peutz, 1–29. Durham, NC: Duke University Press.

Reeves, M. 2015. "Living from the Nerves: Deportability, Indeterminacy, and the 'Feel of Law' in Migrant Moscow." *Social Analysis* 59, no. 4: 119–136. doi: 10.3167/sa.2015.590408.

Republic of South Africa. 2017. Department of Home Affairs Annual Report 2016/17. http://wtww.home-affairs.gov.za/files/Annual%20Reports/Annual%20Report%202017%20WEB.pdf

Roberts, B., C. Menjívar, and N. P. Rodríguez. 2017. *Deportation and Return in a Border-Restricted World. Experiences in Mexico, El Salvador, Guatemala, and Honduras*. New York: Springer

Roitman, J. 2014. *Anti-Crisis*. Durham, NC: Duke University Press.

Rosenberger, S., and J. Winkler. 2014. "Com/passionate Protests: Fighting the Deportation of Asylum Seekers." *Mobilization: An International Quarterly*, 19, no. 2: 165–184.

Schuster, L., and N. Majidi. 2013. "What Happens Post-Deportation? The Experience of Deported Afghans." *Migration Studies*, no. 1 (2): 221–240. doi:10.1093/migration/mns011.

Stumpf, J. P. 2006. "The Crimmigration Crisis: Immigrants, Crime, and Sovereign Power," *American University Law Review*. 56, no. 2: 368–419.

Thronson, D. B. 2008. "Creating Crisis: Immigration Raids and the Destabilization of Immigrant Families." *Wake Forest Law Review* 43, no. 391–418.

Turnbull, S. 2016. "'Stuck in the Middle': Waiting and Uncertainty in Immigration Detention." *Time & Society* 25, no. 1: 61–79. doi: 10.1177/0961463X15604518.

Turnbull, S. 2018. "Starting Again: Life After Deportation from the United Kingdom" in *After Deportation: Ethnographic Perspectives*, edited by S. Khosravi, 37–61. Basingstoke, UK: Palgrave Macmillan.

Turnbull, S., and I. Hasselberg. 2017. "From Prison to Detention: The Carceral Trajectories of Foreign-National Prisoners in the United Kingdom." *Punishment & Society-International Journal of Penology* 19, no. 2: 135–154. doi: 10.1177/1462474516660695.

Walters, W. 2002. "Deportation, Expulsion, and the International Police of Aliens." *Citizenship Studies* 6, no. 3: 265–292. doi:10.1080/1362102022000011612.

Walters, W. 2016. "The Flight of the Deported: Aircraft, Deportation, and Politics." *Geopolitics* 21, no. 2: 435–458. doi:10.1080/14650045.2015.1089234

Willen, S. S. 2007. "Toward a Critical Phenomenology of 'Illegality': State Power, Criminalization, and Abjectivity among Undocumented Migrant Workers in Tel Aviv, Israel." *International Migration* 45, no. 3: 8–38. doi:10.1111/j.1468-2435.2007.00409.x.

Wooding, B., and R. Moseley-Williams. 2004. *Needed but Unwanted: Haitian Immigrants and Their Descendants in the Dominican Republic*. London: Catholic Institute for International Relations.

Zilberg, E. 2004. "Fools Banished from the Kingdom: Remapping Geographies of Gang Violence between the Americas," *American Quarterly* 56, no. 3: 759–779.

PART VII

MEDIA CONSTRUCTIONS AND VISUAL CULTURES

CHAPTER 33

ETHICS AND MIGRATION CRISES

ALEX SAGER

THE language of crisis pervades how politicians, scholars, the media, and humanitarian organizations discuss migration. The BBC explains migration to Europe in seven charts under the heading "Migrant Crisis." An op-ed from *Politico* insists that "The EU Can't Solve Italy's Migration Crisis" (Stefanini 2017). The *Washington Post* tells us that "Europe's refugee crisis strengthens far-right parties" (Tharoor 2015). Even more alarmingly, a headline from *The Telegraph* proclaims that "'Millions of Africans' will flood Europe unless it acts now, warns European chief, as Paris evacuates huge migrant camp" (Samuel and Squires 2017). Reports of migration crises are not restricted to Europe. *The Guardian* informs us how "Central America's rampant violence fuels an invisible refugee crisis" (Lakhani 2016).

The language of crisis is not just a rhetorical device to sell papers. It permeates academic research and policy. A Google scholar search turns up 956 works with "migration crisis" in the title. The International Organization for Migration's Migration Crisis Operation Framework "combines IOM humanitarian activities and migration management services to help tackle migration aspects of a crisis more effectively" (IOM 2018). The Migration Policy Institute program "Moving Europe Beyond Crisis" asserts that "Europe is facing its worst refugee crisis since the Second World War, with more than 1 million people applying for asylum in 2015 and again in 2016" putting "the systems that were designed to manage these flows are under intense pressure" (MPI 2017). Human Rights Watch has a page on "Europe's Migration Crisis" that frequently documents the abuses EU member states and their proxies commit against migrants (Human Rights Watch 2017). Though the United Nations High Commissioner on Refugees (UNHCR) does not explicitly refer to a crisis, it proclaims that "the number of refugees in the world is the highest ever seen," a point illustrated with a graphic of the "unprecedented" 65.6 million forcibly displaced people, including 40.3 million internally displaced persons, 2.8 million asylum seekers, and 22.5 million refugees (UNHCR 2017).

This chapter surveys some of the major ethical issues involved in responding to migration crises, in particular issues about the moral responsibilities of states and other actors when faced with forced migration. It is necessary first, though, to problematize the category of "migration crisis." What constitutes a migration crisis is far less clear than often recognized. Moreover, the identification of migration as a "crisis" is a value judgement, not a straightforward description of a state of affairs. The term "crisis" is frequently mobilized for political and ideological reasons. Humanitarian organizations frame migration as a crisis in an attempt to shape policy and secure resources. More alarmingly, the language of "crisis" is often connected to securitization of migration (Huysmans 2000), as well to racist and xenophobic ideologies. Identifying migration as a crisis can justify harsh policy measures aimed at deterrence, detention, and expulsion, as well as contribute to the illegalization of migrant populations.

The first part of this chapter raises questions about the ethics of representing migration as a crisis. The second section raises ethical questions about the role of practices and institutions in shaping and contributing to migration crises. It focuses on duties to *respect*, to *protect*, and to *fulfill* the rights of migrants and contends that receiving states often directly violate the rights of migrants in crisis, as well as fail to adequately protect them. It also critically analyzes the common distinction between immigrants and refugees which is proposed as grounds for deciding which duties to migrants to fulfill.

Migration Crises and the Ethics of Representation

Consider the following scenarios. First: the UNHCR reports that 270,000 Rohingya Muslims have fled persecution and violence in Myanmar to Bangladesh (*Al Jazeera* 2017). New arrivals are in desperate need of water, food, and shelter. Second: the *LA Times* tells us that "Europe's unrelenting migrant crisis is threatening to overwhelm Italy," citing the "more than 85,000 people fleeing poverty and violence [who] have risked the perilous Mediterranean crossing to reach Italy this year . . . " (Zavis and Simmons 2017). Third: 242,998 refugees, mostly from Somalia, are registered with the UNHCR in the Dadaab refugee camp in Kenya (UNHCR 2018). The camp was created in 1991 for Somalis fleeing civil war. It has operated ever since with many residents staying years or decades. The Kenya government has promised to the close the camp and forcibly repatriate its residents, but so far political and legal resistance have stalled its plans. Finally, US Attorney General Jeff Sessions announced that the United States Citizenship and Immigration Services will not accept new applications for Deferred Action for Childhood Arrivals (DACA) after October 5, 2017, effectively ending the program for 800,000 DACA recipients. Barring a legislative solution, legal challenge, or new executive order in the next six months, long-term resident young adults brought to the United States as children will lose their work permits and find themselves subject to deportation.

Which—if any—of these four scenarios is a migration crisis? The first two scenarios are widely represented as crises. Few would dispute that the Rohingya are "crisis migrants," defined as "all those who move and those who remain trapped but in need of relocation in the context of crises" (Martin et al. 2014, 4). In the second scenario, migration is depicted as a crisis on the grounds that Italy—a county with over 60 million people and a GDP (2016) of 1.85 trillion USD—may be "overwhelmed" by the "unrelenting" stream of migrants arriving at its shores. Little is said about this being a crisis for the 85,000 people fleeing poverty and violence.

What about the Dadaab refugee camp and the Dreamers? The Dadaab refugee camp is rarely discussed as a migration crisis,[1] despite ongoing violence in Somalia that prevents voluntary repatriation, violence in the camp itself, and the limited prospects for resettlement for most of its residents. Finally, though the cancelation of the Deferred Action for Childhood Arrivals in the United States is a crisis for the 800,000 Dreamers, as well as for their families and communities, the media has not chosen to represent it in these terms.[2]

What sense can we make of the decision to label migration—or not label it—a crisis? A central dimension of the ethical study of migration concerns the concepts and categories that we use to think about human mobility (Allen et al. 2017, 1; Jones, 2009). Concepts and categories simplify the world, enabling us to measure and to understand it. They also guide our normative judgments, imposing standards of normality and treating some behaviors as deviant. Migration studies includes categories such as "migrant" and "refugee" (both which are "contested" [Connolly 1993]), as well as categories frequently used in social science research or in the media. Examples include "economic migrants," "undocumented/unauthorized/illegal immigrant," "smuggler," "trafficker," and much else. These classifications have social and political implications, affecting how people are perceived and how they perceive themselves, as well as how they are treated. When classifications guide policy or become legal categories, they have a decisive impact on people's freedom, well-being, and lives. Scholars, journalists, and public figures have the moral responsibility to scrutinize the categories they use.

"Crisis" is a particularly problematic category. The word "crisis" attracts strong emotions, but its meaning is frequently vague. The Greek *krisis* (decision) referred to the critical point in an illness that would determine the patient's recovery or death, the point in which the conflict in a drama comes to a head and demands resolution, or a decision (in the sense of a verdict or judgment) (Kosselleck 2006). Over the centuries the word has acquired a bewildering variety of metaphoric senses in different linguistic, social, religious, and political contexts, as well as in academic disciplines. Moreover, "crisis" promiscuously combines with adjectives, so that we are inundated with (alleged) economic, existential, pedagogical, political, societal, and spiritual crises. The language of crisis often retains its emotive and rhetorical force despite lacking the analytic specificity to usefully describe the world (Holton 1987).

What can we say about the meaning of "crisis" today? "Crisis" is a "thick" concept that entails a value judgment about a situation (Williams 2011): to claim something is a crisis is to evaluate it as abnormal and bad. To call an event a crisis is usually to assert that its resolution requires special measures or resources and that it significantly threatens the social or political order. Sometimes crises herald a decisive—usually negative—change in the political, social, or economic orders. In other cases such as ongoing refugee crises, the word has come to describe a normal—though deplorable—state of affairs.

Discussions of migration and crisis often occur in the context of broader "humanitarian crises," defined by Susan F. Martin and her colleagues as "any situation in which there is a widespread threat to life, physical safety, health, or basic subsistence that is beyond the coping capacity of individuals and the communities in which they reside." (Martin et al. 2014, 5). In the case of groups like the Rohingya, the phrase "migration crisis" typically refers to people who are migrating or have migrated because of a humanitarian crisis. Migration itself is also often framed as a crisis—a crisis for receiving states that are reluctant to receive migrants.

Another issue is the choice between referring to the large-scale movement of people as a "refugee crisis" or as "migrant crisis." The term "migrant" is broader and is sometimes tied to the claim that the people coming are "economic migrants." "Economic migrants" are in turn often conflated with the dehumanizing term "illegal immigrants," depicted as self-interested actors using illegal means to further their own ends at the expense of host societies. Many people accept that refugees have at least a *prima facie* claim to assistance on moral and legal grounds (though the term refugee itself is often racialized [Gans 2017] and the distinction between refugees and other migrants is not necessary well understood in the popular imagination).

As should be clear, to declare something a crisis is to evaluate it and to suggest how to address it. Furthermore, when the language of crisis combines with policies such as immigration enforcement, the choice to name an event a crisis can become a self-fulfilling prophecy. The decision to intercept ships or build walls can transform hitherto invisible (at least to the public and to policy makers) migration flows into humanitarian quagmires.

For all of these reasons, labeling the movement of people a crisis is an ethical choice. To represent migration as a crisis suggests that a particular migration flow is unusual and has bad consequences for the migrants themselves or for the people receiving them (or both). Furthermore, crises often justify measures that would otherwise be unacceptable such as the suspension of due process or civil rights. The language of crisis gives credence to the view that migration is largely a matter of national security, as well as (mostly unfounded) accusations that migrants and refugees are connected to terrorist groups (Nowrasteh 2016). This contributes to the securitization of migration at the expense of its economic, social, and human dimensions. It also risks dehumanizing migrants by depicting them as natural disasters such as floods.

In order to justly determine whether to frame migration as a crisis, we need an ethics of representation. An ethics of representation has epistemic dimensions (does the evidence indeed support the identification of a crisis?) and ethical dimensions (what are our intentions in choosing to represent the event as a crisis, and what effects is our representation likely to have)? A number of questions need to be addressed:

1) Is there in fact a crisis? If so, what makes it a crisis?
2) Is it in fact a *migration* crisis (or is the crisis better described as having other sources)?
3) Who is the migration crisis a crisis for? Who decides it is a crisis?

First, whether something ought to count a migration crisis is a matter of interpretation, values, and judgment about the effects of migration and the capacity to respond. Indeed, whether migration becomes or continues to be a crisis to a significant extent depends on receiving country policies, politics, and attitudes. After the Hungarian revolution of 1956, 200,000 refugees arrived in Austria. Thirty-six of the world's (at the time eighty) countries took in Hungarian refugees, averting a long term crisis (Zieck 2013). Although this response is exceptional, it illustrates how different political responses contribute to creating and resolving crises. The source of crisis may rest on the failure to respond to people in need, rather than the original causes of their displacement.

Second, before labeling human movement a migration crisis, we should ask is the crisis in fact a crisis of *migration*? Migration is often viewed through a sedentarist bias: the default position on mobility is that large-scale migration must be a response to bad or abnormal circumstances (Lindley 2014; Malkki 1992). This ignores the role of human agency in migration. It also deflects attention from the violence, environmental degradation, expulsion due to economic transformation, and other factors that cause people to migrate. In many cases, migration crises might be more aptly described as economic crises, crises of governance, or environmental crises in which migration is a predictable byproduct.

We can see this in the so-called "European refugee crisis." Leo Lucassen has observed the apocalyptical tone in the European response to asylum seekers in 2014–2016, especially compared to the in many respects similar refugee crisis in the 1990s. Negative reactions to recent asylum seekers cannot be explained by their greater numbers (in most European countries the numbers are similar to the 1990s), refugees' countries of origin, the failure of current immigrants to integrate, or a rise in the number of people emigrating globally. Instead, Luccassen locates the explanation in a combination of economic insecurity and social risk linked to neoliberal globalization, changing attitudes toward immigrants and toward Islam, incidents of Islamic terrorism, the rise of far-right parties, and the changes in the EU visa regime that encourages highly visible migration by sea (Lucassen 2017). Lucassen's analysis suggests that *migration* itself may not be the primary source of the "European refugee crisis." Migration is a convenient scapegoat that distracts from the more challenging tasks of addressing structural inequities based in economic and political policies, eradicating racism, and responding to terrorism in a way that does not achieve the ends of its perpetrators.

The question of *what* the crisis is relates to the question of *where* the migration crisis is. Phrases such as the "Mediterranean migration crisis" locate the crisis in a geographical setting, in this case the Mediterranean. This ignores the causes of migration in sending countries (which may in turn have their roots in European or international policies). It also allows the EU to conceal how its own policies contribute to people drowning (Pallister-Wilkins n.d., 41).

Third, the phrase "migration crisis" often equivocates between migration as a crisis for the migrants and migration as a crisis for the receiving societies. This raises the question of who has the authority to designate a situation a crisis. The label "migration crisis" is typically imposed from above by actors such as governments or international organizations with a stake in regulating or hindering movement. It is rarely voiced by people on the move. Governments have the epistemic authority and power to invoke the language of crisis and are unlikely to use this authority to draw attention to their role in generating human misery. This is one reason why it is unlikely that DACA will be widely represented as a crisis, even if mass deportations are aptly described as a humanitarian disaster.

It also helps explain why politicians and media frequently discuss migrant camps and unauthorized border crossings in Calais in terms of crisis when the magnitude and burdens are minimal comapred to much larger camps on the borders of conflict zones or much larger refugee populations in countries such as Turkey, Pakistan, Lebanon, Iran, and Ethiopia (De Genova et al. 2016, 13).

All of these questions are useful when contemplating the ethics of representation—in this case, the choice to represent migration as a crisis. We have epistemic responsibilities to ensure that we have evidence that supports treating migration as a crisis. These include properly analyzing the causality so that we do not identify migration as the source of crisis when there are in fact more fundamental and more significant causes. Epistemic responsibilities also have a moral dimension. Academics and journalists have professional duties to judge situations truthfully, as well as to reflect on the function and potential consequences of their representations. We should also be wary of identifying migration as a crisis from a position of power, especially when this denies migrants a voice and control over how they are depicted.

Once we have answered these questions, we need to ask what we hope to achieve by calling migration a crisis. This is never simply a description of events, but also a normative judgment that typically aims at some sort of result. Sometimes crisis language is understandable (for example when NGOs attempt to secure resources and support). Even in these sorts of cases, they must ask if invoking the language of crisis plays into the hands of reactionaries. In other cases, the language of crisis has more cynical roots, creating the perception of a migration threat to appeal to voters or to divert attention from the root causes of poverty, inequality, or insecurity.

Responding to Crises

So far I have focused on the nature and representation of migration crises and argued for the ethical responsibility to exercise caution in labeling migration a crisis. What should we say about the ethics of migration crises once we have determined that the language of crisis is in fact appropriate?

To a significant extent, migration is self-regulating when people are able to freely determine if, when, and how they move. People migrate for reasons such as economic opportunities or family reunification and return or move on when these reasons no longer hold. In contrast, migration crises typically have their source in the failure to respect human rights such as the rights the life, liberty, and security of person; the right not to be subjected to torture or to cruel, inhuman, or degrading treatment or punishment; the right not to face arbitrary arrest, detention, or exile; and the right not to be persecuted. People also move because they lack reliable access to food, clothing, shelter, health, education, or a healthy environment, arguably in violation of human rights to satisfy basic needs or human capabilities (Sen 2000).

Henry Shue (1996, 52) usefully distinguishes between three types of duties that correlate with rights:

1) Duties to avoid depriving people of their rights.
2) Duties to protect people from deprivations of rights caused by other people.
3) Duties to aid the deprived.

These three types of duties have been enshrined in General Comment 12 by the UN Committee on Economic, Social, and Cultural Rights as duties to *respect*, to *protect*, and to *fulfil* (Pogge 2016). In the context of migration crises, we can distinguish these duties as follows:

1) Duties not to cause migration crises by depriving people of their rights (e.g., by persecuting them).
2) Duties to protect migrants and refugees from those who would deprive them of their rights (e.g., at a domestic level by upholding institutions that provide security and opportunity for the population, at an international level by extending asylum or providing safe zones).
3) Duties to provide durable solutions (local integration, resettlement, or voluntary repatriation) for displaced people. There may also be duties to structure immigration policies to ameliorate poverty and promote development.[3]

Let's begin with the duties not to cause migration crises. People have *prima facie* obligations not to cause harm and responsibilities to ameliorate harms that they do cause. One of the challenges regarding the ethics of migration is that the causes of human movement are complex and often murky. Furthermore, causes interact in unpredictable ways. An added dimension of complexity comes from feedback loops when migrants (as well as people in the business of facilitating migration) react to policies designed to direct and hinder their movement. As a result, we can rarely point to *the* cause of a particular migration. In many cases it is impossible to confidently disentangle how multiple causes interact. Nonetheless, this does not prevent generalizations that certain policies and actions have a causal role in migration and that this causal role in some circumstances entails moral responsibilities.

First, we might think that this injunction applies primarily to dictators, militia leaders, and others who persecute or threaten people, causing them to flee their homes. In fact, it is much broader. It is clear that we should condemn actors who violently force people to move. Although an ethical response to these violations is in practice urgent and fraught with uncertainty (e.g., concerning the ethics of humanitarian intervention), identifying wrongdoing is often fairly straightforward (though in many conflict regions, many actors on different sides share blame and there may be no way to hold them accountable).

Second, the roles that *receiving* states play in contributing to and prolonging migration crises also raise challenging ethical questions. Though receiving states often portray their migration policies as a response to crisis, their foreign, economic, and migration policies are often implicated. The migrant rights group slogan "We are here because you were there" reminds us that migration often has its roots in colonial and imperial history. Direct military intervention such as the US-led Iraq and Afghanistan wars have led to millions of refugees and internally displaced people. Intervention—both direct and through proxies—by the United States, Europe, Turkey, Russia, and the Arab League contributes to ongoing displacement in Syria. More broadly, receiving countries are deeply enmeshed in the global arms trade that fuels many conflicts (Feinstein 2011).

Economic factors are also important. Migration in recent years has taken place in the context of neoliberal globalization, driven in part by international institutions such as the International Monetary Fund, the World Bank, and the World Trade Organisation, whose policies are in large part a result of the interests of the world's richer countries which exert disproportionate influence. Neoliberal economic integration has structurally transformed the economies of many less developed countries, particularly in agriculture, displacing people from their land (Castles 2013). We see this process, for example, in the US-Mexico migration system where the North American Free Trade Agreement ushered in structural transformations in the Mexican economy that led to displacement and migration (Hing 2010). Climate change's burdens tend to fall more heavily on less developed countries, contributing to displacement (Piguet et al. 2011).

Another way in which receiving countries contribute to migration crises is through immigration enforcement and the securitization of immigration policy. Government policies decide the legal status of migrants—hence the terminology *illegalized* immigrant (Bauder 2014)—and determine how they are received. Treating immigration as a security issue is a choice—often a lethal one. The fences and increased border patrol at the US-Mexico border under Operation Gatekeeper in the 1990s predictably turned human smuggling into a lucrative business and funneled migrants into the desert, leading to a rise in border deaths (Nail 2016). Similarly, European Union efforts to curtail migration have played a major role in the increase of deaths in the Mediterranean (Shields 2015).

Immigration enforcement may also violate duties to protect people from having their rights violated by other people (Shue's second category of duties). Migration crises are not only caused by actions that directly contribute to displacement. Though the root cause of refugee flows may be sending country violence or economic or environmental devastation, whether this results in a "migration crisis" to a large extent depends on the response to human mobility. For example, enforcement has increasingly moved away from the official borders of powerful states through carrier sanctions and offshore interdictions, as well as through partnerships with foreign governments (Gibney 2006; Nessel 2009). This can directly lead to rights violations (e.g., through human rights abuses committed by proxies contracted to stop migration [United Nations Support Mission in Libya 2016]). But it also prevents migrants from exercising rights to asylum.

Though refugee camps are often not discussed under the rubric of crisis, they are nonetheless tragedies for the millions of people who live for years and decades unable to return to their country of origin, prohibited from integrating into the country where they have found refuge, and deprived of any realistic chance of resettlement in a third country. Refugees in camps are also often vulnerable to militias, sexual violence, disease, and hunger (Parekh 2017). State policies enforce immobility by preventing local integration and refusing to commit to resettlement (Agier 2011). Although they may not violate obligations under international law, these policies point to clear moral failures.

Deportations may also cause considerable harm, sending people back to countries where they may face persecution or torture. Philosophers have also argued that deporting long-term residents, even if they lack the legal status to remain on the territory, may be unjust given their *de facto* membership in the community (Carens 2013). Mass deportation and immigrant raids traumatize immigrants, their families, and communities. Although the fact that deportation is carried out against vulnerable communities with limited political voice prevents them from being labeled crises, they are certainly crises for immigrants exiled from their homes and communities.

In recent years, countries around the world have increasingly detained immigrants, including people claiming asylum (Nethery and Silverman 2015). The interception of migrants at sea, combined with offshore detention—pioneered by the United States in Guantanamo Bay, and by Australia on Christmas Island, Manus Island (Papua New Guinea), and Nauru—is particularly notorious. Although international law prohibits the use of detention as a means of deterring immigration, there is little doubt that this is one of its intended functions.

So far this article has focused on duties to not violate people's rights and to avoid depriving people of their rights. There are also duties to protect people from deprivation of rights caused by other people. Here the primary responsibility is to human need.

If we assume that finite resources or limited political will mean that only some migrants will receive protection or help, how should we allocate resources? One way of demarcating the moral obligations in "migration crises" is to prioritize refugees. Unlike immigrants (often labeled "economic immigrants") whom many people think states can ignore and exclude at will, refugees are commonly recognized as having a legal and moral claim to protection and to asylum—human rights or humanitarian claims to admission that other migrants lack. In debates in political philosophy about freedom of movement, philosophers who support significant state discretion in admitting—or not admitting—immigrants generally support an obligation to grant asylum to refugees (Miller 2016; Walzer 1983). Despite the banality of this distinction, it faces conceptual and ethical objections.

Discussion of refugees usually proceeds from the 1951 Convention Relating to the Status of Refugees and the 1967 Protocol, which base refugee status on a "well-founded fear of being persecuted for reasons of race, religion, nationality, membership of a particular social group or political opinion" (Article 1.A. [2]). The focus on persecution, strictly understood, excludes people who are not members of a persecuted group but nevertheless are fleeing violence or civil war, people escaping environmental degradation, and people migrating because of extreme poverty. A narrow interpretation also appears to exclude people escaping gender-based violence or persecution due to their sexual identity. The 1951 Convention further defines refugees as being outside of their country of citizenship or of habitual residence, neglecting populations displaced within the boundaries of their country (internally displaced people) and populations immobilized in conflict zones. Though highly influential, the 1951 definition of refugee is by no means definitive. The definition of refugee is much broader in Organization of African Unity Convention Governing the Specific Aspects of Refugee Problems in Africa (1969) and Cartagena Declaration on Refugees (1984), and the UNHCR in fact provides assistance to many people who would not qualify as refugees under the Convention's narrow definition.

Most legal scholars and philosophers favor a broader definition of refugees with some philosophers rejecting a principled distinction between refugees and "economic" migrants altogether (Kukathas 2016). Others have continued to argue that refugees are special, often on the grounds that refugees face either state persecution or find their human rights violated because their state is unable or unwilling to guarantee them (Gibney 2004). Refugees have a series of claims on states, most prominently a right to seek asylum and a right to *non-refoulement*—not to be returned to a country where they face persecution.

What duties do states and other agents have toward refugees? A first duty is to respect the right to *non-refoulement* and not return refugees to danger. Even this right has come under question. As discussed above, many states have taken measures such as intercepting migrants at sea and collaborating with foreign governments to prevent migrants from arriving at their borders so that they cannot claim asylum. When this is done knowing full well that it deprives refugees of an opportunity to claim asylum, it surely violates negative rights not to contribute to depriving people of their rights to life, liberty, bodily integrity, and freedom from persecution.

When migrants are able to claim asylum or reach safety, there are still questions about the responsibilities to provide asylum or ensure safety (Kritzman-Amir 2009). Most refugees flee to bordering countries or zones within their country of origin, placing a disproportionate burden on less developed countries to shelter them. Burdens in migration crises are determined by proximity, rather than by countries' financial resources and capacity to help or by the country's role in contributing to forced migration. Due to carrier sanctions that prevent air travel, refugees unable to secure a visa to Europe tend to arrive in countries such as Italy, Greece, and Spain. The Dublin Regulation requires that asylum-seekers process their claims in the country of first entry, so these countries are charged with hosting and adjudicating claims with little assistance from other EU members. An even more fraught issue is the millions of refugees living in camps for years and even decades. Only a few countries accept refugees for resettlement with the United States, Canada, Australia, and the Nordic countries taking most candidates in recent years. As a result, the UNHRC reports only 189,300 refugees were resettled in 2016, a small number compared to the need.

Even if we grant that there are special duties toward refugees not owed to other migrants, even those migrating because of dire poverty, this does not settle matters. To claim that there are special duties does not entail that there are not also duties to migrants who do not qualify as refugees. Since migration flows are mixed, any response to a migration crisis affects everyone on the move. Many migrants may not qualify for asylum. Nonetheless, they retain their human rights, rights that are often endangered by enforcement. Furthermore, there may be positive duties toward nonrefugee migrants such as shaping migration policies to provide economic opportunities (e.g., through temporary labor programs or more generous immigration policies) or by facilitating family migration.

Beyond duties of original states to not deprive people of their rights and to protect and aid people deprived of their rights, we should also think about larger obligations to uphold and work toward just institutions and structures. Political philosophers have argued that those concerned with justice should focus primarily on the underlying principles or rules that structure society's basic social and economic institutions, rather than dwell on individual actions (Rawls 1999).

Migration crises take place within economic and political systems that cross borders, systems that may well fall short of what global justice requires. For this reason, it makes sense to ask about the justice of global (and international) systems. This includes critical reflection on the laws, policies, and norms that regulate migration. The current international system is poorly structured to deal with migration crises in large part because it is premised on the norm that human movement across state borders is largely at states' discretion. Migrants and refugees in crisis have to negotiate a border regime explicitly designed to stymie movement through harsh enforcement and obstructive bureaucratic measures. Duties to minimize the occurrence of migration crises and to ameliorate existing crises include duties to reform the institutions regulating migration so that they align with a more just world.

Notes

1. An exception is Rawlence 2016.
2. One of the possible "crises" tied to rescinding DACA is a mental health crisis among DACA recipients (Patler and Laster Pirtle 2017).

3. I focus primary on the duties of states and state actors, leaving aside complex questions about the role of nongovernmental organizations, private employers, and individual citizens. One particularly area of ethical obligation that has recently begun to receive attention concerns the obligations of citizens when confronted with arguably unjust immigration laws. In Europe, there have been a number of high-profile cases of humanitarian smuggling (Landry 2016). This raises the possibility that citizens confronted with an unjust immigration regime have a duty to civil disobedience or other form of resistance (Hidalgo 2015).

References

Al Jazeera. 2017. "UN: 270,000 Rohingya Fled to Bangladesh in Two Weeks." *Al Jazeera*, September 8. http://www.aljazeera.com/news/2017/09/rohingya-refugee-numbers-bangladesh-surge-270000-170908090357860.html.

Agier, M. 2011. *Managing the Undesirables: Refugee Camps and Humanitarian Governance*. Malden, MA: Polity.

Allen, W., B. Anderson, N. Van Hear, M. Sumption, F. Düvell, J. Hough, L. Rose, R. Humphris, and S. Walker. 2017. "Who Counts in Crises? The New Geopolitics of International Migration and Refugee Governance." *Geopolitics* 23 (1): 1–27. doi:10.1080/14650045.2017.1327740.

Bauder, H. 2014. "Why We Should Use the Term 'Illegalized' Refugee or Immigrant: A Commentary." *International Journal of Refugee Law* 26: 327–332. doi:10.1093/ijrl/eeu032

Carens, J. H. 2013. *The Ethics of Immigration*. New York: Oxford University Press.

Castles, S. 2013. "The Forces Driving Global Migration." *Journal of Intercultural Studies* 34: 122–140. doi:10.1080/07256868.2013.781916

Connolly, W. E. 1993. *The Terms of Political Discourse. 3rd ed.* Princeton, NJ: Princeton University Press.

De Genova, N., and M. Tazzioli. 2016. "Europe/Crisis: New Keywords of 'the Crisis' in and of 'Europe.'" *Near Futures Online: Zone Books*. March 1. http://nearfuturesonline.org/europecrisis-new-keywords-of-crisis-in-and-of-europe/

Feinstein, Andrew. 2011. *The Shadow World: Inside the Global Arms Trade*. New York, NY: Farrar, Straus and Giroux.

Gans, H. J. 2017. "Racialization and Racialization Research." *Ethnic and Racial Studies* 40 (3): 341–352. doi:10.1080/01419870.2017.1238497.

Gibney, M. 2006. "A Thousand Little Guantanamos: Western States and Measures to Prevent the Arrival of Refugees." In *Displacement, Asylum, Migration: The Oxford Amnesty Lectures*, edited by K.E. Tunstall, 139–169. Oxford: Oxford University Press.

Gibney, M. J. 2004. *The Ethics and Politics of Asylum: Liberal Democracy and the Response to Refugees*. Cambridge, UK: Cambridge University Press.

Hing, B. O. 2010. *Ethical Borders: NAFTA, Globalization, and Mexican Migration*. Philadelphia: Temple University Press.

Holton, R. J. 1987. "The Idea of Crisis in Modern Society." *The British Journal of Sociology* 38 (4): 502–520.

Human Rights Watch. 2017. *Europe's Migration Crisis*. https://www.hrw.org/tag/europes-migration-crisis

Huysmans, J. 2000. "The European Union and the Securitization of Migration." *Journal of Common Market Studies* 38 (5): 751–777. doi:10.1111/1468-5965.00263.

International Organization for Migration (IOM). 2018. *Migration Crisis Operational Framework*. https://www.iom.int/mcof.

Jones, R. 2009. "Categories, Borders and Boundaries." *Progress in Human Geography* 33 (2): 174–189. doi:10.1177/0309132508089828.

Kosselleck, R., 2006. "Crisis." *Journal of the History of Ideas* 67: 357–400.

Kritzman-Amir, T. 2009. "Not in My Backyard: On the Morality of Responsibility Sharing in Refugee Law." *Brooklyn Journal of International Law* 34 (2): 355–393.

Kukathas, C. 2016. "Are Refugees Special?" In *Migration in Political Theory: The Ethics of Movement and Membership*, edited by S. Fine and L. Ypi, 249–268. Oxford: Oxford University Press.

Lakhani, N. 2016. "Central America's Rampant Violence Fuels an Invisible Refugee Crisis." *The Guardian*, October 13. https://www.theguardian.com/world/2016/oct/13/central-america-violence-refugee-crisis-gangs-murder.

Landry, R. 2016. "The 'Humanitarian Smuggling' of Refugees: Criminal Offence or Moral Obligation?" *University of Oxford, Refugee Studies Centre*, October. https://www.rsc.ox.ac.uk/publications/the-humanitarian-smuggling-of-refugees-criminal-offence-or-moral-obligation.

Lindley, A., ed. 2014. *Crisis and Migration: Critical Perspectives*. London: Routledge.

Lucassen, L. 2017. "Peeling an Onion: The "Refugee Crisis" from a Historical Perspective." *Ethnic and Racial Studies* 41 (3): 1–28. doi:10.1080/01419870.2017.1355975.

Malkki, L. H. 1992. "National Geographic: The Rooting of Peoples and the Territorialization of National Identity among Scholars and Refugees." *Cultural Anthropology* 7: 24–44.

Martin, S. F., S. S. Weerasinghe, and A. Taylor, eds. 2014. *Humanitarian Crises and Migration: Causes, Consequences and Responses*. New York: Routledge.

Migration Policy Insitute. 2017. *Moving Europe Beyond Crisis*. https://www.migrationpolicy.org/programs/moving-europe-beyond-crisis?gclid=EAIaIQobChMIsLPUhfT31QIVDIB-Ch2V5Q1MEAAYASAAEgK4ofD_BwE

Miller, D. 2016. *Strangers in Our Midst: The Political Philosophy of Immigration*. Cambridge, UK: Harvard University Press.

Nail, T. 2016. *Theory of the Border*. New York: Oxford University Press.

Nessel, L. A. 2009. "Externalized Borders and the Invisible Refugee." *Columbia Human Rights Law Review* 40 (625): 625–699.

Nethery, A., and S. J. Silverman, eds. 2015. *Immigration Detention: The Migration of a Policy and Its Human Impact*. London; New York: Routledge.

Nowrasteh, A. 2016. *"Terrorism and Immigration: A Risk Analysis." Policy Analysis No. 798*. September 13, 2016. Cato Institute. https://www.cato.org/publications/policy-analysis/terrorism-immigration-risk-analysis.

Parekh, S. 2017. *Refugees and the Ethics of Forced Displacement*. New York: Routledge.

Patler, C., and W. L. Pirtle. 2017. "From Undocumented to Lawfully Present: Do Changes to Legal Status Impact Psychological Well-Being among Latino Immigrant Young Adults?" *Social Science & Medicine* 199: 39–48. doi:10.1016/j.socscimed.2017.03.009.

Piguet, E., A. Pécoud, P. F. A. de Guchteneire, eds. 2011. *Migration and Climate Change*. UNESCO. Cambridge, UK: Cambridge University Press.

Pogge, T. 2016. "Are We Violating the Human Rights of the World's Poor?" In *Ethical Issues in Poverty Alleviation*, edited by H. P. Gaisbauer, G. Schweiger, and C. Sedmak, 17–42. Studies in Global Justice 14. Cham, Switzerland: Springer.

Rawlence, B. 2016. *City of Thorns*. New York: Picador.

Rawls, J. 1999. *A Theory of Justice. Revised Edition.* Cambridge, MA: Harvard University Press.
Samuel, H., and N. Squires. 2017. "'Millions of Africans' Will Flood Europe Unless It Acts Now, Warns European Chief, as Paris Evacuates Huge Migrant Camp." *The Telegraph*, July 7. http://www.telegraph.co.uk/news/2017/07/07/millions-africans-will-flood-europe-unless-acts-now-warns-european/.
Sen, A. K. 2000. *Development as Freedom*. New York: Anchor.
Shields, P. 2015. "The Human Cost of the European Union's External Border Regime." *Peace Review* 27 (1): 82–90. doi:10.1080/10402659.2015.1000196.
Shue, H. 1996. *Basic Rights: Subsistence, Affluence, and U.S. Foreign Policy*. 2nd edition. Princeton, NJ: Princeton University Press.
Stefanini, S. 2017. "The EU Can't Solve Italy's Migration Crisis." *Politico*, July 29. http://www.politico.eu/article/eu-cant-solve-italy-migration-crisis-refugees-mediterranean-sea/.
Tharoor, I. 2015. "Europe's Refugee Crisis Strengthens Far-Right Parties." *Washington Post*, October 13. https://www.washingtonpost.com/news/worldviews/wp/2015/10/13/europes-refugee-crisis-strengthens-far-right-parties/?utm_term=.4566aef190c9.
UNHCR. 2017. *Figures at a Glance: Statistical Yearbooks*. http://www.unhcr.org/en-us/figures-at-a-glance.html
UNHCR. 2018. *Dadaab Refugee Complex*. http://www.unhcr.org/ke/dadaab-refugee-complex
United Nations Support Mission in Libya. 2016. "Detained and Dehumanised: Report on Human Rights Abuses against Migrants in Libya." *United Nations Human Rights*. 13 December 2016. https://unsmil.unmissions.org/Portals/unsmil/Documents/Migrants%20report-EN.pdf.
Walzer, M. 1983. *Spheres of Justice: A Defense of Pluralism and Equality*. New York: Basic Books.
Williams, B. A. O. 2011. *Ethics and the Limits of Philosophy*. New York: Routledge.
Zavis, A., and A. M. Simmons. 2017. "Europe's Migrant Crisis Threatens to Overwhelm Italy, Even as Flows to Greece Dry Up." *LA Times*, July 4. http://www.latimes.com/world/europe/la-fg-italy-migrants-20170704-htmlstory.html.
Zieck, M. 2013. "The 1956 Hungarian Refugee Emergency, and Early and Instructive Case of Resettlement." *Amsterdam Law Forum* 5: 45–63.

CHAPTER 34

MIGRATION FLOWS AND MIGRATION CRISIS IN SOUTHERN EUROPE

DOMENICO MADDALONI AND GRAZIA MOFFA

SOUTHERN Europe is now one of the major crossroads of international migration. According to the Eurostat Population Database, in 2015 about 10.9 million people, 8.37 percent of the residents in southern European countries (Cyprus, Greece, Italy, Malta, Portugal, and Spain) were foreign citizens.[1] According to the same source, in 2014 the total flow of immigrants to these countries was about 0.7 million people, and the total flow of emigrants was a little more than this same figure. This chapter will discuss three migration flows concerning this region. The first kind of mobility involves people from wealthier countries, moving toward southern Europe in search of a better quality of life—a process referred to as "lifestyle migration" by a growing literature. The second flow we will focus on is the "new emigration" from southern Europe toward other OECD countries, or even some emerging countries. Finally, the chapter will analyze the flow of (mainly forced) migrants trying to reach northern Europe through the Mediterranean routes. The first of these trends is usually considered more as an opportunity than a "problem" or a "risk" in the public discourse. The "new emigration" is often reduced to a generational problem or a phenomenon affecting particular groups. Only the flow of migrants, refugees, and asylum seekers coming from poorer countries is seen as a serious social and political issue, a "crisis" to be carefully tackled, if necessary with extraordinary measures. These migration flows occur in the midst of wide regional economic, social, and political changes, mostly driven by globalization, financialization, and the implementation of the neoliberal agenda. Apparently, these changes are leading to a decline of southern European countries in the international development and welfare rankings. Besides, these changes seem to affect the social construction of each migration flow by the national and local political elites and the media system. How do the migratory trends we mentioned previously interface with these more general changes?

And why are these mobility flows assessed so differently in the public discourse by local elites and the media? In the following sections of the chapter we will try to give an answer to these questions, both by outlining the essential features of each migration trend, and by highlighting the way in which politicians, administrators and the media use some of these features to construct a shared narrative in their own interest. The hope is that this will be a stimulus for further research on the role played by migration flows—both on the empirical and discourse level—in the changing societies of southern Europe.

Migration from Wealthier Countries: "A Chance for Development"

In recent years, many people from OECD countries have chosen to live in southern Europe. This section will focus on this type of international mobility, mainly using the concept of "lifestyle migration," recently developed in order to capture some of its distinguishing features. Lifestyle migration involves "relatively affluent individuals of all ages, moving either part-time or full-time to places that are meaningful because, for various reasons, they offer the potential of a better quality of life" (Benson and O'Reilly, 2009, 2). Therefore lifestyle migration overlaps other kinds of mobility, such as retirement migration, leisure migration, seasonal migration, or residential tourism—even if it does not entirely coincide with any of them.

Not all migrants coming to southern Europe from wealthier countries should be included in the concept of lifestyle migration. However, most migrants coming from "Northern" countries choose to live in this part of Europe for reasons related to the search of a better quality of life. Thus the data on migration from countries with a similar or higher level of wealth (though inaccurate, as always when studying migration) can be useful in the attempt to measure the extent of lifestyle migration at a macro level. According to the OECD International Migration Database, in 2014 the foreign residents coming from richer countries (or other southern European countries) to Spain were more than one million (21.5 percent of the foreigners in that country). The figures related to this type of mobility, however, are lower when we consider other countries of southern Europe.[2] No surprise that Spain is among the most studied cases in this field of research (O'Reilly 2003; Rodríguez, Casado, and Huber 2005; Huete 2009).

At a macro level, this kind of mobility indicates an ongoing blurring of the boundaries between tourism and migration: in many cases, middle- and upper-class foreigners visiting a Mediterranean country gradually develop the idea of a change in their lifestyle through migration, just because of their experience as tourists abroad. This gives space to different (seasonal or permanent) "residential lifestyles" which, in turn, can fuel new urbanization processes—a feature that lifestyle migration has shown particularly in Spain, where new *urbanizaciones* (housing estates) have been built in order to accommodate the new foreign residents (Gustafson 2009; Huete 2009). Anyway, even in these cases other factors are at stake in the choice to migrate abroad. As Huete (2009) points out, often the presence of environmental improvements, good infrastructures and public and private services, a low cost of the life, and an easy access to property ownership are among the factors behind individual choices of mobility. Thus "lifestyle migration" cannot be explained only by the individual search for self-fulfillment and a new identity, but also by reasons related to the economic and social conditions of both the individual actor and his or her potential destination areas.

Coming now to the political construction of this kind of mobility as a social issue we can say, first, that the migration of elderly people to southern Europe is presented sometimes as a special case of "welfare tourism," with a negative impact on the fragile southern European local welfare systems.[3] On the other side, the property investments and entrepreneurship of lifestyle migrants are considered as an important contribution to local development. For this reason, local political debates have been focusing on how best to *attract* these migratory flows and turn them into *opportunities* for economic growth. What is at stake is a state or regional legislation favorable to the purchase of real estate and the acquisition of a resident status by foreign citizens (for instance through tax breaks). Policies of this kind are at work in Spain, especially in certain regions like the Canary Islands. Recently Portugal has changed its financial regulations in order to benefit foreign citizens who become tax residents, for the first ten years of their stay in the country—even if the foreigners are among the non-habitual tax residents.[4]

Moreover, research on tourism, migration, and local development in Alicante, Spain has shown that the main social actors (politicians and entrepreneurs) involved in the local development processes tend to place residential tourism and immigration from richer countries in the context of a legitimizing dominant discursive model, a "regime of truth" aimed at supporting these processes (Huete, Mantecón, and Mazón 2008). These actors are the same people who most benefit from the current development model, which is mainly centered on building industry and private services. In turn, this produces a "very simplified divide between desirable and undesirable immigrants, or, even better, between the immigrants (a label reserved for labor immigration) and European residents" (2008, 156–157). While the former are associated with difficult economic and social conditions, the latter are seen as a chance for "progress." Besides, since many lifestyle migrants come from other EU countries, and since some southern European countries like Spain recognize voting rights in local elections to EU residents, these migrants have become legitimized political actors on the local scene, contrarily to migrant workers coming from poorer countries (Janoschka and Durán 2014).

Recently, however, the current southern European downturn has been entering the field of study on lifestyle migration as a research issue of growing importance. More specifically, we have empirical evidence that, in Spain, the recession started in 2007 has reduced the inflows of foreigners from wealthier countries and increased the outflows (Huete, Mantecón and Estévez, 2013). According to official data at a national level, the impact of southern European economic recession on the foreign population coming from richer countries (expressed as differences in both absolute values and relative figures over the period 2007–2014) has been negative also in Portugal and Greece, while data relating to Italy appear to be quite stable (Diana and Maddaloni 2018). But since living in Italy is definitely more expensive than in the other southern European countries, we can think that the Italian exception is caused by a different class composition in this segment of the foreign population. These results show, once more, that this kind of international mobility is not impermeable to changes in the local economic and social conditions. Furthermore, these results show that immigration from richer countries cannot make a decisive contribution to boosting economic growth in a declining southern Europe.

The New Emigration: "Youngsters in Search of Adventure"

The second process on which we will focus our attention is the so-called "new emigration" from southern Europe towards other destination areas, including emerging countries. Apparently, this is a return to the past for southern Europe. For a long time, this region was a source area of international migration, and this situation lasted until the 1970s, when it became a destination area for migration from poorer countries (King and Black 1997). The economic recession that began in 2007–2009, and its effects on local labor markets and welfare systems, seem to have caused, therefore, a major change in the mobility flows involving these countries, turning them once again into a source area.

This new flow of emigrants from southern European countries comes from many different groups and social strata (e.g., Domingo and Blanes 2016, for the case of Spain). Actually, the social composition of the new emigration from southern Europe is one of the main reasons why this process is labeled as "new" (Gjergji 2015). For example, the increase in emigration seems to concern former immigrants, insofar as they can move toward the countries of central and northern Europe. Some of them decide to return home because of the southern European economic recession (Triandafyllidou 2013). However, most new emigrants from the countries of southern Europe are young adult people who are not new citizens, nor foreigners with a residence permit. Today, for instance, there is a greater presence of women actively seeking work abroad, especially in other European Union countries, and this can produce also an inversion of traditional gender roles in the context of marriage or family relationships (Moffa 2014). Another difference from the past mobility trends is the urban origin of most southern European emigrants (Lafleur, Stanek, and Veira 2017).

One of the most important features of the new emigration is its composition with regard to skills and educational level. In southern Europe, "job opportunities in the fields of research and professional activities have diminished and young people seek opportunities of this kind abroad, sometimes finding them. Anyway, there are also young people, sometimes highly educated, who migrate in search of any job" (Pugliese

2014, 23). Furthermore, the decline of employment opportunities in the high-skilled labor market is not only about the total amount of jobs offered. It affects also their quality, in terms of stability, autonomy, and income—a topic related to the increasing flexibilization of southern European labor markets. In turn, this has generated a growing amount of research on the "brain drain" (or "brain escape" [*fuga dei cervelli, fuga de cérebros*]) in many southern European debates (as in Portugal—see Machado Gomes 2015). Conventional literature on the topic highlights the classical "push" and "pull" factors at work, at a macro level, in producing the flow of high-skilled young people moving abroad, especially towards the northern core of the European Union—a flow which is not balanced by a trend of the same strength in the opposite direction. On this point, conventional literature maintains that "highly skilled workers often leave their home country in the pursue of better life standards, higher pay as well as better and more challenging work opportunities." Moreover, "highly skilled individuals are overrepresented in the new flows of Southern European migrants because they are the ones who are able to better respond to the labor market needs of Northern EU Member States" (Lafleur and Stanek 2017, 216).

Recently, however, the idea of a linear and direct correlation between the new emigration from southern Europe and the current economic recession has been challenged to some extent. Southern European highly skilled migrants move abroad searching a well-paid work, a career development, but also a better quality of life (see section on migration from wealthier countries). Moreover, the individual choice to migrate is also the result of a strong criticism of the institutional and political culture of their country of origin, charged with familism, clientelism, and corruption (Triandafyllidou and Gropas 2014). These results have been largely confirmed by subsequent research on young high-skilled southern European migrants (Ricucci 2017; Tomei 2017).

Thus in this context the new emigration can be seen as an "exit strategy" from a regional economic recession that, in southern Europe, is widely perceived as a systemic decline (Maddaloni 2017). No surprise that the willingness of young southern European residents to move abroad in order to find a training opportunity or a job is, today, above the EU average (Nancy 2016). This attitude spreads also among medium- and low-skilled people, who can benefit from the western-central-northern European more dynamic and fluid local labor markets, but also from welfare systems which are often more effective, both as a support in periods of unemployment and as a source of new opportunities for training and work. This is an important point, since, as we have seen, many new migrants find jobs that do not meet their expectations, especially at the beginning of their life as expatriates. Besides, in each country of southern Europe the poorer areas show large long-term outflows, in terms of both international migration and internal mobility. Among the long-term effects induced by these processes, there are an excessive aging of the population, a decline in the potential for economic growth, and an increase of the socioeconomic territorial imbalances (for the case of Italy, see SVIMEZ 2013).

These last remarks have to be contrasted with the public debate and the policy initiatives taken by southern European governments to regulate these migration trends.

According to a comparative study on the subject, the southern European political elite is "now very reluctant to even acknowledge the existence of a crisis-related emigration. The Spanish government's insistence on describing new emigrants as 'youngsters in search of adventure' is particularly telling in this respect. This attitude illustrates the dilemma in which southern European governments find themselves with regard to the current emigration flows. On the one hand, these flows may marginally reduce the pressure on social assistance systems and improve unemployment statistics. On the other hand, explicitly encouraging emigration could be interpreted as a failure by the government to provide an adequate response to the crisis" (Lafleur and Stanek 2017, 218; the term "crisis" here refers to the general southern European decline).

In the local public discourse, therefore, what seems to prevail is the *denial* of the new emigration as a social and political issue. This attitude may entail the total absence of debate and initiatives on the subject (as in Greece: see Mavrodi and Moutselos 2017); the reshaping of policies to support emigration carried out in the previous historical period (as in Portugal—Marques and Góis 2017); or the adoption of a neoliberal vision of territorial mobility, according to which this is simply the product of labor globalization (as in Spain—Bermudez and Brey 2017). In some cases, as in Italy, the issue of the "brain drain" has been used also as a rhetorical device to strengthen ethnonationalist and anti-immigrant arguments (Tintori and Romei 2017). Alternatively, young people in southern Europe have been also described (by an Italian minister) as "choosy"—that is, spoiled children who are unable to be satisfied with the opportunities offered by the local labor market. In this kind of narrative, unemployment or emigration are presented as easy alternatives to hard work and personal sacrifice for the good of the country. This seems to be very consistent with the neoliberal rhetoric of individual responsibility, although it fails to properly consider the role played by local politicians and entrepreneurs in the regional decline. Under these circumstances, we believe that the new emigration will go on for a long time, acting as a factor in the deepening of the current southern European decline.

Migrants and Refugees from Poorer Countries: "Strangers at Our Gate"

Coming now to the mobility flows regarding people from "peripheral" or poorer countries (including some eastern European countries that are now part of the European Union), the first point to focus on is their *decline* in southern Europe because of the current regional economic downturn. Apparently, according to the Eurostat Population Database, in the era that opened with the Wall Street financial crisis (2007–2015) the total number of foreign residents living in southern European countries rose from around 9.0 to about 10.9 million. However, this result seems to be mostly related to the massive regularization policies implemented by the Italian government during this same period.[5] The other most important southern European countries are now experiencing a slight decline of the foreign residents, from both wealthier countries (see section on migration from wealthier countries) and the poorer ones. The inversion of migration trends is even more impressive. The immigration flow has been falling, from more than 1.6 million to less than 0.7 million (2007–2014). Together with the parallel rise in the emigration, from about 0.3 million to more than 0.7 million, the process has resulted in a negative net flow, both for the whole area and the single countries, with the exception of Italy and Malta.

Today, therefore, we have *less* foreign residents and *less* migrants coming from the "peripheral" countries than yesterday. In fact, we have already noted that many foreign legal residents and "new citizens" are leaving the countries of southern Europe in search of better job opportunities in other OECD countries (see section on the new emigration).[6]

However, in spite of this reduction in migratory flows, immigration from poorer countries is increasingly considered—by most of the political system and the media industry—as a "crisis" or a "risk" for the stability of southern European societies. In order to gain a better understanding of this process, it is first necessary to consider the role played by immigrant networks and communities in the local context. This role has been defined as "peripheral incorporation" or "subordinate integration" by many scholars (e.g., Reyneri 2001; Ribas-Mateos 2004). According to this stream of literature, immigrants from poorer countries play—in relation to native citizens—more a complementary than an antagonistic role in the local labor market. These migrants still carry out jobs, which are, for the most part, "dirty, dangerous, and demanding," with a major penalization in terms of salary (Reyneri and Fullin 2011). In addition, immigrant domestic workers and caregivers (mostly women) fill the shortcomings of a very poor welfare system as regards the services for elderly and incapacitated people. "Moreover, the often-illegal housing market for immigrants adds a source of income to the household budget of native residents, at a very low cost" (Blanco, Maddaloni, and Moffa 2016a, 27). Therefore migrants coming from poorer countries may be seen as a device allowing the local society to charge a part of the human and economic costs of the growing precariousness of work and life on these groups.

On the other hand, southern European countries still act as a transit area for many migrants. As we said before, they often use their stay in this part of Europe as a first step of a wider mobility process, culminating in the transfer to another country, in northern Europe or North America (Blanco, Maddaloni, and Moffa 2016b).[7] However, the foreign population has also experienced processes of stabilization and inclusion in the host society. In particular, the granting of legal status (including citizenship) and civil and social rights for immigrant workers and their families has become widespread, mainly because of the massive regularization policies pursued by southern European states since the late 1990s (Finotelli and Arango 2011). On this last point, however, it is important to note that the social inclusion of immigrants is not a homogeneous process in this part of Europe, either at a national or local level. In Italy, for instance, the lack of national programming in this policy area has caused growing territorial disparities, and less resistance to transform what could have been an integration strategy into policies of exclusion, depending on the political interests locally prevailing (Ambrosini 2014, 143–168). Moreover the ongoing reduction in public spending, caused by the financial crisis and the economic downturn, has severely affected the field of social and cultural integration of migrants from poorer countries (Blanco, Maddaloni, and Moffa 2016c). In addition there are now symptoms of an incipient crisis of the peripheral incorporation, related to such factors as the return of the marginal strata of the native population to segments of the labor market previously abandoned to immigrants, or the competition with immigrants for access to social welfare—housing, for instance. This may also produce growing inequalities and conflicts among different groups of immigrants along religious, ethnic, or regional lines (Blanco, Maddaloni and Moffa 2016b).

In the field of immigration policy, the sector that appears to be growing today is the management of the flow of asylum seekers and refugees—first reception, controls, distribution throughout the country, staying, and possible expulsion. This emergency affects Italy and Greece more than Spain and Portugal. Indeed, since 2012, there has been a wave of (mainly forced) migrants trying to cross the Mediterranean Sea in search for asylum. This wave has been caused by many factors. The first of them is the fact that the recent economic downturn hit the peripheral countries of sub-Saharan Africa and the Near East more severely than their southern European counterparts, causing the collapse of political regimes that had previously collaborated on border control with southern European states (i.e., Tunisia, Libya, and Syria).[8] In turn, this caused a deepening of regional, ethnic, and religious conflicts in some of these countries. Another factor has been the political usage of migration flows by other, more powerful states like Turkey and Egypt. As a result, many more migrants have traveled central and oriental Mediterranean routes than in the recent past—even if the Balkans route still seems to be the most important one today. According to the United Nations High Commissioner for Refugees, "Seeking safety and protection in Europe, an estimated 362,000 people risked their lives crossing the Mediterranean Sea in 2016, with 181,400 people arriving in Italy and 173,450 in Greece. Children accounted for just over a quarter of arrivals, many of them unaccompanied, separated from caregivers, and needing specific attention." (UNHCR 2017, 89).

Faced with this emergency, the policy response of the southern European States—primarily Italy and Greece—has appeared weak and contradictory. Undoubtedly, this is partly caused by the budgetary constraints stemming from the austerity policies harshly implemented in both countries—even the increase in resources mentioned previously has not been enough to offset the growth of immigrant needs. However, a major role in this ineffective policy response is played also by the political constraints coming from the European Union, which has the power to co-determine state policies on border control after the Schengen Treaty. Indeed, an EU-level governance of this emergence is difficult "for a variety of reasons: the different geopolitical interests of member states, the different migrant and refugee flows they receive, the different financial capabilities and political wills and the commitment to respect human rights in a framework that is designed and oriented more towards security and deterrence" (Triandafyllidou and Dimitriadi 2014, 25). These contradictions have produced a poor implementation of the same EU asylum seekers and refugee policy (the "Dublin regulation": see Cellini 2016), producing relevant discrepancies between policy intentions and the living conditions of migrants in the hotspots created as their temporary reception and identification areas. Thus while poor (sometimes even miserable) living conditions and legal stalemates tend to entrap migrants in these camps, a growing involvement of NGOs is required in order to provide basic health and legal assistance to them (for the case of Syracuse, Italy, see Kersh and Mishtal 2016).

The intensification of this flow of immigrants (a southern European version of a "refugee crisis" which today is much wider elsewhere) strongly contrasts with the stagnation or decline of the foreign population as a whole.[9] The contrast is exacerbated by the ambiguous attitude of the media towards this phenomenon. The media closer to governments and center-left parties are more prone to a proactive discourse toward migrants from poorer countries (Zapata-Barrero 2009)—that is, a discourse based on a human rights approach, which has a special strength in the case of forced migrants. Therefore, they tend to present asylum seekers and refugees as people asking help to the international community for inescapable humanitarian reasons (Tudisca et al. 2017). The local media, and those closer to center-right political forces, are more prone to a reactive, security-based discourse. Consequently, they often present immigrants from poorer countries as a "problem," associating their image with that of health emergencies, criminality, and ethnic or religious conflicts (Calvanese 2011; Vecina 2012).

Moreover, these changes are taking place in the midst of an incipient European political regression on the issues related to migration and multiculturalism. The "societal malaise" induced by neoliberal globalization and its impact on labor market and welfare institutions is generating a growing ethnocentrism among many European citizens (Aschauer 2016). As regards southern Europe, this can be particularly true for Italy and Greece. In recent years, these countries are experiencing both the harsher retrenchment policies and—as discussed previously—larger flows of refugees and asylum seekers. It is not surprising that "Immigrants become easy scapegoats as impoverished Greeks start competing with them for jobs in the low-skill sector and any claims for special measures (for Roma or immigrant children in schooling for instance) are seen through the lens of the budgetary constraints even more than before" (Triandafyllidou and Kokkali 2012, 199). Neither is it surprising that "in the current Italian context two different approaches to migrants have emerged: on the one hand political and public debate is characterized by the intolerance towards migrants; on the other hand, the labor market promotes their economic integration, whereas some civil society actors (Catholic organizations, trade unions, NGOs), also support their social integration. As a result, there is a deep discrepancy between the sphere of the market and migration policy, between the civil society actors and public or political debate" (Ambrosini and Caneva 2012, 228). As regards Spain, "Policy discourses emphasize interculturality, respect and recognition for cultural, religious and ethnic differences. [. . .] At the same time, [. . .] there has been a shift in public debate from not tolerating particular practices to not tolerating particular groups and 'cultures.'" (Zapata-Barrero and Garcés-Mascareñas 2012, 245). Finally, in Portugal "the Lusophone component continues to represent the largest share of the immigration picture in the country, shaping the relationship with 'diversity' and introducing a further form of distinction and discrimination, based on linguistic heritage" (Zanfrini 2015, 24).

In this perspective, the growing perception of immigrants from poorer countries (even more so if they are Muslims: Triandafyllidou 2015) as a "problem" or a "risk" may now enter a causal chain that deepens the southern European decline, with particular reference to the political arena. Ethnonationalist and anti-immigrant parties like the (northern) Italian Lega Nord or the Greek Golden Dawn have emerged in the last years. They are trying to take advantage of the growing anti-system feelings of the electorate, severely hurt by the economic crisis, by means of a strong nationalist and anti-immigrant propaganda. They express a sort of "conformist voice," in the sense that they claim to be advocates of "people affected by the crisis, but willing to charge its costs on other groups. They try to defend their social ties, cultural values and economic resources by excluding others, perceived as outsiders, from the shrinking benefits of the societal inclusion" (Maddaloni 2017, 220). The working classes and low-skilled middle classes (particularly self-employed workers, low-level employees, and law enforcement officers) seem to be the main recipients of these appeals. The reinvention of tradition, the security obsession, and the rejection of foreigners conveyed by these appeals provide a common ground for the emergence, diffusion and consolidation of political identities based on exclusion while supporting the existing social order (Maddaloni 2003). In turn, these changes feed the shift of public discourse in the immigration policy area towards issues such as border control and the expulsion of unwanted people.

Thus the incipient crisis of the peripheral incorporation, the flow of asylum seekers and refugees from Africa and Asia, and the growing and widespread fear of Islamic terrorism may fuel the rise of ideologies, movements, and parties that seemed to belong to the dark past of Europe. Nevertheless, there are still few open conflicts between immigrants and native citizens in southern Europe today. The political issues related to immigration and multiculturalism still seem to be open to different solutions. In this regard, a view shared by many social workers active in immigration policies is that a new citizenship policy, with particular reference to the granting of voting rights in local and regional elections to foreign residents, could rebalance the political debate on immigrant integration (Blanco, Maddaloni, and Moffa, 2016b, 2016c). Finally, there is evidence that the same wave of asylum seekers and refugees is generating somewhere a new collective actor instigating a positive change in the European political landscape (Benli 2017; for the case of Lampedusa, see Vecchi 2016). Local coalitions of migrants, activists, and social workers may open op new possibilities for participation and social and political inclusion.

Conclusion

This chapter has examined some important migratory flows taking place in southern European countries today—the migration from wealthier countries, the so-called "new emigration," and the "refugee crisis." They occur in the midst of a whole set of changes that are apparently leading to a decline of southern Europe in the international development and welfare rankings. These flows do not have the same intensity or scope in all these countries, but it seems to us that, as a whole, they may define the migratory landscape of this part of Europe. However, as we have seen, they are not perceived in the same way: the first one is seen as an opportunity rather than a problem, the second one is neglected, and only the third one is defined as a serious social and political issue, to be tackled by all means. This is because the southern European elites benefit from this political construction of the first and third of these flows. On the contrary, the second one is downplayed because it risks highlighting the negative and, in the long run, devastating effects of neoliberal policies on southern European "semi-peripherial" societies. Moreover, the dominant views on each of these flows are still conforming to neoliberal ideology, with increasing concessions to a security-based approach. Thus there are many different mobility flows in southern Europe, but there is only one "migration crisis" in national and local public discourses.

In conclusion, first, "Southern European countries cannot be regarded as an isolated area; they rather must be examined with regard to their interconnection with Europe as a whole as well as their position within global developments" (Baumeister and Sala 2015, 14). The issues related to migration and multiculturalism in southern Europe, therefore, have to be analyzed with reference to more general processes, such as globalization, financialization, and the local implementation of the neoliberal agenda—not to forget the growing role played by a supranational actor like the European Union. To this end, this chapter has tried to highlight the relationship between the migration trends mentioned previously and a regional decline which can be primarily seen as the combination of changes in southern European societies caused by neoliberal globalization. For some scholars, these trends are, for the most part, the result of wider strategies aimed at disciplining southern European societies in the global neoliberal order, and continuing capital accumulation (Avallone 2013; Tomei 2016). This chapter sees these flows as part of a complex set of processes, in which the strategies defined by global and national or local elites are confronted with the unanticipated effects produced by the agency of other classes and social groups—the middle and the working classes, regional or ethnic minorities, and migrants themselves. The future, therefore, is open—although we certainly cannot say in advance that it will be better than the present.

Notes

1. It is known that any attempt to quantify migration is affected by problems relating to the quality of the data available in relation to the multiple forms of human mobility. In this case,

the data collection was realized in March 2017 and the first results of the data analysis can be found in a paper by Diana and Maddaloni (2018).

2. In Portugal, this kind of foreign resident numbered a little more than 60,000, 15.4 percent of the foreigners; in Greece, a little more than 40,000 (5.7 percent); in Italy, about 200,000 (4.1 percent).
3. It is known that the different quality of local and national welfare systems with regard to meeting the social and working needs of citizens and residents has generated a controversy on "welfare tourism" among EU member states. Moreover, there is evidence that, in EU member states, restrictions in social and employment policy are increasingly used as an instrument for controlling and delegitimizing migration, including that of EU citizens (Lafleur and Stanek 2017).
4. Greece and Italy have no such preferential treatment for foreign residents, although in the current political debate some Greek parties have expressed their intention to introduce it once in power.
5. The Spanish government had already implemented regularization policies shortly before the outbreak of the country's economic crisis.
6. The trend toward the expatriation of immigrants due to the economic recession has been particularly strong in Spain, especially at its beginnings (Domingo i Valls, Coll, and Rivera 2014), while it is less accentuated in the other countries of southern Europe. The emigration trend is stronger among Spanish immigrants with worse employment outcomes and a poorer educational background (Miyar and Comet, 2015).
7. A viable alternative to transit migration is circular migration, which seems to be mainly practiced by immigrants from Eastern Europe. Circular migration (as well as temporary migration) has the effect of cushioning the difficult living conditions imposed on immigrants in the context of peripheral or subordinate incorporation. No surprise that recently policymakers have widely supported these specific types of international mobility (Triandafyllidou 2013).
8. The tremendous human costs imposed on migrants because of these harsh "preventive" border control policies are now widely documented (for the case of Ghanaians in southern Italy, see Lucht 2011).
9. According to Frontex, in 2015 Italy and Greece hosted less than 2 refugees each 1,000 inhabitants. The corresponding figure for Germany is 3.9; for Jordan, 87; for Lebanon, 232 (Frontex 2016).

References

Ambrosini, M. 2014. *Non passa lo straniero? Le politiche migratorie tra sovranità nazionale e diritti umani*. Assisi, Italy: Cittadella.

Ambrosini, M., and E. Caneva. 2012. "Italy." In *Addressing Tolerance and Diversity Discourses in Europe: A Comparative Overview of 16 European Countries*, edited by R. Zapata-Barrero and A. Triandafyllidou, 207–230. Barcelona, Spain: CIDOB.

Aschauer, W. 2016. "Societal Malaise and Ethnocentrism in the European Union: Monitoring Societal Change by Focusing on EU Citizens' Perceptions of Crisis." *Historical Social Research/Historische Sozialforschung*, 41, no. 2: 307–359.

Avallone, G. 2013. "El campo neoliberal y su crisis. Agricultura, sociedad local y migraciones en la Europa del Sur." *Encrucijadas: Revista critica de ciencias sociales* 6: 39–55.

Baumeister, M., and R. Sala. 2015. "Introduction." In *Southern Europe? Italy, Spain, Portugal and Greece from the 1950s until the Present Day*, edited by M. Baumeister and R. Sala, 7–15. Frankfurt am Main: Campus Verlag.

Benli, A. E. 2017. *Refugee Crisis in Europe: The March To Claim Rights*. Rome: Consiglio Nazionale delle Ricerche—Istituto di Ricerche sulla Popolazione e le Politiche Sociali, IRPPS Working papers no. 97. http://irppsepub.altervista.org/ojs/index.php/wp/article/view/97

Benson, M., and K. O'Reilly. 2009. "Lifestyle Migration: Escaping to the Good Life?" In *Lifestyle Migration. Expectations, Aspiration and Experiences*, edited by M. Benson and K. O'Reilly, 1–13. Farnham-Burlington, UK: Ashgate.

Bermudez, A., and E. Brey. 2017. "Is Spain Becoming a Country of Emigration Again? Data Evidence and Public Responses." In *South-North Migration of EU Citizens in Times of Crisis*, edited by J. -M. Lafleur and M. Stanek. Cham, Switzerland: Springer International.

Blanco Gregory, R., D. Maddaloni, and G. Moffa. 2016a. "Still a Place of Hope? Immigration in the Periphery of Southern Europe in an Age of Crisis." *The International Journal of Interdisciplinary Social and Community Studies* 11, no. 1: 17–30.

Blanco Gregory, R., D. Maddaloni, and G. Moffa. 2016b. "Migration in Southern Europe: The Peripheral Incorporation in Crisis." *Arxius de Ciències Socials* 35: 95–108.

Blanco Gregory, R., D. Maddaloni, and G. Moffa. 2016c. "Welfare, immigrazione e crisi nei Paesi dell'Europa meridionale. Un confronto tra due regioni: Campania ed Estremadura." *The Lab's Quarterly* 2, no. 1: 47–71.

Calvanese, Ernesto. 2011. *Media e immigrazione tra stereotipi e pregiudizi. La rappresentazione dello straniero nel racconto giornalistico*. Milan, Italy: FrancoAngeli.

Cellini, Marco. 2016. *The European Refugees Crisis: How To Address It*. Consiglio Nazionale delle Ricerche—Istituto di Ricerche sulla Popolazione e le Politiche Sociali, IRPPS Working papers no. 95. http://irppsepub.altervista.org/ojs/index.php/wp/article/view/95

Diana, P., and D. Maddaloni. 2018. "Lifestyle Migration: Italy in the Southern European Context." ATINER Conference Paper Series no. SOC2017–2388. Athens (Greece): ATINER. https://www.atiner.gr/papers/SOC2017-2388.pdf

Domingo i Valls, A., A. S. Coll, and E. O. Rivera. 2014. "¿Migración neo-hispánica? El impacto de la crisis económica en la emigración española." *Empiria: Revista de Metodología de Ciencias Sociales* 29: 39–66.

Domingo i Valls, A., and A. B. Llorens. 2016. "La nueva emigración española: ¿Una generación perdida?" *Panorama Social* 23: 157–178.

Finotelli, C., and J. Arango. 2011. "Regularisation of Unauthorised Immigrants in Italy and Spain: Determinants and Effects." *Documents d'Anàlisi Geogràfica* 57, no. 3: 495–515.

Frontex. 2016. *Annual Risk Analysis 2016*. Warsaw: Frontex. https://reliefweb.int/report/world/frontex-annual-risk-analysis-2016

Gjergji, I. 2015. "Cause, mete e figure sociali della nuova emigrazione italiana." In *La nuova emigrazione italiana: Cause, mete e figure sociali*, edited by I. Gjergji, 7–23. Venice, Italy: Edizioni Ca' Foscari.

Gustafson, Per. 2009. "Your Home in Spain: Residential Strategies in International Retirement Migration." In *Lifestyle Migration. Expectations, Aspiration and Experiences*, edited by M. Benson and K. O'Reilly, 69–86. Farnham-Burlington, UK: Ashgate.

Huete Nieves, R. 2009. *Turistas que llegan para quedarse: Una explicación sociológica sobre la movilidad residencial*. Alicante, Spain: Universidad de Alicante.

Huete, R., A. Mantecón, and J. F. Estévez. 2013. "Challenges in Lifestyle Migration Research: Reflections and Findings about the Spanish Crisis." *Mobilities* 8, no. 3: 331–348.

Huete, R., A. Mantecón, and T. Mazón. 2008. "Analysing the Social Perception of Residential Tourism Development." In *Proceedings of the IASK International Conference: Advances in Tourism Research*, edited by C. Costa and P. Cravo, 153–161. Aveiro, Portugal: IASK.

Janoschka, M., and R. Durán. 2014. "Lifestyle Migrants in Spain: Contested Realities of Political Participation." In *Contested Spatialities, Lifestyle Migration and Residential Tourism*, edited by M. Janoschka and H. Haas, 1–12. London and New York: Routledge.

Kersh, A., and J. Mishtal. 2016. "Asylum in Crisis: Migrant Policy, Entrapment, and the Role of Non-Governmental Organisations in Siracusa, Italy." *Refugee Survey Quarterly* 60, no. 4: 97–121.

King, R., and R. Black, eds. 1997. *Southern Europe and the New Immigrations*. Brighton, UK: Sussex Academic Press.

Lafleur, J.–M., and M. Stanek. 2017. "Lessons from the South-North Migration of EU Citizens in Times of Crisis." In *South-North Migration of EU Citizens in Times of Crisis*, edited by J-M. Lafleur and M. Stanek, 215–224. Cham, Switzerland: Springer International.

Lafleur, J.-M., M. Stanek, and A. Veira. 2017. "South-North Labour Migration Within the Crisis-Affected European Union: New Patterns, New Contexts and New Challenges." In *South-North Migration of EU Citizens in Times of Crisis*, edited by J.-M. Lafleur and M. Stanek, 193–213. Cham, Switzerland: Springer International.

Lucht, H. 2011. *Darkness Before Daybreak: African Migrants Living on the Margins in Southern Italy Today*. Berkeley: University of California Press.

Machado Gomes, R., ed. 2015. *Fuga de cérebros: Retratos da emigração portuguesa qualificada*. Lisbon, Portugal: Bertrand.

Maddaloni, D. 2003. "Una scelta ragionevole in tempi complicati: Note sull'economia politica delle riforme nell'epoca della crisi dello sviluppo e del welfare." *Quaderni di sociologia* 32: 116–141.

Maddaloni, D. 2017. "Southern European Pathways across the Great Recession." *Athens Journal of Social Sciences* 4, no. 3: 211–227.

Marques, J. C., and P. Góis. 2017. "Structural Emigration: The Revival of Portuguese Outflows." In *South-North Migration of EU Citizens in Times of Crisis*, edited by J.-M. Lafleur and M. Stanek, 65–82. Cham, Switzerland: Springer International.

Mavrodi, G., and M. Moutselos. 2017. "Immobility in Times of Crisis? The Case of Greece." In *South-North Migration of EU Citizens in Times of Crisis*, edited by J.-M. Lafleur and M. Stanek, 33–48. Cham, Switzerland: Springer International.

Miyar Busto, M., and J. M. Comet. 2015. "La salida de inmigrantes en contextos de declive económico ¿Cambia la autoselección durante fases recesivas?" *Revista Española de Investigaciones Sociológicas* 152: 87–104.

Moffa, G. 2014. "Lo scenario di riferimento delle nuove migrazioni." In *Le nuove generazioni tra i nuovi spazi e nuovi tempi delle migrazioni*, edited by FILEF, 41–60. Rome: Ediesse.

Nancy, J. 2016. *European Youth in 2016. Eurobaretmo, European Parliament*. Public Opinion Monitoring Series, European Parliament Research Service, Bruxelles-Luxembourg. http://www.europarl.europa.eu/atyourservice/it/20160504PVL00110/European-youth-in-2016.

O'Reilly, K. 2003. *The British on the Costa del Sol: Transnational Identities and Local Communities*. London and New York: Routledge.

Pugliese, E. 2014. "L'Italia tra emigrazione e immigrazione: tendenze storiche e recenti." In *Le nuove generazioni tra i nuovi spazi e nuovi tempi delle migrazioni*, edited by FILEF, 17–30. Rome: Ediesse.

Reyneri, E. 2001. *Migrants' Involvement in Irregular Employment in the Mediterranean Countries of the European Union*. International Migration Papers, International Labor Organization, Geneva. http://www.ilo.int/wcmsp5/groups/public/---ed_protect/---protrav/---migrant/documents/publication/wcms_201875.pdf

Reyneri, E., and G. Fullin. 2011. "Labour Market Penalties of New Immigrants in New and Old Receiving West European Countries." *International Migration* 49, no. 1: 31–57.

Ribas-Mateos, N. 2004. "How Can We Understand Immigration in Southern Europe?" *Journal of Ethnic and Migration Studies* 30, no. 6: 1045–1063.

Ricucci, R. 2017. *The New Southern European Diaspora: Youth, Unemployment, and Migration*. Lanham, MD: Lexington.

Rodríguez Rodríguez V., M. A. Casado Diaz, and A. Huber, eds. 2005. *La migración de europeos retirados en España*. Madrid: CSIC.

SVIMEZ. 2013. *Rapporto sull'economia del Mezzogiorno*. Bologna, Italy: Il Mulino.

Tintori, G., and V. Romei. 2017. "The Emigration from Italy after the Crisis: The Shortcomings of the Brain Drain Narrative." In *South-North Migration of EU Citizens in Times of Crisis*, edited by J.-M. Lafleur and M. Stanek, 49–64. Cham, Switzerland: Springer International.

Tomei, G. 2016. "Social Transformation, Subjectification, and Labour Migration: Theorizing the Heterogeneity of Migration Flows in the Current Italian Crisis." In *An Anthology of Migration and Social Transformation. European Perspectives*, edited by A. Amelina, K. Horvath, and B. Meeus, 167–181. Berlin: Springer.

Tomei, G., ed. 2017. *Cervelli in circolo: Trasformazioni sociali e nuove migrazioni qualificate*. Milan, Italy: FrancoAngeli.

Triandafyllidou, A. 2013. *Migration Policy in Southern Europe: Challenges, Constraints and Prospects*. A Strategy for Southern Europe, LSE IDEAS Special Report. European Web Site on Integration. https://ec.europa.eu/migrant-integration/librarydoc/migration-policy-in-southern-europe-challenges-constraints-and-prospects

Triandafyllidou, A. 2015. *European Muslims: Caught between Local Integration Challenges and Global Terrorism Discourses*. IAI working papers no. 15. https://www.osce.org/networks/newmedtrackII/166511?download=true.

Triandafyllidou, A., ed. 2013. *Circular Migration between Europe and its Neighbourhood: Choice or Necessity?* Oxford: Oxford University Press.

Triandafyllidou, A., and R. Gropas. 2014. "'Voting With Their Feet': Highly Skilled Emigrants From Southern Europe." *American Behavioral Scientist* 58, no. 12: 1614–1633.

Triandafyllidou, A., and I. Kokkali. 2012. "Greece." In *Addressing Tolerance and Diversity Discourses in Europe: A Comparative Overview of 16 European Countries*, edited by R. Zapata-Barrero and A. Traindafyllidou, 179–206. Barcelona, Spain: CIDOB.

Triandafyllidou, A., and A. Dimitriadi. 2014. "Governing Irregular Migration and Asylum at the Borders of Europe: Between Efficiency and Protection." *Imagining Europe*. Rome: Istituto Affari. http://www.iai.it/sites/default/files/ImaginingEurope_06.pdf.

Tudisca, V., A. Pelliccia, M. G. Caruso, L. Cerbara, A. Valente. 2017. "La rappresentazione dei migranti nelle testate giornalistiche online europee: Una analisi pilota." In *Migrazioni e integrazioni nell'Italia di oggi*, edited C. Bonifazi, 337–351. Rome: CNR-IRPPS.

United Nations High Commissioner on Refugeees. 2017. *Global Report 2016*. Geneva: United Nations High Commissioner on Refugeees. http://reporting.unhcr.org/sites/default/files/gr2016/pdf/Book_GR_2016_ENGLISH_complete.pdf.

Vecchi, I. 2016. "The Experience of the Askavusa Association: Migrant Struggle with Cultural Activities." *Crossings: Journal of Migration and Culture* 7, no. 2: 165–179.

Vecina Merchante, C. 2012. "Un estudio sobre representaciones sociales de la inmigración en la prensa y en una revista de barrio." *Revista Electrónica de Investigación y Docencia* 2: 32–55. http://revistaselectronicas.ujaen.es/index.php/reid/article/view/1149/971.

Zanfrini, L. 2015. "Diversity Improvement as a Viable Enrichment Resource for Society and Economy." In *The Diversity Value: How to Reinvent the European Approach to Immigration*, edited by L. Zanfrini, 1–34. Maidenhead, UK: McGraw Hill Education.

Zapata-Barrero, R. 2009. "Political Discourses about Borders: On the Emergence of an European Political Community." In *A Right to Inclusion and Exclusion? Normative Fault Lines of the EU's Area of Freedom, Security, and Justice*, edited by H. Lindahl, 15–31. Oxford: Hart Publishing.

Zapata-Barrero, R., and B. Garcés-Mascareñas. 2012. "Spain." In *Addressing Tolerance and Diversity Discourses in Europe: A Comparative Overview of 16 European Countries*, edited by R. Zapata-Barrero and A. Triandafyllidou, 231–248. Barcelona, Spain: CIDOB.

CHAPTER 35

NARRATIVES OF CRISIS MIGRATION AND THE POWER OF VISUAL CULTURE

CLAUDIA TAZREITER

THIS chapter proceeds from the premise that human migrations are not only predictable, but are a common feature of contemporary life as people fulfill life desires and needs such as work, education, family, and social relations. Such human desires and needs are not always met or contained within the bounded nation-state an individual is born into or acquires membership of. Violence, persecution, and discrimination are important additional factors driving "forced" migration. Indeed, there are multiple and often intersecting factors that drive migration, factors that are known, well understood, and therefore arguably unsurprising. Yet too often the responses to human migrations are of shock and disbelief. In the contemporary world, the factors that ought to render migration as an integral aspect of life include the rapid and ever-changing flows of global capital; natural and human-produced disasters; new transnational social and political formations facilitated by new technologies; political and other forms of violence; and nation-states that exercise border control as a form of exclusion. With the context of the interlinked, globalized world in mind, the chapter proceeds to outline a conceptual framework to explore crisis in migration before moving to the example of crisis narratives adopted on the issue of asylum-seekers and irregular migrants in the context of Australia.

What this chapter aims to delineate is a typology of crisis narratives of migration not necessarily linked to, or originating in, migration flows. Nor are these dominant crisis narratives of migration linked to arguments or avenues for solutions to the political or cultural problems and tensions that are often linked to migration—as might be expected. Rather, crisis narratives of migration exploit, situate, and relate social and political problems to migration as if there were causal links where none exist. Complex and sustained rhetoric of migration crises are deployed by governments and political elites in many parts of the world, exploiting voter sentiment in waves of populism that often assert a neonationalist turn to closed borders and associated assertions of national sovereignty. It is notable that recent research indicates that for people convinced by neonationalist rhetoric on migration as a problem for nation-states it is cultural questions that occupy the greatest concern rather than economic concerns of loss of jobs or economic status (Grigorieff et al. 2016; Hainmüller and Hopkins 2014; Kaufmann and Harris 2015).

Narratives of crisis migration are attached to many categories of migrants, but notably to refugees and asylum-seekers. A good deal of the "crisis" attached to refugee and other "irregular migrant" arrivals is generated by the spontaneous nature of these arrivals—without the regulated border crossings nation-states have instituted with passports and visas. Or perhaps, more deeply thought through, the generating of a "crisis" response to refugee arrivals appears as a manufactured hysteria, or deliberatively constructed overreaction, orchestrated by and through the same sovereign states tasked to protect refugees. This claim will be explored in more detail in relation to the Australian case study with a focus on the use of affect, emotions, and visual culture.

Globally, the migration context is one of increased prevalence of temporary rather than permanent migration, due to complex factors including less permanent work; increasingly transnational family, friendship, and wider social and political networks; and the demand for a highly mobile, yet dispensable workforce in neoliberal, globally connected economies. Globalized economies are highly adaptive to international forces, yet the consequences of flexibility and quick adaptation for individuals and social groups is manifest in forms of insecurity and precarity. "Individual success or failure is interpreted in terms of entrepreneurial virtues or personal failings . . . rather than being attributed to any systemic property" (Harvey 2005, 65–66). Markets are rewarded for fluidity and mobility, while humans are often constrained and punished for the same qualities. Human mobility is subject to continuous cycles of regulation and reregulation of borders and the bodies that cross them. These processes are manifested profoundly in the uneven flows of authorized or unauthorized, planned, or spontaneous migrants across nation-state borders (Castles 2010; Cresswell 2010; Dauvergne 2016; Sassen 2006). The processes and practices of bordering—spatial, material, cognitive, and conceptual—have entrenched and extended inequalities and exclusions within and between nation-states, though importantly these inequalities and exclusions are also likely to be increasingly hidden and invisible. Temporary migrants, such as those filling labor shortages, are in some ways fortunate on a migration continuum that also includes irregular migrants such as refugees and asylum-seekers, who have little or no access to the documents that allow official, regulated passage across the territorial borders of states as well as to the social recognition, respect, and dignity that accompanies "official" status through visas, passports, and leads to pathways to citizenship, or residency. But this chapter does not intend to delve into the distinguishing features, or boundaries between categories of migrant, but rather make the general observation that though legal categories are important, in the politicized context of "crisis migration" this engages with, it is the fluidity and slippage of categories (migrant, refugee, temporary worker/guestworker, illegal, outsider, foreigner), and the emotive language and visual triggers used to describe them, that are important to explore and to unmask.

The Language and Context of Crisis in Migration

There are events that are correctly referred to as migration or refugee crises. Indeed, the number and scale of such events appear to be increasing rather than diminishing in the twenty-first century. One recent "migration crisis" is that of the latest wave of mass forced displacements and expulsions of the persecuted Rohingya minority from Myanmar. The forced migration of Rohingya has continued for over two decades; however, the most recent spate of violence and killing has led to a rapid and large exodus. Since September 2017, over 620,000 Rohingya have fled to makeshift camps in Bangladesh. The UN has labeled the targeted killing and burning of Rohingya and their villages by the military as ethnic cleansing (Safi 2017).

This chapter will argue, drawing on the Australian case, that tangible, existential migration crises are not properly and robustly addressed to alleviate the suffering of the most marginalized people such as the Rohingya minority. Rather, "crisis migration" is used to divert public attention from issues that sovereign states, political leaders, and political parties loathe to deal with. The argument is built on the rhetorical and politically expedient uses of "migration crisis" as pejorative shorthand for any number of other social and political problems unrelated to migrant and refugee flows, yet drawn together in the communicative repertoires of political elites, populist parties, and some parts of the mass media. These forms of political communication, either consciously or unconsciously, create, exploit, and then nourish further crisis narratives of migration. These processes are systemic, embedded in institutional practices and knowledge, and include economic accumulation and exchange (neoliberal global capital) and legacies of colonial power and related racialized hierarchies mediated through the fast-paced, technologically-led change to social relations and sociability.

The specter of crisis in relation to migrants has resonances in many parts of the world. The pronouncements of US President Donald Trump, of "building a great wall between the US and Mexico" uses the language of crisis, promising to alleviate the concerns and problems of his electorate. The implied message in the regularly repeated pronouncements on the border wall builds a picture of migrant as existential threat without detail (*BBC News* 2017). The so-called Brexit campaign in the United Kingdom was built on similar rhetoric of immigrants as generalized threat, implying cultural, economic, and political impacts from the presence of non-British, nonwhite persons. The Australian case which is explored in most detail in this chapter is perhaps the most wide-ranging, exclusionary, and punitive example of generating crisis in relation to refugees and asylum-seekers when viewed against Australia's historical leading role in the international human rights system and the relatively small number of asylum-seekers seeing Australia's protection relative to the global refugee numbers. For example, the United Nations High Commissioner for Refugees Global Trends show that by the end of 2016 Australia had 71,778 people of concern. By comparison, Sweden had 349,303 and Germany had 1, 268,845 (UNHCR 2016).

This article will now consider how visual culture and visual communication contributes to generating crisis feelings and crisis talk on the issue of migration before moving to an exploration of a theoretical framing of crisis.

Visualization of Crisis Migration

Visual culture and various applications and uses of the visualization of crisis are important aspects of creating and interpreting "migration crises." Indeed, often visual modes are the most prominent and powerful in generating pro, anti, as well as ambivalent images and portrayals of refugees and "irregular" migrants, with the transmission of photographs, video, film, and other visual documentation, as well as artistic interpretation of migration journeys, arrivals, and the relational flows with a receiver society. Moreover, visual evidence can be a crucial trigger for action as well as confirming that an abuse or injustice has occurred. For example, documentary film and photographic evidence have been instrumental in shedding light on the detention "black sites" of Manus Island and Nauru as part of Australia's offshore regime for asylum-seekers arriving by boat, explored later in the chapter.

In 2015, at the height of what was labeled a "migration crisis" in Europe, the tiny body of Syrian toddler Aylan Kurdi washed up on a Turkish beach. The small vessel on which he and his family and other Syrian asylum-seekers were traveling on in an attempt to reach the Greek island of Kos had capsized. Aylan and his family were attempting to enter Europe along with thousands of other Syrians, as well as irregular migrants and asylum-seekers from other countries. For a few short weeks, the images of Aylan's lifeless body caused an outpouring of sentiment in Europe and across the world. The image fueled a call for government intervention to avert people having to take such desperate and dangerous journeys. High profile Chinese artist, Ai Weiwei continues to use his artistic and activist practice to comment on the so-called "migrant crisis" in Europe and globally in a number of art pieces including a photographic restaging of the death of the toddler Aylan Kurdi as a commentary on the weakness of collective action and political will to find lasting solutions to the "refugee crisis." More recently, Ai Weiwei has released a documentary feature film called Human Flow, drawing links between environmental degradation, climate change, and mass human displacement, as well as refugee flows caused by political violence and various forms of persecution.

Visual forms of communication are impactful through the ability to generate deep feelings in response to an image or immersive experiences (Sontag 2003). In Australia, irregular migrant arrivals, notably of asylum-seekers, has resulted in a new kind of "border of disappearance" (Tazreiter 2017), whereby the legal excision of Australian territory and the related policies of offshore removals results in a unique type of national border—used only by the Australia state—where the state has chosen to "disappear" those claiming to be refugees. What is important here is not only the legal utility of disappearing borders as the national territory disappears for those arriving by boat and wishing to lodge a claim for protection, but the disappearance rendered by the removal of asylum-seekers through the "offshore" processes. This becomes a kind of "double disappearance" as the bodies of asylum-seekers are rendered invisible to Australian citizens through distance, detention, media blackouts, and information bans, as well as the rhetorical and visual demonizing of asylum-seekers as devious and undeserving. The uses of visual culture in the Australian case will be explored later in the chapter with evidence that indicates the manner in which visual and material culture has been used by human rights advocates, activists, and artists to draw attention to the circumstances of asylum-seekers detained in offshore locations with a view to changing policy. Visual and material culture has also been utilized by the Australian state to convince domestic populations of the efficacy and legitimacy of state practices, as well as to communicate with asylum-seekers planning migration journeys to seek protection in an attempt to dissuade them from traveling to Australia.

The Conceptual Framing of Crisis

There are several important theoretical vantage points which help to excavate the concept of crisis and its utility in contemporary social and political life. In the context of this chapter which aims to interrogate the crisis narratives of asylum and migration, the theoretical concepts of affect and biopolitics possess explanatory and analytical nuance. Analyzing social relations through the lens of affect brings to the fore the labile and fluid processes that impact our actions (Ahmed 2004; Hoggett and Thompson 2012; Tazreiter 2015), transcending the linear, planned logic and discursive communication of statist bureaucratic order and control. Moreover, writers exploring the "affective turn" provide rich perspectives on the biomediated body, underscoring "body-as-organism" in boundary or boundary-making conditions and processes (Braidotti 2013; Clough 2010; Haraway 1989; Puar 2017). These concepts allow space for new thinking that nourishes more nuanced understandings of immigration control policies and administrative measures—beyond the commonly invoked concepts from which some of the core values in contemporary societies are also derived—of the nation-state as unit of territorial sovereignty and "container" of members and identities, and universal human rights principles and obligations. The popular and populist uses of "crisis migration" and of "crisis in migration" emerge most commonly through defensive politics invoking one of those concepts, or intersections of nation-state and rights arguments. However, both the nation-state form and the practices of rights allocations (through citizenship for example) already contain a historically specified human subject gendered, racialized, and able-bodied. The culture and processes of modernity, post-enlightenment thinking, and the liberal, democratic traditions themselves are steeped in these histories. The "writing back in" of the historically absent and disenfranchised is an ongoing task, and one that is under constant attack. The migrant body—the asylum-seeker, the refugee, the migrant worker—is caught up in contemporary processes, laws, and stories of fear and hatred with their origin in these longer histories of exclusion, invisibility, and of empire and colonialism (Mann 1993, 2003) with long tentacles to the present.

Before elaborating on the Australian case, it's necessary to turn to the meta-concept, modernity, and related complications pertaining to population governance. Modernity and its correlates of scientific rationality and the drive for exponential development or "progress" are facilitated through a bureaucratically complex administrative machinery; the micro-specialization of work with "experts" at the apex (Foucault 2007); and economic diversification through a capitalist system (Boltanski and Chiapello 2005; Edmondson and Mladek 2017). Schinkel, for example, mounts a powerful argument, drawing on the work of Walter Benjamin, that modernity is crisis (2015). In explaining "the political," Schinkel reminds us that the invocation of crisis in contemporary democracies is precisely a depoliticization of contemporary life in that crisis is constituted as if stumbling through a dream rather than an impetus for awakening and attendant critique (Benjamin, cited in Schinkel 2015, 14). That is, crisis is utilized as a political tactic of scapegoating and creating moral panics, deferring attention from existential problems and threats to more everyday, visible issues such as asylum-seekers arriving at the border. Janet Roitman (2014), Lauren Berlant (2011), and Bonnie Honig (2009) offer highly original and instructive theorizations of crisis and emergency that eschew simplistic labeling, blame, and fear.

Capitalist accumulation as a key aspect of modernity is itself fundamentally a crisis-phenomenon, requiring constant change, renewal, and movement. In everyday social life, such factors are internalized and normalized as everyday aspects of life, leading to what the French theorist Pierre Bourdieu labels "misrecognition" where a social group or class fail to identify the root cause of the problems they face (1977). Following on from this briefly characterized historical vantage point of the embeddedness of certain ideas and actions through the project of modernity, it is also critical to remember that the ideas of permanent settlement of migrants and stasis or immobility of local populations remain the dominant tropes that undergird the nation-state as a political entity and as a system of belonging and identity. This despite the lived reality that the mobility of workers is a desired and often imposed aspect of global capital, marked by growth in temporary, not permanent migration (Glick Schiller and Salazar 2013, 188).

In contrast to the needs, desires, and symbols of transnational capital for openness, fluidity, and flexibility, including people as both workers and consumers, national immigration policies in many parts of the world, including Australia, generate the perception of a crisis and loss of control by the state. Policymakers and political leaders regularly communicate about different categories of immigrants as if these categories were fixed, rather than the reality of fluidity between categories as people move between regular and irregular migration, sponsored and spontaneous arrival, and forced and voluntary migrations (Tazreiter et al. 2016). As will be discussed in the following case study, perhaps surprisingly, Australia is a country that has demonstrated extreme crisis narratives in relation to asylum-seeker arrivals. These crisis narratives have been transformed into state policy and comprehensive legal change to ensure those seeking protection in Australia are not permitted to enter the nation-state at any point in the future—even once found to be genuine refugees. In this regard, family reunion has been quarantined for asylum-seekers arriving by boat, with the result that they may not reunite nor visit family members living in Australia at any point, even once granted a protection visa as a "genuine refugee."

The Australian Case

This article will now consider briefly the history of the reception and treatment of asylum-seekers and irregular migrants in Australia in order to build the argument of crisis migration deployed by successive Australian governments. Indeed, there are numerous examples of "crisis narratives of migration" that can be considered in the Australian case. This is perhaps surprising in the context of Australia as a "settler society," demonstrably benefiting in all spheres of public life—social, cultural, economic, and political—from the positive impacts of immigration including refugee arrivals. Ethnic and linguistic diversity in Australia is a key characteristic of contemporary life with immigrant communities coming from all parts of the world. Since the 1980s, immigration from countries in the Asia region has grown considerably. The context of the end of the discriminatory White Australia Policy, which had ended a decade earlier, was one significant factor in this growth. Australia has also received a steady intake of refugee arrivals through resettlement and humanitarian programs.

Key examples focus particularly on the most explicit political utility of "crisis migration": the "offshore" detention of asylum-seekers arriving by boat to claim protection on Nauru and Manus Island. These examples, and the historical context that gave way to the legitimation of the punitive approach to boat arrivals, also has knock-on effects in other national jurisdictions and, importantly, for international legal and human rights norms. Indeed, the international refugee system relies on a delicate balance of cooperation between nation-states to ensure the protection of vulnerable populations. Arguably, the actions of the Australian state render the international refugee system more fragile in Australia's turn away from fundamental principles such as burden-sharing and adherence to the legal norms outlined in the Refugee Convention of 1951.

A brief backdrop to Australia's history as an immigrant settler nation is an important context for understanding the contemporary nation, if focused primarily on examples of crisis narratives and responses in relation to recent irregular and temporary migration flows. Australia is an immigration nation, a "settler society" (Dauvergne 2016), built on waves of immigration since white settlement as a British colony. In recent years

Australia has had a yearly intake of skilled migrants, temporary workers, and students, as well as a yearly humanitarian quota of "resettlement" refugees who are selected by Australian immigration officials mostly from refugee camps, enter on a visa, and are permitted to become permanent residents and citizens. Asylum-seekers, by contrast, arrive spontaneously, without travel documents. It is this unplanned and uninvited arrival that successive Australian Governments have characterized as problematic and generative of crisis, disrupting an ordered, predetermined immigration system.

Australia's approach to asylum-seekers has been widely written about and analyzed as uniquely harsh and punitive, with the harshest treatment reserved for asylum-seekers arriving by boat. While other Western states do resort to the detention of asylum - seekers, it is usually as a last resort with time limits. Since 1992, the Australian approach of mandatory and indefinite detention of all asylum-seekers as "unauthorized arrivals" has had the effect of removing asylum-seekers from the public consciousness and perhaps also conscience, first through their detention in remote facilities on the Australian mainland and, more recently, through offshore detention on Nauru and in Papua New Guinea (Juss 2017; Tazreiter 2004). Asylum-seekers have been systematically dehumanized through the decades long politics of crisis migration, communicated to the Australian public by political leaders from both the major political parties. The detention of all asylum-seekers arriving by boat, including women and children, in often remote locations is justified in the Migration Act 1958 as protecting the sovereignty of the nation as the asylum-seekers have arrived in an "irregular" manner. Twenty-five years of bi-partisan support for Australia's treatment of asylum-seekers because of the manner of their arrival, rather than the veracity of their claim for protection, is the context for Australia's singularly punitive approach, supported through the communicative and visual specters of crisis migration.

The issue of migrants as disruptive and problematic to the nation is primarily an affective construction, deployed powerfully through the political class, where certain migrants, mostly asylum-seekers but also Muslim migrants, are cast as disruptive, dangerous, different. The conservative government of Prime Minister, John Howard, from 1996 to 2007, significantly toughened Australia's approach to asylum-seekers. During the Howard government, the demonization of asylum-seekers as unworthy "queue jumpers" and as taking the places of more deserving refugees entering through the resettlement program escalated in emotive rhetoric, manifest in incrementally more punitive policies. Indeed the last two decades have seen a plethora of legislative and administrative measures introduced and supported by both major political parties: the conservative Liberal/National coalition; and the social democratic Labor party. Arguably, these policies are designed to be as cruel as possible to deter any future asylum-seeker boat arrivals. The political utility of crisis narratives has been a key aspect of political rhetoric, with senior political leaders communicating to the Australian public about asylum-seekers as if they were existential threats to the Australian nation (Tazreiter 2004, 2015, 2017).

A key transitional moment in the contemporary perpetuation of a crisis narrative applied to asylum-seekers is the so-called *Tampa* incident of August 2001. The MV

Tampa is a Norwegian cargo freighter which rescued 433 mainly Hazara Afghani asylum seekers on August 24 who were stranded in international waters close to the coast of Christmas Island which was at the time part of Australian territory. The Australian government refused the repeated requests of the *Tampa*'s captain to land the asylum-seekers on Australian territory. Over several tense days international negotiations failed to reach a solution. Eventually the Australian navy transferred the asylum seekers from the *Tampa* to naval vessels on the high seas and in the weeks following the first iteration of "offshore" processing and detention of asylum-seekers began with the *Tampa* asylum-seekers moved to Nauru. This key moment of a "migration crisis," labeled as the "*Tampa* Crisis" has powerful visual references that are evocative and readily recalled by Australians: the bright red slash of the MV *Tampa* on the clear, blue Indian Ocean: the 433 asylum-seekers huddled under makeshift coverings on the deck of the *Tampa*; and finally, the appearance of a war footing with heavily armed Special Service troops transferring asylum-seekers from the *Tampa* onto naval ships. Following the "*Tampa* Crisis," the Australian Government passed a number of laws that created the legal framework for what came to be known as the "Pacific Solution." This constituted the beginning of offshore detention of asylum seekers who arrived in Australia by boat. The terrorist bombings of the World Trade Center in New York City and the Pentagon in Washington on September 11, 2001, followed only a few weeks after the "*Tampa* Crisis."

A month later, in October 2001, a federal election campaign was in full swing in Australia and questions of border protection and national security were key issues, whereas prior to events of September 11 and the "*Tampa* Crisis" domestic economic issues were of primary concern to the Australian electorate. Where the Howard government had lagged in public opinion polls behind the social democratic opposition for most of 2001, approval ratings for the Howard government soared due to the actions in the *Tampa* issue which were linked to the events of September 11 in the United States, constructing images of asylum-seekers as terrorist threats and Muslim outsiders (Marr and Wilkinson 2004). While campaigning for reelection in October of 2001, John Howard declared; "we shall decide who comes to this country and the manner in which they come," linking government strength and control to the political will to deter asylum-seekers and not allow them to land on Australian territory. This period also marked the beginning of the "externalization" of Australia's borders through the excision of Australian territory for migration purposes and offshore detention and processing of asylum-seekers. As outlined earlier, this issue of the externalization of Australia's borders through offshore arrangements for detaining and processing asylum seekers and the excision of Australia's territorial borders for migration purposes was accompanied by political rhetoric and visual triggers aimed at the domestic Australian population.

In the period between the *Tampa* incident and the Federal election in November 2001, two key developments in migration administration and legislation were enacted: first, the excision of some Australian territory and second, the removal of asylum-seekers to offshore locations for detention while their asylum claims were processed. In September 2001, the Migration Amendment (Excision from Migration Zone) Act 2001 (Cth) was passed to amend the Migration Act 1958 (Cth). This amendment excised Australian territory including Christmas Island, Ashmore, Cartier, and Cocos (Keeling) Islands from Australia's migration zone, placing them outside the remit of Australia's process of judicial review of ministerial decision-making. Through this process, the concept of "third country" offshore processing was introduced. Asylum-seekers who arrived by boat were intercepted at sea and either turned around and returned to Indonesia or removed to "third countries," either Nauru or Manus Island in Papua New Guinea. The political construction of asylum-seekers as an existential problem to an island nation such as Australia is most evident through the recent history externalizing national borders through offshore processing, interdiction at sea, and the use of turnaround policies to the ordered immigration nation beginning from the period of the Tampa crisis.

The history of Australia's treatment of asylum-seekers, with an accumulation of human rights violations, is acutely evident in the return to the so-called "Pacific Solution" of offshore detention and processing which took place under the social democratic government of Prime Minister Julia Gillard in 2012.

On May 17, 2013, the Labor government of Julia Gillard passed the Migration Amendment (Unauthorised Maritime Arrivals and Other Measures) Bill 2012, which excluded the Australian mainland from the migration zone for "irregular" arrivals. In other words, an asylum-seeker arriving on the Australian mainland by boat without a visa, would automatically be removed to a third country for processing of a protection claim rather than having the right to have a protection claim assessed in Australia. The externalization of Australia's territorial borders has extended to the interception of boats on the high seas, to pushback and tow-back actions that move asylum-seeker vessels to international waters, usually closer to the Indonesian mainland, as well as to offshore processing and resettlement deals with third countries, notably Cambodia.

By late 2013, the newly elected government of Prime Minister Tony Abbott launched "Operation Sovereign Borders," led by a military commander with the aim of deterring asylum boat arrivals. Australian Customs purchased an unspecified number of "disposable lifeboats" for $2.5 million; bright orange in colour, the vessels are launched from Naval vessels and then filled with asylum-seekers picked up in Australian waters, towed back to Indonesian waters, and then cut adrift with a supply of water.

Afghani asylum seeker Ali Batoor, who is a photojournalist and video artist, attempted to reach Australia by boat to claim asylum and filmed on a mobile phone the experience of being placed in an Australian Customs lifeboat and pushed back to Indonesia on a mobile phone (Batoor n.d.).

On December 5, 2014, the Australian Parliament passed the Migration and Maritime Powers Legislation Amendment (Resolving the Asylum Legacy Caseload) Bill 2014 (MPLA Bill 2014). These changes reintroduced temporary visas for asylum seekers arriving without prior authorization (renamed "Illegal Maritime Arrivals"), with the result that an individual granted protection may not later apply to have family members join them in Australia, as has previously been the case. The passage of this Bill as an amendment to the Migration Act 1958 (Cth) is troubling in relation to Australia's international legal obligations to the Refugee Convention, as well as the Convention Against

Torture (CAT), the Convention on the Rights of the Child (CRC), and the International Covenant on Civil and Political Rights (ICCPR). The amending legislation also extends the powers of the Minister for Immigration through amendments to the Migration Act 1958 (Cth) and the Maritime Powers Act 2013 (Cth). The new powers not only reintroduce temporary protection visas, but also remove decision-making review processes, make room for removal powers that are independent of assessments of Australia's non-*refoulément* obligations (which previously ensured that refugees are not returned to the source of their persecution), and allow the minister to place a statutory limit on the number of protection visas granted. This bill is the culmination of years of heated political debate on how best to respond to the arrival of asylum seekers by boat. Indeed, the issue of asylum seekers, particularly those arriving by boat, has remained a key election issue in federal elections since 2001.

From the perspective of the international refugee system, Australia's human rights obligations to asylum-seekers are in no way diminished by the number of humanitarian entrants that are accepted as part of the annual immigration intake of refugees. This is however, one of the potent narratives used by successive Australian governments: that Australia is a generous country that has done more than is required in relation to refugees. This argument relates to the so-called "resettlement intake" of refugees living in camps in third countries and waiting to be resettled, often for many years. Australia accepts on average 13,000 resettlement refugees annually through its humanitarian intake. At the same time, countries that neighbor refugee-producing countries bear the greatest burden of caring for refugee populations and the countries of the European Union have received the highest numbers of asylum seekers. For example, the latest figures published by the UNHCR on asylum application show that in 2014 Australia received 6,875 applications for asylum. In the same period Germany received 156,013 applications; the United Kingdom 26,244; France 53,404; Austria 22,881; and the Netherlands 21,968 (UNHCR 2015). Under its second periodic review by the United Nations Human Rights Council in late 2015, Australia received harsh criticism for its border control policies aimed at criminalizing and punishing asylum-seekers including children due to their mode of arrival. The United States delegate to the Human Rights Council called on Australia to "closely monitor" the offshore processing of asylum-seekers saying "we encourage Australia to enter humane treatment and respect for the human rights of asylum-seekers, including those processed offshore in Papua New Guinea and Nauru." The Swedish delegate reminded the session that Australia remains the only country in the world that uses offshore processing and mandatory detention of asylum-seekers (ABC 2015).

Since 2013, the Abbott and subsequently, the Turnbull Governments have also imposed a culture of secrecy and silence in the Australian Department of Immigration and Border Protection (now called Home Affairs), with little information officially available to journalists, lawyers, and the Australian public. The conditions and day-to-day circumstances in offshore detention have also been further distanced from public scrutiny through the process of privatizing service provision. The two places of offshore detention under "Operation Sovereign Borders" are Manus Island under the jurisdiction of Papua New Guinea, and Nauru, the latter being an independent island state. PNG and Nauru are poor, developing countries that receive significant foreign aid from Australia. The Australian Government has attempted to cover up abuses asylum-seekers have faced in offshore detention through federal legislation that restricts press freedom and prevents employees of detention centers blowing the whistle on conditions in detention. Infringements on press freedom have been introduced via amendments made in 2014 to the Australian Security Intelligence Organization Act 1979 (Cth), which prohibit media reporting of "special intelligence operations." Freedom of the press has been limited further by the enactment of the Telecommunications (Interception and Access) Amendment (Data Retention) Act 2015 (Cth), which provides the executive with new powers to apply for "journalist information warrants" that can compel telecommunications accompanies to surrender the metadata of journalists that may reveal a source. Concerns this would stifle investigative journalism were soon realized after documents obtained under freedom of information revealed that "eight stories on Australia's immigration policy [in 2014] were referred to the Australian Federal Police for the purpose of 'identification, and if appropriate, prosecution' of the persons responsible for leaking the information" (Williams 2015). Federal legislation has also criminalized whistleblowing, where under the Border Force Act 2015 (Cth), a prison sentence of up to two years can be imposed on detention center workers who blow the whistle on conditions.

Despite the veil of secrecy that surrounds offshore detention, human rights activists, filmmakers, and the detainees themselves have documented the life of asylum-seekers on Nauru and Manus Island (Gleeson 2016; Orner 2016). In the ensuing years since 2012, the sexual and physical abuse of detainees has been documented by the UN, human rights groups, and the detainees themselves. Guards murdered one asylum-seeker; medical neglect has been documented, leading in several cases to the deaths of asylum-seekers. Self-harm, suicide, and high levels of mental illness are widespread. On February 13, 2017, a group of international legal scholars lodged a Communiqué with the Office of the Prosecutor of the International Criminal Court on the circumstances in Nauru and Manus Island, charging that the detention of refugees and asylum-seekers amounts to a crime against humanity (Stanford Law School 2017). The submission details the range of human rights violations, including systematic and directed attacks amounting to such a crime against humanity. The Papua New Guinea High Court ruled in 2016 that the detention of asylum-seekers on Manus Island was unconstitutional.

The conditions and day-to-day circumstances of life for asylum-seekers on Nauru and Manus Island have only become visible to Australians through the work of human rights activists, filmmakers, and lawyers through unofficial visits and through the efforts of detained asylum-seekers who have documented their lives via mobile phones. At the time of writing, the situation of asylum-seekers sent by the Australian Government to be detained and have protection claims processed in Manus Island in Papua New Guinea in 2012 reached a crisis point. Many of the 1,300 asylum seekers had been detained for over four years, many despite having their protection claims upheld. The detention center run by the governments of Papua New Guinea and Australia and financed by Australia has been well-documented as contravening human rights standards and deliberatively punitive (Cave 2017; Grewcock 2017).

Visual storytelling mediums have been utilized by activists and artists opposed to Australia's policies on refugees and asylum-seekers by mainstream media that seeks to inform the public and by government. Home Affairs has also utilized visual forms of communication in sending messages to Australians about refugees and asylum-seekers and also in communicating to refugees and asylum-seekers about planning and making journeys to Australia. In 2016 Home Affairs commissioned an AUD$6 million telemovie to discourage asylum-seekers from coming to Australia following the story of a group of Afghan asylum seekers attempting to enter Australia by boat. A spokesperson for the Home Affairs in justification for the telemovie said that market research in the key source and transit countries indicate that television soap operas and telemovies are an effective way to reach the target audience when delivering complex messages (Sadaat 2016).

A prominent asylum seeker on Manus Island is Behrouz Boochani, a Kurdish journalist from Iran, detained for over four years. In 2017, Behrouz, along with collaborator and co-director, Arash Kamali Sarvestani, released the film, *Chauka Please Tell Us the Time*, which documents life in the detention center told over time and pieced together with hundreds of mobile phone clips and written texts. This, along with other forms of visual and material culture and communication have allowed the Australian public access to counternarratives to the dominant government narratives. Mainstream media have largely been hamstrung in obtaining permission to travel to Nauru and Manus Island and gain entry to the detention centers. Eva Orner's 2016 film "Chasing Asylum" documents asylum-seekers' journeys through Indonesia, Cambodia, Lebanon, Afghanistan, and Iran and ultimately Manus and Nauru (Orner 2016). Other evidence has been gathered by official visits to Manus and Nauru by the UNHCR, by international and national human rights organizations, and some individuals.

Discussion

The suite of policies that are part of Operation Sovereign Borders: offshore processing and detention; and the interdiction and pushback of boats departing Indonesia have cost an estimated AUD $9.5 billion since 2013. This is more than the total budget of the UNHCR to tackle refugee problems globally for this year. Given the scale of the global refugee and displaced persons issue and the relatively small scale of asylum-seeker arrivals Australia faces relative to similar Western nations, Australia's deterrence approach through indefinite detention in offshore facilities of boat arrivals and the related cost can well be labeled a crisis: a crisis in shared responsibility (the "burden sharing" the UNHCR asks states to engage in); a crisis in political will; and a future crisis for Australians in terms of Australia's leadership role in the Asia-Pacific region and in international standing.

Alternatives to these policies have often been proposed to the Australian government. Most recently, the Australian Human Rights Commission launched a comprehensive report, "Pathways to Protection," which recommends the adoption of a more humane regional cooperation framework as a key plank in protecting asylum seekers and ensuring the horrors of Nauru and Manus Island are never repeated. Australia has also been referred to the International Criminal Court for its treatment of refugees and asylum-seekers.

As outlined previously, the yearly humanitarian resettlement intake of refugees is usually pointed to by the Australian Government as the rationale for the tough approach to boat arrivals. Yet the images of the young boy Aylan Kurdi, of the many other people who have lost their lives seeking asylum in many parts of the world, and images and detail of the life and conditions for asylum seekers on Manus Island and Nauru, are also reminders of the fundamental human rights principle that the life of one person cannot be bartered for another without putting at risk core values and principles that undergird democratic societies. Using asylum-seekers on Nauru and Manus Island as an expendable human shield in a policy regime of deterrence is not consistent with human rights values.

Both the UN meetings' 2030 Agenda for Sustainable Development and President Barack Obama's three-point plan in the 2016 Global Compact on Refugees and Migrants recognize the interdependence of factors that drive large -cale refugee and migration flows: violence and conflict, extreme poverty and inequality, environmental degradation, and adverse impacts of climate change. If this high-level global compact is to have traction and be judged by the international community as offering solutions to the root causes of refugee flow, challenging the dominant and dominating crisis narratives of migration is required. The brief examples of the visualization of crisis explored in the Australian case take us back to the key conceptual ideas the chapter began with, where crisis is located in a broad field of rigorous and thorough critique.

References

Ahmed, S. 2004. *The Cultural Politics of Emotion*. Edinburgh, UK: Edinburgh University Press.

Australian Broadcast Commission—ABC. 2015. "Australia's Asylum-Seeker Policies Heavily Criticised at UN Human Rights Council Review." http://www.abc.net.au/news/2015-11-10/australias-asylum-policies-heavily-criticised-at-united-nations/6926032

B. A. Batoor. N.d. Videos. http://www.batoor.com/#mi=1&pt=0&pi=11&p=-1&a=0&at=0

BBC News. 2017. "Trump Orders Wall To Be Built on Mexican Border." January 26. http://www.bbc.com/news/world-us-canada-38740717)

Berlant, L. 2011. *Cruel Optimism*. Durham, NC: Duke University Press.

Boltanski, L., and E. Chiapello. 2005. *The New Spirit of Capitalism*. London: Verso.

Bourdieu, P. 1977. *Outline of a Theory of Practice*. Cambridge, UK: Cambridge University Press.

Braidotti, R. 2013. *The Posthuman*. Cambridge, UK: Polity.

Castles, S. 2010. "Understanding Global Migration: A Social Transformation Perspective." *Journal of Ethnic and Migration Studies* 36, no. 10: 1565–1586.

Cave, D. 2017. "This Is Manus Island." *New York Times Magazine*, November 18. https://www.nytimes.com/interactive/2017/11/18/world/australia/manus-island-australia-detainees.html

Clough, P. T. 2010. "The Affective Turn: Political Economy, Biomedia, And Bodies." In The Affect Theory Reader, edited by M. Gregg, G. J. Seigwork, 206–225. Durham, NC: Duke University Press.

Cresswell, T. 2010. "Towards a Politics of Mobility." *Environment and Planning; Society and Space* 28:17–31.

Dauvergne, C. 2016. *The New Politics of Immigration and the End of Settler Societies*. Cambridge University Press, Cambridge.

Edmondson, G., and K. Mladek. 2017. "Natural History: Toward a Politics of Crisis." In *Sovereignty in Ruins. A Politics of Crisis*, edited by G. Edmondson and K. Mladek, 21–62. Durham, NC: Duke University Press.

Foucault, M. 2007. *Security, Territory, Population. Lectures at the college de France 1977-1978*. Translated by Graham Burchell. Basingstoke: Palgrave Macmillan.

Gleeson, M. 2016. *Offshore: Behind the Wire on Manus and Nauru*. Sydney, Australia: Newsouth.

Glick Schiller, N. and N. B. Salazar. 2013. "Regimes of mobility across the globe." *Journal of Ethnic and Migration Studies*, 39, no. 2: 183–200.

Grewcock, M. 2017. "'Our Lives Is in Danger': Manus Island and the End of Asylum." *Race & Class* 59, no. 2: 70–89.

Grigorieff, A. et al. 2016. "Does Information Change Attitudes Toward Immigrants? Representative Evidence from Survey Experiments." London School of Economics. http://www.lse.ac.uk/iga/assets/documents/events/2016/does-information-change-attitudes-towards-immigrants.pdf

Hainmüller, J., and D. J. Hopkins. 2014. "Public Attitudes Toward Immigration." *Annual Review of Political Science* 17: 225–249.

Harvey, D. 2005. *A Brief History of Neoliberalism*. New York, Oxford University Press.

Haraway, D. 1989. "The Biopolitics of Postmodern Bodies: Constitutions of Self in Immune System Discourse." *Differences: A Journal of Feminist Cultural Studies* 1, no. 1:3–43.

Hoggett, P., and S. Thompson, eds. 2012. *Politics and the Emotions*. London: Continuum.

Honig, B. 2009. Emergency Politics: *Paradox, Law, Democracy*. Princeton, NJ: Princeton University Press.

Juss, S. 2017. "Detention and Delusion in Australia's Kafkaesque Refugee Law." *Refugee Survey Quarterly*, 36: 146–167.

Kaufmann, E., and G. Harris. 2015. "'White Flight' or Positive Contact? Local Diversity and Attitudes to Immigration in Britain." *Comparative Political Studies* 48, no. 12: 1563–1590.

Mann, M. 1993. *The Sources of Social Power*. Vol. 2., *The Rise of Classes and Nation-States*, 1760–1914. Cambridge, UK: Cambridge University Press.

Mann, M. 2003. *Incoherent Empire*. London: Verso.

Marr, D., and M. Wilkinson. 2004. *Dark Victory*. Sydney, Australia: Allen & Unwin.

Orner, E. 2016. *Chasing Asylum: A Filmmakers's Story*. Sydney, Australia: Harper Collins.

Puar, J. K. 2017. *The Right to Maim: Debility, Capacity, Disability*. Durham, NC: Duke University Press.

Roitman, J. 2014. *Anti-Crisis*. Durham, NC: Duke University Press.

Sadaat, L. 2016. "The $6 Million Telemovie Designed to Discourage Asylum Seekers From Coming to Australia Has Debuted in Afghanistan." *Huffington Post*, July 15. http://www.huffingtonpost.com.au/2016/03/28/asylum-seeker-film_n_9555074.html

Safi, Michael. 2017. "Myanmar Treatment of Rohingya Looks Like 'Textbook Ethnic Cleansing,' Says UN." *The Guardian*, September 11. https://www.theguardian.com/world/2017/sep/11/un-myanmars-treatment-of-rohingya-textbook-example-of-ethnic-cleansing).

Sassen, S. 2006. *Territory, Authority, Rights: From Medieval to Global Assemblages*. Princeton, NJ: Princeton University Press.

Schinkel, W. 2015. "The Image of Crisis" *Thesis Eleven* 127, no. 1: 36–51.

Sontag, S. 2003. *Regarding the Pain of Others*. New York: Farrar, Straus and Giroux.

Stanford Law School. 2017. "Communiqué to the Office of the Prosecutor of the International Criminal Court: Under Article 15 of the Rome Statute." https://www-cdn.law.stanford.edu/wp-content/uploads/2017/02/Communiqué-to-Office-Prosecutor-IntlCrimCt-Art15RomeStat-14Feb2017.pdf

Tazreiter, C. 2004. *Asylum Seekers and the State: The Politics of Protection in a Security-Conscious World*. Aldershot, UK: Ashgate.

Tazreiter, C. 2015. "Lifeboat Politics in the Pacific: Affect and the Ripples and Shimmers of a Migrant Saturated Future." *Emotion, Space and Society* 16: 99–107.

Tazreiter, C. 2016. *Fluid Security in the Asia Pacific, Transnational Lives, Human Rights and State Control*. London: Palgrave.

Tazreiter C. 2017. "The Unlucky in the 'Lucky Country': Asylum Seekers, Irregular Migrants and Refugees and Australia's Politics Of Disappearance." Special Issue of *Australian Journal of Human Rights* 23, no. 2: 242–260.

UNHCR. 2015. "Asylum Levels and Trends in Industrialized Countries, 2014." March 26. http://www.unhcr.org/search?comid=56b087f44&cid=49aea93aba&scid=49aea93a5c&tags=asylumtrends

UNHCR. 2016. "Global Trends: Forced Displacement in 2016." http://www.unhcr.org/globaltrends2016/.

Williams, G. 2015. "The Legal Assault in Australian Democracy." Sir Richard Blackburn Lecture, ACT Law Society, May 12. https://www.actlawsociety.asn.au/documents/item/1304

CHAPTER 36

FRAMING THE SYRIAN REFUGEE

Divergent Discourses in Three National Contexts

DALIA ABDELHADY

THIS chapter provides an understanding of the social construction of the "refugee crisis," particularly of Syrian refugees, in three countries.[1] Focusing on 2015, the year in which perceptions of the current refugee emergency came to the forefront of public discourse in many countries, the analysis provided here disentangles the crisis discourse and shows its contextual formulation. Through a systematic analysis of the two largest national newspapers in three countries, the argument presented here opposes the assumptions about the representation of a refugee crisis often popularized by politicians and international media. Instead, this chapter shows that contradiction and uncertainty are the main building blocks in the construction of the refugee crisis in 2015.

By 2015, many European countries were declared to have reached full capacity and unable to receive more refugees, a process culminating in border closures. As images of undifferentiated masses of Third World refugees arriving illegally to the shores of Europe became an almost daily banality, the "refugee crisis" became a source of concern and popular condemnation for policy and politics at the local, national, and EU levels (Dahlgren 2016). While some of these public criticisms stressed that refugees are better received and settled in hosting countries that share similar cultural and religious backgrounds, a similar problematic was observed in neighboring countries who see refugees as competitors for jobs and as sources of social and cultural conflict. This chapter looks at the specific ways the crisis is constructed, contested, and dealt with in two of the neighboring countries which act as transit points for many refugees (Turkey and Jordan) and one of Europe's most popular destination for refugees (Sweden).[2]

While the aim of the three case studies is not comparative, given the disparate stage of media development and freedoms in the three settings, it is important to account for the differences and similarities in media discourses in order to understand the process of framing the current refugee crisis and the associated responses such processes of framing evoked. By analyzing the three case studies simultaneously, this chapter highlights the public discourses that shape the environments in which many refugees may be assessing their onward migration to Europe (in Jordan and Turkey) alongside an analysis of the discourses that influence their settlement and integration in European societies (Sweden in this case). As the analysis that follows shows, the three case studies demonstrate that media representations of the refugee crisis in general and the Syrian refugee in particular are simultaneously contradictory and complementary. Uncertainty about the position of the refugee in society, and the added confusion the heightened awareness of refugee presence brings about, leads to a sense of crisis understood largely as a crisis in meaning or in the ability to make sense of current conditions. In the end the Syrian refugee is constructed as an undesirable other, who is at times tolerated but is mostly considered a threatening presence.

News media have an influential role in shaping attitudes, thoughts and perceptions about a given issue. With regards to migration, negative media coverage was found to foster similarly negative public attitudes toward immigration (Crawley 2005) and motivate anti-immigrant sentiments (Balch and Balabanova 2014; Innes 2010; Rasinger 2010). At the same time, news coverage of migration, or any topic for that matter, cannot be simply understood as negative or positive (Binder and Allen 2015). Instead, research increasingly shows that news media are sites of contestation and, at times, contradictions. For example, in analyzing French newspaper coverage of immigration, Clare and Abdelhady (2016) find that newspapers portray a complex reality that is neither simply pro- nor anti-immigration and immigrants. Rather, the same newspaper can present contradictory attitudes toward the same group of people depending on context or type of coverage.

In more recent years, social media and citizen journalism have expanded the range of stories and challenged the monopoly of "mainstream media" over forms of representation. At the same time, mainstream media continues to provide a central source of public discourse which government officials and members of the publics still rely on to make sense of and decide on courses of action as events unfold (Georgiou and Zaborowski 2017). In a comparative analysis of European media coverage of the "refugee crisis," Georgiou and Zaborowski (2017) argue that the scale and speed of events taking place in 2015 support the argument for the importance of mainstream media as a source for publics and policymakers who lacked familiarity with the newly arriving refugees as they attempted to understand the nature and scale of the "crisis." More recent research on developing countries also points to the relevance of mainstream media in verifying and amplifying perceptions of crises (see for example Mare 2013).

Methodology

The largest two national daily newspapers were selected for each country. Coincidently, they can be described as centrist and center-right in each context. While labels such as right, center, or left cannot be easily compared across national contexts, they are intended to provide rough representation of different views within the same national context. Understanding that such labels need to be contextualized within their specific political climate, it suffices to say that at least one of the newspapers in each context was not pro-government. In Jordan, *al Rai* newspaper presents the government's official rhetoric, and often cites officials in dealing with the coverage of Syrian refugees. Information is gathered from government reports, and studies conducted by international organizations. *Al Ghad*, on the other hand, is one of the largest and oldest independent Arabic-language newspapers in the region, and at times presents arguments opposing those of the Jordanian government. In Turkey, *Zaman* (the newspaper with the largest circulation in Turkey) was right-leaning; the newspaper was openly Gülenistic, pro-Islamic, and provided a major source of opposition to the AKP ruling party until its recent takeover by the government.[3] *Hürriyet* is the second largest newspaper in Turkey and is categorized as providing mainstream secular coverage that also opposes the Islamic government. In Sweden, *Dagens Nyheter* is described as liberal, while *Svenska Dagbladet* is characterized as moderate. Over the last few decades, however, political affiliations have been reduced and there has been a change toward more market-driven journalism that focuses on newsworthiness rather than political affiliation among Swedish newspapers. Strömbäck and Nord (2008) refer to this change as part of the mediatization process which is characterized by professional journalistic values and the adoption of a media logic (what is newsworthy) as opposed to a political logic in news coverage (see also Nord 2008).

In Sweden, newspaper articles were collected using search words (asylum, refugee, Middle East) in a database of archived newspapers. For Jordan and Turkey, electronic archives were provided on the newspapers' website allowing for the use of similar search terms. In one case (*Al Rai* in Jordan) no such archive was available for the time frame for this study, which was compensated for by reading through each daily issue (see Table 36.1).

The analysis that follows utilizes frames for understanding the ways the different articles communicate specific aspects of the refugee crisis. Understood as a more general form of categorizing stories, Entman (1993, 52) defines media framing:

> To frame is to select some aspects of a perceived reality and make them more salient in a communicating text, in such a way as to promote a particular definition of a problem, causal interpretation, moral evaluation, and/or treatment recommendation for the item described.

Table 36.1 Newspaper Coverage of Syrian Refugees

	Center	Right
Jordan	Al Ghad	Al Rai
Turkey	Hürriyet	Zaman
Sweden	Dagens Nyheter	Svenska Dagbladet

Table 36.2 Thematic distribution of articles analyzed

	Conflict	Human Interest (includes moral responsibility)	Economic Strain	Institutional Responsibility	Total
Jordan	52 (19%)	60 (22%)	111 (40%)	52 (19%)	275
Turkey	82 (33%)	85 (34%)	56 (23%)	24 (10%)	247
Sweden	37 (12%)	109 (36%)	8 (3%)	149 (49%)	303
Total	171 (21%)	254 (31%)	175 (21%)	225 (27%)	825

Research into media frames has demonstrated that news coverage relies on a variety of specific frames to communicate news to audiences, and that different frames can influence readers' or viewers' perceptions of public issues (for reviews see McCombs and Ghanem 2001; McCombs et al. 1997; Scheufele 1999). Semetko and Valkenburg (2000) assert that media reports (on diverse topics) tend to fall within five specific frames: conflict, human interest, economic consequences, morality, and responsibility. In analyzing the articles collected for this chapter, these same frames were found to be of great relevance. However, morality was merged with human interest as the two frames often fused in the coverage of Syrian refugees.[4] Similarly, the responsibility frame was often mixed with narratives calling for institutional reform in order to better put forward solutions to the perceived crisis. Finally, the frame of economic consequences was taken to refer specifically to economic strain caused by the presence of large numbers of refugees.

In Jordan, the articles were distributed almost evenly across three themes (conflict and competition, human interest, and institutional responsibility) with a larger portion (twice as big) of the articles addressing the economic strain brought about by the reception of Syrian refugees. In Turkey, two-thirds of the articles dealt with conflict and human interest evenly, with a third dealing mostly with economic strain and institutional responsibility. In Sweden, half of the articles discussed institutional responsibility with a particular emphasis on civil society initiatives, a little more than a third depicted the humanization of refugees, and a much smaller portion (one-tenth) dealt with conflict. Being the country with the highest economic standards, it is perhaps not surprising that a minimal number of articles in Sweden raised the concern that refugees are straining the economy (3 percent). Table 36.2 shows the distribution of the articles by theme and country.

Frame One: Competition and Conflict

Conflict as a frame speaks the most to the perception of a "refugee crisis" as it emphasizes tensions between individuals, groups, or institutions while reducing complex social and political problems to simple conflicts (d'Haenens and de Lange 2001). Research on immigrants in western media confirms the overwhelming focus on conflict-filled (or hostility-themed) stories (Leudar et al. 2008, 188) where immigrants and immigration are foremost presented as a threat (Benson 2013; van Dijk 2000). The threat frame portrays immigrants threatening wage systems or taking jobs from domestic workers, bringing diseases, draining the welfare system, and depleting national resources (Benson 2013; Greenberg and Hier 2001; Leudar et al. 2008). Often included is some sort of security frame which relates immigration (and especially refugees) with criminality (Bradimore and Bauder 2011; Greenberg and Hier 2001; Leudar et al. 2008; Steimel 2009; Threadgold 2009). While my data shows that conflict is not the largest frame used for portraying Syrian refugees in the wake of the refugee crisis, many of the narratives within this frame parallel findings of previous research on the portrayal of immigrants and refugees.

Jordan

In addition to reporting on criminal activities committed by Syrians, Jordanian newspapers mostly reflect on conflict in economic terms. Unlike articles discussing the strain on economic resources, this set of articles emphasizes competition between Syrians and Jordanians and stresses the economic threat of Syrian labor and investments to the Jordanian economy. For example, Syrian investments in Jordan, mostly in the restaurant industry, are typically presented as a challenge to Jordanian restaurants. Contrasting the rapid rate of growth of Syrian restaurants to the slow growth of their Jordanian counterparts, these articles also stress the challenges faced by Jordanian restaurant owners: "the reduction of the profit rate in the last period because of the increasing rate of wages, plus the increasing number of new restaurants lately." Moreover, Syrian restaurant owners who had to apply for investment licenses, as well as Syrian investors in general, are portrayed as obtaining their licenses through fraud and bribery and thus engaging in illegal activities.[5] Economic competition and rising unemployment are also sources of conflict as portrayed by the newspapers, while Jordanian authorities have to enforce labor laws on the Syrian refugee population which saw one article reporting the Ministry of Labour closing down 3000 Syrian factories.

More frequently than discussing investors, the articles focusing on economic conflict and competition stress unemployment as the major factor threatening the well-being of Jordanian society. Syrians are largely unemployed in Jordan, and until the end of 2015 had no legal right to employment. The newspapers, in turn, discuss the willingness of Syrian refugees to work under substandard conditions such as for low wages, longer hours, and with no days off. We are reminded that these are conditions that Jordanian workers would not agree to and consequently employers prefer to employ Syrian refugees illegally. In the process, the threat of Syrian refugees stealing Jordanian jobs is established. Importantly, whether the Syrian refugee is portrayed as a fraudulent investor or cheap manual worker, the contradictory images are offset by stressing the threat both pose to the Jordanian economy.

Syrian illegal labor is also presented in the phenomena of the street beggars. Under the title "The Numbers of Beggars in *el-Zarqa* Increases . . . and 50% of Them Are Syrians," one article mentions that they are "embarrassing" to Jordanian passers-by. Child beggars are considered by the newspapers to be particularly bothersome and "their numbers have obviously increased with Syrian refugees." One official is cited saying that "a lot of the beggars are there from same category who inhabit the tents, and they were deported [back to the camps] eventually." The ability of government officials to quickly and firmly address conflict is an important feature in this set of articles. This firmness, however, is indirectly perceived as an inability to confront more real threats posed by Syrian refugees who: "have pushed some alien values and traditions onto our local committees." The alien values alluded to in the article are never clearly stated and are left to the readers' imagination to perceive.

While throughout 2015 Syrian refugees did not have the legal right to work in Jordan, in 2016 the EU and Jordan came to a partnership agreement that promised the strengthening of Jordan's economic resilience in dealing with the refugee issue through aid packages. In return, Jordan was to create economic opportunities for Syrian refugees (European Council 2016). These economic opportunities are intended to provide an incentive for Syrian refugees to stay in Jordan, instead of risking their lives at sea with hopes of crossing over to Europe. In building up to the change in Jordanian policy toward the employment of Syrians, a small number of articles published at the end of 2015 (November and December) prepare the way by arguing that Syrian refugees can be utilized in the economic development of the country. For example, an article entitled "Prime Minister Updated on the National Campaign for Employment," which was published in *Al Ghad* on November 19, mentions that the minister of labor argued that Jordan is facing "an exceptional challenge" that requires finding alternative solutions. Different from previous rhetoric that portrays an image of the Syrian refugee stealing Jordanian jobs, the article states that Jordan is facing its lowest unemployment rates in a ten-year period. As a result, the article moves to discuss proposals to change the conditions for employment for Syrian refugees, arguing that they have skills that can be utilized in fields that are in need of them such as education and healthcare. Additionally, a discussion of working with investors and motivating them to create opportunities for vocational training for refugees is also mentioned.

In sum, while stressing the threat posed by Syrian refugees in Jordanian society, largely due to economic competition, newspaper articles in this theme establish the ambiguity of the position of the Syrian refugee in Jordanian society: Is the refugee a wealthy (yet fraudulent) investor, an embarrassing street beggar, or an exceptionally skillful resource? While the articles may argue that all three types may present areas of conflict and threat, the contradictory imagery and lack of a coherent narrative increase uncertainty about Syrian refugees leading to conclusions of an impending crisis.

Turkey

Conflict is portrayed along a few different axes in Turkish newspapers. Crimes committed by or against Syrians are common. Prostitution, for instance, is often associated with Syrian women in need of money. Some Syrians also take part in organizing illegal boat trips to Greece. On the other hand, local people tricking Syrians into moving into apartments about to be demolished, taking money for rent, and then disappearing is another instance of crime involving Syrians.

Anti-Syrian protests and rallies are also reported, reflecting conflict between Syrians and Turks. Some protests would start with a Syrian child getting into a fight with a Turkish child, a Syrian home being suspected of housing ongoing prostitution, or simply because the Syrian lifestyle disturbs the neighborhood. Different lifestyles are often portrayed as a form of disruption. For instance, in a *Hürriyet* article it is claimed that members of a Syrian family "walk at home topless and dance to loud music while the curtains are open," whereas Turks would not even sit in their living rooms with their pajamas on. Somewhat echoing the sentiment in the previous example is one that addressed conflict and competition facing women specifically. In an article entitled "Wrong Syria Policies Darkened the Lives of Turkish and Syrian Women" in *Zaman*, Turkish women are described to be losing to Syrian women in the competition over attractiveness to men.

Syrian beggars are often stressed as "creating an unpleasant view" or "not suiting a touristic season." For instance, in *Zaman's* article "The Beggars in Taksim Do Not Leave Citizens Alone until They Get Money," Syrian children are shown as disturbingly and even physically insisting on passers-by to give them money. In other articles, it is noted that beggars evoke religious feelings and play with Turkish emotions. Zaman, for instance, claims that "the metropolis has become the beggars' city," that Syrian beggars "pollute streets and alleys," and that even the beauty of Istanbul's tulips cannot cover it. Syrian children collecting recyclable materials in the streets or selling things on the busy roads during red lights are also found somewhat disturbing for both the view and the fact that they should be studying instead of engaging in such dangerous activity.

More so than Jordanian newspapers, the discussion of conflict and competition in their Turkish counterparts stresses the moral differences found between Turks and Syrian refugees. In other words, the conflict takes place in the moral realm and, as a result, can be understood as more immutable. According to the Turkish newspapers, Syrian children pollute the streets of Turkish cities, and Syrian women steal Turkish men from their wives. The threat of visual and biological pollution is clearly established in the articles. By contrast, in Jordanian cities Syrian beggars are a problem that can be dealt with and the moral difference is not as stark, as it is mostly left to the reader to establish.

Sweden

The threat of terrorism and radicalization is the main axis around which conflict was represented in Swedish newspapers when discussing the refugee stream. The risk that

"Sweden's generous refugee policy may be abused by terrorist organizations" (*Dagens Nyheter*, April 18, 2015), is echoed in the majority of articles within the conflict frame for 2015. There are numerous warnings that terrorists may be mixing within the refugee stream and that the expedited review process for asylum applications may increase the security threat, as migration board employees do not have the adequate resources to properly investigate the applicants. The threat is presented in mostly general terms and refers to an undifferentiated mass of refugees. One article in *Dagens Nyheter* attempts to explain to the reader the foundations of the security threat presented to Sweden as the author writes that:

> Someone is currently sitting and planning a new terrorist attack on France, Germany, or perhaps on Sweden . . . There are many more that should be on the IS list of targets. One of them may be Sweden, due to the presence of Swedish military forces in northern Iraq, which acts as an adviser to the Kurdish forces that are against IS. That is something that could increase the terrorist threat from IS to Sweden.
>
> (*Dagens Nyheter*, November 11, 2015)

A smaller number of articles in Swedish newspapers highlight the conflict among the refugees themselves, describing religious antagonisms between Muslim and Christian refugees in particular as a threat to the refugees themselves and Swedish cultural and moral values.

In a way that is comparable to the coverage in Jordanian newspapers, the portrayal of the threat of Syrian refugees in Swedish mainstream newspapers stresses uncertainty and lacks the coherence one observes in Turkish news coverage. Articles from Swedish newspapers in this theme describe a threat that is abstract and often imagined, built on the foreignness of the refugee culture. While foreignness is not discussed at any length, it is often equated with Islam and associated with radicalization and terrorism. This foreignness strengthens the perceived threat, and the uncertainty it generates is interpreted as a crisis.

Frame Two: Refugees as Human

Neuman et al. (1992) find the human interest frame to be, next to conflict, the second most common frame across a variety of news content. Valkenburg et al. argue that the human-interest media frame "brings an individual's story or an emotional angle to the presentation of an event, issue or problem" (1999, 551). By doing so, a human-interest frame describes the news in terms that personalize, dramatize and emotionalize the news. D'Haenens and de Lange (2001) find the human interest frame to be the frame most commonly used in their analysis of refugee coverage in Dutch newspapers.

Similarly, the human interest frame is the largest used among the newspaper articles analyzed for this project. As such, an understanding of how the personalized, dramatized, and emotionalized human interest frame depicts refugees is an important area of study.

Jordan

The humanization of Syrian refugees in Jordanian newspapers is often subtle to discern. The general tendency in *Al Rai* is one that addresses Syrian refugees as an undifferentiated mass, emphasizing numerical patterns and therefore dehumanizing the individual refugees. A few exceptions portray individual Syrians expressing their experiences with displacement and quoting their own words. These exceptions still quote anonymous refugees. In one example, an article titled "From the Syrian Hell to the Security of the Jordanian Desert," an anonymous female refugee is quoted saying "We saw hell (*jihanam*) in Syria." The article, however, spends more space humanizing the Jordanian security forces in contrast to the Syrian hell. A Jordanian brigadier explains that "dealing with the Syrian crisis is getting more and more complicated as time goes on because of the high number of refugees that we had to deal with." The article is more focused on conveying the complications brought about by a lengthy border, faced by members of the security forces who perform the difficult task of keeping Jordan safe. Examples of a similar self-congratulatory approach in other articles includes references to the ways members of the security forces "secure refugees in the camps prepared for them," and "offer medical services and the necessary treatment alongside the royal medical service staff." Others emphasize that the refugees arrived after being wounded in Syria, and how therefore the security officers have to quickly transfer them to hospitals. Such articles often include photos of soldiers and refugees within the same frame, mostly as the soldiers are helping women and children. Extending a helping hand is not confined to security personnel but includes the general Jordanian population as well: "Jordanians Are Sharing Bread and Water with the Syrian Refugees" is an example presenting the friendly connection between Syrian refugees and the Jordanian people. It is noteworthy to mention that almost all the articles that are categorized under this frame also convey a sense of victimizing Syrian refugees.

While *Al Ghad* shared a similar approach of victimization of Syrian refugees that called for the benevolence of Jordanian citizens, the newspaper does not emphasize the heroic role played by the national guard and tends to highlight the human predicament faced by Syrian refugees instead. A discussion of the extreme poverty that many Syrians find themselves in, with vivid personal narratives, repeatedly features in this group of articles. In one example, a father has to tie the torsos of his children in their sleep so that they do not wake up hungry in the middle of the night due to the shortage of food. In another, an elderly woman's narrative is discussed in detail showing how she fled Syria leaving behind all her belongings in order to avoid seeing her children getting radicalized and partaking in militia activities. The article stresses, however, that seventy-year old Khalida can only survive financially given the donations provided by a Jordanian charity organization. At the same time, she commutes daily for an hour each way to attend basic literacy classes that are offered by a different NGO specifically for refugees in Jordan.

Similar to the trend in human interest stories observed by d'Haenens and de Lange (2001) in Dutch news coverage of refugees, the humanization of Syrian refugees in Jordanian newspapers relies on depictions of victimization, limited agency despite acts of endurance and perseverance, and moral responsibility on part of the host population toward their protection. While the stories make clear that Jordanians are stepping in to help their Syrian brothers and sisters, the articles quickly shift to stress that the moral responsibility is a global one—which is discussed later under the responsibility frame. While Syrian refugees are often referred to as neighbors or brothers and sisters who are requesting the help of Jordanians, the Jordanian citizen/culture/state that is capable of meeting its moral obligation toward the Syrian victim (whose morality was already put into question using the conflict frame) is positioned in hierarchical binary vis-à-vis the refugee. In short, victimization and othering are important features of the group of articles categorized under human interest in Jordanian newspapers. At the same time, a self-congratulatory attitude stressing the moral responsibility of Jordanian citizens/state/culture is stressed, which simultaneously alludes to a global moral crisis and a Jordanian economic crisis that is further depicted under the institutional responsibility theme.

Turkey

Similar to Sweden, the humanization of refugees is the most dominant frame used in Turkish newspapers in 2015. Humanization features in most of the Turkish articles included in this analysis, including those which are eventually categorized under a different frame. These articles seem to evoke a sense of compassion and sympathy for Syrian refugees by putting their lives in a context of displacement and loss. Examples of humanization include featuring owners of successful Syrian restaurant chains or bookstores, and families struggling with the loss of their family members or poor life conditions. One interesting example focuses on as Syrian fathers (*Zaman's* "The War Hits Fathers the Most"). Generally, this set of articles tends to address Syrians as individuals, instead of a general mass which only leads to their dehumanization. While the example of fathers was only mentioned once, this set of articles seem to present a strong focus on the life conditions of children, especially on the streets, with the Syrian children featured needing to work instead of being able to go to school. In one example, an article in *Zaman* entitled "Seven Differences between a Turkish Beggar and a Syrian Refugee" calls on Turks to be more compassionate toward Syrians as they beg on the streets because they have no other choice. Turkish beggars, on the other hand, can get jobs, as unlike Syrians they do not need any additional documentation for the right to work.

Somewhat similar to Jordan's newspapers featuring the heroic role played by the security forces, humanization in Turkish newspapers features examples of locals who are getting involved with refugee issues and offering helping hands. Humanitarian gestures are stressed by Turkish newspaper coverage of groups of Turks who "take to their duty and host brothers not only coming from Syria but also from Iraq, regardless of their religion, language, ethnic roots, and sect" (*Hürriyet* "The Minister Nabi Avcı: Syrian Children will Graduate Knowing Two Languages"). Of note is that such helping hands are presented "in the face of the so-called democracy of European states and the US, their misleading talks on human rights, we are doing the most humane/humanitarian help" (Zaman). Humanization of refugees goes hand in hand with the humanization of their saviors. Referring to border patrol officers, coast guard personnel, and doctors who save Syrians in various moments, many articles stress the importance of Turks in saving the lives of Syrian refugees. Many of these articles evoke the nationalist Turkish history thesis of 1932, placing the Turks into the center of world civilization and humanitarianism. As such, helping Syrian refugees is an act that is dictated not as a result of the predicament of the refugees themselves but more by the nationalist burden of greatness. In the process, the hierarchical relationship between the Syrian victim and Turkish savior is clearly established. Importantly, and similar to the discussion in Jordanian newspapers, the crisis is stressed as relating to the global order whereby wealthier countries are refusing to lend a helping hand in line with their moral ideals.

Sweden

Articles within this frame, often including photos of women and children and interviews of individuals arriving to Sweden, describe the lives of people seeking refugee status, their stories of why they needed to escape, life in their homeland, their journey, where they want to go, hopes for the future, and their frustration with the Swedish bureaucracy. In an example:

> After 20 days on the run from Syria, Ahmed Almufti has finally reached his goal. Together with his cousin Ahmed Idris, wife Suheila Mandil and their children Ather, 8 years, Hana 4 years and Sena 1 year, he has walked on foot, traveled with unregistered taxis and train. In Hungary, they lived one week in the forest surrounded by police, in Denmark they occupied the train tracks until the police let them continue into Sweden.
>
> ("After 20 Days on the Run, Some Days without Water and Food," *Dagens Nyheter*, September 11, 2015)

In a similar vein, this group of articles describes the individuals behind the efforts made by civil society and private initiatives that work in assisting refugees, telling stories about retirees, former refugees, and children of immigrants helping out. Here is one example:

> Susanna Charboti was one of all the Swedish people who felt a growing frustration. Should she do something and in that case what? For her it fell into place one day when her eyes saw refugees arrive at Stockholm Central station. The need of simple medical care was evident.
>
> ("Healthcare at Central Station: The Important Thing Is That We Do Not Get Stuck in Powerlessness," *Dagens Nyheter*, December 24, 2015)

This set of articles also debates and stresses the unfair and exclusive systems in place throughout Europe, emphasizing that legal and moral responsibility dictates focusing on refugees' international rights, the right to free movement, and human rights, as well as the moral responsibility of giving people the same dignity as citizens with a passport. This set of articles includes a number of testimonies and observations of the chaos and sadness in the central train stations in Malmö and Stockholm when the arriving numbers were at their highest. Many of these articles make historical comparisons, for example with 1930s Germany or refugees from the Balkans to Sweden in the 1990s. Here is an example:

> Can we really stand for the democratic and compassionate values if we do not do something about the current situation? Is a Syrian and Eritrean life really worth so much less than Swedish in today's globalized world? We are already a hardened social climate, with winds reminiscent of Europe's worst history. Do we live in a society where human life has so little value, or where solidarity and compassion mean so little?
>
> ("We Need To Open Our Border—Also for Our Own Sake," *Dagens Nyheter*, September 15, 2015)

These articles try to counter the image of refugees as a cost and a strain for Swedish institutions by emphasizing the importance of seeing them as individuals with a right to a good life, and as a resource to Swedish society. Furthermore, these articles stress the importance of not seeing asylum-seekers as one undifferentiated group or dividing them into bad and good immigrants. At the same time, refugees are represented as utterly grateful for arriving to a place of safety for families and children: "Sweden is the paradise, even if it is difficult to find a place to live" (*Svenska Dagbladet*, December 9, 2015); because, as one refugee is quoted saying, "Swedes are truly kind and respect other people" (*Svenska Dagbladet*, December 31, 2015).

Frame Three: Economic Strain

In discussing the framing of economic consequences, d'Haenens and de Lange (2001) explain that this frame is often used to clarify the economic consequences of an issue to the public and as a result involve the public more closely with the issue.

Jordan

The straining of resources features in the majority of news articles in *Al Rai*, and the problem covers almost all institutions. The education of Syrian children is discussed in terms of numbers that are considered to be endlessly and rapidly increasing. References to the numbers of Jordanian schools that cater to Syrian children, numbers of night schools (or schools that have to offer a second shift specifically for Syrian children), and numbers of additional schools that need to be built all construct an image of unbearable strain on the educational system: "Governmental schools are facing unprecedented pressures due to the presence of 130 thousand Syrian students" (*Al Rai*, August 13, 2015), and two weeks later the number rises to 140 thousands (*Al Rai*, August 31, 2015). In addition to the overwhelming numbers, there are frequent references to schools as crowded, the quality of education as dropping, and violence as rising among the children. The sense of crisis is reflected in statements such as "the education provided in the governmental schools has become dangerous without the separation between the Syrian and the Jordanian students." Occasionally, articles feature concern for the well-being of Syrian children by encouraging the education of girls and nutrition for schoolchildren in general.

Draining Jordanian resources and especially water is a recurrent theme in the articles included under this frame. Detailed statistics are provided to explain the amount of resources spent on Syrian refugees in terms of electricity, water supply, heating, gas consumption, winter clothes, and food subsidies. Syrian consumption rates of bread and water are often compared to those of Jordanians. A few articles stress that *Al Za'atari* camp has to be relocated given its location on a water reservoir. The articles generally depict Syrian refugees as overconsumers who often abuse Jordan's limited resources. Almost every single discussion of economic strain mentions that the high cost of assisting Syrian refugees is being paid for by the Jordanian state despite its limited resources. Details of international aid and budgets of UNHCR and other organizations are provided in complicated ways leaving the reader with a simple conclusion that the budgets are limited and that Jordan is forced to pay the difference. The representation of the burdensome other, the Syrian refugee, is further strengthened when related to the humanitarian discourse of victimization and destitution, and the conflict frame of alien values.

In sum, the theme of economic strain, which is the largest within Jordanian news articles in 2015, stresses a sense of urgency through combining danger with complex statistical descriptions. Depicting a scene where institutions, budgets, and natural resources are all overwhelmed and overstretched, Jordanian mainstream newspapers accentuate a form of public anxiety toward the presence of Syrian refugees.

Turkey

Syrian refugees are often cited as straining the Turkish economy by increasing unemployment and raising rents. Although rarely stated directly, articles dealing with economic strain regularly mention that Syrian refugees "definitely have an impact" on the increasing economic stress. For example, an article by *Hürriyet* on February 2, 2015 argues that unemployment rates rouse as a result of Syrian residents. While increasing unemployment is repeated a few times with reference to statistics, Syrians' needs for education and healthcare are often addressed by featuring the inauguration of new schools and healthcare facilities which also strain the government's budget.

The ambiguity of Turkish news articles within this frame resembles the ambiguity of Jordanian articles in the conflict frame, both leaving the reader to establish their own version of truth based on incomplete information and passing remarks on the certainty of economic burden and moral corruption simultaneously. Similar to articles depicting conflict in the Jordanian mainstream press, articles citing economic strain in Turkish mainstream newspapers lack coherent narratives, which ultimately increase uncertainty about the presence of Syrian refugees, leading to conclusions of an impending crisis.

Sweden

A very small number of articles within the Swedish newspapers tackle the economic problems associated with the refugee stream. Accounting for the fact that Sweden spends more than other European countries on each refugee due to large welfare programs and for the unprecedented number of unaccompanied minors shapes the contours of the debate within this frame. These arguments are often related to the need for an expedited track to labor market integration and, at times, the need to limit the number of refugees arriving in Sweden, concluding that "the committed migration policy will not be maintained for any length of time" (*Svenska Dagbladet*, October 2, 2015). As such the economic debate, while present in Swedish newspapers, ends up resembling the debate for the need for institutional reform, which is integral within Swedish discussions of refugee reception. At the same time, the sense of crisis is maintained through the conclusion that drastic measures need to be introduced in order to meet the challenges of the crisis.

Frame Four: Institutional Reform

Referred to as the responsibility frame by other authors, this frame presents the issue "in such a way that the responsibility for causing or solving a problem lies with the government, an individual or group" (d'Haenens and de Lange 2001: 850). In the analysis provided here, much of the responsibility lies with the government(s) especially when it comes to causing the problem. The articles here often stress the need to share responsibility among the different members of the international community. Frequently however, civil society institutions are portrayed as sharing the responsibility for solving the problems.

Jordan

Institutional focus in both Jordanian newspapers is often presented in a neutral voice, but still leads the reader to believe that the Jordanian government can do more to curb the refugee crisis and limit the negative influence on Jordanian society and economy. The demand for the government to do more refers to imposing more restrictions to curb the economic cost of Syrian refugees and their negative impact on Jordanian society. A small number of articles focuses on other countries, especially Turkey and the EU, and highlights their efforts to enforce more border controls and limit a further influx of Syrians. With regards to the focus on Turkey, the articles stress border controls and the lack of legal or refugee status for Syrians. For example, designating Syrians as guests in Turkey as opposed to legally recognized refugees is discussed in a number of articles, arguably justifying the denial of legal refugee status to Syrians in Jordan as well. Noteworthy is the emphasis on Turkey's budget for refugee efforts and the additional assistance the country receives from Europe in return for restricting their journey across the Mediterranean. Perhaps toward a more humanitarian end, some articles criticize the return of refugees from Turkey back to Syria despite the ongoing war. For example, "Hundreds of refugees are crossing the borders going back to Syria."

A large portion of articles discussing the responsibility for Syrian refugees focuses on how Jordan is carrying the burden on behalf of the international community and often makes explicit calls for other countries to share the cost. Specific aid packages are discussed in some detail and resettlement processes are highlighted to show exemplary incidents when other countries share the responsibility. As already mentioned, toward the end of 2015 and in preparation for the agreement with the EU, a handful of articles addressing institutional reform in Jordan more directly focused on the need to legalize Syrian workers in order to regularize (and tax) their wages and therefore limit their harm to Jordanian workers. Even discussions of child labor are reported from that perspective.

Overall, the discussion of responsibility stresses that Jordan is not backing down from its intent to help Syrian refugees already within its borders. A Muslim sense of responsibility to others in need, and specifically the concept of almsgiving, are sometimes mentioned to stress the importance of Jordanian benevolence in the face of God. Historical explanations of the way Jordan has constructed a self-image of being a safe haven for various groups of refugees in the region, and Palestinians in particular, are also used to stress the ways Jordan always extends a helping hand to their neighbors. Similar to the humanization frame, all of these draw attention to the moral high ground Jordan wishes to be placed in and strengthen the self-congratulatory narrative of acting responsibly even at times of crisis.

Turkey

Bearing in mind that the two Turkish newspapers in this study held antigovernmental stances in 2015, the small number of articles categorized under the responsibility frame use Syrian refugees in Turkey to criticize the government and its actions toward them and the Turkish people more generally. Employment concerns are featured in a few articles which provided criticism to the government for making the employment of foreigners (Syrians) easier, despite the increasing unemployment among Turkish citizens; there is also a need to tax them. Others provide a different kind of criticism, explaining that if designated as guests then Syrians should not be allowed to beg on the streets of Turkish cities, but instead should be offered more hospitality. References to specific cases of arrests of child beggars are highlighted to critique the AKP government. An interesting example refers to the use of Syrian camp refugees in political rallies where the government is criticized for leaving them stranded on the streets following a rally. In sum, this group of articles reports on Syrian refugees in a way that strengthened the existing opposition and perceptions of the government's lack of competence, which arguably augments a sense of crisis when discussing issues related to institutional responsibility.

Sweden

While a major focus in the articles discussing refugees in relation to Swedish institutions concerns institutional exhaustion, especially during autumn 2015 when the numbers of arrivals peaked, the debate is mainly focused around the need for the integration of refugees into the Swedish system and the extent of responsibility that has been taken on by civil society organizations. On the need for integration, this group of articles deals with access to the labor market (minimum wages), and the refusal of some municipalities to take refugees. One article argues for the need to reduce the minimum wage in order to provide employment opportunities for refugees, and directly critiques the unions' strong protectionist discourse, stating:

> Prerequisites for negotiations sprout and are interpreted fundamentally different by different actors. Sweden has labor shortages in skilled occupations. At the same time, many low-skilled, especially foreign-born, have no job. A growing economy is a precondition for increasing employment. If we fail in the integration of refugees, where work is key, this poses risk to the welfare and cohesion of the country.
>
> ("The Unions' Blind Spot," *Dagens Nyheter*, December 23, 2015)

Debating whether Sweden "has more room," the focus of the article quickly shifts to the municipalities, county councils, and the Migration Board's concern over the lack of space in the asylum accommodation, long waiting periods in asylum cases, as well as criticism of the uneven distribution of asylum cases across the country.

A group of articles focuses on political reforms, decisions, and political turns from the government relating to budget changes to support the reception of refugees extracted from international aid budgets. Furthermore, there are discussions of the proposals to reform refugee policies such as reducing the number of permanent residence permits, instituting more restrictive family immigration policies, and imposing border controls (all of which were later implemented by the beginning of 2016). These reforms are intended to "create breathing space in the Swedish refugee reception," after "Sweden undertook the largest refugee operation in its modern history during the autumn months" (*Dagens Nyheter*, November 25, 2015).

The articles relating to civil society (NGOs, new private initiatives, religious groups, etc.) discuss the role it took during the month when most people arrived into Sweden, coordinating and arranging the reception of people when they arrived in Sweden. For example, some articles discuss the organizations and individuals who helped in finding sleeping places for refugees when the Migration Board could not, and who helped in creating a meaningful life for the people waiting for asylum. There are articles that highlight how civil society makes up for the flaws in the Swedish bureaucratic system when it comes to integration in questions of language acquisition, building avenues to social integration, and learning about Swedish norms. One example relates to the inability of the Swedish bureaucracy to deal with those in transit:

> Just a few days ago, there was a new spontaneous voluntary initiative, a key player for the newly arrived refugees and the hub of the reception of refugees in transit on the way to Finland and Norway. No one could imagine that Sweden would become a transit country. The entire organization of society is built for those who come here to seek asylum here and not travel on. When some refugees do not want it, it suddenly becomes illegal to stay here.
>
> ("Sweden Became a Transit Country—Then the Voluntary Stands for the Safety Net," *Dagens Nyheter*, October 3, 2015)

In the Swedish context, the sense of crisis is most clearly detected through the discussion of institutions (which is also the largest theme among the articles for this study). These articles depict a situation where Sweden was largely unprepared to receive such large numbers of refugees arriving in a relatively short period of time. The institutions end up in a state of crisis, unable to cope with the demands of bureaucratically managing and assisting those who came to Sweden seeking help. The unprecedented numbers challenge the system in different ways (lack of available beds, shortage of personnel working with migration, absent systems that deal with special needs such as transit, among others). For example, labor unions being unwilling to negotiate minimum wages to facilitate integration to the labor market, or municipalities refusing to take on a fair share of asylum-seekers, only heightens the sense of crisis as it uncovers problems with Swedish institutions that are an integral part of Swedish identity and welfare. Calling for the closure of the border with Denmark (where most asylum-seekers travel through before reaching Sweden) is offered as the only solution to the crisis, and the absence of a strong public discourse challenging this conclusion speaks to the extent to which the Swedish public shares a view of an unprecedented crisis that requires such an extreme measure.

Discussion and Conclusion

Competition and conflict is often understood as the most dominant frame in newspaper coverage of refugees. In this analysis, alongside the economic consequences and strain frame, it is taken to be the frame most closely portraying the crisis discourse. While a popular frame in the articles analyzed, it is important to observe the different ways conflict is represented. In Jordan, conflict is based on Syrian illegal activity that gives them an unfair economic advantage when compared to Jordanians. In Turkey, conflict is similarly based on criminal or illegal activities, but different cultural traditions are also used to highlight the distance between Turks and Syrians. In Sweden, the discourse shifts completely to address looming fears of terrorism and radicalization within the refugee stream. Importantly, the evidence found here suggests that while significant, this frame is not the most dominant in news coverage of refugees at the peak of the refugee crisis in 2015. At the same time, the ambiguities of unfair economic competition, cultural differences, or pending terror attacks (the dominant arguments in Jordan, Turkey, and Sweden respectively) depict a situation of uncertainty and contribute to a sense of crisis as one is left unable to make sense of the unfolding events.

Human interest stories feature prominently in all three contexts, albeit with different meanings. In Jordan, the strategy is used to highlight the concern of government institutions and interest in dealing with the crisis in a more humane way. In Turkey, the humanization of Syrian refugees quickly gives way to their victimization and the humanization of the Turkish saviors. Emphasis is drawn on the greatness of the Turkish civilization and the importance of living up to the expectations that come with such greatness. In Sweden, the centrist newspapers utilize humanization to set themselves apart from the ultra-right unpopular (yet gaining in popularity) discourse. In itself, this theme does not necessarily convey a crisis discourse, but when analyzed in a context of conflict or threat or bothj and economic strain, articles in this group add to the sense of uncertainty and inability to discern a stance toward the presence of Syrian refugees in increasing numbers. Such uncertainty leads the way in constructing a sense of crisis that urgently needs to be interpreted and dealt with.

Economic strain is the frame most clearly communicated in Jordan. As the country received the equivalent of 10 percent of its population as arriving refugees in the span of four years—in addition to the existing refugee populations from Iraq, Palestine, and to lesser extents Sudan and Eritrea—it is understandable that the burden is substantial especially when taking Jordan's limited natural resources into consideration. Besides the financial burden, emphasis is placed on depicting cultural differences that shape wasteful consumption of food and water, thereby contributing to making Syrian refugees less desirable and more othered. In the Turkish context, refugees are considered to be straining the economy by aggravating unemployment and rents. In Sweden, the economic strain is largely debated with an interest in institutional reform and a call to limit the number of refugees arriving in the country. The ambiguities in which the argument for economic strain is made in the three contexts, however, directly relate to a sense of crisis in meaning that is similar to the one observed within the conflict theme. Jordanian and Turkish newspapers do not explain the actual processes of economic strain. Instead, they allude to consumption habits or claim obscure co-relationships that only communicate the need to act urgently to address the impending crisis.

Finally, the fourth frame addressing institutional responsibility or reform reflects the similar divide between the newspapers. In Jordan, the government is portrayed as more efficient and humane in dealing with Syrian refugees than the wealthier Turkey. In Turkey, the newspapers criticize the government for abusing Syrian refugees and inadequately meeting their needs. Civil society organizations are represented as stepping in and filling the gaps in meeting the needs of refugees. The role of civil society organizations is also emphasized in the Swedish newspapers. Institutional responsibility is the theme most clearly depicting the discussions around crisis in the Swedish context, with remarks to a suffocating social pressure (and hence the need for a breathing space on the border) stressing the need for urgent and extreme forms of action.

The analysis of the four frames in the three countries highlights some important aspects of media representation of the refugee crisis of 2015. Swedish newspapers are less concerned with the economic strain brought about with the arrival of refugees, and more emphasis is placed on the need to integrate them into the job market. Jordanian and Turkish newspapers, however, emphasize the cost and economic competition presented by the large masses of cheap refugee labor. Instead of conflict and competition, Swedish newspapers are more focused on the threat of terrorism increased by the reception of refugees. At the same time, Swedish coverage contributes a large proportion toward the humanization of refugees in ways that counter the economic strain and, at times, cultural threat. Human interest stories are by far a more regular feature within the two Swedish newspapers than Jordanian and Turkish ones. When utilized, human interest stories in Jordanian and Turkish newspapers often stress the role played by locals (individual heroes or a national great civilization) in face of a global human crisis.

Importantly, in comparing the discourses in the three contexts, despite their disparate media institutions, state of economic development, proportion of Syrian refugees received, and general attitudes toward them, the analysis provided here highlights that the "refugee crisis" of 2015 is constructed around uncertainties and inability to fathom the demands and consequences of such inflows of large numbers of people. Arguments presenting conflicts and economic strains are either contradictory or unsupported but stress the need for urgent interventions. Similarly, discussions of institutional responsibility underscore that society in general, and governments in specific, were caught unprepared to deal with the groups of people who were flowing in seeking asylum. The humanization of refugees, while providing a strong basis for supporting the refugees, can contribute to a sense of crisis as it strengthens the uncertainty and ambiguities toward refugees who are still constructed as both an abstract and concrete threatening other.

Acknowledgements

The author is grateful for the research assistance provided by Bilge Coskun, Giedre Danielyte, Nawras Hafez, David Norcross, Gina Fristedt Malmberg, Omar Mokhles, Pernilla Nilsson and Jasser El Sissi in cataloguing the newspaper articles.

Notes

1. Following the Syrian popular uprisings in 2011, the subsequent civil war and the rise of the Islamic State, large numbers of refugees, mostly from Syria and Iraq, sought asylum in neighboring countries and many made their way to Europe leading to a public debate on what was termed the refugee crisis. I use the term refugee crisis to denote the construction of a sense of urgency within the receiving countries as a result of the influx of a large number of refugees.
2. Jordan and Turkey are not countries of settlement for Syrian refugees and do not legally recognize them as refugees. In Turkey, Syrians have temporary protection status, which grants them access to work, health care, and education. In Jordan, educational and health care services are provided to Syrian refugees based on a memorandum of understanding signed between UNHCR and the government, but access constitutes a major challenge (Achilli 2016).
3. As a result of the newspaper's anti-government stance, it was taken over by the government in March 2016 and was later closed by decree four months later (Cunningham 2016).
4. d'Haenens and de Lange (2001, 850) explain that "the morality frame adds a religious or moral charge to an event, problem or subject." The religious charge was seldom observed in the articles referred to in this analysis, perhaps because all but one of the newspapers (Zaman) are secular in nature. The moral charge, whenever strong, was often used in human interest stories.
5. Syrian investors are also considered to have lied about the amount of capital they invest. The newspaper cited a member in the *Mafreq* chamber of commerce: "The real capital for those investors is between 4–10 thousand dinars, despite that the investment law stated that the capital should be not less than 50 thousand dinars minimum."

References

Achilli, L. 2016. "Back to Syria? Conflicting Patterns of Mobility among Syrian Refugees in Jordan." *Orient* 57, no. 1: 7–13.

Balch, A., and E. Balabanova. 2014. "Ethics, Politics and Migration: Public Debates on the Free Movement of Romanians and Bulgarians in the UK, 2006–2013." *Politics* 36, no. 1: 19–35.

Benson, R. 2013. *Shaping Immigration News*. Cambridge, UK: Cambridge University Press.

Binder, S., and W. Allen. 2015. "Constructing Immigrants: Portrayals of Migrant Groups in British National Newspapers, 2010–2012." *International Migration Review* 50, no. 1: 1–38.

Bradimore, A., and H. Bauder. 2011. "Mystery Ships and Risky Boat People: Tamil Refugee Migration in the Newsprint Media." *Canadian Journal of Communication* 36, no. 4: 637–661.

Clare, M., and D. Abdelhady. 2016. "No Longer a Waltz Between Red Wine and Mint Tea: The Portrayal of the Children of Immigrants in French Newspapers (2003–2013)." *International Journal of Intercultural Relations* 50:13–28.

Crawley, H. 2005. "Evidence on Attitudes to Asylum and Immigration: What We Know, Don't Know and Need to Know." *Working Paper Series* 23. Oxford: COMPAS, University of Oxford. http://www.compas.ox.ac.uk/2005/wp-2005-023-crawley_attitudes_asylum_immigration/

Cunningham, E. 2016. "Turkish Authorities to Shut Down Dozens of Media Outlets." *The Washington Post*, July 27, https://www.washingtonpost.com/world/turkish-authorities-to-shut-down-dozens-of-media-outlets/2016/07/27/d1c8454c-542e-11e6-b652-315ae5d4d4dd_story.html?noredirect=on&utm_term=.9ea33014d60e.

Dahlgren, P. 2016. "Moral Spectatorship and Its Discourses: The 'Mediapolis' in the Swedish Refugee Crisis." *Javnost—The Public* 23, no. 4: 382–397.

d'Haenens, L. and M. de Lange. 2001. "Framing of Asylum Seekers in Dutch Regional Newspapers." *Media, Culture and Society* 23, no. 6: 847–860.

Entman, R. 1993. "Framing: Toward Clarification of a Fractured Paradigm." *Journal of Communication* 43:51–58

European Council. 2016. EU and Jordan Adopted Partnership Priorities and Compact. http://www.consilium.europa.eu/en/press/press-releases/2016/12/20/eu-jordan-partnership-priorities-and-compact/

Georgiou, M., and R. Zaborowski. 2017. "*Media Coverage of the 'Refugee Crisis': A Cross-European Perspective*." Council of Europe Report DG1(2017)03. https://rm.coe.int/1680706b00

Greenberg, J., and S. Hier. (2001). "Crisis, Mobilization and Collective Problematization: 'Illegal' Chinese Migrants and the Canadian News Media." *Journalism Studies* 2, no. 4: 563–583.

Innes, A. 2010. "When the Threatened Become the Threat: The Construction of Asylum-Seekers in British Media Narratives." *International Relations,* 24, no. 4: 456–477.

Leudar, I. et al. 2008. "Hostility Themes in Media, Community and Refugee Narratives." *Discourse and Society* 19, no. 2: 187–221.

Mare, A. 2013. "A Complicated but Symbiotic Affair: The Relationship between Mainstream Media and Social Media in the Coverage of Social Protests in Southern Africa." *Ecquid Novi: African Journalism Studies* 34, no. 1: 83–98.

McCombs, M. E., and S. Ghanem. 2001. "The Convergence of Agenda Setting and Framing." In *Framing Public Life: Perspectives on Media and Our Understanding of the Social World*, edited by S. Reese, O. Gandy, and A. Grant, 83–98. Mahwah, NJ: Lawrence Erlbaum.

McCombs, M. E., D. L. Shaw, and D. Weaver. 1997. *Communication and Democracy: Exploring the Intellectual Frontiers in Agenda-Setting Theory*. Hillsdale, NJ: Lawrence Erlbaum.

Nord, L. 2008. "Swedish Media between Politics and Market." *Informacijos Mokslai/ Information Sciences* 47, no. 1: 9–21.

Neuman, W. R., M. R. Just and A. N. Crigler (1992). *Common Knowledge: News and the Construction of Political Meaning*. Chicago: University of Chicago Press.

Rasinger, S. 2010. "'Lithuanian Migrants Send Crime Rocketing': Representation of 'New' Migrants in Regional Print Media." *Media Culture & Society* 32, no. 6: 1021–1030.

Scheufele, D. A. 1999. "Framing as a Theory of Media Effects." *The Journal of Communication* 49:103–122.

Semetko, H. A., and P. M. Valkenburg. 2000. "Framing European Politics: A Content Analysis of Press and Television News." *The Journal of Communication* 50:93–109.

Steimel, S. 2009. "Refugees in the News: A Representative Anecdote of Identification/ Division in Refugee Media Coverage." *Kentucky Journal of Communication* 28, no. 1: 55–75.

Strömbäck, J, and L. W. Nord. 2008. "Media and Politics in Sweden." In *Communicating Politics: Political Communications in the Nordic Countries*, edited by J. Strömback,

M. Örsten, and T. Aalberg, 103–125. Gothenburg, Sweden: Nordicom/University of Gothenburg.

Threadgold, T. 2009. "*The Media and Migration in the United Kingdom, 1999 to 2009.*" Washington, DC: Migration Policy Institute. https://ec.europa.eu/migrant-integration/index.cfm?action=media.download&uuid=2AEC4EBF-B86C-A9C7-BB4FEB4660514EA3.

Valkenburg, P.M., H. A. Semetko and C. H. De Vreese. 1999. "The Effects of News Frames on Readers' Thoughts and Recall." *Communication Research*, *26*, no. 5: 550–569.

Van Dijk, T.A. 2000. "New(s) Racism: A Discourse Analytical Approach." In *Ethnic Minorities and the Media*, edited by S. Cottle, 33–49. London: Open University Press.

PART VIII

GENDERED CONSTRUCTIONS OF CRISES

CHAPTER 37

GENDER AND SOCIAL EXCLUSION IN EUROPEAN MIGRATION CRISIS

A Sociohistorical Perspective

MARLOU SCHROVER

THIS chapter looks from a gender perspective at the question how structural forces repeatedly generated and constructed the idea of a refugee crisis in the past hundred years. Migration is as much part of life as are birth, death, and marriage. From that perspective migration is normal but the normality of migration is seldom emphasized. Sudden and sharp increases in the number of migrants—especially in the number of refugees—lead to the use of the term "refugee crisis," which emphasizes instability and danger, and which leads to calls for changes in policies or support structures. Crises are constructed by the media, by policymakers, and by politicians and organizations. This chapter critically examines what a crisis is, how it is gendered, and how this concept is used in the field of migration research. The chapter takes a historical approach. Strategies and campaigns that were (successfully) developed and conducted in the past continue to determine current campaigns and social exclusions.

Gender is used in this chapter in a dual way. In the first place, there were both men and women among all migrant groups in the past hundred years, although percentages differed per group. The percentage of men among the Hungarian refugees of 1956, and the Tamil refugees in the 1980s, was 80, while the percentage of men among the Vietnamese refugees of the 1970s or the Yugoslavs of the 1990s was 50. The word "migrants" is used in this chapter for all categories of migrants including refugees, on which the "crisis literature" focuses. Secondly, there is a difference according to gender when it comes to claim makers. As will be illustrated in this chapter, women were important as claim makers and advocates of migrant rights. Frequently these activities were part of their emancipatory trajectory. In the 1920s and again after the 1970s nonmigrant women—mostly white, Christian, Western, and middle-class—came out in support of migrant women.

This chapter starts with a comment about the reasons for having a chapter on gender, followed by a section on the problematization of migration in general, and a brief enumeration of the number of refugees in the twentieth century. It is followed by sections on changes in the problematization of (refugee) migrations over the course of the twentieth century.

Why Have a Chapter on Gender?

For several decades reviewers have protested against having a chapter on women or gender in a handbook because it is used as an excuse for ignoring gender in all other chapters (Schrover 2014). However, there is large literature on gender and migration, as well as a societal and political debate (Schrover and Moloney 2013), and that is reason to have a chapter on this subject, despite valid objections.

There are biases in the literature. Texts about gender and migration are frequently only about women, and not about differences between men and women. The literature on gender and migration is also mostly about family, trafficking, and prostitution, and much less about work and opportunities. Furthermore, there is an emphasis on victimhood. The victimhood discourse has successfully been used by organizations and advocates for acquiring rights for immigrant women. However, as a result all migrant women came to be seen as vulnerable and in need of protection. Discourses that use vulnerability and victimhood deny migrant women agency. Since the 1980s, authors have objected to the use of a victimhood discourse in issues concerning women, minorities, or minority women (MacLeod and Saraga 1988). According to Mohanty (1988) Western feminists eagerly bought into the construction of "third-world women" as "powerless," "exploited," and "sexually harassed." "Third-world women" were as a category automatically defined as religious, and as family oriented. Their victimization played a role in the construction of a counter identity of "Western" women, who were everything the "third-world women" were not (Doezema 2001). Walaardt (2013) has shown that refugee men could also play the victimhood card successfully (and acquire rights based on that), but they did so while retaining a masculine hero image. Women were victims but seldom simultaneously heroes. The "success" of the victimhood discourse for migrant women is not only explained by the fact that it fitted key (Western) ideas about femininity. It was also used to give a humanitarian face to restrictive immigration policies (Schrover 2009). The emphasis on victimhood was and is instrumental for the problematization of migration and for enhancing the idea of crisis.

Problematization of Migration

The process of problematization and the creation of a crisis are gendered. How organizations, politicians, and journalists pay attention to men and women differs; migrant men are portrayed as causing problems, and migrant women as having them (Roggeband and Verloo 2007), or men are portrayed as *a* risk (to the labor market, or security) and women as *at* risk (of being trafficked, ending up in prostitution, forced marriages, situations of domestic violence, or becoming the victim of honor killings) (Schrover 2009, 2010).

This section briefly outlines how the process of problematization works in theory and practice (see also Schrover and Schinkel 2013). Problematization is the process in which actors (such as academics, politicians, journalists, and lawyers) analyze a situation, define it as a problem, expand it by attaching issues to it or by exaggerating the number of people or the cost involved, and finally suggest a solution (Foucault 1991). First, the "problem" has to be defined as new: if it is not new it is not news, and there is no need for worries, new policies and new research. Mockery, ridicule, and appeal to common sense are frequently used to stress that "of course" today's problems cannot be compared to those of the past. Secondly, the ownership of the "problem" is relevant: if it is "our" problem, "we" have to offer a solution. Thirdly, the "problem" has to be legitimized. Politicians justify (controversial) policies by pointing out that their actions were legal and benefiting "the people." They stress the normality of policies, and the abnormality of circumstances as well as the seriousness or the "threat" (Martin Rojo and Van Dijk 1997; Walaardt 2013). Fourthly, via "tactical linkage," issues regarding migration are connected to issues like social cohesion, safety, criminality, or terrorism (Rhodes 1997). The "problem" is expanded by making use of the numbers game; the exaggeration of the number of people involved or the costs (Schrover 2009, 2010). In the fifth place, there is the sensationalization and personification of the "problem." In the case of personification one person is singled out to illustrate a certain issue. Personification makes use of detailed stories, full of grueling elements (Schrover 2009; 2010). Personification is used to make claims on behalf of a larger group, but without making that too explicit in order to avoid fueling the argument that a precedent will be created. Lastly, problematization works via the use of metaphors, which suggest causes and consequences without naming them. The water metaphor is favored in the migration discourse. Dams have to be thrown up against the rising tide, the streams and floods which swamp the country and undermine the dykes that keep out the infinite ocean (O'Brien 2003). Water metaphors are popular because, by nature, water is difficult to stop. Through this metaphor, lack of control over movement is equated with lack of control over change (Charteris-Black 2006).

When it comes to problematization in the case of gender, and thus the creation of an idea of crisis, personification is a favoured strategy of claim makers, and scholars tend to reproduce this strategy: the personal story of a woman or a child is put center stage. Stories used for this problematization focus on the issue of trafficking, and therefore it is useful to say a bit more about this issue (Agustin 2005). The result is that the subject of trafficking is *over*-studied (Anderson and O'Connell Davidson 2006; Andrijasevic 2004; Biemann 2002; Chapkis 2003; El-Cherkeh et al. 2004; Gould 2010; Leppänen 2007; Macklin 2003; O'Connell Davidson 2006; Salt and Stein 1997; Schaeffer-Grabiel 2010; Soderlund 2005).

The literature on trafficking shows continuity over time. Around 1900, the figurehead victim of trafficking was called Maria (emphasizing virginity), currently the stereotypical victim is called Natasha (suggesting an almost European origin), and trafficking is called the Natasha trade (Hughes 2001). Stories about trafficked victims include personal stories and heartbreaking details about the lives of the women, who are mostly referred to as girls, even when they are well beyond the age of girlhood. Personification is effective for drawing attention to a problem, but has the disadvantage that it results in attempts to save the victim, rather than to solve the problems.

Debates about trafficking in women were extensive in the 1920s and 1930s, precisely at the moment when many states moved towards more restrictive immigrant regimes. After the 1970s, and at the onset of a new restrictive era, debates about trafficking were rekindled. The new debates were very similar to those from the beginning of the twentieth century, but few cross-references were made, so as not to lose the emphasis on the newness of the problem. Older stereotypes, which were also influenced by the othering and exoticization used in the colonial context, were recombined with newer ones.

Some scholars have taken a critical stance towards the profusion of scholarship about trafficking, which is part of what Agustin (2007) calls "a rescue industry." Authors have pointed out that claims about the number of trafficked women are based on poor and inadequate research, that all migrant women are seen as trafficking victims, and that heartbreaking stories are used to mobilize support for control and restrictions on the mobility of women (Brennan 2008; Brysk 2011; Deane 2010; Fehér 2000; Kapur 2005; Oude Breuil et al. 2011; Weitzer 2010; Wooditch, DuPont-Morales and Hummer 2009).

Trafficking is used to expand the problem and is linked to slavery, human organ harvesting, forced marriages, child abduction, prostitution, and female genital cutting. Already in the 1920s and 1930s trafficking in humans was linked to trafficking in arms and drugs. From the 1990s onwards it was increasingly linked to illegal migration, and later to terrorism. In a 2003 speech US president Bush effortlessly moved from the "War on Terrorism" to the "War Against Trafficking" (Soderlund 2005).

Scholars have repeatedly pointed out that the stories about trafficking are overdramatized. They pointed out that numbers are overestimated and that part of this group of women were prostitutes before they migrated, or they knew they were going to work as prostitutes (Agustin 2007; Bovenkerk et al. 2006; De Vries 2005; Soderlund 2005). These revelations hardly had an effect on the discourse, or on the number of publications about trafficking. Authors who try to counter the overdramatized stories and try to present a more balanced picture are accused of not caring for girls. Overall, what is important for this chapter is that the trafficking discourse involving innocent victims, violated borders, and criminality is part of problematizing migration and feeds into the idea of a migration crisis (Berman 2003).

Number of People on the Move and the Feminization of Migration

The idea of a migration crisis was—of course—also influenced by increases in the number of refugees. In the twentieth century, there were several moments when the number of refugees increased and in all of these periods organizations, politicians and journalists pushed for change and support.

The First World War caused the displacement of twenty million people in Europe. At the outbreak of the war, one million Belgians fled to the Netherlands (which at that time had a population of 6.3 million) while 250,000 Belgians fled to England, with 16,000 of them leaving in rickety boats from Ostend to Folkestone on one single day. These migrations led to panics among the authorities, and also to large-scale societal support.

After the Russian Revolution, 1 to 1.5 million people fled West, while 50,000 Russians fled East. Two million Armenians fled West and South from Turkey, of whom 25,000 eventually got into the United States despite the policy of restrictionism. During the Spanish Civil War, half a million people fled to France, Belgium, the UK, the Soviet Union, and Morocco. After the Nazi takeover about 37,000 German Jews (of the 523,000 Jews living in Germany at the time) fled to neighboring countries, while smaller numbers of German Jews continued to leave after 1933. In 1938, 225,000 German Jews sought to flee, but hardly any country was willing to take them. In the immediate post–Second World War period, there were in Europe 11 million refugees and Displaced Persons (DPs) and 12 million expellees (ethnic Germans) in camps in Europe. In 1956, 225,000 people fled from Hungary after the Hungarian Revolt. In the 1970s, two million people fled Vietnam, and they were partly resettled in European countries and the United States, after a conference in Geneva decided on distribution across countries. The disintegration of Yugoslavia in the 1990s led to the displacement of four million people. Currently there are about 1.2 million refugees from Syria in Europe. Increases in numbers led to debates about crisis.

The idea that there is a migration crisis, however, need not be the result of a (sudden) increase in the number of refugees. The idea also occurred when it was feared that the number of refugees might increase. This for instance happened shortly before the disintegration of the Soviet Union. Western states expected that seven million people would flee from the crumbling state, mostly to the United States (Rosenberg 2002). The twenty-four member states of the Council of Europe gathered in Vienna to develop a joint strategy to receive these refugees. The United States planned to create a Survivors of Totalitarianism Resettlement Fund in order to help them. Attempts were made to control the crisis and regulate this migration, but in the end, no crisis materialized.

The idea of crisis was mostly linked to refugee migration. However, the arrival of large numbers of migrants from the (former) colonies of France (Vietnam and Algeria for instance); the UK (India, Pakistan, Uganda); the Netherlands (Indonesia, Surinam); Portugal (Angola, Mozambique); and to a lesser extent Belgium (Congo, Burundi), during and after the process of decolonization, also led to feelings of crisis, and calls for support and policy change. In the 1970s, after the end of the guest worker regime, the arrival in Belgium, France, Germany, Luxembourg, and the Netherlands of large numbers of family migrants, in a similar manner led to debates about crisis and the need for policy changes.

Debates about numbers are gendered. The idea of a crisis is created or enlarged by emphasizing that especially the number or the percentage of women on the move has increased in recent years. Migration researchers and policymakers endlessly repeat the claim that a feminization of migration has occurred (Schrover 2013a). Authors generally offer no proof for this, and only observe that women today form 50 percent of the migrants. After that, they move on to issues such as migrant women's health hazards, the problems of careworkers, domestic servants, mail order brides, prostitution, trafficking and illegal migration (Biemann 2002; Sassen 2003). The alleged feminization of migration is assumed to create problems (Dannecker 2005; Labadie-Jackson 2008; Lepp 2002; Ryan 2002). The emphasis on the feminization of migration is used to problematize the migration of women, and create an idea of crisis.

In reality there is not so much a feminization of migration but rather a feminization of the literature on migration. Since the 1980s the number of publications on gender and migration, or women and migration, has sharply increased. Migrant women have become more visible in debates, and in the literature. The debate about migration clearly has feminized (Schrover 2013a). Since the 1970s, organizations acting on behalf of migrant women have used highly personalized cases to fight for immigrant rights via media campaigns (Schrover 2009). In an attempt to gain (legal) equality, differences between migrant men and women were stressed. In asylum cases, for example, rape, female circumcision, honor killings, domestic violence, coercive family planning, forced marriages, or repressive social norms have been introduced and recognized as new—women-specific—grounds for asylum. The drafters of the 1951 Refugee Convention conceived of flight motives as political, public, and collective. They did not conceive of women applying for refugee status (Oxford 2005; Spijkerboer 2000). In recent decades, there has been (what can be called) a women-specific enlargement of refugee grounds. It strengthened the idea of crisis.

For Women, By Women

The attention to women on the move has increased but it is by no means new. At the end of the nineteenth century the number of voluntary organizations sharply increased. People felt they could change societies, and organized to save women and children, redeem prostitutes, protect animals, abolish slavery, eradicate alcoholism, and convert the heathens (Davies 2013; Epp 1998). People wanted to protect morale, tradition, and

Christian values, and to fight decadence or modernism. Because of increases in wealth, women and men had more time, energy, and money to spare than before, and they spent it on changing and saving the world. From the end of the nineteenth century onwards, migration was a key issue on which organizations focused: they wanted to increase and regulate migrations, stop and frustrate the movement of undesirable migrants (including prostitutes and paupers), or help protect people on route. Progressive (immigrant supporting) and regressive (restricting migration) organizations were both active. Women especially started to play an important role in these voluntary organizations. At the end of the nineteenth century, European and American women, labeled "maternal imperialists" (Ramusack 1990), traveled to the colonies with—among other motives—the drive to civilize children and save them from their parents, from forced marriages and slavery, and for Christianity. This was very much an emancipatory trajectory for Western, Christian women.

Organizations fighting trafficking were highly visible in the beginning of the twentieth century and its leaders were largely white, Christian, and middle-class. In the extensive campaigns at the beginning of the twentieth century, there was an emphasis on youth, innocence, whiteness, corruption, and foreignness. Numerous conferences were held on the subject of trafficking and campaigners travelled extensively between countries. Organizations in the first decades of the twentieth century used the new medium of motion pictures to create public interest. The number of newspaper articles in this period about trafficking was stunning: thousands of articles were published yearly (Schrover 2015). The issue enabled organizations to gain high visibility and make strong moral claims. Saving women was a cause to which many people could subscribe. Between 1902 and 1919 several conventions were concluded (Lehti and Aromaa 2006). Success was largely symbolic, but the large number of conferences and gatherings on the issue of trafficking did provide opportunities for the development and exchange of strategies among organizations.

Ideas about strategies spilled over into to the campaigns for the Armenian refugees in 1915–1917, which were like those against trafficking largely driven by women (Western, white, Christian women, to be more precise). The American Committee for Armenian and Syrian Relief (ACASR) (later known as the American Committee for Relief in the Near East [ACRNE], Near East Relief [NER], and Near East Foundation [NEF]) was an active organization, led by Mabel Elliot, Mabelle Phillips and Annie T. Allen. They were middle-class, middle-aged, white, Christian women, and also in this case their activities were very much part of their emancipatory agenda. Campaigns were about saving Christian women from Muslim men. NEF ran a highly successful and innovative campaign and created awareness for the Armenian cause on an unprecedented scale. It managed to successfully resettle 25,000 Armenian refugees (most of them women) in the United States at the heyday of restrictionism (Schacher 2013). Anti-immigrant sentiments in the United States were anti-Semitic, anti-Islamic, anti-Asian, and anticommunist (expressing the fear that there might be communists among the people fleeing Russian Revolution). The NEF's forerunner successfully used the media, photographs, motion pictures, posters, and celebrity claim makers. Women were put central stage as victims. The campaign, its leaders, and its results are important because the NEF is one of the oldest NGOs (Nongovernmental Organizations) currently working for refugees which has now partners in forty countries. The Armenian campaign was the world's first large-scale, modern humanitarian project. It set the stage for strategies and models that were followed in later campaigns.

In the 1920s there were also campaigns—again largely run by organizations in which women played a prominent role—for the 250,000 Russian refugees who arrived in China and from there moved to the European colonies in Asia. Organizations feared that the Russian refugees, and especially the few hundred women among them who were believed to work as prostitutes, would undermine colonial hierarchy by giving colonized men access to white women (Richard 2012). In the years before the refugees' arrival, Aletta Jacobs, a Dutch women's rights activist, and Carrie Chapman Catt, an American suffragette, traveled for sixteen months through South Africa, the Middle East, Ceylon, India, the Dutch East Indies, the Philippines, Hong Kong, China, and Japan (Bosch 1999). Catt was the founder of the *International Woman Suffrage Alliance* (founded in 1904). This organization later had strong ties with the League of Nations. Everywhere they went, Jacobs and Catt gave lectures about women's rights and the right to vote. Jacobs and Catt were famous at the time, and newspapers published extensively about their trip announcing their arrival in several countries, while local women's organizations and authorities did their best to provide a warm welcome. Catt and Jacobs campaigned for women's rights, and at the same time constructed strong images of the colonized other as submissive, repressed, indolent, passive, and childlike: everything Western women claimed they were not. These stereotypes influenced a crisis discourse for decades afterwards. In the 1920s, UILFC (International Union of Catholic Women's Leagues) and other important Western women's organizations gathered extensive information on what they called "marriage customs and abuses" in the "South Pacific, Africa, and Asia and the Islamic world" and other "ancestral, male-dominated societies." It bought into the stereotypes created by Jacobs and Catt and fed into later campaigns.

Women's organizations also very actively campaigned against the position of *mui tsai* in China (Pedersen 2001). *Mui tsai* were girls, who were 5 to 14 years old, who were transferred from their parents' household to another household, where they worked as domestic servants until a suitable marriage was arranged for them, or they became a concubine at age 20 (Paddle 2003). Local authorities called it adoption, while Western authorities called it slavery and emphasized that since Britain was a nation of Christian civilization it should not tolerate this "evil" (Ko 2008). The *mui tsai* system became a cause célèbre for the inter-war European feminists. In 1921, organizations addressed the issue of the "child slaves" of Hong Kong with a large British media campaign (Poon 2000). The *mui tsai* issue was also taken up by eugenic organizations—led by women such as Cora Hodson—which linked it to racial mixing, prostitution, and the creation of a Eurasian population, which they considered as a threat to colonialism (Chung 2010).

As has been said previously, there were contacts between organizations and strategies were copied from one organization onto the other. This applies also to Save the Children, which sprang from the British antiwar movement (Mahood and Satzewich 2009). Save the Children copied strategies but was also highly innovative. Eglantyne Jebb and Dorothy Buxton started the Save the Children's predecessor, the Fight the Famine (in Russia) Council, which had good contacts with the International Women's Association for Peace and Freedom. In 1919, Jebb was arrested in England for distributing pictures of starving Soviet children (Sasson 2016). The pictures, and thus the campaign, was considered to be too shocking. After the First World War, the Council became the Save the Children Fund. It continued its striking campaigns, with page-long advertisements with pictures in newspapers. In 1921, Save the Children and the Red Cross tried to coordinate emergency famine relief in the Soviet Union. Opponents—including Russian émigré organizations—claimed they were feeding the children who would kill "us" in twenty-five years. Despite this opposition, Save the Children succeeded and claimed to have saved 250,000 children from starvation. It raised over a million pounds within a year, branched out to other countries, and gained support from Pope Benedict XV and the Red Cross. In 1921, the League of Nations called Save the Children its pioneer (Nehlin 2009).

As said, in the 1920s and 1930s models were developed regarding gendered migration issues which would be used for decades to come. After 1945, organizations—originally called voluntary organizations—were increasingly referred to as NGOs. Societal changes such as secularization, emancipation, and technological change in travel and communication affected the role of NGOs and strengthened their position (Davies 2013; Epp 1998;). During the Cold War escape from behind the Iron Curtain was difficult, and often spectacular. Refugees—frequently labeled escapees—tunneled their way from East to West Berlin, swam across the Danube river, hid in the cold storage compartments of trains, or used a glider driven by a Trabant engine to get to the West. Escapees were few, they were portrayed as heroes, and they were mostly men. When women escaped, they were believed to join husbands or accompany boyfriends. They were seen as apolitical, and as moving for love or to join family members. They were not seen as refugees (Walaardt 2013).

Beginning in the 1960s, in several countries including the UK, Sweden, Germany, and the Netherlands multiculturalism emerged as an ideology and a policy for managing the cultural diversity that resulted from migration (Bhabha 2009). The multiculturalist policies "allowed" immigrants to be different from the rest of the population, and encouraged them to hold on to their language and culture (Moller Okin 1999; Schrover 2010). Part of the policy was subsidy for immigrant organizations that bought into these ideas. The policy created, stressed, and maintained differences between immigrant men and women because it reproduced stereotypical ideas about the roles of men and women in countries of origin. All migrant women were seen as wives and mothers. In the 1980s, the economic crisis led to severe cutbacks on subsidies for immigrant organizations (Schrover 2013b). When subsidies were reduced, the organizations focused on immigrant women rather than on immigrant men, and magnified differences between men and women (Schrover 2010). When the idea of the temporariness of the guest worker migration was dropped, discourse shifted to religion and especially the assumed oppression of women within Islam. Women's issues—such as the wearing of headscarves—took center stage in debates on integration (Rottmann and Marx Ferree 2008).

The role of women in NGOs campaigning for refugee or other migrant rights was reinforced in the 1970s, when the possibilities for labor migration in Europe were reduced at the end of the guest worker migration regime. Since guest worker migration had largely been a migration of men (80 percent of the guest worker migrants were men), the family reunification migration that followed was largely one of women. When men migrated within the framework of marriage their migration was seen as a cover for labor migration, especially when the migrating partner was a non-Western man. In response, countries such as Denmark, Germany, Austria, France, the Netherlands, and the UK introduced age bars (with minimum ages of 18 to 24), dependent resident status, housing and income requirements, and tests to be taken before migration (Bonjour and Block 2013; Grillo 2008). Dependent resident status means partners cannot divorce until a waiting period lapses (one to four years). If they do, the dependent partner must return to the country of origin. From the 1970s onwards, the issue of dependent resident status led to large-scale campaigns (Schrover 2010). As a result, Germany, the UK, and Norway introduced so-called hardship rules, or domestic violence and abuse clauses: migrant women should not be forced to bear inhumane treatment in order to avoid losing their legal status. These campaigns were important because they very much strengthened the victimhood discourse. Organizations *of* migrant women for this reason protested against activities by organizations *for* migrant women, but this had little effect.

The end of the Cold War freed the agenda for "women's issues" (Joachim 2003). Attention shifted away from the male hero, and refugees came from more and different countries than before. The end of the Cold War meant that it was less clear who was "good" and who was "bad." The Cold War refugees had been seen as proving communism wrong and capitalism right, by their flight from the "workers' paradise." After the Cold War, refugee issues could no longer be used to claim the superiority of capitalism over communism. There was no longer a simple distinction between friend or foe. A new dichotomy had to be found.

In the 1960s and 1970s, NGOs gained high visibility with their campaigns for refugees from Biafra (Nigeria) and Vietnam. During the Biafran War, NGOs distributed images of starving children on a very large scale. In 1971, a group of French doctors founded *Médecins Sans Frontières* after experiencing at firsthand the suffering in Biafra. The Biafran crisis also made older NGOs, like Oxfam (est. 1942), Save the Children, and Caritas (est. 1897) more visible than ever before. They were also criticized more for failing to help. NGOs explicitly moved their attention away from political causes, and this made it possible for them to take on the role of crucial mediators. NGOs claimed that states were unable to solve problems, while they as neutral organizations could. Famines and refugee migration in and from Ethiopia and Sudan led to the creation of the international Muslim NGO IIROSA (International Islamic Relief Organization of Saudi Arabia, est. 1979), as well as of Islamic Relief (est. 1984), and Muslim Aid (est. 1985) both based in the UK. Their creation was partly a response to the Band Aid (1984) and Live Aid (1985) campaigns, with their celebrity claim makers. The Islamic organizations called them patronizing and neocolonial. Muslim Aid became one of the largest Muslim NGOs in the world.

Overall, attention for Islam increased. In recent years, oppression of women within Islam emerged as a major issue in several countries. Older orientalist ideas were integrated into a perspective in which European women served as the standard against which women from elsewhere were measured (Lutz 1997). Muslim women are currently viewed in North-Western European countries as the prototype of immigrant women. They are perceived as exploited victims, handicapped by their cultures of origin. Islam and Western values are presented as incompatible and static (Molokotos Liederman 2000). Debates are characterized by gross overestimates of the number of women wearing headscarves, or other forms of veiling. This discourse—to which both Western feminists and right-wing politicians contribute—uses stereotypes about non-Western women as religious, family-oriented, traditional, and backward (Mohanty 1988; Rosenberger and Sauer 2012).

The debate on family migration increasingly intertwined with debates about Islam. Muslim-Christian marriages had already been problematized in colonial contexts, and their stereotypical portrayal as problematic spilled over into the postcolonial contexts. Debates were about polygamy, child abductions by migrant fathers from Muslim majority countries, divorces not being recognized under Islamic Law, and about so-called sharia courts (De Hart 2001). Campaigns were partly conducted by women's NGOs, in which—as before—white Christian middle-class women dominated, while the cases they campaigned for mostly related to lower-class Muslim women (Schrover 2013b). Regressive organizations and populist and right-wing political parties increasingly became the advocates of women's rights as well as of gay rights, and both were made part of their anti-Islamic rhetoric (Korteweg and Yurdakul 2008; Lettinga 2011).

In the 1990s, refugee migration became more difficult. Authorities tried to penalize carriers (ships, airplanes) for bringing people into countries where they wanted to apply for refugee status. Frontex—the joint EU border authority—put up signs in Mauretania to stop people from leaving and applying for refugee status in Western countries. Frontex border control operations partly had the same effect: they reduced the chances of people reaching countries where they could apply for refugee status. Other buffers were also created. In 2008, the Italian Berlusconi government paid the Libyan Khadafi regime five billion dollars to detain people and stop them from crossing the Mediterranean. Protests against the attempts to curtail migrations emphasized the risks women encountered. International NGOs, in response to restrictionism, tried to get more rights for refugee women. In 1984, the European Parliament passed a resolution, recognizing that women are sometimes persecuted for breaking the social or cultural norms assigned to their gender. For the UNHCR this was reason to also put gender persecution on its agenda. Awareness grew that not only armed resistance was reason to flee, but that rape should also be seen as a form of torture and persecution frequently inflicted on women for political, religious, and ethnic reasons. The UNHCR said that women and girls among the refugees had special needs, although it was never clear what these needs were. Women and children were said to form 75 percent of the world's refugees. By grouping women with children, the numbers were increased, and thus the size and the urgency of the problem. It however also put women in the same role as children: in need of support but without power. Several authors have argued that this portrayal of refugee women downplays—as was true in earlier decades—their agency, while constructing the refugee-receiving states as morally superior to refugee-producing states (Baines 2000). Organizations succeeded in getting issues on the agenda, but with little results in practice, as had been the case in the 1920s (Baines 2000). Authorities and organizations tried to stop people from leaving by investing much more than before in humanitarian projects in the countries of origins. The UNHCR became more involved than before in providing development relief: bringing safety to people, instead of people to safety. UN peacekeeping operations sought to stop people moving across borders and becoming refugees. Several NGOs allocated a key role to women in this peacekeeping process. In practice, this meant the reconstruction of communities, via the reconstruction of households, through which key ideas about (mostly Western-style) civil society were to be transmitted. Women and girls who had fled, were made part of new—often fictive—families, in the hope that these would provide shelter and protection, as well as the basis for stability and reconstruction. Men and boys were, however, moved from camps near the areas of conflicts to destinations further away. As "freedom fighters" they were perceived to be in need of a different kind of protection from the women and girls. Men more easily got refugee status than women, as had been the case during the Cold War (Jackson 2010).

Gender mainstreaming became a key phrase at the end of the twentieth century. Larger NGOs, mostly Western and Christian in origin, put gender issues on the international agenda. Trafficking is again one of these issues. European countries aspiring to EU membership had to develop policies regarding trafficking and established NGOs came out in support. They determined to a large extent how these policies were shaped and how the discourse was constructed. Large and established organizations pushed out the initiatives of grass-roots organizations. Since 2000, the new EU Member States have become the special concern of NGOs fighting trafficking (Anderson and O'Connell Andrijasevic 2004; Agustin 2005; Davidson 2006). Prostitution was taboo in communist countries, and it was seen as part of Western decadency. As a result, there was no strong NGO interest in fighting trafficking before the EU borders moved eastwards. Currently, the Czech Republic is named by organizations as a transit and destination country for women trafficked from Ukraine, Russia, Belarus, Moldova, Lithuania, Romania, Bulgaria, Slovakia, China, and Vietnam. Organizations such as La Strada (est. 1995) help new and potential EU Member States to bring their policies in line with EU guidelines. By doing so they exercise a strong influence, and voice old stereotypes. In 2002, a European Conference on Preventing and Combating Trafficking in Human Beings took place in the European Parliament with the cooperation of the IOM (International Organization for Migration), the European Commission, the EU Parliament, and EU Member States (Goodey 2008). It brought together more than one thousand representatives of Member States, EU-candidate countries, developing countries, and numerous organizations (Laczko 2005). The new Member States became a key target for NGOs, and these countries were under the obligation to have a gendered policy, which the NGOs were happy to provide.

Conclusion

This chapter has shown how and why gender played a role in social exclusion in what was commonly referred to as the European migration crises. It has shown how migrant women were continuously over the past hundred years constructed to be at risk and in need of protection. The stereotypes and discourses that were used, and problematization of the migration of women, were different from those of men. Of course migrant men were also portrayed as in need of support, but women (with children) were allocated a key role as victims. It gave urgency to the issue, and created empathy. It also created the idea that women were to be saved from their "own" patriarchal culture and oppressive religion. A sharp contrast was created between the culture of the West and that of the Rest. Women as claim makers played an important role in this construction, and thus in the construction of the idea of migration crisis. The outcome of the campaigns was that the victim was saved, but the problem was seldom solved, despite the large number of conferences, treaties, and letters of intent. The problematization strategies played a role in creating the idea of crisis, empathy and the need for support, but it did not offer a solution beyond the symbolic level.

References

Agustin, L. 2005. "Migrants in the Mistress's House: Other Voices in the 'Trafficking' Debate." *Social Politics: International Studies in Gender, State and Society* 12, no. 1: 96–117.

Agustin, L. 2007. *Sex at the Margins: Migration, Labour Markets and the Rescue Industry*. London: Zed.

Anderson, B., and J. O'Connell Davidson. 2006. "The Trouble with Trafficking." In *Trafficking and Women's Rights*, edited by C. van den Anker and J. Doomernik, 11–26. London: Palgrave.

Andrijasevic, R. 2004. "Trafficking in Women and the Politics of Mobility in Europe." PhD diss., Utrecht University.

Baines, E. 2000. "The Elusiveness of Gender-Related Change in International Organizations: Refugee Women, The United Nations High Commissioner For Refugees and the Political Economy of Gender." PhD diss., Dalhousie University Halifax, Nova Scotia.

Berman, J. 2003. "(Un)popular Strangers and Crises (Un)Bounded: Discourses of Sex-Trafficking, the European Political Community and the Panicked State of the Modern State." *European Journal of International Relations* 9, no. 1: 37–86.

Bhabha, F. 2009. "Between Exclusion and Assimilation: Experimentalizing Multiculturalism." *McGill Law Journal / Revue De Droit De McGill* 54, no. 1: 5445–5490.

Biemann, U. 2002. "Remotely Sensed: A Topography of the Global Sex Trade." *Feminist Review* 70, no. 1: 75–88.

Bonjour, S., and L. Block. 2013. "Fortress Europe or Europe of Rights? The Europeanisation of Family Migration Policies in France, Germany and the Netherlands." *European Journal of Migration and Law* 15, no. 2: 203–224.

Bosch, M. 1999. "Colonial Dimensions of Dutch Women's Suffrage: Aletta Jacobs's Travel Letters from Africa and Asia, 1911–1912." *Journal of Women's History* 11, no. 2: 8–34

Bovenkerk, F., M. van San, M. Boone, T. Boekhout van Solinge, and D.J. Korf. 2006. *"Loverboys" of Modern Pooierschap in Amsterdam.* Utrecht: L.J. Veen.

Brennan, D. 2008. "Competing Claims of Victimhood? Foreign and Domestic Victims of Trafficking in the United States." *Sexuality Research & Social Policy* 5, no. 4: 45–61.

Brysk, A. 2011. "Sex as Slavery? Understanding Private Wrongs." *Human Rights Review* 12, no. 3: 259–270.

Chapkis, W. 2003. "Trafficking, Migration, and the Law: Protecting Innocents, Punishing Immigrants." *Gender and Society* 7, no. 6: 923–937.

Charteris-Black, J. 2006. "Britain as a Container: Immigration Metaphors in the 2005 Election Campaign." *Discourse & Society* 17, no. 5: 563–581.

Chung, Y. J. 2010. "Eugenics in China and Hong Kong: Nationalism and Colonialism 1890–1940." In *The Oxford Handbook of the History of Eugenics*, edited by A. Bashford and P. Levine, 258–273. Oxford: Oxford University Press.

Dannecker, P. 2005. "Transnational Migration and the Transformation of Gender Relations: The Case of Bangladeshi Labour Migrants." *Current Sociology* 53, no. 4: 655–674.

Davies, T. 2013. *NGOs: A New History of Transnational Civil Society*. Oxford: Oxford University Press.

De Vries, P. 2005. "'White Slaves' in a Colonial Nation: The Dutch Campaign against the Traffic in Women in the Early Twentieth Century." *Social & Legal Studies* 14, no. 1: 39–60.

Deane, T. 2010. "Cross-Border Trafficking in Nepal and India: Violating Women's Rights." *Human Rights Review* 11, no. 4: 491–513.

Doezema, J. 2001. "Ouch! Western Feminists' 'wounded attachment' to the 'third world prostitute'." *Feminist Review* 67, no. 1: 16–38.

El-Cherkeh, T., E. Stirbu, S. Lazaroiu, and D. Radu. 2004. "*EU-Enlargement, Migration and the Trafficking of Women: The Case of South Eastern Europe*." *Report 247*. Hamburg, Germany: HWWA. https://ageconsearch.umn.edu/bitstream/26079/1/re040247.pdf

Epp, C. 1998. *The rights revolution. Lawyers, Activists, and Supreme Courts in Comparative Perspective*. Chicago: Chicago University Press.

Fehér, L. 2000. "International Efforts against Trafficking in Human Beings." *Acta Juridica Hungarica* 41, no. 3–4: 181–198.

Foucault, M. 1991. "Governmentality." In *The Foucault Effect: Studies in Governmentality*, edited by G. Burchell, C. Gordon, and P. Miller, 87–104. Chicago: University of Chicago Press.

Goodey, J. 2008. "Human Trafficking: Sketchy Data and Policy Responses." *Criminology & Criminal Justice* 8, no. 4: 421–442.

Gould, C. 2010. "The Problem of Trafficking." In *Gender and Migration: Feminist Interventions*, edited by I. E. Palmary, K. Burman, P. Chantler, and P. Kiguwa, 31–49. London: Zed.

Grillo, R., ed. 2008. *The Family in Question: Immigrant and Ethnic Minorities in Multicultural Europe*. Amsterdam: Amsterdam University Press.

Hart, B. de. 2001. "Not Without my Daughter: On Parental Abduction, Orientalism, and Maternal Melodrama." *European Journal of Women's Studies* 8, no. 1: 51–65.

Hughes, D. 2001. "The 'Natasha' Trade - Transnational Sex Trafficking." *National Institute of Justice Journal* 246, January: 9–15.

Jackson, L. A. 2010. “Where are the Girls? War, Displacement and the Notion of Home Among Sudanese Refugee Children.” In *Gender, Migration and the Public Sphere 1850–2005*, edited by M. Schrover and E. J. Yeo, 160–178. New York: Routledge.

Joachim, J. 2003. “Framing Issues and Seizing Opportunities: The UN, NGOs, and Women’s Rights.” *International Studies Quarterly* 47, no. 2: 247–274.

Kapur, R. 2005. *Erotic Justice: Law and the New Politics of Postcolonialism*. London: Glass House.

Ko, Y. K. 2008. “From ‘Slavery’ to ‘Girlhood’? Age, Gender and Race in Chinese and Western Representations of the *Mui Tsai* Phenomenon, 1879–1941.” PhD diss., University of Hong Kong.

Korteweg, A., and G. Yurdakul. 2008. “Islam, Gender, and Immigrant Integration: Boundary Drawing in Discourses on Honour Killing in the Netherlands and Germany.” *Ethnic and Racial Studies* 32, no. 2: 1–21.

Labadie-Jackson, G. 2008. “Reflections on Domestic Work and the Feminization of Migration.” *Campbell Law Review* 31, no. 1: 67–90.

Laczko, F. 2005. “Introduction.” In Special Issue: *“Data and Research on Human Trafficking: A Global Survey.”* Edited by F. Laczko and E. Gozdziak. *International Migration* 43, no. 1–2: 5–16.

Lehti, M., and K. Aromaa. 2006. “Trafficking For Sexual Exploitation.” *Crime & Justice* 34:133–227.

Lepp, A. 2002. “Trafficking in Women and the Feminization of Migration. The Canadian Context.” *Canadian Woman Studies: Les Cahiers De La Femme* 21, no. 4: 90–99.

Leppänen, K. 2007. “Movement of Women: Trafficking in the Interwar Era.” *Women’s Studies International Forum* 30, no. 6: 523–533.

Lettinga, D. N. 2011. *Framing the Hijab: The Governance of Intersecting Religious, Ethnic, and Gender Differences in France, the Netherlands and Germany.* Amsterdam: VU University Press.

Lutz, H. 1997. “The Limits of European-Ness: Immigrant Women in Fortress Europe.” *Feminist Review* 57, no. 1: 93–111.

Macklin, A. 2003. “Dancing Across Borders: ‘Exotic Dancers’, Tafficking, and Canadian Immigration Policy.” *International Migration Review* 37, no. 2: 464–500.

MacLeod, M. and E. Saraga. 1988. “Challenging Orthodoxy: Towards a Feminist Theory and Practice.” *Feminist Review* 28, no. 1: 16–55.

Mahood, L., and V. Satzewich. 2009. “The Save the Children Fund and the Russian Famine of 1921–23: Claims and Counter-Claims about Feeding ‘Bolshevik’ Children.” *Journal of Historical Sociology* 22, no. 1: 55–83.

Martín Rojo, L., and T. van Dijk. 1997. “ ‘There Was a Problem, and it was Solved!’: Legitimating of the Expulsion of ‘Illegal’ Migrants in Spanish Parliamentary Discourse.” *Discourse & Society* 8, no 4: 523–566.

Mohanty, C. 1988. “Under Western Eyes: Feminist Scholarship and Colonial Discourses.” *Feminist Review* 30, no. 1: 61–88.

Moller Okin, S. 1999. “Is Multiculturalism Bad for Women?” In *Is Multiculturalism Bad for Women?*, edited by J. Cohen, M. Howard and M. Nussbaum, 9–24. Princeton, NJ: Princeton University Press.

Molokotos Liederman, L. 2000. “Religious Diversity in Schools: The Muslim Headscarf Controversy and Beyond.” *Social Compass* 47, no. 3: 367–382.

Nehlin, A. 2009. *Exporting Visions and Saving Children: The Swedish Save the Children Fund.* Linköping, Sweden: Linköping University.

O'Brien, G. V. 2003. "Indigestible Food, Conquering Hordes, and Waste Materials: Metaphors of Immigrants and the Early Immigration Restriction Debate in the United States." *Metaphor and Symbol*, 18, no. 1: 33–47.

O'Connell Davidson, J. 2006. "Will the Real Sex Slave Please Stand Up?" *Feminist Review* 83, no 1., Sexual Moralities: 4–22.

Oude Breuil, B. C., D. Siegel, P. van Reenen, A. Beijer, and L. Roos. 2011. "Human Trafficking Revisited: Legal, Enforcement and Ethnographic Narratives on Sex Trafficking to Western Europe." *Trends Organized Crime* 14, no. 1: 30–46.

Oxford, C. G. 2005. "Protectors and Victims in the Gender Regime of Asylum." *National Women's Studies Association (NWSA) Journal* 17, no. 3: 18–38.

Paddle, S. 2003. "The Limits of Sympathy: International Feminists and the Chinese 'Slave Girl' Campaigns of the 1920s and 1930s." *Journal of Colonialism and Colonial History* 4, no. 3: 1–22.

Pedersen, S. 2001. "The Maternalist Moment in British Colonial Policy: The Controversy over 'Child Slavery' in Hong Kong 1917–1941." *Past & Present* 171, no. 1: 161–202.

Poon, P. 2000. "The *Mui Tsai* Question in Hong Kong (1901–1940), with Special Emphasis on the Role of the Po Leung Kuk." PhD diss., University of Hong Kong.

Ramusack, B. N. 1990. "Cultural Missionaries, Maternal Imperialists, Feminist Allies: British Women Activists in India, 1865–1945." *Women's Studies International Forum* 13, no. 4: 309–312.

Rhodes, R.A.W. 1997. *Understanding Governance: Policy Networks, Governance, Reflexivity and Accountability.* Buckingham, UK: Open University Press.

Richard A. I. 2012. "Competition and Complementarity: Civil Society Networks and the Question of Decentralizing the League of Nations." *Journal of Global History* 7, no. 2: 233–256.

Roggeband, C., and M. Verloo. 2007. "Dutch Women Are Liberated, Migrant Women Are a Problem: The Evolution of Policy Frames on Gender and Migration in the Netherlands, 1995–2005." *Social Policy & Administration* 41, no. 3: 271–288.

Rosenberg, V. 2002. "Refugee Status for Soviet Jewish Immigrants to the United States." *Touro Law* 19, no. 2: 419–450.

Rosenberger, S., and B. Sauer. 2012. *Politics, Religion, and Gender: Framing and Regulating the Veil.* Abingdon, UK: Routledge.

Rottmann, S. B., and M. Marx Ferree. 2008. "Citizenship and Intersectionality: German Feminist Debates about Headscarf and Antidiscrimination Laws." *Social Politics: International Studies in Gender, State, & Society* 15, no. 4: 481–513.

Ryan, J. 2002. "Chinese Women as Transnational Migrants: Gender and Class in Global Migration Narratives." *International Migration* 40, no. 2: 93–116.

Salt, J., and J. Stein. 1997. "Migration as a Business: The Case of Trafficking." *International Migration* 35, no. 4: 467–489.

Sassen, S. 2003. "The Feminization of Survival: Alternative Global Circuits." In *Crossing Borders and Shifting Boundaries, vol. 1, Gender on the Move*, edited by M. Morokvasic, U. Erel, and K. Shinozaki, 59–78. Opladen, Germany: Leske & Budrich.

Sasson T. 2016. "From Empire to Humanity: The Russian Famine and the Imperial Origins of International Humanitarianism." *Journal of British Studies* 55, no. 3: 519–537.

Schacher, Y. 2013. "Refugees and Restrictionism. Armenian Women Immigrants to the USA in the Post-World War I Era." In *Gender, Migration and Categorisation: Making Distinctions between Migrants in Western Countries (1900) 1945-2010*, edited by M. Schrover and D. Moloney, 55–74. Amsterdam: Amsterdam University Press.

Schaeffer-Grabiel, F. 2010. "Sex Trafficking as the 'New Slave Trade'?" *Sexualities* 13, no. 2: 153–160.

Schrover, M. 2009. "Family in Dutch Migration Policy, 1945–2005." *The History of the Family* 14, no. 2: 191–202.

Schrover, M. 2010. "Why Make a Difference? Migration Policy and Making Differences between Migrant Men and Women (The Netherlands 1945–2005)." In *Gender, Migration and the Public Sphere, 1850–2005*, edited by M. Schrover and E.J. Yeo, 76–96. New York: Routledge.

Schrover, M. 2013a. "Feminization and Problematization of Migration: Europe in the Nineteenth and Twentieth Centuries." In *Proletarian and Gendered Mass Migrations: A Global Perspective on Continuities and Discontinuities from the 19th to the 21st Centuries*, edited D. Hoerder and A. Kaur, 103–131. Leiden: Brill.

Schrover, M. 2013b. "Multiculturalism, Dependent Residence Status and Honour Killings: Explaining Current Dutch Intolerance towards Ethnic Minorities from a Gender Perspective (1960–2000)." In *Gender, Migration and Categorisation: Making Distinctions between Migrants in Western Countries 1945–2010*, edited by M. Schrover and D. Moloney, 231–254. Amsterdam: Amsterdam University Press.

Schrover, M. 2014. "Integration and Gender." In *An Introduction to Immigrant Incorporation Studies: European Perspectives*, edited by M. Martiniello and J. Rath, 117–138. Amsterdam: Amsterdam University Press.

Schrover, M. 2015. "History of Slavery, Human Smuggling and Trafficking, 1860–2010." In *Histories of Transnational Crime*, edited by G. Bruinsma, 41–70. Amsterdam: Springer.

Schrover, M., and W. Schinkel. 2013. "Introduction: The Language of Inclusions and Exclusion in the Context of Immigration and Integration." *Ethnic and Racial Studies* 36, no. 7: 1123–1141.

Schrover, M., and D. Moloney, eds. 2013. *Gender, Migration and Categorisation: Making Distinctions amongst Migrants in Western Countries 1945–2010*. Amsterdam: Amsterdam University Press.

Soderlund, G. 2005. "Running from the Rescuers: New US Crusaders against Sex Trafficking and the Rhetoric of Abolition." *National Women's Studies Association (NWSA) Journal* 17, no. 3: 64–87.

Spijkerboer, T. 2000. *Gender and Refugee Status*. Aldershot, UK: Ashgate.

Walaardt, T. 2013. "New Refugees? Manly War Resisters Prevent an Asylum Crisis in the Netherlands, 1968–1973." In *Gender, Migration and Categorisation: Making Distinctions amongst Migrants in Western Countries 1945–2010*, edited by M. Schrover and D.M. Moloney, 75–104. Amsterdam: Amsterdam University Press.

Weitzer, R. 2010. "The Mythology of Prostitution: Advocacy Research and Public Policy." *Sexuality Research and Social Policy* 7, no. 1: 15–29.

Wooditch, A.C., M. A. DuPont-Morales, and D. Hummer 2009. "Traffick Jam: A Policy Review of the United States' Trafficking Victims Protection Act of 2000." *Trends in Organized Crime* 12, no. 3: 235–250.

CHAPTER 38

LGBTQ MIGRATION CRISES

RACHEL A. LEWIS

International interest in the treatment of lesbian, bisexual, gay, transgender, and queer migrants has grown exponentially since the United Nations High Commissioner for Refugees (UNHCR) published its official guidelines on asylum claims related to sexual orientation and gender identity in 2008. While the European Union has recognized sexual orientation as a cause of persecution in Article 10 of the EU Asylum Qualification Directive, the United States issued specific guidelines for the evaluation of asylum claims based on sexual orientation and gender identity in 2011. In response to the UN's identification of LGBTQ refugees as central to its gender-and sexuality-based violence-prevention strategy for 2011–2016, the Obama administration took a leading role in the establishment of Emergency Transit Centers for LGBTQ migrants who were in the process of resettlement. According to the Obama administration, LGBTQ refugees constitute a "priority population of concern," one that is especially vulnerable to danger and abuse at every stage of the displacement cycle (Richard 2012).

The language of emergency that drove the Obama administration's rhetoric on LGBTQ migrants is characteristic of mainstream representations of refugee populations as embodying a humanitarian crisis in need of resolution. Peter Nyers has commented on the ways that emergency discourses determine how refugees are spoken of by governments, international aid organizations, and humanitarian groups: "Unlike the lives of migrants, the condition of refugee has no normality; it is life in a state of emergency and is stripped bare of all cultural and political qualities" (2006, 21). While LGBTQ refugees and asylum-seekers are undoubtedly vulnerable to danger and abuse in the context of the refugee camp, as a number of human rights reports have documented (UNHCR 2008, 2011), they are also at risk of violence as a consequence of political asylum policies. As a result of the fact that sexual orientation and gender identity are still relatively new grounds for political asylum, it is often difficult for LGBTQ refugees to translate their experiences of persecution into the kinds of asylum narratives that are recognizable to the state. Caught between universal human rights and the particularities of state immigration controls, many LGBTQ migrants are condemned to a state of emergency at the border rendered invisible in the Obama administration's discourse on refugee camps. The Obama administration's relegation of LGBTQ refugees to Emergency Transit Centers on the margins of the social order conveniently obscures state violence in the form of the United States' own immigration and asylum policies, policies that continue to leave many LGBTQ migrants legally vulnerable to detention or deportation. The state of crisis facing LGBTQ migrants has only intensified in the aftermath of President Trump's executive order which has resulted in over 1,000 LGBTQ refugees from Syria and Iran becoming permanently displaced in Turkey, many suffering from extreme violence and persecution as a result of their sexual orientation or gender identity or both (Dehghan 2017).

With the exception of the recent media interest in the displacement of LGBTQ migrants in Turkey, however, queer migration itself has rarely been figured in terms of crises resulting from displacement, as with the global refugee crisis more generally, but rather in terms of the specific challenges LGBTQ migrants encounter when navigating state immigration and asylum bureaucracies. As a result, the structural violences that condemn LGBTQ migrants to a state of crisis are often marginalized within the majority of migration research on refugees, asylum seekers, and displaced populations. While there is a growing body of work that explores how detention and deportation condemn migrants to a state of crisis (DeGenova and Peutz 2010), discussions of gender and sexuality are conspicuously absent from such analyses. And yet, as recent scholarship in the field of queer migration studies has shown, LGBTQ refugees, asylum-seekers, and undocumented populations are at particular risk of state violence in the form of the global detention and deportation regime (Lewis 2013; Lewis 2014).

In this essay, my goal is to examine the legal and administrative forms of violence produced by immigration laws and policies that condemn LGBTQ migrants to a state of crisis, leaving them permanently vulnerable to detention, deportation, and in some cases, death. Despite the newly emerging body of scholarship devoted to theorizing deportation (Anderson, Gibney, and Paoletti 2011; DeGenova 2002; DeGenova and Peutz 2010), there has been relatively little attention to the ways that gender and sexuality along with race, class, nationality, and geopolitical location produce particular migrants as deportable subjects. By *deportability*, I am referring to the lived experience of the constant threat of removal, as well as to the ways in which immigration laws and policies render specific migrants legally vulnerable to deportation. Considering the needs of LGBTQ migrants means going beyond an approach that sees detainability and deportability primarily as labor-related issues or in terms of economic migration, but rather taking a feminist and queer approach to the socially constructed processes through which detainability and deportability are experienced by LGBTQ migrants. Building on recent work in queer migration studies that engages with the social construction of the undocumented migrant (Luibhéid 2008, 2011), this essay examines the sociolegal production of LGBTQ migrant deportability and crisis in the context of political asylum policies. As is demonstrated, detainability and deportability structure the experiences of the majority of LGBTQ migrants; for this reason, the political asylum system is a crucial site for addressing the multiple forms of precarity endured by LGBTQ migrant populations.

The first part of the essay considers the historically specific asylum regimes that transform LGBTQ migrants into deportable subjects. An analysis of the challenges to successful LGBTQ migration and asylum claims illustrates how state practices of deportation and detention are linked to gendered, racial, and class-based norms of sexual citizenship. The second part of the article examines the various forms of legal and administrative violence inflicted upon LGBTQ migrants by the global detention and deportation regime. While current scholarship on migrant precarity has begun to address the material forms of violence inflicted upon refugees and asylum seekers by the global deportation regime (DeGenova and Peutz 2010), less attention has been paid to the psychic forms of violence and dispossession that repeated exposure to deportability produces. And yet, dispossession from a political community often results in an inability to participate in the kinds of social activities that provide a sense of security and comfort in the familiarity and regularity of everyday life—these are less visible but no less meaningful forms of violence to which migrants are subjected by the global detention and deportation regime. The third and final part of the essay discusses LGBTQ migrant activism that is emerging from these spaces of deportability and crisis to contest the global detention and deportation regime.

LGBTQ Migration and Asylum Policies

The primary challenge to LGBTQ asylum claims lies in the fact that the 1951 Refugee Convention was designed to protect individuals from racial, religious, or political persecution, and the category "particular social group" included neither women nor individuals persecuted for their sexual orientation or gender identity. Like all political asylum applicants, LGBTQ migrants must prove both that they have a "well-founded fear of persecution" and that they are members of a particular social group. Article 1 of the 1951 Refugee Convention provides the following definition of a refugee:

> Any person who . . . owing to well-founded fear of being persecuted for reasons of race, religion, nationality, membership of a particular social group or political opinion, is outside the country of *his* nationality and is unable or, owing to such fear, is unwilling to avail *him*self of the protection of that country; or who, not having a nationality and being outside the country of *his* former habitual residence as a result of such events, is unable or, owing to such fear, is unwilling to return to it (emphasis added).
>
> (UNHCR 1950)

LGBTQ migrants have experienced a number of obstacles in demonstrating that they have faced persecution on account of their sexual orientation or gender identity, and in arguing against the idea that they should hide or change their sexual orientation or gender identity in order to avoid persecution. While sexual orientation and gender identity have been included in the category "membership of a particular social group" since the mid-to-late 1990s, it is still the case that the closer one's application conforms to the traditional model of the male activist fleeing an oppressive political regime, the more likely one is able to obtain asylum (Bohmer and Shuman 2008).

Lesbians have encountered particular challenges in translating their experiences of gender-based persecution into narratives that are recognizable to the state. Women's and lesbians' claims for asylum are often dismissed as insufficiently meeting the Refugee Convention requirements. Whereas gay men often experience violence within the public sphere, lesbians' experiences of violence in the private sphere do not conform to immigration officials' preconceptions and expectations about the nature of political persecution. In lesbian asylum cases, courts still have a tendency to equate the lack of documented evidence of human rights abuses against lesbians in country-of-origin reports with an absence of persecution (Lewis 2013). The result is that it is often difficult for lesbians to produce successful asylum claims when their experiences are perceived by judges to be "too private," the assumption being that they can return to their countries of origin and be "discreet" about their sexual orientation.

Although a number of countries (for example, the United Kingdom, the Netherlands, the Czech Republic, and Australia) have now rejected the "discretion" requirement, or the notion that LGBTQ asylum applicants can return to their country of origin and be "discreet" about their sexual orientation or gender identity, a growing number of lesbian and gay asylum claims are being refused on the grounds that the applicant's claimed sexual orientation is disbelieved (Jansen and Spijkerboer 2011). In assessing the credibility of a political asylum applicant's claim, immigration officials often rely upon stereotypical assumptions and expectations. For example, asylum adjudicators tend to assume that all lesbians and gay men engage in practices of cross-gender identification, that they all form part of a common social group with shared cultural tastes and social spaces, and that they will all come out as gay or lesbian immediately upon arrival in the receiving country (Jansen and Spijkerboer 2011). Unlike other refugee claimants who are not compelled to "perform" a visible identity in the country to which they migrate, lesbian and gay asylum applicants are expected to conform to Western stereotypes of male homosexual behavior based on visibility, consumption, and an identity in the public sphere in order to be considered worthy candidates for asylum (Lewis 2013).

The privileging of stereotypical markers of identity in LGBTQ asylum claims continues to pose significant challenges for lesbian migrants. Although the discretion requirement is no longer explicitly stated in most countries' asylum policies, it remains implicit in the treatment of lesbian asylum cases and is evident in terms of the increasing burden of proof placed on lesbian asylum applicants to make their sexual orientation visible. In many asylum hearings, individuals have been interrogated regarding the degree of visibility of their sexual orientation, and lesbians are often declared to be insufficiently visible, as measured by the expectations of gay men. The problems of claiming asylum are often compounded for lesbian and bisexual women, who may be asked to "prove" their sexual orientation and who are frequently disbelieved, especially if they have children or have been married. In her recent work with lesbian refugees in the

United Kingdom, Claire Bennett (2013) has observed the hypersexualization of lesbian and bisexual women in the political asylum process. While one of the women Bennett interviewed was interrogated about whether or not she "used sex toys" and which sexual positions she liked to adopt in bed, another woman was questioned about the novels of Oscar Wilde and "which [lesbian] shows she watched" (2013). Judges also told some of the women Bennett interviewed that they did not "look like" lesbians, that lesbians "don't have children," and that all lesbians "enjoy the gay scene" and like to go on "Pride marches" (2013). Failure to conform to these heteronormative stereotypes about lesbian identity meant that the women were disbelieved, their asylum claims denied. As one lesbian migrant in the UK commented regarding the absurdity of having to prove lesbian identity in the context of the political asylum process:

> Before I ended up in detention I didn't feel the need to go outside and shout yes I'm a lesbian. Now everything I do I have to prove something. If I don't put pictures of myself or my new haircut up on my Facebook, they will be saying I'm not open enough. That's how it is: "how much of a lesbian are you? Do you go to gay clubs? Do you hang around with other lesbians? How many lesbians can write a letter for you to say yes I know her she's a lesbian? And of those lesbians how many of those lesbians have been accepted by the Home Office or are British?".
>
> (UK Lesbian and Gay Immigration Group 2016)

Many lesbian asylum applicants now feel compelled to produce sex tapes in order to "prove" their sexual orientation in asylum hearings (Lewis 2014). Because of the successful use of such evidence in a number of gay male asylum cases, lesbian migrants feel that immigration officials will not believe that they are lesbians unless they film themselves having sex with another woman. As Ugandan LGBT activist Aderonke Apata who was disbelieved to be a lesbian because she had been married and had a child commented, "It's dehumanizing for me to even mention it. What you do in your room with your lover should not be shared with anybody. So, if you have to share that, it's like pornography" (2016).

Recent work on LGBTQ migration claims in Europe and Canada has shown that bisexual and transgender identities tend to be similarly judged in relation to heteronormative assumptions about gender and sexuality in the political asylum process. While transgender and intersex identities are commonly misunderstood by immigration officials and conflated with sexual orientation, bisexual asylum applicants are deemed unworthy of protection because of the biphobic assumption that it is possible for them to return to their country of origin and assume a heterosexual orientation (Rehaag 2009; Jansen and Spijkerboer 2011). In their analysis of how transgender identities are incorporated into the category of "particular social group," Laurie Berg and Jenni Millbank have observed that, unlike bisexual asylum claims, transgender asylum claims are relatively successful in terms of establishing credibility regarding gender identity. They suggest that this is due to the privileging of visual markers of difference and gender performance within the political asylum process (2013). While transgender asylum applicants tend to be more successful in establishing credibility than gay and lesbian asylum seekers, however, the reasoning behind this success is often the result of misunderstanding on the part of immigration officials about the differences between sexual orientation and gender identity. Berg and Millbank have noted that transgender claims are frequently treated as a "subset" of sexual orientation claims, leading to inappropriate applications of country of origin reports in documenting transgender persecution (2013). Such misunderstandings have the potential to exclude transgender claimants who identify as heterosexual from refugee protection and marginalize forms of persecution experienced by gay and lesbian claimants who do not engage in practices of cross-gender identification.

The fact that LGBTQ migrants are forced to fit into Western identity categories that only signify from legal and bureaucratic perspectives means that they often find themselves in a catch-22 situation whereby they are either perceived by the officials to be "too gay" and thus "faking it," or simply not "gay enough." In this way, we can see how political asylum regimes frequently operate as a site of legalized violence by which the majority of LGBTQ migrants are differentially deprived of the resources needed to make credible asylum claims. This denial of LGBTQ asylum claims results in the reclassification of queer migrants as illegal and thus, by extension, vulnerable to state-sanctioned forms of violence such as detention and deportation. As I discuss in the next section of the essay, the experiences of detention and deportation resulting from the denial of their asylum claims condemns LGBTQ migrants to a state of crisis rarely examined in current scholarship on migration and asylum.

LGBTQ Detention, Deportation, and Asylum

The massive global expansion of deportation regimes in the West during the past couple of decades has led to a related growth in immigrant detention. Indeed, the latter has become an increasingly significant feature of the ways in which Western states seek to govern contemporary migration control. This new "economy of detainability" (DeGenova 2016), attempts to strip migrants of their rights by holding them in custody for often indefinite periods of time; as a result, many migrants held in detention would prefer to be deported immediately rather than to remain in detention indefinitely. Faced with the unsettling reality of potential deportation, many deportable migrants suffer from the precarity created by living with an uncertain sense of time, one that simultaneously confines them to an endless present within detention, but that can also bring change (i.e., deportation) at any moment.

LGBTQ migrant populations are especially vulnerable to state regulations of their temporal existence in the form of indefinite detention and the constant risk of deportation. In the United Kingdom, for example, which has one of the largest detention estates in Europe and is the only European country to detain migrants indefinitely, over 1,000

LGBTQ migrants are placed in detention every year.[1] In their 2016 report, "No Safe Refuge: Experiences of LGBT Asylum Seekers in Detention," the UK Lesbian and Gay Immigration Group has documented the acute vulnerability faced by LGBTQ migrants in detention. As they note, LGBTQ migrants in detention frequently experience discrimination, harassment, and violence both from other detainees and from members of staff (2016). Moreover, it is incredibly difficult for LGBTQ migrants to gather the documentation needed for their asylum claims while in detention, as they are denied even the kind of basic internet access that would help them to collate information about the conditions facing LGBTQ individuals in their country of origin. Furthermore, LGBTQ migrants are required to provide witness statements as evidence of their sexual orientation or gender identity in their asylum hearings. And yet being in detention makes it virtually impossible to contact potential witnesses and to gather their statements. The cruel irony of this global detention and deportation regime is that while many LGBTQ migrants have been imprisoned in their home countries for being "too queer," they are imprisoned in the West for not being "queer enough."

In addition to the challenges to their asylum claims posed by the experience of indefinite detention, many LGBTQ migrants live under a constant fear of being forcibly removed. This fear is exacerbated by seeing other detainees being injected with sedatives in order to be forcibly removed. As two lesbian asylum seekers commented to the UK Lesbian and Gay Immigration Group regarding the experience of witnessing violent forced removals of fellow lesbian migrants:

> This girl had mental problems. She had come from Africa where she got raped. In detention they injected her and dragged her like a piece of cloth to deport her. While they were doing it they locked us down.
>
> (UK Lesbian and Gay Immigration Group 2016)

> Yarl's Wood is not safe. They inject people, if they say you must go and you refuse. They have injected people in front of me. When they want to inject people they lock all doors. They lock everybody inside their rooms. They come and collect the person and take you to the airport.
>
> (UK Lesbian and Gay Immigration Group 2016)

As is evident from the above narratives, lesbian migrants are especially vulnerable to violence within immigrant detention as well as during the deportation process itself. And yet the UK charity Women for Refugee Women documents that at least 340 lesbian women are placed in detention every year (2016). While in detention, queer women are frequently subjected to sexual harassment from male officers. As Brianna, a lesbian asylum seeker from Jamaica commented regarding the potential for abuse of power on the part of male officers,

> What I found really disgusting: it is a woman's detention center and 99% of the security were men. Come on we're ladies. I don't care where we're from, what kind of

> sexual orientation we have; we're ladies you can't have mostly men guarding us. I am in the room naked and they just open the door and come in on me.
>
> (UK Lesbian and Gay Immigration Group 2016)

LGBTQ migrants are also denied access to much-needed medical treatment while in detention. All medicine is taken away from migrants upon arrival at detention centers and it can often take weeks to receive replacement medications. As the UK Lesbian and Gay Immigration Group has documented, many queer migrants have described a pervasive culture of disbelief when talking to health staff in detention about their physical and mental health issues, leading to long-term effects on their emotional and physical well-being (2016). Indeed, transgender migrants are especially vulnerable while in detention. Not only are transgender migrants like all migrants subjected to the mental stress of indefinite detention, but they are frequently denied access to crucial hormone treatment and other medications while simultaneously being placed in detention facilities that do not match their chosen gender. This can be particularly traumatic for transgender female migrants who are subjected to relentless sexual abuse both from cisgender male detainees and from male prison officers. In the United States, for example, Mexican transgender female migrant Christina Madraso who sought asylum in the United States but was detained at the Krome Detention Center in Florida, was raped twice by a prison guard, leading her to attempt to sue the US government for 15 million dollars (Soloman 2005). In some cases, depriving transgender migrants of essential medical treatment while in detention can result in their death. This is precisely what happened in the tragic case of Victoria Arellano, a transgender HIV positive migrant in the United States who was placed in a men's detention facility and denied access to HIV medication needed to save her life. Victoria subsequently died in hospital, shackled to her bed, as a result of being denied access to her HIV medication while in Immigration and Customs Enforcement detention (Chavez 2010).

The violence of the global detention and deportation regime is evident not only in terms of the actual treatment LGBTQ migrants receive while in detention, but within the deportation or forced removal process itself. The Movement for Justice Campaign, a radical queer migrant activist organization that campaigns on behalf of LGBTQ refugees and asylum seekers in the United Kingdom, is in the process of producing a documentary about the forced deportation of a Ugandan lesbian asylum seeker known as "Prossy N." Prossy was raped by her uncle and was forced to witness the murder of her grandmother in Uganda before she fled to the United Kingdom to seek asylum. While awaiting a decision in her asylum case, Prossy was randomly detained in Yarlswood immigration detention center after a violent raid on her home that left her physically beaten and badly traumatized. Prossy was put on the detained fast track system, which meant that she was given no time to contact witnesses for her case; she was also denied access to all medical treatment. During her violent deportation from Britain, the removal agents attempted to force feed Prossy medication that could have killed her. They also deprived Prossy of food and threatened her with suffocation despite numerous protests from other passengers on the flight. The removal agents then left Prossy in Entebbe airport in Uganda without the required identity documents needed to inform the Ugandan government of her citizenship. As Prossy commented to the Movement for Justice Campaign in 2014, as a known lesbian in Uganda she is forced to live in permanent hiding, leaving her vulnerable both to persecution and to extreme poverty (2014).

The kinds of violent, necropolitical border mechanisms produced by the global detention and deportation regime that condemn queer migrants to a state of crisis lead some LGBTQ migrants to consider avoiding the political asylum bureaucracy altogether. This was the case for Ugandan lesbian refugee Jacqui Nanyonjo in the United Kingdom who fled an attempted forced marriage in Uganda but who was forced by the UK asylum system into undocumented status and an exploitative underground labor market. Jacqui rightly understood the Catch-22 situation facing LGBTQ asylum applicants whereby if you apply for asylum immediately upon arrival you are told that you do not have sufficient evidence of your sexual orientation, whereas if you apply for asylum after you have had an opportunity to gather the required documentation, your evidence is often discounted and you are assumed to be "bogus" because you failed to make an asylum claim immediately upon arrival.[2] Eventually, however, Jacqui was advised by the Movement for Justice group to apply for political asylum in Britain. Despite having lived openly as a lesbian in the UK for a number of years, though, Jacqui, like many lesbian migrants, was denied political asylum on the grounds that she could not provide sufficient "proof" of her sexual orientation. Jackie was subsequently sent to Yarl's Wood detention center in November, 2012. Facing deportation to Uganda on January 10, 2013, Jackie's only option was physical resistance but she was outnumbered by the four removal agents charged to assist with the deportation. Jackie struggled for as long as she could against the removal agents until, badly beaten and half-strangled, she was overcome by the pain in her chest and was unable to breathe. When Jackie arrived at Entebbe Airport in Uganda, the removal agents handed her over to the Ugandan authorities, who held her for many more hours without any medical attention. Family members finally met Jackie long after her flight had landed, at which point she was vomiting blood. Her family rushed her to a clinic, but Jackie was unable to get the medical attention she desperately needed. Since Jackie was also in hiding as a lesbian, every visit to a doctor or hospital involved a risk not only to her life but to the safety of her family. Jackie's health rapidly deteriorated and she died two months later as a result of the injuries inflicted upon her by the UK removal agents.

Cases such as those of Jacqui Nanyonjo and Victoria Arrellano attest to the state violence inflicted upon queer female migrants of color by the global detention and deportation regime. This is a necropolitical form of border violence that frequently condemns LGBTQ migrants to states of crisis and, in some cases, premature death.

LGBTQ Migrant Rights Activism

Given the ways in which LGBTQ migration and asylum policies condemn LGBTQ migrants to states of crisis and precarity, it is perhaps not surprising that new forms of queer antideportation activism are emerging to contest the ways in which state immigration controls produce queer migrants as detainable and deportable subjects. In the United Kingdom, for example, the Movement for Justice group has repeatedly protested the death of lesbian asylum seeker Jacqui Nanjonyo as a result of state-sanctioned forms of racism and violence (2013). The more recent "Rivers of Blood" protest in the United Kingdom in 2015 has similarly sought to call attention to the deadly forms of violence produced by European and UK border regimes that condemn LGBTQ migrants to states of extreme crisis. During the protest, LGBTQ migrant activists cut their arms in a graphic protest outside the Home Office in opposition to the UK's racist immigration and asylum policies. With masks covering their faces, activists from the group Lesbians and Gays support the Migrants (LGSM) stood in front of the Home Office and made small cuts to their arms. This symbolic act of self-harming was designed to create a "river of blood," in reference to the notorious anti-immigration speech given by Enoch Powell in 1968. As LGSM commented in a public statement regarding the "deadly" nature of UK asylum policies:

> We created "rivers of blood" to show that the real river of blood flows from the Home Office. Our society is becoming divided, not by diversity, but by our government forcing ordinary people to become border guards. The MPs voting for the Immigration Bill have blood on their hands. The Bill will leave people unable to access adequate housing and [will] force workers into perilous working conditions. People fleeing persecution will be left with nothing to live on.
>
> (RT 2015)

By using the example of the UK's treatment of LGBTQ migrants to call attention to racism and xenophobia in twenty-first century Britain, both the Movement for Justice and Rivers of Blood Campaigns seek to situate the detention and deportation of queer migrants in relation to larger histories of racism, colonialism, and xenophobia in Britain. Through framing the challenges to LGBTQ migration and asylum in relation to civil rights and immigrant rights struggles more generally, both the Movement for Justice and Rivers of Blood campaigns call attention to the multiple and intersecting forms of violence experienced by queer migrants of color. Bringing together a critique of LGBTQ migration and asylum policies with a critique of domestic forms of racism, they show how transnational structures of antiblack racism intersect with sexism and homophobia in the UK's treatment of LGBTQ migrants.

Undocumented queer migrant resistance movements for social justice and immigration reform are also beginning to emerge in the United States to protest the treatment of LGBTQ migrants. More recently, queer migrant activism in the United States has been led by undocumented trans women of color, such as Jennicet Guiterrez, who disrupted White House celebrations of gay pride month in 2015 to protest and call for an end to the detention and deportation of LGBTQ migrants in the United States. As President Obama began a speech on the civil rights of LGBT Americans, Jennicet Gutiérrez called for the President to, "release all LGBTQ immigrants from detention and stop all deportations!" She continued chanting, "not one more deportation" as she was forcibly escorted from the room. Guiterrez is a founding member of *La Familia: Trans Queer Liberation Movement* (TQLM), a trans queer Latinx rights movement based in Los Angeles advocating at national and local levels on issues that affect the LGBTQ Latinx population. TQLM is also part of UndocuQueer—a coalition of organizations supporting queer migrant rights that advocates for an end to the prison industrial complex and the detention of queer and transgender migrants. And yet, as Guiterrez clearly demonstrated through her protest at the White House, the global detention and deportation regime that condemns LGBTQ migrants to states of crisis and precarity is rendered invisible in mainstream gay rights advocacy in the United States.

Recent antideportation activism produced by the Movement for Justice Campaign in the United Kingdom and by transgender migrants such as Jennicet Guiterrez in the United States is crucial in terms of calling attention to state immigration controls as sites of legalized violence by which LGBTQ migrants of color are differentially deprived of the resources needed to make credible asylum claims. Moreover, these protests demonstrate the complicity of Western states and immigration law enforcement agencies with the neoliberal for-profit prison industry. Queer migrant resistance movements, such as these, show how the institution of asylum, an institution initially created to safeguard human rights, has become a tool for further entrenching the coercive, racist powers of the neoliberal state and strengthening its reach through the incarceration of LGBTQ migrant populations. By showing how Western immigration policies are structured in a way that renders LGBTQ migrants detainable and deportable populations, queer migrant antideportation activism points toward the need for coalitions between feminist, queer, immigrant, and antiracist advocates. Such activism, which demonstrates how state immigration controls seek to make racism and its effects invisible, illustrates the need to approach LGBTQ migration and asylum policies from an intersectional perspective. As these activist campaigns suggest, only then will queer migration scholars and activists be in a position to effectively comprehend—and ultimately counteract—the multiple ways in which Western immigration controls seek to produce LGBTQ migrants as deportable and, ultimately, disposable populations.

Conclusion

As I have demonstrated throughout this essay, the social construction of queer detainability and deportability in the context of state immigration controls results in crisis for the vast majority of LGBTQ migrants who are forced to navigate the political asylum bureaucracy. For many LGBTQ migrants confronting the daily threat of detention and deportation, their sense of time becomes fractured and their private lives become ruptured. Such indefinite uncertainty condemns LGBTQ migrants to a state of precarious temporality, removing them from the familiar rhythms of everyday life. Numerous studies on the mental health of refugees have shown how the restructuring of temporal relations for those navigating the political asylum bureaucracy contributes to profound emotional crisis and to a lack of mental well-being (Griffiths 2014). In this way, we can see how the condition of deportability—or being condemned to live in a state of precarious temporality—works to regulate the psychic life and emotional well-being of queer migrant populations. These are some of the less visible—but no less meaningful—forms of violence to which LGBTQ migrants are subjected by the global detention and deportation regime.

Given the challenges to LGBTQ migration and asylum in the Global North, coupled with the violence enacted by the global detention and deportation regime, it is not surprising that the majority of LGBTQ migrants choose to remain in the Global South. As recent reports by the Organization for Refuge, Asylum, and Migration (2013) have shown, the Global South is host to the vast majority of the world's queer refugees, many of whom are forced to remain undocumented. ORAM reports that LGBTQ migrants in Mexico, Uganda, and South Africa are often isolated, with no social networks, leaving them vulnerable to violence and unable to secure even basic food and shelter (2013). Many LGBTQ migrants in the Global South have experienced violence as a response to their visibility and do not have the networks that would establish their participation in a "particular social group" that is necessary for producing a credible claim to asylum. Instead of evidence of their public performances of their sexuality, they report the opposite, efforts to conceal their sexuality as a matter of safety (Lewis and Shuman 2016). These conditions of vulnerability in the world weaken, rather than strengthen, their claims for political asylum. While a number of organizations are involved in assisting LGBTQ migrants in the Global South, however, scholarship on queer migration has not, for the most part, situated the challenges to LGBTQ migration in relation to questions of human rights and development. Future work on LGBTQ migrants in the Global South needs to connect queer migration to human rights and development issues in order to effectively grapple with the impact of histories of colonialism on contemporary forms of queer migration, displacement, and crisis.

Notes

1. There are currently nine detention centers in the United Kingdom. Between 2015 and 2016, the UK Lesbian and Gay Immigration Group conducted 22 interviews with detained LGBTQ migrants. The detention times of the LGBTQ migrants they interviewed ranged from between 3 days to 18 months. Many were detained under the UK's Detained Fast Track system which has subsequently been ruled unlawful. While prohibited to work outside of detention, LGBTQ migrant detainees can work inside the detention facility for £1 per hour (UKLGIG 2016).

2. As I have argued elsewhere, there are numerous LGBTQ asylum cases in which UKBA officials have denied an applicant's claim on the basis that they failed to attend gay bars immediately upon arrival in the United Kingdom (Lewis 2014).

References

Anderson, B., M. J. Gibney, and E. Paoletti. 2011. "Citizenship, Deportation and the Boundaries of Belonging." *Citizenship Studies* 15, no. 5: 547–63.

Bennett, C. 2013. "Claiming Asylum on the Basis of Your Sexuality: The Views of Lesbians in the UK." *Women's Asylum News* 115: 1–4.

Berg, L., and J. Millbank. 2013. "Developing a Jurisprudence of Transgender Particular Social Group." In *Fleeing Homophobia: Sexual Orientation, Gender Identity and Asylum*, edited by Thomas Spijkerboer, 121–153. New York and London: Routledge.

Bohmer, C., and A. Shuman. 2008. *Rejecting Refugees: Political Asylum in the Twenty-First Century*. New York: Routledge.

Chavez, K. 2010. "Spatializing Gender Performativity: Ecstasy and Possibilities for Livable Life in the Tragic Case of Victoria Arellano." *Women's Studies in Communication* 33, no. 1: 1–15.

DeGenova, N. 2016. "Detention, Deportation, and Waiting: Toward a Theory of Migrant Detainability." Global Detention Project. Working Paper 18. https://www.globaldetentionproject.org/detention-deportation-waiting-toward-theory-migrant-detainability-gdp-working-paper-no-18

DeGenova, N. 2002. "Migrant 'Illegality' and Deportability in Everyday Life." *Annual Review of Anthropology* 31 (October): 419–47.

DeGenova, N., and N. Peutz, eds. 2010. *The Deportation Regime: Sovereignty, Space, and the Freedom of Movement*. Durham, NC: Duke University Press.

Dehghan, S. K. 2017. "US Travel Ban Leaves Iranian LGBT Refugees in Limbo." *The Guardian*, February 1. https://www.theguardian.com/world/2017/feb/01/us-travel-ban-leaves-iranian-lgbt-refugees-in-limbo

Griffiths, M. 2014. "Out of Time: The Temporal Uncertainties of Refused Asylum Seekers and Immigration Detainees." *Journal of Ethnic and Migration Studies* 40, no. 12: 1991–2009.

Jansen, S., and T. Spijkerboer. 2011. "Fleeing Homophobia: Asylum Claims Related to Sexual Orientation and Gender Identity in Europe." In *Fleeing Homophobia: Sexual Orientation, Gender Identity and Asylum*, edited by Thomas Spijkerboer, 121–153. New York and London: Routledge.

Lewis, R., and A. Shuman. 2016. "Asylum, Sexual Orientation and Gender Identity." In *Encyclopedia of Gender and Sexuality Studies*, edited by Nancy A. Naples. Oxford: Wiley-Blackwell.

Lewis, R. 2013. "Deportable Subjects: Lesbians and Political Asylum." *Feminist Formations* 25, no. 2: 174–194.

Lewis, R. 2014. "'Gay? Prove It': The Politics of Queer Anti-Deportation Activism," *Sexualities* 17, no. 8: 958–975.

Luibhéid, E. 2008. "Sexuality, Migration, and the Shifting Lines Between Legal and Illegal Status." *GLQ: A Journal of Lesbian and Gay Studies* 14, no. 2–3: 289–315.

Luibhéid, E. 2011. "Nationalist Heterosexuality, Migrant (Il)legality, and Irish Citizenship Law: Queering the Connections." *South Atlantic Quarterly* 110, no. 1: 179–204.

Movement for Justice. 2012. "Shut Down Yarls Wood: Asylum For Women Now." Facebook. https://www.facebook.com/pages/SHUT-DOWN-Yarls-Wood-Asylum-for-Women-NOW/126966244120907?notif_t1/4page_new_likes

Organization for Refuge, Asylum, and Migration (ORAM). 2013. "Blind Alleys: The Unseen Struggles of Lesbian, Gay, Bisexual, Transgender and Intersex Urban Refugees in Mexico, Uganda, and South Africa." http://www.refworld.org/docid/524d46864.html

Rehaag, S. 2009. "Patrolling the Borders of Sexual Orientation: Bisexual Refugee Claims in Canada." *McGill Law Journal* 53: 59–102.

Richard, A. C. 2012. "Strengthening Protection for LGBT Refugees." Human Rights First Campaign Office. US Department of State, Washington, DC, May 17. https://2009-2017.state.gov/j/prm/releases/remarks/2012/190280.htm

RT. 2015. "LGBT Activists Self-Harm, Create 'Rivers Of Blood' To Protest Immigration Bill." December 1, 2015. https://www.rt.com/uk/324127-lgbt-blood-immigration-protest/

Soloman, Alisa. 2005. "Trans/Migrant: Christina Madrazo's All-American Story". In *Queer Migrations: Sexuality, U.S. Citizenship and Border Crossings*, edited by Eithne Luibhéid and Lionel Cantu, 3–29. Minneapolis and London: University of Minnesota Press.

UK Lesbian and Gay Immigration Group. 2016. Stonewall. "No Safe Refuge: Experiences of LGBT Asylum Seekers in Detention." https://www.stonewall.org.uk/sites/default/files/no_safe_refuge.pdf

UNHCR: The UN Refugee Agency. 2008. *UNHCR Guidance Note on Refugee Claims Relating to Sexual Orientation and Gender Identity*. Geneva, Switzerland: UNHCR. http://www.refworld.org/docid/48abd5660.html

UNHCR. 2011. *Working with Lesbian, Gay, Bisexual, Transgender & Intersex Persons in Forced Displacement*. Geneva, Switzerland: UNHCR. http://www.refworld.org/docid/4e6073972.html

UNHCR. 1950. "Statute of the Office of the UNHCR." General Assembly Resolution 428 (V) of 14 December 1950. http://www.unhcr.org/3b66c39e1.pdf

CHAPTER 39

THE POST-COMMUNIST IDENTITY CRISIS AND QUEER MIGRATION FROM POLAND

RICHARD C.M. MOLE

UNTIL relatively recently, the academic study of migration did not explicitly deal with sexual difference, implicitly assuming the 'typical migrant' to be heterosexual. Since the mid-1990s these assumptions have been challenged by scholars who have produced a small but growing literature on the migration experiences of lesbian, gay, bisexual, trans* and queer (LGBTQ) subjects. This body of work comprises theoretical analyses of the relationship between migration and sexuality (Binnie 1997; Mai and King 2009; Manalansan 2006); queer rural-to-urban domestic migration (Gorman-Murray 2009); border crossing by queer migrants and the legal hurdles which they have to overcome (Cantu 2009; Luibhéid 2008); the construction and reconstruction of sexual identities following migration (Kuntsman 2009); and the emergence and the lived experience of queer diasporas (Eng 1997; Fortier 2002; Manalansan 2003; Mole 2018; Watney 1995). Moreover, while much has been written in the migration literature about population movements arising from crises related to economic downturns, natural disasters, or conflict, the impact of ideational crises on mass mobility has been underexplored.

This chapter will use the experiences of Polish queer migrants in London to show how a crisis in Polish identity following the collapse of communism in 1989 constructed nonheterosexuals as a threat to Polish norms and values, fueling homophobic rhetoric, violence, and discrimination and prompting LGBTQ Poles to view migration as "a means of escape and of self-realisation" (Binnie 1997, 240). The chapter examines how homosexuality was constructed in postcommunist Poland, with a view to gaining a sense of the social environment in which the interview respondents grew up and also to understanding why attitudes towards sexual minorities unexpectedly became more negative following Poland's accession to the European Union. This section will be followed by a brief explication of methods and an analysis of the factors prompting queer Poles to migrate, with a focus on both domestic and cross-border migration.

Homophobia and the Crisis of Identity in Postcommunist Poland

In many ways, 1989 marked a watershed in the lives of LGBTQ Poles. While homosexuality was not criminalized during the communist era, it had nevertheless been presented by the state as "a symptom of 'Western depravity'" and as inconsistent with "socialist morality" (Kliszyński 2001, 161).[1] Homosexuals were frequently kept under observation by the Civic Militia or the Security Services, with an individual's homosexuality becoming of interest to the authorities if this could be used "as a means of recruitment or blackmail" (Tomasik 2012, 20). After 1989, Polish gays and lesbians had far less to fear from the police and other state authorities, gay and lesbian venues were opened throughout the country—at least in the larger cities—and magazines aimed specifically at LGBTQ individuals were launched. However, the long-hoped-for liberation for gays and lesbians soon came into conflict with attempts by the state and society to redefine Polish identity after fifty years of communist rule.

The collapse of state socialism set in train a process of unparalleled social, economic, and political transformation. Not only did the Soviet-style economic system need to be dismantled and new democratic political institutions rebuilt from scratch but a new cognitive framework had to be found through which citizens could make sense of the world around them and guide their decisions about whom to trust and with whom to cooperate. In the context of the social turmoil triggered by the end of the communist system and the "shock therapy" economic policies introduced thereafter, both nationalism and religion provided a sense of cohesion and stability by offering a credible explanation of the past and a guide for the present and the future. In many cases, it was the past itself that served as the guide for the present and the future. In rejecting the hated communist era, Polish political elites harked back to the interwar Second Republic and its traditional norms and values. As this period was held up as the opposite of the abnormal communist era, *traditional* became equated with *normal*, with traditional gender and sexual roles thus seen as "an important aspect of the nostalgia for 'normality'" (Watson 1993, 472–473). However, what was seen as 'normal' was defined strictly in national, Catholic, and heterosexual terms. In the Polish context, the three concepts are largely understood as indivisible: to be Polish is to be Catholic and heterosexual. In the search for stability, any form of diversity (such as ethnic, religious, or sexual minorities) can therefore seem threatening (Inglehart and Baker 2000, 28). In Poland, as in much of Central and Eastern Europe, there was thus a tendency among individuals disoriented by the social, economic, and political changes triggered by the collapse of communism to "cling to traditional gender roles and sexual norms, and emphasize absolute rules and familiar norms in an attempt to maximise predictability in an uncertain world" (Inglehart and Baker 2000, 28). The rise in nationalist feeling after 1989 further exacerbated social antipathy towards homosexuality.

While most academics understand nations as social constructs, the prevailing view outside of academia is that they are natural phenomena, growing out of extended kin groups, united by shared biology, culture, history, norms and values, stretching back centuries if not millennia. To ensure the nation maintains its internal homogeneity and clear demarcation from the Other, nationalists put considerable effort into promoting its biological and cultural reproduction, a process that can be ensured only by naturalizing the patriarchal family and associated public and private roles of men and women. As I argue elsewhere, individuals performing nonnormative sexualities "are thought to threaten this national narrative by undermining the patriarchal family, failing to adhere to national stereotypes of masculinity and femininity, confusing the public/private roles of men and women, undermining the nation's internal homogeneity, and deviating from its shared norms, especially those derived from religious teaching" (Mole 2016, 109–110). Given that Polish-ness is understood to be inextricably linked with Catholicism and heterosexuality, homosexuality was represented by nationalist politicians as a threat to national values, thereby legitimizing the marginalization of Polish LGBTQ citizens and attempts to restrict them to the private sphere.

While most political institutions in Poland were weakened by the collapse of communism, the one institution which emerged stronger after 1989 was the Polish Catholic Church. Having acted as the *de facto* political opposition to the Polish Communist Party throughout the period of state socialism and, following the election of Karol Wojtyła to the papacy in 1978, credited by some with precipitating the fall of the regime, the Catholic Church acquired enhanced legitimacy and political power after 1989, acting as the ultimate arbiter of national values—particularly with reference to issues of gender and sexuality. While intellectual debates about sexual orientation did appear in the 1990s in Catholic journals such as *Tygodnik Powszechny* and *Więź*, they did not stray far from the position set out in the Catechism of the Catholic Church, namely that same-sex acts are sinful in that they "close the sexual act to the gift of life. They do not proceed from a genuine affective and sexual complementarity. Under no circumstances can they be approved." (Catechism of the Catholic Church, 2357) Far from restricting its views to the pulpit, the Church actively lobbied successive governments in the 1990s to ensure that their position on issues relating to sexuality was in line with Catholic dogma. According to former Polish MP Robert Biedroń, the Catholic Church succeeded, for example, in ensuring that there was no reference to sexual orientation in the non-discrimination clause of the Polish Constitution (Selinger 2008, 25).

The accession of Poland to the European Union in 2004 led to an intensification of political debate about the place of LGBTQ individuals in Polish society. Given the EU's introduction of various measures aimed at promoting the legal equality of sexual minorities—including the incorporation of sexual orientation into the Equalities Agenda through Article 19 of Treaty on the European Union and the requirement that member states ban sexual orientation discrimination in employment—nationalist politicians presented the EU's more liberal position toward LGBTQ rights as a threat to Polish values. In the run-up to the 2005 parliamentary elections, nationalist and populist parties used the issue of LGBTQ rights to draw a boundary between the "decadent

West" and the "traditional East," with attitudes toward sexuality in Poland becoming "a reference point for political self-definition and national pride" (Graff 2010, 584). While homosexuality could perhaps be tolerated in private, there were various attempts to clamp down on manifestations of nonnormative sexuality in the public sphere, with Pride marches a particular target. In the summer of 2005, Lech Kaczyński, the Mayor of Warsaw, refused to issue a permit for an Equality Parade on the grounds that it was "obscene" and "would upset the feelings of the religious" (Selinger 2008, 19). The march went ahead anyway and participants were attacked by members of All-Polish Youth, a right-wing nationalist organization, which was given permission by Kaczyński to hold a "parade of normality" a week after the Equality Parade (Selinger 2008, 19).[2] The influence of religion on Polish politics became even more pronounced from October 2005, following the election of the Law and Justice Party, led by Jarosław Kaczyński, the brother of the Mayor of Warsaw, and its coalition partners, Self-Defence and the League of Polish Families, which embraced an ultra-Catholic and highly nationalist political agenda. The coalition came to power, in part, on a campaign to protect Polish national values from the perceived secular and liberal principles of the European Union. The perception in Poland of a marked cleavage between Polish and European values was strengthened by the publication by the European Parliament of three resolutions in January and June 2006 and April 2007, in which Poland is either implicitly or quite explicitly criticized for its failure to respect the rights of its LGBT citizens (European Parliament 2006a, 2006b, 2007). The tone of the resolutions was interpreted in Poland as being highly patronising and resulted in a feeling of wounded national pride and a backlash against both the EU and the promotion of LGBT rights, the two now seen as inextricably linked. Following criticism from the European Parliament, therefore, it became a matter of national sovereignty that Poland be allowed to criticize sexual minorities, with homophobia thereby becoming "the new voice of patriotism" (Graff, 2010, 590).

The outcome of this politicization of homophobia in tandem with the negative rhetoric from the Church and stereotypical portrayal of sexual minorities in the media was an environment in which homophobic attitudes dominated and many LGBTQ Poles faced discrimination, verbal abuse, and physical violence. A Eurobarometer survey conducted by the EU in 2006 found that 76 percent of Poles opposed same-sex marriage (the third-highest in the EU) and 89 percent were against the adoption of children by homosexual couples (the highest in the EU) (Eurobarometer 2007, 43). A survey of more than 1,000 LGBTQ Poles published by the Campaign Against Homophobia in 2007 showed that 17.6 percent of respondents had experienced physical violence, with 40 percent of those having been attacked three or more times, while over half of those surveyed reported suffering psychological abuse, including verbal harassment, threats, blackmail, insults and graffiti (Abramowicz 2007, 15–17). Homophobia in Poland had reached crisis point.

In such contexts, sexual minorities have to decide how to respond to situations in which they are constructed as a threat to society, national mores, and religious values. One could argue that for sexual dissidents, the basic response is one of loyalty, voice, or exit, to use Hirschman's classic paradigm (i.e. attempt to remain invisible, engage in public protest to bring about change, or leave the country) (Hirschman 1970). While the three strategies are not mutually exclusive and individuals can certainly adopt all three at different stages of their lives, in the section that follows the brief discussion of my methodology I focus on the "exit" strategy adopted by LGBTQ Poles, analysing how for many migration became "a means of escape and of self-realisation" (Binnie 1997, 240).

Methodology

The qualitative research upon which this chapter is based is drawn from a larger project conducted in 2012–2014 on LGBTQ migration from Eastern Europe and Latin America to London and Berlin. Eligible respondents for the specific research that follows were literate men and women aged 18 years or over who self-identified as nonheterosexual migrants from Poland and who lived or worked in London. The sample was recruited through dating and community websites on the Internet, community venues, and through snowballing. Informed consent was sought using information sheets in both Polish and English. In total, 25 in-depth interviews were conducted. The interviewees were aged between 23 and 39; 16 were men and 9 were women. As none of the interviewees identified as trans*, I refer to my respondents collectively as LGBQ but to nonheterosexual Poles in general as LGBTQ. The interviews were carried out in English, took place in a university office and lasted, on average, 45–50 minutes. Participants were offered GBP 25 as an incentive. The interviews were recorded and transcribed verbatim. Data management and analysis were facilitated by the use of the qualitative software N-Vivo. The verbatim data was coded and ordered within a thematic matrix, which emerged both from reviewing extant literature and from the interview data itself. N-Vivo helped identify key themes in the respondents' narratives, around which the chapter has been structured: growing up LGBQ in Poland, social attitudes towards homosexuality, experience of homophobia, the decision to migrate, and relations with the ethno-national diaspora in the UK and with friends and family at home in Poland. Pseudonyms have been used to protect participants' identities.

Queer Migration

A few words about terminology. When referring to my interview respondents as queer, I use the term as an alternative for lesbian, gay, and bisexual to reflect the fact that the latter terms were not adopted by all the migrants I interviewed.[3] It is noteworthy that the idea of "queer" was to a large extent brought about by migration in that the mass movement of people to the West from various non-Western cultures brought into sharp relief the numerous "sexual identity categories and practices that [did] not depend on Western conceptions of selfhood and community," thus producing a range of queer identities and subjectivities (Manalansan 2006, 229). With reference to queer migration, queer is used in part to take account of the queer subjects of the processes of migration but also to refer to the role of nonnormative sexualities in the migration experience and the ways in which the presence of nonheterosexuals problematizes the dominant understandings of migration. While "queer migration," according to Andrew Gorman-Murray (2009, 443), relates exclusively to cases where "the needs or desires of non-heterosexual identities, practices and performances" are implicated in the queer migrant's *decision to move*, I argue, following Hector Carillo, that to conceptualize queer migration fully, we also need to consider the lives of queers "in their places of origin, their exposure to local and foreign sexual ideologies prior to migrating, their agency in adapting and appropriating ideologies and practices prevalent in both home and host countries, and the transformations in sexual identities and behaviors that they experience after migration" (2004, 58).

In the academic literature, the dominant explanation for migration sees the main motivation as economic, with individuals moving abroad to gain higher wages or acquire marketable skills (Stark and Bloom 1985). While economic considerations certainly do play a role in queer migrants' decisions to move abroad, they are often far less important than social and political factors. Indeed, less than a quarter of the respondents in this study mentioned economic factors, whereas 23 of the 25 interviewees referred to their sexual orientation as a reason influencing their decision to leave Poland. As Iryna explained: "I didn't migrate because I wanted to visit another country or I wanted to earn more money or I wanted to have a better job, I did it because I was gay and I didn't live good (sic.) in my country." It is important to stress that issues related to sexuality were not always the primary reason for migrating but sexuality was nevertheless the single most cited factor directly or indirectly influencing the decision to move abroad.

From the migration experiences of my respondents, it was possible to make out two main pathways from Poland to the UK. While a number of my interviewees moved directly from their home towns to London, most relocated from the smaller towns they grew up in to larger cities—primarily to the nation's capital, Warsaw—before subsequently moving to Britain. As Ryszard succinctly put it, "[If] you're gay, you move to Warsaw or you can move abroad, or you move to Warsaw and *then* you move abroad!"

Domestic Queer Migration

Migration from small towns to cities is a common experience of LGBTQ people the world over (see Weston 1995) and the motivations of the queer Poles in this study in many ways mapped on to those identified by scholars working on other societies. In his study of queer migration in Australia, Gorman-Murray (2009) identifies three main patterns. The first is "coming-out migration," whereby LGBQ people migrate with the aim of "self-reinvention as non-heterosexual and to explore bodily sexual desires in the process"; the second is "gravitational group migration" (i.e., "moving to be near a neighbourhood with a gay and lesbian presence"); the third is "relationship migration," where individuals move "with a partner to consolidate a same-sex relationship—or conversely, moving away after a relationship breakdown" (446). As the experiences of my respondents show, these motivations were in many ways intertwined.

While all respondents did eventually come out to their parents (in most cases prior to migrating to the UK), moving away from their home towns enabled those who had not yet come out to extricate themselves from the social control of their families to perform their sexuality in line with their own desires and reduce the risk that their sexual behavior and identity would be reported back to their parents before they felt ready to tell them. For those who were not ready to come out but who wanted to explore their sexuality, living in their home towns might increase the risk of word getting out that they were gay or lesbian. The fact that, according to Bartosz, "everybody knows everyone," in small towns in particular but also to some extent in cities, meant that it was difficult to ensure that your private life stayed private. As Konrad explained: "[I]f you want to live in the closet, you really need to watch out, because [. . .] people are not very, you know, they don't care that it's your secret."

Migration to Warsaw, which was frequently referred to as the most liberal city and its inhabitants the most open-minded in the country, offered an unparalleled gay scene, providing queer Poles with a sense of community and the opportunity to engage in sexual relationships—often for the first time. It was the fact that Feliks "didn't know any gay people" in his small home town, that there were "no gay places" and he was not out to his parents that prompted him to move to the capital with the aim of "looking for guys." For many respondents, domestic migration to Warsaw and other large cities was thus motivated by the desire to come out, reinvent themselves as nonheterosexual and explore bodily sexual desires in cities with a gay and lesbian presence—rather than enhance their economic capital, as the dominant theories of migration would suggest.

Yet for others domestic migration to Warsaw or one of Poland's other cities only *partly* enabled them to live their lives on their own terms—particularly when it came to long-term relationships. For Ireneusz, access to the gay bars and clubs that opened in the mid-1990s did enable him to meet other men but, for him, the sexualization of the gay scene and even of gay magazines ("every kind of advertisement was about sex"), in tandem with the dominant media discourse about gays and lesbians presented as being in opposition to the "traditional family," led him to believe that being in a same-sex relationship on the same terms as a heterosexual relationship would not be possible in Poland: "Being gay [in Poland] is not about being in a relationship. It's about sex only because everyone says so." Even for those, like Adam, who were in a same-sex relationship, the dominant discourses around appropriate gender and sexual behavior and the heterosexualization of public space placed restrictions on his ability to express his feelings towards his boyfriend in ways that would have gone unnoticed had his partner been a woman:

> When I started dating and I had a partner that I wanted to go out with, yeah, I didn't ever feel comfortable about, I don't know, showing our affection in public places, so to speak. And I didn't mean like just snogging in the middle of a square or something but I mean, you know, those little gestures, like holding hands or just sitting close to each other on a bench somewhere, things like that or holding hands in the cinema.

What my findings suggest is that domestic queer migration only met some of the needs of queer Poles in terms of their ability to live their lives on their own terms, due in large part to the retraditionalization of gender and sexual norms following the identity crisis triggered by the collapse of communism. The general impression given by my respondents—even those who had moved to Warsaw or other big cities—was that they felt that they did not fit into Polish society, which, I argue, is due to the fact that hegemonic discourses of Polish identity constructed LGBQ Poles as a threat to national norms and values. Even presenting a gender image that did not adhere to the traditional ideas of how Polish men and women should behave and even what they should wear was a source of disquiet. As Adam explained: "Poland is very rigid in terms of maintaining certain gender identities. [. . .] More often than not, there's no malice in the remarks people make [but] it still makes you feel kind of uncomfortable." Bartosz, for example, reminisced that pressure to conform to traditional norms in Poland forced him to regulate his own gender performance to such an extent that he would not have dared wear the skinny jeans he had on during the interview in the medium-sized Polish town he grew up in. He did not fear for his personal safety, but rather he felt a sense of unease and was thus unable to live his life on his own terms. Thus, whether or not LGBQ Poles migrated to more liberal cities such as Warsaw, their freedom would still be constrained to some degree by hegemonic discourses of "acceptable" gender and sexual norms. One way to extricate themselves from these constraining forces was to leave Poland.

Cross-Border Queer Migration

It is important to emphasize that, contrary to some Western media reports (e.g. Graham 2007) and unlike a number of the Russian migrants whom I interviewed as part of the larger project (Mole 2019), none of the Polish respondents reported fleeing the country in fear of state persecution, with only two having personally experienced physical violence. Rather, the general impression given by the respondents was that their decision to migrate was prompted by the belief that moving to London would grant them greater freedom to perform their sexuality in line with their own desires. As Grzegorz explained: "I think homosexuality just plants this thing in your head that you're not going to be free until you go somewhere where you're accepted, you know." And if Poland was seen as the place where homosexuals are "not going to be free," the "somewhere you're accepted" was clearly understood to be the West, an idea implanted in Grzegorz's head from an early age. The fact that the first gay character he saw on Polish television was in an American TV series established in his mind a link between more positive attitudes towards homosexuality and the West:

> I remember when I was a child and we were watching *Dawson's Creek* and they had a—do you remember that?—they had an openly gay character there and that was, I guess, a big thing, to know that in the Western media, this actually happens.

This belief that the West was more accepting of sexual diversity was also produced through direct experience. Once they became EU citizens in 2004, Poles were able to travel freely through the European Union and queer Poles saw for themselves what life was like for LGBQ people outside of Poland. It was this that led Feliks to conclude that people were "more relaxed" about sexuality in countries like Germany or Britain, prompting him to decide "to live a normal life somewhere else."

While for most respondents, like Feliks above, their sexuality had a direct impact on their decision to move abroad, largely in line with the motivations identified by Gorman-Murray, for others the influence was more indirect. Grzegorz, for example, argued that being gay means that you are more open to difference ("you have to accept the fact you're different and it has to open your mind somehow, otherwise you'd end up hating yourself"), which makes gay people more open to trying different things, such as experiencing foreign cultures. For Jacek, it was more to do with the fact that, as a gay man, he did not have the responsibilities of a husband and father to tie him down: "I can be a bit selfish and do what I really want. So maybe that was the idea. That's why I want to live abroad, to do different things."

Unlike the factors motivating migration within Poland, very few of the respondents decided to move to the UK to come out. Almost all had come out to their friends and families in Poland prior to moving to London and, in most cases, the reaction had been quite positive—again in contrast to the experience of many of the Russian-speaking respondents in the larger project (Mole 2018). Only Irena used cross-border migration for self-redefinition purposes. As she explained: "I never wanted to admit still then that I'm gay and [. . .] the easiest way for me was to just leave Poland and start my life somewhere else as an openly gay person." While not exactly "coming out migration," for Agnieszka, it was migration to London that gave her the space to come to terms with her own sexual identity: "I think it was the migration that allowed me to, kind of, engage with my sexuality and then, once I was conscious of it, then I think, but I guess I saw things abroad that made me feel like, well, that's a lot better than being at home because they have all these resources and it's not such a big deal."

While very few respondents cited the desire *to come out* as a factor motivating them to move to Britain, the ability *to be out* to most people beyond a small circle of friends and family was identified as a factor which, if not prompting them to move to the UK in the first place, was at least seen as a reason to stay. To Dariusz, this was tied up with the perception that people in London were more accepting of sexual difference.[4]

> I feel much more comfortable being out here at work, everywhere I go, I do feel that, you know, I don't have to be ashamed of it any more, there's nothing to hide. [. . .] I know that people here will understand, if they don't, no problem. So, this is the attitude that, you know, I didn't have in Poland. I just felt like if someone has a problem with me being gay, they'd probably beat me up or something.

Compared with "coming out migration," "gravitational group migration" was cited more frequently as a motivation—particularly for those who had moved directly from small towns to London, rather than first moving to Warsaw or other major Polish cities. Florentyna, who grew up in a town of just 50,000 people, initially wanted to move to Edinburgh but eventually opted for London because of the greater range of LGBTQ venues there: "I wanted [. . .] to go to a town that has a bigger gay scene than the one I experienced at home." While those respondents who moved from Warsaw or other big cities were less likely to refer to London's gay scene as a motivating factor, they did notice the impact access to a gay scene like London's had on LGBTQ Poles who had migrated from the Polish countryside:

> I think a lot of Polish gays, when they come from villages, [. . .] come here and they absolutely explode with freedom. [. . .] They're from places where it's really frowned upon and it's really tough. [. . .] It's interesting how when they come here, you know, they just, it's nice to see, they just explode with gayness.
>
> (Grzegorz)

Although none of the respondents was motivated to move to London to consolidate a relationship or to deal with the effects of a break-up in line with Gorman-Murray's "relationship migration" pattern (2009, 446), a number of the men and women I interviewed were prompted to migrate by the sexual citizenship rights for couples available in the UK compared with Poland. Ireneusz explained that, as Poland does not legally recognize same-sex couples, neither he nor his partner would be able to inherit the property they co-owned in Kraków in the event one of them died. The children of Ireneusz's niece would have a greater legal claim to his inheritance than his partner. A number of my respondents also planned to take the opportunity to adopt, get married, or enter into civil partnerships in the UK, and this was cited as a reason for wanting to stay in Britain. As Norbert reminisced: "I remember in 2005, that was the Civil Partnership Act, and that was the first news I read when I was in the country, the first newspaper that I purchased, it was about the Civil Partnership Act and I literally cried on the bus to Manchester."

In general, and contrary to dominant theories of migration, it was thus the draw of London's gay scene, sexual citizenship rights, and the perception that there was greater acceptance of difference that drew most of my respondents to the British capital, rather than the opportunity to earn money. Ireneuz and his partner specifically ruled out moving to some countries, such as Russia, "even if it would be really good because of the economy" as it was not perceived as being "gay friendly." Freedom to be oneself trumped all other motivating factors. And, even though a number of respondents still referred to Poland as 'home', it was clear many felt more *at home* in London:

> At home, as I walk down the street, there's a chance that, like, I'll get a lot of looks, that people will stare because of my hair, because of what I'm wearing or I don't know what, to be honest, I don't always know what it is, but then every time I came to London, I felt like nobody really thinks that there's anything weird about me and I felt freer to wear clothes that I wanted to wear. [. . .] I just felt like at home in the sense that I didn't feel different, like I didn't feel strange.
>
> (Czesław)

Given the size of the Polish diaspora in London and the number of Polish shops, restaurants, and bars in the city, it would not have been difficult for the respondents to move between their Polish and British worlds but few did, with many of my respondents pointing out that they would not associate with Polish people in Britain just because they shared a nationality with them. While most of the people I interviewed did have some Polish friends in London and enjoyed the opportunity to speak Polish with them and make jokes they knew would be understood ("I just have a different sense of humor when I'm with my English friends and a different one when I'm with my Polish friends." [Bartosz]), they tended to avoid Polish venues because they felt they had little in common with most Polish economic migrants—in part due to the perception that the latter were "very closed minded and very traditional" and "don't like gay people" (Norbert).[5] Unlike the Russian-speakers in the larger study, none of the Polish respondents sought out other queers of the same nationality as a way to perform their sexual identities in a specifically Polish environment and thereby create a community of belonging in the UK, defined in both sexual and national terms. In any case, most of the respondents made frequent use new technologies, such as Skype, and cheap flights to enable them to maintain interpersonal ties with the homeland and a sense of Polishness, although in some cases this required some respondents to police their behavior to bring it more into line with Polish norms:

> I realized that the closer to Poland I am, I become more reserved, more closed, like we go to Stansted[6] and we're a couple and apparently when we are at the airport already, we don't speak, we don't hold hands, we stay in the line for the plane like two friends, not a couple. We're surrounded by all those Polish people and we are, like, separated. (Dariusz)

Conclusion

In the context of the academic analysis of migration crises, the experiences of queer migrants allow us to challenge dominant economic understandings for population movements and at the same time consider, alongside economic downturns, natural disasters, or conflict, the impact on mass mobility of ideational crises—in this case, the identity crisis in Poland that followed the collapse of state socialism in 1989. As religion and nationalism emerged as the cognitive frameworks through which Poles made sense of the world, sexual norms underwent a process of retraditionalization, with homosexuality largely rendered invisible and queers marginalized and expected to restrict themselves to the private sphere. This process was exacerbated by Poland's accession to the European Union and the latter's denunciation of Warsaw's treatment of its queer citizens, with the result that criticism of sexual minorities became a matter of national sovereignty and homophobia a new form of patriotism. The crisis of homophobia that ensued prompted LGBTQ Poles to see migration as a way to escape the repressive discourses of politicians, the Catholic Church, and the media and live their lives on their own terms.

In analyzing the narratives of the LGBQ Polish migrants in this study, a number of patterns emerged. Firstly, it was possible to make out two modes of queer migration, domestic and cross-border, as well as both an indirect and direct influence of sexuality on the decision to migrate. Indirectly, queer migrants' sexuality made them more open to difference and to trying different things, such as experiencing foreign cultures, which was facilitated by the fact that gays and lesbians are less likely to be tied down by spouses and children. A range of sexuality-related factors having a direct impact on queer migrants' decisions to relocate could be identified in the interviews, although it was clear that the factors motivating domestic and cross-border queer migration were different. Domestic migration to Warsaw and other large cities in Poland was motivated primarily by the desire to come out as LGBQ and explore bodily sexual desires in cities with gay and lesbian venues. Yet, in many ways, they were still relegated to the private sphere of the home or gay and lesbian clubs in that their freedom to perform their sexuality on their own terms in the public sphere was constrained to some degree by hegemonic Polish discourses of acceptable gender and sexual norms.

With cross-border queer migrants, very few of the respondents moved abroad to come out, as almost all had done so in Poland. In addition, it was noticeable that the London queer scene was less of a draw for those who had first migrated to Warsaw or other big Polish cities before moving to the UK. The main differences in the factors prompting domestic vs. cross-border migration were twofold: firstly, the sexual citizenship rights available in the UK but not in Poland (primarily, civil partnership or marriage and adoption) and, most frequently cited, the perception that there was greater social acceptance of difference, including of sexual difference. Whereas migrating to Warsaw did allow the respondents to perform their sexuality in line with their own desires in the private sphere, migrating to London enabled them to perform their sexuality to a greater extent in line with their own desires in the public sphere as well.

Notes

1. No laws criminalizing homosexual activity between consenting adults were ever introduced in independent Poland, although such laws were enacted on Polish territory by the occupying powers during the country's partition (1795–1918) and remained in force until 1932.
2. In September 2005 the Regional Administrative Court in Warsaw ruled that the ban was unconstitutional and in 2007 the European Court of Human Rights announced that Kaczyński's refusal to allow the parade to go ahead had violated "several principles covered by the European human rights conventions, such as freedom of assembly and prohibition of discrimination" (Kubosova 2007).
3. Queer is also used to refer to non-cisgender individuals, although trans* migrants are not part of this research.

4. It is important to emphasize that attitudes toward homosexuality outside London are not always as positive as in the capital and that anti-LGBT hate crime remains a serious problem throughout the UK.
5. Recent research shows that migration to London by Central and East Europeans can result in their attitudes towards homosexuality softening (see Mole et al., 2017).
6. One of the international airports serving London.

References

Abramowicz, M., ed. 2007. *Situation of Bisexual and Homosexual Persons in Poland: 2005 and 2006 Report*. Warsaw: Campaign Against Homophobia and Lambda Warsaw Association. http://www.kph.org.pl/publikacje/sytuacja_bi_homo_2007_EN.pdf

Binnie, J. 1997. "Invisible Europeans: Sexual Citizenship in the New Europe." *Environment and Planning A*, 29:237–248

Cantu, L. 2009. *The Sexuality of Migration: Border Crossings and Mexican Immigrant Men*. New York: New York University Press

Carillo, H. 2004. "Sexual Migration: Cross-Cultural Sexual Encounters, and Sexual Health." *Sexuality Research & Social Policy* 1, no. 3: 58–70.

Catechism of the Catholic Church. http://www.vatican.va/archive/ENG0015/_INDEX.HTM. Accessed July 27, 2017.

Eng, D. 1997. "Out Here and Over There: Queerness and Diaspora in Asian American Studies." *Social Text* 15:31–52

Eurobarometer. 2007. *Public Opinion in the European Union*. No. 66. http://ec.europa.eu/commfrontoffice/publicopinion/archives/eb/eb66/eb66_en.pdf. Accessed August 2, 2017.

European Parliament. 2006a. *European Parliament Resolution on Homophobia in Europe*, 18 January 2006, P6_TA(2006)0018. http://www.europarl.europa.eu/sides/getDoc.do?pubRef=-//EP//TEXT+TA+P6-TA-2006-0018+0+DOC+XML+V0//EN. Accessed August 13, 2017.

European Parliament. 2006b. *European Parliament Resolution on the Increase in Racists and Homophobic Violence in Europe*, 15 June 2006, P6_TA(2006)0273. http://www.europarl.europa.eu/sides/getDoc.do?type=TA&reference=P6-TA-2006-0273&language=EN&ring=B6-2006-0333. Accessed 13 August 2017.

European Parliament. 2007. *European Parliament Resolution of 26 April 2007 on Homophobia in Europe*, 26 April 2007, P6_TA(2007)0167. http://www.europarl.europa.eu/sides/getDoc.do?pubRef=-//EP//TEXT+TA+P6-TA-2007-0167+0+DOC+XML+V0//EN. Accessed 13 August 2017.

Fortier, A. M. 2002. "Queer Diaspora." In *Handbook of Gay and Lesbian Studies*, edited by D. Richardson and S. Seidman, 183–197. London: SAGE.

Gorman-Murray, A. 2009. "Intimate Mobilities: Emotional Embodiment and Queer Migration." *Social and Cultural Geography* 10:441–460

Graff, A. 2010. "Looking at Pictures of Gay Men: Political Uses of Homophobia in Contemporary Poland." *Public Culture* 22, no. 3: 583–603

Graham, C. 2007. "Gay Poles Head for UK to Escape State Crackdown." *The Guardian*, 1 July: http://www.guardian.co.uk/world/2007/jul/01/gayrights.uk. Accessed 4 August 2017.

Hirschman, A. O. 1970. *Exit, Voice, and Loyalty: Responses to Decline in Firms, Organizations, and States*. Cambridge: MA: Harvard University Press.

Inglehart, R., and W. E. Baker. 2000. "Modernization, Cultural Change, and the Persistence of Traditional Values." *American Sociological Review* 65, no. 1: 19–51.

Kliszyński, K. 2001. "A Child of a Young Democracy: The Polish Gay Movement, 1989–1999." In *Pink, Purple, Green: Women's, Religious, Environmental and Gay/Lesbian Movements in Central Europe Today*, edited by H. Flam, 161–168. New York: Columbia University Press.

Kubosova, L. 2007. "Poland's Ban of Gay Parade Ruled Illegal." *EU Observer*, 4 May 2007. https://euobserver.com/social/23995. Accessed August 1, 2017.

Kuntsman, A. 2009. *Figurations of Violence and Belonging: Queerness, Migranthood, and Nationalism in Cyberspace and Beyond*. Oxford: Peter Lang.

Luibhéid, E. 2008. "Sexuality, Migration and the Shifting Line between Legal and Illegal Status." *GLQ: A Journal of Lesbian and Gay Studies* 14, no. 2–3: 289–315.

Mai, N., and R. King. 2009. "Love, Sexuality and Migration: Mapping the Issues." *Mobilities* 4, no. 3: 295–307.

Manalansan, M. F. 2003. *Global Divas: Filipino Gay Men in the Diaspora*. Durham, NC: Duke University Press

Manalansan, M.F. 2006. "Queer Intersections: Sexuality and Gender in Migration Studies." *International Migration Review* 40: 224–249.

Mole, R. C. M. 2019. "Queer Russian Asylum-Seekers in Germany: Worthy Refugees and Acceptable Forms of Harm?" In *Refuge in a Moving World*, edited by E. Fiddian-Qasmiyeh. London: UCL Press (forthcoming).

Mole, R. C. M. 2018. "Identity, Belonging and Solidarity among Russian-Speaking Queer Migrants in Berlin." *Slavic Review* 77, no. 1: 77–98.

Mole, R. C. M., C. J. Gerry, V. Parutis, and F. M. Burns. 2017. "Migration and Sexual Resocialization: The Case of Central and East Europeans in London." *East European Politics and Societies* 31, no. 1: 201–222.

Mole, R. C. M. 2016. "Nationalism and Homophobia in Central and Eastern Europe." In *EU Enlargement and Lesbian and Gay Politics: The Impact of Eastern Enlargement on Rights, Activism and Prejudice*, edited by K. Slootmaekers, H. Touquet, and P. Vermeersch, 99–12. Basingstoke, UK: Palgrave Macmillan.

Selinger, M. 2008. "Intolerance Toward Gays and Lesbians in Poland." *Human Rights Review* 9: 15–27.

Stark, O. and D. E. Bloom. 1985. "The New Economics of Labor Migration." *American Economic Review* 75:173–178.

Tomasik, K. 2012. *Gejerel. Mnieszości Seksualne w PRL-u*. Warsaw, Poland: Krytyka Polityczna

Watney, S. 1995. "AIDS and the Politics of Queer Diaspora." In *Negotiating Lesbian and Gay Subjects*, edited by M. Dorenkamp and R. Henke, 53–70. New York and Abingdon, UK: Routledge.

Watson, P. 1993. "Eastern Europe's Silent Revolution: Gender." *Sociology* 27, no. 3: 471–487.

Weston, K. 1995. "Get Thee to a Big City: Sexual Imaginary and the Great Gay Migration." *GLQ: A Journal of Lesbian and Gay Studies* 2, no. 3: 253–277.

CHAPTER 40

A GENDERED ANALYSIS OF THE EUROPEAN REFUGEE "CRISIS"

JANE FREEDMAN

In 2015 over one million refugees arrived in Europe, many of them seeking protection from armed conflict and violence in their countries of origin including Syria, Iraq, and Afghanistan.[1] While the flow of arrivals has since diminished, there are still hundreds of thousands of refugees attempting to reach the EU and living in varying conditions of insecurity within Europe. As the EU has previously put in place measures that have made it more and more difficult to arrive in Europe across a land border, the majority of these refugees arrive by sea, and many lose their lives in the process. The huge numbers of arrivals on the coasts of Greece and Italy (and to a lesser degree Spain) has led the EU to label this a refugee "crisis." However, it may be argued that it is not so much a crisis of refugees, but more a crisis of the EU itself. The influx of refugees from 2015 onwards is not the first time that European leaders have evoked a 'crisis' of migration, and indeed, the term was already employed in 2011 when migration increased following the Arab Spring uprisings (Jeandesboz and Pallister-Wilkins 2014). The use of the term "crisis" may seem banal, but we would argue that this labeling is serving a powerful political and symbolic purpose. As Edelman has argued "crisis labeling" signals a claim that a particular situation is "different from political social and issues that we routinely confront" and that it came about for reasons outside of the control of political leaders (Edelman 1977). In the current situation, EU leaders have repeatedly stressed the unprecedented nature of the flows of refugees trying to reach the EU, and the way that the causes of migration are "out of their hands." They have invoked crisis to justify exceptional measures such as closing of borders or the signature of the EU-Turkey agreement which have been argued to be contrary to international and European law. This crisis labeling has served to reinforce an ongoing process of securitization of migration to the EU, and at the same time to raise pressure for a humanitarian (rather than a mainly political) response to the refugees' arrival. In fact, we could argue that the labeling of the current migration flows as a "crisis" has served the interests of political leaders in EU member states and in EU institutions, by diverting attention away from their failures to find any real political solutions to this problem and focusing attention on the humanitarian emergency and the increasingly insecure conditions in which refugees are living (and dying) in their attempts to reach the EU. While studies of the securitization of migration in the EU have previously pointed to the way in which the level of the "crisis labeling" and political spectacle operate at the same time as the ongoing bureaucratic and technical processes of migration management, in the current situation it seems that everyday bureaucratic procedure has been largely overridden by the politically spectacular. In the process, the level of regional politics, and the threat to the European Union's own political existence, has been highlighted. But this focus on the spectacular politics of crisis has also obscured another dimension, that of the experiences of the individual refugees themselves, including the gendered experiences of men and women attempting to reach Europe.

While increasing numbers of women are among these refugees, there has been little attention paid to the gendered dimensions of this migration. Those involved in the humanitarian response to the "crisis" seem to employ the family as a unit of analysis, and have largely overlooked gendered dynamics within groups of refugees traveling together (often these are only "families" in a very loose sense of the term), thus obscuring specific relations of power, inequality, and violence within these groups. And if gender issues are discussed, either by politicians or by the media, the security and crisis discourses employed tend to reinforce stereotypical representations of refugee men as a "threat," and refugee women as "vulnerable." This chapter will examine the experiences of refugee women in order to try and provide a more nuanced and complex understanding of issues of gender in the current "crisis." It will examine sources of insecurity and violence for these women, as well as strategies and choices made during their journeys. It will also analyze gendered representations and constructions of refugee migration in EU policies and in the responses by EU agencies and institutions and national and international humanitarian organizations.

The chapter is based on field research carried out on the Greek island of Kos, in Serbia, in Paris, and in the various migrant camps around Calais in France, including interviews with male and female refugees from Syria, Afghanistan, Iraq, Iran, Eritrea, Ethiopia, and the DRC, as well as with representatives of UNHCR, of international humanitarian organizations such as MSF and Médecins du Monde, and with locally based migrant support groups. These locations were chosen to reflect different stages on the refugees' journeys, countries within and exterior to the EU, and transit and destination countries. There are also interviews (by telephone or in person) with key informants from UNHCR, the European Parliament, Frontex, and the European Asylum Support Office. The rapidly changing nature of the national and EU responses to the current refugee flows mean that some of the local information provided may have changed between the time of research/writing of this chapter and today, although the chapter has tried to provide the most up to date information possible.

Security and Crisis in Migration to Europe

The current European refugee "crisis" is not new and has not developed out of nowhere but is the culmination and combination of on the one hand the growing restriction of legal channels of migration to Europe and securitization of the European borders (de Haas 2007; Lutterbeck 2009, and on the other hand, huge instability and conflict in certain areas of the Middle East and Africa, and in particular Syria, which is causing more and more desperate people to flee their countries and seek protection within the EU. While some European leaders have been quick to point to the existence of trafficking and smuggling gangs as the cause of the increased numbers of refugees attempting to cross the Aegean and Mediterranean, in fact it can be argued these traffickers and smugglers are only gaining more work as the regular and safer routes to Europe are progressively blocked, leading refugees to take riskier journeys and to pay more to do so. As EU countries have increasingly tried to restrict entry so refugees have been forced to find new and more perilous routes. As Lutterbeck points out: "Plugging one hole in the EU perimeter quickly leads to enhanced pressure on other parts of its external borders" (Lutterbeck 2009, 123).

The outbreak of conflict in Syria has clearly increased the numbers of refugees trying to reach the EU. Since the beginning of the conflict in Syria, millions have been displaced, either becoming IDPs, fleeing to neighboring countries, or seeking asylum in Europe or one of the other industrialized states. UNHCR estimates that in 2016 there are 4.8 million Syrian refugees dispersed throughout the region and in the EU. Faced with the scale of the refugee crisis in Syria and its neighboring countries, there have been many criticisms of the EU's failure to do enough to support neighboring states and to offer protection to those seeking to reach Europe (Fargues and Fandrich 2012). As the numbers arriving have increased, more and more EU member states have closed their borders and refused to take any further refugees, while attempts at regional resettlement agreements have been largely unsuccessful. Refugees are also arriving in large numbers from other areas where conflict is ongoing such as Afghanistan, Iraq, Iran, Somalia, and Eritrea. On April 23, 2015, the European Council held a special meeting in response to the "crisis" situation in the Mediterranean during which they acknowledged that the situation has become a "tragedy," and promised to take measures including strengthening the EU's presence at sea, fighting against traffickers, preventing illegal migration flows, and reinforcing international solidarity and responsibility (European Council 2015). The EU's approach has been heavily criticized, however, by human rights and refugee support groups for its focus on repression of trafficking and prevention of illegal migration rather than that of protecting the rights and lives of refugees who are desperate to reach Europe (Giuffre and Costello 2015). In principle, a plan was agreed under which each EU state should resettle a certain number of Syrian refugees, but this plan was met with negative reactions from some of the Eastern European member states who refused outright to take any refugees for resettlement. And even where member states have agreed to the plan, the numbers of refugees actually resettled has been minimal, and far below the (already modest) targets. The failure of the EU to agree on and implement regional plans or policies for facilitating legal migration of refugees and organizing resettlement has increased the insecurities and dangers of refugees' journeys, insecurities which may take specific forms for women.

Gender, Migration, and (In)Security

The interconnections between gender, migration, violence, and insecurity have been highlighted by research in various regions of the world (Freedman 2012; Marchand 2008). Different push and pull factors, migration control regimes, as well as social and economic conditions in countries of origin, transit, and destination create varying types of insecurity and violence for men and women, depending on their varying social and economic positions and the relations of power between them. As Marchand argues: "It goes without saying that the migration–violence nexus is gendered. Men and women are affected in different ways and the violence to which they are exposed is related to their position with respect to the migration–violence nexus." (Marchand 2008, 1387) Recent research has also highlighted the physical risks of border crossing for women, and the higher rate of mortality at the borders for women than for men (Pickering and Cochrane 2012). Despite these risks, however, refugee women continue to try to reach Europe desperate to escape conflict, violence, and persecution in their home countries and to find a safer home for them and their families. There are no completely accurate statistics on the numbers of women among the refugees arriving in Europe, but all existing data and evidence points to an increase in the proportion of women, and of women traveling alone (Freedman, Kivilcim and Ozgur Baklacioglu, 2017).

Experiences of violence are common to refugees. All of the Syrian women I spoke to on Kos, had experienced violence directly in Syria or had a close family member who had experienced violence. They talked about violence from all sides in the conflict, both the official Syrian army and the Islamic State and rebel forces. One woman, for example, had lost her husband who had been killed in Aleppo and had fled with her two children, aged twenty and twelve. She said that she no longer felt safe in Syria and felt that she had lost her home and everything she had. She explained in addition to the direct insecurities arising from the fighting, she experienced another layer of insecurity as a woman alone without a husband. There were many similar stories of women and families who no longer felt safe and had fled to protect themselves and their children, determined to reach Europe to find a place where they could be safe and restart their lives. Many had little hope of ever being able to return to Syria. "I feel as though I have lost my home forever," said one woman, echoing the feelings of many others (Interview July 2015).

All of the refugees interviewed in Greece had traveled through Turkey, some taking longer than others to finally reach Greece. Some of the Syrians had stayed in Turkey for several years, and had attempted to "settle" there, but had then moved on due to a deteriorating situation for Syrian refugees in Turkey (Amnesty International 2015), and lack of opportunities for employment and for their children's education. Turkey currently hosts nearly three million Syrian refugees, far more than can be hosted in the refugee camps constructed by the Turkish government, and thus the majority of these refugees have to fend for themselves. There are frequent stories of exploitative and insecure work and housing conditions for these refugees, conditions which again may be worse for women and especially those traveling alone (Ozgur Baklacioglu 2015). In addition, many families are worried that their children are not going to school, and are missing out on vital years of their education. One family I talked to had been living in Turkey for five years, and the two children had learned to speak fluent Turkish. The mother explained, however, that they had encountered increasing hostility from the Turkish authorities and population, and that she could not find any work, meaning that they were living in squalid conditions. She wanted to move to Europe to try and find a better future for her children. "I want my children to go to school, to have an education. And I want to work. There was nothing left for us in Turkey, and I can't go back to Syria," she said.

There are demographic differences in the migrant populations arriving in Europe, so that while Syrian, Afghan, Iraqi, and Iranian women arrive mainly accompanied by their husbands or in family groups (although the number of women traveling alone from these countries is also increasing), and often children, women from other countries such as Eritrea or Ethiopia are more likely to arrive alone. Traveling in family groups may provide some degree of security for women refugees but it can also be a source of other problems. One of the tendencies of those providing aid and assistance to refugees is to classify any group of people of mixed sex traveling together as a family. Many of these are very extended families or loose groupings of unrelated people who are traveling together in order to, for example, increase their security on the route or to share resources. Several NGO representatives that I interviewed said, however, that they did not seek to understand the composition of the groups but just spoke to the group's leader, who was always a man. They acknowledged that women and children usually stayed back and kept out of any interactions or discussions with aid workers, NGO representatives, etc., but although this was seen as problematic by some, they argued that in the current "crisis" situation and with the large number of refugees arriving and passing through, they did not have time to try and approach women separately, or to try and establish contact with them to find out if they had any specific problems or needs. This assumption about women's dependence on men, and the implication that men would ensure the security of the women traveling with them, can be seen as problematic in gender terms, reinforcing the idea of women's lack of agency and dependency, and the role of men as "protectors." In fact, as discussed further below, there have been growing reports of violence within these family groups and of conjugal violence against women refugees. Failure to consider these possibilities and to seek out women's voices can exacerbate this problem, or lead to a nonrecognition of the issue.

Although the majority of Syrian, Afghan, Iraqi, and Iranian women do still arrive within these "family" groups, it does seem that there are now increasing numbers of Syrian women traveling without a husband or male partner, in particular those women whose husbands have been killed in the conflict, or women who are sent ahead by their families to try and claim asylum in a safe country, before trying to bring other family members across to join them. Some families have been separated during the migratory journey, others have deliberately played on representations of women's greater vulnerability and need for protection to seek an easier point of entry for the family into Europe. Those women I met who were traveling without a husband or male partner spoke of the particular difficulties and insecurities they faced. "It is certainly very difficult to be a woman alone. It is hard to cope on my own, people look badly at me, I have to protect my children and do everything for them on my own" (Interview July 2015), said one woman interviewed in Kos, whose husband had been killed in Syria, and who was traveling with two teenage children, attempting to reach her brother in Hamburg, Germany. Another woman who I met in the migrant camp at Grande-Synthe in Dunkerque, France, had traveled from Iraq with her three young children. She told me that her husband had been injured during fighting in Iraq, and that she was trying to bring her children to safety in Europe before attempting to get her husband to join them. She said that she spent most of her day inside her tent, as she was scared for her safety and that of her children, and underlined the difficulties of traveling without a male companion (Interview January 2016).

Smugglers: Source of Insecurity or Service Providers and Allies?

European leaders have been quick to try and blame smugglers and traffickers for the "refugee crisis" and the increasing numbers of refugees attempting sea crossings to reach Europe, but as argued above, the role played by smugglers in the refugees' journeys is more complex than that of simple "exploitation" and any analysis of the relationship between refugees and smugglers thus needs to be more nuanced. All of the refugees interviewed had used the services of smugglers to cross borders and the sea. For some this was a "normal" part of the journey, while others complained about being victims of exploitation. The price of the passage varied but some quoted prices of up to one thousand euros for the short crossing between Turkey and Kos. For many, the prices were unexpectedly high, and had eaten into the money they had saved for the journey, making them fearful of running out of money before they reached their final destination. The worry about money meant that they were reluctant to buy anything other than very basic necessities from the shops in Kos, and were even limiting the amount of food they bought for themselves and their families. They complained about the high prices on the island which were driven up by the fact that it was a tourist destination. They were also worried about the price they would have to pay to complete their journeys and to travel across the borders from Greece on their onward trips. The Greek economic crisis of 2015 and the closure of banks for several weeks in June and July had also affected refugees badly, meaning that they were unable to access money transferred from abroad, or to change their currency or withdraw euros, thus creating even greater economic insecurity for them.

Apart from being worried about the price they had to pay to the smugglers, some refugees felt that they had been cheated by these smugglers, or had suffered violence or harm. There were several families who complained that the smugglers had thrown all their possessions into the sea because there was no room in the boat, or because they thought the boat might sink. One woman told me she had lost everything, including all her clothes and her children's clothes, money, and papers during the crossing, and was now relying on the help of local people to clothe and feed her family (Interview July 2015). Others had been promised passage in a "real" boat but had found themselves in a small rubber dinghy overcrowded with too many people. One Syrian family with two young children had paid one thousand dollars for the crossing on the assurance that they would be making the crossing in a proper fibreglass boat. They found themselves in a three-meter-long rubber dinghy with fourteen other people. Halfway across the 5km stretch of water the motor stopped working and they found themselves floating helplessly until they were eventually rescued by the Greek coastguard after nine hours at sea. "I would never do that again, I thought I was going to die, and my children too. It was the worst experience of my life. I would never do that again", this woman told me, close to tears as she recounted her experience (Interview July 2015). The women I met all seemed very distressed by the memory of the journey and the sea crossing, and indeed the MSF psychologist to whom I spoke told me that, in her experience, women seemed more traumatized by the experience of the journey and the crossing than men did. Or in any case women expressed their feelings of trauma and fear more readily.

Women traveling alone, or just with children, are particularly vulnerable to attack, and there were several accounts of women who had been raped or sexually assaulted on their journeys. One woman was traveling with a woman friend who had been raped by smugglers and badly injured. She expressed fear about continuing their journey in case this type of incident occurred again. Danger comes not only from smugglers, but also from police and military in the countries that the refugees have to cross to reach Europe. Women alluded to attacks and harassment by police and military in Turkey. A psychologist working with MSF and providing psychological support and counseling to refugees on Kos, recounted how one Syrian woman had told her of her experience of being separated from her husband and children and held in a Turkish prison for forty-five days on her own. The woman would not talk about the detail of the abuse she had suffered, but was showing signs of severe trauma from this experience (Interview with MSF psychologist on Kos, July 2015).

Smugglers are also a key part of the migratory landscape in the camps around Calais. Most of the refugees interviewed in these camps had been brought or directed there by smugglers. Although in recent years it has reportedly been possible to cross the Channel from France to the UK without paying for the services of a smuggler, all of those interviewed, both refugees and representatives of humanitarian organizations and local support groups, said that is it now completely impossible to cross without paying someone to help you. The average cost of a crossing is said to be currently about 5000 euros. As in other locations, the relations between smugglers and refugees are gendered, and women who have no resources to pay for their crossing may find themselves being asked for sexual services instead by the smugglers. Several prostitution networks have been reported in the camps, and medical NGOs who I interviewed reported that they regularly accompanied treated young women for sexually related injuries and accompanied them to hospital for abortions. However, there has been no formal investigation into sexual violence or prostitution, and no official claims have been made.

Living in Limbo

There is a huge pressure on the refugees to move onwards and through different countries to try and get to their preferred European destination before another border closes. But paradoxically, there is also much time spent not traveling but waiting. Refugees arriving on one of the Greek islands must wait for a permit to travel on to Athens, others wait at borders to be allowed to cross, and those who have arrived in Calais wait (sometimes for years) for the chance to cross from France to the UK.

While waiting for their permit to leave and travel onwards to Athens, refugees face extremely difficult living conditions on Kos. The living conditions for all refugees are precarious and insalubrious in the extreme. Kos has no official reception facilities and provides no basic services (such as food or healthcare) for refugees. Basic health and psychosocial support is provided by MSF, while a local support group, Kos Solidarity, provides food (one cooked meal a day plus milk and other essentials for children), clothing, and basic hygiene necessities such as toothbrushes and soap for the refugees. The local authorities have requisitioned an abandoned hotel, the Captain Elias, on the outskirts of Kos Town, to house the arriving refugees. As they land on the island, and once they have been registered by the coastguard and police, they are led out on in a procession and left here. The building, which has twenty-five bedrooms and was originally built to house a hundred or so people at the maximum, is now "home" to around seven hundred men, women, and children. Mattresses line the floor not only of the bedrooms but of all the corridors and communal areas, and more tents and mattresses are crammed in to the garden outside. Still more refugees have made camps in the nearby fields, apparently worried about the security for their families within the crowded "hotel." There is no electricity in the building and no cooking facilities. Some refugees make fires outside in the garden to cook, others eat only cold food, and the meal distributed in the evening by local volunteers. There are only two working toilets and running water comes from standpipes outside in the garden. Medecins Sans Frontières have also installed a few shower cubicles outside the building in order to try and provide some private washing facilities for the refugees. MSF provide basic health services, sanitary services, and psychological support to refugees, but faced with the huge numbers of people arriving in Kos every day, the support that they can offer is limited. Local people, formed into a group called Kos Solidarity, collect clothes, food, and sanitary supplies which they distribute to refugees, but as one of the local volunteers explained to me, they are a small group who are also overwhelmed by the number of people needing help (Interview with a Member of Kos Solidarity, July 2015). The volunteers are angry that the local authorities on the island have not done more to help meet the needs of refugees.

More recently, following a big fight in the Captain Elias between groups of Afghan and Pakistani refugees over the food that was being distributed by volunteers, some families have chosen to move out and are now sleeping in nearby fields or in a park in the center of the town. One Afghan family sleeping in a field with their three daughters told me that they felt it was unsafe for their daughters to sleep in the Captain Elias with all the other refugees, especially the single men whom they saw as a threat to the girls. In the local park several Syrian families were sleeping on pieces of cardboard, with a few blankets donated by local people. There are no toilets or running water, and one interviewee told me that they had been using water from the park's irrigation system to wash, and even drinking this, until some local volunteers provided bottled water for them.

This lack of access to basic facilities and services provides a source of insecurity for all refugees, but women may be particularly affected, particularly by the lack of sanitary facilities and lack of cooking facilities. While it would be wrong to essentialize women's role in cooking and caring for children, in reality, these responsibilities are generally placed on them both by the men with whom they may be traveling and the NGOs and international organizations working to help or support refugees. Women I spoke to who were living in the Captain Elias complained about the fact that they felt unable to take a shower because the shower facilities that existed were not private enough and they felt scared going to wash in front of the men. Those that were "lucky" enough to have been able to find a room to share with their family could ask husbands or male friends to bring buckets of (cold) water upstairs for them to wash in the relative privacy of these rooms, but others sleeping outside or in corridors were not so fortunate. Women also complained about the lack of cooking facilities and the fact that they could not provide meals for their families. "We have to wait for the local people to bring us food. It is only one meal a day, not enough for my children. We are hungry all the time," said one woman.

There seems to be a de facto division of space, with women refugees trying to remain in bedrooms or other more "private" spaces and to avoid the more crowded "public" areas of the Captain Elias. Women spoke of their fear of being attacked or harassed when they tried to use the toilets or the showers outside, and most said that they refrained from using the toilets or from going outside of their rooms at night time because there was no lighting and they were very scared of moving around in the dark in case they were attacked. One young seventeen-year-old Afghan woman, traveling with her mother and young sister, described how she and her family spent their days and nights barricaded in their room with another two Afghan families, only venturing out when they were desperate to use the toilets, or when they had to walk into town to the police station to see if they were on the list of refugees who could go and collect their permits to leave.

Those waiting in Calais are also faced with insalubrious and dangerous living conditions. Women interviewed described the precariousness and insecurity of their living conditions in makeshift tents in muddy and swamped fields, with a few dirty communal toilets and showers. Once again a gendered division of space is clearly visible. Men are clearly visible walking around the camps and occupying the public spaces such as cafés and shops that have been built there. Women are far less visible and during my time in the camps, it was necessary to go and visit individual tents to find and talk to women. Several women whom I spoke to said that they preferred to go out as little as possible, and certainly did not venture out of their tents at night when they described the conditions in the camp as "very dangerous" for them.[2]

Shifting Gender Relations

Migration can also lead to changes in relations of power and gender relations within families and couples, and in some cases to increasing incidences of domestic violence. As pointed out above, the known dangers and risks of the refugee journey mean that many women choose to travel in a "family" group with men that they may not have known previously. This formation of "family" groups may offer protection to some women but may also lead to varying forms of violence and exploitation within the groups, which are overlooked by those outside who assume that men will protect women traveling with them. Violence occurs also within "real" families. MSF, for example, has reported cases of both psychological and physical violence within families, and women have spoken about the fact that they were victims of violence from their husbands during their journeys. These women suffered both the insecurities of their journey, and from their own husbands, who not only did not protect them, but also offered a threat. Women in this situation find it almost impossible to leave their abusive husbands or partners because the idea of continuing the journey alone, or just with their children, is too difficult. So, they find themselves stuck in a violent relationship. There have also been reports that women who have arrived in an EU country have had little help or support in escaping violence from their husbands or partners. One report in Germany, for example, recounted the story of a Syrian woman whose husband raped and beat her while they were living in a temporary camp set up to house newly arrived refugees. When the woman tried to file a complaint with the police they would not listen to her, and there was no real help either from social work or refugee support services. A group founded to help refugee women in Berlin explained that: "There is no real security for asylum-seeking women because whenever they are attacked, either physically or sexually harassed, nobody knows what to do. There is no clear policy" (Moore 2015).

Gendered Strategies of Migration

Having spoken of specific sources of insecurity and violence for women, it would be wrong to paint these women merely as passive victims without their own migratory strategies and their own systems for coping with insecurity. In some cases, women expressed the feeling that migration had in fact improved their security and well-being despite the difficult conditions they faced on the journey and on arrival. For some this had meant escaping from family violence and constraints in their countries of origin. One Afghan woman, who had traveled with her children, told me that she felt much freer in Kos, despite the difficult living conditions (she was sleeping with them in a field). She was also very positive about the possibilities for her children's schooling, explaining that the school in her village had been destroyed by the Taliban, and that she was enthusiastic about the opportunities for her children in Europe. Another Syrian woman explained that she was pleased to be alone with her husband and children, and no longer "controlled" by her husband's family.

And although in the division of space, women refugees seemed to be more relegated to private and "safer" spaces, they also proved to be taking initiatives in some areas, and to be more central to some areas of their families' well-being. The MSF psychologist I talked to noted, for example, that women are far more willing than their husbands to come and ask for medical and psychological help. According to her, while many refugee men are constrained by norms of masculinity and are reluctant to admit trauma, illness, or weakness and to ask for help for this, their wives are much more forthcoming in requesting help for themselves and their husbands. So, in some ways these women are ensuring the health and well-being of all of their families by seeking help, particularly for illness and stress.

Women also had definite strategies for onward migration, and had clear ideas about where they wished to go and what they wanted to achieve through their migration. Nearly all of the women whom I spoke to were hoping to reach Germany with their families, although a few said that they were just aiming for countries in the north of Europe. All planned to continue their journeys as soon as possible via Athens, and then through Macedonia, Serbia, and Hungary to reach Germany. None of the refugees interviewed intended to stay in Kos or to remain in Greece at all, citing the lack of facilities and welcome for refugees, as well as very limited opportunities for integration and employment. One of the women remarked that "Greece has its own crisis, there is nothing here for us, we need to go elsewhere where we'll be safe and have a life" (Interview July 2015). The choice of destination seems to be governed by several factors including the presence of family or friends already living in Germany (or another country), the idea that other countries have better reception conditions for refugees, including fairer and more rapid asylum procedures, and perceptions about the economic conditions in other EU countries where refugees may more easily find work to support themselves and their families. The issue of language was also raised, as although the refugees did not speak German, many spoke some English (in some cases quite good English) and hoped that this would help the process of settling and integration in northern European states.

Some women also played on the idea of their vulnerability to advance their migratory strategies. Some of the NGO representatives I talked to discussed the idea that women might be encouraged to migrate ahead of their family or husbands because there was a belief that it was easier for them to cross borders. Others talked of the way in which women, and particularly pregnant women, would be placed at the front of refugee boats as they were perceived as highly vulnerable and thus the boat was more likely to be rescued by the coastguard if they saw these women. There were families I talked to in Greece, for example, who planned to stay in Athens and send their wives on ahead to Germany, or other European destinations. They believed that the women would have an easier time negotiating with border guards and immigration authorities because of their perceived vulnerability, and that an asylum claim made by a woman on her own would have more chance of success than a claim by a man. These families hope that their wives or mothers or both will be able to obtain refugee status and will then be able to safely bring their families to join them. The perception that women are more "vulnerable" and in greater need of protection can therefore be used strategically by refugees to help them to further their goals of securing protection for themselves and their families within the European Union.

Integrating Gender into EU Reponses

Theoretically, gender equality issues have been mainstreamed both into the Common European Asylum System (CEAS) and the Frontex operations. The CEAS directives which have recently been recast on paper oblige EU member states to take gender issues into consideration both in reception conditions for asylum seekers and refugees, and in the refugee status determination process (Freedman 2015). Frontex has also recently integrated gender guidelines into its Fundamental Rights Training. An official for Frontex told me that "based on the manual the European border guards are trained that their work requires gender sensitivity at all stages of dealing with a migrant: interception, reception, assistance, interviewing, and deprivation of liberty. Practical examples and guidelines are given in all the modules" (Email Interview July 2015).

The Frontex training also includes guidelines on how to treat women where there is a suspicion that they may have been victims of sexual violence. It states with regard to interviews by border guards that "Women should not be pushed to talk about problems related to sexual violence nor to provide any details on the substance of their claim for international protection. If border officials suspect that a woman has been a victim of sexual violence, or if she is unable or unwilling to discuss certain events relating to such an incident, they should ask discreet and indirect questions that could enable them to identify what appropriate protection measures could be taken and to what specialized agency they should be referred to. It is important to ensure the presence of female border guards in field control operations and in the course of routine border tasks" (Frontex, 2015). In an interview it was also underlined that if border guards suspect that there has been any kind of violence or coercion within a family group, they should interview all members of the family separately (Email Interview July 2015). However, despite these written guarantees both with the CEAS directives and in the Frontex training and operations, it seems clear that in practice there is no such attention paid to issues of gender, and border guards have not been offering specific protection to any women, including those who they suspect may have been victims of violence. In several interviews, both officials and representatives of NGOs and of the UNHCR talked about the "crisis" situation and the impacts this was having on their ability to actually implement any of the existing guidelines. As one interviewee explained, "there are so many people, and they are so desperate to move on as quickly as possible, that we just can't really do much for them" (Interview with UNHCR official, July 2015). In answer to my questions others just responded that "this is a crisis," as though this label took away all responsibility for trying to implement the gender policies and guidelines that exist. As mentioned above, the "crisis labeling" of this migration can be argued to have enabled the application of a range of measures of exception and the abandonment of "normal" procedures, including norms and policies on gender equality in the border and asylum procedures.

Representations of Threat and Vulnerability

The representations of the current influx of refugees in the media and in political discourse are highly gendered. For men, and particularly young men, there is a persistent representation of the threat that they pose to Europe, both at a regional and an individual level. The fact that some of those involved in the Bataclan attacks in Paris in November 2015 may have traveled through Turkey and Greece with the other refugees added fuel to these representations of threat, as did the supposed involvement of some refugees in the sexual violence perpetrated against women in Cologne during the 2016 New Year celebrations. Following the Cologne attacks there were many articles in the media and statements by political leaders drawing on discourses of the lack of respect for women's rights in "other" cultures, and the need to "educate" refugees on "European values" concerning women's rights and gender equality.

Women, on the other hand, when they are made visible in discourses on refugees, are portrayed largely as "vulnerable" and in need of protection. As mentioned earlier, many humanitarian and aid organizations deal with the refugees as "family" groups, and assume that the men will protect the women with whom they are traveling. As well as obscuring relations of domination and violence within these groups, this also acts to silence the voice of women, and to take away the possibilities for them to express their own needs and wishes. Women who travel alone are categorized as vulnerable because of the lack of this male protection. As noted earlier, this supposed "vulnerability" can be used as a strategy for women to try and gain easier access to Europe and to facilitate the entry of the rest of their family, but it is also a label which may have negative connotations in that women are overlooked as independent agents. And although women have been labeled as "vulnerable" there is still a real lack of any kind of systematic consideration of their specific needs within the refugee and asylum systems in place in Europe.

Women interviewed, while highlighting the insecurity they felt, and the lack of support which they were receiving from European authorities, also claimed that they often felt diminished because of a lack of respect from the officials or from aid workers with whom they came into contact. Although being treated as "vulnerable" may be seen as an advantage, it also reduces women to what they feel is an "inferior" status where their own autonomous strategies and projects are undermined. This was particularly marked in the case of women who were wearing a headscarf who felt that they were treated as "other" and less educated, enlightened, or intelligent than both European women and refugee men. One woman told me that "they think that all Syrian women are stupid and oppressed. They don't understand how it was for us before in Syria." This woman was an architect who had had a well-respected career before the outbreak of the Syrian conflict; she felt that she was treated just as an "oppressed victim" by those working with refugees, even though the efforts to help her may have been well-intentioned. Another Syrian woman interviewed in Paris explained how she had been treated by the Croix Rouge when she went to ask for food. "They gave me 1kg of chocolate biscuits, and I told them I don't like chocolate. But then they said 'I thought you said you were hungry. If you're hungry you'll eat them.' I felt so humiliated. They just treated me as if I was stupid, nothing." This type of symbolic violence seems unfortunately to be a common experience of women refugees arriving in Europe, and particularly those who are easily identified as Muslim. These representations of women (and particularly Muslim women) as "vulnerable" or "victims" devoid of agency combine a racialized and gendered discourse which reduced their ability to express and make heard their own needs, wishes, and opinions.

Conclusion

The current refugee "crisis" is exposing the failure of EU countries to offer real protection to those fleeing from conflict, including the hundreds of thousands of Syrians who have been forced to flee their homes and who are seeking refuge. In this respect, the "crisis" is not one of refugees, but of the EU itself (Gilbert 2015). The journey to Europe can provide particular insecurities for women, who appear to be affected in specific ways by the dangers of the journey and the lack of facilities in countries of reception such as Greece. However, these women also show resilience and have in many cases adopted their own strategies for coping with the insecurities of migration. There is little real analysis of the gendered experiences of refugees, and thus stereotypes of the "dangerous" male refugee or the "vulnerable" female refugee prevail both in media and political discourse. In order to move beyond such stereotypes a more careful analysis of the experiences and needs of female and male refugees should be undertaken, including an analysis of the ways in which gendered relations may change during the migratory process. The EU must now react to ensure that those seeking protection are able to access this, and rather than blaming smugglers and traffickers must look to the root causes of migration and see how they can offer regular and safe routes to Europe for those who can no longer remain in their home countries, and safe places to stay and live for both men and women once they arrive in the EU.

Notes

1. There has been much debate among politicians and in the media as to whether those people entering (or attempting to enter) Europe in the current "crisis" should be referred to as refugees. While some argue that they cannot be correctly called refugees as they have not as yet obtained official refugee status from the UNHCR or from one of the EU member states, others point to the fact that they have been forced to flee from their home countries because of conflict and persecution, and are thus de facto refugees. This chapter has chosen to use the term "refugees" to indicate that while all of these people may not have formal refugee status, they are attempting to reach Europe to gain refuge and protection from various forms of persecution and insecurity.
2. Since completion of this research, the main "Jungle" camp at Calais has been dismantled by the French authorities, but refugees still remain in the area, in even more precarious conditions, camping out wherever they find some shelter and constantly moved on by French police.

References

Amnesty International. 2015. *Struggling to Survive: Refugees from Syria in Turkey*. London: Amnesty International.

De Haas, H. 2007. "The Myth of Invasion: Irregular Migration from West Africa to the Maghreb and the European Union." Oxford: International Migration Institute http://www.temaasyl.se/Documents/Forskning/Forskningsstudier/The%20Myth%20of%20Invasion%20%20%20Irregular%20migration%20from%20West%20Africa%20to%20the%20Maghreb%20and%20the%20European%20Union.pdf

Edelman, M. 1977. *Constructing the Political Spectacle*, Chicago, IL: University of Chicago Press.

European Council. 2015. *EC Statement: Special Meeting, 23 April 2015*. http://www.consilium.europa.eu/en/press/press-releases/2015/04/23-special-euco-statement.

Fargues, P., and C. Fandrich. 2012. "The European Response to the Syrian Refugee Crisis, What Next?" Migration Policy Centre Research Report; 2012/14. Florence, Italy: European University Institute.

Freedman, J. 2012. "Analysing the Gendered Insecurities of Migration: A Case Study of Female Sub-Saharan African Migrants in Morocco." *International Feminist Journal of Politics*, 14, no. 1: 36–55.

Freedman, J. 2015. *Gendering the International Asylum and Refugee Debate*. 2nd ed. Basingstoke, UK: Palgrave Macmillan.

Freedman, J., Z. Kivilcim, and N. O. Baklacioglu, N. 2017. *A Gendered Approach to the Syrian Refugee Crisis*. London: Routledge.

Gilbert, G. 2015. "Why Europe Does Not Have a Refugee Crisis." *Journal of Refugee Law* 27, no. 4: 531–535.

Giuffre, C., and M. Costello. 2015. "'Tragedy' and Responsibility in the Mediterranean." *Open Democracy*, April 27, 2015. https://www.opendemocracy.net/can-europe-make-it/mariagiulia-giuffr%C3%A9-cathryn-costello/crocodile-tears-tragedy-and-responsibility-i

Jeandesboz, J. and Pallister- Wilkins, P. 2014. 'Crisis, Enforcement and Control at the EU Borders', in A. Lindley (ed.), Crisis and Migration: Critical Perspectives, London and New York: Routledge, 115–135.

Lutterbeck, D. 2009. "Small Frontier Island: Malta and the Challenge of Irregular Migration." *Mediterranean Quarterly* 20, no. 1: 119–144.

Marchand, M. 2008. "The Violence of Development and the Migration/Insecurities Nexus: Labour Migration in a North American Context." *Third World Quarterly* 29, no. 7: 1375–1388.

Moore, J. 2015. "When You're a Refugee and Your Husband Beats You, You're Basically On Your Own," *Buzzfeed*, October 29, 2015. http://www.buzzfeed.com/jinamoore/when-youre-a-refugee-and-your-husband-beats-...

Ozgur Baklacioglu, N. 2015. "The Violence of Tolerated Temporality: Syrian Women and LGBTI Refugees in Istanbul." Paper presented at a Conference on Gender and Exile: Syrian Women and LGBTI Refugees in the Middle East, Kadir Has University, Istanbul, 9 May 2015.

Pickering, S., and B. Cochrane. 2012. "Irregular Border-Crossing Deaths and Gender: Where, How and Why Women Die Crossing Borders". *Theoretical Criminology* 17, no. 1: 27–48.

CHAPTER 41

HUMAN TRAFFICKING AS A MIGRATION CRISIS

Gender, Precariousness, and Access to Labor Rights

INGA K. THIEMANN

This chapter approaches human trafficking as a phenomenon in gendered migration. Whereas human trafficking is nearly always described as a contemporary crisis, it is hardly ever perceived as a crisis of gendered migration, let alone a crisis caused by migrants' exclusions from rights.

The chapter will first identify root causes of human trafficking in gendered approaches to migration. Not only has a male norm of "migrant" influenced the way migration is perceived and regulated, but gender norms also influence, sometimes purposefully, sometimes only consequentially, nationalist sentiments and policies to prevent women from traveling.

The second part of this chapter then illustrates the interplay of migration policies, on the one hand, and migrants' perceived and actual access to labor rights, on the other. It links precarious and feminized labour and demonstrates how trafficked persons constitute the ultimate exploitable workers. By viewing immigrant status as a legal category, which fosters precarious working conditions, it will demonstrate that the combination of insufficient labor protections and increased vulnerability can culminate in human trafficking as one of the most severe forms of exploitation.

Gendered Assumptions about Migration

Migration theory has always assumed migration to be a male-dominated process (Bludau and Ezzeddine 2013; Boucher 2009; Boyd 1986). Women traditionally are seen as migrating only as spouses or children of migrating men. However, since the early 1980s, more women have been migrating independently in search of jobs, rather than traveling with their husbands or joining them abroad (Zhyvytsya and Keil 2012). According to data from the United Nations Population Division between 1965 and 1990 the number of female migrants grew faster than the number of male migrants in most receiving countries. It is assumed that at least half of all international migrants today are women (Zhyvytsya and Keil 2012). The International Labour Organization (from here on ILO) even argues that, if the numbers of official and unofficial flows of migrants are added, the proportion of women migrants is likely to be much higher than that of men (Chammartin 2002). The increase in female migration is due to a combination of factors, including the feminization of the labor market, a greater demand for women's labor (particularly their care work, domestic work, and sex work) as well as changing views on women's mobility (Dhar 2012). However, this increase in female migration is insufficiently reflected in discourse about migration. Human trafficking in particular is seen as a separate phenomenon, rather than as part of broader migratory patterns.

The lack of focus on women's participation in the migratory process is connected to assumptions about labor. An emphasis on the human capital model values productive labor conducted by men outside the house and neglects the importance of women's reproductive labor at home and in private households in terms of economic activity and labor force participation (Dhar 2012). Women are estimated to spend around 70 percent of their unpaid time caring for family members. Due to its classification as unpaid, reproductive work, this contribution to the global economy remains largely unrecognized (Zhyvytsya and Keil 2012), as does women's paid work in the informal sector and private households. In addition to ignoring reproductive labor, the focus on productive labor in migration research neglects the impact of family life, gender norms in countries of origin and destination, and the interdependence of productive and reproductive spheres on the migratory process (Meares 2010).

There is a need to understand the unique challenges of female migration such as the poor working conditions in the female-dominated fields of domestic work and care-giving jobs (Anderson 2000; Mantouvalou 2012); the changing role of women in the family and in their community due to migration; and the vulnerability and exposure of migrant women to different kinds of risks, including trafficking (Kawar 2004; Zhyvytsya and Keil 2012).

The Discriminatory Effects of Gendered Migration Policies

Migration policy based on a male norm also reinforces gender norms and contributes to some of the risks of female migration by creating female dependency and denying official access to women-dominated fields of work (Chuang 2006; True 2012). In combination with a migration theory that is gender-neutral on the surface, but founded on the concept of a male (migrant) worker, gendered institutions in receiving countries, which are also based on a male norm, further affect migrant women's well-being. The assumption of an independent male migrant and a dependent female migrant increases women's vulnerability. The idea of the male breadwinner means that women's legal status in a country is often tied to the status of their spouse, which creates a situation in which women are indeed dependent on their spouses and this dependency increases their vulnerability (Boyle and Halfacree 2002). For example, in many countries, if domestic violence occurs, women risk losing their residence rights if they decide to leave their spouses or are forced to stay with the abuser (True 2012, 60).

Discrimination in Immigration Policy

Migration policies of Western countries are not normally openly gender-biased. However, legal, official recruitment efforts are frequently indirectly aimed at male workers through minimum income, education, or work experience requirements (Agustín 2007; Boucher 2009; OSCE 2009). Additionally, some countries have imposed restrictions on admissions of migrants for feminized occupations and the demand for domestic, care, and sex workers does not translate into legal immigration routes for these occupations (León 2010; Murphy 2015; van Hooren 2010). Therefore women's opportunities for legal migration are limited to the extent to which they are able to meet the male norms both in the ability to move and in the work they are able to do. These limits mean that women's migration is more limited than men's in most countries (Chammartin 2002). Partly due to these male-focussed migration policies, much of the feminization of migration will go undocumented. Furthermore, female migrants will struggle even more than their male counterparts to receive decent remuneration for their work, acceptable working conditions, or labor protection as a whole (Chammartin 2002).

When women are able to migrate legally, they often take up positions at the lowest end of the economy, jobs that male migrants and female nationals refuse to do, such as work in the domestic and sex industries (Anderson 2000; Truong 1996). Therefore, even when they migrate through legal channels, women end up working in sectors in which they can easily become subject to discrimination and arbitrary employment terms, as well as abuses, exploitation, and human trafficking (Anderson 2012; Zhyvytsya and Keil 2012).

Gender also affects the industries both nationals and migrants end up working in. Men still form the majority of workers in the information technology and scientific sectors, while women more often work in welfare and care professions, including the education and health sectors, which are closer to traditional "women's work" (Morris 2009; True 2012). Since policy in receiving countries assumes a male migrant, these female-dominated sectors are only rarely open to official migration. Additionally, they tend to be marked by low wages, by absence of social services, and by poor working conditions (Lutz 2012; Mantouvalou 2012).

Since women have a lesser chance of migrating legally, they are more vulnerable to discrimination, abuse, and violence than male migrants are in the migration process (Chammartin 2002). The policies of some receiving countries include bans and restrictions on female migration in order to "prevent" women from falling into the hands of traffickers and smugglers (Adams 2003; Andrijasevic and Anderson 2009; Doezema 2010). Contrary to its intention, restrictive regulation often drives the migratory process further underground and forces women migrants into even more vulnerable positions, since it increases their need for assistance to migrate clandestinely (Chammartin 2002). For women, this trend of migration regulation and tightened border controls causes increased vulnerability to exploitation and abuse, and continuing inequality with men (Zhyvytsya and Keil 2012).

Women migrants are already at a higher risk of exploitation *during* their migrant journey, due to being both a woman and a migrant. This risk is aggravated by policies limiting the forms of migration available to women, meaning their migratory journeys often include flight, trafficking, and undocumented migration. While protecting women is at the forefront of the debate, especially with regard to trafficking (Adams 2003; Chapkis 2003), policy responses still adhere to male categories and the trafficking debate has failed to translate into a migration policy that takes the specific needs and rights of women into consideration and offers women-specific migration routes. This makes them more likely to utilize the services of smugglers and other intermediaries, and ultimately renders them more vulnerable to traffickers (Andrijasevic 2009; Costello 2014; Zhyvytsya and Keil 2012).

Once they have arrived in a receiving country, women's immigration status often does not allow them to work legally. They are therefore forced to work in the informal sectors of the economy, where there is less regulation and protection. At the same time they are not considered active participants in the labor market by the state (Morris 2009). Such continuous exclusion then also leads to women being unable to claim residency or citizenship, as their "informal" labor in the underground economy does not qualify them for residency in most countries (Calavita 2006).

Some of these informal, feminized jobs, particularly domestic and sex work, make female migrants more vulnerable to exploitation than male migrants. The lack of regulations and labor controls regarding work in private houses and in the sex industry (Mantouvalou 2012; Thiemann 2016b), coupled with the solitude of individualized work environments in these sectors, creates greater precariousness than the work environments of migrant men, who tend to work in groups on construction sites or on farms. This lack of scrutiny in the private sphere is a gender-specific issue affecting migrant women (Chammartin 2002; Piper 2003). Work in private households (e.g., as a care, domestic, or sex worker) involves greater risks of being exploited and/or being treated badly due to the lack of laws and standards regulating it. Therefore, it often involves unregulated, long work hours with too few rest days, no monitoring of workplace conditions, and a heightened risk of abuse by employers.

Discrimination in Emigration Policy

Both in destination countries and in countries of origin, women's migration is often viewed more critically and is perceived as less "normal" than men's. Countries of origin have concerns about the migration of "their" women. Particularly when countries experience a so-called "brain-drain" (Docquier and Rapoport 2011), a case of the most highly educated and skilled young people leaving a country to work elsewhere, this may correlate with fears of also losing the young women most able to raise the nation (Docquier et al 2009). In some countries male emigration is completely unregulated, but female migration is restricted or even banned (Oishi 2002).

Restrictive emigration policies of developing countries are not just the simple products of economic concerns. Instead, Nana Oishi's case studies show that both policy on and public perception of female migration is different from male migration and limits female migration (Oishi 2002). Whereas economic concerns form the main reason for policies on male migration, emigration policies for women are "value-driven." Women's migration is more emotionally laden for the state than men's migration, because women are not considered a value-neutral workforce. Women are considered the nurturers of the nation, as well as the symbols of national dignity and pride. Due to this, the number of female emigrants is low in countries in which independent female migration carries social prejudice, despite economic hardship. This indicates a social stigma of women's migration that is strong enough to effectively discourage a significant number of women from leaving the country, despite the economic effects of such a decision (Oishi 2002).

The phenomenon of human trafficking has exacerbated the problem insofar as the governments of some countries of origin have taken steps to curb or outright prevent women's migration in order to "protect" women from abuse and exploitation (Kapur 2002; Kapur and Sanghera 2000; Lepp 2002). Annalee Lepp explains this phenomenon with the example of Thailand:

> On the one hand, the Ministry of Labour and Social Welfare tends to encourage Thai people, especially men, to seek employment abroad through various program and government-endorsed employment agencies, it promotes and facilitates "safe" and legal labor migration, because the remittances sent from workers abroad contribute to boosting the economy, especially in terms of earning foreign currency. At the same time, other government agencies, such as the Department of Public Welfare, tend to discourage female migration, by providing information about potential abuses and warning women about the difficulties they may encounter abroad.
>
> (Lepp 2002, 94)

Some countertrafficking organizations, such as the Global Alliance Against Trafficking in Women (GAATW) condemn such policies, as they operate on the assumption that trafficking will be reduced if the flow of female migration is reduced. This occurs without taking into account the root causes of migration, such as a need to provide for their families and the absence of employment in the country of origin (Lepp 2002).

Such restrictive approaches echo historical "protective" policies, in which women were excluded from night work as a protective measure to prevent them from being attacked or sexually assaulted (Wikander et al. 1995). There is significant feminist scholarship criticizing "protective" approaches to prevent women's vulnerability in the public sphere (Baer 1978; Miller 2004; Nakanishi 1983; Wikander et al 1995). Protective measures essentially result in excluding women from that sphere. In this, they fail to provide any real protection for women and fail to create the public sphere as a space that is safe for all members of society. Instead, such measures perpetuate the idea that for women only the home (the literal home, but also the home community, or, in this case the home country) is a safe space, rendering women's attempts to operate in the public sphere as risky and ultimately shifting the blame for violence against women onto the victims of such violence (Andrijasevic 2003; Chapman and Hockey 1999; Goldsack 1999; Price 2002).

Labor Migration: Human Smuggling or Human Trafficking?

While women experience particular exclusion due to their gender, all migrant workers share vulnerabilities created through their immigration status. Equally, other groups of workers, who are not restricted to certain sectors or employers, such as working holidaymakers and students, may instead be limited to part time or temporary work (Anderson 2000). Again, this creates an imbalance between employers and employees, as both part-time and short-term work come with fewer labor protections than full-time work in the standard employment contract.

Irregular migrants are likely to stay with their employer due to fears of deportation and lack of other options (Andrijasevic and Anderson 2009), making them even more vulnerable to exploitation than regular migrants. Instead of rendering migrant labor undesirable, immigration law's restrictions on the sector, the length, the number of hours, and for whom migrant laborers can work actively contribute to creating precarious labor conditions for workers (Fudge 2012).

This leads us to one of the definitional problems in migration—when does migration turn into irregular migration, where are the lines between irregular migration and human smuggling and how do smuggling and human trafficking differ? There are definitions of human trafficking in the 2000 UN Trafficking Protocol and of human smuggling in its sister protocol, the 2000 UN Smuggling Protocol. However, these definitions are vague and in reality, the experiences of trafficked and smuggled persons cannot easily be distinguished. Smuggled persons can become trafficked persons and the early stages of a person being trafficked may look like smuggling (Gallagher

2006; O'Connell Davidson 2010; Thiemann 2016a; van Liempt 2007). Equally, common concepts of legal or illegal migration are challenged through people who enter a country legally, overstay their visa, or lose their status by violating their visa regulations (Anderson 2013). Governments' policies that aim to deter both illegal migration and human trafficking through means of stricter border controls might thus be ineffective in curbing migratory flows. Instead, they might increase the vulnerabilities of irregular migrants in general and trafficked persons in particular. By nonetheless describing human trafficking as a phenomenon that is separate from other forms of migration, and one that predominantly affects women, an artificial barrier is created.

Links Between Trafficking and "Normal" Migration

In fact, there are continuities between someone holding regular migrant status and a person with the most precarious form of irregular migrant status, a trafficked person. Immigration and labor policies contribute to creating the specific vulnerabilities among migrants, which then lead to an exploitability in precarious labor and human trafficking.

Already the lines between migration, smuggling of humans and human trafficking are blurry. Trafficking is often presented as being different from other kinds of migration or not a migratory process at all (Derks et al. 2006). Trafficked persons, unlike migrants, are assumed to have been coerced into crossing borders. As a result, trafficked persons receive greater sympathy and official concern than those who are considered illegal immigrants (Basok and Piper 2012; Pérez 2012). However, it also means that the solution to trafficking becomes the removal or arrest of traffickers and repatriation of trafficked persons (Sharma 2005). Thus, the result is largely the same as for irregular migration, but it is presented as helping a victim, rather than expelling an irregular migrant. Idealizing victimhood, particularly female victimhood, in this context, creates a further loss of rights, which will be discussed subsequently.

Furthermore, framing the problem as voluntary vs. involuntary migration shifts attention away from immigration laws in Western host countries and ignores the close links between migration and trafficking which have been demonstrated in studies based on primary interviews (Rao and Presenti 2012). If, for example, human smuggling is considered to be only "*largely* voluntary," human smuggling and human trafficking have to be viewed on a scale such that the difference between the two might be in the different levels of abuse experienced by trafficked persons and smuggled persons rather than viewing the two as separate phenomena with different responses (Rao and Presenti 2012). This distinction might be difficult to make, both legally and practically.

Equally, other kinds of irregular and even legal migration can and often do involve violence, confinement, coercion, deception, and exploitation (Anderson and O'Connell Davidson 2002; Andrijasevic 2010; Derks et al 2006). As we have seen, employers actively seek migrant workers because they are exploitable. In this context, creating a distinction between trafficking and exploited migrant labor then means defining what constitutes acceptable and unacceptable levels of exploitation (Anderson and Andrijasevic 2008). This distinction is both difficult to make and morally questionable, as it creates hierarchies of suffering which "may reflect more the preconceptions and feelings of those who devise them than those who experience them" (Andrijasevic and Anderson 2009, 154).

In addition to exploitation of trafficked persons and other migrants being on a scale rather than existing in distinct categories, there are additional features that make trafficking appear similar to migration rather than being a distinct category. For example, a study conducted by Smriti Rao and Christina Presenti found a significantly higher likelihood of a state having high numbers of persons trafficked out of the country if said state is a transition economy, in which women have already achieved some level of economic mobility and independence (Rao and Presenti 2012). Equally, Rutvica Andrijasevic found in interviews conducted with trafficked women that their accounts of why and how they migrated did not differ significantly from other female migrants, mostly quoting dire economic conditions, problems at home, and desire for independence (Andrijasevic 2010, 56).

Immigration controls and stronger border protections are more likely to keep out women trying to migrate into the sex industry (as well as domestic work), which makes them more likely to engage third parties in the migration process, further amplifying their vulnerability. Depending on their involvement and on their willingness to exploit others, these third parties could in retrospect turn out to be agents, smugglers, or traffickers. Additionally, long traveling distances to consulates and embassies, and the difficulties of obtaining visas through regular channels, often leads to women (and men) requesting services from a third party, regardless of whether or not they qualify for an official visa and regardless of the third party charging more than official consulate's visa rates (Andrijasevic 2010, 38–40).

Thus visa regulations and border controls that attempt to channel migration into legally sanctioned schemes often increase the likelihood of third party involvement in facilitating travel and employment and consequently increase migrants' vulnerability to abuse and exploitation (Andrijasevic 2010, 45). Rutvica Andrijasevic reports from her interviews the recurring case of female migrants incurring debt and becoming dependent on third parties due to their status as undocumented migrants. In addition to being vulnerable to abuse by third parties exploiting their labor, undocumented status also exposes migrants to potential ill-treatment by border police (Andrijasevic 2010, 44).

Stricter immigration controls often unintentionally serve the economic interests of third parties. Paying third parties for irregular migration, as well as being apprehended by border police en route and the journey being prolonged, increases the migrants' debt to the third party and increases third parties' levels of control over migrants. Andrijasevic goes as far as to say that in an EU context "immigration regulations that aim at suppressing 'trafficking' and hampering the illegal movements of people work in favor of third parties as these become an alternative to the formally sanctioned EU migratory channels" (Andrijasevic 2010, 45).

Trafficked persons, like other undocumented migrants, choose not to seek help from the police due to fears of deportation. Some trafficked women report that they would only go to the police once all attempts to get hold of their passports failed, as it would mean accepting the risk of getting deported (Andrijasevic 2010, 75). This further demonstrates that immigration status plays a key factor in creating vulnerability and exploitation, one which trafficking narratives aim to erase, but countertrafficking policies reinforce.

The Problem with Current Countertrafficking Approaches

Countertrafficking policies often affect immigration policy in ways that result in more tightly controlled borders and more restrictive visa regulations as well as more extensive police investigations and raids, claiming that they will control or at least deter trafficking by reducing the involvement of organized crime in migratory processes (Chacon 2005; Lepp 2002; Kinney 2015). Evidence, however, points toward the opposite. Stronger borders force migration further underground, increase the potential violence and abuse to which women are subjected, and make facilitating cross-border movement, forced labor, and exploitative practices more profitable (Anderson and Andrijasevic 2008; Lepp 2002). Equally, rescue missions in red light districts often lead to a criminalization of migrant sex workers who are unwilling to be "rescued" as victims of trafficking, but may nonetheless find themselves in exploitative working conditions.

Instead of focusing on the exclusions that lead to exploitation and human trafficking, human trafficking is normally treated as an exceptional crime, which requires criminal law solutions, with victims who require "rescue" and temporary paternalistic protections. Thus, traffickers' explicit exploitation—of the vulnerabilities and implicit exclusions of trafficked persons from the political community—is maintained in trafficked persons continued status as non-rights holders and as "rescued" victims of trafficking.

The Criminal Law Approach and Idealized Victimhood

Today human trafficking is predominantly conceptualized within a criminal law framework at international level and in most domestic legislation. The UN Trafficking Protocol, the key international agreement on human trafficking, is part of the UN Convention Against Transnational Organized Crime, establishing the focus of counter-human trafficking action as both cross-border/transnational and crime-focused. In this, the UN Trafficking protocol takes the so-called "3P"-approach, focussing on a combination of prosecution, prevention, and victim protection. Both on international and domestic levels, the focus within this approach is on the criminalization of human trafficking and the prosecution of its perpetrators.

The criminal law approach then sets trafficking up as a binary criminal act with two polar opposites, the trafficker as the perpetrator and the trafficked person as the victim. By defining trafficking as a phenomenon that only concerns criminals in their active role as traffickers and trafficked persons as their passive victims, trafficking is placed outside of any larger societal context and trafficked persons are defined as mere props to the traffickers' crimes. Additionally, this binary approach obscures state contributions to conditions, which foster trafficking (Anderson and Andrijasevic 2008), such as exclusionary immigration regimes and lack of laborr controls (Costello 2015; Costello and Freedland 2014; Fudge 2012). This approach is problematic, as it ignores governments' involvements through the complex interplay of economic inequalities between countries of origin and destination countries, as well as the role of destination countries' immigration controls and labor regulations in creating the conditions that render people vulnerable to human trafficking (Andrijasevic and Anderson 2009).

The UN Protocol's definition of trafficking is founded on a narrow historic concept of human trafficking as "sexual slavery in migrant prostitution" (Doezema 2010; Thiemann 2016a). However, its definition encompasses both human trafficking for sexual exploitation and human trafficking for labor exploitation and services, as well as the exploitation of organ trading. Such a broad definition, built on such a narrow original victim category, makes it both too wide and too narrow, if trafficking is to be distinguished from other forms of exploitation, and from human smuggling.

The UN Trafficking Protocol also builds on a legacy of highly gendered countertrafficking legislation. On the surface, the UN Trafficking Protocol defines trafficking in gender-neutral terms and seems to apply it to all persons equally. However, there are a number of instances in which it blatantly or indirectly continues narratives of idealized victimhood and is gendered in problematic ways.

The text mentions the category of "women and children" on several occasions, switching from the wider construction of exploitation of all persons to a narrower category, which focuses on the vulnerability of women and children. The phrase "especially women and children" in the Preamble, but also throughout the text of the Protocol, echoes older white slavery and trafficking treaties, and satisfies the concerns of lobbying groups, which wanted to particularly highlight the situation of women and children in order to maintain the connection between trafficking and prostitution (Ditmore and Wijers 2003).

By mentioning the vulnerability of women and children without acknowledging the structural factors which create their vulnerability, the Protocol presents their vulnerability as inherent. Thus, while the inclusion of the term "especially women and children" in the title and the definition of the Protocol seems to recognize the gendered history and trafficking, it perpetuates a view of trafficking that conflates trafficking and prostitution and casts all trafficked persons into one mould, that of innocent women and children. Such a categorization makes it harder for "atypical" victims to receive assistance. Instead, this focus on prostitution and vulnerable, idealized victims ignores the global economic dimension of human trafficking. It lets us view human trafficking as a migration crisis of an exceptional exploitation committed by criminal organizations against very few individuals, which it sets up as a binary of absolute victims and absolute perpetrators. This assumption ignores that exploitative labor situations are common, rather than exceptional, and that exploitative forms of labor, including human trafficking, play a role in maintaining the global economy (Raigrodski 2015).

Thus, whereas gender is omnipresent in the focus on women and children in the Protocol, it acts to idealize women as victims, rather than to address their gendered vulnerabilities and to empower them as agents in their own right. The approach of focusing on trafficked persons only as victims, not as persons with agency, including the focus on prostitution and on "women and children," can be seen throughout the Protocol.

Similarly, the 2005 Council of Europe Convention on Action against Trafficking in Human Beings, while shifting its focus away from traffickers as criminals and from intercepting trafficking at the border, still maintains a focus of feminised victimhood. In fact, while using more gender-neutral language than the UN Protocol, the explanatory report of the Convention makes special note of the historic "White Slave Traffic" and—uncritically—sees human trafficking as a continuation of that legacy. Thus, it maintains the problematic notion of both conflating human trafficking and sex work and separating human trafficking from other migratory patterns.

In some passages, such as the following, the Convention seems to acknowledge the connection of women's global disadvantages and gendered issues in migration more broadly, for example when it states that the "[. . .] development of communications and the economic imbalances in the world have made trafficking in women, mainly for sexual exploitation purposes, more international than ever. There was first the 'white slave traffic', then trafficking from South to North, and now there is trafficking in human beings from the more disadvantaged regions to the more prosperous regions, whatever their geographical location (but in particular to western Europe)." (Council of Europe Convention on Action Against Trafficking in Human Beings and its Explanatory Report 2005, 209).

Equally, the report further points out that "women, according to existing data, are the main target group of trafficking in human beings and to the fact that women, who are susceptible to being victims, are often marginalized even before becoming victims of trafficking and find themselves victims of poverty and unemployment more often than men. Therefore, measures to protect and promote the rights of women victims of trafficking must take into account this double marginalization, as women and as victims [. . .]" (Council of Europe Convention on Action Against Trafficking in Human Beings and its Explanatory Report 2005, 210).

Whereas the acknowledgement of women's different needs from men is positive, particularly in light of male-focussed international legal and policy norms, the way in which womanhood and victimhood are linked is nonetheless problematic. The wording "who are susceptible to being victims" seems to imply that women are inherently more likely to be victims, reiterating the UN Trafficking Protocol's problematic notion of "women and children" as one passive, agency-free entity.

Just like the UN Trafficking Protocol, the Council of Europe explanation implies that being "susceptible" to victimhood is intrinsically linked to womanhood, rather than created by existing societal exclusions women face due to the gendered effects of policymaking and legislation on labor, migration, and the regulation of reproductive work—sex work in particular. As a consequence, while the Convention suggests a gender-sensitive response to dealing with women victims of trafficking, it nonetheless ignores gender as a factor which affects all labor and migration regulations and therefore creates women's vulnerability. Thus, the Convention's seemingly gender-aware response is too limited in its scope to be meaningful in its effects.

In political rhetoric in member states, human trafficking has been portrayed as one of the main methods through which people enter Western countries. The British Home Office Minister stated in March 2007 that "three quarters of illegal immigrants to Britain are trafficked" (Andrijasevic and Anderson 2009, 153–154), giving an impression that the government wants to help all these victims of a terrible crime, while at the same time protecting Britain's borders. Thus for the general discourse in the media "Victim of Trafficking" creates both fears of floods of irregular migrants, and pity for trafficked persons. This ambiguity helps to contribute to political claims for remedies for "real victims" rather than for rights for all irregular migrants as human beings and for (irregular) migrant workers as workers.

The categorization of trafficked persons is difficult, and, as mentioned earlier, the differentiation between smuggled persons, exploited illegal migrants, and victims of trafficking is almost impossible to make in practice (Andrijasevic and Anderson, 2009). Even when exploited migrants meet the official and implied criteria of a "real" victim of trafficking, this does not necessarily afford them improved treatment. Those who meet the legal requirements of the victim of trafficking category can only access temporary and conditional protections, for example temporary leave to remain. Attempts to "rescue" trafficked persons, particularly in feminized jobs such as in nail bars, massage parlors and brothels, usually includes first arresting and detaining suspected trafficked persons, and ultimately repatriating them. Thus, women migrant workers, particularly sex workers, are often the ones who bear the cost of a perception of human trafficking as a unique migration crisis. They are excluded from labor protections, while being not only at risk of exploitation, but also at risk of unwelcome "rescue" and return to their country of origin.

Some argue that this is favourable to alternative outcomes, as it saves women from their captors. However, this approach ignores the fact that a large number of "victims of trafficking" do not want to be rescued—and in fact do not perceive their situation as requiring this kind of interference. This line of argument also overlooks women's socioeconomic and family conditions, which caused them to migrate in the first place and often have not changed since, making trafficked women likely to remigrate (Lepp 2002). Through the continuous stress of the criminal-victim dichotomy, trafficking policy reiterates ideas of women as passive and naïve victims who need such "rescue" from traffickers, even if "rescue" means forcible return to their home country. Equally, women need "protection" by the state, even though this may include the "protection" of being kept out by Western countries or being forced to stay "at home" by countries of origin.

Additionally, making so-called protections in destination countries dependent on either a persons' worthiness as a victim (by fulfilling the narrow victim category) or their usefulness to the prosecution (by being a credible victim) makes help for trafficked persons conditional. This conditionality of services, together with the time limits imposed on both residency and access to services, leads to a normalization of victims of trafficking as recipients of charitable gifts. They are not perceived as rights-holders whose rights have been violated, but instead as passive victims receiving generous care that they are not entitled to.

By casting trafficked women in particular as helpless, agency-free victims, who are forced into prostitution and unable to escape, they are rendered simultaneously powerless and innocent. By implying that these women never had a choice and never wanted to be in the destination country, they are also absolved from crossing state borders by migrating (supposedly against their will) and from engaging in prostitution (again, against their will).

By creating this narrative, trafficked women are set them apart from (other) exploited migrants (O'Connell Davidson, 2010).

In creating this victim of trafficking narrative of absolute helplessness, governments can be seen as saving innocent victims, while at the same time to be maintaining exclusion and restrictions in immigration regimes and silencing criticism of restrictive immigration policies. Thus the trafficking narrative keeps in place the structures that create human trafficking, while "rescuing" those who are able and willing to present themselves as absolute victims. Furthermore, such an approach ignores the underlying structures in labor and migration created by government policy and legislation, as well as the effect of social structures and prejudice, and the harmful exclusions and stigmatization faced by (migrant) sex workers in particular.

As a result, criminal law based antitrafficking initiatives are based on "regulating women's sexuality, curtailing migration processes and protecting the State by responding to a popular idea of trafficking as transnational organized crime. [. . .] These interventions [are] not only futile in terms of eradicating and preventing trafficking, but also ultimately harmful for women, and for both potential and actual victims of labor and sexual exploitation," (Daglistani and Milivojevic 2013) as they perpetuate gendered concepts of victimhood and exclude women from truly rights-based responses.

Thus the victim category, which requires absolute and passive victims, maintains trafficked persons' exclusion from labor rights and human rights at the hand of the traffickers and ignores the underlying exclusions they face as women, migrants and sex workers, which facilitated their initial alienation from those rights.

Alternative Approaches

The victim protection measures in the criminal law approach are sometimes conflated with a so-called human rights approach. Critical voices have long stated that this approach has failed to take into account root causes, both in supply and in demand, of human trafficking.

Instead, a labor rights approach could address "structural labor market conditions and practices that shape workers' vulnerability and inferior bargaining power in the workplace" (Shamir 2012). In order to do so one has to understand human trafficking as existing at one end of a spectrum of exploitation, not as a separate labor or migration crisis. Additionally, trafficking has to be seen as a feature of a neoliberal capitalist market, which has created a demand for cheap labor, deregulation of working practices and malleable precarious workers. In this context, employers, and traffickers benefit from underregulated working conditions, which make exploitation likely for workers, particularly for those rendered vulnerable by their immigration or minority status.

Whereas this critique is crucially important, in order to address the situation of trafficked persons, particularly in the sex industry, such an approach also needs to engage with women's gendered exclusions from workers' rights on the basis of the binary notion of "productive vs. reproductive labor." In this, sex workers' exclusions from people's notions of what constitutes work, is particularly pervasive. Alternative approaches to human trafficking thus not only need to link human trafficking with exploitative work conditions more broadly, but need to particularly embrace women's work in nonstandard occupations, including sex work, as labor. Furthermore, such policies need to reimagine trafficked persons, including those in the sex industry, as workers with both rights and agency.

Conclusion

Focusing on trafficking as a category distinct from other forms of irregular migration shifts the focus away from a larger picture of underlying vulnerabilities. Equally, casting women migrants' vulnerability in the trafficking context as inherent ignores the contribution policy and legislation make to the creation of gendered vulnerability in the migration process. Whereas some countries favor family migration, routes for skilled, regular migration often exclude women, as there is a perceived higher demand for migrants in male-dominated professions (Briddick 2015; Kofman 2014). Women are thus more likely to enter precarious working conditions in the informal sector, particularly in domestic work and prostitution, since additional stereotypes attributed to women are those of providing care at home and of providing sexual gratification (Chammartín 2002). Ignoring such gendered differences in migration and labor policies and instead focusing on human trafficking approaches the phenomenon from the wrong angle. It restricts the dimension of harm that is experienced by trafficked women to that perpetrated by traffickers and—in the context of sex work—by pimps.

Whereas traffickers, pimps, and employers exploit migrants' vulnerabilities, they do not create them. Not only exclusionary immigration and emigration policies, but also government-sanctioned restrictions of vulnerable migrants' access to social rights, such as a possibility to sue for wages not received, create the basis for exploitability. In the case of human trafficking for sexual exploitation, this exploitability is exacerbated as the gains from prostitution are not considered to be wages at all, as prostitution is not considered work in most countries' legislation. Equally, sex workers experience fear of criminalization in their profession in addition to their immigration status. By directing the attention to the individual culpability of traffickers and by casting trafficked persons as passive victims, states can obscure their own role in creating the vulnerable status of trafficked persons. This leads to a perception of human trafficking as a crime with clear victims and perpetrators, a migration crisis in which states play the role of rescuers, rather than contributors to the phenomenon.

Instead, an approach focused on gendered exclusions in access to labor rights would enable us to see trafficked persons as on a continuum of vulnerability. Citizen-employees, regular migrant workers, irregular migrant workers, smuggled or trafficked workers all experience vulnerabilities, with added layers of vulnerability for those who belong to gendered, religious, or ethnic minorities. A response to the crises of workers' rights, with particular focus on gender and migration status, could alleviate some of the root causes of human trafficking. Treating trafficked persons as a unique category just isolates them.

References

Adams, N. 2003. "Anti-Trafficking Legislation: Protection or Deportation?" *Feminist Review* 73:135–139.

Agustín, L. M. 2007. *Sex at the Margins: Migration, Labour Markets and the Rescue Industry*. New York: Zed Books.

Anderson, B. 2000. *Doing the Dirty Work? The Global Politics of Domestic Labour* London: Palgrave Macmillan.

Anderson, B. 2012. "Where's the Harm in That? Immigration Enforcement, Trafficking, and the Protection of Migrants' Rights." *American Behavioral Scientist*, 56, no. 9: 1241–1257.

Anderson, B. 2013. *Us and Them? The Dangerous Politics of Immigration Control.* New York: Oxford University Press.

Anderson, B., and R. Andrijasevic. 2008. "Sex, Slaves and Citizens: The Politics of Anti-Trafficking." *Soundings* 40: 135–145.

Anderson, B., and J. O'Connell Davidson. 2002. "Trafficking—A Demand Led Problem?: A Multi-Country Pilot Study." Save the Children.

Andrijasevic, R. 2003. "The Difference Borders Make: (Il)legality, Migration and Trafficking in Italy among Eastern European Women in Prostitution." In *Uprootings/Regroundings: Questions of Home and Migration*, edited by S. Ahmed, C. Castaneda, and A.-M. Fortie, 251–272. Berg Publishers.

Andrijasevic, R. 2009. "Sex on the Move: Gender, Subjectivity and Differential Inclusion." *Subjectivity* 29, no. 1: 389–406.

Andrijasevic, R. 2010. *Migration, Agency and Citizenship in Sex Trafficking.* London: Palgrave Macmillan.

Andrijasevic, R., and B. Anderson. 2009a. "Anti-Trafficking Campaigns: Decent? Honest? Truthful?" *Feminist Review* 92: 151–155.

Andrijasevic, R., and B. Anderson. 2009b. "Conflicts of Mobility: Migration, Labour and Political Subjectivities." *Subjectivity* 29: 363–366.

Baer, J. A. 1978. *The Chains of Protection: The Judicial Response to Women's Protective Legislation.* Westport, CT: Greenwood.

Basok, T., and N. Piper. 2012. "Management Versus Rights: Women's Migration and Global Governance in Latin America and the Caribbean." *Feminist Economics* 18, no. 2: 35–61.

Boucher, A. K. 2009. "Picking the Best and the Brightest: Gendering Skilled Immigration Policy in Australia and Canada." Conference paper presented at The European Consortium of Political Research (ECPR), First European Conference on Politics and Gender. Queen's University Belfast, Ireland.

Boyd, M. 1986. "Immigrant Women in Canada" In *International Migration: The Female Experience*, edited by R. Simon and C. Brettell, 45–61. Totowa, NJ: Rowman & Allanheld.

Boyle, P., and K. Halfacree. 2002. *Migration and Gender in the Developed World.* New York: Routledge.

Bludau, H., and P. Ezzeddine. 2013. "Seeing Gender in Migration. An Introduction." In *Special Issue: "Gender and Family in Migration." Lidé Města/Urban People:* 15, no. 2: 179–184.

Briddick, C. 2015. "Sex Discrimination and UK Immigration Law." COMPAS Blog http://compasoxfordblog.co.uk/2015/07/sex-discrimination-and-uk-immigration-law/

Calavita, K. 2006. "Gender, Migration, and Law: Crossing Borders and Bridging Disciplines." *International Migration Review* 40, no. 1. doi:10.1111/j.1747-7379.2006.00005.x

Chacon, J. M. 2005. "Misery and Myopia: Understanding the Failures of U.S. Efforts to Stop Human Trafficking." *Fordham Law Review* 74: 2977–3029.

Chammartin, G, 2002. "The Feminization of International Migration." ILO Report 37. http://www.eif.gov.cy/mlsi/dl/genderequality.nsf/0/AFBE56C70CCE41DFC22579A70031B56A/$file/feminization_of_migration.pdf

Chapkis, W. 2003. "Trafficking, Migration, and the Law Protecting Innocents, Punishing Immigrants." *Gender & Society* 17, no. 6: 923–937.

Chapman, T., and J. L. Hockey. 1999. "The Ideal Home as It Is Imagined and as It Is Lived." In *Ideal Homes? Social Change and Domestic Life*, edited by Tony Chapman and Jennifer Lorna Hockey, 1–14. New York: Routledge.

Chuang, J. 2006. "Beyond a Snapshot: Preventing Human Trafficking in the Global Economy." *Indiana Journal of Global Legal Studies* 13, no. 1: 137–163.

Costello, C. 2014. "Migrants and Forced Labour: A Labour Law Response." In *The Autonomy of Labour Law*, edited by Alan Bogg et al. New York: Hart; 189–228.

Costello, C., and M. Freedland, eds. *Migrants at Work: Immigration and Vulnerability in Labour Law*. New York: Oxford University Press.

Daglistani, S., and S. Milivojevic. 2013. "Appropriating the Rights of Women: Moral Panics, Victims and Exclusionary Agendas in Domestic and Cross-Border Sex Crimes." *Women's Studies International Forum* 40: 230–242.

Dhar, R. 2012. "Women and International Migration: A Cross-Cultural Analysis." *Social Change* 42, no. 1: 93–102.

Derks, A., R. Henke, and L. Vanna. 2006. "Review of a Decade of Research on Trafficking in Persons, Cambodia." The Asia Foundation, https://asiafoundation.org/resources/pdfs/CBTIPreview.pdf

Ditmore, M., and M. Wijers. 2003. "The Negotiations on the UN Protocol on Trafficking in Persons." *Nemesis* 79. doi:10.14197/atr.20121544

Docquier, F., and H. Rapoport. 2011. "Globalization, Brain Drain and Development." *Institute for the Study of Labor Discussion Paper* 5590. http://ftp.iza.org/dp5590.pdf

Docquier, F., L. Lowell, and A. Marfouk. 2009. "A Gendered Assessment of Highly Skilled Emigration." *Population and Development Review* 35, no. 2: 297–321.

Doezema, J. 2010. *Sex Slaves and Discourse Masters: The Construction of Trafficking.* London: Zed.

Fudge, J. 2012. "Precarious Migrant Status and Precarious Employment: The Paradox of International Rights for Migrant Workers." *Comparative Labor Law & Policy Journal* 34, no. 1: 95–132.

Gallagher, A. 2006. "Recent Legal Developments in the Field of Human Trafficking: A Critical Review of the 2005 European Convention and Related Instruments." *European Journal of Migration and Law* 8: 163–189.

Goldsack, L. 1999. "A Haven in a Heartless World? Women and Domestic Violence." In *Ideal Homes?: Social Change and Domestic Life*, edited by T. Chapman and Jennifer Lorna Hockey. London: Routledge: 121–132.

Kapur, R. 2002. "The Tragedy of Victimization Rhetoric: Ressurecting the 'Native' Subject in International/Post-Colonial Feminist Legal Politics." *Harvard Human Rights Journal* 15.1: 131–138.

Kapur, R., and J. Sanghera. 2000. "An Assessment of Laws and Policies for the Prevention and Control of Trafficking in Nepal." The Asia Foundation. Policy Analysis. https://asiafoundation.org/resources/pdfs/nepaltraffickingassesment.pdf

Kawar, M. 2004. "Gender and Migration: Why Are Women More Vulnerable?" In *Femmes en mouvement: genre, migrations et nouvelle division internationale du travail*, edited by F. Reysoo and C. J. Verschuur. Geneva: IUED.

Kinney, E. 2015. "Victims, Villains, and Valiant Rescuers: Unpacking Sociolegal Constructions of Human Trafficking and Crimmigration in Popular Culture." In *The Illegal Business of Human Trafficking*, edited by M. J. Guia. New York: Springer, 87–108.

Kofman, E. 2014. "Towards a Gendered Evaluation of (Highly) Skilled Immigration Policies in Europe." *International Migration* 52, no. 3: 116–128.

León, M. 2010. "Migration and Care Work in Spain: The Domestic Sector Revisited." *Social Policy and Society* 9, no. 3: 409–418.

Lepp, A. 2002. "Trafficking in Women and the Feminization of Migration: The Canadian Context" *Canadian Woman Studies* 21, no. 4: 90–99.

Lutz, H. 2012. *Migration and Domestic Work: A European Perspective on a Global Theme.* Aldershot, UK: Ashgate.

Mantouvalou, V. 2012. "Human Rights for Precarious Workers: The Legislative Precariousness of Domestic Labor." *Comparative Labor Law & Policy Journal* 34, no. 1: 133–166.

Meares, C. 2010. "A Fine Balance: Women, Work and Skilled Migration." *Women's Studies International Forum* 33, no. 5: 473–481.

Miller, A. M. 2004. "Sexuality, Violence Against Women, and Human Rights: Women Make Demands and Ladies Get Protection." *Health and Human Rights Journal* 7, no. 2: 16–47.

Morris, E. 2009. *Second Class Migrants? Gender and Migration in the European Union: Explaining Gender (In)Equality in EU Immigration, Asylum, and Trafficking Policymaking*. Saarbrucken, Germany: VDM.

Murphy, C. 2015. "Access to Justice for Undocumented Migrant Domestic Workers in Europe: The Consequenes of Constructed Illegality." In *Care, Migration, and Human Rights: Law and Practice*, edited by Siobhán Mullally. London: Routledge; 120–140.

Nakanishi, T. 1983. "Equality or Protection—Protective Legislation for Women in Japan." *International Labour Review* 122, no. 5: 609–622.

O'Connell Davidson, J. 2010. "New Slavery, Old Binaries: Human Trafficking and the Borders of 'Freedom.'" *Global Networks* 10.2. doi:10.1111/j.1471-0374.2010.00284.x

Oishi, N, 2002. "Gender and Migration: An Integrative Approach." Center for Comparative Immigration Studies. https://ccis.ucsd.edu/_files/wp49.pdf

OSCE. 2009. *Guide to Gender-Sensitive Labour Market Policies*. Vienna: OSCE.

Pérez, M. 2012. "Emergency Frames: Gender Violence and Immigration Status in Spain." *Feminist Economics* 18, no. 2: 265–290.

Piper, N. 2003. "Feminization of Labor Migration as Violence Against Women International, Regional, and Local Nongovernmental Organization Responses in Asia." *Violence Against Women* 9, no. 6: 723–745.

Price, J. M. 2002. "The Apotheosis of Home and the Maintenance of Spaces of Violence" *17 Hypatia* 17, no. 4: 39–70.

Raigrodski, D. 2015. "Economic Migration Gone Wrong: Trafficking in Persons Through the Lens of Gender, Labor and Globalization." *Indiana International & Comparative Law Review* 25, no. 1: 79–114.

Rao, S., and C. Presenti. 2012. "Understanding Human Trafficking Origin: A Cross-Country Empirical Analysis." *Feminist Economics* 18, no. 2: 231–263.

Shamir, H. 2012 "A Labor Paradigm for Human Trafficking" *UCLA Law Review* 60: 76–136.

Sharma, N. 2005. "Anti-Trafficking Rhetoric and the Making of a Global Apartheid." *NWSA Journal* 17, no. 3: 88–111

Thiemann, I.K. 2016a. "Villains and Victims, but No Workers—Why a Prosecution-Focussed Approach to Human Trafficking Fails Trafficked Persons." In Special Issue: Prosecuting Human Trafficking. *Anti-Trafficking Review* 6: 126–129.

Thiemann, I.K. 2016b. "She Is Not Just a Victim: An Intersectional Feminist Labour Law Approach to Human Trafficking into the Sex Industry." PhD diss., University College London.

True, J. 2012. *The Political Economy of Violence against Women*. New York: Oxford University Press.

Truong, T-D. 1996. "Gender, International Migration and Social Reproduction: Implications for Theory, Policy, Research and Networking." *Asian and Pacific Migration Journal* 5, no. 1: 27–52.

van Hooren, F. 2010. "When Families Need Immigrants: The Exceptional Position of Migrant Domestic Workers and Care Assistants in Italian Immigration Policy." *Bulletin of Italian Politics* 2, no. 2: 21–38.

van Liempt, I. 2007. *Navigating Borders: Inside Perspectives on the Process of Human Smuggling into the Netherlands*. Amsterdam: Amsterdam University Press.

Wikander, U., A. Kessler-Harris, and J. E. Lewis. 1995. *Protecting Women: Labor Legislation in Europe, the United States, and Australia, 1880–1920*. Champaign: University of Illinois Press.

Zhyvytsya, O., and K. Keil. 2012. "The Female Face Of Migration." Caritas Internationalis. https://www.caritas.org/2012/03/female-face-of-migration/

PART IX

INTEGRATION, MULTICULTURALISM, AND MEMBERSHIP

CHAPTER 42

SANCTUARY AND UNSETTLING "THE" REFUGEE CRISIS

JEN BAGELMAN

"The" Crisis: Setting a Political Stage

In the summer of 2015 the image of a drowned toddler, Aylan Kurdi, galvanized concern about the problems and perils of displacement. In the weeks, months—and now years—that have followed, harrowing visuals and stories have pervaded media, depicting what has been widely articulated as "the refugee crisis."

In keeping with the spirit of this *Handbook*, the chapter approaches this now-common phrase ("the refugee crisis") not as a given starting point but, rather, a powerful discourse to be questioned. What are the political contours of this discourse—how do they affectively shape political imaginations, and what do they expose and conceal? I would like to suggest that there are two especially salient discursive features worth unpacking: first, the narrative of newness, and second, the implied notion of a singular crisis.

With regards to the first dimension, it is vital to consider how this phrase orients us toward imagining displacement as a sudden, or even unexpected, event, rather than an enduring condition. We see this articulated by media outlets like *The Guardian* who mark "the" crisis as a phenomenon "suddenly born" in 2015 (Kingsley 2015). While the forced migrations which many experience today are intensifying (indeed, UNHCR estimates that over sixty million people are currently displaced, a figure which is unprecedented) to presume this is, in any way, new eclipses the persistent genealogies that give rise to contemporary forms of forced migration. As scholars, from various disciplines have argued, critically interrogating this narrative of "the new" remains important political work (Isin 2008; Walker 2010).

In addition to framing displacement as new, this discourse, which places primacy on "the" crisis, presents displacement as if this were a singular issue impacting a distinct group.

As the world's media focuses on "the" refugee, what other (sometimes internally) displaced groups are being left out of the discussion? Reese Jones, in his text *Violent Borders*, makes the case that while drawing attention to refugee struggles through signifiers like #RefugeesWelcome may unite a cause, it also serves to distract from the plight of many other migrants who never get even get counted as refugees (Jones 2016) Figure 42.1.

In a similar vein, activist Harsha Walia argues in *Undoing Border Imperialism* that exclusively focusing on particular refugee routes (notably Syrian refugees crossing the Med to Europe), invisibilizes the many other migrant journeys taking place in forgotten corridors (Walia 2014). Furthermore, in highlighting the struggles entailed in movements across particular routes, we remain insensitive to the challenges of being held still. As a narrowing of attention gets placed on movement, how can we begin to understand the struggles facing people indefinitely held in detention, such as the countless asylum-seekers detained on remote islands like Nauru? Their deaths, as Alison Mountz has argued, in putrid prison cells are invisibilized when we focus simply on the question of the refugee (Mountz 2015).

The singular framing not only obscures the violence experienced by many who do not fit within the refugee category, it also evades the persistent colonial legacies that play a role in producing intractable forms of violence. It positions certain nation-states (such as Canada where the author grew up as a settler) as a benevolent host, welcoming refugees, rather than as an endemic part of a settler-colonial logic producing displacement and dispossession. By way of example: at the very same moment that the Canadian government celebrates welcoming approximately 30,000 Syrian refugees, it actively denies permanent citizenship to countless temporary migrant laborers who are separated from their families and it continues to develop and expand energy projects that displace Indigenous communities from their unceded territories.

Finally, the singular framing of crisis paints a misleading picture that displacement is delimited to contained geographies. As critical border scholars have long-argued, given

FIGURE 42.1 "Refugees Welcome"

Source: walterw.a on Flickr. Graffiti: *Refugees Welcome*. Retrieved from https://www.flickr.com/photos/walterwa/13904424715. Licensed under CC BY-SA 2.0.

the increasingly interconnected and diffuse ways in which bodies/objects/energies are managed through harmonized control it is problematic to assume "the crisis" belongs to a one particular region (Amoore 2006; Bigo 2000). International agreements, such as Canada's Safe Third Country Agreement with the United States, are but one example whereby hostile bordering is externalized, rendering it impossible to locate "the" crisis within tidy geographical lines. Refusing this statist approach, geographers like Nick Gill, Deirdre Conlon, Dominique Moran and Andrew Burridge have suggested that it is vital to examine entangled border regimes and carceral logics, or "circuits," that produce intersecting forms of violence (2017). To unsettle the singularity of crisis and instead address intersecting circuits of violence (colonial, environmental, economic, gendered) is to more radically imagine both collective culpability and routes toward change.

In a geopolitical context wherein a delimited crisis rhetoric pervades how can we orient ourselves toward more expansive political routes? It is one thing to suggest that we need to move beyond the crisis frame, but how do we meaningfully engage to do this work in our lives? This chapter suggests that sanctuary (as a lexicon and grounded movement) offers some generative possibilities here. Sanctuary can interrupt dangerously myopic framings of "the refugee crisis" and, in so doing, provide more robust possibilities for responding to intersecting forms of violence.

In its most political form sanctuary offers an incisive and practice-oriented critique to the narrowness of a crisis lens that reduces global displacement to a new or somehow singular event. The long-standing practices of sanctuary—with complex and even conflicting roots—have a capacity to shake us from the grip of presentism that constructs today's violence as fresh and instead situates contemporary displacement within a much longer and fermenting historicity. Moreover, sanctuary can provide us with a powerful set of examples which expose how hostility and violence can be actively challenged.

To make this case, it is first necessary to provide some historical traces that are part of the rich concept of sanctuary. Second, this chapter will explore how sanctuary reemerges and becomes mobilized in contemporary geopolitical landscapes through diverse tactics. Third, building on a growing field of sanctuary scholarship, it argues that while these expressions are varied, they are best understood as representing a collective movement. However, diverging from recent sanctuary scholarship, this chapter makes the argument that this movement cannot be understood through conventional scalar logics of the city, the nation, or even the planetary. Instead, I contend that emergent sanctuary practices are better approached as a *global-intimate movement* that seeks to challenge global inequities by building solidarities in and through the places we inhabit everyday: our neighborhoods, modes of public transit, schools, hospitals . . .

Roots

Sanctuary is a complex lexicon and practice that belies simple starting points. For thousands of years sanctuary has been expressed through various religious and spiritual traditions such as Christianity, Islam, Judaism, Buddhism, Baha'I, Sikhism, and Hinduism. As diverse as these traces are, one connective tissue that runs through is the desire to provide a form of safety—or refuge—to prosecuted peoples within a sacred space and time (Rabben 2011). As Michael Chmielewski has explored in his recent study, these practices of protection also extend to the more-than-human world, with sanctuary as an expression of providing protection to animals and wildlife (Chmielewski 2017).

Although posing a singular trajectory of sanctuary or origin of would be misleading, some of the earliest expressions of sanctuary can be traced back to Hebrew traditions of the six contained Cities of Refuge. These enclosed cities have been described as providing "refuge to anyone, including a foreigner who was accused of manslaughter, thus preventing the automatic use of blood feud as a rough and ready and often indiscriminately unfair route to justice" (Barnett and Bhogal 2009). This is illuminated in passage from Numbers 35: 9–15, "these six towns will be a refuge for Israelites, aliens and any other people living among them, so that anyone who has killed accidentally can flee there." Such safety, however, was not extended to all. When the slayer reached the city "he had to first prove through a trial by the 'congregation,' probably the elders of the city that acted as a court, that the killing had indeed been accidental" (Bau 1985, 125). If accepted, the subject was offered protection from revenge as long they stayed within the sanctuary's municipal confines; however, if they failed the test the subject was left to their fate (*Numbers* 35: 12). Here, it is important to note the ways in which an exclusionary logic is entwined with seemingly inclusive practice of welcome (Bagelman 2016).

Another significant trace of sanctuary emerges in ancient Roman law dating back to 392 CE, where sanctuary privileges were granted to churches rather than cities (Lippert 2005). The practice of church sanctuary continued in medieval Europe whereby those accused of crimes could be offered protection from the sovereign forms of power through church asylum. Those people seeking sanctuary (called suppliants), were required to perform their abjection: tolling a bell and kneeling to religious authorities, and making their claim in passive terms. So too, the suppliant was often expected to bear a mark of inferiority on his or her body in the form of a letter branded on upon the skin. In other instances, those entering sanctuary were required to "wear a black gown with a large yellow cross" to clearly mark out the vulnerability, and passivity, of the person seeking refuge (Bagelman 2016, 81). This ritual of sanctuary was recognized in English law for over a thousand years (Shoemaker 2011). With the growth of liberalism in Europe in the seventeenth and eighteenth centuries most sanctuary practices in the West were abolished.

Reemergences

With the increasing illegalization of migrants and refugees through exclusionary national immigration policies in Western countries, the second half of the twentieth century has seen the reemergence of sanctuary practices. Churches in Denmark, France,

Finland, Germany, Norway, the United States and other countries began to offer sanctuary to irregularized migrants (Bauder 2017).[1] In this context sanctuary emerges as a response to an intensifying problem: the criminalization of certain types of migration. While church sanctuary no longer held legal weight, the collective memory of it as a religiously sanctioned form of alternative justice persists in these church-based expressions. Indeed, this historical resonance is weighty enough that most governments and legal authorities avoided entering into the confines of a church said to harbor people seeking sanctuary (Rabben 2011).

In addition to church-based expressions of sanctuary, which tend to entail protecting people facing imminent arrest or deportation by immigration authorities in a physical shelter (Lippert 2005), there was, in the 1980s, a revival of whole cities emerging as spaces of sanctuary. The following section explores how these practices have manifested in the three national contexts often cited as particularly vibrant expressions of city-based sanctuary—namely the United States, Canada, and the United Kingdom—focusing on these particular cases, in part, because of their international significance and also the author's own personal activist involvement and grounded knowledge of these movements.

San Francisco's 1985 "City of Refuge" resolution represents a significant crystallization of contemporary city-based sanctuary, and is even referred to as the emergence of a contemporary urban-based movement (Bauder 2017; Mancina 2016; Ridgley 2008). This resolution, and the subsequent 1989 "City of Refuge" Ordinance, was designed to ensure a safe-haven for Central American refugees fleeing civil conflict. While the initial resolution was in many ways largely "symbolic," the Ordinance concretely prohibited the use of city funds and resources to assist in federal immigration enforcement (Mancina 2016). Moreover, this Ordinance rejected the cooperation with investigations by or surveillance request from foreign government. The intention was to undermine the exclusionary municipal administration against, primarily, El Salvadorian and Guatemalan refugees who were not extended residency status.

The 2007 New Sanctuary Movement in the United States expanded its focus from "newly arrived" refugees toward illegalized migrants residing in the United States. The purpose of this movement was to insist that all residents, regardless of their legal citizenship status, have a right to the city. Dozens of cities in the United States followed. Concrete policies, such as Don't Ask Don't Tell (DADT), emerged to prohibit the use of municipal police funds and city administration from "requesting, recording, or disseminating status information and deny cooperation with federal immigration authorities unless required by federal or state law" (Bauder 2017, 3). Municipal ID cards have also been issued by a number of cities—such as San Franscico—to allow all residents to identify themselves regardless of whether they hold state-issued ID such as a drivers license.

Of course, in the context of President Donald Trump's controversial threat to defund sanctuary cities, we have seen these sanctuary practices under increased pressure. Yet, in this context, we have also seen an intensification of sanctuary activism: San Francisco has become the first sanctuary city to file a lawsuit against the Trump's Executive Order

13769, which requires cities to either comply with immigration authorities or lose federal funding. A number of other cities have responded similarly, Mayor Martin J. Walsh of Boston declared: "We will do everything lawful in our power to protect you. If necessary, we will use City Hall itself to shelter and protect anyone who's targeted unjustly." Although the particularities of how sanctuary cities are responding to harsh immigration policies differs greatly, we are witnessing efforts by sanctuary organizers to insist on the divisions between federal and local forms of governance.

During the 1980s many urban-sanctuary initiatives similarly emerged in Canada. Toronto was the first city in Canada to declare itself a sanctuary city, with Toronto City council voting in 2013 to adopt a formal policy allowing undocumented migrants to access city services, such as emergency medical services, public health programs, emergency shelters, fire protection, and libraries. Following Toronto's declaration Hamilton, Ontario also declared itself a sanctuary city 2014. Here the Hamilton City Council voted unanimously to allow undocumented immigrants to access city-funded services such as housing and food banks.[2] And, in response to Trump's Executive Order, the city council of London, Ontario unanimously declared London a sanctuary city in January 2017, with Montreal following suit shortly thereafter. Currently, a number of other cities—and rural places—are considering motions to declare themselves places of sanctuary (Marshall, Schmid-Scott, Gill, and Bagelman, in preparation).

The United Kingdom (UK) has also experienced a robust sanctuary city revival, beginning in Sheffield in 2005. The emergence of this movement was largely animated as a response to the national policy adopted in 1999 to disperse asylum-seekers to different towns and cities in the UK (Darling 2010). In 2009, the city council of Sheffield crafted a manifesto outlining key areas of concern and one hundred supporting organizations signed on. A city's status as a place of sanctuary is not necessarily a formal governmental designation. The organization City of Sanctuary encourages local grassroots groups throughout the UK and Ireland to build a culture of hospitality toward asylum-seekers (Squire and Bagelman 2012). According to its latest report, there are now over ninety City of Sanctuary initiatives in cities, towns, villages, and boroughs across UK and Ireland.

It is important to note that the sanctuary designation has not been taken up evenly among migrant justice activists. Many organizers (in Vancouver, Canada, for instance) have resisted the full implementation of this term, concerned that it can serve as a bland symbolic gesture rather than a tangible response to the precariousness of many residents. Some organizers in Vancouver have, instead, adopted the language and policy of "Access to City Services without Fear" (Sanctuary City, n.d.). In April 2016, through grassroots mobilization, led by groups like No One is Illegal, City of Vancouver councilors unanimously approved this policy to provide "residents with Uncertain or No Immigration Status" access to services without fear that employees will share their information with public agencies that could deport them. This means that City staff will not ask for immigration status in the provision of City services and the City will not pass information about immigration status to other orders of government unless required by law. The policy's power rests in its principle of noncompliance or noncooperation with Canadian Border Services Agency (CBSA) enforcement. While this resembles the forms of sanctuary organizing in cities like Toronto, what distinguishes this approach is the ambivalence attitude toward the term "sanctuary city." Rather than refer to "the city" as if it were a totalizing entity that has or has not achieved safety, organizers approach particular aspects of and services in the city such as: health, transit, food, and housing. This targeted multisectorial approach, which addresses specific services, illuminates a more variegated urban reality wherein certain sites are understood safe to differing degrees at different times. And, rather than address how lack of services impact only particular residents (i.e., refugees) organizers identify how these services are experienced differently, depending on one's gender, age, citizenship, or sexuality. This mode of organizing therefore more explicitly seeks to take on an intersectional approach, building solidarities between the growing number of people negatively impacted by Vancouver which—though often celebrated as Canada's most livable city—is also an occupied, gentrified, carceral city.

Vitally, the Vancouver example illuminates how sanctuary can be mobilized as an ongoing *process,* rather than a product. Vancouver-based organizers have not entirely rejected the ambition of sanctuary; rather, they are clear that their orientation to sanctuary is dynamic, ongoing rather than static or complete (Walia 2014). By insisting on a policy that does not rely on a language of "sanctuary city," this movement insists that sanctuary is a work-in-progress. This progress is occurring at different speeds, in different places. Victories across services are not evenly won, and so attention is placed on particular (minor) success in specific sectors. Grassroots organizers have urged the city to drop the term "sanctuary" from this policy because there exist substantial gaps and attending to these gaps through focused campaigns, such as "Transportation Not Deportation," is vital. Indeed this campaign recently uncovered a Memorandum of Understanding (MOU) between transit police and the Canadian Border Services Agency—a document that transit police had previously said did not exist. Through pointed campaigning there has been a cancellation of the MOU and a commitment to change policing procedures that will (hopefully) make transit a safer place for migrants.

Resignifying

There are significant differences between these various sanctuary expressions. For instance, whereas some sanctuary cities in the United States tend to place primacy on sanctuary policies, the UK has tended to place emphasis on cultural activities. As Bauder points out, in the UK the emphasis is perhaps more on creating "hospitable urban environments for refugees and asylum-seekers" (Bauder 2017, 7). It is vital to consider how differences exist not simply between national contexts but within them. Moreover, there are tensions in terms of how sanctuary is mobilized even within cities and services. This is evidenced in the tensions at play in Vancouver where there have been ongoing debates regarding how sanctuary might be enacted as a product (a designation determined by the city) or a more ongoing process (through grassroots organizing). And then, of course, there are those sanctuary spaces—such as villages and boroughs—which do not even fit neatly within a "city" designation (Marshall, Schmid-Scott, Gill, and Bagelman, in preparation). Given this diversity, perhaps, it would be misleading to refer to sanctuary as any kind of coherent "movement."

However, observing the words of sanctuary organizers, such as Marisa Franco, in her call for a "Radical Expansion of Sanctuary," one can note an intensifying effort to intentionally connect these practices as part of a linked movement that crisscrosses organizations and localities. Drawing inspiration from Engin Isin's provocation to think about the power of naming, claiming, and resignifying seemingly distinct political acts collectively to embolden collective action illuminates links between diverse sanctuary expressions in order to imagine change (Isin 2017). In pointing to these shared dimensions of sanctuary the idea is not to flatten-out the richness of sanctuary expressions that we witness today. Instead, we seek to remain attuned to these differences while also pointing to how there may be some shared ground through which to build a more robust politics. There are three shared commitments that might link sanctuary expressions today: solidarity, contextualization, and a questioning of the political.

To return to the assertion made at the beginning of this chapter, one feature that links diverse sanctuary expressions is a refusal to reduce displacement to a singular issue. Increasingly what we are witnessing are expressions of sanctuary that refuse to place emphasis on a particular "crisis," and rather illuminate the various conditions (of capitalism, of patriarchy, of colonialism) that give rise to intersecting forms of violence. Rather than focus exclusively on "the" refugee, which can too easily polarize a movement between those positioned as most or least deserving, one can see a deepened insistence on a language of solidarity. As Phoenix-based sanctuary organizer and writer Marisa Franco has powerfully put it:

> Sanctuary is not a single-issue. We have multiple targets on our backs. There is no time for our ideas of sanctuaries to be exclusive. Sanctuaries must include not only undocumented people, but also nonimmigrant Muslims, LGBTQ people, black and Indigenous folks and political dissents . . . Not only of our movements or organizations is strong enough alone: without shared force we will be disseminated. Our sanctuary organizing must include this expanded understanding.
>
> (Franco 2017)

In these words, we hear an appeal to a more expansive politics that emphasizes the importance of providing access to services without fear to all residents. Sanctuary movements are increasingly embodying this type of intersectional politics in their struggles. One particularly notable example is the "Access Without Fear" sanctuary politics mobilized in Vancouver. This movement promotes cooperation between various organizations and service providers that often remain otherwise siloed given the retreat of state funds and the therefore increasingly competitive nonprofit grant landscape. By creating shared space through web platforms and meetings, this movement ensures a commitment to coalition-building across sectors. On their website, for instance, resources are shared for people systematically failed by the state and experiencing different forms of precariousness (Walia 2014). For instance, this site provides support for refugees, asylum-seekers, refused asylum-seekers, temporary foreign workers, LGBT communities, people facing domestic abuse . . . Vitally, these groups also explicitly organize as a form of anticolonial migrant justice, fostering relationships between Indigenous peoples whose lands were stolen by the very colonial powers that bomb today and then fail to unconditionally welcome the refugees it produces tomorrow. In the words of Access Without Fear:

> Honouring the land and actions of the First Nations that have lived on this land since time immemorial, we want to build communities that are in solidarity with Indigenous land defenders on Turtle Island and with global movements against dispossession . . . we seek to collaborate with communities and service providers to create safer access to services for all people based on need rather than status.
>
> (Access Without Fear 2017)

Such movements also identify the links between environmental degradation and displacement. These grassroots organizations draw important connections between, for instance, the 1.5 million Syrians forced to leave their homes in 2007 due to a historic draught caused in part by climate change. These intersectional politics upend narrow notions of crisis, and instead expose the complex conditions inciting various forms of precarity: from statelessness to homelessness. In so doing this work knits a response that is anything but singular in focus.

The second aspect that increasingly connects sanctuary efforts today is a commitment to situate questions of displacement within a wider historical and geopolitical horizon of significance. Evoking the discourse of sanctuary emplaces contemporary struggles within struggles for hospitality that extend to biblical times. Insisting on deepened critical attention to histories of violence and refuge, and logics of insider/outside, remains important work within many sanctuary movements. This is a step to both acknowledge historic and persistent persecution. For instance in the UK City of Sanctuary Handbook *Becoming a City of Sanctuary* written by organizers Craig Barnett and Inderjit Bhogal we see this aspiration to delve into the historical precedents of sanctuary. In a chapter entitled "Sanctuary, Hospitality, and Refuge in World Faiths" the authors illustrate how sanctuary has emerged in response to forms of violence and exile over thousands of years (Barnett and Bhogal 2009). We see a similar desire to contextualize sanctuary practices when we look to the growing number of "sanctuary schools" in the UK, United States, and Canada—where teachers, students, and communities place primacy on the role of education in challenging xenophobic attitudes. A central way in which this is achieved is through lesson plans that address histories that give rise to contemporary displacement, and the persistent violent realities that many communities face today. Rather than shy away from difficult conversations, students are encouraged to think about, for instance, how military interventions have led to children (sometimes classmates) being forced to flee beloved homes. Creative reading lists (or "sanctuary syllabi") also provide resources for students, teachers, and parents alike to learn how communities have, historically, courageously challenged violence against persecuted peoples. Especially in a context where there is a denial of facticity and history, the ambition—it seems—in many sanctuary efforts is to both understand histories of violence, and also learn from those more hopeful traces we might build upon today. Again, to quote Marisa Franco: "Our defiance must not simply be to recreate what existed, but instead expand, reimagine, and breathe life into its possibilities" (2017).

The third dimension that links sanctuary efforts today is a deep questioning of what counts as the political. Implied in many sanctuary expressions is a questioning of where, when, and who gets counted as political. With regards to the "who gets counted as political?," sanctuary—in its various articulations—unsettles the simple statist equation that legal citizen = political citizen. Sanctuary challenges this legalistic notion that citizenship is bestowed by the nation-state and instead insists that *all* residents, regardless of status, should be considered citizens with an equal right to the places they inhabit (Isin 2008; Nyers 2010). We see this in sanctuary organizing which emphasizes the meaningful contributions of all residents to a vibrant urban life, as well as more explicitly in "Access Without Fear" sanctuary policies which seek to actually carve out safe space for such contributions (and contestations) to flourish.

In addition to challenging statist assumptions about who gets counted as political, sanctuary efforts also explicitly expand the where-ness of the political. Contemporary sanctuary practices, in their various iterations, tend to share one thing in common: they exceed the confines of conventionally recognized political fora (Ridgley 2008). Indeed, sanctuary organizing is not confined to parliament or polling booths. Sanctuary organizing takes and makes new places to be political, creating opportunities for all to publicly enact their political "right to have rights" (Arendt 1973). For instance, increasingly we see the university campus enacted as an energetic public place where migrant rights are mobilized and asserted. In the UK, Warwick University—located on the outskirts of the city of Coventry, which is recognized as a "City of Sanctuary"—has become the first official University of Sanctuary. This initiative celebrates the good practices of Universities welcoming asylum-seekers and refugees in Higher Education. A key dimension of this initiative is to channel University resources to tangibly supports people with precarious status; one example of this has been the creation of "sanctuary scholarships" which cover tuition costs (Handbook). In the United States we have seen the proliferation of the sanctuary campus—that is, any college or university that adopts policies to protect members of the campus community who are irregularized. In November 2016, students around the country staged demos, walkouts, and sit-ins to demand this sanctuary designation. One of the first university presidents to declare a sanctuary campus explicitly was Michael S. Roth of Wesleyan who, in November 2016, announced that it "will not voluntarily assist" any efforts by federal authorities to deport students. Soon after, John Coatsworth, the provost of Columbia University, said that it would not allow immigration agents on campus without a warrant. Reflective of the processual nature of sanctuary being explicitly articulated in cities like Vancouver many sanctuary campus proponents remain critical to how this term "sanctuary" becomes mobilized. As Berkely PhD student Joel Sati writes:

> Sanctuary campuses must have a front-facing quality to them; they must engage with the world that they claim to prepare us for. That being said, there is a danger that the whole exercise could be self-congratulatory absent a deep political analysis and a sustained grassroots push. Merely protecting a subset of the undocumented population, without a critical engagement of the political situation that brought us to this point, will not get undocumented persons anywhere but in grave danger.
>
> (Sati 2016)

In these framings of sanctuary, politics is not confined to traditional places of deliberative democracy (such as parliament), nor in the so-called "hot-spots" of crisis (such as camps), but altogether in seemingly quotidian places (such as the campus). Moreover, as expressed by Sati, sanctuary is a politics whose temporality is not confined to the strictures of election countdowns or news cycles. Sanctuary is not a politics that ends when recognized from above; but rather, a continually process which only has meaning if it resonates with those people on the ground whose lives are directly impacted by the harsh edges of border control. It may be tempting to see sanctuary "like a state"—that is, a power struggle between hierarchically arranged authorities such as the head of a university or municipality or state (Magnusson 2013). However, by insisting on a different notion of the who/what/where of the political, sanctuary exceeds this conventional framing. Rather than a legal feud simply between (for instance) majors and presidents, sanctuary is as much found in the ongoing relationship building and quiet work that organizers do day-on-day to support people in precarious living conditions. As Harsha Walia has argued in her article "Sanctuary from Below," complex solidarities are sustained through intimate (and often slow) modes of organizing such as intergenerational conversation, art, song, and other loving ways of being together (Walia 2014).

Forging a Global-Intimate Movement beyond Crisis

So, if contemporary expressions of sanctuary can be linked as a movement—what type of movement is this? This act of resignifying diverse sanctuary as part of a wider movement is clearly articulated by sanctuary activists mentioned previously like Mariso Franco. It is also articulated by academics seeking to understand sanctuary as a form of political action that links diverse communities. These more expansive frames tend to imagine sanctuary as wider process that is: urban (Cordes 2017; Ridgley 2008); national (Darling 2010); international (Bauder 2017); and—increasingly—planetary (Carney et al., 2017). In his article "City Sovereignty: Urban Resistance and Rebel Cities

Reconsidered" Vojislava Filipcevic Cordes makes the persuasive case that we should consider sanctuary at the urban scale. That sanctuary is not simply haphazard activity, but rather a collective form of action that becomes realized through shared urban living. Jonathan Darling, calling upon geographer Doreen Massey, carefully argues that urban sanctuary efforts in the UK cannot be understood as bound to particular cities, but rather are part of a more interconnected, and "outward-looking," national movement (Massey 2010). Harald Bauder argues in his recent article "Sanctuary Cities: Policies and Practices in International Perspective" that this outward-looking quality is not only within national sanctuary contexts, but *across* them. What we see today, as the title of Bauder's piece implies, is an international movement (Bauder 2017). In a recent, joint-authored piece, "Sanctuary Planet," this scale is extended further. This article provides a direct call to imagine sanctuary as a planetary movement (Carney et al., 2017). In each of these cases, there is an appeal to view sanctuary as a kind of movement that links various actors, at different scales.

While understanding sanctuary through the scale of the city, nation, international, or even planetary helps expand our political horizons, these frames also have a tendency to reduce our political imaginations. When we defer to these scalar logics we inherit certain assumptions of the what, where, and how politics might be. There are solidarities we see emerging between migrant and Indigenous communities and environmental movements which stand (sometimes uncomfortably) together to challenge the sovereignty of the state, and settler colonial logics of the city, Figure 42.2; when we hear the rallying cries "No Ban on Stolen Land" can we truly understand this as a *national* movement? Artists, like Dylan Miner whose work is featured below are illustrating the limits of our geopolitical imaginaries through creative cartographies like this:

FIGURE 42.2 "No Ban on Stolen Land"

Source: Dylan Miner. Used with permission

When we acknowledge the complex modes of sanctuary organizing that are taking place within and beyond urban environments that explicitly address environmental concerns—such as climate change—can we really understand this as a city-based movement? And while the ambition may be toward a broader sense of political community, can this appeal be understood as aspiring for the planetary? To assume so risks recoding complex political activity within conventional, hierarchical, still-statist logics. What if these sanctuary practices cannot squeeze within these categories? What if they are doing something . . . different?

As we witness sanctuary expand in exciting ways, we need to develop more expansive ways to articulate and engage with these politics. A different analytical lens might be helpful in approaching diverse sanctuary expressions; namely, the global-intimate. Building on feminist geographical scholarship the global-intimate is a lens which attends to the ways in which our lives take shape in particular localities and also how these intimate lives are globally connected to extended geographies (Conlon and Heimstra 2017; Pratt and Rosner 2006). The analytical task set out here is to trace how people and places are connected through political process—such as globalizing capitalism—often in highly uneven and exploitative ways. There are a few principal ways this lens is vital in helping us understand and carefully build sanctuary movements today.

First, retaining the language of global-intimate is important because it explicitly draws our attention to the lived, felt, visceral dimensions of both the need for and manifestations of sanctuary. In practice, approaching sanctuary through a global-intimate lens means being attentive to how movements are being organized day-on-day (not just the spectacular Major Moment [i.e., the moment that a city is designated "safe" by an official ordinance]). It draws our attention to the *slow* work and (often gendered) emotional labor that goes into building and sustaining places of safety for people with precarious status, the sustained energy that goes into listening, being silent with and holding space for those people who have experienced trauma resulting from exile. Or the emotional labor that goes into organizing public vigils for the lives lost due to hostile border control. Or the quiet organizing that goes into finding temporary homes for people facing deportation orders, or the fierce work of fundraising that is done to support legal cases for people in precarious situations. These acts are perhaps not always seen or heard—but they are vital to a sanctuary movement that seeks to make all residents feel welcome. All of this work and energy, we must remember, is not peripheral to but the beating heart animating sanctuary.

Additionally, attending to intimacy compels us to ask not only "what is sanctuary" but *how* is sanctuary enacted and felt by those with precarious status? And, importantly, how are the limits of sanctuary's sacred promise experienced by those who do not hold legal rights? Placing primacy on intimacy ensures that we keep asking these questions. An intimate register keeps our focus on building a movement that remains in step with those who are most immediately impacted by intensifying hostile border politics. Moreover, examining the intimacies of sanctuary repositions people with precarious status as experts with diverse knowledge and reorients us toward hard questions like: how can we bring these voices to the fore in ways that create safe platforms, and that support communities in the ways they wish to be supported?

To think about intimacy is not to suggest a turning attention away from wider geopolitical forces: capitalism, colonialism, and the many other "isms." Rather, this global-intimate lens insists on tracing and exposing the ways in which our everyday lives are tangibly and inexorably entwined with wider forces and struggles while remaining responsible to our everyday relationships (Conlon and Hiemstra 2017). As Geraldine Pratt has shown in her over-decade-long work with temporary foreign workers in Canada, the global-intimate exposes how a reliance on cheap care or labor in one place (namely Vancouver) produces the displacement of women elsewhere (namely the Philippines) (Pratt and Johnston 2013). And, this lens provides a point of entry into sensing the myriad ways in which sanctuary organizing responds to these uneven global relations. For instance, it exposes how sanctuary is doing the political work to link purportedly distinct crises (environmental, economic, colonial) across seemingly disparate geographies. This global-intimate lens calls upon us to acknowledge how these modes of organizing are being performed across multiple sites, often at the same time. At once we are called to grasp, for instance, the street protests; the policies; the fund-raising; the doctor refusing to ask for status; the lobbying of governmental officials; the sanctuary school reading-lists; the meals quietly being made together. Rather than prioritizing some of these modes of political activity as higher and designating some as lower, the relational lens of the global-intimate incites us to interrogate how these politics are functioning *together* to promote more generative places. As an analytical lens, the intimate-global provides us with a more nuanced way to stay with—and even contribute to—these complex sanctuary expressions that upend familiar spatial hierarchies and oppositions to make space for the complex ways we inhabit our worlds.

We must pay greater attention to these global-intimacies in our research on and participation in sanctuary movements. For, in a geopolitical context where the language of crisis tends toward shock and simplicity, this prismatic lens draws us toward more textured and intersectional struggles: struggles that exceed traditional modes and scales of political belonging, struggles that are both intensely depressing but also—always—surprising.

Notes

1. Following Bauder, rather than undocumented, unauthorized, irregular, or nonstatus migrant I prefer the term "irregularized" to draw attention to the laws, policies, and practices that deny migrants full status or legal residency (2014).
2. However, as a recent (2015) report by No One Is Illegal—Toronto, "Often Asking, Always Telling: The Toronto Police Service and the Sanctuary City Policy" reveals, DADT policies are not consistently actualized in practice. Confusion still exists as to the nature and extent to which municipal programs cohere with federal and provincial law. Consequently, fear of arrest, detention, and removal from Canada still results in marginalization of undocumented migrants, and susceptibility to exploitation and abuse.

REFERENCES

Arendt, H. 1973. *Origins of Totalitarianism*. New ed. New York: Harcourt Brace Jovanovich.

Amoore, L. 2006. "Biometric Borders: Governing Mobilities in the War on Terror." *Political Geography* 25:336–351.

Bagelman, J. 2016. *Sanctuary City: A Suspended State*. New York: Springer.

Barnett, C, and Bhogal, I. 2009. *Becoming a City of Sanctuary: A Practical Handbook with Inspiring Examples*. Ripon, WI: Plug and Tap.

Bau, I. 1985. *This Ground Is Holy: Church Sanctuary and Central American Refugees*. Mahwah, NJ: Paulist Press.

Bauder, H. 2017. "Sanctuary Cities: Policies and Practices in International Perspective." *International Migration* 55, no. 2: 174–187.

Bigo, D. 2000. "When Two Becomes One: Internal and External Securitisations in Europe" In *International Relations Theory and the Politics of European Integration: Power, Security and Community*, edited by Morten Kelstrup and Michael C. Williams, 185. London: Routledge.

Carney, M. A., et al. 2017. "Sanctuary Planet: A Global Sanctuary Movement for the Time of Trump." *Society and Space*. http://societyandspace.org/2017/05/16/sanctuary-planet-a-global-sanctuary-movement-for-the-time-of-trump/

Chmielewski, M., 2017. "In Church and City: Canadian Political Sanctuary's Four Characteristics, Questions About Its Success, and Its Relationship with the State." PhD diss.,

Conlon, D., and Heimstra, N, ed. 2017. *Intimate Economies of Immigration Detention: Critical Perspectives*. London: Routledge.

Darling, J. 2010. "A City of Sanctuary: The Relational Re-Imagining of Sheffield's Asylum Politics." *Transactions of the Institute of British Geographers* 35, no. 1: 125–140.

Don't Ask, Don't Tell Coalition. 2005. Proposed DADT policy, accessed May 9, 2017. http://www.dadttoronto.org.

Filipcevic Cordes, V. 2017. "City Sovereignty: Urban Resistance and Rebel Cities Reconsidered." *Urban Science* 1, no. 3: 22.

Franco, M. 2017. "Radical Expansion of Sanctuary." *Truthout*, September 1. truth-out.org.

Gill, N., Conlon, D., Moran, D., and Burridge, A. 2017. "Carceral Circuitry: New Directions in Carceral Geography." *Progress in Human Geography* 42, no. 2: 183–204.

Isin, E. 2008. *Acts of Citizenship*. London: Zed.

Isin, E. F. 2017. "Enacting International Citizenship." In *International Political Sociology: Transversal Lines*, edited by T. Basaran, D. Bigo; E.-P. Guittet, and R. B. J Walker,185–204. London: Routledge.

Jones, R. 2016. *Violent Borders: Refugees and the Right To Move*. London: Verso.

Kingsley, P. 2015. "The Syrian Refugee Crisis." *The Guardian*, September 4. https://www.theguardian.com/world/2015/sep/04/syrian-refugee-crisis-why-has-it-become-so-bad

Lippert, R. 2005. *Sanctuary, Sovereignty, Sacrifice: Canadian Sanctuary Incidents, Power, and Law*. Vancouver: UBC Press.

Magnusson, W. 2013. *Politics of Urbanism: Seeing Like a City*. London: Routledge.

Mancina, P. 2016. *In the Spirit of Sanctuary: Sanctuary-City Policy Advocacy and the Production of Sanctuary-Power in San Francisco, California*. PhD. diss., Vanderbilt University.

Mountz, A. 2015. "In/Visibility and the Securitization of Migration: Shaping Publics Through Border Enforcement on Islands." *Cultural Politics* 11, no. 2: 184–200.

Nyers, P. 2010. "No One Is Illegal between City and Nation." *Studies in Social Justice* 4, no. 2: 127.

Pratt, G., and C. Johnston, 2013. "Staging testimony in Nanay." *Geographical Review* 103, no. 2: 288–303.

Pratt, G., and V. Rosner. 2006. "The Global and the Intimate." *Women's Studies Quarterly* 34, no. 1: 13–24.

Rabben, L. 2011. *Give Refuge to the Stranger: The Past, Present, and Future of Sanctuary*. Walnut Creek, CA: Left Coast Press.

Ridgley, J. 2008. "Cities of Refuge: Immigration Enforcement, Police, and the Insurgent Genealogies of Citizenship in U.S. Sanctuary Cities." *Urban Geography* 29, no. 1: 53–77.

Sanctuary City Vancouver (n.d.). http://www.sanctuarycityvan.com.

Sati, J. 2016. "No Church in the Wild: The Politics of the Sanctuary Campus." BerkeleyBlog, November23,2016.http://blogs.berkeley.edu/2016/11/23/no-church-in-the-wild-the-politics-of-the-sanctuary-campus/

Shoemaker, K. *Sanctuary and Crime in the Middle Ages, 400–1500*. New York: Fordham University Press, 2011.

Squire, V., and J. Bagelman. 2012. "Taking not waiting : space, temporality and politics in the city of sanctuary movement." In *Citizenship, migrant activism and the politics of movement. Routledge research on the global politics of migration (No. 2)*, edited by Peter Nyers and Kim Rygiel. London: Routledge.

Walia, H. 2014 "Sanctuary from Below." Rabble.ca, accessed: April 21, 2016. http://bit.ly/1SnebIe

Walker, R.B. 2010. *After the globe, before the world*. London: Routledge.

CHAPTER 43

THE SYRIAN REFUGEE CRISIS, MULTICULTURALISM ISSUES, AND INTEGRATION IN CANADA

LAURENCE CROS

THERE were many ways of defining what migration crises mean. This chapter will look into one particular category of migration, that of refugees. Since 1951, when the United Nations adopted the "Convention Relating to the Status of Refugees," the term "refugees" has had a precise legal meaning. The convention was "grounded in Article 14 of the Universal Declaration of Human Rights of 1948, which recognizes the right of persons to seek asylum from persecution in other countries," and defines a refugee as "someone who is unable or unwilling to return to their country of origin owing to a well-founded fear of being persecuted for reasons of race, religion, nationality, membership of a particular social group, or political opinion" (UNHCR 1951). While persecution can occur under regular circumstances and force individual refugees to leave, extraordinary circumstances in certain areas of world, especially linked to war, create such horrific conditions that large numbers of civilians have no choice but to flee in the hope to survive. Hence the first meaning of "crises" in relation to refugees refers to the contextual factors that trigger large movements of displaced persons. This meaning is found over and over in reports of the United Nations Refugee Agency (hereafter, UNHCR). For example, the subtitle of the UNHCR's *Global Trends for 2011* is: "A Year of Crises." But as some passages for reports indicate, while they are born from the context of crises, exceptionally large numbers of displaced persons constitute crises in themselves: "During this year of spiralling crises, with millions of people already forced to flee from their homes (. . .) the global humanitarian system has been severely stretched" (UNHCR 2014, 5). As UN High Commissioner for Refugees Antonio Guterres warned in June 2015: "The world is facing a staggering crisis as the number of forcibly displaced people rises to record numbers—59.5 million at the end of 2014." (Murray 2015) This was reiterated the following year by United Nations Secretary General Ban Ki Moon, who stated: "We are facing the biggest refugee and displacement crisis of our time. Above all, this is not just a crisis of numbers; it is also a crisis of solidarity" (UNHCR 2015, 5).

It is this second meaning of the term "crises" (i.e., the humanitarian challenges and issues of solidarity posed by exceptional mass movements of refugees) that this chapter will examine. More precisely it will focus on a particular case study, that of the Canadian plan to resettle Syrian refugees from 2015 to 2017. The Canadian plan will be analyzed to assess its effectiveness both in welcoming Syrian refugees (i.e., in bringing some relief to a global humanitarian crisis) and in doing so without creating a "crisis of solidarity" at home (i.e., by winning over the Canadian people's support for the project). The factors that allowed Canada to represent the resettlement of Syrian refugees as a "non-crisis" will be examined to reflect whether the Canadian method can be transposed to other potential host countries to help remedy global refugee crises without causing political crises at home.

The Context of Canada's Syrian Refugee Resettlement Plan

The Canadian plan to resettle Syrian refugees took place in a particularly critical global context. The first two decades of the 21st century have seen a major increase in refugees. The UNHCR indicates that "the global population of forcibly displaced people has grown substantially from 33.9 million in 1997 to 65.6 million in 2016" (UNHCR 2016, 5). It states that the present number of displaced persons is "the highest since the aftermath of World War II" (UNHCR 2015, 5) and that "most of this increase was concentrated between 2012 and 2015, driven mainly by the Syrian conflict" (UNHCR 2016, 5). This massive and brutal increase of refugees in turn created "crises of solidarity" in many countries. Syria's immediate neighbors (mostly Turkey but also Lebanon and Jordan) host the bulk of the almost 5 million Syrians forced to flee their homes. This represents an enormous burden and has strong implications for the stability of the entire region. But hundreds of thousands of Syrians have also tried to reach Europe, embarking on the dangerous journey across the Mediterranean Sea, where many died (UNHCR 2015, 7).

Reactions in Europe to the flood of asylum-seekers ranged from generosity and open-door policy to fear and the temptation to close down borders.[1] In November 2013, Bulgaria began to build a 30km fence on its border with Turkey to stop asylum seekers. In July 2015, it was Hungary's turn to start building a fence along its border with Serbia, which was completely closed in September, thus blocking the main land route of migrants into Western Europe and ending two decades of open borders in the EU. On the other hand, in August 2015, Germany declared it would accept asylum seekers no matter what European countries they arrived in, and called for other EU countries to do the same. In September 2015, the European Commission presented a plan to relocate 160,000 asylum seekers from the most affected ports of entry in Italy and Greece to other EU member states. However, Hungary and other EU states refused to implement the Commission's relocation measures. And as the flood of refugees continued, even countries which had originally adopted a generous policy began restricting access. In January 2016, Sweden, which had previously received the highest number of asylum seekers in Europe in proportion to its population, established border checks to block their arrival. Likewise, in February 2016, Austria, which like Germany and Sweden had been taking in large numbers of refugees since 2014, introduced limits on the number of refugees allowed into the country. In August 2016, a poll in Germany showed that two-thirds of respondents did not approve of Angela Merkel's "open door" policy (BBC News 2016; Dempsey 2016; Migration Policy Centre 2016).

In Canada, 2015 was an election year. Canadians, like everyone else in the world, could not ignore the ongoing tragedy of Syria and the terrible stories of fleeing refugees dying as they tried to cross the Mediterranean to Europe. The shocking event that made the Syrian refugee crisis a central issue in the Canadian election was the drowning of 3-year-old Alan Kurdi during his family's failed attempt to reach Greece in early September 2015. As images of the drowned toddler went viral, Canadians discovered that his aunt Tima Kurdi, a recent immigrant to Canada, had been trying to help the Kurdi family to resettle in Canada. It turned out that Citizenship and Immigration Canada had rejected the application of Alan's uncle, Mohammad Kurdi, as incomplete because it lacked the proper documentation to certify refugee status.

The Alan Kurdi tragedy made the Syrian refugee crisis a key issue in the Canadian election, although there had already been some debates on this issue. In mid-2013, Canada had announced that by the end of the following year, it would resettle 1,300 Syrian refugees identified by the UNHCR as being in need of immediate assistance. However, by the end of 2014, only 457 Syrian refugees had been resettled in relation to the 2013 plan, although some 1,150 more had arrived in Canada on their own and claimed asylum (Nuttall 2015). Critics denounced the Conservative answer as slow and ineffective, and there were accusations that administrative reorganization was deliberately slowing down the application process of Syrian refugees (Goodspeed 2014). In January 2015, the Conservatives promised that another 10,000 Syrian refugees would be resettled in Canada by the end of 2018, with a focus on religious minorities (Canadian Press 2015).

Immediately after the death of Alan Kurdi, Conservative PM Stephen Harper promised to speed up the resettlement of the Syrian refugees, but added that taking in more people was not the only solution; it was also necessary to continue to "fight the root cause of the problem and that is the violent campaign being waged against these people by ISIS" CBC News 2015). This did not prevent the opposition parties, particularly the Liberal leader Justin Trudeau, from attacking the Conservatives for their lack of compassion and betrayal of Canada's tradition of welcoming refugees (CBC News 2015). By contrast, the Liberals reiterated their promise to bring in 25,000 refugees and pledged to do it before the end of 2015.

Implementation of the Syrian Refugee Resettlement Plan

The Liberal government of Justin Trudeau took power on November 4, 2015 after winning the election. Originally the government announced it would keep its promise not only of a target of 25,000 Syrian refugees, but also of the deadline of the end of 2015. Things did not go exactly as planned, since the original target of 25,000 people by the end of 2015 could not be met. However, by the end of February 2016, the newly renamed department of Immigration, Refugees and Citizenship Canada (hereafter, IRCC) had indeed resettled 26,172 Syrian refugees (IRCC 2017c). Moveover, the Liberal government continued its commitment beyond its original promise, since Canada resettled 53,620 Syrian refugees between November 4, 2015 and 2017 April 30,2018 (IRCC 2017d).[2]

Several important changes to the original plan were made to ensure that the resettlement would be acceptable to Canadians. First, within a week of the Paris attacks by Islamic terrorists on November 13, 2015, Justin Trudeau pushed back the deadline to the end of February 2016. He gave as a reason the need to complete thorough security screening of the applicants "to reassure Canadians that absolutely everything is being done to keep Canadians safe, and therefore ensure that these refugees are welcomed as new Canadians and not a cause for anxiety or division within the population" (Levitz 2016). Another change was the decision to select candidates abroad and bring to Canada only refugees whose applications had been reviewed and accepted. Originally the idea had been to bring candidates on temporary residence permits, and to proceed with the security checks after applicants arrived in Canada (Proctor 2015).

These early changes in the resettlement plan are crucial because they demonstrate how the Canadian program reconciled generosity in welcoming refugees, thus relieving the global humanitarian crisis caused by the Syrian war, and pragmatism in ensuring that the process would not cause a national crisis in Canada by scaring people and dividing public opinion. This was achieved by proving to Canadians that the plan was safe and kept under control, thus reassuring people and making the resettlement acceptable to them.

Security was promoted in two main ways, through the method of selection and through the criteria of selection, both of which were presented on the website of IRCC. The method was to choose candidates among people already registered with the United Nations in Jordan and Lebanon and review their applications on location, by sending a large delegation of several hundreds of "experienced visa officers" (IRCC 2017a). This method ensured that the government was firmly in control of selecting those who came to the country. Contrary to European countries which received thousands of asylum-seekers and then had to determine who to keep, Canada selected candidates abroad and only "safe" refugees were allowed in the country. There was no risk of being overrun by unwanted candidates, no additional cost of housing them while the lengthy process of reviewing their applications went on, and no difficult and potentially divisive decisions to be made regarding the fate of those whose applications were eventually rejected.

The selection criteria also were a crucial contribution to making the plan safe and acceptable. The plan targeted people who were particularly vulnerable, but also considered a low security risk: "We focused on on identifying vulnerable refugees who are a lower security risk such as women, complete families, and persons identified as vulnerable due to membership in the LGBTI community" (IRCC 2017a).

As a result, single men were mostly excluded from the process. This exclusion of men (especially young single men) from the Canadian resettlement plan conforms to popular stereotypes that this category of population is more likely to be a source of trouble, either as terrorists or as disruptive social elements. By eliminating this category of population from the pool of potential refugees, the government of Canada thus addressed public fears, conscious or unconscious, that refugees could cause crises. The refugees targeted by the Canadian resettlement plan were deliberately chosen to be nonthreatening and easy to empathize with, with the purpose of reassuring Canadians and making the initiative acceptable to them.

Indeed, polls showed that reassuring Canadians that the plan was safe was a crucial element to gain support for it. A November 2015 poll showed that only 42 percent of Canadians supported the refugee resettlement plan while 54 percent of Canadians opposed it, and that for 53 percent of those, the reason was that the timelines were too short to ensure necessary security checks (Angus Reid Institute 2015). However, results were reversed after the government pushed back the deadline to the end of February 2016. In February 2016 support reached 52 percent while opposition decreased to 44 percent (Angus Reid Institute 2016a).

Therefore, communication with the Canadian public was a crucial element. The perception of security was just as important as the reality of security in making sure that the Canadian citizens would support the resettlement program. The government of Canada made remarkable efforts to promote perceptions both of safe refugees and of a transparent and controlled process. The IRCC website provided the public with extremely clear and detailed explanations of how the program was carried out. Great emphasis was placed on the "safety, security and health" elements of the program and each step in the security screening was presented in detail, insisting on the fact that they all would be completed before refuges arrived in Canada (IRCC 2017a).

The selection criteria that targeted women, children, and families are reflected in the stories, videos, and photos presented on the website (IRCC 2017b). Indeed, the same tendency is visible in recent UNHCR reports, which portray women and children to the almost complete exclusion of men. This exclusion of men from the visual representation of refugees helps to construct an image of the ideal refugee, one that is not likely to create crises, one that people can empathize with rather than fear.

Another element that encouraged Canadians to support the Syrian resettlement plan was the resort to private sponsorship, another change made to the original project. During the campaign, the Liberals had criticized the Conservatives for relying mostly on private sponsorship, and had promised to bring government-assisted refugees. However, when it came to implementing their electoral promise, and doing it fast, the newly elected Liberal government realized that it would need private sponsors. By then, private sponsors had already started selecting refugees to meet the quota of 10,000 Syrian refugees authorized by the Conservatives in January 2015. In fact, before the Liberals took power on November 4, about 1,263 Syrians had arrived in Canada under the Conservatives' commitment. In the end, rather than 25,000 government-assisted Syrian refugees to arrive by December 31, the Liberal plan called for 10,000 privately sponsored refugees by early 2016 and a further 15,000 government-assisted ones by spring 2016. Between November 4, 2015 and January 1, 2016, 6,064 privately-sponsored refugees arrived, most of them cases opened under the Conservatives, with another 4,000 scheduled to arrive in early January 2016 (Levitz 2016).

Private sponsorship played a great part in making the Syrian resettlement plan successful. First, it placed the Syrian plan within the tradition of Canadian hospitality and civic engagement. The Canadian Private Sponsorship of Refugees Program began in 1979 and allows nongovernmental groups to bring individuals and families to Canada, on condition that they provide resettlement support for at least one year (Epp 2017, 17). It played a key role in resettling about 77,000 "boat people" from Southeast Asia from 1979 to 1981. The share of refugees among immigrants rose to 25 percent during this period, a record never equaled since. The key role of private sponsors continued in the 1980s as more refugees arrived from Latin America. In 1986, the contribution of Canada's private sponsors was honored when the Nansen Refugee Award of the UNHCR was awarded to "the people of Canada" (Epp 2017, 18–20). The important role of private sponsorship appears on the IRCC website, which presents a clear and detailed description of how Canadians can sponsor refugees, simply by creating a "group of five" persons working together (IRCC 2018).

From a practical point of view, private sponsorship was a great help to resettle Syrian refugees. It allowed refugee assistance agencies extra time to find and process the large number of government-assisted refugees called for by the Liberal initiative. Private sponsorship also helped to reduce the major cost of the resettlement plan; while the electoral promise had announced a cost of $250 million, the first budget of the Liberal government gave an estimate of $678 million over six years (Levitz 2016). Private sponsorship spread part of the financial burden not only to private citizens, but also to the business community, which was targeted by special fund-raising appeals. Moreover, studies point out that privately sponsored refugees tend to do better economically in the first years after arrival (Friesen 2017). This is not only because they often came through family networks and had a higher level of education, but also because the sponsorship program "provides so much support, emotional, social and financial" (Kantor and Einhorn 2017).

Most importantly, private sponsorship was a very efficient way to implicating the Canadian people in the Syrian resettlement plan. As happened in 1979–1981 with the welcoming of "boat people," Canadian citizens were very generous in answering the call for sponsors for Syrian refugees. There were so many applications that they could not be processed quickly enough to be among the government's initial target of 25,000. As a result, in March 2016, Immigration Minister John McCallum announced that Canada would take in an additional 10,000 privately-sponsored Syrian refugees (Mas 2016). Private sponsorship was therefore crucial to generate social cohesion and consensus around the plan, by making Canadian citizens feel that they were actors and decision makers in the refugee resettlement process (Taub 2017).

In summary, the Syrian resettlement plan was very carefully orchestrated not only to ensure the successful arrival of refugees, but to win Canadian support for the initiative. Pushing back the deadlines to ensure full security checks, targeting nonthreatening categories of people, processing the applications from abroad, maintaining complete transparency of the process through careful communication, and enlisting popular support through private sponsorship, were all elements that contributed to a positive perception of the event. The Syrian refugee resettlement plan could thus be presented as an opportunity to demonstrate national solidarity and promote national self-interest, rather than a potentially disruptive crisis.

Multiculturalism and Integration in Canada: Building Migration as a Non-Crisis

The positive construct around the Syrian refugee crisis was greatly facilitated by the Canadian model of multiculturalism and integration, a model in which migration benefits from a very positive image. History and geography are crucial elements that contribute to this view; however, it is important to recognize that it is built on very pragmatic considerations, and that there can be, as a result, serious limits to Canada's generous policy towards immigrants or refugees.

Canadian History and the Acceptance of Diversity

Canada was the first country in the world to adopt an official policy of multiculturalism, when in 1971, Pierre Elliot Trudeau's government promulgated the "Announcement of Implementation of Policy of Multiculturalism within Bilingual Framework." Multiculturalism aims at accommodating and promoting diversity, by meeting the claims of ethnocultural minorities within the context of liberalism. It became part of the Canadian Constitution in 1982 through the Charter of Rights and Freedoms, which enshrines group-specific rights, such as language rights or self-government rights. Section 27 states that "This Charter shall be interpreted in a manner consistent with the preservation and enhancement of the multicultural heritage of Canadians."

Since the 1970s, many countries in the world have adopted policy instruments comparable to those of Canada to promote diversity. But academics and politicians alike stress that "Canada's policy of accommodating diversity" has been incorporated into the Canadian "sense of national identity" (Kymlicka 2003, 1). In a symbolic way, the 2015 electoral victory of Justin Trudeau, son of Pierre Elliot Trudeau, has reaffirmed the centrality of multiculturalism for Canada. During a campaign interview, he described Canada as "the first postnational state" and explained that in Canada, there is "no core identity," but only "shared values" (Trudeau 2015).

Thus, after fifty years of not only pursuing multiculturalism policies, but of increasingly defining itself through multiculturalism, Canada has created a political culture that minimizes fear and rejection of the migrant/refugee. To use Edward Shils' terms (1961), in the Canadian multicultural society, the migrant/refugee is no longer relegated to the periphery but has become an important symbol of the center and its values. As Justin Trudeau said, in Canada no one can claim to be "a typical citizen" (2015); all forms of ethnicity are equally acceptable; and therefore acceptance of different groups, and particularly of immigrant groups, is facilitated. Not only has multiculturalism become a central element of the national identity, it has encouraged the development of structural forces that influence the perception of migrants and their contribution to the host society. Comparing the incorporation of immigrants in Canada and the US, Irene Bloemraad (2006, 2–3) pointed out that 72 percent of foreign-born residents of Canada acquire the Canadian citizenship, double the proportion in the United States. She explains this difference by the existence in Canada of the official policy of multiculturalism which promotes an interventionist stance toward the incorporation of immigrants by public bureaucracies at the federal, provincial, and municipal levels. Polls confirm the centrality of multiculturalism for Canadians. In 2015, 54 percent considered it a very important symbol of Canadian identity. The number was up five points since a previous poll in 2012 (Environics Institute 2015, 2).

For the past fifty years, multiculturalism and the acceptance of immigration as a crucial agent of national development have been at the heart of the Canadian identity. But long before this, Canadian history paved the way for the success of multiculturalism, thanks to Canada's long tradition of defining itself in terms of its capacity to accommodate diversity. In this country born from two competing imperial powers and based on two "founding peoples," the federal project of 1867 emerged from the need of accommodating regional diversity and the cultural demands of the French Canadian minority. Most Canadian thinkers rejected John Stuart Mill's definition of a "Nation-State" based on an identity of race and a community of language and religion. They preferred Lord Acton's definition of the ideal nationality as heterogeneous and ethnically diverse, because such a state is, by necessity, forced to compromise and therefore is less likely to become intolerant.[3]

This trend accelerated in the 1960s, as the country moved toward multiculturalism. Canadian thinkers came up with the notion of "limited identities" (Careless 1971; Cook 1966)—the possibility that Canadian citizens should define themselves through diverse experiences of region, class and ethnicity. There is an obvious convergence between the concept of "limited identities" and the Actonian model, which work together to transform the multiplicity of identities available to the Canadian citizens from a weakness into an asset. In a world that is more and more transnational and global, it turns Canada into a model, as one Canadian historian expressed in 1969: "We are a highly pluralistic society in a bi-national union. That is our problem, our weakness, our distinction, and reason to exist" (Careless 1969, 26).

Canadian Geography and the Sense of Control over Immigration

The specific geographical conditions enjoyed by Canada have also contributed to the construct of immigration as a positive force. Immigration is comparatively easy to control because Canada is a country isolated on three sides by thousands of miles of open ocean (the Atlantic, the Pacific, and the Arctic). Its only land border is with the United States, a more prosperous country which does not produce mass immigration to Canada. On the contrary, the thousands of miles of the US landmass act as a barrier that stops immigrants from the less developed southern parts of the continent from reaching Canada. As a result, Canada has relatively little illegal immigration. The great majority of immigrants are accepted into the country after undergoing selection under Canada's program of economic immigration, family reunification, or refugees. This obviously creates a very reassuring feeling that immigration is under control. The importance of this factor in the Canadian perception of immigration has been underlined by academic thinkers and political actors. As Will Kymlicka (2004, 847) wrote, "it's impossible to exaggerate the importance of this fact [geography] for the success of 'the Canadian model' of immigrant multiculturalism." Recently Canada's Liberal immigration minister, Ahmed Hussen (himself of immigrant origin), recognized that "the luck of geography" helps Canada to control immigrants who enter the country (Taub 2017). Conservatives of course share this view, which Howard Anglin, previously chief of staff to former Conservative immigration minister Jason Kenney, recently summed up:

> Bounded by three oceans and a large absorbent southern neighbour, we could afford to be selective about who we invited to become Canadians. This allowed us to maintain among the highest levels of immigration with little of the controversy that immigration policy generates in other countries.
>
> (Anglin 2017)

But when this geographical protection is breached, the Canadian sense of control which generates a usually serene support of immigration quickly evaporates to be replaced by a feeling of crisis. This is clearly demonstrated by the different attitudes of Canadians toward asylum seekers who enter Canada illegally (either arriving by ships or crossing the US-Canada border), as compared to refugees who apply from abroad.

The link between the fear of losing control and a negative opinion of immigration has been the topic of several recent studies in social psychology. They show that low perceived control in the sociopolitical domain may lead to prejudice against outgroups and global ethnocentrism (Fritsche et al. 2011, 109). The rise of ethnocentrism as compensation after experiences of control deprivation has been used to explain, for example, the recent rise of far-right anti-immigrant parties in Austria (Agroskin and Jonas 2010, 79). In the case of Canada, geographical conditions tend to work toward providing Canadians with a sense of control over who or how many enter the country, which may have prevented the growth of anti-immigrant sentiment in Canada. This explains, in part, why immigration in general and the Syrian resettlement plan in particular did not result in political crises.

Limits to the Canadian Model of Multiculturalism and Integration

While Canada has developed a model of multiculturalism and integration that promotes a positive view of immigration as a "non-crisis," it is important not to fall into an overly romantic view of the system. There is nothing particularly idealistic about Canadian multiculturalism; to borrow the terms of a recent *New York Times* article, it is "ruthlessly rational" (Tepperman 2017) and based on national self-interest. One could apply to Canadian multiculturalism the words that David Haglund (2009, 350) used to qualify Canadian foreign policy: "Canada, it transpired, would do well by doing good." As a government initiative rooted within the official framework of immigration policy, the Syrian resettlement plan sheds light on the underlying principles of the Canadian model: the insistence on integration, and the priorities given to national self-interest and economic prosperity. By contrast, it highlights the fact that immigration patterns that fall outside of the official framework, such as the arrival of irregular asylum seekers, do not enjoy the same popular acceptance and are ruthlessly discouraged.

The Integrative Nature of Canadian Multiculturalism

One key element of the Canadian model is the integrative nature of Canadian multiculturalism. As Will Kymlicka explained, Canada's form of multiculturalism is grounded on the theories of liberal egalitarian justice developed by John Rawls in particular, with the idea that liberal justice can defend the group-specific rights that minorities need. Canadian multiculturalism, however, has stopped short of communitarianism, whose supporters, like Charles Taylor, consider that the liberal-democratic approach is too individualistic to protect minorities from assimilation (Kymlicka and Peonidis 2008). Canadian multiculturalism works within a liberal framework to protect minority rights while reaffirming core values of individual freedom and democracy. This is illustrated by the way the Canadian Charter mixes individual rights and group rights within the same document. This means that there are limits to how far Canadians are willing to go to accommodate minority groups and immigrant groups. Accommodation must be reasonable, so that the core values of Canadian political culture should be protected. In other words, if Canadian multiculturalism protects immigrants from assimilation, it nonetheless encourages them to integrate. This approach is reflected in the findings of a 2016 poll, which indicated that 68 percent of respondents thought that minorities should do more to fit in better with mainstream Canadian society. Only 32 percent thought that Canada should encourage cultural diversity with different groups keeping their own customs and languages (Angus Reid Institute 2016b, 16). This poll is one of a regular series that investigates Canada's values and a similar poll in 1993 had found that 57 percent of respondents thought minority groups should be encouraged to try to change to be more like most Canadians. So with time insistence on the need for integration into the Canadian political culture has in fact increased. It shows very clearly that Canadian multiculturalism enjoys popular support only as long as it is successful in incorporating immigrants into the national fabric.

Canada's Pragmatic Approach to Immigration: The Priorities of National Self-Interest and Economic Prosperity

The same hardheaded pragmatism lies at the core of the Canadian system of immigration. Canada's multicultural model and its immigration system are closely linked and support each other. Immigration is a success because multiculturalism helps immigrants to adjust smoothly to life in Canada, but multiculturalism enjoys popular support because immigration is felt to contribute positively to Canada. The two systems were elaborated around the same time. While the foundations of multiculturalism date back to 1971, the main principle that governs immigration to Canada was adopted in 1967, when a points system was introduced to rank potential immigrants for eligibility. This system no longer took into account race, color, or nationality; it rather focused on work skills, education levels, and language ability. Thus Canada was adopting an approach to immigration that was both progressive (by refusing all types of discrimination) and pragmatic (in promoting immigrants likely to boost the economy of the country). In 1976, a new Immigration Act made refugees a distinct group of immigrants, while defining the priorities of Canada's immigration policy to be the promotion of Canada's demographic and economic interests as well as family reunion. Since then, immigration to Canada has been distributed between the three categories of economy class, family class, and refugees. The economic class is by far the largest, making up around 60 percent of the total of immigrants since the mid-1990s. This supports the claim that "immigration under Canada's skilled worker point system (. . .) is a cold calculation based on domestic economic requirements with little consideration for humanitarianism" (Khan 2017).

Canada is often represented in the media as an exception to the current mistrust toward immigration in the developed world. And indeed, there is an overall strong support for immigration in Canada, with only 35 percent agreeing that immigration levels are too high, and 62 percent disagreeing. Moreover, 82 percent of respondents believe that the economic impact of immigration is positive (Environics Institute 2017, 2–3). However, support for immigration is conditional on priority being given to economic immigrants: 79 percent of Canadians think that Canada's immigration and refugees policies should give priority to Canada's own economic and workforce needs, while only 21 percent think it should give priority to people "in crisis" abroad (Angus Reid Institute 2016b, 18).

A good illustration of this is the reaction to the Liberal government's decision to increase the annual target of immigrants to 300,000 for 2017, from an average of 250,000 since the mid-1990s. This was approved by 62 percent of Canadians (Environics Institute 2017, 2). However, it is important to note that the increase of the share of refugees and family class immigrants, announced by the Liberals during the campaign, turned out to be minimal: the economy class still makes up 58 percent of the total, as compared to a maximum of 62 percent under the Conservatives from 2011 to 2015 (Canadian Council for Refugees 2017). It seems clear that most Canadians do not want to see a major increase of refugees: while 47 percent approve of the target of 40,000 set by the government for 2017, 41 percent think it's too high, and only 11 percent think it's too low (Angus Reid Institute 2017a, 1). The government recently announced that Canada would admit nearly 1 million immigrants over next 3 years.[4] However, the economic class will make up about 60 percent of the newcomers; the Canadian Council of Refugees has deplored the fact that the share for refugees was only increased slightly from 13 percent in 2017 to 14 percent in each of the next three years (Harris et al. 2017).

While there is a major difference between Canadians' strong support of economic immigration and their much less enthusiastic support of refugees, even this group benefits for the general idea that immigration is good for the Canadian economy. Canada's choice to primarily target Syrian families not only answered humanitarian needs (by protecting the most vulnerable people), and security needs (by weeding out higher-risk individuals), it was also a "generational investment" (Kantor and Einhorn 2017). Almost 50 percent of the Syrian refugees resettled in Canada are children under the age of 18, from large, uneducated families, primarily farmers. It seems clear that the integration of the first generation of Syrian refugees will be difficult for them and costly for Canada.

However, while the parents may find it hard to adapt to Canadian society, the children will benefit from the Canadian school system, a system geared toward the integration of immigrant children, where language acquisition and social integration are emphasized (Friesen 2017). The fact that previous groups of refugees, like the Vietnamese, have done so well in Canada encourages Canadians to welcome refugees "as an investment in the future" (Harper 2015). The Senate Standing Committee on Human Rights recently published a report that recommends that more resources be allocated to help the Syrian refugees to integrate, especially through the funding of language training classes (2016, 9). This investment in future generations is particularly justified in a huge country with a small, aging population with a low birth rate, where some regions, like the Atlantic Provinces, are actually losing population. This argument is at the core of the Liberal decision to increase immigrant targets in the next years (Harris 2017). This shows that Canada's generous policy towards immigrants and refugees is primarily based on national self-interest and the desire to ensure the present and future economic prosperity of the country.

Official Refugees versus Irregular Asylum Seekers: The Double Standards of Canadian Generosity

The Syrian Resettlement Plan is a good example of Canada's generous, if pragmatic, immigration policy. By contrast, irregular asylum seekers, who apply for protection in Canada after arriving on Canadian soil, most of the time illegally, receive a much colder welcome.

In 2010 and 2012, the Conservative government of Stephen Harper passed the Balanced Refugee Reform Act (Bill C-11) and the Protecting Canada's Immigration System Act (Bill C-31), which amended the determination of refugee status. Rick Dykstra, then parliamentary secretary to the Minister of Citizenship and Immigration, summed up the double purpose of Bill C-31: to "make Canada's refugee determination process faster and fairer" and to "ensure faster removal of those whose claims (. . .) are bogus" or "have been rejected" (Dykstra 2012, 1025). Dykstra made clear that the bill was a reaction to the irregular arrival of 76 Tamil asylum seekers aboard the *MV Ocean Lady* in 2009, followed by 492 more aboard the *MV Sun Sea* in 2010. He condemned the human smugglers and described the migrants themselves as potential terrorists and criminals (Dykstra 2012, 1030). He also insisted that the bill was an answer to the Canadians' desire for "a stop (. . .) to the abuse which exists within our immigration system" (Dykstra 2012, 1020). Indeed, according to a 2010 poll, 63 percent of Canadians believed that the ship carrying the Tamil migrants should have been turned back and not allowed to reach Canada. Even in the case their claims were proved to be legitimate, almost half of Canadians (48 percent) said that passengers and crew should be deported to their country of origin, while only one third (35 percent) would allow them to stay in Canada as refugees (Angus Reid Institute 2010).

Many advocates of refugees criticized the Conservatives' amendments of 2010 and 2012. We can mention in particular a working paper of the Canadian Association for Refugees and Forced Migration Studies (CARFMS), based on a five-year research project funded by the Social Sciences and Humanities Research Council of Canada (Atak et al. 2017). The CARFMS working paper argues that the new legislation violates the human rights of refugee claimants by reducing the time limit to submit a claim, instituting different categories of applicants with different procedures, mandating the detention of people who arrive with the help of a smuggler, and finally denying the deliverance of a work permit while the claim is pending (Atak *et al.* 2017, 3–10). Moreover, the paper argues that the bills started a process of "criminalization of asylum seekers" by integrating criminal law processes into immigration control. The governmental rhetoric, originating from the United States and adopted by the Conservatives, tends to increasingly associate immigration to threats to national security and community safety, thus encouraging a negative opinion of asylum seekers (Atak *et al.* 2017, 26).

The Syrian resettlement plan stands as a clear contrast to the negative view of asylum seekers promoted by the recent Conservative legislation. One key reason is that the plan, as a governmental initiative, obviously conforms to the principles of immigration as established by the government of Canada. Refugees who respect the rules benefit from a positive image while irregular asylum seekers are viewed with suspicion, even though their plight might be just as desperate as that of "legitimate" refugees. The CARFMS working paper points out that the Conservative government of Stephen Harper disparaged the 2010 Tamil asylum-seekers as "queue jumpers," as opposed to refugees who apply overseas (Atak *et al.* 2017, 12). In the same way, the 2010 poll revealed that 83 percent of respondents thought the Tamil migrants were "jumping the immigration queue and should apply like any other foreigner who wants to relocate to Canada" (Angus Reid Institute 2010). At work here is a mistrust born from the feeling that irregular asylum seekers, even if their claims are legitimate, abuse the system by bending the rules and unfairly taking the place of more disciplined applicants. Therefore a clear difference is made between "deserving" refugees and asylum seekers, who are seen as somehow "underserving," not because their claims are illegitimate, but because they did not respect the rules. A striking illustration of this is the difference made between refugees and asylum seekers, even after they are granted protection: the CARFMS working paper points out even after they obtain refugee status, asylum seekers who entered the country irregularly are "required to wait five years before applying for permanent residence and before they can sponsor their family members," while people who obtain the status of refugees from abroad can do this after 180 days (Atak *et al.* 2017, 10). It is almost as if, even after winning their claim for protection, irregular asylum seekers are still regarded with suspicion and punished for abusing the system.

This difference in perception and treatment of regular refugees and irregular asylum seekers comes in part from the fear that Canada could lose control of the immigration process if the protection provided by the geographical situation of the country in the past was breached. A study of the 2009 Tamil crisis pointed out that the arrival of irregular asylum seekers by boat has happened only once around a decade in recent Canadian history, making them rare and striking events that inevitably trigger heated debate and an overwhelming negative representation of asylum seekers (Bradimore and Bauder 2011, 639). Public Safety Minister Vic Toews said at the time that the arrival of the ships should be not seen as isolated, independent acts, but as a test of Canada's determination to turn back irregular asylum-seekers (Chase 2010). In the 2010 poll, 72 percent of respondents agreed that the ship was a "test boat" and that more ships carrying migrants could be expected to attempt to reach Canadian waters in the future (Angus Reid Institute 2010).

This negative view of "bad" asylum-seekers as opposed to "good" refugees is not limited to a time when Conservatives dominated the political life of Canada. Since January 2017, when United States President Donald Trump signed several executive orders that restricted the rights of immigrants and refugees, in particular access to asylum,[5] Canada has had to deal with an increasing number of asylum seekers who fear being turned away by the United States. Statistics show a steady increase in the number of refugee protection claims since 2013 (from 10,465 to 23,350 in 2016), with a sharp spike in 2017 (32,938), especially considering that the temporary figure for that year includes only January to September (IRB 2017). This is very likely a reaction to the new US legislation. The number of asylum-seekers apprehended by the Royal Canadian Mounted Police is particularly high in Quebec, where the small town of Hemmingford is reported as the busiest illegal crossing point of Canada's border with the US.[6] It is difficult to assess how lasting this increase of asylum seekers crossing from the United States will be, but the media speculate that it will continue if the Temporary Protected Status of migrant groups in the United States such as the Salvadorans, Hondurans, and Nicaraguans is lifted (Anglin and House 2017). This is what happened with the Haitians, causing them to arrive in large numbers in 2017: 6,249 Haitians claimed refugee protection in Canada from January to September 2017, as opposed to only 631 for the whole year 2016 (IRB 2017).

At first the Liberal government seemed willing to take in asylum seekers turned away from the United States. Prime Minister Trudeau tweeted that Canada would welcome those "fleeing persecution, terror and war, regardless of your faith" (Trudeau 2017). However, the government decided not to increase its target of 40,000 refugees for 2017, a decision that was approved by 57 percent of Canadians. 25 percent thought that Canada should have adopted a ban similar to the US policy, and only 18 percent thought Canada should take in more refugees in response to the US policy (Angus Reid Institute 2017a, 5). Later in the year 2017, clearly in reaction to the spike in illegal border-crossings, the government increased its efforts to discourage asylum seekers. Through their Twitter account, the IRCC has launched an aggressive campaign under the hashtag #cdnref to dispel the false information about refugee status in Canada Tweets made striking by eye-catching red or orange signs menacingly warn that "Asylum-seekers who do not meet requirements to be considered a refugee will be removed" (@CitImmCanada. 2017a) or that "Crossing into Canada between designated ports of entry is against the law. You will be arrested and detained if you cross here" (@CitImmCanada. 2017b). They repeat over and over that "Temporary Protected Status in the US does not give you any status or privilege to come claim asylum in Canada" (@CitImmCanada. 2018).In addition, on the IRCC website, a page explains about "Irregular border crossings and asylum in Canada", with a video in Creole which clearly indicates that Haitian asylum-seekers are especially targeted (IRCC 2017g).

Even the Prime Minister was forced to backtrack on his January tweet. In August 2017, he stated that "entering Canada irregularly is not an advantage. There are rigorous immigration and customs rules that will be followed" (Lampert 2017). The government's policy was no doubt in part the consequence of Canadians' negative view of asylum seekers who cross illegally from the United States into Canada. An April 2017 poll revealed that Canadians were more likely to say their country should be "concerned about the threat posed by these arrivals" (37 percent) than "focused on the opportunity to help" them (24 percent). To the question: "It's not fair that people can cross into Canada illegally and apply for refugee status here," 72 percent agreed and 28 percent disagreed (Angus Reid Institute 2017b).

The current attitude of the Canadian government toward irregular asylum seekers may convey the impression that Trudeau's Canada is no more welcoming to migrants than Trump's United States, as one commentator claims (Khan 2017). This critical view has recently been developed by several academic studies that link Canada's nature as a settler-colonial state responsible for the destruction of Indigenous nations to its treatment of migrants, depicted as exploitative and discriminatory despite an official rhetoric of openness and welcome. For example, Julie Kaye challenges the separation between international and domestic antitrafficking policies, which function similarly in harming the persons they are supposed to protect, particularly migrant and Indigenous women (Kaye 2017). Jennifer Bagelman also emphasizes this parallel discrimination when she writes about "indigenous peoples whose lands were stolen by the very colonial powers that bomb today and then fail to unconditionally welcome the refugees it produces tomorrow" (Bagelman 2015). In her study of British sanctuary cities, she argues that even the sanctuary movement, through which cities choose not to cooperate with state authorities in enforcing immigration laws[7] in fact contributes to reducing asylum seekers to abject supplicant figures (Bagelman 2016).

Militant associations and militant academics are right to point out that Canada's treatment of refugees is less than perfect. Nonetheless, it is important to remember that the immigration policy of the present government of Canada does conform to the long Liberal tradition that has built a relatively generous immigration and integration system since the 1960s, although admittedly for pragmatic reasons rather than pure humanitarianism. For example, although it will not throw the border with the United States wide open, the present Liberal government is making an effort to reduce popular prejudices against irregular asylum seekers. Instead of leading the charge that they are "queue jumpers" who take the place of more deserving and disciplined refugees, as the Conservatives did, the present government created a page on the IRCC website to dispel this "myth." It clearly explains that "asylum seekers are (. . .) a separate category and are neither ahead nor behind applicants for immigration, permanent residence, or citizenship" (IRCC 2017h). And to return to our original topic, the Syrian Resettlement Plan, militant associations like the CARFMS do praise it as a generous and effective policy that illustrates the difference in attitudes toward refugees between the Conservatives and the Liberals (Atak *et al.* 2017, 4).

Canada's Syrian Resettlement Plan: A Global Model for Refugee Crises?

Canada's plan to resettle Syrian refugees is still going on, but already over 50,000 Syrians have benefitted from it. While this remains a modest figure compared to the almost 5 million Syrian people languishing in refugee camps in Turkey, Lebanon, and Jordan, the Canadian plan was a success because it will give these chosen few a true chance at making a good life in a stable and prosperous democracy, and because it enjoyed the support of the great majority of Canadian citizens.

It is this national consensus around the plan that has caught the attention of media around the world. They drew comparisons with the reluctance of other developed countries to resettle Syrian refugees and presented the Canadian initiative as an example that should guide and inspire them. The *New York Times* argued that "Canada's generosity (...) can serve as a beacon for others" (Editorial Board 2015) while *Le Monde* praised the achievement of the "Canadian model" (Kauffmann 2016).

But can the Canadian plan really serve as model for other countries? As we have seen, part of the plan's success in winning support from the Canadian people came from working within the context of a long established social construct where multiculturalism is a structural force for the harmonious integration of immigrants. This construct rests on historical and geographical conditions that are specific to Canada and cannot be reproduced by other countries. It is difficult to assess whether the resettlement plan would have worked so effectively outside of this specific national context.

However, close examination of the way the Syrian resettlement plan was implemented reveal several elements that were developed to reassure Canadians and convince them to support the plan. These elements, contrary to the more global historical and geographical context from which Canada benefits, may be reproduced by other countries. The first element is the pragmatic recognition that a key priority of refugee resettlement programs is to reassure citizens of the host country that everything is done to make them safe and beneficial. In Canada, this was achieved by setting up a selection process that guaranteed that the people accepted as refugees would integrate into the host society without incidents. However, the perception of safety and control is just as important as the reality; hence communication is a key element in this process of winning over the citizens' support. In the case of Canada, this aim was achieved by an exemplary use of participative democracy, especially in the way communication through the IRCC website was kept transparent and open. Finally, and most importantly, the Canadian private sponsorship system is one element that could certainly be adopted by other countries since it has proven effective both to facilitate the resettlement of refugees and to give private citizens the opportunity to appropriate and therefore support the process. Indeed several countries, including the UK, have indicated their interest in the Canadian private sponsorship program (Canadian Press 2016).

These three elements (the pragmatic approach and willingness to address citizens' fears; participative democracy through transparent and open communication; the sponsorship program) are undoubtedly part of the larger Canadian political culture. Nonetheless, contrary to Canada's geography and its 50-year-old tradition of multiculturalism, they can be borrowed by other countries to create conditions where the arrival of refugees will be considered as an investment for the future rather than a national crisis.

Notes

1. There is a legal difference between asylum seekers and refugees. Asylum seekers request protection when they arrive on the receiving country's soil; their applications are assessed individually and may be refused. Refugees, on the other hand, belong to a group which an agency has already defined as needing protection; their applications are processed and accepted prior to arrival. The term "migrants" refers to a much larger category that include people who fear persecution and seek refugee status, and people whose motivations are primarily economic and seek a better life outside of their home country.
2. 25,210 people came as government-assisted refugees, 20,440 as privately sponsored refugees, and 4,720 as blended visa office-referred refugees (a mix of private sponsorship and government assistance).
3. As they worked to propose definitions of the Canadian nation, many historians quoted this passage by Lord Acton: "The co-existence of several nations under the same State is a test, as well as the best security of its freedom. It is also one of the chief instruments of civilization, and, as such, belongs to the natural and providential order, and indicates a state of greater advancement than the natural unity which is the ideal of modern liberalism." See John Emerich Acton, *Essays on Freedom and Power* (Boston: Beacon, 1948), 185.

   For several quotes of this passages, see W. P. M. Kennedy, "Nationalism and Self-Determination," *Canadian Historical Review* 2, no. 1 (1921): 17; R. Cook, *Canada and the French-Canadian Question* (New York: Macmillan, 1966), 102–103; W. Morton, "Clio in Canada; The Interpretation of Canadian History," in *Approaches to Canadian History*, ed. C. Berger (Toronto, ON: University of Toronto Press, 1967 [1946]), 48; K. McNaught, "Canada's European Ambiance," *The Round Table* 310 (1989): 148; D. Morton, "History and Nationality in Canada: Variations on an Old Theme," *Report of the Canadian Historical Association* 14, no. 1 (1979): 7.
4. 310,000 in 2018, up from 300,000 in 2017. That number will rise to 330,000 in 2019 and 340,000 in 2020.
5. Executive Order 13767, "Border Security and Immigration Enforcement Improvements," 25 January 2017, https://www.whitehouse.gov/presidential-actions/executive-order-border-security-immigration-enforcement-improvements/. Executive

Order 13768, "Enhancing Public Safety in the Interior of the United States," 25 January 2017, https://www.whitehouse.gov/presidential-actions/executive-order-enhancing-public-safety-interior-united-states/. Executive Order 13769, "Protecting the Nation from Foreign Terrorist Entry into the United States," 27 January 2017, https://www.nytimes.com/2017/01/27/us/politics/refugee-muslim-executive-order-trump.html. See also (CMS 2017).

6. Between January and November 2017 there were 16,920 RCMP interceptions in Quebec out of a total of 18,615 (IRCC 2017f). In 2002, Canada and the United States signed the Safe Third Country Agreement, which requires asylum seekers to apply for status in the country where they first arrive. However, this applies only to persons who enter Canada at official land border crossings or ports of entry (IRCC 2017e). Persons who enter Canada irregularly, once in custody, are entitled to an oral hearing and fair procedures, regardless of whether they entered through a safe third country. This legal loophole is seen as encouraging asylum seekers who fear their claim will be rejected in the United States under the Trump legislation to cross illegally into Canada to make another claim for asylum (Annett 2017).
7. In the United States, many large cities, such as New York, Los Angeles, and Chicago, as well as smaller cities and communities have declared themselves sanctuary cities and refuse to implement the federal immigration policies introduced by President Trump (CMS 2017). In Canada, Montreal, Vancouver, Toronto and other smaller cities have declared themselves sanctuary cities to ensure that irregular migrants are able to obtain municipal services without fear of being deported. This may imply that municipal law enforcement agencies limit their cooperation with federal immigration officials (Montpetit 2017).

References

@CitImmCanada. "Asylum seekers who do not meet requirements to be considered a refugee will be removed." Tweeter. October 28, 2017a. https://twitter.com/CitImmCanada/status/924380380924448769

@CitImmCanada. "STOP! Crossing into Canada between designated ports of entry is against the law." Tweeter. November 1, 2017b. https://twitter.com/CanBorder/status/925738057868902401

@CitImmCanada. "The Immigration and Refugee Board of Canada decides whether or not someone is in need of Canada's protection". Tweeter, January 3, 2018. https://twitter.com/CitImmCanada/status/948630136571727873

Agroskin, D., and E. Jonas. 2010. "Out of Control: How and Why Does Perceived Lack of Control Lead To Ethnocentrism?" *Review of Psychology* 17, no. 2: 79–90.

Anglin, H. 2017. "How Canada Can Restore Order to its Immigration System." *Maclean's*, September 1. http://www.macleans.ca/opinion/how-canada-can-restore-order-to-its-immigration-system/

Anglin, H., and A. House. 2017. "How Canada Could Prepare for Potential New Wave of Asylum-Seekers." *Maclean's*, November 10. http://www.macleans.ca/opinion/how-canada-could-prepare-for-potential-new-wave-of-asylum-seekers/

Angus Reid Institute. 2010. "Almost Half of Canadians Believe Tamil Migrants Should Be Deported." August 18. http://angusreid.org/almost-half-of-canadians-believe-tamil-migrants-should-be-deported/

Angus Reid Institute. 2015. "Syrian Refugee Resettlement: Tight Timelines Are Key Driver of Opposition to Ottawa's New Year Plan." November 18. http://angusreid.org/refugee-resettlement/

Angus Reid Institute. 2016a. "Canadians Divided on Legacy of Syrian Refugee Resettlement Plan." February 19. http://angusreid.org/canada-refugee-resettlement-plan/

Angus Reid Institute. 2016b. "What Makes Us Canadian? A Study of Values, Beliefs, Priorities and Identity." October 3. http://angusreid.org/canada-values/

Angus Reid Institute. 2017a. "Open-Door Policy? Majority Support Government Decision Not To Increase 2017 Refugee Targets." February 20. http://angusreid.org/syrian-refugee-travel-ban/

Angus Reid Institute. 2017b. "Canadians Prioritize Border Security over Aid to Those Crossing Illegally." April 10. http://angusreid.org/illegal-border-crossing/

Annett, E. 2017. "Asylum Seekers from the U.S: A Guide to the Saga So Far, and What Canadians Think of It." *The Globe and Mail*, February 21. https://www.theglobeandmail.com/news/national/asylum-seekers-from-the-us/article34095595/

Atak, I., G. Hudson, and D. Nakache. 2017. "Making Canada's Refugee System Faster and Fairer: Reviewing the Stated Goals and Unintended Consequences of the 2012 Refugee Reform." CARFMS Working Paper No. 2017/3, Toronto. http://carfms.org/wp-content/uploads/2017/05/CARFMS-WPS-No11-Idil-Atak.pdf

Bagelman, J. 2015. "Foucault and the 'Current' Refugee Crisis." *OpenDemocracy*, November 13. https://www.opendemocracy.net/jen-bagelman/foucault-and-current-refugee-crisis

Bagelman, J. 2016. *Sanctuary City: A Suspended State*. New York: Palgrave Macmillan.

BBC News. 2016. "Migrant Crisis: Migration to Europe Explained in Seven Charts." *BBC News*, March 4. http://www.bbc.com/news/world-europe-34131911

Bloemraad, I. 2006. *Becoming a Citizen: Incorporating Immigrants and Refugees in the United States and Canada*. Berkeley: University of California Press, 2006.

Bradimore, A., and H. Bauder. 2011. "Mystery Ships and Risky Boat People: Tamil Refugee Migration in the Newsprint Media." *Canadian Journal of Communication* 36, no. 4: 637–661.

Canadian Council for Refugees. 2017. "2017 Immigration Level—Comments." http://ccrweb.ca/en/2017-immigration-levels-comments

Canadian Press. 2015. "Timeline: Canada and the Syrian Refugee Crisis." *Maclean's*, November 24. http://www.macleans.ca/politics/ottawa/timeline-canada-and-the-syrian-refugee-crisis/

Canadian Press. 2016. "Trudeau Urges More Help for Syrian Refugees at UN Summit." *Toronto Star*, September 19. https://www.thestar.com/news/canada/2016/09/19/trudeau-in-new-york-for-un-meetings.html

Careless, M. 1969. "Nationalism, Pluralism and Canadian History." *Culture* 30: 19–26.

Careless, M. 1987 [1971]. "'Limited Identities' in Canada." Reprinted in *Contemporary Approaches to Canadian History*, edited by Carl Berger, 5–12. Toronto: Copp Clark.

CBC News. 2015. "Refugee Crisis, Drowned Syrian Boy Shift Focus of Election Campaign." *CBC News*, September 3. http://www.cbc.ca/news/politics/syria-migrants-canada-drowned-migrants-leaders-respond-1.3213878

CMS (Center for Migration Studies of New York). 2017. *President Trump's Executive Orders on Immigration and Refugees*. http://cmsny.org/trumps-executive-orders-immigration-refugees/

Chase, S. 2010. "Tamil Migrant Ship Is a Test, Toews Says, and More Boats Are on the Way." *The Globe and Mail*, August 13. https://www.theglobeandmail.com/news/politics/tamil-migrant-ship-is-a-test-toews-says-and-more-boats-are-on-the-way/article1319927/

Cook, R. 1966. *Canada and the French-Canadian Question*. Toronto: Macmillan.
Dempsey, J. 2016. "The Tide of Syrian Refugees Is Unraveling Europe." *Newsweek*, February 25. http://www.newsweek.com/tide-syrian-refugees-unraveling-europe-430460
Dykstra, R. 2012. Bill C-31, third reading. *House of Commons Debates*, 41st Parliament, 1st session, Edited Hansard, No. 137, June 8. http://www.ourcommons.ca/DocumentViewer/en/41-1/house/sitting-137/hansard
Editorial Board. 2015. "Canada's Warm Embrace of Refugees," *New York Times*, December 11. https://www.nytimes.com/2015/12/12/opinion/canadas-warm-embrace-of-refugees.html
Environics Institute. 2015. "Focus Canada—Spring 2015: Canadian Public Opinion about Immigration and Multiculturalism." June. https://www.environicsinstitute.org/docs/default-source/project-documents/focus-canada-2015-survey-on-immigration-and-multiculturalism/final-report.pdf?sfvrsn=71f7c79e_2
Environics Institute. 2017. "Focus Canada—Spring 2017. Canadian Public Opinion about Immigration and the USA." April. https://www.environicsinstitute.org/docs/default-source/project-documents/focus-canada-canadian-public-opinion-on-immigration-and-the-usa/final-report.pdf?sfvrsn=2e7076b1_2
Epp, M. 2017. "Refugees in Canada." Immigration and Ethnicity in Canada Series 35. Ottawa, ON: The Canadian Historical Association. http://www.cha-shc.ca/download.php?id=2488
Friesen, J. 2017. "Syrian Exodus to Canada: One Year Later, a Look at Who the Refugees Are and Where They Went." *The Globe and Mail*, November 12, 2017. https://www.theglobeandmail.com/news/national/syrian-refugees-in-canada-by-the-numbers/article33120934/
Fritsche, I., E. Jonas, and T. Kessler. 2011. "Collective Reactions to Threat: Implications for Intergroup Conflict and Solving Societal Crises." *Social Issues and Policy Review*, 5: 101–136.
Goodspeed, P. 2014. "Why Has Canada Only Taken In 200 Syrian Refugees?" *Toronto Star*, September 19. https://www.thestar.com/news/atkinsonseries/2014/09/22/delay_delay_delay.html
Haglund, D. 2009. "And the Beat Goes On: 'Identity' and Canadian Foreign Policy." In *Canada among Nations, 2008: 100 Years of Canadian Foreign Policy*, edited by R. Bothwell and J. Daudelin, 343–367. Montreal and Kingston: McGill-Queen's University Press.
Harper, T. 2015. "Refugees as a Long-Term Investment in the Country." *Toronto Star*, November 11. https://www.thestar.com/news/canada/2015/11/11/refugees-as-a-long-term-investment-in-the-country-tim-harper.html
Harris, K., C. Hall, and P. Zimonjic. 2017. "Canada to Admit Nearly 1 Million Immigrants over Next 3 Years." *CBC News*, November 1. http://www.cbc.ca/news/politics/immigration-canada-2018-1.4371146
IRB (Immigration and Refugee Board of Canada). 2017. "Refugee Protection Claims Statistics." http://www.irb-cisr.gc.ca/Eng/RefClaDem/stats/Pages/index.aspx
IRCC (Immigration, Refugees, and Citizenship Canada). 2017a. "#WelcomeRefugees: Security and Health Screening." http://www.cic.gc.ca/english/refugees/welcome/overview/security.asp
IRCC (Immigration, Refugees, and Citizenship Canada). 2017b. "#WelcomeRefugees: Photos from the Journey." http://www.cic.gc.ca/english/refugees/welcome/photos.asp
IRCC (Immigration, Refugees, and Citizenship Canada). 2017c. "Canada's Syrian Commitments." http://www.cic.gc.ca/english/refugees/welcome/commitment.asp
IRCC (Immigration, Refugees, and Citizenship Canada). 2017d. "Immigration: Syrian Refugees—Monthly IRCC Updates." http://open.canada.ca/data/en/dataset/01c85d28-2a81-4295-9c06-4af792a7c209

IRCC (Immigration, Refugees, and Citizenship Canada). 2017e. "Canada-U.S. Safe Third Country Agreement." https://www.canada.ca/en/immigration-refugees-citizenship/corporate/mandate/policies-operational-instructions-agreements/agreements/safe-third-country-agreement.html

IRCC (Immigration, Refugees, and Citizenship Canada). 2017f. "Asylum Claims: Key Figures on Asylum Claims Made in Canada." https://www.canada.ca/en/immigration-refugees-citizenship/services/refugees/asylum-claims.html

IRCC (Immigration, Refugees, and Citizenship Canada). 2017g. "Irregular Border Crossings and Asylum in Canada." https://www.canada.ca/en/immigration-refugees-citizenship/campaigns/irregular-border-crossings-asylum.html

IRCC (Immigration, Refugees, and Citizenship Canada). 2017h. "Myth: Are Asylum-Seekers Queue Jumpers?" https://www.canada.ca/en/immigration-refugees-citizenship/campaigns/irregular-border-crossings-asylum/myth.html

IRCC (Immigration, Refugees, and Citizenship Canada). 2018. "Sponsor a Refugee." https://www.canada.ca/en/immigration-refugees-citizenship/services/refugees/help-outside-canada/private-sponsorship-program.html

Kantor, J. and C. Einhorn. 2017. "Canadians Adopted Refugee Families for a Year. Then Came 'Month 13.'" *New York Times*, March 25. https://www.nytimes.com/2017/03/25/world/canada/syrian-refugees.html

Kauffmann, S. 2016. "Réfugiés: L'exception canadienne." *Le Monde*, March 26. http://www.lemonde.fr/idees/article/2016/03/26/l-exception-canadienne_4890452_3232.html

Kaye, J. 2017. *Responding to Human Trafficking: Dispossession, Colonial Violence, and Resistance among Indigenous and Racialized Women*. Toronto: University of Toronto Press.

Khan, A. 2017. "Canada's Immigration System Is No Kinder Than America's." *Maclean's*, August 11. http://www.macleans.ca/opinion/canadas-immigration-system-is-no-kinder-than-americas/

Kymlicka, W. 2003. "Canadian Multiculturalism in Historical and Comparative Perspective: Is Canada Unique?" *Forum Constitutionnel* 13, no. 1: 1–8. doi: http://dx.doi.org/10.21991/C9W37Q

Kymlicka, W. 2004. "Marketing Canadian Pluralism in the International Arena." *International Journal* 59, no. 4: 829–852.

Kymlicka, W., and F. Peonidis. 2008. "Multiculturalism and Liberal Democracy" *Eurozine*, July 25. http://www.eurozine.com/multiculturalism-and-liberal-democracy-2/

Lampert, A. 2017. "Canada's Trudeau Warns Against Entering Country 'Irregularly' "; *Reuters*. August 20. https://ca.reuters.com/article/topNews/idCAKCN1B00M9-OCATP

Levitz, S. 2016. "Canada's Ever-Changing Response to Syrian Refugee Crisis." *Toronto Star*, January 1. https://www.thestar.com/news/canada/2016/01/01/canadas-ever-changing-response-to-syrian-refugee-crisis.html

Mas, S. 2016. "McCallum Promise To Boost Privately Sponsored Syrian Refugees Spawns Confusion." *CBC News*, April 3. http://www.cbc.ca/news/politics/john-mccallum-more-room-for-privately-sponsored-refugees-1.3514058

Migration Policy Centre. 2016. *Syrian Refugees—A Snapshot of the Crisis—in the Middle East and Europe*. European University Institute, updated September 2016. http://syrianrefugees.eu/

Montpetit, J. 2017. "Sanctuary City Movement Grows in Canada, But Could Bring Tension with Police, Immigration Officials." *CBC News*. February 21. http://www.cbc.ca/news/canada/montreal/sanctuary-cities-montreal-canada-toronto-vancouver-1.3991321

Murray, D. 2015. "World Faces Major Crisis as Number of Displaced Hits Record High." *UNHCR*. June 18. http://www.unhcr.org/news/latest/2015/6/5582c2f46/world-faces-major-crisis-number-displaced-hits-record-high.html

Nuttall, J. 2015. "Will Canada Meet Its Target to Bring in 10,000 Syrian Refugees?" *The Tyee*, January 22. https://thetyee.ca/News/2015/01/22/Canada-Syrian-Refugee-Target/

Proctor, J. 2015. "Syrian Refugee Screening Will Be a Challenge, But One Canada Can Meet." *CBC News*, November 17. http://www.cbc.ca/news/canada/british-columbia/syrian-refugee-screening-will-be-a-challenge-but-one-canada-can-meet-1.3321889

Senate Standing Committee on Human Rights. 2016. *Finding Refuge in Canada: A Syrian Resettlement Story*. 42nd Parliament, 1st Session, Report No. 5. December. https://sencanada.ca/content/sen/committee/421/RIDR/Reports/RIDR_RPT_SyrianResettlement_FINAL_E.pdf

Shils, E. 1961. "Centre and Periphery." In *The Logic of Personal Knowledge: Essays Presented to Michael Polanyi*, edited by Michael Polyani and Paul Ignotus, 117–130. London: Routledge.

Taub, A. 2017. "Canada's Secret to Resisting the West's Populist Wave." *The New York Times*, June 27. https://www.nytimes.com/2017/06/27/world/canada/canadas-secret-to-resisting-the-wests-populist-wave.html

Tepperman, J. 2017. "Canada's Ruthlessly Smart Immigration Policy." *The New York Times*, June 28. https://www.nytimes.com/2017/06/28/opinion/canada-immigration-policy-trump.html

Trudeau, J. 2015. "Interview with Justin Trudeau." In "Trudeau's Canada, Again," by Lawson Guy, .*New York Times Magazine*. December 8. https://www.nytimes.com/2015/12/13/magazine/trudeaus-canada-again.html

Trudeau, J. 2017. #WelcomeToCanada. Twitter. January 28. https://twitter.com/justintrudeau/status/825438460265762816

UNHCR. 1951. The 1951 United Nations Refugee Convention. http://www.unhcr.org/1951-refugee-convention.html

UNHCR. 2014. *World at War*. "Global Trends: Forced Displacements in 2014." http://www.unhcr.org/556725e69.html

UNHCR. 2015. *Global Trends: Forced Displacements in 2015*. http://www.unhcr.org/576408cd7.pdf

UNHCR. 2016. *Global Trends: Forced Displacements in 2016*. http://www.unhcr.org/globaltrends2016/

CHAPTER 44

MIGRATION AND INTEGRATION IN CHINA

ERIC FONG, YINGTONG LAI, AND AIJIA LI

OVER the last three decades, China has experienced the largest internal migration from rural areas to cities in human history (Liang 2016). Since the 1980s, fueled by the urgent and high demand for labor in the city because of economic reform, the central government has loosened the strict household registration system of "hukou," which was formally lifted in 1985 (Xu et al. 2011). The hukou system controls population movement, by systematically allowing people in rural areas to move into cities (Chan 2009). Consequently, China has witnessed massive human migration on an unprecedented scale from rural to urban areas and from less developed to more developed towns and cities (Liu and Xu 2017). According to the sixth and latest Chinese census, in 2010, the migrant population reached 221 million (NBS 2012). This number is close to 70 percent of the total population of the United States in 2016, and close to six times the population of Canada in 2016.

This large-scale human migration, with the majority of the migrants moving from rural areas to major cities in China (Fan 2011; Hao et al. 2011; Yue et al. 2013), has had a broad and drastic impact on China's economic and social development in cities as well as rural areas (Hao et al. 2011; Liang 2016; Yan et al. 2014). An obvious consequence of the internal migration is that it has contributed directly to rapid industrialization and urbanization in China in the last few decades (Cai and Wang 2008; Yan et al. 2014). The GDP grew 9.8 percent annually between 1978 and 2007 (Cao et al. 2012), compared to 6.1 percent between 1952 and 1978 (Chan et al. 2011). In 2010, China's economy became the second largest in the world (The World Bank 2011). Meanwhile, the urban population jumped from 26.41 percent of the total population in 1990 to 56.10 percent in 2015 (Chan and Hu 2003; NBS 2016).

Although this unprecedented internal migration has brought positive economic development and urban growth, it also exerts a lot of pressure on cities to accommodate such a large influx of population. Local governments have worked to meet the need for more housing in urban areas and to address the hollowing phenomenon in the countryside (Hao et al. 2011; Huang 2012; Liu et al. 2010; Long 2014). At the same time, most rural migrants face challenges in the labor and housing markets, and in gaining access to public resources (Chen et al. 2017; Fan et al. 2009; Huang and Tao 2015; Song 2016; Zhu 2016). New demographic patterns have emerged both in the cities and rural areas due to the adjustment of this internal migration (Fan 2011; Fan et al. 2011; Fang et al. 2016; He and Ye 2014; Hu 2017; Zhang and Wu 2017).

Most studies have explored migration from rural areas to cities, due to the sheer size of that movement (Fang et al. 2016; Hao and Tang 2015; Liu and Xu 2017; Wu and Treiman 2007; Yue et al. 2013). However, there are an increasing number of studies that mention urban migrants, those who move from one city to another without local hukou, and discover that they also encounter difficulties (J. Chen 2011; Gagnon et al. 2014; Lian 2009; Zhang 2013). And with the growing economy, more individuals from overseas have settled in the cities (Bodomo 2010; Mathews and Yang 2012; He 2008; Lee et al. 2014; Li et al. 2008; Liang 2014; Pieke 2012; Zhou and Yang 2014).

Both internal migration (to cities from rural areas or other cities), especially rural migrants, and international migration (to China from other countries) have gained considerable attention over the decades. Many studies have been published to address their economic, social, and psychological difficulties (Chen et al. 2017; Wong et al. 2007; Wu and Treiman 2007; Zhang and Wu 2017). This chapter's discussion will detail the predicaments faced by rural migrants, and the adaptation challenges encountered by urban migrants and individuals from overseas in Chinese cities, giving more attention to rural migration to the city, because it is the key concern among academics, government officials, and the public (Huang and Guo 2017; Song et al. 2008; Yan et al. 2014; Zhang and Wu 2017). The discussion highlights that the influx of rural migrants to the city has emerged as a crisis and that the situation is framed as being beyond control of the government. The issue has indeed become a crisis as the situation poses difficulties and uncertainties for the government's ability to govern, and especially the situation of migrant workers in the city has become a crisis as it demands the government to do something. Finally, the public anxiety over the controversy creates a clear boundary between "us" and "them" which facilitates the perpetuation of the crisis.

Rural-to-Urban Migration in China

Rural-to-urban migrants have formed the largest proportion of the internal migration tide in China for the last four decades (Fan 2011; Hao et al. 2011; Yue et al. 2013). They have become the backbone of the labor force in urban China. By 2010, according to Chan (2010b), rural migrants represented 70 percent to 80 percent of the total labor force in some major coastal cities, such as Shenzhen and Dongguan. To appreciate the impact of this rural-urban migration, it's first necessary to provide a brief historical overview of the economic and political developments that contributed to this massive internal migration.

After the Communist government took control of mainland China in 1949, geographic mobility was strictly controlled. Individuals were not allowed to move without official approval. There was particular restriction on migration from rural to urban areas. This control was possible because individuals required local household registration, hukou, to obtain local welfare and social benefits. In the 1950s, even food was rationed through the hukou system (Liang 2016).

The economic reforms that began in 1978 prioritized the development of urban areas. Preferential governmental policies were introduced, foreign investment was invited, and better welfare schemes were recommended. China began to initiate labor-intensive and export-oriented growth strategies. Many low-skilled jobs were created (Huang et al. 2017). With this drastic change in economic policies, in 1985 the rural population was officially allowed to move to cities to meet the huge demand for labor (Liu and Xu 2017). There was a massive influx of rural migrant workers that increased the urban population at an incredible rate. The percentage of urban population in China jumped from 17.92 percent in 1978 to 56.10 percent in 2015 (NBS 2016).

The top destinations for rural migrant workers always are coastal areas and major metropolises that have vibrant markets with major foreign investment, such as Guangdong, Zhejiang, Fujian, Shanghai, and Beijing. Although a large proportion of migrants come from the same provinces, there is a substantial proportion from other provinces. Migrants from provinces in the central and western regions especially have been attracted to work in cities in the eastern part of China (Shen 2012). However, there is an emerging trend in recent years that migrants also seek cities in the western part of the country, where local urban hukou is easier to attain (Zhang and Tao 2012).

Although most rural migrants chose to work in the coastal areas, they are attracted to different tiers of the urban hierarchy in the region with different social and demographic characteristics. In a case study in Jiangsu Province, Hao and Tang (2015) have found that the choice of destination is shaped by regional preferences, gender, educational attainment, and rural landholdings, as well as other typical factors which drive the migration such as age, marital status, and earning differentials. Although individual experiences in the city may vary, our discussion focuses on the general patterns and experiences in the major cities where the data for most studies were collected.

Regardless of destination, the migration of rural workers is characterized by its circular pattern. Most migrants move back and forth between their rural villages and cities, since they are prohibited by the hukou system from settling in cities. Faced with an uncertain social and economic future in the city, rural migrants are motivated to adopt a strategy of flexible mobilization, which can maximize economic returns, diversify risks, and mitigate hukou-based constraints (Fan 2011; Fan et al. 2011; Liu et al. 2017). Even when they are participating fully in the urban economy, some migrants are socially and economically tied to their rural roots and willing to move between rural and urban areas to obtain the best of both worlds. Subsequently, many migrant families are "split-household," as some members are left behind in the rural home (Fan 2011, 12). Split households can persist for long periods of time, sometimes even more than twenty years (Fan et al. 2011). A split family with long distance relationships can develop many problems, including issues related to the children and elderly who are left behind (Fan 2011; He and Ye 2014; Hu 2017).

As parents work in the city, over 61 million children in rural China have been left behind by their parents according to an estimate in 2013 (Duan et al. 2013). The large number of left-behind children are portrayed as a situation beyond the control of the government and as a crisis threatening the future of China. Most of these migrants return home infrequently, typically once a year, during the Spring Festival in the beginning of the year, and sometimes less often (Fan et al. 2011). Many of their children reside with grandparents. They often lack supervision because of parental absence and their grandparents' limitations (Lu 2012; Ye and Lu 2011). There is consistent evidence of consequences such as cognitive delay, poor academic performance, and poor physical and mental health outcomes (Chang et al. 2017; Wang et al. 2015; Ye and Lu 2011; Zhang et al. 2014). As a result, their accumulation of human capital is seriously affected (Chang et al. 2017). Some observers argue that outmigration directly increases educational inequality in the short run and income inequality in the long run (Lu 2012; Zhang et al. 2014).

As adults leave their village, the large exodus to cities has drastically changed farming behavior (Hao and Tang 2015). Land abandonment has become a widespread phenomenon. Although more land is being subcontracted by farmers, land abandonment is still substantial (Cai and Wang 2008; Mullan et al. 2011). In 2016, the Ministry of Land and Resources estimated that about 66,000 hectares of arable land had been lost annually from 2011 to 2015 (MLR 2016). Such a drastic decline could consequently threaten food security crisis in China (Long 2014).

Rural migrants working in the city faced a lot of hardship. The first generation of rural migrants, pushed by rural poverty and tempted by the emerging urban market, moved to cities for economic opportunities in order to subsidize their household farming activities (Yue et al. 2010). However, with low levels of education and without professional skills, migrant workers could only take low-skilled jobs in the manufacturing, construction, and low-level service sectors (Liu and Xu 2017). In the city, they were labeled as "peasant workers" or "rural migrant workers" (*nongmingong* 农民工). The label highlighted their rural origins and their transient status. Emphasizing these characteristics strengthened the group boundaries between rural migrants and local residents. These clear boundaries were further reinforced by negative stereotyping of migrant workers imposed by local residents. Migrant workers were viewed as rude and uneducated, with bad manners and shabby dress (Chung 2018). Such stereotyping created tremendous barriers for migrant workers to integrate socially. Because they had only agricultural hukou, migrant workers were not granted resources or services under urban-based policies and suffered discrimination from their urban counterparts (Chan and Buckingham 2008).

Discrimination against rural migrants in the city has continued since the economic reform. Although the socioeconomic profile of rural migrant workers has changed and become more diversified in the past three decades, the labeling and discrimination still help to maintain a clear strong boundary between rural migrants and local residents (Cheng et al. 2013; Wang 2008; Yue et al. 2010). In particular, there is a new generation of rural migrants born in or after the 1980s who have higher levels of education and skill, but little to no agricultural experience (Yue et al. 2010). Their rural status still prevents them from enjoying services within urban communities, and leaves them with many of the same economic and social disadvantages that the older generation faced, despite being more competitive in the labor market (Wang 2008).

Earning Differential, Workplace Discrimination

Studies have consistently found that rural migrants in the city earn significantly less than their urban counterparts (Song 2016; Zhang and Wu 2017). Many attribute the earning disparities to the hukou status of workers, compounded by the role of the state in generating institutional inequality among social groups (Y. Chen 2011; Song 2016; Zhang and Wu 2017).

Analyses suggest that the income difference between rural migrants and local residents is due to three sources of inequality. First, part of the pay gap is related to differences in human capital (Song 2016). Most rural migrants have low levels of education that lead them to be employed only in jobs that require minimal skill and education.

Second, the pay gap partly results from inequality within occupations. Workers with rural hukou earn less within the same occupation. However, income inequality within occupational groups varies. Song (2016) investigated the heterogeneity of discrimination in relation to wage distribution, and discovered that hukou-based wage discrimination mainly affects middle- and high-wage workers. Access to high-paid occupations in various work units differs for rural migrants and urban workers, not only because the former lack human capital such as education and professional experience, but also due to the hukou-based exclusionary policy. The human capital returns for rural migrants suffer considerably (Y. Chen 2011; Fan et al. 2009; Zhang and Wu 2017).

Third, based on the analysis of sample data from the mini-census in China in 2005 Zhang and Wu (2017) have identified that rural migrants' overall earnings disadvantage is derived from occupational segregation. Workers with rural hukou are less likely to participate in certain occupations even after controlling for education and other factors. The findings seem to suggest that rural migrant workers, because of their non-local hukou status, are systematically blocked from certain occupations. Rural migrants are relegated to occupations that urban locals are reluctant to pursue (i.e., occupations that are physically demanding, low-skilled, and/or potentially dangerous [Chan and Buckingham 2008; Zhang and Wu 2017]). Studies also show that the occupational segregation of rural hukou holders varies among different ownership sectors. Discrimination is more severe in state agencies and enterprises than in the private sector (Song 2016; Zhang and Wu 2017).

In addition to wage and occupational discrimination, some rural migrants are asked to work in unfavorable environments. They are expected to work longer hours and are treated negatively in the workplace (Cheo 2017). They are assigned to work in dangerous environments or are asked to perform high-risk tasks (Zhang and Wu 2017). In some situations, some of them were not paid. Given their limited knowledge of their rights, they rarely complained or refused to work under such circumstances. Pun's research on factory female workers in Shenzhen, a special economic zone where many foreign factories are located, showed that they were subjected to long hours of work (Pun 2005). Many of them suffered from chronic backaches and headaches.

Rural migrants in the city face disadvantages in the workplace due to their non-local hukou, and their children suffer from the same institutional arrangements. Many of their children grow up in the city and are well oriented to city culture, but are not able to convert their rural hukou to urban hukou (Fang et al. 2016; Liang and Chen 2007). Subsequently, they suffer as much as their parents in the workplace (Pun 2005). The hukou system reproduces poverty and lack of opportunity for the next generation of rural migrants (Fang et al. 2016). Therefore, Y. Chen (2011) and Wu and Treiman (2007) question the potential for social mobility in urban areas as long as the hukou system persists. There have been persistent calls over the years for the government to do something with the hukou of rural migrants in the city.

Housing and Residential Segregation

Rural migrants face a segmented housing market when dormitories are not provided (Liu et al. 2017). Without local urban hukou, rural migrants have no access to subsidized housing provided by local governments (Huang 2012; Huang and Tao 2015). They have difficulty finding decent affordable residences as they face discrimination in the housing market. With limited resources and choices, migrant workers live in inexpensive rental housing such as urban villages and basements (Huang and Yi 2015; Liu et al. 2015; Zhu 2016). In fact, the housing experience of rural migrants not only is the direct result of discrimination in the housing market, but also, as discussed earlier, an indirect result of discrimination in the workplace where they occupy mostly low-paying jobs (Hao et al. 2011). With low incomes, they have little choice but to cluster in poor rental housing. Consequently, the hukou-based exclusion from housing opportunities leads to the proliferation of rural migrant enclaves, usually located in poor areas of Chinese cities (Wu 2004).

Living conditions for rural migrants usually are at a subsistence level, with crowded living space, poor hygiene conditions, lack of proper ventilation, and lack of fire equipment in underground residences (Huang and Tao 2015; Huang and Yi 2015; Song et al. 2008). The poor physical environment has negative consequences for migrants' subjective well-being (Liu et al. 2017). Studies have documented that a poor physical environment and overcrowded conditions are related to higher levels of psychological distress and behavioral problems (Hao et al. 2011; Huang and Tao 2015; Song et al. 2008). The poor living conditions also reduce the migrants' settlement intentions as they feel that they are living on the fringe, spatially and socially isolated (Liu et al. 2017). Because they shelter a socially marginal group, migrant enclaves have been labeled as dirty, chaotic, and dangerous (Huang and Yi 2015). The label further intensifies the clear boundary between rural migrants and local residents.

However, some researchers see the positive aspect of migrant enclaves. Living close to their relatives, friends from the same hometown, fellow villagers, or with their workmates from the same industry, migrants develop social ties that can provide social and even financial support if needed (Zhu 2016). Liu et al. (2015) found that rural migrants living in a migrant enclave in Guangzhou, through social networks developed in the enclave, were more likely to experience upward social mobilization than did those not living in the enclave. In this regard, the massive demolition of migrant enclaves and clean-up of underground spaces in major cities in recent years may have a negative effect on the social support and integration of rural migrants in cities (Liu et al. 2015; Song et al. 2008; Zhu 2016).

Health Care and Social Services

In addition to discrimination in workplace and housing, rural migrants also experience exclusion from social services. Employment-based social insurance programs were not made available to rural migrant workers until the end of the 1990s (Huang and Guo 2017; Xu et al. 2011). Despite this change, migrant workers still have fewer insurance benefits than local residents (Wang, Guo and Cheng 2015). They also participate less in welfare programs (Huang and Guo 2017).

The situation experienced by rural migrants is reflective of a welfare system in China that is far from universal given the trends of welfare decentralization and marketization (Huang and Guo 2017). Although fiscal decentralization has significantly improved individual satisfaction with care for the sick, elderly, and poor, most rural migrants are considered a potential fiscal burden, and are denied entitlements including the decentralized delivery of social services (Chan and Buckingham 2008; Chen et al. 2017). Only migrants who are better educated, highly skilled or economically well-off and expected to enhance economic competitiveness are more likely to be granted local hukou and welfare opportunities, which means there is differentiation among rural migrants regarding access to social services (Huang and Guo 2017). In addition, Xu et al. (2011) have suggested that individual factors are critical in determining migrant workers' participation in welfare programs, such as lack of knowledge of welfare programs and distrust of local governments, and macro-level factors, including employer's support and industry.

With limited access to public services, lack of health services, and facing family disruption and a tough urban environment, rural migrants have a higher than average chance of depression (Wong et al. 2007). Based on the Centre for Epidemiologic Depression Scale (CES-D), a recent study of migrant workers in Chengdu, reported in

2011, showed that 24 percent of migrant workers displayed clinically relevant symptoms of depression, and 13 percent had a clinical diagnosis of depression (Qiu et al. 2011). Difficulty in adapting to the city was one of the key factors contributing to their depression. Another study collected data in Shenzhen in 2009 and reported similar findings (Mou et al. 2011). There have been consistent calls from the public that something has to be done to improve public services provided to rural migrants.

Settlement Intention and Return Migration

Under the Chinese hukou system, it would be very hard for migrant workers to settle in the city permanently. In addition, if they want to change their status to urban hukou, rural migrants have to abandon their land in their home community. Because of the barriers to changing status, and the increase in land value back home, many rural migrants do not intend to change their household registration and do not plan to stay in the city permanently. According to Cai and Wang's study in the Pearl Delta (2008), they estimated only one quarter of the total migrants (about 30 million) wanted to transfer their household registration to their city of employment. Zhu's study (2004) of Fujian Province showed that only 24 percent of the migrant population surveyed wanted to move to the city permanently with their entire families. Most migrants prefer to stay in the city without changing their hukou status, or continue to circulate between urban destinations and their rural homes.

As shown in the 2010 Chinese Census, China's floating population rose to 221 million by 2010 (NBS 2012). For most migrant workers, the key factor to staying in the city is economic gain. Despite low income, poor working environments, and undesirable living environments, many still arrive in the city and work there largely because their income is still better than it would be in rural areas.

In recent years, the settlement of rural migrants has become a more pressing concern. In 2014, the government set up a single national resident registration system (*jumin hukou*) for both rural and urban populations. Rural migrants are encouraged to settle in small and medium cities. It is hoped that this reform will provide services and welfare to residents who stay for long periods in the city, especially small and medium cities. However, larger cities require longer duration and allow applications of changing hukou status from a smaller number of occupations.

As well as a low intention to stay permanently and economic recession after financial crisis, a new trend emerging in internal migration is a growing number of migrant workers returning to their villages and hometowns (Bai and Song 2002; Chan 2010a; Piotrowski and Tong 2013; Zhao 2002). Liang et al. (2014) showed that interprovincial return migration from Guangdong to Sichuan was 1.88 percent from 1995 to 2000, and 3.27 percent from 2005 to 2010. For Hunan province (which sends the largest number of interprovincial migrants to Guangdong), interprovincial return migration from Guangdong was 1.61 percent from 1995 to 2000, and 4 percent from 2005 to 2010. There is no doubt the number of return migrants is increasing. As the supply of rural migrants declines, it remains to be seen whether their working and living environments in the city will improve.

Urban-to-Urban Migration in China

The previous discussion described how the economic and social well-being of rural migrants in cities is affected by their rural hukou status. Migrants moving from another city with urban hukou encountered minimal issue in adaptation. Yet for all migrants without local hukou status, the hukou system blocks them from gaining access to housing subsidies, educational resources, and many urban welfare programs (Chan and Buckingham 2008; Gagnon et al. 2014; Hui et al. 2014).

Urban migrants are those who move from one town or city to another without local hukou status at the destination. Since 1990, a growing number of urban migrants has moved to other cities. The 2000 census revealed that 37.2 percent of all migrants in China moved between urban areas in 2000 (Cai and Wang 2003). Even though they differ from their rural counterparts as they have higher educational qualifications and understand urban contexts, urban migrants still face challenges in occupational attainment and upward mobility.

Among them, a large number of college graduates came from other cities. They have problems securing a desirable job despite their educational credentials. The term "colony of ants," is commonly used in the local media and discourse to describe low-income college graduates who are working in low-paying jobs and living in subsistence circumstances (Lian 2009). A survey of college students in Beijing and Zhengzhou conducted by Zhang (2013) showed that of college students in major cities, about 27.3 percent came from county-level towns and 12.1 percent from medium-sized and small-sized cities. These college graduates, without local houku, may encounter discrimination in the labor market (Gagnon et al. 2014) and housing market (Logan et al. 2009; Hui et al. 2014; Stephens 2010). The situation is even worse for those who have only high school education. Y. Chen (2011) found that those with educational levels below senior high school, including those from other cities, face discrimination in their job search.

Migrants from other urban areas also face health issues and experience lower life satisfaction. Their experiences are related partly to the tough urban environment they face (Gee and Takeuchi 2004). A study conducted in Beijing in 2009 demonstrated that the physical health advantage diminished significantly among urban migrants from townships or small cities the longer they stayed in Beijing. Furthermore, those who grew up in townships or small cities showed a significantly higher level of distress (Chen 2011).

Migrants from other urban areas are more likely to emphasize improvement in their social status and want to establish themselves in the new place. Such expectations may increase the pressure to adapt and create anxiety. Most of them want to stay in the new city, and develop a sense of attachment after spending years there. Yet, given the difficulty of transferring to local hukou, these urban migrants may feel frustrated and confused about their future (J. Chen 2011; Du 2017).

Despite the fact that urban migrants without local hukou face a similar situation as rural migrants, their situation has never been considered as serious as that of rural migrants and their issue has never been elevated to become a national crisis. This is partly because the sheer number of urban migrants without hukou is much smaller than the number of rural migrants. It is also partly because urban migrants are not so distinctive in terms of social behavior and demeanor compared to rural migrants

International Migration in China

China has gradually become a new destination for many people to look for jobs and to settle. The trend is largely related to the rapid growth of the Chinese economy in recent decades. This newly emerged pattern has raised considerable discussion among scholars in China in recent years (Lee et al. 2014). Foreigners have come from diverse regions and countries, from Africa to Southeast Asia, as well as Korea and Taiwan. Some are children of Chinese living overseas. Some married local Chinese and decided to stay. They have settled in major cities, such as Guangzhou, Beijing, Shanghai, and Dongguan, where jobs and opportunities are easily found. Despite the growing number of foreigners staying in China, the country does not have a legal framework for immigration. Therefore, foreigners find it hard to settle. By 2011, only 4,752 foreigners had obtained Chinese green cards (Gan 2013). Many foreigners have to renew their visa outside the country when their visa periods have expired. This arrangement has created many problems for foreign residents. The institutional barriers to settling leads foreigners in China to develop strong transient attitudes. A recent study conducted in Guangzhou in 2015 showed that only 14.1 percent migrants planned to stay in China permanently (Liang and Li 2016).

However, not every foreigner follows the requirements to renew their visa outside the country. Many stay without status. These illegal foreigners have become a major issue for the government of China. Local governments usually do not have the enforcement capacity in place to manage high immigration pressure (Haugen 2012). In 2006, the Ministry of Public Security handled 36,000 cases of individuals who had entered, stayed, or worked in China illegally. (These three categories of illegal status are referred to as *san fei*.) 9,560 of those individuals were repatriated (Pieke 2012).

Africans in Guangzhou have raised much academic concern in recent years (Bodomo 2010; Mathews and Yang 2012; Li et al. 2008; Zhou et al. 2016). The city of Guangzhou, China's most important manufacturing center, attracts many traders from Africa. In 2008, it was conservatively estimated that between 50,000 and 130,000 African migrants were residing in Guangzhou (Cai and Huang 2008). After 2008, both the Chinese central government and the Guangzhou provincial government began to issue or extend fewer visas for Africans in the province because of the high security requirements of the

Olympic Games and the economic recession caused by the financial crisis (Bodomo and Ma 2010; Liang 2014). Many African traders assumed illegal status in Guangzhou. The government responded to the situation by conducting frequent status checks in African communities. Many were pushed to other places such as Yiwu, a city with a heavy concentration of small commodity trade in Zhejiang Province (Bodomo and Ma 2010).

Another major group outside mainland China is from Taiwan. A large number of businessmen from Taiwan, known as Taishang, have settled in China. In 2015, the Directorate-General of Budget, Accounting, and Statistics of Taiwan estimated about 420,000 left Taiwan and worked in China (National Statistics R.O.C [Taiwan] 2017). The exact number of Taiwanese working in China would far exceed that number. However, estimation is difficult because workers from Taiwan travel back and forth. Taiwanese businessmen and workers have taken advantage of the common language and close cultural ties and established factories and companies in major cities in the coastal region. These Taiwanese communities established their own schools and some have their own hospitals (Ng 2004). Even in the workplace, the interaction between Taiwanese and mainland Chinese remains remote (Deng 2002). There is limited integration of Taiwanese businessmen and workers with the local communities. This pattern also applies to Koreans in China. Many of them cluster in the Wangjing area in Beijing and the Yuanjing area in Guangzhou with limited social integration (He 2008; Zhou and Yang 2014).

Conclusion

Whether internal or international, human migration in China is an important social issue. To the extent possible, this chapter has reviewed existing literature about the issues facing both internal migrants and non-Chinese in China. It is clear that institutional arrangements impede the adaptation of rural migrants in the city. Largely due to their rural hukou status, rural migrants face discrimination in the labor and housing markets, and they have limited access to local services and welfare. Their children experience the same predicament in the city. In short, rural migrants are treated largely as second-class citizens because of their hukou.

This chapter further suggests that the presence of rural migrants and associated uncertainties have created a crisis beyond control of the government. Therefore, there has been a call from the public to ameliorate the problem. Given the heightened public anxiety and cultural and economic difference between rural migrants and urban residents, local residents have maintained a clear boundary between themselves and rural migrants. Such a situation has facilitated the perpetuation of the crisis.

Studies also show that migrants without hukou from other cities experience difficulties in cities. Without local hukou, they experience discrimination in the labor and housing markets. However, the group has never been constructed as a serious crisis as much as rural migrants. As for individuals from other countries, China does not have a legal framework for them to apply for residential status. Studies suggest that many non-Chinese cluster and have limited social integration.

China seems to stand at a historical crossroads with respect to human migration. Since the relaxation of hukou policies with respect to migration, millions of rural migrants and a considerable number of migrants from other cities have arrived in Chinese cities. At the same time, the growth of China's economy has attracted many foreigners. Some observers see great challenges. However, some also see great opportunities for urbanization and economic growth. The most important challenge or opportunity is to provide each individual with equal opportunities and fair treatment no matter whether they are from rural or urban areas, from other parts of China, or other parts of the world.

References

Bai, N. and H. Song. 2002. *Out to the City or Back to the Village: Return Migration in China*. Beijing: China Finance and Economics Press. (in Chinese)

Bodomo, A. B. 2010. "The African Trading Community in Guangzhou: An Emerging Bridge for Africa–China Relations." *The China Quarterly* 203:693–707.

Bodomo, A. and G. Ma. 2010. "From Guangzhou to Yiwu: Emerging Facets of the African Diaspora in China." *International Journal of African Renaissance Studies* 5, no. 2: 283–289.

Cai, G. and Y. Huang. 2008. *African Merchants and their Activities in Guangzhou: The Case of China-Africa Trading Post in Dengfeng Community*. Guangzhou, China: Guangzhou Academy of Social Sciences. (in Chinese)

Cai, F. and D. Wang. 2003. "Population Movement by Market Forces: Data Analysis Based on the Fifth Census." *Chinese Journal of Population Science* 5:11–19. (in Chinese)

Cai, H. and J. Wang. 2008. "Factors Influencing the Migration Intentions of Rural Workers in the Pearl River Delta." *Social Sciences in China* 29, no. 3: 157–171.

Cao, J., M. Ho, and D. Jorgensen. 2012. "An Integrated Assessment of the Economic Costs and Environmental Benefits of Pollution and Carbon Control." In *The Chinese Economy: A New Transition*, edited by M. Aoki and J. Wu, 231–258. Basingstoke, UK: Palgrave MacMillian.

Chan, K. W. 2009. "The Chinese Hukou System at 50." *Eurasian Geography and Economics* 50, no. 2: 197–221.

Chan, K. W. 2010a. "The Global Financial Crisis and Migrant Workers in China: 'There Is No Future as a Labourer; Returning to the Village Has No Meaning.'" *International Journal of Urban and Regional Research* 34, no. 3: 659–677.

Chan, K.W. 2010b. "The Household Registration System and Migrant Labor in China: Notes on a Debate." *Population and Development Review* 36, no. 2: 357–364.

Chan, K.W. and W. Buckingham. 2008. "Is China Abolishing the Hukou System?" *The China Quarterly* 195: 582–606.

Chan, L. H., G. Chan, and F. Kwan. 2011. "China at Sixty: Global-Local Interactions." In *China at 60: Global-local Interactions*, edited by L- H. Chan, G. Chan, and F. Kwan, 1–14. Singapore: World Scientific Publishing.

Chan, K.W., and Y. Hu. 2003. "Urbanization in China in the 1990s: New Definition, Different Series, and Revised Trends." *China Review* 3, no. 2: 49–71.

Chang, F., Y. Shi, A. Shen, A. Kohrman, K. Li, Q. Wan et al. 2017. "Understanding the Situation of China's Left-Behind Children: A Mixed-Methods Analysis." Working Paper 315, Rural

Education Action Program, Freeman Spogli Institute for International Studies, Stanford University. https://fsi-live.s3.us-west-1.amazonaws.com/s3fs-public/315_-_understanding_the_situation_of_chinas_left-behind_children.pdf

Chen, J. 2011. "Internal Migration and Health: Reexamining the Healthy Migrant Phenomenon in China." *Social Science and Medicine* 72, no. 8: 1294–1301.

Chen, Y. 2011. "Occupational Attainment of Migrants and Local Workers: Findings from a Survey in Shanghai's Manufacturing Sector." *Urban Studies* 48, no. 1: 3–21.

Chen, L., J. Huang, and J. Li. 2017. "Fiscal Decentralization, Satisfaction with Social Services, and Inequality Under the Hukou System." *Social Indicators Research* 132, no. 1: 377–394.

Cheng, Z., H. Wang, and R. Smyth. 2013. "Happiness and Job Satisfaction in Urban China: A Comparative Study of Two Generations of Migrants and Urban Locals." *Urban Studies* 51, no. 10: 2160–2184.

Cheo, R. 2017. "Migrant Workers and Workplace Bullying in Urban China." *Social Indicators Research* 132, no. 1: 87–115.

Chung, H. 2018. "Rural Migrants in Villages-In-The-City in Guangzhou, China: Multipositionality and Negotiated Living Strategies." *Urban Studies* 55, no. 10: 2245–2260.

Deng, J. B. 2002. "Close Distance: Taiwanese Entrepreneurs and Mainland Core Employees in Taiwanese Factory in China." *Taiwanese* Sociology 3 (June): 211–251. (in Chinese)

Du, H. 2017. "Place Attachment and Belonging among Educated Young Migrants and Returnees: The Case of Chaohu, China." *Population, Space and Place* 23, no. 1: doi: 10.1002/psp.1967.

Duan, C. R., L. D. Lv, J. Guo, and Z. P. Wang. 2013. "Survival and Development of Left-Behind Children in Rural China: Based on the Analysis of Sixth Census Data." *Population Journal* 35, no. 3: 37–49. (in Chinese)

Fan, C. 2011. "Settlement Intention and Split Households: Findings from a Survey of Migrants in Beijing's Urban Villages." *China Review* 11, no. 2: 11–41.

Fan, C., P. Hall, and G. Wall. 2009. "Migration, Hukou Status, and Labor-Market Segmentation: The Case of High-Tech Development in Dalian." *Environment and Planning* A41, no. 7: 1647–1666.

Fan, C., M. Sun, and S. Zheng. 2011. "Migration and Split Households: A Comparison of Sole, Couple, and Family Migrants in Beijing, China." *Environment and Planning* A 43, no. 9: 2164–2185.

Fang, L., R. Sun, and M. Yuen. 2016. "Acculturation, Economic Stress, Social Relationships and School Satisfaction among Migrant Children in Urban China." *Journal of Happiness Studies* 17, no. 2: 507–531.

Gagnon, J., T. Xenogiani, and C. Xing. 2014. "Are Migrants Discriminated against in Chinese Urban Labour Markets?" *IZA Journal of Labor & Development* 3, no. 1: 17–40.

Gan, J. 2013. "Research on the Right of Permanent Residences of Foreigners System in China." MLaw diss., Hunan Normal University.

Gee, G. and D. Takeuchi. 2004. "Traffic Stress, Vehicular Burden, and Well-Being: A Multilevel Analysis." *Social Science and Medicine* 59, no. 2: 405–414.

Hao, P. and Tang, S. 2015. "Floating or Settling Down: The Effect of Rural Landholdings on the Settlement Intention of Rural Migrants in Urban China." *Environment and Planning* A 47, no. 9: 1979–1999.

Hao, P., R. Sliuzas, and S. Geertman. 2011. "The Development and Redevelopment of Urban Villages in Shenzhen." *Habitat International* 35, no. 2: 214–224.

Haugen, H. 2012. "Nigerians in China: A Second State of Immobility." *International Migration* 50, no. 2: 65–80.
He, B. 2008. "The Characteristics and Integration Of South Koreans' Enclave in Beijing–A Case Study of South Koreans' Village in Wangjing." *Urban Problems* 10: 59–64. (in Chinese)
He, C. and J. Ye. 2014. "Lonely Sunsets: Impacts of Rural–Urban Migration on the Left-Behind Elderly in Rural China." *Population, Space and Place* 20, no. 4: 352–369.
Hu, S. 2017. "It's for Our Education": Perception of Parental Migration and Resilience Among Left-behind Children in Rural China." *Social Indicators Research*. doi: 10.1007/s11205-017-1725-y.
Huang, X., M. Dijst, J. Weesep, Y. Jiao, and Y. Sun. 2017. "Residential Choice among Rural–Urban Migrants after Hukou Reform: Evidence from Suzhou, China." *Population, Space and Place* 23, no. 4: e2035. doi: 10.1002/psp.2035.
Huang, Y. 2012. "Low-Income Housing in Chinese Cities: Policies and Practices." *The China Quarterly* 212:941–964.
Huang, Y. and F. Guo. 2017. "Welfare Programme Participation and the Wellbeing of Non-local Rural Migrants in Metropolitan China: A Social Exclusion Perspective." *Social Indicators Research* 132, no. 1: 63–85.
Huang, Y. and R. Tao. 2015. "Housing Migrants in Chinese cities: Current Status and Policy Design." *Environment and Planning C: Government and Policy*, 33, no. 3: 640–660.
Huang, Y. and C. Yi. 2015. "Invisible Migrant Enclaves in Chinese Cities: Underground Living in Beijing, China." *Urban Studies* 52, no. 15: 2948–2973.
Hui, E., K. Yu, and Y. Ye. 2014. "Housing Preferences of Temporary Migrants in Urban China in the Wake of Gradual Hukou Reform: A Case Study of Shenzhen." *International Journal of Urban and Regional Research* 38, no. 4: 1384–1398.
Lee, J., J. Carling, and P. Orrenius. 2014. "The International Migration Review at 50: Reflecting on Half a Century of International Migration Research and Looking Ahead." *International Migration Review* 48, s1: 3–36
Li, Z., D. Xue, M. Lyons, and A.M.B. Brown. 2008. "The African Enclave of Guangzhou: A Case Study of Xiaobeilu." *Acta Geographica Sinica* 63, no. 2: 208–218.
Lian, S. 2009. *Ant Tribe: A Record of Inhabited Village of University Graduates*. Guilin: Guangxi Normal University Press. (in Chinese).
Liang, Y. 2014. "The Causal Mechanism of Migration Behaviors of African Immigrants in Guangzhou: From the Perspective of Cumulative Causation Theory." *The Journal of Chinese Sociology* 1, no. 1: 1–25
Liang, Z. 2016. "China's Great Migration and the Prospects of a More Integrated Society." *Annual Review of Sociology* 42:451–471.
Liang, Z. and Y. P. Chen. 2007. "The Educational Consequences of Migration for Children in China." *Social Science Research* 36, no. 1: 28–47.
Liang, Y. and A. Li. 2016. "The Report of Survey on Foreigners in Guangzhou 2016." *Chinese Social Science Newspaper*, 28 January 2016. (in Chinese)
Liang, Z., Z. Li, and Z. Ma. 2014. "Changing Patterns of the Floating Population in China, 2000–2010." *Population and Development Review* 40, no. 4: 695–716.
Liu, Y., Z. Li, Y. Liu, and H. Chen. 2015. "Growth of Rural Migrant Enclaves in Guangzhou, China: Agency, Everyday Practice and Social Mobility." *Urban Studies*, 52, no. 16: 3086–3105.
Liu, Y., Y. Liu, Y. Chen, H. Long. 2010. "The Process and Driving Forces of Rural Hollowing in China under Rapid Urbanization." *Journal of Geographical Sciences* 20, no. 6: 876–888.

Liu, Y. and W. Xu. 2017. "Destination Choices of Permanent and Temporary Migrants in China, 1985–2005." *Population, Space and Place* 23, no. 1. doi: 10.1002/psp.1963.

Liu, Z., Y. Wang, and S. Chen. 2017. "Does Formal Housing Encourage Settlement Intention of Rural Migrants in Chinese Cities? A Structural Equation Model Analysis." *Urban Studies* 54, no. 8: 1834–1850.

Logan, J. R., Y. Fang, and Z. Zhang. 2009. "Access to Housing in Urban China." *International Journal of Urban and Regional Research* 33, no. 4: 914–935.

Long, H., 2014. "Land Consolidation: An Indispensable Way of Spatial Restructuring in Rural China." *Journal of Geographical Sciences* 24, no. 2: 211–225.

Lu, Y., 2012. "Education of Children Left Behind in Rural China." *Journal of Marriage and Family* 74, no. 2: 328–341.

Mathews, G., Y. Yang. 2012. "How Africans Pursue Low-End Globalization in Hong Kong and Mainland China." *Journal of Current Chinese Affairs* 41, no. 2: 95–120.

MLR (Ministry of Land and Resources). 2016. *Communiqué on Land and Resources of China 2016*. (in Chinese) http://data.mlr.gov.cn/gtzygb/201704/P020170428532821702501.pdf

Mou, J., J. Cheng, S. M. Griffiths, S. Wong, S. Hillier, and D. Zhang. 2011. "Internal Migration and Depressive Symptoms among Migrant Factory Workers in Shenzhen, China." *Journal of Community Psychology* 39, no. 2: 212–230.

Mullan, K., P. Grosjean, A. Kontoleon. 2011. "Land Tenure Arrangements and Rural–Urban Migration in China." *World Development* 39, no. 1: 123–133.

National Statistics R.O.C. (Taiwan). 2017. "Taiwanese Working Overseas." Taiwan: National Statistics, Republic of China (Taiwan). https://www.stat.gov.tw/public/Attachment/813018211L3E53FL6.pdf (in Chinese)

NBS (National Bureau of Statistics). 2012. *Tabulation on the 2010 Population Census of the People's Republic of China*. Beijing: China Statistics Press. http://www.stats.gov.cn/english/statisticaldata/censusdata/rkpc2010/indexch.htm

NBS (National Bureau of Statistics). 2016. *China Statistical Yearbook 2016*. Beijing: China Statistics Press. www.stats.gov.cn/tjsj/ndsj/2016/indexeh.htm.

Ng, S. 2004. "Taiwanese Gold Rush to China." *Asia Times*. June 30. www.atimes.com/atimes/China/FF30Ad04.html.

Pieke, F. N. 2012. "Immigrant China." *Modern China* 38, no. 1: 40–77.

Piotrowski, M., and Y. Tong. 2013. "Straddling Two Geographic Regions: The Impact of Place of Origin and Destination on Return Migration Intentions in China." *Population, Space and Place* 19, no. 3: 329–349.

Pun, N. 2005. *Made in China: Women Factory Workers in a Global Workplace*. Durham, NC: Duke University Press.

Qiu, P., E. Caine, Y. Yang, Q. Chen, J. Li, and X. Ma. 2011. "Depression and Associated Factors in Internal Migrant Workers in China." *Journal of Affective Disorders* 134, no. 1: 198–207.

Shen, J. 2012. "Changing Patterns and Determinants of Interprovincial Migration in China 1985–2000." *Population, Space and Place* 18, no. 3: 384–402.

Song, Y. 2016. "Hukou-Based Labour Market Discrimination and Ownership Structure in Urban China." *Urban Studies* 53, no. 8: 1657–1673.

Song, Y., Y. Zenou, C. Ding. 2008. "Let's Not Throw the Baby Out with the Bath Water: The Role of Urban Villages in Housing Rural Migrants in China." *Urban Studies* 45, no. 2: 313–330.

Stephens, M. 2010. "Locating Chinese Urban Housing Policy in an International Context." *Urban Studies* 47, no. 14: 2965–2982.

The World Bank. "Gross Domestic Product." World Development Indicators. 2011. https://siteresources.worldbank.org/DATASTATISTICS/Resources/GDP.pdf

Wang, X. 2008. "An Investigation into Intergenerational Differences between Two Generations of Migrant Workers." *Social Sciences in China* 29, no. 3: 136–156. (in Chinese)

Wang, H., F. Guo, and Z. Cheng. 2015. "A Distributional Analysis of Wage Discrimination against Migrant Workers in China's Urban Labour Market." *Urban Studies* 52, no. 13: 2383–2403.

Wang, X., L. Ling, H. Su, J. Cheng, L. Jin, and Y. H. Sun. 2015. "Self-Concept of Left-Behind Children in China: A Systematic Review of the Literature." *Child: Care, Health and Development* 41, no. 3: 346–355.

Wong, K., D. Fu, C.Y. Li, and H. X. Song. 2007. "Rural Migrant Workers in Urban China: Living a Marginalised Life." *International Journal of Social Welfare* 16, no. 1: 32–40.

Wu, W. 2004. "Sources of Migrant Housing Disadvantage in Urban China." *Environment and Planning A* 36, no. 7: 1285–1304.

Wu, X., and D. J. Treiman. 2007. "Inequality and Equality under Chinese Socialism: The Hukou System and Intergenerational Occupational Mobility." *American Journal of Sociology* 113, no. 2: 415–445.

Xu, Q., X. Guan, and F. Yao. 2011. "Welfare Program Participation among Rural-To-Urban Migrant Workers in China." *International Journal of Social Welfare* 20, no. 1: 10–21.

Yan, X., S. Bauer, and X. Huo. 2014. "Farm Size, Land Reallocation, and Labour Migration in Rural China." *Population, Space and Place* 20, no. 4: 303–315.

Ye, J., and P. Lu. 2011. "Differentiated Childhoods: Impacts of Rural Labor Migration on Left-Behind Children in China." *The Journal of Peasant Studies* 38, no. 2: 355–377.

Yue, Z., S. Li, M. W. Feldman, and H. Du. 2010. "Floating Choices: A Generational Perspective on Intentions of Rural–Urban Migrants in China." *Environment and Planning A* 42, no. 3: 545–562.

Yue, Z., S. Li, X. Jin, and M. W. Feldman. 2013. "The Role of Social Networks in the Integration of Chinese Rural–Urban Migrants: A Migrant–Resident Tie Perspective." *Urban Studies* 50, no. 9: 1704–1723.

Zhang, X. 2013. "China's 'Ant Tribe' Present Social Survival Situation and Personal Financial Advice." *Asian Social Science* 9, no. 2: 24–35.

Zhang, H., J. R. Behrman, C. S. Fan, X. Wei, and J. Zhang. 2014. "Does Parental Absence Reduce Cognitive Achievements? Evidence from RURAL CHINA." *Journal of Development Economics* 111: 181–195.

Zhang, L., and L. Tao. 2012. "Barriers to the Acquisition of Urban Hukou in Chinese Cities." *Environment and Planning A* 44, no. 12: 2883–2900.

Zhang, Z., and Wu, X. 2017. "Occupational Segregation and Earnings Inequality: Rural Migrants and Local Workers in Urban China." *Social Science Research* 61:57–74.

Zhao, Y. 2002. "Causes and Consequences of Return Migration: Recent Evidence from China." *Journal of Comparative Economics* 30, no. 2: 376–394.

Zhou, D., and X. Yang. 2014. "Assimilating Superficially and Segregating Deeply—The Study about Cultural Adaption of South Koreans in Guangzhou." *Ethnic Studies* 2: 51–60. (in Chinese)

Zhou, M., T. Xu, and S. Shenasi. 2016. "Entrepreneurship and Interracial Dynamics: A Case Study of Self-Employed Africans and Chinese in Guangzhou, China." *Ethnic and Racial Studies* 39, no. 9: 1566–1586.

Zhu, P. 2016. "Residential Segregation and Employment Outcomes of Rural Migrant Workers in China." *Urban Studies* 53, no. 8: 1635–1656.

Zhu, Y. 2004. "The Household Registration System Reform, the Floating Population's Intention to Settle in Destinations, and the Restriction Mechanism." *South China Population* 19, no. 3: 21–28. (in Chinese)

CHAPTER 45

THE PARADOX OF IMMIGRANT POLITICAL PARTICIPATION IN EUROPE AMIDST CRISES OF MULTICULTURALISM

FLORIS VERMEULEN

THE Netherlands' general elections in March 2017 resulted in three immigrants joining Dutch parliament under a new party known as Denk (literally meaning "think" in Dutch and "equal" in Turkish). The entrance of three members from a brand new party is unprecedented and shows how much clout Denk quickly came to carry. Having MPs of immigrant background is not unusual in the Netherlands, which in the three decades has had the highest percentages of migrant representatives compared with the rest of Europe (Bloemraad 2013). What was extraordinary was that the three politicians entered on their own pro-immigrant party. Moreover, it was one in which primarily immigrant politicians campaigned on behalf of a primarily immigrant constituency.

Under a pronounced antidiscrimination, pro-diversity campaign, Denk, with strong links to the more conservative religious constituency of the Dutch-Turkish community, mobilized voters largely of Turkish and Moroccan origins. Across the Netherlands' largest cities—Amsterdam, Rotterdam, and The Hague—Denk got most votes in poor neighborhoods inhabited predominantly by Muslim immigrants and their descendants. Poor neighborhoods whose majority of residents were low-skilled majoritarian inhabitants mostly voted for the anti-Islam and anti-immigrant Freedom Party (PVV), led by populist Geert Wilders. Wealthy neighborhoods whose majority of residents were highly skilled cosmopolitan dwellers voted mostly for the Green Left (GroenLinks) and social progressive liberals Democrats 66 (D66). And wealthy neighborhoods whose majority of residents were middle-class majoritarian inhabitants voted for the conservative liberals, the People's Party for Freedom and Democracy (VVD). Each group, it seems, had a party to represent its interests. Meanwhile, the social democratic Labour Party (PvdA)—which once was a catchall for most of these groups, and since World War II, dominated local politics in the big Dutch cities—seemed to nearly vanish. In both The Hague and Rotterdam, the PvdA was simply outvoted by Denk.

The Netherlands' current urban political landscape is an example of extreme group polarization. It is primarily the outcome of identity politics for more than a decade. Other European cities and countries, however, are also polarized, following years of nativist and anti-Islamic discourse churned by populist politicians, including Wilders and France's Marine LePen, but also more moderate left-wing politicians. In Germany, for instance, prominent Socialist Democratic Party (SPD) politician Thilo Sarrazin authored *Deutschland schafft sich ab* [*Germany is Doing Itself In*]. Published in 2010, the book ties changing demographics in German society with the country's Muslim population, who, says Sarrazin, are unwilling to integrate. In Berlin, former SPD borough mayor Heinz Buschkowsky made similar points in *Neukölln ist uberall* [*Neukölln Is Everywhere*], published in 2012. Naming one of Berlin's immigrant neighborhoods in its title, the book correlates immigration with low educational levels, high poverty, and high rates of criminal behavior. Buschkowsky draws on very local examples to make national generalizations, giving the impression that his analysis of Neukölln applies to the majority of Germany (Vermeulen and Doğan 2015).

This chapter identifies common elements in Europe's anti-immigrant, anti-Muslim discourses and examines how they have impacted immigrants' political participation. Denk's electoral accomplishments may be seen as the outcome of an immigrant emancipation process, wherein a constituency votes for a party claiming to represent the constituency's interests and the party is formed and led by politicians who share the constituency's background. At the same time, Denk's success may be understood as a reaction to the fear that integration in the Netherlands has failed and, more concretely, the anti-immigrant, anti-Muslim attitudes that have compelled a "civic turn" in the last decade's integration debates and policies. As I argue in this chapter, the civic turn is itself an effect of the crisis-of-multiculturalism narrative (herein "crisis narrative" for short), which after 11 September 2001, gained traction in many European countries and was especially pronounced in the Netherlands, where the narrative surfaced even earlier.

The Netherlands and capital city Amsterdam, in particular, provide a robust case study for understanding the situation across Europe today. Dutch society was always held up as a paragon of multiculturalism and tolerance. The Netherlands, it was broadly acknowledged, fostered a national context in which immigrants could integrate fairly easy. The fact that the Netherlands' own attitudes towards and consequent discourse surrounding immigrants was changed under influence of the crisis narrative, which was popular in almost every other European city, allows a study of its effects on how immigrants and their descendants participate politically in Europe.

I begin this chapter by identifying elements present in immigration debates across the continent. One common thread is the notion that immigration, primarily of Muslims, has pushed Europe into some kind of state of emergency. Responding to the ostensible crisis, politicians developed policies to size up the civicness of Muslim immigrants.

Such policies have had a significant effect on how Muslims, as a group, participate politically. After briefly discussing the civic turn, the chapter gives an overview of the extent to which immigrants have entered Amsterdam's local political system. The case study invites a detailed analysis of the civic turn's effects and some immigrant politicians' response to them. The chapter concludes with reflections on this development in Amsterdam, and then presents a broader perspective to make better sense of how the crisis narrative has significantly impacted European countries and cities in a relatively short time span.

The Crisis of Multiculturalism and the Civic Turn in Integration Policies

By now, most European leaders such as Angela Merkel, David Cameron, Nicolas Sarkozy, and Dutch prime-minister Mark Rutte have publically decried the failure of multiculturalism in one way or the other. Regardless of what "multiculturalism" actually means or whether true multiculturalism has ever existed anywhere, many European politicians' proclamations at the national or local level reflect a persistent belief: European societies are characterized and segregated by rife cultural and religious conflicts—and it is a crisis. The narrative maintains that countries have been too generous and too tolerant towards immigrants who settled in Europe during the 1970s and 1980s. According to the discourse, generosity and tolerance emerged from a multiculturalist ideology that served to accommodate guest workers and postcolonial immigrants after the oil crisis of 1973. Purportedly, the problem is that most of "these immigrants" do not share liberal values and have exploited the tolerant multicultural ethos from which they themselves benefitted. They took advantage of it to live their separate lives, thus able to nurture their illiberal ideologies and develop their own institutions. Integration, consequently, has failed; its hope is dimmer than ever. Kundnani (2012) argues that almost all issues addressed by this narrative and cited as evidence of a crisis of multiculturalism are linked to perceived values of Muslim communities in Europe. In debates, their values are pitted against the liberal stances of women's rights, gay rights, freedom of expression, secularism, and antitotalitarianism. Kundnani (2012) concludes that Muslims have come to symbolize the debate and the danger of cultural difference; they have, moreover, become the focus of a project by most mainstream parties to produce good, liberal individuals who have absorbed Western values.

To troubleshoot this crisis, the narrative goes on, Europe must take a more repressive stance against illiberal values of the immigrants. Such fortitude should prevent their communities from further institutionalizing their value-based culture, but also shape it to fit in, if not blend in, with majoritarian Western culture. Mouritsen (2008) notes that throughout Europe, similar solutions have been proposed with two main features in common. First, to resolve perceived cultural conflicts, political solutions must come to the rescue. Western majorities are associated with modernity, rationality, individualism, and universal values; Western societies converge on these civic understandings of national communities. Conceptualizations of Dutch, French, and German national cultures, for example, are therefore based on similar neoliberal civic values. Furthermore, politicians who perpetuate this narrative accept the idea that these civic interpretations of European national cultures should be forcefully implemented in immigrant communities; they believe that doing so can alter traditional illiberal value systems imported from their Muslim countries of origin. Second, and relatedly, cultural and religious identities and their linked illiberal communities become highly problematized, often presented as security problems. Stigmatizing these communities so drastically and on a daily basis produces suspect communities throughout Europe. In such a policy framework, an entire group is treated very differently from the rest of the population when it comes to enforcing laws, policies, and policing. Viewing a whole group as inherently dangerous and therefore suspicious is detrimental, often resulting in increasingly intrusive and heavy-handed policies that stigmatize entire communities (Vermeulen 2014).

Politicians in different European countries thus push for, and often implement, the civic turn in integration policies (Joppke 2004). The turn assigns greater individual responsibility to immigrants, demanding they become compatible with, and integrate into, a liberal European context in which the nation-state and its majoritarian culture are privileged. Breaking existing bonds and links with immigrant ethnic and religious communities is deemed essential for integration and, consequently, for resolving the crisis of multiculturalism. The logic is that cutting such ties corrects for any illiberal value systems and converts communities into autonomous liberal individuals. Joppke (2007) regards the liberalization of civic integration as negative group targeting. In being so preoccupied with preventing ethnic separatism, which is predominantly identified as a Muslim issue, civic integration "furthers the normatively questionable vision of the liberal state as one for liberal people only" (Joppke 2007, 271).

Kudnani (2012) argues that there is a strong sense of pessimism as to the possibility of implementing this civic turn through conventional democratic processes of representation and negotiation. Rather, many European politicians believe the crisis should be resolved outside the normal functioning of politics, which has huge implications for the groups involved. As Kudnani (2012, 160) states:

> [T]o be "Muslim" in this discourse is to belong to a group with common origins, a shared culture and a monolithic identity that can be held collectively responsible for the failure of European multiculturalism. The much-vaunted distinction between "moderate" and "extremist" Muslims is perfectly consistent with such a position: it is precisely the "moderates" who are held responsible for their failure to stop the "extremists." This failure of the "moderates," then, is taken to be proof of the general failure of Muslims to adjust to modernity.

So the political message is relatively straightforward: immigrants who willingly opt for inclusion are to be accepted on the condition that they successfully demonstrate having internalized prevailing values and reject allegedly backward religious ideas. Muslims deemed to have rejected liberal democratic norms are to be excluded from the public sphere through stigmatization, discrimination and, in extreme circumstances, revocation of their rights to citizenship and residency (Triadafilopoulos 2011).

That said, this chapter is less concerned with whether there actually was, or currently is, a crisis of multiculturalism, whether any European country ever implemented a policy of full multiculturalist tolerance, or whether immigrants from predominantly Muslim countries are intrinsically unable to integrate into European liberal democracies. Instead, the focus is on the political effects of a civic turn, wherein majoritarian politicians are preoccupied by the project of ensuring immigrants are or become autonomous individuals free of any ties to illiberal ethnic or religious communities. Lentin and Titley (2011) warn that the civic turn's effects on immigrants' opportunities to participate politically are omnipresent. The effects have severe ramifications on the extent to which immigrants and minorities gain access to democratic political processes. As Lentin and Titley (2011, 192) observe:

> The ethno-national variant of culture promoted by the state is legitimate and neutral, while the assertion of minoritarian culture difference on the contrary has no place in public sphere. This continues to present minorities with an equally familiar double bind, as compliant integration into a prescribed national way of doing things depends on being recognized as integrating.

"[B]eing recognized as integrating," as Lentin and Titley state, is of crucial significance here because it is others—the majoritarian people in power—who assess the level and legitimacy of integration. Moreover, anything and everything can be cited as proof of failing to integrate. Any identification with someone or something related to immigrant origin can and often is used as evidence of unwillingness or inability to internalize liberal values.

This double bind also compels immigrants to exempt themselves from group-based resources. They might, for instance, steer clear of immigrant organizations and religious networks despite the group-based resources they could tap within them. These resources include tools granting access to political systems by mobilizing constituencies and enabling different collective actions (Fennema and Tillie 1999; Vermeulen and Berger 2008). Within the crisis narrative, these capacities are considered obstacles to immigrants' successful integration as individuals into liberal democratic societies. Moreover, they are seen as recurrent examples of the failure of multiculturalism and its ensuing crisis. Collective identities, organizational capacities, and political activities that emerge from ethnic or religious communities are seen as signs of crisis-causing failure. This compounds stigmatization. Stigmatization can provoke a reactive assertion of identity, thereby boosting forms of political participation among marginalized minorities. In other contexts and for some individuals, however, stigmatization and group identification can promote in-group solidarity and further separation from mainstream society. That can lead to apathy, segregation, and exclusion, which lowers formal forms of political participation and integration (Kranendonk et al. 2017). In the next paragraph the case of Amsterdam is taken as an illustration of whether and when the crisis narrative and related double bind leads to a reactive assertion among immigrants, increasing the political participation of these groups, or whether it leads to political apathy and decreasing levels of political participation among immigrant voters.

Immigrants' Formal Politics

In this chapter formal political representation and voting become the main elements for studying the workings of the double bind. Studies on immigrants' political integration in Europe have emphasized the importance of voting and subsequent political representation and political integration. These factors determine the opportunities immigrant communities get to influence policies affecting their lives in many different ways, for example, in terms of social welfare, education, housing, the labor market, and security. A political appointment allows the representative to have a direct voice in political decisions that affect constituencies (Heath et al. 2013). Alba and Foner (2009) therefore regard the election of politicians of immigrant background as the "gold standard" of immigrant groups' political integration. At the same time, a political party's nomination or selection on party lists also signals something about the party. For example, including fewer candidates of Muslim background can be taken as a sign of little interest in diversity or of that particular party's more secular orientation. As Katz (2001, 278) notes:

> [C]andidates define the public face of the party in elections. Collectively, they manifest the demographic, geographic, and ideological dimensions of the party. The nomination of more women or more minority group members or more members of some religious sect signals something about the party as a whole.

Studying turnout rates, voting patterns, and levels of representation over time, as the research for this chapter entailed, allows detailed analysis of the specific effects of the Netherlands' civic turn on immigrants' political position in the country. Ramakrishnan et al. (2008, 21) differentiate between, on the one hand, political presence or access to the political system (i.e., ability and willingness to participate in the political process and to be represented) and, on the other hand, political weight or power and influence in the political system (i.e., rank within the local political hierarchy and ability to make political decisions). I abided by this distinction in assessing the development of political participation and representation in Amsterdam as a generalizable example for developments across Europe. To analyze the different groups' political presence, this chapter examines participation (turnout rates in local elections) and level of representation (immigrant politicians on city council); political weight is manifested by immigrant politicians holding executive positions (city district mayor and city aldermen). Hochschild and Mollenkopf (2009, 16) find that the political incorporation of immigrants is a process in which groups move from less to more incorporation, or the other way around. The process of political incorporation is not automatically linear, they argue, nor is there any guarantee it will continue once started. In dynamic situations—in this case, the many societal changes tied up with the crisis narrative and the civic turn—it is especially interesting to see if indeed the crisis narrative has a negative nonlinear effect on the different groups' political participation and representation.

Amsterdam: Context and Groups

Amsterdam constitutes in general a favorable context for minority representation because specific features of the city's political system (and, for that matter, of the Netherlands overall) permit minority groups to mobilize easily. Elections occur through a party list system, with pure proportionality and very low thresholds. Parties make lists of candidates to be elected, and seats are allocated to each party in proportion to the number of votes. Effectively, there is a low threshold so that a party or a candidate must receive a minimum percentage of votes to obtain seats. Another important feature fostering a favorable context for minority groups is the ability to cast preferential votes; this means that on election day, the voter not only chooses a party, but also votes for a specific candidate within it. Prior to elections, each party is responsible for ranking their candidates and determining the order in which they appear on the ballot; however, voters can select any listed candidate, who will simply earn a seat if enough votes are cast. The ability to cast a preferential vote implies that minority candidates who are placed at seemingly hopelessly low positions on electoral lists might still win if a significant group of voters mobilizes for their election. Furthermore, in 1985, the Netherlands began allowing non-citizens to participate in local elections after completing five years of legal residence in the country. It is unnecessary for them to even register: the municipal administration automatically mails voter registration cards to all inhabitants entitled to vote. The enfranchisement of foreigners has had a direct effect on electoral politics via participation in elections, as well as an indirect effect in that parties list immigrants to appeal to the foreign electorate. Amsterdam is furthermore a prime example of a European city that implemented multicultural policies in the 1980s by which official minority groups are eligible for subsidies, such as to fund ethnic organizations (Vermeulen 2006). And yet, the civic turn was introduced earlier and with more fervour in the Netherlands than elsewhere in Europe (Bloemraad and Wright 2014; Joppke 2004, 2007).

This chapter compares the politics of Amsterdam's three main immigrant groups: Turks, Moroccans, and Surinamese. These categories as shorthand to refer to three communities comprising migrants from Turkey, Morocco, and Suriname to the Netherlands as well as their Dutch-born descendants. These single-word labels are oversimplified descriptors, though used for linguistic efficiency. Each group has its own migration history and levels of in-group solidarity, self-identification, and immigrant organization density. Furthermore, the fact that representatives or executives are of a certain ethnic background does not necessarily mean they represent that particular group; they may have other more significant political identities for their political objectives than immigrant origin. As Hochschild and Mollenkopf (2009, 22) observe, politicians of immigrant background face a classic dilemma. A representative from an immigrant group is expected to work on behalf of his or her whole group, regardless of whether its members are part of that person's constituency; meanwhile, constituencies outside the immigrant group want their elected representative to show no ethnic favoritism.

Detailing Amsterdam's main immigrant groups, their varied backgrounds, and unique characteristics goes beyond this chapter's scope, although some key features merit mention. Immigration from Suriname to the Netherlands has a long history, intimately tied to the countries' colonial relationship. Suriname's population comprises several distinct ethnic groups, the largest being Afro-Surinamese or "Creoles" (descendants of African slaves) and the Indo-Surinamese or "Hindustanis" (descendants of contract laborers brought mainly from India to Suriname after the Dutch colonies abolished slavery in 1863). After the Second World War, Surinamese migration became more ethnically diverse and economically driven. The prospect of Suriname becoming independent, which it did in 1975, caused great economic and political uncertainty, resulting in more people leaving the country. An exodus of over 50,000 people occurred between 1974 and 1975. Many moved to Amsterdam, with over 10,000 settling in the Dutch capital in 1975 alone (Vermeulen 2006). As of 2017, about 8 percent of Amsterdam's population was of Surinamese origin.

Both Turks and Moroccans, mainly males, arrived as guest workers in the late 1960s to take up low-skilled jobs in Amsterdam's heavy industry. After the economic crisis of the early 1970s and the closure of most of the city's factories, many became unemployed. At the same time, a large percentage decided not to return, but rather to send for their families to join them in Amsterdam, which was enabled through family reunification. The presence of Turks and Moroccans thus grew rapidly over the next decades, mostly in similar postwar neighborhoods in the city's west. Turks now represent about 5 percent of Amsterdam's population and Moroccans, about 9 percent. Both groups are predominantly Muslim, making them a religious minority in a predominantly secular city. There is ample evidence that Turks still constitute the ethnic community with the strongest ties in Amsterdam, followed by Moroccans, with Surinamese showing the lowest level of ethnic identification among the three groups (Vermeulen et al. 2014). The Turkish immigrant community is characterized by strong ideological polarization between religious and secular groups, multiple ethnic subgroups, and different religious denominations; at the same time, a majority of the community strongly identifies with their national origin. The Turkish community is also the most organized immigrant group in Amsterdam, having formed the most immigrant organizations. These are densely connected through interorganizational networks (Michon and Vermeulen 2013; Vermeulen 2006), and Turks are significantly more often members of an immigrant organization than Moroccans and Surinamese (Vermeulen et al. 2014).

Immigrant Political Participation in Amsterdam: An Overview

Figures on electoral turnout for immigrants—defined as individuals who are foreign-born or have at least one foreign-born parent—for six consecutive local elections (1994–2014) demonstrate that immigrant turnout is almost always lower than overall turnout. The overall average turnout rate in these elections is around the 50 percent, whereas the rate of immigrant groups consistently ranges between 20 percent and 40 percent. The figures also reveal that Turks participate significantly more in elections than do Moroccans or Surinamese. In 1994 and 2006, their turnout rate was comparable to, if not higher than, overall turnout. The Moroccan turnout rate has been substantially lower (often below 30 percent) than the overall rate, while the Surinamese turnout rate was lowest (always below 30 percent) among all immigrant groups in the city and showed little variation. A final observation is that since 2006, the turnout rates of all immigrant groups have decreased significantly. The finding, thus, is that more and more immigrant voters are refraining from political participation. Moreover, the overwhelming majority of immigrants—comprising around 75 percent of all eligible Moroccan voters and around 75 percent of all eligible Surinamese voters—does not participate politically. The conclusion is that a large group of the immigrant electorate appears excluded from the political system. These immigrants would be better described as displaying apathy than reactive resistance (Kranendonk et al. 2014; Vermeulen et al. 2014).

Amsterdam's 45-seat city council, the city's legislative body, sets the policy agenda, passes regulations, and controls the actions taken by the executive branch. Comprising the mayor and the deputy mayors, the executive branch must abide by council decisions, and it relies on the council's support. Amsterdam's number of councilors of immigrant origin has risen gradually since the early 1990s. The highest share elected to city council was in 2006 and 2014, when a fifth of local councillors were either born abroad or were the children of immigrants. Relative to their share in Amsterdam's general population, Turks were proportionately represented in city council between 1994 and 2010. This is a direct effect of Amsterdam's favorable political context for immigrants: higher turnout rates and a significantly higher number of Dutch-Turkish voters voting for Dutch-Turkish politicians led to a higher number of Dutch-Turkish politicians being elected (Vermeulen et al. 2014). By contrast, in these six elections, Moroccans were statistically underrepresented. Although in the 1990s, Surinamese were well represented in city council, relative to their share in Amsterdam's population, since 2002, they too have been statistically underrepresented (Kranendonk et al. 2014). Michon (2011) concludes in her study on minority politicians' careers in Amsterdam that many immigrant politicians are unlike their co-ethnics in the city. Their family background and migration history deviate from those of most other immigrants, and they are often members of ethnic or religious minority groups in their or their parents' country of origin. These circumstances tend to set them apart from the larger immigrant community in Amsterdam, making it difficult or, at times, undesirable to represent the interests of immigrant constituencies. This puts in perspective the high percentage of immigrant representatives on Amsterdam's city council—these politicians are immigrants though they have weak, or no, links with the city's immigrant electorate.

As for political influence, measured by number of individuals of an immigrant background who hold executive positions, a different picture emerges than that suggested by representative figures in city and district councils. Besides showing how far such individuals have climbed up a ladder, their status also reflects political parties' responsiveness towards immigrant groups. Executive positions include mayor, deputy mayor at the city level, district mayor, and district deputy mayor at the city district level. The last two positions existed up until 2014. The mayors of Dutch municipalities are not elected by either the population or city council. Instead, they are appointed for a six-year period on the basis of choices made by a council committee. In 2002, the Netherlands introduced a strict separation between the council (the legislative branch controlling the executive branch) and the mayor and the deputy mayors (the executive branch). As a result, it is now possible to appoint someone who is not on a party list as deputy mayor—and this happens quite often. Deputy mayors are appointed by the winning coalition. A coalition consists of those political parties that agree to govern the city until the next election and who together hold the majority (at least 23) of city council seats. Deputy mayors have different domains for which they are responsible. It is striking that since the early 1990s, there have been many more Dutch-Moroccan and Dutch-Surinamese than Dutch-Turkish executive-level politicians. Amsterdam has thrice had Moroccan city-level deputy mayors and thrice had Surinamese city-level deputy mayors, though never Turkish. After the 2010 elections, two of the seven district mayors were Moroccan and one was Surinamese, though no Turk has yet been elected.

On account of these trends, Michon and Vermeulen (2013) argue that the political weight of the Dutch-Turkish group, despite being well-represented and displaying high levels of participation, is primarily due to political parties' wariness of strong ethnic communities and ethnic politics. That study finds:

> Parties fear that giving politicians of Turkish descent an influential position will automatically bring in ethnic group-based interests. The recent hostility of parties towards immigrant group-based mobilization therefore has a negative effect on political weight: Turkish politicians' access to politically influential positions becomes obstructed. The electoral system, in contrast, is less influenced by the backlash against multiculturalism: given that the electoral system includes party lists and preferential voting, group-based resources can still help garner votes and seats on council, thus keeping the door relatively open to Turkish immigrants' political participation and representation in Amsterdam.
>
> (Michon and Vermeulen 2013, 608)

Strong ties to an ethnic or a religious community that is considered to have different or incompatible values or both are reason enough for political parties to not support politicians of Turkish origin. And this holds even in a political context generally characterized as favorable to minority group representation, such as Amsterdam. So while the number of Dutch-Turkish politicians on the city council has stayed steady, their influence has diminished, since many had lower, less prestigious positions on party lists for 2014's local elections (Kranendonk et al. 2014).

The Amsterdam Case in Perspective

A dozen immigrant politicians in the Netherlands, both at national and local levels, have in the last couple of years left mainstream parties to form their own parties. In them, ethnic and religious identifications and ties to related communities are not problematized, but rather celebrated as an asset and a tool for immigrants to succeed. Denk embodies such a party. Its two founders are Turkish immigrants and former Labour Party (PvdA) MPs. They frame themselves as successful Dutch-Turks who embrace their connections to Dutch society and Turkish society, both. By contrast, Dutch-Turkish politicians in mainstream parties are often viewed by parties like Denk as traitors who claim to represent an immigrant community's interests but fail. Denk warns their immigrant constituency against losing ties to their ethnic and religious communities because they provide indispensable resources in a hostile environment.

In their own explanation of why immigrant politicians have left mainstream parties, several elements take centre stage. Religion is almost always a major factor. These politicians' former mainstream parties are almost always progressive and secular, whereas they themselves are frequently religious; they maintain strong links with the more conservative religious factions of the Netherlands' Turkish and Moroccan communities. Their decision to leave is often validated by their experiences of political debates around religion, for example, concerning possible bans on certain religious traditions or types of schooling. Ritual slaughtering and religious education are meaningful to conservative constituents in the immigrant electorate in the Netherlands. Yet, progressive secular parties, primarily since the civic turn, have changed their position on these issues in recent years and oppose them in debates. Immigrant politicians who belong to mainstream parties have gone on record, saying discussions about Islam within their own party are highly paternalistic and often offensive (Santing and Vermeulen 2015). Similar sentiments are expressed by immigrant politicians in other contexts in other European cities (Vermeulen and Doğan 2015). Any mobilizing of an immigrant constituency in order to engage in these debates is not only made controversial within the secular parties, but is often grounds to marginalize immigrant politicians within the party structure if not altogether push them out.

Another point of dispute involves issues connected to origin countries. Present-day Turkey offers a glaring example. In Germany, the Netherlands, Belgium, and

France, Turkish politicians of mainstream parties have been explicitly asked to pledge loyalty to European, Western norms and values by rejecting any financial, moral, or logistical endorsement that would show support for Turkey's current president, Recep Tayyip Erdoğan. These European mainstream parties often hold Erdoğan up as an emblem of illiberal Muslim leadership promulgating an ideology that is opposite from, and incompatible with, the civic liberal terms they uphold. The crisis narrative is extended to European-residing supporters of Erdoğan and his party. Its reading goes like this: religious Turkish immigrants strongly supporting the illiberal AKP party are exploiting the West's ethos of tolerance as they practise intolerance towards minorities, women, and secular people. Conservative Turkish immigrants' allegedly illiberal behavior is problematized almost daily and groups are castigated for not internalizing prevailing civic values or rejecting backward religious ideas. This places them outside the civic conception of the nation-state and essentially shames them within the public sphere.

To reiterate, it is no coincidence that Turkish politicians in Amsterdam have not held positions of political influence even though Turks, as a group, have been overrepresented on city councils for the last twenty-five years. The links they presumably hold with well-organized, often conservatively religious communities and constituencies make parties not only cautious, but also unreceptive to their claims and ideas. This is a political response to a perceived cultural conflict—but is there really a cultural conflict? Assumed and, at best, circumstantial evidence helps perpetuate these perceptions in a polarized context, in which everything can be taken as proof of cultures clashing. It is also no coincidence that Denk spawned from this group of conservatively religious Turks. The elements that make it difficult for them to function within mainstream political parties are precisely the elements that allow them to reactively resist the crisis narrative. This is the double bind at work.

Similar developments are unfolding in other European countries. In Belgium, Turkish politicians have confirmed plans to found a similar party. Or to take an example from Berlin where the largest Turkish immigrant group outside Turkey resides. A study was conducted in which almost all local politicians with a Turkish background were interviewed about their experiences and perceptions of local politics in Berlin (Vermeulen and Doğan 2015; Santing and Vermeulen 2015). One of the SPD politicians active at the city district level explained how he often speaks with young German-Turks in his neighborhood and encountered several initiatives of young second-generation Muslim immigrants establishing their own religious identity-based parties. At first, the politician reacted negatively, asking: "Why would you start an Islamic party in Berlin? The founders of these initiatives involved are not that religious to begin with." The answers he received from them in daily conversations, often from women, made him reconsider. They included responses such as "people have been feeling they are left without any option but to join such a party." In a hostile environment, it is their only coping mechanism, thus one they feel is largely forced upon them. Religion plays a role in their lives, but in many ways they lead their lives very differently from their parents; the second generation feels more cosmopolitan, less traditional, and more individualistic. In reflecting on the situation of young German-Turks in Berlin the politician states:

> We are categorized, excluded and stigmatized as Muslims on a daily basis. We are seen as strangers who do not belong here. We are forced to play the religious card. It almost is an inevitable choice whether you want it or not.
>
> (Santing and Vermeulen 2015)

This double bind—defined by Lentin and Titley (2011) as the "compliant integration into a prescribed national way of doing things that depends on being recognized as integrating"—presents many of Europe's Muslim immigrants with a dilemma. On the one hand, they must prove their ability to integrate into liberal European societies by convincing the secular progressive liberal majority that they have denounced their religious and ethnic affiliations. Any signs of collective identification or action can and often are used as evidence of the contrary. On the other hand, the crisis narrative emphasizes the presence of cultural and religious conflicts in Europe. Muslim immigrants are categorized and stigmatized by this crisis narrative every day. That exacerbates existing suspicion, discrimination, and isolation. The Amsterdam example illustrates that the crisis narrative and subsequent civic turn in Dutch debates and policies on immigration, integration and Islam did indeed have a negative effect on the political participation of immigrants, especially those originating from Muslim countries. One of the few possible ways they see to resist this narrative is by strengthening their ethnic and religious ties, developing tools and resources to collectively resist and mobilize, as has been done by some Turkish immigrant communities in Europe. Still, in the current polarized political climate and within public debate, resistance and mobilization exacerbates marginalization and segregation. That, in turn, strengthens the narrative of the crisis of multiculturalism because these examples are used again as evidence of these groups' inability to integrate. The double bind therefore gives way to a vicious circle, that affects many European cities.

References

Alba, R., and N. Foner. 2009. "Entering the Precincts of Power: Do National Differences Matter for Immigrant Minority Political Representation?" In *Bringing Outsiders In: Transatlantic Perspectives on Immigrant Political Incorporation*, edited by J. Hochschild and J. Mollenkopf, 277–293. Ithaca, NY: Cornell University Press.

Bloemraad, I. 2013. "Accessing the Corridors of Power: Puzzles and Pathways to UnderstandingMinority Representation." *West European Politics* 36, no. 3: 652–670. doi:10.1080/01402382.2013.773733.

Bloemraad, I., and M. Wright. 2014. "'Utter Failure' or Unity out of Diversity? Debating and Evaluating Policies of Multiculturalism." *International Migration Review* 48, no. 1: 292–334. doi:10.1111/imre.12135.

Fennema, M., and J. Tillie. 1999. "Political Participation and Political Trust in Amsterdam: Civic Communities and Ethnic Networks." *Journal of Ethnic and Migration Studies* 25, no. 4: 703–726. doi:10.1080/1369183X.1999.9976711.

Heath, A. F., S. D. Fisher, G. Rosenblatt, D. Sanders, and M. Sobolewska. 2013. *The Political Integration of Ethnic Minorities in Britain*. Oxford: Oxford University Press.

Hochschild, J., and J. Mollenkopf. 2009. "Modeling Immigrant Political Incorporation." In *Bringing Outsiders In: Transatlantic Perspectives on Immigrant Political Incorporation*, edited by J. Hochschild and J. Mollenkopf, 15–30. Ithaca, NY: Cornell University Press.

Joppke, C. 2004. "The Retreat of Multiculturalism in the Liberal State: Theory and Policy." *The British Journal of Sociology* 55, no. 2: 237–257. doi:10.1111/j.1468-4446.2004.00017.x.

Joppke, C. 2007. "Transformation of Immigrant Integration: Civic Integration and Antidiscrimination in the Netherlands, France, and Germany." *World Politics* 59. no. 2: 243–273. doi:10.1353/wp.2007.0022.

Katz, R. S. 2001. "The Problem of Candidate Selection and Models of Party Democracy." *Party Politics* 7, no. 3: 277–296. doi:10.1177/1354068801007003002.

Kranendonk, M., L. Michon, H. Schwarz, and F. Vermeulen. 2014. *Opkomst en stemgedrag van Amsterdammers met een migratie-achtergrond tijdens de gemeenteraadsverkiezingen van 19 maart 2014*. Amsterdam: OIS.

Kranendonk, M., F. Vermeulen, and A. van Heelsum. 2017. "'Unpacking' the Identity-to-Politics Link: The Effects of Social Identification on Voting among Muslim Immigrants in Western Europe." *Political Psychology* 39, no. 1. https://doi.org/10.1111/pops.12397

Kundnani, A. 2012. "Multiculturalism and Its Discontents: Left, Right and Liberal." *European Journal of Cultural Studies* 15, no. 2: 155–166. doi:10.1177/1367549411432027.

Lentin, A., and G. Titley. 2011. *The Crises of Multiculturalism: Racism in a Neoliberal Age*. London: Zed.

Michon, L. B. 2011. "*Ethnic Minorities in Local Politics: Comparing Amsterdam and Paris*." PhD diss., Universiteit van Amsterdam.

Michon, L., and F. Vermeulen. 2013. "Explaining Different Trajectories in Immigrant Political Integration: Moroccans and Turks in Amsterdam." *West European Politics* 36, no. 3: 597–614. doi:10.1080/01402382.2013.773727.

Mouritsen, P. 2008. "Political Responses to Cultural Conflict: Reflections on the Ambiguities of the Civic Turn." In *Constituting Communities: Political Solutions to Cultural Conflict*, edited by P. Mouritsen and K. E. Jørgensen, 1–30. New York: Palgrave MacMillan

Ramakrishnan, K., and I. Bloemraad. 2008. "Introduction." In *Civic Hopes and Political Realities: Immigrants, Community Organizations and Political Engagement*, edited by S. K. Ramakrishnan and I. Bloemraad, 1–44. New York: Russell Sage Foundation.

Santing, F., and F. Vermeulen. 2015. "'O wee als wij in de raad komen': Immigranten keren de gevestigde politiek de rug toe." *De Groene Amsterdammer*, 18 February. https://www.groene.nl/artikel/o-wee-als-wij-in-de-raad-komen.

Triadafilopoulos, T. 2011. "Illiberal Means to Liberal Ends? Understanding Recent Immigrant Integration Policies in Europe." *Journal of Ethnic and Migration Studies* 37, no. 6: 861–880. doi:10.1080/1369183X.2011.576189.

Vermeulen, F. 2006. *The Immigrant Organising Process: Turkish Organisations in Amsterdamand Berlin and Surinamese Organisations in Amsterdam, 1960–2000*. Amsterdam: Amsterdam University Press.

Vermeulen, F. 2014. "Suspect Communities—Targeting Violent Extremism at the Local Level:Policies of Engagement in Amsterdam, Berlin, and London." *Terrorism and Political Violence* 26, no. 2: 286–306. doi:10.1080/09546553.2012.705254.

Vermeulen, F., and M. Berger. 2008. "Turkish Civic Networks and Political Behavior in Amsterdam and Berlin." In *Civic Hopes and Political Realities: Community Organizations *and Political Engagement among Immigrants in the United States and Abroad*, edited by S. K. Ramakrishnan and I. Bloemraad, 160–192. New York: Russell Sage Foundation.

Vermeulen, F., L. Michon, and J. Tillie. 2014. "Immigrant Political Engagement and Incorporation in Amsterdam." In *Immigration and the New Urban Landscape: New Yorkand Amsterdam*, edited by N. Foner, J. Rath, J. W. Duyvendak, and R. van Reekum, 230–256. New York: New York University Press.

Vermeulen, F., and A. Doğan. 2015. "How Berlin's Local Politicians of Turkish Background Perceive Their Access to Party Networks and Ability to Succeed?" In *Politics and Law in Turkish Migration*, edited by I. Sirkeci, D. Elçin, and G. Şeker, 79–92. London: Transnational Press.

CHAPTER 46

MIGRATION TO AUSTRALIA IN TIMES OF CRISIS

JOCK COLLINS

AUSTRALIA has been one of the western world's major migration nations for the past seven decades. Since the end of the second world war Australia has embarked on a sustained settler immigration program designed to contribute significantly to population growth and nation building. As the OECD reported (2017, 36) "The proportion of foreign-born is highest in Luxembourg (46 percent of the total population), Switzerland (29 percent), Australia (28 percent) and New Zealand (23 percent)." Together with their Australian-born children—second-generation immigrants—immigrants comprise more than 60 percent of the population of Australian's largest cities today (Salt 2017). As a consequence Australia's largest and most cosmopolitan city, Sydney, has become the fourth greatest immigrant city in the western world today (IOM 2015, 39).

Immigrants have contributed half of Australia's population and workforce growth in the last seven decades (Productivity Commission 2016) and transformed Australian society in general—and its major cities like Sydney, Melbourne, Brisbane, Perth and Adelaide in particular—into cosmopolitan, cultural, linguistic, and religiously diverse places. As one of the four major settler immigration countries—with the United States, Canada, and New Zealand—Australia is shaped by and defined by immigration in a way that few other contemporary western nations have been. Australia's history of a large-scale and geographically diverse immigration intake and immigration policy fine-tuned over time to maximize its economic benefits was complimented by a multiculturalism policy that could claim to be a world leader in immigrant settlement outcomes since the 1980s.

This claim cannot be sustained today. Periods of economic, political, and social crises in Australia and internationally—and Australian government responses to them—have disrupted these long-term postwar immigration trends and challenged Australia's immigration reputation.

In the formative years of Australia's new immigration program it had to abandon its promise that nine out of every ten postwar immigrants would be British because the crisis of people displaced from the Second World War meant that only half of the intake in the late 1940s were British: the rest were European refugees (or "displaced peoples"). The fall of Saigon in 1975 triggered an outflow of Vietnamese boat people who began arriving on northern Australian shores soon after, testing for the first time the reality, rather than rhetoric, of Australia's abandonment of "white Australia." It also tested once again Australian's appetite for refugees, a recurring narrative that, while numerically small, loomed large in Australia's postwar immigration history. More recent chapters of this narrative arose following a series of conflicts in the Middle East: from the Israeli invasions of Lebanon in the late 1970s and early 1980s, the first and second invasion of Iraq by the United States and allies (including Australia) up to the recent conflict in Syria. Countries like Canada and Australia also opened their doors to Syrian-conflict refugees.

Globally, a refugee anxiety had been transformed into a migration anxiety, ironically at the very moment that significant progress was made on global governance of migration with the historic 2016 New York Declaration for Refugees and Migrants and the establishment of the UN Global Compacts on Refugees and Migrants. Launching the *International Migration Outlook 2016* (OECD 2016a) at the United Nations General Assembly in New York, OECD Secretary-General Angel Gurríawas worried that "Too many people in too many countries are losing faith in how we manage migration, and the refugee crisis has exacerbated this." (OECD 2016b). Gurria warned about "the rising tide of anti-immigration voices" and urged OECD governments to develop more effective migration and integration policies. Undocumented migration and the arrival of asylum-seekers generated migration anxieties and controversial policy responses from governments in North America (Donald Trump's wall between Mexico and the United States) and Europe (the rise of the anti-immigrant far-right and the resurrection of hitherto dismantled borders triggered by the Syrian conflict and refugee flows in 2015–2016).

This century in Australia the political anxieties related to undocumented arrivals and asylum-seekers who arrived on the northwestern shores by boat triggered unprecedented, draconian immigration policies of mandatory detention and offshore processing of boat people as the Australian navy was called on to push boatloads of asylum seekers back to sea. This was an Australian-made crisis characterized by political bipartisanship.

The Syrian conflict generated massive flows of refugees to European countries and to Syria's neighbors in the Middle East of a speed, magnitude, and unpredictability not seen since the end of the Second World War (Betts and Collier 2017; Crawley et al. 2017; Kingsley 2016). This triggered a wave of political tremors. Countries struggled at first to develop policies and infrastructure to deal with the arrival stage. Anti-immigrant populist parties exploited the situation to peddle the politics of xenophobia. Borders long dormant began to be resurrected in Europe. At the same time Brexit fractured the progress that Europe had made in the free movement of people and labor within its boundaries and the Shengen Agreement that underwrote this immigrant mobility began to teeter. At the same time in the United States Donald Trump was elected on a promise—among others—of building a wall to stop the entry of people and workers from the Mexican border. Trump also withdrew US support for the Trans Pacific Partnership's free trade reforms and, more recently, from the UN Global Compacts on Refugees and Migrants.

These developments in Europe and North America can be viewed as manifestations of a crisis in globalization. Australia is geographically a long way from Europe, North America, and the Middle East, yet, at the same time, is very close economically, politically, socially, and culturally to these regions after successive Australian governments enthusiastically embraced globalization since the 1980s. The Achilles heel of globalization has been the free global movement of labor which, unlike the global movement of capital and goods and services, continues to be severely constrained. Migrant laborers become neighbors and workmates, triggering prejudice, xenophobia, and nationalism. Populist antimigration parties proclaim that migrant workers take the jobs of locals. In Australia, this contradiction played out in a slightly different way. The massive growth in temporary migration engineered by Australian migration policy over the past two decades was very welcome by employers, but the increasing evidence of the exploitation of temporary migrant labor by employers in the small-business sector in particular has triggered a public backlash. A political crisis related to lack of governmental oversight of and regulation of employer exploitation of temporary migrant labor has emerged, leading to a major revision of temporary skilled labor migration policy.

Like the current so-called refugee crisis, the global financial crisis of a decade ago disrupted and challenged immigration policy across the western world as immigration intakes plummeted in Australia and other countries. The fallout extended beyond the economy and onto Australian immigration debates, just as the global downturn of 1982–1983 led not only to a significant reduction in immigration intakes in Australia but was also a catalyst for the Blainey debate about Asian immigration in Australia.

Middle Eastern Conflict: Boat People and the Crisis in Australian Immigration Policy

There is no more controversial aspect of Australia's contemporary immigration policy than that of the "boat people" (Maley 2016), the term in political and popular discourses used to describe what the Australian government calls irregular maritime arrivals. Boat people have been arriving on Australian shores seeking asylum at least since the *Dunera* arrived prior to the Second World War with Jews escaping the impending Nazi holocaust. Many refugees who had been displaced by the Second World War—the so-called displaced peoples –arrived in boats from Poland and the Baltic States in the late 1940s, though with reluctant consent of the Australian Government's first Minister for Immigration, Arthur Caldwell (Collins 1991, 53–56). Following the fall of Saigon in 1975, thousands of Vietnamese arrived after a dangerous, perilous journey by small fishing boats on Australia's northern shores (Vivianni 1984). They were asylum-seekers seeking protection by Australia under the 1956 UNHCR Convention of Refugees and were welcomed by the Fraser Conservative government, which—against public opinion at the time—argued that refugee boats should not be allowed to become an election issue because "human suffering transcends partisan advantage" (Higgins 2017). From the 1990s small boats of asylum seekers once again began to arrive on northwest Australian shores, this time mostly people escaping conflict and persecution in the Middle East. They made their way to Indonesia and secured the services of smugglers for their long and hazardous journey to Australian shores, usually by fishing boat. The response to these boat people from the Middle East was very different from the reception of those Lebanese refugees who arrived by plane after 1976 displaced by conflict with Israel and very different from the response to the Vietnamese boat people.

The Keating Labor Government (1991–1996) responded to the humanitarian claims of these boat people displaced by conflict in the Middle East by introducing mandatory detention for boat people—men, women and their children—until their claims for refugee status were assessed. The conservative Howard government (1996–2007) took controversy surrounding boat people to a very different level of negativity compared to the response of his counterpart on the mid-1970s. In August 2001 the Howard government dispatched vessels of the Australian navy to prevent the Norwegian freighter—the *MV Tampa*—which had rescued 438 Middle Eastern refugees whose boat—the 20-meter Indonesian fishing boat KM *Palapa 1*—had foundered before reaching Australian shores where they could have had their claims for protection assessed (Marr and Wilkinson 2003). This was despite the fact that more than 300 of those aboard *Palapa 1* were Afghanis escaping persecution from the Taliban and the fact that the Howard government had committed Australian troops to Afghanistan to fight the Taliban in coalition with US-led forces.

The Howard government introduced a "turn back the boats" policy, a race card that played on negative stereotypes and falsehoods about boat people to develop a moral panic about refugees (Marr 2011) that was decisive in the Conservative coalition victory at the November 2001 national election (Marr and Wilkinson 2003, 277–286; Nakhoul 2011). This was the beginning of the politicization of the boat people issue. The Stop the Boats and policy of offshore processing—sending asylum-seekers to other countries for detention and determination of their claim to refugee status—of refugees was also central to the campaign and victory of the Abbott Conservative government (2013–15) and remains a central plank of the current Turnbull (2015–) Conservative government to this day.

Labor Governments have been complicit in this moral panic about boat people in Australia. The Keating Labor Government (1991–1996) had introduced mandatory detention for boat arrivals. The Rudd (2007–2010 and 2013) and Gillard (2010–2013) maintained mandatory detention and offshore processing policy. As Prime Minister Rudd declared on July 19, 2013, any asylum-seeker who arrived in Australia by boat would have no chance of being settled in Australia even when confirmed as a refugee.

Under Coalition and Labor governments boat people have been pilloried as queue-jumpers unsuitable for life in Australia as the boat people issue became a political football. Today the offshore processing of boat people, including young children, on Manus Island—found to be illegal by the PNG High Court and currently being challenged in the Australian High Court (Gleeson 2016; Hasham and Gordon 2016); O'Brien Solicitors 2017)—and Nauru continues to underline the narrative that boat people are a danger to Australian society. Australia receives around 200,000 permanent immigrant arrivals and over 700,000 temporary immigrant arrivals each year (Department of Immigration and Border Protection 2017. Comparatively, the humanitarian program is just 1.7 percent of the total immigration intake or 12 percent of the permanent program intake. Boat arrivals are a fraction of the humanitarian intake, though the Abbott government announced an additional intake of 12,000 refugees from the Syrian conflict (Bourke 2015). Despite this, Australia's refugee "problem" has captured most of the oxygen generated by public debate and political discourses on Australian immigration policy, particularly when asylum-seekers arrive on Australian shores by boat.

In the lead-up to the 2016 Federal election the Minister for Immigration and Border Protection, Peter Dutton, claimed that "illiterate and innumerate" refugees would "swamp welfare queues and take the jobs of locals" if the annual humanitarian intake was substantially increased (Baxendale and Lewis 2016). It is remarkable that an Immigration Minister would make such a claim. It is also clear evidence in itself of the role that Australian politics has played in constructing the refugee crisis in Australia.

Yet the evidence suggests that while refugees do face higher unemployment rates than other migrants, they also demonstrate twice the rate of self-employment and entrepreneurship than immigrants who arrive under a skilled or family visa. 2009–2010 data shows that "Humanitarian migrants displayed greater entrepreneurial qualities and reported a higher proportion of income from their own unincorporated businesses and this income increased sharply after five years of residency" (Australian Bureau of Statistics 2016).

Minister Dutton might have been speaking about the Hazara refugees who were denied education by the Taliban and other political regimes in Afghanistan where they were relentlessly persecuted (Malley 2016, 4–5). For many Hazaras there was no alternative but to flee Afghanistan and seek a better life for their families in the refugee camps in Syria and other neighboring countries. Some decided to take the greatest risk for their future: to embark on the costly, uncertain, and dangerous journey by boat from Indonesia to Australia. Many of them settled in Adelaide after periods of detention in processing camps across Australia before receiving refugee status. Fieldwork with 31 Hazara refugee entrepreneurs (29 males and 2 females) who had established a business in Adelaide, the capital city of South Australia, found that they overcame the highest imaginable barriers to establish a business in Adelaide. They overcame their lack of start-up capital by saving from meager wages over many years, often in factories and unskilled manual jobs. They built strong Hazara community networks in Adelaide to overcome the lack of social capital that refugee entrepreneurs face in Australia. In a strange contradiction, a number of Hazara refugee entrepreneurs developed friendships with other Hazara they met during their period of mandatory detention in Australia, building their social capital and, in a number of instances, lifelong friendships and business partnerships with them. These Hazara refugee entrepreneurs were very positive about the future of themselves and their families—and their children—in Adelaide. They were very thankful for the opportunity given to them to seek refuge in Australia, eternally grateful and at the same time determined to make a success of their lives (Collins et al. 2017: 109–110).

While most refugees will not become entrepreneurs, refugee entrepreneurship in countries like Australia (Collins 2017a); Canada (Klingbeil 2017); the UK (Lyon, Sepulveda, and Syrett 2007); Belgium (Wauters and Lambrech 2006); the United States (Grey, Rodríguez, and Conrad 2004); and Uganda (Betts, Bloom, and Weaver 2015) demonstrates the innovation, resilience, and agency of refugees—including those who arrived by boat—and their capacity for what Betts and his colleagues (2015) call "bottom-up innovation . . . the way in which crisis-affected communities engage in creative problem solving, adapting products and processes to address challenges and create opportunities." This evidence-based research on refugee entrepreneurship refutes the narrative in Australia that boat people are a danger to Australian society and the narrative around the world that refugees threaten the economic and social future of host societies.

The Global Financial Crisis and Australian Immigration

International economic crises have had substantial reverberations on Australian immigration policy and politics. Immigration intakes to Australia have always responded to the business cycle, increasing during boom times and being reduced during economic downturns and periods of economic recession. The late Australian demographer and immigration scholar, Charles Price, likened this aspect of Australian immigration policy to a "boa constrictor" which followed a huge food intakes (such a pig or some other large animal) with a long period of little food intake at all (Collins 2008).

The Australian economy had a long boom following the Second World War until it was interrupted by the first postwar global recession in 1974–1975. Immigration intakes were reduced as unemployment rates escalated to record postwar levels. The subsequent economic recovery and boom saw immigration intakes climb until the 1982–1983 global recession (Collins 1991, 115–119), a pattern repeated following the 1990–1992 recession (Collins, Morrissey, and Grogan 1995). At the same time, as unemployment rates rose post-recession male and female immigrant minorities experienced significantly higher rates of unemployment than the Australian-born. This was a consequence of their over-representation in jobs in the industries (manufacturing and building and construction) that were most impacted by economic downturn.

Australia's permanent immigration intake declined after the 1990–1991 economic recession (when the annual intake was 107,400) to a low of 69,800 in 1993–1994. With subsequent economic recovery immigration intakes were increased to 184,837 in 2007–2008. The 2007–2008 global financial crisis (GFC) led to severe economic recession in most western countries (Cassidy 2009; Stiglitz, 2010). While Australia was an exception—quick and effective large fiscal stimulus together with sustained demand for minerals exports from China helped the country stave off economic recession (Quiggin 2010)—the Australian economy experienced a severe economic downturn. Unemployment rose and economic output fell. Prior to the GFC Australia's permanent immigration intake reached record levels postwar levels—the 2007–2008 intake of 114, 777 was the largest skilled migration intake ever (DIAC 2009)—while temporary immigrant intakes rose to unprecedented levels, significantly outstripping permanent immigrant intakes. In May 2009 Australia's Immigration Minister, Chris Evans, announced that the skilled migration programme would be reduced by 14 percent, or 18,500 jobs, over the following three years. The total number of immigrants was reduced from 133,500 in 2009 to 115,000 in 2010. Further cuts to immigration were announced in the 2009 annual budget with a number of occupations removed from the permanent immigration list. Restrictions on international students gaining temporary student visas were also introduced. Despite these announced cuts, the Australian skilled migration intake for 2008–2009 increased by 5.7 percent due to the "pipeline" effect of immigration and the lag between immigrant application approvals and immigrant arrivals in Australia (Collins 2011). The immigration tap takes some time to respond to policy changes. Following the GFC, Australia's skilled permanent immigration intakes were reduced from a record 133,500 in 2008–2009 to 108,780 for the 2009–2010 year (Hugo 2011, 36). However, permanent immigration actually increased in Australia by 7 percent in 2008–2009 when it fell in most other OECD countries (OECD 2011, 41)—mainly because Australia escaped economic recession following the GFC (Collins 2011)—but declined by 7 percent in 2009–2010 (Phillips and Simon-Davies 2017, 3).

At the same time, the experience of recession was fertile ground for immigration critics. Not coincidentally, the greatest national debate about postwar immigration and multiculturalism—the Blainey debate—occurred in the immediate aftermath of the 1982–1983 global recession. Similarly, the rise of anti-Asian immigration politician Pauline Hanson and the establishment of her One Nation political party in 1996 followed in the aftermath of the 1991–1992 recession because the Australian economy took many years before unemployment began to fall after this recession (Markus 2001).

Another dimension of the relationship of the GFC to Australian immigration relates to the share of burden of the increasing unemployment rates following the economic downturn that accrued to immigrant minorities. Data on immigrant unemployment rates for all ages over the 2008–2009 period shows that immigrants born in North Africa and the Middle East and Asian countries experienced significantly higher unemployment rates than other immigrants such as those born in European countries (Collins 2011).

This is a reminder that crises that impact on immigration and immigrants do so in uneven and sometimes complex ways. In Australia it has been immigrants from racialized minority backgrounds and not immigrants from the UK, New Zealand, and North America who have borne the brunt of economic crises and negative migrant discourses and who have been the target of anti-immigrant far-right populist parties. In Australia the nomenclature for immigrants from racialized minority backgrounds is CALD (culturally and linguistically diverse) migrants, though post 9/11 Muslim immigrants have been particularly singled out as the object of most anti-immigrant discourses. At the same time it is important to remember that intersections of class and gender are also at play.

Temporary Migration Unsettling Australian Immigration

A political crisis is emerging around Australia's temporary migration policy. In the past two decades Australia, one of the world's few post-1945 settler immigration nations, has switched to strongly preferring temporary over permanent immigration (Markus et al. 2009). This historical shift in Australian immigration policy away from an exclusive focus on permanent settlers to one that heavily prioritizes temporary immigrants is, according to Mares (2009, 2017), the biggest change in migration to Australian since the end of the White Australia Policy. Markus, Jupp, and McDonald (2009) refer to this change as Australia's immigration revolution. Today the annual intake of temporary immigrants is three times as large as Australia's permanent immigrant intake (Collins 2014). This change in Australian immigration policy has opened the door to three quarters of a million temporary immigrants annually. They arrive under international student, working holiday maker or temporary skilled worker (457) visas. In 2015–2016, for example, the Australian permanent migration program was 207,325 (of which 17,555 were humanitarian entrants). The temporary program intake in 2016 was 654,480: 150,220 Temporary Work (Skilled) (subclass 457) visa holders, 355,760 Student visa holders, and 148,500 Working Holiday Maker visa holders (Phillips and Simon-Davies 2017). The main source countries were New Zealand, PRC, India, the UK, and the United States (DIBP 2017, 1–2).

It is not true to say that Australia has completely abandoned settler immigration and replaced it with guest worker migration. Some 200,000 permanent immigrants arrive each year. In addition, temporary migration is a pathway to permanent migration for many immigrants. This is a new form of circular migration (Massey 2015) circulating through a number of different temporary migration visas on the pathway to reach the ultimate immigrant objective: permanent residence in Australia. As the Productivity Commission (2016, 418) put it: "For many immigrants, the pathway to permanent residency involves multiple temporary visas before obtaining permanent residency. On average, multi-step immigrants receive 3.3 visa grants, including extensions or renewals. The average duration of multi-step pathways is approximately 6.4 years, although some pathways are significantly quicker than others." So not all temporary migrants to Australia remain temporary, although only the minority of temporary migrants achieve their ultimate goal of permanent residence in Australia (Collins 2017b).

This historic shift in Australian immigration policy to dramatically increase temporary immigrants has far reaching implications that have surprisingly been ignored in public immigration debates and discourses in Australia. At the most basic level is the question of the place of temporary immigrants in the Australian nation. When it was a settler immigration nation in the first fifty years of postwar immigration history the answer was clear: immigrants will contribute to long-term nation building in Australia by bringing their extended families with them via the process of chain migration, filling about half of the new jobs created and generating half of the population growth in Australia. Immigrants transformed the Australian nation into the cosmopolitan nation it is today (Castles et al. 2015). As part of this grand bargain, immigrants can claim, as North American political philosopher Joseph Carens (2008, 419) put it, "full membership in [Australian] society and to the enjoyment of the same rights as citizens, including, eventually, citizenship itself." But the new emphasis on temporary migration unsettles this arrangement since temporary migrants have few of the political and social rights of permanent residents. Is this ethical, Carens (2013) asks? For Mares (2017, 294), paraphrasing Carens, the question becomes: "what is the place of long-term temporary migrants on the 'normative map' of Australian democracy (Mares 2017, 23–24)?"

On average, Australia's skill-stream permanent immigrants have relatively good labor market and settlement outcomes (Productivity Commission 2016, 421). The Productivity Commission is justifiably concerned about the lack of research into temporary immigration, calling for "a better understanding of the labor market impacts of temporary migration programs." The surprising fact, then, is that the most significant change to Australia immigration policy in the past seven decades has occurred in an absence of evidence-based research on its impact on the Australian economy and society and on Australia's new immigrant arrivals themselves. In addition, until recently there has been little political or public debate about the dramatic increase in the Australian temporary migration intake. This can mainly be explained by the disproportionate attention to the boat people issue in Australia—addressed previously in this chapter—which has captured most of the oxygen in contemporary immigration debates.

There has, however, been increasing evidence of, and public concern about, the widespread and systematic exploitation of temporary migrants—those on skilled 457 visas and working holiday and student visas—in the Australian labor market. Because the international student visa permits international students to work up to 20 hours per week, it is also a temporary migrant worker visa. Assuming all international tertiary students work 20 hours per week, this is the equivalent workforce impact of an extra 146,677 temporary migrants working a 37-hour week, or more than three times the total intake (45,400) of 457 visas workers last year. This is a conservative estimate, since research suggests that many are forced to work longer hours to make ends meet in Australia (Robertson 2013).

According to many judgements and reports made by the Australian Fair Work Commission, the evidence suggests that many international students, 457 visa holders and international students are exploited, paid under-award wages in often substandard workplaces. In 2013–2014 the Fair Work Ombudsman (FWO) assessed 1029 workplaces employing a total of almost 2000 temporary skilled visa holders and found that wages or employment obligations were not being met for 338 employees (FWO 2014, 30). The FWO found 457 workers at Baiada Chicken, one of the largest chicken processors in Australia, were paid about half the minimum hourly wage and worked up to 18 hours a day without paid overtime (Om 2015). As is often the case with the employment of temporary migrants, Baiada contracts six intermediary "labor hire companies" who in turn contract a large number of other intermediaries to provide temporary migrant labor for its factories. Another study reported that 18.4 percent of 457 visa holders from non-English-speaking backgrounds reported experiencing discrimination because of their "skill, colour, ethnic origin, or religious beliefs" (Migration Council of Australia, 2013, 32). Another survey found that 16 percent of 457 workers reported discrimination on these grounds (DIBP 2013, 35).

More recently, the most comprehensive study of wage theft and working conditions among international students, backpackers, and other temporary migrants in Australia reported on the responses from 4,322 temporary migrants across 107 nationalities of every region in the world, working in a range of jobs in all states and territories (Berg and Farbenblum 2017). The survey indicates that Australia has a large silent underclass of migrant workers, primarily made up of international students and backpackers, who are paid well below the minimum wage. In the words of the authors "The study confirms that wage theft is endemic among international students, backpackers and other temporary migrants in Australia" (Berg and Farbenblum 2017, 7). It found that 30 percent of international students and backpackers earned $12 per hour or less with at least one in five Americans, British, Indians, Brazilians, and Chinese temporary migrant workers earning roughly half the legal minimum wage for their jobs.

There is also evidence that the other major component of temporary migrant workers—those on 457 visas—are also subject to exploitation in the workplace. Submissions to a 2008 federal review of the integrity of the 457 program (the Deegan Report) provided "numerous examples of the exploitation of workers on Subclass 457 visas," including: lack of overtime payments; working longer hours than Australian co-workers; limited access to sick leave and threat of firing if the visa holder takes it; being fired because of pregnancy; being fired for taking leave; sexual harassment; and being overcharged rent and other costs by the employer (Deegan 2008, 6). A three-year survey of the experiences of Indian temporary skilled migrants in Australia illuminated significant levels of vulnerability arising from visa conditions, recruitment processes, illegal employment practices, and living arrangements (Velayutham 2013).

A continuing series of media reports and television documentaries into exploitative working conditions and pay arrangements experienced by 457 visa temporary skilled workers led the conservative Australian government to establish an inquiry into the program (Azarias et al. 2014). Following this review the conservative Turnbull government took the decision in April 2017 to scrap the 457 skilled temporary worker visa and replace it with a TSS temporary skilled workers visa which had two components: a two-year short-term stream prohibiting a transfer to permanent residence and a medium-term four-year stream that keeps the permanent residence pathway open

(Department of Home Affairs 2017). There is no guarantee that this change will end exploitation of temporary skilled migrant workers. The ability for migrants to transition from temporary to permanent visas is the strongest argument against the claim that Australia has abandoned the settler immigration model in favour of a guest-worker immigration model. Hence the decision to replace the 457 visa and replace it—in part—with a short-term stream that does not permit a pathway to permanent residence reinforces the increasingly guest-worker character of Australia's current immigration program.

The shifting emphasis to temporary migrant workers in Australia is the outcome of government attempts to fine-tune Australian immigration policy and—in the age of globalization—to maximize the short term economic benefits of a flexible and internationally mobile workforce. Not all temporary migrant workers are exploited, and those who do experience exploitation in some jobs do not experience exploitation in the other jobs that they take in Australia (Collins 2017b 80–83). The "crisis" of temporary migrant worker exploitation in Australia is a consequence of immigration authorities believing in globalization and the inherent efficiency of deregulated global labor markets while putting few resources into compliance matters. This is another example of the inherent inequalities of globalization.

Conclusion

Global economic and political crises and global conflict reverberate in Australia, an enthusiastic player in the globalization game. As one of the world's major postwar immigration nations where immigration is both popular and controversial, these crises play out if the field of immigration policy and practice and the public and political immigration discourses. For the second half of the twentieth century Australia had a well-earned reputation for world-leading immigration policy, practices, and outcomes related to immigrant settlement. This reputation has been displaced in the first decades of the twenty-first century when Australia is now infamous for its unhumanitarian policies and practices related to asylum-seekers who arrive by boat. While small in number relative to the 900,000 or so annual permanent and temporary immigrant arrivals, a bipartisan political obsession about boat people means that both major political parties in Australia (Conservative Coalition and Labor) are wedged into jointly refusing boat people the human and legal rights to processing in Australia and the right to settle in Australia once they receive refugee status. Refugee families, including children, face indeterminant detention in camps in offshore countries that were described by Patrick McGorry, the Australian of the Year in 2010, as "factories for producing mental illness" (Robotham 2011). This is a crisis made in Australia in response to the displacement of people from conflict and crises in the Middle East. The negative stereotypes of boat people as unsuitable for Australian life and settlement—amplified by, of all people, the Minister for Immigration and Border Protection—are at odds with the evidence-based research. The political opportunism is rife: elections are won and lost in Australia on these politics of prejudice. Hence the Labor opposition has proved reluctant to take a human rights stand on the issue.

This chapter has also considered the impact of the global financial crisis on Australian immigration. Because immigration is increasingly about providing migrant workers in Australia, immigration intakes fell, though more slowly and by less than in other countries, in part because Australia did not fall into economic recession and in part because of the time lags involved in immigration policy. Immigrant minorities took the greatest share of the burden of the increasing unemployment that accompanied the downturn.

The historical shift in Australian immigration from settler immigration toward temporary immigration also reflects Australia's enthusiastic embracing of globalization and the short-term neoliberal focus on efficient labor markets (Collins 2013). While the boat people issue deflected public and political attention from this historical shift, mounting evidence about the exploitation of temporary migrants eventually forced the Turnbull government to scrap the skilled worker temporary 457 visa. The contradiction here is that the profit motive of small-business owners—at the heart of free market economics and the desirable "economic man"—overrode legal conventions of minimum wages and conditions of employment. Wage theft was exposed as rampant across the Australian small-business sector, with temporary migrant workers the most vulnerable. The "greed is good" unrestricted free market mantra—at the heart of neoliberalism, economic rationalism, and globalization—hit back at a government that had its immigration eye focused on the security and border protection issues related to boat people and away from the excessive greed of its private sector employers.

References

ABS. 2016. *Humanitarian Migrants the Most Entrepreneurial: ABS Report*. http://www.abs.gov.au/AUSSTATS/abs@.nsf/Previousproducts/3418.0Media%20Release12009-10

Azarias, J., J. Lambert, P. McDonald, and P. Malyon. 2014. "Robust New Foundations: A Streamlined, Transparent and Responsive System for the 457 Programme." https://www.homeaffairs.gov.au/about/reports-publications/reviews-inquiries/independent-review-of-the-457-programme

Baxendale, R. and R. Lewis. 2016. "Federal Election 2016: Dutton on Refugees". *The Australian*, May 18. http://www.theaustralian.com.au/federal-election-2016/federal-election-2016-dutton-on-refugees-shorten-in-sydney-turnbull-in-cairns/news-story/16e8096aa3081a62dc9cd306a25f9158

Berg, L. and B. Farbenblum. 2017. "Wage Theft in Australia: Findings of the National Temporary Work Survey." *MWJI*. https://www.mwji.org/highlights/2017/11/14/report-released-wage-theft-in-australia-findings-of-the-national-temporary-migrant-work-survey

Betts, A., L. Bloom, and N. Weaver. 2015. "Refugee Innovation: Humanitarian Innovation that Starts with Communities." Refugee Studies Centre, University of Oxford, July 2015. https://reliefweb.int/sites/reliefweb.int/files/resources/refugee-innovation-web-5-3mb.pdf.

Betts, A., and P. Collier. 2017. *Refuge: Transforming a Broken Refugee System*. London: Allen Lane and Penguin.

Bourke, L. 2015. "Abbott Government Agrees To Resettle 12,000 Syrian Refugees in Australia. *Sydney Morning Herald*, September 9. http://www.smh.com.au/federal-politics/political-news/abbott-government-agrees-to-resettle-12000-syrian-refugees-in-australia-20150909-gjibqz.html

Carens, J. 2008. "Live in Domestics, Seasonal Workers, and Others Hard to Locate on the Map of Democracy." *Journal of Political Philosophy* 16, no. 4: 419–445.

Carens, J. 2013. *The Ethics of Immigration*. New York: Oxford University Press.

Cassidy, J. 2009. *How Markets Fail: The Logic of Economic Calamities*. New York: Farrar, Strauss, and Giroux.

Castles, S., D. Ozkul, and M. Arias Cubas, eds. 2015. *Social Transformation and Migration: National and Local Experiences in South Korea, Turkey, Mexico and Australia*. London: Palgrave Macmillan.

Collins, J. 1991. *Migrant Hands in a Distant Land: Australia's Postwar Immigration*. Sydney and London: Pluto.

Collins, J. 2008. "Globalisation, Immigration and the Second Long Postwar Boom in Australia." *Journal of Australian Political Economy* 61 (June 2008): 244–266.

Collins, J. 2011. "The Global Financial Crisis, Immigration and Immigrant Unemployment, and Social Inclusion in Australia." In *Immigration And The Financial Crisis The United States and Australia Compared*, edited by J. Higley, J. Nieuwenhuysen, and S. Neerup, 145–158. Monash Studies in Global Movements Series. Cheltennam, UK: Edward Elgar.

Collins, J. 2013. "Rethinking Australian Immigration and Immigrant Settlement Policy." *Journal of Intercultural Studies*, 34, no. 22: 160–177.

Collins, J. 2014. "Report Marks Australia's Shift from Settler to Temporary Migrant Nation." *The Conversation*, December 2. https://theconversation.com/report-marks-australias-shift-from-settler-to-temporary-migrant-nation-34794

Collins J. 2017a. *From Refugee to Entrepreneur in Sydney in Less Than Three Years*. UTS Business School, Sydney, Australia. https://www.ssi.org.au/images/stories/documents/Ignite/SSI_Ignite_evaluation_report_2017.pdf

Collins, J. 2017b. "Australia's New Guest Workers: Opportunity or Exploitation?" In *Critical Reflections on Migration, "Race," and Multiculturalism*, edited by M. Boese and V. Marotta, 71–87. London and New York: Routledge.

Collins, J., M. Morrissey, and L. Grogan. 1995. "Employment." *1995 State of the Nation: A Report on People of non-English Speaking Background, Federal Race Discrimination Commissioner*. Canberra, Australia: AGPS.

Collins, J., K. Watson, and B. Krivokapic-Skoko. 2017. *From Boats to Businesses: the Remarkable Journey of Hazara Refugee Entrepreneurs in Adelaide*. UTS Centre for Business and Social Innovation. https://www.uts.edu.au/sites/default/files/2017-10/From%20Boats%20to%20Businesses%20Full%20Report%20-%20Web.pdf

Crawley, H., F. Duvell, K. Jones, S. McMahon, and N. Sigona. 2017. *Unravelling Europe's "Migration Crisis."* Bristol, UK: Policy.

Deegan, B. 2008. *Visa Subclass 457 Integrity Review Final Report*. https://www.border.gov.au/WorkinginAustralia/Documents/457-integrity-review.pdf.

Department of Home Affairs, Australian Government. 2017. *Abolition and Replacement of the 457 Visa—Government Reforms to Employer Sponsored Skilled Migration Visas*. https://www.homeaffairs.gov.au/Trav/Work/457-abolition-replacement

Department of Immigration and Citizenship (DIAC). 2009. *Population Flows: Immigration Aspects 2008–2009 Edition*. National Library of Australia. https://trove.nla.gov.au/work/11514835?selectedversion=NBD27062712

DIBP. 2013. *Filling the Gaps: Findings from the 2012 Survey of Subclass 457 Employers and Employees*. Australian Government. Canberra: Australia. https://www.homeaffairs.gov.au/ReportsandPublications/Documents/research/filling-gaps.pdf

DIBP. 2017: Temporary entrants in Australia: At 31. December 2016 https://www.border.gov.au/about/reports-publications/research-statistics/statistics/live-in-australia/temporary-entrants-in-australia

FWO (Fair Work Ombudsman). 2014. *Fair Work Ombudsman to Review Entitlements of Overseas Visa-Holders on Working Holidays*, www.fairwork.gov.au/about-us/news-and-media-releases/2014-media-releases/august-2014/20140804-working-holiday-entitlements-review

Gleeson, M. 2016. *Offshore: Behind the Wire on Manus and Nauru*. Sydney, Australia: Newsouth.

Grey, M., N. Rodríguez, and A. Conrad. 2004. *Immigrant and Refugee Small-Business Development in Iowa: A Research Report with Recommendations*. New Iowans Program, University of Northern Iowa.

Hasham, N. and M. Gordon. 2016. "Papua New Guinea Court Finds Australia's Detention of Asylum-Seekers on Manus Island is Illegal." *Sydney Morning Herald*, April 26, 2016. http://www.smh.com.au/federal-politics/political-news/papua-new-guinea-court-finds-australias-detention-of-asylum-seekers-on-manus-island-is-illegal-20160426-gofaaj.html

Higgins, C. 2017. *Asylum by Boat: Origins of Australia's Refugee Policy*. Kensington, Australia: UNSW Press.

Hugo, G. 2011. "International Migration in Australian and the Global Financial Crisis." In *Immigration And The Financial Crisis: The United States and Australia Compared*, edited by J Higley, J Nieuwenhuysen, and S Neeru, 35–56. Monash Studies in Global Movements Series. Cheltenham, UK: Edward Elgar.

IOM. 2015. World Migration Report. Geneva, Switzerland. https://www.iom.int/world-migration-report-2015

Kingsley, P. 2016. *The New Odyssey: The Story of the Twenty-First Century Refugee Crisis*. New York: WW Norton & Company.

Klingbeil, C. 2017. "Despite Struggles, Many Syrian Refugees Businesses Are Gaining Traction." *The Globe and Mail*, April 25. https://www.theglobeandmail.com/report-on-business/small-business/sb-managing/manysyrian-refugees-launched-businesses-when-they-came-to-canada-how-are-they-faring-now/article34799676/.

Lyon, F., L. Sepulveda, and S. Syrett. 2007. "Enterprising Humanitarian Immigrants: Contributions and Challenges in Deprived Urban Areas," *Local Economy* 22, no. 4: 362–375.

Maley, W. 2016. *What is a Refugee?* New York: Oxford University Press.

Mares, P. 2009. "Temporary Migration and Its Implications for Australia." Paper Presented at the Senate Occasional Lecture Series, Parliament House, Number 57. Canberra: Australia. https://www.aph.gov.au/~/~/link.aspx?_id=06B96F584FD0483D9F369F0B5186C6A9&_z=z

Mares, P. 2017. *Not Quite Australian: How Temporary Migration is Changing the Nation*. Melbourne, Australia: Text Publishing.

Markus, A. 2001. *Race: John Howard and the Remaking of Australia*. Crows Nest, Australia: Allen and Unwin.

Markus, A., J. Jupp, and P. McDonald. 2009. *Australia's Immigration Revolution*. Sydney, Australia: Allen and Unwin.

Marr, D. 2011. *Panic*. Melbourne, Australia: Black Books.

Marr, D., and M. Wilkinson. 2003. *Dark Victory*. Sydney, Australia: Allen & Unwin.

Massey, D. 2015. "A Missing Element in Migration Theories." *Migration Letters* 12, no. 3: 279–299.

Migration Council of Australia. 2013. "More Than Temporary: Australia's 457 Visa Program." http://migrationcouncil.org.au/2013/05/11/457-visa-program-is-more-than-temporary/

Nakhoul, G. 2011. *Overboard: You Would Not Believe What Really Triggered Australia's Controversial Policy on Boat People*. Merrylands, NSW, Australia: Dar Meera.

O'Brien Solicitors. 2017. "Asylum-Seekers on Manus Island: The New High Court Case and Why It's Important." May 8. http://obriensolicitors.com.au/asylum-seekers-on-manus-island-the-new-high-court-case-why-its-important/

OECD. 2011. *Trends in International Migration: Annual Report 2010*. Paris: OECD.

OECD. 2016a. *International Migration Outlook 2016*. Paris: OECD.

OECD. 2016b. *Launch of the 2016 International Migration Outlook*. September 20. http://www.oecd.org/migration/launch-of-the-2016-international-migration-outlook.htm

OECD. 2017. *International Migration Outlook 2017*. Paris: OECD.

Om, J. 2015. "Foreign Workers Exploited at Baiada Chicken Processing Plants: Fair Work Ombudsman Finds." *ABC News*, June 17. http://www.abc.net.au/news/2015-06-17/foreign-workers-exploited-at-baiada-plant-investigation-reveals/6554570

Phillips, J., and J. Simon-Davies. 2017. "Migration to Australia: A Quick Guide to the Statistics." https://www.aph.gov.au/About_Parliament/Parliamentary_Departments/Parliamentary_Library/pubs/rp/rp1617/Quick_Guides/MigrationStatistics

Productivity Commission. 2016. *Migrant Intake into Australia*. https://www.pc.gov.au/inquiries/completed/migrant-intake/report

Quiggin, J. 2010. "Australia and the Global Financial Crisis." In *Goodbye to All That? On the Failure of Neoliberalism and the Urgency of Change*, edited by R. Manne and D. McKnight, 99–122. Melbourne, Australia: Black Inc. Agenda.

Robertson, S. 2013. *Transnational Student-Migrants and the State: The Education Migration Nexus*. Melbourne, Australia: Palgrave Macmillan.

Robotham, J. 2011. "Psychiatrist Shines Light on Neglected Mental Health Services." *Sydney Morning Herald*, January 26. http://www.smh.com.au/national/psychiatrist-shines-light-on-neglected-mental-health-services-20110125-1a4bf.html

Salt, B. 2017. "2016 Census: City Launch Pads Project Migrants Far and Wide." *The Weekend Australian*, October 14. http://www.theaustralian.com.au/news/inquirer/2016-census-city-launch-pads-project-migrants-far-and-wide/news-story/ef9a7e9ccdecaf8485143358c59957df

Stiglitz, J. E. 2010. *Freefall: America, Free Markets, and the Sinking of the World Economy*. New York: W.W. Norton.

Velayutham, S. 2013. "Precarious Experiences of Indians in Australia on 457 Temporary Work Visas." *The Economic and Labour Relations Review* 24, no. 3: 340–361. doi: 10.1177/1035304613495268

Viviani, N. (1984) *The Long Journey: Vietnamese Migration and Settlement in Australia*. Carlton, Australia: Melbourne University Press.

Wauters, B., and J. Lambrech. 2006. "Refugee Entrepreneurship in Belgium: Potential and Practice." *International Entrepreneurship and Management Journal* 2, no. 4: 509–525.

CHAPTER 47

MIGRATION CRISIS AND SOCIAL TRAUMA

PASCALE BALIGAND

The expression "migrant crisis" has been making its way into the French public debate and the French media since 2015 (Beauchemin and Ichou 2016). Associated with images of shipwrecks on the Mediterranean, people living in hardship, or countries at war, it conveys the idea of a sharp and massive influx of impoverished people fleeing all sorts of difficulties, an influx that would threaten to exceed critical thresholds for French and European reception capacities (Bevelander and Bo 2014; Bigo 2002; Bigo and Guid 2006). The number of immigrants arriving in Europe and France was indeed very high in 2015, the highest it has been since the 1950s (Withol de Wenden 2016). There is nevertheless a case for putting this situation into perspective and asking ourselves what factors have led to its being constituted as a "migrant crisis," especially in France. Many authors consider this "migrant crisis" to be the product of another crisis: that of migration and asylum policies (Akoka, Carlier and Coussemaker 2017; Withol de Wenden 2017), specifically the failure of certain security policies and policies of deterrence that have been in place in Europe and France since the early 2000s (Withol de Wenden 2016, 2017). In France, the advent of a "management of undesirables" (Agier 2011) in connection with security policies led the Ministry of the Interior to close the Sangatte center in 2002 as well as to a reform of the right to asylum in 2003 (Sadik, Bourgoing, and Jourdan 2010). Meanwhile, the introduction of *Frontex* in 2007 could be considered as one of the peaks of the bureaucratization of the treatment of migration issues across Europe (Withol de Wenden 2017).[1] In keeping with these trends, French politics has witnessed the arrival of a question concerning "national identity," for which a ministry was created in 2007. These events constitute a turning point in migration and asylum policies in France, so much so that we no longer only observe the implementation of restrictive policies, but also the emergence of a form of "externalization" with respect to the treatment of migrants, who would be kept at the borders of the European Union (Delouvin 2003). In addition to the construal of the arrival of migrant populations as a "crisis" in host countries, the second term in the expression "migrant crisis" should also capture our attention. Since the early 2000s there has been a shift in migration and asylum policies in France, if not in Europe as whole, that has led to the recategorization of asylum-seekers as migrants. "Migrant crisis" rhetoric thus refers to the constitution of a "migrant" condition for those populations excluded "from and through registration" (Bigo 2002) and carries with it traumatic repercussions on the subjective and social levels. Treated as undesirables, their reasons for being on French soil and the aspirations of these "migrant" populations matter very little, their primary characteristic now being that they are not destined to settle nor, consequently, to be welcomed. For asylum-seekers, for associations involved in the reception of exiled populations, and more generally for the whole of French society, the treatment reserved for asylum-seekers turned migrants calls into question one of the essential foundations of the social bond, one that is intimately linked to the question of trauma. The difficulty associated with finding and providing a refuge for migrants thus leads to questioning trust in the figure of the other of the social bond, the guarantor of social integration (Edkins 2006; Waintrater 2003). It is this other that Freud once designated as the "fellow human being" (Freud 1895). Based on studying the experiences of asylum-seekers based on semistructured interviews carried out in 2007 in Ile-de-France, this chapter proposes several stages in which the shift toward this migrant status took place and analyzes its traumatic consequences not only for the migrants themselves, but also for the populations of host countries.

Being an Asylum-Seeker in France in 2007

At the time of this chapter's field survey, asylum policies had seen major restrictions imposed over several years. These restrictions went hand in hand with the implementation of restrictive and security policies on migratory issues in general (Crisp 2003; Price 2009) and may be regarded as underlying causes for the "migrant crisis." As early as the 1960s and 1970s, the promotion of the figure of the exile, linked to the creation of the Geneva Convention, left room for a distinction between political refugees struggling for freedom in the face of communism and "migrant" workers who arrived to reconstruct postwar France (Sayad 1999). This first distinction, associated with a disjunction between migration policies and asylum policies (Noiriel 2006; Sayad 1997, 1999), would later diverge against the backdrop of decolonization, economic crisis, and the end of the Cold War. A division within the refugee category itself gradually emerged. General restrictions in the reception of migrant populations led to a logic of "sorting" migrant populations according to their reasons for migrating, as well as according to the identities to which they found themselves assigned (Agier 2011), ultimately resulting in a sorting of the migrants themselves. At the same time, the number of administrative categories identifying those authorized or not authorized to stay in the territory multiplied (Agier 2011), and the mistrust of applicants intensified. It is in this context that, beginning in 1980, a distinction was gradually made between asylum-seekers and refugees and that "asylum-seeker" came to be considered an administrative category (Kobelinsky 2010). In a mechanical fashion, those who had previously been admitted as refugees now became asylum-seekers. In other words, they became people requesting refugee status, but who had an increasingly arbitrary possibility of obtaining it (Agier 2011). In practice, and right up until the 2000s, the administrative category of "asylum-seeker" as regulated by the legal framework pertaining to the right to asylum as defined by the Geneva Convention, referred to a specific social position that can be qualified as a "situation-based category" (Bertaux 1997). This "situation-based category" is defined by the fact that individuals within it share a situation that is characterized by common social traits, namely "insofar as it engenders constraints and logics of action that present many points in common, where it is perceived through collective schemas, and where it may be treated by a single institution" (Bertaux 1997, 15). Although it is not always considered as such by those who share it, the situation-based category "request for asylum" is indeed defined according several common traits, the main trait being one's dependence on the decision of an institution in order to be able to enjoy a "free life in society" (Legoux 2004, 10). In this case, the institution in question is the French Office for the Protection of Refugees and Stateless People (OFPRA).

Even though asylum has designated an inviolable place since ancient Greece and the status of refugee as defined by the United Nations Geneva Convention of 1951 promotes a "universalist message . . . of 'protecting' the stateless" (Agier 2011, 11), the OFPRA has over time been caught up in paradoxes concerning the restrictive impacts of migration and asylum policies (Sadik, de Bougoing, and Jourdan, 2010). With the 2003 reform, and in the context of the Interior Ministry's growing influence on this institution initially attached to the Ministry of Foreign Affairs, we began to see a security-based approach to asylum-seeker populations, which went hand in hand with an equally security-based treatment of migration issues (Sadik, de Bourgoing, and Jourdan, 2010). The primary function of " 'protecting' the stateless" with which OFPRA was tasked, gave way to a "function of control" (Agier 2011, 11). With increasingly long processing times for applications, resulting from a lack of staff dedicated to this task (Sadik, de Bourgoing, and Jourdan, 2010), and against a backdrop of a growing bureaucratization of processing procedures on the European scale (Bigo 2002), people applying for refugee status were increasingly assigned to a common position of waiting (Kobelinsky 2010). This position entailed social assistance and regulated housing options as well as an increasing obligation to prove the legitimacy of their request. This new situation has had multiple effects on applicants' trajectories, and when this logic reached its climax, we entered into the "migrant crisis"—an era of externalizing the treatment of people now referred to as "migrants." This is reflected in immigration data from 2007, when "the rejection rate of asylum applications in France, as in Europe, generally rose above 90 percent, at which point it is legitimate to believe that the Geneva convention of 1951 that defined the status of refugee has today been challenged by the facts on the ground" (Agier 2011, 24). The asylum application process plays a central role in excluding applications "from and through registration" (Bigo 2002, 63–92), the consequences of which associations have tried to overcome (Franguiadakis, Jaillardon and Belkis 2004). In doing so they have become a primary point of interest in the analysis of the "migrant crisis." As a result, the situation-based category for requesting asylum, such as it emerged in 2007, can retrospectively be seen as a landmark category in the externalization of asylum and thus in the construction of the "migrant crisis." It has, moreover, come to undermine asylum- seekers' trust in the social bond over the course of their journeys. Through the suspicion of applicants that it fostered, the precariousness and extraterritoriality in which it placed asylum-seekers, and the endless waiting times to which it subjected them, this situation-based category has become the site on which the "migrant crisis" has been constructed, constituting the scene of a socially orchestrated reenactment of the traumas asylum-seekers experienced during the growing peril that preceded their departure from their country of origin (Agier 2002).

In order to shed light on these different points, this article will draw upon the journeys of two asylum-seekers, Mr. R and Mr. C, in conjunction with brief extracts from other interviews and with data from the scientific literature. Their stories are particularly helpful for revealing the mechanisms behind the construction of the "migrant crisis." The interview with Mr. R evidenced a pronounced distress that led to questions as to whether trust would still be possible for him in his relationships with others. Mr. R is a 25-year-old Central African Republic student encountered through a student union that supports the cause of foreign students facing difficulties in administrative enrollment in universities. He grew up in the Central African Republic with his parents and several siblings. In 1997, rebellions against the ruling government were organized by soldiers, most of whom, he explained, came from the same ethnic group as him. During the interview, he spoke of an escalation of violence against the government, saying that "it practically turned into an ethnic war." After fleeing to a neighboring country for several years in order to distance himself from the most radical of the rebels, he attempted to return. After this, there was a coup d'état, and the army raided his family home, killing his older brother. He was imprisoned and tortured but nevertheless succeeded in escaping, exchanging his identity for the identity of one of his brothers living in France, and later found himself separated from his parents. Since his arrival in France in 2005, when his application for asylum was initially refused, and up until the time of his interview, he had been hosted by his older sister in difficult living conditions. In the interview with Mr. C, which took place while he was in the process of obtaining refugee status, it was his retrospection on the years he spent waiting that was particularly useful for identifying what is at stake for those in the situation-based category for requesting asylum. Mr. C is a Cameroonian refugee, aged 37 at the time of the interview, which took place on the premises of Cimade, an association that provides social assistance and legal support for migrants. Mr. C lived in the countryside in Cameroon before going to study in Yaoundé. During that time, he had participated in several strikes and had been arrested and tortured. During a strike in 2000, soldiers conducted a violent on-campus raid, resulting in numerous arrests. Mr. C escaped to the village where his mother lived, obtained papers through a friend, and began a journey of several months that would ultimately take him to Paris in May 2000. At the time of the interview, he had just been granted refugee status after a lengthy seven-year process for which he had gathered a wealth of evidence to support his story. At this time, he was still subject to a deportation order in connection with the initial refusal of his request and he no longer had any livelihood. Unable to work legally during this process, he worked under the table giving private lessons. He had lived in many different places, ranging from centers run by the Samu Social to makeshift accommodations and the homes of friends or people he encountered in the street. During his life in France, he met a woman who became his companion and with whom he had a daughter in 2003. They lived in a furnished hotel for several months before his daughter and companion were housed in a dedicated reception center, where he was not able to be accommodated. At the time of the interview, he was living in a Salvation Army center. Drawing on the interviews conducted with these two asylum seekers in order to trace their journeys from a bottom-up perspective (Lindley 2014), this article will analyze how their paths both reveal the mechanisms that have produced the "migrant crisis" and pose questions for the institutions of the host society, in particular through their traumatic social and subjective consequences.

Age of Suspicion and Trauma

An event likely to have a traumatic impact can be understood as one that exceeds the subject's processing abilities (Ferenczi 1934) or that colludes with disturbing fantasies (Freud 1919h). It also disrupts the symbolic universe to which the subject may ascribe (Smelser 2004), especially when it comes to mass violence (Waintrater 2003). Thus questioning the possibility of establishing a relationship of trust with others represents a main source of psychic and social trauma. An event becomes traumatic when it makes the environment uncertain for the subject, while also undermining the possibility of a social bond and the emergence of a daily life. As Jenny Edkins points out:

> It seems that trauma is more than a shock encounter with brutality or death; in an important sense, trauma is the betrayal of a promise or an expectation. Trauma can be seen as an encounter that betrays our faith in previously established personal and social worlds and calls into question the resolutions of impossible questions that people have arrived at in order to continue with day-to-day life.
>
> (Edkins 2006, 109)

At the level of individual trajectories, we are able observe in detail how a logic of engendering suspicion and undesirability is played out through the situation-based asylum-seeker category (Agier 2011). We also see how it resonates with the question of a traumatic exclusion from the social bond, a distinguishing feature of the "migrant crisis." In the journeys of the asylum-seekers interviewed, the figure of the other of the social bond (Freud 1895; Lacan 1986) was distorted by the persecutions suffered in the country of origin, creating a breach in their relationship with the world. It appears then that the "crisis" related to migration at the level of asylum-seeker journeys comes at a time when asylum-seekers have become undesirables in their own country. This crisis is then repeated and prolonged in the country meant to welcome them. In the context of the asylum application process, whose bureaucratic logic has been pushed to the point of absurdity, their situation in France renews for them the potentially painful challenge of establishing a relationship of trust with others. Suspected of stirring up trouble against the authorities in their country, Mr. R and Mr. C both found themselves excluded or threatened by these authorities. They thus fell outside of the social bond, or to quote Michel Agier, "outside the *nomos*, outside the ordinary human law" (Agier 2008, 29). As such, they have experienced a radical distress that constitutes a founding element of the loss of confidence in one's environment. For Mr. R, the threat has overtaken his daily life, causing him to lose his status as citizen in order to reduce him to the status of a "killable" man (Agamben 1995): "There were several months . . . of truces, of assassinations. So, it changed, it practically turned into an ethnic war [. . .] you could kill any Yakoma [the ethnic group to which he belongs]." In the case of Mr. C., the robbing of the privacy of his home constituted a traumatic attack. The situation-based category for requesting asylum and the related procedure, which encourages suspicion toward applicants, violently enacts this moment of faltering trust in one's fellow human being. By making asylum-seekers dependent on the authorities and their potential vagaries, the asylum application process returns asylum-seekers to the state of mistrust of others that they experienced when leaving their country. This mistrust is extended to the point of its crystallization with the "migrant crisis."

In the context of these interviews, there was a concordance, experienced as a repetition, between the violence suffered at the time of migration and the bureaucratization of the procedure that induces a suspicion of potentially "fake asylum-seekers." The question of proof, for example, was repeatedly posed in Mr. C's journey. He was required to gather proof from multiple sources, including sources recognized by the host country:

> I went over there [to an association to get a medical certificate]. They sent me to get different examinations. I gave my explanations. They established in their medical certificate the accounting of the facts declared and the physical examination that was done.[2] And I also had the report of the international mission, who visited when there was this strike, and who recorded, and who saw the conditions under which people were beaten in prison [. . .]. And I also had the report from ACAT, the Christian Association for the Abolition of Torture [. . .] and I already had newspapers in Africa . . . so there you go.

The feeling of invisibility in the host country and the threat of arbitrariness on the part of institutions is strikingly apparent, revealing a correlation between the application procedure and the dimension of lost confidence in the other of the social bond:

> What I said to the Court of Appeals is that they have everything they asked for, but no matter, they went to check. They asked the general police. You have to do some

> looking for information, you have to do this, you have to do that . . . I went and I was told "Yeah, we're still doing some research", and all that stuff, [by] the general police . . . I said [. . .] "I'm not a thief, I'm not a killer, I'm not anything at all. It's just because we filed a file [that] you will refuse!"

Mr. C went so far as to denounce a slight maliciousness in the administrative and legal twists and turns to which he has been consigned to struggle for several years. His attempts to show his goodwill or to find help seem to systematically turn against him:

> And then, the representative of the prefecture said that "yes, he came himself." I said, "Yes, indeed, because it was already the main objective of the memorandum that aimed precisely at people who were under a deportation order, and I said unfortunately, that's it, that's why we did it.[3] If only I had known it was a strategy for capturing people and sending them back under such conditions . . ."

Here again we see the dehumanizing dimension of the bureaucratic treatment that is constitutive of the situation-based asylum-seeker category as identifying an undesirable population. This bureaucratization constitutes a foundation of the "migrant crisis." In the interviews, the dehumanization experienced by asylum-seekers echoes the first attacks they suffered when leaving their country, repeating once again in the host country the trauma that permeated the social bond in the country of origin. This question of arbitrariness and the difficulty of restoring trust in others also figured at the forefront of the interview with Mr. R, albeit in a more insidious way. In Mr. R's trajectory, it was at the level of the links with those who hosted him that this mistrust was most perceptible. While being hosted by his sister, he was beset by a hostility that made him feel he was not welcome:

> [. . .] I miss my parents a lot. And so, me, I said to myself, I live in France as if I'm alone, [. . .], as though I've been thrown into a place where I know no one, so there you go. Because my sister, I do not see her as my sister. It's true, I know she's my sister—same father, same mother—but you know . . . We've never lived together, and so there is no . . . since we can't seem to talk to each other.

This fear of arbitrariness was reflected in the interview relationship itself, which Mr. R questioned, telling me about France's foreign policy toward his country. Asking me implicitly if I was on the side of those who had brutalized him, he seemed to enact in the interview the question of trust that is posed throughout the notion of asylum (Franguiadakis, Jaillardon, and Belkis 2004). This shows how the experience in the host country is likely to prolong a previously encountered arbitrariness that led asylum-seekers to leave their country. We also see to what extent the systems put in place for receiving them are a deciding factor in this respect, as well as how systems that perpetuate arbitrariness have had a hand in the creation of the "migrant crisis."

Faced with the emergence of this age of suspicion—one that makes individual journeys the scene of a traumatic repetition of the loss of trust in one's fellow human-being—associations find themselves in a complex position. They endeavor to preserve zones of trust in order to facilitate the existence of a social bond and soften the effects of restrictive policies (Franguiadakis, Jaillardon, and Belkis 2004). In this sense, they serve a specific role in the societal consideration of the traumatic dimension of the "crises" linked to migration. However, just like the situation-based asylum-seeker category, the role of associations is precarious and they are likely to be caught up in political decisions over which they have little control. Thus associations previously dedicated to receiving exiles are also being affected by the emergence of new categories in connection with restrictive migration policies. The debate between "real" and "fake" asylum-seekers has repercussions for these associations, some of which will ultimately specialize in the care of exiles who have been victims of torture, proposing the idea that torture must be distinguished from other forms of trauma (Fassin and Rechtman 2009). These associations are in the process of redefining themselves and the nature of their work, which raises the question of how vulnerable they are to prevailing policies. A debate has also emerged regarding the issue of drafting certificates that are used to attest to violence suffered, and for which there is an increasing demand among asylum-seekers as part of the bureaucratization of the procedure (Fassin and Rechtman 2007). For associations working to accompany migrants, this issue is both ethical and pragmatic. Applicants and those who put together applications have progressively confirmed the increasing requirement of attaching medical certificates to these files in order to document physical and psychological evidence of violence suffered, echoing the suspicion that now looms over the examination of asylum applications. The case of Mr C is emblematic here: he recounts how it was explained to him that medical certificates issued by the Committee for the Health of Exiles (COMEDE) would be regarded as trustworthy. He also mentioned that seeking help from this association was an opportunity for him to begin psychological treatment and that this support proved to be a decisive factor in confronting his situation on a subjective level. This demonstrates that the issue of trust in connection with the treatment of a traumatic dimension surfaces in the journeys of asylum-seekers on many levels. It also demonstrates how, in dealing with institutions in the host society, associations play a role that could be described as mediation, which goes together with socially and subjectively working through trauma. In this way, it is possible to see how the transformations and failures in dealing with this questioning of trust in the social bond lie at the heart of the emergence of the "migrant crisis."

Finally, it should be pointed out that, as a result of the reduction in the number of people obtaining refugee status at the end of the procedure, a new intermediate category has emerged: that of the rejected asylum-seeker, which has led to the development of informal asylum. The emergence of this form of "black asylum" [*asile au noir*] (Brachet 1997) constitutes a new step in the shift toward the social construction of a migrant condition, one based on a permanent threat of having to leave the country. It thus repeats in a new form the arbitrariness that originally pushed migrants to leave and is clearly demonstrated in the "migrant crisis."

EXTRATERRITORIALITY AND TRAUMA

The traumatic dimension of losing confidence in one's fellow human beings, which is consistently found in the suspicious treatment reserved for asylum-seekers, goes hand in hand with an extraterritorial position specific to this situation-based category. With the advent of the "migrant crisis," this position has become one of a radical externalization (Delouvin 2003). Restrictive asylum policies and the development of "refugee management" (Agier 2011) tend to confine applicants to a position of liminality (Murphy et al. 1989), or a territorial and symbolic in-between. On the social level, asylum-seekers have a difficult time finding a place to live and rebuilding anchors for their identity, while on the psychic and symbolic level, they lack a space in which they can recount their stories. Concretely, this results in the impossibility of establishing permanent housing and being confined to marginal locations (Kobelinsky 2010). As a corollary to the distinction between refugees and asylum-seekers, asylum accommodation centers (CADA) were created in the 1990s in order to provide accommodation for people waiting for their application to be processed (Kobelinsky 2010). These accommodations may be communal or offered in the form of self-contained housing. Statistically, those housed at CADAs are more likely to receive favorable responses to their applications (Franguiadakis, Jaillardon, and Belkis 2004). In this way, such welcome centers are similar to other associations insofar as they manage to support the hope of a renewed home for those interviewed and play a supporting role in both redefining their identity and working through their traumatic journey. Mr. and Mrs. J, who have just been granted asylum after fleeing war in Sri Lanka, bear witness to this, saying they feel that their accommodation at the CADA has brought them "peace" and hope for a future for their daughter: "there where [our] house was, there is nothing left but dirt." However, it must be noted that the CADA's intermediary role with respect to other associations raises some paradoxes, and people housed at the CADA live in a state of dependency and monitoring with regard to the authorities. They are, moreover, subject to security measures if their asylum application is rejected. Evolutions in policy for the reception of refugees thus have a very strong impact both on asylum-seekers' attempts to rebuild a home and on the work of associations. The fact that the people interviewed by Carolina Kobelinsky who were living in the CADA identified themselves as "traveling prisoners" (Kobelinsky 2010) is very telling in this respect. It highlights the paradoxes of this system, which in part institutionalizes "zones of indistinction" (Agamben 1995; Edkins 2006) in which asylum-seekers are reminded that they are "bare lives" after being rejected by their countries of origin. Although they are free to move about in the host country while waiting for their asylum application to be processed, and although the host country provides some of their basic needs, they do not have the right to settle nor take part in the economic life or institutions of society.

Moreover, as the number of places in these centers remains very limited compared to the number of applicants (Kobelinsky 2010), a divide is established between those who benefit from them and everyone else. The asylum system thus tends toward an extraterritoriality for the majority of applicants, who find themselves condemned to vagrancy. We find this in the journeys of the two interviewees, whose stories have been selected for their significance. Mr C first lived for a while with a fellow countryman whom he met at the prefecture. He then lived with a man he met by chance in a fast food restaurant, before going on to stay in different accommodation centers for the homeless. The multiple mobilities that preceded his migration to the host country were thus followed by multiple mobilities within the host country, leading to frequent changes in living quarters and nights spent at hotels, in emergency shelters, or even in public spaces. Such moves are likely to occur unexpectedly and can take place on the European scale, depending on the expected possibility of obtaining asylum or of a less precarious life in a given country. They echo the distress of the first mobilities that took place in the context of crisis in the country of origin and reveal the dependence of asylum-seekers on sometimes unscrupulous people or mafia networks. Ultimately, this vagrancy must be put into perspective in conjunction with the question of trust in relationships with others, something that is intimately associated with the possibility of feeling at home in any given place (Baligand 2013; Bernard 1998). Thus, although he currently enjoys a stable accommodation, Mr. R is vulnerable to a vagrancy that reenacts the rejection he suffered in his country. Subjectively, he lives as a homeless person:

> [I have] no bed as such, I sleep on some foam [. . .] In Africa, we would have said "he's bed-less." And then sometimes, it's complicated because with small blankets, when it's cold, you have to bend in order to cover yourself well. So, it's hard, you know. You're forced to spend the night like that.

He also spends as much time as possible outside the housing where he is supposed to be accommodated in order to escape the negative comments he receives and the instability that he experiences there:

> So, on Saturday, I always went [to the university] to . . . well, there you go . . . not to be at home. Often on weekends, just like that, if I have nothing to do, I go out, I go to Paris, I walk a little [. . .] On the weekends when I can't go out, I stay in my bed.

We observe the effects of the uncanny (Freud 1919h) in relationships with family members or interlocutors from the host country, relationships that seem to have been infiltrated by the violence that has made the home disturbing and pushed these interviewees to flee. For Mr. R., it is as though he must recreate his family in a foreign country, with people he considers to be strangers, who constantly remind him of what he has gone through, and for whom he embodies the memory of the violence that decimated their families. The vagrancy that was precipitated in the country of origin is thus prolonged within the host country, invading the very heart of their living quarters, which acquire a status of extimacy (Lacan 1986). Consequently, in place of a helping other who would open up the social bond and the possibility of rebuilding a home, is substituted a hostile other who threatens social exclusion. Even when it is sustainable, the only way that housing can be invested as a home that mobilizes relationships of trust (Bernard 1998) and provides a social bond is if the specific position of asylum-seekers is recognized in some way other than as a purely administrative category and if a collective processing of trauma can begin. Here again we observe how, right up until the 2000s, evolutions in asylum policy and in the associated mechanisms tended toward an externalization of the treatment of asylum-seekers. Asylum-seekers were for the most part living in a situation of vagrancy and extraterritoriality with regard to the *socius*, gradually adopting a migrant condition. It was this that ultimately led to the "migrant crisis" of 2015.

Waiting and Traumatic Temporality(s)

It is not only a spatial and subjective vagrancy that asylum-seekers experience. Their relationship with time is also altered, as the "migrant crisis" signals the social and subjective construction of a position "outside time" for migrants (Agier 2002). As a corollary to the ever-increasing demand for the justification of their motives for migration and the rise of the category of asylum-seeker over the category of refugee, the length of processing times had, until the 2003 reform, increased to the point that in 2007 it could last for up to several years (Sadik, de Bourgoing, and Jourdan 2010). For Mr. C, this wait has been the source of a difficult alternation between hope and disappointment, imbued with a serious concern about the future and a feeling of not being able to find a reliable interlocutor. He concluded a description of the vagaries of the procedure with a striking sentence: "I lost seven years just like that." For Mr R, the time it has taken to process his request for an appeal exceeds the time limit in which he could have collected asylum-seeker benefits. At the time of our interview, he no longer had any resources and found himself dependent on his family, which only escalated the existing tensions:

> [My sister's husband] has no financial problems, because first of all, I hardly eat. Maybe it can be seen, even physically [. . .] I hardly eat so as to avoid problems [. . .] because I see that every time I eat at home, he talks about it, and then it really makes me feel uncomfortable . . . so here, I come to the university, and I stay like that until the evening . . .

Even when they were not enacting it in the interview itself, both Mr. R and Mr. C testified to the feeling of suffering from a distorted temporality and a perpetual anxiety about the future. This context made the interview with Mr. R rather trying: he seemed as though frozen in his chair during an interview that lasted more than two hours, which brought my attention to the waiting and the distress that he constantly confronts. He spoke of a journey that led to a stripping away of his previous anchors, leaving him "empty-handed," "like a tourist," immersed in his wait for a safe place and always disappointed in the result. This precariousness corresponds to his position of waiting vis-à-vis the authorities, who will hand down a ruling on his request for asylum, and to his dependence on associations that provide humanitarian relief. The daily life of asylum-seekers is thus marked by a vulnerability, the height of which is evidenced by the "migrant crisis." Distorted temporalities and this position of dependency, which are induced by the situation-based category for requesting asylum are, just like loss of trust in others and spatial vagrancy, elements that can prolong or repeat traumatic elements from asylum-seekers' journeys. Confronted with an event that has taken on traumatic significance, the subject will indeed be caught in an identical and repetitive reenactment of the original scene, inducing a temporal register that cannot be integrated into the psyche and which remains heterogeneous to him—unless, that is, the process of working through it can take place (Altounian 2005). This work notably involves the historically and socially offered possibility of finding an interlocutor and a language for formulating what is behind this trauma (Altounian 2005). This also supposes a shared questioning of the phenomenon of the collective dimension of memory (Edkins 2006; Waintrater 2003). In constructing a temporal space marked by waiting and precariousness, the situation-based category for requesting asylum makes it impossible for asylum-seekers to give a place to lived events, thereby allowing these events to have a potentially critical impact. The stages of the application process preside over daily life and represent so many occasions that could potentially lead to yet another collapse. This is especially the case when an unfavorable outcome seems to be emerging or is confirmed after an appeal. Mr R spoke of the future in very somber terms, stating that, in the event that he did not obtain refugee status, he believed he would prefer to "die and have [his] ashes taken back to the Central African Republic" because there he would finally be "at peace." Here, it is the entanglement of asylum policy with socially and subjectively processing trauma that is in play. Moreover, we perceive here the potential for a crisis of the systems put in place to receive migrants who are not able to assume this process.

It should be added that applicants are asked to provide a complete and detailed account of their journey, including supporting documentation that would make it possible to verify the coherence and veracity of their statements. This constitutes an additional violence toward them, one that does not respect the temporality specific to the subjective processing of trauma (Pestre 2010). The procedure constrains asylum-seekers to a narrative of their trajectory that aims at transcribing a reality they have not been able to make their own, and for an interlocutor in whom trust is not guaranteed. This is the case despite the fact that the trajectories of asylum-seekers are first of all the product of their social erasure and the denial of the violence they have suffered (Pestre 2010). The fantasy of a complete narrative, promulgated by the administrative requirements of the asylum-seeker category, supposes that the asylum-seeker is able to remember events that he may instead wish to put out of his mind, and this can be considered as a source of violence for applicants. It also generates misunderstanding among the people who, charged with evaluating the applications, treat inconsistencies in the story as falling into the category of "false" asylum claims (Kobelinsky 2010). The associations involved in this work have also been alarmed by the request for proof of not only physical but also psychological sequelae and have become worried about the effects that this evidentiary requirement may have on their work ethic (Fassin and Rechtman 2009). They see it as a particularly intrusive modality for controlling migrant populations, as well as an obstacle to the implementation of psychotherapeutic care for patients. As a consequence of these dehumanizing procedures, they also express the feeling that they are being used by asylum-seekers who solicit their support only to cease contact when the certificates are issued. The underlying question concerns the power conferred by the control of the temporality of memory, and therefore of the subjectivity of the applicants via the process. It also concerns the control of a temporality that may be played out at the social level. In this sense, the "migrant crisis" is the result of a short-circuit of temporalities that is induced by the systems in place for treating asylum applications, forcing a return to traumatic events both for subjects seeking to forget them and for those processing these applications, and who may not be prepared to deal with the content they contain. We hear this in the question addressed to me by Mr. R concerning the social treatment, at the level of the national narrative, of the political positions taken by France in the face of historical events:

> [. . .] France plays a very negative role in Africa, supporting dictators and then intervening militarily to support dictatorial regimes [. . .] I do not see what living here brings me today. But at the same time, I cannot [return to Africa] because France supports dictators who are there while simultaneously refusing to grant asylum to those who flee from this kind of regime.

In this way, as Jenny Edkins points out, trauma and its treatment imply a collective dimension (Edkins 2006), one that may encounter resistance from political authorities in order to construct a national narrative that privileges certain identities or a certain historical account:

> The form of political authority that the nation represents is intimately tied up with, and made possible by, the way in which it invokes its memories, and with what it remembers and why.
>
> (Edkins 2006, 101)

With the creation of a Ministry of National Identity in 2007, this has emerged as an important issue in the public debate in France, bringing the links between migration policy, asylum policy, and national belonging to the fore (Noiriel 2006). One wonders, like Didier Fassin, whether what played out at that time had to do with the return of certain elements of French history, hitherto denied, and which concern the racialist component of the definition of nationality (Fassin 2006, 2010). Promoting the idea of a "migrant crisis" would thus constitute a denial of the stakes and struggles that led to the establishment of nationality criteria, while simultaneously proposing an "univocal" version of French history (Fierke 2006, 31) that ignores this racialist dimension, especially where the former colonies are concerned. In this context, the externalization of asylum could place particular focus on the foundations of the nation state as defined by the 1889 nationality laws (Noiriel 2006) and once again raise the question of the link between migration and asylum policies, only this time confusing them through a systematic rejection of "migrants."

Conclusion

The crisis that emerged in France in 2015 under the name of "migrant crisis" can be understood as a crisis of migration and asylum policies in their shift toward an externalization of the treatment of migrant populations. This seems to indicate that it is no longer possible for French institutions to confront the reality of the existence of these populations living in difficulty, representing a return to a collection of migration and asylum policies characterized by a universal rejection of all migrants. The category of "migrant," referring to someone constrained to perpetual mobility while being simultaneously subject to an increasing degree of marginalization, can be considered as the product of these developments. In recent years, the category of "migrant" seems to have replaced that of the asylum-seeker who was at the mercy of a State implementing reluctant reception policies. This category was itself supplanted by the category of refugee, designating a person who was received as a matter of principle, which emerged as the product of a distinction between exiles and migrant workers. The "migrant crisis" thus constitutes the product of these successive shifts, a paroxysmal moment in a long-term process that has both social and individual impacts. Asylum-seekers who are caught up in a heightened bureaucratization of procedures and an age of suspicion, relegated to marginal and monitored spaces, and kept waiting in a literal time-lessness, find themselves in the grips of an institutionalized repetition of the violence they experienced at the moment of their original departure. There are many aspects to the traumatic significance of this shift. They concern asylum-seekers just as much as they concern the associations engaged in providing them care and assistance, or French society as a whole. Today, these traumatic effects still leave unresolved the possibility of both constructing a collective and nonunivocal narrative about migration and working through the traumatic elements associated with it, thus making a critical examination of "migrant crises" all the more necessary.

Notes

1. A European agency that monitors the external borders of EU member states.
2. The idea here is that the correspondence between the traces of physical injuries observed during the medical examination and the violence that asylum claimants declare they have experienced must be verified, or vice versa.

3. The December 7, 2006 Memorandum pertaining to repatriation assistance for irregular and destitute foreigners.

References

Agamben, G. 1998 [1995]. *Homo Sacer: Sovereign Power and Bare Life*. Translated by D. Heller-Roazen. Stanford, CA: Stanford University Press.

Agier, M. 2002. *Aux bords du monde, les réfugiés*. Paris: Flammarion.

Agier, M. 2008. *On the Margins of the World. The Refugee Experience Today*. Translated by D. Fernbach. Cambridge, UK: Polity.

Agier, M. 2011. *Managing the Undesirables: Refugee Camps and Humanitarian Government*. Translated by D. Fernbach. Cambridge, UK: Polity.

Akoka, K., M. Carlier, and S. de Coussemaker. 2017. "Ce n'est pas une crise des migrants mais une crise des politiques d'hospitalité." *Revue Projet* 5, no. 360: 77–83. doi: 10.3917/pro.360.0077.

Altounian, J. 2005. *L'intraduisible: Deuil, mémoire, transmission*. Paris: Dunod.

Baligand, P. 2013. "La demande d'asile: l'attente du lieu d'un lien social?" *Topique* 122, no. 1: 61–70. doi: 10.3917/top.122.0061.

Beauchemin, C., and M. Ichou. 2016. *Au-delà de la crise des migrants: décentrer le regard*. Paris: Karthala.

Bevelander P., and P. Bo. 2014. Crisis and Migration: Implications of the Eurozone Crisis for Perceptions, Politics, and Policies of Migration, Lund, Sweden: Nordic Academic Press.

Bernard, Y. 1998. "Du logement au chez-soi." In *Le logement et l'habitat: L'état des savoirs*, edited by M. Segaud, C. Bonvalet, and J. Brun, 374–382. Paris: La Découverte.

Bertaux, D. 1997. *Les récits de vie*. Paris: Nathan Université.

Bigo, D. 2002 "Security and Immigration: Toward a Critique of the Governmentality of Unease." *Alternatives: Global, Political, Local* 27, no. 1: 63–92.

Bigo, D., and E. Guid. 2006. *Controlling Frontiers: Free Movement into or Within Europe*. Aldershot, UK: Ashgate.

Brachet, O. 1997. "L'impossible organigramme de l'asile en France: Le développement de l'asile au noir." In *Revue Européenne des Migrations Internationales* 13: 7–36. doi: 10.3406/remi.1997.1530.

Crisp, J. 2003. "New Asylum Paradigm? Globalization, Migration and the Uncertain Future of the International Refugee Regime." *New Issues in Refugee Research Working Papers 100*, UNHCR. http://www.unhcr.org/en-us/research/working/3fe16d835/new-asylum-paradigm-globalization-migration-uncertain-future-international.html

Delouvin, P. 2003. "Europe: vers une externalisation des procédures d'asile?" In Special Issue: "Le temps des vacances." *Hommes et* migrations 1243:88–93. doi: 10.3406/homig.2003.4010.

Edkins, J. 2006. "Remembering Relationality. Trauma, Time and Politics." In *Memory, Trauma and World Politics: Reflection on the Relationship between Past and Present*, edited by D. Bell, 99–115. London: Palgrave Macmillan.

Fassin, D. 2006. *Du déni à la denegation: Psychologie politique de la représentation des discriminations*. Paris: La Découverte.

Fassin, D. 2010. Les nouvelles frontières de la société française. Paris: La Découverte.

Fassin, D., and R. Rechtman. 2007. *L'empire du traumatisme: Enquête sur la condition de victime*. Paris: Flammarion.

Fassin, D., and R. Rechtman. 2009. *The Empire of Trauma:An Inquiry Into the Condition of Victimhood*. Princeton, NJ: Princeton University Press.

Ferenczi, S. 2006 [1934]. *Le Traumatisme*. Paris: Payot.

Fierke, K. M. 2006. "Bewitched by the Past." In *Memory, Trauma and World Politics. Reflection on the Relationship between Past and Present*, edited by D. Bell, 116–134. London: Palgrave Macmillan.

Franguiadakis S., E. Jaillardon, and D. Belkis. 2004. *En quête d'asile: Aide associative et accès aux droits*. Paris: Ed. Lgdj.

Freud, S. 1895. *Project for a Scientific Psychology: Standard Edition, 1.*

Freud, S. 1950. [1895]. L'esquisse d'une psychologie scientifique, dans la naissance de la psychanalyse. Traduire par A. Berman. Paris: PUF.

Freud, S. 1985 [1919]. "L'inquiétante étrangeté [Das Unheimliche, GW XII]." In *L'inquiétante étrangeté et autres essais*, traducteur B. Féron, 209–263. Paris: Gallimard.

Kobelinsky, C. 2010. "Les limites de l'hospitalité. Accueil et dépendance des demandeurs d'asile." In *Les nouvelles frontières de la société française*, dir. D. Fassin, 2385–2402. Paris: La Découverte.

Lacan, J. 1986. *L'éthique de la psychanalyse: Le séminaire livre VII (1959–1960)*. Paris: Seuil, 1986.

Lindley, A. 2014. "Exploring Crisis and Migration: Concepts and Issues." In *Crisis and Migration: Critical Perspectives*, edited by A. Lyndley, 1–23. New York: Routledge.

Legoux, L. 2004. "Changements et permanence dans la protection des réfugiés." *Revue Européenne des Migrations Internationales, L'asile politique en Europe depuis l'entre-deux guerres*. 20, no. 2: 9–22.

Murphy, R., J. Sheer, Y. Murphy, and R. Mack. 1989. Physical disability and social liminality: A study in the rituals of adversity. Social Science and Medecin 26, no. 2:235–242.

Noiriel, G. *Réfugiés et sans-papiers: la République face au droit d'asile (XIXe-XXe)*. Paris: Hachette, 2006.

Pestre, E. 2010. *La vie psychique des réfugiés*. Paris: Payot.

Price, M. 2009. *Rethinking Asylum. History, Purpose and Limits*. Cambridge, UK: Cambridge University Press, 2009.

Sadik G., S. de Bourgoing, and M. Jourdan. 2010. *Voyage au centre de l'asile. Enquête sur la procédure de détermination d'asile. Rapport d'observation*. Paris: La Cimade, 2010.

Sayad, A. 1997. *L'immigration ou les paradoxes de l'altérité*. Brussels: De Boeck.

Sayad, A. 1999. *La double absence: Des illusions de l'émigré aux souffrances de l'immigré*. Paris: Seuil.

Smelser, N. J. 2004. "Psychological Trauma and Cultural Trauma." In *Cultural Trauma and Collective Identity*, edited by J. C. Alexander, et al., 31–59. Berkeley: University of California Press.

Waintrater, R. 2003. *Sortir du genocide: Témoigner pour réapprendre à vivre*. Paris: Payot.

Withol de Wenden, C. 2017. *La question migratoire au XXIème siècle: Migrants, réfugiés, et relations internationales*. 3rd edition. Paris: Les Presses de la Fondation Nationale des Sciences Politiques.

Withol de Wenden, C. 2016. *Migrations, une nouvelle donne*. Paris: Éditions de la Maison des Sciences de l'Homme.

CHAPTER 48

THE CRISIS OF GULF MIGRATION

S. IRUDAYA RAJAN

THE estimate of the world's stock of migrants in 2015 was 244 million, according to the United Nations Population Division. Between 1990 and 2015, the number of international migrants worldwide rose by 91 million, with developed regions accounting for more numbers of migrants. Europe and Asia together hosted nearly 70 percent of all international migrants. Between 1990 and 2015, the increase in international migrants in Asia was 27 million; the majority of them or about 90 percent were born in other Asian countries (United Nations 2015). In 2015, Asia-to-Asia migration came to be described as the largest regional migration corridor among world migration regions, with 59 million migrants born and residing in another country of Asia. Europe-to-Europe was the second largest migration corridor with 20 million international migrants.

Among countries, the United Arab Emirates (UAE) recorded the largest migrant population during 1990–2015 (7 million), followed by Germany (6 million) and Saudi Arabia (5 million). For instance, as per the census conducted in 1968, UAE had a population of 1.80 lakh of which 63.5 percent were enumerated as nationals. However, by 1995, the total number of international migrants was estimated at 17.7 lakh and constituted 75 percent of the total population of UAE. In 2005, the six Gulf countries—namely Bahrain, Kuwait, Oman, Qatar, Saudi Arabia, and United Arab Emirates—altogether had about 12.8 million nonnationals, which comprised 64 percent of their population (Shah 2009). This working population of nonnationals had created a population crisis in the Gulf countries. The increasing share of nonnationals in Gulf countries in the early 1990s and decreasing share of nationals over the years made tremendous changes to the age-sex composition of population of Gulf countries.

Objectives

The article examines the impact of migration on population growth in Gulf countries using the data published by United Nations over the last fifty years (1973–2015) in the context of migration policies implemented in the Gulf to reduce immigration as well as unemployment of nationals in the Gulf. In addition, it also discusses the crisis of undocumented migration in the Gulf and the amnesty schemes introduced to ameliorate the situation.

Migration Crisis in the Gulf

Six Gulf countries, which constitute Gulf Cooperation Council, together had a population of 55 million persons (0.7 percent of the world's population) in 2017 (United Nations 2017). Historically, workers migrated to Gulf countries for employment reasons, especially after 1973–1974 due to the rise in oil prices. The discovery of oil and gas resources resulted in tremendous economic growth in all GCC countries and thus increased demand for human resources for development as there was scarcity among nationals to meet the demand for work in oil-related industries (Kapiszewski 2006; United Nations 2006, 2007). Initially, those human resources were sourced from mainly from Arab countries, such as Egypt, Jordan, Sudan, the Syrian Arab Republic, and Yemen, but gradually these migrants were replaced by south Asian workers. Although migrant workers come to work in the Gulf from all around the world, Asia remains the primary sending region for the majority of workers (Rajan 2010, 2012). One of the main reasons for the large presence of Asians is because they were considered to be both cheaper and safer to employ. The top three destinations for international workers are the UAE (Narayana and Abraham 2012); Saudi Arabia (Rajan and Joseph 2013, 2015, 2016; Zachariah, Rajan, and Joseph 2014) and Kuwait (Pushpangdan and Parameswaram 2012). The majority of the workers from south Asia work as low-skilled labor confined to "blue-collar" occupations (ILO 2015; Rajan and Narayana 2012; Rajan 2015, 2016).

Migration-Led Population Growth Crisis

The abundance of migrants created changes not only in the economy of the Gulf countries but also in the age-sex population structure, especially in the working age group of 15–59. Generally, changes in population of any particular country occur either because of natural growth rate (birth rate minus death rate) or because of net migration (immigration minus emigration). The major reasons for the population growth in all Gulf countries are owing to immigration or net migration. The natural growth rate and migration rate together influence the rate of growth of total population while keeping other things constant. In this chapter an extensive analysis has been done using the United Nations publication of World Population Prospects to examine the migration rate along with natural growth rate and population growth rate over the last thirty years.

The results are presented in Table 1 for all the Gulf countries. In its population assessment report, United Nations (1990) had provided the population of all the countries prior to assessment year and then projected the population for longer periods (United Nations 1990). The analysis in this report is limited to the period 1950–2015. In the later assessment reports, there were larger differences between the actual and the earlier projected population due to large-scale migration to the Gulf which was not predicted correctly in the projections (United Nations 2002a, 2015).

According to the latest assessment, three countries (Bahrain, Saudi Arabia, and United Arab Emirates) have reported their migration rate as below one percent during 2010–2015 due to the extensive restrictions imposed by them regarding immigration. We will discuss this in detail in the next section. Oman is currently the only country which reported the highest migration rate of 6.6 percent per annum, followed by Kuwait with 3.0 and Qatar with 2.8. However, if we review the migration rates from 1950–2015, each country in the Gulf has its own migration rate. The UAE reported the highest migration rate of 11.3 percent just prior to global financial crisis (2005–2010) but now it hovers around 0.9 percent per annum, which is one of the lowest migration rates over the last seventy years. Similarly, Saudi Arabia, Oman, and Kuwait reported the negative migration rates during 1999–2000. In Qatar, the migration rate was as high as 13.8 in 2005–2010, but declined to 2.8 in 2010–2015. Saudi Arabia is maintaining a migration rate below 1 percent per annum due to its strict implementation of the Nitaqat since the year 2000.

Figures 48.1 to 48.3 explores the population, natural growth, and migration rate for Bahrain as a case study using the three United Nations publications on World

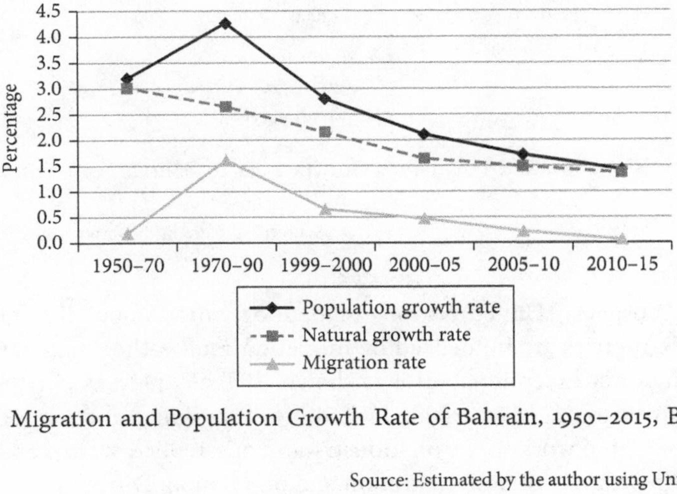

FIGURE 48.1 Migration and Population Growth Rate of Bahrain, 1950–2015, Based on 1990 Assessment

Source: Estimated by the author using United Nations 1990.

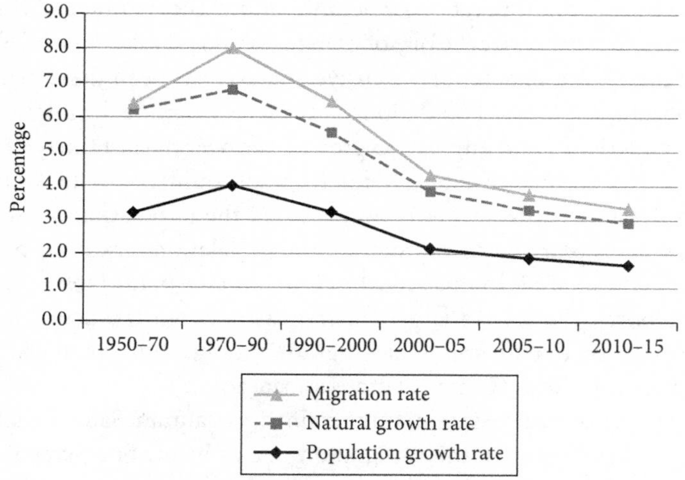

FIGURE 48.2 Migration and Population Growth Rate of Bahrain, 1950–2015 Based on 2002 Assessment

Source: Estimated by the author using United Nations 2002b.

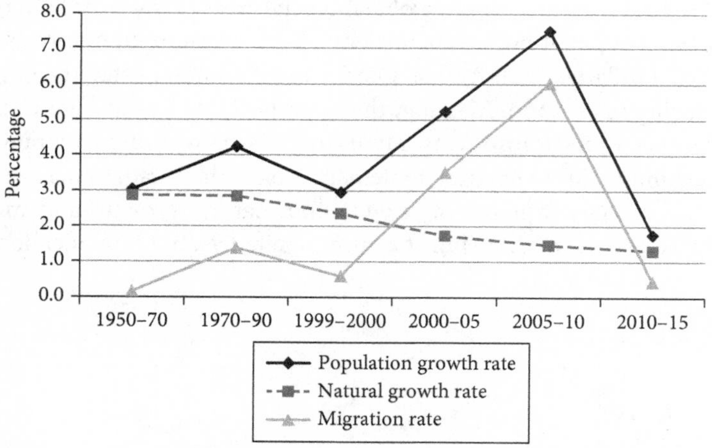

FIGURE 48.3 Migration and Population Growth Rate of Bahrain, 1950–2015 Based on 2015 Assessment

Source: Estimated by the author using United Nations 2002b.

Population Prospects (United Nations 1990, 2002, 2015). Population growth rates of all the Gulf countries are influenced by migration rates rather than natural increases and Bahrain is not exceptional. This is shown in Table 48.1. As per the 1990 assessment, Bahrain encouraged migration by inviting more skilled and semiskilled migrants around the world to work in the oil industry and other allied sectors and it is reflected in the high growth rate of both migration and population. During 1970–1990, Bahrain

Table 48.1 Population Growth, Natural Growth and Migration Rates for Gulf Countries, 1950–2015 as Assessed in 2015

	1950–1970	1970–1990	1990–2000	2000–2005	2005–2010	2010–2015
Bahrain						
Population growth rate	3.0	4.2	3.0	5.2	7.5	1.8
Natural growth rate	2.9	2.9	2.4	1.7	1.5	1.3
Migration rate	0.1	1.3	0.6	3.5	6.0	0.5
Kuwait						
Population growth rate	8.0	5.0	–0.7	3.2	6.0	4.8
Natural growth rate	3.6	3.3	2.1	1.9	2.1	1.8
Migration rate	4.4	1.7	-2.8	1.3	3.9	3.0
Oman						
Population growth rate	2.3	4.6	2.1	2.3	3.2	8.4
Natural growth rate	2.7	3.6	2.9	1.9	1.8	1.8
Migration rate	–0.4	1.0	–0.8	0.4	1.4	6.6
Qatar						
Population growth rate	7.4	7.4	2.2	6.9	14.9	4.7
Natural growth rate	3.2	2.8	2.0	1.6	1.1	2.0
Migration rate	4.2	4.6	0.2	5.3	13.8	2.7
Saudi Arabia						
Population growth rate	3.1	5.2	2.7	2.9	2.5	2.3
Natural growth rate	2.9	3.4	2.9	2.1	1.9	1.7
Migration rate	0.2	1.8	–0.2	0.8	0.6	0.6
UAE						
Population growth rate	6.1	10.2	5.2	7.7	12.4	1.9
Natural growth rate	2.9	2.6	2.1	1.3	1.1	1.0
Migration rate	3.2	7.6	3.1	6.4	11.3	0.9

Source: Estimated by the author using United Nations 2015.

experienced a population growth rate of 4.3 percent whereas the migration growth rate of Bahrain increased from 0.2 percent in 1950–1970 to 1.6 percent during 1970–1990 and it was projected that Bahrain would experience a decline in migration in the decades to come and a subsequent reduction in the population. However, not only the projections made during the 1990s but also the beginning of the twenty-first century have been proved wrong.

According to the World Population Prospects 2015, there was a constant increase in the migration rate which led to the increase in population growth rate since 1990–2000 that continued until 2005–2010, but which then witnessed a sharp decline in migration. Along with migration growth rate, the natural growth rate continually declined over the decades. Thus the population growth rate was influenced by migration, and migration led to a crisis in the population of Bahrain, generating more nonnational than nationals. This is also true for all countries in the GCC region.

Bahrain experienced population growth rate of 7.5 percent along with a migration rate of 6.0 percent during 2005–2010. Kuwait experienced the largest negative population growth rate of 2.7 percent during 1990–2000, which can be attributed to the Kuwait war in 1990. There was a tremendous population growth rate in Qatar (13.8 percent) and in UAE (11.3 percent) during 2005–2010 due to migration. The growth of nonnationals in the Gulf countries along with the unemployment rate among nationals led most of the countries to follow the policies of reducing immigration through innovative migration policies.

Irregular Migration in the Gulf as a Crisis

In one of our earlier studies on irregular migrants in the Gulf, we concluded that a conservative estimate of irregular migration in Gulf ranged from 20 percent to 40 percent of the total migrants in the region (Fargues and Shah 2017; Rajan and Joseph 2017). For countries with a relatively lower stock of migrants (Oman, Kuwait, Qatar, and Bahrain) our estimate ranged from about 20 percent to 30 percent. However, in the leading regional migrant destinations, both UAE and Saudi Arabia, our lowest estimate is about 30 percent and the higher estimate is about 40 percent. From our calculations, based on recent population figures from the Gulf Labour Markets and Migration (GLMM) database, Saudi Arabia is the primary destination for irregular migrants in the GCC, hosting between 3 million and 4 million irregular migrants. The UAE also hosts a large number of irregular migrants ranging from 2.2 million to 3 million (Rajan and Joseph 2017). We estimate that the number of irregular migrants in the Gulf ranges between 6.5 million to 9 million—that is, approximately a third (and potentially half) of all migrants in the GCC are irregular.

With respect to the share of irregular migrants to GCC populations and labor force, Kapiszewski (2006) estimates that irregular migrants comprise at minimum 10 percent of the total population or 15 percent of the workforce in GCC countries, with numbers as high as 700,000 in Saudi Arabia. Our estimates indicate that the labor force share of irregular migrants is between 20 percent to 40 percent in GCC countries, and up to 50 percent in some countries (UAE, Kuwait). The proportion of irregular migrants to the total population of GCC countries lies between 10 percent to 20 percent, constituting up to 25 percent to 35 percent of UAE's population, with numbers as high as 4 million in Saudi Arabia (Table 48.2).

Table 48.2 Irregular Migrants in the Gulf as a Percentage of GCC Labor Force and Total Population

Country	Labor Force*	Lower range (Labor force)	Upper range (Labor force)	Total Population**	Lower Range (Population)	Upper Range (Population)
Saudi Arabia	11,232,277	26.9	35.9	30,770,375	9.8	13.1
UAE	6,325,502	34.7	46.3	8,264,070	26.6	35.4
Oman	1,809,462	20.2	30.3	4,149,917	8.8	13.2
Kuwait	1,733,184	33.2	49.8	4,161,404	13.8	20.7
Qatar	1,624,057	17.9	26.9	1,699,435	17.1	25.7
Bahrain	738,890	18.5	27.8	1,314,562	10.4	15.6
Total	23,463,372	28.1	38.4	50,359,763	13.1	18.0

Source: Estimated by Rajan and Joseph 2017 based on

* World Bank Labor Force Database (2010–2014) and

** Gulf Labour Markets and Migration, Gulf Cooperation Council, POP 1.1

Managing Irregular Migration Crisis: Introduction of Amnesty Schemes in the Gulf

Amnesty schemes aimed at reducing or eliminating undocumented immigrants and allowed window periods for immigrants to go back to their respective countries without facing any legal implications or hurdles. Reliable data on the numbers of irregular migrants are almost nonexistent. Newspaper reports and newsletters by different international agencies provide useful information (Shah 2009). In this section, we briefly review the history of amnesty schemes implemented in the countries in the Gulf (see Table 48.3).

According to the available information, the UAE and Bahrain have implemented amnesty schemes four times over the last twenty years, both Oman and Saudi Arabia gave amnesty three times, Qatar two times, and Kuwait just once. For instance, for the first time amnesty schemes were organized by both Bahrain and Saudi Arabia as early as 1995, followed by UAE in 1997 and Qatar in 1997 and Oman in 1998 (Ghafour 2013).

In 2017, Saudi Arabia had granted a 90-day amnesty period to all undocumented immigrants to return to their homes. The Indian embassy reported that around 20,000 Indian nationals had applied under this scheme. More than 2.5 million visa violators had

Table 48.3 Review of Amnesty Schemes in Gulf

Country	Amnesty year	Outcomes
Bahrain	1995	32,365 in 1995 and 52,000 in 1997 either left or regularized.
	2000	23,632 left.
	2007	5,000 foreign workers corrected their status with 1,300 returning to their countries and 3,700 were regularized.
	2015	Announced a six-month amnesty for all illegal workers.
Kuwait	2011	42,000 undocumented expatiates had benefitted.
Oman	1998	24,000 left.
	2001	13,000 left.
	2015	23,653 left.
Qatar	1997	3,000 left.
	2016	3,500 left.
Saudi Arabia	1995	2.3 million left during October 1997 to July 2000; 70000 deported per year.
	2013	2.5 million left.
	2017	Ninety-day amnesty scheme: results awaited.
United Arab Emirates	1996	200,000 left.
	2003	300,000 left.
	2007	342,000 undocumented regularized; 175,000 left.
	2010	Fined more than 1,000 for residency breaches.
	2012	Announced that illegal immigrants will be provided extension permits to remain in the UAE to regularize their immigration papers or leave the country without paying penalty.

Sources: Saudi Arabia: *Migration News*, January 7, 2003; *The Associated Press*, July 3, 2000; *Arab News*, February 25, 2013; *Arab News*, March 21, 2017; UAE: *Kuwait Times*, December 1996; *Gulf News*, December 26, 2002; *Khaleej Times* December 5, 2012; *Arabian Business* September 23, 2010; *Asian Migrant News*, Nov 30, 2007: Bahrain: *Bahrain Tribune*, December 28, 2000; *Trade Arabia Business News Information* April 26, 2015: Oman: *CISNEWS*, June 1998; *Times of India*, Oct 30, 2002; *Khaleej Times* April 29, 2015: Kuwait: *Kuwait Times*, Saturday, December 20, 1997; *Al Bawaba*, August 21, 2002; Batistella and Asis, 2003; *Kuwait Times*, December 13, 2013; Qatar: *Overseas Migration News*, August 1998; *Gulf Times*, August 24, 2016.

left the kingdom during the amnesty declared three years ago. Among them, there were 1.5 lakh of Indians, while another 1 million Indians rectified their status and remained in the kingdom (Shalhoub and Hameed 2017; Rajan and Joseph 2017). The main aim of these amnesty schemes is not only to regularize or deport the undocumented workers but also to reduce the share of nonnationals in the workforce.

In 2012, the UAE immigration authorities announced an amnesty scheme stating that all undocumented immigrants should regularize their visas with payment or leave the country without paying anything. The initiative was to reduce the illegal migrants in the country without any negative consequences both for immigrants and the UAE. However, this policy was only for visa overstayers and not for those who arrived illegally. Two years back, in 2010, UAE announced an amnesty scheme which had benefited 30,000 Indians (*The Economic Times* 2010). The UAE declared a three-month amnesty scheme by late 2007 and it benefited 3.4 lakh undocumented migrants. Of them, 70,000 were Indians. Out of 70,000 undocumented Indian migrants, 40,000 workers legalized their status under this scheme to stay in the UAE. The Andhra Pradesh Government had given free air tickets to 1,135 laborers, who could not afford to buy their tickets to travel from UAE to India (*The Economic Times* 2007).

In 2015, Bahrain announced a six-month amnesty for all undocumented foreign workers who wished to leave the country. Previously in 2007, Bahrain announced an amnesty in which 1,300 returned to their home countries and 3,700 stayed back in Bahrain after completion of legal documentation (*Khaleej Times* 2015; Toumi 2007). This scheme was implemented by the Labour Market Regulatory Authority (LMRA) in association with the Interior Ministry. More than 11,000 migrant workers were sent back to their home countries by end of 2007 because of staying irregularly in the country. The irregular migrant workers were mainly from India, Pakistan, Bangladesh, Sri Lanka, and the Philippines (Toumi 2007).

Demographic Dividend as a Crisis

Most of the countries in the region have the possibility to reap rich demographic dividends as many of them currently enjoy a high proportion of the population that is of working age population (Table 48.4). After few decades, the working age population will shrink and the problem of ageing will emerge in the Gulf. According to the

Table 48.4 Percentage of Working age (15–59) to Total Population in Gulf Countries

	1950	1980	2000	2015	2035	2050
Bahrain	53.1	61.7	65.5	74.7	32.4	29.6
Kuwait	59.4	57.0	69.2	74.2	50.3	46.6
Oman	52.7	50.7	58.8	75.1	50.6	44.0
Qatar	52.1	63.7	71.1	82.2	44.5	41.5
Saudi Arabia	52.4	50.8	58.4	66.4	61.7	57.8
United Arab Emirates	52.1	70.0	72.8	83.7	62.5	55.9
Gulf	52.7	53.3	61.0	71.6	65.7	60.0

Source: United Nations 2015.

recent United Nations (2015) assessment, the Gulf countries as a whole have increased their proportion of working-age population from 52.7 percent in 1950 to 71.6 percent in 2015 and thereafter it is expected to decline to 65.7 percent in 2035 and 60.0 percent in 2050. As of 2015, United Arab Emirates has reported the highest working population with 84 percent, followed by 82 percent in Qatar and 75 percent in Oman (Rajan 2017; Zachariah, Prakash, and Rajan 2004)

Shaped by institutions, rules, and norms governing the labor market and education system, youth unemployment is a complex structural problem, driven by deep-rooted social and economic behavior. Figure 48.4 shows the overall unemployment and youth unemployment rate of GCC member states and this is emerging as one of the crises among the Gulf countries, with at least some feeling that migrants are taking away the jobs of the nationals. This has led most countries to regulate their migration policies which will be discussed later.

It is clear from Figure 48.4 and Table 48.5 that unemployment is on an increase over the years in the GCC economies.According to the World Bank (2012), one-fourth of the youth in Bahrain and Saudi Arabia are unemployed. The hiring of both skilled and unskilled nonnational labor, which has been needed to sustain the rapid oil-based growth of GCC economies, has also helped to shape the employment situation of Gulf States, with nonnationals filling the majority of jobs in the private sector. In 2016, 41.3 percent of men and 81.0 percent of women among the youth were unemployed (Table 48.5). Gulf countries do not want to experience an Arab spring scenario in their countries and therefore have attempted to alleviate the problem of unemployment among the youth in

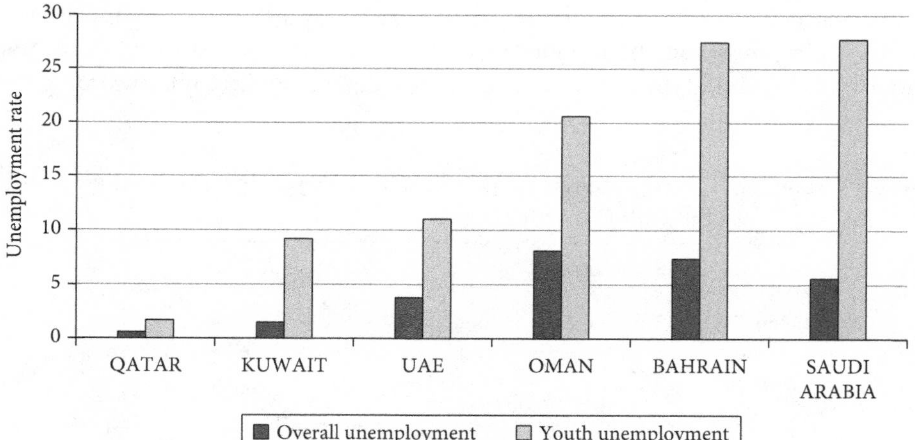

FIGURE 48.4 Overall Unemployment and Youth Unemployment in Gulf, 2012

Source: World Bank 2012

Table 48.5 Unemployment in Age Group 15–24 (Male and Female)

	Male		Female	
GCC Member States	1991	2016	1991	2016
Bahrain	2.6	2.9	13.4	13.4
Saudi Arabia	25.0	22.0	47.8	58.1
Kuwait	5.1	15.3	3.0	10.0
UAE	7.2	9.3	16.5	19.7
Oman	36.8	41.3	72.0	81.0
Qatar	1.0	0.3	11.9	3.4

Source: ILO 2016.

the Gulf; to avoid a crisis, all countries are reworking their earlier pro-migration policies to more challenging migration ones (World Bank 2017).

Migration Policy Crisis

The six GCC member states currently comprise the third largest hub of international migration. Managing the delicate balance between population constraints and development needs continue to be the crucial test of policies of the governments in this region. In this context, this article has reviewed the perceived governments' policies on immigration documented by the United Nations over the last forty years (United Nations 2005, 2013a, 2013b, 2013c). All governments were requested for their views on fertility, mortality, and migration policies. Migration policies include immigration for permanent settlement and temporary work or family reunification. Government views toward asylum-seekers, refugees, and undocumented immigrants are not considered. Three categories of views on the level of immigration are distinguished by the United Nations: (1) too low; (2) satisfactory; and (3) too high. In 1976, almost forty years back, the perception regarding Saudi Arabia on immigration was that it was too low while all other countries expressed their immigration levels as satisfactory (see Table 48.6). By 1986, United Arab Emirates, Kuwait, and Bahrain reported to the United Nations that their immigration levels were too high and they had policies to reduce immigration. In 1996, three of the Gulf countries reported their immigration levels as too high whereas the other three reported that their immigration levels were satisfactory. Since 2005, all countries except Bahrain have reported their immigration levels were too high;

Table 48.6 Views on Immigration by Gulf Countries, 1976–2013

		1976	1986	1996	2005	2011	2013
United Arab Emirates	Satisfactory	✓					
	Too high		✓	✓	✓	✓	✓
Saudi Arabia	Too low	✓					
	Satisfactory		✓				
	Too high			✓	✓	✓	✓
Kuwait	Satisfactory	✓		✓			
	Too high		✓		✓	✓	✓
Qatar	Satisfactory	✓	✓	✓			
	Too high				✓	✓	✓
Bahrain	Satisfactory	✓		✓	✓		
	Too high		✓			✓	✓
Oman	Satisfactory	✓	✓			✓	✓
	Too high			✓	✓		

Source: United Nations 2005, 2013.

now only Oman says that immigration levels are satisfactory and all other countries report that they are too high and they have inculcated policies to reduce immigrant crisis, which are discussed in the next section.

Manipulating Migration Policies in the Gulf

International migration for employment is known, but little information exists on the immigration policies of the GCC countries. Winckler (1997) tries to identify the policies adopted by these governments.

The *Kafala*

The *kafala* system was practiced in the 1950s in GCC countries.The *kafala* is bound by the contractual agreements which are signed between foreign workers and their sponsors. This system creates a direct relationship between each labor migrant and their sponsor or *kafeel* (see Migrant Forum in Asia, n.d.). These contracts particularly for the lower-skill categories of migrants are drawn up for a two-year period of employment and residency but may be renewed or extended. Upon the completion of the contracted period of employment sponsors are responsible for ensuring that workers are immediately repatriated to their country of origin. The *kafala* system forces the migrant worker to depend upon the sponsor for employment. For several decades this system was used as a means to regulate the flow of labor migrants to the Gulf.

The Transnational Labor Recruitment System

Recruitment agencies and labor brokerages in both labor receiving and sending countries play a critical role in this system. Recruiters in sending countries, along with a host of sub-agents, serve to link migrants in remote locations of Asia and Africa with manpower agencies and employers based in the GCC (Rajan, Varghese, and Jayakumar 2011). Recruiters and labor brokerages at both ends of the system financially benefit from the costs they extract from potential migrants.

Labor Nationalization Program of GCC Countries

Bahrain

Bahrain was the earliest to inaugurate the nationalization program in GCC, and it aimed at creating 6000 employment opportunities annually for the nationals (Gardner 2010). Firms were asked to increase the employment of nationals by 5 percent until it reached 50 percent of the total workforce of the company. New firms must have a workforce that has 20 percent of nationals (Del Bel-Air 2015; Zahra 2015). Since 1994, the nation started a human resource development program to offer financial incentives to small and mid-sized firms in the manufacturing sector that employ 30 percent of Bahrainis (Hussain 2011).

After the creation of the Economic Development Board under the Bahraini Crown Prince in 2001, a comprehensive policy review was initiated which concluded that labor market nationalization could be possible only through the integration of he labor market (Dito 2007, 2008). In 2007, Bahrain introduced its labor reforms, which aimed at,

- Deregulating the labor market.
- Eliminating the cost differential between foreign and local labor.
- Giving equal rights and choices to foreigners and locals
- Upgrading working environment standards.

Kuwait

Kuwait targets to create 10,000 jobs a year for Kuwaitis during next five years and to raise the share of nationals to 25 percent of the labor force. In addition to policies to increase the cost of work permits for immigrant workers, the latter are barred from employment in certain professions. Policies further seek to develop certain skills of the national workforce. The regulatory capacity of the labor administration has been insufficient for either implementing consistent Kuwaitization or effectively controlling the foreign workforce.

Oman

Under its fifth five-year plan (1996–2000), Oman set labor market policies with an aim of creating 17,400 new job opportunities actually and increasing the proportion of national labor from the total work force from 36 to 42 percent. It has pursued a dedicated "Omanization" policy since 1994, when it set a number of fairly high quotas for different sectors of business and reserved several job categories for nationals. The implementation of several of the steps had to be postponed, and during the first few years, Omanization was seen as a relative failure. This perception changed at least somewhat after the mid-2000s, when the government broadened its policies beyond the mere imposition of quotas. Omanization has always had a market-based component. The government reformed the sponsorship system in the country. Since late 2006, nonnatives have no longer needed the permission of the current employer to switch to a new one. In February 2011, the Omani government increased the official minimum wage for nationals from 120 to 200 Omani riyal. In March 2011, it also created an unemployment benefit to nationals of 150 Omani riyal per month, which was greater than the monthly wage of about half of the Omani private workforce in 2010. The minimum wage, which does not apply to foreigners, was further increased to OR325 in February 2013. Since 2012 annual wage increases have been made mandatory for Omani private sector employees (Hertog 2014).

Saudi Arabia

Saudi Arabia was the first country in GCC which started experimenting on employment rules. The Saudisation started in late 1940s but that was not properly implemented. The renewed push was given to the quota system in 1995, which resulted in a 5 percent increase in the employment share of Saudis in all companies with more than twenty employees.

Nitaqat was introduced in 2011 to achieve targeted nationalization of private sector employment via sanctions, subsidies, and incentives. Nitaqat also aimed at ending illegal visa trading and also intended to reduce the economic drain in the form of remittances. In the medium to long term, the government also expects to train and nurture skilled national workers and thereby reduce dependency on foreign labors (Hussain 2011). As a result of an unprecedented monitoring and sanctioning campaign, about half a million Saudis have been added to the private payroll from 2011 to 2013, constituting a stunning 70 percent increase. However, *nitaqat* efforts have been largely unsuccessful; Saudi Arabia recently announced the rollout of the third phase of the *nitaqat* program to include a range of amendments, including higher quotas of private sector Saudisation, new methods to assess the accurate number locals employed in private companies, and changes to incentives package available to local workers. A new *nitaqat* program aspiring to set recruitment standards—such as cost-ceiling, 60-day turnaround for recruitment procedures and inducement of much needed private sector structural adjustments—was also announced in June 2015. It ended with a period of amnesty and a subsequent crackdown on visa irregularities (Rajan and Joseph 2016; Alhasan 2017; *Khaleej Times* 2017).

Recently, the Saudi government has raised the expatriate dependent fee, which is effective from July 1, 2017. The Saudi General Authority for Statistics estimates that there are 100 lakh migrant workers and 24 lakh dependents in Saudi Arabia. This is viewed as a burden for the economy. An increase in tax will affect the migrant workers; the tax will generate 65 billion riyals by 2020. Apart from revenue, the real aim of the tax is to decrease migrant workers in Saudi Arabia (Basheer 2017).

Conclusion

As per the Population Division of United Nations, the number of international migrants globally reached 232 million with an annual growth rate of 1.6 percent per year. The changes in population of any particular area are mainly due to two reasons—natural increase and migration. Migration played a major role in the demographic, social, and economic changes in Gulf countries. Migration policies do play an important role in determining the flows, trends, conditions, and consequences of immigration. According to the IMF reports, the oil revenues accounted for between 70 and 95 percent of total government revenues during 2011–2014 across the six countries in the country. The emergence of oil resulted in demand for not only highly qualified technical workers but also semiskilled and unskilled workers. There was also a demand for large number of laborers to work in the oil industry as well as the construction industry. Since the indigenous labor was not sufficiently available, they had to invite nonnationals from different countries. The GCC countries looked to employ cheap sources of labor and the highest numbers of immigrants were engaged in health, education, construction, and manufacturing sectors. Both origin and destination countries face different problems in regard to migration flows.

Initially, migrants from Arab-speaking countries moved to the Gulf legally and later were replaced by Asians. Asians were found to be less expensive to employ and more efficient in the workplace and manageable in GCC countries. In addition, Asians were willing to migrate without their families, whereas Arab migrants, in contrast, bring their families and settle permanently in the Gulf. These tendencies of the Arabs were perceived as a potential threat to Gulf countries. This led to an enormous increase in the population of the Gulf countries in general and an increase in foreign workers in the labor force in both public and private sectors in particular. The Gulf countries also invited skilled migrants from different countries, especially Asia, which not only amounted to brain drain in the countries of origin but also helped them to achieve the highest human development indicators in terms of health and education. The majority of the South Asian migrants are mainly confined to blue-collar occupations where the demand for the labor from the GCC member states is met with the labor supply from the Asian countries. These were supplied by South Asian countries, especially India, Pakistan, and Bangladesh (Rajan and Kumar 2010).

Over a period of time, especially after the oil price decline, the number of migrants in Gulf countries has declined and showed a decreasing growth rate in terms of the total population of Gulf countries. Given the small size of native population, it is clear that the GCC countries cannot sustain their present economic activities and future growth, even if their populations continue to grow and if more nationals (both men and women) are ready to participate in the labor market. It is evident that all GCC countries will depend on nonnationals in maintaining economic development. Migrant labor has played an important role in the economies of Gulf countries. Thus by giving citizens an entitlement on oil wealth without promoting the productive use of national labor resources, the social contract has led to low labor force participation rates among GCC nationals and a high proportion of nonworking dependents per employed person. Among the GCC countries Oman has a high proportion of unemployed youth (both male and female). The World Bank (2012) predicted that the overall unemployment is at its peak in Oman. In terms of dealing with unemployment among the youth of the Gulf, the countries do not want to experience an Arab spring scenario; the Gulf countries are thus reworking earlier pro-migration policies to antimigration policies in order to avoid a migration crisis.

Within the GCC countries, the authorities are fully aware of the high number of irregular resident workers, especially overstayers (Babar 2013). Amnesty schemes are designed to provide an opportunity for such persons to depart or regularize their status. The latest amnesty in Saudi Arabia appears to have been relatively more successful, although irregular workers still persist. Localization policies in most countries restrict employment of nonnationals in the public sector while also coercing the private sector to employ the nationals. In this context, this article considers the government's policy on immigration documented by the United Nations over the last forty years (United Nations 2005, 2013a, 2013b, 2013c). All governments were requested to report their view on fertility, mortality, and migration policies. Migration policies include immigration for permanent settlement, temporary work, or family reunification. All Gulf countries report that they perceive immigration levels to be too high and they are working on policies to reduce immigration to satisfactory or low levels. The *kafala* system operated in the Gulf in which every laborer depends upon the sponsor for employment and livelihood. As a whole the GCC member states are trying to nationalize their economies by implementing amnesty schemes and renewing their labor migration policies to reduce immigration because they believe migrants and migration both directly and indirectly create crises in their economies and societies.

References

Alhasan, H. 2017. "Irregular Migration in Bahrain: Legislations, Policies, and Practices." In *Skillful Survivals: Irregular Migration to the Gulf*, edited by P. Fargues and N. M. Shah, 77–94. Cambridge, UK: Gulf Research Center.

Babar, Z. 2013. "A Regional Perspective: Migration Policy and Governance in the GCC." Emirates Centre for Strategic Studies and Research. http://eservices.mol.gov.ae/LabourMobility/attachments/babar-theme4E.pdf

Basheer, K. P. M. 2017. "Tax Forces Indian Families to Exit Saudi." *The Hindu*, July 7. http://www.thehindu.com/news/national/kerala/tax-forces-indian-families-to-exit-saudi/article19226671.ece

Del Bel-Air, F. 2015. "Demography, Migration and the Labor Market in Bahrain." GLMM, Gulf Research Centre, Florence.

Dito, M. E. 2007. "Migration Policies and Challenges in the Kingdom of Bahrain." Paper Prepared for the Migration and Refugee Movements in the Middle East and North Africa. The Forced Migration & Refugee Studies Program. The American University in Cairo, Egypt, October 23–25. http://schools.aucegypt.edu/GAPP/cmrs/reports/Documents/Mohammed_Dito.p

Dito, M. E. 2008. "GCC Labor Migration Governance." Paper Presented at the UN Expert Group Meeting on International Migration and Development in Asia and the Pacific, Bangkok, Thailand.

The Economic Times. 2007. "70,000 Indian Workers benefited from UAE Amnesty Scheme." November 5. http://economictimes.indiatimes.com/news/politics-and-nation/70000-indian-workers-benefited-from-uae-amnesty-scheme/articleshow/2517873.cms

The Economic Times. 2010. "UAE Amnesty Scheme to Benefit 30,000 Indians." September 22. http://economictimes.indiatimes.com/visa-power/uae-amnesty-scheme-to-benefit-30000-indians/articleshow/6607453.cms

Fargues, P., and N. M. Shah (eds). 2017. *Skillful Survivals: Irregular Migration to the Gulf*. Cambridge, UK: Gulf Labor Market and Migration.

Gardner, A. M. 2010. "Engulfed: Indian Guest Workers, Bahraini Citizens, and the Structural Violence of the Kafala System." In *The Deportation Regime: Soverignty, Space and the Freedmom Movement*, edited by Nicholas De Genova and Nathalie Peutz, Chapter 6, 196–223. Durham, NC: Duke University Press.

Ghafour, A. P. K. 2013. "Amnesty: Illegals Can Leave with No Penalty." *Arab News*, February 25. http://www.arabnews.com/saudi-arabia/amnesty-illegals-can-leave-no-penalty

Hertog, S. 2014. "Arab Gulf States: An Assessment of Nationalization Policies." GLMM-Research Paper-No 1/2014. http://cadmus.eui.eu/handle/1814/32156

Hussain, Z. 2011. "Immigration Policies of the GCC Countries: Implications and Responses." In *Dynamics of Indian Migration, Historical and Current Perspectives*, edited by S. I. Rajan and M. Percot, 93–163. London: Routledge.

International Labor Organization. 2015. Labor Market Trend Analysis and Labor Migration from South Asia to Gulf Cooperation Council Countries, India, and Malaysia. International Labor Organization, Kathmandu, Nepal. http://www.ilo.org/global/topics/labour-migration/publications/WCMS_378239/lang--en/index.htm

Kapiszewski, A. 2006. "Arab Versus Asian Migrant Workers in the GCC Countries." Department of Economics and Social Affairs, Population division, United Nations secretariat, Beirut, May 15-17. UN/POP/EGM/2006/02

Khaleej Times. 2015. "Bahrain Launches Six-Month Amnesty Scheme." June 29. http://www.khaleejtimes.com/region/bahrain-launches-six-month-amnesty-scheme

Khaleej Times. 2017. "Saudi Amnesty Scheme: 20,000 Indians to Return Home." May 3. http://www.khaleejtimes.com/region/saudi-arabia/saudi-amnesty-scheme-20000-indians-to-return-home

Migration Forum in Asia. n.d. Reform of the Kafala (Sponsorship System). Policy Brief No. 2. Migration Forum in Asia, Quezon City, Philippines.

Narayana, D. and V. Abraham. 2012. "Dubai Model and the Impact of the Financial Crisis on South Asian Migrant Workers in the United Arab Emirates." In *India Migration Report 2012: Global Finacial Crisis, Migration and Remittances*, edited by S. I. Rajan, Chapter 6, 94–121. New Delhi, India: Routledge.

Pushpangdan K., and M. Parameswaram. 2012. "Global Financial Crisis and the Migrant Labor Market: A Study of Kuwait." In *India Migration Report 2012: Global Financial Crisis, Migration and Remittance*, edited by S. I. Rajan, 131–150. New Delhi, India: Routledge.

Rajan, S. I., ed. 2010. *India Migration Report 2010: Governance and Labor Migration*. New Delhi, India: Routledge.

Rajan, S. I., ed. 2012. *India Migration Report 2012: Global Crisis, Migration and Remittances*. New Delhi, India: Routledge.

Rajan, S. I., ed. 2015. *India Migration Report 2015: Gender and Migration*. New Delhi, India: Routledge.

Rajan, S. I., ed. 2016. *India Migration Report 2016: Gulf Migration*. New Delhi, India: Routledge.

Rajan, S. I. 2017. "Demography of the Gulf Region." In *South Asian Migration in the Gulf: Causes and Consequences*, edited by M. Chowdhuri and S. I. Rajan. London: Palgrave.

Rajan, S. I. and J. Joseph. 2013. "Adapting, Adjusting and Accommodating: Social Costs of Migration to Saudi Arabia." In *Global Financial Crisis, Migration and Remittances: India Migration Report 2013*, edited by S. I. Rajan, Chapter 9, 139–153. New Delhi, India: Routledge.

Rajan, S. I., and J. Joseph. 2015. "Migrant Women at the Discourse–Policy Nexus: Indian Domestic Workers in Saudi Arabia." In *India Migration Report 2015: Gender and Migration*, edited by S. I. Rajan, 9–25. New Delhi, India: Routledge.

Rajan, S. I., and J. Joseph. 2016. "Gulf Migration in a Time of Regulation: Do Migration Controls and Labour Market Restrictions in Saudi Arabia Produce Irregularity?" In *India Migration Report 2016: Gulf Migration*, edited by S. I. Rajan. New Delhi, India: Routledge.

Rajan, S. I., and J. Joseph. 2017. "Migration (In)flux: Impact of Legislation on Patterns and Quantum of Irregular Mobility between India and Saudi Arabia." In *Skillful Survivals: Irregular Migration to the Gulf*, edited by P. Fargues and N. M. Shah Cambridge, UK: Gulf Labor Market and Migration.

Rajan, S. I., and P. Kumar. 2010. "Historical Overview of International Migration." In *India Migration Report 2010: Governance and Labor Migration*, edited by S. I. Rajan. New Delhi, India: Routledge.

Rajan, S. I., and D. Narayana. 2012. "The Financial Crisis in the Gulf and its Impact on South Asian Migrant Workers." In *India Migration Report 2012: Global Financial Crisis, Migration and Remittance*, edited by S. I. Rajan. New Delhi, India: Routledge.

Rajan, S. I., V. J. Varghese, and M. S. Jayakumar. 2011. *Dreaming Mobility and Buying Vulnerability: Overseas Recruitment Practices in India*. London: Routledge.

Shah, N. M. 2009. "The Management of Irregular Migration and its Consequences for Development: Gulf Cooperation Council." ILO Asia Regional Programme on Governance of Labor Migration, Working Paper No. 19. http://www.ilo.org/asia/publications/WCMS_105105/lang--en/index.htm

Shalhoub, L. and N. Hameed. 2017. "90-Day Amnesty Period Allows Illegal Workers To Return to Saudi Arabia." *Arab News*, March 21. http://www.arabnews.com/node/1071511/saudi-arabia

Toumi, H. 2007. "11,000 Workers get Amnesty in Bahrain." *Gulf News*, December 25. http://gulfnews.com/news/gulf/bahrain/11-000-workers-get-amnesty-in-bahrain-1.219409

Trade Arabia Business News Information. 2015. "Bahrain Mulls Amnesty Plans for Migrant Workers." April 26. http://www.tradearabia.com/news/EDU_280582.html

United Nations. 1990. *World Population Prospects 1990*. Department of Economics and Social Affairs, Population Division, United Nations, New York.

United Nations. 2002a. *International Migration Report 2002*. Department of Economics and Social Affairs. Population Division, United Nations, New York. http://www.un.org/esa/population/publications/ittmig2002/2002ITTMIGTEXT22-11.pdf

United Nations. 2002b. *World Population Prospects 2002*. New York: Department of Economics and Social Affairs, Population Division, United Nations.

United Nations. 2005. *World Population Policies 2005*. ST/ESA/SER.A/254. New York: Department of Economics and Social Affairs. Population Division, United Nations. http://www.un.org/en/development/desa/population/publications/pdf/policy/WPP2005/WPP2005_full.pdf

United Nations. 2006. *International Migration in the Arab Region*. UN/POP/EGM/2006/14. New York: Department of Economics and Social Affairs. Population Division, United Nations. http://www.un.org/esa/population/meetings/EGM_Ittmig_Arab/P14_PopDiv.pdf

United Nations. 2007. *International Migration in GCC Countries*. Regional Symposium on Foreign Workers in the GCC: Towards a Common Strategy. Doha, Qatar. 17–19 April 2007. http://www.un.org/en/development/desa/population/migration/events/docs/IttMig_170407.pdf

United Nations. 2013a. *International Migration Policies, Government Views and Priorities*. ST/ESA/SER.A/342. New York: Department of Economics and Social Affairs. Population Division, United Nations. http://www.un.org/en/development/desa/population/publications/pdf/policy/InternationalMigrationPolicies2013/Report%20PDFs/z_International%20Migration%20Policies%20Full%20Report.pdf

United Nations. 2013b. *World Population Policies 2013*. ST/ESA/SER/341. New York: Department of Economics and Social Affairs. Population Division, United Nations. http://www.un.org/en/development/desa/population/publications/pdf/policy/WPP2013/wpp2013.pdf

United Nations. 2013c. *International Migration Policies 2013*. New York: Department of Economics and Social Affairs. Population Division, United Nations, New York. http://www.un.org/en/development/desa/population/publications/policy/international-migration-policies-2013.shtml

United Nations. 2015. *International Migration Report 2015*. New York: Population Division, United Nations. http://www.un.org/en/development/desa/population/migration/publications/migrationreport/docs/MigrationReport2015.pdf

United Nations. 2017. *World Population Prospects: The 2017 Revision: Key Findings and Tables*. ESA/PWP/248. New York: Department of Economic and Social Affairs, Population Division. United Nations. https://www.compassion.com/multimedia/world-population-prospects.pdf

Winckler, O. 1997. "The Immigration Policy of the Gulf Cooperation Council (GCC) States." *Middle Eastern Studies* 33, no. 3: 480–493.

World Bank. 2012. *World Development Report: Gender Equality and Development*. Washington, DC: World Bank. https://siteresources.worldbank.org/INTWDR2012/Resources/7778105-1299699968583/7786210-1315936222006/Complete-Report.pdf

World Bank. 2017. *Sustaining Fiscal Reforms in the Long Run*. Gulf Economic Monitor 1. Washington, DC: World Bank.

Zachariah, K. C., S. I. Rajan, and J. Joseph. 2014. "Kerala Emigration to Saudi Arabia: Prospects under the Nitaqat Law." In *India Migration Report 2014: Diaspora and Development*, edited by S. I. Rajan. New Delhi, India: Routledge.

Zachariah, K. C., B. A. Prakash, and S. I. Rajan. 2004. "Indian Workers in UAE: Employment, Wages and Working Conditions." *Economic and Political Weekly*, 39, no. 22: 2227–2234.

Zahra, M. 2015. "Bahrain's Legal Framework of Migration." GLMM- EN - No. 1/2015, Gulf Research Centre, European University Institute. http://cadmus.eui.eu/bitstream/handle/1814/34579/GLMM_ExpNote_01_2015.pdf?sequence=1

Index

Figures, maps, notes, and tables are indicated by *f*, *m*, *n*, and *t* following page numbers.